Douglas Moo is one of the leading New Testament scholars of our generation, and his many books on the apostle Paul have benefited students and pastors all over the world. This volume on Paul's theology is arguably Moo's *magnum opus*, as it presents an analytic summary of the theology of Paul's individual letters as well as a synthesis of Paul's overall thought. Moo has produced here a massive and monumental work on Pauline theology that will teach readers for decades to come.

Rev. Dr. Michael F. Bird, academic dean and lecturer in theology,
Ridley College in Melbourne, Australia

Doug Moo's *A Theology of Paul and His Letters* is a book all scholars and pastors should have on their shelves. First, it gives an updated discussion (interacting with the most recent and relevant secondary sources) of all the major topics and issues in Pauline studies. Second, it also gives a sane and very well-reasoned interpretation of the key topics in Paul's theology. Among the outstanding discussions, as one would expect, are those dealing with the "New Perspective," justification, grace, and the necessary transformation of true believers. One will gain many insights into various Pauline passages by reading this book (e.g., on various uses of the Old Testament). Even when one may disagree with Moo, he gives an evenhanded, fair, and balanced discussion of debated issues. This, in fact, is a hallmark of the book. I heartily recommend Moo's work. I will consult it often.

G. K. Beale, professor of New Testament, Reformed Theological Seminary

The ideal person to write a Pauline theology is someone who has been immersed in his letters for decades and has a strong grasp on the wild world of Pauline studies. There are few scholars alive today who could rival Doug Moo on this score. Moo's careful analysis and synthesis of the entire Pauline canon is an invaluable addition to the field, as *A Theology of Paul and His Letters* helpfully presents the apostle's thought organized around the concept of the new realm in Christ, permeated by union with Christ. This wonderful resource will quickly become a standard reference work for anyone interested in Christianity's greatest missionary-pastor-theologian.

Constantine R. Campbell, author, *Paul and the Hope of Glory* and
Paul and Union with Christ

Doug Moo has had a distinguished career as an outstanding commentator on the Pauline epistles. Now we are treated to his theology of Paul. All the virtues that characterize Moo's work are on display here, including thorough research, careful exegesis, theological synthesis, and balanced judgment. Moo learns from and interacts with all sectors of scholarship, and he invariably respects other viewpoints. At the same time, he presents his own views with arguments and evidence. Moo's *A Theology of Paul and His Letters* is marked by a close reading of the text, and he warns against constructs of Paul's theology that are imposed upon the text instead of being derived from the text.

We are treated to both a theology of each Pauline letter (and he includes all thirteen letters as authentically Pauline) and also a synthesis of Paul's theology. As is often the case in Pauline theologies, the importance of the "already and not yet" as well as "union with Christ" are stressed. Moo also highlights "realm" in Paul's thought, featuring it as one of the key Pauline themes. This is a crucial book for understanding Paul's theology, and I am confident that Moo's work will impact scholarship for years to come.

Thomas Schreiner, James Buchanan Harrison Professor of New Testament
Interpretation, The Southern Baptist Theological Seminary

Humility is an essential virtue of any biblical scholar, but especially—given the contemporary context—for Pauline scholarship. Doug Moo neither founds nor follows fads. While recognizing wider assumptions in the apostle's consciousness in the history of Israel, he points out where Paul goes his own way, interpreting the new covenant according to the historical advent of Christ.

I have found Moo's work to be a marvelous blend of biblical-theological breadth and careful exegetical spadework. *A Theology of Paul and His Letters* is the crown of that exemplary approach.

Michael Horton, J. Gresham Machen Professor of Systematic Theology and
Apologetics, Westminster Seminary California

Doug Moo is one of the few scholars who can be trusted to write a theology of Paul's letters that is exegetically rigorous, philologically informed, theologically and biblically consistent, and at the same time written in a style that scholars, pastors, as well as believers interested in advanced explanations of Scripture will read with pleasure. Surveying the life of Paul as missionary theologian, Moo provides analyses of each of Paul's thirteen letters before explaining Paul's convictions regarding Jesus Christ, Jesus's substitutionary death, human beings and sin, the blessings of what Moo calls the "new realm," God's election and the faith response, Jesus's return and judgment, the nature and life of the church, and the ethical behavior of believers in Jesus.

On the last page of this *magnum opus,* Moo records his desire that readers would come away with the "renewed mind" that Paul wishes for the believers in the city of Rome. One does not need to be a prophet to be convinced that anyone who reads *A Theology of Paul and His Letters* attentively will gain a consolidated understanding of the gospel and a new perspective for Christian living that is faithful to Scripture.

Eckhard J. Schnabel, Mary F. Rockefeller Distinguished Professor of
New Testament Studies, Gordon-Conwell Theological Seminary

This superb work of New Testament scholarship will serve the church for years to come as a reliable guide to Paul's letters and their theological substructure. It is methodologically rigorous, robust in its engagement with the best scholarship, and reasonable in its conclusions. It is also written with the humility and reverence of one whose life has itself been shaped by Paul's theology.

Frank Thielman, Presbyterian Professor of Divinity, Beeson Divinity School

Doug Moo has been at the forefront of Pauline studies for four decades, and this book could only arise out of years of mature reflection. *A Theology of Paul and His Letters* is at the same time both panoramic in scope and attentive to the details of individual words and phrases. Moo draws on a vast wealth of scholarship, interacting fairly and charitably with others, and invariably clarifying not just Paul's thought but also his emphases and balance. I can recommend it with pleasure—and with envy of the learning and good judgment evident throughout this book.

Simon Gathercole, professor of New Testament and early Christianity,
University of Cambridge

A THEOLOGY OF
PAUL AND HIS
LETTERS

The Gift of the New Realm in Christ

A THEOLOGY OF PAUL AND HIS LETTERS

BIBLICAL THEOLOGY OF THE NEW TESTAMENT

DOUGLAS J. MOO

Andreas J. Köstenberger,
general editor

ZONDERVAN ACADEMIC

ZONDERVAN ACADEMIC

A Theology of Paul and His Letters
Copyright © 2021 by Douglas J. Moo

Requests for information should be addressed to:
Zondervan, *3900 Sparks Dr. SE, Grand Rapids, Michigan 49546*

Zondervan titles may be purchased in bulk for educational, business, fundraising, or sales promotional use. For information, please email SpecialMarkets@Zondervan.com.

Library of Congress Cataloging-in-Publication Data

Names: Moo, Douglas J., author. | Köstenberger, Andreas J., 1957- editor.
Title: A theology of Paul and his letters : the gift of the new realm in Christ / Douglas J. Moo, Andreas J. Köstenberger, general editor
Other titles: Biblical theology of the New Testament
Description: Grand Rapids : Zondervan, 2021. | Series: Biblical theology of the New Testament | Includes bibliographical references and index.
Identifiers: LCCN 2021003626 (print) | LCCN 2021003627 (ebook) | ISBN 9780310270904 (hardcover) | ISBN 9780310128502 (ebook)
Subjects: LCSH: Paul, the Apostle, Saint--Theology. | Bible. Epistles of Paul--Theology. | Bible. Epistles of Paul--Criticism, interpretation, etc.
Classification: LCC BS2651 .M665 2021 (print) | LCC BS2651 (ebook) | DDC 227/.06--dc23
LC record available at https://lccn.loc.gov/2021003626
LC ebook record available at https://lccn.loc.gov/2021003627

Cover design: Rob Monacelli
Cover image: ©BenetS
Interior design: Kait Lamphere

To Jenny
Wife and fellow-worker in Christ

CONTENTS

PART 4: *Final Matters*

Contents (Detailed)

PART 3: *The Theology of Paul*

19. The Old Realm: The Context for the Good News 405

PART 4: *Final Matters*

SERIES PREFACE

THE BIBLICAL THEOLOGY of the New Testament series consists of eight distinct volumes covering the entire New Testament. Each volume is devoted to an in-depth exploration of a given New Testament writing, or group of writings, within the context of the theology of the New Testament, and ultimately of the entire Bible. While each corpus requires an approach that is suitable for the writing(s) studied, all volumes include:

(1) a survey of recent scholarship and of the state of research
(2) a treatment of the relevant introductory issues
(3) a thematic commentary following the narrative flow of the document(s)
(4) a treatment of important individual themes
(5) discussions of the relationship between a particular writing and the rest of the New Testament and the Bible

While Biblical Theology is a relatively new academic discipline and one that has often been hindered by questionable presuppositions, doubtful methodology, and/ or flawed execution, the field is one of the most promising avenues of biblical and theological research today. In essence, Biblical Theology engages in the study of the biblical texts while giving careful consideration to the historical setting in which a given piece of writing originated. It seeks to locate and relate the contributions of the respective biblical documents along the lines of the continuum of God's salvation-historical program centered in the coming and salvific work of Christ. It also endeavors to ground the theological exploration of a given document in a close reading of the respective text(s), whether narrative, discourse, or some other type of literature.

By providing in-depth studies of the diverse, yet complementary perspectives of the New Testament writings, the Biblical Theology of the New Testament series aims to make a significant contribution to the study of the major interrelated themes of Scripture in a holistic, context-sensitive, and spiritually nurturing manner. Each volume is written by a scholar who has written a major commentary or monograph on the corpus covered. The generous page allotment allows for an in-depth investigation. While coming from diverse academic backgrounds and institutional affiliations, the contributors share a commitment to an evangelical faith and a respect for the authority of Scripture. They also have in common a conviction that the canon of Scripture is ultimately unified, not contradictory.

In addition to contributing to the study of individual New Testament writings and to the study of the New Testament and ultimately of Scripture as a whole, the series also seeks to make a methodological contribution, showing how Biblical Theology ought to be conducted. In each case, the way in which the volume is conceived reflects careful consideration of the nature of a given piece or body of writings. The complex interrelationships between the three so-called "Synoptic Gospels"; the two-volume nature of Luke-Acts; the relationship between John's Gospel, letters, and the book of Revelation; the thirteen letters making up the Pauline corpus; and the theologies of Peter, James, and Jude, as well as Hebrews, each present unique challenges and opportunities.

In the end, it is hoped that the volumes will pay tribute to the multifaceted nature of divine revelation contained in Scripture. As G. B. Caird put it:

> The question we must ask is not whether these books all say the same thing, but whether they all bear witness to the same Jesus and through him to the many splendoured wisdom of the one God. . . . We shall neither attempt to press all our witnesses into a single mould nor captiously complain that one seems at some points deficient in comparison with another. What we shall do is rejoice that God has seen fit to establish His gospel at the mouth of so many independent witnesses. The music of the New Testament choir is not written to be sung in unison.[1]

In this spirit, the contributors offer their work as a humble aid to a greater appreciation of the magnificent scriptural symphony of God.

Andreas J. Köstenberger, series editor
Wake Forest, NC

---

1. G. B. Caird, *New Testament Theology*, compl. and ed. L. D. Hurst (Oxford: Clarendon, 1995), 24.

Author's Preface

WRITING THIS BOOK on Paul's theology has been a burden and a joy. A burden because I am not naturally good at synthesis (give me analysis any day!) and because the amount of scholarly material on Paul is overwhelming. For every book I read on Paul, it seemed as if two more were published. But, in the end, the joy outweighed the burden. Writing this book forced me to delve into the thought world of one of the greatest thinkers in the history of Christianity—an experience that, I trust, has "renewed my mind" and, as a consequence, directed my life into a more Christlike pattern.

Since I signed the contract to write this book in 2005 (!), much of my teaching, writing, and thinking has been focused on Paul and his letters. I have written commentaries on four of Paul's letters and written articles on several texts and themes in Paul. These books and articles naturally overlap at places with topics in this volume. Rather than writing afresh on these topics, I have sometimes used the wording of these earlier projects in this volume—almost always revised to some degree. I indicate in footnotes where this is the case.

The length of time I have been working on this project means that several generations of students have assisted me in this work. I have had the privilege of working with gifted PhD students at both Trinity Evangelical Divinity School and Wheaton College. Many of them wrote dissertations on Paul that helped shape my own thinking. I mention here Ardel Caneday, Stephen Pegler, Russ Lovett, Jay Smith, Wendell Hollis (at TEDS), and Chris Vlachos, Chris Bruno, Dane Ortlund, Chee-Chiew Lee, Elisée Ouoba, Laurie Norris, Matt Harmon, Paul Cable, Jared Brown, Ben Dally, Matthew Monkemeier, and Johnathan Harris (at Wheaton). I refer to the work of most of these students (sometimes in the form of published dissertations) in footnotes and the bibliography. In addition to their written work, these students, as well as others (e.g., Ben Ribbens, Mike Kibbe, Ben Mandley, Josh Maurer, Stephen Wunrow, Jason Liu, Grant Flynn, and Felipe Chamy) have assisted in this work by securing scholarly material, editing, proofreading, and compiling indices.

My thinking has also been significantly shaped by interaction with students and colleagues in classes at both Wheaton and several other institutions: Westminster Theological Seminary, Western Theological Seminary West, Regent College, Sovereign

Grace Pastors' College, Carolina Graduate School of Theology (Greensboro, NC), Oakhill College (London, England), Proclamation Trust Pastors' Conferences, Pastors' Conference in Oradea, Romania, McMaster Seminary Conference on Christology, Nairobi Evangelical Graduate School of Theology, the John Bunyan Conference, Denver Seminary, Liberty University, the Faraday Institute (Cambridge, England), London Theological Seminary, Cru Conference in Pordoroz, Slovenia, E. W. Wahl Lectures at Taylor Seminary (Edmonton, Canada), Australian College of Theology, Queensland Theological College, Presbyterian Theological College (Sydney, Australia), Caskey Divinity School, Blackhawk Evangelical Free Church (Madison, WI), Huntington College (Huntington, IN), Séminaire Baptiste Evangélique du Québec, Bible Institute of South Africa (Kalk Bay), Rosebank Union Church (Johannesburg, South Africa), Seminario Teologico Institutio Biblica (Buenos Aires, Argentina), Bible Study Fellowship Conference (San Antonio, TX), Hughes Unit Prison (Hughes, TX), Asia Biblical Theological Seminary (in Manila, Philippines), Temple Bible Church (Temple, TX), California Baptist University, Greer-Heard Forum (New Orleans Baptist Seminary), Gateway Seminary, Sibima-Fortaleza Seminary (Fortaleza, Brazil), Bethel West Seminary, Griffith-Thomas Lectures, Dallas Theological Seminary, Henry Center Creation Conference (Trinity Evangelical Divinity School, Deerfield, IL), Berean Bible Church (Hilo, HI), and various sessions of the Evangelical Theological Society, the Society of Biblical Literature, and the Institute for Biblical Research.

I appreciate the patience of the editor of this series, Andreas Köstenberger, and the Zondervan Academic editor, Katya Covrett, as they waited many long years for this book to be finished. I am thankful for their input. Most of all, however, I thank my wife Jenny for her many discussions with me about issues in Paul and for her direct contributions to this book: she compiled the bibliography, most of the indexes, and—most importantly—edited the entire volume. This book is dedicated to her.

Wheaton, Illinois
February 2020

ABBREVIATIONS

1QpHab	Pesher on Habakkuk (Habakkuk Commentary)
1QS	Serek Hayaḥad (Rule of the Community)
2 Bar.	2 Baruch
4Q266	Damascus Document[a]
4Q174	Florilegium, also Midrash on Eschatology (also abbreviated 4QFlor[a])
4QMMT	Miqṣat Maʿaśê ha-Torah
11QMelch	Melchizedek text
AARSR	American Academy of Religion Studies in Religion Series
AB	Anchor Bible
ABR	*Australian Biblical Review*
AcBib	Academia Biblica
ACCS	Ancient Christian Commentary on Scripture
AGJU	Arbeiten zur Geschichte des antiken Judentums und des Urchristentums
ALBO	Analecta Lovaniensia Biblica et Orientalia
Alleg. Interp.	*Allegorical Interpretation* (Philo)
AnBib	Analecta Biblica
Ann.	*Annales* (Tacitus)
Ant.	*Jewish Antiquities* (Josephus)
AOTC	Abingdon Old Testament Commentaries
Apol.	*Apology* (Tertullian)
ATANT	Abhandlungen zur Theologie des Alten und Neuen Testaments
AV	Authorized Version
b. Šabb.	Babylonian Talmud, Šabbat
b. Yoma	Babylonian Talmud, Yoma
BBMS	Baker Biblical Monograph Series
BBR	*Bulletin for Biblical Research*
BDAG	Danker, Frederick W., Walter Bauer, William F. Arndt, F. Wilbur Gingrich. *Greek-English Lexicon of the New Testament and Other Early Christian Literature.* 3rd ed. Chicago: University of Chicago Press, 2000
BECNT	Baker Exegetical Commentary on the New Testament
BETL	Bibliotheca Ephemeridum Theologicarum Lovaniensium

BEvT	Beiträge zur evangelischen Theologie
BHT	Beiträge zur historischen Theologie
Bib	*Biblica*
BibInt	Biblical Interpretation Series
BJRL	*Bulletin of the John Rylands University Library of Manchester*
BJS	Brown Judaic Studies
BNTC	Black's New Testament Commentaries
BSac	*Bibliotheca Sacra*
BTCP	Biblical Theology for Christian Proclamation
BTS	Biblical Tools and Studies
BZNW	Beihefte zur Zeitschrift für die neutestamentliche Wissenschaft
CBC	Cambridge Bible Commentary
CBQ	*Catholic Biblical Quarterly*
CBQMS	Catholic Biblical Quarterly Monograph Series
CD	Cairo Genizah copy of the Damascus Document
CEB	Common English Bible
CGTC	Cambridge Greek Testament Commentary
CNT	Commentaire du Nouveau Testament
ConBNT	Coniectanea Biblica: New Testament Series
CRINT	Compendia Rerum Iudaicarum ad Novum Testamentum
CSB	Christian Standard Bible
CTQ	*Concordia Theological Quarterly*
CTR	*Criswell Theological Review*
CurBR	*Currents in Biblical Research*
Diatr.	*Diatribai (Dissertationes)* (Epictetus)
EB	Echter Bibel
ECC	Eerdmans Critical Commentary
ECL	Early Christianity and Its Literature
EFN	Estudios de filología neotestamentaria
EGGNT	Exegetical Guide to the Greek New Testament
EKKNT	Evangelisch-katholischer Kommentar zum Neuen Testament
ESV	English Standard Version
ETS	Erfurter theologische Studien
EvQ	*Evangelical Quarterly*
EvT	*Evangelische Theologie*
ExpTim	*Expository Times*
FB	Forschung zur Bibel
FRLANT	Forschungen zur Religion und Literatur des Alten und Neuen Testaments
GBS	Guides to Biblical Scholarship

Ger.	German
Gk.	Greek
Haer.	*Adversus Haereses* (Irenaeus)
HBT	*Horizons in Biblical Theology*
Heb.	Hebrew
HNT	Handbuch zum Neuen Testament
HNTC	Harper's New Testament Commentaries
HThKNT	Herders Theologischer Kommentar zum Neuen Testament
HTR	*Harvard Theological Review*
HTS	Harvard Theological Studies
ICC	International Critical Commentary
IDB	*The Interpreter's Dictionary of the Bible.* Edited by George A. Buttrick. 4 vols. New York: Abingdon, 1962
IKZ	*Internationale kirchliche Zeitschrift*
IVPNTC	InterVarsity Press New Testament Commentary
JAAR	*Journal of the American Academy of Religion*
JBL	*Journal of Biblical Literature*
JETS	*Journal of the Evangelical Theological Society*
JRH	*Journal of Religious History*
JSJ	*Journal for the Study of Judaism in the Persian, Hellenistic, and Roman Periods*
JSNT	*Journal for the Study of the New Testament*
JSNTSup	Journal for the Study of the New Testament Supplement Series
JSPL	*Journal for the Study of Paul and His Letters*
JTISup	Journal for Theological Interpretation, Supplements
JTS	*Journal of Theological Studies*
Jub.	Jubilees
J.W.	*Jewish War* (Josephus)
KEK	Kritisch-exegetischer Kommentar über das Neue Testament (Meyer-Kommentar)
KJV	King James Version
LAB	Liber antiquitatum biblicarum (Pseudo-Philo)
LD	Lectio Divina
Let. Aris.	Letter of Aristeas
LNTS	Library of New Testament Studies
LS	*Louvain Studies*
LSJ	Liddell, Henry George, Robert Scott, Henry Stuart Jones. *A Greek-English Lexicon.* 9th ed. with revised supplement. Oxford: Clarendon, 1996
LUÅ	Lunds universitets årsskrift
LXX	Septuagint (Greek translation of the Old Testament)

m. 'Abot	Mishnah, 'Abot
m. Yoma	Mishnah, Yoma
NAB	New American Bible
NAC	New American Commentary
NASB	New American Standard Bible
NCB	New Century Bible
NET	New English Translation
NETS	New English Translation of the Septuagint
NewDocs	*New Documents Illustrating Early Christianity.* Edited by Greg H. R. Horsley and Stephen Llewelyn. North Ryde, NSW: The Ancient History Documentary Research Centre, Macquarie University, 1981–
NIB	*The New Interpreter's Bible.* Edited by Leander E. Keck. 12 vols. Nashville: Abingdon, 1994–2004
NICNT	New International Commentary on the New Testament
NIDNTTE	*New International Dictionary of New Testament Theology and Exegesis.* Edited by Moisés Silva. 5 vols. Grand Rapids: Zondervan, 2014
NIGTC	New International Greek Testament Commentary
NIV	New International Version
NIVAC	New International Version Application Commentary
NJB	New Jerusalem Bible
NLT	New Living Translation
NovT	*Novum Testamentum*
NovTSup	Supplements to Novum Testamentum
NPNF¹	*Nicene and Post-Nicene Fathers*, Series 1
NRSV	New Revised Standard Version
NSBT	New Studies in Biblical Theology
NT	New Testament
NTAbh	Neutestamentliche Abhandlungen
NTD	Das Neue Testament Deutsch
NTG	New Testament Guides
NTL	New Testament Library
NTOA	Novum Testamentum et Orbis Antiquus
NTS	*New Testament Studies*
NTTS	New Testament Tools and Studies
ÖBS	Österreichische biblische Studien
OT	Old Testament
ÖTK	Ökumenischer Taschenbuch-Kommentar
OTP	*Old Testament Pseudepigrapha.* Edited by James H. Charlesworth. 2 vols. New York: Doubleday, 1983, 1985

par.	parallel(s)
PNTC	Pillar New Testament Commentary
Pr. Man.	Prayer of Manasseh
Prelim. Studies	*On the Preliminary Studies* (Philo)
Presb	*Presbyterion*
ProEccl	*Pro Ecclesia*
Pss. Sol.	Psalms of Solomon
ResQ	*Restoration Quarterly*
RevExp	*Review and Expositor*
Rewards	*On Rewards and Punishments* (Philo)
RHPR	*Revue d'histoire et de philosophie religieuses*
RSV	Revised Standard Version
RTR	*Reformed Theological Review*
SANT	Studien zum Alten und Neuen Testaments
SBLDS	Society of Biblical Literature Dissertation Series
SBS	Stuttgarter Bibelstudien
SBT	Studies in Biblical Theology
SE	*Studia Evangelica*
SFSHJ	South Florida Studies in the History of Judaism
SGBC	Story of God Bible Commentary
Sir	Sirach
SJT	*Scottish Journal of Theology*
SNT	Studien zum Neuen Testament
SNTSMS	Society for New Testament Studies Monograph Series
SNTSU	Studien zum Neuen Testament und seiner Umwelt
SNTW	Studies of the New Testament and Its World
SP	Sacra Pagina
Spec. Laws 1, 2	*On the Special Laws* 1, 2 (Philo)
SR	*Studies in Religion*
ST	*Studia Theologica*
StBibLit	Studies in Biblical Literature (Lang)
STI	Studies in Theological Interpretation
Str-B	Strack, H. L., and P. Billerbeck. *Kommentar zum Neuen Testament aus Talmud und Midrasch.* 6 vols. Munich, 1922–1961
StudNeot	Studia Neotestamentica
SUNT	Studien zur Umwelt des Neuen Testaments
T. Levi	Testament of Levi
T. Mos.	Testament of Moses
TBei	*Theologische Beiträge*

TDNT	*Theological Dictionary of the New Testament.* Edited by Gerhard Kittel and Gerhard Friedrich. Translated by Geoffrey W. Bromiley. 10 vols. Grand Rapids: Eerdmans, 1964–1976
Them	*Themelios*
THKNT	Theologischer Handkommentar zum Neuen Testament
TNTC	Tyndale New Testament Commentaries
TOTC	Tyndale Old Testament Commentaries
TrinJ	*Trinity Journal*
TU	Texte und Untersuchungen
TynBul	*Tyndale Bulletin*
TZ	*Theologische Zeitschrift*
UBS⁵	*The Greek New Testament*, United Bible Societies, 5th ed.
Virtues	*On the Virtues* (Philo)
WBC	Word Biblical Commentary
Wis	Wisdom of Solomon
WMANT	Wissenschaftliche Monographien zum Alten und Neuen Testament
WTJ	*Westminster Theological Journal*
WUNT	Wissenschaftliche Untersuchungen zum Neuen Testament
ZBK	Zürcher Bibelkommentare
ZECNT	Zondervan Exegetical Commentary on the New Testament
ZNW	*Zeitschrift für die neutestamentliche Wissenschaft*
ZTK	*Zeitschrift für Theologie und Kirche*

Unless otherwise noted, I have used the New International Version (rev. ed., 2011) for quotations from the Scriptures, *Novum Testamentum Graece* (ed. Kurt Aland, Johannes Karavidopoulos, Carlo M. Martini, and Bruce M. Metzger; 28th ed., 2012) for the Greek text of the New Testament, *Biblia Hebraica Stuttgartensia* (ed. K. Elliger and W. Rudolf, 5th ed., 1997) for the Hebrew OT, *Septuaginta* (ed. A. Rahlfs, 1971) for the Septuagint, the Loeb Classical Library editions for the works of Josephus and Philo, *The New Revised Standard Version* (1989) for English translations of the Apocrypha, *The Old Testament Pseudepigrapha* (ed. J. Charlesworth; 2 vols., 1983, 1985) for English translations of the Pseudepigrapha, and *The Dead Sea Scrolls Reader* (ed. Donald W. Parry and Emanuel Tov, 6 vols.) for the Dead Sea Scrolls.

I have cited texts from the OT according to the versification of the English translations, even when the MT or LXX verse number differs.

Part 1

INTRODUCTORY ISSUES

Chapter 1

APPROACHING PAUL'S THEOLOGY

THE APOSTLE PAUL has arguably had a greater impact on Christianity than any figure other than Jesus Christ himself. His words and the ideas those words point to are woven into the fabric of our faith, our hymns, and our sermons. His influence has varied over time, and some parts of the church are more influenced by his teaching than others. And, of course, an overreliance on Paul's writings to the detriment of the rest of the canon can create an imbalance in our understanding of the faith. Yet with all appropriate caveats introduced, we still need to treasure the rich deposit of teaching Paul has left for us. I know I do. I have had the inestimable privilege of spending at least thirty years in intense study of Paul. I cannot even estimate the number of articles and books about Paul I have read over these years. (Please: could someone call a moratorium on books on Paul?) However, without in any way minimizing all that I have learned from this extensive reading, the heart of my study has been reading, and rereading, and rereading, the letters of Paul. I pray that what I have written in these pages reflects what is found in those letters.

Nevertheless, writing a book on Paul's theology is a daunting task. Over the last fifteen years, I have more than once regretted that I ever agreed to something so foolish. But I persevered, despite my doubts (which have not gone away). Readers will have to decide how justified those doubts might be.

"Doing" Paul's theology is hard for several reasons. In this opening chapter, I want to deal briefly with some of these challenges and to explain my own approach in this book.

1 BIBLICAL THEOLOGY[1]

This volume appears in a series entitled "Biblical Theology of the New Testament," so I begin with this big issue: What do we mean by "biblical theology"? While taking quite diverse forms, theology for most of church history was not consciously divided into different types or styles. However, it is important, in contrast to some construals of the history, to emphasize that Christian theologians had been doing some form of what

---

1. The content, and occasionally the wording, of this section, is taken from a paper read at the 2012 national Evangelical Theological Society conference and is found also in Douglas J. Moo and Jonathan A. Moo, *Creation Care: A Biblical Theology of the Natural World* (Grand Rapids: Zondervan, 2018), 34–38. Used by permission.

we might call "biblical" theology for a long time—if we define it as a close reading of Scripture focused on drawing out the theological meaning of the text. This enterprise, generally viewed simply as "theology," took on a new aspect in the late 1700s under the impact of Enlightenment-influenced academic study of the Bible. As academic study of the biblical text became increasingly separated from the church, it was felt necessary to isolate this kind of theology from "doctrinal" or "systematic" theology. I have neither the space nor the ability to pursue the history of this new discipline of "biblical theology."[2] To fastforward to the present, we now find ourselves in a time when "biblical theology" has lost any agreed-upon meaning. As Klink and Lockett comment, "*Biblical theology* has become a catchphrase, a wax nose that can mean anything from the historical-critical method applied to the Bible to a theological interpretation of Scripture that in practice appears to leave history out of the equation altogether."[3] As this quotation suggests, one key tension in current discussions of biblical theology is the one between historical reconstructions of early Christianity, on the one hand, and the final, canonical shape of Scripture on the other. This tension is closely tied to a second issue: How should we "locate" biblical theology with respect to exegesis, on the one hand, and systematic theology on the other?[4]

Addressing this latter question (and implicitly, perhaps the former one also), Charles Scobie, in his breathtakingly ambitious whole-Bible theology, advocates an "intermediate" biblical theology. Representing what is probably the dominant view among contemporary scholars, he compares biblical theology to a bridge, with one pier sunk in a close reading of the text and the other in systematic theology and, by implication, the ministry of applying the text. The bridge metaphor, while it has drawbacks (see below), is a good starting point to use in pinning down biblical theology.

A biblical-theological bridge capable of carrying traffic from text to application will need to be built of four materials in particular. These materials are, in fact, inherent in the words "biblical" and "theological."

First, to be truly *biblical*, our biblical theology must be *descriptive*. This element of biblical theology is widely recognized and relatively uncontroversial. As a second-level activity, one step removed from the text, biblical theology seeks to summarize and synthesize the teaching of the Bible using the Bible's own categories and with attention to its redemptive-historical movement.[5]

---

2. The first clearly to enunciate the idea of "biblical theology" was apparently J. P. Gabler in 1797. A useful survey of this history is provided by Charles H. H. Scobie, "History of Biblical Theology," in *New Dictionary of Biblical Theology*, ed. T. Desmond Alexander and Brian S. Rosner (Downers Grove, IL: InterVarsity Press, 2000), 11–20.

3. Edward W. Klink and Darian R. Lockett, *Understanding Biblical Theology: A Comparison of Theory and Practice* (Grand Rapids: Zondervan, 2012), 13. Christopher R. Seitz agrees: "'Biblical theology' is an elastic and imprecise term" (*The Character of Christian Scripture: The Significance of a Two-Testament Bible*, STI [Grand Rapids: Baker, 2011], 95).

4. For helpful reflection on this issue, see D. A. Carson, "Systematic Theology and Biblical Theology," in Alexander and Rosner, *New Dictionary of Biblical Theology*, 89–104.

5. This general description of biblical theology is ubiquitous;

Second, to be truly *theological*, our biblical theology should also be *prescriptive*. Biblical theologians have not always recognized this aspect in their work. Indeed, it has often been actively resisted. This resistance has its basis in an appropriate concern to root theology in history and exegesis, requiring, it is thought, a strict separation between "what the text meant" in distinction to "what the text means"—to use the familiar terminology from Krister Stendahl's programmatic dictionary article.[6] While sometimes rejected today in the name of postmodernism, the concern to distinguish these and to ground "what it means" firmly in "what it meant" is a valid one, necessary if our theology is to have any authority.[7] However, without in any way neglecting the absolutely indispensable descriptive exegetical task, a prescriptive aspect in our biblical theology seems to me to be implied in the word "theology"—at least as I understand it.[8] No "theology," whatever adjective we put in front of it, can fully avoid the task of addressing the people of God today. The very nature of the Word of God discourages us from confining our study, whatever we call it, to description only. The biblical theologian rightly focuses on the horizon of the text, while the systematic theologian gives more attention to the horizon of our own world. But focus should not become tunnel vision. The dividing line between the one task and the other will not be a neat one. We biblical theologians must build our bridge far enough toward the land of systematic theology and application, so that our colleagues in theology will have the necessary biblical-construction materials to build their structures, and pastors will be given the kind of biblical material they need to address their congregations.

Third, to turn back again to the word "biblical": our biblical theology must be *inclusive*. Discussions of biblical theology often focus on whether "biblical" here means that we study the theology found in the Bible or that we develop a theology that does justice to the Bible. But the adjective implies something more fundamental: It suggests that the theologian operates as a Christian who assumes that the thirty-nine books of

---

see, e.g., Brian S. Rosner, "Biblical Theology," in Alexander and Rosner, *New Dictionary of Biblical Theology*, 10: "*Biblical theology can be defined as theological interpretation of Scripture in and for the church. It proceeds with historical and literary sensitivity and seeks to analyse and synthesize the Bible's teaching about God and his relations with the world on its own terms, maintaining sight of the Bible's overarching narrative and Christocentric focus*" (emphasis original).

6. Krister Stendahl, "Biblical Theology, Contemporary," *IDB* 1:418–32. Making similar points are James Barr, *The Concept of Biblical Theology: An Old Testament Perspective* (Minneapolis: Augsburg Fortress, 1999), esp. 196–205; Peter Balla, *Challenges to New Testament Theology* (Peabody, MA: Hendrickson, 1997), e.g., 249.

7. I therefore endorse the claim of Gordon Fee and Douglas Stuart in their popular book on biblical interpretation that "what it means" must be grounded in "what it meant" (*How to Read the Bible for All Its Worth*, 4th ed. [Grand Rapids: Zondervan, 2014], 34).

8. Stephen Motyer's definition of biblical theology is similar: "That creative theological discipline whereby the church seeks to hear the integrated voice of the whole Bible addressing us today" ("Two Testaments, One Biblical Theology," in *Between Two Horizons: Spanning New Testament Studies and Systematic Theology*, ed. Joel B. Green and Max Turner [Grand Rapids: Eerdmans, 2000], 158). For a vigorous assertion of this point, see Kevin Vanhoozer: "To limit biblical theology to historical description is to abandon the attempt to read the Bible as theologically normative for the church and to reject the notion of divine inspiration and divine authorship, and thus to refuse to read the Bible as the word of God" ("Exegesis and Hermeneutics," in Alexander and Rosner, *New Dictionary of Biblical Theology*, 63). See also especially Peter Stuhlmacher, *Biblical Theology of the New Testament* (Grand Rapids: Eerdmans, 2018), 13; Dan O. Via, *What Is New Testament Theology?*, GBS (Minneapolis: Fortress, 2002), e.g., 43.

the Old Testament and the twenty-seven books of the New Testament canon form a distinctive set of books that are worthy of study and synthesis. The *evangelical* biblical theologian fleshes out this assumption by taking a further vital step: he or she assumes that these thirty-nine, or twenty-seven, or sixty-six, books ultimately speak with a single voice. I often remind my students that we evangelicals face a special challenge in our biblical theology: to develop a theology that does full justice to all the data of Scripture. We don't have the luxury of throwing out inconvenient bits of text or of forcing interpretations on them in the interest of harmonization. Of course, our concern in this volume is with the thirteen letters of Paul we find in the New Testament. As I will briefly argue elsewhere, I consider all thirteen of these letters to be authentically Pauline. The voice of each letter must be heard in its appropriate volume and tone as we construct a theology of Paul.

Fourth, our biblical theology must be *canonical*. The word "theology" reminds us that we engage in our task as "people of the book"—the whole book. Paul's teaching must ultimately be seen in relationship to the other books of the canon. The relationship of his teaching to the Old Testament will therefore be a constant concern in this book. And, while we will have less opportunity to do so, his theology must ultimately be compared and integrated with the teaching of the rest of the New Testament.

Our biblical theology must, then, be descriptive, prescriptive, inclusive, and canonical. These are what we might call the essential characteristics of the interpretive bridge that we are building. But there are some other interpretive matters that need to be added before we are finished, matters that have to do not so much with the basic structure as the way we navigate it. To describe these additional matters, I need to change our ruling metaphor. After comparing biblical theology to a bridge between the text and systematic theology, Scobie goes on to argue that this bridge must be able to "carry traffic in both directions."[9] The basic image is widespread in this context, and those who use it are not pressing the analogy beyond the simple point of mutual interaction and enrichment. Still, if we take a closer look at the two-way traffic analogy, its limitations become clear. We picture either two lanes of traffic passing each other with little or no contact; or, more disturbingly, a head-on accident. Perhaps a better image, then, at least for my purposes, is the roundabout that one finds along some highways, especially in the United Kingdom. The road from exegesis to systematics and application is not an uninterrupted super highway. Feeding into our biblical theology are several roads, which we may compare to the traffic from secondary roads that merge into the main through road at a roundabout. My point here, then, is that we perhaps have to abandon, or at least modify, the notion that our biblical work proceeds in a linear fashion from

9. Charles H. H. Scobie, *The Ways of Our God: An Approach to Biblical Theology* (Grand Rapids: Eerdmans, 2003), 46–49, 77.

exegesis to biblical theology to systematic theology. These disciplines are inevitably mixed up with each other. The diverse movement labeled "theological interpretation of Scripture" has drawn attention to these matters. I do not view this movement as clearly espousing a specific methodology; I view it rather as insisting on certain values that should characterize our methodology: the importance of bringing the resources of historical and systematic theology to bear on our exegesis and biblical theology, the importance that we "do" theology for the sake of the church, and the importance of humility in light of our location in time, place, and theological tradition.

So my study of Paul's theology will unashamedly draw on the resources of systematic theology and historical theology. Of course, I recognize that I thereby open myself to the charge that I am simply reading my own theological preferences into the text. The response, however, is not to try to escape the roundabout; it should be, rather, to make sure that the road emerging from the text is always given its appropriate priority. In sum, then, I would characterize my own method as an exegetically based biblical theology informed by some of the values of the "theological interpretation of Scripture" movement.[10]

2 Pauline Theology

My outline of Pauline theology in this volume is an instantiation of the biblical theology I have described above. Several issues specific to our study of Paul's theology emerge at this point.

2.1 What Is "Pauline Theology"?

A question that continuously surfaced in a years-long discussion of Pauline theology at the annual Society of Biblical Literature meetings was a deceptively simple one: Where do we find Paul's theology? Specifically, do we find his theology *in* his letters or *behind* his letters? Should "Pauline theology" be a summary of what he says in his letters? Or should Pauline theology be a reconstruction of Paul's thought that we can discern behind his letters? Introducing an approach that will surface repeatedly in this chapter, I answer yes. We have no access to Paul's thought outside the letters he wrote, preserved for us in Scripture. But Pauline theology must be more than a simple repetition of what we find on the surface of Paul's letters—otherwise, it would be hard to distinguish theology from exegesis. The Pauline theologian must penetrate "behind" the text in an effort to uncover the basic framework and content of Paul's thinking. Jouette Bassler summarizes the process and the desired theological outcome:

---

10. See, for an overview of this movement, Daniel J. Treier, *Introducing Theological Interpretation of Scripture: Recovering a Christian Practice* (Grand Rapids: Baker, 2008). Generally, this movement emphasizes the importance of interpreting Scripture in conversation with voices from throughout Christian history, interpreting Scripture with a focus on its ultimate theological claim, and interpreting Scripture for the church.

The *raw material of Paul's theology* (the kerygmatic story, scripture, traditions, etc.) passed through the *lens of Paul's experience* (his common Christian experience as well as his unique experience as one "set apart by God for the gospel") and generated a *coherent (and characteristic) set of convictions*. These convictions, then, were refracted through a prism, Paul's *perception of the situations that obtained in various communities*, where they were resolved into specific *words on target for those communities*.[11]

In a sense, this is simply the move from exegesis—describing what is in the text—to theology—synthesizing what is in the text. This is what "Pauline theology" is.

The minute we make this move "behind" or "beyond" the text, however, we inevitably introduce a strong measure of subjectivity. This is most obvious among scholars who self-consciously choose a perspective from our own context to use in interpreting Paul: for example, feminism,[12] postcolonialism,[13] or "post-Holocaust hermeneutics."[14] I acknowledge that the interpreter of Paul will inevitably bring some of their own "baggage" into their interpretation. Nor is that baggage always a problem. For instance, Lisa M. Bowens has documented how black interpreters of Paul in North America in the late nineteenth and early twentieth centuries "resisted" a certain biased perspective on Paul as endorsing slavery.[15] The experience and social position of these interpreters brought valid and important corrections to a certain dominant view of Paul. My own experience of teaching Paul in various parts of the world has shown again and again how perspectives from different geographic, social, and cultural contexts can shed light on texts—light that my limited perspective might not have seen so clearly. To use the terms often heard in this discussion, our task is not to "resist" the text—quite the contrary, I am called to submit to the text. But I *am* called to resist distortions of the text or imbalances in our synthesis that have crept into our theology. And listening to voices from different eras of the church and from different parts of the contemporary church helps to identify where this kind of "resistance" is needed.

I am a North American, white evangelical whose thinking has been strongly influenced by Reformation theology. Biases stemming from my identity are undoubtedly present in this volume. But, through sympathetic listening to the voices of others, both ancient and modern, and—not least!—the ministry of God's Spirit as I read and

11. Jouette M. Bassler, "Paul's Theology: Whence and Whither?," in *Pauline Theology, Volume 2: 1 and 2 Corinthians*, ed. David M. Hay (Minneapolis: Augsburg Fortress, 1993), 11.

12. E.g., Cynthia Briggs Kittredge, "Feminist Approaches: Rethinking History and Resisting Ideologies," in *Studying Paul's Letters: Contemporary Perspectives and Methods*, ed. Joseph A. Marchal (Minneapolis: Fortress, 2012), 117–33; Sandra Hack Polaski, *A Feminist Introduction to Paul* (St. Louis: Chalice, 2005).

13. Davina Casperina Lopez, *Apostle to the Conquered: Reimagining Paul's Mission* (Minneapolis: Fortress, 2008).

14. See, e.g., Angus Paddison, *Theological Hermeneutics and 1 Thessalonians*, SNTSMS 133 (Cambridge: Cambridge University Press, 2005).

15. Lisa M. Bowens, *African American Readings of Paul: Reception, Resistance, and Transformation* (Grand Rapids: Eerdmans, 2020); see, for a broader hermeneutical perspective, Esau McCaulley, *Reading While Black: African American Biblical Interpretation as an Exercise in Hope* (Downers Grove, IL: InterVarsity Press, 2020).

reread Paul, I am also hopeful, if not confident, that what I claim to find in the text really is in the text.

2.2 How Do We Describe Paul's Theology?

To state the obvious: Paul wrote thirteen letters to churches and individuals spread across the eastern Mediterranean over at least fifteen years. Moreover, what Paul teaches in these letters is generated by the circumstances of his readers. No other biblical author confronts the interpreter with materials so diverse. N. T. Wright comments: "Trying to describe what was going on in Pauline theology used to be like trying to board a moving train. It is now more like trying to describe a box of fireworks seven seconds after someone has thrown a match in it."[16]

Containing and categorizing the offshoots of this explosion of diverse material is a classic problem. J. C. Beker popularized the alliterative terms "contingency" and "coherence" to describe this challenge;[17] another pair of terms is "diversity" and "unity."[18] The problem, of course, is more than a Pauline one; indeed, the challenge is ratcheted up when we seek to integrate the twenty-seven books written by at least nine different authors (NT theology) or the sixty-six books of the canon ("whole Bible" theology).

I might note here one other aspect of the "contingency" issue: the chronological spread of Paul's letters that I alluded to above. Many interpreters of Paul think his theology developed in significant ways over the time he was writing letters—and developed to such an extent that we find outright contradictions in his teaching on various issues. I will only say here that I am convinced that a sympathetic reading of his letters suggests that, while of course his thinking developed, that development did not entail contradiction of earlier views.[19] The differences in the theology expressed in the letters have far more to do with the occasional circumstances of those letters than their placement in a chronology of Paul's life.[20] Moreover, on the assumption (see pp. 49–51) that Paul wrote all thirteen letters attributed to him in the canon, the period of his letter-writing is no longer than the period between his conversion and the writing of his first letter. The point is that we should not think of Paul's foray into letter writing as an enterprise of a neophyte who does not yet really understand Christian reality.

---

16. N. T. Wright, *Paul and His Recent Interpreters: Some Contemporary Debates* (Minneapolis: Fortress, 2015), 26. I am taking a bit of a liberty in my application of this comment; N. T. Wright is referring to the scholarly landscape.

17. J. Christiaan Beker, *Paul the Apostle: The Triumph of God in Life and Thought* (Philadelphia: Fortress, 1980), 23–36. Beker clarified his thinking on these categories in a subsequent article: "Recasting Pauline Theology: The Coherence-Contingency Scheme as Interpretive Model," in *Pauline Theology, Volume 1: Thessalonians, Philippians, Galatians, Philemon*, ed. Jouette M. Bassler (Minneapolis: Augsburg Fortress, 1991), 15–24.

18. See, e.g., James D. G. Dunn, *Unity and Diversity in the New Testament: An Inquiry into the Character of Earliest Christianity*, 3rd ed. (London: SCM, 2006).

19. Sanders refers to "organic growth" in Paul's thought (E. P. Sanders, "Did Paul's Theology Develop?," in *The Word Leaps the Gap: Essays on Scripture and Theology in Honor of Richard B. Hays*, ed. J. Ross Wagner, C. Kavin Rowe, and Katherine Grieb [Grand Rapids: Eerdmans, 2008], 325–50).

20. Martin Hengel and Anna Maria Schwemer, *Paul between Damascus and Antioch: The Unknown Years* (Louisville: Westminster John Knox, 1997), 308–9.

A decade and a half of study, preaching, and interaction with other believers was behind Paul before he first put quill to parchment.

However, the problem of the diverse nature of Paul's contingent letters remains. It is tempting to sidestep this problem by contenting ourselves with a description of each author's theology (when producing a NT theology)[21] or the theological teaching of each individual letter (in the case of Pauline theology).[22] This style of biblical theology has the advantage of keeping us closer to the occasion that called forth each book, helping us avoid taking what the author says out of its context in ways that distort what he is saying. The problem, however, with this approach is that "it leaves all the most important work of collective comparison still to be done."[23] Of course, some would say that this limitation is built into the nature of biblical theology: further synthesis is in the hands of the systematic theologian. However, as I indicated above, while recognizing that the work of the systematic theologian is absolutely indispensable, I think the biblical theologian is called to enter into the work of synthesis. Most recent biblical theologians agree, as can be seen in both recent New Testament theologies[24] and Pauline theologies.[25]

If we are to attempt a synthesis of Paul's thought, to identify a "syntax of Paul's thought," as Hays puts it,[26] what are the categories we should use to do this? One option, which seems at first sight to keep us from imposing too much on Paul, is to use his own theological vocabulary as our structure. However, a second look quickly reveals fatal limitations in any kind of lexical approach. The point is a simple one: Paul gives key theological words different meanings in different contexts and letters. For instance, to lump together everything Paul says about *dikaiosynē*, "righteousness," would be to confuse what Paul says about forensic justification and what he says about the moral life of the believer (as I will argue on pp. 475–79). Writing about the *word* "righteousness" is quite appropriate; but this is not at all the same thing as writing about the theological

21. George Barker Stevens, *The Theology of the New Testament* (New York: Scribner's Sons, 1947); Rudolf Bultmann, *Theology of the New Testament*, 2 vols. (New York: Scribner's Sons, 1951, 1955); Werner Georg Kümmel, *The Theology of the New Testament* (Nashville: Abingdon, 1973); Hans Conzelmann, *An Outline of the Theology of the New Testament* (London: SCM, 1969); Leonhard Goppelt, *Theology of the New Testament*, 2 vols. (Grand Rapids: Eerdmans, 1981, 1982); Georg Strecker, *Theology of the New Testament* (Louisville: Westminster John Knox, 1996); Frank J. Matera, *New Testament Theology: Exploring Diversity and Unity* (Louisville: Westminster John Knox, 2007); I. Howard Marshall, *New Testament Theology: Many Witnesses, One Gospel* (Downers Grove, IL: InterVarsity Press, 2010); Stuhlmacher, *Biblical Theology of the New Testament*. A variant of this approach is to attempt to describe the chronological development of NT theology; see, e.g., Udo Schnelle, *The Theology of the New Testament* (Grand Rapids: Baker, 2007).

22. See, e.g., Paul Barnett, *Paul: Missionary of Jesus* (Grand Rapids: Eerdmans, 2008), 7–8.

23. G. B. Caird, *New Testament Theology*, ed. L. D. Hurst (Oxford: Clarendon, 1994), 18.

24. George Eldon Ladd, *A Theology of the New Testament*, rev. ed., ed. Donald A. Hagner (Grand Rapids: Eerdmans, 1993); Donald Guthrie, *New Testament Theology* (Downers Grove, IL: InterVarsity Press, 1981).

25. Hans Joachim Schoeps, *Paul: The Theology of the Apostle in the Light of Jewish Religious History* (Philadelphia: Westminster, 1961); Leander E. Keck, *Christ's First Theologian: The Shape of Paul's Thought* (Waco, TX: Baylor University Press, 2015) (with a separate chapter on Romans); Frank J. Matera, *God's Saving Grace: A Pauline Theology* (Grand Rapids: Eerdmans, 2012).

26. Richard B. Hays, "Crucified with Christ: A Synthesis of the Theology of 1 and 2 Thessalonians, Philemon, Philippians, and Galatians," in Bassler, *Pauline Theology*, 227–29.

concept to which that word—and, of course, other words as well—points. To write a theology of Paul, then, requires that we employ categories that are not provided to us in so many words by the text itself, and some distortion of Paul's thought is therefore an inevitable risk.

Most syntheses of Paul's theology are organized by topics that the authors of these syntheses think are key foci for Paul's theology; for example, "The Holy Spirit," "The Person of Jesus Christ," "The New Obedience," "The Whole Work of Christ," "The Destiny of Israel."[27] Another option, sometimes used to structure Paul's thought, at other times identified as a key substructure of this thought, is narrative or story. Scholars in recent years have shown keen interest in the possibilities of narrative to explain Paul's thought and to commend his thought to modern audiences.[28] This interest is bolstered by studies of the workings of the human brain that have drawn attention to the fundamental role of stories in shaping our thinking. But the more forceful argument is that the Jewish Paul would certainly have thought about Christ and his significance in narrative terms. Indeed, this point is somewhat self-evident. Paul proclaims Christ as the "climax" of Israel's history (Rom 10:4), who has fulfilled God's redemptive purposes. Paul's theology is also, of course, grounded in the gospel narrative: the Christ he proclaims is the one who was "sent" into this world, who died and rose again, and who, now ascended into heaven, will return in glory. And Paul's own story, especially his transformation from persecuting Jewish zealot to persecuted apostle of Christ, influences his theology in various ways.

The two most significant advocates of a narrative approach to Paul are Richard B. Hays and N. T. Wright. In his 1983 monograph on Galatians, Hays argued that chapter 3 of that letter could best be understood as a kind of running interaction with the story of Jesus. And Wright has made the story of Israel, continued and brought to climax in Jesus, the key framework for his understanding of Paul's theology. These seminal narrative construals have opened the floodgates to many other scholars, who have studied parts of Paul's letters or his letters as a whole within a narrative framework.

Narratives undoubtedly shape Paul's theology. However, I must register four reservations about the way narrative approaches are being used to interpret Paul. First, and most important, is the danger of imposing an underlying narrative on a text. We can

---

27. Another option for our synthesis is to use the template supplied by a single Pauline letter. James Dunn has taken this route in his magisterial survey of Paul's theology, using the argument of Romans as the framework for his discussion (James D. G. Dunn, *A Theology of Paul the Apostle* [Grand Rapids: Eerdmans, 1998]). The advantage of this approach is that it uses the categories that Paul himself uses rather than imposing categories on Paul that might distort his teaching. The disadvantage, of course, is that it privileges one contingent expression of Paul's theology over

others. Bruce Longenecker and Todd Still select a few themes to get a sense of Paul's theology (*Thinking through Paul: A Survey of His Life, Letters, and Theology* [Grand Rapids: Zondervan, 2015]).

28. J. R. Daniel Kirk therefore argues that we need to take a narrative approach to Paul in order to gain a hearing for his theology among modern readers (*Jesus Have I Loved, but Paul? A Narrative Approach to the Problem of Pauline Christianity* [Grand Rapids: Baker, 2010]).

grant that narratives are usually lurking somewhere behind Paul's teaching. But since he uses various narratives and gives them very different degrees of prominence, we need to make sure there are adequate textual indicators pointing to the use of a particular narrative. I am not convinced, for instance, that Galatians 3 has enough indicators to justify the claim that Paul is structuring his teaching according to the narrative of Jesus's life.

My second reservation about narrative approaches is the difficulty of determining the particular form of a narrative that Paul might be using. N. T. Wright, for instance, interprets Paul's theology in terms of his own particular reading of the story of Israel, some of whose elements are controversial—for example, that many, or most, Jews in Paul's day viewed the nation as still in exile (see further on this issue, pp. 420–22).[29]

Third, we have to recognize that Paul uses narrative in various ways. We might here borrow and apply to this issue a distinction made in literary studies: a distinction between a "linear plot" and an "episodic plot." Paul, of course, is familiar with the linear plot of the continuous narrative of God's redemptive plan. However, his actual reference to that narrative is usually episodic: that is, he uses various incidents from the story as a basis for his theologizing.[30] This is not to deny that Paul sometimes makes a point about the sequence of Israel's story. Galatians 3 is the most obvious case in point. Here Paul reminds his readers that the law was given "430 years" after God's promise to Abraham (Gal 3:17). However, while reminding his readers of the sequence of the story in this way, his actual "theologizing" takes the form of propositional conclusions drawn from that sequence: for example, the "inheritance" is based on promise (and its corollary, faith) and not on the law. Another explicit reminder of the Israel story comes in 1 Corinthians 10:1–5. Paul briefly narrates Israel's passing through the sea (their "baptism into Moses"), their eating and drinking of the spiritual food and drink God supplied in the wilderness, and their subsequent lapse into unbelief and consequent judgment by God. Again, Paul cites this episode from Israel's experience as a warning "example" (or "type," *typos*) for his readers (v. 6). The story itself is not Paul's theologizing; it provides the basis for his theology: here, that spiritual experiences will not shield God's people from his judgment. The Corinthians therefore must "be careful that

---

29. N. T. Wright enunciates his view in the first volume of his Christian Origins and the Question of God series: "Paul presupposes this story even when he does not expound it directly, and it is arguable that we can only understand the more limited narrative worlds of the different letters if we locate them at their appropriate points within this overall story-world, and indeed within the symbolic universe that accompanies it" (*The New Testament and the People of God* [Minneapolis: Fortress, 1992], 405). Note L. T. Johnson's warning: N. T. Wright has "the tendency to create an artificially unified worldview out of the complex world of first-century Judaism" (Luke Timothy Johnson, "A Historiographical

Response to Wright's Jesus," in *Jesus and the Restoration of Israel: A Critical Assessment of N. T. Wright's Jesus and the Victory of God*, ed. Carey C. Newman [Downers Grove, IL: InterVarsity Press, 1999], 210).

30. As Francis Watson puts it, "Paul's appeal to scriptural narrative does not incorporate the gospel into that narrative; rather, it aims to show how the narratives in their different ways attest this or that aspect of the gospel" ("Is There a Story in These Texts?," in *Narrative Dynamics in Paul: A Critical Assessment*, ed. Bruce Longenecker [Louisville: Westminster John Knox, 2002], 235).

you don't fall!" (v. 12). Of course, this "episodic" approach is evident in Paul's use of the gospel story also. Episodes from Christ's life become the basis for his theologizing, whether these be Christ's incarnation (2 Cor 8:9; Phil 2:5–8), his death (e.g., Rom 5:6–8), his resurrection (Rom 4:25), or his coming again in glory (1 Thess 4:13–18).

A fourth reservation is related to this last point. Paul simply does not (usually) use narrative as a form, or genre, to communicate his theology. The "narrative turn" in biblical theology has taken us too far down this new road. Michael Gorman claims, for instance, that Paul is "always telling stories"; Timothy Gombis argues that Ephesians "is a drama."[31] Yet I submit that a natural reading of Paul's letters rather suggests that they are organized not by a sequence of events in a story but by the issues Paul needs to address or by the logic of his own theology.[32] Narratives often lie at the base of Paul's letters, but the evidence that they shape his letters is not, in my view, compelling.[33] As I. Howard Marshall says, "Paul, however, does not so much tell a story in his letters as rather comment on the story and its implications for his readers."[34]

My point, to say it again, is not that narratives are unimportant for Paul's theology. The events the scriptural stories narrate determine the nature of the world Paul and his readers inhabit. It is a world locked in sin and death because of Adam's fall into sin. It is a world that remains under sin and death despite God's work in and through Israel. It is a world offered wonderful new hope on the basis of what God did through his Son on a Roman cross and in his victorious resurrection. And it is a world still sadly subject to the ravages of sin and death until God's Son returns from heaven to put all things right. My point, rather, is that while these stories, or, more accurately, key events in these stories, provide the raw material of Paul's theology, his theology itself takes the form of commentary on these events. Too often, an alleged narrative structure, or substructure, is used to interpret Pauline texts in ways that seem to me to distort or suppress points that he seems to be making in the text itself.[35] Mark Seifrid observes, "Those who adopt this sort of [narrative] reading generally appeal to

---

31. Michael Gorman, *Apostle of the Crucified Lord: A Theological Introduction to Paul and His Letters*, 2nd ed. (Grand Rapids: Eerdmans, 2017), 75; Timothy Gombis, *The Drama of Ephesians* (Downers Grove, IL: InterVarsity Press, 2010), 15. Ian Scott goes too far in claiming that "Paul's theological knowledge is *structured as* a grand unified story" (Ian W. Scott, *Paul's Way of Knowing: Story, Experience, and the Spirit* [Grand Rapids: Baker, 2009], 108; see esp. 89–156).

32. We may take as an example N. T. Wright's claim that the story of Israel is the substructure of Romans 3–8: exodus/redemption (ch. 3); covenant establishment (ch. 4); baptism/Red Sea (ch. 6); Sinai (ch. 7); Inheritance/Promised Land (ch. 8) ("New Exodus, New Inheritance: The Narrative Substructure of Romans 3–8," in *Romans and the People of God: Essays in Honor of Gordon D. Fee on the Occasion of His 65th Birthday*, ed. Sven

Soderlund and N. T. Wright [Grand Rapids: Eerdmans, 1999], 26–35). I am not convinced that Paul furnishes sufficient clues to direct our attention to this Israel story in these chapters.

33. For others who question the primacy of narrative, or story, in Paul, see esp. R. Barry Matlock, "The Arrow and the Web: Critical Reflections on a Narrative Approach to Paul," in B. Longenecker, *Narrative Dynamics in Paul*, 44–57; Watson, "Is There a Story in These Texts?," 231–39. On Galatians, see A. Andrew Das, *Paul and the Stories of Israel: Grand Thematic Narratives in Galatians* (Minneapolis: Fortress, 2016).

34. Marshall, *New Testament Theology*, 423.

35. See also, e.g., James D. G. Dunn, *New Testament Theology: An Introduction*, Library of Biblical Theology (Nashville: Abingdon, 2009), 14–16.

an implicit narrative that informs the statements which appear in the text. The text stands in constant danger of being overrun by the imagination of the interpreter, rather than being illuminated by a story to which it alludes."[36] While, therefore, giving due attention to the way narratives inform Paul's theology, I will not use any particular narrative as the lens through which we view Paul's teaching.

As I noted above, there is virtue in both a letter-by-letter exposition of Paul's thought and in a more inclusive synthesis of his thought. Some recent New Testament theologies[37] and Pauline theologies[38] take this combined approach, and this is also the approach I adopt in this book.[39] My synthesis, additionally, uses the category of "realm" as a basic organizational rubric (see the chapter headings for part 3 of the book). Of course, I need to justify the use of this concept, but I cannot do so until we have a sense of the basic contours, or framework, of Paul's thinking.

36. Mark A. Seifrid, "The Narrative of Scripture and Justification by Faith: A Fresh Response to N. T. Wright," *CTQ* 72 (2008): 26–27.

37. Ben Witherington III, *The Indelible Image: The Theology and Ethical Thought World of the New Testament*, 2 vols. (Downers Grove, IL: InterVarsity Press, 2009, 2010); Ferdinand Hahn, *Theologie des Neuen Testaments*, 3rd ed.; 2 vols. (Tübingen: Mohr Siebeck, 2011); Ulrich Wilckens, *Theologie des Neuen Testaments*, 6 vols.; 2nd–4th ed. (Neukirchen-Vluyn: Neukirchener, 2014)

(his first four volumes ["Band I"] survey the thought of early Christianity in general chronological sequence; the second two ["Band II"] provide a synthesis of NT thought).

38. Udo Schnelle, *Apostle Paul: His Life and Theology* (Grand Rapids: Baker, 2005).

39. I strongly endorse this two-pronged approach. But, to give credit where credit is due, the editor of this series required this dual approach.

Chapter 2

THE SHAPE OF PAUL'S THOUGHT

1 SOME METHODOLOGICAL ISSUES

In the pages that follow, I will be examining trees—Paul's teaching about issues such as justification, the church, or the gospel. Indeed, I will often peer more closely to scrutinize the bark on the trees—verses and paragraphs that contribute to his teaching about specific issues. The old adage applies here: It will be easy to lose sight of the forest in our focus on bark and trees. The danger is not only that we might lose sight of the "big issues" that Paul wants to communicate to the church. The danger is also that we will fail to recognize the nature of the trees by not keeping them in their appropriate forest context.

The importance of interpreting a person's language against the background of their own culture and worldview is obvious. In the case of Paul, we can readily identify this general background: the first-century Greco-Roman world, and, within that world, the Judaism in which he grew up and by which he was formed. His Jewish faith was, of course, grounded in the Old Testament, which Paul would have learned from an early age—perhaps in Hebrew but certainly, as his references to it attest, in Greek. Moreover, as a Jew who became a Jesus follower, Paul's thinking, as we find it in his letters, is decisively shaped by his encounter with the risen Christ and by early Christian teaching to which he was exposed after his conversion.

The relevance of these several inputs into Paul's thinking is universally acknowledged. Consensus quickly disappears, however, when we probe further to determine the balance among these several inputs and to identify the more specific forms each of these inputs might have taken. Indeed, it is not much of an exaggeration to say that many influential interpretations of Paul's theology are rooted in a decision to prioritize one particular background input over another. Some might argue, then, that a truly "objective" reading of Paul would avoid using background data to interpret his language and letters. However, as we widely recognize today, we all inevitably bring such data to the reading of the text, whether the data be taken from the first-century Greco-Roman/ Jewish world or subtly, and perhaps unconsciously, from the modern church world. Reading Paul without a background is impossible and, as I noted above, unwise: Paul's words, like anyone else's, are shaped by the various influences on his thinking.

I do worry, however, that extratextual factors have played an outsize role in interpretations of the apostle in recent years. Modern scholars have access to an incredible store of information about the world of Paul's day and have developed sophisticated interpretive methods to process and apply that information. All this is very good. The danger, however, is that we might illegitimately privilege one particular stream of information over another—often determined by the material with which the particular interpreter is most familiar. A scholar such as Troels Engberg-Pedersen, for instance, brings his expertise in the world of the Greek Stoics to bear on our understanding of Paul—with obvious benefits but also with the potential of distorting the apostle's teaching in a certain direction. Another danger is that one might interpret Paul's teaching in the context of one particular view of a background source. N. T. Wright, for instance, sheds light on Paul's theology by setting it in the context of the story of Israel. But, for all its strengths, I worry that Wright's interpretation of Paul is too strongly influenced by a particular form of Israel's story that he adopts.

What is needed, then, is to give the text of Paul's letters hermeneutical priority. Of course, virtually all interpreters of Paul would agree in principle. But it is very difficult to put into practice—simply because the text *always* has a context. There is no such thing as a "bare text" that can sit in judgment over the context in which we interpret it. However, while recognizing the challenge, I nonetheless am convinced that the text itself still has a fundamental role to play in our assessments of the background data we bring to it. The interpretation resulting from reading within a certain perspective must be evaluated in terms of its ability to provide a natural reading of the text—"text" being understood broadly to include (in this case) *all* the relevant words in all thirteen letters of Paul.

With these brief and, no doubt, somewhat naïve, methodological musings behind us, I now turn to considering two large issues as we attempt to read Paul's "trees" in terms of the "forest." I will first briefly survey some of the most important influences on the way Paul is using his words. Second, I will offer my own view on the particular way of thinking that shapes Paul's words.

2 FORMATIVE INFLUENCES

What we call "Paul's theology" is our attempt to describe the coherent set of beliefs that lie behind and generate the various specific teachings found in his letters. This set of beliefs, in turn, is Paul's reflection on the Christ event. It is that event, whose significance was brought home to Paul at his conversion, that generated Paul's theology. However, Paul developed his theology in constant interaction with several shaping influences: most notably the Old Testament, Second Temple Jewish thought, early Christian teaching, and the teaching of Jesus.

2.1 The Old Testament[1]

Paul's theological reasoning could almost be characterized as a dialogue with Scripture. As Francis Watson puts it, "Engagement with scripture is fundamental to Pauline" teaching.[2] Paul, of course, was shaped by the Old Testament from birth. His parents undoubtedly taught him the Scriptures (they were "Hebrews"; see Phil 3:5). His education under Gamaliel (Acts 22:3) would have involved careful study of the Old Testament. When he replaced Torah with Christ at the center of his thinking, his understanding of the Old Testament underwent a radical revision, but his commitment to its authority remained as strong as ever—as the well-known text in 2 Timothy 3:16 indicates: "All Scripture is God-breathed and is useful for teaching, rebuking, correcting and training in righteousness."[3] Paul can envisage no Messiah, no "good news," that is not anchored in the Scriptures (e.g., Rom 1:2). The "use of the Old Testament in the New Testament" is, of course, a vast area of study, even when we pare it down to the "use of the Old Testament in Paul." I will comment on particular texts as they arise in our expository survey; here I want simply to provide a few orientation markers.

2.1.1 Forms of Reference

Paul uses the language of "old covenant" only once (2 Cor 3:14), but he does not quite mean the same thing we do when we use this phrase to denote the first part of the canon of Scripture.[4] There was, of course, no "new covenant" or "New Testament" in the canonical sense in Paul's day (although there is evidence of some movement toward one; see p. 17). Paul refers to what we would call the "Old Testament" simply as the "Scriptures" (*graphai*—five times: Rom 1:2; 15:4; 16:26; 1 Cor 15:3, 4) or "Scripture" (*graphē*—nine times: Rom 4:3; 9:17; 10:11; 11:2; Gal 3:8, 22; 4:30; 1 Tim 5:18; 2 Tim 3:16).

Paul integrates these Scriptures into his theology in several ways.[5]

2.1.1.1 Explicit References and Quotations

Paul appeals to the Old Testament explicitly in two ways. First, he refers to people, events, and institutions: for example, "just as Eve was deceived by the serpent's cunning" (2 Cor 11:3); "the promises were spoken to Abraham and to his seed" (Gal 3:16); "they all [Israelites] passed through the sea" (1 Cor 10:1). Second, he quotes from the Old Testament. A quotation is marked either by an introductory formula

---

1. On the general subject, see the comparatively recent overview in J. Ross Wagner, "Paul and Scripture," in *The Blackwell Companion to Paul*, ed. Stephen Westerholm (Chichester: Wiley-Blackwell, 2011), 154–71; and also Steve Moyise, *Paul and Scripture: Studying the New Testament Use of the Old Testament* (Grand Rapids: Baker, 2010).

2. Francis Watson, *Paul and the Hermeneutics of Faith*, 2nd ed. (Edinburgh: T&T Clark, 2016), 5.

3. For discussion and defense of this translation, see pp. 344–45.

4. As Harris argues, it is basically equivalent to "Moses" (v. 15), referring to "the Sinaitic covenant in its written form" (Murray J. Harris, *The Second Epistle to the Corinthians: A Commentary on the Greek Text*, NIGTC [Grand Rapids: Eerdmans, 2005], 302).

5. See E. Earle Ellis, *Paul's Use of the Old Testament* (Grand Rapids: Baker, 1957), 11–20.

(e.g., "as Scripture says" [Rom 10:11]; "Isaiah boldly says" [Rom 10:20]) or by the use of language so well-known that listeners or readers would recognize its source (see, e.g., Rom 10:13; 1 Cor 10:26). Paul's quotations are spread very unevenly across his letters:

Romans: 51 (25 in chs. 9–11)
1 Corinthians: 14
2 Corinthians: 11
Galatians: 10
Ephesians: 3–4
Colossians: 0
Philippians: 0
1 Thessalonians: 0
2 Thessalonians: 0
1 Timothy: 1
2 Timothy: 1
Philemon: 0[6]

Paul's favorite sources for these quotations are Isaiah (21), the Psalms (17), Genesis (13), and Deuteronomy (9). Paul's quotations usually follow closely the Greek textual tradition that became enshrined in the Septuagint, although there are notable exceptions (e.g., Isa 59:20 in Rom 11:26; Ps 68:18 in Eph 4:8).[7] Scholars wonder about what kind of Old Testament text Paul might have had available to him. Do the "scrolls" of 2 Timothy 4:13 refer to Old Testament texts, or compilations of Old Testament texts? Did the availability of texts have something to do with the uneven distribution of his quotations? Did Paul have texts memorized? These and related questions have occupied scholars for centuries, with no definite conclusions having been reached.[8]

2.1.1.2 Allusions (and "Echoes")

The absence of quotations in some of Paul's letters does not mean that these letters are unaffected by the Scriptures. Paul has many other ways of bringing Scripture

---

6. These numbers can vary depending on what one counts as a quotation and how one counts places where Paul combines quotations. See, in general, Christopher D. Stanley, *Paul and the Language of Scripture: Citation Techniques in the Pauline Epistles and Contemporary Literature*, SNTSMS 69 (Cambridge: Cambridge University Press, 1992).

7. For the "consensus" that Paul was working almost exclusively with a Greek text of the OT, see Dietrich-Alex Koch, *Die Schrift als Zeuge des Evangeliums: Untersuchungen zur Verwendung und zum Verständnis der Schrift bei Paulus*, BHT (Tübingen: Mohr Siebeck, 1986); Christopher D. Stanley, *Arguing with Scripture:*

The Rhetoric of Quotations in the Letters of Paul (New York: T&T Clark, 2004); J. Ross Wagner, *Heralds of the Good News: Isaiah and Paul "in Concert" in the Letter to the Romans*, NovTSup 101 (Leiden: Brill, 2002), 5–8. For a contrary view, see Timothy H. Lim, *Holy Scripture in the Qumran Commentaries and Pauline Letters* (Oxford: Clarendon, 1997), who thinks that Paul may occasionally be using Hebrew or Aramaic texts.

8. For a recent survey, see Leonard Greenspoon, "By the Letter? Word for Word? Scriptural Citation in Paul," in *Paul and Scripture: Extending the Conversation*, ed. Christopher D. Stanley; ECL 9 (Atlanta: SBL, 2012), 9–24.

into his theologizing. The most notable of these is by means of "allusion," which we might define in a general way as a conscious and deliberate choice of language that is designed to draw listeners' or readers' attention to a particular text, or series of texts, in Scripture. A good example of an allusion in this sense is the language of "bearing fruit and growing" in Colossians 1:6, 10. In my commentary on Colossians, I say:

> The language *bearing fruit and growing* is reminiscent of the Genesis creation story, where God commands human beings to "be fruitful and increase in number" (Gen. 1:28; see also 1:22). After the Flood, the mandate is reiterated (Gen. 8:17; 9:1, 7), and the same language is later used in God's promises to Abraham and the patriarchs that he would "increase" their number and "multiply" their seed (e.g., Gen. 17:20; 28:3; 35:11). The nation Israel attains this blessing in Egypt (Gen. 48:4; Exod. 1:7) but then, of course, suffers judgment and dispersal. So the formula appears again in God's promises to re-gather his people after the exile (Jer. 3:16; 23:3). Paul may, then, be deliberately echoing a biblical-theological motif according to which God's original mandate to humans finds preliminary fulfillment in the nation Israel but ultimate fulfillment in the world-wide transformation of people into the image of God by means of their incorporation into Christ, *the* "image of God."[9]

The presence of this allusion, and many others, in Colossians reveals that the Old Testament remains here an important source and dialogue partner for Paul—even though there are no quotations in this letter.[10]

Following the groundbreaking study of Richard Hays on Paul's use of the Old Testament, many scholars are now also identifying what they call "echoes" of Scripture in Paul.[11] There does not seem to be an agreed-upon definition of "echo" among scholars, but it generally refers to an allusion to Scripture that may not be consciously intended by the author. Moreover, some view "echoes" as reverberating back and forth between the text and its readers. I am not convinced that "echo" in this somewhat technical sense is a useful category to use in thinking of Paul's use of Scripture.[12] I am also a bit skeptical of the popular current use of "intertextuality" to refer to Paul's engagement with Scripture, since this word often carries with it quite a bit of philosophical and hermeneutical baggage that I find questionable.[13]

---

9. *The Letters to the Colossians and to Philemon*, PNTC (Grand Rapids: Eerdmans, 2008), 88.

10. For these allusions in Colossians, see esp. Christopher A. Beetham, *Echoes of Scripture in the Letter of Paul to the Colossians*, BibInt 96 (Leiden: Brill, 2009; repr., Atlanta: SBL, 2010).

11. Richard B. Hays, *Echoes of Scripture in the Letters of Paul* (New Haven: Yale University Press, 1989), 14–29.

12. See the discussions in Das, *Paul and the Stories of Israel*,

4–16; Matthew Scott, *The Hermeneutics of Christological Psalmody in Paul: An Intertextual Enquiry*, SNTSMS 158 (Cambridge: Cambridge University Press, 2014), 11–18.

13. For some useful distinctions, see Russell L. Meek, "Intertexuality, Inner-Biblical Exegesis, and Inner-Biblical Allusion: The Ethics of a Methodology," *Bib* 95 (2014): 280–91; and for warnings about the implications of the term *intertextuality*, see esp. Richard J. Schultz, "Intertextuality, Canon and 'Undecidability':

Detecting allusions in Paul's letters is an inevitably subjective, and therefore very contested enterprise. How many words must an Old Testament text and New Testament text have in common to justify an allusion? How unusual must these words be? To what extent should we consider audience capacity? How much Old Testament did Paul's mainly gentile readers know? Richard Hays has sought to bring a bit more objectivity to the task by setting forth seven criteria.[14] However, the criteria he identifies are, for the most part, those that scholars have been using for centuries to identify allusions. And the evaluation of these criteria remains quite subjective, so that I am not sure his method takes us very far forward.

2.1.1.3 Conceptual Influence

Paul's theological vocabulary was shaped by the Old Testament and his Jewish environment. It is therefore generally agreed that, overall, the first and best place to look when we want to unpack the meaning of a key term in Paul is the Old Testament, especially in Greek. Thus, for instance, I argue that the word *hilastērion* in Romans 3:25 is an allusion to the "atonement cover" in Israel's tabernacle, a piece of furniture that figured prominently in the Day of Atonement ceremony (Lev 16). Through its association with this feature of the tabernacle and its prominence on the Day of Atonement, this word, then, would have communicated to Paul and other first-cenury Jews the concept of God's atoning work. As Anthony Thiselton reminds us, the significance of the words Paul uses is enriched by the way in which they are used to refer to particular experiences in the history of Israel.[15] However, we should not limit the influence to vocabulary only. Paul will sometimes use a word not found in the Greek Old Testament to describe an Old Testament concept. The word *huiothesia*—"adoption"—is not found in the Greek Old Testament and obviously has a background in Paul's Greco-Roman world. However, it also refers to the Old Testament motif of Israel as God's son. Paul's reading of the Old Testament shapes his "big picture" ideas also. The God he regularly refers to is the God Paul has come to know through Scripture. The salvation-historical framework within which Paul does his theologizing (see above, pp. 27–34) is rooted in the scriptural story.

2.1.1.4 Structural Influence

Matthew may arrange his story of Jesus by highlighting five discourses of Jesus in imitation of the five books of Torah. Does Paul do anything like this? Some scholars have thought so,[16] but I am not convinced by the arguments I have seen. In another

---

Understanding Isaiah's 'New Heavens and New Earth' (Isaiah 65:17–25)," *BBR* 20 (2010): 19–38.

14. Hays, *Echoes*, 29–32.

15. Anthony C. Thiselton, *The Hermeneutics of Doctrine* (Grand Rapids: Eerdmans, 2007), 320–21.

16. E.g., N. T. Wright's identification of an OT narrative substructure behind Romans 3–8 (see above, p. 13n32). Tom Holland argues that Romans is structured around the sequence of "new exodus" prophecies in Isaiah (*Contours of Pauline Theology: A Radical New Survey of the Influences on Paul's Biblical Writings* [Fearn, Ross-shire: Mentor, 2004], 31–34).

sense, however, the structure of the Old Testament and its story is obviously important in shaping Paul's theological convictions. Promise, and its corollary, faith, is central because it came before the giving of the law (Gal 3). For a similar reason, God, Paul assumes everywhere, acts in grace toward his creation—as his initiative in calling Israel reveals.

2.1.1.5 Appropriating the Story

I noted above that it has become popular to think that Paul's theology is under-girded and informed by a continuation of the story of Israel. In a general sense, this is certainly true: Christ, and the people gathered around him, bring the story begun in the garden of Eden and continued in the experience of Israel to its culmination: New Testament events "fill up" (*plēroō*) the Old Testament story.[17] However, we must be cautious when we press for the detailed contours of that story as Paul understands it; some approaches have dropped down on Paul a particular form of the story that may not have adequate support from his letters. At the same time, as we have argued, Paul also appeals to particular episodes in the story of Israel to illuminate gospel events. That appeal sometimes takes the form of what is usually called "typology," according to which Paul sees Old Testament people and events as foreshadowings of gospel people and events. Adam, for instance, is a "type" (*typos*) of Christ (Rom 5:14); disobedient Israelites wandering in the wilderness were potential "types" (*typoi*) of the Corinthians, should they fall into sin (1 Cor 10:6).

2.1.2 Paul and the Old Testament: Continuity and Discontinuity

The connections Paul draws between Old Testament texts and New Testament circumstances sometimes appear rather arbitrary. He claims that the inclusion of gentiles in the new-realm people of God was predicted by Hosea (Rom 9:25–26; see Hos 1:10; 2:23), but Hosea was referring to Jews—the ten northern tribes of Israel. Paul contrasts the "righteousness of the law" with the "righteousness of faith" in Romans 10:5–8, arguing that the latter is prefigured in Deuteronomy 30:11–14—yet Moses in the Deuteronomy passage is speaking of the gracious provision of the law. He appears to change the verb in Psalm 68:18 from "receive" to "give" so that he can apply the verse to the risen Christ's provision of gifted people for the edification of the church (Eph 4:8). Texts such as these have given rise to the claim that Paul simply reads his own ideas into the Old Testament, changing its meaning or its text to suit his own interests. It is often suggested, moreover, that this way of reading the Old Testament is historically plausible, with Paul simply following the methods of Jewish exegetes of his day.[18]

---

17. Paul does not use "fulfillment" language often to refer to the relationship of OT and NT: "fulfill" (*plēroō*) in Rom 13:8; Gal 5:14; "fullness" (*plērōma*) in Rom 13:10; Gal 4:4; Eph 1:10.

18. E.g., Peter Enns, *The Evolution of Adam: What the Bible Does and Doesn't Say about Human Origins* (Grand Rapids: Brazos, 2012), 101–17.

On this latter point, we must note, first, that "Jewish methods" of interpreting the Old Testament were quite diverse, and certainly not as arbitrary as is sometimes suggested. Second, while Paul at times appears to imitate his Jewish contemporaries in some of his methods,[19] there are also considerable differences in approach. Here I find it helpful to distinguish between two levels in the process of contemporizing Scripture.[20] One level is the "appropriation technique"—the specific, textually oriented means by which Old Testament texts are applied to new circumstances. The second level is the "hermeneutical axiom"—the set of theological suppositions that lie behind and guide the contemporizing process. Paul's appropriation of Scripture sometimes uses appropriation techniques popular in his day. But, of course, he disagrees with most of his Jewish contemporaries on the second issue. For instance, the covenanters responsible for the Dead Sea Scrolls were convinced that their community was what the prophets were talking about, and they naturally therefore applied the prophets' predictions to the circumstances of their community. Paul, on the other hand, was convinced that Christ was the ultimate goal of Old Testament teaching, and he therefore claims these prophecies found their fulfillment in Jesus and his followers.

The apparent arbitrariness of Paul's Old Testament interpretation is considerably mitigated when we take his hermeneutical axioms into account (see my discussion of the specific passages cited above in my exposition). When we view Paul's use of the Old Testament as a whole, I am generally persuaded of the view argued so ably by scholars such as Greg Beale: Paul usually shows sensitivity to the context and meaning of the Old Testament passages he quotes and to which he alludes.[21] Fairness to the data in Paul's letters demands balance on this matter. Scripture must be read both "forward" and "backward."[22] On the one hand, therefore, Paul inserts Christ and the community he founds into the existing Old Testament story of redemption. As John M. G. Barclay puts it, reversing the direction of language Hays made so prominent, "Paul finds *echoes*

---

19. E.g., Paul's use of "consider" (*logizomai*) to join a text from the Torah (Gen 15:6) with one from the Writings (Ps 32:1–2) in Rom 4:1–8.

20. I develop this idea in my dissertation, now in published form: Douglas J. Moo, *The Old Testament in the Gospel Passion Narratives* (Eugene, OR: Wipf & Stock, 2007 [1983]), 25–74. Dunn (*Theology of Paul*, 172–73) makes a similar distinction.

21. See esp. G. K. Beale, *The Right Doctrine from the Wrong Texts? Essays on the Use of the Old Testament in the New* (Grand Rapids: Baker, 1994); see also idem, *Handbook on the New Testament Use of the Old Testament: Exegesis and Interpretation* (Grand Rapids: Baker, 2012); idem, "The Cognitive Peripheral Vision of Biblical Authors," *WTJ* 76 (2014): 263–93; Mitchell Kim, "Respect for Context and Authorial Intention: Setting the Epistemological Bar," in Stanley, *Paul and Scripture: Extending the Conversation*, 115–29. For a contrary view, see esp. Steve Moyise,

"Does Paul Respect the Context of His Quotations?," in Stanley, *Paul and Scripture: Extending the Conversation*, 106–13. Beale, and others who argue as he does, are carrying forward the seminal insights of C. H. Dodd in his small, but enormously influential book, *According to the Scriptures: The Substructure of New Testament Theology* (London: Nisbet, 1953). The specifics of what this reading of the OT in the NT looks like are worked out in G. K. Beale and D. A. Carson, eds., *Commentary on the New Testament Use of the Old Testament* (Grand Rapids: Baker, 2007).

22. See esp. Watson, *Paul and the Hermeneutics of Faith*, 273–74. As Luke Timothy Johnson puts it, "In the Pauline dialectic, Scripture is at least as much read in light of Christ as Christ is read in light of Scripture" (Luke Timothy Johnson, "The Paul of the Letters: A Catholic Perspective," in *Four Views of the Apostle Paul* [ed. Michael F. Bird; Grand Rapids: Zondervan, 2012], 49).

of the gospel in the Scriptures of Israel."[23] But, on the other hand, he also interprets that story in light of the climax of that story in Christ. If we eliminate any "forward" reading in Paul, we end up with no genuine continuity between Old Testament and New: if Paul shapes the story entirely in light of Christ, he can hardly be seen as its climax or fulfillment in any meaningful sense. However, we cannot eliminate the "backward" reading of the story either. Stories make sense, ultimately, when we see the whole picture. To eliminate Christ from that picture would be to try to understand only a part of the story. The Judaism that was the matrix of the early Christians provided several and, to some extent, mutually conflicting "forward" readings of the Old Testament story.[24] Paul's claim is that a "true" reading of that story must take its hermeneutical key from the significance of the Christ event. It is the cross that sheds light "backward" on what the Old Testament ultimately "means."

On the basis of his understanding of the whole story, and especially in light of its consummation in Christ, Paul often discovers what we might call a "fuller sense" (*sensus plenior*) in the Old Testament. This "fuller sense" usually has an organic relationship to the "original sense" and can be seen as fitting in light of the hermeneutical axioms Paul assumes.[25] In light of these complications, our assessment of the "validity" of Paul's use of the Old Testament must be somewhat nuanced. We will have to be careful about claims that we can *prove* that Paul's interpretation of the Old Testament is correct at every point. Our approach should be governed by what Kevin Vanhoozer, speaking of general hermeneutics, calls "fallibilism."[26] In contrast to the tendency of some "modernist" interpretations to insist that we can draw a straight line from *the* meaning of the Old Testament to Christ, a "fallibilistic" approach to the use of the Old Testament in the New admits that the Old Testament text does not always provide enough information for us to be certain about the precise shape of its fulfillment; we could not know that Deuteronomy 30:11–14 was speaking ultimately about the word of the gospel (Rom 10:6–8). But in contrast to the tendency of postmodern hermeneutical nihilism, "fallibilism" also insists that our interpretation of the Old Testament,

---

23. John M. G. Barclay, *Paul and the Gift* (Grand Rapids: Eerdmans, 2015), 418 (emphasis original).

24. I need briefly to justify my use here and throughout this volume of the appellation "Christian." Recent study of Paul has emphasized his continuing allegiance to Judaism (in some sense) and noted that "the parting of the ways" between Judaism and Christianity took place many years after Paul's life. To call him a "Christian," then, it is alleged, is anachronistic and misleading. I deal with these issues elsewhere (pp. 573–75). Here, I will simply note that, without ignoring Paul's concern to maintain continuity with Judaism, the view he adopted after his confrontation with Christ differed dramatically from most forms of Judaism in his day—to such an extent, indeed, that Paul felt it necessary to persecute the new movement. In light of this obvious discontinuity, then, I think it appropriate to use the NT-sanctioned word "Christian" (Acts 11:26; 26:28; 1 Pet 4:16) to describe Paul and other Jesus followers of his day.

25. See Douglas J. Moo and Andrew David Naselli, "The Problem of the New Testament's Use of the Old Testament," in *The Enduring Authority of the Christian Scriptures*, ed. D. A. Carson (Grand Rapids: Eerdmans, 2016), 702–46.

26. Kevin J. Vanhoozer, "Christ and Concept: Doing Theology and the 'Ministry' of Philosophy," in *Doing Theology in Today's World: Essays in Honor of Kenneth S. Kantzer*, ed. John D. Woodbridge and Thomas Edward McComiskey (Grand Rapids: Zondervan, 1991), 99–145, esp. 103.

while often derived from the New Testament, must be subject to testing. We may not be able to explain a particular appropriation of the Old in the New from the ground up, each step following inevitably and rationally from the previous one, and all resting on an unshakable foundation of agreed-upon propositions. But any explanation of the use of the Old Testament in the New must nevertheless be able to survive the test of rationality and adequacy. Does it make sense? Does it make better sense than the interpretation of the Old Testament found at Qumran, or in the rabbis? We still may not be able to "prove" that the New Testament is the fulfillment of the Old Testament. But what we can do is ask whether the overall framework of biblical truth established by the New Testament interpretation of the Old Testament validates the assumption of their unity.[27] Evangelicals dare not give up the quest to demonstrate this fundamental biblical unity.[28]

2.2 Second Temple Jewish Teaching

Paul grew up with an intimate understanding of the Scriptures. But that understanding was mediated by the Second Temple Jewish reading of Scripture that Paul was exposed to as a child in his home and in his education under Gamaliel in Jerusalem. As has been pertinently stressed in recent decades, Judaism in Paul's day held a variety of viewpoints on the meaning of Scripture. Paul claims to be a Pharisee, so we can be fairly confident that it was the Pharisaic approach to Scripture that Paul would have adopted. However, even Pharisaism in Paul's day was diverse, with a more "liberal" wing open to new approaches and movements (in Jewish tradition associated with the rabbi Hillel) and a stricter wing (identified with the teaching of the rabbi Shammai). Gamaliel's attitude to the early Christian movement (Acts 5:34–39) suggests that he was a "Hillelite," and we might have expected Paul to fall into line with this open view. However, Paul's own emphasis on his "zeal," a zeal that led him to persecute the early church, suggests that he may have been identified with the "Shammai wing" of Pharisaism. The fact is that we simply don't have enough data to draw certain conclusions about the particular shape of Paul's own Judaism.[29]

What we can be sure about is that Paul's "Copernican revolution"—replacing the Torah with Jesus the Son of God as the center of his worldview—required him to reread all the Scriptures in light of their fulfillment in Christ. His new perspective on Scripture plays a role in both his development and application of his theology almost everywhere, to one degree or another. Of course, this rereading does not mean that Paul abandoned all the views he had held as a Pharisaic Jew. After all, many aspects of

---

27. See my essay, "Paul's Universalizing Hermeneutic in Romans," *The Southern Baptist Journal of Theology* 11 (Fall 2007): 62–90.

28. This point has been made by Greg Beale in dialogue with Peter Enns ("Myth, History, and Inspiration: A Review Article of Inspiration and Incarnation," *JETS* 49 [2006]: 287–312).

29. On this issue see, e.g., Schnelle, *Apostle Paul*, 69.

Jewish theology simply reproduced the teaching of the Scriptures themselves. Paul's rereading obviously confirmed standard Jewish teachings, such as the oneness of God, the unique role of Israel in God's plan of salvation, the covenant-based structure of that plan, the necessity of sacrifice to deal with sins, etc. However, there were, of course, points of discontinuity as well, as Paul's rereading in light of Christ shifted his earlier Jewish perspective. Indeed, some parts of Paul letters rather explicitly take the form of a debate with Jewish views of his time over the meaning and ultimate significance of Scripture: for example, Galatians 3:14–25; 4:21–31; Romans 4, 9–11; 2 Corinthians 3:7–18.

2.3 Early Christian Tradition

Paul makes two points about his dependence on the teaching of other early Christians. On the one hand, he says in Galatians, "I did not receive [the gospel] from any man, nor was I taught it; rather, I received it by revelation from Jesus Christ" (Gal 1:12). He then goes on in this letter to proclaim his independence from the Jerusalem apostles, "those who seemed to be pillars" (Gal 2:9; my translation). On the other hand, Paul also claims that the basic gospel outline of Christ's death, burial, and resurrection that he "passed on" to the Corinthians was something he in turn "received" (1 Cor 15:3). The language of "receive" generally indicated receiving traditional teaching in Paul's day (*paralambanō*; see also 1 Cor 11:23; Gal 1:9; Phil 4:9). We can resolve this tension if we read Paul as claiming that he was taught "truths" about Christ and the gospel by others, but that he was convinced of *the* "truth" of these matters because he had himself encountered the risen Christ. Paul "passes on" tradition that he himself has verified via his own experience of Christ.[30]

Paul's inclusion of fellow workers in the salutations of his letters also implies that his theology was, to some degree, a collaborative effort. I do not think that these salutations indicate coauthorship (pp. 52–53). But they do show that Paul includes other important early Christian leaders in his theologizing—or, at least, as giving their stamp of approval to the theology he communicates to his churches. Another way Paul brings other early Christians into his theologizing is by quoting hymns or confessional statements that were apparently already circulating in the church. Paul appeals explicitly (probably) to this kind of tradition in Ephesians 5:14: "This is why it is said: 'Wake up, sleeper, rise from the dead, and Christ will shine on you.'"

Scholars have, however, identified many other such quotations in the Pauline letters that are not explicitly introduced as such. There is considerable debate about where these are found, the degree to which Paul may have redacted them, and their exact place of origin in the church. The texts most often cited in this regard are Romans 1:3–4;

---

30. See Ladd, *Theology of the New Testament*, 425–32.

Philippians 2:6–11; Colossians 1:15–20; and 1 Timothy 3:16.[31] But there are almost certainly others as well. One important point relating to the theology of these passages should be made: unless Paul indicates otherwise, we must assume that Paul agrees with what he quotes from these hymns and confessions. Whatever their source (and we must recognize how little we can know of the sources Paul may have used), these passages are fair game for a reconstruction of Paul's theology.

2.4 Jesus

A longstanding tradition of interpretation sees a deep gulf between the teaching of Jesus and the theology of Paul.[32] Paul, on this view, has turned the simple ethical call of the teacher of Nazareth into a speculative, philosophically influenced system. Paul, then, is the "second founder of Christianity," with an impact on later theology far more important than that of the "first founder."[33] Few hold this view in so radical a form anymore, although many still presume a considerable degree of independence between the two.[34]

However, it must be said that Paul's letters can, at first sight, give the impression that he developed his theology in relative independence from Jesus. He seldom cites Jesus's teaching explicitly (1 Cor 7:10; 9:14; 11:23–26; 14:37; 1 Thess 4:15–16 [?]; 1 Tim 5:18). Nor does he very often refer to events in Jesus's life—apart, of course, from Jesus's death and resurrection (see pp. 358–60 for fuller discussion of this point). A closer look at the letters, however, suggests more connections between Paul and Jesus than first thought.

In addition to the explicit references mentioned above, there are a fair number of texts in which verbal resemblances point to Paul's dependence on the teaching of Jesus (see esp. Rom 12:14; 14:4; 1 Cor 13:2; and 1 Thess 5:2, 4).[35] The teaching of Jesus may also have informed Paul's theology in a number of other ways.[36] Dependence is difficult to prove, for some of the similarities could be explained by Paul's reliance on early Christian tradition. Moreover, at the end of the day, as James Dunn puts it, "Even when the evidence of the Jesus tradition is pressed as hard as it seems to bear,

---

31. On so-called NT "hymns," see e.g., Ralph P. Martin, "New Testament Hymns: Background and Development," *ExpTim* 94 (1983): 132–36; Stephen E. Fowl, *The Story of Christ in the Ethics of Paul: An Analysis of the Hymnic Material in the Pauline Corpus*, JSNTSup 36 (Sheffield: Sheffield Academic, 1990); Matthew E. Gordley, *New Testament Christological Hymns: Exploring Texts, Contexts, and Significance* (Downers Grove, IL: InterVarsity Press, 2018); Benjamin Edsall and Jennifer R. Strawbridge, "The Songs We Used to Sing? Hymn 'Traditions' and Reception in the Pauline Letters," *JSNT* 37 (2015): 290–311.

32. See a survey of options from mid-nineteenth to early twentieth century in Victor Paul Furnish, "The Jesus-Paul Debate: From Baur to Bultmann," *BJRL* 47 (1965): 342–81.

33. Wilhelm Wrede, *Paul* (Boston: American Unitarian Association, 1908), 180.

34. See, e.g., Jürgen Becker, *Paul: Apostle to the Gentiles* (Louisville: Westminster John Knox, 1993), 112–24.

35. See the survey in Craig L. Blomberg, "Quotations, Allusions, and Echoes of Jesus in Paul," in *Studies in the Pauline Epistles: Essays in Honor of Douglas J. Moo*, ed. Matthew S. Harmon and Jay E. Smith (Grand Rapids: Zondervan, 2014), 129–43.

36. See David Wenham, *Paul: Follower of Jesus or Founder of Christianity?* (Grand Rapids: Eerdmans, 1995); idem, *From Good News to Gospels: What Did the First Christians Say about Jesus?* (Grand Rapids: Eerdmans, 2018); Detlef Häusser, *Christusbekenntnis und Jesusüberliefung bei Paulus*, WUNT 2/210 (Tübingen: Mohr Siebeck, 2006), 351–52, passim; Barnett, *Paul*; Dunn, *Theology of Paul*, 189–95.

there is still a substantial gap between Jesus's own remembered self-estimation and the proclamation of Paul."[37] Yet the important point is that, however developed, Paul's teaching stands in continuity with the teaching of Jesus. Paul probably assumes a fair degree of acquaintance among his listeners with the story and teaching of Jesus. But the needs of his churches, living in such a different environment than first-century Palestine, required new formulations of Christian truth.

3 CONCEPTUAL CATEGORIES

In this section, I attempt to survey the "forest" in which Paul's theological "trees" are found—to sketch the broad outline of his way of thinking as a context for interpreting specific elements of his theology. I identify three components to this outline. First, I argue that Paul's *theological worldview* takes the shape of a history of salvation. Second, I suggest that the *organizing concept* he uses to unpack this worldview is "realm." And, third, I propose that union with Christ is the *webbing* that knits together Paul's diverse theological teaching. I will also look briefly at some of the key formative influences on the development and expression of Paul's theology.

3.1 Theological Framework: Salvation History

The phrase "salvation history," or "redemptive history" (Ger. *Heilsgeschichte*), is used to designate several different and sometimes contradictory concepts.[38] I am using the phrase in a rather untechnical fashion to denote, as the phrase suggests, that Paul thinks of the salvation brought by Christ as taking place in the context of a historical process. He understands Christ and his significance as the culmination of God's saving plan. This plan was initiated after the Fall, declared in his promise to Abraham, and continued in the vicissitudes of Israel's history. Paul, of course, was strongly conditioned to think in these terms by his intimate knowledge of the Hebrew Bible and by his formative education in the Jewish "academy." Paul, like other Jews of his time, would have longed for God's promised deliverance of Israel when he would vindicate his chosen people and, in doing so, magnify his own name. Jewish salvation history was divided into two "ages," with the old age of Israel's subjection and sinfulness giving way to a new age of Israel's exaltation and the abolishment of idolatry and sin.[39] Paul's letters

<hr/>

37. James D. G. Dunn, *Beginning from Jerusalem*, Christianity in the Making 2 (Grand Rapids: Eerdmans, 2009), 24–25.

38. See, e.g., Robert W. Yarbrough, "Salvation History (*Heilsgeschichte*) and Paul: Comments on a Disputed but Essential Category," in Harmon and Smith, *Studies in the Pauline Epistles*, 181–97.

39. This "two-age" scheme is sometimes associated specifically with apocalyptic Judaism. However, as N. T. Wright has noted, this scheme was quite widespread among Jews of Paul's day (*Paul and His Recent Interpreters*, 157–58). It should also be noted that some Jewish schemes of salvation history were more complex than a simple "two-age" outlook (Loren T. Stuckenbruck, "Posturing 'Apocalyptic' in Pauline Theology: How Much Contrast to Jewish Tradition?," in *The Myth of the Rebellious Angels: Studies in Second Temple Judaism and New Testament Texts*, WUNT 2/355 [Tübingen: Mohr Siebeck, 2014], 245–56).

reveal on virtually every page that this historically oriented way of thinking was an assumed framework for the expression of his theology.

However, the revelation to Paul of Christ as the risen Son of God required a significant revision to this two-age salvation history. Messiah had come, as promised, but Israel was still under Roman power and sin was still rampant. The cross and resurrection of Christ truly fulfilled the plan of God—but, to use familiar language, it was a fulfillment that awaited a further consummation. The "new age" had dawned, but the "old age" had not disappeared—these two "ages" overlap at the present time. Believers, while decisively transferred into the new age, are still affected by the old age. We therefore live in the tension between the "already" of what God has done and the "not yet" of what he still has to do. As we will see below, this overlap means that we cannot confine Paul's salvation-historical scheme to "history" in the narrow sense. I will suggest below a further step we can take in conceptualizing Paul's worldview.

The brief sketch I have given above of "salvation history" is rather standard in recent studies of Paul and of the New Testament more generally. An influential statement of this view came in George Eldon Ladd's advocacy of "inaugurated eschatology" in his description of the kingdom in the teaching of Jesus.[40] Many scholars, far too numerous to mention, have carried forward this basic conception,[41] but I mention two who have especially influenced me: Herman Ridderbos in his theology of Paul and Greg Beale in several writings, perhaps most clearly in his essay "The Eschatological Conception of New Testament Theology."[42]

As this last paragraph suggests, Paul's salvation-historical worldview is closely related to his eschatology. Other scholars have amply developed the fundamental nature of Paul's eschatology (see Beale's above-cited article), and I will come back to the issue many times in this volume. So here I will simply note some of the evidence that justifies Dunn's claim about Paul's eschatology: *"Paul's gospel was eschatological not because of what he still hoped would happen, but because of what he believed had already happened."*[43]

"Eschatology" is the teaching (*logos*) about "last things" (*eschata*). Fundamental to all New Testament theology is the claim that the "last things"—those matters predicted in

40. Ladd, *Theology of the New Testament*, esp. 55–67.

41. E.g., Oscar Cullmann, *Christ and Time: The Primitive Christian Conception of Time and History* (Philadelphia: Westminster, 1950); and idem, *Salvation in History* (London: SCM, 1967); Goppelt, *Theology of the New Testament*, e.g., 1:280–81; Martin Hengel, "Heilsgeschichte," in *Theologicsche, Historische und Biographische Skizzen: Kleine Schriften VII*, ed. Claus-Jürgen Thorton; WUNT 2/253 (Tübingen: Mohr Siebeck, 2010), 1–33. A useful introduction to some of these perspectives at a more popular level is Lewis B. Smedes's *Union with Christ: A Biblical View of the New Life in Jesus Christ* (Grand Rapids: Eerdmans, 1983).

42. See the chapter "Fundamental Structures" in Herman Ridderbos, *Paul, An Outline of His Theology* (Grand Rapids: Eerdmans, 1975), 44–90; G. K. Beale, "The Eschatological Conception of New Testament Theology," in *"The Reader Must Understand": Eschatology in Bible and Theology*, ed. K. E. Brower and M. W. Elliott (Leicester: Inter-Varsity, 1997), 11–52.

43. Dunn, *Theology of Paul*, 465 (emphasis original).

the Old Testament to come to pass in the "last days"—had arrived. The conviction of the first Christians that they were living in the era of fulfillment is central to their way of thinking about themselves and the history of which they were a part. Paul shares this perspective. Referring to Israelites in the wilderness, he says, "These things happened to them as examples and were written down as warnings for us, on whom the culmination of the ages has come" (1 Cor 10:11). Paul and the believers to whom he writes are living in the "new creation" (2 Cor 5:17; Gal 6:15), the era when God's mysteries were being revealed (e.g., Col 1:26–27), the law was reaching its culmination (Rom 10:4), and the Old Testament was being fulfilled (see below, pp. 354–56). This emphasis on the "already" must not, of course, ignore or minimize the "not yet"—indeed, I suggest that it is the failure to keep these in appropriate balance that leads to some of the theological and behavioral problems Paul addresses in his letters.

In addition to eschatology, "covenant" is another concept integrally tied to salvation history. It is, after all, the canonical label that Christians have traditionally used to describe "old" and "new." Paul does not use the language of covenant often, although the concept of covenant arguably lies beneath some of his key emphases (see pp. 464–65). Paul never uses "covenant"—nor do other biblical authors—in the way it is used in the Reformed concept of "covenant theology": that is, to describe a single administration of God's grace extending from the garden of Eden to the new heaven and earth.[44] This is not to contest the valid emphasis on continuity in covenant theology, but it is to suggest that the biblical use of "covenant" language focuses more on discontinuity than continuity.[45] In other words, "covenant" is not the biblical word that describes salvation history generally; rather, it refers to the distinct phases I have labeled "old age" and "new age." It is important, then, to give space to both continuity and discontinuity in mapping out the unfolding plan of God. Of course, everyone would agree with this; differences arise when one tries to weigh accurately the balance between continuity and discontinuity and to apply that balance to specific doctrines. I am happy to think of myself as belonging to the broadly Reformed theological tradition (although some might want to contest my membership as they read parts of this book!). However, I also think that Paul's theology tilts us to a bit more discontinuity than has been typical in Reformed theology. This discontinuity comes to the surface, for instance, in my preference for believer's baptism over infant baptism—my view being that the church is constituted by believers only, and my conclusion that the Mosaic law does not apply directly to the new covenant people of God. I am pleased that several other scholars in recent years have initiated perspectives on the mix of

---

44. Jeffrey J. Niehaus has argued that covenants in Scripture always institute new arrangements rather than continuing existing ones (Jeffrey J. Niehaus, "An Argument against Theologically Constructed Covenants," *JETS* 50 [2007]: 259–73).

45. See, on this point, among many others, Henri A. G. Blocher, "Old Covenant, New Covenant," in *Always Reforming: Explorations in Systematic Theology*, ed. A. T. B. McGowan (Downers Grove, IL: InterVarsity Press, 2006), 240–70.

continuity and discontinuity that align to some degree with my own tweaking of Reformed theology.[46]

As I noted above, the general salvation-historical perspective I have sketched here is widely adopted among scholars of Paul. Of course, no perspective on Paul's theology commands unanimous support, and salvation history is no exception. A number of scholars in recent years have expressed a greater or lesser degree of hostility to salvation history, arguing that the idea of a continuous progress of history toward fulfillment in Christ is ruled out by Paul's presentation of the coming of Christ as a sudden, unexpected irruption into history. As Charles Cousar puts it, the issue is "whether there is a discernible line of continuity between Israel's story in the past and the death and resurrection of Christ or whether the apocalyptic character of God's disclosure in Christ precipitates an irreparable rupture in the story that makes any smooth notion of continuity difficult to discern."[47] As Cousar's language suggests, many interpreters use the label "apocalyptic" to characterize this discontinuous focus, and this word has been adopted by a number of scholars who describe their approach as the "apocalyptic Paul" movement.[48] I will bypass here the debate over just what is meant by "apocalyptic" and whether, in turn, the word is appropriately applied to the distinctive emphases of this movement.[49] What I need to do, rather, is justify my preference for "salvation history" in light of the objections of scholars in this movement.

First, though, it is important to recognize the valid insight into Paul's theology that this movement highlights. As D. A. Carson helpfully points out, Paul's appropriation of

---

46. See, e.g., Tom Wells and Fred Zaspel, *New Covenant Theology: Description, Definition, Defense* (Frederick, MD: New Covenant Media, 2002); Peter J. Gentry, and Stephen J. Wellum, *Kingdom through Covenant: A Biblical-Theological Understanding of the Covenants* (Wheaton, IL: Crossway, 2012) (see my review of this latter volume: www.thegospelcoalition.org/reviews/kingdom-covenant-douglas-moo).

47. Charles B. Cousar, "Continuity and Discontinuity: Reflections on Romans 5–8," in *Pauline Theology, Volume 3: Romans*, ed. David M. Hay and E. Elizabeth Johnson (Minneapolis: Fortress, 1995), 196.

48. Some of the key proponents of this view (though they differ on many specifics) are J. Louis Martyn, "Apocalyptic Antinomies in Paul's Letter to the Galatians," *NTS* 31 (1985): 410–24; idem, *Galatians: A New Translation with Introduction and Commentary*, AB 33A (New York: Doubleday, 1997); Beverly Roberts Gaventa, "The Singularity of the Gospel: A Reading of Galatians," in Bassler, *Pauline Theology*, 147–59; idem, *When in Romans: An Invitation to Linger with the Gospel according to Paul* (Grand Rapids: Baker, 2016); Douglas A. Campbell, *The Quest for Paul's Gospel: A Suggested Strategy* (London: T&T Clark, 2005), idem, *Pauline Dogmatics: The Triumph of God's Love* (Grand Rapids: Eerdmans, 2020). For a good overview of the understanding

of apocalyptic in Paul's theology, see J. P. Davies, *Paul among the Apocalypses? An Evaluation of the "Apocalyptic Paul" in the Context of Jewish and Christian Apocalyptic*, LNTS 562 (London: Bloomsbury, 2016), 3–22. Ernst Käsemann famously claimed that apocalyptic was "the mother of all Christian theology" (*New Testament Questions of Today* [Philadelphia: Fortress, 1969], 102).

49. R. Barry Matlock justly objects that the word "apocalyptic" is often used in Pauline studies in a way that has a very questionable basis in the actual way that language was being used in Paul's day (*Unveiling the Apocalyptic Paul: Paul's Interpreters and the Rhetoric of Criticism*, JSNTSup 127 [Sheffield: Sheffield Academic Press, 1996], esp. 257–316). See also N. T. Wright, *Paul and His Recent Interpreters*, 155–89. It should be noted that in D. Campbell especially, "apocalyptic" becomes a way of referring to a certain epistemology, arguably more closely tied to the theology of Barth than to anything we find in ancient Judaism. A running battle with what Campbell calls "foundationalism" marks his latest book, *Pauline Dogmatics*. On this issue, see Ben C. Blackwell, John K. Goodrich, and Jason Maston, "Paul and the Apocalyptic Imagination: An Introduction," in *Paul and the Apocalyptic Imagination*, ed. Ben C. Blackwell, John K. Goodrich, and Jason Maston (Minneapolis: Fortress, 2016), 6–11.

the Old Testament is characterized by both a "promise-fulfillment" scheme as well as a "mystery-revelation" scheme.[50] If the former suggests some kind of continuity between the Old Testament and Paul's teaching, the latter sounds a note of discontinuity. God has acted in ways that could not have been expected. This degree of unexpectedness applies even to some of Paul's claims about the fulfillment of the Old Testament. Paul's own dramatic encounter with the risen Christ is a paradigm for his Christ-centered approach. He does not simply plug Christ into the story of salvation history that he was already working with; Christ reconfigures that history. As Bruce Longenecker says, "Paul provides a radical rereading of Israel's history and scriptures in terms of the revealed gospel. It is the latter that defines and determines the former, and not vice versa."[51]

However, this does not mean that the "apocalyptic" Christ event erases salvation history. Paul continues to recognize that Christ fits into a story that begins and is carried forward in the Old Testament. Continuity *and* discontinuity, in the right proportion, must be given their proper place in Paul's theology. The Christ-event, with all its ramifications, is the center and hermeneutical linchpin of salvation history. Paul's theology is to a great extent a reflection on this "apocalyptic" ("revelatory") event. But at the same time, Paul's theology, for it to be a genuine *theo-logy* (a "message about God") must relate to, and be continuous with, the revelation of the only God Paul knows: "the God of Abraham, Isaac, and Jacob." As several scholars have therefore argued, we are not forced to make a choice between "salvation history" and "apocalyptic" when characterizing Paul's theology.[52] His is a salvation history with a central and hermeneutically explosive apocalyptic event at its heart. We do well to remember here that "salvation history" is a broad category. To claim that Paul's worldview is characterized by "salvation history" demands that we go further in pinning down the exact nature of Paul's perspective. While advocates of the "apocalyptic Paul" movement, therefore, tilt the scales too heavily toward discontinuity, they rightly highlight the overwhelming significance of the Christ event in configuring that history.

One important byproduct of Paul's salvation-historical worldview is that he is often more concerned with corporate history than with individual history. Those of

50. D. A. Carson, "Mystery and Fulfillment: Toward a More Comprehensive Paradigm of Paul's Understanding of the Old and the New," in *The Paradoxes of Paul*, vol. 2 of *Justification and Variegated Nomism*, ed. D. A. Carson, Peter T. O'Brien, and Mark A. Seifrid; WUNT 2/140 (Tübingen: Mohr Siebeck, 2004), 393–436. See also Blocher, "Old Covenant, New Covenant," 245–54, who stresses the complexity involved in tracing continuity and discontinuity in Paul.

51. Bruce W. Longenecker, *The Triumph of Abraham's God: The Transformation of Identity in Galatians* (Edinburgh: T&T Clark, 1998), 210.

52. E.g., Barclay, *Paul and the Gift*, 143–49, 414–18; D. A.

Shaw, "Apocalyptic and Covenant: Perspectives on Paul or Antinomies at War?," *JSNT* 36 (2013): 155–71; N. T. Wright, "A New Perspective on Käsemann? Apocalyptic, Covenant, and the Righteousenss of God," in Harmon and Smith, *Studies in the Pauline Epistles*, 116–23; see also three articles taking different perspectives on this issue in vol. 2 of *JSPL* (2012): Bruce W. Longenecker, "Salvation History in Galatians and the Making of a Pauline Discourse," 65–87; Jason Maston, "The Nature of Salvation History in Galatians," 89–103; and Martinus C. de Boer, "Salvation History in Galatians: A Response to Bruce W. Longenecker and Jason Maston," 105–14.

us who are heirs of the Western individualist mentality may need to adjust our perspective if we are to understand Paul's teaching. A good example is Paul's teaching about the law in Galatians 3:23–25: "Before the coming of this faith, we were held in custody under the law, locked up until the faith that was to come would be revealed. So the law was our guardian until Christ came that we might be justified by faith. Now that this faith has come, we are no longer under a guardian." This sequence is often thought to refer to the individual, who, before he or she comes to faith in Christ, is held under God's law; or with a different reading, is led by the law itself to find justification in Christ. However, it is almost certain that Paul is not here rehearsing the experience of an individual but the experience of Israel, confined under the law until the new stage of salvation history, when faith in Christ became possible. Another place where an appropriate regard for corporate ways of thinking help us understand Paul rightly is in his language of "old man" versus "new man" (Rom 6:6; Eph 4:22, 24; Col 3:9–11). Many popular discussions of Paul's doctrine of the Christian life argue, or assume, that Paul distinguishes with these phrases between two parts or "natures" of a person. With this interpretation as the premise, it is then debated whether the "old nature" is replaced with the "new nature" at conversion, or whether the "new nature" is added to the "old nature." But the assumption that "old man" and "new man" refer to parts, or natures, of a person is incorrect, betraying an assumption of individualism not shared by Paul. Rather, they designate the person as a whole, considered in relation to the corporate structure to which he or she belongs (see pp. 607–8).

The need to shed our modernist notions of individualism and get back to Paul's own "corporate" way of thinking was the burden of Krister Stendhal's influencial 1963 article, "The Apostle Paul and the Introspective Conscience of the West."[53] Since Stendahl's article, however, opinions about the relative degree of individual versus corporate focus have been all over the place. Gary Burnett, for instance, has shown that people in Paul's day thought in terms of the individual more than Stendahl recognized.[54] A concern with the individual is not a modernist innovation. More recently, without returning to Stendahl's approach, scholars have highlighted the corporate dimension of Paul's thought, especially among those trying to reclaim and give prominence to the importance of the Christian community in Paul.[55] Refocusing our attention on the

53. Krister Stendhal, "The Apostle Paul and the Introspective Conscience of the West," *HTR* 56 (1963): 199–215.

54. Gary W. Burnett, *Paul and the Salvation of the Individual*, BibInt 57 (Leiden: Brill, 2001). Stephen J. Chester claims: "Stendahl's work on the introspective conscience represents a misleading dead end for contemporary scholarship" (*Reading Paul with the Reformers* [Grand Rapids: Eerdmans, 2017], 346).

55. See, e.g., James W. Thompson, *The Church according to*

Paul: Rediscovering the Community Conformed for Christ (Grand Rapids: Baker, 2014); Timothy G. Gombis, "Participation in the New-Creation People of God in Christ by the Spirit," in *The Apostle Paul and the Christian Life: Ethical and Missional Implications of the New Perspective*, ed. Scot McKnight and Joseph B. Modica (Grand Rapids: Baker, 2016), 103–24. See also further discussion of this point in relation to the church on pp. 568, 587–88.

church is a welcome emphasis, sorely needed in some Christian circles. However, here again, a valid and important point can be taken too far.

For instance, a corporate focus in Paul's thought is often based on his use of plural pronouns. However, the presence of a plural pronoun is not, in itself, an indication of a corporate focus. Several recent writers on Paul's theology appear to make this mistake. We may take Susan Eastman's essay on Romans 8 as an example. She draws attention to the plural pronoun in Romans 8:9 and translates, "The spirit of God dwells in the midst of your life together." Likewise, the plural pronouns in verses 15–16 point to a "communal prayer": "We cry Abba, Father."[56] The problem here, of course, is that plural words and pronouns, in both Greek and English, function in two very different ways. In their massive *Cambridge Grammar of the English Language*, Rodney Huddleston and Geoffrey Pullum illustrate these two uses with the example of the difference between "five students voted against the proposal" and "five students lifted the piano onto the stage."[57] In the latter sentence, the five students are conceived as acting together, as a unit. In the former, however, they are conceived as acting individually. This "distributive" sense is quite common in the use of plural pronouns. Thus, it is not at all clear that Romans 8:9 should be understood as "the spirit of God dwells in the midst of your life together." It could also be interpreted to mean "the Spirit of God dwells in each one of you." Only context and parallel passages elsewhere can decide the issue.[58]

A happy balance between extremes on this issue is struck by Ben Dunson in his 2012 published dissertation. On the one hand, he accuses Burnett of going too far in removing the significance of community in Paul. On the other, however, he seeks to vindicate the individual focus of Rudolf Bultmann over against the corporate emphasis of Ernst Käsemann. He accuses Käsemann and others of constructing a modern notion of the "individual" and then, failing to find it in Paul, claiming Paul is unconcerned about the individual. In fact, Dunson concludes, "The individual and the community are thoroughly and inextricably integrated in Paul's letters. *The individual and the community imply each other.*"[59] Recent scholarship is right to point to the Pauline churches as places where a new group identity, founded in the gospel of Christ, resocializes converts into a new worldview and mindset. Individual Christians are transformed into holy persons as they identify with, and participate in, the holy people God is creating. As Dunson has rightly argued, Paul never thinks of individuals in an isolated sense but as

---

56. Susan Grove Eastman, "Oneself in Another: Participation and the Spirit in Romans 8," in *"In Christ" in Paul: Explorations in Paul's Theology of Union and Participation*, ed. Michael J. Thate, Kevin J. Vanhoozer, and Constantine R. Campbell, WUNT 2/384 (Tübingen: Mohr Siebeck, 2014), 112, 114.

57. Rodney Huddleston and Geoffrey K. Pullum, *The Cambridge Grammar of the English Language* (Cambridge: Cambridge University Press, 2002), 362.

58. On this general point, see Gerald W. Peterman, "Plural You: On the Use and Abuse of the Second Person," *BBR* 20 (2010): 201–14.

59. Ben C. Dunson, *Individual and Community in Paul's Letter to the Romans*, WUNT 2/332 (Tübingen: Mohr Siebeck, 2012); quotation from p. 17.

"individuals in community." But Paul does often think of and describe individuals.[60] As Bauckham notes, "The claim that ancient people perceived the self in relational terms, as essentially related to others or to the group, rather than as autonomous and atomized individuals that modern individualism envisages, presupposes selves that were distinguishable, however closely related."[61]

3.2 Organizing Concept: Realm

As I noted above, the overlap between old age and new in Paul's view of salvation history inevitably means that his two-age perspective cannot be explained in solely historical terms.[62] The "change of aeons," while occurring historically at the cross, becomes real for the individual only at the point of faith. The "change of aeons" that took place in Christ is experienced only "in Christ." Therefore, the person who lives *after* Christ's death and resurrection but has not yet appropriated the benefits of those events by faith still lives in the old era—enslaved to sin, in the flesh, and doomed to eternal death. On the other hand, Abraham, for example, though living many centuries *before* Christ, must, in light of Romans 4, be considered to belong, in some sense at least, to the new era. This circumstance introduces a confusing factor, making it difficult to come up with an overall system that is capable of integrating all of Paul's applications of salvation history.

However, without making inappropriately grandiose claims for it, the category "realm" may be a useful way of conceptualizing the matter.[63] Why "realm"? It appears to be a strange choice, since the NIV uses the singular "realm" only four times in Paul's letters, and none of these straightforwardly renders a single Greek word (Rom 7:5; 8:8, 9 [twice]); and it does not appear at all in the ESV or NRSV of Paul's letters. My reason for choosing this term is that it builds neatly on the salvation-historical worldview I outlined above. I maintain the "historical" element in this scheme by using the contrast of "old realm" and "new realm." At the same time, however, this language is more amenable to handling the presence of both these "realms" at the same time. Furthermore, the idea of "realm" helpfully ties in to an important focus in Paul's theology: the contrasting "powers" that war for control over people. This scheme of conflicting powers is highlighted in the "apocalyptic Paul" movement (see above,

---

60. See also, e.g., Michael S. Horton, *Rediscovering the Holy Spirit: God's Perfecting Presence in Creation, Redemption, and Everyday Life* (Grand Rapids: Zondervan, 2017), 178; Thiselton, *Hermeneutics of Doctrine*, 185–92; Troels Engberg-Pedersen, *Paul and the Stoics* (Louisville: Westminster John Knox, 2000), 293–94.

61. Richard Bauckham, *Gospel of Glory: Major Themes in Johannine Theology* (Grand Rapids: Eerdmans, 2015), 3.

62. See esp. K. Stalder, *Das Werk des Geistes in der Heiligung bei Paulus* (Zürich: EVZ, 1962), 240–48; Victor Paul Furnish, *Theology and Ethics in Paul* (Nashville: Abingdon, 1968), 134–35; John M. G. Barclay, *Obeying the Truth: Paul's Ethics*

in Galatians (Edinburgh: T&T Clark, 1988), 99, 104–5; Beker, *Paul the Apostle*, 135–81. As Moisés Silva points out, "Paul is not concerned about purely chronological differences but about the difference in *character* between the two ages: the age of the flesh (= self-confidence and sin) and the age of the Spirit (= promise and salvation)" (*Philippians*, BECNT [Grand Rapids: Baker, 2005], 160–61n10).

63. Constantine R. Campbell also singles out the category "realm" as his framework for describing Paul's eschatology (*Paul and the Hope of Glory: An Exegetical and Theological Study* [Grand Rapids: Zondervan Academic, 2020], 65–102).

pp. 30–31). I think this movement goes too far in viewing Paul's soteriology almost exclusively through this lens. At the same time, however, they have drawn attention to a recurring emphasis in Paul's theology. Note, for instance, the summary statement at the end of Romans 5: "So that, just as sin *reigned* in death, so also grace might *reign* through righteousness to bring eternal life through Jesus Christ our Lord" (v. 21, my emphases). People outside of Christ are "under [the power of] sin" (e.g., Rom 3:9); when they come to Christ, they are no longer "under the law" but are "under grace" (Rom 6:14, 15). Paul frequently uses the language of slavery and lordship to denote the situation of humans both outside Christ and in him—not least, of course, in his ubiquitous reference to Christ as "Lord." "Realm" language also has the benefit of tying into other key canonical witnesses. "Realm" is similar to "kingdom," which many Old Testament scholars identify as a unifying theme of Old Testament theology, and which Gospels scholars often single out as the central theme of Jesus's teaching.

The spatial imagery of "realm," then, serves as a useful way of conceptualizing and working out Paul's salvation-historical scheme. Geerhardus Vos, a pioneering voice in biblical theology, endorses this basically spatial conceptualization:

> There has been created a totally new environment, or, more accurately speaking, a totally new world, in which the person spoken of is an inhabitant and participator. It is not in the first place the interiority of the subject that has undergone the change, although that, of course, is not to be excluded. The whole surrounding world has assumed a new aspect and complexion.[64]

However, the "in the first place" in this quotation is an important reminder that the use of a spatial conception must not overwhelm or exclude other conceptual schemes, such as the work of inner transformation and empowerment. Forcing all of Paul's thought into the conceptualization of realm will distort him at various points, and I hope I am sensitive enough to this problem so that I "back off" when this begins to happen. With all due caveats noted, however, I still think the basic scheme of conflict between "old realm" and "new realm" provides a helpful unifying perspective on Paul's theology.

3.3 "Center": Union with Christ

I have suggested that we should think of salvation history as the framing worldview of Paul's theology and "realm" as the conceptual category Paul uses to express his theology. I turn now to a question Pauline scholars love to debate: What is the "center"

---

64. *The Pauline Eschatology* (Princeton: Princeton University Press, 1930; repr., Phillipsburg, NJ: P&R, 1994), 47. Edith Humphrey also argues for the need to use spatial categories in conceptualizing Paul's theology ("Apocalyptic as Theoria in the Letters of St. Paul: A New Perspective on Apocalyptic as Mother of Theology," in Blackwell, Goodrich, and Maston, *Paul and the Apocalyptic Imagination*, 87–110).

of Paul's theology?[65] One reason the question is so popular is that it allows us students of Paul to propose speculative answers that can never be proved or disproved. But the question is of more than just academic importance, since the answer could either illuminate Paul's teaching or throw us off track.

Right at the outset we must pause to consider just what we are talking about: specifically, what do we mean by "center"? The word could refer to three distinct ideas. First, we might identify the "center" of Paul's theology as the concept he most often talks about. We could envisage a horizontally aligned bar graph, each bar a plot of one of Paul's concepts. The bar extending furthest to the right would be the "center" of Paul's thought. While I have not actually worked out such a graph, I strongly suspect that if we were to do so, the bar with the name "Christ" on it would be by far the longest one. This is really a no-brainer (one thinks of the child in Sunday school always having the right answer if he or she responds "Jesus!"). Christ, or perhaps more particularly the "Christ event" (emphasizing what God has done through him) is clearly what Paul is usually talking about, whether directly or indirectly.[66]

However true this might be, it does not get us very far—and it may not even do justice to the word "center." By "center," we usually mean more than "most common" or even "most important." We usually use it to refer to something that is the locus of a set of ideas or activities; as when we refer, for instance, to "the center of the controversy." "Center" in this sense has an integrating function. This is how "center" is usually used in discussions of Paul's theology. A good example is the long-standing debate about whether "participation in Christ" or "justification by faith" is the "center" of Paul's theology. Classic Reformation theologians often singled out the latter as the "center" of Paul's theology (although far less often than critics of this approach recognize). In the early 1900s, however, Albert Schweitzer argued that "Christ mysticism," participation in Christ, was the center of Paul's thought.[67] Many contemporary scholars argue similarly. They note that we can draw clear lines of connection from participation to Paul's other teaching, whereas this is much harder to do if we put justification at the center. "Center," here, then, is used in a way suggesting the imagery of the hub of a wheel, with spokes radiating out from it—or, to press my realm imagery to the breaking point, the urban hub of a particular realm or nation. Of course, many other candidates have been

---

65. Some scholars suggest that salvation history might be the "center." However, I think D. Campbell is correct: the framework of Paul's thinking cannot really be its "center" (*Quest for Paul's Gospel*, 27).

66. See Schnelle, who claims that the beginning point and center of Paul's thought and life was "an unshakable theological conviction: the eschatological presence of salvation from God in Jesus Christ" (*Apostle Paul*, 389). See also Peter Stuhlmacher, *Grundlegung: Von Jesus zu Paulus*, vol. 2 of *Biblische Theologie des*

Neuen Testaments (Göttingen: Vandenhoeck & Ruprecht, 2005), 283. Beker's claim that "the coherent center of Paul's gospel is constituted by the apocalyptic interpretation of the Christ-event" (*Paul the Apostle*, 135) is similar.

67. Albert Schweitzer famously described the concept of participation as the "main crater" and justification as a "subsidiary crater" (*Paul and His Interpreters: A Critical History* [London: Adam and Charles Black, 1912], 225–26; see also idem, *The Mysticism of Paul the Apostle* [London: Adam & Charles Black, 1931]).

put forward for the role of "center" in this sense: among them, anthropology,[68] Paul's gentile mission,[69] the word of the cross,[70] the *Shema* confession,[71] dying and rising with Christ,[72] gospel,[73] salvation,[74] reconciliation,[75] God in Christ,[76] and new creation.[77]

Of these, "gospel" and "reconciliation" perhaps have the best claims to represent the "center" of Paul's thought. However, we again face the question of what we mean by "center." "Gospel" is, in my view, the central theme of Paul's most significant theological letter, Romans (see pp. 195–96), but it is more an overarching concept than a "center" in the sense of a hub. The same is true of "reconciliation," although it is certainly one of Paul's most significant and all-embracing soteriological concepts. I should also note that, while I do not mention "justification" as a good candidate for "center," it is certainly an important, even critical, enunciation of Paul's gospel.

One key point has perhaps become clear by this point: identifying the "center" of Paul's gospel is confusing and capable of having several "right" answers because of the confusion over the meaning of "center." We must be careful not to allow a semantic debate to cloud our analysis of what stands out as especially significant in Paul's theology. I shift the meaning, then, yet again, and suggest that "center" might also have the sense of a recurring motif that knits together much of Paul's thought. Constantine Campbell suggests the analogy of a "web"; to revert again to my realm imagery, we might also think of a network of roads that links all the parts of a nation or territory. Along with Campbell and many others, I suggest that participation in Christ, or union with Christ, might serve as the web that holds Paul's theology together.[78] This union

---

68. This suggestion is associated particularly with Rudolf Bultmann's existential approach (*Theology of the New Testament*). He divides his treatment of Paul into two parts: "Man Prior to the Revelation of Faith" and "Man under Faith."

69. Krister Stendahl, *Final Account: Paul's Letter to the Romans* (Minneapolis: Fortress, 1995), 11–12.

70. Pascale Rondez, "Ein Zentrum Paulinischer Theologie? Eine Pneumatologische Erschliessung des Zusammenhangs von Soteriologie und Christologie anhand von Gal 5,25," in *Kreuztheologie im Neuen Testament*, ed. Andreas Dettwiler and Jean Zumstein (Tübingen: Mohr Siebeck, 2002), 59–79; Jean Zumstein, "Das Wort von Kreuz als Mitte der Paulinischen Theologie," in Dettwiler and Zumstein, *Kreuztheologie im Neuen Testament*, 27–41.

71. Mark D. Nanos, "Paul and the Jewish Tradition: The Ideology of the *Shema*," in *Celebrating Paul: Festschrift in Honor of Jerome Murphy-O'Connor, O.P., and Joseph A. Fitzmyer, S. J.*, ed. P. Spitaler, CBQMS 48 (Washington, DC: Catholic Biblical Association of America, 2011), 65.

72. Terrance Callan, *Dying and Rising with Christ: The Theology of Paul the Apostle* (New York: Paulist, 2006), 8–9, 92–93.

73. Hahn, *Theologie des Neuen Testaments*, 1:181–91.

74. C. A. Anderson Scott, *Christianity according to St. Paul* (Cambridge: Cambridge University Press, 1927).

75. See the discussion on pp. 491–97.

76. Thomas R. Schreiner, *Paul, Apostle of God's Glory in Christ: A Pauline Theology* (Downers Grove, IL: InterVarsity Press, 2001), 15–35.

77. Beale, "Eschatological Conception."

78. Constantine R. Campbell, *Paul and Union with Christ: An Exegetical and Theological Study* (Grand Rapids: Zondervan, 2012), 437–41. See also André du Toit, "'In Christ,' 'in the Spirit' and Related Prepositional Phrases: Their Relevance for a Discussion on Pauline Mysticism," in *Focusing on Paul: Persuasion and Theological Design in Romans and Galatians*, ed. Cilliers Breytenbach and David S. du Toit (New York: de Gruyter, 2007), 139; Emmanuel L. Rehfeld, *Relationale Ontologie bei Paulus: Die ontische Wirksamkeit des Christusbezogenheit im Denkend des Heidenapostels*, WUNT 2/326 (Tübingen: Mohr Siebeck, 2012), 52, 289. Others who stress the participatory element in Paul's theology are E. P. Sanders, *Paul and Palestinian Judaism: A Comparison of Patterns of Religion* (Philadelphia: Fortress, 1977), esp. 502–8; Michael J. Gorman, *Inhabiting the Cruciform God: Kenosis, Justification, and Theosis in Paul's Narrative Soteriology* (Grand Rapids: Eerdmans, 2009), 22–55; Terence L. Donaldson, "The Juridical, the Participatory and the 'New Perspective' on Paul," in *Reading Paul in Context: Explorations in Identity Formation. Essays in Honour of William S. Campbell*, ed. Kathy Ehrensperger and J. Brian Tucker (London: T&T Clark, 2010), 233–40.

with Christ concept comes to expression in many ways in Paul. For instance, he uses "with" (usually Gk. *syn*) to associate Christians with Christ in his redemptive work: we die "with" Christ, are crucified "with" Christ, live now "with" Christ, are (and will be) raised "with" Christ, suffer "with" Christ, and look forward to being glorified "with" Christ (e.g., Rom 6:1–10; 8:17; Gal 2:19–20; Col 2:12, 20; 3:1, 3). But his most common way of indicating this union is in his ubiquitous "in" (*en*) Christ language (approximately 130x in his letters). Paul uses this phrase to refer to virtually every aspect of Christian existence and theology, as the following smattering of occurrences illustrates:

Gal 5:6: "In Christ Jesus neither circumcision nor uncircumcision has any value"
1 Cor 1:2: "to those sanctified in Christ Jesus"
1 Cor 1:4: "his grace given you in Christ Jesus"
1 Cor 1:30: "It is because of him that you are in Christ Jesus"
1 Cor 3:1: "mere infants in Christ"
1 Cor 4:15: "Even if you had ten thousand guardians in Christ, you do not have many fathers, for in Christ Jesus I became your father through the gospel"
1 Cor 4:17: "my way of life in Christ Jesus"
2 Cor 1:20: "no matter how many promises God has made, they are 'Yes' in Christ"
2 Cor 5:17: "Therefore, if anyone is in Christ, the new creation has come"
2 Cor 12:2: "a man in Christ"
Rom 16:7: "They were in Christ before I was"

The phrase is attached to a breathtaking range of ideas. We should also note, before we place too much weight on specific connotations of the "in Christ" idea, that Paul can reverse the relationship at times without any apparent difference in meaning; for example, "Do you not realize that Christ Jesus is in you?" (2 Cor 13:5), and similarly, "If Christ is in you" (Rom 8:10).

The language of "in Christ" and the broader concept of union with Christ to which it points have played an important role in historical theology.[79] Modern study of the phrase was set on its course by Adolf Deissmann, who understood the Greek *en* in the

79. For a historical survey, see Robert Letham, *Union with Christ in Scripture, History, and Theology* (Phillipsburg, NJ: P&R, 2011); for both history and theology, see esp. Grant Macaskill, *Union with Christ in the New Testament* (Oxford: Oxford University Press, 2013). "Union with Christ" is especially important for the theology of John Calvin (see, e.g., J. T. Billings, *Calvin, Participation, and the Gift: The Activity of Believers in Union with Christ*, Changing Paradigms in Historical and Systematic Theology [Oxford: Oxford University Press, 2007]). Some interpreters who single out Paul's participation-in-Christ theme as fundamental to his theology have argued that it may be seen in relation to the widespread concept in Orthodox theology of *theosis* (see esp. Gorman, *Inhabiting the Cruciform God*; idem, "Romans: The First Christian Treatise on Theosis," *Journal of Theological Interpretation* 5 [2011]: 13–34). However, the particular expression of this idea in Orthodox theology is so closely tied to other doctrines in that tradition that it is probably not helpful to label Paul's teaching with this word (e.g., N. Russell, *The Doctrine of Deification in the Greek Patristic Tradition* [Oxford: Oxford University Press, 2004], 79–85; Macaskill, *Union with Christ*, 44–76; Gösta Hallonsten, "Theosis in Recent Research: A Renewal of Interest and a Need for Clarity," in *Partakers in the Divine Nature: The History and*

phrase as locative and interpreted Christ as a kind of "medium" or "ether" in which the Christian lives.[80] This mystical approach to the phrase, while considerably popular in the history-of-religions school, is now widely discounted. But the view that the phrase basically, in some sense, "locates" us in Christ is widespread. A perusal of the list of occurrences above reveals that most seem to have this sense. However, it would be pressing matters to force all these phrases into the same sense.[81] Some of them, for instance, appear to have a more instrumental sense, specifying Christ as the means by which something is accomplished.[82] Some interpreters, indeed, suggest that both the locative and instrumental senses are often found together, in what J. C. Beker calls a "participatory-instrumental" sense: What Christians do and who they are is "in and through Christ."[83] I do think, however, that the locative predominates.[84] Paul insists that everything the believer is and experiences has relation to Christ: we have been "incorporated in the Christ reality."[85]

The idea of incorporation into Christ and the benefits he has won for us in his redemptive work probably finds its home in Paul's broader salvation-historical world-view. As Adam "heads up" the old realm, incorporating us into the reality of sin and death he inaugurated, so Christ heads up the new realm. Through our identification with him, we are brought out from under Adam's reign, set free from the powers of the old realm, and destined for the glory Christ has already entered.[86]

Development of Deification in the Christian Traditions, ed. M. J. Christensen and J. A. Wittung [Cranbury, NJ: Farleigh Dickinson University Press, 2007], 281–93).

80. The content and wording of the following paragraph is a revision of Douglas J. Moo, *The Epistle to the Romans*, 2nd ed., NICNT (Grand Rapids: Eerdmans, 2018), 420–21. Unless otherwise noted, future references to *Romans* (NICNT) will refer to the 2nd edition.

81. E.g., for an argument that some of Paul's phrases are instrumental, see A. J. M. Wedderburn, "Some Observations on Paul's Use of the Phrases 'in Christ' and 'with Christ,'" *JSNT* 25 (1985): 83–90. Campbell (*Paul and Union with Christ*, 413) stresses the various specific nuances found in the relevant phrases; he concludes that ideas of union, participation, identification, and incorporation are the key ones.

82. See, e.g., F. Neugebauer, *In Christus (EN ΧΡΙΣΤΩΙ). Eine Untersuchung zum paulinischen Glaubensverständnis* (Göttingen:

Vandenhoeck & Ruprecht, 1961). For a history of research (now a bit dated), see Michel Bouttier, *En Christ: Étude d'exégèse et de Théologie Pauliniennes*, Etudes d'histoire et de philosophie religieuses 54 (Paris: Presses universitaires de France, 1962), 5–22.

83. *Paul the Apostle*, 272.

84. A fundamentally local sense for this phrase resonates with those who claim that ἐν generally encodes the idea of space or locality. I am indebted for this emphasis to Steven Runge, who shared a presentation on this matter with me (his work brings together the linguistic approaches found in Dirk Geeraerts, ed., *Cognitive Linguistics: Basic Readings* [New York: Mouton de Gruyter, 2006], and S. Luraghi, *On the Meaning of Prepositions and Cases: The Expression of Semantic Roles in Ancient Greek*, Studies in Language Companion Series [Amsterdam: John Benjamin, 2003]).

85. Strecker, *Theology*, 118.

86. See esp. Ridderbos, *Paul*, 57–62; Beker, *Paul the Apostle*, 272–73; Schreiner, *Paul*, 156–59.

Part 2

THE THEOLOGY OF THE LETTERS

Chapter 3

PAUL, MISSIONARY THEOLOGIAN[1]

"A man in Christ"

—2 CORINTHIANS 12:2[2]

PAUL'S GREATEST CONTRIBUTION to the faith is his theology. However, as we well know, Paul did not write a "theology"—that is, a single book, or series of books, in which he systematically set out his teaching (think of Calvin's *Institutes* or Barth's *Church Dogmatics*). Rather, as a missionary and pastor, Paul wrote thirteen letters. Synthesizing Paul's "theology" from these letters is a serious challenge, as I noted in the first chapter. And while I have argued that the biblical theologian needs to engage in the synthetic task of putting the various pieces of Paul's theologizing together, it is also essential that we understand his letters in their own right. So, in the first part of this book, I situate each of Paul's letters in the context of his missionary career and briefly summarize their teaching. This chapter clears the way for that task by looking generally at the life and letters of Paul.

1 LIFE

I begin with an overview of Paul's life. This kind of overview is difficult to construct on the basis of Paul's letters only, since he seldom provides the kind of specific information needed to figure out an even generally accurate chronology. Chronologies of Paul's life, based only on his letters, therefore, go in many directions.[3] However, once we

---

1. While I am not aware that I drew this title from him, Robert L. Reymond uses this same terminology in the title of his book on Paul: *Paul, Missionary Theologian: A Survey of His Missionary Labours and Theology* (Fearn, Ross-shire: Christian Focus, 2000). Schreiner also devotes a chapter of his Pauline theology to the apostle's mission: "Proclaiming a Magnificent God: The Pauline Mission" (*Paul*, 37–72).

2. I was influenced in choosing this epigraph by James Stuart Stewart's book on Paul with this title (*A Man in Christ: The Vital Elements of St. Paul's Religion* [New York: Harper & Row, 1935]).

3. See, e.g., Charles Buck and Greer Taylor, *Saint Paul:*

A Study of the Development of His Thought (New York: Charles Scribner's Sons, 1969); Robert Jewett, *A Chronology of Paul's Life* (Philadelphia: Fortress, 1979); Gerd Lüdemann, *Paul, Apostle to the Gentiles: Studies in Chronology* (Philadelphia: Fortress, 1984); Jerome Murphy-O'Connor, *Paul: A Critical Life* (Oxford: Oxford University Press, 1996), 1–31; Gregory Tatum, *New Chapters in the Life of Paul: The Relative Chronology of His Career*, CBQMS 41 (Washington, DC: Catholic Biblical Association of America, 2006); Douglas A. Campbell, *Framing Paul: An Epistolary Biography* (Grand Rapids: Eerdmans, 2014).

supplement Paul's occasional references with the chronological account of Paul's life in Acts, a much clearer picture emerges.[4] Since I consider Acts to be a reliable guide to the history of Paul's life, I use it as a basic framework in the following overview. Of course, Luke himself is far from precise about chronology, often using transitional phrases such as "after many days" (e.g., Acts 9:23). Nevertheless, using his account as a basis and fitting in the letters as seems appropriate enables us to assemble a fairly accurate account. Moreover, Luke and Paul refer to enough datable events and known persons from secular history to enable us to assign at least approximate dates to the key events of Paul's life. The overview that follows, then, corresponds closely to the ones proposed by other scholars who integrate the evidence from Acts into the picture.[5]

Two events in this chronology, marked with an asterisk, require further comment, which I provide following the chart. I should also note that my location of the letters of Paul in this chronology will receive explanation and justification in the book surveys found throughout the rest of part 2. The two letters whose dates I consider most uncertain (Galatians and Philippians) appear twice, each at their most probable locations (with brief indication of my estimation of their relative likelihood).

PAUL: CHRONOLOGICAL OVERVIEW

Event	Date	Acts	Epistles
Birth—Tarsus of Cilicia	5–12?	22:3	
*"Brought up" in Jerusalem		22:3	
Educated in Jerusalem	20–30?	cf. 22:3	
Hillel versus Shammai debate			
Persecutor of the church	30–34	8:1; 9:1–2	Gal 1:13–14; Phil 3:6
*Conversion	34	9:1–19	Gal 1:15–16
Preaching in Damascus	33–35		Gal 1:17
Preaching(?) in "Arabia"	33–35		Gal 1:17
Escape from Damascus	36		2 Cor 11:32–35

---

4. The presentation of Paul in Acts is a long-standing controversy. See, for a recent overview, the essays in David P. Moessner et al., eds., *Paul and the Heritage of Israel: Paul's Claim upon Israel's Legacy in Luke and Acts in the Light of the Pauline Letters*, LNTS 452 (London: T&T Clark, 2012). For a defense of the essential accuracy of Luke's picture of Paul, see Stanley E. Porter, *Paul in Acts*, Library of Pauline Studies (Grand Rapids: Baker, 2000).

5. See, e.g., F. F. Bruce, *Paul: Apostle of the Heart Set Free* (Grand Rapids: Eerdmans, 1977), 475; Rainer Riesner, "Pauline Chronology," in Westerholm, *Blackwell Companion to Paul*, 23 (see table of alternatives on p. 24); Stanley E. Porter, *The Apostle Paul: His Life, Thought, and Letters* (Grand Rapids: Eerdmans, 2016), 50–60; Ben Witherington III, *The Paul Quest: The Renewed Search for the Jew of Tarsus* (Downers Grove, IL: InterVarsity Press, 1998), 327–31. I should note that specific dates are often off by a year or two, reflecting inevitable uncertainty relative to both the meaning of NT texts and to the dates of external events.

Event	Date	Acts	Epistles
First Jerusalem visit	36	9:26–29	Gal 1:18–19
Stay in Syria and Cilicia	36–45	cf. 9:30	Gal 1:21
Ministry in Antioch	45–46	11:25–26	
Second Jerusalem visit ("famine relief")	46	11:27–30	Gal 2:1–10
First Missionary Journey	46–47	13:1–14:26	
Stay in Antioch	47–48	14:27–28	Gal 2:11–14
GALATIANS (?)			
Jerusalem Council	48	15:1–29	
Stay in Antioch	48–49	15:35	
Second Missionary Journey	49–52	15:36–18:22	
Galatia, Macedonia, Athens	Early 49		
Corinth	Autumn 49–Summer 51		
1 & 2 THESSALONIANS			
Third Missionary Journey	52–57	18:23–21:16	
Ephesus	52–55		
GALATIANS (?)			
1 CORINTHIANS			
PHILIPPIANS (?)			
Northern Greece	55–56		
2 CORINTHIANS			
Corinth	Winter, 56–57		
ROMANS			
Return to Judea	Spring 57		
Imprisonment in Judea	57–59	21:27–26:32	
"Shipwreck" voyage	Fall 59–Spring 60	27:1–28:14	
First Roman Imprisonment	60–62	28:15–31	
EPHESIANS			
COLOSSIANS			

(continued)

Event	Date	Acts	Epistles
PHILEMON			
PHILIPPIANS (?)			
Ministry	62–64?		Pastorals
1 TIMOTHY			
TITUS			
Second Roman imprisonment	64?		cf. 2 Tim 1:8
2 TIMOTHY			
Death	64/65 (67?)		

1.1 "Brought Up in Jerusalem"

After Paul is rescued by the Romans from Jews who were protesting what they thought was his desecration of the temple (Acts 21:27–36), the Roman commander gives him the opportunity to address the crowd (22:1–21). Paul begins with a brief overview of his childhood and education: "I am a Jew, born in Tarsus of Cilicia, but brought up in this city. I studied under Gamaliel and was thoroughly trained in the law of our ancestors" (22:3). Three stages in Paul's early life appear to be indicated here. *First*, he was born in Tarsus, an important and cosmopolitan city in the Roman province of Cilicia, in southeast Asia Minor. The *third* stage is also quite clear: Paul was trained in the Jewish faith by Gamaliel, one of the leading rabbis of Paul's day (see Acts 5:34). Just what Paul is claiming in the *second* stage of this sequence is not so clear. "This city" might refer to Tarsus, but a reference to Jerusalem is more likely. Harder to determine is what is entailed in the language "brought up" (*anatrephō* is the verb). One option is that the verb refers to the kind of training that one might receive in the teenage years. On this reading, Paul may have moved to Jerusalem only in his early teens.[6] However, the only other relevant occurrence of this verb in the New Testament refers to earlier childhood (Acts 7:21). Probably, then, Paul claims that he moved to Jerusalem at a fairly early age.[7] No other autobiographical references of Paul contradict this scenario.

The reason this apparently incidental reference has attracted attention is because it becomes embroiled in the larger debate about the relative influence of Paul's Hellenistic environment and Jewish training on his life and thought. Earlier stages in the study of Paul were marked by pitched battles over this issue, some arguing that Paul's Hellenistic

---

6. E.g., Eckhard J. Schnabel, *Acts*, ZECNT (Grand Rapids: Zondervan, 2016), 900.

7. See esp. Willem C. van Unnik, *Tarsus or Jerusalem: The City of Paul's Youth*, 2nd ed. (Eugene, OR: Wipf & Stock, 2009);

Craig S. Keener, *Acts: An Exegetical Commentary, Volume 3: Acts 13:1–23:35* (Grand Rapids: Baker, 2014), 3207–8; Rainer Riesner, *Paul's Early Period: Chronology, Mission Strategy, Theology* (Grand Rapids: Eerdmans, 1998), 268.

background exposed him to a peculiar form of Judaism and that his theology owes a great deal to the Greco-Roman world,[8] while others insisted Paul was trained in "orthodox" Judaism. These battles, while they have not disappeared, have subsided. For one thing, any sharp divide between "Hellenism" and "Judaism" has been shown to be simplistic; Judaism, even in Palestine, was strongly influenced by Hellenism.[9] Second, the attempt in some older treatments of Paul to attribute many of his key theological ideas to the Greco-Roman world has now been widely seen as a failure. Apart from his appeal to his Tarsian or general diaspora heritage for apologetic reasons, Paul rather consistently stresses his Jewish background; he is, he claims, a "Hebrew of Hebrews" (Phil 3:5). Paul's thinking is fundamentally Jewish, though debates continue over the specific stream of Judaism to which he is most indebted. However, this fundamentally Jewish core in Paul's thinking should not be allowed to push out all influence from his Greco-Roman environment. Paul was a man of two worlds; or, perhaps better, a man who moved in a world open to influences from a variety of sources, both Jewish and Hellenistic. In light of all this, it is not ultimately all that important where Paul was "brought up."

1.2 "Conversion"

A second debated matter in my outline of Paul's life is the reference to Paul's "conversion." Luke narrates this event in Acts 9:1–19, and Paul describes it in Acts 22:6–16, 26:12–18, and Galatians 1:15–16. Some recent interpreters doubt the appropriateness of this language, arguing that what Paul experienced on the Damascus Road was a "call," not a conversion. The accounts of this event do stress God's call on Paul to preach Christ (Acts 9:15; 22:15; 26:16–18; Gal 1:16), and Paul alludes to descriptions of prophetic calls in Galatians 1:15. "Conversion," it is argued, implies that Paul moved from one religion to another, and this would not be an accurate description of what happened on the Damascus Road. For one thing, Paul continued to emphasize his Jewish identity long after this event (e.g., Rom 9:3; cf. Acts 23:6). For another, there simply was no such thing at this early date as a Christian religion to which Paul could have been converted. The "separation of the ways" between Jews and Christians was some decades away.

The insistence that Paul was not converted, then, is often part of a larger movement to stress the continuity between Paul and Judaism. The titles of several recent volumes suggest the direction of scholarly thinking: *Paul: A New Covenant Jew*,[10] *Paul:*

---

8. See, e.g., C. G. Montefiore, *Judaism and St. Paul: Two Essays* (New York: E. P. Dutton, 1915), 93; Schoeps, *Paul*, 214, passim; Samuel Sandmel, *The Genius of Paul: A Study in History* (Philadelphia: Fortress, 1958), 30–33 (Schoeps and Sandmel see Hellenistic influence especially in Paul's view of the law). See the response in William D. Davies, *Paul and Rabbinic Judaism: Some Rabbinic Elements in Pauline Theology*, 4th ed. (Philadelphia: Fortress, 1980), 1–16.

9. The classic study is Martin Hengel, *Judaism and Hellenism: Studies in Their Encounter in Palestine during the Early Hellenistic Period*, 2 vols. (Tübingen: Mohr Siebeck, 1974).

10. Brant Pitre, Michael P. Barber, and John A. Kincaid, *Paul, a New Covenant Jew: Rethinking Pauline Theology* (Grand Rapids: Eerdmans, 2019).

An Anomalous Jew,[11] *Paul the Jew,*[12] *Paul Was Not a Christian.*[13] The latter two titles exemplify the more extreme form of this line of thought, which takes shape in the "Paul within Judaism" movement. I will deal with this movement and the issues it raises at a later point (pp. 433–35). Here I simply want to note the importance of steering a careful course between continuity and discontinuity in Paul's religious experience. As a Jesus follower, Paul continued to affirm the one God of the Old Testament and Judaism, to revere the Scriptures of Israel as authoritative, and to look for the salvation of Israel (adopting a certain view of Rom 11:25–28). On the other hand, he renounced matters central to Judaism as it was understood and practiced in his day: election as bound to the Torah covenant, the people of God identified in terms of Torah observance, and eschatological deliverance in terms of Israel's salvation first.

I would argue, then, that while Paul certainly experienced a call when Christ appeared to him, there were also elements of "conversion" involved as well. In Galatians 1:13–16, Paul suggests that the revelation of God's Son led him to contrast his new faith with his earlier "Judaism" (vv. 13, 14). To be sure, it is not entirely clear what Paul means by this word. James Dunn, for instance, noting the reference to "zeal" in this context, argues that it refers to a nationalistic, gentile-hostile form of Judaism. On the Damascus Road, then, Paul shifted his position within what we might broadly call Judaism.[14] Labels can be reductive and misleading, of course. What is especially important to note here is that (1) Jews themselves, if Luke is to be believed, rather consistently treated Paul's view as outside the bounds of "Judaism" as they understood it (e.g., Acts 13:45, 49–51; 14:2, 19; 17:5–9, 13; 18:6, 12–14; 20:3; 1 Thess 2:14–16); (2) Paul's language about his conversion in texts such as Philippians 3:2–11 suggests a fundamental shift from how Judaism was understood in his day to a very different set of priorities and values; and (3), as we will see elsewhere (pp. 573–75), Paul portrays the movement he was so instrumental in furthering as something that required a new category (e.g., "Jews, Greeks or the church of God"; 1 Cor 10:32). To label Paul's experience simply as a "call" drastically underplays Paul's own claim about the dramatic change that this event triggered for him.[15] Paul's letters make clear that his

11. Michael F. Bird, *An Anomalous Jew: Paul among Jews, Greeks, and Romans* (Grand Rapids: Eerdmans, 2016). See also Luke Timothy Johnson's "prophetic Jew" (*Constructing Paul*, vol. 1 of *The Canonical Paul* [Grand Rapids: Eerdmans, 2020], 143).

12. Gabriele Boccaccini and Carlos A. Segovia, eds., *Paul the Jew: Rereading the Apostle as a Figure of Second Temple Judaism* (Minneapolis: Fortress, 2016).

13. Pamela Eisenbaum, *Paul Was Not a Christian: The Original Message of a Misunderstood Apostle* (New York: HarperOne, 2009).

14. James D. G. Dunn, *The Epistle to the Galatians*, BNTC (Peabody, MA: Hendrickson, 1993), 56–65. For a different

suggestion severely limiting the scope of the word "Judaism," see Steve Mason, "Jews, Judaeans, Judaizing, Judaism: Problems of Categorization in Ancient History," *JSJ* 38 (2007): 457–512 (but see the critical evaluation of Matthew V. Novenson, "Paul's Former Occupation in *Ioudaismos*," in *Galatians and Christian Theology: Justification, the Gospel, and Ethics in Paul's Letter*, ed. Mark W. Elliott et al. [Grand Rapids: Baker, 2014], 24–39).

15. See, e.g., Terence L. Donaldson, *Paul and the Gentiles: Remapping the Apostle's Convictional World* (Minneapolis: Fortress, 1997), 249–60; Seyoon Kim, *Paul and the New Perspective: Second Thoughts on the Origin of Paul's Gospel* (Grand Rapids: Eerdmans, 2002), 1–19.

experience led him to leave behind "Judaism" as it was then practiced and in which Paul was raised. The word "conversion" is appropriately applied to this thoroughgoing change. Only a difference of fundamental importance can explain why Paul would have persecuted the early Christians and then gone to suffer persecution himself after embracing Christianity. When God revealed his Son to Paul, he was both converted *and* called: "Conversion and commission came together."[16] As John M. G. Barclay put it, "As a believer, Paul is a 'Jew' who (in his terms) no longer remains 'in Judaism'—his ethnicity has not been renounced but subsumed within an identity and an allegiance governed by the event of Christ."[17]

Paul's Damascus Road experience was a significant generating force in his theology. Paul underwent a "Copernican revolution," replacing Torah with Christ as the center of his intellectual and religious universe. Many of Paul's fundamental convictions, which emerge in various ways in his letters, can be traced in their basic thrust back to this event in his own life.[18] Damascus is "the fundamental point of departure for Pauline meaning formation."[19] As we study Paul's theology, we must not eliminate Paul himself from the picture. His own experience of Christ, both initially on the Damascus Road and continually throughout his life, inevitably colored his theology.

2 LETTERS

Our access to Paul's theology comes predominantly (thinking of Acts as a secondary source) through the letters he wrote to churches and individuals. Several issues pertaining to those letters need brief airing here.

2.1 Number

The shape of our theology of Paul will be significantly affected by our decision about what should "count" as evidence for Paul's views. This decision will have relatively little impact on some aspects of the apostle's teaching (e.g., justification), while it will quite

---

16. F. F. Bruce, *The Epistle to the Galatians: A Commentary on the Greek Text*, NIGTC (Grand Rapids: Eerdmans, 1982), 93; and see esp. Peter T. O'Brien, "Was Paul Converted?," in Carson, O'Brien, and Seifrid, *The Paradoxes of Paul*, 361–91; Bruce Corley, "Interpreting Paul's Conversion: Then and Now," in *The Road from Damascus: The Impact of Paul's Conversion on His Life, Thought and Ministry*, ed. Richard N. Longenecker (Grand Rapids: Eerdmans, 1997), 1–17; Larry W. Hurtado, "Convert, Apostate or Apostle to the Nations: The 'Conversion' of Paul in Recent Scholarship," *SR* 22 (1993): 273–84; Stephen J. Chester, *Conversion at Corinth: Perspectives on Conversion in Paul's Theology and the Corinthian Church*, SNTW (London: T&T Clark, 2003), 3–42, 153–72.

17. *Paul and the Gift*, 359–60; see also idem, "Paul, Judaism,

and the Jewish People," in Westerholm, *Blackwell Companion to Paul*, 188–201. A recent brief survey of options for Paul's "Jewishness" is found in Pitre, Barber, and Kincaid, *Paul, a New Covenant Jew*, 13–63.

18. This insight is pressed strongly (a bit too strongly?) by Seyoon Kim, *The Origin of Paul's Gospel*, WUNT 2/4 (Tübingen: Mohr Siebeck, 1981). See also, among others, Josef Blank, *Paulus und Jesus: Eine Theologische Grundlegung*, SANT 18 (Munich: Kösel, 1968), 184–238; Stuhlmacher, *Grundlegung*, 242–49; Christian Dietzfelbinger, *Der Sohn: Skizzen zur Christologie und Anthropologie des Paulus*, BTS 118 (Neukirchen-Vluyn: Neukirchener, 2011), 57–97.

19. Schnelle, *Apostle Paul*, 101.

seriously affect others (e.g., church leadership). I refer here, of course, to the modern debate about the authenticity of the letters of Paul. Scholars today often consider several of the letters ascribed to Paul to have been written by followers of Paul after his death. Most think the Pastoral Epistles fall into this category, many think Ephesians does, and quite a few also include Colossians and 2 Thessalonians. The "scholarly consensus," then, is that we can be relatively assured that Paul wrote seven letters, and many studies of Paul's theology or of particular Pauline theological themes are based on these letters alone. The effect this decision has on one's conclusions vary significantly. Some scholars, while doubting the Pauline authorship of some of the letters, will nonetheless view them as providing genuine insight into Paul's thinking. At the other extreme are those who find a sharp division between the authentic letters and the others. An example of the latter approach is found in the book by Marcus J. Borg and Dominic Crossan, who view post-Pauline letters as "anti-Paul," propagating "a taming of Paul, a domestication of Paul's passion."[20]

This is not the place to assess the debate about "pseudepigraphical" New Testament letters. My opinion is that the widely held view that many of our New Testament letters were written by others than the letters themselves claim faces far more difficulties than is usually admitted. The evidence we possess suggests that people in Paul's day and later looked askance at letters written in someone else's name. Armin Baum, after a thorough analysis of the data from the ancient world, concludes that "a statement is not viewed as inauthentic if its wording is not from the author but will be ascribed to him; it is viewed however as false, if one can not trace its content back to the person whose name it bears."[21] Neil Elliott, who thinks many of Paul's letters are inauthentic, similarly concludes, "Pseudepigrapha are forgeries, however devoutly motivated they may have been."[22] If we grant that early Christians shared these perspectives, it is difficult to imagine how they would have admitted into the canon letters that they knew to be pseudepigraphical. Of course, it is still possible that they were duped into thinking letters were genuinely Pauline when they were not. However, while we do not know a lot about the process of collecting and authenticating Paul's letters, we do know that early Christians recognized the possibility of fraudulent letters and rejected those so identified as having any authority in forming Christian teaching.

20. Marcus J. Borg, and John Dominic Crossan, *The First Paul: Reclaiming the Radical Visionary behind the Church's Conservative Icon* (New York: HarperCollins, 2009), 15.

21. Armin D. Baum, *Pseudepigraphie und literarische Falschung Im Frühen Christentum*, WUNT 2/138 (Tübingen: Mohr Siebeck, 2001), 92; idem, "Content and Form: Authorship Attribution and Pseudonymity in Ancient Speeches, Letters, Lectures, and Translations: A Rejoinder to Bart Ehrman," *JBL* 136 (2017): 381–403. For other criticisms of the pseudepigraphical hypothesis, see Terry Lee Wilder, *Pseudonymity, the New Testament and*

Deception: An Inquiry into Intention and Reception (Lanham, MD: University Press of America, 2004); Lee Martin MacDonald and Stanley E. Porter, *Early Christianity and Its Sacred Literature* (Peabody, MA: Hendrickson, 2000), 388–93; D. A. Carson and Douglas J. Moo, *An Introduction to the New Testament*, 2nd ed. (Grand Rapids: Zondervan, 2005), 337–50. See also Johnson, *Constructing Paul*, 33–41, 74–92.

22. Neil Elliott, *Liberating Paul: The Justice of God and the Politics of the Apostle* (Minneapolis: Fortress, 1994), 29.

While several lines of evidence are often cited for regarding a Pauline letter as pseudepigraphical, the most important by far is theological consistency. Put simply, many scholars are convinced that the theology taught in some of the disputed letters simply cannot be reconciled with the theology found in the authentic Pauline letters. Evaluating this line of evidence is inevitably a very subjective matter. It is also important to be clear what the issue is. It is not whether Paul's theology developed. Of course it did. The issue is, rather, if that development led to irreconcilable contradictions. My own view is that it did not. Tensions between the seven "authentic" Pauline letters and the disputed letters are significantly eased once we allow for (1) the inevitable growth in Paul's thinking as he matured; (2) the need to address new issues as the church itself matured; and (3) the very different circumstances addressed in the letters.

In this book, then, I attempt to ground Paul's theological teaching in all thirteen canonical letters.

2.2 Genre and Rhetoric

The "letter" was a recognized form of communication in the ancient world, and Paul's letters share generic features with these other ancient letters. To be sure, the length of some of Paul's letters strains the genre a bit: the longest of the many letters of Cicero is 2,530 words, that of Seneca 4,134 words, while Paul's Romans is 7,101 words in length.[23] Some scholars therefore suggest that Paul's correspondence breaks boundaries into a new genre: the "apostolic/pastoral letter," "the apostle in absentia."[24] As this language suggests, Paul's letters seem to have been an attempt to bring Paul's "presence" into pastoral situations even when he was distant physically from the situation (see, e.g., his reference to being "with you in spirit" and therefore "present with you in this way" in 1 Cor 5:3). However, rather than classifying Paul's correspondence as a new genre, it might be better to see them as extensions or applications of the standard letter form. In any case, it seems appropriate to consider them in the context of other letters of their day. Various rather sophisticated models for the "form" of a letter have been suggested, but ancient letters, taken as a whole, display a rather simple and straightforward form, consisting of an opening, a thanksgiving, the body of the letter, and a closing.[25] These categories are obviously so general that useful interpretive conclusions from this division are minimal.

The Greek world of Paul's day was "into" rhetoric. Methods and styles of persuasive argument were developed, studied, and applied. It is natural, then, that scholars would

23. Larry W. Hurtado, *Destroyer of the Gods: Early Christian Distinctiveness in the Roman World* (Waco, TX: Baylor University Press, 2016), 120.

24. Gorman, *Apostle of the Crucified Lord*, 92–98.

25. Jeffrey A. D. Weima, *Paul the Ancient Letter Writer: An Introduction to Epistolary Analysis* (Grand Rapids: Baker, 2016), 10–26. See also the collection of essays in Stanley E. Porter and Sean A. Adams, eds., *Paul and the Ancient Letter Form*, Pauline Studies 6 (Leiden: Brill, 2010).

use these widespread styles and forms of rhetoric to analyze the letters of Paul. For instance, there were three main forms of ancient rhetoric: (1) "forensic," focused on defending or criticizing past activity; (2) "deliberative," designed to persuade or dissuade people from adopting a course of action; and (3) "epideictic," raising the question of whether something or someone should be praised or blamed. Scholars have argued about which of these Paul may have been using in his letters, or at particular places in his letters. However, the diversity of conclusions reached by these scholars strongly suggests that Paul's argument(s) cannot neatly be put into one of these categories. As Murray Harris puts it with respect to 2 Corinthians:

> Any document of the length of 2 Corinthians . . . that is (1) written by a highly edu-cated person, (2) apologetic in character, (3) logical in presentation, and (4) aimed at winning over an audience and influencing their way of thinking and acting is likely to display the basic ingredients of forensic, deliberative, or epideictic rhetoric—but not necessarily in a recognizable or schematic sequence.[26]

As a man of his world, Paul naturally uses many of the rhetorical forms, devices, and language of his day. Yet there is no evidence that he had any special training in rhetoric, and on the whole, analyzing Paul's letters in terms of specific rhetorical techniques and categories is not particularly helpful.[27]

2.3 Coauthors?

I have been referring, as others do, to the "letters of Paul." In fact, however, most of the letters we usually attribute simply to Paul include in their opening verses references to other Christian leaders:

Paul and Sosthenes (1 Cor 1:1)
Paul and Timothy (2 Cor 1:1; Phil 1:1; Col 1:1; Phlm 1)
Paul, Silas, and Timothy (1 Thess 1:1; 2 Thess 1:1)

Some interpreters argue that the intention of these openings is to identify the per-sons named as genuine coauthors.[28] However, the frequent use of first-person singular

---

26. Harris, *Second Epistle to the Corinthians*, 109.

27. See esp. Stanley E. Porter, "Paul of Tarsus and His Let-ters," in *Handbook of Classical Rhetoric in the Hellenistic Period (330 B.C.–A.D. 400)*, ed. Stanley E. Porter (Leiden: Brill, 2001), 533–85; Weima, *Paul the Ancient Letter Writer*, 8–9; Paul M. Robertson, *Paul's Letters and Contemporary Greco-Roman Liter-ature: Theorizing a New Taxonomy*, NovTSup 167 (Leiden: Brill, 2016), 40–56; Ryan S. Schellenberg, "Rhetorical Terminology in Paul: A Critical Reappraisal," *ZNW* 104 (2013): 177–91. For a useful series of essays giving a spectrum of opinion on rhetoric in Paul, see Stanley E. Porter and Bryan R. Dyer, eds., *Paul and Ancient Rhetoric: Theory and Practice in the Hellenistic Context* (Cambridge: Cambridge University Press, 2016).

28. See esp. E. R. Richards, *Paul and First-Century Letter Writing: Secretaries, Composition and Collection* (Downers Grove, IL: InterVarsity Press, 2004), 32–36.

forms in the letters as well as personal allusions to Paul only (never to the alleged coauthor) strongly suggest that we should view these individuals as "cosenders."[29] Paul is responsible for the content of the letter, although we also have to allow that Paul's amanuenses may have had a role in the wording.[30] Paul includes reference to coworkers in the introductions to many of the letters to remind his readers that what Paul says in the letter has the backing and authority of other key Christian leaders. Often, of course, these leaders are included because they played a significant role in the life of the church or individual Paul is addressing.[31]

29. Weima, *Paul the Ancient Letter Writer*, 27–32. Paul, of course, often uses first-person plural verbs in his letters. These may be genuine plurals, referring to Paul and others like him (sometimes fellow Jews, more often fellow Christians) and perhaps also at times to himself and his cosender. However, some of these plurals probably refer to Paul only (see, e.g., Karl Dick, *Der Schriftstellerische Plural bei Paulus* [Halle: Ehrhardt Karras, 1899]).

30. On amanuenses and the nature of their involvement in the letter, see E. R. Richards, *Paul and First-Century Letter Writing*, 81–93. Armin Baum successfully argues, contra Bart Ehrman, that letters would have been considered authentic as long as the *content* (not necessarily the wording) of the letter could be traced to the named author (Baum, "Content and Form," 381–403).

31. Samuel Byrskog, "Co-Senders, Co-Authors and Paul's Use of the First Person Plural," *ZNW* 87 (1996): 230–50.

Chapter 4

GALATIANS

GALATIANS, in my view the earliest letter Paul wrote, introduces some of his most distinctive theological ideas: salvation history as an overall framework for interpreting God's plan and our place in it; justification by faith alone; the place and function of the law in God's purposes; the terrific power of the Spirit to transform God's people.[1] All this theology, as always in Paul, has a practical aim: seeking to keep new Christians on the path of righteousness in the face of temptations to stray from the sufficiency of Christ and the Spirit.

LOCATING THE LETTER

We can better understand how the teaching of Galatians on these, and other issues, contributes to Paul's theology if we are able to accurately locate the letter within the trajectory of Paul's mission. Unfortunately, the date of Galatians is uncertain—and this is because the destination of the letter is also uncertain. *When* Paul wrote hinges on to *whom* he wrote.

Paul is explicit about writing "to the churches in Galatia" (1:2; cf. "you foolish Galatians" in 3:1). But "Galatia" could refer either to a *region* in north-central Asia Minor or to a *province* in the Roman Empire that derived its name from this region. If Paul is referring to the former, then the earliest possible date for the letter would be around AD 51 or 52, when Paul was on his second missionary journey. Indeed, if "Galatia" refers to the region by that name, Paul is probably writing during his third missionary journey, and the letter would have to be dated sometime in AD 54–57.[2] On the other hand, if Paul writes to the *province* of Galatia, which included the cities of Pisidian Antioch, Lystra, Iconium, and Derbe, then he could be writing as early as AD 48 or 49, just after the first missionary journey.[3] Note, however, my language:

---

1. This chapter draws heavily (in concepts and occasionally in wording) from Douglas J. Moo, *Galatians*, BECNT (Grand Rapids: Baker, 2013). Used by permission.

2. Galatians makes clear that Paul had ministered in Galatia before he wrote the letter. Luke's record of Paul's movements strongly suggests that the apostle did not enter the *region* of Galatia until the beginning of the second missionary journey—at the

earliest: see Acts 16:6. Moreover, if Gal 4:13 implies that Paul had visited the Galatians twice before he wrote the letter (*proteron* in that verse meaning "former of two" visits), then he probably could not have written until the third missionary journey, since Paul next visited "Galatia" at the beginning of that journey (Acts 18:3).

3. The two visits perhaps hinted at in Gal 4:13 would then include the initial founding visit along with the follow-up visit

"as early as." A "south" Galatian destination does not entail an early date: Paul could be writing any time after AD 48 or so. The key difference is that a provincial Galatian destination for the letter *allows* a very early date, while the regional identification does not.

Considerable academic energy has been expended evaluating and arguing for a range of options.[4] In my view, the deciding issue is the implication of Paul's rehearsal of his relationship with the Jerusalem church in 1:11–2:10. Paul mentions two visits: one shortly after his conversion and before his return to his hometown of Tarsus (1:18); and a second some years later (2:1). There are three possible incidents in the book of Acts with which these visits might line up: Paul's brief, initial visit shortly after his conversion (Acts 9:26–30); his "famine relief" visit (11:27–30); and the Jerusalem Council visit (15:1–21). The first visit Paul mentions pretty clearly lines up with Acts 9:26–30. But what about Galatians 2:1–10? The general similarities between Paul's description of his conference with the "pillar" apostles and Luke's narrative of the Jerusalem Council are clear, and it is not surprising that many scholars conclude that they must be describing the same event.[5] There are, however, some notable discrepancies between these accounts as well. More seriously, an identification of 2:1–10 with Acts 15 implies that Paul has omitted any reference to the "famine relief" visit. Perhaps Paul does not intend to mention every one of his visits to Jerusalem between his conversion and his writing to the Galatians. But I think the polemical context of the letter would make it unlikely

as Paul retraced his steps (Acts 14:21–25). But it is not at all clear that Gal 4:13 requires two previous visits to Galatia (*proteron* can mean simply "previous"; see Moo, *Galatians*, 283–84).

4. The range of options is:
  i. Paul wrote to churches in the southern part of provincial Galatia
    a. just before the Jerusalem Council (AD 48; e.g., Bruce, *Galatians*, 3–18, 43–56; Richard N. Longenecker, *Galatians*, WBC [Dallas: Word, 1990], lxi–lxxxviii; Richard Bauckham, "Barnabas in Galatians," *JSNT* 2 [1979]: 61–70; Colin J. Hemer, *The Book of Acts in the Setting of Hellenistic History*, ed. Conrad H. Gempf, WUNT 2/49 [Tübingen: Mohr Siebeck, 1989], 260–71; David A. deSilva, *The Letter to the Galatians*, NICNT [Grand Rapids: Eerdmans, 2018], 39–62);
    b. early on the second missionary journey (AD 50–51; e.g., James D. G. Dunn, *The Theology of Paul's Letter to the Galatians* [Cambridge: Cambridge University Press, 1993], 12–17; Craig S. Keener, *Galatians: A Commentary* [Grand Rapids: Baker, 2019], 8–22);
    c. during the third missionary journey (AD 54–57; e.g., Ernest de Witt Burton, *A Critical and Exegetical Commentary on the Epistle to the Galatians*, ICC [Edinburgh: T&T Clark, 1921], xlvii–xlix (hesitantly); Gordon D. Fee, *Galatians*, Pentecostal Commentary [Blandford Forum, UK: Deo, 2007], 4;

Frank J. Matera, *Galatians*, SP 9 [Collegeville, MN: Liturgical, 1992], 19–26).
  ii. Paul wrote to churches in regional ("North") Galatia
    a. during the second missionary journey (AD 50–51; Martyn, *Galatians*, 19–20; Martinus C. de Boer, *Galatians: A Commentary*, NTL [Louisville: Westminster John Knox, 2011], 5–11);
    b. early on the third missionary journey (AD 54–55; Raymond E. Brown, *An Introduction to the New Testament* [New York: Doubleday, 1997], 474–77; Werner G. Kümmel, *Introduction to the New Testament*, 2nd ed. [London: SCM, 1975], 296–304; Murphy-O'Connor, *Paul*, 159–62, 180–82);
    c. late on the third missionary journey (AD 57; this is the "classic" form of the "north Galatian" view; see, e.g., J. B. Lightfoot, *Saint Paul's Epistle to the Galatians: A Revised Text with Introduction, Notes, and Dissertations*, 7th ed. [London: Macmillan, 1881], 48–49; Joachim Rohde, *Der Brief des Paulus an die Galater*, THKNT 9 [Berlin: Evangelische Verlagsanstalt, 1989], 10; Franz Mussner, *Der Galaterbrief*, 5th ed., HThKNT 9 [Freiburg: Herder, 1988], 9–10).

5. See esp. the clear and succinct summary of Moisés Silva, *Interpreting Galatians: Explorations in Exegetical Method*, 2nd ed. (Grand Rapids: Baker Academic, 2001), 129–39.

that he would omit a visit. Assuming, then, the historical accuracy of Luke on this matter, it is more likely that Galatians 2:1–10 lines up with Acts 11:27–30—implying that Paul writes Galatians before the Jerusalem Council, and therefore to the first missionary cities in the southern part of the Roman province of Galatia. The failure of Paul to mention the conclusion of the Jerusalem Council—a matter quite significant for the issue in Galatians—tends to confirm this conclusion.[6]

I therefore conclude that Galatians should be located between the end of the first missionary journey and before the Jerusalem Council (Acts 14:26–28). On this view, Galatians would be the first letter Paul wrote. I also, however, acknowledge that the location of Galatians is not all that certain, meaning that we will have to be cautious about using this location to draw conclusions about the development of Paul's theology.

ISOLATING THE ISSUES

The issue sparking Paul's writing of the letter to Galatian gentile Christians is clear: at stake is nothing less than the gospel. People preaching "another gospel" (1:6–10) have appeared on the scene. They are "confusing" (see the verb *tarassō* in 1:7 and 5:10) the Galatians by insisting that these converted gentiles could belong to the "seed" or be "children" of Abraham only by being circumcised (5:2–4) and by committing themselves to a lifestyle set forth by the law of Moses (3:15–4:7). The rhetorically central paragraph 3:1–5 reveals Paul's view of the matter: having begun well with faith and the Spirit, the Galatians were being urged to "finish by means of the flesh" (3:3). Dunn, speaking for most interpreters of the letter, succinctly summarizes the situation: "The letter makes clearest and fullest sense if we see it as a response to a challenge from *Christian-Jewish missionaries* who had come to Galatia to improve or correct Paul's gospel and to 'complete' his converts by integrating them fully into the heirs of Abraham through circumcision and by thus bringing them 'under the law.'"[7] By using the word "complete," Dunn points to another issue:[8] that the agitators' (see 5:12) efforts were focused on what we might call the "second phase" of Christian experience. Perhaps the distinction made famous by E. P. Sanders would be applicable here: the issue was not on how one "gets in" but on how one "stays in." I think this general reading of the letter is accurate. However, the argument of the letter suggests that Paul's concern was not only, or perhaps even mainly, on "staying in" but on ultimate vindication in the final judgment.

The "missionaries" who had come to Galatia probably claimed some relationship to the apostles in Jerusalem. Paul's focus on his own relationship with Jerusalem and "those who were apostles before [he] was" in 1:13–2:10 points in this direction. But this

---

6. See esp. R. Longenecker, *Galatians*, lxxxviii–lxxx, for a clear presentation of these arguments.

7. Dunn, *Epistle to the Galatians*, 11.

8. Dunn, *Theology of Paul's Letter to the Galatians*, 16–17.

identification becomes quite explicit in Paul's "allegory" based on the narrative about Sarah and Hagar (Gal 4:21–31). Paul contrasts the free children of Abraham, descendants of Sarah through Isaac, with those who are descendants of Hagar, "the present city of Jerusalem," "in slavery with her children" (4:25). Not only, then, did the agitators claim to represent Jerusalem; their perspective is one that Paul identifies with Judaism in general.[9]

Keeping in mind the polemical situation in which Paul writes Galatians is vital to appreciating his teaching in this letter and the way it is integrated in his theology. Take, for instance, the issue of the law in Galatians. This letter has the highest proportion of occurrences of *nomos* ("law") of any Pauline letter.[10] Galatians rightly therefore is a key source for our understanding of Paul's theology of the law. Yet our use of the evidence of Galatians on this point must be directed by the polemical stance Paul adopts in the letter. Paul's teaching about the law is designed to right an imbalance that the agitators had created. He is engaged in a balancing operation, putting all his weight on the negative side of the law in order to bring the Galatians back to an even keel in their theology. This does not mean, of course, as some have alleged, that Paul's teaching about the law in Galatians must be dismissed as a pastorally motivated overreaction in favor of the more "neutral" stance of Romans. In fact, all the negative points about the law in Galatians are repeated in Romans. The difference is that Romans does not have in view the same polemical issues as Galatians and hence has more positive things to say about the law.

ANALYZING THE ARGUMENT

Paul responds to the challenge of the agitators in three stages. First, he uses his own experience to illustrate the relationship between "the truth of the gospel" (2:5, 14) and the law of Moses (1:11–2:21), with a particular focus on his relationship to the Jerusalem apostles (1:17–2:14). Second, he uses the Galatians' own experience and especially Scripture, to argue that the justification that accompanies belonging to the "seed" of Abraham is by faith, apart from Torah observance (3:1–5:12). Third, he shows that conduct pleasing to God is secured by that same faith and the work of God's Spirit apart from Torah (5:13–6:18).

---

9. Contra, e.g., Martyn, *Galatians*, 457–66, who virtually limits Paul's debate to Christian opponents; see, e.g., Thomas R. Schreiner, "Paul and Perfect Obedience to the Law: An Evaluation of the View of E. P. Sanders," *WTJ* 47 (1985): 254–55. Mark Nanos thinks the "influencers" (his term) had not come from outside the community but were Jews who were charged with admitting new members into Jewish communities (*The Irony of Galatians: Paul's Letter in First-Century Context* [Minneapolis: Fortress, 2002], 110–99). But this view makes no sense of Paul's claim that the agitators were preaching "another gospel" (1:6–9).

See, e.g., Dunn, *Beginning from Jerusalem*, 721–22; John M. G. Barclay, "Paul, the Gift and the Battle over Gentile Circumcision: Revisiting the Logic of Galatians," *ABR* 58 [2010]: 37). Neil Martin has recently argued that the emphasis on Jewish religious practices (innocuous in themselves) was tempting the Galatians to "regress" into their former pagan idolatrous habits (*Regression in Galatians*, WUNT 2/530 [Tübingen: Mohr Siebeck, 2020]).

10. *Nomos* occurs once for every 4.7 verses in Galatians. Romans is a close second, with *nomos* coming once every 5.8 verses.

Justification by faith, while perhaps not the main theme of Galatians, is a critical aspect about the truth of the gospel that Paul needs to establish. What is not as often appreciated, but which is made clear by the justification language in 5:4–5, is that the justification involved here is not simply entrance into the Christian life. The issue in Galatia, as 3:1–5 reveals so clearly, is not how one begins the Christian life but on how one continues it. Paul challenges the Galatians to "continue" in the same way that they have begun. He does not deny that the Galatians have been justified when they first came to faith in Christ—a point that Romans makes quite clearly. But the rhetorical exigencies of the Galatian crisis require Paul to focus on the continuation and culmination of the Christian life. The focus in the letter, then, is on what we might call "ultimate justification," vindication on the day of judgment.[11]

1 INTRODUCTION: THE CROSS AND THE NEW AGE (1:1–10)

Galatians follows the usual pattern of letters in the Greco-Roman world, with an opening, body, and closing. The letter opening (Galatians 1:1–10) falls into two parts: the typical epistolary salutation (vv. 1–5) and an identification of the letter's occasion (vv. 6–10).

As usual, Paul identifies himself as "an apostle." But he elaborates this claim with a defense of the divine authority of his office, with an initial hint in v. 1 of an important argument in the letter (1:11–2:10). Also reflecting his polemical concerns in the letter are two other unusual elements in this introduction. First, after (unusually) including "God the Father" as one from whom his apostleship comes, Paul adds "who raised him [Jesus Christ, earlier in the verse] from the dead" (v. 1). Second, Paul adds to his typical "grace and peace" wish (v. 3) a description of the Lord Jesus Christ: "Who gave himself for our sins to rescue us from the present evil age, according to the will of our God and Father" (v. 4). In this latter verse, Paul picks up language from Isaiah 53 to depict the sacrificial offering of Christ for "sins."[12] These elements combine to draw attention to the decisive turn in salvation history that has taken place with the coming of Christ: the end-time resurrection has been inaugurated, and Christ-followers experience an "apocalyptic rescue operation."[13] These additions serve to remind the Galatians that

---

11. Simon Gathercole has drawn attention to the importance of this future "getting in" in Jewish literature and its comparative neglect in the debate (*Where Is Boasting? Early Jewish Soteriology and Paul's Response in Romans 1–5* [Grand Rapids: Eerdmans, 2002], 113–19). On Galatians, see also Graham N. Stanton, "The Law of Moses and the Law of Christ: Galatians 3:1–6:2," in *Paul and the Mosaic Law*, ed. by James D. G. Dunn (Tübingen: Mohr Siebeck, 1996), 99–116, 103–4.

12. See esp. Isa 53:6, 10, 12; and see Matthew S. Harmon, *She Must and Shall Go Free: Paul's Isaianic Gospel in Galatians*, BZNW 168 (Berlin: de Gruyter, 2010), 56–66.

13. Richard Hays, "Galatians," *NIB* 11 (Nashville: Abingdon, 2000), 202.

the agitators have failed to reckon seriously enough with the radical implications of Christ's death and resurrection.

Paul's omission of his usual thanksgiving for his readers and his abrupt turn to the situation in the Galatian churches suggests the strength of Paul's concern. The issue in the Galatian churches so concerns Paul that he skips any commendatory language to launch directly into his polemic; as Chrysostom puts it, the letter "breathes an indignant spirit."[14] Paul is amazed at how "quickly" (perhaps meaning so soon after their conversion) the Galatian believers are "turning to a different gospel" (v. 6). The impetus for this exchange is the arrival of "some people" who have confused the Galatians about the meaning of the true gospel of Christ (v. 7). Specific references elsewhere in the letter (see esp. 5:2–4), as well as the general argument, reveal that these false teachers were insisting that the Galatian gentiles be circumcised and submit to the law of Moses in order to be counted among the true people of God and to achieve the righteous standing that they would need to go free in the judgment (see *Isolating the Issues* above). Paul warns the Galatians not to succumb to this teaching. He accomplishes this by using the strongest language he can muster to paint the false teachers as people who have perverted the gospel of Christ and who are thereby destined for eternal condemnation (1:8–9). The threat of divine judgment for following false teaching in the beginning of the letter stands in antithetical contrast to the blessing promised for those who continue to follow the apostolic "rule" at the end of the letter (6:16).[15] Paul concludes the paragraph by contrasting himself, as a true servant of Christ, with these false teachers (1:10).[16]

2 THE TRUTH OF THE GOSPEL (1:11–2:21)

Paul uses a disclosure formula—"I want you to know"—to signal the transition from the letter opening to the body of the letter. This letter body falls into three parts. The first begins at 1:11 (or 1:10) and ends either at 2:14 or 2:21 (see my comments at that point). Paul has used the language of the gospel to set up the basic issue of the letter in 1:6–10. The long section that begins in 1:11 has five more references to the gospel (1:11; 2:2, 5, 7, 14). Paul clearly focuses on his own apostleship in this section, but that apostleship is, in turn, focused on, and to some extent determined by, the gospel that he preaches.

---

14. *Commentary on Galatians* on 1:1 (*NPNF¹* 13:1).

15. Hans Dieter Betz, *Galatians: A Commentary on Paul's Letter to the Churches in Galatia*, Hermeneia (Minneapolis: Fortress, 1979), 50–51; Todd A. Wilson, *The Curse of the Law and the Crisis in Galatia: Reassessing the Purpose of Galatians*, WUNT 225 (Tübingen: Mohr Siebeck, 2007), 26–27.

16. Some texts (e.g., NA²⁷) and interpreters (e.g., Mussner, *Galaterbrief*, 62; François Vouga, *An die Galater*, HNT [Tübingen: Mohr Siebeck, 1998], 25) take this verse with what follows.

2.1 How Paul Received and Defended the Gospel: Paul and the "Pillars" (1:11–2:14)

Paul's argument in this first section of the letter body comes in two parts: a thesis statement in 1:11–12, and elaboration and justification for that statement in 1:13–2:14 (21). We can divide this long second section into four parts (with 2:15–21 as a transitional section). He tells the story of his own conversion and ministry, using his relationship to Jerusalem and the apostles resident there as his structuring element. In 1:13–17 he celebrates God's initiative in turning him from persecutor of the church to evangelist of the gentiles. But his relationship with Jerusalem surfaces here, as he comments that he did not "go up to Jerusalem to see those who were apostles before" him immediately after his conversion (v. 17a). In Galatians 1:18–24 Paul briefly describes his subsequent ministry, with a focus again on his contacts with Jerusalem: "Then after three years, I went up to Jerusalem . . ." (v. 18); "I was personally unknown to the churches of Judea" (v. 22). Note also that Paul transitions to his description of the "apostolic conference" in 2:1–10 with a formula similar to the one in 1:18: "Then after fourteen years, I went up again to Jerusalem" (2:1). In his description of this conference (vv. 2–10), Paul shifts from the negative—"I did not have much contact with the Jerusalem apostles"—to the positive—"the Jerusalem apostles agreed with me about the nature of the gospel."[17] The final narrative stage, the incident at Antioch (2:11–14), does not neatly fit into the chronological narrative of 1:18–2:10 and abandons the Jerusalem focus. But the general theme of Paul's relationship with the "pillars" continues, and the Antioch incident thus becomes a kind of "add-on" to the narrative.

Paul's rhetorical purpose in 1:13–2:14 (21) is to assure the Galatians that they have, indeed, received (see 1:9) the true gospel. "The truth of the gospel" (2:5, 14) is Paul's focus in this section. Since the Galatians received this gospel from Paul, their confidence in the former is bound up with the latter: message and messenger are closely related. The truth of the gospel and Paul's credentials as an authoritative messenger of that gospel are therefore woven together in this part of the letter. But the focus on Jerusalem in this argument is notable and demands an explanation.

Those who argue that Paul is simply rehearsing his experience as an example for the Galatians have some basis in the text (see 4:12).[18] However, they are unable to account satisfactorily for this focus on Jerusalem.[19] This focus is best explained if Paul in this section is making a polemical thrust against the agitators, who were asserting

---

17. Silva, *Interpreting Galatians*, 99–100.

18. See esp. George Lyons, *Pauline Autobiography: Toward a New Understanding*, SBLDS 73 (Atlanta: Scholars Press, 1985), 123–76; Beverly Roberts Gaventa, "Galatians 1 and 2: Autobiography as Paradigm," *NovT* 28 (1986): 311–19; Stephen A. Cummins, *Paul and the Crucified Christ: Maccabean Martyrdom and Galatians 1 and 2*, SNTSMS 114 (Cambridge: Cambridge

University Press, 2001), 98–101, 114–37; Donald J. Verseput, "Paul's Gentile Mission and the Jewish Christian Community: A Study of the Narrative in Galatians 1 and 2," *NTS* 39 (1993): 36–58.

19. James D. G. Dunn, *Did the First Christians Worship Jesus? The New Testament Evidence* (Louisville: Westminster John Knox, 2010), 29–34; deSilva, *Galatians*, 137.

that Paul was under the authority of the Jerusalem apostles and that therefore they, the (self-claimed) representatives of those apostles, should be listened to rather than Paul. Paul's purpose, then, is to establish his independent authority as an apostle, in response to the false claims of the agitators, so that the gospel that he has preached to the Galatians might retain its truth and authority.[20]

If we turn now to the thesis statement in 1:11–12, we find that Paul combines and elaborates on two important claims that he has made in 1:1–10: that his apostleship, and thus his authority, is not of human origin but came through Jesus Christ (v. 1); and that "the gospel of Christ" the Galatians have received should not be exchanged for any other "gospel," no matter what the claims about its origin might be (vv. 6–9). Especially important is Paul's use of the language of "revelation" (*apokalypsis*) to depict his encounter with Christ (v. 12). It is debated whether Paul means that Christ himself was revealed to him (taking the genitive *Iēsou Christou* as objective),[21] that Christ revealed the gospel to him (a subjective genitive),[22] or, perhaps most likely, that Paul's gospel is rooted in "Christ's revelation" (a "general" genitive).[23] In any case, the use of this terminology reinforces Paul's emphasis on the determinative nature of Christ's appearance.[24]

As many interpreters have pointed out, the narrative of Paul's conversion and early travels is structured by temporal indicators: *pote*, "at one time" (1:13, my own translation), *hote*, "when" (1:15), *epeita*, "then" (1:18, 21; 2:1). Paul focuses throughout on the Jerusalem apostles, those he calls "pillars" in 2:9. He insists that his understanding of the gospel did not depend on the pillars (1:13–24), that the pillars themselves agreed with his version of the gospel (2:1–10), and that he defended the gospel when it came under attack from one of those pillars (2:11–14).

Paul sets the stage for the narration of his contacts with Jerusalem by reminding his readers of his own radical conversion from persecutor to apostle. Particularly striking in Paul's narrative is his emphasis on the divine initiative in the whole matter. Far from being "prepared" for his conversion by a time of soul-searching, Paul testifies that he was a convinced, indeed "zealous," Jew until God called him "by his grace" (1:15) and revealed his Son to him (1:16). While not the main point in these verses, then, a concern on Paul's part to present himself as one to emulate is present.[25] Like Paul, the

---

20. See, e.g., D. François Tolmie, *Persuading the Galatians: A Text-Centred Rhetorical Analysis of a Pauline Letter*, WUNT 2/190 (Tübingen: Mohr Siebeck, 2005), 32–47; Moisés Silva, "Galatians 1:1–2:16a" (unpublished manuscript, 2003), 38–39; Karl Olav Sandnes, *Paul—One of the Prophets? A Contribution to the Apostle's Self-Understanding*, WUNT 43 (Tübingen: Mohr Siebeck, 1991), 49–51; Jost Eckert, *Die Urchristliche Verkündigung im Streit zwischen Paulus und seinen Gegnern nach dem Galaterbrief* (Regensburg: Friedrich Pustet, 1971), 163–228.

21. E.g., Burton, *Galatians*, 41–43.

22. This interpretation is expressed in the English "from Jesus Christ" in, e.g., NIV; CSB; NLT; and see Simon Légasse, *L'épître de Paul aux Galates*, LD 9 (Paris: Cerf, 2000), 80; R. Longenecker, *Galatians*, 24; Pierre Bonnard, *L'épître de saint Paul aux Galates*, 2nd ed., CNT 9 (Neuchatel: Delachaux & Niestle, 1972), 28.

23. Silva, "Galatians 1:1–2:16a," 45.

24. See the discussion on pp. 25–26 for the relationship between direct apprehension of the gospel and Paul's claim to have "received" the gospel (e.g., 1 Cor 15:3).

25. E.g., Verseput, "Paul's Gentile Mission."

Galatians have been "called" to live in "grace" (1:6), and, like Paul, they should stay firmly rooted in this gracious gospel and not exchange it for any "other" gospel. At the same time, the very syntax of the paragraph points to the overarching apologetic focus. For, remarkably, Paul narrates his conversion in the subordinate clause of a sentence whose main clause is about his contact with other humans: "When God . . . was pleased . . . to reveal his Son in me . . . my immediate response was not to consult any human being. I did not go up to Jerusalem" (vv. 15–17a). These two basic parts of the paragraph develop chiastically the thesis of verses 11–12:

(a) my gospel is not from any human source (vv. 11–12a), rather
   (b) it came by revelation (v. 12b);
   (b') when God revealed his Son to me (vv. 13–16a),
(a') I did not consult with any human being (vv. 16b–17).

As he does elsewhere (e.g., Phil 3:2–11), Paul stresses that he was a pious, indeed, passionate Jew when Christ encountered him on the road to Damascus: Paul's "previous way of life in Judaism" was characterized by religious diligence and persecuting zeal (Gal 1:13–14). Paul's apparent claim that he had left "Judaism" behind in favor of Christ has been a matter of controversy in recent years. Scholars, with some reason, note that Paul elsewhere (e.g., Acts 23:6) can suggest that his following of Christ does not mean leaving Judaism and that indeed in Paul's day, there was not yet something one could call "Christianity" that Paul might have embraced in place of Judaism. It is therefore argued that "Judaism" (*Ioudaismos*) refers not to "Judaism" in general but to a distinctive form of nationalistic Judaism.[26] At the same time, then, what happened on the Damascus Road should not be characterized as a "conversion" (as if Paul replaced one religion with another) but a "call" (to proclaim Christ among the gentiles; see Gal 1:16). However, restricting "Judaism" in this way is not warranted; in both verses 13 and 14 "Judaism" appears to refer broadly to the Jewish faith as a whole. Embracing Christ, as Paul makes clear in Philippians 3:2–11, means renouncing *all* other religious distinctions and accomplishments. To label Paul's experience simply a "call" drastically underplays Paul's own claim about the dramatic change that his conversion involved. And while it would indeed be anachronistic to claim that Paul "converted to Christianity," it does seem appropriate to depict his Damascus Road encounter as

---

26. See esp. Dunn, *Epistle to the Galatians*, 56–65 (though Dunn is a bit more nuanced in a more recent work, where he speaks of Paul's "conversion" from Judaism, understood in terms of a cultural emphasis on gentile distinctiveness: "Paul's Conversion: A Light to Twentieth Century Disputes," in James D. G. Dunn, *The New Perspective on Paul: Collected Essays*, WUNT 2/185 [Tübingen: Mohr Siebeck, 2005], 351–58); see also Hays, "Galatians," 214–15; Eisenbaum, *Paul Was Not a Christian*, 132–49; Mark D. Nanos, "Paul and Judaism: Why Not Paul's Judaism?," in *Paul Unbound: Other Perspectives on the Apostle*, ed. Mark D. Given (Peabody, MA: Hendrickson, 2010), 117–60.

a "conversion" to a new perception of God's purposes and people, centered on Christ rather than Torah. (For more on this issue, see pp. 355–56). When God revealed his Son to Paul, he was both converted *and* called.

The language Paul uses to describe his own apostolic "commission" or "call" in verse 15 alludes to the call of God's Servant in Isaiah 49:1—"Before I was born the LORD called me; from my mother's womb he has spoken my name"—and Jeremiah's call in Jeremiah 1:5—"Before I formed you in the womb I knew you, before you were born I set you apart; I appointed you as a prophet to the nations."[27]

The chronological indicators in Galatians 1:18 and 21 mark out the next stages in Paul's travelogue: a visit to Jerusalem and a move to the regions of "Syria and Cilicia" (v. 21). Paul spends no time describing his ministry during these years (the events he narrates in this paragraph may have covered as many as ten years). He concentrates, rather, on the negative point that he introduced in verse 17a: his minimal contact with Jerusalem and the apostles resident there.

Paul's sketch of his relationship with the Jerusalem authorities shifts direction at 2:1. Paul's account of his meeting with the "pillar" apostles in Jerusalem in 2:1–10 has in common with the previous narrative a focus on Jerusalem. And it is bound to that narrative also by an explicit temporal connection: "Then after fourteen years" (v. 1; see "then after three years" in 1:18; "then" in 1:21). But if Paul in chapter 1 shows that he did not *learn* his gospel *from* the Jerusalem apostles, he now demonstrates that those apostles did not *add anything* to his gospel (2:6). In fact, there was unanimity on the matter at issue both in this Jerusalem meeting and in the churches of Galatia—the inclusion of gentiles in the people of God without the law. Paul's independence was not the independence of a maverick or a cultist. His sphere of ministry might have differed from that of the Jerusalem apostles, but there was no fundamental difference among Paul and the others over the essence of that gospel.

As I suggest above, the meeting Paul describes here probably took place around AD 45–47 and would, then, have preceded Paul's initial church-planting ministry in Galatia (Acts 13–14). Only after that trip did there arise a further dispute on these matters in Antioch (Gal 2:11–14; cf. Acts 15:1–2), an incident that probably provided ammunition to the agitators in Galatia.[28] Galatians 2:1–10 features some of the most convoluted language found anywhere in Paul. He begins straightforwardly, describing his journey to Jerusalem and his companions in verse 1, the reason for going— "by revelation"—the general issue to be discussed—"the gospel I preach among the Gentiles"—and his concern—"I wanted to be sure I was not running and had not been

---

27. See esp. the careful analysis of Roy E. Ciampa, *The Presence and Function of Scripture in Galatians 1 and 2*, WUNT 2/102 (Tübingen: Mohr Siebeck, 1998), 111–18.

28. On this chronology, see esp. Richard Bauckham, "James and the Jerusalem Church," in *The Book of Acts in Its Palestinian Setting*, ed. Richard Bauckham, vol. 4 of *The Book of Acts in Its First Century Setting* (Grand Rapids: Eerdmans, 1995), 468–70.

running my race in vain"—in verse 2. But he then abruptly mentions that Titus was not compelled to be circumcised (v. 3). An even more serious interruption of the narrative occurs in verses 4–5, an extended parenthesis about "false brothers" who infiltrated the church. Paul picks up the main course of the narrative in verse 6, which begins a long sentence that extends to the end of the paragraph. Paul observes that the Jerusalem apostles, negatively, "added nothing" to his gospel (v. 6) and, positively, recognized that they and Paul were all animated in their ministries by the same grace of God and were preaching the same gospel (vv. 8–9a). But the conference participants also agreed to recognize different spheres of ministry—Paul going to the gentiles/the "uncircumcised" and Peter, James, and John to "the circumcised" (vv. 7, 9b). The unit concludes with another point of agreement: Paul gladly agreed to the Jerusalem apostles' request that he continue to "remember the poor" (v. 10).[29]

The syntactical and logical difficulties in this narrative reveal Paul's concern to walk a tightrope here. On the one hand, he does not want to undercut the special position and legitimate authority of the Jerusalem apostles. Indeed, as he implies, their endorsement of his law-free gospel is important (for this latter point, see esp. v. 2b). Paul perhaps hints at this special place for the Jerusalem apostles by calling them "pillars" (v. 9), which may be an allusion to the motif of an eschatological temple. Paul, then, wants "to have his divine commission to preach the gospel affirmed in the center of the eschatological community of the Messiah, in the 'eschatological temple' in Jerusalem."[30] However, Paul does not want to fall off the other side of the tightrope and give the Jerusalem apostles any final say over the gospel that Christ revealed to him. One of his purposes seems to be, then, to reduce the overly slavish regard for these "pillars" among the agitators.

The most important point that we have to pin down is the specific matter of debate. Clearly, this point of contention had something to do with "the gospel that I preach among the Gentiles" (v. 2)—a gospel ministry that the Jerusalem apostles clearly endorse (v. 6). The abrupt introduction of Titus and the fact that he was not circumcised (v. 3) along with the contrast between "the circumcised" and "the uncircumcision" in verse 9 makes it pretty clear that the underlying issue was: Should gentile Christians be circumcised? And the specific issue of circumcision carried with it the larger issue of the law of Moses. The offer of salvation to gentiles, apart from adherence to the law (either at conversion or later on), was the issue at this meeting in Jerusalem. And it is the Jerusalem apostles' agreement with this gospel that is the key rhetorical point of

---

29. This is therefore probably a reference to his current practice rather than to the "collection," which on my dating is still some years off (see, e.g., Verlyn D. Verbrugge and Keith R. Krell, *Paul and Money: A Biblical and Theological Analysis of the Apostle's Teachings and Practices* [Grand Rapids: Zondervan, 2015], 125–29).

30. Eckhard J. Schnabel, *Paul and the Early Church*, vol. 2 of *Early Christian Mission* (Downers Grove, IL: InterVarsity Press, 2004), 991.

the story, as verse 5b reveals: Paul's refusal to submit to the "false brothers" means that "the truth of the gospel might be preserved *for you.*" The Jerusalem apostles' agreement with Paul's law-free gospel for the gentiles shows how wrong the Galatians would be to succumb to the agitators' perversion of the gospel into a gospel-plus-law message.

This narrative concludes the section of the letter written in first-person narrative style. In Jerusalem, Paul wins agreement from the Jerusalem apostles for his version of the law-free gospel, and so "the truth of the gospel" is maintained for gentile Christians (v. 5). In Antioch, by contrast, Paul fights for the truth of the gospel against at least one of those same Jerusalem apostles (Peter), and the outcome of that fight is not at all clear. In fact, there is a lot that is unclear about this narrative.[31] We cannot be sure whether this incident takes place before or after the consultation in 2:1–10, although after is more likely.[32] Indeed, it is quite possible that Acts 15:1—"Certain people came down from Judea to Antioch and were teaching the believers: 'Unless you are circumcised, according to the custom taught by Moses, you cannot be saved'"—is Luke's summary of this same incident.[33] More important is the question of what the specific issue may have been. What is clear is that Paul is deeply upset with the decision of Peter (and Barnabas also) to stop eating with gentiles. There were apparently diverse views among first-century Jews over how much contact with gentiles was allowed.[34] But we have good reason to think that the viewpoint reflected in the Antioch incident was a rigorous one that urged pious Jews to avoid as much contact with gentiles as possible.[35] I follow Bauckham on this matter, who argues that Peter, and perhaps the emissaries from James also, feared contact, and especially the intimate contact of eating together, with gentiles, out of fear that they might be contaminated by their immorality.[36] Questions about the nature and degree of these relationships were bound to arise in a community such as the one at Antioch. For here a "new race" of people, neither Jews nor gentiles, was formed, requiring that they be given a new name: "Christians" (Acts 11:19–26). This unity was enshrined in common meals. Peter, who had at first taken part in such meals, withdrew under pressure from some emissaries claiming to represent James in Jerusalem. He perhaps viewed this retreat simply as a prudent accomodation to honor the concerns of stricter Jewish Christians. Paul, obviously, disagreed. For him, Peter's

---

31. For a history of interpretation, see Mussner, *Galaterbrief,* 146–67.

32. E.g., Murphy-O'Connor, *Paul,* 132.

33. See, e.g., David Wenham, "Acts and the Pauline Corpus, II: The Evidence of Parallels," in *The Book of Acts in Its Literary Setting,* ed. Bruce W. Winter and Andrew D. Clarke, vol. 1 of *The Book of Acts in Its First Century Setting* (Grand Rapids: Eerdmans, 1993), 241; Paul Barnett, *Jesus and the Rise of Early Christianity: A History of New Testament Times* (Downers Grove, IL: InterVarsity Press, 1999), 285; Richard Bauckham, "James, Peter, and the Gentiles," in *The Missions of James, Peter and Paul: Tensions in*

Early Christianity, ed. Bruce Chilton and Craig Evans (Leiden: Brill, 2004), 136.

34. See esp. Bauckham, "James, Peter, and the Gentiles," 91–142; James D. G. Dunn, "The Incident at Antioch (Gal 2:11–18)," *JSNT* 18 (1983): 3–57; E. P. Sanders, "Jewish Association with Gentiles and Galatians 2:11–14," in *The Conversation Continues: Studies in Paul and John in Honor of J. Louis Martyn,* ed. Robert T. Fortna and Beverly R. Gaventa (Nashville: Abingdon, 1990), 170–88.

35. See esp. Let. Aris. 142; Jub. 22.16; Acts 10:28.

36. Bauckham, "James, Peter, and the Gentiles," 3–57.

retreat sent the signal that gentiles in Christ are not truly and fully cleansed from sin in Christ, that they remain morally stained and must be avoided, and that they can finally remove that stain only by taking on Jewish customs. And all this is a flat contradiction to "the truth of the gospel."

2.2 The Truth of the Gospel Defined (2:15–21)

The gospel is front and center in the first major section of the letter body. His ministry autobiography focuses on "the truth of the gospel" (2:5 and 14). However, while there are hints along the way, Paul has not explained what that "truth" is. The paragraph 2:15–21 is a positive assertion of this truth of the gospel. The key point is expressed in verse 16, where Paul asserts that justification before God comes through faith in Jesus Christ and not through "works of the law." In this context, this claim about the truth of the gospel applies particularly to the situation at Antioch that Paul has just described (vv. 11–14). This connection is clear from Paul's introduction in verse 15: "We who are Jews by birth." The "we" includes Paul and Cephas (or Peter)—see verse 14. And this "we," then, is the subject of the verbs in verse 16—"know," "we have put [our faith]" "that we may be justified." The first-person plural is continued in verse 17 ("we Jews find"), and verses 18–21 are logically tied to verse 17. There is good reason, then, to think that Paul continues to "quote" his speech at Antioch right up through the end of verse 21.[37]

However, if this central assertion about the truth of the gospel looks back to the Antioch incident, it also looks ahead to the following teaching that Paul directs to the Galatians. Key words central to that argument are introduced here: "law" (*nomos*); "works of the law" (*erga nomou*); "justify" (*dikaioō*); "righteousness" (*dikaiosynē*). These considerations make it clear that 2:15–21 is a transitional passage, continuing Paul's speech from Antioch while focusing on the Galatians.

In this paragraph, Paul argues in three steps.

In verses 15–16, he enunciates the essential theological point: Jewish Christians like Paul and Peter understand that they have been justified by faith and not by the law. With the early dating of Galatians I have advocated, this is the first time Paul in his letters speaks of "justification" (*dikaioō* in vv. 16 and 17; cf. *dikaiosynē* in v. 21). Yet it is important to note that Paul introduces this important soteriological idea as if it were common in early Christianity ("we . . . know that . . ."). I discuss justification at length elsewhere (see pp. 469–91). Here I note simply that I think the Reformers were basically right in interpreting justification as a purely forensic declaration of God, a declaration that powerfully effects what it declares, putting the person who believes

---

37. So NIV; NASB; other versions (e.g., NRSV; ESV; CSB; NET; CEB) end the quotation at the end of v. 14 (NLT at the end of v. 16).

in right relationship with God. We should note the present tense that Paul uses here, suggesting a timeless, "gnomic" idea, and also the hint at a future focus in verse 17 ("seeking to be justified"). Justification in Galatians is not simply a declaration that occurs at conversion; it is also a verdict that awaits the last day of judgment (see 5:4–5 and comments there).[38]

The agitators, we can surmise from the letter, were arguing for a synthesis: faith in Christ *and* the law. In response, Paul insists on an antithesis: it is Christ and therefore *not* the law. To determine more precisely the nature of this antithesis requires decisions about two ambiguous phrases (both using the Greek genitive) that might be roughly and minimally translated as "law works" and "Christ faith." The ultimate theological connotations suggested by the phrase "law works," usually translated "works of the law," has been a key point of contention between defenders and critics of the New Perspective (the phrase, *erga nomou*, occurs three times in this verse and again in 3:2, 5, 10; Rom 3:20, 28). It is now generally agreed that the phrase *denotes* "things done in obedience to the Mosaic law."[39] The debate is over its connotations: Is the phrase to be confined to *Torah* works, viewed as maintaining one's position in God's covenant (à la most New Perspective advocates)? Or is it legitimate to extend the sense of the phrase to works in general (as the Reformers did)? On the other side of the antithesis, does "[Jesus] Christ faith" (twice in this verse) refer to Christ's own faith or faithfulness (a subjective genitive), to the Christian's faith "in" Christ (an objective genitive), or, perhaps more generally and ambiguously, to a faith "bound up with Christ" (a "general" genitive)? I treat these issues fully elsewhere (see pp. 379–82). Suffice it for now to say that I think the Reformers were theologically on the right track here also, seeing in this verse a basic contrast between two ways of appropriating justification: "works," or doing, on the one hand, and faith ("in Christ"), on the other.

The rest of the paragraph elaborates the negative side of verse 16 (justification does *not* come via works of the law). Verses 17–20 spell out the implications of finding justification "in Christ" for the law. While its meaning is debated, verse 17 makes best sense if we posit a shift in the meaning of "sin" between its beginning and its end. Some Jewish-Christians were apparently arguing that to abandon "works of the law" would put them into the same category as "gentile sinners" (see v. 15). Christ would then, in effect, be promoting sin. Paul rejects this logic (v. 17b), arguing that only when the law is elevated again to an absolute standard of right conduct (as Peter effectively did in Antioch) can Jewish-Christians who do not follow all its requirements be considered sinners (v. 18). Jewish-Christians need to imitate Paul, who, in order to truly live for God, has replaced his attachment to the law with an attachment to Christ (vv. 19–20).

38. Indeed, deSilva claims justification is entirely future in Galatians (*Galatians*, 218–19).

39. Douglas J. Moo, "'Law,' 'Works of the Law,' and Legalism in Paul," *WTJ* 45 (1983): 73–100; see also Moo, *Epistle to the Romans* (NICNT), 215–20.

In verse 21, then, Paul effectively urges the Galatians to adopt his own attitude and practice. He will not reject the grace of God, which has been climactically exhibited in the death of Christ. To seek righteousness by the law is, in effect, to deny that death—or at least that death in the epochal significance with which Paul views it. The grace of God exhibited in the death of his own Son is the central event in salvation history, and this event relativizes every other means of righteousness or justification.

Paul in this paragraph brings together two of his great theological themes: justification (v. 16 esp.) and union with Christ (vv. 19–20). The close association of these two concepts has sparked considerable discussion among modern Pauline theologians. The relationship between the judicial (justification) and the participatory ("crucified with Christ") cuts to the heart of Paul's theology. In my view, the passage does not identify these ideas; rather, they are associated. It is important to connect the participatory and the forensic, but equally important to recognize the distinct ideas each connotes (see, for discussion, pp. 486–87).

3 THE DEFENSE OF THE GOSPEL (3:1–5:12)

Galatians 3:1–5:12 is the central argument of the letter. This second major part of the letter body is framed by passages of rebuke and exhortation (3:1–6; 5:1–12). Sandwiched between these bookend paragraphs are two distinct units: theological argument (3:7–4:7) and an appeal based on that argument (4:8–31).[40] Both units argue from the life of Abraham. The whole section is a prolonged defense of the "truth of the gospel." This defense focuses on the key distinction that Paul introduced in 2:16: "works of the law" versus "believing"/"faith" (3:2, 5, 10–12). The opening paragraph, which sets the tone for the argument to follow, has just this contrast at its heart: Did you, Paul asks the Galatians, experience the Spirit by "works of the law" or by "believing what you heard" (3:2, 5)? This contrast, enunciated with several different words and combinations ("law," "doing" versus "faith," "believing," "[Jesus] Christ faith"), is basic to the argument that follows. We find this same antithesis is central to 5:1–6, which is the rhetorical climax of the letter. The exact nature of this contrast has great significance for recent interpretations of Paul. It has become increasingly popular to think that the contrast is fundamentally a salvation-historical one: the law, or Torah, the focal point of the old covenant, versus "Christ faith" or "Christ's faithfulness," the animating force of the new covenant. There is no doubt that salvation history is basic to the argument of Galatians: 3:15–29 is a classic expression of this perspective. However, as I will argue at greater length elsewhere (see pp. 435–39), the key contrast

---

40. While their overall structural proposal and its rhetorical underpinnings are not entirely convincing, G. Walter Hansen, *Abraham in Galatians: Epistolary and Rhetorical Contexts,* JSNTSup 29 (Sheffield: JSOT, 1989), 78–79, and R. Longenecker, *Galatians,* 97, also emphasize the hortatory character of all of 4:12–6:20.

in these phrases is not between eras of salvation history but between two different ways for humans to appropriate the benefits of the new covenant: by "works," or doing, on the one hand, or by faith, on the other. The ultimate issue Paul deals with in Galatians is not limited to the salvation-historical movement from one testament to another. As Stephen Westerholm has nicely put it, "The fundamental question addressed by Galatians thus is not 'What is wrong with Judaism (or the Sinaitic law)?' but 'What is wrong with humanity that Judaism (and the Sinaitic law) cannot remedy?'"[41]

3.1 Rebuke and Reminder: Faith, Spirit, and Righteousness (3:1–6)

The rebuke and exhortation of these verses set the rhetorical direction for the whole argument. "You foolish Galatians" is the first direct address of the readers since 1:11 and signals Paul's return to his rebuking mode from 1:6–9. Central to this rebuke is Paul's appeal to the experience of the Galatians (v. 4). Christ was "placarded" among them (v. 1, my translation); they have received the Spirit (vv. 3, 5); they have experienced the Spirit's power (v. 5). As he often does, Paul sets forth the powerful presence of the Spirit as a clear mark of the coming of a new era of salvation.

But the key point in the paragraph, which Paul will develop in the theological argument that follows, is the means by which the Galatians have experienced these signs and blessings of the era of fulfillment: not by "works of the law" but by means of "believing what [they] heard" (vv. 2, 5). As I argue elsewhere, "works of the law" is Paul's shorthand for "doing what the law requires." The second phrase is variously understood, with the genitive case in Greek again the point of debate. Paul uses the noun *akoē* (which can mean either "hearing" or "what is heard" [e.g., a report]) and then adds to it a genitive: *pisteōs* ("faith"). Some interpreters think it refers to "the message about [Christ's] faith."[42] However, as I argue at length elsewhere (pp. 379–82), it is doubtful that Paul uses that "faith" to refer to Christ's faith. "Faith" more likely refers to human believing, the phrase meaning something like "hearing accompanied by faith," or even "the hearing Christians call faith"—the true attentive "hearing" that the Old Testament often praises (Exod 15:26; 19:5; 23:22; Deut 11:13, 22; 15:5; 28:1, 2; 2 Sam 22:45; Jer 17:24; cf. 1 Sam 15:22: "To hear [*akoē*] is better than sacrifice").[43] Paul's concern is how

41. Stephen Westerholm, *Perspectives Old and New on Paul: The 'Lutheran' Paul and His Critics* (Grand Rapids: Eerdmans, 2004), 381; see his whole argument on pp. 371–84; see also esp. Moisés Silva, "Faith Versus Works of the Law in Galatians," in Carson, O'Brien, and Seifrid, *Paradoxes of Paul*, 217–48; Robert H. Gundry, "Grace, Works, and Staying Saved in Paul," *Bib* 66 (1985): 15–32.

42. Frank J. Matera, "The Death of Christ and the Cross in Paul's Letter to the Galatians," *LS* 18 (1993): 290; Douglas A. Campbell, *The Deliverance of God: An Apocalyptic Reading of Justification in Paul* (Grand Rapids: Eerdmans, 2009), 853–56; cf. de Boer, *Galatians*, 174–76.

43. The NIV translates most of these Hebrew words for "hear" with some form of the English "obey," making the point. See on this Don B. Garlington, *An Exposition of Galatians: A New Perspectival/Reformational Reading* (Eugene, OR: Wipf & Stock, 2003), 134; Oliver O'Donovan, *Resurrection and the Moral Order: An Outline for Evangelical Ethics*, 2nd ed. (Grand Rapids: Eerdmans, 1994), 110; Sam K. Williams, "The Hearing of Faith: ΑΚΟΗ ΠΙΣΤΕΩΣ in Galatians 3," *NTS* 35 (1989): 82–93; In-Gyu Hong, *The Law in Galatians*, JSNTSup 81 (Sheffield: JSOT, 1993), 129–31.

the Galatians "finish" or "complete" their course (v. 3). His confirmatory reference to Abraham's experience in verse 6, while obviously introducing what follows, also functions to corroborate the importance of faith in the Galatians' experience.[44]

3.2 Argument: Abraham's Children through Incorporation into Christ by Faith (3:7–4:7)

In this second major unit with 3:7–4:31, Abraham is especially significant. Abraham occurs in vv. 7, 8, 9, 14, 16, 18, 29; and reference to the promise[s] in vv. 8, 14, 16, 17, 18, 19, 21, 22, 29. His prominence in this part of the letter is not surprising. Paul is arguing from the history of salvation and Abraham plays a foundational role in that unfolding drama of redemption. There is evidence, however, that a more urgent reason for Paul's appeal to Abraham is polemical. The Jewish appropriation of the Abraham story tended to magnify the patriarch's own virtues and accomplishments to explain his prominence. For instance, he was said to have obeyed the whole law before it had been given. However, another, more basic fact about Abraham is more important in explaining his prominence in Paul's argument. Jews in Paul's day identified themselves by virtue of their biological relationship to Abraham, the "father of the nation." Paul reflects this tradition by introducing the language of "children of Abraham" in 3:7. The agitators were undoubtedly citing the Abraham story along these lines, arguing that the Galatian Christians could secure their righteous status before God by becoming "children of Abraham" through the time-honored means of submission to the Torah.

Paul attacks this logic in two ways in 3:7–4:7. First, beginning, as we saw, in verse 6, he focuses on Abraham's faith rather than his obedience. Paul's Jewish antagonists may have agreed with him on this point. But Paul quickly moves on to highlight two aspects of Abraham's faith that would have been more controversial. First, he notes that the "blessing" of faith for righteousness was always intended to include gentiles (vv. 8, 14; cf. "you . . . all" in v. 26). Second, he insists that faith was in itself adequate to secure his righteous standing with God. The former point is not critical to Paul's argument, since we have no reason to think that the agitators were disputing the *fact* that gentiles could be included in Abraham's family. The point at issue, rather, was the *means* through which they could be included in that family. As a result, it is this second aspect of Abraham's faith that receives the most attention in the verses that follow. This focus is especially prominent in verses 10–12, where Paul insists that "works of the law"—and, by extension, "works" of any kind—add nothing to the adequacy of faith as a means of righteousness.[45] Paul's confidence in the ability of faith to justify rests

44. The verse should, then, probably be linked to vv. 1–5, as in, e.g., ESV, NIV, and see Bruce, *Galatians*, 152–53; Silva, *Interpreting Galatians*, 253; Andrew H. Wakefield, *Where to Live: The Hermeneutical Significance of Paul's Citations from Scripture in Galatians 3:1–14*, AcBib 14 (Atlanta: SBL, 2003), 136. Contra, e.g., NRSV, NLT, and Burton, *Galatians*, 153; R. Longenecker, *Galatians*, 112.

45. See de Boer, *Galatians*, 167.

not in the power of human believing as such. As the unfolding argument will make clear, it is the fact that faith brings people into union with Christ (vv. 14, 26–29) that gives it its significance. Paul's conviction therefore about the utter adequacy of *Christ* engenders his insistence on the adequacy of *faith*.

Galatians 3:7–14 is governed by the antithesis that Paul introduced in 2:16 (see also 3:2, 5): faith versus "works of the law." Paul expounds the positive side in 3:7–9 (justified by faith), and then turns in 3:10–14 to the negative side (*not* justified by works of the law). Woven together in this paragraph, as in the preceding one, is the general principle that "faith" is the means of finding righteousness/blessing (vv. 7, 9, 11, 14) *and* that faith also enables the inclusion of gentiles within the people of God (vv. 8, 14).

"Those who have faith" (*hoi ek pisteōs*) in verse 7 refers to those who, like Abraham, trusted God for righteousness.[46] Moreover, because this blessing is secured by faith, it is open to gentiles as well as Jews (v. 8, quoting Gen 12:3). "Blessing" brings to Paul's mind its opposite: curse. The curse comes on those who are "out of" (*ex*) "works of the law" (v. 10). This phrase might simply denote Jews in general. But it more likely refers to those who "rely" on works of the law for justification (see 2:16; 3:2, 5). Paul adds a quotation from Deuteronomy 27:26 to support this point. At first glance, the quotation would appear to prove the opposite of what Paul says in the first part of the verse. For the text in Deuteronomy encourages obedience to the law as a means of avoiding the curse; yet Paul claims that it is just those people who are bound up with the law who suffer that curse. The traditional way of explaining this is to assume a key point in Paul's logic:

Only those who do everything written in the law will escape the curse (v. 10b).
No one can do everything written in the law (assumed).
Therefore: No one who depends on doing the law will escape the curse (v. 10a).

Many recent interpreters have objected to this reading, arguing that it is illegitimate to read this assumption into the text. They argue that Paul is making a simple point about Jews (those who are "out of the works of the law"): they stand under the curse promised in Deuteronomy for Israel's disobedience. The Galatian gentiles should not therefore identify with Israel by putting themselves under the law, for they would then be also joining Israel under the curse.[47] However, I prefer the usual view.

---

46. Following his overall interpretation of Galatians 3 as a history of Christ, Hays suggests that this phrase might mean "those who are given life on the basis of [Christ's] faith" (Richard B. Hays, *The Faith of Jesus Christ: The Narrative Substructure of Galatians 3:1–4:11*, 2nd ed. [Grand Rapids: Eerdmans, 2002], 170–73; he thinks human believing may be a subordinate idea). But this interpretation does not give enough weight to the

connection between vv. 6 and 7. It is human believing that is in view here. Dunn is quite forthright; he finds Hays's view "frankly incredible" (*Beginning from Jerusalem*, 733n352).

47. See esp. Christopher D. Stanley, "'Under a Curse': A Fresh Reading of Galatians 3:10–14," *NTS 36* (1990): 481–511; James M. Scott, "'For as Many as Are of Works of the Law Are under a Curse' (Galatians 3:10)," in *Paul and the Scriptures of Israel*, ed.

"Those who are of works of the law" would be a very strange way of describing Jews *per se*. Moreover, Paul emphasizes the "works," or "doing" part of the phrase: his quotation from Deuteronomy ends on this note, and he picks up this emphasis again in verse 12 and in 5:3: "Again I declare to every man who lets himself be circumcised that he is obligated to obey the whole law." While the "law" in view is, of course, the law of Moses, and much of Paul's argument in Galatians rests on the contrast between the era of the law and the era of fulfillment in Christ, this verse in context suggests that Paul is also concerned with what is in many ways the more fundamental issue of "doing." A simple claim that Christ has superseded the law may be adequate for Paul's purposes, but we might expect him to push further and ask why it was necessary for Christ to supersede the law. In other words, while much of Paul's argument in this letter could be summarized as "doing is wrong because (and when) it is tied to an outmoded law," Paul here suggests that he has moved to a deeper and more universal issue: the law provides no basis for the blessing because it involves "doing": a "doing" that humans find to be impossible.

In verses 11–12, Paul uses quotations from the Old Testament to reinforce the "faith" versus "(works of the) law" distinction. Habakkuk highlighted faith as the means by which the righteous were to live (v. 11; see Hab 2:4); and so, Paul argues, the person who is righteous in Christ will also live by faith.[48] And this faith, Paul insists, stands in contrast to the law, which is "not of faith"—that is, it operates in a different sphere (v. 12). Paul again uses the Old Testament to make his point, quoting Leviticus 18:5. The language of this text was widely used in the Old Testament and Judaism to state a fundamental aspect of the Mosaic covenant: it was "doing" that would secure the life promised in that covenant.[49] Paul therefore appropriately cites the text to summarize his understanding of the Mosaic covenant: it certainly expects and assumes faith, but its blessings are clearly contingent on obedience, on works (see also the quotation of this same text in Rom 10:5).[50] Verse 13 then returns to the issue of curse introduced in verse 12: Christ "redeems" those who are under the curse, those who fail to do what the law demands, by taking the curse on their behalf. It is hard to know whether the

Craig A. Evans and James A. Sanders, JSNTSup 83 (Sheffield: JSOT, 1993), 187–221; N. T. Wright, "Curse and Covenant: Galatians 3.10–14," in *The Climax of the Covenant: Christ and the Law in Pauline Theology* (Minneapolis: Fortress, 1991), 141–48.

48. The interpretation of Hab 2:4 and the point that Paul wants to derive from it are debated. For an interpretation along the lines I am suggesting, see Moisés Silva, "Galatians," in Beale and Carson, *Commentary on the New Testament Use of the Old Testament*, 800–802.

49. For this view of this very contested verse, see Preston M. Sprinkle, *Law and Life: The Interpretation of Leviticus 18:5 in Early Judaism and in Paul*, WUNT 2/241 (Tübingen: Mohr Siebeck, 2008); and also Simon J. Gathercole, "Torah, Life, and Salvation:

Leviticus 18:5 in Early Judaism and the New Testament," in *From Prophecy to Testament: The Function of the Old Testament in the New*, ed. Craig A. Evans (Peabody, MA: Hendrickson, 2004), 126–45.

50. See esp. Sprinkle, *Law and Life*, 136–42, and Gathercole, "Torah, Life, and Salvation," 126–45; see also Francis Watson, "Constructing an Antithesis: Pauline and Other Jewish Perspectives on Divine and Human Agency," in *Divine and Human Agency in Paul and His Cultural Environment*, ed. John M. G. Barclay and Simon Gathercole (Edinburgh: T&T Clark, 2006), 101. Note allusions to Lev 18:5 in Ezek 20:11, 13, 21; Neh 9:29; CD 3.14–16; 4Q266; Philo, *Prelim. Studies* 86–87; LAB 23.10; Pss. Sol. 14.1–2.

"us" in this verse refers to Paul and his fellow Jews[51] or to Paul and his fellow Christians generally[52]—but the latter might be slightly more likely. For the fourth verse in a row, Paul uses the Old Testament to support his point. Christ was hung on a tree in his crucifixion, and Deuteronomy 21:23 pronounces a curse on anyone who hangs on a tree (meaning, in its original context, the exposure on a pole of the bodies of executed criminals). In verse 14, Paul brings to a climax two of the key themes of 3:1–9: the extension of the blessing of Abraham to the gentiles (vv. 7–9), and the gift of God's Spirit as the evidence of the arrival of the new age of redemption (vv. 1–6).

Paul's second argument, with Abraham at its center, focuses on salvation history (3:15–4:7). "Works of the law" are unable to justify not only because they are "works" (implied in the argument of vv. 10–14) but also because they are "of the law." This law (*nomos*), the Torah, only came on the scene after God's promise to Abraham (vv. 15–18); it had a narrowly focused purpose, and it was always intended to end at some point. The sequence of argument here in Galatians is similar to the one in Romans 4, Paul beginning with principial arguments about faith versus works/law (Rom 4:1–8; Gal 3:7–14) and then moving on to an argument from salvation history (Rom 4:9–25; Gal 3:15–25).

In contrast to the agitators, who undoubtedly highlighted the enduring importance of the giving of the Torah at Sinai, Paul uses a chronological argument to relegate Torah to a subordinate role. As is the case in a human will, the initial terms are decisive (v. 15). God's covenant was established with Abraham 430 years before the Torah was given (v. 17): it cannot change the original terms, which took the form of a promise (vv. 16, 18). And, for Paul, promise and grace (see v. 18) on God's part are tied to faith on the part of humans. Paul also introduces an important christological note here. The promise "spoken to Abraham" was for him and his "seed" (v. 16; see esp. Gen 15:18 and 17:7–8, both of which also refer to "covenant"). Controversially, Paul notes the singular form of the word "seed" and argues that it refers to Christ. Paul's reading might not be as arbitrary as it seems at first, for some of the Genesis promise texts might have in view a singular individual, such as Isaac.[53] In any case, Paul's argument here more broadly reflects his overall understanding that all God's promises finally have Christ in view. Note also that verse 29 shows that Paul is very well aware of the collective sense of "seed": Christ is *the* seed, and all who belong to him are "seed," or descendants, of Abraham.

Paul's exposition of salvation history raises obvious questions, which Paul deals with in verses 19–25. The biggest question is this: If the law did not add anything to the promise, why, then, did God give it to Israel (see v. 19a)? First, Paul responds, the law and the promise were given to serve different purposes. God gave the law to exacerbate

---

51. See, e.g., Lightfoot, *Galatians*, 139; Betz, *Galatians*, 148.

52. E.g., Bruce, *Galatians*, 166–67; Martyn, *Galatians*, 334–36; Dunn, *Epistle to the Galatians*, 176–77.

53. T. Desmond Alexander, "Further Observations on the Term 'Seed' in Genesis," *TynBul* 48 (1997): 363–67; C. John Collins, "Galatians 3:16: What Kind of Exegete Was Paul?," *TynBul* 54 (2003): 75–86.

and reveal sin (vv. 19b, 22a). It was never intended to—or even able to—awaken spiritual life. Only the promise and faith were able to do that (v. 21). Second, God gave the law with a definite "shelf life": it was to have authority over the people of God only until the promised Messiah came (vv. 19b, 23–25). The law, Paul adds, was like the ancient *paidagōgos*, a "guardian" (vv. 24, 25) who watched over a young child.[54] Paul obviously holds to a single, continuous history of salvation.[55] But at the same time, he also presents the coming of Christ—"Christ crucified" (3:1; cf. also 2:19–20; 6:14)—as a climactic moment that shifts the course of that single history of salvation. At base, Paul's disagreement with the agitators focuses on this crucial point: How significant is the shift in salvation history that Christ's coming has inaugurated?

Verses 26–29 are the rhetorical and theological heart of 3:7–4:11. Paul circles back to the beginning of his argument in verses 7–9, even as he gathers up some of the key themes of verses 15–25. He alludes to the inclusion of gentiles that was touched on in verse 8 (see also v. 14). Identifying these believers as "sons"/"children" harks back to verse 7 ("sons/children of Abraham"). Key language from verses 15–25 is also integrated into this paragraph: "faith," "seed," "heir"/"inheritance," "promise." Central to all these points is the believer's union with Christ: "In Christ Jesus you are all children of God through faith" (v. 26). If this paragraph is central to this part of Galatians, this verse is central to this paragraph and arguably the single most important point Paul makes in this letter. *All*, Jew and gentile alike, can belong to God's people by belonging to Christ, and belonging to Christ comes by faith (alone). Belonging to Christ transcends all the earthly distinctions that separate humans (v. 28).

Paul concludes his central theological argument in 4:1–7 by reinforcing his salvation-historical argument, using the metaphor of slavery and sonship that he introduces in 3:22–25. This new paragraph, like 3:15–25, is dominated by a temporal contrast between a time of confinement and a time of freedom and inheritance. But 4:1–7 adds a significant feature not found in 3:23–29: the Spirit (4:6). This reminder of the Galatians' experience of the Spirit takes us back to the beginning of his argument in 3:1–5.[56]

In 4:1–2, Paul refers to an inheritance custom, but none we know of in the ancient world quite corresponds to his description. Probably, then, he takes liberties with some of the details of that experience in order to facilitate its application to their spiritual situation.[57] It is also possible that Paul refers to the foundational "adoption" event

---

54. Some interpreters think the word suggests that the law was given to "teach" Israel and thus to be their "schoolmaster to bring us unto Christ" (AV/KJV). But this is almost certainly wrong. The *paidagōgos* in the ancient world was a slave who was responsible to watch over a young child. He was not a teacher but a guardian, or "nanny." The imagery Paul uses here, therefore, suggests the idea of the law as a guardian over the people of Israel in their "minority."

55. This point needs to be made in response to those, like Martyn (*Galatians*, esp. 161–79), who argue that in Galatians Paul holds to such antithetical contrasts that any notion of a continuous salvation history is abandoned. See on this issue pp. 27–34.

56. Hays, "Galatians," 280.

57. Betz, *Galatians*, 203–4; R. Longenecker, *Galatians*, 163–64.

in the history of Israel: the people's liberation from their taskmasters in Egypt (the "guardians and trustees") at the time determined by God, a liberation that led to their "inheritance" (the promised land).[58]

In 4:3–7, then, Paul applies his illustration from inheritance practice to the situation of believers in Christ—taking the first-plural pronoun ("we," *hēmeis*, v. 3) as referring to Christians generally. In contrast to 3:22–25, where the law is the dominating power, Paul here refers to "the elemental spiritual forces of the world" (*ta stoicheia tou kosmou*). The meaning of this phrase, which occurs again in abbreviated form in verse 9 and in Colossians 2:8, 20, is unclear. The word *stoicheion* has a "formal" sense, meaning "fundamental component" or "element," and thus can take on a wide variety of specific senses, depending on the context in which it is used.[59] Three options are proposed here: (1) the "elements" that comprise the universe; (2) basic or elementary "principles" (cf. NRSV; ESV); or (3) spiritual powers (NIV). The last option is very popular, but there is some question if the word was being used with this reference in Paul's day. The sense best supported is the first, and this can make good sense here. The material components of the universe were often associated with spiritual beings or the gods. In light of this background, then, a reference to the material elements of the universe would almost certainly include some reference to those deities or spirits who were so closely associated with the elements.[60] In this sense, those who suggest that the phrase is a general way of describing the situation of humans before and outside of Christ are not far off the mark.[61]

Paul uses the inheritance illustration primarily to illuminate the dire condition of the Galatians in their pre-Christian state (v. 3). But the illustration hints also at the change that occurs when the underage boy enters into his inheritance. In verses 4–5, Paul applies this side of the illustration. Paul borrows the idea of God "sending" his Son from early Christian tradition (often in the Johannine writings; e.g., John 3:16; 1 John 4:9), although the closest parallel to these verses in general is Romans 8:1–17. At the right moment in salvation history ("when the set time had fully come," Gal 4:4), God sent his Son—and sent him as fully human, born of a woman, and under the law. Paul uses the

58. James M. Scott, *Adoption as Sons of God: An Exegetical Investigation into the Background of ΥΙΟΘΕΣΙΑ in the Pauline Corpus*, WUNT 2/48 (Tübingen: Mohr Siebeck, 1992), 122–45. See also, with some modifications, Scott J. Hafemann, "Paul and the Exile of Israel in Galatians 3–4," in *Exile: Old Testament, Jewish, and Christian Conceptions*, ed. James M. Scott, Journal for the Study of Judaism Supplement 56 (Leiden: Brill, 1997), 333–51.

59. See especially Andrew J. Bandstra, *The Law and the Elements of the World: An Exegetical Study in Aspects of Paul's Teaching* (Kampen: Kok, 1964), 31–46; and also Neil Martin, "Returning to the *Stoicheia Tou Kosmou*: Enslavement to the Physical Elements in Galatians 4.3 and 9?," *JSNT* 40 (2018): 434–52.

60. For this view in general, see esp. Joseph Blinzler, "Zur Auslegung von I Kor 7,14," in *Neutestamentliche Aufsätze: Festschrift für Josef Schmid*, ed. Joseph Blinzler, Otto Kuss, and Franz Mussner (Regensburg: Friedrich Puster, 1963), 23–41; Dietrich Rusam, "Neue Belege zu den *Stoicheia tou Kosmou* (Gal 4,3.9, Kol 2,8.20)," *ZNW* 83 (1992): 119–25; Eduard Schweizer, "Die 'Elemente der Welt' Gal 4,3.9; Kol 2,8.20," in *Verborum Veritas: Festschrift für Gustav Stählin zum 70. Geburtstag*, ed. Otto Böcher and Klaus Haacker (Wuppertal: Brockhaus, 1970), 245–59.

61. E.g., Bruce, *Galatians*, 204; Dunn, *Epistle to the Galatians*, 213.

phrase "under the law" to refer generally to the situation of Israel under Torah. Christ was a Jewish human—and in his identification with us and with Israel was able to redeem those "under the law." Those so designated may be Jews; but Paul can also associate gentiles with being "under the law" (cf. Rom 6:14, 15; 7:4–5), so it may also be possible that he has both Jews and gentiles in view here.[62] If redemption means, negatively, being released from the law's condemnation, it also means, positively, "adoption to sonship" (*huiothesia*; the word occurs also in Rom 8:15, 23; 9:4; Eph 1:5). This language, while borrowed from Paul's Greco-Roman world, is rooted also in the Old Testament, which portrays Israel as God's "son" (Exod 4:22; see also Jer 31:20). Paul is claiming not only that we become God's adopted children, with all the rights and privileges pertaining to that status, but also that we have become his own people, inheriting the status and blessings promised to his people Israel. As he does in Romans 8:14–15, Paul associates possession of the Spirit with adoption (Gal 4:6): as "sons," we receive God's Spirit, leading us to exclaim "Abba, Father." Our sonship follows and parallels, in some ways, Jesus's own sonship (see Mark 14:36). And being sons means that we are also heirs, awaiting with confidence the completion of God's work in us and in the world (v. 7).

3.3 Appeal (4:8–31)

These verses can be considered together because, in contrast to what has come before, they are dominated by exhortations, or implied exhortations: "How is it that you are turning back to those weak and miserable forces? Do you wish to be enslaved by them all over again?" (4:9); "I fear . . . that somehow I have wasted my efforts on you" (v. 11); "Become like me" (v. 12); "You who want to be under the law, are you not aware of what the law says?" (v. 21); "Get rid of the slave woman" (v. 30). Paul's appeal proceeds in three stages. The first two focus on the past, as Paul implicitly and explicitly urges the Galatians to resist the agitators' insistence on law observance by reminding them of their own past (4:8–11) and of Paul's relationship with them (4:12–20). The climax of his appeal comes in the third stage (4:21–31), where Paul creatively cites Scripture to warn his readers about the agitators and to reassure them about their status as God's people.

The first paragraph (4:8–11) continues some of the key imagery found in 4:1–7. But it ranges widely, serving as the application of all of 3:7–4:7.[63] Paul urges the Galatians not to return again to the slavery of their non-Christian past by embracing the law. To put themselves under the law, Paul suggests—quite provocatively!—is in some sense

---

62. E.g., Burton, *Galatians*, 219–20; Bruce, *Galatians*, 197; Martyn, *Galatians*, 390; Brendan Byrne, *"Sons of God"—"Seed of Abraham": A Study of the Idea of the Sonship of God of All Christians in Paul against the Jewish Background*, AnBib 83 (Rome: Biblical Institute Press, 1979), 182; Scott, *Adoption as Sons*, 173–74.

63. R. Longenecker, *Galatians*, 178–79; G. Walter Hansen, *Galatians*, IVPNTC 9 (Downers Grove, IL: InterVarsity Press, 1994), 124–25.

the same as returning to their paganism (v. 9). "Observing special days and months and seasons and years" (v. 10) probably alludes to their inclination to follow the agitators and begin observing ritual elements of the Torah.

The second paragraph (4:12–20) is a strong personal appeal based on Paul's previous relationship with the Galatians. The tone of these verses is characteristic of the ancient rhetorical device called "pathos," by which a speaker sought to move his or her audience by appealing to the emotions and to shared personal experience.[64] Paul appeals directly to his audience at the beginning and the end: "brothers and sisters" in verse 12; "my dear children" in verse 19. Paul explicitly (v. 12) or implicitly (vv. 19–20) urges the Galatians to turn away from the agitators and their message and reassert their adherence to Paul and the gospel that he preaches. Toward this end, Paul contrasts the response he received when he first preached the gospel among them with their current attitude (vv. 12–16). In verses 17–18, Paul urges his audience to display the kind of zeal the agitators have for their viewpoint toward Paul.

The story of Abraham, which is so prominent in 3:6–18, is again the backdrop for Paul's argument in the third stage of his appeal (4:21–31). Paul uses the two wives of Abraham, Sarah and Hagar, as the basis for what he calls an "allegory." This word had a wider range in Paul's day than it does in ours—but elements of what we call allegory, with components of the scriptural story given symbolic meaning, are certainly present. This unusual way of appealing to Scripture probably suggests that he cites this OT narrative to counter the agitators' own appeal to the story.[65] They were probably arguing for a continuous reading of salvation history. Israel is to be identified as the true children of Abraham. Israel was given the law, and the people of God therefore remain under that law. Only law-observant people can be children of Abraham or children of Sarah.

Paul counters this argument by reading the story about Abraham's wives quite differently, focusing on the contrast between slavery and freedom:

"the slave woman"/"the free woman" (v. 22 and 23)
"bears children who are to be slaves" (v. 24b)
"the present city of Jerusalem . . . in slavery with her children" (v. 25)
"the Jerusalem that is above is free" (v. 26)
"the slave woman's son will never share in the inheritance with the free woman's son" (v. 30)
"we are not children of the slave woman, but of the free woman" (v. 31)

---

64. See esp. Ben Witherington III, *Grace in Galatia: A Commentary on Paul's Letter to the Galatians* (Grand Rapids: Eerdmans, 1998), 295–96, 305–7.

65. See esp. C. K. Barrett, "The Allegory of Abraham, Sarah, and Hagar in the Argument of Galatians," in *Rechtfertigung:*

Festschrift für Ernst Käsemann zum 70. Geburtstag, ed. Johannes Friedrich, Wolfgang Pöhlmann, and Peter Stuhlmacher (Göttingen: Vandenhoeck & Ruprecht, 1976), 1–16; contra, e.g., Watson, *Paul and the Hermeneutics of Faith*, 190.

The portrayal of Hagar in Genesis 16–21 as a "slave woman" (*paidiskē*) is the basis for Paul's development of this slave/free contrast. Paul is not, of course, simply surveying the surface meaning of the OT passage. His reading is governed by his conviction that the coming of Christ marks the center of salvation history and that all of Scripture must be read in light of that event. As so often in Paul, a prophetic text from Isaiah is the starting point for Paul's interpretation. This text refers to the joy of a barren woman who ends up having many children. In the context, this barren woman is Jerusalem, promised, despite her current captivity, "many children."[66] On the reverse side of the situation, then, it is Israel's failure to obey the law that has led the people into their current "barrenness." Paul moves from Isaiah to the story in Genesis on the basis of his reading of the broader Old Testament context. Isaiah implies that the "barren woman" who rejoices, identified with Jerusalem in Isaiah 54:1, also has in view Sarah, the "barren woman" who ultimately gives birth par excellence (Isa 51:1–2). If, then, Sarah is identified with the Jerusalem that rejoices over many children, Hagar can be identified with the current barren state of Jerusalem. Paul's christological reading of Isaiah gives him the scriptural basis to align Sarah with the law-free gospel that has given birth to the "Jerusalem above," while conversely Hagar becomes associated with subjection to the law.

We can identify three steps in Paul's "allegorical" reading: an introduction (v. 21); the interpretation of the narrative of Sarah and Hagar (vv. 22–27), a section bounded by occurrences of "it is written" (*gegraptai*—vv. 22, 27); and the application and appeal (vv. 28–31). The argument proceeds by means of a series of contrasts (perhaps alluded to in the verb *systoichei*, "corresponds," in v. 25).

v. 22	"Abraham had two sons"	
v. 22	"by the slave woman"	"by the free woman"
v. 23	"born according to the flesh"	"born as the result of a divine promise"
v. 24	"one covenant is from Mount Sinai and bears children who are to be slaves"	
vv. 25–26	"the present city of Jerusalem, because she is in slavery with her children"	"the Jerusalem that is above is free"
v. 27 [Isa 54:1]	"[the children] of her who has a husband"	"more are the children of the desolate woman"
v. 29	"the son born according to the flesh"	"the son born by the power of the Spirit"
v. 30	"the slave woman's son"	"the free woman's son"
v. 31	"we are not children of the slave woman"	"but [children] of the free woman"

---

66. See esp. Harmon, *She Must and Shall Go Free*, 173–85; Joel Willitts, "Isa 54,1 in Gal 4,27b–27: Reading Genesis in Light of Isaiah," *ZNW* 96 (2005): 188–210.

As I have noted, the paragraph continues Paul's concern with the hermeutical and salvation-historical significance of Abraham (see 3:6–15). Christians, Paul has argued, are, in Christ, the true "seed" of Abraham, heirs to the promises he was given. But, as he now demonstrates, they are also the children of the free woman, Sarah. Like Isaac, then, Christains are heirs of all the promises that God made to the patriarchs. Christians can trace their status as God's people to both their paternity and their maternity. In addition, however, as the antithetical form of his conclusion makes clear—children of the free woman, *not* of the slave woman (4:31)—Paul also contrasts the children of Abraham through Sarah with the children of Abraham through Hagar. He therefore counters the agitators' view of salvation history, for whom law observance is essential to defining the people of God, with his own version, according to which faith in Christ, "the seed" of Abraham, is fully sufficient to guarantee the inheritance.

3.4 Exhortation and Warning: Faith, Spirit, and Righteousness (5:1–12)

In the two paragraphs that compose this section (vv. 1–6, 7–12), Paul brings his rhetoric in the letter to its climax. The first paragraph, especially, picks up key emphases from 3:1–6; these two paragraphs, then, bracket the central section of the letter. Both passages highlight the importance of faith and the Spirit (3:2, 3, 5, 6) in contrast to the law (3:2, 5; 5:2–4) and stress the complete sufficiency of faith (and the Spirit) as the means of righteousness (3:6; 5:5).

In verse 1, Paul warns his readers not to submit again to "a yoke of slavery." This verse is transitional, picking up the central contrast in 4:21–31—slavery versus freedom—and applying it to the readers. The NIV echoes the emphasis of the Greek by putting "for freedom" (a dative in Gk.) at the beginning of the verse. Putting themselves under the law would be to retreat from the freedom that Christ has purchased for his people. Paul unpacks this general exhortation in three roughly parallel warnings in verses 2–4: if the Galatians are circumcised or seek justification in the law, "Christ will be of no value" to them (v. 2), they will have to do all the law (v. 3), and they will be cut off from grace (v. 4). Although Paul has hinted that circumcision might be an issue in the Galatian churches (2:3), this is the first time that Paul mentions it as a key point of contention. Withholding the pivotal issue of a writing until the key moment was a common rhetorical strategy[67] and gave it special prominence. Circumcision was, of course, given by God to Abraham and his descendants as a "sign of the covenant" (Gen 17:11) and took on special importance as a "marker" of Jewishness in the pluralistic, Greco-Roman, first-century world. The agitators therefore were probably insisting

---

67. Ben Witherington III, *Jesus the Seer: The Progress of Prophecy* (Peabody, MA: Hendrickson, 1999), 364.

on circumcision as a necessary step if the Galatian Christians were to be considered as belonging to the people of the covenant and therefore to be found "righteous" on the day of judgment. Paul warns bluntly about the consequences of such a move: circumcision, in this religious sense, signals belonging to the old covenant, with the consequent requirement to obey the law. Yet, as Paul has shown, the law was outmoded (Gal 3:15–18; 4:1–3); it demands works that sinful humans cannot adequately produce (cf. 3:10, 12), and it therefore subjects its "doers" to a curse (3:10, 13; 4:4–5). Thus the acceptance of circumcision would mean losing Christ's benefits (v. 2), being alienated from him, and falling away from the grace of the new covenant (v. 4).

In verse 5, Paul moves to a positive argument. The new focus is marked by the shift from the second-person formulation in verses 2–4 to the first-person language in verses 5–6: Christians have the secure expectation of being justified in the final day through the Spirit and through their faith, a faith that produces works pleasing to God. Verse 5 reiterates a key point he has made earlier: righteousness comes via the work of the Spirit and by faith. Paul here also adds a new nuance by referring to "the hope of righteousness." Paul may mean that the believer's faith secures our hope, which "springs from [the] righteousness [we already possess]" (construing *dikaiosynēs* as a source or subjective genitive).[68] However, it is more likely that he portrays righteousness as the content of our hope: "The hope that consists in righteousness" or "the righteousness for which we hope" (NIV; a genitive of apposition).[69] In this case, Paul focuses attention, as he does elsewhere in the letter, on the ultimate attaining of "righteousness"—vindication in the judgment. In verse 6, finally, Paul again highlights the dramatically new situation that Christ has inaugurated: being circumcised—or not—matters not at all; what counts, he says, is "faith expressing itself through love." This does not mean "faith that has genuine power only when love is added" but "faith that, because it brings us in relationship to Christ and is accompanied by God's Spirit, leads inevitably to a life of love." Calvin's expression of the point is classic: "It is not our doctrine that the faith which justifies is alone; we maintain that it is invariably accompanied by good works; only we contend that faith alone is sufficient for justification."[70]

Paul brings the great central theological argument of the letter (3:1–5:12) to an end with a concluding exhortation. To be sure, the exhortation in these verses is more implicit than explicit. As he does elsewhere (3:7–4:7 in light of 4:8–20), Paul moves from theological argument to personal appeal ("pathos"). He describes the agitators in

68. E.g., Ronald Y. K. Fung, *The Epistle to the Galatians*, NICNT (Grand Rapids: Eerdmans, 1988), 226; Matera, *Galatians*, 182; Timothy George, *Galatians*, NAC 10 (Nashville: Broadman & Holman, 1994), 361; John A. Ziesler, *The Meaning of Righteousness in Paul: A Linguistic and Theological Enquiry*, SNTSMS 20 (Cambridge: Cambridge University Press, 1972),

179; Hans-Joachim Eckstein, *Verheissung und Gesetz: Eine exegetische Untersuchung zu Galater 2,15–4,7*, WUNT 86 (Tübingen: Mohr Siebeck, 1996), 142.

69. See Moo, *Galatians*, 327–28.

70. John Calvin, *Commentaries on the Epistles of Paul to the Galatians and Ephesians* (Edinburgh: Thomas Clark, 1854), 132.

biting polemical language (vv. 7b–9, 10b, 12), refers to his own ministry (v. 11), and implicitly appeals to the Galatians to stay the course (vv. 7a, 10a). In this paragraph as a whole, he makes two closely related points: (1) the agitators are not worth listening to; they are themselves under condemnation; and (2) the Galatians, Paul suggests, will at the end come around to embracing Paul and the gospel he preaches. This last point echoes a key rhetorical emphasis from 3:1–6, where his concern also was to encourage the Galatians to "finish" their course as they had begun it (see 3:3).

4 THE LIFE OF THE GOSPEL (5:13–6:10)

The third main part of Paul's letter to the Galatians is characterized by a shift in vocabulary and, by extension, a shift in subject matter also. Two words dominate this new section: "Spirit" and "love." The Spirit is mentioned ten times, very often set in contrast with the flesh (5:17, 19/22, 24–25; 6:8). The word "love" occurs only twice (5:13, 22) but the concept of love is a key motif (see also 5:14 [the verb]; 6:1–2, 9–10). Interwoven with these two key motifs is another, carried over from earlier in the letter: the law (5:14, 18, 23; 6:2). Putting these key motifs together reveals the central thrust of this section: the Spirit enables believers to overcome the power of the flesh and, by stimulating love for others, provides for the true fulfillment of the law. The continuing focus on the law is natural in a letter that has been dominated by polemics over this issue. The agitators may well have been setting forth the law as an objective set of moral requirements and at the same time as a means of avoiding sin. In response, Paul argues that the Spirit-filled life is not only fully adequate to maintain and confirm one's status of righteousness before God; the Spirit also provides fully for the life of righteousness that God expects of his people.

We can identify four distinct stages of argument.

In 5:13–15, Paul warns his readers about the danger posed to the Christian living by the "flesh" and reminds them of the vital need for love of others. The "freedom" Christ wins for us (see v. 1) is to lead not to selfish conduct but to love for others. Following Jesus (Matt 22:39//Mark 12:31//Luke 10:27; cf. also Matt 5:43–44; 19:19), and in keeping with other New Testament authors (Jas 2:8; and see the "new command" of John 13:34; 1 John 2:7–8 [cf. 3:23; 4:21]; see also Rom 13:8–10), Paul singles out the love command of Leviticus 19:18 as central to Christian ethics. Loving, Paul claims, "fulfills" the law. But how? He might mean that Christians bring the whole law to its conclusive and intended "end" by loving others.[71] But another view, which might fit the wording here a bit better, sees the implied agent of the passive verb to be Jesus Christ. On this view, Paul would be teaching that Jesus himself "fulfills" the whole law.

---

71. See, e.g., Mussner, *Galaterbrief,* 370.

He does so in his teaching by highlighting love for the neighbor as the true and ultimate completion and/or "filling up" of the law and in his life by going to the cross as the ultimate embodiment and pattern of sacrificial love.[72]

The second stage of the section, 5:16–24, introduces the dominant "actor" in the drama of Christian living: the Spirit. It is the Spirit who enables us to overcome the continuing influence of the "flesh" (*sarx*). This key theological term in Paul is notoriously difficult to define, but in general refers to "man insofar as he belongs to the mode of existence of this world and perishes with it."[73] "Flesh" in this sense is a dominant force of the old realm, whose desires we must resist (v. 16); it engages in perpetual conflict with the Spirit (v. 17). The Spirit also enables believers to meet all the demands of the law (v. 18).

Paul elaborates the flesh/Spirit antithesis by detailing some of the acts and attitudes that each of them produces in humans (vv. 19–23a). In contrast to the "works" of the flesh stands the "fruit" of the Spirit. The shift in vocabulary may highlight the powerful working of the Spirit to produce those virtues that God commends; it is also possible, though less likely, that there is a contrast between the diverse "works" of the flesh and the single focus of the Spirit.[74]

It is striking that Paul returns again to the law after this contrast (v. 23b). Again, his concern appears to be to show how the Spirit can fully provide for the conduct that the law itself seeks to inculcate. Paul ends this paragraph by returning to the point where he began. In verse 16, he exhorted believers to "walk by the Spirit" so that they might not "gratify the desires of the flesh." Now he claims that "those who belong to Christ Jesus have crucified the flesh with its passions and desires" (v. 24). Calling believers "those who are of Christ" (*hoi tou Christou*) alludes to the "inclusive Christology" that is the bedrock of Paul's theology in Galatians (see esp. 3:26–29). This same point is underscored by the verb "crucify," which clearly alludes to Christ's own crucifixion, in which the believer shares by God's decree.

In the third paragraph of this section, Paul spells out some specific ways in which believers can "keep in step" with the Spirit (5:25–6:6). While Paul's exhortations appear to move in several directions, we can identify a concern for appropriate relationships within the community as a key motif. Negatively, Paul warns about undue pride (5:26; 6:3–5). Positively, he encourages believers to restore people caught in sin (6:1) and to carry the burdens of others (6:2). Paul encourages believers to support one another with his claim that such people fulfill "the law of Christ." What is this "law of Christ"? Many interpreters argue that Paul is referring to the Mosaic law interpreted and fulfilled by

---

72. See esp. Hays, "Galatians," 322–24; also Martyn, *Galatians*, 480–90; Susan Grove Eastman, *Recovering Paul's Mother Tongue: Language and Theology in Galatians* (Grand Rapids: Eerdmans, 2007), 173.

73. Ridderbos, *Paul*, 104. See also pp. 452–54.

74. Heinrich Schlier, *Der Brief an die Galater*, 15th ed., KEK 7 (Göttingen: Vandenhoeck & Ruprecht, 1989), 256.

Christ.[75] However, I think it more likely that "of Christ" is used in deliberate contrast with "of Moses": as Torah is associated with Moses, so there is a new "law" associated with Christ. Paul may be thinking in particular of the love command (5:13–15),[76] but perhaps a more general reference to the ethical demands of the gospel is more likely. R. Longenecker summarizes it especially well: "Prescriptive principles stemming from the heart of the gospel (usually embodied in the example and teachings of Jesus), which are meant to be applied to specific situations by the direction and enablement of the Holy Spirit, being always motivated and conditioned by love."[77]

Verses 3–5, while not tied closely together, have a certain coherence in their focus on the need for self-examination.[78] Paul warns about the inappropriate pride that people can have when they don't truly understand themselves (v. 3). Any pride that we might have should be based on critical self-reflection and not on a comparison with others (v. 4). On the day of judgment, Paul reminds us, we will each have to answer for ourselves (v. 5). Verse 6, with its exhortation to support those who instruct believers in the word, is difficult to integrate into the context. Probably, however, it goes with the immediately preceding verses. Paul's strong emphasis on individual responsibility in verses 4–5 could be used by some as an excuse to stop supporting those who teach. His purpose in verse 6, then, might be to cut off this misapplication of his teaching.[79]

The larger section ends appropriately with a reminder of the importance of Christian obedience for the eschatological judgment and a final call to love all people, but especially "the family of believers" (6:7–10). Appeal to the prospect of God's scrutiny of our lives on the day of judgment often culminates Paul's exhortations (see esp. Rom 13:11–14 within 12:1–13:14; and also Phil 3:12–21). The flesh/Spirit antithesis is picked up here again (see 5:13–25). Human effort, Paul makes clear—as he does elsewhere (e.g, Rom 8:12–13)—is required if a believer expects to attain ultimate salvation.

---

75. In his survey of interpretation, Todd A. Wilson notes that this interpretation has become especially popular in recent years ("The Law of Christ and the Law of Moses: Reflections on a Recent Trend in Interpretation," *CurBR* 5 [2006]: 123–44). And see also, e.g., Ridderbos, *Paul*, 284–85; Barclay, *Obeying the Truth*, 126–41; Karl Kertelge, "Gesetz und Freiheit im Galaterbrief," *NTS* 30 (1984): 389–90; Thomas R. Schreiner, *The Law and Its Fulfillment: A Pauline Theology of Law* (Grand Rapids: Baker, 1993), 158–59; E. P. Sanders, *Paul, the Law, and the Jewish People* (Minneapolis: Fortress, 1983), 97–98; Matera, *Galatians*, 219–21; Stanton, "Law of Moses," 115–16; Frank S. Thielman, *Paul and the Law: A Contextual Approach* (Downers Grove, IL: InterVarsity Press, 1994), 141 (the "law of Christ" is both "something new" yet also "a reference to Christ's summary of the Mosaic law"); T. Wilson, *Curse of the Law*, 100–104; Dunn, *Epistle to the Galatians*, 323 ("that law [the Torah] as interpreted by the love command in the light of the Jesus-tradition and the Christ-event").

76. Furnish, *Theology and Ethics in Paul*, 60–64; Mussner, *Galaterbrief*, 399; Wolfgang Schrage, "Probleme paulinischer Ethik anhand von Gal 5,25–6,10," in *La foi agissant par l'amour (Galates 4,12–6,16)*, ed. Albert Vanhoye (Rome: Abbaye de S. Paul, 1996), 183–88.

77. R. Longenecker, *Galatians*, 275–76. See also, e.g., Andrea van Dülmen, *Die Theologie des Gesetzes bei Paulus*, SBM 5 (Stuttgart: Katholisches Bibelwerk, 1968), 66–68; Lauri Thurén, *Derhetorizing Paul: A Dynamic Perspective on Pauline Theology and the Law* (WUNT 124; Tübingen: Mohr Siebeck, 2000), 86–87; T. J. Deidun, *New Covenant Morality in Paul* (AnBib 89; Rome: Pontifical Biblical Institute, 1981), 210; Bruce, *Galatians*, 261; Garlington, *Exposition of Galatians*, 269; Fung, *Galatians*, 287. On the larger issue of "law," see pp. 615–22.

78. Barclay, *Obeying the Truth*, 159.

79. Barclay, *Obeying the Truth*, 162–63; Dunn, *Epistle to the Galatians*, 326.

This insistence on the indispensability of human works for the attaining of eternal life must, of course, be integrated with Paul's equally clearly insistence in Galatians that our ultimate justification rests on our faith and the work of the Spirit. Paul himself highlights the importance of the Spirit in this verse: it is "from the Spirit" that believers will reap eternal life.

Paul wraps up the paraenetic section of the letter with a general call for believers to "do good" (vv. 9–10). "All people" (v. 10) are to be included in this doing good. As the next phrase makes clear, this "all" is without boundaries, including unbelievers as well as believers. Amid the vital theological issue they are wrestling with and the internal divisions this issue has created, the Galatian Christians are to continue to manifest the love of Christ and grace of God to all the people they come into contact with.[80] When Paul then adds, "especially to the household of faith," this is meant "not as a narrowing of the general obligation, but as the most immediate way of giving it effect."[81]

5 CLOSING: CROSS AND NEW CREATION (6:11–18)

Various studies, some of which compare Paul's letters with those in the wider Greco-Roman world, have shown that Paul's letter endings fall into a clear pattern, marked by certain standard features. The ending of Galatians, however, omits some of these standard features, such as greetings of other believers, requests to greet others, notification of travel plans, requests for prayer, and doxologies. In their place, Paul has included a final rebuke of the agitators (vv. 12–13) and significant theological comment on the situation and status of his readers: with Paul (the apostle implies), they have been crucified to the world and the world to them (v. 14); they live in the new creation (v. 15), and they constitute the "Israel of God" (v. 16). The urgency of the situation in Galatia leads Paul to dispense with some of the usual "polite" formulas and to cut right to the heart of the life-and-death issue confronting the churches.[82] The ending of the letter reflects the strong sense of eschatological context with which the letter begins and which permeates the argument throughout.[83] God's rescue of humans from the "present evil age" (1:4) has a general counterpart in Paul's claim to have been separated from "the world" by means of his co-crucifixion with Christ (6:14). The positive side of this eschatological rescue is the "new creation" in which believers now live (v. 15). Christ's death has broken the power of the old age/the world and inaugurated God's all-embracing work of making the universe new.

---

80. Bruce W. Longenecker, *Remember the Poor: Paul, Poverty, and the Greco-Roman World* (Grand Rapids: Eerdmans, 2010), 141–42, sees here a particular focus on helping the poor.

81. Dunn, *Epistle to the Galatians*, 333.

82. See esp. Jeffrey A. D. Weima, *Neglected Endings: The Significance of the Pauline Letter Closings*, JSNTSup 101 (Sheffield: Sheffield Academic, 1994), 159–60.

83. B. Longenecker, *Triumph of Abraham's God*, 36–46.

The passage seems to have a concentric structure. Paul's "signature" in verse 11 and the grace wish in verse 18 provide a formal frame around the passage. The apostle's rebuke of the agitators in verses 12–13 is, similarly, matched by his plea that such people no longer "cause [him] trouble" in verse 17. Evocative and wide-ranging theological images dominate the center of the passage: crucifixion to the world, new creation, and maintaining, as the "Israel of God," this new-creation perspective.

Paul begins his concluding remarks by adding his own signature as a means of authenticating the letter (v. 11). He then engages in one final blast against the agitators, accusing them of selfish motives (to avoid "being persecuted for the cross of Christ," v. 12) and hypocrisy (while seeking to impose the law on the Galatians, they themselves do not keep it, v. 13). The cross has been a central focus in Galatians (see also 2:19–20; 3:1), for it powerfully signals the new state of affairs that the new covenant has introduced. It is no surprise, then, that Paul returns to it again here at the end (v. 14). Christ's crucifixion is a redemptive-historical event in which believers participate (see Gal 2:20; Rom 6:1–6). Through their co-crucifixion with Christ, Paul and other believers are definitively freed from the baneful influence of this world and no longer owe that world their allegiance. Christ's crucifixion is "the transformative event that ended the old order of things."[84]

Verses 14 and 15 are closely related.[85] The first, negative, part of the sentence elaborates "world" in verse 14, and "new creation" in the second part describes that which has taken the place of the world. Paul refers to "new creation" (*kainē ktisis*) once elsewhere: "Therefore, if anyone is in Christ, new creation! The old has gone, the new is here!" (2 Cor 5:17; my translation). The phrase itself never occurs in the Old Testament, but its equivalent is found in several Jewish texts. As in the Pauline texts, "new creation" is introduced in these Jewish texts without explanation, but the concept seems to denote the final state of affairs after God's climactic intervention on behalf of his people.[86] "New creation" is set in contrast to the "world" (v. 14) and the "old age" (1:4). It describes the new state of affairs that the cross signifies and inaugurates. Strictly speaking, as Theodoret notes, "*new creation* is the transformation of all things which will occur after the resurrection of the dead."[87] But, typical of New Testament "inaugurated eschatology," Paul celebrates the breaking into this world of that new creation in the gospel events. I argue, then, that "new creation" is an all-embracing

---

84. Hays, "Galatians," 344.

85. Dunn, *Epistle to the Galatians*, 342.

86. For surveys of the background, see Peter Stuhlmacher, "Erwägungen zum ontologischen Charakter der *kainē ktisis* bei Paulus," *EvT* 27 (1967): 1–35; Ulrich Mell, *Neue Schöpfung: Eine traditionsgeschichtliche und exegetische Studie zu einem soteriologischen Grundsatz paulinischer Theologie*, BZNW 56 (Berlin: de Gruyter, 1989); Edward Adams, *Constructing the World: A Study of Paul's Cosmological Language*, SNTW (Edinburgh: T&T Clark, 2000), 225–28; Joel White, "Paul's Cosmology: The Witness of Romans, 1 and 2 Corinthians, and Galatians," in *Cosmology and New Testament Theology*, ed. Jonathan T. Pennington and Sean M. McDonough, LNTS 355 (London: T&T Clark, 2008), 90–106.

87. Mark J. Edwards, ed., *Galatians, Ephesians, Philippians*, ACCS 8 (Downers Grove, IL: InterVarsity Press, 1999), 98.

phrase that refers to the conversion of individuals, the new community of Jew and gentile (see Gal 3:28 and the argument of Eph 2:11–22), and, ultimately, the renovation of the universe ("a new heaven and new earth").[88]

A reference to "peace" is typical in Paul's letter endings (Rom 15:33; 16:20; 2 Cor 13:11; Eph 6:23; Phil 4:9; 1 Thess 5:23; 2 Thess 3:16). "Peace" is mentioned in verse 16, but Paul includes the word "mercy." While cast in the form of a wish for peace and mercy, the verse essentially becomes an exhortation: you Galatians, Paul is saying, must join the unbounded group ("all," or "or as many as" [hosoi]) who will experience God's peace and mercy. Those who belong to this group are those who will follow "this rule"—the values of the kingdom that Paul has been outlining in this part of the letter. Paul's addition of the phrase "the Israel of God" is difficult to integrate into the syntax of the verse. Specifically, the kai that comes immediately before it could be:

1. Conjunctive ("and"). On this view, "the Israel of God" might be a separate, or overlapping, group with respect to "all who follow this rule": "And as for all who walk by this rule, peace and mercy be upon them, and upon the Israel of God" (ESV; see also NAB); or
2. Epexegetic ("even"). In this case, "the Israel of God" would be identical to "all who follow this rule"—"Peace and mercy to all who follow this rule—to the Israel of God" (NIV; cf. also NLT).

On the former reading, "Israel" probably has an ethnic sense, referring either to Jewish Christians or to the "Israel" that will one day be saved (on one reading of Rom 11:26).[89] On the latter reading, Paul here uses "Israel" to refer to the true people of God, composed of both faithful Jews and gentiles.[90]

---

88. For further detail on "new creation" and its cosmic scope, see Douglas J. Moo, "Nature in the New Creation: New Testament Eschatology and the Environment," *JETS* 49 (2006): 449–88, and Douglas J. Moo, "Creation and New Creation," *BBR* 20 (2010): 39–60. See also pp. 645–47.

89. With differences in detail, (1) Michael Bachmann, "The Church and the Israel of God: On the Meaning and Ecclesiastical Relevance of the Benediction at the End of Galatians," in *Anti-Judaism in Galatians? Exegetical Studies on a Polemical Letter and on Paul's Theology* (Grand Rapids: Eerdmans, 2008), 101–23; Dunn, *Epistle to the Galatians*, 345 (the covenant people of God as redefined in Gal 2–4); (2) Jewish Christians (Gottlob Schrenk, "Was bedeutet 'Israel Gottes'?," *Judaica* 5 [1949]: 81–94; idem, "Der Segenwunsch nach der Kampfepistel," *Judaica* 6 [1950]: 170–90; Betz, *Galatians*, 322–23); (3) the Israel destined for salvation (see Rom 11:26; Peter Richardson, *Israel in the Apostolic Church*, SNTSMS 10 [Cambridge: Cambridge University Press, 1969], 74–84; Bruce, *Galatians*, 274–75; Mussner, *Galaterbrief*, 416–17).

90. See esp. Andreas J. Köstenberger, "The Identity of the ΙΣΡΑΗΛ ΤΟΥ ΘΕΟΥ (Israel of God) in Galatians 6:16," *Faith & Mission* 19 (2001): 3–24; Nils Alstrup Dahl, "Der Name Israel: Zur Auslegung von Gal 6,16," *Judaica* 6 (1950): 161–70; and also, e.g, Chrysostom, *Commentary on Galatians* (*NPNF¹* 13:47), on 6:15–16; Calvin, *Galatians and Ephesians*, 186; Martin Luther, *Lectures on Galatians 1535, Chapters 5–6, and Lectures on Galatians 1519, Chapters 1–6*, vol. 27 of *Luther's Works*, ed. Jaroslav Pelikan (Saint Louis: Concordia, 1964), 142; Lightfoot, *Galatians*, 224–25; Albrecht Oepke, *Der Brief des Paulus an die Galater*, THKNT; Berlin: Evangelische Verlagsanstalt, 1973), 204–5; Barclay, *Obeying the Truth*, 98; Schlier, *Galater*, 283; Fung, *Galatians*, 311; Garlington, *Exposition of Galatians*, 292–93; Hays, "Galatians," 345–46; R. Longenecker, *Galatians*, 297–98; Martyn, *Galatians*, 574–77; Thomas R. Schreiner, *Galatians*, ZECNT (Grand Rapids: Zondervan, 2010), 381–83; G. K. Beale, "Peace and Mercy upon the Israel of God: The Old Testament Background of Galatians 6,16b," *Bib* 80 (1999): 204–23; Ridderbos, *Paul*, 336.

While the decision is not an easy one, I think the second option is the most likely. Paul's whole focus in Galatians has been on the one people of God who are created in and by Christ. Paul redefines the "seed of Abraham," insisting that his heirs consist of all who believe (3:7–29) and that the gentile Galatians "like Isaac, are children of promise" (4:28). Granted this central and critical argument, it makes best sense to think he ends his letter with a final reminder that Jews and gentiles together, in Christ, constitute a "new Israel."

Paul alludes to the agitators one last time (v. 17). However, while directed to the agitators, Paul undoubtedly wants it to be "overheard" by the Galatians themselves. Paul cannot do much to stop the agitators from their preaching and teaching heresy. But they will not "trouble" Paul if Christians for whom he feels spiritual responsibility, such as the Galatians, stop paying attention to them. Paul grounds his request in an intriguing personal remark: "I bear on my body the marks of Jesus." The reference is probably to scars and other marks on Paul's body that are the result of his persecution on behalf of Christ. Paul probably intends these physical scars to stand in contrast to the physical mark of circumcision. As Eastman paraphrases Paul's point, "You want something to brag about? You want identity markers? I'll give you identity markers! You see these scars? I'm branded for Jesus. Become like me!"[91]

Paul concludes his letter with a "grace" wish (v. 18), a standard literary feature that marks the endings of all Paul's letters.

---

91. Eastman, *Recovering Paul's Mother Tongue*, 109.

Chapter 5

1 THESSALONIANS

PAUL'S FIRST LETTER to the Thessalonians is famous for its teaching about
eschatology. Concern among the Thessalonians for brothers and sisters who have
died sparks Paul's important description of the parousia of Christ and events associated with it. However, this letter also offers important insights into the nature and
antecedents of conversion, as Paul celebrates the new life that God's word, faithfully
proclaimed by Paul and his coworkers, has awakened in these Thessalonian gentiles.

LOCATING THE LETTER

Paul wrote his first letter to the Thessalonian Christians shortly after founding the
church on his first missionary journey (Acts 17:1–9). As was his custom, Paul proclaimed the good news of Jesus on three Sabbaths and perhaps stayed in the city for a
longer time. His preaching drew a positive response from "some of the Jews" as well as
from "a large number of God-fearing Greeks and quite a few prominent women" (v. 4).
But some other Jewish people resisted Paul's message, instigating a riot that the city
officials had to quell. As a result, Paul was spirited away at nighttime to Berea, where
some of the Thessalonian Jews again sparked resistance to Paul and his message, as a
result of which Paul moved on to Athens. From Athens, Paul went on to Corinth, where
he spent a year and a half establishing and building up the church. Paul had left Silas
and Timothy in Berea, and Timothy also traveled back to Thessalonica to check on
the young believers there. Timothy eventually arrived in Corinth, and his good report
about the Thessalonians was the immediate stimulus for the writing of 1 Thessalonians,
probably in AD 50 or 51 (1 Thess 2:17–3:10).

ISOLATING THE ISSUES

Paul writes to the Thessalonian Christians for three reasons. First, he celebrates both
their faithfulness to Christ and to the message he, Silas, and Timothy preached to them
and exhorts them to continue on this same path (chs. 1–3). The persecution that was
continuing to put pressure on the new believers rendered this exhortation especially
urgent. An additional complicating factor was Paul's own conduct. One can imagine

that the Thessalonians might have harbored some doubts about Paul, the chief herald of the message they had embraced, since, when persecution arose, he simply fled the scene. And so, in 2:1–12 Paul asserts his sincerity and the purity of his motives. Second, Paul reminds the Thessalonians of some basic ways in which they need to continue to live out their new faith (4:1–12). Paul focuses on gentiles in the letter and is keenly aware of the pressures for conformity to their culture that they face.[1] Third, Paul has heard (almost certainly from Timothy) that the Thessalonians were worried about the fate of their brothers and sisters who had died (in the persecution?[2]) and were generally confused about the events surrounding Jesus's return. In 4:13–5:11, then, Paul turns to eschatology, with a view to comforting and instructing the Thessalonians. However, focus on Jesus's return in glory is not confined to this text; it punctuates the letter throughout (1:9b–10; 2:19; 3:13; 5:23).[3]

The circumstances in which Paul writes dictate the theological shape of the letter. Paul's need to address the specific situation in Thessalonica means that the letter is especially helpful in enhancing our appreciation for the inherent power of the gospel message and in revealing details about eschatology. Some scholars think the "apocalyptic" style of 4:13–18 especially, with its laying out of specific events and their sequence, reveals Paul's early views that he later came to modify or at least tone down.[4] But it is the circumstances of the Thessalonians that require Paul to teach here as he does. As Barclay says, "For Paul, apocalyptic is one part of his mental landscape which can be accorded more or less prominence in different circumstances, but for the Thessalonians, the apocalyptic contours of Paul's message stand out as a ready explanation of their *thlipsis* and provide the necessary means for enduring it."[5] We should also note parallels to the eschatological teaching here in later letters (e.g., 1 Cor 15:20–28, 50–57).

ANALYZING THE ARGUMENT

This early letter of Paul clearly works within an eschatological framework that is fundamental to the apostle's theology and pastoral teaching. As Donfried summarizes, "God's choice of the Thessalonian Christians, then, announced by Paul through the

---

1. Some recent interpreters think that an important part of this culture that Paul addresses in the letter is Roman imperial propaganda (e.g., James R. Harrison, "Paul and the Imperial Gospel in Thessalonika," *JSNT* 25 [2002]: 71–96).

2. A number of scholars think the best explanation for a number of people in the Thessalonian church dying would be that they were martyred (e.g., Nijay K. Gupta, *1 & 2 Thessalonians*, Zondervan Critical Introductions to the New Testament [Grand Rapids: Zondervan Academic, 2019], 61–62).

3. Robert Jewett, *The Thessalonian Correspondence: Pauline Rhetoric and Millenarian Piety* (Philadelphia: Fortress, 1986), 161–78, identifies a basic problem that gives rise to the different issues treated in the letter: "millenarian radicalism."

4. E.g., Dunn, *Beginning from Jerusalem*, 713.

5. John M. G. Barclay, "Conflict in Thessalonica," *CBQ* 55 (1993): 519.

gospel and responded to in faith, is to be realised and actualised, despite all external adversities, through a lifestyle informed by love and established in hope."[6] Eschatology is an obvious focal point of the letter, but we should not overlook other important themes. For example, as Paddison has noticed, Paul's juxtaposition of God and Christ reveals an incipient trinitarianism: compare "the church . . . in God the Father and the Lord Jesus Christ" (1:1); "God's churches . . . which are in Christ Jesus" (2:14); "the gospel of God" (2:8, 9); "the gospel of Christ" (3:2; cf. 1:8: "the Lord's message"); "those approved by God" (2:4); "apostles of Christ" (2:6); "now may our God and Father himself and our Lord Jesus clear the way [a singular verb in Gk.]" (3:11); "God's will for you in Christ Jesus" (5:18).[7] The holiness of God's people, both attained as a status (perhaps 3:13), but more importantly set forth as a standard for living (4:3, 4, 7; 5:23), is important.[8]

The circumstances I have outlined account for the absence of certain theological motifs in the letter. Thus, while assuming the foundational importance of Jesus's death and resurrection (1:10; 4:14; 5:10), Paul says little about them—not because they are unimportant but because Paul is convinced his teaching on these matters when he was with the Thessalonians requires no supplement at this point. Also missing from 1 Thessalonians is any mention of justification. For many scholars who think 1 Thessalonians is the first letter Paul wrote, this absence suggests that this doctrinal concern only arose later in Paul's ministry. However, Galatians, in my view, predates 1 Thessalonians, and Galatians, of course, has a lot to say about justification. We must assume again that the circumstances of the letter did not require Paul to address the matter.[9] Whether Paul integrated justification into his preaching of the gospel in Thessalonica, we simply cannot know.

1 PAUL AND THE THESSALONIANS (1:1–3:13)

The epistolary prescript indicates the letter is from "Paul, Silas and Timothy" (1:1). Some scholars, noting the high frequency of first-plural forms in this letter, think that we need to view all three as genuine authors of the letter.[10] However, the abrupt shift

---

6. Karl P. Donfried and I. Howard Marshall, *The Theology of the Shorter Pauline Letters* (Cambridge: Cambridge University Press, 1993), 30.

7. Paddison, *Theological Hermeneutics and 1 Thessalonians*, 150–51.

8. Jeffrey A. D. Weima, "'How You Must Walk to Please God': Holiness and Discipleship in 1 Thessalonians," in *Patterns of Discipleship in the New Testament*, ed. Richard N. Longenecker, McMaster NT Studies (Grand Rapids: Eerdmans, 1996), 98–119.

9. Hengel and Schwemer, *Paul between Damascus and Antioch*, 304–10, stress the continuity between the theology of 1 Thessalonians and later Pauline letters.

10. Gene L. Green, *The Letters to the Thessalonians*, PNTC (Grand Rapids: Eerdmans, 2002), 57–58 (he notes that 96 percent of the first-person verbs in 1 Thess are plural); see also, on the issue in general, E. R. Richards, *Paul and First-Century Letter Writing*, 32–36; Steve Walton, *Leadership and Lifestyle: The Portrait of Paul in the Miletus Speech and 1 Thessalonians*, SNTSMS 108 (Cambridge: Cambridge University Press, 2000), 142–44. See also pp. 52–53.

to Paul's personal situation (2:18) suggests rather that Silas and Timothy should be considered co*senders* rather than co*authors*.[11]

As per his custom, Paul immediately turns to thanksgiving (1:2). What is not customary, however, is Paul's return to thanksgiving in 2:13 and 3:9. It is possible, then, that the "thanksgiving" section of the letter extends all the way from 1:2 through 3:13.[12] Whether this is so or not[13]—and we must be careful not to force Paul's letter-writing into a straitjacketed form of our own devising—all of 1:2–3:13 coheres around the dual theme of the apostles' faithful preaching of God's word and the Thessalonians' faithful reception of it. The latter motif is the focus of 1:2–10. Touching on a theological point basic to Paul's teaching about conversion, he traces the Thessalonians' spiritual standing to their election (v. 4). The evidence for this election is the powerful way the gospel was embraced by them (v. 5). A key theme of chapters 1–2, a kind of intermediary step between the apostles' preaching and the Thessalonians' response, is the word or message (*logos*, "message" or "word" in 1:5, 6, 8; 2:5, 13 [3x]; *euangelion*, "gospel" in 1:5; 2:2, 4, 8, 9)—a word that carries with it power, a word "at work in you who believe" (2:13). This message "rang out from you" (1:8). This may mean only that the Thessalonians, because of their transformed lives, were examples of the power of that word. However, it is likely that Paul hints here at the way the Thessalonians were also actively proclaiming the message.[14] This initial thanksgiving section concludes with a beautiful summary of the Thessalonians' conversion experience. They "turned to God from idols to serve the living and true God, and to wait for his Son from heaven, whom he raised from the dead—Jesus, who rescues us from the coming wrath" (1:9b–10). The language suggests that Paul has gentiles in view, whose past was characterized by the various idols that so dominated the culture of that time. The suitability of the wording of this brief summary to the Thessalonian situation, dominated by concerns about eschatology, strongly suggests that this is not a pre-Pauline formula—as many think—but Paul's own composition.[15]

In chapter 2, Paul's focus shifts from the way the Thessalonians *received* the gospel message (1:2–10) to the way Paul and his associates *proclaimed* the gospel to them (2:1–12, a point anticipated in 1:5b). They preached with pure motives, seeking to please God rather than people (2:3–5). They did not vaunt their authority over them but

11. M. Eugene Boring, *I and II Thessalonians: A Commentary*, NTL (Louisville: Westminster John Knox, 2015), 48–49; Jeffrey A. D. Weima, *1–2 Thessalonians*, BECNT (Grand Rapids: Baker Academic, 2014), 66.

12. Peter Thomas O'Brien, *Introductory Thanksgivings in the Letters of Paul*, NovTSup 49 (Leiden: Brill, 1977; repr., Eugene, OR: Wipf & Stock, 2009), 141–61; cf. also Abraham J. Malherbe, *The Letters to the Thessalonians*, AB 32B (New Haven: Yale University Press, 2004), 103–5.

13. Most scholars doubt that it is appropriate to classify all of 1:2–3:13 as thanksgiving (e.g., Boring, *I and II Thessalonians*, 56; Weima, *1–2 Thessalonians*, 77).

14. Gary S. Shogren, *1 & 2 Thessalonians*, ZECNT (Grand Rapids: Zondervan, 2012), 70–72; Weima, *1–2 Thessalonians*, 105.

15. E.g., Weima, *1–2 Thessalonians*, 115–18; contra, e.g., Ernest Best, *The First and Second Epistles to the Thessalonians*, BNTC (Peabody, MA: Hendrickson, 1993), 86.

lived with them in love and with deep concern for them (vv. 6–8), sharing with them not just the gospel but themselves as well. In a remarkable series of familial images, Paul compares himself to the Thessalonians' father (v. 11), their mother (v. 7b), and, perhaps, to young children (v. 7a; the text is uncertain).[16] They worked at their own secular jobs so that they would not be a burden to the Thessalonians (v. 9). They lived "righteous and blameless" lives among them (v. 10). The length Paul goes to in making this point, along with the negative way he frames some of it ("not trying to please people," "never used flattery," "did not put on a mask to cover greed," "not looking for praise from people") suggests that the apostles were being accused of this kind of conduct and that Paul is therefore defending himself and his associates. However, Malherbe initiated a different way of looking at the passage. Noting that the general outline of conduct that Paul distances himself from is similar to that of particular wandering teachers in his day (known as Cynics), he argued that Paul's purpose here is not apologetic but paraenetic.[17] However, it makes better sense of the passage if Paul is, in fact, defending his conduct in the face of accusations leveled against the apostles not by false teachers but by the Thessalonians' fellow citizens (see 2:14)—and perhaps suspicions harbored by some of the Christians themselves.[18] We can well imagine that Paul's hasty departure from Thessalonica in the face of opposition might have cast doubt on his motives and sincerity—especially since the Cynic teachers provided a well-known pattern of just such duplicitous and greedy motives and immoral behavior.[19] Paul therefore reminds the Thessalonians of the nature of his "entrance" (*eisodon*, 2:1; also translated "visit" [NIV]; "coming" [NET]).

Paul repeats his thanksgiving for the way the Thessalonians received the word of God that Paul and his associates faithfully and selflessly proclaimed (2:13). That word, which had the power to convert them, now continues to work powerfully in and among them (v. 14). As evidence, Paul cites the suffering they are undergoing—suffering that marks God's true people. They have been persecuted by their fellow citizens, just as their brothers and sisters in Judea have been persecuted by "the Jews" (v. 14).

---

16. On these images, see Trevor J. Burke, *Family Matters: A Socio-Historical Study of Kinship Metaphors in 1 Thessalonians*, JSNTSup 247 (London: T&T Clark, 2003), 13–62.

In v. 7 it is unclear whether Paul says that "we were like young children among you" (NIV) or "we were gentle among you" (ESV). The difference is a text-critical one, some MSS reading *nēpioi*, "young children," and others *ēpioi*, "gentle." For the former, see Gupta, *1 and 2 Thessalonians*, 106–14; Weima, *1–2 Thessalonians*, 180–87; and Gordon D. Fee, *The First and Second Letters to the Thessalonians*, NICNT (Grand Rapids: Eerdmans, 2009), 65–71; and for the latter, Malherbe, *Thessalonians*, 145–46. In either case, Paul stresses the apostles' mild tone with the Thessalonians.

17. Abraham J. Malherbe, "'Gentle as a Nurse': The Cynic Background to 1 Thess 2," *NovT* 12 (1970): 203–17; idem, *Thessalonians*, 154–56; Charles A. Wanamaker, *The Epistles to the Thessalonians*, NIGTC (Grand Rapids: Eerdmans, 1990), 93.

18. Todd D. Still, *Conflict at Thessalonica: A Pauline Church and Its Neighbors*, JSNTSup 183 (Sheffield: JSOT Press, 1999); Seyoon Kim, "Paul's Entry (εἴσοδος) and the Thessalonians' Faith (1 Thessalonians 1–3)," *NTS* 51 (2005): 519–42; Colin Nicholl, *From Hope to Despair in Thessalonica: Situating 1 and 2 Thessalonians*, SNTSMS 126 (Cambridge: Cambridge University Press, 2004), 91–93; Fee, *Thessalonians*, 53; Weima, *1–2 Thessalonians*, 122–25.

19. Green, *Thessalonians*, 114.

The persecution Paul has in mind is not clear, and also unclear is the meaning of his reference to "Jews" (*Ioudaioi*). The word could refer narrowly to Judeans, but despite the reference to Judea earlier, so restricted a sense is unlikely in light of the way Paul goes on to describe them in four parallel clauses in vv. 15–16a:

"who killed the Lord Jesus and the prophets"
who "drove us out"
who "displease God and are hostile to everyone"
who "keep us from speaking to the Gentiles so that they may be saved"

A critical issue is whether these clauses are restrictive—the "Jews" are *restricted* to those with these characteristics—or nonrestrictive—"Jews" are *defined* in general by these characteristics. (A restrictive clause is not preceded by a comma [cf. NIV; CSB]; a nonrestrictive clause has the comma [cf. RSV; NRSV; ESV; NET].) To put it another way: Is Paul describing a subset of the Jewish people who have been actively hostile to Paul and his ministry, or is he describing the Jewish people in general?[20] A decision is difficult, since Paul elsewhere can speak quite generally about "the Jews" or "Israel" in a corporate sense as having deserted true worship of God by failing to embrace Jesus as the Messiah (see, e.g., Rom 9:1–3, 31; 10:9, 21; 2 Cor 11:24). On the other hand, Paul would obviously exclude from "the Jews" those, like him, who were Christians; and the focus on active resistance of the gospel in these descriptions probably suggests that we should think that Paul refers to a subset of the Jews.[21]

These Jews, Paul goes on to say, are accumulating an intolerable burden of sin, and this means that "the wrath of God has come upon them at last" (v. 16). Some think the verb here means not "has come" but "is impending,"[22] but this would not be the normal sense of the verb. The translation of the last phrase in the verse (*eis telos*) is also debated, and the debate is an important one because, on certain interpretations of the verse, it would appear that Paul contradicts what he later says in Romans 11:25–28. In this latter text, Paul appears to predict that many Jews will be saved in the last day. Here, however, it could appear that he has pronounced a final doom on the Jews: wrath has come upon them—end of story. Some avoid the problem by claiming the text has been introduced into the text of 1 Thessalonians after AD 70, when, it might be argued,

20. For the former, see, e.g., Still, *Conflict at Thessalonica*, 41–42; Frank D. Gilliard, "The Problem of the Antisemitic Comma between 1 Thessalonians 2.14 and 15," *NTS* 35 (1989): 481–502; Fee, *Thessalonians*, 94–96; Boring, *I and II Thessalonians*, 99; I. Howard Marshall, *1 & 2 Thessalonians*, NCB (Grand Rapids: Eerdmans, 1983), 82; Malherbe, *Thessalonians*, 169; Weima, *1–2 Thessalonians*, 168; for the latter, e.g., F. F. Bruce, *1 and 2 Thessalonians*, WBC 45 (Dallas: Word, 1982), 46.

21. This subset cannot, however, be restricted to "Judeans," another possible meaning of *Ioudaioi* (contra, e.g., Fee, *Thessalonians*, 94–96; Weima, *1–2 Thessalonians*, 168).

22. James E. Frame, *A Critical and Exegetical Commentary on the Epistles of St. Paul to the Thessalonians*, ICC 36 (New York: Scribner's Sons, 1912), 114; Fee, *Thessalonians*, 102; Marshall, *1 & 2 Thessalonians*, 80; Best, *Thessalonians*, 119–20.

God's wrath did indeed come upon the Jews in the form of the Roman invasion of Judea.[23] However, there are no grounds for thinking verses have been added here, and the passage fits its context quite well.[24]

The key problem is the Greek phrase ending the verse, *eis telos*. The Greek word *telos* can have a temporal sense ("end, termination") or a telic sense ("goal, outcome"), while the preposition *eis* can mean "in," "unto," or "until." These options can be combined in different ways to produce at least four translations. (1) Most versions and many commentators think the idea is that (in response to the heaping up of their sins), God's wrath has finally, "at last," fallen on the Jews (cf. NIV; RSV; NRSV; ESV; NLT; CSB; CEB; NJB).[25] (2) Other interpreters think the idea is that God's wrath rests on the Jews permanently, forever.[26] (3) Paul might mean that God's wrath will rest on the Jews right up until the end (see Matt 24:13). This interpretation would allow, but does not require, a removal of that wrath at the end.[27] (4) Finally, the phrase might focus on degree rather than time, meaning something like "God's wrath has come upon them completely" (NET).[28] A choice among these options is difficult to make, but I slightly prefer the third.[29] On this view, it is tempting to take one more step and interpret Paul to be suggesting that there will be a change of circumstances at "the end": for example, God's wrath remains on the Jews right up to the end, when God removes it and opens the way for "all Israel to be saved" (Rom 11:26). But this is probably to read too much into this verse. And, in any case, we must remember that the antecedent of "them" in this clause would be those particular Jews Paul has in view in verses 15–16a, not all Jews. The bottom line here is that Paul's claim about wrath and the Jews is far too brief and allusive to build any kind of case for tension or contradiction with his fuller statements elsewhere.

Paul's direct address of the Thessalonians—"brothers and sisters"—signals a shift from the initial preaching of the gospel in Thessalonica to the subsequent history of their relationship (2:17–3:13; see *Locating the Letter* above). What does carry over

23. See esp. Birger A. Pearson, "1 Thessalonians 2:13–16: A Deutero-Pauline Interpolation," *HTR* 64 (1971): 79–94; also, e.g., William O. Walker Jr., *Interpolations in the Pauline Letters*, JSNTSup 213 (London: Sheffield Academic, 2001), 210–20.

24. Wanamaker, *Thessalonians*, 30–33. See also Carol J. Schlueter, *Filling Up the Measure: Polemical Hyperbole in 1 Thessalonians 2.14–16*, JSNTSup 98 (Sheffield: JSOT, 1994); and esp. Still, *Conflict at Thessalonica*, 24–45.

25. Frame, *Thessalonians*, 114; Green, *Thessalonians*, 149; Best, *Thessalonians*, 121. Defenders of this view often cite as a possible parallel T. Levi 6.11: "The wrath of God ultimately [*eis telos*] came upon [the Shechemites]."

26. See Matt 24:13. The LXX often uses the phrase in this way (e.g., 1 Chr 28:9; Ps 9:19).

27. Malherbe, *Thessalonians*, 171. Johannes Munck takes this view and thinks it allows for a removal of wrath at the end (*Christ and Israel: An Interpretation of Romans 9–11* [Philadelphia: Fortress, 1967], 63–64); cf. also Bruce, *Thessalonians*, 49; Ben Witherington III, *1 and 2 Thessalonians: A Socio-Rhetorical Commentary* (Grand Rapids: Eerdmans, 2006), 84; Donfried and Marshall, *Theology of the Shorter Pauline Epistles*, 69–70.

28. Traugott Holtz, *Der erste Brief an die Thessalonicher*, EKKNT 13 (Zürich: Benziger, 1986), 108.

29. This interpretation gives *eis* its normal sense in Paul ("toward," "with a view toward") and is arguably the meaning of the phrase in its three other NT occurrences (Matt 24:13; John 13:1; 2 Cor 3:13).

from chapters 1–2, however, is the apologetic tone. Paul is again anxious to assure the Thessalonians of his deep concern for them and that his absence from them was not his own choice but the work of Satan (2:18). The whole passage, Nicholl suggests, is "an apology for the missionaries' absence."[30] He reminds them that the persecutions they are experiencing should be no surprise, since he warned them that "we are destined for them" (3:3). And he rejoices at Timothy's news—that the Thessalonian believers are remaining steadfast in their faith, despite these troubles (3:6–10). The prayer report in 3:11–13 both brings to a close the first part of the letter and anticipates some of the themes in the next part (see below).

2 EXHORTATIONS TO HOLY LIVING (4:1–12)

The exhortations in 4:1–5:11 elaborate brief references earlier in the letter. In 1:9–10, Paul notes that the Thessalonians have been converted so that they might "serve the living and true God"—elaborated in 4:1–12—and so that they might "wait for his Son from heaven"—the theme of 4:13–5:11.[31] Probably more relevant, because it functions as the transition from the first to the second part of the letter, is the conclusion of Paul's prayer in 3:13, where he prays that the Thessalonians might be "blameless and holy" (= 4:1–12) "when our Lord Jesus comes with all his holy ones" (= 4:13–5:11).[32]

The theme of this section is clearly stated at the outset: "How to live in order to please God" (4:1). Paul focuses on two matters: sexual fidelity (vv. 3–8) and love for one another (vv. 9–12). Singling out these two matters for attention here reflects the priority of these concerns throughout Paul as he seeks to instill in converted pagans basic priorities and values of the kingdom of God. At the same time, while explicit reference to the Old Testament is lacking (indeed, there are no quotations from the OT anywhere in the letter), Paul's exhortations here in fact reflect central old-covenant values. Paul's call for "holiness" (*hagiosmos*, v. 3; NIV "be sanctified") echoes the famous refrain at the heart of the law of Moses: "You yourselves must be holy, because I am holy" (Lev 11:44a, etc.). Indeed, "holiness" language is sprinkled throughout the following passage (vv. 4, 7). Paul's elaboration of this central demand in terms of a contrast with the pagan past (see 1:9–10) and of purity and the empowering presence of the Spirit reflects a well-known prophecy in Ezekiel 36:25–27:

> I will sprinkle clean water on you, and you will be clean; I will cleanse you from all your impurities and from all your idols. I will give you a new heart and put a new spirit in you; I will remove from you your heart of stone and give you a heart

---

30. Nicholl, *From Hope to Despair*, 96.
31. Gorman, *Apostle of the Crucified Lord*, 195–96.
32. Fee, *Thessalonians*, 129.

of flesh. And I will put my Spirit in you and move you to follow my decrees and be careful to keep my laws.[33]

Central to verses 3–8 is the demand that the Thessalonians "control your own body" (v. 4). The word translated "body" (*skeuos*, "vessel") could also mean "wife," an option adopted by some translations (NAB; RSV) and commentators.[34] It is more likely, however, that Paul, like other Greek writers of his day, uses the word as a euphemism for the male sexual organ.[35] "Body," which in this context has a sexual nuance, adequately conveys the meaning. Of course, Scripture often addresses the male as representative, so his point applies equally to women. Verses 6–8 do not introduce a new issue (business relationships) but continue the focus on sex from verses 3–5. Believers should not "wrong or take advantage" of a brother or sister by engaging in illicit sex.

Paul is confident that the Thessalonians have been well taught about the importance of love for one another—indeed, reflecting his distinctive new-covenant perspective, he thinks that God himself, resident in their hearts as the Spirit, has taught them (v. 9). But he reminds them anyway, urging them to continue to express their love for brothers and sisters throughout the province of Macedonia. The exhortations in verses 11–12 to lead quiet lives, mind their own business, and work with their own hands continue the general theme of love—now, however, warning about its abuse.[36] The problem, which will come up again in Paul's letters to the Thessalonians (1 Thess 5:13; 2 Thess 3:6–10), probably is that some believers are taking advantage of others, not being diligent in their own work and expecting others to support them. Such behavior not only puts stress on the loving relationships that should characterize the Christian community but also brings the church into ill repute with outsiders (v. 12).

3 LIVING IN LIGHT OF CHRIST'S RETURN (4:13–5:11)

The bulk of the body of 1 Thessalonians is devoted to eschatology—specifically, the relationship of believers to the parousia (4:15) or day of the Lord (5:2). In 4:13–18 Paul

---

33. See Weima, "'How You Must Walk to Please God,'" 98–119, for these parallels.

34. Frame, *Thessalonians*, 149–50; Raymond F. Collins, *Studies on the First Letter to the Thessalonians*, BETL 66 (Leuven: Leuven University Press, 1984), 311–13; T. Holtz, *An die Thessalonicher*, 157; Best, *Thessalonians*, 161–63; Burke, *Family Matters*, 187–90.

35. See esp. Robert W. Yarbrough, "Sexual Gratification in 1 Thess 4,1–8," *TrinJ* 20 (1999): 215–32; Jay E. Smith, "Another Look at 4Q416 2 ii.21: A Critical Parallel to First Thessalonians 4:4," *CBQ* 63 (2001): 499–504; Fee, *Thessalonians*, 146–49; Weima, *1–2 Thessalonians*, 272.

36. Wanamaker, *Thessalonians*, 163; Boring, *I and II Thessalonians*, 153. Winter, on the other hand, thinks the issue might be that some of the Thessalonians were thinking of their relationship to others in terms of the typical patron-client pattern of that day, the "clients" using dependence on a patron as an excuse not to work (*Seek the Welfare of the City: Christians as Benefactors and Citizens*, First-Century Christians in the Graeco-Roman World [Grand Rapids: Eerdmans, 1994], 41–60; cf. also Green, *Thessalonians*, 210–11). Barclay argues that the problem may be that believers have abandoned their normal work in order to preach the gospel ("Conflict in Thessalonica," 521–22).

outlines the basic sequence of events accompanying the parousia; then, in 5:1–11 he exhorts his readers to live in light of the coming of the day of the Lord—a "day" that is, in fact, already exercising its power over believers.

The eschatological teaching of 4:13–18 is designed to meet a pastoral problem: believers in Thessalonica were grieving over the death of some of their brothers and sisters. What was causing the believers to grieve "like the rest of mankind, who have no hope" is unclear. Scholars have speculated endlessly. Some think, for instance, that the Thessalonians thought their dead brothers and sisters would not experience the bliss of the afterlife because they would not be alive to greet Christ at his return.[37] But this assumes that Paul would not have taught the Thessalonians about the resurrection—an omission hard to believe, even if persecution forced Paul to leave suddenly.[38] We should probably take our clue from the stress that the text puts on chronology: living believers "will certainly *not precede*" those who have died (v. 15); "the dead in Christ will rise *first*"; only after that will living believers join them (vv. 16b–17). For some reason—which we cannot now identify—the Thessalonians thought that those who had died, though eventually to be raised, might miss out on the joyful reunion with the Lord at the time of his return.[39]

Paul describes the believers who had died as those who had "fallen asleep" (NIV "sleep in death"; vv. 13, 14). While it is tempting to think that this word choice might imply a distinctly Christian view of death—believers sleep because they will be awakened one day in resurrection—it was in fact fairly widely used in Paul's day as a euphemism for dying. Paul reminds his readers of basic gospel teaching, that Christ "died and rose again," and then builds on this reality the solid hope that "God will bring with Jesus those who have fallen asleep in him" (v. 14).[40] As he does elsewhere (see esp. 1 Cor 15:20–28), Paul views the resurrection of believers as, in a sense, included in the resurrection of Christ himself. In his effort to bring solid comfort to the Thessalonians, Paul grounds his teaching on a "word of the Lord" (v. 15). Paul may refer to a prophecy uttered in the Lord's name,[41] but it is perhaps more likely that he refers to teaching of

---

37. See, e.g., Nicholl, *From Hope to Despair*, 35–38; Vos, *Pauline Eschatology*, 247–51.

38. Though this view is defended by, e.g., Vos, *Pauline Eschatology*, 247–51; Nicholl, *From Hope to Despair*, 19–48.

39. So, essentially, Best, *Thessalonians*, 180–84; Wanamaker, *Thessalonians*, 165–66; Marshall, *1 & 2 Thessalonians*, 120–22; Malherbe, *Thessalonians*, 283–85; Shogren, *1 & 2 Thessalonians*, 34.

40. The placement of the phrase "in him" (*dia tou Iēsou*) is debated. The NIV takes it with the verb "fall asleep" and gives the preposition *dia* (usually "through" when governing a genitive) an unusual sense ("attendant circumstances"; see Green, *Thessalonians*, 221; Murray J. Harris, *Raised Immortal: Resurrection and Immortality in the New Testament* [Grand Rapids: Eerdmans,

1985], 113, for this option). Most who construe the phrase with "fall asleep" retain the usual instrumental sense, sometimes giving the aorist form used here an inceptive sense: "Those who fall asleep through Jesus," i.e., those who die as believers (see Wanamaker, *Thessalonians*, 169). Despite the awkwardness of taking both prepositional phrases with the same verb, others think *dia tou Iēsou* modifies "will bring" (*axei*): "Through Jesus, God will bring with him those who have fallen asleep" (ESV; see Fee, *Thessalonians*, 170–72; Best, *Thessalonians*, 189).

41. E.g., David Luckensmeyer, *The Eschatology of First Thessalonians*, NTOA/SUNT 71 (Göttingen: Vandenhoeck & Ruprecht, 2009), 186–90; Boring, *I and II Thessalonians*, 164; Dunn, *Theology of Paul*, 303–4.

the historical Jesus. Since the words in this context do not match anything we find in the Gospels, the teaching may be an unrecorded "word" of Jesus.[42] But it is possible that the "word" or "message" (*logos*) is not a single quotation but a summary of Jesus's teaching, now found in the Gospels, on these issues.[43] Supporting this last idea are the many resonances between Paul's teaching here in 4:13–5:11 with eschatological teaching in our Gospels.[44]

The heart of Paul's teaching here, as we noted above, is the sequence of events: When the Lord returns, dead believers will be resurrected, and only living believers will be "caught up together . . . to meet the Lord in the air" (vv. 16–17). Paul refers to Jesus's return with the Greek word *parousia*, which means "presence" or "coming," and which becomes a technical theological term for Christ's return in glory and events accompanying that return.[45] The resurrection of believers is, of course, standard teaching in Paul and is the ultimate hope of God's people. Much more unusual is reference to those believers who will be alive when the Lord returns. Our theological term "rapture" comes from the Latin verb *rapio*, used here to translate *harpazō*, "caught up." This "catching up," in a context that refers to clouds and joining the Lord "in the air," naturally could suggest physical movement. However, the main point about the rapture, made especially clear in 1 Corinthians 15:51, is that through it believers who are alive will have their bodies transformed so that they are suited for life in the new creation. There has, of course, been much speculation about the timing of these events, especially in terms of the relationship between an alleged great tribulation at the close of this age and the rapture of the saints. Paul is clearly not addressing that kind of detail here, although he does obviously link believers' rapture and resurrection with the parousia, viewing them as a single event.[46]

The word used by Paul to describe the "meeting" between the living saints and their Lord in the air (*apantēsis*, v. 17) occurs in references to the visit of dignitaries and generally implies that the "delegation" accompanies the dignitary *back to* the delegation's point of origin.[47] The two other occurrences of this term in the New

---

42. Frame, *Thessalonians*, 171–72; Nicholl, *From Hope to Despair*, 38–41.

43. Shogren, *1 & 2 Thessalonians*, 32; Weima, *1–2 Thessalonians*, 321.

44. For these parallels, see especially J. B. Orchard, "Thessalonians and the Synoptic Gospels," *Bib* 19 (1938): 19–42; Lars Hartman, *Prophecy Interpreted: The Formation of Some Jewish Apocalyptic Texts and of the Eschatological Discourse Mark 13 Par.*, ConBNT 1 (Lund: Gleerup, 1966), 188–89; David Wenham, "Paul and the Synoptic Apocalypse," in *Studies of History and Tradition in the Four Gospels*, ed. R. T. France and David Wenham, Gospel Perspectives 2 (Sheffield: JSOT, 1981), 4–5; idem, *Paul: Follower of Jesus or Founder of Christianity?* (Grand Rapids: Eerdmans, 1995), 305–16.

45. The word occurs 18x in the NT in this sense, eight of them in Paul, and seven of those, in turn, in 1 and 2 Thessalonians. See the discussion on pp. 537–39.

46. For this issue, and my own view on it, see Craig A. Blaising, Alan Hultberg, and Douglas J. Moo, *Three Views on the Rapture: Pretribulation, Prewrath, or Posttribulation*, ed. Alan Hultberg, Counterpoints (Grand Rapids: Zondervan, 2010), esp. 185–241.

47. See esp. Green, *Thessalonians*, 226–28; N. T. Wright, *The Resurrection of the Son of God*, Christian Origins and the Question of God 3 (Minneapolis: Fortress, 2003), 217–18; Nicholl, *From Hope to Despair*, 43–45.

Testament seem to bear this meaning (Matt 25:6; Acts 28:15). This would suggest that the saints, after meeting the Lord in the air, accompany him back to earth, instead of going with him to heaven.[48]

Paul apparently includes himself in their number: "We who are still alive" (v. 15). This way of speaking has fueled the widespread theory that Paul in his early ministry believed the parousia would definitely occur in his lifetime, only to abandon this hope later on. However, it is easy to make too much of this casual "we who are still alive." As Thiselton suggests, Paul is here using "participant logic," according to which he speaks "in solidarity with the readers," hoping thereby that they will "take the possibility at issue seriously."[49] He probably hopes that he will live to see Jesus's parousia; but this verse cannot be used to claim he knew he would. Paul clearly teaches "imminency"—Christ could come at any time—but it is not clear that he holds to "immediacy"—Christ *will* come within *x* number of years. Paul's pastoral concern in this passage emerges again at its end: "Therefore encourage one another with these words" (v. 18).

"Whereas 4:13–18 deals with eschatology and those who are asleep, 5:1–11 focuses on the impact of eschatological hope on those who are awake—or who ought to be."[50] Paul also shifts his language: whereas he spoke about the rapture and parousia in chapter 4, Paul discusses in chapter 5 the "day of the Lord." In the Old Testament, the day of the Lord (also "that day," etc.) denotes the time when God would decisively intervene in history to judge his enemies and deliver his people.[51] It can refer to a relatively *near* event or to the *final* climactic event; it is not always clear that the prophets distinguished the two. Although the day is usually described as one *of judgment*, deliverance for the people of God is often involved as well (cf. Isa 27; Jer 30:8–9; Joel 2:32; 3:18; Obad 15–17; etc.). In the New Testament, the term is almost universally related to the end. In a move typical of his high Christology, however, the "Lord" of the day is now Jesus Christ (see, e.g., 1 Cor 1:8; 2 Cor 1:14; Phil 1:6). Clearly, the parousia of Christ is closely related to the "day of the Lord" (see also 2 Thess 2:1–2), but perhaps we can view the latter as slightly broader than the former[52] and also more clearly connoting the judgment aspect.[53]

There is also a rhetorical shift as we move from one chapter to the other. In 4:13–18, Paul has comforted believers about the position of the *dead* at the parousia; in 5:1–11,

---

48. Some doubt if the idea of accompanying the dignitary back to the point of departure would be carried over here (Wanamaker, *Thessalonians*, 175; Malherbe, *Thessalonians*, 275).

49. Anthony C. Thiselton, *The First Epistle to the Corinthians*, NIGTC (Eerdmans: Grand Rapids, 2000), 581; cf. also idem, *Life after Death: A New Approach to the Last Things* (Grand Rapids: Eerdmans, 2012), 95–99. Arthur L. Moore (*The Parousia in the New Testament*, NovTSup 13 [Leiden: Brill, 1966], 109–10) thinks the "we" refers to Christians in general.

50. Gorman, *Apostle of the Crucified Lord*, 204.

51. Cf. H. H. Rowley, *The Faith of Israel: Aspects of Old Testament Thought* (London: SCM, 1956), 178–200.

52. E.g., Boring, *I and II Thessalonians*, 266; Best, *Thessalonians*, 272. On the other hand, others see the two terms as essentially interchangeable (Nicholl, *From Hope to Despair*, 51, 115–43).

53. Weima, *1–2 Thessalonians*, 346.

he exhorts the *living* about their responsibilities in light of that parousia. At the same time, as 5:9–10 make especially clear, Paul is reassuring the believers in Thessalonica that, despite their present sufferings, they will not be subject to the wrath to be poured out on the day of the Lord: they are destined for salvation.[54]

As in the Old Testament, the day of the Lord brings ultimate judgment on unbelievers: "Destruction will come on them suddenly" (v. 3); it will bring wrath (v. 9). That day will come suddenly, even as they comfort themselves by saying it is a time of "peace and safety" (v. 3). This language may reflect Old Testament texts that similarly refer to people who think they live in a time of peace even as the disastrous invasion of foreign troops is imminent (e.g., Jer 6:14). But the phrase may more relevantly echo Roman imperial propaganda that boasted of the famous *pax Romana*.[55]

Paul's focus, however, is on how believers should respond. Reflecting his typical inaugurated eschatological perspective, Paul makes clear that, while the day itself is future, believers already enjoy initial benefits of that day: they are "children of the light" (v. 5). Paul therefore morphs from "day" in a technical sense to "day" in a prosaic sense (he makes a similar move in Rom 13:11–14).[56] The nighttime is when evil acts are committed; but believers, who live in the light of the "day," need to live pure and moral lives. They are not to sleep, ignoring the realities of the time in which they live, but to be "awake and sober" (v. 6). "Wakefulness," then, does not here refer to a posture of watching for the Lord's return but to an alert posture that guards Christian values.[57] Believers will experience salvation, not wrath, when Christ returns, so that when he appears, "we may live together with him" (v. 10). Paul's pastoral focus emerges again at the end of this paragraph, echoing 4:18: "Therefore encourage one another and build each other up, just as in fact you are doing" (v. 11).

Before leaving this paragraph, we should note the close relationship between this text and two Gospel passages that encourage watchfulness in view of the parousia—Matthew 24:42–44 and Luke 21:34–36. The parallels between the latter text and 1 Thessalonians 5:2–6 are particularly compelling—both have as their subject the day, which, it is warned, will come suddenly and unexpectedly upon those unprepared ("like a trap," Luke 21:34); both warn that the day will bring widespread devastation (cf. Luke 21:35); both encourage believers to watch in light of that coming "day"; and both use the same verb (*ephistēmi*, "come upon") and the same adjective (*aiphnidios*, "suddenly") about the day (the latter word occurs only in these two passages in canonical Greek).[58]

---

54. Nicholl, *From Hope to Despair*, 63–77, stresses this point.

55. See esp. Jeffrey A. D. Weima, "'Peace and Security' (1 Thess 5.3): Prophetic Warning or Political Propaganda?," *NTS* 58 (2012): 33–59; disputed by Joel White, "Anti-Imperial Subtexts in Paul: An Attempt at Building a Firmer Foundation," *Bib* 90 (2009): 313–14.

56. Boring, *I and II Thessalonians*, 182. Evald Lövestam

(*Spiritual Wakefulness in the New Testament*, LUÅ 55.3 [Lund: Gleerup, 1963], 49) claims "day" means "the sphere of light and salvation in which the Christian lives."

57. On this meaning of the terms *grēgoreō* ("watch") and *nēphō* ("be sober"), see especially Lövestam, *Spiritual Wakefulness*.

58. For these parallels, see esp. David Wenham, *The Rediscovery of Jesus' Eschatological Discourse*, Gospel Perspectives 4

4 FINAL EXHORTATIONS AND
LETTER CLOSING (5:12–28)

The letter concludes with a series of brief exhortations covering many aspects of the believer's individual piety and, especially, the community's relationships.[59] In this early letter, it is worth noting that Paul specifically mentions some "who work hard among you, who care for you in the Lord and who admonish you" (vv. 12–13). The verb translated "care for you" might also have the nuance of leadership (NET, "preside over you"). This text suggests that even a very new church had some kind of leadership structure in place. In a probable allusion back to 4:11–12, Paul rebukes those among them who are "idle and disruptive" (5:14). This appears at first sight to be a double translation in the NIV, since a single word, *ataktous*, lies behind it. However, the NIV reflects here a certain view of this word, according to which, while it *means* "disruptive" or "disorderly" people,[60] in this context (since it is elsewhere elaborated in terms of "not working"), it *refers* to a disorderliness that takes the form of idleness.[61] Paul moves on to rather clear and self-explanatory encouragements and exhortations (vv. 15–24) before issuing some final remarks (vv. 25–28).

(Sheffield: JSOT Press, 1984; repr., Eugene, OR: Wipf & Stock, 2003), 54–55, 110–14; idem, *Paul*, 307–11; Hartman, *Prophecy Interpreted*, 192; Yongbom Lee, *Paul, Scribe of Old and New: Intertextual Insights for the Jesus-Paul Debate*, LNTS 512 (London: Bloomsbury, 2015), 139–51.

59. This passage has many parallels with Rom 12:9–18; see the chart in Boring, *I and II Thessalonians*, 186.

60. E.g., Boring, *I and II Thessalonians*, 189; Fee, *Thessalonians*, 209–10.

61. Weima, *1–2 Thessalonians*, 391–93.

Chapter 6

2 THESSALONIANS

P AUL'S THEOLOGY comes to expression in letters designed to challenge, encourage, and edify believers in the specific circumstances they face. Second Thessalonians, like 1 Thessalonians, is rightly known for its eschatology. But that eschatology is directed toward believers who are suffering persecution. Paul's purpose, then, is to deploy his teaching about the hope Christians have to encourage his readers. The just God "will pay back trouble to those who trouble you and give relief to you who are troubled" (1:6–7a); "the Lord Jesus will overthrow [the lawless one] with the breath of his mouth and destroy [him] by the splendor of his coming" (2:8b).

LOCATING THE LETTER

On the assumption that Paul is the author of 2 Thessalonians (see below), we can locate this letter at a time very shortly after 1 Thessalonians.[1] It will also have been written from Corinth during the second missionary journey, in AD 50 or 51.

ISOLATING THE ISSUES

Many scholars argue that 2 Thessalonians is one of six pseudepigraphical letters attributed to the apostle Paul. As is usually the case in these discussions of authorship, several arguments are put forward to justify this conclusion. It is argued, for instance, that the many parallels between 1 and 2 Thessalonians suggest that a later writer has borrowed extensively from the first (authentic) letter. But scholars generally agree that the key issue is an alleged contradiction in eschatological teaching. There is, on the one hand, a more "apocalyptic" atmosphere.[2] At the same time, 2 Thessalonians, it is argued, leaves behind the strong sense of imminence in 1 Thessalonians (e.g., "we who are still alive" [1 Thess 4:15]) in favor of a postponement of an end preceded

---

1. A few interpreters reverse the order of the letters (e.g., Wanamaker, *Thessalonians*, 37–45), but the usual order makes better sense of the letters and is defended by the vast majority of Thessalonians scholars (see esp. the reconstruction of Nicholl, *From Hope To Despair*).

2. "Paul speaks with the voice of an apocalyptic visionary" (Beker, *Paul the Apostle*, 305).

by a series of signs. As Beker puts it, 2 Thessalonians "inserts a specific apocalyptic program between the present and the Parousia."[3] We have already suggested that the imminence, which, appropriately defined, is surely present in 1 Thessalonians, has often been illegitimately stretched to what we have called "immediacy." In addition,

> Many Jewish apocalypses contain the same mixture of imminence and warning signs. More to the point, we find this same mixture in the eschatology of the gospels. Compare, for instance, Matthew 24:33—"When you see all these things, you know that it is near, right at the door"—with Matthew 24:44b—"The Son of Man will come at an hour when you do not expect him." Paul's focus on imminence in 1 Thessalonians and on preliminary events in 2 Thessalonians arises because of the different pastoral situations he is addressing. There is no good reason to deny that he could have held the two views at the same time as part of his overall eschatology. The different problems being addressed in the two letters require Paul to stress different sides of his stable eschatological teaching.[4]

What was the occasion that sparked the particular eschatological teaching found in the letter? Chapter 2:1–2 provides the answer:

> Concerning the coming of our Lord Jesus Christ and our being gathered to him, we ask you, brothers and sisters, not to become easily unsettled or alarmed by the teaching allegedly from us—whether by a prophecy or by word of mouth or by letter—asserting that the day of the Lord has already come.

While there are uncertainties in this text, the following scenario seems relatively clear. The Thessalonian Christians are "unsettled" and "alarmed" because they think that the day of the Lord had come. They have been led to this conclusion by some kind of communication that they attribute to Paul himself. (Detailed discussion of this text is found below.) Paul therefore writes to disabuse the Thessalonians of this notion. Two other subsidiary issues can be detected from the content of the letter. First, the Thessalonians are continuing to suffer persecution, and Paul writes to comfort them and exhort them to remain faithful to Christ amid their suffering (1:4–10; 2:15–17; 3:3–5). Second, the

---

3. Beker, *Paul the Apostle*, 161. The contemporary scholarly doubts about Pauline authorship rest especially on the work of Wolfgang Trilling, *Untersuchungen zum zweiten Thessalonicherbrief*, ETS 27 (Leipzig: St.-Benno, 1972). For a more recent argument, see Christina M. Kreinecker, *2 Thessaloniker*, Papyrologische Kommentare zum Neuen Testament 3 (Göttingen: Vandenhoeck & Ruprecht, 2010), 38–99.

4. Carson and Moo, *Introduction to the New Testament*, 536–42; see also Luke Timothy Johnson, *The Writings of the New Testament: An Interpretation*, 3rd ed. (Minneapolis: Fortress, 2010), 287–88; Malherbe, *Thessalonians*, 368–69. For other arguments for authenticity, see esp. Beda Rigaux, *Saint Paul: Les Epitres aux Thessaloniciens*, EB (Paris: Gabalda, 1956), 124–52. See also Stuhlmacher, *Biblical Theology of the New Testament*, 492, who rightly notes that Paul in 2 Thessalonians clarifies (not annuls) the imminent expectation of 1 Thessalonians.

problem of unruliness/idleness, mentioned in the first letter (4:11; 5:14), has apparently worsened; Paul rebukes those within the community acting in this way (3:6–13).

Analyzing the Argument

Second Thessalonians resembles 1 Thessalonians in both opening (after the usual epistolary opening, 1:1–2) with a thanksgiving statement (1:3) and then returning to thanksgiving later in the letter (2:13). It is even clearer in the case of 2 Thessalonians, however, that the formal thanksgiving section should be confined to 1:3–12. Paul then deals with the central issue in the letter, explaining to the Thessalonians why they are wrong in thinking that the day of the Lord had begun (2:1–12). Paul ends this passage with a renewed condemnation of those who refuse to love the truth. Paul contrasts these people with the Thessalonians, as he celebrates their salvation, exhorts and encourages them, and requests prayer for his own struggle with "wicked and evil people" (2:13–3:5). Paul concludes with a rebuke of unruly and idle people within the community (3:6–13), a warning about disobedience (3:14–15), and an epistolary conclusion (3:16–18).

Second Thessalonians, of course, makes its most important theological contribution in the area of eschatology. The Thessalonians' suffering leads Paul to encourage them by reminding them that the day of judgment, when Christ returns in glory to punish the wicked and reward the righteous, is coming (1:5–10; 2:10–12, 13–14). The passage in chapter 1 is the strongest assertion of judgment on the wicked that we find in Paul. At the same time, the Thessalonians' alarm over their belief that the day of the Lord had arrived requires Paul to go into some detail about the events of the end. In order to dissuade the Thessalonians of this notion, Paul mentions events that must take place before that day arrives. These events are sometimes thought to have occurred at the time of the Roman suppression of the Jewish rebellion in AD 67–73 (a so-called "preterist" view). However, it is far more likely that Paul refers to events that will immediately precede the parousia. The obscurity of many of the specifics of this passage means that attempts to outline a specific scenario of "end-time" events are doomed to failure. But the text does suggest that a time of unprecedented satanic oppression will immediately precede the return of Christ to destroy "the lawless one" and deliver God's people.

As always, this theology has a pastoral purpose, not only to assuage the anxiety of the Thessalonians about the day of the Lord but positively to reassure them of God's settled purpose for them. This note is sounded clearly in 2:13–17, a passage that as clearly as any summarizes the letter—indeed, it is not a bad candidate to choose as a summary of Paul's theology.[5]

---

5. David Peterson, *Possessed by God: A New Testament Theology of Sanctification and Holiness*, NSBT 1 (Downers Grove, IL: InterVarsity Press, 1995), 60–61.

But we ought always to thank God for you, brothers and sisters loved by the Lord, because God chose you as firstfruits to be saved through the sanctifying work of the Spirit and through belief in the truth. He called you to this through our gospel, that you might share in the glory of our Lord Jesus Christ.

So then, brothers and sisters, stand firm and hold fast to the teachings we passed on to you, whether by word of mouth or by letter.

May our Lord Jesus Christ himself and God our Father, who loved us and by his grace gave us eternal encouragement and good hope, encourage your hearts and strengthen you in every good deed and word.

This passage sets the Thessalonians' current status—"loved by the Lord"—within the typical "already-not yet" eschatological tension: "God chose you" and "called you," on the one hand, and "to be saved" and to "share in the glory of our Lord Jesus Christ," on the other. The means of God's calling is the gospel Paul preached, while they maintain their status by both divine means—"the sanctifying work of the Spirit"[6]— and human means—"belief in the truth." In addition to the work of the Spirit, the Lord Jesus Christ and God the Father, in a Trinitarian work of grace, are also active in preserving and encouraging the believers. Yet the believers are not only to wait passively for their ultimate deliverance but are also actively to live out their faith "in every good deed and word."

1 GOD'S RETRIBUTIVE JUDGMENT (1:1–12)

As in 1 Thessalonians, Paul includes Silas and Timothy as cosenders of the letter (v. 1; see the note on 1 Thess 1:1). He then moves to a typical thanksgiving section (v. 3), noting the Thessalonians' "faith" and "love." His attention then turns to the severe trial the Thessalonians are facing. Their perseverance amid these persecutions is, Paul claims, "evidence that God's judgment is right" [*dikaios*] (v. 5).[7] This clause effects a transition from Paul's commendation to consolation, as Paul elaborates on the "rightness" or "justness" of God's judgment (vv. 5b–10). Paul picks up imagery and language from the Old Testament to draw a picture of a cataclysmic time of final reckoning.[8] That judgment will take place when "the Lord Jesus is revealed from heaven in blazing fire with his powerful angels" (v. 7b), "on the day he [the Lord] comes to be glorified" (v. 10). The justice of God's judgment is seen in the way two sets of people

---

6. Peterson, *Possessed by God*, 60–61, however, takes the Spirit's sanctifying work to refer to conversion.

7. I take "evidence" (*endeigma*) as the predicate of an implied clause—as in NIV, "all this is evidence." It is harder to know what the "all this" refers back to. I am taking it as referring to

the Thessalonians' endurance or *hypomonē* (Frame, *Thessalonians*, 226; Best, *Thessalonians*, 254–55 [with Paul's boasting]), but it could also refer to the persecutions themselves (Wanamaker, *Thessalonians*, 220–21; Nicholl, *From Hope to Despair*, 149–50).

8. See esp. Rigaux, *Thessaloniciens*, 623–24, for these allusions.

will be treated. Believers, such as the Thessalonians, will experience "relief" (v. 7); as God's chosen people, they will be "counted worthy of the kingdom of God" (v. 5). But the focus of the passage is on the fate of the wicked—those who "do not know God and do not obey the gospel of our Lord Jesus" (v. 8), represented by the Thessalonians' persecutors.[9] In a clear display of God's justice (*dikaios* again), he will mete out "trouble" (*thlipsis*) to those who are "troubling" (*thlibō*) the Thessalonians (v. 6). Specifically, "they will be punished with everlasting destruction and shut out from the presence of the Lord and from the glory of his might" (v. 9). This language raises questions about just how Paul thinks of the ultimate fate of unbelievers. Some think the punishment Paul refers to consists mainly, or even entirely, in the exclusion of unbelievers from the presence of Christ.[10] However, it is not clear that this focus on negation can do justice to the word "punishment." Other interpreters have focused on the word "destruction" (*olethros*), arguing that the fate of the unbeliever is annihilation—either immediately at the judgment or after a period of punishment. However, the word Paul uses here does not need to have the sense of annihilation,[11] and "eternal" (*aiōnios*) suggests continuing existence.[12] Probably, then, Paul falls into step with Jesus (e.g., Matt 25:46) in portraying the fate of the wicked in terms of eternal punishment (see, further, pp. 548–51).

Paul ends his thanksgiving, as he often does, with a prayer for his readers (vv. 11–12), in this case asking God to help them remain faithful and to continue to be active in good works. We can well imagine that the persecution the believers are suffering might lead some in the church to respond in kind, abandoning the gospel imperative to "do good to all people" (Gal 6:10).

2 THE DAY OF THE LORD (2:1–12)

Paul's focus turns from the outcome of Jesus's "coming" (see 1:10) to the timing of that coming (Gk. *parousia* in v. 1). Paul takes up this issue in order to correct the Thessalonians' belief that the day of the Lord had come (v. 2).[13] The move from

---

9. The Greek syntax, which repeats the article in the clause describing the second clause, could suggest that Paul has two groups in view—presumably gentiles and Jews (e.g., Marshall, *1 & 2 Thessalonians*, 177–78). But the syntax does not require this, and there is nothing in 2 Thessalonians that would support a reference to two groups (see, e.g., Weima, *1–2 Thessalonians*, 472–73). Advocates of annihilationism argue that "eternal" refers to the unending effects of the destruction (e.g., Edward Fudge, *The Fire That Consumes: A Biblical and Historical Study of Final Judgment* [Houston: Providential, 1982], 37–50).

10. Fee's treatment (*Thessalonians*, 259–60) moves in this direction. Paul probably alludes to Isa 2:10: "Go into the rocks, hide in the ground from the fearful presence of the LORD and the splendor of his majesty!"

11. The word Paul uses, *olethros*, occurs elsewhere in the NT in 1 Cor 5:5; 1 Thess 5:3; and 1 Tim 6:9. "Annihilation" is a possible meaning in each text but is not required in any of them. Best claims that *olethros* never has the meaning "annihilation" in the LXX (*Thessalonians*, 261–62, though he admits Wis 1:14 might be an exception).

12. Weima, *1–2 Thessalonians*, 474.

13. Contemporary scholars are virtually unanimous in thinking that the verb *enestēken* (a perfect form of *enistēmi*) means "has come" rather than, e.g., "is impending" (e.g., KJV, NAB, "is at hand"; see Leon Morris, *The First and Second Epistles to the Thessalonians*, rev. ed., NICNT [Grand Rapids: Eerdmans, 1991], 216–17; Green, *Thessalonians*, 305; Shogren, *1 & 2 Thessalonians*, 276–77, for this view).

parousia in verse 1 to "the day of the Lord" in verse 2 makes clear that they both refer to the same event (cf. also 1 Thess 4:15; 5:2). The Thessalonians have been led to this belief on the basis of a "teaching allegedly from us—whether by a prophecy or by word of mouth or by letter."[14] Paul is obviously uncertain about the specific source of this misapprehension. But he does know that it has "unsettled" and "alarmed" them. It is not clear whether these words connote an excited, agitated state or a state of alarm and fear.[15] But the latter word, *throeō*, is used elsewhere in the NT only in the Olivet Discourse, where Jesus urges the disciples not to be "alarmed" about "wars and rumors of wars," because "such things must happen, but the end is still to come" (Matt 24:6//Mark 13:7). Paul's point in 2 Thessalonians 2 is roughly similar: he urges the Thessalonians not to become alarmed about "the coming of our Lord Jesus and our being gathered to him" (v. 1). Besides the alleged communication from Paul, it is uncertain what might have led the Thessalonians to think this. But the severity of their persecution might have convinced them they were living in the last great outbreak of tribulation in the last days.[16]

Among the many difficulties presented by the following verse 3 is a very basic one: Paul moves into a protasis—"if" clause—without ever using an apodosis—a "then" clause. However, English versions are united in assuming that Paul must have meant that apodosis to be something like "that day will not come." The "if" clause then states the condition that must be met before the "then" clause can become true: the day of the Lord cannot come until the "rebellion occurs and the man of lawlessness is revealed" (v. 3b). "Rebellion" (*apostasia*) translates a word that can refer to either a political revolt or to a religious "apostasy," but the latter is probably the referent here, granted biblical use of the word and the context.[17] The "man of lawlessness" is probably to be identified as the eschatological antichrist, a figure also described in Revelation 13:1–8 and based on the depiction of the usurper of God in the book of Daniel (Dan 7:8,

14. The NIV assumes, probably correctly, that "allegedly from us" (*hōs di hēmōn*) modifies all three forms of communication (Weima, *1–2 Thessalonians*, 505). Malherbe (*Thessalonians*, 417) thinks that the reference might be to Paul's claim that believers were "of the day" (1 Thess 5:5, 8). See also Trilling, *Thessalonicherbrief*, 76–77; Bruce, *Thessalonians*, 164; Ulrich Wilckens, *Die Briefe des Urchristentums: Paulus und seine Schüler, Theologen aus dem Bereich judenchristlicher Heidenmission*, vol. 3 of *Geschichte der urchristlichen Theologie*, part 1 of *Theologie des Neuen Testaments*, 3rd ed. (Neukirchen-Vluyn: Neukirchener, 2014), 65–66.

15. The verb translated "unsettled" is from *saleuō* and means "shake." It is usually applied in the NT to physical phenomena, but note Acts 17:13, where Luke says that the Jews in Thessalonica were "agitating" the crowds against Paul. The second verb, "alarmed," translates a form of *throeō*, which means "to be aroused" or "frightened" (BDAG). Many interpreters think that the verbs together connote "a continuous state of nervous

excitement and anxiety" (Best, *Thessalonians*, 275), while others think they suggest fear (Nicholl, *From Hope to Despair*, 126–32).

16. This passage has been a battleground in (now much muted) debates over the timing of the rapture in relationship to an alleged last great tribulation period. For my own view on these issues with respect to this text, see Blaising, Hultberg, and Moo, *Three Views on the Rapture*, 185–241.

17. For the use of the word in biblical Greek, see, e.g., Josh 22:22; 2 Chr 29:19; Jer 2:19; Acts 21:21. A religious rebellion was frequently associated with the time of the end (as in Mark 13:6ff). Most modern commentators take this view; see, e.g., Malherbe, *Thessalonians*, 418; G. K. Beale, *1–2 Thessalonians*, IVPNTC 13 (Downers Grove, IL: InterVarsity Press, 2003), 203; and also, e.g., Robert H. Gundry, *Church and Tribulation: A Biblical Examination of Posttribulationism* (Grand Rapids: Zondervan, 1999), 115–16; Desmond Ford, *The Abomination of Desolation in Biblical Eschatology* (Washington, DC: University Press of America, 1979), 201–3.

20–25; 11:36–39).[18] Paul claims that this antichrist will "oppose and will exalt himself over everything that is called God or is worshiped, so that he sets himself up in God's temple, proclaiming himself to be God" (v. 4). This language is reminiscent of Daniel's prediction of an ungodly king who will "exalt and magnify himself above every god" (Dan 11:36). This same king, Daniel also says, will "with flattery" "corrupt those who have violated the covenant" (11:32), and this sounds a lot like the "rebellion" to which Paul alludes. Paul's prediction here, then, appears to reflect a reading of Daniel that sees in his language a reference to an end-time anti-god leader. Paul's claim that this last and greatest antichrist will take his seat in the temple may suggest that this antichrist will work from within the church, since the New Testament suggests that the presence of God that was formerly found in the temple is now found in the new-covenant community, the body of Christ.[19] But it is also possible that Paul envisages the antichrist revealing himself in a literal Jerusalem temple.[20]

Paul's reminder that he had already taught these things to the Thessalonians when he was with them (v. 5) signals a transition from Paul's basic point—the day of the Lord cannot be here because the great religious rebellion, perhaps led by the antichrist, has not yet occurred—to an elaboration of the timing and results of these events. There is a "proper time" for the events of these last days, a time God has determined (v. 6b). In the meantime, someone or something is now "holding him back," "the one who now holds it back" (vv. 6a, 7b). The identity of this "restrainer" (as the verb is often translated) is notoriously obscure. The verb that Paul uses (*katechō*) can be translated "hold back" or "hold fast," or "occupy,"[21] and has been understood as signifying, among other things, the Holy Spirit, Rome/the emperor,[22] civil government,[23] God and his power,[24] Michael the archangel,[25] the preaching of the gospel/Paul,[26] Satan,[27] general

18. Ford, *Abomination of Desolation*, 199–200, 207, provides a good discussion of the parallels between Daniel and the portrayal of the antichrist in the NT.

19. See esp. Beale, *1–2 Thessalonians*, 207–10; idem, *The Temple and the Church's Mission: A Biblical Theology of the Dwelling Place of God*, NSBT 17 (Downers Grove, IL: InterVarsity Press, 2004), 269–92.

20. Most interpreters think the reference is to the Jerusalem temple, perhaps used as a metaphor for usurping God's position (see esp. Weima, *1–2 Thessalonians*, 518–23; and also, e.g., Bruce, *Thessalonians*, 168–69; Wanamaker, *Thessalonians*, 247; Rigaux, *Thessaloniciens*, 660–61). It is unlikely that Paul refers to the heavenly temple (contra, e.g., Frame, *Thessalonians*, 256–57).

21. Frame, *Thessalonians*, 259–61; Best, *Thessalonians*, 301; D. W. B. Robinson, "II Thess. 2:6: 'That Which Restrains' or 'That Which Holds Sway'?," in *Studia Evangelica II*, ed. Frank L. Cross, TU 87 (Berlin: Akademie, 1964), 635–38.

22. Tertullian, *Apol.* 32, and many other church fathers; Otto Betz, "Der Katechon," *NTS* 9 (1963): 283–85; Bruce, *Thessalonians*, 171–72.

23. George Milligan, *St. Paul's Epistles to the Thessalonians*

(London: Macmillan, 1908), 101; William Hendriksen, *Exposition of I and II Thessalonians*, NT Commentary (Grand Rapids: Baker, 1955), 181–82.

24. George Eldon Ladd, *The Blessed Hope* (Grand Rapids: Eerdmans, 1956), 95; Ridderbos, *Paul*, 524–25.

25. See esp. Nicholl, *From Hope to Despair*, 225–49; and Weima, *1–2 Thessalonians*, 532, 567–77; Gupta, *1 and 2 Thessalonians*, 250–57; see also Beale, *1–2 Thessalonians*, 214–17; Witherington, *Thessalonians*, 208–11; Orchard, "Thessalonians," 40–41; Ferdinand Prat, *The Theology of Saint Paul*, 2 vols. (Westminster, MD: Newman, 1952), 1:80–83.

26. In the early church, Theodoret and Theodore of Mopsuestia; Cullmann, *Christ and Time*, 164–66; Johannes Munck, *Paul and the Salvation of Mankind* (Richmond, VA: John Knox, 1959), 36–43; Moore, *Parousia in the New Testament*, 112–13; Beker, *Paul the Apostle*, 161.

27. The view of J. Coppens, according to Charles Homer Giblin, *The Threat to Faith: An Exegetical and Theological Reexamination of 2 Thessalonians 2*, AnBib 31 (Rome: Pontifical Biblical Institute, 1967), 14.

evil forces,[28] or a mythic symbol with no particular content. Clearly we cannot identify this figure, although the obvious reliance on Daniel in this passage might favor Michael (see Dan 10:13, 21; 12:1; cf. Rev 12:7).[29]

Paul concludes his brief and somewhat obscure outline of eschatological events by comparing and contrasting two "comings" (*parousia*). The first is the coming of the antichrist, who embodies the power and strategy of Satan, that great "deceiver," to lead people astray and consign them to condemnation (vv. 9–12). The second "coming" is that of the Lord Jesus, who wins the ultimate victory over the antichrist (v. 8).

3 GOD'S FAITHFULNESS TO HIS CHOSEN ONES (2:13–3:5)

In contrast to the people whom the antichrist deceives and leads to condemnation (2:10–12) are Paul's "brother and sisters" in Thessalonica, for whom he again gives thanks (v. 13). We briefly summarized the theology of this rich and strategic passage in the section *Analyzing the Argument*. We might add here that Paul contrasts the false information the Thessalonians wrongly assume came from Paul (v. 2) with the authentic "traditions" (*paradoseis*) that Paul taught them (v. 15). Following the former leads to wrong ideas and ultimately wrong behavior; following the latter brings confirmation of their identity as God's people.

In 3:1–5, Paul begins by requesting prayer for himself (and Silas and Timothy) so that they might be "delivered from wicked and evil people" (vv. 1–2). The Lord, Paul is sure, will be "faithful" (v. 3a)—both to him and his associates and to the Thessalonians as they continue to struggle with persecution, itself a manifestation of the attacks of "the evil one" (vv. 3b–5; see 2:9–12).

4 REBUKE OF DISRUPTIVE IDLERS AND LETTER CONCLUSION (3:6–18)

The related themes of persecution and eschatology have dominated the letter to this point. Now Paul turns to a different matter: the behavior of some in the church who are not following the traditions that Paul passed on to them (3:6; cf. 2:15). Interestingly, this "tradition" (*paradosis*, NIV "teaching") involves not only verbal communication but the way of life of Paul and his associates. Following his usual practice (see also 1 Cor

---

28. Wanamaker, *Thessalonians*, 252; Leas Sirard, "La Parousie de l'Antéchrist, 2 Thess 2, 3–9," in *Studiorum Paulinorum Congressus Internationalis Catholicus 1961*, AnBib 17–18 (Rome: Pontifical Biblical Institute, 1963), 2:94–99; Giblin, *Threat to Faith*, 164–246.

29. I assume, with all the translations and most of the commentators, that the somewhat obscure clause *heōs ek mesou genētai* of v. 7 ("until out of the midst it becomes") refers to the removal of the restraining force. For a very different reading of this clause, and the paragraph as a whole, see Giblin, *Threat to Faith*.

9:6; 2 Cor 11:7–9; 1 Thess 2:9), Paul, Silas, and Timothy worked to support themselves so that they would not place any burden on the Thessalonians (vv. 7b–9a). Bracketing Paul's description of this way of life are claims that this behavior was intended to set an example for the Thessalonians (vv. 7a, 9b). And, in case the point of their behavior was not clear, Paul backs it up with a severe principle: "The one who is unwilling to work shall not eat" (v. 10). Some, apparently, are ignoring Paul's example and violating this principle. They are, Paul says twice, living *ataktōs* (vv. 6, 11). This adverb, cognate to the adjective *ataktos* that we encountered in 1 Thessalonians 5:14, means to act in a disruptive or unruly way. Many interpreters therefore insist that any translation of the word should stick to this meaning. However, while the word pretty clearly *means* to live "in an unruly way," the context here makes abundantly clear that the unruliness in this case *refers to* believers disobeying the apostolic example and dictum by ceasing to work and, perhaps, depending on others for their daily needs (see also 1 Thess 4:11–12), hence the NIV's "idle and disruptive."[30] Interpreters have often speculated that this idleness may have been related to the Thessalonians' basic eschatological error: thinking the day of the Lord was upon them, some of them decided that there was no point in going to work every day. However, the letter does not make this connection, and it is unclear if the kind of "unsettledness" Paul refers to (2:2) would naturally have led to this attitude.[31]

Paul concludes the letter by urging that the faithful Thessalonians stop associating with people like these idlers who ignore apostolic teaching. Such disassociation, an instance of "church discipline," will, it is hoped, lead to shame and potential restoration (as in 1 Cor 5:1–5). Paul adds his "signature" (v. 17) as a guarantor of this letter (to distinguish it, perhaps, from the bogus ones circulating? [see 2:2]).

---

30. Weima, *1–2 Thessalonians*, 600–601, translates "rebellious idlers."

31. Nicholl, *From Hope to Despair*, 157–75. Nicholl, plausibly, thinks the problem might be manual laborers who were abusing the church's mercy. Others suggest the problem might have been compounded by believers who were interpreting their relationship to wealthy believers in terms of the culture's client/patron relationship (Winter, *Seek the Welfare*, 41–60; Green, *Thessalonians*, 341–42).

Chapter 7

1 CORINTHIANS

PAUL'S FIRST LETTER to the Corinthians has a stronger explicit focus on particular problems in the church than any of his other letters. These problems structure the letter, as Paul moves from issue to issue. However, as a good pastor, Paul deploys theology to respond to these issues. As Anthony Thiselton puts it, the letter is a *"reproclamation of the different value system of grace, gifts, the cross, and the resurrection as divine verdict, criterion, and status bestowal within the new framework of respect and love for the less esteemed 'other.' Glorying in the Lord and receiving status derived from identification with the crucified Christ (1:30–31) lead to a new value system demonstrable in a wide array of issues."*[1]

LOCATING THE LETTER

First Corinthians is one of the so-called "chief epistles" (Ger. *Hauptbriefe*), a letter that is universally attributed to Paul the apostle. Locating the letter in Paul's ministry is quite straightforward. In chapter 16, he claims to be writing from Ephesus, where "a great door for effective work has opened" for him. He therefore plans to remain there until Pentecost and then, after traveling through Macedonia, to visit the Corinthians (16:5–9). These data make clear that Paul writes on his third missionary journey, during which he spent about three years in Ephesus (Acts 19). From Ephesus, he traveled through Macedonia to Corinth, where he spent the winter (Acts 20:1–3). It is likely this winter was in AD 56–57, in which case Paul would have left Ephesus either in the summer of 55 (if he traveled in Illyricum and surrounding areas before going to Corinth)[2] or 56 (if he went directly to Corinth). But it is possible that problems with the Corinthians (see the introduction to 2 Corinthians) may have forced Paul to stay longer in Ephesus than he first planned. Most interpreters, then, date 1 Corinthians to AD 54–55.[3] However, Paul wrote 2 Corinthians shortly after leaving Ephesus, and this

---

1. Thiselton, *First Epistle to the Corinthians*, 40 (emphasis original).

2. See Rom 15:19; and, for discussion, Schnabel, *Paul and the Early Church*, 1250–51.

3. See Wolfgang Schrage, *Der erste Brief an die Korinther*, 2nd ed., 4 vols., EKKNT 7 (Zürich: Benziger, 2008), 1:36–38; Thiselton, *First Epistle to the Corinthians*, 31. Joseph A. Fitzmyer, on the other hand, puts the letter early in AD 57 (*First Corinthians: A New Translation with Introduction and Commentary*, AB 32 [New Haven: Yale University Press, 2008], 48).

letter presumes travels and correspondence between Paul and the Corinthians not reflected in 1 Corinthians. We should perhaps, then, date 1 Corinthians a bit earlier, in AD 53.

ISOLATING THE ISSUES

Identifying the issues that stimulated Paul to write 1 Corinthians appears, on the one hand, very straightforward. In six passages, Paul introduces his teaching with the formula, "now for the matters you wrote about" (*peri de hōn egrapsate*), or its abbreviation, "now about" (*peri de*):

> 7:1: "Now for the matters you wrote about: 'It is good for a man not to have sexual relations with a woman'"
> 7:25: "Now about virgins"
> 8:1: "Now about food sacrificed to idols"
> 12:1: "Now about the gifts of the Spirit"
> 16:1: "Now about the collection for the Lord's people"
> 16:12: "Now about our brother Apollos"

We are not sure about the Corinthians' posture in raising these issues. They may have simply been asking for Paul's perspective. On the other hand, they were perhaps challenging Paul by advancing their own views.[4] Or, perhaps most likely, their letter occupied a middle position: "Paul, here is what we think about this matter. You agree, don't you?"

A second explicit indicator of occasion is the information about schisms in the church that Paul hears about from "Chloe's household" (1:11)—probably slaves of a wealthy Corinthian who have encountered Paul in Ephesus. Finally, third, Paul undoubtedly learned much about the church from Stephanas, Fortunatus, and Achaicus (1 Cor 16:17). Trying to decide just what Paul might have heard from Chloe's slaves (beyond the issue of schisms) and what he learned from these three Corinthian men is impossible and unnecessary. What is clear is that Paul had at least three good sources of information about the Corinthian church, and this information was disturbing. The Corinthians held views and were acting in ways that Paul views as incompatible with their Christian profession—and Paul tackles these one by one. Of all the letters of Paul, then, 1 Corinthians is the most "occasional" in the sense that almost everything Paul says in it is explicitly generated by a problem in the Corinthian church.

---

4. See, e.g., John Coolidge Hurd, *The Origin of 1 Corinthians* (New York: Seabury, 1965), 163–65, passim; and esp. Gordon D. Fee, *The First Epistle to the Corinthians*, 2nd ed., NICNT (Grand Rapids: Eerdmans, 2014), 5–6.

If, then, the specifics of the issues Paul addresses are fairly clear, the overall picture is far from certain. To put it another way, if it is easy to "isolate the *issues*," it is more difficult to "isolate the *issue*." Scholars have focused on three general scenarios: (1) the Corinthians were influenced by a particular ideology or set of ideologies from the Greco-Roman or Jewish world; (2) the Corinthians had misunderstood, or perverted, Christian teaching; or (3) the Corinthians were allowing their view of the gospel to be shaped by their general culture. Under the first heading are suggestions that Gnosticism or, more likely, "proto-Gnosticism"[5] or Hellenistic Jewish wisdom teaching[6] were influencing the Corinthians. A popular option under the second heading, advanced by A. Thiselton in an influential article (and modified a bit in his commentary), is that the Corinthians were guilty of an "overrealized eschatology." By putting too much emphasis on their present spiritual status at the expense of transformation yet to occur, they were guilty of triumphalism (see 4:8–10), a focus on "spirit" existence that ignored the body (e.g., 5:1–12; 6:12–20; 15), and a privatized spirituality that ignored the rights and needs of others (1:10–4:21; 8:1–11:1; 11:17–34; 12–14).[7] Recent scholarship has put particular stress on the third general category, manifesting what is on the whole a salutary move to situate the letters of Paul more firmly in their own world. Influence from the Greek world, for instance, is plausibly behind the Corinthians' doubts about a resurrection body (ch. 15), and social tensions typical of the Roman world between rich and poor may lie behind some of the problems Paul addresses (e.g., lawsuits in 6:1–11; meat sacrificed to idols in 8:1–11:1; more clearly, abuses at the Lord's Supper in 11:17–34).[8]

Of course, one need not choose between these options, and in fact most scholars probably end up arguing for some combination of two or three of them. At the risk of adopting an easy "all-of-the-above" approach, I think a combination of influences is most likely. Some of Paul's letters react against a relatively coherent "false teaching," with explicit mention of the false teachers themselves (e.g., Galatians and Colossians).

---

5. For Gnosticism, see Walter Schmithals, *Gnosticism in Corinth: An Investigation of the Letters to the Corinthians* (Nashville: Abingdon, 1971); for "proto-Gnosticism," see Victor Paul Furnish, "Theology in 1 Corinthians," in Hay, *Pauline Theology*, 62; Harris, *Second Epistle to the Corinthians*, 80–84.

6. Birger A. Pearson, *The Pneumatikos-Psychikos Terminology in 1 Corinthians: A Study in The Theology of the Corinthian Opponents of Paul and Its Relationship to Gnosticism*, SBLDS 12 (Missoula, MT: Scholars Press, 1973); James A. Davis, *Wisdom and Spirit: An Investigation of 1 Cor. 1:18–3:20 against the Background of Jewish Sapiential Traditions in the Greco-Roman World* (Lanham, MD: University Press of America, 1984).

7. Anthony C. Thiselton, "Realized Eschatology at Corinth," *NTS* 24 (1977–78): 510–26; cf. idem, *First Epistle to the Corinthians*, 40. Scholars who doubt that "overrealized eschatology" was a factor include Richard B. Hays, *The Conversion of the Imagination: Paul as Interpreter of Israel's Scripture* (Grand Rapids: Eerdmans,

2005), 5–6, 18–19; David E. Garland, *1 Corinthians*, BECNT (Grand Rapids: Baker, 2003), 13–14. Indeed, Hays suggests the problem in Corinth was too little eschatology, in the sense that the Corinthians were not strongly enough integrating their Christian worldview into their culture (Richard B. Hays, "The Conversion of the Imagination: Scripture and Eschatology in 1 Corinthians," *NTS* 45 [1999]: 391–412; cf. also Wright, *Resurrection*, 279).

8. See esp. Bruce W. Winter, *After Paul Left Corinth: The Influence of Secular Ethics and Social Change* (Grand Rapids: Eerdmans, 2001), 7–28; cf. also, for this general approach, Garland, *1 Corinthians*, 3–9; Roy E. Ciampa and Brian S. Rosner, *The First Letter to the Corinthians*, PNTC (Grand Rapids: Eerdmans, 2010), 4; John K. Chow, *Patronage and Power: A Study of Social Networks in Corinth*, JSNTSup 75 (Sheffield: JSOT, 1992); Thomas R. Schreiner, *1 Corinthians: An Introduction and Commentary*, TNTC 7 (Downers Grove, IL: InterVarsity Press, 2018), 8–16.

We find nothing like that in 1 Corinthians. The problems in the Corinthian community, then, arise from their environment, broadly understood. As in our day, so the Christians in Corinth are allowing their perspective to be influenced by their culture, a culture itself undoubtedly fed from many specific streams of thought. Ciampa and Rosner refer to a "rough consensus" that "the problems Paul addresses in 1 Corinthians reflect the infiltration of Corinthian social values into the church."[9] At the same time, I think that standard early Christian teaching about eschatology was being interpreted by the Corinthians in an imbalanced way. The tension between the initial "already" breaking in of the kingdom ("D-Day") and the ultimate "not yet" of that kingdom's full realization ("V-Day") was being dissolved in favor of the "already." "A D-Day without an impending V-Day loses its character as D-Day. Likewise a D-Day that is celebrated as if it were V-Day loses sight of the reality of things. . . . The Corinthians, however, with their spiritual pride, celebrate D-Day as if it were V-Day."[10]

ANALYZING THE ARGUMENT

Paul responds to the smorgasbord of issues in the Corinthian church with a powerful and coherent theological message. As I suggested above, the wide array of issues provides the basic outline of the letter, as Paul tackles each in turn, sometimes briefly (e.g., lawsuits, 6:1–11), sometimes at some length (e.g., meat sacrificed to idols, 8:1–11:1). Discerning larger thematic movements in the letter is more difficult, as revealed in the very different outlines offered by commentators.[11] It seems best, then, in general, to avoid identifying a single theme that binds together Paul's sequence of topics, noting rather various themes that emerge in each larger section.

1 THE NEW IDENTITY: DIVISIONS, WISDOM, AND THE MESSAGE OF THE CROSS (1:1–4:21)

1.1 Introduction and Appeal for Unity (1:1–17)

Following his usual "A to B" letter address form, Paul associates Sosthenes, the converted synagogue leader (Acts 18:17), with the writing of the letter and stresses the holiness of the church in Corinth (vv. 1–2). Also following his pattern, Paul gives thanks to God for the Corinthians (v. 4). Strikingly, however, what Paul gives thanks for is not the Corinthians' faith or obedience but God's provision for the Corinthians' spiritual needs: they have received God's grace (v. 4); have been "enriched in every way" (v. 5); do not lack any spiritual gift (v. 7); and can be confident that God will

---

9. Ciampa and Rosner, *First Letter to the Corinthians*, 4.
10. Beker, *Paul the Apostle*, 177.

11. See Andrew David Naselli, "The Structure and Theological Message of 1 Corinthians," *Presb* 44 (2018): 98–114.

keep them firm "to the end" (v. 8). Whatever the Corinthians' failings—and they are many—Paul is convinced of God's continuing faithfulness to them.

The body of the letter begins in 1:10. The tone of 1 Corinthians is set right from the start, as Paul turns immediately to exhortation ("I appeal" [NIV], *parakaleō*). He has heard from members of Chloe's "household" (probably slaves) that the Corinthians are divided, choosing different leaders to follow. This issue sets the agenda for chapters 1–4, as Paul criticizes the Corinthians for misunderstanding both the nature of the Christian message (1:18–2:16) and the nature of the Christian messenger (3:1–4:13).[12] Some interpreters, indeed, think that factionalism is the basic issue Paul addresses in the letter.[13] However, while it comes up explicitly once more (11:18) and is a factor in other matters Paul takes up, it is going too far to make it the central issue in the letter.[14] As Fee notes, the disunity in the church is a symptom of a deeper problem.[15]

The schisms in Corinth take the form of four "parties," each of which is tied to a particular Christian leader. Since at least the time of the "Tübingen School" in the nineteenth century, scholars have invested these parties with specific ideologies, sometimes constructing on this basis rather elaborate scenarios of theological conflict. In fact, however, Paul never criticizes any of the parties for theological deviation. The problem appears to be more a matter of style than content, as the Corinthians, perhaps under the influence of the "personality cults" fostered by sophist teachers, latched onto one leader or another with a special focus on their rhetorical skill (*sophia logou* in v. 17b probably has a focus on rhetoric; note NIV's "wisdom and eloquence").[16] Nevertheless, this divisiveness cannot finally be divorced from theology. As Paul makes clear in his rebuttal of the Corinthians' quarreling, a false understanding of the gospel, with the gospel's focus on "strength in weakness," manifested most notably in the cross, is also involved.[17]

1.2 The Christian Message (1:18–2:16)

Paul's rebuke of the Corinthians' quarrelling continues in 3:1. Before returning to his rebuke, however, Paul lays the groundwork in theology. Three themes, which are interwoven, dominate this passage: wisdom, the Spirit, and the cross. Paul uses the word "wisdom" (*sophia*) twenty-eight times in his letters; fifteen of them occur in 1:17–2:16. Scholars debate the source of what appears to have been a kind of "wisdom theology"

---

12. See Leon Morris, *The First Epistle of Paul to the Corinthians*, TNTC (Grand Rapids: Eerdmans, 1985), 57.

13. See esp. Margaret M. Mitchell, *Paul and the Rhetoric of Reconciliation: An Exegetical Investigation of the Language and Composition of 1 Corinthians* (Louisville: Westminster John Knox, 1991).

14. See, e.g., Thiselton, *First Epistle to the Corinthians*, 33–34.

15. Fee, *First Epistle to the Corinthians*, 49–51.

16. See Andrew D. Clarke, *Secular and Christian Leadership in Corinth: A Socio-Historical and Exegetical Study of 1 Corinthians*

1–6, AGJU 18 (Leiden: Brill, 1993), 90–94; see also Bruce W. Winter, *Philo and Paul among the Sophists: Alexandrian and Corinthian Responses to a Julio-Claudian Movement* (Grand Rapids: Eerdmans, 2002), 180–202; Duane Litfin, *St. Paul's Theology of Proclamation: 1 Corinthians 1–4 and Greco-Roman Rhetoric*, SNTSMS 79 (Cambridge: Cambridge University Press, 1994).

17. See Sigurd Grindheim, "Wisdom for the Perfect: Paul's Challenge to the Corinthian Church (1 Corinthians 2:6–16)," *JBL* 121 (2002): 689–709.

in Corinth.[18] Essentially, Paul argues that true wisdom must be defined not by worldly standards of status and outward importance but by divine standards, defined by the cross and mediated by the Spirit. As David Garland puts it, "Paul seeks to replace a pagan paradigm, fascinated by displays of status and power, with God's paradigm, exhibited in the weakness of the cross."[19]

In 1:18–2:5, Paul explains why worldly wisdom and eloquence rob the cross of Christ of its power (v. 17b). The wisdom the Corinthians prized was bound up with displays of power and with clever, sophisticated rhetorical techniques. But God's wisdom, Paul asserts, is defined by the cross. It is "Christ crucified" that Paul preached (v. 23); indeed, Paul "resolved to know nothing while I was with you except Jesus Christ and him crucified" (2:2)—not that he talked of nothing else but that everything he talked about was related to and seen in light of the cross. Jesus's crucifixion in this paragraph has a paradigmatic function: it symbolizes the most unusual way in which God has chosen to accomplish his purposes and reveal his power, exemplifying what the world would deem "foolishness" (1:20–23, 25, 27).[20] "In the theology of the cross, the cross is not the object of discussion, but through the cross everything simply comes up for a new discussion."[21] The Corinthians, Paul suggests, are allowing themselves to be captivated by worldly wisdom and eloquence, thereby running the danger of cutting themselves off from the very means by which God has chosen to save people (1:21). Christ crucified is the embodiment of "wisdom from God" and, as such, mediates "righteousness, holiness, and redemption" to those who embrace him in faith (1:30).

Paul's own preaching follows this same pattern (2:1–5). He has renounced the typical rhetorical modes of his day, which involved an attempt to persuade one's audience by adapting the message appropriately. Paul, by contrast, views himself as a herald, announcing an unchanging message, and allowing God's Spirit to accomplish the work of persuasion.[22] Paul wanted to make sure that his hearers' faith would be based on God's power, not human wisdom (2:5).

As the cross in 1:17 anticipates the focus of 1:18–2:5, so reference to the Spirit in 2:4 anticipates the focus of 2:6–16. Paul did not use "wise and persuasive words" when he preached the gospel; rather his message came "with a demonstration of the Spirit's power."[23] Paul is not criticizing reason or orderly presentation of the gospel message; his polemic is directed against flashy and manipulative techniques that do not bring hearers

---

18. Hellenistic Jewish "religiosity" (Richard A. Horsley, "Gnosis in Corinth: 1 Corinthians 8:1–6," *NTS* 27 [1980]: 37–39).

19. Garland, *1 Corinthians*, 100.

20. The paradigmatic nature of the cross in Paul is stressed by, e.g., Gorman, *Inhabiting the Cruciform God*.

21. Becker, *Paul: Apostle to the Gentiles*, 208.

22. See esp. Duane Litfin, *Paul's Theology of Preaching: The Apostle's Challenge to the Art of Persuasion in Ancient Corinth* (Downers Grove, IL: IVP Academic, 2015), esp. 259–84.

23. NIV "wise and persuasive words" translates *peithoi[s] sophias [logois]* (the final sigma on *peithois* and the word *logois* are textually uncertain).

into contact with the transforming message of the cross.[24] Paul therefore exhibits skill in rhetoric; what he opposes is what Gorman labels "rhetorical showmanship."[25] In fact, Paul now makes clear that he—and Cephas and Apollos; note the plural "we"—"speak a message of wisdom among the mature" (2:6). These "mature" or "perfect" people (Gk. *teleioi*) may be Christians in general. But Paul's use of this terminology elsewhere (e.g., 1 Cor 14:20; Phil 3:15) might suggest that he invites his readers to make sure they are themselves "mature": "We speak wisdom among the 'mature'—and you need to examine yourselves to see if, indeed, you belong to this group."[26] In the following verses, Paul develops both sides of this claim: the nature and source of the wisdom that the apostles "speak" and the kind of people who are able to understand this message. On both sides, it is the ministry of the Spirit that is the critical matter.[27]

First, the wisdom the apostles "speak" is not the product of human reasoning; nor can it be understood by the "rulers" (*archontōn*, perhaps human rulers who reflect the spiritual "powers"[28]). Divine wisdom, with its focus on God's plan manifested in the cross, is "hidden" until the Spirit reveals it (vv. 7, 10). The "hidden"/"revealed" language here reflects one of Paul's foundational theological schemes (see pp. 30–31). So the Spirit is instrumental in revealing God's wisdom to its proclaimers: this is probably the point Paul is making in the contested verse 13b: "We speak . . . in words taught by the Spirit, explaining spiritual realities with Spirit-taught words." The main alternative reading of the verse, reflected in the NIV footnote (and, e.g., ESV), "interpreting spiritual truths to those who are spiritual," also fits the context, since Paul goes on in verses 14–16 to focus on the vital role of the Spirit in receiving and understanding the message of divine wisdom.[29] Only those "with the Spirit" (the *pneumatikoi*) can discern spiritual realities. In addition, then, to the rhetorical purpose this passage serves with respect to the Corinthian problem of division, this passage gives important insight into Paul's theology of "knowing." Peter Stuhlmacher identifies three critical points. First, "the word of God" is given by revelation from God, not formulated by human preachers. Second, "theological thought" is not first of all critical thought; it proceeds from faith. Third, "spiritual knowledge of the gospel is not only a matter of the intellect; it is at the same time also a matter of the heart."[30]

24. See esp. Litfin, *Paul's Theology of Preaching*; also Ian W. Scott, *Implicit Epistemology in the Letters of Paul: Story, Experience and the Spirit*, WUNT 2/205 (Tübingen: Mohr Siebeck, 2006), 30–48.

25. Gorman, *Apostle of the Crucified Lord*, 63.

26. See Grindheim, "Wisdom for the Perfect," 702–7. Among those who think "mature" simply = "Christian," are Fee, *First Epistle to the Corinthians*, 109–10; Ciampa and Rosner, *First Letter to the Corinthians*, 122.

27. Here I follow, with minor differences, the structure suggested by Ciampa and Rosner, *First Letter to the Corinthians*, 121.

28. See, e.g., Garland, *1 Corinthians*, 96–97; Thiselton, *First Epistle to the Corinthians*, 246. Clarke argues for a reference to human rulers in light of the focus on leadership throughout this part of the letter (*Secular and Christian Leadership*, 113–17).

29. In defense of the translation in the NIV text, see esp. Fee, *First Epistle to the Corinthians*, 122–23. The differing translations reflect uncertainty about two matters: (1) the meaning of *synkrinontes* ("combine" or "explain"?); and (2) the function of the dative *pneumatikois* (instrumental ["with Spirit-taught words"] or advantage ["to those who are spiritual"]).

30. Peter Stuhlmacher, "The Hermeneutical Significance of 1 Cor 2:6–16," in *Tradition and Interpretation in the New Testament: Essays in Honor of E. Earle Ellis*, ed. Gerald F. Hawthorne and Otto Betz (Grand Rapids: Eerdmans, 1987), 328–43 (342).

1.3 The Christian Messenger (3:1–17)

Paul begins his criticism of the "party spirit" in Corinth by reminding the Corinthians of the nature of the Christian message, which embodies a wisdom focused on the cross and both revealed and received through the Spirit. He continues his critique in this section by reminding the Corinthians that the Christian messengers they are exalting are coworkers in God's kingdom, each called to faithful work in service of the building of God's new temple, a temple that rests on the only possible foundation, Jesus Christ himself. Periodic references to the issue of divisions (3:3–5, 21–22; 4:6) reveal that this issue continues to drive Paul's teaching.

In the opening paragraph of this section, 3:1–4, Paul picks up the first-person singular form of speaking from 1:10–17 and 2:1–5 and returns to the issue that sparked his discourse on Christian wisdom: divisions in the church. The "jealousy and quarreling" among the Corinthians (v. 3) reveal that the Christians in Corinth are "worldly" in their outlook. The NIV "worldly" translates the Greek *sarkinos* (v. 1)/*sarkikos* (v. 3), obvious antonyms to *pneumatikos* in verse 1, a word that in turn picks up the emphasis on the Spirit in 2:6–16.[31] "Flesh" and Spirit is a common contrast in Paul, the former word looking at humans *qua* humans, as people not only living in this world but as people who are following the values of this world. The fact that Paul appears to apply both terms to believers in this context has led many to think that Paul contrasts two levels of Christian experience: "carnal" (KJV) Christians versus "spiritual" Christians. However, possession of the Spirit is an inalienable mark of being a Christian for Paul. Probably, then, Paul is shaming the Corinthians by claiming that their preoccupation with popular wisdom and party spirit betrays a way of thinking that is inconsistent with their true status as "people of the Spirit." Paul thus polemically expresses his difference of opinion with the Corinthians over their spiritual state. They were priding themselves on being "spiritual people," feeding on the "solid food" of secular wisdom. For Paul, on the other hand, they are "fleshly" and immature, like very young children who still need milk.[32]

Following the pattern of 1:10–2:16, Paul grounds his rebuke of the Corinthians' divisiveness in theology. In the earlier section, the theology focused on the Christian message; here the focus is on the Christian messenger (3:5–17).

In 3:5–9, Paul relativizes the significance of Christian leaders by stressing their utter dependence on God. God alone causes the seed planted by Christian messengers to grow (vv. 6–7); Christian leaders are coworkers "in God's service," laboring in "God's

---

31. It is unlikely that *sarkinos* and *sarkikos* have any difference in meaning in this paragraph (see, e.g., Schrage, *Der Erste Brief an die Korinther*, 1:281–82). The two words appear to be interchangeable elsewhere in Paul also (cf. Rom 7:14 [*sarkinos*] with 2 Cor 1:12; 10:4 [*sarkikos*]).

32. Fitzmyer, *First Corinthians*, 187. The *psychikos* person

(2:14) is probably another way of designating this "fleshly" person. Paul's use of anthropological language in this context is notoriously difficult to pin down; as Margaret M. Mitchell puts it, "Paul left anthropological hermeneutics tantalizingly unresolved" (*Paul, the Corinthians and the Birth of Christian Hermeneutics* [Cambridge: Cambridge University Press, 2010], 45).

field" to erect "God's building" (v. 9).[33] The Corinthians' preference for one leader over another misses the fact that these leaders are "servants" assigned specific and often differing tasks in a cooperative effort to do God's work by God's power. Paul's focus on himself and Apollos here and in what follows (4:6; cf. 16:12) suggests that Apollos had a particularly strong following in Corinth—perhaps because of his rhetorical skills (see Acts 18:24).[34]

In 3:10–17, Paul continues to "put leaders in their place" by stressing that what matters is not the leader as such but how the leader is contributing to the building up of God's people.[35] And only on the day of the Lord, when all things are brought to light (v. 13), will the quality of what the Christian servant has built be clear. These verses, then, are not, as has often been thought, about the "works" of the individual believer and how those works will affect their status on the day of judgment. Nor is there any suggestion that God will apportion different degrees of reward in keeping with the varying degrees of faithfulness in this life.[36] Rather, these verses are about the product of one's Christian ministry. Those who have built well by faithfully serving God and proclaiming the "message of the cross" (1:18) will receive a reward, while those who build badly, focusing on their own status or building their own empire will "suffer loss"—that is, will not receive a reward (3:15). Their "work," the product of their ministry, will be "burned up" (even though they themselves may still be saved). The seriousness of the work Christian ministers are called to do is underscored by the fact that the "building" they are working on is nothing less than God's own dwelling place: his temple (vv. 16–17). Here Paul touches on a great biblical-theological theme that spans redemptive history from beginning to end.[37] The promise of God's presence with his people is climactically fulfilled in Jesus Christ (see John 2:21) and is now, Paul makes clear, expressed in Christ's body, the church (see also 2 Cor 6:16; Eph 2:21). Recognizing the church as the very dwelling place of God, through the Spirit (v. 16), is all the more reason for the Christian servant to build it well.

In 3:18–23, Paul exhorts the Corinthians again to stop "boasting about human leaders" (v. 21). He grounds this exhortation by returning to the contrast he introduced in

---

33. Fitzmyer, *First Corinthians*, 192. Paul may depend on OT texts that also compared God's people to both a field and a building (e.g., Jer 24:6: "I will bring them back to this land. I will build them up and not tear them down; I will plant them and not uproot them"). Jean Noël Aletti, *Essai sur l'ecclesiologie des lettres de Saint-Paul*, Études Bibliques 2/60 (Pendé: J. Gabalda, 2009), 29–30, draws attention to the Jeremiah background here.

34. Ben Witherington III thinks that Apollos's familiarity with Hellenistic wisdom was attractive to the Corinthians (*Jesus the Sage: The Pilgrimage of Wisdom* [Minneapolis: Fortress, 1994], 300–302).

35. "God's servants are for the church, not the church for God's servants" (Craig S. Keener, *1–2 Corinthians*, New Cambridge Bible Commentary [Cambridge: Cambridge University Press, 2005], 43).

36. See, e.g., Craig Blomberg, "Degrees of Reward in the Kingdom of Heaven," *JETS* 35 (1992): 159–72; Ciampa and Rosner, *First Letter to the Corinthians*, 156–57; Andrew J. Wilson, *The Warning-Assurance Relationship in 1 Corinthians*, WUNT 2/452 (Tübingen: Mohr Siebeck, 2017), 46–52. Likewise, there is no basis in this text for the doctrine of purgatory (contra, e.g., E. Bernard Allo, *Saint Paul: Première épître aux Corinthiens*, Études Bibliques [Paris: Gabalda, 1934], 66–67).

37. See esp. Beale, *Temple and the Church's Mission*.

1:18–31 between God's wisdom—"foolishness" in the eyes of the world—and human wisdom. The Corinthians need to view themselves as being "of Christ," who, in turn, is "of God" (3:23). As Paul has stressed in 3:5–9 especially, it is God, not human leaders, who should be the focus of attention; and God has made Jesus Christ the foundation on which the church must be built.

1.4 Paul and the Corinthians (4:1–21)

Paul has not entirely left the issue of divisions behind (see 4:5–6), but the new chapter marks a shift from leaders in general to Paul in particular. Paul applies to himself in his relationship with the Corinthians two principles that he has brought to bear on the issue of leaders and divisions in Corinth: (1) that God's wisdom is manifested in human weakness, allowing God's power to emerge all the more clearly (1:25, 27–29; 2:3–5; see 4:8–13); and (2) that God, not humans, will evaluate the effectiveness of his servant's work (3:12–15; see 4:3–5).

The first paragraph (4:1–5) is bracketed by remarks about leaders in general (vv. 1–2a, 5), within which Paul focuses on his own circumstances. These verses suggest that the Corinthians' debates about their leaders have a negative side, with Paul being judged by the Corinthians (v. 3). Gordon Fee thinks this issue of Paul's contested authority looms large in 1 Corinthians,[38] but it does not elsewhere appear as a significant point of difference. Picking up the teaching of 3:10–15, Paul insists that it is "the Lord who judges me," a judgment that awaits the time when the Lord comes (4:4–5).

Paul returns to the matter of the Corinthian divisions, continuing his focus on himself and Apollos (v. 6) and then broadening his focus to the Corinthians themselves (v. 7). In the context, Paul's citation of a probably proverbial warning about not "going beyond what is written" is best seen as a reminder of the scriptural warnings about arrogance (see, e.g., 1:31, quoting Jer 9:23–24).[39] Paul's warning about their boasting is elaborated in verse 8, where Paul uses irony to mock their claim to have "become rich" and to have "begun to reign." These sarcastic comments provide the strongest single textual base for the assumption that one of the Corinthians' fundamental theological problems was their "overrealized eschatology"—an overemphasis on the presence of the kingdom that fostered a triumphal spirit and disdain for the continuing realities and demands of this life.[40] The Corinthians' apparent claim to be "wise," "strong," and "honored" (v. 10) contrasts strangely, Paul points out, with the situation of himself and other apostles in the world: treated as "fools," "weak," and "dishonored." His point in elaborating the suffering and scorn endured by the apostles is to suggest that the Corinthians' evaluation of matters is far off base. Their relatively easy circumstances

---

38. See, e.g., Fee, *First Epistle to the Corinthians*, 6–7.
39. Hays, *Conversion of the Imagination*, 17.

40. See esp. Thiselton, *First Epistle to the Corinthians*, and the introduction to 1 Corinthians above.

reveal not that they are enjoying the full experience of the kingdom but that they are failing rightly to follow Christ.

The ironic rebukes of verses 6–13 give way to a much different tone in verses 14–17, where Paul addresses the Corinthians as a loving father who sets an example for his children to follow.[41] Yet he quickly adopts a sterner tone, concluding this section on divisions and wisdom with a warning about his imminent return to the Corinthians (vv. 18–21).

2 A NEW IDENTITY AND A NEW LIFESTYLE (5:1–6:20)

Charting the course of Paul's argument in chapter 5 and following chapters is difficult, as the many different structural proposals proposed by scholars make clear. Furnish, for instance, thinks all of 5:1 through 11:1 is broadly unified around the theme of Christian interaction with the pagan world.[42] Others isolate chapters 5–7 as a section focusing (mainly) on Christians and sexual conduct (with the inclusion of 6:1–11 explained in various ways). Still others think the literary marker in 7:1—"Now for the matters you wrote about"—should be determinative, with chapters 5–6 distinguished from what follows by a focus on clear-cut issues.[43] While a decision is difficult—and, more importantly, somewhat artificial (must Paul have had one clear structure in mind?)—I slightly prefer this last option. The fundamental issue in chapters 5–6 is the failure to recognize that "conversion to the new loyalty to Christ meant a complete break with the old mores and patterns of social relationship and with all self-indulgent behavior."[44] In three separate matters (5:1–13; 6:1–11, 12–20), Paul forcefully reminds the Corinthian Christians that certain kinds of behavior are incompatible with the kingdom they take so much pride in. A common feature in the chapters also is Paul's focus on future eschatology as a criterion for present Christian behavior (5:5; 6:2, 14).[45]

2.1 Preserving the Purity of the Community (5:1–13)

Paul is horrified at a report he has heard about the Corinthians' tolerance of a gross sexual sin, of a kind that even pagans deplore: a Christian man within the community is having sex with his stepmother (presumably what Paul means by the circumlocution "his father's wife").[46] But the Corinthians are not only tolerating this sin; they are, Paul claims, "proud." The Greek behind this NIV translation is the verb *physioō*, "puffed

---

41. For the emphasis on love in the father-child imagery here, see esp. Jonathan A. Moo, "Of Parents and Children: 1 Corinthians 4:15–16 and Life in the Family of God," in Harmon and Smith, *Studies in the Pauline Epistles*, 57–73. Ciampa and Rosner, *First Letter to the Corinthians*, think the change in tone signals that 4:18 is the beginning of a new phase in Paul's argument (190–91).

42. Furnish, "Theology in 1 Corinthians," 50–51.

43. E.g., Thiselton, *First Epistle to the Corinthians*, 381.

44. Dunn, *Beginning from Jerusalem*, 798.

45. Garland, *1 Corinthians*, 101.

46. The OT also, of course, prohibits sex with "your father's wife" (Lev 18:7–8).

up," a word that identifies a fundamental spiritual problem in the Corinthian church (six of the seven NT occurrences of the word are found in this letter: 4:6, 18, 19; 5:2; 8:1; 13:4). What were the Corinthians proud of? They may have seen this blatant disregard of common morality as an indication of the degree to which, as "spiritual" people in the age to come, they had been set free from the conventions of this world. It is also possible that the man committing the sin had prominence in the Corinthian community that made them reluctant to take any action against him.[47] Yet the text suggests that the Corinthians were proud of the sin, not the man.[48]

Though absent, Paul is present "in spirit" and demands that the church take action: they are to "hand this man over to Satan" (v. 5), meaning that they are to expel him from Christian fellowship (see v. 2), removing him from the protective sphere of the church and consigning him to the realm that Satan rules (see also 1 Tim 1:20; cf. Job 2:6). Yet the ultimate purpose of this severe disciplinary action is a positive one: that his "spirit may be saved on the day of the Lord" (v. 5). The means by which this purpose is accomplished is debated, the matter hinging on the meaning of one of Paul's most challenging theological words: *sarx*, often translated "flesh." Will the effect of handing over this sinner be that "his sinful nature [*sarx*] will be destroyed" (NLT)[49]—or that his physical body (*sarx*) will undergo serious suffering, a suffering that might, in turn, lead him to repent and so be saved (cf. 1 Cor 11:30; NJB)?[50] A decision is difficult, but the former interpretation of *sarx* might provide a more natural contrast with "spirit" (*pneuma*).

Paul's critique of the Corinthians' "boasting" (v. 6) signals a break and return to the starting point in verses 1–2. The disciplinary action the church is to take is not only ultimately for the benefit of the sinner himself—it is also vitally necessary for the health of the church.[51] Paul uses the popular analogy of yeast leavening a batch of dough to make his point: allowing serious sin to go unpunished means that sin, once tolerated, will spread to the whole community (v. 6). Reference to leaven leads Paul naturally to think of the Jewish Festival of Unleavened Bread, with its centerpiece in Passover. Christians celebrate their own Passover, focused on the sacrifice of the ultimate Passover lamb, Christ himself (vv. 7–8). Paul concludes with a general exhortation to cut off fellowship with those in the community who are guilty of serious sexual sins (vv. 9–13).

---

47. See, e.g., Clarke, *Secular and Christian Leadership*, 73–88; Chow, *Patronage and Power*, 130–41; Ciampa and Rosner, *First Letter to the Corinthians*, 203; Thiselton, *First Epistle to the Corinthians*, 388–90.

48. Fee, *First Epistle to the Corinthians*, 221–22.

49. Fee, *First Epistle to the Corinthians*, 232–33; Garland, *1 Corinthians*, 169–77; Thiselton, *First Epistle to the Corinthians*, 395–97. Thiselton and a few other scholars also think this

act might include the "fleshly" tendencies of the community as a whole.

50. Allo, *Saint Paul*, 124–27; C. K. Barrett, *The First Epistle to the Corinthians*, BNTC (London: Black, 1993), 125–27; Fitzmyer, *First Corinthians*, 239.

51. See esp. Calvin J. Roetzel, *Judgment in the Community: A Study of the Relationship between Eschatology and Ecclesiology in Paul* (Leiden: Brill, 1972), 118–22, for this emphasis.

2.2 Lawsuits and Inheriting the Kingdom (6:1–11)

It is no surprise that the matter of lawsuits should arise in a letter written to a community guilty of compromising with their Greco-Roman culture. For going to court was an extraordinarily popular "spectator sport" in the world of the Corinthians. However, why Paul brings this issue up in this context is not so clear. Sean McDonough has suggested that the sequence might be influenced by Paul's deeply rooted knowledge of Scripture.[52] As he points out, it may not be a coincidence that Deuteronomy 17 moves from the call to remove transgressors from Israel (vv. 2–7) to the topic of difficult cases in Israelite lawcourts (vv. 8–13). Paul has quoted from this very context at the end of chapter 5 (v. 13 quotes from Deut 17:7), lending plausibility to this connection.

What distresses Paul is that the Corinthians were relying on secular law courts to resolve differences among them. They should rather settle such matters among themselves. After all, Paul reminds them, Christians will "judge the world"—including even angels (6:2–3). The involvement of God's people in judging the world was taught in Judaism—"God will judge all the nations by the hand of his elect" (1QHab 5:4; cf. Dan 7:22)[53]—and is reflected in the NT elsewhere (Rev 2:26; 20:4). Paul therefore views recourse to secular legal institutions as a failure to give the Christian community the central place it is to have in the lives of believers. Surely, Paul suggests, the distinctive values that characterize that community make it the place to resolve differences among believers (vv. 4–5)—rather than airing "dirty linen" in front of the world (v. 6). As God's presence in the tabernacle/temple of Israel made it the appropriate place for judgments to be rendered, so it is the Christian community, where God now resides (3:16), that should be the forum for judgments to be made.[54]

Paul goes on to penetrate to a deeper issue: the very fact that believers are pursuing lawsuits against each other is itself a "defeat" for the community and its witness to the world (6:7). Many recent interpreters are convinced that another issue lies behind Paul's rebuke. They note that our knowledge of the pervasive corruption in Roman-era law courts would strongly suggest that the situation Paul addresses involves upper-class Christians using the law courts to gain advantage over others in the community.[55] However, while it was undoubtedly true that only the well-to-do would have the option of taking cases to court, Paul gives no hint that the problem here was the rich exploiting the poor. Moreover, his exhortations in verses 7–8 send a mixed signal. On the one hand, his exhortation to believers tempted to resort to the courts that they should

52. Sean M. McDonough, "Competent to Judge: The Old Testament Connection between 1 Corinthians 5 and 6," *JTS* 56 (2005): 99–102.

53. Paul D. Gardner, *1 Corinthians*, ZECNT (Grand Rapids: Zondervan, 2018), 251–53, argues that Paul derives the idea from Dan 7:22.

54. McDonough, "Competent to Judge," 101.

55. See esp. Winter, *Seek the Welfare*; A. C. Mitchell, "Rich and Poor in the Courts of Corinth: Litigiousness and Status in 1 Corinthians," *NTS* 39 (1993): 562–86; and also David G. Horrell, *The Social Ethos of the Corinthian Correspondence: Interests and Ideology from 1 Corinthians to 1 Clement* (Edinburgh: T&T Clark, 1996), 137–42; Clarke, *Secular and Christian Leadership*, 59–69.

be willing to be "wronged" and "cheated" (v. 7) would suggest that those going to court had a valid reason to do so. On the other hand, however, his claim that those going to court are "cheating" and "doing wrong" (v. 8) supports the scenario of rich believers using the courts to defraud others. It is best, then, to be cautious about finding economic factors in the situation here.

As he did at the climax of his exhortation in chapter 5, Paul in verses 9–11 reminds the Corinthians that God will not include among his people those who persistently behave in certain ways. Paul's emphasis on this point makes clear that the Corinthians were guilty of thinking that their status as "spiritual" people, already enjoying their reign in the kingdom, rendered sin a trivial matter. On the contrary, Paul reminds them: God's kingdom, while present to some extent, is also future, something to be "inherited," and persistent sin can exclude people from that inheritance. Our contemporary context has drawn special attention to the inclusion in this list of both active (*arsenokoitai*) and passive (*malakoi*) partners in homosexual relations.[56] However, while this context justifies attention to these sins, it is important to maintain perspective by reminding ourselves of the breadth of sinful behavior encompassed by this list (e.g., greed, slander). For all the strength of Paul's denunciations of the Corinthians, he regularly affirms their status as genuine believers. Here then, again (v. 11), Paul contrasts their past lives with who they have now been made by God's grace: "washed," "sanctified," and "justified." The order here is significant: their legal standing as justified, while fundamental, takes second place to their having been transformed.

2.3 Glorifying God with the Body (6:12–20)

Paul abruptly introduces a new issue, although one that is clearly related to the overall theme of chapters 5–6. Thus, while the immediate issue is that some of the Corinthian men are going to prostitutes for sex (v. 16), the deeper problem is that the Corinthians appear to be tolerating this situation on the basis of bad theology.[57] Paul therefore condemns the practice of going to prostitutes, labeling it a form of serious sexual sin (*porneia*; v. 18). More fundamentally, he criticizes the Corinthians' disregard for the body. As most modern English versions recognize, following the lead of most scholars, Paul quotes and rebuts the Corinthian position on this matter. Thus, in verses 12–13 it is almost certainly the Corinthians who are saying "I have the right to do anything" and "food for the stomach and the stomach for food, and God will destroy

---

56. The former term is well attested in this sense in Paul's day; the latter is rare and is probably derived from OT texts such as Lev 18:22 and 20:13, which use the Gk. words *arsenos* ("man") and *koitēn* ("sexual intercourse"), thus "men lying with a male." See esp. Robert A. J. Gagnon, *The Bible and Homosexual Practice: Texts and Hermeneutics* (Nashville: Abingdon, 2001), 303–39; Fitzmyer, *First Corinthians*, 256. As Winter points out, reference to both partners in a homosexual relationship was typical in Paul's day (*After Paul Left Corinth*, 110–20).

57. It is possible that here again wealth and influence may be involved; Winter notes that it was particularly the rich and powerful who took advantage of a permissive attitude toward prostitutes (*After Paul Left Corinth*, 76–109).

them both."[58] More controversially, it is also possible that the difficulties of verse 18 are to be resolved by attributing the middle of the verse to the Corinthians, who are saying, in effect, "every sin that a man commits is outside the body"; that is, sin, by definition, has nothing to do with the body.[59] This disdain for the body is, of course, deeply rooted in the Greek culture. The Corinthians have erred again by bringing this cultural attitude into their Christian faith.

Paul responds to these Corinthian claims by qualifying or rejecting them. Christians do, indeed, have a newfound freedom; but that freedom, Paul insists, should be exercised within limits imposed by what is sensible. Certain forms of behavior, while perhaps not actually sinful, have the power to enslave people and to lead them away from complete devotion to Christ (v. 12). Paul outright rejects the Corinthian claim that the body is destined to be destroyed. Anticipating his much longer discussion of the issue in chapter 15, Paul reminds the Corinthians that God has destined the body to be raised, as Christ's body was raised (v. 14). Christians—and, indeed, people in general—have an embodied existence that is permanent and basic to what it means to be human. The body is not going to be thrown away, nor is it uninvolved in the struggle between sin and holiness. Sin is *not* "apart from the body"; those who engage in inappropriate sexual behavior are sinning "against their own body" (v. 18). Paul stresses the significance of the body in two other ways. First, believers, in their bodies, are "members of Christ himself" (v. 15). Joining that body with a prostitute in a "one-flesh" union would be to violate that union with Christ (vv. 16–17; cf. Gen 2:24). Second, the body of believers is a temple, indwelt by the Holy Spirit. Temple imagery in chapter 3 was applied to the community; here Paul applies it to individual believers (v. 19).[60] All this means that believers must use their bodies to glorify God (v. 20).

3 IMPLICATIONS OF THE NEW IDENTITY FOR MARRIAGE AND SEX (7:1–40)

This chapter is a discrete unit, focusing on issues the Corinthians have raised concerning marriage. Paul's response falls into an A-B-A pattern, with Paul's response to their two questions (vv. 1–16, 25–40) bracketing a section providing theological grounding for his responses (vv. 17–24). It is unclear how this chapter fits into the development

---

58. There is some doubt whether this last phrase—"God will destroy them both"—is part of the Corinthians' speech. For the view that the phrase should be included in the quote, see, e.g., Fee, *First Epistle to the Corinthians*, 280; Thiselton, *First Epistle to the Corinthians*, 462–63.

59. Jay E. Smith, "A Slogan in 1 Corinthians 6:18b: Pressing the Case," in Harmon and Smith, *Studies in the Pauline Epistles*, 74–98; Andrew David Naselli, "Is Every Sin outside the Body

except Immoral Sex? Weighing Whether 1 Corinthians 6:18b Is Paul's Statement or a Corinthian Slogan," *JBL* 136 (2017): 969–87; Charles H. Talbert, *Reading Corinthians: A Literary and Theological Commentary on 1 and 2 Corinthians* (New York: Crossroad, 1987), 34; Fitzmyer, *First Corinthians*, 269.

60. See, e.g., Fee, *First Epistle to the Corinthians*, 291. It is unlikely that a corporate idea is to be found here (contra J. Thompson, *Church according to Paul*, 68–69).

of the letter. On the one hand, we might attach it to what follows. Literary markers support this option, since 7:1 marks the first reference to the letter the Corinthians wrote to Paul, a feature that recurs regularly in the following chapters (7:25; 8:1; 12:1; 16:1, 12). Fee therefore identifies 7:1–16:12 as one large letter unit.[61] Thiselton includes this chapter with 8:1–11:1 under the rubric "Paul's pastoral sensitivity to grey areas of difficulty."[62] Others put the chapter with what precedes (4:18–6:20 or 5:1–6:20), since chapter 7 has in common with these previous chapters a focus on sex.[63] I think this latter connection is materially the most important.[64] Yet the indication of a break at 7:1 cannot be ignored. I therefore treat the chapter as its own stage in the argument of the letter, noting, of course, its connections with what comes before and after.

One of the most important theological and ethical issues arising from this chapter is its generally bleak view of sex and marriage. Paul seems grudgingly to allow marriage as the better option to unbridled passion; his preference, it seems, would be for all Christians to remain unmarried, as he is (vv. 7–9): "Those who marry will face many troubles in this life" (v. 28); they will find it more difficult to be fully devoted to the Lord (vv. 32–35). It is no wonder, then, that this chapter has figured prominently in Christian arguments for celibacy.[65] Two things may be said in response. First, Paul is by no means "anti-marriage" in this chapter. He makes it clear that it is not sin to marry (v. 36), and encourages those who are married to remain married (vv. 10–16). And sex, within marriage, is not only an option but something of an expectation (vv. 2–5). It is the Corinthians, not Paul, who are saying that "it is good for a man not to have sexual relations with a woman" (v. 1). Second, Paul's advice in this chapter is very much directed to the particular stance the Corinthians are taking on these issues. It is their underlying false view of the body that stimulates both their libertinism (the body doesn't matter: do with it whatever you want; 6:12–20) and their asceticism (the body doesn't matter: don't indulge it; ch. 7). Paul's response is calibrated to meet this underlying issue.[66] Therefore, while agreeing with the Corinthians that there are valid grounds for remaining unmarried, he replaces their false theological grounds with Christian principles. Against their tendencies toward asceticism, he firmly asserts not only the validity but the appropriateness of sex within marriage. And he strongly

61. *First Epistle to the Corinthians*, 295–96. Fitzmyer advocates a similar structure, but with the section ending at 14:40 (*First Corinthians*, 273).

62. Thiselton, *First Epistle to the Corinthians*, 483.

63. E.g., Ciampa and Rosner, *First Letter to the Corinthians*, 22–25.

64. See Schrage, *Der erste Brief an die Korinther*, 2:50.

65. See, e.g., the brief overview in Eckhard J. Schnabel, *Der erste Brief des Paulus an die Korinther*, Historisch Theologische Auslegung: Neues Testament (Giessen: Brockhaus, 2006), 349–50.

66. Judith M. Gundry Volf, "Male and Female in Creation and New Creation: Interpretations of Galatians 3:28c in 1 Corinthians 7," in *To Tell the Mystery: Essays on New Testament Eschatology in Honor of Robert H. Gundry*, ed. T. E. Schmidt and Moisés Silva (Sheffield: JSOT, 1994), 95–121; Will Deming, *Paul in Marriage and Celibacy*, SNTSMS 83 (Cambridge: Cambridge University Press, 1995), 211–20.

rejects any notion that life in the new realm of Christ and the Spirit requires married Christians to separate.

As he has done in 6:12–13, 18, Paul initiates a new topic by quoting the Corinthians: "It is good for a man not to have sexual relations with a woman."[67] In this case, however, Paul attributes this slogan to a letter the Corinthians have written. Whether this letter had a neutral tone—"Hey, Paul, what do you think about . . . ?"—or a polemical one— "Here's what we think, Paul"—is unclear. In any case, as we have seen, Paul responds by implicitly rejecting the premise of their slogan. Sex—at least within marriage—is not only appropriate but is expected (vv. 2–3). Significantly, reflecting a theme that runs through this letter, Paul implicitly rebukes the Corinthians for thinking they have ultimate control over their bodies. Rather, Paul argues that marriage brings people into a union in which each partner cedes "authority" over their body to their spouse (vv. 3–4). Significantly, and unusually for that time and place, Paul gives the wife just as much authority in this matter as the husband. As the bodies of Christians are to be used to glorify Christ, so the bodies of believing spouses are to be used for the benefit of the partner. Touching on another theme important in this chapter, Paul also encourages the Corinthians to be realistic about the power of the sexual impulse and to view marriage as the appropriate venue for sexual gratification (vv. 5–9). His appeal to his own state (of being unmarried) may be because the Corinthians were appealing to his example.[68]

After addressing the "unmarried" (or "widowers"; see NIV note) and widows in these terms in verses 8–9, Paul returns to married partners in verse 10. Paul's command that those who are married stay married is probably directed against the assumption of some of the Corinthians that the "fleshly" joining of man and woman in marriage is incompatible with the spiritual existence of believers.[69] Against such a view, Paul cites Jesus's own command: It is "not I, but the Lord" who prohibits married partners from separating. Paul indirectly incorporates Jesus's teaching into his own teaching fairly often, but he rarely explicitly cites Jesus. Perhaps he does so here because, unlike some of the other issues Paul treats in this context, the prohibition of divorce does not have clear Old Testament support.[70] When Paul turns next to Christians married to unbelievers (vv. 12–16), he therefore makes clear that it is he, not the Lord, who is speaking. The force of the command remains, for, as Paul notes in verse 40, he speaks

---

67. Paul uses the idiom "touch" a woman, which probably refers to sex in general (see most English translations)—though Ciampa and Rosner argue that the idiom refers more specifically to sex motivated by passion or pleasure (*First Letter to the Corinthians*, 274).

68. Fee, *First Epistle to the Corinthians*, 315; Talbert, *Reading Corinthians*, 38–39.

69. Noting that Paul addresses wives first, Fee suggests that the view being propagated among the Corinthians comes from "eschatological women"—women who took to an extreme their new freedom in Christ because of an overrealized eschatology (see also 11:2–16; 14:33b–35; *First Epistle to the Corinthians*, 322–23; cf. Robin Scroggs, "Paul and the Eschatological Women," *JAAR* 40 [1972]: 283–303).

70. See, e.g., Ciampa and Rosner, *First Letter to the Corinthians*, 291.

as one indwelt by the Spirit. Again in probable direct response to the Corinthians, who might have been arguing that at least unions between the sanctified and the "unholy" should be terminated, Paul urges Christian spouses to stick with the marriage. Rather than the Christian being contaminated by the unbeliever, it is the unbeliever who is "sanctified" by the union—probably in the sense that they (and their children) enjoy the benefit of God's grace in the household. Verse 16, then, is probably to be read with this encouraging word, holding out hope for the salvation of those under this gracious influence.[71] Verse 15 is best read as an aside, as Paul takes into account a situation in which the unbelieving partner, not wanting perhaps to be joined to someone who has embraced what many would have viewed as a strange cult, insists on leaving the marriage. It has long been debated whether the language of "not bound" applied to the believer in these circumstances means that they are not "bound" to Paul's commands in verses 10, 12–13[72] or that they are no longer "bound" to the marriage—permitting remarriage.[73] I slightly prefer the latter option.

Sandwiched between Paul's teaching on a Christian view of marriage in the new realm (7:1–16, 7:25–40) is a section laying out a fundamental theological principle informing that advice. Basically, that principle, stated three times in this paragraph, is "each person should remain in the situation they were in when God called them" (v. 20; see also vv. 17, 24). "Call" (Gk. *kaleō*) is a key theological term in this paragraph, occurring eight times. Paul does not develop the idea inherent in the word in this context. Yet his "casual" use of the word in this context speaks volumes about the theological significance of the language. Clearly here it denotes the entrance point into Christian existence; it is equivalent to "converted" (see also 1:9). In this context, at least, it is applied to individuals, as Paul differentiates the varied circumstances people were in when God called them. It does not mean "invite" but refers to what in theology we call the "effectual call": God's determinative decision to bring a person into relationship with Christ (a notion closely related to election; see further pp. 511–15).[74] Paul illustrates his key point about "remain[ing] in the situation they were in when God called them" with the religious/ethnic polarity of "circumcised"/"uncircumcised" (vv. 18–19) and the social polarity of slave/free (vv. 21–23). In encouraging the circumcised to remain in their original state, Paul is not requiring them to remain Torah observant; the issue is simply physical.[75] Indeed, reflecting an important theological point for Paul,

71. Barrett, *First Epistle to the Corinthians*, 167; Garland, *1 Corinthians*, 293; Fee, *First Epistle to the Corinthians*, 337–38 (hesitantly). Others think the verse is pessimistic toward eventual salvation (Morris, *Corinthians*, 111; Archibald Robertson and Alfred Plummer, *A Critical and Exegetical Commentary on the First Epistle of St. Paul to the Corinthians*, ICC [Edinburgh: T&T Clark, 1914], 144); still others that it is neutral on the matter (Thiselton, *First Epistle to the Corinthians*, 538–40).

72. Fee, *First Epistle to the Corinthians*, 334–35.

73. Ciampa and Rosner, *First Letter to the Corinthians*, 302; David Instone-Brewer, "1 Corinthians 7 in the Light of the Graeco-Roman Marriage and Divorce Papyri," *TynBul* 52 (2001): 238–43.

74. S. Chester, *Conversion at Corinth*, 77–112.

75. N. T. Wright, *Paul and the Faithfulness of God*, 2 vols. (Minneapolis: Fortress, 2013), 2:1434–35; contra, e.g., Peter J.

he claims that "circumcision is nothing and uncircumcision is nothing" (v. 19a; cf. Gal 6:15; see also Gal 3:28). For both Jew and gentile, what is important is "keeping God's commands" (v. 19b). Many think the reference here is to the commands of Torah as they are filtered through Christ's fulfillment of the law.[76] It may be preferable, however, to think that Paul is referring here not to the law of Moses but to Christ's law (1 Cor 9:19–21).[77] Likewise, Paul exhorts slaves not to "trouble" about their state of slavery, focusing rather on their new spiritual status as "the Lord's freed person" (vv. 21–22). Paul's advice to slaves in verse 21b is much debated. Is he urging them to "use [the opportunity to gain their freedom] rather [than remain a slave]"[78] or to "use [their existing state of slavery] all the more" (the debated Gk. is *mallon chrēsai*)?[79] Most English versions and a slight majority of commentators favor the former. In any case, Paul urges slaves not to transfer their earthly state into the spiritual sphere and become "slaves of human beings"—for, Paul reminds them, "you were bought at a price" (v. 23). Paul here echoes the similar exhortation and theological rationale he applied to sex in 6:12–20: "I will not be mastered by anything" (v. 12b); "you were bought at a price" (v. 20). Again, Paul's "casual" reference to being purchased by God suggests that the notion of Christ's death paying a price to purchase the freedom of those who were slaves (to sin) is deeply rooted in Paul's teaching of his churches.

We should not think that Paul completely ignores the reality of believers' earthly situation. Nevertheless, these circumstances do not finally determine who we are: our true identity arises from our identification with Christ. As Furnish puts it, "Believers are conditioned but not claimed by their particular circumstances."[80] This principle needs to be taken on board by the Corinthians so that they cease thinking that their new Christian identity compels them to change their marital status or plans.

The "now about" (*peri de*) that introduces this paragraph (vv. 25–40) indicates that Paul is again dealing with a matter the Corinthians have raised in their letter. Paul directs

---

Tomson, *Paul and the Jewish Law: Halakha in the Letters of the Apostle to the Gentiles*, CRINT (Minneapolis: Fortress, 1990), 271–72; Mark S. Kinzer, *Post-Missionary Messianic Judaism: Redefining Christian Engagement with the Jewish People* (Grand Rapids: Baker, 2005), 72–73.

76. E.g., Schreiner, *Law and Its Fulfillment*, 155–56. He notes, following Frank Thielman (*Paul and the Law*, 101), that "commandments" in both Paul and the Jewish world of his day usually referred to commandments of the Mosaic law.

77. Brian S. Rosner thinks "commandments of God" would refer to Paul's own instructions in this letter (*Paul and the Law: Keeping the Commandments of God*, NSBT 31 [Downers Grove, IL: InterVarsity Press, 2013], 32–39; 128–29). See also Douglas de Lacey, "The Sabbath/Sunday Question and the Law in the Pauline Corpus," in *From Sabbath to Lord's Day: A Biblical, Historical and Theological Investigation*, ed. D. A. Carson (Grand Rapids: Zondervan, 1982), 176–77.

78. E.g., Fee, *First Epistle to the Corinthians*, 350–51. As Bartchy has made clear, slaves in Paul's day did not themselves have the choice of remaining a slave or being manumitted; it was up to the master (S. Scott Bartchy, *Mallon Chrēsai: First-Century Slavery and the Interpretation of 1 Corinthians 7:21*, SBLDS 11 [Missoula: SBL, 1973]). See also Ben Witherington III, *Conflict & Community in Corinth: A Socio-Rhetorical Commentary on 1 and 2 Corinthians* (Grand Rapids: Eerdmans, 1995), 181–85.

79. E.g., Barrett, *First Epistle to the Corinthians*, 170–71. Bartchy, however, thinks the issue is how a manumitted slave is to live: "If you are set free, then by all means (as a freedman) live according to God's calling" (*Mallon Chrēsai*, 155–59).

80. Victor Paul Furnish, *The Theology of the First Letter to the Corinthians*, NT Theology (Cambridge: Cambridge University Press, 1999), 62.

attention to this particular issue in verses 25–28 and 36–40, with verses 29–35 an explanatory digression. Just what this matter is, however, is very unclear. "Virgins" in English inevitably suggests women; but the Greek word (*parthenoi*) can refer to either men or women (see BDAG). A few interpreters therefore think that the issue Paul addresses is the status of both men and women who are not yet married.[81] The word in Paul's day was normally used of women, however, and it is likely this is the referent here also. Supporting this is the shift in verse 28 from "you," which refers to a man (v. 27), to "virgin." It is much more difficult to decide if Paul's advice is directed to a man who is engaged to be married or to a father who must decide whether to give his daughter in marriage. Verse 36 is critical but poses a nest of exegetical problems. The verse can be read as directed to a man who is engaged; hence NIV: "If anyone is worried that he might not be acting honorably toward the virgin he is engaged to, and if his passions are too strong and he feels he ought to marry, he should do as he wants. He is not sinning." But it could also be read as referring to a father; as in NASB: "But if any man thinks that he is acting unbecomingly toward his virgin *daughter*, if she is past her youth, and if it must be so, let him do what he wishes, he does not sin" (note also the long note in NIV offering this alternative rendering).[82] On the whole, along with a slight majority of commentators and most versions, I think a reference to an engaged man might be the best option.[83]

As he has done in verses 1–16, Paul steers a careful course between affirming marriage as a valid option for believers while at the same time suggesting that remaining single—for those who have the "gift"—might be the preferable option. He gives two reasons for this judgment. First, unmarried believers can give greater time and focus to the Lord; those who are married must of necessity divide their attention (vv. 32–35). Second, believers need to consider their marital options in light of the time they live in: "Because of the present crisis" (v. 26); "the time is short" (v. 29). These references might manifest Paul's view that, at least at this early stage of letter-writing, the return of Christ would be happening in the very near future. However, it is not clear that this is what Paul means. The "crisis" may refer to a particular circumstance in first-century Corinth; Winter, for instance, suggests Paul may be thinking of a grain shortage.[84] Even if the reference is more general, Paul may be referring to the entire time between the first and second comings of Christ as a time of "pressure" (*anankē*) for believers (v. 26).

---

81. E.g., Thiselton, *First Epistle to the Corinthians*, 570–71, although he thinks the emphasis is on women. See also Talbert, *Reading Corinthians*, 47.

82. Fee, though he does not himself hold this view, claims that this was the "nearly universal tradition of the church up to the twentieth century" (*First Epistle to the Corinthians*, 360).

83. See, e.g., Fee, *First Epistle to the Corinthians*, 361–62;

Garland, *1 Corinthians*, 320–21; Thiselton, *First Epistle to the Corinthians*, 568–71. The debated word *hyperakmos* in v. 36 will then probably mean "with strong passion" rather than "past marriageable age" (BAGD gives both options).

84. Winter, *After Paul Left Corinth*, 216–25; Schnabel, *Der Erste Brief des Paulus an die Korinther*, 403.

"The time is short," moreover, could also be translated "the time is constrained."[85] In any case, as Gorman puts it, Paul's perspective on the issues he treats here "is indebted as much to the *quality* of the present time as to the *quantity* of time remaining."[86] Or Garland: "He is not talking about how little time is left but about how Christ's death and resurrection have changed how Christians should look at the time that is left."[87]

4 THE NEW IDENTITY: LIBERTY AND LOVE (8:1–11:1)

In these chapters, Paul addresses another issue the Corinthians have raised in their letter ("now about" [*peri de*], 8:1): What should they think about buying and eating "food sacrificed to idols" (*eidōlothytos*; 8:1, 4, 7, 10; 10:19)? In first-century Corinth, meat (which is probably what is mainly in view)[88] would have been sacrificed for a meal in a pagan temple before being offered for sale in the marketplace. Can Christians consume such meat? Paul says, basically, "Yes, but . . . ." Christians have the freedom to eat this marketplace food, but their freedom must be tempered by concern for believers who have not yet entirely shed their pagan worldview and who might therefore be spiritually harmed by seeing fellow believers eat such food. This concern for the conscience of a "weak" brother or sister is the topic of 8:1–13. In chapter 9, then, Paul presents himself as an example of one who, as an apostle, has numerous "rights," but who has chosen not to exercise many of those rights for the sake of the gospel. The tone changes in 10:1–22. Here, using the Israelites in the wilderness as an illustration, Paul warns about idolatry itself, culminating in the command to "flee from idolatry" (v. 14). The contrast between this uncompromising command and Paul's openness to believers to eat meat sacrificed to idols (8:9; 10:25–26) raises questions about the coherence of these chapters. A few interpreters think that 10:1–22 sets the basic agenda and that Paul is warning about committing idolatry by participating in meals in a pagan temple.[89] But it is better, with most interpreters, to think that Paul deals with two—or perhaps three—related issues in these chapters: (1) Christians have the freedom to eat meat sacrificed to idols (ch. 8; or perhaps 8:1–6); (2) Christians must, however,

---

85. John M. G. Barclay, "Apocalyptic Allegiance and Disinvestment in the World: A Reading of 1 Corinthians 7:25–35," in Blackwell, Goodrich, and Maston, *Paul and the Apocalyptic Imagination*, 260. The only other NT occurrence of the relevant verb, *systellō*, refers to a corpse being "wrapped up" (Acts 5:6).

86. Gorman, *Apostle of the Crucified Lord*, 254.

87. Garland, *1 Corinthians*, 328–29; see also Schreiner, *1 Corinthians*, 154.

88. See 10:25, where the word *makellon* probably means "meat market" (BDAG).

89. Fee, *First Epistle to the Corinthians*, 396–97; see also John Fotopoulos, *Food Offered to Idols in Roman Corinth: A Social-Rhetorical Reconsideration of 1 Corinthians 8:1–11:1*, WUNT 2/151 (Tübingen: Mohr Siebeck, 2003); Sean M. McDonough, *Christ as Creator: Origins of a New Testament Doctrine* (Oxford: Oxford University Press, 2009), 150–71; Schnabel, *Der Erste Brief des Paulus an die Korinther*, 427–33; Richard B. Hays, *First Corinthians*, Interpretation (Louisville; Westminster John Knox, 1997), 135; and, with minor differences, Alex T. Cheung, *Idol Food in Corinth: Jewish Background and Pauline Legacy*, JSNTSup 176 (Sheffield: Sheffield Academic, 1999). Bruce W. Winter (*Divine Honours for the Caesars: The First Christians' Responses* [Grand Rapids: Eerdmans, 2015], 209–25) thinks that eating meals in pagan temples in honor of the emperor was involved.

avoid idolatry, which eating in a temple would involve (10:1–22; perhaps also 8:7–13); (3) Christians can eat meat set before them in a pagan household (10:23–11:1).[90] In any case, the variety of views on this matter among competent scholars over many years warns us about dogmatism. And this variety may well echo the variety and complexity of opinions on these issues in Corinth. As Derek Newton reminds us, "There could be no easily attained consensus . . . on precisely what constituted *idolatry* and *worship* in such complicated contexts."[91]

This section again exhibits an A-B-A pattern (see also 5:1–13/6:1–11/6:12–20; 7:1–16/17–24/25–40), with chapter 9 providing basic background theology. These chapters are usually viewed as a section of the letter in their own right, although there are connections with what precedes and especially with what follows. Thus, Ciampa and Rosner think the topics of idolatry and the proper worship of God unite chapters 8–14, while Thiselton identifies concern for the "other" as a key issue in these same chapters.[92] Certainly the latter theme is important in these chapters, as it is indeed throughout the letter.[93] One of the root sins of the Corinthians, which is bearing fruit in many specific sins, is their focus on self at the expense of others. "Rights" are real, and valuable—but they are not ultimate.[94] Theologically, these chapters also provide insight into the pastoral challenge of translating theology into practice.

4.1 Knowledge and the "Other" (8:1–13)

"Food sacrificed to idols" (*eidōlothytos*) was a common phenomenon in the Greek world of Paul's day.[95] It was natural, then, that early Christians would have to deal with the issue. The Council in Jerusalem urged gentile converts to abstain from such food (Acts 15:29), and the risen Jesus appears to view eating such food as a sinful accommodation to the culture (Rev 2:14, 20). These texts appear to adopt a position that appears to be at odds with Paul's more "liberal" attitude in these chapters. However,

---

90. See esp. Ciampa and Rosner, *First Letter to the Corinthians*, 368–71. Making "food sacrificed to idols" the basic issue provides a much better basis for integrating Paul's *exemplum* about his own view toward "rights" in ch. 9 into the flow of argument.

91. Derek Newton, *Deity and Diet: The Dilemma of Sacrificial Food at Corinth*, JSNTSup 169 (Sheffield: Sheffield Academic Press, 1998), 384. See his helpful survey of views on the relationship of ch. 8 and 10:1–22 on pp. 387–90. He also suggests that the various attitudes among some Asian Christians to ancestor worship may provide something of a modern parallel.

92. Ciampa and Rosner, *First Letter to the Corinthians*, 367; Thiselton, *First Epistle to the Corinthians*, 607. James W. Thompson (*Moral Formation according to Paul: The Context and Coherence of Pauline Ethics* [Grand Rapids: Baker, 2011], 161–66) likewise thinks 8:1–11:1 and chs. 12–14 are outworkings of Paul's demand for love.

93. Recent interpreters have suggested another dimension to this self-regarding sin. They point out that it would have been particularly, indeed perhaps only, the rich who could have afforded to buy meat. The theological tension between "strong" and "weak," then, may be at least partially rooted in socio-economic tensions. See esp. Thiselton, *First Epistle to the Corinthians*, 608–11. Chow, further, thinks that eating idol food would have been tied to the imperial cult; the strong were eating idol food to secure their social standing (*Patronage and Power*, 141–57; see also Winter, *Divine Honours for the Caesars*, 196–225).

94. Dunn (*Beginning from Jerusalem*, 802) thinks these chapters are held together by a focus on "rights."

95. The usual word for something offered to a deity was *hierothyton*; Paul may use a different word to highlight the idolatry potentially involved (Garland, *1 Corinthians*, 364–65).

Paul himself qualifies the liberty he allows the Corinthians on this issue in a number of ways: context is everything with respect to these kinds of issues. Probably, then, the Council's decree was intended as a temporary measure to ease tensions between Jewish and gentile believers, and the churches of Revelation appear to be facing a situation in which growing pressure on believers to conform to the world of their day meant that eating idol food could no longer be distinguished from idolatry itself.

As he has done in 6:12–20 and 7:1–2, Paul advances his argument by means of a dialogue between the Corinthians and himself. They are vaunting themselves on their "knowledge" (8:1); Paul does not disparage knowledge as such, but he does warn that, by itself, knowledge can "puff up" (*physioō*, a key word in 1 Corinthians: see also 4:6, 18, 19; 5:2; 13:4). And, in what becomes a key contrast in the letter, Paul opposes that kind of knowledge to love. Only those who accompany their knowledge with love "know as they ought to know" (v. 2). In the rest of the chapter, Paul elaborates on these two key ideas, turning first to knowledge (vv. 4–8) and then to love (vv. 9–13).

With respect to knowledge, Paul agrees with what the Corinthians claim to "know": that "an idol is nothing at all in the world" and "there is no God but one" (vv. 4–6). See, for example, Deuteronomy 10:17: "For the LORD your God is God of gods and Lord of lords, the great God, mighty and awesome." Paul's elaboration of this latter point in verse 6 constitutes one of the most important christological claims in the New Testament. Here Paul divides the Jewish confession of the Shema (Deut 6:4) in half, with *theos* referring to the Father and *kyrios* (Lord) referring to Christ.[96] Paul thereby, as Richard Bauckham has noted, includes Jesus within the divine identity.[97] However, this "objective" truth about the one God is not the end of the story. As Paul notes, "not everyone possesses this knowledge" (v. 7); that is, some believers, while intellectually agreeing with these propositions, cannot divest themselves of the worldview with which they have lived all their lives—a worldview in which the gods who are labeled "idols" are very real indeed. They have head knowledge but not heart knowledge, and as a result their "conscience is weak."

While the word "love" does not appear in verses 9–13, love, or concern for the other, is the key point here. Believers have certain "rights" (or "authority" to do things: *exousia*), but those rights must be used (or not used) in light of how one's actions are affecting other believers. The spiritual vitality of a fellow Christian is far more important than the kind of food someone is eating. Paul's warning that exercising one's rights might "destroy" (the verb is *apollymi*) a "brother or sister" for whom Christ died (v. 11; see the close parallel in Rom 14:15) is a strong one: Paul uses this verb to

96. Gordon D. Fee, *Pauline Christology: An Exegetical-Theological Study* (Peabody, MA: Hendrickson, 2007), 90.

97. Richard Bauckham, *Jesus and the God of Israel: God*

Crucified and Other Studies on the New Testament's Christology of Divine Identity (Grand Rapids: Eerdmans, 2008), 212–15; cf. also Hurtado, *Destroyer of the Gods*, 71–72.

denote ultimate spiritual ruin (see, e.g., 1 Cor 1:18 and 15:18).[98] Those who argue that Paul allows for the possibility of a genuine believer being forever lost can find support in this verse. The problem, of course, is that other verses in Paul appear strongly to assert that true believers will infallibly be saved. This is not the place to reconcile these conflicting perspectives. But those who hold the latter view—so-called "eternal security" or "perseverance of the saints"—argue that Paul might hold the door open to repentance and restoration[99] or that he is exaggerating for rhetorical effect.[100] Paul's reference here to the believer "eating in an idol's temple" (v. 10) has led some to conclude that the basic issue in these chapters is eating in a temple.[101] However, it makes better sense of the chapters as a whole if we see this simply as an extreme example of the behavior that Paul is warning about.

4.2 On Giving Up "Rights" (9:1–27)

Paul's abrupt turn in 9:1 to an impassioned defense of his own apostolic ministry has led some scholars to view chapter 9 as an interpolation or at least as awkwardly placed. However, the chapter makes perfect sense in its context when we see Paul using the common Greco-Roman rhetorical device of "proof from example."[102] As an apostle, Paul has certain "rights" (*exousia*; vv. 4, 12, 18), but he has chosen often not to use those rights in order that he might commend the gospel to people. As Winter and others have noted, Paul probably is contrasting himself with the sophist teachers of his day, who were known for their unscrupulous tactics and personal presence.[103] Gorman points out that Paul is here imitating his Lord, who also did not use his "rights" for his own benefit but for the sake of others.[104]

Paul begins by asserting the "rights" he enjoys as an apostle (cf. v. 1, "Am I not an apostle?"; vv. 1–14). The polemical tone in which Paul asserts his apostleship and the privileges that go along with it has led some scholars to think that chapter 9 is basically a defense of Paul's apostleship in the face of Corinthian attacks on him.[105] However, while Paul does sound this note, it is the penultimate point he makes; the ultimate point is the way he views his apostleship and the rights that accompany it.[106] Paul's apostleship has been manifested in the results of his work among the Corinthians; "to them," at least, he is an apostle (vv. 1–2).[107] Nevertheless, criticisms of his apostleship compel him

---

98. Contra those who weaken the verb here to mean "is spiritually harmed" (e.g., F. W. Grosheide, *Commentary on the First Epistle to the Corinthians*, NICNT [Grand Rapids: Eerdmans, 1953], 197; F. F. Bruce, *I and II Corinthians*, NCB [Grand Rapids: Eerdmans, 1971], 82).

99. Schnabel, *Der Erste Brief des Paulus an die Korinther*, 465–66.

100. E.g., Schreiner, *1 Corinthians*, 177–78.

101. See esp. Fee, *First Epistle to the Corinthians*, 395–97.

102. See esp. Thiselton, *First Epistle to the Corinthians*, 662; Schrage, *Der erste Brief an die Korinther*, 2:278–81.

103. Winter, *Philo and Paul*, 164–72.

104. Gorman, *Apostle of the Crucified Lord*, 308.

105. See esp. Fee, *First Epistle to the Corinthians*, 434–35.

106. See esp. Thiselton, *First Epistle to the Corinthians*, 666; Garland, *1 Corinthians*, 396–400.

107. The dative *allois*, on this reading, is a dative of advantage. It could also mean "in the eyes of others" (see NLT: "Even

to mount a "defense" (*apologia*). This defense is the focus of verses 4–27. He begins by asserting the rights he enjoys along with the other apostles, such as enjoying provision of food and drink, bringing a wife along with him, and, in general, being supported (vv. 4–6). Paul illustrates with examples from everyday life (v. 7) and then caps off his argument with appeal to Scripture (vv. 8–10). Apostles have the right to be provided for while they work, in the same way that oxen are not to be muzzled while they tread the grain (Deut 25:4). As a general analogy, the appeal to this text makes perfect sense, but Paul confuses the matter by asking, "Is it about oxen that God is concerned?" (a question whose form in Greek [with *mē*] indicates Paul expects a negative answer). Is Paul then claiming that the law has no concern with oxen? Perhaps—and Paul would have some Jewish precedent for this view.[108] It is also possible, however, that Paul simply wants to stress the ultimate application of the principle assumed in this text to humans.[109] In the case of Paul and Barnabas, however (cf. v. 6), their spiritual labor among the Corinthians makes it appropriate for them to expect a return in the form of material benefits (v. 11). In verse 12, Paul anticipates his key point, asserting his genuine rights (the main point of vv. 4–11) but stressing that he has chosen not to use these rights for the sake of the gospel. This section ends with a final illustration to bolster the right Paul and other apostles have to support (vv. 13–14).

The basic thrust of verses 15–23 (perhaps extending through v. 27) is stated in the opening and closing sentence of the first paragraph: "But I have not used any of these rights" (v. 15a); "[I do] not make full use of my rights as a preacher of the gospel" (v. 18b; the point is anticipated in v. 12b). His purpose in not using his rights is that he might offer the gospel "free of charge" (v. 18). He does not want people to reject his message because they think the preacher—like the sophists of Paul's day—is preaching for his own financial gain. Nor does Paul want the Corinthians to think that he is covertly asking them to begin supporting him (v. 15). His reward in discharging his call to proclaim the gospel is the proclamation itself (vv. 16–18a).

In verses 19–23, Paul illustrates the central principle of giving up rights for the sake of the gospel with a matter central to Paul's ministry and teaching: the status of the Torah for the new covenant people of God. Paul's focus on gentile evangelism thrust him into the role of proponent for a gospel message that did not require submission to the law in order to be a faithful member of God's people. Paul therefore, while a Jew and therefore born "under the law," as a Christian preacher treats submission to the law as optional, to be determined on the basis of its usefulness in ministry. Therefore when

---

if others think I am not an apostle"; cf. Ciampa and Rosner, *First Letter to the Corinthians*, 399).

108. See, e.g., Philo: "For the law does not prescribe for unreasoning creatures, but for those who have mind and reason" (*Spec. Laws* 1.260). See esp. David Instone-Brewer, "1 Corinthians 9:9–11: A Literal Interpretation of 'Do Not Muzzle the Ox,'" *NTS* 38 (1992): 225–43. It is also possible to take v. 9a as a hesitant question (Ciampa and Rosner, *First Letter to the Corinthians*, 405).

109. As Hays notes, Deuteronomy 24–25 is all about provision for humans (*First Corinthians*, 151).

evangelizing Jews, Paul follows a Torah-faithful lifestyle (v. 20). But when evangelizing gentiles, he abandons that lifestyle, since he is no longer "under the law" (vv. 20, 21).[110] Nevertheless, Paul adds, he is "not free from God's law but [is] under Christ's law [*ennomos Christou*]." This passage is a window into Paul's general view of the law. On the one hand, the text reflects Paul's basic conviction that the turn of salvation history that occurs in the coming of Christ means that God's old-covenant law, the law of Moses, no longer has direct binding authority on God's people. Christians are no longer "under the law"—including Jewish Christians like Paul.[111] At the same time, Paul wants to make clear that Christians are not "lawless" (*anomos*), left without concrete direction for their lives. As new-covenant believers, they are under new-covenant law: the "law of Christ" (see Gal 6:2).[112] This new "law" is found in the teaching of Jesus and the apostles and exhibited in Christ's example of sacrificial love (see discussion of the law in Paul on pp. 614–22). Paul's subordination of his own lifestyle choices to the needs of the gospel illustrates the way the Corinthians should view their "rights" with respect to food offered to idols. This application is hinted at clearly in verse 22, where he claims that he "to the weak . . . became weak."

Paul concludes his "proof from example" by evoking athletic imagery to show how he works hard and sacrificially for others (vv. 24–27). The Corinthians are, therefore, like Paul, to "run in such a way as to get the prize" (v. 24b).

4.3 Warning about Idolatry (10:1–22)

Paul pursues his ministry with discipline and self-sacrificial love so that he "will not be disqualified for the prize" (9:27). In contrast to Paul are the people of Israel, who failed to attain the "prize" of the promised land (10:1–13). One of the main reasons they fell short was their idolatry (v. 7). The warning about idolatry is the central theme of verses 1–22: "Do not be idolaters" (v. 7); "flee from idolatry" (v. 14). Paul probably uses the wilderness generation of Israel as his warning example because it was a common source of instruction in early Christianity (see esp. Heb 3:7–4:12). Paul shared with early Christians the conviction that their own experience had a typological relationship to the Old Testament, a point Paul makes twice in this section: "Now these things occurred as examples [*typoi*]" (v. 6); "These things happened to them as examples

---

110. I take "Jews" and "those under the law" to be descriptions of the same group of people (for Jews as those "under/in the law" see, e.g., Rom 2:12; 3:19; Fee, *First Epistle to the Corinthians*, 473). Ciampa and Rosner think "those under the law" might include proselytes along with Jews (*First Letter to the Corinthians*, 426).

111. Contra contemporary movements such as the "Paul within Judaism" school, which argues that Paul and Jewish Christians generally remain bound to Torah (e.g., Mark D. Nanos

and Magnus Zetterholm, eds., *Paul within Judaism: Restoring the First-Century Context to the Apostle* [Minneapolis: Fortress, 2015]). For an interpretation of this text along these lines, see esp. David J. Rudolph, *A Jew to the Jews: Jewish Contours of Pauline Flexibility in 1 Corinthians 9.19–23*, WUNT 2/304 (Tübingen: Mohr Siebeck, 2011), 90–173.

112. This phrase in Galatians is quite debated. For a brief discussion and defense of my own view, see pp. 82–83.

[*typikōs*, "in a typological way"] and were written down as warnings for us, on whom the culmination of the ages has come" (v. 11). The Greek terms here give us our vocabulary of "typology," which refers to the way God had so orchestrated Old Testament salvation history that it could provide encouragement, warnings, and anticipations of the "fullness of time" in which the church lived.[113]

The wilderness generation serves as a particularly appropriate warning example for the Corinthians because the Corinthians share with the Israelites particularly clear evidence of God's working in their midst. Paul accentuates this parallel by describing the experiences of Israel with the language of Christian sacraments. They underwent a "baptism," when Moses brought them through the water of the Red Sea (v. 2); and they had their own "Lord's Supper," when they ate spiritual food (manna) and drank from "the spiritual rock that accompanied them (vv. 3–4). "All" the Israelites[114] enjoyed these gracious gifts from God; yet "God was not pleased with most of them," evident in the death of most of that generation before the promised land was entered (v. 5). God's judgment fell on "some of them" because they were idolaters (v. 7), committed sexual immorality (v. 8), tested Christ (v. 9), and grumbled (v. 10).[115] To illustrate Israel's idolatry, Paul cites Exodus 32:6 in verse 7, a text that suggests the people were indulging in pagan meals and sexual sin; to illustrate their sexual immorality, he refers to Numbers 25:1–9 in verse 8 (see Num 26:62 for the number 23,000). The reference to being killed by snakes makes clear the "testing" Paul has in view is the incident in Numbers 21:4–7 (cf. Ps 78:18). The "grumbling" occurs so often during that period of Israel's history that Paul is probably referring to the general phenomenon. Since this grumbling was often against Israel's leaders, it is possible that here again Paul reflects the Corinthians' tendency to question his authority (see 9:1–3).[116] One of the startling elements in this passage is Paul's reading "Christ" into Israel's story: he was the rock that accompanied Israel (v. 4); he was the one the Israelites "tested" (v. 9).[117] This, of course, serves Paul's rhetorical purpose by lining up Israel's experience with that of the Corinthians. But it also reflects the degree to which Paul (and other early Christians) saw the preexistent Christ at work in Israel's history.[118]

---

113. The language of this text strongly suggests that typology has a prospective focus: God caused these events to happen so that they could serve to instruct the people of God (see esp. Richard M. Davidson, *Typology in Scripture: A Study of Hermeneutical Typos Structures*, Andrews University Seminary Doctoral Dissertation Series [Berrien Springs, MI: Andrews University Press, 1981]).

114. "All" (*pantes*) reverberates through these verses: vv. 1 [twice], 2, 3, 4.

115. "Some of them" (*tines autōn*) acts as a narrative marker in vv. 7–10 as "all of them" does in vv. 1–4 (see vv. 7, 8, 9, 10; see Ciampa and Rosner, *First Letter to the Corinthians*, 455).

116. Fee, *First Epistle to the Corinthians*, 505–6.

117. It is possible, however, that Paul means here "we should not test Christ, as some of them tested the Lord" (Hays, *First Corinthians*, 165).

118. On the "rock that accompanied" the Israelites, see esp. Peter D. Spychalla, "The Use of the Old Testament in 1 Corinthians 10:4: Paul's Combining of the Water-from-Rock and YHWH-as-Rock Motifs" (PhD diss., Wheaton College, 2008).

The sad history of the wilderness generation of Israel, then, should warn the Corinthians about placing false confidence in the gracious work of God among them, as if that grace did not demand a response of faithfulness.[119] The Corinthians need to avoid the example of the Israelites by avoiding any taint of idolatry (v. 12). And they can do so because God is working to help them overcome the temptations (NIV; or "trials" [NET]—the Gk. *peirasmos/peirazō* can mean either) of their pagan environment (v. 13).[120]

As I suggested in the introduction to 8:1–11:1, the issue Paul addresses in 10:1–22 is whether Christians can eat meals in idol temples. The fact that these temples were the setting for many civic and social events made the question a pressing one. Paul is open to Christians eating marketplace meat even if it has been associated with idols; he is flat out opposed to Christians eating in a pagan temple (v. 14). Reminding the Corinthians again of the example of the Israelites (v. 18),[121] he argues that eating meals in an idol temple would be to be "participants with demons" (v. 20).[122] While Paul therefore agrees with the Corinthians that "an idol is nothing at all in the world"—in the sense that they are not gods or "lords" (8:4)—an idol may be a locus of evil spiritual influence. Clearly, Christians should avoid any contact with such influences—they "cannot have a part in both the Lord's table and the table of demons" (v. 21). Following up the allusion to the Lord's Supper in verses 3–4, Paul explicitly introduces Christians' participation in the sacrament as a point of argument in verses 16–17, 21. In the context of the Supper, believers participate in the blood and body of Christ—that is, they benefit from his sacrificial death on their behalf. This "participation" (*koinōnia*) runs both vertically (believers and Christ) and horizontally (believers with one another);[123] hence, in an anticipation of the argument of 11:17–32, Paul mentions this last point in verse 17. Paul ends his brief exhortation to avoid temple meals with two rhetorical questions. The first—"Are we trying to arouse the Lord's jealousy?"—alludes to Deuteronomy 32:21a: "They [Israelites] made me jealous by what is no god / and angered me with their worthless idols." The second—"Are we stronger than he?"—is a sarcastic rebuke to those among the Corinthians who were probably calling themselves, in contrast to the "weak" (8:7, 9, 11, 12; cf. 9:22), "the strong": "Do you 'strong' think you can eat idol meals with impunity—when the Lord himself warns about them?"

---

119. The theological implications of the warning "be careful that you don't fall!" (v. 12) are debated; does this imply that genuine believers can lose their salvation?

120. For the translation "temptation"/"tempt," see, e.g., Thiselton, *First Epistle to the Corinthians*, 747; Ciampa and Rosner, *First Letter to the Corinthians*, 467–68.

121. The NIV's "people of Israel" translates *ton Israēl kata sarka*, which could be rendered "the Israel according to the

flesh"—possibly suggesting another "Israel," one "according to the Spirit" (see Gal 4:26; 6:16; Rom 9:6[?]).

122. Paul's concern about eating in temples may also be motivated by the frequent sexual excesses associated with temple meals (note the reference to the Israelites' "sexual immorality" in v. 8; Witherington, *Conflict and Community in Corinth*, 191–95).

123. Fee, *First Epistle to the Corinthians*, 514; Thiselton, *First Epistle to the Corinthians*, 761–62.

4.4 Food Sacrificed to Idols Again (10:23–11:1)

Paul closes off this section of the letter by returning to where he began, with the issue of Christians eating food sacrificed to idols.[124] He reiterates his opinion that a believer can "eat anything sold in the meat market without raising questions of conscience" (v. 25). Yet before he gives this opinion, he reminds the Corinthians that the exercise of this "right" must be informed by what is "constructive" (what "builds up" [*oikodomeō*]) and by consideration of the good of others (vv. 23–24). Paul then applies this advice to a specific situation: a believer invited to a meal in a pagan's home. The believer again has liberty—"eat whatever is put before you" (v. 27; cf. v. 30)—but should refrain if someone raises the issue (v. 28). Matters of food and drink are, Paul concludes, secondary: glorifying God (v. 31) and the spiritual state of others (v. 32) is primary.

5 THE NEW IDENTITY AND GENDER RELATIONSHIPS (11:2–16)

The issue Paul now takes up is clear enough: women were inappropriately "uncovering" their heads in the worship service (vv. 5–6, 10, 13–15).[125] However, just what this uncovering involves is unclear: Were the women discarding the veil,[126] or were they no longer "putting up" their hair on the top of their heads?[127] The former may be the more likely scenario, but in either case the problem appears to be that Corinthian women were flaunting cultural expectations with respect to the appropriate dress for respectable wives. Evidence from Roman Corinth and the larger Roman world of that time indicates that women kept their heads covered with some kind of clothing in public as a signal that they were respectable. Flouting such conventions would have brought shame on their husbands and families.[128] Bruce Winter has argued that this spirit of independence tied into a kind of sexual revolution going on in Paul's day.[129]

---

124. Thiselton, *First Epistle to the Corinthians*, 782. Fee and Garland, however, think a new issue is raised here (marketplace meat for Fee [*First Epistle to the Corinthians*, 525–26]; meat of unknown origin for Garland [*1 Corinthians*, 489–90]).

125. Garland (*1 Corinthians*, 505–7) argues convincingly that the focus of the passage is on women, not men and women equally. See also Fitzmyer, *First Corinthians*, 405–6; contra Philip B. Payne, *Man and Woman, One in Christ: An Exegetical and Theological Study of Paul's Letters* (Grand Rapids: Zondervan, 2009), 115–16.

126. Winter, *After Paul Left Corinth*, 126–41; Fee, *First Epistle to the Corinthians*, 547–50. Craig S. Keener (*Paul, Women and Wives: Marriage and Women's Ministry in the Letters of Paul* [Peabody, MA: Hendrickson, 1992], 22–31) suggests that social status may here again also play a role: it would perhaps have been the wealthier women who were most emboldened to flaunt normal style.

127. James B. Hurley, *Man and Woman in Biblical Perspective* (Grand Rapids: Zondervan, 1981), 168–71; Hays, *First Corinthians*, 185–86; Schrage, *Der erste Brief an die Korinther*, 3:492–93.

128. See esp. Thiselton, *First Epistle to the Corinthians*, 823–26, quoting Aline Rousselle, "Body Politics in Ancient Rome," in *From Ancient Goddesses to Christian Saints*, ed. Pauline Schmitt Pantel, vol. 1 of *A History of Women in the West*, ed. Georges Duby and Michelle Perrot (Cambridge: Harvard University Press, 1992), 296–337; Schnabel, *Der Erste Brief des Paulus an die Korinther*, 589–93.

129. Winter, *After Paul Left Corinth*, 127–30. Cynthia Long Westfall, on the other hand, argues that it was the men who were insisting that the women go unveiled (*Paul and Gender: Reclaiming the Apostle's Vision for Men and Women in Christ* [Grand Rapids: Baker, 2016], 32–37).

It is also likely, however, that this tendency toward independence reflects the overrealized eschatology that we have seen lying behind several of the Corinthians' sinful activities.[130] Indeed, it is possible that with respect to this issue, as others in this letter, the Corinthians were basing their conduct on their own reading of Paul's teaching (e.g., Gal 3:28: "There is neither Jew nor Gentile, neither slave nor free, nor is there male and female, for you are all one in Christ Jesus").

How this passage fits into the development of the letter is unclear. A coherent line of argument is again elusive, as the sequence of topics appears to be dictated by the issues that Paul has heard about and that the Corinthians have written about.[131] However, two lines of continuity, one backward and one forward, can be discerned. First, the women whom Paul rebukes here were probably basing their behavior on their new spiritual status—taking a false or extreme view of what it means to live as Spirit-filled people in the new age of redemption. Similar attitudes probably lie to some extent behind the issues in 5:1–13; 6:12–20; ch. 7; 8:1–11:1. Second, the setting for the behavior Paul criticizes is the worship service (v. 5), loosely associating this passage with the abuses of the Lord's Supper (11:17–34) and the use of gifts (chs. 12–14).[132]

Paul deploys a theology of gender relationships in response to this issue. As most translations recognize, the Greek binary pair that is at the heart of this passage, *gynē* and *anēr*, probably refer most of the time to "woman" and "man" rather than "wife" and "husband."[133] The very general scope of verse 3, where the words are introduced, suggests this. However, the presenting problem Paul deals with probably relates to the marital relationship. The ESV decision to use "wife"/"wives" in verses 5, 6, and 10 is probably justified.[134]

Paul's response falls into three stages. The basic thrust of Paul's argument comes in verses 3–6, where he urges women (wives?) to keep their heads covered in worship because of the relationship in which they stand to men (their husbands?). Paul explores this relationship further in verses 7–12, where he stresses the interdependence of husband and wife. Finally, in verses 13–15, Paul appeals to nature to make his point. The text is framed by implicit (v. 2) and explicit (v. 16) appeals to maintain common early Christian traditional teaching about these matters.

Verses 3–6 are held together by the thematic word "head" (*kephalē*). In verses 4–6, the word refers simply to the physical head. In verse 3, however, it obviously has metaphorical significance, being used to characterize the relationship of men to God, women

---

130. Fee, *First Epistle to the Corinthians*, 549–50; Ciampa and Rosner, *First Letter to the Corinthians*, 501–2.

131. It is difficult to know whether the Corinthians have raised this issue in their letter (as Fee, *First Epistle to the Corinthians*, 552, thinks) or whether Paul has heard about this behavior from one of his other sources. But the lack of the typical introductory phrase ("now concerning") might suggest the latter.

132. Allo, *Saint Paul*, 253; Schrage, *Der erste Brief an die Korinther*, 3:487.

133. As Thiselton notes, this is also the view of most commentators (*First Epistle to the Corinthians*, 822). However, Garland, *1 Corinthians*, 514, and Ciampa and Rosner, *First Letter to the Corinthians*, 508, think the focus is on wives and husbands.

134. See, e.g., Gardner, *1 Corinthians*, 480.

to men, and Christ to God. The difficulty is to find an extant metaphorical sense that can "fit" these varied relationships. At one stage of the discussion, two opposing options were popular: "source" or "authority over."[135] Most interpreters today are inclined to steer something of a middle course. The ancients understandably viewed the physical "head" as the most prominent part of the body and attributed to it controlling and directing power over the body. As a metaphor, then, "head" can connote "prominence," "preeminence." However, this preeminence is expressed at times in having control or authority, and it is difficult in this passage to avoid connotations of "authority over" in the way "head" is used.[136] Here, then, Paul's basic point is that the man (or the husband) has a preeminence with respect to the woman (or his wife) that is similar (though of course not identical) to the relationship of Christ to a man and of God to Christ.[137] In first-century Roman society, men who covered their heads with their togas as they worshiped were claiming a kind of elite status. In Christian worship, therefore, men who covered their (physical) heads were, in effect, dishonoring their (metaphorical) head, Christ (v. 4). Similarly, women who failed to cover their (physical) heads when they prayed and prophesied in public worship were dishonoring their (metaphorical) heads, their husbands (v. 5).[138] They were, in effect, proclaiming their independence from their husbands.

In verses 7–11, Paul further supports his command that women should not be "uncovered" in the worship service. But the focus shifts to the interrelatedness of men and women. Paul's claim that man is the "image and glory of God" does not deny that both men and women are created in God's image (Gen 1:26–28). Paul is using the language in a limited sense to emphasize that wives bring glory to their husbands by their comportment in public. This relationship between husband and wife is manifested

---

135. These options were thoroughly explored in the back-and-forth between Wayne A. Grudem and Richard Cervin (Grudem, "Does Κεφαλή Mean 'Source' or 'Authority Over' in Greek Literature? A Survey of 2,336 Examples," *TrinJ* 6 [1985]: 38–59; Cervin, "Does Κεφαλή Mean 'Source' or 'Authority Over' in Greek Literature? A Rebuttal," *TrinJ* 10 [1989]: 85–112; Grudem, "The Meaning of Κεφαλή ('Head'): A Response to Recent Studies," *TrinJ* 11 [1990]: 3–72). In addition, see Grudem's response to further studies in "The Meaning of Κεφαλή ('Head'): An Evaluation of New Evidence, Real and Alleged," *JETS* 44 (2001): 25–65. For the metaphorical sense of "source," see esp. Payne, *Man and Woman*, 117–37; and also Westfall, *Paul and Gender*, 38–40.

136. See esp. Andrew C. Perriman, "The Head of a Woman: The Meaning of Κεφαλή in 1 Cor 11:3," *JTS* 45 (1994): 602–22; and also Thiselton, *First Epistle to the Corinthians*, 812–22; Garland, *1 Corinthians*, 514–16; Schreiner, *1 Corinthians*, 222–24. As Gardner notes (*1 Corinthians*, 480–85), the notion of "authority" is hard to separate from the notion of "preeminence." The LXX use of *kephalē* to translate *rosh* in the sense "leader," "ruler" has

probably also influenced Paul (cf. Judg 11:11: "So Jephthah went with the elders of Gilead, and the people made him head [*rosh*; *kephalē*] and commander [*archēgon*] over them").

137. The claim that "the head of Christ is God" has sparked a debate over whether this language (interpreted in terms of "subordination") applies to the eternal relations with the Trinity or only to the "economic" Trinity. The former view, often labelled "eternal functional subordination," is defended as both biblical and fully orthodox by some but criticized as being neither by others (see, e.g., the selection of essays in Dennis W. Jowers and H. Wayne House, eds., *The New Evangelical Subordinationism? Perspectives on the Equality of God the Father and God the Son* [Eugene, OR: Pickwick, 2012]). While I am not well qualified to adjudicate this issue, I am slightly inclined to think "eternal functional subordination" creates some problems for orthodox Trinitarian theology (see, e.g., Michael F. Bird and Scott Harrower, eds., *Trinity without Hierarchy: Reclaiming Nicene Orthodoxy in Evangelical Theology* [Grand Rapids: Kregel, 2018]).

138. E.g., Garland, *1 Corinthians*, 520–21.

in the sequence of creation (vv. 8–9). It is, then, "for this reason that a woman ought to have authority [*exousian*] over [or "on," *epi*] her own head because of the angels" (v. 10). The interpretation of this verse is contested. Some understand the authority in a passive sense: the woman's covering symbolizes her authority under her husband.[139] However, the Greek more likely has an active sense, referring to her own authority. The reference, then, might be to the covering of the head as a symbol of the woman's right to participate publicly in the worship ("pray and prophesy") of the church.[140] But it might be more likely that the phrase means that the woman should maintain "power" or "control" over her own head by covering it and not exposing it, herself, and her family to shame.[141] "Because of the angels" is equally unclear. Of the several options, two are the most likely, with the second perhaps preferable. (1) Granted the early Jewish tradition based on Genesis 6 about evil angels lusting after "the daughters of men," it may mean that the women's dress is tempting those angels.[142] (2) Early Jewish sources also speak of angels present during worship. Perhaps Paul is concerned that these holy angels, often viewed as guardians of the created order, would be offended by the women's flouting of convention.[143] The paragraph ends with explicit reference to the interdependence of men and women "in the Lord" (vv. 11–12).

Paul concludes with reference to convention—what is "proper" (v. 13); "nature" (vv. 14–15)—and to general Christian practice (v. 16).

6 The New Identity and the New Community: Celebrating the Lord's Supper (11:17–34)

Paul's sources have informed him (v. 18) of another manifestation of the Corinthians' self-focus: selfishness and factionalism in celebrating the Lord's Supper. The NIV, along with most other major English translations, suggests that the problem may have been that some believers were "go[ing] ahead with your own private suppers" (v. 21). This translation suggests the problem in Corinth was that some were eating before others, and this reading of the passage is reinforced if the verb *ekdechomai* in verse 33 means "to wait for" (e.g., ESV and most versions). However, the translation of both these words is debated, some arguing that the former means simply "consume" and the latter "receive." On this reading, there is no evidence that the problem in Corinth was that some were eating *before* others; the problem, rather, was that some were eating their own "private"

139. E.g., Allo, *Saint Paul*, 263–67. See NJB: "This is why it is right for a woman to wear on her head a sign of the authority over her."

140. See esp. Morna D. Hooker, "Authority on Her Head: An Examination of 1 Corinthians 11.10," *NTS* 10 (1963–1964): 410–16.

141. Fee, *First Epistle to the Corinthians*, 574–76; Schrage,

Der erste Brief an die Korinther, 2:513; Garland, *1 Corinthians*, 524–26; Schnabel, *Der Erste Brief des Paulus an die Korinther*, 610.

142. Tertullian, *The Veiling of Virgins* 7.

143. This view was held by Augustine (*The Trinity* 12.7.10); and see, e.g., Thiselton, *First Epistle to the Corinthians*, 839–41; Fitzmyer, *First Corinthians*, 418.

meals (v. 21), thereby violating the unity of the body of Christ, the church, which was so integral to the meaning of the body of Christ, his own physical body. I think there is much to be said for the view that sees the essential problem to be a division between rich and poor. Paul explicitly criticizes the Corinthians' factionalism here again (vv. 18–19), and his accusation that the Corinthians were "humiliating those who have nothing" (v. 22) makes clear that these divisions were drawn along socioeconomic lines. These divisions were probably being manifested in the very space where the meal was celebrated. We can surmise that the wealthier Christians were going ahead with their own meals in a special dining room (the "triclinium") while others, less wealthy and lower on the social scale, had to make do with whatever was offered in the larger public room (the "atrium").[144] However, I am not convinced that the lexical data allow us to dispose entirely with the problem of temporal priority. The key verbs in verses 21 and 33 probably have some temporal force.[145] Therefore a kind of combination view seems best: wealthier Corinthians were eating their own private meals before less well-to-do believers arrived to eat their own meals, consisting of less food of lower quality and consumed in a more modest space. In any case, this behavior is yet another violation of regard for the "other" that is so central a theme in the letter.[146]

The passage begins (vv. 17–22) and ends (vv. 27–34) with stinging rebukes of the Corinthians' selfish and arrogant behavior. At its center, Paul cites the well-known tradition of the words of institution that are recited at the celebration of the Lord's Supper (vv. 23–26).[147]

The "coming together" (*synerchomai*; vv. 17, 18, 20) of the Christians in such circumstances does "more harm than good" (v. 17) and calls into question any benefit they might have from their celebration (v. 20). Indeed, Paul goes so far as to conclude that they are not eating "the Lord's Supper" (*kyriakon deipnon*) when they gather; rather, they are turning a community meal whose host is ultimately Christ himself into their "own private suppers" (vv. 20–21). When we read this text in the light of the argument of 10:1–13, we may also surmise that the Corinthians may have had a kind of "magical" view of the sacraments, as if they would confer spiritual benefit without regard to the attitude of the celebrant. We learn very little from this passage about Paul's "theology" of the Lord's Supper. As is the case with baptism also (cf. Rom 6:3–5),

---

144. See esp. Gerd Theissen, *The Social Setting of Pauline Christianity: Essays on Corinth* (Philadelphia: Fortress, 1982), 145–74; Bruce W. Winter, "The Lord's Supper at Corinth: An Alternative Reconstruction," *RTR* 37 (1978): 73–82; Garland, *1 Corinthians*, 540–41; Gardner, *1 Corinthians*, 506–8. Talbert (*Reading Corinthians*, 75) notes that Juvenal mentions the practice of providing different levels of food to different people, according to their social standing. I note that some scholars are not convinced that we have adequate evidence for the physical space in homes in Roman Corinth (see, e.g., Fitzmyer, *First Corinthians*, 428).

145. The verb *prolambanō* (v. 21) retains a temporal sense in its only other equivalent context (Mark 14:8), while the verb *ekdechomai* usually has a temporal sense also ("wait for," "expect"; see Acts 17:16; 1 Cor 16:11; Heb 10:13; 11:10; Jas 5:7). See, e.g., Fitzmyer, *First Corinthians*, 434–35.

146. Talbert (*Reading Corinthians*, 74) quotes Plutarch: "Where each guest has his own private portion, fellowship perishes" (*Quaest. conv.* 644C).

147. See Fee, *First Epistle to the Corinthians*, 588–89, for this outline.

Paul assumes that the sacraments are being observed in his churches, but he does not engage in theologizing about them (see pp. 588–92). What he does say here, however, makes clear that any benefits arising from the celebration of the Supper depend on the attitude of the person who takes part.

In responding, Paul begins by reminding the Corinthians of the "words of institution," passed down to Paul from the Lord himself and, in turn, from Paul to them (v. 23a). The wording is similar to what we find in our first three Gospels, although Paul's version is closer to Luke's than to Matthew's and Mark's.[148] The word over the bread—"this is my body"—probably has sacrificial connotations; the word over the cup—"this cup is the new covenant in my blood"—certainly does. This latter word also alludes to the initial covenant-establishing ritual (see Exod 24:8) as well as to the new-covenant prophecy of Jeremiah 31:31–34.[149] At the same time, the sacrificial element in the words was probably still associated with Passover, the context in which Jesus inaugurated the meal. Perhaps particularly significant for Paul's application is the emphasis on what is done in the meal as being "in remembrance of me" (vv. 24, 25). As Thiselton notes, "Paul's point" is "that such *remembrance* constitutes a self-involving *proclamation of Christ's death* through a life and a lifestyle which derives from understanding our identity as Christians in terms of sharing the identity of Christ who is *for* the 'other.'"[150]

Paul's rebuke of the Corinthians' selfish conduct (vv. 27–32) takes up the language of the Supper. His point in general is that the efficacy of the Supper is tied to the attitude and behavior of the believer who celebrates. Eating an elaborate meal before others and/or while others go without is to sin against the Lord's body and blood, who is "present" in some form in the elements of the Supper.[151] Each believer needs to "examine" or "test" (*dokimazō*) themselves (v. 28). Paul's exhortation here can certainly include a degree of introspection, as it is often interpreted. But what Paul is encouraging is less "looking within" than "looking around"—assessing our conduct toward fellow believers.[152] The precise balance here depends partly on the meaning of "discerning the body" in verse 29. This might refer to the need to (1) recognize the significance of Christ's own body, given for us in death and "remembered" in the Supper; or (2) recognize the body of the church by acting appropriately toward its members.[153] The former may be more

---

148. See, in general, Joachim Jeremias, *The Eucharistic Words of Jesus* (London: SCM, 1966), 106–203.

149. Moo, *Old Testament in the Gospel Passion Narratives*, 301–10.

150. Thiselton, *First Epistle to the Corinthians*, 880 (emphasis original; two bold words changed to italics).

151. While the precise scenario is unclear (Otfried Hofius, "The Lord's Supper and the Lord's Supper Tradition: Reflections on 1 Cor 11:23b–25," in *One Loaf, One Cup: Ecumenical Studies*

of *1 Cor 11 and Other Eucharistic Texts*, ed. Ben F. Meyer [Macon: Mercer University Press, 1988], 75–115), Paul appears to assume that a regular meal was consumed in the context of the eucharistic celebration.

152. Fee, *First Epistle to the Corinthians*, 620–22.

153. A less popular option is that Paul is urging the Corinthians to be cognizant of the ways in which the Supper "differs" or "is distinguished" (*diakrinō*) from other meals (e.g., Morris, *Corinthians*, 164).

likely in light of the rough parallel in verse 27, where "body and blood of the Lord" is used. Those who are properly "discerning [*diakrinō*] the body" or who are "discerning" (*diakrinō*) about themselves in their relation to fellow believers (v. 31) will not come under judgment—a judgment signaled by the illness and even death of some in the community (v. 30). As he does throughout biblical history, God uses physical distress to manifest his judgment over his people's sinful conduct. These physical manifestations of judgment are, in fact, the Lord's discipline (*paideuō*, v. 32), intended to wake God's people up so that they will avoid final judgment (see, perhaps, also 5:5).

Returning to a key word from the beginning of the passage, Paul concludes by urging that the Corinthians' "coming together" (*synerchomai*) should be marked by unity in eating so that this judgment might be avoided (vv. 33–34).[154]

7 THE NEW IDENTITY AND THE NEW COMMUNITY: ONE SPIRIT, ONE BODY, MANY GIFTS (12:1–14:40)

This next topic, apparently raised by the Corinthians themselves ("now about"; *peri de* [12:1]) and treated at length in chapters 12–14, has much in common with what has come before. On the one hand, the general theme and/or setting of the worship service joins these chapters with both 11:2–16 and 11:17–34. More important, on the other hand, is the underlying theme of a focus on the self at the expense of others. The Corinthians were eating idol food without concern for its effect on other believers; some of the women were "liberating themselves" in worship at the expense of their husbands; some were going ahead and eating their own meals while others went without; and now we find that the Corinthians were focusing on gifts that elevated themselves rather than on those that build up the community.[155] The persistence of this problem in the Corinthian church explains why the famous "love chapter" comes here in this letter: it is love that will lead to the "other regard" that will fix many of the Corinthians' problems. These three chapters again display an A-B-A order, with the poetic encomium on love (ch. 13) sandwiched between extensive exhortations about the use of gifts in the community (chs. 12 and 14).

These chapters reveal Paul's "charismatic"-oriented view of church ministry—ministry guided by and empowered by "charisms" (Gk. *charisma*, "gift"—12:4, 9, 28, 30, 31). The Spirit gives these gifts as "he determines" (v. 11); they are "manifestations" of the Spirit, or "spiritual gifts" (v. 7; cf. v. 1 NIV [and below]). Paul never defines what he means by "spiritual gift," although he gives examples of at least fourteen

---

154. The NIV translates as if it is simply "eating together" that Paul is urging (v. 33; see Fee, *First Epistle to the Corinthians*, 628). But the verb Paul uses here (*ekdechomai*) more likely means "wait" (e.g., ESV; NLT; and see above). Still, the basic point is the same: the Corinthians should "eat together" when they "come together."

155. See esp. Thiselton, *First Epistle to the Corinthians*, 900. Ciampa and Rosner emphasize the continuity in the worship theme (*First Letter to the Corinthians*, 560).

gifts in chapter 12 (vv. 8–10; 28–29). In chapter 14, he concentrates on two of them, prophecy and tongues, recommending the former over the latter because prophecy more effectively builds up the church. Paul refers to the gift of tongues only in these chapters, and the exact nature of the gift is unclear. The Greek *glōssa* can refer simply to "language," and some think the gift here, as is probably the case in Acts (see Acts 2:3–4, 11), is a Spirit-given ability to speak in a known human language.[156] But 14:2 rather implies a "private" language: language-like utterances prompted by the Spirit and comprehensible only via a Spirit-given interpretation.[157] Such ecstatic speech had parallels in the Hellenistic world, and reference to "tongues . . . of angels" in 13:1 might suggest that the Corinthians valued tongues as a heavenly language, available to them because they now live in the eschatological age (perhaps "overrealized eschatology" again).[158] In any case, the Corinthians viewed this gift as one that gave them status in the community.[159] Paul mentions the New Testament gift of prophecy (or "prophet") more often (Eph 4:11; 2 Thess 2:2; 1 Tim 4:14; possibly Eph 2:20 and 3:5) but offers no definition. The gift may encompass a wide range of speaking ministries, including, for example, preaching.[160] However, the alternation with "revelation" in 1 Corinthians 14:26, 30 may suggest that prophecy involves a more immediate and spontaneous insight given by God and communicated to believers.[161]

Paul's focus on gifts here stands in some contrast to the instructions about church "offices" and procedures in the Pastoral Epistles. A difference in focus is indeed obvious; but the two need not be contradictory. Those "appointed" to particular positions of ministry leadership will (ideally) be those who manifest in the community particular gifts given by the Spirit (see pp. 592–602).

Paul's perspective on the gifts is driven by his view of the church. These chapters, and especially chapter 12, therefore contribute significantly to Paul's ecclesiology, as he uses the imagery of the "body" to stress the diversity within unity of the church (see pp. 581–87).

7.1 The Unity and Diversity of the Body (12:1–31)

Again citing the Corinthians' letter ("now about"), Paul introduces the next topic with the word *pneumatikōn*. This word might refer to "spiritual people" (masc.) or, more

---

156. E.g., Max Turner, *The Holy Spirit and Spiritual Gifts: Then and Now* (Carlisle: Paternoster, 1996), 221–39. See further pp. 595–97.

157. So most interpreters. See, e.g., Christopher Forbes, *Prophecy and Inspired Speech in Early Christianity and Its Hellenistic Environment*, WUNT 2/75 (Tübingen: Mohr Siebeck, 1995), 56–65. On the variety of interpretations of the gift of tongues, see Vern S. Poythress, "The Nature of Corinthian Glossolalia: Possible Options," *WTJ* 40 (1977): 130–36.

158. Fee, *First Epistle to the Corinthians*, 699; Garland, *1 Corinthians*, 584–87.

159. Some interpreters find here again evidence of social/economic division, it being alleged that ecstatic speech was especially associated with the upper classes (Dale B. Martin, *The Corinthian Body* [New Haven: Yale University Press, 1999], 87–92).

160. E.g., Thiselton, *First Epistle to the Corinthians*, 964; Ciampa and Rosner, *First Letter to the Corinthians*, 581. The latter suggest that "prophecy" is more "situation-focused" than preaching.

161. See comments on 14:26 and also pp. 594–96.

likely, to "spiritual things" (neut.)—that is, as the context will make clear, spiritual gifts (so most English translations). In verses 2–3, Paul makes an important preliminary point: the Spirit of God does not produce mindless ecstatic utterances but speech consistent with Christian truth.

The rest of the chapter begins to address the Corinthian imbalance in assessing spiritual gifts by stressing the necessary and salutary diversity of gifts the Spirit has given within the single body of Christ. Verses 4–11 introduce this argument by contrasting the variety of gifts with the single giver: the "same Spirit" distributes them (v. 4); they honor the "same Lord" (v. 5); in them all the "same God" is at work (v. 6). Paul elaborates this basic point in verses 7–11, illustrating the variety of gifts by listing nine of them. The repeated phrase, picked up from verses 4–6, makes the basic point: it is the "same Spirit" who distributes all the gifts.

The second stage of the "diversity within unity" argument introduces and elaborates the simile/metaphor of the body. The Spirit is again the agent who creates and sustains the unity of the body: "We were all baptized by one Spirit so as to form one body—whether Jews or Gentiles, slave or free—and we were all given the one Spirit to drink" (v. 13). In the NIV, the Spirit in the first part of the verse is the agent active in water baptism.[162] However, it is also possible that the Spirit is the "substance" in which a person is immersed (the issue is whether the Gk. preposition *en* is instrumental—*by* one Spirit—or local—*in* one Spirit).[163] The former is probably slightly more likely. In either case, the "one Spirit" creates "one body," a body with many parts (vv. 12, 14). This diversity within a single body is elaborated with respect to an analogy with the physical body in verses 15–26.

The first part of this passage lays the groundwork for Paul's application by elaborating the theme "many parts," "one body" (vv. 15–20; cf. v. 20). The focus shifts in verses 21–26 to the relative merits of each body part, the point being that even "weaker" or less presentable body parts are essential to the healthy functioning of the body. With obvious application to the Corinthians' bragging about certain gifts, Paul concludes that the parts of the body "should have equal concern for each other" (v. 25). Thiselton appropriately comments, "Those whom the church likes to put 'on display' as our 'best' people (whether because of their supposed wisdom and knowledge, or more visible gifts of the Spirit such as tongues or 'mighty works') are far from being the essence of the church."[164]

---

162. For this interpretation, see, e.g., Thiselton, *First Epistle to the Corinthians*, 997; G. R. Beasley-Murray, *Baptism in the New Testament* (Grand Rapids: Eerdmans, 1962), 167–71; Volker Rabens, *The Holy Spirit and Ethics in Paul: Transformation and Empowering for Religious-Ethical Life*, WUNT 2/283 (Tübingen: Mohr Siebeck, 2010), 99–108.

163. See, e.g., Fee, *First Epistle to the Corinthians*, 670–72; Ciampa and Rosner, *First Letter to the Corinthians*, 592–93. See NIV footnote.

164. Thiselton, *First Epistle to the Corinthians*, 1009.

The simile of the body becomes a metaphor in verse 27: "You are the body of Christ, and each one of you is a part of it." The source of Paul's imagery of the body for the church is debated, but perhaps the most important is the comparison, widespread in Paul's day, between society and the human body (see pp. 581–87). This comparison was often made to support the status quo, stressing the need to respect the more important members of society. As verses 15–26 make clear, Paul uses the metaphor for quite a different purpose, stressing that even the most "insignificant" members play a vital role in the body.[165] However, in addition to the influence of the widespread use of "body" as a metaphor in Paul's culture, we also have to allow for distinctive Christian theological influence on Paul's "body" language—especially when he refers to "the body *of Christ*." The context suggests that the eucharistic celebration of Christ's "body" may have influenced the metaphor (11:24, 27, 29)—particularly in light of 10:16b–17: "And is not the bread that we break a participation in the body of Christ? Because there is one loaf, we, who are many, are one body, for we all share the one loaf." Another influence, perhaps not as evident in this context, is Paul's portrayal of Adam and Christ as corporate figures.

Paul concludes this section with some specifics, again detailing some of the gifts God has given the body (vv. 28–30). He mentions eight gifts, divided into two parts. In the first part, he focuses on the person exercising the gift: "First of all apostles, second prophets, third teachers." In the second part he focuses on the gifts: "Then miracles, then gifts of healing, of helping, of guidance, and of different kinds of tongues." Paul's several listings of gifts are not the same, suggesting that in each case the choice of gifts mentioned is somewhat incidental. However, the prominence here given to apostles, prophets, and teachers is probably significant: apostles and prophets are listed first also in Ephesians 4:11 (with teachers mentioned also), while in Romans 12:6–8, prophesying is mentioned first, while teaching is third. Placing tongues at the end of the list is also almost certainly significant, suggesting Paul's relative depreciation of this gift—as the argument in chapter 14 makes clear. Verse 31 also anticipates the coming argument, as Paul exhorts the Corinthians to "eagerly desire" the "greater gifts"—and Paul will explain what are the greater gifts and why they are in chapter 14.[166] But before Paul does this, he outlines "the most excellent way."

7.2 Greater Than the Gifts (13:1–13)

As I have noted, there is every reason for this famous chapter on love to appear where it does. One of the most fundamental errors of the Corinthians, manifested in several

---

165. Mitchell, *Paul and the Rhetoric of Reconciliation*, 157–64.

166. The verb *zēloute* in v. 31 could be indicative, in which case Paul may be offering an implicit rebuke of the Corinthians: "You are [wrongly] desiring [what you consider] greater gifts" (cf. the Message; and Talbert, *Reading Corinthians*, 85). But most English versions translate *zēloute* as an imperative: "Eagerly desire the greater gifts" (NIV), and this seems to be the better option (e.g., D. A. Carson, *Showing the Spirit: A Theological Exposition of 1 Corinthians 12–14* [Grand Rapids: Baker, 1987], 56–58).

of the issues Paul treats in this letter, is self-regard—pride, arrogance, unconcern about others. The "way of love," then, is not only a basic perspective the Corinthians must have as they evaluate gifts; it needs also to become basic to their outlook on everything.

The passage falls into four parts. In verses 1–3, we find three parallel conditional sentences indicating how useless even the best abilities and accomplishments are without love. The first two appropriately highlight gifts Paul has mentioned in the context: "Tongues of . . . angels" (12:10, 28),[167] prophecy (12:10, 28), knowledge (12:8), and faith (12:9). Verse three shifts from gifts one possesses to sacrificial acts: giving all one possesses to the poor and giving over one's body "that I may boast."[168] The second part of the passage features fifteen brief assertions about what love is, or is not (vv. 4–7). Then, in verses 8–12 Paul magnifies love as a virtue that, in contrast to prophecies, tongues, and knowledge, will endure even beyond the end of this age. All these gifts will pass away when "completeness" (*to teleion*) comes (v. 10). This text has sometimes been used to support what is today known as "cessationism"—the view that certain of the gifts were given by God only for the early years of the church, only to "cease" at some point. However, while it has an ancient and respectable pedigree, this view is inadequately grounded in the New Testament.[169] Certainly "completeness" in verse 10 refers not to the close of the canon or the "maturity" of the church but to the culmination of this age (see the cognate *telos* in 1 Cor 1:8; 15:24). In that new age, the gifts necessary to build the church will no longer be needed—we will "know fully, even as I am fully known" (v. 12). But love will remain. Fee puts it well: "[Paul] is not here condemning the gifts; he is relativizing them."[170] In the present time, Paul concludes (v. 13), there remain three great virtues: faith, hope, and love. And the greatest of them is love. The triad of faith, hope, and love is common in the New Testament (e.g., Heb 10:19–25; 1 Pet 1:3–9); see especially 1 Thessalonians 1:3, where Paul gives thanks for the Thessalonians' "work produced by faith," "labor prompted by love," and "endurance inspired by hope." Even more common is the focus on love as the key Christian virtue throughout the New Testament (Matt 22:34–40 and par.; Luke 10:25–37; John 13:34–35; Rom 13:8–10; Gal 5:13–14; Jas 2:8; 1 John 2:7–11).

7.3 Prophecy and Tongues (14:1–40)

In this chapter, Paul applies his criterion of love from chapter 13 and his vision of the unity and diversity of the church from chapter 12. The opening section, verses 1–25, picks up this first point: love, or concern for the other, should guide the choice and use

---

167. The whole phrase might refer simply to human and angelic "languages" (NIV fn.; NLT).

168. A famous textual variant here has *kauthēsomai* (or *kauthēsōmai*), "that I might be burned" (see, e.g., ESV) in place of *kauchēsōmai*, "that I might boast."

169. Some notable cessationists were Origen, Chrysostom, Aquinas, and B. B. Warfield. It should be noted that many of those who argued this view in the past did not appeal to 1 Cor 13:10 (see Thiselton, *First Epistle to the Corinthians*, 1063–64).

170. Fee, *First Epistle to the Corinthians*, 711.

of gifts.[171] This criterion, Paul argues, sets prophecy over tongues in the hierarchy of "greatest" gifts. The diversity-in-unity principle undergirds verses 26–40, where Paul cautions the Corinthians to use their variety of gifts in ways that preserve the orderly functioning of the church.

7.3.1 *Building Up the Church (14:1–25)*

Verses 1–12 are framed by encouragements to seek the gifts that will "build up" the church (see *oikodomeō* in v. 4 [twice]; and *oikodomē* in vv. 3, 5, and 12). Paul criticizes the Corinthians not because they were seeking gifts but because they were seeking particular gifts for the wrong reasons. As becomes clear in this paragraph, the Corinthians are prizing the gift of tongues, presumably because the ecstatic speech of the tongues-speaker would enhance their status and prominence in the community. They are once again guilty of self-regard when "the way of love" should turn them to consider others first. And when the church as a whole is considered, the gift of prophecy becomes obviously more of a priority than tongues. Paul makes the basic point in verses 1–5 and then develops it with a series of illustrations in verses 6–12: tongues, because they are not understood by others (unless they are interpreted), edify the speaker only; prophecy, on the other hand, "edifies the church" (v. 4). As I noted earlier, Paul's argument here appears to rule out the idea that tongues may refer to known human languages. Rather, spontaneous language-like utterances in private "prayer language" seem to be indicated.[172]

This understanding of tongues appears to be confirmed by Paul's application ("for this reason," v. 13) of his teaching about tongues in verses 13–17. The one who "prays in a tongue," Paul says, is praying in their spirit, but the mind is "unfruitful" (v. 14). Only if the tongues-speaker is able to interpret the tongue will the gift illuminate mind as well as spirit and be useful for those who hear as well (vv. 16–17).[173] It is not that Paul disparages the gift of tongues (v. 18); it is rather that using "intelligible words to instruct others" is a much better option (v. 19).

The address "brothers and sisters" (*adelphoi*) in verse 20 introduces the closing exhortation in this section (vv. 20–25). As he has done in chapter 13 (vv. 10–12), Paul again hints that the Corinthians' attitude toward tongues betrays not a sophisticated view but a rather childish one: "Stop thinking like children. In regard to evil be infants, but in your thinking be adults" (v. 20). He is probably here alluding to Isaiah 28:9, where the prophet mocks the teaching of immoral teachers in Judah as if their audience were

---

171. E.g., Thiselton, *First Epistle to the Corinthians*, 1074.

172. This view receives some mild confirmation from Paul's use of the phrase *genē phōnōn* (instead of *glōssa*) to refer to human languages in v. 10 (Fee, *First Epistle to the Corinthians*, 736–37; Garland, *1 Corinthians*, 637).

173. Paul's reference in v. 16 to an *idiōtēs* is debated (see also 14:23–24). The word can refer to a "person who is relatively unskilled or inexperienced in some activity or field of knowledge" (cf. Acts 4:11) or "to someone 'not in the know,' outsider" (BDAG). The latter fits the occurrences here in ch. 14, but it is not clear whether these people are unbelievers (Barrett, *First Epistle to the Corinthians*, 321), part of a particular class of "seekers," or simply people who don't understand the tongue speaking (Garland, *1 Corinthians*, 641).

"children weaned from their milk," "those just taken from the breast." Paul then goes on to quote from this same passage in verse 21: "With other tongues and through the lips of foreigners I will speak to this people, but even then they will not listen to me, says the Lord" (cf. Isa 28:11). The reference is to Assyrian, the incomprehensible language the people of Israel will hear in their exile. It is this Old Testament context that explains Paul's otherwise puzzling assertion that "tongues, then, are a sign, not for believers but for unbelievers": when "outsiders" come into the worship service and hear incomprehensible tongues being spoken, they will be confirmed in their "outsider" status.[174]

7.3.2 Order in Worship (14:26–40)

The second half of chapter 14 moves from the particular focus on the superiority of prophecy over tongues to a more general concern with the "orderly" functioning of the Corinthian worship service (vv. 33, 40), something Paul is concerned with because it facilitates the ultimate goal of "building up" the church (see v. 26). Therefore, when the church "comes together," and believers are exercising their gifts, the service should be conducted in a way that fosters mutual edification. Reflecting the Corinthians' preoccupation with the gift once again, Paul applies this principle to tongues, urging that those who have this gift should take turns speaking, one at a time, and then only if an interpreter can make the tongue comprehensible to the church (vv. 27–28). Paul exhorts the church to exercise similar restraint with respect to the gift of prophecy (vv. 29–33). The apparent equivalence between prophecy and "revelation" (*apokalyptō*, v. 30) may suggest that the gift of prophecy involves communicating to others a word that God spontaneously reveals to the prophet.[175] This "revelation" is not the revelation that God gives authoritatively to his people, as in the case of Old Testament prophets or New Testament apostles. The fact that prophetic speech is subject to evaluation of other believers (or other prophets[176]) makes this clear.[177] Nevertheless, this text must be set alongside others that suggest the importance of prophets in communicating the truth on which the church is built (see esp. Eph 2:20).

Paul's exhortations about disruptive women in verses 34–36 fit generally into his overall concern about order in the worship service. Nevertheless, the introduction of this issue is somewhat abrupt, and there is some textual evidence that verses 34–35 were not an original part of 1 Corinthians.[178] On the whole, however, evidence for an interpolation falls short of being convincing; these verses should be considered

---

174. For this interpretation, see, e.g., Thiselton, *First Epistle to the Corinthians*, 1122; Fee, *First Epistle to the Corinthians*, 755–56.

175. E.g., Wayne A. Grudem, *The Gift of Prophecy in the New Testament and Today* (Wheaton, IL: Crossway, 1988), esp. 115–31.

176. The "others" (*hoi alloi*) who evaluate prophecy in v. 29 may be other Christians in general (e.g., Garland, *1 Corinthians*, 663; Thiselton, *First Epistle to the Corinthians*, 1140–41; cf.

1 Thess 5:20–21) or other prophets (see v. 32; and see G. Friedrich, *TDNT* 6:851).

177. See, e.g., Grudem, *Gift of Prophecy*, 78–79.

178. See especially Payne, *Man and Woman*, 225–67; Fee, *First Epistle to the Corinthians*, 780–92; idem, *God's Empowering Presence: The Holy Spirit in the Letters of Paul* (Peabody, MA: Hendrickson, 2007), 272–81.

authentic.[179] Paul's recognition that women pray and prophesy (almost certainly in the worship service) in 11:5 makes clear that the prohibition of women "speaking" (*lalein*) in the "churches" (that is, worship gatherings) cannot be absolute.[180] Of the many suggestions for interpreting this somewhat opaque text, the most likely is that women are again (as in 11:2–16) straining cultural boundaries by raising issues and asking questions of men who are not their husbands.[181]

The chapter concludes with a final warning about heeding Paul's teaching in verses 26–35 (vv. 36–38) and a summarizing admonition that takes up all of chapter 14 (vv. 39–40).

8 THE FUTURE OF THE NEW IDENTITY: RESURRECTION (15:1–58)

This chapter is, as Furnish puts it, about both "the necessity and plausibility" of resurrection from the dead.[182] We do not know how Paul heard about the skepticism on this matter among the Corinthian Christians. Nor are we sure why the Corinthians may have been so skeptical. Some scholars have focused on "overrealized eschatology,"[183] which, I have argued, is indeed one of the Corinthians' root theological problems. However, while the passage does reveal some interest in chronology (vv. 23–28), the repeated emphasis is on the issue of resurrection of the body *per se* (vv. 12–13, 16, 29–32).[184] Granted the dominance of dualism among the Greeks, it is probable that the Corinthians' problem with the resurrection was once again the result of their failure to replace their background worldview with a thoroughly Christian one. They had absorbed their culture's criticism of—indeed, disdain for—the notion that the physical body would exist in any form in the afterlife.

179. See especially the judicious evaluation of Thiselton, *First Epistle to the Corinthians*, 1150–52. It is also unlikely that vv. 34–35 is a Corinthian view that Paul is rejecting (as, e.g., Talbert, *Reading Corinthians*, 91–93, thinks).

180. Contra, e.g., Gillian Beattie, *Women and Marriage in Paul and His Early Interpreters*, JSNTSup 296 (London: T&T Clark, 2005), 56–57, who thinks different women may be involved.

181. See esp. Ciampa and Rosner, *First Letter to the Corinthians*, 718–30. They cite the Roman Marcus Porcius Cato (c. 195 BC): "Indeed I blushed when, a short while ago, I walked through the midst of a band of women. Had not respect for the dignity and modesty of certain ones (not them all!) restrained me (so they would not be seen being scolded by a consul), I should have said, 'What kind of behaviour is this? Running around in public, blocking streets, and speaking to other women's husbands! Could you not have asked your own husbands the same thing at home?'" See also Keener, *Paul, Women, and Wives*, 70–100; Armin D. Baum, "Paul's Conflicting Statements on Female Public

Speaking (1 Cor 11:5) and Silence (1 Cor 14:34–35): A New Suggestion," *TynBul* 65 (2014): 247–74. Others think the women were being prohibited from judging prophecies (Thiselton, *First Epistle to the Corinthians*, 1158; Hurley, *Man and Woman*, 188–93).

182. Furnish, *Theology of the First Letter to the Corinthians*, 109.

183. Talbert, *Reading Corinthians*, 98; Christopher M. Tuckett, "The Corinthians Who Say 'There Is No Resurrection of the Dead' (1 Cor 15,12)," in *The Corinthian Correspondence*, ed. Reimund Bieringer, BETL 125 (Leuven: Leuven University Press, 1996), 251–74. For a strong criticism of this view, see A. J. M. Wedderburn, *Baptism and Resurrection: Studies in Pauline Theology against Its Graeco-Roman Background*, WUNT 2/44 (Tübingen: Mohr Siebeck, 1987), 164–295.

184. Joost Holleman, *Resurrection and Parousia: A Traditio-Historical Study of Paul's Eschatology in 1 Corinthians 15*, NovTSup 84 (Leiden: Brill, 1996), 35–40; Martin, *Corinthian Body*, 105–7; Garland, *1 Corinthians*, 698–701.

It is unclear why Paul decides to take up this important theological issue—indeed, perhaps the only "purely" theological issue he deals with—at the very end of the letter.[185] But perhaps the placement is climactic, drawing appropriate attention to this crucial matter of basic Christian belief. Indeed, as, for example, Schrage has noted, the letter is suffused with references to future eschatology, often deployed to counter an overrealized focus (see esp. 1:7–8; and 3:13–15; 4:5; 5:5; 6:2–3, 14; 7:29–31; 10:11; 11:12; 13:8–13). In that sense, the topic of this chapter is not one among many but "the presupposition and basis" for the whole.[186] Paul's argument falls into two obvious parts, the first part of the chapter (vv. 1–34) concentrating on the *fact* of resurrection and the second part (vv. 35–58) on the *how* of resurrection. In addition to its obviously important contribution to the theology of resurrection, this chapter is also important theologically for its eschatology and, secondarily, for the light it sheds on the gospel, the Spirit, and the Adam/Christ parallel.

8.1 The Fact of Resurrection (15:1–34)

Paul approaches the issue of resurrection obliquely but significantly by first reminding the Corinthians of "the gospel I preached to you" (v. 1). This gospel has the power to bring those who hold firmly to it to eventual salvation (v. 2). And this gospel is a "word" or "message" (*logos*) that Paul himself "received" (v. 3). The language of "receiving" and "passing on" (*paradidōmi*) here refers to the handing down of tradition. The gospel Paul preaches has its ultimate source in the revelation of Christ (Gal 1). However, as he makes clear here, Paul also stands in a line of faithful transmitters of the truth of that gospel. Paul rapidly touches on four key points in the gospel he preaches: Christ "died for our sins according to the Scriptures," "he was buried," "he was raised on the third day according to the Scriptures," he "appeared" to Cephas, then to the Twelve, to five hundred believers at once, to James, to "all the apostles," and, finally, to Paul (vv. 3b–8). The sequence of death, burial, and resurrection is echoed elsewhere in Paul (Rom 6:3–5; Col 2:11–12), suggesting it was a standard summary of the foundational redemptive events. The focus on Jesus's appearances here has the obvious purpose of demonstrating the historical reality of the resurrection.

Recent scholarship has stressed the breadth of Paul's gospel, seeing it as encompassing broadly the central truth that Christ is Lord and all the implications that flow from that truth. There is much to be said for this more expansive view of the gospel. However, this breadth should not take the focus of the gospel away from where Paul puts it: on the salvation made available to humans through Christ's death and resurrection.

---

185. Ciampa and Rosner, *First Letter to the Corinthians*, 736–37, theorize that Paul is following a sequence found elsewhere in his letters, from idolatry to worship to eschatology (e.g., 1 Thess 1:9–10).

186. Schrage, *Der erste Brief an die Korinther*, 3:7–8; Schnabel, *Der Erste Brief des Paulus an die Korinther*, 864. N. T. Wright calls resurrection a "unifying theme" of the letter (*Resurrection*, 278).

This emphasis, obviously seen in this text, is found throughout his writings. (On "gospel" in Paul, see 349–51.)

Early Christians from the beginning stressed that Christ's death was no historical accident; it took place "by God's deliberate plan and foreknowledge" (Acts 2:23). This crucial apologetic point was buttressed by reference to many Old Testament texts and patterns. Here, then, the "Scriptures" that attest to Christ's death may include many texts, although there is reason to think that the fourth servant song, Isaiah 52:13–53:12, was especially significant.[187] Pinning down the Old Testament text, or texts, that Paul may have in view when he claims that Christ's third-day resurrection was "according to the Scriptures" is more difficult, but many scholars think that Hosea 6:2 should be given pride of place.[188] This text refers to God's judgment of his people Israel and his subsequent purpose to restore them again:

> Come, let us return to the LORD.
> He has torn us to pieces
>   but he will heal us;
> he has injured us
>   but he will bind up our wounds.
> After two days he will revive us;
>   on the third day he will restore us,
>   that we may live in his presence. (Hos 6:1–2)

The typological relationship of Christ to the nation of Israel was a fundamental basis for New Testament interpretation of the Old Testament in terms of Christ.

By referring to himself as one "abnormally born" (v. 8), Paul is probably hinting at the unusual nature of the "appearance" of Christ to him: one not occurring during the time between Christ's resurrection and ascension but later on. In verses 9–11, Paul elaborates, stressing that it is God's grace that has qualified him to be the apostle that he has become.

Paul now turns to the resurrection. He first argues that the general idea of resurrection is a necessary entailment of the fundamental reality of Christ's resurrection (vv. 12–19). To deny Christ's resurrection would be to evacuate Christian faith of any meaning: there would be nothing to preach, and the dead in Christ would have no hope (vv. 14, 18–19). Clearly Paul sees Christ's bodily resurrection as essential to Christian faith. And, as Wright has massively shown, it is indeed *bodily* resurrection to which Paul is referring.[189] Second, Paul elaborates the connection of Christ's resurrection and the

---

187. Detlef Häusser, *Christusbekenntnis und Jesusüberlieferung bei Paulus*, WUNT 2/210 (Tübingen: Mohr Siebeck, 2006), 61–158; Schnabel, *Der Erste Brief des Paulus an die Korinther*, 881.

188. See, e.g., Schnabel, *Der Erste Brief des Paulus an die Korinther*, 884.

189. Wright, *Resurrection*.

resurrection of those who belong to him by briefly setting out the course of redemptive events (vv. 20–28). Christ is "the firstfruits of those who have fallen asleep" (v. 20), meaning that his resurrection, in a sense, "contains" the resurrection of all who belong to him. Here for the first time in his letters Paul introduces one of his fundamental theological building blocks: the comparison between Adam and Christ. "As in Adam all die, so in Christ all will be made alive" (v. 22). Death here is mainly, if not exclusively, "spiritual death": condemnation, leading to ultimate judgment. "Life," on the other hand, refers in this context to resurrection life: the transformation from the state of physical death to new, eschatological life. The "all" in the second part of verse 22 might be inclusive of all humans, since all will indeed be raised: some to eternal life and some to judgment (see, e.g., John 5:28–29).[190] But the following verses suggest rather that Christians only are in view; we could perhaps translate "all who are in Christ will be made alive."[191] This resurrection of Christians will take place "when he comes," that is, at his ultimate "coming" or "appearance" at the end of history (v. 23; see also 1 Thess 4:13–18). After that will come "the end," "when he hands over the kingdom to God the Father after he has destroyed all dominion, authority and power" (v. 24). As Fee notes, Paul employs Psalm 110:1 in verses 25–26 to explain "after he has destroyed," and Psalm 8:6 in verses 27–28 to elaborate "when he hands over the kingdom." These two psalm verses are linked by the language of "under his/your feet," and they are used together elsewhere in the New Testament (Heb 1:13; 2:5–9; cf. Eph 1:20–22). The goal of this unfolding plan of God is that he might be "all in all" (v. 28). The idea that the Son "himself will be made subject to him who put everything under him" (v. 28) has naturally spawned considerable theological debate over the centuries. There is here an obvious note of subordination, but, as most agree, it is not ontological but relational or functional subordination, as each person of the Trinity carries out his particular part in the economy of redemption. Wesley Hill, moreover, has noted how this text also equates Father and Son in terms of identity.[192]

In the last part of this first part of the chapter, Paul argues that Christ's resurrection is a necessary inference from the Corinthians' own belief and behavior (vv. 29–32), before adding a final exhortation (vv. 33–34). Paul's appeal to his own sacrificial ministry is clear enough: if "there is no resurrection" (v. 29), no continuity of the body into the world to come, it makes little sense for Paul to give himself in ministry as he does (vv. 30–33).[193] By contrast, Paul's first appeal is anything but clear: "If the dead are not raised at all, why are people baptized for them?" Of the many interpretations

---

190. Schrage, *Der erste Brief an die Korinther*, 3:163–66.

191. E.g., Fee, *First Epistle to the Corinthians*, 831; Fitzmyer, *First Corinthians*, 570; Harris, *Raised Immortal*, 179–80.

192. Wesley Hill, *Paul and the Trinity: Persons, Relations, and the Pauline Letters* (Grand Rapids: Eerdmans, 2015), 120–33.

193. Paul's fighting with wild beasts in Ephesus is taken by some literally, as he was thrown into the arena by Roman authorities. Most, however, take the language as a metaphor for his struggle with enemies of the gospel (Fee, *First Epistle to the Corinthians*, 852–53; Garland, *1 Corinthians*, 720).

that have been suggested, one of three is most likely. (1) Christians are being baptized vicariously for (*hyper*, "on behalf of") those who are physically dead; (2) Christians are being baptized on behalf of believing friends who died without being baptized; (3) Christians are being baptized with the purpose (*hyper* in a final sense) of being joined with believing relatives who have died.[194] Whatever the situation, the main point is clear: Why be concerned with dead people if their corpses will simply rot in the grave?

8.2 The How of Resurrection (15:35–58)

The two questions in verse 35—"How are the dead raised? With what kind of body will they come?"—set the agenda for verses 35–58. The form in which Paul poses these questions ("someone will ask") suggests he is engaging in an argument with the Corinthians. Their skepticism about resurrection probably included incredulity about the nature and composition of a resurrection body. Paul responds with two basic points. First, and most fundamentally, God is quite capable of providing exactly the kind of body that is needed for any circumstance, including the kingdom of God (v. 38). Second, there are a great variety of bodies, and God is giving resurrected believers the appropriate body for their life in the kingdom.

Paul begins with the illustration of the seed planted by the farmer (vv. 36–37). That seed is quite different than the final "body" that will come from it. So, Paul implies, we should not think the fraility and dissolution of our earthly bodies prevents them, once they have died, from being transformed into something quite different. And, Paul goes on, there are different kinds of "flesh" (v. 39), which he illustrates by referring to humans, animals, birds, and fish—deliberately reversing the order of creation on the fifth and sixth days (Gen 1:20–28). But not only does the created order display diversity in the "stuff" of creation ("flesh"); it also exhibits variety in form and character ("bodies"; vv. 40–41).[195]

Paul draws his conclusion in verse 42: "So will it be with the resurrection of the dead." Verses 42b–44 elaborate the contrast between the bodies believers have in this life and the bodies they will have in the kingdom: perishable versus imperishable; dishonorable versus glorious; weak versus powerful; natural versus spiritual. This last contrast is particularly important to get right. The Greek terms are *psychikos* and *pneumatikos*. The former word, derived from *psychē*, "soul," means "natural," "pertaining to this life" (see 2:14, where the same word is again contrasted with "Spirit"). The latter word, "spiritual," is from a word group that Paul consistently relates to the Holy Spirit as the distinctive gift of new-covenant life. Paul, then, does not mean here that God is going to give believers a body composed of "spirit" (a nonsensical notion in

---

194. For a survey of options, see Thiselton, *First Epistle to the Corinthians*, 1242–49; he thinks the third view might be the least problematic (1248–49).

195. Thiselton, *First Epistle to the Corinthians*, 1267.

itself) but that he is giving believers a body provided by the Spirit and suited for life in the Spirit.[196] Paul explains this basic contrast (note the "so" [*houtōs*] in v. 45) by appeal to the creation of the first man, Adam. Paul has already employed his Adam/Christ contrast to make a point in this chapter (vv. 21–22); and, indeed, as Wright has noted, Genesis 1–2 appear to lie behind much of what Paul is teaching in this chapter.[197] He begins with the last contrast he drew in verse 44: "The first man Adam became a living being"/"the last Adam a life-giving spirit." The Greek behind the NIV "being" in Paul's quotation of Genesis 2:7 is *psychēn*, "soul," while "spirit," of course, renders *pneuma*. Adam was created as a "natural" human and put that stamp on all who came from him. Christ, on the other hand, probably at his resurrection, entered into the realm of the Spirit, leading the way for those who would follow. I therefore think that NLT may be correct to capitalize "Spirit" here.[198] Paul, of course, does not ontologically identify Christ with the Spirit, but he does often speak of their work in such a way as to bring them in close relationship. In contrast to some speculation among his Jewish contemporaries, who posited that God created both a "heavenly" and an "earthly" man in the beginning,[199] Paul maintains a typical eschatological perspective. The first man, made from the dust of the earth (Gen 2:7), came first; after him came the "spiritual" or "heavenly" man. All humans are tied to Adam as their representative head and prototype; we "bear his image." But believers, who become "sons of God" by their relationship to *the* Son of God, who is *the* "image of God," will bear that image in their resurrection bodies (v. 49).

Paul marks a transition to a new paragraph with the formula "I declare to you" (or "this I say," *touto de phēmi*) and a direct address of his readers ("brothers and sisters") (v. 50). We may, then, view vv. 50–58 as a concluding paragraph of the chapter as a whole. But its opening verses, at least, continue the contrasting imagery of verses 42–49, and we should perhaps then relate it more closely to these verses. The reason that believers need transformed bodies is made clear in v. 50: "Flesh and blood [earthly bodies] cannot inherit the kingdom of God." Believers need different kinds of bodies to live in the kingdom that Christ definitively establishes at his coming. When that moment comes, some believers will already be dead ("sleeping"), while others will remain alive. But they all must be "changed," discarding the perishable and mortal bodies of this world for imperishable and immortal bodies suited to the new existence (vv. 51–54). When this happens, "death" will be "swallowed up in victory" (v. 54, quoting Isa 25:8), and believers will be able to taunt death itself (v. 55, quoting Hos 13:14). Death "stings" because of sin: physical death after the introduction of sin into the world becomes a painful and uncertain matter. Moreover, alluding to a familiar theme in his teaching,

---

196. See esp. Wright, *Resurrection*, 348–54; also Rabens, *Holy Spirit and Ethics in Paul*, 86–96.

197. Wright, *Resurrection*, 340.

198. See Fitzmyer, *First Corinthians*, 597–98.

199. Philo, *Alleg. Interp.* 1.31.

Paul ties sin's power to the law. By setting forth God's requirements in great detail, God's law manifests and empowers sin (Rom 5:20; 7:7–12; Gal 3:19). But in Christ, God wins the victory over both sin and death (v. 57). Paul concludes this lengthy discussion with an exhortation to "stand firm" and to be involved in the work of ministry (v. 58). Hope for a resurrection body should not detract from our commitments in this world; rather, that hope should stimulate us to even greater effort.

Sean McDonough helpfully summarizes Paul's main points about resurrection in this crucial chapter on the subject:

> Paul does provide a theologically refined defence of bodily resurrection that undercuts all manner of objections to the doctrine: bodies are a good gift from God, and thus one need not shy away from their materiality; the new body will not be subject to the limitations governing the present one, so one need not worry about disfigured corpses stumbling their way through eternity; and God's creative power is such that no amount of decay or dispersion can prevent him from raising his people to eternal embodied life.[200]

9 FINAL WORDS (16:1–24)

Chapter 16 is the letter closing. As such, it includes matters typical of these closings: travel plans (vv. 5–9), references to fellow workers (vv. 10–12, 15, 17–18), and greetings (vv. 19–20). Paul also adds his "autograph" (v. 21), giving confirmation that, whoever might have been his amanuensis, the content is Paul's. See 2 Thessalonians 3:17: "I, Paul, write this greeting in my own hand, which is the distinguishing mark in all my letters. This is how I write" (cf. Gal 6:11; Phlm 19). Somewhat distinctive of this closing (though see Rom 15:24–29) are Paul's instructions about procedures for the "collection," his project of raising money from gentile churches to aid the impoverished Jewish believers in Israel (vv. 1–4). Paul mentions this project in each of his third-missionary-journey letters (see also Rom 15:24–29; 2 Cor 8–9), and his reference here suggests the Corinthians are already well aware of it (note that v. 1 begins with "now about," implying that the Corinthians may have written Paul about it). Also unusual is the curse formula in verse 22 and the wish, "Come, Lord!" This latter is found in Aramaic transliteration in the Greek text: *marana tha*. Divided in this way, the formula means, "Come, Lord!" (an imperative), whereas it could also be divided *maran atha*, "Our Lord has come." But the former is more likely, and is followed by almost all the English translations.[201]

---

200. Sean McDonough, *Creation and New Creation: Understanding God's Creation Project* (Peabody, MA: Hendrickson, 2016), 196.

201. Oscar Cullmann, *The Christology of the New Testament* (Philadelphia: Westminster, 1963), 209–10; Richard N. Longenecker, *The Christology of Early Jewish Christianity* (Grand Rapids: Baker, 1970), 121–24.

Chapter 8

2 CORINTHIANS

P̶AUL THE THEOLOGIAN cannot be separated from Paul the person. Like the rest of us, what Paul believes and teaches is tied in various ways to his own experiences. Taking an appropriately robust view of providence, we believe that a sovereign God orchestrated these experiences so that Paul would, under the influence of the Spirit, teach precisely what God wanted him to. Paul's own experience is closer to the surface of his theologizing in 2 Corinthians than in any of his other letters. Circumstances (see below) dictated that Paul would in this letter have to reflect on the nature and implications of his own apostolic ministry. Several key theological issues get drawn into his reflections on his apostleship—the relationship between old covenant and new, the "life in the midst of death" character of this in-between period of salvation history, the central message of reconciliation that Paul proclaims—but the overall theme of the letter is the glory and nature of new-covenant ministry.

LOCATING THE LETTER

Paul wrote his second (canonical) letter to the Corinthians only one to three years after his first—most scholars date 2 Corinthians to AD 56. Yet, as the focus and tone of the letters indicate, a lot changed over the course of this short period of time. In his first letter, Paul implies that the Corinthians may have been chafing under his authority (4:3–4; 9:2–3), and the manner in which Paul treats the issues that the Corinthians raise also could imply some distance between them. But Paul's authority is not a major issue.[1] In 2 Corinthians, by contrast, the issue of Paul's authority governs the letter from beginning to end. Even while giving thanks for the Corinthians' repentance, Paul continues to defend and explain his ministry throughout chapters 1–9, and in chapters 10–13 this defense, which now takes into account rival missionaries, becomes impassioned. These circumstances lead Paul to say more about his own ministry—and ministry in general—in this letter than in any of his other letters.

We cannot identify for certain Paul's rivals for the Corinthians' attention. But he

---

1. Contra, e.g., Fee, who stresses this issue throughout his commentary (*First Epistle to the Corinthians*).

does fill out pretty well the other circumstances that led to the writing of this letter. These circumstances are best set in the wider context of Paul's relations with the Corinthians:[2]

Paul plants a church in Corinth on the second missionary journey.   AD 51–52

The "Previous Letter" (Letter A)

Paul writes a letter to the Corinthians warning them to avoid immorality (see 1 Cor 5:9).

First Corinthians (Letter B)   AD 53–55?

The "painful visit"   (see 2 Cor 2:1)

In response to deteriorating relations between Paul and the Corinthians (perhaps exacerbated by the arrival of rival teachers), Paul visits Corinth. The visit does not go well.

The "Severe Letter" (Letter C)   See 2 Corinthians 2:4; 7:8–12

After returning to Ephesus, Paul sends another letter via Titus in which he takes them to task for their rebellious posture toward him.

Second Corinthians (Letter D)   See 2 Cor 2:12–14; 7:5–7

Anxiously awaiting word about the Corinthians' response from Titus, Paul leaves Ephesus, traveling north to Troas and then west into Macedonia. Here Titus meets Paul with the good news that the Corinthians have (largely) repented and reaffirmed their commitment to Paul's authority.

Paul spends the winter in Corinth   See Acts 20:2b–3a

Many interpreters are convinced that we should add a "Letter E" to this list. They argue that the sudden change in tone at 10:1 is best explained if chapters 10–13 were originally a separate letter, written either before chapters 1–9 (in which case it might be the "severe letter")[3] or after them.[4] Some want to take a further step and add a "Letter F." These scholars note that 6:14–7:1 fits very awkwardly in our present letter and may also have once existed as a separate letter (some identify this fragment with "Letter A"). Thorough discussion of these matters is best left to the commentaries and introductions.[5] But I think it is, on the whole, easier to explain the changes in tone and

---

2. The best outline and analysis of these events is found in Harris, *Second Epistle to the Corinthians*, 101–5.

3. E.g., E. P. Sanders, *Paul: The Apostle's Life, Letters, and Thought* (Minneapolis: Fortress, 2015), 228–38; Munck, *Paul and the Salvation of Mankind*, 168–75 (this is the standard "critical" view).

4. E.g., Victor Paul Furnish, *II Corinthians*, AB 32A (Garden City: Doubleday, 1984), 44; Margaret E. Thrall, *Second Epistle*

to the Corinthians, 2 vols., ICC (London: T&T Clark, 1994), 2:3–20; Ralph P. Martin, *2 Corinthians*, WBC 40 (Nashville: Thomas Nelson, 2010), 48–49, 60–62.

5. See esp. Harris, *Second Epistle to the Corinthians*, 8–51; Peter Arzt-Grabner, *2. Korinther*, Papyrologische Kommentare zum Neuen Testament 4 (Göttingen: Vandenhoeck & Ruprecht, 2014), 73–154; Carson and Moo, *Introduction to the New Testament*, 430–35.

subject matter on the assumption that we are dealing with a single letter than to explain how two or more letters would have been stitched together (leaving no textual evidence). The "break" between chapters 9 and 10 may reflect Paul's switch in rhetorical strategy and/or a lapse of time between the writing (or dictating) of chapters 1–9 and 10–13.[6] As N. T. Wright puts it, "Paul may well have been writing while on the move, and while in turmoil of spirit. I am inclined to agree with those recent commentators who have regarded it as more plausible to think that 2 Corinthians always was a bits-and-pieces letter, in more or less this order, than to suppose that some later editor has stitched together a number of fragments into the present patchwork quilt."[7]

ISOLATING THE ISSUES

The single major issue that led to the writing of 2 Corinthians, then, is a crisis of authority. The crisis probably had its origins among the Corinthians themselves, since, as I noted above, 1 Corinthians implies this may already then have been a problem. But chapters 10–13 make clear that outsiders have exacerbated the problem. Who these people were is hard to say, since Paul focuses on their character and manner rather than on any specific theological teaching.[8] It is clear, however, that, whatever their message, it is contrary to the gospel Paul preaches. He calls them "false apostles" (11:13) and claims that they are teaching a different Jesus and a different gospel (11:4). They are Jewish, perhaps coming from Palestine (which labeling them "Hebrews" may indicate; see 11:22). They were appealing to the apostles in Jerusalem for their authority (see his reference to "super-apostles" [*tōn hyperlian apostolōn*] in 11:5 and 12:11). These characterizations remind us inevitably of the situation in Galatians, where Paul's opponents apparently claimed support from the Jerusalem apostles (Paul's description of them as "those esteemed as pillars" there [Gal 2:9; cf. 2:6] sounds a lot like the semi-ironical "super-apostles" here) and were preaching a "different gospel" (Gal 1:6–9). It may, then, be appropriate to label the opponents in Corinth as "Judaizers."[9] However, this is a label that might conceal more than it reveals. Many Jewish-Christians advocated

---

6. For the former, see esp. Witherington, *Conflict & Community in Corinth*, 338–39; Paul Barnett, *The Second Epistle to the Corinthians*, NICNT (Grand Rapids: Eerdmans, 1997), 17–23; David E. Garland, *2 Corinthians*, NAC 29 (Nashville: Broadman & Holman, 1999), 38–44; George H. Guthrie, *2 Corinthians*, BECNT (Grand Rapids: Baker Academic, 2015), 30–32; for the latter, Harris, *Second Epistle to the Corinthians*, 29–51; Schnelle, *Apostle Paul*, 237–45. If, as seems likely, Paul's claim to have preached the gospel "all the way around to Illyricum" (Rom 15:19) means that he preached in this Roman province, then Paul may have finished 2 Corinthians there (see, e.g., Murphy-O'Connor, *Paul*, 316–17; Schnabel, *Paul and the Early Church*, 1250–51).

7. Wright, *Paul and the Faithfulness of God*, 2:713. See also Dunn, *Beginning from Jerusalem*, 835–36.

8. For a summary of Paul's characterization of these teachers, see Harris, *Second Epistle to the Corinthians*, 69–77. See also Dieter Georgi, *The Opponents of Paul in Second Corinthians* (Philadelphia: Fortress, 1986), who thinks the false teachers were Hellenistic-Jewish apologists with a "divine man" Christology.

9. See esp. C. K. Barrett, "Paul's Opponents in II Corinthians," *NTS* 17 (1971): 233–54; Harris, *Second Epistle to the Corinthians*, 67–87.

for more continuity with Judaism than Paul did; and their views fall at different places on the spectrum of continuity and discontinuity between Judaism (in various forms) and the nascent Christian movement. Thus, for instance, Paul says nothing about circumcision or the law in dealing with the opponents in Corinth (though see 2 Cor 3:7–18). While probably advocating some degree of "Judaizing," then, we cannot know the specific doctrinal posture of these "false apostles." In any case, Paul is far more concerned with their style of ministry, which they are contrasting with Paul's as a basis for their attack on his authority. His opponents are apparently presenting themselves as "powerful" and attractive, perhaps demanding support from the Corinthians (see 11:20). Paul stands in contrast to this slick and attractive posture. His frequent sufferings (11:23–29), his humiliating escape from Damascus in a basket (11:32–33), his refusal to receive support from the Corinthians—these might seem like "weakness" in the eyes of the world—as indeed they do. However, Paul's "weakness" allows Christ's power to become all the more evident and effective, attesting therefore to his own authentic apostolic credentials.

The lack of clear evidence about these "false apostles" has naturally led to many different proposals about their identity. Schnelle's characterization is representative of the identification suggested by a fair number of scholars: "Christian itinerant missionaries of Jewish-Hellenistic origin who charged Paul with lacking spiritual power and who wanted to legitimate themselves as authentic apostles and bearers of the Spirit."[10]

Of course, the false teachers appear explicitly only in chapters 10–13, and chapters 1–9 have a different flavor. A tone of joy at the Corinthians' repentance is prominent (2:14; 7:5, 13–16). Nevertheless, the issue of authority is hinted at also in these chapters, and much of Paul's teaching in chapters 1–7 focuses on his own ministry. What becomes explicit and personalized in chapters 10–13 is therefore also present in these earlier chapters. The issue throughout is the nature of Paul's ministry, the gospel he preaches, and the authority he bears as an emissary of Christ.

ANALYZING THE ARGUMENT

Second Corinthians focuses from beginning to end on Paul's apostolic ministry.[11] Chapters 10–13 make clear that this focus on his ministry is stimulated by his need to defend himself and his methods over against interlopers. Yet, while implicit rather than explicit, this defensive posture is evident in chapters 1–7 also. As we have seen, Paul

---

10. Schnelle, *Apostle Paul*, 260–61; see also, with more emphasis on a "Judaizing" focus, Harris, *Second Epistle to the Corinthians*, 67–87; Barrett, "Paul's Opponents."

11. Paul's frequent use of the first-person plural in the letter raises the question of the degree to which he speaks of his own authority vis-à-vis apostolic authority in general (Wilckens refers to "the apostolic we" in 2 Corinthians [*Die Briefe des Urchristentums*, 114]).

provides almost no specifics about the content of the interlopers' teaching; his focus is almost entirely on their style. Paul's purpose, then, is to vindicate his own ministry and authority vis-à-vis these false teachers. While Paul eventually is willing to play their own game by boasting in his own accomplishments, his general approach is to argue that, paradoxically, the power and authority of his ministry are manifested exactly in his humble and even embarrassing persona and experiences.[12] Toward this end, two contrasts dominate his argument: death versus life in chapters 1–7, and weakness versus power in chapters 10–13. This pattern of life *through death* and power *through weakness* is the inevitable product of Paul's conformity to Christ, who dispenses power and new life through his own weakness, poverty (11:9), and death. As Gorman notes, "What unifies the shifting rhetoric of 2 Corinthians is its ultimate focus on the Spirit-filled cruciform shape of transformed life in Christ."[13] Throughout the letter, as Wright puts it, "Paul is drawing on the controlling narrative of the Messiah's death and resurrection."[14] The clearest expression of this theme comes in 13:4: "For to be sure, he was crucified in weakness, yet he lives by God's power. Likewise, we are weak in him, yet by God's power we will live with him in our dealing with you." Second Corinthians therefore sets in contrast to a "theology of glory" a "theology of the cross," bringing to expression in many ways this distinctive focus in Paul's theology.[15] Yet Paul also stresses his conformity to Christ in his resurrection, echoing what is theological bedrock for Paul: the death-resurrection pattern stamped on Paul's self-perception and teaching. "The life of the apostle is the *existential illustration of the kerygma*."[16] And, of course, it is this same pattern, manifested in the foundational Christ-event and exemplified in Paul's life and ministry that the Corinthians are also to imitate.

Paul's impassioned defense and explanation of his ministry falls into three obvious parts. In chapters 1–7, Paul describes and defends his ministry vis-à-vis the Corinthians and the fraught history between them and the apostle. In chapters 8–9, he exhorts the Corinthians to participate in a specific ministry of Paul's: his collection for the struggling believers in Judea. Finally, in chapters 10–13, Paul defends his ministry in the face of competition for the Corinthians' attention from rival apostles who have entered into the community.

---

12. Alexander N. Kirk has argued that "encouragement in affliction" is a key theme (he translates *paraklēsis* as "encouragement" rather than "comfort" [1:3–7]) (*The Departure of an Apostle: Paul's Death Anticipated and Remembered*, WUNT 2/406 [Tübingen: Mohr Siebeck, 2015], 159–63).

13. Gorman, *Apostle of the Crucified Lord*, 346; see also Jerome Murphy-O'Connor, *The Theology of the Second Letter to the Corinthians* (Cambridge: Cambridge University Press, 1996), 142–43.

14. Wright, *Resurrection*, 310.

15. For this emphasis, see esp. Mark A. Seifrid, *The Second Letter to the Corinthians*, PNTC (Grand Rapids: Eerdmans, 2014), e.g., 100–109.

16. Schnelle, *Apostle Paul*, 247 (emphasis original). A key contrast in 2 Corinthians 1–7, therefore, is between "life" and "death" (1:8–9; 2:16; 3:6; 4:10–12, 14; 5:4, 14–15; 6:9).

1 PAUL'S BOLDNESS IN MINISTRY (1:1–7:16)

This first section of the letter is, according to Paul himself, sparked by the favorable report of Titus, whom Paul had sent to reconcile the Corinthians to his gospel and ministry. Yet it would be a mistake to think that this joyful tone characterizes these chapters as a whole. Paul seems to be wary of the sincerity or perhaps the extent of the Corinthians' repentance, because the tone of his ministry description is often defensive (as if he has to rebut charges against him) and aggressive (as if he thinks he still needs to win over some of the Corinthians). Thus, he continues to defend his conduct (3:1–3; 4:2, 13–15; 5:11–13; 6:3–11; cf. 1:12, 15–23), sometimes focusing on the strong tone of his "severe letter" (2:4; 7:4, 8–10). He exhorts them to "open wide" their hearts to him (6:13; cf. 7:2). A motif running through this section is Paul's "commending" of himself (3:1; 4:2; 5:12; 6:4).[17] Perhaps, if I had to single out one verse as setting the tone for the whole, it would be 3:12: "Therefore, since we have such a hope, we are very bold."[18]

1.1 Introduction and Initial Defense of Conduct (1:1–2:13)

After the usual identification of sender and audience, along with a greeting (1:1–2), Paul praises God for the comfort he brings to his people in Christ (1:3–7). This "praise" or "blessing" (*eulogētos*) replaces Paul's usual thanksgiving for his readers—perhaps an indication of continuing tension. At the same time, Paul, as he often does, uses this opening section to touch on themes that we will see throughout the letter: the close interdependence of Paul and the Corinthians—"if we are distressed, it is for your comfort" (v. 6)—rooted in Paul's own interdependence with Christ: he shares abundantly in the "sufferings of Christ" (v. 5: *ta pathēmata tou Christou*, "sufferings experienced in association with Christ").[19] Paul's use of the plural "we" creates difficulties for the interpreter throughout his letters, and this text is a prime case in point. The plural might be "editorial," Paul using it to refer to himself alone.[20] However, the shift to the singular in verse 15 might suggest rather that Paul, while referring perhaps especially to himself, refers not only to himself. As Guthrie puts it, "The 'we' of ministry carried out as a team must be considered as a significant 'voice' in 2 Corinthians alongside the 'I' of Paul's personal plans, experiences, perspectives, authority, and defense."[21] Having given thanks for the comfort he (and others) receive from God generally, Paul goes on to single out a particular time of distress when that divine comfort was very evident

---

17. As Talbert, *Reading Corinthians*, 133, notes. See also Linda Belleville for the emphasis on reciprocity and importance of "commendation" language (*Reflections of Glory: Paul's Polemical Use of the Moses-Doxa Tradition in 2 Corinthians 3:1–18*, JSNTSup 52 [Sheffield: JSOT, 1991], 120–35, 165).

18. Garland, *2 Corinthians*, 135–36.

19. Harris, *Second Epistle to the Corinthians*, 71, 75. See also Belleville, *Reflections of Glory*, 112–14; Gorman, *Apostle of the Crucified Lord*, 349–50.

20. E.g., Harris, *Second Epistle to the Corinthians*, 140; Seifrid, *Second Letter to the Corinthians*, 23.

21. Guthrie, *2 Corinthians*, 38; see discussion on pp. 32–38.

to him. The "troubles [or better "trial"—the Gk. is singular] we experienced in the province of Asia" (v. 8; cf. vv. 8–11) cannot be identified: Was it a serious illness,[22] the riot in Ephesus (Acts 19:23–41), or some other unknown persecution? Whatever it was, God delivered Paul from it, and so Paul now begins his letter by reflecting on the "comfort" that God brings amid "trials."

The opening paragraph of the letter body, verses 12–14, reveals the apologetic tone of the letter. It is framed by "boast," a word that is especially prominent in the letter.[23] Verse 12 exemplifies the tone and focus of the letter: "Now this is our boast: Our conscience testifies that we have conducted ourselves in the world, and especially in our relations with you, with integrity and godly sincerity. We have done so, relying not on worldly wisdom but on God's grace."[24] Paul immediately provides an example of his integrity in his relations with the Corinthians (1:15–2:4). The Corinthians were apparently citing Paul's change in travel plans to accuse him of being fickle and undependable. Paul had originally hoped to travel from Ephesus by sea to Corinth, then to move overland to Macedonia before returning to Corinth again to set sail for Judea (1:15–16). However, the seriousness of the rift between Paul and the Corinthians forced Paul to change those plans. He made an emergency trip to Corinth, a visit that exacerbated rather than solved the problem; hence he labels this a "painful" visit (2:1; cf. 1:23). After returning to Ephesus, he wrote a harsh letter of rebuke and sent it with Titus (2:3–4, 9; cf. 7:8–12). He is now in Macedonia, from whence he plans to visit Corinth once more. This change in plans, Paul stresses, was not the result of indecision or his own whim. He revised his itinerary because the situation in Corinth had changed: he wanted to "spare them" another "painful" visit to them (1:23; 2:1). Paul therefore has acted in integrity in his change of plans, revising his itinerary for the sake of his ministry to the Corinthians. His consistency toward them mirrors the consistency in God's dealings with his people in Christ. Just as Paul does not say both yes and no at the same time, so in Christ God's posture toward his promises and his people is always yes in Christ (1:17–20). Indeed, Paul argues, in a kind of theological excursus, all God's promises are "yes" in Christ (1:20). Here Paul reflects his foundational conviction about the way all God's promises in the Old Testament—be they prophecies, typological prefigurements, or general teaching—find their fulfillment and ultimate meaning in Christ (cf. Rom 3:21; 10:4; 15:4; 1 Cor 10:6, 11). The Corinthians have seen a realization of these promises in God's "anointing" of them (2 Cor 1:21). This anointing, as Chrysostom suggests, transfers to all believers the special "setting

---

22. E.g., E. Bernard Allo, *Saint Paul: Seconde épître aux Corinthiens*, Études Bibliques (Paris: Gabalda, 1937), 10–11.

23. Six of Paul's ten uses of *kauchēsis* ("boasting") and twenty of his thirty-five uses of *kauchaomai* ("boast") are in 2 Corinthians. On the importance of "boasting" in the letter, see Timothy

B. Savage, *Power through Weakness: Paul's Understanding of the Christian Ministry in 2 Corinthians*, SNTSMS 86 (Cambridge: Cambridge University Press, 1996), 58–61.

24. Belleville suggests that this verse states the theme of the letter (*Reflections of Glory*, 119).

apart" reserved for prophets, priests, and kings in the Old Testament.[25] This anointing causes believers to have confidence that they will stand firm in Christ. Bridging the time between this inaugural "anointing" and the full realization of the promises is the Spirit, given to believers as a "deposit [*arrabōn*], guaranteeing what is to come" (v. 22).

Paul's reminiscence about his previous experience with the Corinthians leads him to bring up a particularly difficult matter on which he wants closure. A certain person (Gk. *tis*) had created difficulty for the church and for Paul in particular (2:5). The perpetrator has apparently been punished in some way, and Paul insists that this punishment is adequate (v. 6). He is concerned that continuing discipline may overwhelm this person with sorrow, perhaps leading them permanently to turn their back on Christ and the church and giving Satan the ultimate victory in this matter (vv. 7–11). Paul therefore urges the community to forgive him, as he himself has (vv. 7, 10) and to reassert their love for him (v. 8). A few interpreters think that the person Paul now wants to restore is the man Paul urged the church to discipline in 1 Corinthians 5:1–13. But the focus on injury to Paul especially (2 Cor 2:5) suggests rather an otherwise unknown instance of a person prominent in leading the rebellion against Paul's authority.[26]

1.2 Paul's New-Covenant Ministry (2:14–7:4)

In 2:12–13, Paul returns to his discussion of his travels, now bringing the readers up to date on his latest movements: he has traveled from Ephesus to Troas, but, not yet finding Titus there, he has moved on to Macedonia. At this point, he abruptly breaks off his outline of travel to express thanks to God (v. 14). He does not return to his travels until 7:5, which picks up right where he left off in 2:13: "So I said goodbye to them and went on to Macedonia" (2:13b); "For when we came into Macedonia" (7:5a). Therefore, the lengthy and involved description of Paul's apostolic ministry in 2:14–7:4 is, from a literary standpoint, a digression. As I have noted, joy at the good report of Titus is prominent, framing this long section of the letter (2:14; 7:5–7). However, as already noted, Paul's relief is tempered by his apparent continuing concern about the depth and/or extent of the Corinthians' repentance. At least it is difficult otherwise to explain Paul's robust defense of his apostolic ministry among them. And it should be noted that the whole section culminates in his exhortation that the Corinthians "make room for us in your hearts" (7:2).

Paul's concern, then, is to "commend" himself to the Corinthians with a view to them fully acknowledging his authority and completely buying into the gospel he preaches. For, as we will see, Paul's ministry and the gospel he preaches are inextricably tied together. Paul's case for his authority and gospel proceeds in four stages. After the transitional

25. *NPNF¹* 12:290; cf. Philip Edgcumbe Hughes, *The Second Epistle to the Corinthians*, NICNT (Grand Rapids: Eerdmans, 1962), 43.

26. E.g., Harris, *Second Epistle to the Corinthians*, 227;

Guthrie, *2 Corinthians*, 139–40; cf. Roetzel, *Judgement in the Community*, 120–22. Garland, however, thinks the identification with the person in 1 Corinthians 5 is possible (*2 Corinthians*, 117–25).

travel note in 2:12–13, Paul commends himself as a minister of the new covenant, boldly proclaiming a message that brings either salvation or damnation (2:14–4:6). In 4:7–5:10, Paul develops a theme central to the letter: that the life God offers in Christ comes through mortality and death. Paul then expands on the nature of his ministry, calling on the Corinthians to respond to the grace of God's salvation (5:11–6:2). Finally, Paul turns again to his own experience, pleading with the Corinthians to avoid compromise with the world and to return to the fold of his gospel ministry (6:3–7:4). A key contrast throughout these chapters is that between life and death:

> For we are to God the pleasing aroma of Christ among those who are being saved and those who are perishing. To the one we are an aroma that brings death; to the other, an aroma that brings life. (2:15–16a)

> The letter kills, but the Spirit gives life. (3:6b)

> We always carry around in our body the death of Jesus, so that the life of Jesus may also be revealed in our body. For we who are alive are always being given over to death for Jesus' sake, so that his life may also be revealed in our mortal body. So then, death is at work in us, but life is at work in you. (4:10–12)

> For while we are in this tent, we groan and are burdened, because we do not wish to be unclothed but to be clothed instead with our heavenly dwelling, so that what is mortal may be swallowed up by life. (5:4)

> For Christ's love compels us, because we are convinced that one died for all, and therefore all died. And he died for all, that those who live should no longer live for themselves but for him who died for them and was raised again. (5:14–15)

> Dying, and yet we live on . . . (6:9b)

Christ's death and resurrection provide the template for his followers and servants. Paul's ministry is therefore characterized by that life-through-death pattern.

1.2.1 Paul's New-Covenant Boldness (2:14–4:6)

Paul's argument here has three movements: 2:14–3:6, 3:7–18, and 4:1–6—the first and the third featuring parallel vocabulary and ideas in a ring composition.

Before Paul can even mention the arrival of Titus, with the good news he brings (see 7:6–7), he breaks out in an expression of thanks to God (v. 14). He celebrates God as the one who "always leads us as captives in Christ's triumphal procession." Paul here alludes to the familiar Roman custom of celebrating the military victory of a general through a "triumph," a kind of parade in which the victorious conqueror would lead captives from his campaign in a public display. Paul puts himself, and other Christian ministers, in the place of these captives, led in Christ's victory parade.[27] The imagery might suggest that Paul was led to death, since this was often the fate of captives in a triumph—and, as we have seen, this would fit with the focus on life in the midst of and through dying that marks these verses.[28] However, captives in a triumph were not always, and perhaps not even usually, put to death,[29] so we cannot press this point.[30] But it is significant for the argument of the letter that Paul casts himself in the role of the degraded captive, whose condition of suffering and humility, he will argue, is precisely the means by which Christ wins the victory and by which his power is unleashed in ministry.

The Roman triumphal procession also featured the use of censers to spread incense. It is therefore possible that Paul's claim to be an "aroma" of Christ, bringing either death or life, carries on the imagery of the triumph (vv. 14b–16).[31] Paul's defensive posture in speaking of his ministry becomes obvious in verse 17, where he contrasts his sincere and forthright spirit with those "who peddle the word of God for profit." This contrast carries over into 3:1–3. We may surmise that Paul's opponents were bragging about letters of commendation they carried with them. Paul, however, needs no such letters: the work of God's Spirit, written on their hearts, is all the commendation the Corinthians should require. Paul's reference to "tablets of stone" (v. 3) reveals that he is already morphing into his discussion of the contrast between old covenant, with its focus on the law, and new covenant, with its focus on the Spirit. He is obviously reflecting new-covenant prophecies about the internal work of God's Spirit and the interiorization of his law in the last days:

> I will give you a new heart and put a new spirit in you; I will remove from you your heart of stone and give you a heart of flesh. And I will put my Spirit in you and move you to follow my decrees and be careful to keep my laws. (Ezek 36:26–27)

> I will put my law in their minds and write it on their hearts. (Jer 31:33b)[32]

---

27. Many older interpreters struggled with the idea that Paul would be comparing himself to a degraded prisoner and took the verb *thriambeuonti* to mean "cause to triumph" (see KJV). But almost all modern scholars agree that this verb with an accusative following (*hēmas*) must mean "lead [us] in triumphal procession" (see also Col 2:15).

28. See esp. Scott J. Hafemann, *Suffering and Ministry in the Spirit: Paul's Defense of His Ministry in II Corinthians 2:14–3:3* (Grand Rapids: Eerdmans, 1990), 19–34.

29. Mary Beard, *The Roman Triumph* (Cambridge: Harvard University Press, 2007), 129–32.

30. See, e.g., Harris, *Second Epistle to the Corinthians*, 245–46.

31. Indeed, Guthrie thinks that Paul might be comparing himself to the incense bearers (*2 Corinthians*, 167).

32. For the influence of Ezekiel's new-covenant prophecies on 2 Corinthians, see esp. Jeffrey W. Aernie, "Tablets of Fleshly Hearts: Paul and Ezekiel in Concert," *JSPL* 6 (2016): 55–73; Carol Kern Stockhausen, *Moses' Veil and the Glory of the New Covenant: The Exegetical Substructure of II Cor. 3,1–4,6*, AnBib 116 (Rome: Pontifical Biblical Institute, 1989).

It is the Spirit, whose power is unleashed in unprecedented ways, that gives Paul his "competence" in ministry (vv. 4–6). Paul climaxes this section with a contrast between "letter" (*gramma*), which "kills," and the Spirit, which "gives life" (v. 6). The letter-Spirit contrast is found twice else in Paul, in Romans 2:29 (see also v. 27) and 7:6. This contrast, as is well known, took on for many centuries in the church a hermeneutical thrust, setting a "literal" reading of the text against a "S/spiritual" one. But, however valid a strategy for interpreting the text this approach might be, it has no basis in Paul's contrast. For him, as this context makes quite clear, the contrast is between the old era dominated by God's "written" law and the new dominated by God's Spirit. Some interpreters soften the contrast between old and new by arguing that Paul's choice of "letter" (instead, for instance, of "law") shows his contrast is between the Spirit and the old covenant when it is read legalistically or apart from the Spirit.[33] But Paul's use of "letter" here is governed by the context, in which he is speaking of letters of commendation. And Paul typically views the Spirit as a distinctive new-covenant gift. It is therefore more likely that "letter" refers straightforwardly to the Old Testament law that, for him, is, in itself, an inevitably external, written document.[34]

Reference to the Old Testament law in terms of "letter" leads Paul to highlight his ministry and its power by contrasting it with the ministry of Moses (vv. 7–18). This passage is one of the most difficult in the Pauline letters, due to a number of ambiguous words and constructions and to the debate about how Paul is appropriating the Old Testament. But it is also an important text theologically, since it is one of the only places where Paul specifically discusses the salvation-historical movement from old covenant to new. So, while it is true that Paul's focus is on the relationship between his *ministry* and that of Moses, he also contrasts those ministries by contrasting the two covenants that give those ministries their basis and power. Paul's main point—indeed, one of the main points of the whole letter—comes in verse 12: "Since we have such a hope, we are very bold." Paul's confidence in ministry arises not from his own person or talents but from the new-covenant ministry, empowered by the Spirit. This extensive discussion of a contrast in covenants may simply arise from Paul's own concerns. But it is perhaps more likely that Paul is already here launching a strike against the "false apostles" with whom he deals in chapters 10–13.[35]

Paul explains and defends his own ministry by way of contrast with the ministry of Moses, drawing freely on the narrative about Moses veiling his face in Exodus

---

33. See, e.g., Thomas Schmeller, *Der zweite Brief an die Korinther*, 2 vols., EKKNT 8 (Neukirchen-Vluyn: Neukirchener, 2010, 2015), 1:184–87; Martin, *2 Corinthians*, 195.

34. See, e.g., Ridderbos, *Paul*, 215–19; Sigurd Grindheim, "The Law Kills But the Gospel Gives Life: The Letter-Spirit Dualism in 2 Corinthians 3.5–18," *JSNT* 84 (2001): 97–115. As Michael Winger argues, *gramma* and *nomos* refer to the same

thing—the law of Moses—but view it in different ways (*By What Law? The Meaning of Nomos in the Letters of Paul*, SBLDS 128 [Atlanta: Scholars Press, 1992], 41).

35. E.g., Belleville, *Reflections of Glory*, 165; Murphy-O'Connor, *Theology of the Second Letter to the Corinthians*, 32–33; Hays, *Echoes*, 126; contra, e.g., Thrall, *Second Epistle to the Corinthians*, 1:240–41.

34:29–35. This narrative comes immediately after the second giving of the law (Exod 34:1–28), occasioned by the Israelites' fall into sin at the golden-calf incident (Exod 32:1–33:6). Moses's face was "radiant" after his encounter with God on the mountain, causing Aaron and all the Israelites to fear. But Moses insisted that they draw near so that he could relay to the people the Lord's commandments. After Moses spoke with the people, he put a veil over his face until he entered to speak with the Lord again. The LXX uses the verb *doxazō*, "glorify," three times in this paragraph to denote the radiance of Moses's face (34:29, 30, 35). Paul uses this word to contrast old and new covenants in verses 7–11, and then picks up the veil imagery to continue this contrast in verses 12–18.

The ministries of Moses and of Paul both "came with glory," Paul affirms, but that of Moses brought "death" (v. 7)/"condemnation" (v. 9), while his brings "righteousness" (v. 9)—used here, in contrast to condemnation, in the forensic sense of "right standing" with God. Paul does not here explain why Moses's ministry brought death. But he elsewhere teaches that the law, while God's good gift to his people, could not be obeyed because of pervasive human sin.[36] Rather than bringing the life it promised, therefore, it brought, or perhaps better, confirmed the sentence of death pronounced on humankind because of Adam's sin (Rom 5:12–21; 7:7–25; Gal 3:10, 15–29). Paul's commentary on the text of Exodus at the end of verse 7 is difficult to unravel. Drawing an inference from the Old Testament text, he claims that "the Israelites could not look steadily at the face of Moses because of its glory, transitory though it was." "Transitory though it was" translates the participle *katargoumenēn*, which comes from a distinctive Pauline verb (*katargeō*) that means "abolish, render impotent" (it refers again to the old covenant in vv. 11 and 13; see also v. 14). Many argue that the verb must have this meaning here: the glory of the old covenant is being "rendered null and void" by the advent of new-covenant realities.[37] However, despite protests to the contrary, this verb, used in the present tense to modify "glory," quite naturally takes the sense of "fading"—hence NIV's "transitory."[38] The glory of the old covenant was not permanent, in contrast to the "greater glory" "which lasts" of Paul's new-covenant ministry (v. 11).

If Paul's ministry has more glory than that of Moses, it is also characterized by openness and boldness, in contrast to hiddenness, signified by the veil worn by Moses. Paul's comment on this in verse 13 is again difficult to understand: "We are not like Moses, who would put a veil over his face to prevent the Israelites from seeing the end of what was passing away." Paul again uses a participial form of *katargeō*, and the controversy over its meaning arises here again. In this particular context, it is possible that it modifies "veil," so that Paul would be suggesting that it is the veiling that is

---

36. Hays, *Echoes*, 131.
37. E.g., Garland, *2 Corinthians*, 211–12; Hays, *Echoes*, 134.
38. "Fading" is the translation in RSV; CEB; NAB; NASB;

NLT. See on this point, Harris, *Second Epistle to the Corinthians*, 284–85.

"brought to an end" with the advent of the new covenant (see vv. 14–16).[39] However, it is likely that this participle picks up the use of the same form in verse 7 (see also v. 11) and refers to the glory: Moses did not want the Israelites to see the "end" of the glory that was fading. The translation "end" here in verse 13 in the NIV is also controversial. While most English translations adopt a reading similar to the NIV, the word Paul uses here, *telos*, could also mean "result" (NET) or "outcome" (ESV) or even "goal." If this is its meaning, then Paul would be suggesting that Moses had a beneficent purpose in wearing the veil: he wanted to keep the Israelites from seeing the ultimate significance of the glory on his face—namely death (v. 7). However, it perhaps makes better sense to follow most translations and give *telos* the meaning "end." Paul would then be suggesting that Moses veiled his face so that the Israelites would not recognize that the glory of his face, and hence his old-covenant ministry, would be coming to an end. While the promised new covenant became a hope for the people of Israel, Moses, at this point in time, wanted the people to deal with the realities of the old-covenant ministry they had been put under and not simply ignore the law he was revealing to them. This reading of verse 13 is preferable, among other reasons, for the continuity it establishes with verses 14–16, where "veiling" is used to denote the inability of the people to understand the true meaning of the old-covenant Scriptures. Only in Christ is that veil taken away.

In verses 17–18, Paul wraps up this complicated "midrash" on Exodus by returning to the key theme of the Spirit. The simple claim that "the Lord is the Spirit" is a well-known text that has been used to speculate about the relationship of Christ and the Spirit. However, there is considerable debate about what "lord" (*kyrios*) refers to in these verses. The word occurs five times in verses 16–18:

> But whenever anyone turns to *the Lord* [*kyrion*], the veil is taken away. [17]Now *the Lord* [*ho kyrios*] is the Spirit, and where the Spirit of *the Lord* [*kyriou*] is, there is freedom. [18]And we all, who with unveiled faces contemplate *the Lord's* [*kyriou*] glory, are being transformed into his image with ever-increasing glory, which comes from *the Lord* [*kyriou*], who is the Spirit.

On the one hand, most scholars in recent years think that "Lord" refers at least initially to Yahweh in these verses. Verse 16 may be a kind of interpretive rendering of Exodus 34:34a: "But whenever he [Moses] entered the LORD's presence to speak with him, he removed the veil until he came out."[40] The articular *kyrios* in verse 17 would then be resumptive: "This Lord [in Exodus] is the Spirit"; and the other references

---

39. Scott J. Hafemann, *2 Corinthians*, NIVAC (Grand Rapids: Zondervan, 2000), 153–56.

40. See esp. Harris, *Second Epistle to the Corinthians*, 306.

First Thessalonians 1:9b might also support this reading: "They tell how you turned [*epestrepsate*] to God from idols to serve the living and true God."

would then follow.[41] However, it is more natural to think that the Lord to whom one turns in verse 16 is Christ. Paul's point in verse 17 and verse 18b, then, is to identify the work of this Lord with the work of the Spirit. He is not identifying the persons; but he is equating the Lord with "the Spirit's *work* of moving believers into freedom from Torah observance."[42]

Verse 18 continues, implicitly identifying Yahweh's glory with Christ's, in a way typical of Paul's high Christology.[43] A possible objection to this interpretation is 4:5, which claims that Christ is "the image of God." "His image," then, in verse 18, it is argued, must mean "the image of God," with "Lord" being Yahweh. However, "his image" might simply refer to Christ's own image, as in Romans 8:29: "The image of his Son." Paul's point would not be, of course, that the two are identical in person but that what turning to the Lord meant for Moses—removal of the veil, contemplating God's glory—is now possible for the people of God through the Spirit.[44] It is this "Spirit of the Lord" who brings "freedom"—perhaps, in context, especially freedom from the condemning power of the "letter" (see vv. 6, 7–9).[45] Unlike the Israelites, the new-covenant people of God are able, by the Spirit, to encounter permanently the glory of the Lord, and, in doing so, are being transformed into his image (v. 18).

Paul concludes his initial defense of his ministry in 4:1–6, a paragraph that picks up key vocabulary from 2:16–3:18. Because of the ministry he has been given (see 3:7, 8, 9), Paul does not "lose heart"—he is not timid.[46] Rather he "commends" himself (see 3:1) as a minister who proclaims the truth clearly and without pretense (4:2–3). As Guthrie notes, the theme of commendation is "an important thread that weaves its way through the book" (see also 5:12; 6:4; 7:11; 10:12, 18; 12:11).[47] To be sure, not everyone responds. But this is because "the god of this age" has blinded people (v. 4), causing Paul's gospel proclamation to be veiled (see 3:14–16). They therefore cannot see "the light that emanates from the gospel, that light being the glory of Christ himself" (my own paraphrase, following Guthrie; for "glory," see 3:7, 8, 9, 10, 11, 18). In what almost appears as an add-on, Paul notes that Christ is himself "the image of God." As in Colossians 1:15, where we find a similar claim (cf. Rom 8:29; note again 2 Cor 3:18),

---

41. James D. G. Dunn, "2 Corinthians III.17—'The Lord Is the Spirit,'" *JTS* 21 (1970): 309–20; Harris, *Second Epistle to the Corinthians*, 310–11; Belleville, *Reflections of Glory*, 257–67. Some who take this view think that Paul supposes that Christ is included in the person of the Lord in Exodus (e.g., C. Kavin Rowe, "Biblical Pressure and Trinitarian Hermeneutics," *ProEccl* 11 [2002]: 303–4; Hill, *Paul and the Trinity*, 143–49; Guthrie, *2 Corinthians*, 225).

42. Fee, *Pauline Christology*, 179.

43. See, e.g., Barnett, *Second Epistle to the Corinthians*, 196–200; Thrall, *Second Epistle to the Corinthians*, 1:278–82; David B. Capes, *The Divine Christ: Paul, the Lord Jesus, and the*

Scriptures of Israel (Grand Rapids: Baker, 2018), 143–46; Fee, *Pauline Christology*, 177–80.

44. Thrall, *Second Epistle to the Corinthians*, 1:278–82.

45. Neill Quinn Hamilton, *The Holy Spirit and Eschatology in Paul*, Scottish Journal of Theology Occasional Papers 6 (Edinburgh: Oliver & Boyd, 1957), 4–8. It is also possible that "freedom" here is virtually equivalent to Paul's ministerial "boldness" (v. 12; Paul B. Duff, "Transformed 'From Glory to Glory': Paul's Appeal to the Experience of His Readers in 2 Corinthians 3:18," *JBL* 127 [2008]: 767).

46. See Garland, *2 Corinthians*, 204, on the verb *enkakeō*.

47. Guthrie, *2 Corinthians*, 237.

the point is that Christ is in the closest possible relationship to God. After the somewhat parenthetical verse 5, Paul elaborates on verse 4 in verse 6, identifying God as the one "who said 'Let light shine out of darkness' [*ek skotous phōs lampsei*]." The Old Testament text Paul cites is usually thought to be Genesis 1:3, so that we find here a creation/new-creation link. However, a good case can be made that the reference is to Isaiah 9:2 (LXX 9:1): "The people walking in darkness have seen a great light; on those living in the land of deep darkness *a light has dawned* [*phōs lampsei eph hymas*]." In this case, Paul, as he often does, would be viewing his own ministry in the light of the Isaianic vision for the future.[48] In the last part of verse 6, Paul brings this vision of light to bear on Christ; God "made his light shine in our hearts to give us the light of the knowledge of God's glory displayed in the face of Christ." In addition to the obvious allusions to the new-covenant glory of Christ (3:17–18), Paul may also be alluding to his own conversion experience. Common to this text and the narratives of that experience are light, a heavenly voice, and a commission to service (see, e.g., Acts 9:3–16; 22:6–11; 26:12–17), when "a light from heaven flashed around him" (Acts 9:3) and Paul was given a revelation of the risen Christ.[49]

1.2.2 The Interplay of Life and Death (4:7–5:10)

The transition from 2:14–4:6 to this next section is captured by Margaret Thrall: "If Paul has truly experienced the revelation of the divine glory (4.6), why is his own condition so conspicuously lacking in glory?"[50] Paul's answer comes immediately in verse 7, which introduces the theme of verses 7–15: "But we have this treasure in jars of clay to show that this all-surpassing power is from God and not from us."[51] The "treasure" of the "gospel that displays the glory of Christ" (v. 4) is contained in fragile and impermanent human bodies. Yet it is that humble state of the vessel that makes it all the more clear that it is God's power that is at work in the gospel. "The fragility of the human minister thus serves to keep the focus on the God of the gospel, not his messenger."[52] Paul provides examples of the weakness of himself and other gospel ministers in verses 8–9 and then, in verses 10–12, adds a theological commentary. The trials faced by Paul and others are because they carry around in their bodies "the death [*nekrōsin*] of Jesus"—probably a reference to the daily humiliations and trials Paul experiences in his apostolic ministry. These difficulties are related to Jesus in that it is his conformity to Christ, who sets the pattern of dying followed by new life, that explains and gives meaning to these trials. It is precisely through the apostle's dying "every day"

---

48. See esp. Savage, *Power through Weakness*, 112–13.

49. Martin, *2 Corinthians*, 224; Thrall, *Second Epistle to the Corinthians*, 1:316–17; Schnelle, *Apostle Paul*, 92. On the importance of Paul's conversion in informing this language in Paul, see esp. Kim, *Origin of Paul's Gospel*, 7–11. Some doubt that the reference is to Paul's conversion (e.g., Furnish, *II Corinthians*, 251).

50. Thrall, *Second Epistle to the Corinthians*, 1:321.

51. Schmeller, *Der zweite Brief an die Korinther*, 1:253.

52. Guthrie, *2 Corinthians*, 254.

(1 Cor 15:31) that the life of Jesus is revealed in Paul and that the Corinthians themselves experience that new life also (2 Cor 4:11–12). These verses, Savage notes, are "the nucleus of the apostle's understanding of Christian ministry."[53] Paul uses a quotation from Psalm 116:10 (115:1 LXX) to draw a connection between his faith in the reality of Christ's death and resurrection and his bold proclamation of the gospel (vv. 13–15).[54] Verses 14–16 are transitional.[55] "Therefore we do not lose heart" repeats 4:1, and verses 16–17 summarize the contrast between the humble form of the human body and its inward renewal, leading to "an eternal glory." But there is also introduced a contrast between the "momentary" troubles of this life (see also "temporary" in v. 18) and the glory that is yet to come (v. 17). This contrast introduces the subject matter of 5:1–10.

In these verses, Paul focuses on the hope that God will replace the "earthly tent we live in" with "an eternal house in heaven" (5:1). While a few interpreters have argued that Paul is referring to corporate entities (e.g., the people of God represented by the temple),[56] most agree that it is the body of individual believers that Paul is talking about. The passage is therefore a bit of an aside, interrupting Paul's discussion of his ministry (4:7–15; 5:11ff.) with an elaboration of the contrast between the "wasting away" and troubles of the believer's earthly body and the yet unseen glory to come (4:16–18). Picking up this theme, Paul notes that "while we are in this tent [our earthly bodies]" where "we groan and are burdened" (5:4), we have God's promise that we will be "clothed . . . with our heavenly dwelling" (the resurrection body; vv. 2, 4). The present tense that Paul uses in verse 1—"we *have* a building from God"—and the verb he uses in verses 2 and 4—*ependyomai*, which might be rendered "put on *over*"—could indicate that Paul thinks this new resurrection body is given to us immediately after our earthly body is "destroyed."[57] However, Paul seems pretty clear in other texts that the resurrection body is given only at the time of the parousia (e.g., 1 Thess 4:13–18). We can read this present text legitimately in conformity with this perspective, the present tense stressing the certainty of what God will give us, and the verb *ependyomai* meaning simply "clothe" (e.g., NIV).[58] In light of this, believers can be confident in knowing that, while in our earthly bodies, "we are away from Lord," we look forward to the time when we will not be "naked" (v. 3) but will be "away from the body and at home with the Lord" (vv. 6–8). Paul is obviously using "away from the Lord" and "at home with

---

53. Savage, *Power through Weakness*, 172.

54. As Peter Balla points out, Paul probably quotes Ps 115:1 LXX with the wider context in view, a context that focuses on the suffering of the psalmist ("2 Corinthians," in Beale and Carson, *Commentary on the New Testament Use of the Old Testament*, 765; cf. Wright, *Resurrection*, 363).

55. Most scholars (and Bibles) put a major break between 4:18 and 5:1, but a minority (e.g., Furnish, *II Corinthians*, 288; Garland, *2 Corinthians*, 238) put the break between 4:15 and 4:16.

56. E. Earle Ellis, "II Corinthians V.1–10 in Pauline Eschatology," *NTS* 6 (1960): 211–24.

57. Harris, *Raised Immortal*, 219–26.

58. E.g., Harris, *Second Epistle to the Corinthians*, 378–79 ("an ideal possession"); Andrew T. Lincoln, *Paradise Now and Not Yet: Studies in the Role of the Heavenly Dimension in Paul's Thought with Special Reference to His Eschatology*, SNTSMS 43 (Cambridge: Cambridge University Press, 1981), 62–63; Kirk, *Departure of an Apostle*, 177–78.

the Lord" in a particular relative sense. The believer's entire existence is "in Christ," whether in this life or the next. Yet our life in these earthly bodies, with all the trials, doubts, and continuing sin that goes with this life, means we are not "at home" with the Lord in the way we someday will be.[59]

Interpreted in this way (which follows the majority of scholarly assessments), this paragraph both stresses the certainty of being given a new resurrected body and implies the possibility of a transitional period of "nakedness"—that is, of being without a body. Paul, of course, often expresses his hope that he will be alive, to be "taken up" with Christ at the moment of his appearing, exchanging in an instant the earthly body for the heavenly. But this paragraph suggests he also reckons with the possibility that he will die before the parousia and will therefore have to endure a period of time without a body. This is also, of course, a time of great joy, being "with Christ" (Phil 1:23). But, in keeping with the biblical perspective on human beings, which views the body as basic to human identity, a time without a body is less than ideal. Being with Christ after death is a good thing, but living in the new heaven and new earth in resurrection bodies is better.[60]

Paul concludes this passage with an exhortation and warning: whether in this body or not, we should always "make it our goal to please him" (v. 9) because "we must all appear before the judgment seat of Christ, so that each of us may receive what is due us for the things done while in the body, whether good or bad" (v. 10). The judgment Paul refers to in this verse is often interpreted as a matter of the rewards that Christians will receive when we appear before Christ. The judgment about being saved, it is argued, has already been finalized for believers in the declaration of justification at the time of initial faith. So what Paul is warning about here is the reality that the work believers do after conversion will be assessed and that this assessment will determine the degree of reward that we receive.[61] However, there is some question about whether Paul speaks elsewhere about degrees of rewards (see my comments on 1 Cor 3:12–15 and pp. 554–57). And there is little in this context to suggest that Paul is referring to anything else but his usual focus in judgment texts: the salvation or damnation of the individual.[62] To be sure, if this is what Paul means here, we face a certain tension in his teaching in terms of the relationship between an initial and definitive judgment of justification and a final assessment of status at the judgment. But this tension runs through many passages and themes in Paul, and we should probably not try to dissolve it here by interpreting 5:10 in terms of "degrees of reward" (see pp. 554–57).

59. For discussion of the tension in Paul between the "presence" and "absence" of Christ, see esp. Peter Orr, *Christ Absent and Present: A Study in Pauline Christology*, WUNT 2/354 (Tübingen: Mohr Siebeck, 2014).

60. For this emphasis, see esp. Wright, *Resurrection*, passim.

61. See, e.g., Furnish, *II Corinthians*, 305; Barnett, *Second Epistle to the Corinthians*, 276–77; Liselotte Mattern, *Das Verständnis des Gerichtes bei Paulus*, ATANT 47 (Zürich: Zwingli, 1966), 157–58; Harris, *Second Epistle to the Corinthians*, 408–9; cf. also idem, *Raised Immortal*, 155–57; Hughes, *Second Epistle to the Corinthians*, 181–82; Guthrie, *2 Corinthians*, 289–90.

62. See, e.g., Hafemann, *2 Corinthians*, 216–26; Thrall, *Second Epistle to the Corinthians*, 1:395; Seifrid, *Second Letter to the Corinthians*, 237–38.

1.2.3 Responding to Paul, God's Ambassador (5:11–6:10)

After the slight detour in 5:1–10, Paul returns to the main highway: his explanation and defense of his apostolic ministry. This next section is framed by two related points:

1. Paul again "commends" himself to the Corinthians as a credentialed ambassador of the ministry of reconciliation (5:12; 6:4);
2. Paul pleads with the Corinthians to "take pride" in him (v. 12) and to "not . . . receive God's grace in vain" (6:1).

In between, Paul elaborates on the nature and content of his preaching, weaving together a number of threads that express key aspects of Paul's theology.

The influence of his opponents can again be detected, as Paul defends himself against the charge that he is "out of [his] mind" (5:13). He deflects this criticism simply by asserting the constancy of his concern for the Corinthians and their spiritual welfare. Paul is impelled in his attitude by the love of Christ, exhibited, as Paul so often emphasizes, in Christ's death for us: "We are convinced that one died for all, and therefore all died" (v. 14). The preposition "for" (Gk. *hyper*) probably has the sense of "in place of," as the second part of the verse implies: Paul is thinking of Christ as the "second Adam," the head of all humans, whose death is, then, our death as well. He dies "for [*hyper*] us" in that we all died, in God's sight, in and with him.[63] Some proponents of "limited atonement" insist that the "all" in this verse is implicitly qualified in the sense of "all believers." There is certainly some basis for this limitation, since the "all died" in the second part of the verse is most naturally taken to be limited to Christians. However, it is also possible that Paul thinks of Christ's death as having potentially universal effects and that he can express this in terms both of Christ's dying "for" (*hyper*) all and, reciprocally, of all themselves dying. It is, then, in verse 15, with the reference to "those who live" that the limitation to believers is expressed: only those who "receive the gift" of God's universally available atoning grace live in this sense.[64]

Paul resumes his defense in verse 16: Although he used to regard Christ "according to the flesh" (*kata sarka*), he no longer views him or anyone in this "worldly" (NIV) way. Rudolf Bultmann famously read this verse as if Paul were saying that he no longer had any concern about the physical or "historical" Jesus. But "according to the flesh" modifies Paul's way of perceiving, not Christ.[65] Paul's conversion meant a turnaround

---

63. Hughes, *Second Epistle to the Corinthians*, 192–95. On the use of *hyper* as having a substitutionary sense, see, e.g., R. E. Davies, "Christ in Our Place—The Contribution of the Prepositions," *TynBul* 21 (1970): 82; Murray J. Harris, *Prepositions and Theology in the Greek New Testament* (Grand Rapids: Zondervan, 2012), 211–16.

64. See, e.g., Guthrie, *2 Corinthians*, 304–5, for a good explanation of this view; also Harris, *Second Epistle to the Corinthians*, 420–21.

65. Bultmann acknowledged that *kata sarka* ("according to the flesh") probably modified the verb rather than "Jesus" but claimed that the point about Paul's lack of interest in the earthly

in his perception of all things, including Christ.[66] Indeed, so radical is this turnaround that it can be expressed in the language of "new creation" (v. 17). This phrase, which appears only here and in Galatians 6:15 in the New Testament, is often taken to refer to the individual believer, who, "in Christ," is a "new creation" (*kainē ktisis*).[67] However, Old Testament and Jewish antecedents of this phrase suggest a broader connotation: the entire new state of affairs inaugurated at Christ's first coming and to be consummated at his second.[68] The language at the end of verse 17—"the old has gone, the new is here"—picks up language from Isaiah 43:18–19, where the prophet is celebrating the new "exodus" that God will accomplish for his people. Paul elaborates this new work of redemption with the language of "reconciliation" in verses 18–20. While not widely used in Paul (see also Rom 5:10–11; 11:15; Eph 2:16; Col 1:20–22), reconciliation is a key concept in unpacking the significance of God's work in Christ. The word group is rare in the LXX (only five occurrences), but the idea communicated by it, in association with some of the other Old Testament allusions in this context, may include reference to the return from Israel's exile that is now occurring in the proclamation of the gospel.[69] Thus here Paul uses this word to sum up the message he proclaims.[70] Specifically, he says, he proclaims that "God was reconciling the world to himself in Christ, not counting people's sins against them" (v. 19). The first part of this verse could also be translated "For God was in Christ, reconciling the world to himself" (NLT), putting a bit more stress on the incarnation.[71] But the former rendering, adopted in most English translations, fits the contextual focus on reconciliation. The extent of the meaning of "world" is also debated. The reference to human sins in the second part of the verse suggests a limitation to the "world of humans." But the partial parallel in Colossians 1:20 could suggest that the reference is to the universe—the "all things" that God created.[72] In verse 20, Paul yet again returns to his focus on his own ministry: "We are therefore Christ's ambassadors, as though God were making his appeal through us. We implore you on Christ's behalf: Be reconciled to God."

Jesus was present in any case (*Theology of the New Testament*, 1:238–39). But this presumes an unlikely sense of "knowing."

66. Christian Wolff, "True Apostolic Knowledge of Christ: Exegetical Reflections on 2 Corinthians 5:14ff," in *Paul and Jesus: Collected Essays*, ed. A. J. M. Wedderburn (Sheffield: Sheffield Academic, 1989), 87–91.

67. Moyer V. Hubbard, *New Creation in Paul's Letters and Thought*, SNTSMS 119 (Cambridge: Cambridge University Press, 2002), 178–82; Harris, *Second Epistle to the Corinthians*, 432–33.

68. See Moo, "Creation and New Creation"; and also, e.g., Martin, *2 Corinthians*, 146; Garland, *2 Corinthians*, 287.

69. See esp. G. K. Beale, *A New Testament Biblical Theology: The Unfolding of the Old Testament in the New* (Grand Rapids: Baker, 2011), 528–38.

70. Despite the first-person plural forms, there is good reason to think that Paul in this passage focuses on his own apostolic ministry (Bruce Clark, *Completing Christ's Afflictions: Christ, Paul, and the Reconciliation of All Things*, WUNT 2/383 [Tübingen: Mohr Siebeck, 2015], 134–50).

71. Allo, *Seconde épître aux Corinthiens*, 170; Harris, *Second Epistle to the Corinthians*, 441–42; Richard H. Bell, "Sacrifice and Christology in Paul," *JTS* 53 (2002): 9–11.

72. Richard Bauckham, *The Bible and Ecology: Rediscovering the Community of Creation* (Waco, TX: Baylor University Press, 2010), 175; Joseph A. Fitzmyer, "Reconciliation in Pauline Theology," in *No Famine in the Land: Studies in Honor of John L. McKenzie*, ed. James W. Flanagan and Anita Weisbrod Robinson (Missoula, MT: Scholars Press, 1975), 161–67.

It is possible that Paul here is simply summarizing the message he preaches as Christ's ambassador.[73] But his concern for the Corinthians and their response to him might suggest, rather, that he is directing his plea directly to them: they need to be reconciled to God and, along with it, to Paul as God's accredited "ambassador." It would therefore parallel 6:1, where Paul urges the Corinthians not to accept God's grace in vain.[74] In verse 21, Paul finishes his brief outline of his preaching points by stating a key motif of his message, what some scholars have labeled "interchange." The principle was a staple of patristic theology, formulated as early as Irenaeus: "The Word of God, our Lord Jesus Christ, who did, through His transcendent love, become what we are, that He might bring us to be even what He is Himself."[75] On one side of the interchange, Christ, who "had no sin" (or "did not know sin" [*ton mē gnonta hamartian*]), was "made . . . to be sin for us." Paul might mean simply that Jesus became a sinner.[76] But it is perhaps more likely he means that Jesus became a "sin offering" on our behalf.[77] The other side of the "interchange" is only implied, and many would argue it is not present at all. Certainly Paul's language here is puzzling: How can humans "become the righteousness of God" in Christ? In Romans, where the other eight occurrences of the phrase *dikaiosynē theou* ("righteousness of God") appear, the reference is to an "enacted attribute of God": the way his own character of "doing right" comes to expression in his saving acts to put sinful humans in a new relationship with him.[78] Some interpreters give the phrase the sense of "divine saving justice" and argue that "become" in this verse implies that we are invited to participate in God's program of "making right."[79] However, Paul's other occurrences of "righteousness of God" focus on human status rather than behavior. It is better, then, to give the phrase a forensic sense here: humans attain a righteous standing, given by God, "in him [Christ]." This "in him" might imply the other part of the interchange logic: in Christ, who is *the* righteous one, we are given righteousness.[80]

---

73. Stanley E. Porter, Καταλλάσσω *in Ancient Greek Literature, with Reference to the Pauline Writings*, EFN 5 (Cordoba: Ediciones el Almendro, 1994), 139–40; Harris, *Second Epistle to the Corinthians*, 447–48.

74. E.g, Guthrie, *2 Corinthians*, 312.

75. Irenaeus, *Haer.*, book 5, preface (*ANF* 1:526).

76. Bell, "Sacrifice and Christology," 13–14; Charles Lee Irons, *The Righteousness of God: A Lexical Examination of the Covenant-Faithfulness Interpretation*, WUNT 2/386 (Tübingen: Mohr Siebeck, 2015), 292–93.

77. E.g., Talbert, *Reading Corinthians*, 167–68; Harris, *Second Epistle to the Corinthians*, 442–56; Brian Vickers, *Jesus' Blood and Righteousness: Paul's Theology of Imputation* (Wheaton, IL: Crossway, 2006), 160–70.

78. See pp. 476–79.

79. E.g., Michael J. Gorman, *Becoming the Gospel: Paul,* *Participation, and Mission* (Grand Rapids: Eerdmans, 2015), 246–49; Morna D. Hooker, "On Becoming the Righteousness of God: Another Look at 2 Corinthians 5:21," *NovT* 50 (2008): 364–75. Edith Humphrey usefully surveys and analyzes some of the key views ("Becoming the Righteousness of God: The Potency of the New Creation in the World (2 Cor 5:16–21)," in *Participation, Justification, and Conversion: Eastern Orthodox Interpretation of Paul and the Debate between "Old and New Perspectives on Paul,"* ed. Athanasios Despotis, WUNT 2/442 [Tübingen: Mohr Siebeck, 2017], 125–57).

80. Theologians such as John Piper therefore think this passage gives support to the notion of Christ's "imputed righteousness" (John Piper, *Counted Righteous in Christ: Should We Abandon the Imputation of Christ's Righteousness?* [Wheaton, IL: Crossway, 2002], 68–69).

Paul is working along with God (the probable implied reference in *synergountes*) in this great work of redemption. The Corinthians need to recognize this and respond accordingly, not receiving God's grace in vain (6:1). Paul then quotes Isaiah 49:8, a passage in which the Lord assures his Servant that he will continue to support and equip him for his chosen ministry. Paul may be applying this text to himself, for he certainly sees his ministry as an extension of the ministry of the Servant.[81] But, while Paul implies some degree of identification between himself and the Servant, the focus is probably on the Corinthians, as he reminds them of the grace that God had already displayed among them.[82] His point, then, is to emphasize that their "time of favor" and "day of salvation" remains open—hence the need for decisive action (6:2).

Paul ends this second major section in his description and defense of his apostolic ministry (5:11–6:10) by once again "commending" himself to the Corinthians (6:3–4a), rapidly touching on various aspects of that ministry (vv. 4b–10).[83] This rather haphazard and varied list sounds two notes that characterize the letter: Paul's suffering and, related to it, his conformity to his Lord in the paradoxical way that life emerges from death.

1.2.4 Embracing Paul and Renouncing Idolatry (6:11–7:4)

The last part of the "great digression" (2:14–7:4) has an obvious A-B-A structure. The passage begins and ends with Paul's impassioned plea that the Corinthians "open their hearts" to him (6:11–13; 7:2–4) as the appropriate response to his own deep love for them. Between these exhortations is a passage about avoiding idolatry (6:14–7:1) that has sparked considerable speculation as to its origins and placement here in the letter. The transitions from the exhortation in 6:11–13 to this warning about idolatry and then back to exhortation again are abrupt. These sudden shifts might mean that the passage has been inserted into this context from somewhere else. Perhaps the compiler of Paul's letters inserted at this point part of the "severe letter" (see the "Isolating the Issues" section above). Or, more radically, perhaps the passage is not Pauline at all. This is not the place to engage in these issues, but (1) the absence of any textual evidence for an insertion, and (2) the difficulty of imagining how (and why) someone would have inserted a fragment of teaching into the middle of a letter, argue for accepting this section as Paul's own digression as he dictated 2 Corinthians. Perhaps Paul composed this warning about idolatry on another occasion, as the shift in tone and vocabulary might suggest.[84]

---

81. See G. K. Beale, "The Old Testament Background of Reconciliation in 2 Corinthians 4–7 and Its Bearing on the Literary Problem of 2 Corinthians 6.14–7.1," *NTS* 35 (1989): 561–64; Garland, *2 Corinthians*, 305.

82. See, e.g., Thrall, *Second Epistle to the Corinthians*, 1:453.

83. For placing a major break between vv. 10 and 11, see, e.g., Jan Lambrecht, "'Reconcile Yourselves . . .': A Reading

of 2 Corinthians 5:11–21," in *Studies on 2 Corinthian*, ed. R. Bieringer and J. Lambrecht, BETL 112 (Leuven: Leuven University Press, 1994), 364.

84. See, e.g., Guthrie, *2 Corinthians*, 349; Harris, *Second Epistle to the Corinthians*, 492; Richards, *Paul and First-Century Letter Writing*, 111–18.

The focus of the passage is the warning in verse 14 about being "yoked together with unbelievers." Scholars have suggested a number of specific situations that Paul might be referring to. The two most likely are (1) a plea to avoid inappropriate associations with idolatry in the context of eating food sacrificed to idols (1 Cor 8–10),[85] and (2) a plea to cut off association with the false teachers ("unbelievers" here) that Paul harshly criticizes in chapters 10–13.[86] However, the text does not offer enough data to confirm or deny such specific scenarios. As Thrall notes, the command is "unspecific, and therefore widely comprehensive."[87] The traditional application of this warning to mixed marriages or to entering into business associations with unbelievers may then be justified. But we can't restrict the application to these specific matters.

Paul grounds his warning in both a negative and a positive argument. Negatively, Paul reminds us that the supreme and total claim Christ makes on our lives is incompatibile with dalliance with the world. Positively, Paul reminds us that the new community we are a part of is nothing less than the "temple of the living God" (v. 16). Paul explicitly compares the church to a temple elsewhere (see esp. 1 Cor 3:16; Eph 2:21–22) and probably alludes to the notion in many other places.[88] God's presence is now manifested in a people, not a building. Paul confirms this idea and elaborates on the connection between this reality and the need to avoid too close an association with unbelievers with a series of Old Testament quotations (vv. 16b–18).

Verse 16b
Lev 26:11–12: "***I will put my dwelling place among you***, and I will not abhor you. I <u>will walk among you and be your God, and you will be my people</u>. I am the LORD your God, who brought you out of Egypt so that you would no longer be slaves to the Egyptians; I broke the bars of your yoke and enabled you to walk with heads held high."

Ezek 37:26–27: "I will make a covenant of peace with them; it will be an everlasting covenant. I will establish them and increase their numbers, and ***I will put my sanctuary among them forever. My dwelling place will be with them;*** I <u>will be their God, and they will be my people</u>. Then the nations will know that I the LORD make Israel holy, when my sanctuary is among them forever."

Verse 17
Isa 52:11: "Depart, depart, go out from there! <u>Touch no unclean thing! Come out from it and be pure</u>, you who carry the articles of the LORD's house."

85. See especially Gordon D. Fee, "II Corinthians VI.14–VII.1 and Food Offered to Idols," *NTS* 23 (1977): 140–61; Garland, *2 Corinthians*, 315–27.

86. Gorman, *Apostle of the Crucified Lord*, 367.
87. Thrall, *Second Epistle to the Corinthians*, 1:473.
88. See esp. Beale, *Temple and the Church's Mission*, 245–68.

Verse 18

> 2 Sam 7:14: "I <u>will be his father, and he will be</u> my son. When he does wrong, I will punish him with a rod wielded by men, with floggings inflicted by human hands."
>
> (See also Isa 60:4: "Lift up your eyes and look about you: All assemble and come to you; <u>your sons</u> come from afar, and <u>your daughters</u> are carried on the hip.")
>
> Ezek 20:41: "I <u>will accept you</u> as fragrant incense when I bring you out from the nations and <u>gather you</u> from the countries where you have been scattered, and I will be proved holy through you in the sight of the nations."
>
> 2 Sam 7:8: "Now then, tell my servant David, 'This is <u>what the *Lord* Almighty says</u>: I took you from the pasture, from tending the flock, and appointed you ruler over my people Israel.'"[89]

The rapid move from text to text suggests that Paul is here reproducing a standard combination of ideas that was fundamental to his own preaching and, perhaps, in the early church in general.

1.3 Joy Over the Corinthians' Repentance (7:5–16)

Paul's appeal in 7:2–4 brings his digression about his ministry to its exhortatory conclusion; it also prepares the way for Paul's return to his "travelogue" in verse 5. As we have seen, Paul here picks up where he left off in 2:13: Paul has moved on to Macedonia, where he lacks "peace of mind" (2:13)/"rest" (7:5) because he has not yet heard Titus's report about the delivery of his "severe letter" to the Corinthians. Paul's burst of praise to God in 2:14 is echoed in verses 6–7 with specific reference to Titus's positive report about the Corinthians' response. Despite this welcome news, Paul feels the need to explain again why he wrote so severely to them (vv. 8–13a). Paul's motives were entirely pure, seeking to bring them to acknowledge again Paul's authority and, therefore, their obedience to the gospel with which Paul is entrusted. Pain and sorrow, such as that caused by Paul's letter, can have a beneficial end when it is genuine "godly sorrow" (v. 11). He concludes with his delight in the way Titus himself has now also been encouraged by the Corinthians' response (vv. 13b–16).

2 THE COLLECTION (8:1–9:15)

The second major section of 2 Corinthians is devoted to a project that occupied Paul's attention throughout the third missionary journey: his collection of money from the

---

89. On these allusions, see Beale, *Temple and the Church's Mission*, 253–56.

largely gentile churches he established in the eastern Mediterranean for the struggling Christians in Jerusalem. He urges participation in it and prayers for it in 1 Corinthians 16:1–4 and Romans 15:25–33. It is possible, though not perhaps likely, that this enterprise had its origins in the Jerusalem apostles' request to Paul to "remember the poor" (Gal 2:10).[90] In chapters 8–9, Paul is trying to renew the Corinthians' interest in the collection, an interest that had undoubtedly waned during the time of their estrangement.

Scholars generally recognize that the collection had two main motivations. The first, naturally enough, was simple material help to believers who were facing difficult times—an act of Christian charity. It is this motivation that dominates Paul's exhortations here. The second motivation, pretty clearly alluded to in Romans 15 but entirely absent in these chapters, is the easing of tensions between Jewish and gentile Christians. If Paul could get his gentile converts to give money to their Jewish brothers and sisters, and if he could get those Jewish brothers and sisters to accept it (not a given, as Paul's request for prayer about this in Rom 15:31 indicates), it would go some way toward healing this rift. Other aspects of the collection that scholars have often speculated about are not clear. Did Paul view the collection as a continuation in a new vein of the requirement that Jews in the diaspora support Jerusalem?[91] Perhaps, but Paul says nothing to indicate it. Did Paul stress the selection of gentiles to accompany the collection to Jerusalem because he saw this as the fulfillment of Old Testament prophecies about gentiles streaming into a restored Zion in the last days? Perhaps—but the more specific notion that Paul also saw this "pilgrimage of the nations" as the stimulus for the coming of the Lord is unlikely.[92]

These chapters break down into three distinct units. In 8:1–15, Paul urges the Corinthians to renew their commitment to the collection, citing Macedonian believers as an example. In 8:16–25, he turns to administrative matters, asking the Corinthians to respect and welcome Titus and several unnamed "brothers" who are apparently in charge of logistics. After this focus on administration, Paul turns back to the collection itself, tying the Corinthians' commitment to the collection to their larger commitment to Christ (9:1–15). Throughout, Paul exhibits the reticence he often displays in dealing with money matters. As N. T. Wright notes, the chapters are "remarkable for Paul writing thirty-nine verses about money without mentioning the word."[93]

2.1 Exhortation to Renew Commitment to the Collection (8:1–15)

Paul's reticence in asking for money is revealed in his approach in this section. It is only in verses 6 and 10–12 that Paul explicitly requests that the Corinthians "finish the work," by renewing the zeal they had shown for the project the previous

90. Moo, *Galatians*, 139.

91. See, e.g., Keith F. Nickle, *The Collection: A Study in Paul's Strategy*, SBT 48 (London: SCM, 1966), 74–99.

92. See esp. Munck, *Paul and the Salvation of Mankind*, 303–5.

93. Wright, *Resurrection*, 307.

year (presumably before the break in relations that occasioned Paul's "painful visit" and "severe letter"). He paves the way for this request by holding out the Macedonian believers as an example of people who, despite suffering a "severe trial" (v. 2; perhaps a continuation of the persecution described in Acts 16:19–24; 17:5–9, 13–15), pleaded with Paul for the "privilege of sharing in this service" (*tēn charin kai tēn koinōnian tēs diakonias*; 2 Cor 8:4). This is the first occurrence of two words that carry much of the rhetorical force of these two chapters. The Greek *charis* occurs ten times here, referring to at least four different but related ideas: God's favor, the privilege of participating in the collection (as here in v. 4), the collection itself, and a verbal thanks.[94] Especially important is the connection between God's grace, bestowed on undeserving people, and their appropriate response of "grace" to others. The Greek word *diakonia*, in contrast, occurs only four times in these two chapters (see also 9:1, 12, 13), but in important places, denoting the collection as a "service" or "ministry" to the believers in Jerusalem. Paul here introduces another theme that will be important in these chapters: his concern that the Corinthians give not because Paul commands it but out of genuine love for God and his people (8:8). Paul grounds this concern in the example of "the grace of our Lord Jesus Christ": he "was rich, yet for your sake he became poor, so that you through his poverty might become rich" (v. 9). A few interpreters suggest that Paul might be thinking of Christ becoming materially poor or that he is thinking of Jesus's death on the cross[95] or his lifetime of obedience.[96] But it is quite clear that here, as in Philippians 2:6–8, Paul is referring to the contrast between Christ's preexistent glory and his incarnation, a "becoming poor" for the sake of others.[97] The complementary movement by which believers who were "poor" (because of sin—implied here) become "rich" (spiritually) reflects Paul's familiar "interchange" pattern, according to which Christ becomes what we are so that we might become what he is.

2.2 Administering the Collection (8:16–25)

In this middle part of the collection exhortation, Paul assures the Corinthians that the enterprise will be carried out with integrity (see vv. 20–21) by mentioning several fellow Christians who be involved in collecting and delivering the money. Titus (8:16–17) is, of course, well known to the Corinthians by now. He will be accompanied by "the brother who is praised by all the churches" who has, in fact, been chosen by the churches for this ministry (vv. 18–19).[98] Yet another "brother" is mentioned in verse 22, and Paul then commends all three to the Corinthians (vv. 23–25).

---

94. Guthrie, *2 Corinthians*, 392.

95. E.g, Murphy-O'Connor, *Theology of the Second Letter to the Corinthians*, 83–84.

96. See, e.g, James D. G. Dunn, *Christology in the Making: A New Testament Inquiry into the Origins of the Doctrine of the Incarnation* (London: SCM, 1980), 121–23.

97. See, e.g., Fee, *Pauline Christology*, 162–65. The aorist *eptōcheusen* is ingressive (as the NIV renders it: "became poor").

98. We cannot determine the identity of this unnamed "brother," although scholars love to speculate: Luke, Barnabas, Apollos, Mark, Erastus, Silas, or one of the brothers mentioned in Acts 20:4 (see the note in Harris, *Second Epistle to the Corinthians*,

2.3 Completing the Work (9:1–15)

The beginning of chapter 9—"there is no need for me to write to you about this service to the Lord's people"—suggests to some that Paul is now only here beginning to talk about the collection, implying that chapter 9 belongs to a separate letter than chapter 8.[99] But the formula Paul uses here is, in fact, often used to resume a subject (e.g., 1 Cor 8:4; 1 Thess 5:1). The concern for integrity in the way the collection is administered (8:16–25) interrupts Paul's exhortations about participating in the work. Paul now both explains why those arrangements are needed[100] and resumes his exhortation to participate in the collection.[101]

Paul has used the Macedonians' example to exhort the Corinthians (8:1–5); now he turns the tables and praises the Corinthians for setting an example for the Macedonians (9:2). However, this "eagerness to help" was in the past. Paul is concerned now to renew that eagerness, and he is sending "the brothers" (see 8:16–25) to encourage that renewal (vv. 3–5). Paul again expresses his wish that the Corinthians give generously and not grudgingly (v. 5). A minor break, signaled by "remember this" (a felicitous rendering of *touto de*), occurs at verse 6. Paul makes three basic points as the climax to his exhortations about the collection. First, picking up the focus in verse 5b, Paul urges that the Corinthians should give willingly, not "under compulsion" (v. 7). Second, Paul encourages generous giving by noting the reciprocity between giving and receiving: those who give generously will also "reap generously" (vv. 6, 8–11). God responds to believers who are generous by giving gifts generously to them. Third, Paul stresses that the gifts the Corinthians give to the Lord's people ultimately bring glory to God, as others praise him because of their example (vv. 12–15).

3 PAUL AND THE FALSE APOSTLES (10:1–12:13)

As I noted in "Locating the Letter" above, the sudden shift from Paul's celebration of the Corinthians' anticipated generosity in giving to the collection (9:14–15) to impassioned defense of his own apostleship along with strong denunciations of "false apostles" (chs. 10–13) has sparked considerable speculation. I suggested earlier that the best explanation for this break may lie in Paul's having received fresh news or, perhaps more likely, in his having employed a rhetorical strategy where one withholds this kind of blunt warning until the end of one's argument. One reason to doubt that the receiving of fresh information explains the shift is the fact that Paul clearly alludes to rival teachers in chapters 1–9 (e.g., 3:1), and their presence may be lurking

---

602; and also the discussion in Thrall, *Second Epistle to the Corinthians*, 2:557–62).

99. E.g., Martin, *2 Corinthians*, 430.

100. Allo, *Seconde épître aux Corinthiens*, 229.

101. I think the form of v. 1 suggests, therefore, that a break occurs here rather than between 9:5 and 6 (the latter is the preference of most English Bibles and commentators [e.g., Guthrie, *2 Corinthians*, 383; Garland, *2 Corinthians*, 390]).

in the background of other passages as well (e.g., 3:7–18; 4:1–2; in both texts Paul is probably defending himself against their criticism).[102] I concluded above that these rivals were probably advocating some degree of "Judaizing," were claiming authority from the Jerusalem apostles, and were adopting the trappings of typical, powerful, and rhetorically effective speakers from their Greco-Roman culture.

Paul's imminent "third visit" to the Corinthians, mentioned at the beginning (10:2) and elaborated at the end (12:1–13:10), looms over these chapters. The strength of Paul's rhetoric is explained by his desire to make that visit a happy rather than an unpleasant one.[103] This will happen only if the Corinthians renounce any loyalty to Paul's rivals and fully embrace his own apostolic ministry. The central theme of these chapters is that, in conformity to the pattern established in Christ's own death and resurrection, "power" in ministry springs from "weakness."[104] We may divide Paul's argument into three large sections: 10:1–18; 11:1–12:13; 12:14–13:14.

3.1 Paul Defends His Ministry Style (10:1–18)

In this opening section, Paul begins rebutting charges that "certain people" have made against him (vv. 2, 7, 10, 11, 12). While not explicitly identifying them at this point, Paul's reference is obviously to those he will label "false apostles" later (11:13). Verses 1–11 are framed by the contrast of "face to face" and "present" with "away" and "absent" (vv. 1, 11).[105] Paul's rivals are apparently ridiculing his personal "presence": he is "bold" when away from Corinth, writing his letters (vv. 1, 10–11), but "timid" when he is with them. The issue probably has to do with expectations created by popular teachers in Paul's day (called "sophists") who capitalized on their appearance, dress, and demeanor to sway audiences.[106] Paul's rivals apparently have adopted this approach and are mocking him for failing to conform to this expected cultural norm. As Thrall puts it, Paul's rivals were arguing that "he lacks the charismatic power necessary to effective apostolic leadership."[107]

Paul warns the Corinthians that, if they continue to follow these rivals, the "boldness" he exhibits in his letters (perhaps with specific reference to the "severe letter"; 7:8–15) will be on display when he arrives for his visit (10:2). Paul is also being accused of living "according to the flesh" (v. 2 ESV; *kata sarka*). "Flesh" (*sarx*) has its usual Pauline sense of "the world" (hence NIV "by the standards of this world" in v. 2 and "world" in v. 3

---

102. Garland has a good summary of the many connections between chs. 1–9 and 10–13 (*2 Corinthians*, 419–22).

103. On this point, see esp. Allo, *Seconde épître aux Corinthiens*, 239; Harris, *Second Epistle to the Corinthians*, 662.

104. See esp. on this theme, D. A. Carson, *From Triumphalism to Maturity: An Exposition of 2 Corinthians 10–13* (Grand Rapids: Baker, 1984).

105. Paul's reference to "the humility and gentleness of

Christ" (*tēs prautētos kai epieikeias tou Christou*) is sometimes thought to refer to Christ's preexistent attitude (see Phil 2:6; Furnish, *II Corinthians*, 460; Thrall, *Second Epistle to the Corinthians*, 2:600), but more likely refers to his earthly life (Harris, *Second Epistle to the Corinthians*, 668).

106. Winter, *Philo and Paul*, 203–39. See the reference to the importance of dress for the orator in Epictetus, *Diatr.* 3.22.86–89.

107. Thrall, *Second Epistle to the Corinthians*, 2:607.

[2x])—the values and behaviors characteristic of those who have no knowledge of, or concern with, the heavenly realm. We are unsure just what Paul's rivals might have meant by this claim, but Paul responds by claiming that the weapons he uses to wage spiritual warfare are not "worldly" but possess God's own power to refute any ideas contrary to knowledge of God and thereby to "take captive every thought to make it obedient to Christ."[108] Paul's martial imagery here reveals his sense of being engaged in spiritual warfare with rival teachers who are battling for the hearts and minds of the Corinthians. After a minor break, Paul accuses the Corinthians of "judging by appearances" (v. 7). His rivals are confident that they are "of Christ" (Gk. *Christou*), perhaps here meaning that they are authoritative representatives of Christ.[109] But Paul can claim the same authority, given to him by God, and he warns the Corinthians that that authority will be on full display if they are still following his rivals when he arrives (vv. 8–11).

The last section of this paragraph is again marked by an *inclusio* focused on the language of "commending" (vv. 11, 18).[110] Paul unpacks this word (which has figured earlier in his defense of his ministry [3:1; 4:2; 5:12; 6:4; 7:11]) with the language of "boasting" (*kauchaomai*). This word occurs five times in this short paragraph (vv. 13, 15, 16, 17 [2x]), while the word group it is a part of is prominent throughout the letter.[111] Paul's basic point is expressed via a paraphrastic quotation of Jeremiah 9:24 in verse 17: "Let the one who boasts boast in the Lord." Paul accordingly will confine his boasting to "the sphere of service God himself has assigned to us" (v. 13). The Greek of this phrase is notoriously difficult, but it is perhaps best to think that Paul is thinking of the original call to ministry issued to him by the risen Lord, which, while not omitting Jews, focused on gentiles—a calling he later acknowledged in agreement with the Jerusalem apostles (Gal 2:7–8).[112] Paul is apparently again responding to accusations of his rivals that he has been transgressing on others' territory.

3.2 Paul Boasts as a "Fool" (11:1–12:13)

This longish section is marked by the language of "fool"/"foolishness."[113] The word group frames the passage (11:1; 12:11), while the heart of it contains what is generally known as the "fool's speech." Scholars differ about where this speech begins, but a good case can be made for thinking it begins in 11:21b. Chapter 11:1–21a can then

---

108. The last phrase translates a genitive phrase in Gk., *tēn hypakoēn tou Christou*, that is occasionally interpreted in a subjective sense, "the obedience displayed by Christ" (Michael Kibbe, "'The Obedience of Christ': A Reassessment of Τὴν Ὑπακοὴν Τοῦ Χριστοῦ in 2 Corinthians 10:5," *JSPL* 2 [2012]: 41–56). But an objective sense, "obedience directed toward Christ," fits the context better.

109. E.g., Martin, *2 Corinthians*, 490–91; Harris, *Second Epistle to the Corinthians*, 689.

110. Guthrie, *2 Corinthians*, 486.

111. The verb *kauchaomai*: 5:12; 7:14; 9:2; 10:8; 11:12, 16, 18 [2x], 30 [2x]; the noun *kauchēsis*: 1:12; 7:4, 14; 8:24; 11:10, 17; the noun *kauchēma*: 1:14; 5:12; 9:3. See, e.g., Guthrie, *2 Corinthians*, 479.

112. Barnett, *Second Epistle to the Corinthians*, 485.

113. The noun *aphrosynē*, "foolishness," occurs in 11:1, 17, 21; the noun *aphrōn*, "fool," in 11:16 [2x], 19; 12:6, 11.

be seen as a long and discursive introduction to the speech. This introduction reveals Paul's strong degree of discomfort in taking on the role of a fool and "boasting" in his status and accomplishments. He is clearly embarrassed to do so, but feels compelled to do so by the rival claims of the false apostles.[114] Harris appropriately quotes Proverbs 26:4–5—"Do not answer a fool according to his folly, or you yourself will be just like him. Answer a fool according to his folly, or he will be wise in his own eyes"—noting that "both ignoring the fool and trying to answer the fool are procedures fraught with danger."[115] Paul thus goes to great lengths to explain his motivations for such boasting.

This introduction to the "fool's speech" can be divided into two parts: verses 1–15 and 16–21a. Paul is motivated, positively, by his deep concern for the Corinthians' spiritual welfare and, negatively, by the need to wean them away from their infatuation with his rivals. His "jealousy" for the Corinthians is a "godly jealousy" (v. 2), a jealousy such as that of a father who gives his daughter (the Corinthians) away to a bridegroom (Christ). His rivals are seeking to break up this marriage, leading the Corinthians away from their "sincere and pure devotion to Christ" (v. 3). Verse 4 is one of the few places in these chapters where Paul gives any information about the content of his rivals' message, and even here that information is very general: they are preaching "a Jesus other than the Jesus we preached"; they are trying to persuade the Corinthians to receive "a different spirit from the Spirit you received,"[116] and a "different gospel from the one you accepted." Jesus, the Spirit, the gospel—Paul chooses three of the central elements of the new covenant to emphasize how seriously astray is the teaching of his opponents.[117] Clearly Paul is pulling out all the rhetorical stops to warn the Corinthians of the danger these rivals pose to their spiritual well-being.[118] However, neither here nor elsewhere does Paul elaborate, leaving us very much in the dark about what the specifics of their heresy may have been.

Paul instead turns again to the contrast between himself and his rivals in terms of style of ministry. In verse 5, he claims to be in no way inferior to "those 'super-apostles.'" As the NIV quote marks suggest, the designation is probably one that the apostles themselves have used for themselves or that the Corinthians have bestowed on them. But who are they? An obvious possibility is that Paul is again referring to his rivals, whom he will call "false apostles" in verse 13.[119] However, it is also possible that the "super-apostles" are the Jerusalem apostles, whose authority the false teachers are (falsely) claiming.[120] Paul's other reference to "super-apostles" (12:11) may favor the

---

114. Furnish, *II Corinthians*, 498.

115. Harris, *Second Epistle to the Corinthians*, 729–30.

116. "Spirit" (*pneuma*, used just once in the Gk. in v. 4) is sometimes taken to refer to a general "spirit of the faith," or something of the sort (Martin, *2 Corinthians*, 521). But, set in parallel to Jesus and the gospel, *pneuma* almost certainly refers to the Holy Spirit.

117. Harris, *Second Epistle to the Corinthians*, 744.

118. Schmeller, *Der zweite Brief an die Korinther*, 2:170.

119. This is the majority view. See, e.g., Guthrie, *2 Corinthians*, 516.

120. Barrett, "Paul's Opponents," 242–46; Harris, *Second Epistle to the Corinthians*, 746–47.

former view, but the parallel between the semi-ironic label here and the similar way Paul describes Peter, James, and John in Galatians 2 ("those esteemed as leaders" [v. 2; cf. v. 6], "those esteemed as pillars" [v. 9]) might point to the latter option.

One issue of ministry style that emerges in these verses has to do with financial support. Paul's rivals have apparently received support from the Corinthians (v. 20), perhaps viewing it as no more than their due as such superior and talented speakers. Paul, however, following his usual policy, refused to accept support from the Corinthians as he ministered with them—not wanting anyone to be able to question his motives (see esp. 1 Thess 2:1–12). In a passage dripping with irony, Paul asks the Corinthians to forgive him for not being a burden to them in this way (vv. 7–11). Paul concludes this section with a scathing description of his rivals as "false apostles, deceitful workers," allies of Satan, destined for judgment (vv. 13–15).

In the short second part of this introduction, Paul sets up his speech by returning to the language of "fool," focusing on the boasting he feels compelled to engage in because of the circumstances (vv. 16–21a).

This "boasting like a fool" is the theme of the speech, which divides into three basic parts (11:21b–29; 11:30–33; 12:1–10). The first part consists of a long list of Paul's apostolic credentials and experiences. The false teachers were apparently claiming authority on the basis of their authentic "Jewish" status. Paul counters by claiming to be just as much of a "Hebrew," "Israelite," and descendant of Abraham as they (v. 22; cf. Phil 3:4b–6). They are also claiming to be "servants of Christ," but Paul has a better claim on that status—a status, however, paradoxically revealed in his "weakness" (vv. 23a, 29). Paul illustrates his "weakness" in a long list of the difficulties and challenges he has faced in ministry (vv. 23b–28). Here Paul touches on a theme that has been central to his defense of apostleship throughout the letter. As Christ's death was the route to his resurrection and salvific power, so his true followers will be marked by a similar pattern of life in and through death, and power in and through weakness.

This theme of (God's) power through weakness is exhibited in the story of Paul's escape from Damascus, the topic of the second part of the speech (11:30–33). We may for our purposes leave to the side the geographical and chronological issues raised by this description and simply note that being "lowered in a basket from a window" is hardly a heroic means of escaping from the clutches of the authorities.

"I must go on boasting" effects the transition to the third part of the speech (12:1–10). Paul boasts of "visions and revelations from the Lord" (or "of" the Lord).[121] The plurals suggest that Paul had more than one visionary experience, although he here mentions only one. Paul claims it took place "fourteen years ago," placing it during

---

121. The genitive modifier *kyriou* might denote source (NIV), but it could also denote content, "the Lord" being the object of Paul's visions. Perhaps we should avoid classifying the genitive one way or the other, so that some nuance of each might be involved (Schmeller, *Der zweite Brief an die Korinther*, 2:282; Lincoln, *Paradise Now and Not Yet*, 72–73).

Paul's stay in Antioch after his conversion and before his first missionary journey (v. 2; AD 41–42). Paul's reticence to brag in his own experiences combined with the clearly mystical nature of the experience is why he speaks in the third person: "I know a man in Christ." So strange was the experience that Paul cannot even be sure whether he was "in the body" or not. God's action is undoubtedly behind his being "caught up" (v. 4; the passive verb *hērpagē*). When Paul was "caught up," he entered "the third heaven" (v. 2)/"paradise" (v. 4). Here he heard "inexpressible things" (v. 4). Whether this means that the things were impossible to express in words or that he was forbidden to express them in words is unclear. In either case, the point is that these words were holy.[122] It is possible that Paul thinks of a two-stage experience—from the third heaven on to paradise[123]—but perhaps it is more likely that he describes the same place in two ways.[124] Second Temple Jews often speculated about the number and nature of the "heavens," and "paradise," used in various ways, came to describe the place of dead believers (see Luke 23:43). We should probably avoid thinking that this passage provides any information about Paul's view of the configuration of the spiritual realm. Both "third heaven" and "paradise" may be language he rather unreflectingly picks up from his environment.[125]

The pull in two directions with respect to his boasting is indicated by Paul again in verse 5: "I will boast about a man like that, but I will not boast about myself, except about my weaknesses." This could be taken to mean that it was not Paul who saw this vision. However, verses 7–9 make pretty clear that all of verses 1–10 refer to Paul's own experiences. What he means is that, while Paul can boast with his rivals about receiving visions, the experience is, in a sense, distant from his own person and no cause for particular pride or basis for apostolic authority. As Hughes notes, "The man who experienced the ineffable 'ascent' even to the third heaven was the same man who had experienced the undistinguished 'descent' from a window in the Damascus wall."[126] However great the revelations (v. 7), it is, again, weakness that Paul brags about. And in order to keep Paul in line on this matter, God brought into his life a "thorn in the flesh." The longstanding debate about just what this was goes on without any hope of being settled. Was it a serious physical problem? A mental problem? Opponents? We cannot be sure, athough a slight majority of contemporary scholars, echoing the preference of interpreters throughout church history, favors a reference to illness. Perhaps, indeed, as has often been suggested, the text is deliberately vague so that any believer, whatever difficulty they are facing, can find comfort in Paul's experience. His repeated prayer that it be taken away went unanswered. Rather, God was preventing Paul from becoming

---

122. Schmeller, *Der zweite Brief an die Korinther*, 2:291.

123. E.g., Schmeller, *Der zweite Brief an die Korinther*, 2:288.

124. Second Enoch 8.1 appears to locate paradise in the "third heaven."

125. See esp. the discussion in Lincoln, *Paradise Now and Not Yet*, 78–81.

126. Hughes, *Second Epistle to the Corinthians*, 422.

conceited (v. 7) and teaching him that "my grace is sufficient for you" (v. 9a). Verses 9b–10 offer a final comment on this thorn-in-the-flesh experience and summarize at the same time the central theme of the "fool's speech": "I will boast all the more gladly about my weaknesses, so that Christ's power may rest on me. That is why, for Christ's sake, I delight in weaknesses, in insults, in hardships, in persecutions, in difficulties. For when I am weak, then I am strong."

Verses 11–13 match 11:1–21a as the concluding comment on the "fool's speech." Paul again expresses the tension that marks this whole section. On the one hand, he is "nothing" (v. 11b). On the other hand, he is in no way inferior to the "super-apostles" (v. 11a), and has worked "signs, wonders and miracles" among the Corinthians (v. 12). The point seems to be again that Paul's authority and power in ministry has nothing to do with him as such and everything to do with the power that God works in and through him.

4 PREPARING FOR PAUL'S VISIT (12:14–13:14)

The first two sections of this concluding part of the letter mention Paul's "third visit" (12:14; 13:1).[127] The prospect of this visit has been a driving force throughout chapters 10–13, and that visit now receives more direct attention.

The matter of Paul's financial independence from the Corinthians is the central theme of verses 14–18. Paul has not burdened them with requests for support (v. 16), nor have the emissaries he has sent to them (vv. 17–18). This refusal to accept support was not a "trick" designed to enlist their loyalty but an expression of Paul's fatherly concern for his spiritual children (v. 14). Paul then warns the Corinthians about his impending visit, seeking to stimulate them to full repentance (vv. 19–21).

The tone of warning continues and increases in strength in 13:1–10. If he is met with continuing rebellion on the part of the Corinthians, Paul will show them just how "bold" he can be in their presence (see 10:1–11). Paul again follows the cruciform path of his Savior, demonstrating power amid weakness (13:3–4).[128] Faced with Paul's impending visit, Paul urges the Corinthians to "examine yourselves to see whether you are in the faith" (v. 5). This warning, along with the conclusion of the verse— "Christ Jesus is in you—unless, of course, you fail the test"—must be factored into our interpretation of Paul's theology of perseverance (see pp. 554–57). Serious warnings about the danger of falling away are certainly common in Paul. Here, however, the issue appears to be not a falling away from the faith but the question whether they were ever truly "in the faith." Perseverance is the sign that they do belong; failing the test

127. Guthrie, *2 Corinthians*, 607.
128. Raymond Pickett, *The Cross in Corinth: The Social*   *Significance of the Death of Jesus*, JSNTSup 143 (Sheffield: Sheffield Academic, 1997).

would indicate that they never had Christ Jesus in them. Paul is apparently concerned that the sinfulness and rebellious attitudes of some in Corinth may reveal a lack of true saving faith. Paul often follows a severe warning with reassurance, and he does so here, but with a twist: it is Paul himself who will pass the test (v. 6). He hopes that his own weakness will result in greater spiritual strength for the Corinthians (v. 9).

Paul concludes the letter in his usual way (vv. 11–14), with brief exhortations, a promise of God's presence, an encouragement to greet each other, greetings from Christians in Paul's place of writing, and a wish that the readers might experience the "the grace of the Lord Jesus Christ, and the love of God, and the fellowship of the Holy Spirit" (an obvious allusion to incipient trinitarian thinking).

Chapter 9

ROMANS

ROMANS IS THE FIRST Pauline letter that springs to mind when we think of the theology of the apostle.[1] The seventeenth-century Puritan Thomas Draxe called Romans "the quintessence and perfection of saving doctrine"; Luther, "the purest gospel."[2] No biblical book has had a greater impact on the church's theology: Romans has had a formative influence on theologians from Augustine to Calvin to Barth. "Romans," comments C. Kavin Rowe, is "where he says what Christianity is most basically about."[3] The far-reaching influence of Romans is not surprising. The context in which Paul wrote led him to write a letter that covered a significant number of basic theological issues from a relatively neutral perspective. Nevertheless, we must never forget that Romans is a *letter*, written in a particular set of circumstances and addressed to a particular set of issues. The message of Romans is, indeed, timeless; but to understand its message aright, we must appreciate the specific context out of which Romans was written.

LOCATING THE LETTER

Locating Romans within the ministry of Paul is straightforward. In the epistolary closing, Paul tells us that he has "fully proclaimed [or 'fulfilled,' *plēroō*] the gospel of Christ" "from Jerusalem all the way around to Illyricum" (15:19). He is planning on missionary work next in Spain (v. 24), but must first visit Jerusalem "in the service of the Lord's people there" (v. 25). On his way to Spain, Paul is hoping to stop in Rome "to have you assist me on my journey there" (v. 24). These details reveal that Paul writes toward the end of his third missionary journey, when he had wrapped up his pioneering church-planting ministry in the eastern Mediterranean area ("from Jerusalem all the way around to Illyricum") and his focus had shifted to the west (cf. Acts 19:21). It was

---

1. Concepts (and occasionally wording) are taken from my other writings on Romans; esp. *Epistle to the Romans* (NICNT) and *Romans*, NIVAC (Grand Rapids: Zondervan, 2000). Both are used by permission.

2. The Draxe quotation is from William Haller, *The Rise of Puritanism* (Philadelphia: University of Pennsylvania Press, 1972), 87; the Luther reference from Luther's "Preface to the

Epistle of St. Paul to the Romans," in *Word and Sacrament 1*, vol. 35 of *Luther's Works*, ed. E. Theodore Bachmann (Philadelphia: Muhlenberg, 1960), 365.

3. C. Kavin Rowe, *One True Life: The Stoics and Early Christians as Rival Traditions* (New Haven: Yale University Press, 2016), 87.

probably then, during Paul's three-month stay in Corinth (Acts 20:2–3), that he wrote Romans—a supposition that receives some support from his reference in Romans 16:1–2 to Cenchreae (a city next to Corinth). Assuming the chronology of Paul's life that we outlined earlier (pp. 43–49), the date of Romans would therefore be AD 57.

ISOLATING THE ISSUES

If the circumstances in which Paul wrote Romans are fairly clear, the particular issues that led him to write this wide-ranging theological treatise are not. More specifically, the purpose of the letter is not immediately clear. Explicit claims about the purpose of the letter are few and so general as to be ultimately rather unhelpful. In the letter opening, as Paul introduces himself to Christians living in a city Paul has never visited, he refers to "preaching the gospel" to them (1:14–15), but he refers here to his reasons for coming to Rome, not for his writing of a letter to them. The only reference to the purpose of the letter comes in the letter closing, where Paul speaks vaguely of writing to "remind" them about certain matters (15:15). But *why* he chooses to remind them about these particular topics is not clear.

The silence of Romans on its purpose and the issues it addresses has opened the door to an intense and wide-ranging debate about the "reason—or reasons—for Romans."[4] The geographic information I surveyed above provides some useful pegs on which we can hang my survey and evaluation of options.

As we have seen, Paul probably writes from *Corinth* and at a turning point in his ministry. We can therefore imagine Paul taking advantage of a pause in ministry to reflect on over a decade of church-planting, pastoral ministry, and theological conflict. Paul may, in other words, be writing Romans as a way of summarizing his own theological convictions. The nature of Romans could support this way of looking at it. The letter moves along according to its own internal logic with little explicit reference to the readers or their issues. Moreover, Paul's balanced stance on issues such as the law and circumcision might suggest that no particular viewpoint was forcing Paul into a polemical position on these matters.[5] However, while Romans probably has deep roots in Paul's own circumstances, this scenario cannot explain why Paul chooses to send this "last will and testament" (as Günther Bornkamm calls it) to Rome.

Paul's ultimate destination, *Spain*, may explain why Paul sends this letter to the

---

4. I refer to the title of A. J. M. Wedderburn's useful (though now dated) survey: *The Reasons for Romans* (London: T&T Clark, 1991).

5. Günther Bornkamm, "The Letter to the Romans as Paul's Last Will and Testament," in *The Romans Debate*, ed. Karl P. Donfried, rev. ed. (Grand Rapids: Baker Academic, 1991), 25; Munck, *Paul and the Salvation of Mankind*, 199; Kümmel, *Introduction*, 312–13 (with, however, some modifications); T. W. Manson, "St. Paul's Letter to the Romans—and Others," in Donfried, *Romans Debate*, 4. Michael Wolter thinks Romans focuses on Paul's own theological concerns, put in terms of a debate between "Paul the Jew" and "Paul the Apostle" (*Der Brief an die Römer*, EKKNT 6 [Neukirchen-Vluyn: Neukirchener, 2014], 41–56).

Romans. Paul's choice of verbs in 15:24 (*propempō*, "assist me on my journey," quoted above) suggests that he is hoping the Roman Christians will support his Spanish ministry, with their money and perhaps just as importantly, with logistics, such as assistants and translators. Romans, as L. T. Johnson has put it, "is Paul's letter of recommendation *for Paul*" (emphasis original).[6] But Paul cannot hope to garner their support unless they are supportive of Paul's understanding of the gospel. So he uses the letter to set forth his gospel theology—aware, as, for example, 3:7–8 makes clear, that the Romans have probably heard from detractors of Paul's ministry and gospel.

Preparation for the mission to Spain was certainly one of Paul's purposes in writing, probably even a major purpose. But it is probably not his only purpose. Had this been Paul's sole concern, we would have expected him to mention the visit to Spain more prominently—in the introduction, not just in the conclusion of the letter.[7] Moreover, while much of the theology of the letter could be explained as necessary to introduce Paul and defend his "orthodoxy," the sustained interest in relationship between Jews and gentiles seems to be more than would be needed for this purpose alone.

The intermediate stop in Paul's itinerary could explain this focus. Paul, as we have seen, is stopping first in *Jerusalem*, in "service of the Lord's people" there (15:25; see further vv. 26–29). This service involves his delivering contributions gathered from his gentile churches to impoverished Jewish believers in Jerusalem. What we call the "collection," an important concern of Paul's on his third missionary journey (see also 1 Cor 16:1–4; 2 Cor 8–9), was intended to do more than ease the Jerusalem believers' poverty—it was intended also to shrink the growing fissure between Paul's gentile converts and the "mother" church in Jerusalem. Paul's urging of the Roman Christians to be praying for this enterprise (15:30–32) makes clear that this matter loomed large in his mind as he wrote Romans. Therefore, while it is a considerable exaggeration to view Romans as a kind of rehearsal for the speech Paul plans to deliver in Jerusalem, his impending visit to Rome undoubtedly plays a role in the attention Paul gives to the Jewish-gentile issue in Romans.

As I noted above, it is important to remember that Romans is indeed a *letter*, and a letter is usually written with the intended readers of the letter in view. So, finally, we need to consider the role that *Rome* itself plays in the issues that give rise to Romans. Although Paul had never visited Rome, he is clearly acquainted with the situation there (see 1:8; 7:1; 11:13; 14–15; Prisca [Priscilla] and Aquila would have been good sources of information). Several aspects of that situation might have sparked this letter, but the most obvious is the rift in the community between the "weak" and the "strong" that Paul addresses in 14:1–15:13. As most scholars now recognize, this passage addresses

---

6. Johnson, *Writings of the New Testament*, 304; see also F. F. Bruce, "Romans Debate—Continued," in Donfried, *Romans Debate*, 182–83.

7. A. Andrew Das, *Solving the Romans Debate* (Minneapolis: Fortress, 2007), 32–34.

a debate between those (mainly Jews) who thought Christian identity needed to be worked out in terms of Torah piety and others (mainly gentiles) who saw no need to bring the Torah into their Christian experience. Much of what Paul says in Romans can be seen as preparation for this exhortation.[8] Granted this purpose, it is probable that Paul directs his teaching to both Jewish and gentile Christians, with perhaps a greater focus on the gentile element—as Paul's tendency to highlight the gentiles within his audience suggests (1:5–6, 13; 11:13; see above).[9]

The tensions between Jewish and gentile believers in Rome were probably accentuated by the particular history of the community. In AD 49 the emperor Claudius, the Roman historian Suetonius tells us, expelled the Jews from Rome (*Life of Claudius* 25.2; see Acts 18:2). At one blow, then, what up to then had been a community rooted in the synagogue became a largely, or exclusively, gentile community. By the time Paul writes Romans eight years later, Jews have been allowed to return to Rome, and the community is once again a mixed one—with Jewish believers perhaps resentful at the new domination of gentiles, and gentiles perhaps dismissive of Jews and their focus on Torah. Paul would then be writing to correct the gentiles' indifference, even arrogance, toward the Jewish minority, at the same time that he tries to show the Jews that they must not insist on the law as a normative factor in the church.[10]

I think that Paul does, indeed, write with an eye on specific problems in the community at Rome. However, this is not to deny the other reasons that I have surveyed above. Tensions in Rome between Jews and gentiles mirror the larger issue that Paul seeks to confront with his collection for the Lord's people in Jerusalem. The disunity these tensions at Rome create could make it difficult for Paul to gain support from them for his ministry to Spain. At the same time, the tension between Jewish and gentile believers is the single greatest issue that Paul had to confront as he preached the gospel. In Romans, then, Paul rehearses many of the central gospel perspectives that he had developed over the course of his ministry. The purpose of Paul in Romans, then, cannot be confined to any single issue. Romans has several purposes.[11] But the various purposes share a common denominator: Paul's missionary situation.[12] The past battles in Galatia and Corinth, the coming crisis in Jerusalem, the need to unify the Romans around "his" gospel to support his work in Spain—all these led Paul to write

8. Francis Watson, *Paul, Judaism, and the Gentiles: A Sociological Approach*, SNTSMS 56 (Cambridge: Cambridge University Press, 1986); see also Thorleif Boman, "Die dreifache Würde des Völkerapostels," *ST* 29 (1975): 69.

9. Das, *Solving the Romans Debate*, argues that Paul's intended audience is entirely gentile. Mark D. Nanos thinks that Paul urges gentile Christians to recognize the enduring heritage of Israel and to embody that recognition in deference to Jewish customs (*The Mystery of Romans: The Jewish Context of Paul's Letter* [Minneapolis: Fortress, 1996]).

10. Willi Marxsen, *Introduction to the New Testament: An Approach to Its Problems* (Philadelphia: Fortress, 1968), 92–104; William S. Campbell, "Why Did Paul Write Romans?," *ExpTim* 85 (1974): 264–69.

11. Probably most modern interpreters see several purposes for Romans. See esp. Wedderburn, *Reasons for Romans*.

12. For a similar suggestion, see L. Ann Jervis, *The Purpose of Romans: A Comparative Letter Structure Investigation*, JSNTSup 55 (Sheffield: JSOT, 1991), esp. 158–63 (summary).

a letter in which he carefully rehearsed his understanding of the gospel, especially as it related to the salvation-historical questions of Jew and gentile and the continuity of the plan of salvation.[13]

Contemporary estimates of the theological focus in Romans are sharply divided over the relative stress to be placed on the two elements of this last sentence: "the gospel" and "the salvation-historical questions of Jew and gentile and the continuity of the plan of salvation." Historically, interpreters of Romans have emphasized the first point, finding in Romans the most systematic exposition of the New Testament gospel, the "good news" that God in Christ has provided for the justification (chs. 1–5) and sanctification and ultimate glory (chs. 6–8) of any human being who responds to the good news in faith. This construal of the argument of Romans often had difficulty explaining why chapters 9–11, with their focus on Israel, were included in this exposition of the gospel. It is precisely this part of the letter that many modern interpreters think is the heart of Romans. On this view, associated especially with the "New Perspective on Paul," Romans is not focused on individuals—their sin, their justification, their sanctification—but on people groups. In response to the issues we noted above (the collection, tensions in Rome), Paul writes to explain how God has acted in Christ to provide a way for gentiles to be integrated into the people of God without disenfranchising God's "original" people, the Jews. It was this "people" question that confronted the Jewish apostle Paul in the first century as he sought to explain and defend the gospel. The problem with the law, then, about which Paul says so much in Romans, was that it was a barrier not to individuals finding a relationship with God but to the full and equal inclusion of gentiles in the people of God.

A full discussion of the New Perspective is found elsewhere (pp. 430–31, 439–48). Here I simply echo with respect to Romans the verdict I render there. While highlighting a key element in the theology of Romans that some interpreters have missed, the New Perspective in turn goes too far in elevating the "people" issue at the expense of the "individual" question. In other words, I want to preserve the balance in the sentence I used above to describe Romans's theme: It is a letter about "the gospel, especially as it related to the salvation-historical questions of Jew and gentile and the continuity of the plan of salvation." The "gospel" is a key focus in both the letter introduction and closing and takes pride of place in the letter's thematic introduction. Indeed, this overview of Paul's argument in Romans nicely captures the balance I want to preserve: "For I

13. Many interpreters take this approach. See, e.g., Charles E. B. Cranfield, *A Critical and Exegetical Commentary on the Epistle to the Romans*, 2 vols., ICC (Edinburgh: T&T Clark, 1975–1979), 2:814; Joseph A. Fitzmyer, *Romans: A New Translation with Introduction and Commentary*, AB 33 (Garden City: Doubleday, 1993), 68–83; John Drane, "Why Did Paul Write Romans?," in *Pauline Studies: Essays Presented to F. F. Bruce*, ed. Donald A. Hagner and Murray J. Harris (Exeter: Paternoster, 1980), 212–23; Ulrich Wilckens, "Über Abfassungszweck und Aufbau des Römerbriefes," in *Rechtfertigung als Freiheit: Paulusstudien* (Neukirchen-Vluyn: Neukirchener, 1974), 110–43; Beker, *Paul the Apostle*, 71–74; James D. G. Dunn, *Romans 1–8*, WBC 38A (Dallas: Word, 1988), lv–lviii.

am not ashamed of the gospel, because it is the power of God that brings salvation to everyone who believes [the individual focus]: first to the Jew, then to the Gentile [the 'people' focus]" (1:16).

ANALYZING THE ARGUMENT

Paul, then, writes with particular circumstances of his day in view. But it is good to be reminded that, for all its specific historical rootedness, Romans is at the end of the day a piece of Holy Scripture with a message that addresses the people of God of every age. While exaggerated, then, Luther's claim that Romans is "purest gospel" has more than an element of truth. Romans is far less tied to issues bound up with a particular church than is any other Pauline letter (with the possible exception of Ephesians). The legitimate desire to pin down as precisely as possible the historical background and purpose of the letter should not obscure the degree to which Romans deals with theological issues raised by the nature of God's revelation itself. Perhaps the earliest comment on the purpose of Romans comes in the Muratorian Canon (AD 200?): "To the Romans he [Paul] wrote at length, explaining the order (or plan) of the Scriptures, and also that Christ is their principle (or, main theme)."[14] We moderns—especially we modern scholars!—must beware the tendency to over-historicize: to focus so much on specific local and personal situations that we miss the larger theological and philosophical concerns of the biblical authors.[15] Paul was certainly responding in Romans to immediate concerns in the early church of his day. But these issues are ultimately those of the church—and the world—of all ages: the continuity of God's plan of salvation, the sin and need of human beings, God's provision for the problem of our sin in Christ, the means to a life of holiness, and security in the face of suffering and death.[16] Barth saw this in his day as he fought to reclaim Romans for its contemporary theological significance:

> Paul, as a child of his age, addressed his contemporaries. It is, however, far more important that, as Prophet and Apostle of the Kingdom of God, he veritably speaks to all men of every age. The differences between then and now, there and here, no doubt require careful investigation and consideration. But the purpose of

---

14. Muratorian Fragment 44–46. Translation taken from Peter Kirby, "The Muratorian Fragment," *Early Christian Writings*, www.earlychristianwritings.com/text/muratorian-metzger.html.

15. For all the problems with "canonical criticism," Brevard S. Childs has a point when he warns about the danger of allowing specific historical contexts to blot out the larger theological dimensions of Romans (*The New Testament as Canon: An Introduction* [Philadelphia: Fortress, 1985], 51).

16. Cf. James Denney ("St. Paul's Epistle to the Romans," in *The Expositor's Greek Testament*, ed. W. Robertson Nicoll [London: Hodder & Stoughton, 1900], 2:570): "Is it not manifest that when we give [the 'conditions' under which Paul wrote] all the historical definiteness of which they are capable, there is something in them which rises above the casualness of time and place, something which might easily give the epistle not an accidental or occasional character, but the character of an exposition of principles?"

such investigation can only be to demonstrate that these differences are, in fact, purely trivial.[17]

Augustine, Luther, Calvin, and Wesley, whatever their failings as exegetes, saw this also, and perhaps they understood more clearly than many of their latter-day critics.[18] We need to recognize that Romans is God's word to *us* and read it seeking to discover the message that God has for us in it. As Luther said, "[Romans] is worthy not only that every Christian should know it word for word, by heart, but occupy himself with it every day, as the daily bread of the soul. It can never be read or pondered too much, and the more it is dealt with the more precious it becomes, and the better it tastes."[19]

Romans follows the simple "form" of ancient letters, with a letter opening (1:1–17), a letter body (1:18–15:13), and a letter closing (15:14–16:26). Each of these parts is considerably longer than their counterparts in most ancient letters, as Paul adapts the letter form to the needs of theological reflection and pastoral exhortation.

1 THE LETTER OPENING (1:1–17)

Following the letter-writing conventions of his day, Paul begins Romans by identifying himself as the sender (1:1–6), the Roman Christians as his addressees (1:7a), and by extending a greeting to them (1:7b). But Paul stretches those conventions by going into much detail in describing himself. Clearly he sees the need to establish his credentials with Christians worshiping in churches that he did not plant and which he has never visited. Paul draws particular attention to his status as an "apostle" and as one "set apart for the gospel of God" (v. 1). He elaborates on each of these, in reverse order.

As I suggested above, "gospel" is the theme of Romans. In verses 2–4, Paul makes two points about this gospel that will be fundamental to his argument. First, it is rooted in the Old Testament (v. 2). While certainly not ignoring the discontinuities between Old Testament and New, Paul's purpose in this letter is to defend the basic continuity in God's plan of salvation. Second, the gospel, the "good news," is about what God has accomplished in his Son, the Lord Jesus (vv. 3–4). Perhaps building on an early Christian confession, Paul highlights the move from Jesus's earthly identity as Messiah ("descendant of David") to his current exalted status as "Son of God in power."[20] Eternally the Son, Jesus, as a result of his resurrection, has entered into a

---

17. These are the first sentences in the preface to the first edition of Karl Barth's commentary (*The Epistle to the Romans* [London: Oxford University Press, 1933], 1). John Webster alerted me to this passage: "Karl Barth," in *Reading Romans through the Centuries: From the Early Church to Karl Barth*, ed. Jeffrey P. Greenman and Timothy Larsen (Grand Rapids: Baker, 2011), 217.

18. For similar remarks, although in a different context, see Westerholm, *Perspectives*, 445.

19. Luther, "Preface to the Epistle to the Romans," 365.

20. The fact that Jesus has already been identified as God's Son (v. 3a) makes it likely that "in power" (*en dynamei*) should be taken with the title "Son of God" rather than with the verb "appointed."

new state in which he has the power to mediate salvation to all who believe (see v. 16). While Romans features no great christological passage such as we find in, for example, Philippians 2:6–11, we should not overlook the way Paul grounds his gospel—and by extension, the entire argument of Romans—in the "Christology of events" in 1:3–4.

It is through this exalted Lord that Paul has received his commission to be an apostle (v. 5). Paul's apostolic ministry is focused on gentiles (v. 5), a point he makes partly to justify his right to write an authoritative message to the Romans (dominated by gentiles; v. 6).[21] Paul claims, specifically, that his goal is to call gentiles to "the obedience of faith" (my translation). The phrase seems to be important for the argument of Romans, since Paul, in an *inclusio*, repeats it in 16:26 (see also 15:18), and it occurs nowhere else in his letters. The phrase (a genitive construction in Greek) might be translated "the obedience that now consists in faith," suggesting that faith is the new-covenant equivalent to the Old Testament (and Jewish) obedience.[22] Others think we should translate "the obedience that comes from faith" (NIV): Paul calls gentiles both to believe and also to demonstrate that faith in obedience. But it might be better to avoid being too specific about the relationship of these two key words. Faith and obedience, for Paul, are two sides of the same coin, distinct yet inseparable. Barth puts it well: "Faith is not obedience, but as obedience is not obedience without faith, faith is not faith without obedience. They belong together, as do thunder and lightning in a thunderstorm."[23]

Again following Greco-Roman epistolary form and Paul's own habit, the apostle gives thanks for the Roman Christians. But his thanksgiving quickly turns to an assurance of Paul's deep concern for them. He prays for them regularly, and only pressing ministry issues have kept him from visiting. What is theologically especially interesting is Paul's expressed desire to "preach the gospel also [in addition to gentiles elsewhere] to you who are in Rome" (v. 15). Paul's plan to "preach the gospel" to people who are already Christian is a reminder that the gospel for Paul involves much more than the initial call for sinners to embrace Christ. The "good news" about Jesus affects all of life, including of course conversion but extending to the new life ("obedience"; see v. 5) that a relationship with Christ ("faith") demands and makes possible (see pp. 349–51 on the gospel).

In verses 16–17, Paul announces the theme of the letter (the verses are therefore transitional, linking the letter opening with the letter body). They comprise one long sentence in Greek carried forward by a series of subordinate clauses:

---

21. The claim that this verse shows that Paul's "implied audience" is entirely gentile (e.g., Das, *Solving the Romans Debate*, 54–60) is overstated. It need imply no more than that his audience is mainly gentile.

22. See esp. Don B. Garlington, *"The Obedience of Faith": A Pauline Phrase in Historical Context*, WUNT 2/38 (Tübingen: Mohr Siebeck, 1991).

23. Karl Barth, *CD* IV/2, 438 (*Church Dogmatics*, 14 vols. [Edinburgh: T&T Clark, 1936–77]). For a thorough discussion of this phrase in its Roman context, see Jared Brown, "'The Obedience of Faith' in Romans: An Exegetical and Rhetorical Case for Polyvalence" (PhD diss., Wheaton College, 2019).

> For I am not ashamed of the gospel,
> *because* it is the power of God that brings salvation to everyone who believes:
> first to the Jew, then to the Gentile.
> *For* in the gospel the righteousness of God is revealed—a righteousness that is by
>   faith from first to last,
> *just as* it is written: "The righteous will live by faith."

"Gospel" is the dominant concept, signaling its importance in the letter as a whole. The result of the preaching of the good news about Christ is "salvation." This word is the broadest of the terms Paul uses to describe the benefits of God's work in Christ. It often has a negative focus (e.g., being saved *from* wrath) and, as Romans 5:9–10 (see also 13:11) illustrates particularly well, usually denotes not the initiation of God's work in humans ("conversion") but its completion. The striking juxtaposition of universality and particularity we meet at the end of verse 16 encapsulates a distinctive motif in Romans: salvation is for "*everyone* who believes," but it also comes "*first* to the Jew, *then* to the Gentile." Interpreters since the advent of the New Perspective in the 1970s and 1980s have rightly drawn attention to the importance of the "people" issue in Romans and in Paul's theology generally. As the apostle to the gentiles, Paul's special call was to preach the good news to gentiles and so integrate them fully into the people of God. He stresses this mission throughout Romans, returning again and again to the everyone-who-believes theme. But appropriate attention to what we might call this "horizontal" focus (gentiles alongside Jews) should not blind us to the importance of the "vertical" focus: the good news of Jesus is first of all about "salvation" for every individual who believes.

The reason (see the "for" introducing v. 17) the gospel has this power to save is because the "righteousness of God" is revealed in it. "Righteousness of God" is a particularly distinctive phrase in Romans, occurring seven other times in the letter (in various formulations; see 3:5, 21, 22, 25, 26; 10:3 [2x]) and only once outside it (2 Cor 5:21). The phrase has been one of the most debated in all of Paul's writings. We are confronted here again with the genitive construction in Greek, a very flexible form that is open to a wide variety of specific interpretations. Some argue here for a genitive of source, viewing "righteousness" as a gift that God gives those who respond to the gospel.[24] Paul certainly uses the word "righteousness" in this sense (Rom 4; and cf. Phil 3:9: "righteousness *from* [*ek*] God"), but it is hard to see how our own status of righteousness can be "revealed" in the gospel. An interpretation that better explains this focus is to give "righteousness" an active sense and interpret the genitive as subjective:

---

24. See, e.g., Mark A. Seifrid, *Justification by Faith: The Origin and Development of a Central Pauline Theme*, NovTSup 68 (Leiden: Brill, 1992), 214–15; Irons, *Righteousness of God*, 311–18.

"the righteous, or justifying, activity that God is doing." Support for this view is found in the way certain Old Testament texts set "righteousness" and "salvation" in parallel (e.g., Isa 51:5, 8) and by the way Paul can move seamlessly from references to God's "righteousness" to references to his justifying work (e.g., Rom 3:21–24).[25] However, the form of the Greek word for "righteousness," *dikaiosyne*, would not generally connote an action. Moreover, the Old Testament usage of the phrase makes it more likely that the phrase connotes an attribute of God. N. T. Wright has argued that this attribute is God's "covenant faithfulness."[26] However, Old Testament references to God's righteousness, especially those that would arguably have had the greatest influence on Paul (Ps 98:2; 143:1, 11; Isa 45:21; 51:5, 8), refer to a more basic character of God: his always doing "what is right," "right" being defined in terms of God's own nature and in terms of his expressed commitments. God, then, "reveals" his righteousness when he fulfills his promises to save his people—his people now, however, not being defined as Israel but as all those who in faith respond to the good news about Jesus Christ.[27]

It is this crucial point of faith that Paul draws attention to in the last part of verse 17. The NIV "by faith from first to last" translates a phrase that could also be rendered "from faith for faith." The NIV reflects a popular option according to which the phrase stresses how faith is always fundamental to our relationship with God. Some recent interpreters have argued that the phrase should be translated "from the faithfulness [of God] to the faith [exercised by humans]" (cf. CEB), as Paul exploits the dual meaning of the Greek word used twice here (*pistis*) to foreshadow an important theological theme in the letter: that God's work in Christ, while appropriated by humans in faith, is based on the faithfulness of God and/or Christ.[28] But the strong emphasis on human faith throughout Romans makes it more likely that the focus in the phrase as a whole is on faith. Perhaps, then, Paul intends to return to the salvation-historical sequence he touched on in verse 16: faith begins with Israel and then extends to the gentiles.[29] As Paul is keen to do throughout Romans, he grounds his opening summary statement about the gospel in the Old Testament. Habakkuk 2:4 is an appropriate text for Paul's purpose because it is one of the only Old Testament verses that brings together two of Paul's key theological concepts: "righteousness"/"righteous"/"justify" and "faith." Moreover, like the prophet, Paul is faced with the need to respond to accusations that God is acting out of

25. While a bit more nuanced, Ernst Käsemann's very influential view fits here ("'The Righteousness of God' in Paul," in Käsemann, *New Testament Questions of Today* [Philadelphia: Fortress, 1969], 168–82).

26. N. T. Wright argues for this view in many places in his writings. See, e.g., "Romans," in *NIB* 8:403–6.

27. Moo, *Romans* (NICNT), 73–78.

28. Richard N. Longenecker, *The Epistle to the Romans: A Commentary on the Greek Text*, NIGTC (Grand Rapids:

Eerdmans, 2016), 178; Scott, *Implicit Epistemology in the Letters of Paul*, 55. Teresa Morgan (*Roman Faith and Christian Faith: Pistis and Fides in the Early Roman Empire and Early Christianity* [Oxford: Oxford University Press, 2015], 286–87) argues, on the basis of broad Greco-Roman usage, that the word has a broad sense, referring to trustworthiness as central to relationships.

29. See Colin G. Kruse, *Paul's Letter to the Romans*, PNTC (Grand Rapids: Eerdmans, 2012), 76–78; Moo, *Romans* (NICNT), 78–80.

character: in Habakkuk's day by using a pagan nation to punish Israel; in Paul's day by opening the doors to people who were never part of God's historical people Israel.[30] As a response to this circumstance, it might make sense if Paul (as Habbakuk apparently does) announces that "the righteous person will live [out his or her life before God] by faith." However, it is also possible, considering the way Paul uses the key words in Romans, that he wants to say that "it is the person who is righteous by faith who will find life."

2 THE LETTER BODY (1:18–15:13)

2.1 The Heart of the Gospel: Justification by Faith (1:18–4:25)

The revelation of God's righteousness (1:17) dominates the first major section of the letter body. "Righteousness" and related words occur twenty-nine times in this section. But even more prominent is "faith" language (twenty-seven occurrences), as Paul elaborates the concern revealed already in 1:16–17 to tie the experience of God's righteousness to faith. Paul has two reasons for stressing faith so strongly. First, the depth of the human predicament means that humans can do nothing to find God's righteousness on their own: it is only God's own grace that can overcome the power of sin, and faith is the only right response to that grace (see esp. 4:4–5). Second, faith is a response that all humans can render to God—unlike the law, which, as God's special gift to Israel, privileges Jews. Faith, then, overcomes both the innate inability of humans to respond rightly to God ("faith versus works") *and* the barrier erected against gentiles by the law ("faith versus works of the law").

2.1.1 The Universal Reign of Sin (1:18–3:20)

The book of Acts and Paul's own testimony indicate that, for him, solution preceded plight: that is, Paul was suddenly and unexpectedly confronted with the fact that the crucified Jesus of Nazareth was indeed God's Son and Messiah; and from that "solution," he worked back to the "plight" that must have required such a radical solution. Here in Romans, however, Paul exposits the gospel by first setting forth the plight of humanity. The revelation of God's righteousness (1:17) is paralleled by a quite different revelation: of God's wrath (1:18).[31] In this lengthy first part of the first major section of Romans, Paul elaborates this theme, showing that gentiles and Jews have both failed to respond rightly to the revelation God has given them and are thus, equally, enslaved to sin (3:9).

---

30. Rikki E. Watts, "'For I Am Not Ashamed of the Gospel': Romans 1:16–17 and Habakkuk 2:4," in Soderlund and Wright, *Romans and the People of God*, 3–25.

31. An alternative understanding takes the revelation of God's wrath to be an aspect of God's righteousness (see, e.g., Jonathan A. Linebaugh, *God, Grace, and Righteousness in Wisdom of Solomon and Paul's Letter to the Romans: Texts in Conversation*, NovTSup 152 [Leiden: Brill, 2013], 105–8; Michael F. Bird, *Romans*, SGBC [Grand Rapids: Zondervan, 2016], 53–54). Barth, on the other hand, thinks that God's righteousness and God's wrath are parallel aspects of the gospel (*Romans*, 42–43).

2.1.1.1 Humans Disobey God's Revelation in Nature (1:18–32)

Verses 18–20 establish the theme of the whole section: God's wrath falls on humans who sin and who suppress the truth about God that has been revealed to them. In verses 21–31, Paul elaborates on the ways humans have suppressed God's truth and the way God has reacted to that rejection. Verse 32 is a concluding indictment. Paul never identifies the humans he describes in this paragraph as gentiles; however, his focus on natural revelation (vv. 19–20) and the sins he highlights (idolatry and sexual sin) suggest he has mainly gentiles in view.

Four points of particular theological interest are found in this paragraph. First, the wrath of God is a present reality as well as a future judgment (cf. 2:5). God's wrath in Scripture is his inevitable judging reaction to sin, rooted in his own holy character. Paul thinks that God's "giving over" of people is one of the present manifestations of that wrath.[32]

Second, Paul teaches that God has revealed his existence and basic nature to humans in general (vv. 19–20). This text then buttresses the biblical idea of a "natural revelation."[33] However, Paul also makes clear that this revelation does not lead to saving knowledge of God; rather, confronted with the reality of God, people turn away from him, choosing to worship their own gods rather than the true God (vv. 21–23). People "suppress" (v. 18) the truth they are given and so are "without excuse" (v. 20b).

Third, God reacts to the human decision to reject him with his own rejection. Three times in this paragraph Paul claims that God "gave [people] over" in response to their own decision to "exchange" God's person and truth for their own gods and the sins that result from that exchange (vv. 23–24, 25–26a, 26b–28).[34] This "giving over" on God's part is not simply a passive allowing people to go the way they have chosen; it is a judicial decision that manifests God's wrath against humans.[35]

Fourth, following Jewish precedents (see esp. Wis 13–15), Paul singles out idolatry and sexual sin as the most obvious manifestations of the gentiles' distance from the God of the Bible. Paul famously highlights same-sex activity in his description (vv. 26–27). In doing so, he again follows Jewish precedent, but this does not mean that Paul does not himself "own" what he is saying here. These verses rather reveal a New Testament

---

32. Dunn, *Theology of Paul*, 42.

33. Thomas C. Oden has shown that a robust view of natural revelation was common in the early church (although this revelation was not viewed as salvific) ("Without Excuse: Classic Christian Exegesis of General Revelation," *JETS* 41 [1998]: 55–68). See also Richard H. Bell, *No One Seeks for God: An Exegetical and Theological Study of Romans 1.18–3.20*, WUNT 2/106 (Tübingen: Mohr Siebeck, 1998), 90–118. Barth famously denied any truly natural revelation (*CD* II/1, 107–41).

34. The fact that this human fall into idolatry echoes some

OT texts about Israel (Ps 106:20: "They exchanged their glorious God for an image of a bull, which eats grass"; Jer 2:11: "Has a nation ever changed its gods? . . . But my people have exchanged their glorious God for worthless idols") suggests that we cannot entirely eliminate Jews from Paul's polemic in 1:18–32.

35. See, e.g., John Calvin, *Commentaries on the Epistle of Paul the Apostle to the Romans* (repr., Grand Rapids: Eerdmans, 1947), 76–77; contra, e.g., Chrysostom, "Homily III on Romans" (*NPNF¹* 11:354).

endorsement of the typical Old Testament and Jewish perspective on same-sex activity as contrary to the will of God for his people.[36]

2.1.1.2 God's Equity in Judging All Humans (2:1–16)

For the first of many times in Romans, Paul uses the "diatribe" style to help the Roman Christians understand key principles of the gospel. This style, popular with some philosophers and teachers (e.g., the Stoic philosopher Epictetus, who lived just after Paul's time), uses a dialogical format to get one's points across. The second-singular "you" forms that are used throughout 2:1–5 (and resumed in 2:17–29), then, do not address a particular Roman Christian but a fictional dialogue partner. Several indications make clear that this dialogue partner is a Jew who, in typical fashion, claims exemption from punishment for his sins because of his membership in the covenant people of God.[37] And it is this accusation of guilt despite covenant membership that is the point of chapter 2.

Paul begins by rejecting a basic Jewish assumption of his day, namely, that the people of Israel, because of God's covenant with them, were basically immune from God's judgment. "Do you think you will escape God's judgment?" Paul asks (2:3). Not at all: you are doing "the same things" as the gentile (probably referring to the list of sins in 1:29–31). Long before Paul, of course, the prophets had condemned this kind of presumption (see, e.g., Jer 7), as did John the Baptist (e.g., Matt 3:7–10). But Second Temple books such as Wisdom 13–15 reveal that a complacent attitude toward God's judgment was widespread among the Jewish people in Paul's day. Paul alludes to language such as that found in Wisdom of Solomon to scold his Jewish compatriots for their assumption that God's "kindness, forbearance and patience" gives them immunity from judgment (v. 4). But Paul takes the prophetic criticism a significant step further. Sincere repentance or recommitment to do the law is no longer adequate. One could escape the condemnatory judgment of God only by embracing God's new-covenant work in Christ (see, e.g., 2:28–29).

Paul shifts focus in the next two paragraphs, using third-person forms to establish two basic points: God's judgment is based on what a person actually does (vv. 6–11), and possession of the law does not provide Jews with immunity from judgment (vv. 12–16).

---

36. On this text, see esp. Mark D. Smith, "Ancient Bisexuality and the Interpretation of Romans 1:26–27," *JAAR* 64 (1996): 223–56; Preston M. Sprinkle, "Romans 1 and Homosexuality: A Critical Review of James Brownson's *Bible, Gender, Sexuality*," *BBR* 24 (2014): 515–28; contra, e.g., Robin Scroggs, *The New Testament and Homosexuality: Contextual Background for Contemporary Debate* (Philadelphia: Fortress, 1983), 17–118; James V. Brownson, *Bible, Gender, Sexuality: Reframing the Church's Debate on Same-Sex Relationships* (Grand Rapids: Eerdmans, 2013), 224–31. On the larger issue, see esp. Gagnon, *Bible and Homosexual Practice*; Richard B. Hays, *The Moral Vision of the New Testament: A Contemporary*

Introduction to New Testament Ethics (San Francisco: HarperSanFrancisco, 1996), 379–406; and my discussion on pp. 632–33.

37. Watson, *Paul, Judaism, and the Gentiles*, 197–99; Moo, *Romans* (NICNT), 136–37. Others think Paul is addressing any self-righteous person (Calvin, *Romans*, 83–84; Runar M. Thorsteinsson, *Paul's Interlocutor in Romans 2: Function and Identity in the Context of Ancient Epistolography*, ConBNT 40 [Stockholm: Almqvist & Wiksell, 2003], 177–94) or perhaps a proud gentile (William S. Campbell, *Paul and the Creation of Christian Identity* [London: T&T Clark, 2008], 107–9; Matthew Thiessen, *Paul and the Gentile Problem* [Oxford: Oxford University Press, 2016], 52–54).

Verses 6–11 form a neat chiasm:

A ⁶God "will repay each person according to what they have done."

>B ⁷To those who by persistence in doing good seek glory, honor and immortality, he will give eternal life.

>>C ⁸But for those who are self-seeking and who reject the truth and follow evil, there will be wrath and anger.

>>C' ⁹There will be trouble and distress for every human being who does evil: first for the Jew, then for the Gentile;

>B' ¹⁰but glory, honor and peace for everyone who does good: first for the Jew, then for the Gentile.

A' ¹¹For God does not show favoritism.

Unlike some chiasms, the main point comes at the outer (A) lines: God impartially judges every person according to what they do. The inner (C) lines state a well-known biblical point: Sinful acts bring God's condemnatory judgment. Controversy, however, surrounds the point Paul appears to make in the (B) lines: that a person can achieve eternal life by doing good. Some interpreters think that this might suggest that God graciously accepts humans who, even apart from knowledge of Christ, lead good lives.[38] But such a conclusion would seem to contradict Paul's claim about universal sinfulness and condemnation apart from Christ (1:19–21; 3:9, 19–20). A more widely held and theologically unobjectionable view is that Paul is here implicitly describing Christians. As he will make clear later in this passage, those who persist in "doing good" are Spirit-filled believers (vv. 28–29).[39] However, the best option is to think that Paul is simply spelling out here the two possible outcomes that result from God's scrutiny of all humans. He does not here claim that anyone actually belongs to the class of those who achieve eternal life by doing good; and he will make clear that this is, in fact, an empty set in his subsequent argument (3:9).[40]

A similar debate surrounds the "Gentiles" to whom Paul refers in verse 14. Are these gentile Christians who illustrate verse 13b people who are declared righteous by obeying the law—in this case the new-covenant law written on the heart (Jer 31:31–34)?[41] Or does Paul refer to gentile unbelievers who, because they possess "law" in some form,

---

38. Augustine, *On Grace* 7.17; Klyne R. Snodgrass, "Justification by Grace—to the Doers: An Analysis of the Place of Romans 2 in the Theology of Paul," *NTS* 32 (1986): 72–93.

39. See esp. N. T. Wright, *Paul and the Faithfulness of God*, 2:937–39; Thomas R. Schreiner, *Romans*, 2nd ed., BECNT (Grand Rapids: Baker Academic, 2018), 123–24; idem, "Did Paul Believe in Justification by Works? Another Look at Romans 2," *BBR* 3 (1993): 131–55.

40. Longenecker, *Romans*, 261–62; Kevin M. McFadden, *Judgment according to Works in Romans: The Meaning and Function of Divine Judgment in Paul's Most Important Letter* (Minneapolis: Fortress, 2013), 139–53; Moo, *Romans* (NICNT), 150–52.

41. E.g., Simon J. Gathercole, "A Law unto Themselves: The Gentiles in Romans 2.14–15 Revisited," *JSNT* 85 (2002): 27–49; Wright, "Romans," 441; idem, *Paul and the Faithfulness of God*, 2:1379–81.

undermine the Jewish claim to be the only ones who have God's law?[42] I think the latter is a bit more likely. Paul continues to "level the playing field" between Jew and gentile, reiterating again that God's judgment (at which time one might hope to be "declared righteous") is based on what a person actually does and stressing that the Jewish presumption of privilege based on the law is not absolute: gentiles have "law" in some form also. It is important to note why I have put this last occurrence of law in quotes. Verse 12, with its distinction between those who have the law and those who do not, illustrates Paul's normal use of the word "law" (Gk. *nomos*): it is a reference to the law of Moses, the *Torah*, that God gave to his people Israel at Sinai. This is overwhelmingly what the word means in Romans and in Paul's letters generally. But there are exceptions, and I think the third occurrence of *nomos* in verse 14 is one of those: unbelieving gentiles have "law" in the sense that God reveals to all humans something of his basic moral expectations. Overall, Paul's purpose here is again to stress that for all people, whether they have law in the specific and detailed form of Torah or in the general sense of "right and wrong" that God has placed in every person, it is only the actual doing of the law that will count before God in the judgment.

2.1.1.3 The Covenant Cannot Protect the Jewish People from Judgment (2:17–29)

Returning to the diatribe style of 2:1–5, Paul continues to press home his argument with a typical Jew. It would be normal for Jews in Paul's day to appeal to their unique status as the covenant people of God as reason for them to be treated in quite a different manner than gentiles. While not referring to the covenant *per se*, Paul now brings up two of the most important signs of that covenant: the law (2:17–24) and circumcision (2:25–29). In each case, as Paul has done throughout this chapter, he stresses that the covenant to which these two markers point will be salvifically significant only if the covenant member obeys that law. Jews have a right to "boast" about their privileges: they have been signally blessed by God. But when the law is broken, these privileges simply stand in judgment over them (v. 23). Likewise, the covenant sign of circumcision has value, Paul says, if the law is obeyed. But when it is not followed, Jews are no better off than gentiles. In fact, gentiles who keep the law will themselves be regarded by God as if they were circumcised. This is the third time in this chapter Paul refers to people who appear to be considered righteous through their obedience (2:7 and 10; 2:13). Reference to the Spirit in this context (v. 29) is the strongest evidence that Paul may be referring in these texts to gentiles whose "fulfillment" of the law by the Spirit (see 8:4) marks them out as people who have entered into relationship with God by faith

---

42. Calvin; Schreiner, "Did Paul Believe in Justification by Works?," 131–58.

in Christ.[43] However, while there is here some looking ahead to where Paul's argument is going—true "doers of the law" are those who walk by the Spirit—I continue to think that Paul is using a hypothetical circumstance (gentiles who do the law) to undermine the Jewish sense of automatic protection from judgment.[44]

2.1.1.4 God's Faithfulness and the Judgment of Jews (3:1–8)

A fair conclusion to be drawn from chapter 2 is that God has erased all ethnic or national distinctions in the new age that has dawned. But Paul confounds us: In 3:1–2a, he strongly rebuts any notion that Jewish privilege has been erased. On the other hand, however, the note about "first for the Jew" in the theme statement of 1:16–17 should perhaps mitigate any surprise at this turn in the argument. Paul continues to balance continuing Jewish precedence (in both positive [1:16; 2:10] and negative [2:9] ways) with full inclusion of gentiles. A full discussion of the somewhat perplexing juxtaposition of "no distinction" (3:22 NRSV) and "first for the Jew" will await chapters 9–11. At this point, Paul simply rejects an incorrect inference from his argument in chapter 2, asserting a continuing precedence for Jews (3:1–2). However, the bulk of the paragraph picks up the theme of Jewish disobedience from chapter 2, asserting that God's judgment of such disobedience in no way negates God's faithfulness and righteousness (vv. 3–8). We see here that, in keeping with the Old Testament, God's righteousness (v. 5) for Paul is not simply a saving righteousness but a judging righteousness as well. For God's righteousness, as we have seen (1:17) is basically God's doing what is right—in terms of his own person and his commitments. God's covenant with Israel promised blessing for obedience—but cursing for disobedience.

2.1.1.5 The Guilt of All Humanity (3:9–20)

Paul completes his sketch of the human plight by summarizing the situation (v. 9), adducing scriptural support for that conclusion (vv. 10–18), and making clear the implications of this argument (vv. 19–20). Paul continues the question-and-answer style of 3:1–8 (another feature of the diatribe style) in verse 9, asking, "Do we [Jews] have any advantage [see vv. 1–2]?" and answering quickly and emphatically, "Not at all!" In fact, Paul concludes, Jews and gentiles are alike in all being "under the power of sin." This NIV rendering appropriately draws out the significance of the Greek "under sin" (*hyph hamartian*) here. The human predicament is not that people commit sins; the problem is that they are helpless slaves of sin. While taken too far by some Pauline scholars (see my discussion of the "Apocalyptic Paul" movement on pp. 30–31), this notion of

---

43. See, again, Schreiner, *Romans*, 150–51; idem, "Did Paul Believe in Justification by Works?"; Wright, "Romans," 448; idem, *Paul and the Faithfulness of God*, 2:1432.

44. See also, e.g., Frank Thielman, *Romans*, ZECNT 6 (Grand Rapids: Zondervan Academic, 2018), 130.

enslavement to a power is vital to an understanding of Paul's view of humanity and, by implication, the solution to the human problem.

The series of Old Testament quotations in verses 10–18, drawn from various parts of Scripture, reinforce this sense of universal human sinfulness. As verse 19 reveals, Paul wants especially to make clear again that what these texts say has special application to Jews. Indeed, throughout 1:18–3:20 Paul's focus has been on demonstrating why it is that Jews, God's covenant people, need the righteousness of God available in Christ. Verse 20 draws an important conclusion that begins the transition into the next stage of Paul's argument: "No one will be declared righteous in God's sight by the works of the law." The little phrase "works of the law," used a total of eight times in Paul (see also 3:28; Gal 2:16 [three times]; 3:2, 5, 10) bears theological significance quite out of proportion to its length or frequency. Indeed, one might say that the debate between "old" and "new" perspectives on Paul focuses on this phrase. Interpreters throughout the history of the church have interpreted the phrase to refer to doing what the Jewish law commands but—and this is the vital point—as ultimately connoting any human work. On the basis of this phrase (and others like it), then, interpreters concluded that Paul was denying the possibility that any human work could put one in right relationship with God.[45] However, while not necessarily denying this last point, advocates of the New Perspective have insisted that Paul has quite a different and more restricted point in view. They claim that the phrase refers not so much to human doing of the law as to the law in general. What Paul is denying, then, is any continuing ability for Jews to be put right with God under the old Sinai covenant.[46] I will engage in a full discussion of this phrase and its wider theological significance later (pp. 435–39). For now, I will just say that I think the older view of this phrase is the more accurate one—Paul concludes his survey of human sinfulness by asserting that nothing a human does can gain him or her favor with God. Hence all depends on the benefits of the revelation of God's righteousness in Christ (v. 21).

2.1.2 God's Righteousness and Justification by Faith (3:21–4:25)

With a clear picture of human helplessness now in view, Paul can turn from "plight" to "solution," as he elaborates the notion of God's righteousness, introduced in 1:17. Romans 3:21–26 introduces the key terminology and concepts, which are then developed (especially with respect to faith) in 3:27–31 and 4:1–25.

---

45. See, e.g., Calvin, *Romans*, 130–33; Adolf Schlatter, *Romans: The Righteousness of God* (Peabody, MA: Hendrickson, 1995); Cranfield, *Romans*, 1:197–99 (and his article "'The Works of the Law' in the Epistle to the Romans," *JSNT* 43 [1991]: 89–101); Schreiner, *Romans*, 177–83 (and his article "'Works of the Law' in Paul," *NovT* 33 [1991]: 217–44); Longenecker, *Romans*, 360–70; Eckhard J. Schnabel, *Der Brief des Paulus an die Römer*, 2 vols., Historisch Theologische Auslegung: Neues Testament (Giessen: Brunnen, 2015, 2016), 1:362–65; Westerholm, *Perspectives*, 300–21.

46. See, e.g., Dunn, *Theology of Paul*, 354–59; Wright, "Romans," 458–61.

2.1.2.1 God's Righteousness Displayed and Vindicated (3:21–26)

Luther famously characterized verses 21–26 as "the chief point, and the very central place of the Epistle, and of the whole Bible."[47] He is not far off the mark. Not many other texts juxtapose so many important theological ideas in so short a space. Words from the Greek root *dik-* dominate the paragraph: "righteousness" (*dikaiosynē*) in verses 21, 22, 25, 26; "justify" (*dikaioō*) in verses 24 and 26; "just" (or "righteous") (*dikaios*) in verse 26. The manifestation of God's righteousness, the climactic, eschatological display of his "saving character" (vv. 21, 22), brings those who believe, Jew or gentile, into a state of righteousness ("justified," v. 24). This divine rescue operation ("redemption") is an act of God's grace, made possible because God in Christ was finally and forever taking care of people's sins (v. 24). And, by acting in this way, God in turn displays the fact that he acts entirely in accord with his own righteous character (vv. 25b–26).

A point of particular emphasis in these verses, and the two sections that follow (3:27–31 and 4:1–25), is "faith." Traditionally, the faith Paul refers to in all these texts was attributed to humans—it is by exercising faith, or "believing," that a person can enjoy the benefits of God's righteousness in Christ. However, a strong trend in recent interpretation has been to attribute several references to faith as connoting Christ's faithfulness (esp. "faith of Christ" in v. 22; and often also "faith" in vv. 25 and 26).[48] Advocates of this interpretation argue that such an interpretation makes good linguistic sense and restores a theological balance by bringing to the forefront the christological basis for justification. This interpretation is certainly theologically unobjectionable. However, the linguistic basis is not especially strong. The key phrase in verse 22 (*pisteōs Iēsou Christou*) uses the Greek genitive construction. We might straightforwardly render it in English as "Jesus Christ faith/faithfulness." All that the syntax tells us is that faith, or faithfulness, has some relationship to Jesus Christ. Defenders of the "faithfulness of Christ" view think the genitive is subjective ("faithfulness exhibited *by* Jesus Christ"). But when Paul uses the cognate verb *pisteuō* ("believe"), he never makes Christ its subject, whereas he regularly makes humans it subject. This pattern in the verb strongly suggests we should treat the ambiguous noun construction the same way: *pistis* is what humans do. I think, then, that "faith" in this paragraph (and in 3:27–4:25) refers consistently to human believing.[49] Of course, as Paul stresses, this belief is "in Jesus Christ." For Paul, the object of faith is what gives faith its power, and so Christology is hardly missing in this traditional way of viewing the text.

Characteristic of Paul's theological concerns in Romans, he stresses that the manifestation of God's righteousness stands in both continuity and discontinuity with

---

47. Luther, margin of the Luther Bible, on 3:23ff.

48. Longenecker's defense of the subjective-genitive reading is particularly clear, balanced, and theologically sensitive (*Romans*, 408–13).

49. Moo, *Galatians*, 38–48; and see the full discussion on pp. 379–82.

the Old Testament. It comes "apart from the law," but is testified to by "the Law and the Prophets" (v. 21). Also characteristic of Romans is Paul's insistence that God's righteousness is available for "all who believe" (v. 22), a universal note that, as the somewhat parenthetical verse 23 makes clear, focuses again on the breaking down of the barrier between Jews and gentiles. As Paul's three earlier uses of the verb "justify" reveal (2:13; 3:4, 20), the word indicates forensic approval: the verdict of "acquitted" in the law court (see my full discussion on pp. 469–91). Sounding one of the fundamental notes in the melody of the gospel, Paul reminds us that this justifying work of God is a free gift, an act of grace. Shifting conceptual contexts a bit, Paul then notes that our justification is possible because of an act of liberation, a "redemption" (v. 24). This word (*apolytrōsis*; cf. also 8:23; 1 Cor 1:30; Eph 1:7, 14; 4:30; Col 1:14) and its cognates (Paul uses the verb *lytroō* in Titus 2:14 and *antilytron* in 1 Tim 2:6) connotes a liberating act. It was used in the Old Testament to describe the exodus. Paul, then, suggests that as God delivered his people from slavery in Egypt, he now in Christ rescues his people from slavery to sin (see Rom 3:9). But "redemption" also implies that the liberation involved takes place by the payment of a price.[50]

It is therefore natural for Paul to go on and refer to that "price paid" by referring to Christ as a *hilastērion*. Just what Paul wants to say about Christ's death by using this word is considerably debated. Does it mean "expiation," the wiping away of sin (RSV; NAB)?[51] Or "propitiation," the act of propitiating God's wrath (see 1:18; 2:5; e.g., ESV; NASB)?[52] Or, more broadly, does it refer to the "mercy seat" or "atonement cover" in the Old Testament tabernacle (see NET)?[53] This last option is the best: *hilastērion* refers to this atonement cover in its one other New Testament occurrence (Heb 9:5) and in most of its occurrences in the LXX. As this atonement cover was, in a sense, the place where God dealt with his people's sins in the old covenant (it was especially prominent in the Day of Atonement ritual—Leviticus 16), so Christ, set forth on the cross, is now the "place" where God takes care, once and for all (the particular emphasis of Hebrews, of course), of his people's sins.[54] At the end of the day, however, I would

50. The classic argument is made by Leon Morris, *The Apostolic Preaching of the Cross* (Grand Rapids: Eerdmans, 1955), 9–26.

51. C. H. Dodd, "Ἱλασκεσθαι, Its Cognates, Derivatives, and Synonyms, in the Septuagint," *JTS* 32 (1931): 352–60 (repr. in C. H. Dodd, *The Bible and the Greeks* [London: Hodder & Stoughton, 1935], 82–95); Alexander J. M. Wedderburn, *The Death of Jesus: Some Reflections on Jesus-Traditions and Paul*, WUNT 2/299 (Tübingen: Mohr Siebeck, 2013), 113–25.

52. Adolf Deissmann, "ἱλαστήριος und ἱλαστήριον: Eine lexikalische Studie," *ZNW* 4 (1903): 195–211. See also Schreiner, *Paul*, 234–36.

53. The English "mercy seat" comes from Tyndale's translation, which was in turn influenced by Luther's German "Gnadenstuhl."

54. Arland J. Hultgren, *Paul's Gospel and Mission: The Outlook from His Letter to the Romans* (Philadelphia: Fortress, 1985), 47–72, and Peter Stuhlmacher, "Recent Exegesis on Romans 3:24–26," in *Reconciliation, Law, and Righteousness: Essays in Biblical Theology* (Philadelphia: Fortress, 1986), 94–109. Via an extensive lexical analysis, Daniel Bailey has shown that the word here almost certainly means "place of atonement" ("Biblical and Greco-Roman Uses of Hilastērion in Romans 3:25 and 4 Maccabees 17:22 (Codex S)," in Stuhlmacher, *Biblical Theology of the New Testament*, 824–67; see also, e.g., Stephen Hultgren, "Hilasterion (Rom. 3:25) and the Union of Divine Justice and Mercy Part II: Atonement in the Old Testament and in Romans 1–5," *JTS* 70 [2019]: 566–74).

like to have my cake and eat it twice: *hilastērion*, I think, *refers* to the atonement cover, and by extension to the Day of Atonement ritual, but, considering the Old Testament meaning of this ritual, the word also *means* both expiation (sins are "sent away") and propitiation (God's wrath against sin is removed).[55]

In a kind of *inclusio*, Paul returns at the end of this paragraph to where he began: the "righteousness of God." Many interpreters think all four occurrences of this phrase in verses 21–26 have the same meaning, a particularly popular option being that it refers throughout to the "covenant faithfulness" of God. But, as we saw in my comments on 1:17 (and see also pp. 476–79), the phrase is better understood as referring to God's character of "doing right." In verses 21–22, as Longenecker helpfully notes, the phrase focuses more on a "communicative" aspect of this righteousness: the expression of God's doing right for his people when he delivers them. In these last two occurrences (vv. 25b, 26a), however, the focus is on the "attributive" sense of righteousness: God's commitment, rooted in his nature, to always do what is right.[56] God cannot, then, simply overlook sin when he justifies human beings; the problem of sin must be taken care of. By sending Christ as the one who dies in our place, to take the wrath we deserved on himself, God has been able to "justify" us while remaining "just" (v. 26b).

2.1.2.2 "By Faith Alone" (3:27–4:25)

In 3:27–31 and then again in 4:1–25, Paul elaborates on one key element from 3:21–26: faith as the means by which humans are justified and therefore experience the benefits of the revelation of God's righteousness. In this paragraph, Paul briefly outlines the key points. As he does in 4:1–2, he uses the subject of "boasting" as an entrée into his teaching. The boasting Paul has in view may, especially in light of 2:17, be the pride of Jews in their covenant relationship with God.[57] However, while Jewish pride may be an important aspect of what Paul criticizes, the idea is probably broader than this, touching on the general human tendency to take pride in achievement and status.[58]

---

55. A good case can be made that the martyrdoms of faithful Jews in the Maccabean period were presented with language drawn from the Levitical sacrificial texts (2 Macc 7:37–38; 4 Macc 6:27–29; and see esp. 4 Macc 17:21–22, which characterizes the martyrs' deaths as "a ransom for the sin of our nation" and "an atoning sacrifice" [NRSV; *tou hilastēriou*]). See especially Eduard Lohse, who rejects any connection with the mercy seat (*Der Brief an die Römer*, KEK [Göttingen: Vandenhoeck & Ruprecht, 2003], 134–35; and, in greater detail, idem, *Märtyrer und Gottesknecht: Untersuchungen zur urchristlichen Verkündigung vom Sühntod Jesu Christi*, FRLANT 46 [Göttingen: Vandenhoeck & Ruprecht, 1963]). A better and more balanced approach is taken by Jarvis J. Williams, who argues that Paul is using these martyr traditions, which themselves pick up language from Leviticus (*Maccabean Martyr Traditions in Paul's Theology of Atonement: Did Martyr*

Theology Shape Paul's Conception of Jesus's Death? [Eugene, OR: Wipf & Stock, 2010]). I argue that the main reference is to Leviticus, with the Maccabean martyr tradition exercising some additional influence.

56. James Denney, *The Death of Christ: Its Place and Interpretation in the New Testament* (New York: A. C. Armstrong and Son, 1903), 96–107, and the succinct exegetical defense of John Piper, *The Justification of God: An Exegetical and Theological Study of Romans 9:1–23* (Grand Rapids: Baker, 1993), 115–30. See also Thielman, *Romans*, 212.

57. Sanders, *Paul, the Law and the Jewish People*, 33; Dunn, *Romans 1–8*, 185. See also Wright: "The Jewish claim to be the means through which God would rescue the world from its plight" (*Paul and the Faithfulness of God*, 2:847).

58. See esp. Gathercole, *Where Is Boasting?*, 225–26, passim.

All such boasting is excluded when one understands the new-covenant "principle" ("the law of faith" [my translation])[59]: a person can be justified before God only by faith and not by obedience to the law ("works of the law") or by any other form of obedience (see my comments on 3:20). Romans 3:28 does not, to be sure, use the word "only"; yet it has been widely recognized that the famous Reformation cry of *sola fide* is, indeed, the point Paul is making here. Signaling an important and often overlooked aspect of Paul's teaching about the gospel in Romans is Paul's reminder in verses 29–30 that faith is important because it enables gentiles to access God's grace equally with Jews. Paul ends the paragraph in a characteristic way by heading off possible misunderstanding of his teaching. God's righteousness is manifested "apart from the law" (v. 21); people are justified "apart from the works of the law" (v. 28). But Paul in no way wants his readers to conclude that the law of God is therefore a bad thing or a false move in salvation history. No, he insists, "we uphold the law" (v. 31). We can expect that Paul will explain this brief claim later in the letter. But where? Chapter 4, where he shows that the "law" (in the sense of the Pentateuch) testifies to justification by faith?[60] In 13:8–10 and elsewhere, where he suggests that the law remains a standard of behavior for Christians?[61] Or in 8:4, understood in the sense that Christ's work enables believers to be those who find the law "fulfilled" in them? Paul never makes this clear. Yet I think the last option is probably best.

In chapter 4, Paul elaborates the basic points he has made in 3:27–31 with reference to Abraham:

Boasting is excluded (3:27a)	Abraham has no right to boast (4:1–2)
. . . because one is justified	. . . because Abraham was justified
by faith, not works of the law (3:27b–28)	by faith, not works (4:3–8)
Circumcised and uncircumcised	Circumcised and uncircumcised
are united under the one God	are united as children of
through faith (3:29–30)	Abraham through faith (4:9–17)

There are two related reasons for Paul to focus on Abraham to elaborate his point about justification by faith alone. First, of course, Abraham is a key figure in salvation history, the one to whom God promised an immense family, drawn from many nations, and the one who would form the nucleus of the people whom God rescues

---

59. I understand "law" here, then, to mean "principle" (see also, basically, Schreiner, *Romans*, 210–11). A popular option among recent interpreters is to see a reference to the OT law, in terms of the faith it calls for (e.g., Cranfield, *Romans*, 1:219–20).

60. So most interpreters; see, e.g., C. Thomas Rhyne, *Faith Establishes the Law*, SBLDS 55 (Chico, CA: Scholars Press, 1981).

61. John Murray, *The Epistle to the Romans*, 2 vols. in 1, NICNT (Grand Rapids: Eerdmans, 1968), 1:126; Schreiner, *Romans*, 216.

from the sin and death of Adam. Second, Paul must show how his emphasis on faith fits with this basic foundational Old Testament and Jewish narrative, in contrast to the tendency in many Jewish sources to praise Abraham for his piety and faithfulness to the law (see, e.g., Jub. 23.10; Pr. Man. 8; Sir 44:19). Paul's counternarrative is built on his interpretation of Genesis 15:6, the Old Testament text that provides the jumping-off point for almost everything Paul says about Abraham in chapter 4. He frames the chapter by quoting it in verses 3 and 23 and uses it to develop his argument via a series of antitheses: Abraham's righteousness was a matter of faith—not works (vv. 4–8), not circumcision (vv. 9–12), and not the law (vv. 13–17). This latter text morphs into an exposition of the nature of Abraham's faith (vv. 18–22). While Abraham's faith and its significance for his justification/relationship to God is the dominant note in this chapter, we should not overlook a significant second theme: Abraham's inclusive significance. His faith and later circumcision means that he can represent both believing Jews and believing gentiles (vv. 11–12); he is "the father of many nations" (vv. 16–18).

The basic points about "faith alone" that Paul has made in 3:27–31 are now elaborated with respect to Abraham. As all "boasting is excluded" in light of the truth that people are justified by faith and not works of the law (3:27–28), so Abraham has no reason to boast because his "righteousness" was also based on faith (4:1–3). Paul cites Genesis 15:6 as the evidence for Abraham's experience. This Old Testament text, one of the few in which "righteousness" language and "faith" are brought together, stitches the argument of the chapter together, as Paul draws out the significance of this "crediting" of Abraham's faith.[62] As 3:28 contrasts faith with "works of the law," so Paul now contrasts faith and "works" (vv. 4–5). Some interpreters think that we should view "works" as shorthand for "works of the law," with limited application, therefore, to the Jewish Torah. However, the breadth of the language Paul uses here suggests that "works" includes any human "doing." As I have argued above, then (see the note on 3:20 and also pp. 435–39), rather than narrowing "works" to "works of the law," it is better to expand "works of the law" to ultimately refer to works of any kind.[63] The argument of verses 4–5, while clearly stated in this way, involves a simple logic: (1) a relationship based on "works" involves obligation; (2) God cannot be under obligation to any of his creatures; (3) therefore "works" cannot be the basis of our relationship with God. The assumption Paul makes that enables this logic to work is that God always acts by grace, never being constrained by forces outside himself. Faith, then, because it is a

---

62. On the meaning of Gen 15:6 and the NT use of it, see Douglas J. Moo, "Genesis 15:6 in the New Testament," in *From Creation to New Creation: Biblical Theology and Exegesis. Essays in Honor of G. K. Beale*, ed. Daniel M. Gurtner and Benjamin L. Gladd (Peabody, MA: Hendrickson, 2013), 147–62.

63. Moo, *Romans* (NICNT), 285; contra, e.g., Dunn, *Romans 1–8*, 206.

matter of holding out our hands to receive God's gift (to use the imagery employed by both Luther and Calvin), aligns with grace—whereas works do not.

In typical Jewish fashion, Paul supports his basic point from the "law" (the Pentateuch) and from "the prophets and the writings." Paul also follows Jewish custom by linking the two passages he quotes by means of a word common to both: Genesis 15:6 (quoted earlier) and Psalm 32:1–2, which Paul quotes in verses 7–8, share the Greek word *logizomai* (translated "credited" in Gen 15:6 and "count" in Psalm 32). But the texts have more than this word in common. Like Genesis 15:6, David in Psalm 32 makes clear that God's blessing comes not as a result of human merit but because of God's gracious decision not to "count" sins against a person.

If Abraham's righteous standing with God was based on faith "apart from works" (vv. 1–8), it was also based on faith "apart from circumcision" (vv. 9–12). Paul's argument here is a simple chronological one: Abraham believed (Gen 15) and was pronounced righteous *before* he was circumcised (Gen 17). He is therefore uniquely qualified to be the spiritual ancestor of both believing Jews (who, like Abraham, are both circumcised and believe) and believing gentiles (who, like Abraham, exercise their faith without being circumcised).

While the argument shifts a bit at verse 16 and again at verse 18, verses 13–25 are bound together by the theme of "promise" (vv. 13, 14, 16, 20, 21). The opening verses (13–15) are marked by another opposition: Abraham's righteousness is a matter of faith, not the law. Dependence on the law, Paul argues, would eviscerate the whole point of faith, making it worthless and keeping people from experiencing what God has promised. The law, Paul claims, has other functions: It "brings wrath" (v. 15). Paul's use of the word "transgression" (Gk. *parabasis*) in verse 15 is the key to his meaning. Paul uses this word to refer to disobedience of a known command for which someone has been made responsible (see also Rom 2:23; 5:14; Gal 3:19; 1 Tim 2:14). The law brings wrath, then, by imposing specific commandments on Israel, rendering their sinning more reprehensible and thus bringing more wrath.

While Paul's main line of argument in Romans 4 focuses on his "faith alone" claim about receiving God's righteousness, he also continues to stress (as he did in 3:29–30) the significance of faith as a basis for integrating Jews and gentiles into a single new-covenant people of God. Thus, in verse 16 Paul teaches that the promise that comes by faith and by grace means all Abraham's "offspring" can be included— both believing Jews ("those who are of the law")[64] and gentiles ("those who have the faith of Abraham"). For, in addition to stimulating wrath, the law, as a gift uniquely

---

64. This interpretation is more likely than the view (which, to be sure, has some support in the Greek) that "those who are of the law" refers to unbelieving Jews.

given to Israel, functions as a kind of barrier, keeping gentiles apart from the people of God. Yet, as Paul makes clear with another citation of Genesis, Abraham was promised that he would be the "father of many nations" (v. 17; Gen 17:5)—including the gentiles in his interpretation of the text. A second shift in our text occurs in verse 18, as Paul adds a brief excursus on the nature of Abraham's faith. It was a faith that rested in God's hope and promise but that flew in the face of "hope" in a worldly sense ("against all hope . . . in hope," v. 18). Abraham's advanced age and Sarah's "dead" womb made the idea of their giving birth to a child to fulfill the promise quite impossible. Yet Abraham's faith looked beyond the physical barrier; he "was strengthened in his faith" (v. 20), "being fully persuaded that God had power to do what he had promised" (v. 21).

In verse 22, Paul comes back to where he began: with Genesis 15:6. In verses 23–25, he concludes this discussion of Abraham by reminding his readers that this text has relevance to them as well as to Abraham. For Christians, like Abraham, believe in a God who "gives life to the dead" (v. 17)—specifically, the God who "raised Jesus our Lord from the dead" (v. 24). The chapter ends with the apostle's citation of what may be an early tradition about Jesus's death and resurrection. Note the parallelism:

He	was handed over	for[65]	our trespasses
He	was raised	for	our justification

Paul obviously does not intend to communicate that Jesus's resurrection, in contrast to his death, provides for our justification. He connects justification with Jesus's death far too often for this to be the idea. We should not, then, press the literary parallelism here too far: Jesus's death and resurrection are both vital to his taking care of his people's sin problem and to their justification. Yet some relationship between Jesus's resurrection specifically and their justification is indicated here. What this connection involves is not clear. Perhaps, however, the claim in 1 Timothy 3:16 that Jesus was "vindicated [or 'justified'; *edikaiōthē*] by the Spirit" may help fill out the picture. Jesus's resurrection vindicated him and freed him from the influence of sin (Rom 6:10); so we who share in Jesus's resurrection likewise experience that vindication, or "justification."[66]

---

65. The Greek is the preposition *dia*, which often (when followed by the accusative, as here), means "because of." But the preposition can have a prospective sense—"because of the need to," and thus "for the sake of" (most English versions follow this interpretation).

66. See esp. Richard B. Gaffin Jr., *Resurrection and Redemption: A Study in Paul's Soteriology*, BBMS (Grand Rapids: Baker,

1987; repr. of *The Centrality of Resurrection: A Study in Paul's Soteriology* [Grand Rapids: Baker, 1978]), esp. 123; see also, e.g., I. Howard Marshall, *Aspects of the Atonement: Cross and Resurrection in the Reconciling of God and Humanity* (London: Paternoster, 2007), 68–97; Beale, *New Testament Biblical Theology*, 297, 490–97, passim; Campbell, *Paul and the Hope of Glory*, 335–39.

2.2 Assurance and the Gospel (5:1–8:39)

Interpreters of Romans disagree about where Paul transitions from one stage of his argument to another. One option, with a long history in the tradition, places the transitional point at the end of chapter 5, the idea often being that Paul here moves from the topic of justification to sanctification.[67] Less often, the break is placed at 5:12, or chapter 5 is viewed as a transition between major sections.[68] But Paul's argument makes better sense if we see the transition taking place at the beginning of chapter 5.[69] The strongest indicator of a break in Paul's argument at 5:1 is the remarkable similarity in vocabulary and theme in 5:1–11 and 8:18–39. Both passages teach that God's love, his justifying act in Christ, and the work of the Spirit will produce ultimate salvation and glory despite the tribulations that believers encounter in this life. With these two passages as the outer frame, chapters 5–8 form a clear ring composition:

A. 5:1–11 —assurance of future glory
  B. 5:12–21 —basis for assurance in work of Christ
    C. 6:1–23 —the problem of sin
    C'. 7:1–25 —the problem of the law
  B'. 8:1–17 —ground of assurance in the work of Christ, mediated by the Spirit
A'. 8:18–39 —assurance of future glory[70]

This ring composition suggests that the overarching topic of chapters 5–8 is assurance.[71] The verdict of "justified" pronounced over the sinner who puts their faith in Christ will infallibly eventuate in ultimate salvation—sharing in the glory of God himself. The second "ring" (5:12–21; 8:1–17) focuses on the believer's experience of Christ and the Spirit as the basis for this assurance. And the inner ring, finally, takes up two potential threats to this assurance: sin (ch. 6) and the law (ch. 7).

67. E.g., Ulrich Wilckens, *Der Brief an die Römer*, 3 vols., EKKNT (Neukirchen-Vluyn: Neukirchener; Zürich: Benziger, 1978–81), 2:286–87; Dunn, *Romans 1–8*, 242–44.

68. For the former, see Melanchthon (who comments on 5:12: "Now there follows, as it were, a new book"; P. Melanchthon, *Commentary on Romans* [repr., St. Louis: Concordia, 1992], 131–32); for the latter, Bruce Norman Kaye, *The Thought Structure of Romans with Special Reference to Chapter 6* (Austin, TX: Schola, 1979), 1–13.

69. See, e.g., Anders Nygren, *Commentary on Romans* (repr., Philadelphia: Fortress, 1949), 187–89; Cranfield, *Romans* 1:252–54; Longenecker, *Romans* 539–43; Moo, *Romans* (NICNT), 318–20.

70. See esp. Nils Alstrup Dahl, *Studies in Paul: Theology for the Early Christian Mission* (Minneapolis: Augsburg, 1977), 82–91.

N. T. Wright suggests an alternate structure, according to which Paul imitates the sequence of Israel's history to tell the story of the new exodus, from the rescue from Egypt by means of, or in the context of water (ch. 6), to the giving of the law (ch. 7), and leading, ultimately, to deliverance in the promised land (ch. 8) ("New Exodus," 26–35. See also, with some differences, Frank S. Thielman, "The Story of Israel and the Theology of Romans 5–8," in Hay and Johnson, *Pauline Theology*, 169–95). The text, however, does not provide adequate evidence for this structure (see, e.g., Ben Witherington III, with D. Hyatt, *Paul's Letter to the Romans: A Socio-Rhetorical Commentary* [Grand Rapids: Eerdmans, 2004], 92–93; and on narrative in Paul generally, pp. 11–14 of the present volume).

71. See also Wright, "Romans," 509.

2.2.1 The Hope of Glory (5:1–11)

The variety of benefits arising from justification ("having been justified" in v. 1) that Paul rapidly touches on in this paragraph makes it difficult to discern the overall theme. One strong candidate is reconciliation. This theme brackets the paragraph, "peace with God" in verse 1 being conceptually similar to, if not identical with, the focus on reconciliation at the end of the paragraph (v. 11).[72] Moreover, "being reconciled" is highlighted also in verse 10. Stanley Porter thinks reconciliation is not only the key theme in this paragraph but also thinks chapter 5, with this focus on reconciliation, is the climax of Romans.[73] And other interpreters think reconciliation is the concept that can best stand at the center of Paul's theology as a whole.[74] However, I think another theme stands out as even more prominent in this paragraph: hope. The hope of sharing God's glory (v. 2b) is the theme that Paul develops in verses 3–10. Believers boast, or rejoice in, tribulations because God is using their sufferings to create in them a series of virtues, a series that climaxes in hope (vv. 3–4). The beautiful celebration of God's love in verses 5b–8, a love experienced in our hearts through the Spirit (v. 5b) and revealed in the death of Christ for sinful and ungodly people (vv. 6–8), explains why we can be sure that we will not be put "to shame" (v. 5a)—that is, condemned on the final day of judgment. The climax of the paragraph and, to some degree, the central point of all of chapters 5–8 comes in the parallel "how much more" arguments of verses 9 and 10. Here Paul anchors hope for future salvation in the believer's justification (v. 9) and reconciliation (v. 10). Surely, Paul argues, we can be certain of ultimate vindication in the judgment when God has already done the more difficult thing, sending his Son to die for ungodly, sinful people.

The key theological idea that emerges from this paragraph is therefore the inextricable connection between initial justification and ultimate salvation. As he does frequently in his writings, Paul uses the language of salvation (*sōzō*, "save" in vv. 9b and 10b) to refer to the ultimate deliverance of believers at the end of time.[75] Paul's teaching about an initial, definitive verdict of justification in our union with Christ does not remove his adherence to the traditional Old Testament and Jewish teaching about a decisive judgment yet to come, a time when God's wrath is poured out on sinners (see 2:5). Believers will not avoid that judgment, but they can be certain of being vindicated on that day—not only because they have been justified and reconciled but also because they continue to enjoy the benefits of Christ's life (v. 10b, anticipating vv. 12–21).[76]

72. If, as I think likely, the original reading in v. 1 is the indicative *echomen* ("we have [peace]") rather than the subjunctive *echōmen* ("let us have, or enjoy [peace]"), Paul is celebrating the believer's possession of peace/reconciliation in both verses.

73. Stanley Porter, *The Letter to the Romans: A Linguistic and Literary Commentary*, New Testament Monographs 37 (Sheffield: Sheffield Phoenix, 2015), 112–13.

74. E.g., Ralph P. Martin, *Reconciliation: A Study of Paul's Theology*, New Foundations Theological Library (Atlanta: John Knox, 1981); Marshall, *Aspects of the Atonement*, 98–127; see pp. 491–97 of the present volume.

75. The vocabulary of salvation occurs elsewhere in Romans in 1:16; 8:24; 9:27; 10:1, 9, 10, 13; 11:11, 14, 26; 13:11.

76. Contra almost all the English translations (which render

2.2.2 The Reign of Grace and Life (5:12–21)

Throughout Romans 5–8, Paul uses the imagery of realm transfer to depict the situation of believers. In 5:12–21, Paul contrasts the reign of death, inaugurated by Adam, with the reign of life, inaugurated by the second Adam, Jesus Christ (v. 21; see also v. 17). Adam and Christ are representative figures, whose actions determine the fate of all whom they represent. Adam's sin and disobedience brings death, or condemnation, into the world, a fate that affects all people, who themselves sin and are caught up at the same time in the sin of Adam (vv. 12, 18–19). Christ's act of obedience reverses and more than cancels the effect of Adam's disobedience, with the result that all who belong to him enjoy righteousness and eternal life (vv. 18–19, 21).

We can rightly situate this famous comparison, or "synkrisis," of the two heads of the human race in the argument of the letter by attending to the focus of this comparison and to the transitional phrase that connects it to what precedes. Paul uses the framework of "just as . . . so also" (vv. 18, 19, 21; v. 12 has the first half only) to create his comparison. In the very nature of this kind of comparison, the emphasis, the point being argued for, comes in the "so also" part of the argument. While, therefore, Paul's teaching about Adam, sin, and death is theologically very important, this side of the matter is not his main point. Rather, his focus is on how Christ has won righteousness and life for all whom he represents. The phrase Paul uses to introduce this argument in verse 12a, *dia touto*, is usually translated "therefore" (so most English versions). On this reading, 5:12–21 draws a conclusion from something Paul has said earlier in the letter. It makes far better sense, however, to give the phrase the sense "in order to accomplish this," the "this" referring back to the attaining of salvation and ultimate glory in 5:1–11.[77] Believers can be absolutely certain that they will be saved from wrath because they are "in Christ" (see v. 10b, "in his life"; see the note above).

Theologians throughout Christian history have argued about the nature of the connection that Paul makes between the sin of Adam and this sin of all other humans. Comparing verse 12b and verse 18a encapsulates the issue:

people die because[78] people sin (v. 12b)
people are condemned because of Adam's transgression (v. 18a)

"by" or "through"), the preposition *en* in this phrase does not indicate instrument ("through his life") but sphere: "in Christ's life," i.e., in union with his resurrected person, we are certain of ultimate salvation. I am indebted to Steve Runge, in a private paper and conversation, for highlighting this sense of the preposition here and elsewhere.

77. The preposition *dia* often has this kind of telic force (see the note on 4:25), and the phrase *dia touto* states a "final cause"

or purpose in several verses (2 Cor 13:10; Col 1:9[?]; 2 Thess 2:11; 1 Tim 1:16; 2 Tim 2:10[?]; Phlm 15).

78. The meaning of the Greek phrase behind our English "because" (*eph hō*) is debated. With almost all English versions and most interpreters, I think it has a causal sense here. See 1 Cor 5:4; Phil 3:12; 4:10; and F. Blass, A. Debrunner, and R. W. Funk, *A Greek Grammar of the New Testament* (Chicago: University of Chicago Press, 1961), §235(2) (though note the question mark);

Some interpreters think these two statements can be reconciled if we assume a middle stage in the sequence: Adam's sin introduces the "virus" of sin into the human race, a virus that inevitably leads every human to sin and therefore die.[79] The notion that humans have a fatal "bent" away from God and toward their own gratification is a thoroughly Pauline idea (see, e.g., 1:22–23; and his use of "flesh"). However, Paul's direct comparison of Adam's sin and the sin of all people, in the context of the corporate ways of thinking typical of Paul's world and the world of the Bible, suggests that Paul views Adam as a representative of all humanity, such that his sin is at the same time the sin of all humans. Adam's sin is, indeed, the "original sin," the sin that brings the shadow of death into the world for all humans[80]—this "death" being, as the language of "condemnation" in verse 18 reveals, primarily what we call "spiritual death."

In verses 12 and 18a Paul argues that Adam's sin has condemned all humans to this spiritual death, a point reinforced by the simple claim that Adam's sin, and the death his sin brought into the world, "reign" (vv. 17, 21). The shift to "many" in verses 16 and 19 does not necessarily detract from this universal emphasis. While the word often refers to a limited number in Paul, the number intended can only be determined by context. Here the alternation with "all" suggests an unlimited scope. However, how about the universality on the other side? As Adam's sin brings condemnation to all, so Christ's "righteous act" brings "justification and life" to all (v. 18; see also 1 Cor 15:22). Verses such as these have provided the basis to claim that Paul's ultimate perspective (however much he may depart from it elsewhere) is that all humans will ultimately be saved. However, Pauline soteriological universalism requires that we pick and choose among Paul's various statements on this matter—a procedure best avoided. And Paul himself in this context implies that the situation on the Adam and Christ side of this matter are not the same. In verse 17, while sin simply "reigns" because of Adam's sin, it is only "those who receive" the gift that enjoy the reign of life. On the Christ side, then, it is possible that verse 18 teaches that all humans are in principle the recipients

---

Nigel Turner, *Syntax*, vol. 3 of *A Grammar of New Testament Greek*, by J. H. Moulton (Edinburgh: T&T Clark, 1963), 272; H. von Siebenthal, *Griechische Grammatik zum Neuen Testament* (Giessen: Brunnen, 2011), §277c. See the discussion in Moo, *Romans* (NICNT), 321–22. The most likely alternative is that it indicates result (the entrance of death led to sinning; see esp. Joseph A. Fitzmyer, "The Consecutive Meaning of *eph' hō* in Romans 5.12," *NTS* 39 [1993]: 321–39; and also Thielman, *Romans*, 283. Schreiner, who held this view in the first edition of his commentary, has now opted for the usual interpretation [*Romans*, 279–80]).

79. The seventeenth-century theologian Johannes Wollebius stated it this way: "As person has infected nature, so in turn the nature has infected persons" (quoted in Heinrich Heppe, *Reformed Dogmatics: Set Out and Illustrated from the Source*, ed. and rev. Ernst Bizer [Grand Rapids: Baker, 1978], 314). See also, e.g., Chrysostom, *Homilies on Romans* (*NPNF¹* 11:335–564, at loc.); Cranfield, *Romans*, 1:278; Longenecker, *Romans*, 590.

80. For the best defenses of this view, see Joseph Freundorfer, *Erbsünde und Erbtod beim Apostel Paulus: Eine religionsgeschichtliche und exegetische Untersuchung über Römerbrief 5,12–21*, NTAbh 13 (Münster: Aschendorff, 1927), 240–55; John Murray, *The Imputation of Adam's Sin* (Phillipsburg, NJ: P&R, 1959), 7–21, 64–70. A detailed historical survey (up to 1925) is found in Freundorfer, *Erbsünde*, 105–214; more recent surveys are found in essays in Hans Madueme and Michael Reeves, eds., *Adam, the Fall, and Original Sin: Theological, Biblical, and Scientific Perspectives* (Grand Rapids: Baker, 2014).

of God's good gift in Christ, but that only those who "receive" the gift actually benefit from it.[81] Or the "all" might be restricted to "all who are in Christ."[82]

This paragraph takes the broadest possible view of salvation history, showing how the spiritual state and destiny of all humanity are determined by the two contrasting figures of Adam and Christ. The good news Paul preaches, which he wants the Romans to understand, is that Christ has more than reversed the consequences of Adam's act—hence the "how much more" language of verses 15 and 17 (and see vv. 16 and 21). At the same time, Paul has not forgotten the "intermediate" stages of salvation history. Intervening between Adam and Christ, of course, is a long series of events especially relating to Israel and the law that God gave Israel. Thus, in verses 13–14 and again in verse 20a, Paul injects the law into his sweeping overview. Following the pattern established in Romans to this point (see esp. 3:20 and 4:15), Paul indicates that the law has been unable to change the fundamental state of affairs introduced into the world by Adam. Like Adam, confronted with the command of God, Israel is also confronted with a clear expression of God's demand in the law. Yet even before the law was given, death was reigning over human beings because of Adam (vv. 13–14). Even those who had God's law did not find release from Adam's sin and its consequences; indeed, the law, Paul claims in verse 20, had the purpose (*hina*) of increasing the trespass: turning sin into transgression, making sin even more sinful (7:13) by deepening Israel's accountability.[83]

2.2.3 Freedom from Bondage to Sin (6:1–23)

The inner ring in the ring composition of chapters 5–8 focuses on two possible hindrances to the assurance that Paul argues for in this section: sin (ch. 6) and the law (ch. 7). Paul signals at least a rough parallel between them by making the central claim in each chapter that believers have been released from bondage to them: Christians have "died to sin" (6:2) and have "also died to the law" (7:4). Chapter 6 is divided into two main parts, marked by the parallel sequence of question and answer: "What shall we say, then? Shall we go on sinning so that grace may increase? By no means!" (6:1–2a) and "What then? Shall we sin because we are not under the law but under grace? By no means!" (6:15).

The question that opens this chapter is stimulated immediately by 5:20b—"But where sin increased, grace increased all the more"—but, of greater theological importance,

81. Mark Rapinchuk, "Universal Sin and Salvation in Romans 5:12–21," *JETS* 42 (1999): 427–41.

82. Augustine suggests that the "all" in v. 18b means that all who are justified are justified in Christ (*Nat. grat.* 41.48; see *NPNF¹* 5:137–38).

83. The *hina* is occasionally interpreted as indicating result (e.g., Chrysostom, *Homilies on Romans* 10 [*NPNF¹* 11:404]) or

even cause (Chrys C. Caragounis, *The Development of Greek and the New Testament: Morphology, Syntax, Phonology, and Textual Transmission*, WUNT 2/167 [Tübingen: Mohr Siebeck, 2004], 223–25), but there is no good reason to abandon the usual final sense of the word (see, e.g., C. F. D. Moule, *An Idiom Book of New Testament Greek* [Cambridge: Cambridge University Press, 1953], 143).

ultimately by Paul's insistence that our standing with God ("justification") is through faith alone. As Martyn Lloyd-Jones points out, the doctrine of justification by faith alone is bound to spark this question—one that has, indeed, frequently been asked by those wrestling with the Reformation *sola fide*.[84] Paul justifies his strong negation—*mē genoito* ("by no means!")—by reminding us that believers are people who have "died to sin" (6:2). This is the central teaching of the chapter and is unpacked by Paul with the language of release from slavery (vv. 6, 14, 17, 18, 19, 20, 22). To be "dead to sin" means to be set free from its mastery (v. 14). Paul uses the image of death because 1) it connotes a radical break; and 2) it ties into our participation in Christ's death.

We die to sin, then, because Christ has himself "died to sin" (v. 10), and we die "with him." The language of "with" (*syn*) Christ is central to Paul's teaching here, as he includes believers in Christ's death (vv. 5a, 6, 8a; cf. 11), burial (v. 4), and resurrection (vv. 5b, 8b). It is surely no accident that Jesus's death, burial, and resurrection feature in Paul's famous summary of his gospel (1 Cor 15:1–3); and participation with Christ in baptism, death, and resurrection is found also in Colossians 2:12–14, 20. Participation with Christ in these key redemptive events is also closely tied to what, following Con Campbell,[85] we might call the webbing that holds Paul's theology together: union with Christ (see "in Christ Jesus" in Rom 6:11). Elsewhere I investigate the meaning of this conception of union with Christ and its relationship to other key elements in Paul's theology (see pp. 35–39). Here it is important to comment on the relationship between this participation with Christ and baptism (vv. 3–4). In contrast to a widely held view, baptism here functions not as a picture or symbol of the believer's prior spiritual experience but as the means by which (see the *dia*, "through," in v. 4) the believer is brought into relationship with these events.[86] Rather than concluding, with many, that baptism then has a strongly sacramental significance (the water as the "place" where Christians meet Christ), it is better to respect Paul's great emphasis on faith throughout Romans and his other letters and view baptism as one component of the larger complex of events dubbed by James Dunn as "conversion-initiation."[87] As the varied form of the apostolic preaching in Acts makes especially clear, the early Christians viewed repentance, faith, water baptism, and the gift of the Spirit as components of one complex event, coming to Christ and being integrated into his body. Baptism in Romans 6, then, signals this

84. D. Martyn Lloyd-Jones, *Romans: Exposition of Chapter 6, The New Man* (Edinburgh: Banner of Truth, 1972), 8–9.

85. Campbell, *Paul and Union with Christ*, 437–39.

86. For the "symbolic" view, see, e.g., F. F. Bruce, *The Letter of Paul to the Romans*, TNTC (Grand Rapids: Eerdmans, 1985), 129; William Frederick Flemington, *The New Testament Doctrine of Baptism* (London: SPCK, 1957), 59. The apparent soteriological significance of baptism here is one reason some interpreters think that Paul refers to "Spirit baptism" (e.g., Lloyd-Jones, *Romans 6*, 35–36; cf. Tom Holland, *Romans: The Divine Marriage. A Biblical Theological Commentary* [Eugene, OR: Pickwick, 2011], 183). But the noun *baptisma* especially, used in v. 4, always refers to an experience with water. Paul consistently uses the verb *baptizō* ("baptize") also to refer to an event with water (although 1 Cor 12:13 is debated).

87. James D. G. Dunn, *Baptism in the Holy Spirit: A Re-Examination of the New Testament Teaching on the Gift of the Spirit in Relation to Pentecostalism Today*, SBT 15 (London: SCM, 1970), 145, passim.

whole complex, with faith, of course, being of central importance.[88] In this light, then, Christ's death, burial, and resurrection are not present in the water of baptism; nor is the focus on the believer's own spiritual death, burial, and resurrection symbolized in baptism. Rather, faith/baptism is the means by which believers are joined to, or secure the benefit of, their participation in Christ's own death, burial, and resurrection.[89] As humans, we participate in Adam's sin and its consequences. As those who belong to Christ, we participate in the benefits of Christ's "righteous obedience."[90]

As we have seen, Paul teaches that believers participate in Christ's resurrection/new life: "United with him in a resurrection like his" (v. 5); "we will also live with him" (v. 8). Since Paul's concern in this context is to remind believers that, having died to sin, they have already entered into a new life (vv. 4, 11, 13), the future tenses in these two verses may have a "logical" force, indicating simply that participation in Christ's resurrection follows participation in his death. In this case, Paul would be implying the notion of a present, spiritual resurrection with Christ such as he asserts in Ephesians 2:6 and Colossians 3:1.[91] In contrast to many Pauline interpreters, I think these texts are authentically Pauline and therefore can legitimately be used to illuminate Romans 6. However, it is more natural to read these future tenses as genuine temporal futures. Christ's resurrection guarantees the future resurrection of believers' bodies (see esp. 1 Cor 15:20–23). Yet the new life that Christ entered as a result of his resurrection is one that believers now share.

But this new life is also one that believers *must* share. Romans 6 classically expresses the famous "indicative-imperative" mode of Paul's exhortations. God takes the initiative in transferring us out of the realm in which sin holds sway—who we were in Adam. "The old self," or "old man," has been "crucified with Christ" (v. 6; for the meaning of "old man" see p. 492). God's act empowers and requires a response from believers: "Count yourselves dead to sin but alive to God in Christ Jesus" (v. 11) and "do not let sin reign in your mortal body" (v. 12).

As in 5:12–21, Paul's broad theological focus does not mean that his concern to explain his gospel in terms of Israel's history and the law has been left behind. At the end of the paragraph, he traces the believer's freedom from sin's power to their being "under grace" and not "under the law" (v. 14). This grace-law contrast is salvation-historical: The law, as regularly in Romans, is the Mosaic law, which ruled over the people of God in the old-covenant era; grace typifies the new-covenant era (see esp. 5:2).

---

88. In his *Theology of Paul* (p. 445), Dunn calls "baptism" a "concertina" word that can be "squeezed" to refer to the rite alone but also expanded to include the process of coming to Christ.

89. For this general line of interpretation, see esp. Beasley-Murray, *Baptism in the New Testament*, 130–40.

90. In keeping with his conviction that the story of Israel massively impacts Paul's teaching, N. T. Wright suggests a different reason for the mention of baptism here: It carries connotations of the exodus event (see 1 Cor 10:2; see Wright, "Romans," 533–35).

91. See, e.g., Wright, "Romans," 539.

The law, as Paul has indicated in 4:15 and 5:20, has not solved the problem of sin but made it worse, and it is a key element of the age that has now passed away.[92] Only by being brought out from under its ruling authority can the people of God experience freedom from sin.[93]

The second part of Romans 6, like the first part, is triggered by an assertion in the immediate context: If Christians are under grace and not under the law (v. 14), can they sin with impunity? Paul's response is parallel to what he said earlier. Christians are no longer slaves of sin (v. 18) and should therefore stop offering themselves as "slaves to impurity and to ever-increasing wickedness" (v. 19). The imperative again grows out of the indicative. What distinguishes verses 15–23 from verses 1–14 is Paul's balanced focus on the transfer from one state of slavery to another. The believer's freedom from sin entails a new slavery: to God and to righteousness (vv. 18, 22). Believers have been handed over to a new "pattern" (*typos*) of teaching, that is, a teaching that forms them for God's purposes (v. 17).[94] Paul recognizes that calling believers "slaves" is far from the whole story (v. 19a)—but it is, he insists, part of the story. There is no such thing as human autonomy. All people are slaves to something; the only question is whether that master will be sin and unrighteousness or God and righteousness.

The occurrence of righteousness language in this chapter has potential implications for Paul's teaching on justification. In verse 7, Paul claims that believers are "justified from sin" (*dedikaiōtai apo tēs hamartias*; my translation), with apparent reference to sin's power. Then, in verses 13, 16, 18, 19, and 20, Paul refers to "righteousness" (*dikaiosynē*), which he sets in contrast to "death" and which is, he claims, the result of obedience (v. 16). Some interpreters insist that the language of righteousness in this chapter must refer to the same thing it refers to in chapters 1–5: justification. If so, then justification would include an element of transformation (v. 7) and be the product of "obedience"—perhaps "the obedience of faith" (1:5).[95] However, it is questionable if the righteousness language in this text should "count" toward the doctrine

---

92. Douglas J. Moo, "The Law of Moses or the Law of Christ," in *Continuity and Discontinuity: Perspectives on the Relationship between the Old and New Testaments. Essays in Honor of S. Lewis Johnson Jr.*, ed. John S. Feinberg (Westchester, IL: Crossway, 1988), 210–17.

93. In taking this view, I disagree with the long tradition in Reformed theology to interpret not being "under the law" to mean not being under the condemning power of the law (the law being viewed in terms of the "covenant of works"). For this view, see, e.g., Samuel Bolton, *The True Bounds of Christian Freedom* (repr., London: Banner of Truth, 1964 [1645]), 28; John Cotton, *A Treatise of the Covenant of Grace*, 3rd ed. (London, 1671), 87; and see the discussion in J. von Rohr, *The Covenant of Grace in Puritan Thought*, AARSR 45 (Atlanta: Scholars Press, 1986), 110. See also my discussion of the law in Paul on pp. 614–22.

94. On the meaning of "the pattern of teaching that has now claimed your allegiance" (cf. CSB: "that pattern of teaching you were transferred to"), see esp. Robert A. J. Gagnon, "Heart of Wax and a Teaching That Stamps: ΤΥΠΟΣ ΔΙΔΑΧΗΣ (Rom 6:17b) Once More," *JBL* 112 (1994): 671–73.

95. See, e.g., Scott Hafemann, "Reading Paul's ΔΙΚΑΙΟ-Language: A Response to Douglas Campbell's 'Rereading Paul's ΔΙΚΑΙΟ-Language,'" in *Beyond Old and New Perspectives on Paul: Reflections on the Work of Douglas Campbell*, ed. Chris Tilling (Eugene, OR: Cascade, 2014), 214–29; and, on the wider methodical issue, Gorman, *Becoming the Gospel*, 222–54. I discuss this issue more fully on pp. 472–73.

of justification. The doctrine is, of course, built on words using the Greek root *dik-*. But not all occurrences of *dik*-words should be used to construct the doctrine; we must observe the distinction between lexeme and concept. We admittedly enter into a bit of a circular argument here, the temptation being to define the concept arbitrarily and then on that basis include or exclude key vocabulary. However, I think there is good reason to define justification as a doctrine that is about a person's standing, or judicial position, before God. In this particular paragraph, however, the language Paul uses to contrast with "righteousness" ("wickedness" in v. 13; "sin" in vv. 18 and 20; "impurity" and "ever-increasing wickedness" in v. 19; see, however, "death" in v. 16) suggests he is using the word with a moral force, in its standard Old Testament and Jewish sense, meaning behavior pleasing to God.

2.2.4 Freedom from Bondage to the Law (7:1–25)

After stating a general principle—death severs obligation to the law (v. 1)—and giving an illustration of the principle—a woman can remarry only after the death of her husband (vv. 2–3)—Paul expresses the key theological point of chapter 7: believers in Christ have been "put to death with respect to the law" (v. 4; my translation). Picking up the marital imagery of verses 2–3, Paul claims that separation from the law is necessary so that believers can be joined to Christ. Verses 5–6 elaborate, contrasting the state of people "in the realm of the flesh," where sinful passions, aroused by the law, brought death, and the state of those who have been released from the law's lordship, who serve in the new way of the Spirit.

Strikingly, Paul uses the same imagery here that he used in chapter 6 to depict the believer's new relationship to sin. One can appreciate why Christians need to be freed from bondage to sin. But to claim they need to be freed from bondage to the law— God's law!—is a bold claim, one that generates most of the discussion in the rest of this chapter. The believer's death "with respect to the law" (my translation: *ethanatōthēte tō nomō*) is apparently that act of God (the verb is a "divine passive") that puts them in the state referred to in 6:14, 15—no longer "under the law." As those verses, I have argued, refer to the believer's freedom from the binding authority of the law, so also this "dying" to the law will mean separation, in general, from Torah's authority (see also 7:6, "released from the law"). As the contrast between "letter" (*gramma*) and "Spirit" in verse 6 suggests, Paul is operating within his usual salvation-historical contrast. The law, or Torah, belongs to the earlier era of salvation history, when it governed the life of God's people. Now that God has inaugurated the new era, that law is no longer directly applicable to the people of God (see also 6:14, 15; cf. 1 Cor 9:20–21; Gal 3:15–25). Rather, believers enjoy the distinctive new-covenant blessing of God's Spirit.

Paul's brief mention of the Spirit in verse 6 is taken up in considerable detail in Romans 8. The section in between, then, 7:7–25, is something of an aside in the flow of Paul's argument. The passage falls into two parts, the first (vv. 7–12 or 13) focusing on the entrance of the law into salvation history and the second (vv. 13 or 14–25) on the continuing effects of the law. This long and complex "apology for the law" is stimulated immediately by Paul's controversial claim that God's own law has been responsible for arousing "sinful passions" (v. 5). But the stimulus for this apology is rooted more broadly in Paul's rather negative portrayal of the law throughout Romans thus far (3:20, 28; 4:15; 5:13–14, 21; 6:14, 15). His main point is straightforward: Israel, and humans in general, have experienced "death" because sin has coopted the law for its own purposes (vv. 7–12), a takeover made possible by the sinful state of humans (vv. 14–25). "What the law was powerless to do because it was weakened by the flesh" (8:3) is a neat summary of Paul's main point here.

Famously, Paul presents his theology of the law in this passage through a story: "I" was "alive apart from the law" and died "when the commandment came" (vv. 9–10); this happened because, while the law is "spiritual," "I" am "unspiritual" (v. 14), a "prisoner of the law of sin" (v. 23). Whose story is Paul telling? Parallels between what Paul says here and what he elsewhere says about Adam and Israel suggest that he might be telling the story of Adam (and humankind) or of Israel. These parallels are significant and indeed suggest that the story of "I" is genuinely influenced by Adam's experience in the garden and Israel's at Sinai. It is hard, however, to avoid the conclusion that the "I" has some reference to Paul himself: Paul is telling his own story. However, the focus is not so much on Paul as an individual but Paul in solidarity with Adam and his own people, Israel. As a Jew under the law, Paul is bound up with the experience of his people: in parallel with Adam's experience in the garden, the coming of "law" did not bring life—it confirmed the people in death. And it did so because Israel, and humans in general, received God's good law when they were already ruled by sin, unable to obey that good law and therefore condemned by their failure (vv. 13–25).[96]

This famously debated passage at the end of Romans 7 therefore probably describes the experience of the Jewish person under the law[97] rather than a mature Christian[98] or believer who is not living by the Spirit.[99] To be sure, the struggle Paul movingly describes (vv. 15–20) is one that believers experience as they struggle to live out their

---

96. See, for this view, Moo, *Romans* (NICNT), 448–56; and for debate about the main options, see Terry L. Wilder, ed., *Perspectives on Our Struggle with Sin: 3 Views of Romans 7* (Nashville: B&H, 2011).

97. A good recent defense of this view is Stephen J. Chester, "The Retrospective View of Romans 7: Paul's Past in Present Perspective," in Wilder, *Perspectives on Our Struggle with Sin*, 57–103.

98. Some of the best defenses of this view include Will Timmins, *Romans 7 and Christian Identity: A Study of the "I" in Its Literary Context*, SNTSMS 170 (Cambridge: Cambridge University Press, 2017); Timo Laato, "*Simul Iustus et Peccator* through the

Lenses of Paul," *JETS* 61 (2018): 735–66; Grant R. Osborne, "The Flesh without the Spirit: Romans 7 and Christian Experience," in Wilder, *Perspectives on Our Struggle with Sin*, 6–48; Cranfield, *Romans*, 1:344–47; Dunn, *Romans 1–8*, 387–89, 403–12; idem, "Rom 7,14–25 in the Theology of Paul," *TZ* 5 (1975): 257–73.

99. E.g., J. A. Bengel identified the subject of these verses as a person in the transition from the state of law to the state of grace (*Gnomon of the New Testament*, 5 vols. [repr., Edinburgh: T&T Clark, 1860], 91–92). Longenecker's view may fit here; he argues that Paul is depicting any person who attempts to live their life "under their own steam" (e.g., *Romans*, 650).

new life in Christ. But the defeat that is the result of that struggle is not typical of the believer. Paul depicts this defeat by again playing on the word "law": the law of God is a power or force that is countered by another "law" or force—sin.[100] Contrary to the believer, who has died to sin's power (ch. 6) and been liberated from the "law of sin" (8:2), the person here is held captive by that law of sin (vv. 23, 25).

Romans 7 is therefore primarily about the law: the Torah that God gave Israel first of all, but it also refers implicitly to any "law." God's demand that his creatures live by his guidelines comes to people already locked up under sin's power as a result of Adam's disobedience (5:12–21). "Law," therefore, cannot liberate humans from sin's control or rescue them from "death." God's intervention in Christ is the means of liberation.

2.2.5 Life, Sonship, and Glory in and through the Spirit (8:1–39)

The Spirit is the dominant figure in Romans 8. The word *pneuma* occurs twenty-one times in the chapter, and all but two (those in vv. 15a and 16b) refer to the Holy Spirit. Nevertheless, the focus of the chapter is not on the Spirit as such but on what the Spirit does. In a word, what he does is give assurance to believers: "life" both now and in the future (vv. 1–13), "adoption as sons" now (vv. 14–17), and "glory" in the future (vv. 18–30). Paul caps off this exposition of assurance with a hymn-like paragraph celebrating this assurance (vv. 31–39).

"No condemnation for those in Christ Jesus" (v. 1) takes us back to the end of chapter 5, which recounts the "condemnation" introduced into the human race by Adam. Paul now reiterates the certainty of life for those in Christ in light of the threats of sin (ch. 6) and the law (ch. 7): In Christ, he claims, "the law of the Spirit who gives life has set you free from the law of sin and death" (v. 2). The two laws in this verse are sometimes thought to refer to two aspects or effects of the law of Moses.[101] On this view, a strong "law"/"gospel" contrast is weakened by putting the law on both the imprisoning and liberating sides of the human predicament. But it is more likely that *nomos* in both instances has its established sense of "power" or "principle."[102] The focus, then, is on the Spirit's deliverance of people from the "rule," or "law," that sin must lead to death. This deliverance comes through Christ's incarnation ("sending his own Son in the likeness of sinful flesh") and sacrificial death on the cross ("to be a sin offering"[103]; "condemned sin," v. 3). Dominating verses 4–13 is the contrast between "flesh" (*sarx*) and Spirit. As the NIV brings out with its translation "realm of the flesh"

---

100. Some interpreters, however, think that all the occurrences of "law" (*nomos*) in these verses refer to the law of Moses, viewed from different perspectives. See, e.g., Klyne Snodgrass, "Spheres of Influence: A Possible Solution for the Problem of Paul and the Law," *JSNT* 32 (1988): 106–7; Dunn, *Romans 1–8*, 409; Wright, "Romans," 570.

101. See, e.g., Dunn, *Romans 1–8*, 416–17; Robert Jewett, with Roy D. Kotansky, *Romans*, Hermeneia (Minneapolis: Fortress, 2007), 481; Wright, "Romans," 576–77. See above for a similar issue in Rom 7:22–23.

102. E.g., Schreiner, *Romans*, 396–97.

103. The NIV translation here is based on the use of the Gk. phrase *peri hamartias* in the LXX to denote the sin offering (the phrase has this meaning in forty-four of its fifty-four occurrences).

(vv. 8, 9), *sarx* takes its theological sense from Paul's overarching salvation-historical conception, with its focus on two contrasting realms, one dominated by "flesh" (that which belongs to this world) and the other by the Spirit. Believers, Paul argues, are now "located" in this new realm (v. 9), are oriented in their thinking toward it (vv. 5–7), and consequently live according to its values (v. 4). The Spirit, therefore, "gives life" now "because of righteousness" (v. 10) and will "also give life to your mortal bodies" in the future (v. 11). Nevertheless, in a tension typical of his theology, Paul warns, capping off this paragraph, that believers must respond to make this life their own: only as they "put to death the misdeeds of the body" will they "live" (v. 13).

Being God's children, or "sons," is the focus of verses 14–17.[104] Israel was known as God's "son" (Exod 4:22; Jer 3:19; 31:9; Hos 11:1; and, e.g., Sir 36:12; 4 Ezra 6.58), so calling Christians God's sons undoubtedly makes a point about a certain "transfer" of privilege from Israel to the church. Paul may also be picking up the wider Old Testament story of God leading his children from bondage (in Egypt) to sonship.[105] Being God's children, Paul makes clear, is an intensely personal and even emotional matter; we cry "Abba, Father," imitating Jesus's own address of God (v. 15; cf. Mark 14:36). At the same time, however, the reference to the Spirit as "the Spirit of adoption" (my translation) clearly alludes to the Roman practice of adoption—a legal procedure whereby one can "adopt" a child and confer on that child all the legal rights and privileges that would ordinarily accrue to a natural child.[106] Paul's move from the present state of believers to their future (from adoption to inheritance, v. 17) is quite natural (see also Gal 4:1–7).

"Glory" frames verses 18–30: it will be "revealed in us" (v. 18); "those he justified, he also glorified" (v. 30). Assurance of ultimate glory brings the text back to where this section began, with the hope that we will share the glory of God (5:2). In verses 18–25, Paul focuses on the importance of believers' glory in God's plan. First, it is only when believers are glorified that the created world will be "liberated from its bondage to decay" (v. 21). Paul seldom refers to the created world, and even here he brings God's wider creation purposes into the picture to illustrate and accentuate believers' ultimate redemption. Nevertheless, these verses importantly reveal that Paul maintained the

---

104. Paul uses *tekna*, "children," in vv. 16–17 but *huioi*, "sons," in v. 14 and *huiothesia* in v. 15. In contrast to the NIV, it is preferable to translate *huioi* as "sons" in order to preserve the significant allusion to the first-century Roman practice of adoption.

105. See esp. Silvia C. Keesmaat, "Exodus and the Intertextual Transformation of Tradition in Romans 8.14–30," *JSNT* 54 (1994): 29–56; Wright, *Paul and the Faithfulness of God*, 2:721.

106. See esp. Francis Lyall, "Roman Law in the Writings of Paul: Adoption," *JBL* 88 (1969): 458–66; idem, *Slaves, Citizens, Sons: Legal Metaphors in the Epistles* (Grand Rapids: Academie, 1984), 67–99; Trevor J. Burke, *Adopted into God's Family: Exploring a Pauline Metaphor*, NSBT 22 (Downers Grove, IL:

InterVarsity Press, 2006), 46–71. Scholars debate whether the term *huiothesia*, as Paul uses it, denotes the *act* of adoption (see, e.g., Cranfield, *Romans*, 1:397) or the *status* of "sonship" (Byrne, *"Sons of God,"* 215). In Rom 9:4, status appears to be the focus, and probably also in Gal 4:5 (since we "receive" it), and the contrast with *douleia* ("slavery") may tip the scales in this direction here at Rom 8:15. But in 8:23 the stress seems to be on the act of adopting, and since the word almost invariably has this meaning outside the NT (Scott, *Adoption as Sons*, 3–57), this is probably Paul's main focus (Paul also uses the word in Eph 1:5, but it cannot be certain whether "act" or "status" is primary).

robust Old Testament hope that God's purposes extend beyond the sphere of humans to encompass all of his creation.[107] In response to Adam's original sin—a sin repeated and extended by humans who have failed to steward creation as God intended—God has "subjected" the creation (v. 20). But that act of subjection itself was carried out in a context of hope—hope that creation itself would enjoy the freedom "related to the glory that God's children will one day enjoy" (my own rendering of v. 21b). If hope conditions God's decree about creation, hope is also foundational in God's salvation of his people (vv. 24–25). Indeed, believers have the Spirit as God's "downpayment" on all he has yet to accomplish for them and in them and therefore "groan" as they long for their hope to come to fruition (v. 23).

Hope therefore is part and parcel of our experience of God's salvation. The "already" of new life, adoption as God's sons, and possession of the Spirit is conditioned by the "not yet" of our complete inheritance as God's children. In the second, and last, part of this passage, Paul explains why believers can wait for the fulfillment of this hope with "persevering confidence" (v. 25, NJB). First, God's Spirit supplies what is lacking in our "weakness," interceding on our behalf in prayer for us in perfect accordance with God's purposes (vv. 26–27). Second, God is himself ensuring that all things touching our lives work "for good"—our spiritual maturing and ultimate glory (v. 28). Third, God has a purpose for us that he is infallibly carrying out (v. 28b). Paul elaborates this purpose in a series of five verbs, each of them debated and soteriologically significant (vv. 29–30). The first, God's "foreknowing," is especially contentious. Many scholars insist that the verb must have here the meaning it invariably has in secular Greek: God "knew something about" believers ahead of time—perhaps that they would choose to respond in faith to the gospel message.[108] On this view, then, God's saving purposes for a particular individual are conditioned by that individual's decision to believe. Other scholars, however, think that the verb here carries the connotation of the verb "to know" as it is used in Scripture: God deciding to enter into relationship with people. See, for example, Amos 3:2: "You [Israel] only have I known [ESV; NIV: "chosen"] of all the families of the earth." On this reading, God's salvific purposes are determined by his own determination to choose, or elect, certain people to be his own. I think, partly because of the personal object of the verb here, that this latter meaning is the more likely. We should also note that the plural objects of the verbs in this context make it difficult to think that Paul refers here more generally to God's choosing of a people to be his own.[109]

---

107. See esp. D. Moo and J. Moo, *Creation Care*, 147–52.

108. See, e.g., Frederic Louis Godet, *Commentary on Romans* (repr., Grand Rapids: Kregel, 1977), 324–25; Jack W. Cottrell, "Conditional Election," in *Grace Unlimited*, ed. Clark H. Pinnock (Minneapolis: Bethany, 1975), 57–62.

109. A view associated with Barth (*CD* II/2); see also esp.

Robert Shank, *Elect in the Son: A Study of the Doctrine of Election* (Springfield: Westcott, 1970), 45–55, 154–55; B. J. Oropeza, *Jews, Gentiles, and the Opponents of Paul: The Pauline Letters*, vol. 2 of *Apostasy in the New Testament Communities* (Eugene, OR: Cascade, 2012), 168–74.

God's foreknowing leads to his "predestining," his "calling," his "justifying," and finally (returning to the overall focus of this paragraph) to his "glorifying." Amid discussion of these significant verbs, it is easy to miss a key component of this passage: God's "predestining" is specifically directed to christological conformity. Verse 29 then is the climax of a series of important "Son" references in this chapter: God sends the Son to rescue his people (v. 3), we are given a sonship that parallels in some way Christ's own (vv. 15–16), and our ultimate destiny is to be conformed to that Son.

Paul brings his argument for assurance in chapters 5–8 to its conclusion in verses 31–39, grounding that assurance in both the work of God in Christ for us (vv. 31–34) and the love of God in Christ for us (vv. 35–39).

2.3 The Gospel and Israel (9:1–11:36)

In contrast to some interpreters in the past, who tended to view these chapters as, at best, an excursus or, at worst, an awkward detour detracting from the "real focus" of the letter, modern interpreters rightly understand that the argument of these chapters is integral to Paul's purposes in Romans. In these chapters, he addresses the relationship between the gospel—the overall theme of Romans—and Israel. And he must do so because the preaching of the gospel in Paul's day had created an unexpected and potentially problematic situation: the church was increasingly being dominated by gentiles. In this respect, the Roman church, with its "gentile" flavor (see 1:6, 15), was a microcosm of the larger church in Paul's day.

Paul's theology, as we have seen, is particularly oriented to this issue of the relationship of Jews and gentiles in the new realm. Interpreters sometimes gravitate to two rather extreme options in explaining Paul's view of this relationship. At one extreme is the attempt to avoid the problem by putting Israel and the gentiles on two separate tracks to salvation. Gentiles are saved by embracing Christ, but Jews are saved in the context of their own Torah covenant, a covenant that remains in place for the Jews after the coming of Christ for the gentiles. Paul's problem with Jews in his day, then, was simply that they were refusing to acknowledge the mission to the gentiles.[110] At the other extreme is the solution that some of the gentiles in the Roman church (and undoubtedly elsewhere) were apparently advocating: turn the church into its own self-contained entity by cutting the cord connecting the Old Testament and the gospel. Neither option is one that Paul can entertain. The former misses the fact that the gospel, and the Christ it proclaims, is directed first of all to Jews (1:16). Salvation is now found in him only (10:9–13), and it is this state of salvation that stimulates Paul's deep concern (9:1–3) and fervent prayer for the Jewish people (10:1). The latter

---

110. This view is sometimes call "bi-covenantalism," since it posits two distinct soteriological covenants, or *Sonderweg*, because it argues for a "special way" of salvation for Jews. See, further, on this issue, pp. 558–65 and 572–73.

solution is no more attractive, because it means that the gospel can no longer be "the gospel of God"—"the God of Abraham, Isaac, and Jacob." The promises God made to Israel must be seen to be in concert with the situation that the preaching of the gospel in Paul's day has created.

In Romans 9–11, then, Paul offers an extended explanation of the relationship between the gospel and the effects it has created, and Israel, especially the promises God made to Israel. "It is not as though God's word had failed" (9:6a) is a fitting summary of Paul's overall argument in these chapters.

2.3.1 Israel's Privileges and Position (9:1–5)

As apostle to the gentiles, Paul may well have been accused of having abandoned concern for his own people. In verses 1–3, therefore, Paul goes out of his way to express his continuing deep concern for Israel. Indeed, like Moses (Exod 32:30–32), he offers to take the place of Israel under the curse (v. 3). These verses indirectly reveal the problem Paul confronts: Israel, by rejecting God's salvation in Christ, has put itself under the curse. This position conflicts significantly with the many privileges Israel has been given (vv. 4–5). The climax of these privileges is the Messiah himself. The most likely interpretation of the end of verse 5 is reflected in the punctuation adopted in the NIV (and, substantially, in most modern versions): "The Messiah, who is God over all, forever praised!"[111] This is, then, the first time a New Testament author uses *theos* ("God") to refer to Jesus.

2.3.2 Defining the Promise (1): God's Sovereign Election (9:6–29)

Paul's first step in aligning God's Old Testament promises to Israel with the gentile-dominated church of his day is to define just what those promises entail. Essentially, his argument is that God's people have always been constituted on the basis of God's call—not simply biological relationship to Abraham. God is free to choose only some Israelites to be saved (vv. 6b–13; 27–29), and he is also free to include gentiles in that people (vv. 24–26). In reading the passage this way, I take issue with many recent interpreters who insist that Romans 9 is concerned with the way God has sovereignly chosen certain people, or nations, to have a certain role in his plan of salvation. On this reading, "election" as Paul unpacks it has nothing to do with the election to salvation of individuals.[112] While there are certainly verses in this chapter that could suggest that Paul focuses on Israel as a nation (e.g., v. 13, with its quotation of Mal 1:2, 3) and that

---

111. See esp. Murray J. Harris, *Jesus as "God": The New Testament Use of Theos in Reference to Jesus* (Grand Rapids: Baker, 1992), 144–72; George Carraway, *Christ Is God over All: Romans 9:5 in the Context of Romans 9–11*, LNTS 489 (London: Bloomsbury, 2013).
112. A good, fairly recent summary of this view is found in

Brian J. Abasciano, "Corporate Election in Romans 9: A Reply to Thomas Schreiner," *JETS* 49 (2006): 351–71. On the broader theological issue, see also A. Chadwick Thornhill, *The Chosen People: Election, Paul and Second Temple Judaism* (Downers Grove, IL: InterVarsity Press, 2015).

his concern is with the history of God's people (e.g., Pharaoh in v. 17), three points in particular argue for some application to the salvation of individuals.[113] First, much of the language Paul uses here is used elsewhere to refer to salvation: children of God (v. 8), descendants (vv. 7–8), counted or "regarded" (v. 8), "children of the promise" (v. 8), "reckon" or "call" (vv. 7, 12), "not by works" (v. 12), "wrath" (v. 22), and "mercy" and "glory" (v. 23). Second, the larger argument of chapters 9–11 requires such a focus. Paul's concern is not with the status of nations or about how God has used people in salvation history but with the question of who is included in God's people. Only by explaining God's choosing in terms of that issue—the issue of salvation—can Paul meet the demands of the situation. Third, and admittedly less compelling, is the nature of the questions Paul himself raises about his emphasis on God's sovereign call: "Is God unjust?" (v. 14); "Why does God still blame us?" (v. 19). These questions, and the answers (or lack of answers!) Paul gives, make most sense if Paul has been describing God's sovereign election to salvation.

Paul sets the agenda for what is coming in verse 6b: "For not all who are descended from Israel are Israel." This distinction of two Israels, a "physical" and a "spiritual" one, is controversial. Paul might mean that there is *within* physical Israel a spiritual nucleus of those whom God has truly called, constituting the "remnant" (see v. 27). Paul's immediate argument, in verses 7–13, would match this thesis quite well. On the other hand, Paul might mean that there is a spiritual Israel that overlaps physical Israel but that also extends beyond it to include gentiles. This reading would summarize Paul's larger argument (see esp. vv. 24–26) quite well.[114] A choice between these two options is difficult, being complicated by the highly charged debate over Paul's conception of "Israel" (see pp. 572–73). While I think Paul does indeed sometimes use Israel to denote the new-covenant people of God as a whole (esp. Gal 6:16), it might be preferable here to see verse 6b as governing verses 7–13 only—in which case a reference to the remnant is more likely.[115]

Verses 7–13 touch on two key moments in the patriarchal salvation history: God's choosing of Isaac over Ishmael and his choosing of Jacob over Esau. The principle Paul derives from this history is the sovereignty of God in making these choices: everything rests on "him who calls" (v. 12)—a principle Paul applies to the surprising turn of salvation history in his day, with many Jews outside the people of God and many gentiles within. The strength of Paul's claim about God's role in this process

---

113. For these points and others, see esp. Piper, *Justification of God*; Thomas R. Schreiner, "Does Romans 9 Teach Individual Election unto Salvation? Some Exegetical and Theological Reflections," *JETS* 36 (1993): 25–40; idem, "Corporate and Individual Election in Romans 9: A Response to Brian Abasciano," *JETS* 49 (2006): 373–86.

114. See esp. Günther Juncker, "'Children of Promise': Spiritual Paternity and Patriarch Theology in Galatians and Romans," *BBR* 17 (2007): 131–60.

115. See, e.g., Susan Grove Eastman, "Israel and the Mercy of God: A Re-Reading of Galatians 6.16 and Romans 9–11," *NTS* 56 (2010): 381–83.

stimulates questions (vv. 14–23). It is telling that Paul does not answer these questions by reminding his readers that he is referring only to nations or to the roles people play in salvation history. Nor does he say that God's sovereign decision is conditioned by human choice. Just the opposite. He denies that it is a matter of "human desire or effort" and asserts instead that it is a matter of "God's mercy" (v. 16). He responds to any suggestion that God's ways are open to question by asserting God's right to do what he chooses with his creatures (vv. 20–21). God bestows that mercy on whomever he chooses and also (with reference to the exodus story) "hardens" whomever he chooses (v. 18). Some people are "prepared for destruction," and others are prepared by God for glory (vv. 21–23). Some interpreters see in this text a reference to "double predestination." However, I think there are reasons to be cautious about drawing this conclusion (see on this issue, pp. 511–15).[116]

After this slight detour to deal with objections, Paul makes his way back to his main focus on God's "calling" in verse 24. In verses 7–13, Paul cited the patriarchs to show that God has called only some within Israel; now, in verses 27–29, he cites the prophets to make the same point.[117] But in verses 24b–26, Paul begins to moves beyond the history of physical Israel, suggesting that Hosea's prediction of "not my people" becoming "my people" has ultimate reference to the gentiles. It is, we must remember, not only, or even mainly, the small number of Jews being saved that stimulates Paul's discussion; it is especially the large-scale entrance of gentiles that creates the problem.

2.3.3 Understanding Israel's Plight: Christ as the Climax of Salvation History (9:30–10:21)

The dual reality that stimulates Paul's argument in these chapters is stated again at the opening of this section: while Israel, pursuing the law "as the way of righteousness," has "not attained their goal," gentiles, who have not been pursuing righteousness, have obtained it—by faith (9:30–31). This contrast is reiterated at the end of this next stage of Paul's argument: God has been "found" by "those who did not seek me" (10:20, quoting Isa 65:1), while Israel is "a disobedient and obstinate people" (10:21, quoting Isa 65:2). In 9:6–29, Paul explains this turn of events in terms of God's sovereign choosing. In this second stage of his argument, he puts the responsibility for Israel's failure on their own shoulders, faulting their stubborn failure to respond appropriately to God's revelation in Christ.

The first part of the passage (9:30–10:13) is dominated by a contrast between two kinds of "righteousness":

---

116. See, recently, Stephen N. Williams, *The Election of Grace: A Riddle without a Resolution?* (Grand Rapids: Eerdmans, 2015), 108–52; and also pp. 511–15.

117. On the way Paul applies texts from Hosea 1–2 in vv. 25–26 to gentiles, see Moo, "Paul's Universalizing Hermeneutic in Romans," 71–72, 76.

"a righteousness that is by faith" versus "the law as the way of righteousness"
   (9:30–31)
"the righteousness of God" versus "their own [righteousness]" (10:3)
"the righteousness that is by the law" versus "the righteousness that is by faith"
   (10:5–6)

Paul employs the key vocabulary he introduced earlier in the letter to explain now the
puzzling turn in salvation history. "Righteousness" in this context clearly refers to "right
standing," "forensic" righteousness. Even "the righteousness of God" (10:3), which,
as we have seen, refers basically to God's own character, focuses here, as the contrast
with "their own righteousness" and the close parallel in Philippians 3:9 suggest, on the
connotation of a status conferred by God. The way in which the law, or the Torah,
is bound up with Israel's failure to attain righteousness is debated. Arguing that the
natural antecedent of "it" in 9:32 (an object inferred from the Greek here) is "the law"
from verse 31, some interpreters think that Paul faults Israel for not recognizing that the
law was not just to be "done" but also "believed."[118] However, the context puts the focus
on righteousness, not the law. The implied object in verse 32, then, is not the law *per se*,
but "the righteousness bound up with the law" (cf. "the law as the way of righteousness"
in v. 31). Moreover, at the risk of circular argument, Paul elsewhere, I would argue,
maintains a principial distinction between the law, which is to be obeyed, done, or
practiced on the one hand, and the gospel, or the promises, which is to be believed, on
the other. Another popular option is that Paul faults Israel here for focusing on the law
as a means of maintaining her unique and special status with God. On this view, "their
own righteousness" in 10:3 means not "the righteousness each Israelite tries to establish
by his or her own doing of the law" but "the righteousness that belongs exclusively to
Israel."[119] As we have seen throughout Romans, Paul is keen to show how the good news
extends to gentiles. That theme is clear in the present text as well, as the emphasis on
"for everyone who believes" demonstrates (v. 4; see also vv. 11–13). However, while this
emphasis is present here and is important, it is not the main focus of Paul's criticism of
Israel. As the closely parallel text in Philippians 3:9 suggests, "their own righteousness"
here probably means "a righteous standing with God that a person seeks to establish,
or maintain, by doing the law."[120] This focus on "doing" is seen also in Paul's quotation
of Leviticus 18:5 in Romans 10:5. As I have argued he does elsewhere in Romans, then,

---

118. See Daniel P. Fuller, *Gospel and Law: Contrast or Continuum? The Hermeneutics of Dispensationalism and Covenant Theology* (Grand Rapids: Eerdmans, 1980), 71–79; Cranfield, *Romans*, 2:509–10.

119. See esp. James D. G. Dunn, *Romans 9–16*, WBC 38B (Dallas: Word, 1988), 595; Wright, "Romans," 654–55.

120. To be sure, the Philippians text refers to "the righteousness from [*ek*] God" (versus "my own [e.g., Paul's] righteousness") rather than the "righteousness of [genitive] God," but this difference does not materially affect the parallel.

I think that Paul again here is criticizing Israel for thinking that her right standing with God could be maintained by doing the law.

At the same time, Paul also faults Israel in this passage for failing to reckon with the shift in salvation history that has taken place with the coming of Christ. Israel has "stumbled" over the stone God has placed in Zion (9:33, quoting Isa 8:14 and 28:16). This salvation-historical shift is probably also what Paul asserts in the famous words of 10:4: "Christ is the *telos* of the law." The word *telos* can mean simply "end" in the sense of termination, and many take the word this way here.[121] However, the word often has a telic force, and we should probably see something of this nuance here as well. Christ does not simply "end" the law; he brings it to its intended climax and culmination (see NIV).[122] One key reason, then, for so many Jews failing to embrace the good news in Christ was their tunnel vision—their continuing exclusive focus on the law that kept them from seeing the culmination of God's purposes in Christ.

Romans 9–11 is in general remarkable for the density of Old Testament quotations: one-third of all Paul's quotations occur in these chapters. Many of his quotations are relatively straightforward, once Paul's hermeneutical axioms, rooted in his conviction that Christ is the ultimate fulfillment and true meaning of the Old Testament, are factored in. But others are not so easily understood. Especially challenging is Paul's use of language from Deuteronomy 30:11–14 to describe key elements of the gospel in 10:6–8. How can Paul take language describing the law to depict the "righteousness that is by faith" *in contrast to* "the righteousness that is by the law"? Of the many answers to this question proposed in the literature, the simplest and probably best is to think that Paul finds in Deuteronomy 30 a description of the grace of God in establishing a relationship with his people.[123] As God brought his word "near" to Israel through Moses at Horeb, so he now climactically brings his decisive word of salvation "near" to Israel in Paul's day—and not only to Israel. "Anyone" who believes—Jew and gentile alike—can call on the name of the Lord and be saved (10:11–13, quoting Joel 2:32 [3:5 LXX]).

Paul uses this language to transition to the last part of this section (10:14–21). One can "call on" the Lord only if they "believe"; people can believe only if they hear; people can hear only if someone preaches the message; and people will preach the message only if they are sent to do so. Paul affirms that all these steps are in place (vv. 14–15). The problem, therefore, lies with Israel, who has not responded (vv. 16–17), even though God's purposes have been revealed long ago (vv. 18–19).

---

121. E.g., Ulrich Luz, *Das Geschichtsverständnis des Paulus*, BEvT 49 (Munich: Kaiser, 1968), 139–57; Otto Michel, *Der Brief an die Römer*, KEK 4 (Göttingen: Vandenhoeck & Ruprecht, 1966), 326–27; Brice L. Martin, *Christ and the Law in Paul*, NovTSup 62 (Leiden: Brill, 1989), 129–34.

122. See, e.g., Dunn, *Romans 9–16*, 596–98; Longenecker, *Romans*, 850; Bandstra, *Law and the Elements*, 105–6.

123. For a similar approach see, e.g., Calvin, *Romans*, 388.

2.3.4 Transitional Summary: Israel, the "Elect," and the "Hardened" (11:1–10)

A single topic dominates 11:1–32, introduced at the beginning and reiterated at the end: "God did not reject his people, whom he foreknew" (v. 2a); "as far as election is concerned, they [Israelites] are loved on account of the patriarchs" (v. 28b). The second section, verses 11–32, looks to the future of Israel, while the first section of verses 1–10 focuses on the present. Paul's basic point in this first section is that God has preserved a remnant of Jews who continue to be faithful to God by embracing his Messiah, Jesus. As in the days of Elijah (vv. 3–4), there is "at the present time . . . a remnant chosen by grace" (v. 5). Paul, a Jew who is a Christian, is himself living proof of the existence of this remnant (v. 1). Still, the majority of his fellow Jews have not followed him in embracing Jesus. These "others" "were hardened" (vv. 7–10).

2.3.5 Defining the Promise (2): The Future of Israel (11:11–32)

Is the current state of Israel—a small number being saved, most being insensitive to God's revelation in Christ—permanent? This is the question that dominates this second section of chapter 11. Paul answers no, and he bases his answer on a salvation-historical process that God is using to embrace both Jew and gentile in his saving mercy (see v. 32). Paul goes over this process several times in slightly different ways.

vv. 11–12: "their [Israel's] transgression" leads to "salvation" for gentiles, stimulating jealousy among Israel and leading to their "full inclusion"

v. 15: "their [Israel's] rejection" brought "reconciliation to the world"; "their acceptance" will mean "life from the dead"

vv. 17–23: "natural branches" (Israel) have been broken off, and wild shoots (gentiles) "have been grafted in"; so God can graft back in "natural branches"

vv. 25–26: "hardening in part" of Israel "until the full number of Gentiles has come in"; "in this way all Israel will be saved"

vv. 30–31: "you [gentiles] . . . have received mercy as a result of their [Jews'] disobedience"; "they too have now become disobedient in order that they too may now receive mercy as a result of God's mercy to you"

The first two steps in this process—Jewish disobedience and gentile inclusion—have already taken place. What Paul clearly wants to emphasize is that the infusion of gentiles is designed by God ultimately to affect Jews—stimulating them to "envy" or "jealousy" and bringing many of them to salvation.

Interpreters debate the timing and nature of this last step. I can focus my discussion of this theologically important issue on the famous debated claim in verse 26: "In this way all Israel will be saved." One option that I mention only to dismiss is that Paul envisages the salvation of all, or most, Jews by means of their own Torah covenant.[124] While this option has gained some traction among the "Paul within Judaism" school of interpreters, it is foreign to Paul's express and repeated claim that a person—Jew or gentile—can be saved only through faith in Christ (e.g., 1:16; 10:9–13). A second interpretation has deep roots in the history of interpretation: that the process Paul has described is the way (note "in this way" in v. 26) that God will bring all his elect, Jew and gentile, to salvation.[125] As I noted in my comments on 9:6, there is some basis in Paul for interpreting "Israel" to refer to the church as a whole, and the addition of "all" to Israel here might signal this broader meaning. However, the immediate context uses "Israel" in a national, or ethnic, sense (v. 25), and the addition of "all" does not change the meaning of the word it modifies. While theologically attractive, then, this option probably does not have adequate exegetical basis. A third option also stresses that Paul in verse 26 is summarizing the manner ("in this way"; Gk. *houtōs*) in which God is bringing "all Israel" to salvation. However, defenders of this view think that "all Israel" is ethnic Israel, in terms of "all elect Jews." The salvation of Jews on this view takes place over the course of salvation history, as the oscillation between Jews and gentiles results in the salvation of Jews.[126] This reading also has much to be said for it, but I think it finally fails to deal adequately with the "until" in verse 25: Israel is hardened in part *"until* the full number of Gentiles has come in, and in this way all Israel will be saved." The most natural reading of this sequence sees all Israel being saved as a new stage in salvation history that comes after all elect gentiles have come into the kingdom.[127] Indeed, the key word translated "in this way" (*houtōs*) could also be translated "then," although this is not necessary to establish this view.[128] On this reading, which I hesitantly think is the best option, Paul is revealing a "mystery" (v. 25) having to do with the way God will in the future bring many of his chosen people Israel to salvation. While debated, the deliverer "coming from Zion" (quoting Isa 59:20) probably refers to Jesus's return in glory, establishing the general time frame in which this salvation will happen. "All Israel," it is important to note, need not mean "every single Israelite" alive at that time. The phrase is used in the Old Testament often as a representative summary of the people (see, e.g., Josh 7:25; 2 Sam 16:22).

My reading of this famously debated passage has several important implications for

---

124. A key earlier scholar arguing this view was Krister Stendahl, "Paul among Jews and Gentiles," in *Paul among Jews and Gentiles, and Other Essays* (Philadelphia: Fortress, 1976), 1–77; idem, "The Apostle Paul and the Introspective Conscience of the West," 199–215; and idem, "Christ's Lordship and Religious Pluralism," in *Meanings: The Bible as Document and as Guide* (Philadelphia: Fortress, 1984), 233–44.

125. E.g., Calvin, *Romans*, 437; Barth, *CD* IV/1:671; Wright, "Romans," 688–91; idem, *Climax of the Covenant*, 249–50.

126. E.g., Ben L. Merkle, "Romans 11 and the Future of Ethnic Israel," *JETS* 43 (2000): 709–21.

127. This is the majority view among contemporary scholars. See, e.g., Murray, *Romans*, 93–96; Cranfield, *Romans*, 2:576–77; Dunn, *Romans 9–16*, 679–81; Schreiner, *Romans*, 597–605.

128. For a defense of the translation "then," see Peter W. van der Horst, "Only Then Will All Israel Be Saved: A Short Note on the Meaning of Καὶ Οὕτως in Romans 11:26," *JBL* 119 (2000): 521–25.

Paul's theology—implications that I will explore in another context (see pp. 558–65, 272–73). Here I simply note that Paul's "transfer" of privilege and blessing from Israel to the church (which is clearly an important emphasis in his theology) does not mean that Israel, as a nation, is erased from God's salvation-historical plan. The increasingly gentile-dominated nature of the church in Paul's day is no threat to the integrity of God's promises to Israel. Indeed, gentile inclusion is one of the means by which God is fulfilling his promises to national Israel. We should also note that Paul makes clear that his purpose in describing this salvation-historical process is to critique gentile arrogance (11:13–14, 20, 25).

2.3.6 Conclusion: Praise to God in Light of His Awesome Plan (11:33–36)

As he did in 8:31–39, Paul concludes a lengthy and involved theological discourse with praise and celebration. Borrowing extensively from Old Testament wisdom traditions, apocalyptic, and Hellenistic-Jewish teachings, Paul composes a hymn in praise to God for his awesome plan. His expression of praise falls into three strophes: verse 33, containing three exclamations about God's wise plan; verses 34–35, featuring three rhetorical questions that emphasize human inability to understand God's ways; and verse 36, containing a declaration about the ultimacy of God that calls forth a final doxology.

2.4 The Transforming Power of the Gospel: Christian Conduct (12:1–15:13)

Paul does not stop "doing theology" at the end of chapter 11; he simply shifts into a different mode. In 12:1–15:13, the imperative carries the discourse as Paul spells out some of the implications of the gospel for Christian living. The imperative of a transformed life is not an optional second step after we embrace the gospel: it is rooted in and, indeed, part of the gospel itself. The topics Paul touches on in these chapters are ones we find elsewhere in his letters:

The need for transformation by the renewing of the mind (12:1–2)	Eph 4:17–24
The unity of the body of Christ despite its diversity of gifts (12:3–8)	1 Cor 12; see Eph 4:11–17
The central demand of love (12:9–21)	1 Cor 13; 1 Thess 4:9–12
—as the fulfillment of the law (13:8–10)	Gal 5:13–15
The need for spiritual wakefulness in light of the day of the Lord (13:11–14)	1 Thess 5:1–11
Reconciliation between weak and strong Christians over issues of food (14:1–15:13)	1 Cor 8–10

At the same time, there is good reason to think that Paul is also choosing topics and treating them in a fashion that fits the situation he is addressing in Rome.

2.4.1 The Heart of the Matter: Total Transformation (12:1–2)

Paul's gospel exhortations fall into two parts: a section treating fundamental issues in Christian living (12:1–13:14) and a section focusing on a particular issue in the Roman Christian community (14:1–15:13). Paul begins and ends the first section by urging Christians to be transformed in light of the new era of salvation history that has dawned: "Do not conform to the pattern of this age" (12:2, my translation); "let us . . . put on the armor of light" because "the day is almost here" (13:12). The opening transitional words of this entire part of the letter root Paul's exhortations in the gospel itself: he exhorts believers "in view of God's mercy" (12:1). As we saw in chapter 6, Paul's "imperative" is grounded in, and stimulated by, the indicative. Transformed living, Paul makes clear, comes via a transformed mindset—"the renewing of your mind"—and encompasses all of life—"offer your bodies [that is, your whole person 'embodied' in the world; see pp. 455–56] as a living sacrifice."

2.4.2 Humility, Mutual Service, and Love (12:3–21)

The main point of verses 3–8 is expressed in verses 3 and 5: don't think too highly of yourselves because you are all members of the one body of Christ. True, the "members" have different gifts and therefore function in different ways (vv. 6–8), but this is no reason for some of the members to think of themselves as superior to others. As 1 Corinthians 12 and Ephesians 4:1–16 reveal, this call for believers to recognize the "diversity in unity" of the body of Christ is fundamental to Paul's view of the gospel and its outworking. At the same time, Paul's warning that believers should not "think [hyperphronein] of yourself more highly than you ought" (v. 3) reminds us of Paul's rebuke of gentile believers in relation to Jewish believers in 11:20: "Do not be arrogant [mē hypsēla phronei]." Paul, then, deploys a common theme of his paraenesis to address the situation in Rome: "strong" believers should not view themselves as superior to "weak" believers.

Love for others is the heart of the new life in Christ, as Jesus himself made clear (e.g., Mark 12:28–34 par.; John 13:31–35; cf. also 1 Cor 13; Gal 5:13–14; 1 Thess 4:9; Jas 2:8–9; 1 Pet 1:22; 1 John 2:7–11; 3:10–18; 4:7–12, 18–21). It is unsurprising that it has a prominent place in this series of general exhortations (see also 13:8–10). "Love must be sincere," or simply, "sincere love" (there is no verb in the Gk.), is the topic of verses 9–21. The varied exhortations of these verses therefore are best seen as attempts to elaborate the variegated form that sincere Christian love can take. Paul makes clear that Christian love has moral direction and content. He frames his exhortations with this focus: "hate what is evil" and "cling to what is good" (v. 9b); "do not be overcome by evil, but overcome evil with good" (v. 21). Paul stresses the "vertical" dimension of our love (alluding to the "first" of the "two great commandments"?): we are to maintain our spiritual passion while "serving the Lord" (v. 11). The scope of our love, on the human plane, is to be unlimited. The "others" we are to love include both "insiders"

(vv. 13, 15–16) and "outsiders" (vv. 14, 17–20). One noteworthy aspect of this passage is its clear dependence on the teaching of Jesus: compare especially verse 14, "Bless those who persecute you; bless and do not curse," with the Sermon on the Mount:

Matt 5:44: "Love your enemies and pray for *those who persecute you*."
Luke 6:27–28: "Love your enemies, do good to those who hate you, *bless* those who curse you, pray for those who mistreat you."

The paucity of explicit references to Jesus's teaching in Paul's letters has generated considerable discussion, but passages such as this reveal that Paul has absorbed much of Jesus's teaching into his own paraenesis (see pp. 26–27).[129]

2.4.3 Secular Rulers and Love (Again) (13:1–10)

Paul's basic point in verses 1–7 is clear: believers are to be "subject to the governing authorities" (v. 1; see also v. 5). While there have been famous dissenters (e.g., Barth), the view that Paul is referring to secular rulers is now almost universal.[130] Paul's apparently unqualified call for submission to government has, as might be expected, generated an avalanche of discussion and criticism. The passage has an important role to play, then, in constructing Paul's political theology (see pp. 641–43). It is quite possible, even probable, that Paul addresses a particular problem in Rome with this paragraph—perhaps a "tax revolt" for which we have evidence from Roman historians (see vv. 6–7).[131] But it is clear that Paul's admonition cannot be confined to the first-century Roman community, for he goes out of his way to universalize his teaching ("everyone" in v. 1). In general, then, this paragraph shows that Paul strongly believed the secular authorities were set in place by God and therefore deserved respect. However, the conflicting views concerning authorities that we find elsewhere in the New Testament (esp. Acts 4:19–20; the book of Revelation) justifies our searching for exceptions to Paul's apparent requirement of absolute and unquestioned obedience. Two bases in the text itself might be mentioned. First, "submission" in Paul (Paul uses

---

129. See esp. Blomberg, "Quotations, Allusions, and Echoes of Jesus in Paul," 129–43; and also James D. G. Dunn, "Paul's Knowledge of the Jesus Tradition: The Evidence of Romans," in *Christus Bezeugen: Festschrift für Wolfgang Trilling zum 65. Geburtstag*, ed. Karl Kertelge, Traugott Holtz, and Claus-Peter März (Leipzig: Benno, 1989), 193–207; Peter Stuhlmacher, "Jesustradition im Römerbrief? Eine Skizze," *TBei* 14 (1983): 240–50; and, in greatest detail, Michael B. Thompson, *Clothed with Christ: The Example and Teaching of Jesus in Romans 12.1–15.13*, JSNTSup 59 (Sheffield: Sheffield Academic, 1991).

130. Karl Barth (*Church and State* [London: SCM, 1939], 23–36) argued that the Gk. *exousiai* referred to both human rulers and the spiritual "authorities" that stand behind them. Christians are absolved from their call to obey the authorities when they rebel against Christ, who has subjected them. See also Oscar Cullmann, *The State in the New Testament* (New York: Scribner's Sons, 1956), 55–70. For a rebuttal of this view, see Wesley Carr, *Angels and Principalities: The Background, Meaning, and Development of the Pauline Phrase hai archai kai hai exousiai*, SNTSMS 42 (Cambridge: Cambridge University Press, 1981), 115–21.

131. The Roman historian Tacitus refers to resistance against the payment of indirect taxes in the middle 50s, culminating in a tax revolt in AD 58 (*Ann.* 13.50ff.).

the verb *hypotassō* in vv. 1 and 5) involves a general "ordering under" that reflects a divinely ordained hierarchy (Paul uses the same verb in calling on wives to "submit" to their husbands). At the top of this hierarchy is God himself. When any "lower" authority requires a believer to do something in conflict with the will of that ultimate authority, disobedience at that point (while remaining "submissive" in general) may be appropriate. Second, Paul's description of authorities as rewarding good and punishing evil (vv. 3–4) appears to ignore the many times when the authorities act in just the opposite manner, rewarding evil and punishing good. It may be, then, that Paul is implicitly describing government as it ought to function—perhaps justifying the believer's disobedience when government fails to carry out its divine mandate.[132]

In verses 8–10 Paul returns to his discussion of Christian love (see 12:9–21). In another probable instance of dependence on Jesus's teaching, Paul quotes the command to love one's neighbor as oneself (Lev 19:18) as a basic summing up of the intent of the law of Moses (see Matt 22:34–40//Mark 12:28–34//Luke 10:25–28; and see the close parallel to this passage in Gal 5:13–15). Loving others "fulfills" the law (vv. 8 and 10). Paul may mean by this that love for others must accompany obedience to the other Mosaic commandments. But his use of the key salvation-historical technical word *plēroō* ("fulfill") suggests that he is making a more radical claim. Christians, Paul has asserted, are "not under the law" (Rom 6:14, 15). Does this freedom from the law open the door to unbridled licentiousness? Not at all. As Paul argues also in Galatians (5:13–6:10), believers are directed and empowered by the new-covenant gift of the Spirit (see esp. Rom 8:4) and, by obeying the central Christian demand that we love others, we end up actually accomplishing all that the Mosaic law demands.

2.4.4 Living in Light of "the Day" (13:11–14)

Paul concludes the first part of his gospel exhortations with a reminder about the nature of the time that believers live in. Central to this paragraph is a double entendre with respect to the word "day." On the one hand, the word connotes "daytime" (as the NIV translates in v. 13). Believers are to pursue activities that occur "in the light of day" and not those that typically occur under cover of darkness. On the other hand, Paul's claim that "the night is nearly over; the day is almost here" (v. 12) makes clear that "day" here has the typical salvation-historical sense of the "day of the Lord." Believers need to understand "the present time" (v. 11), remembering that they live in the era when God's promises have found an initial, decisive fulfillment, even as they wait for the culmination of the new era that has dawned. In this "already/not yet" situation, they must live in Christ, "clothing themselves" with him (v. 14).

---

132. This view is widespread. See, e.g., Jean Hering, "'Serviteurs de Dieu': Contribution à L'exégèse pratique de Romains 13,3–4," *RHPR* 30 (1950): 31–40.

2.4.5 A Plea for Unity (14:1–15:13)

Appreciating the theology taught in this passage depends on identifying the nature of the issue that Paul is addressing. Fortunately, contemporary scholars generally agree that the conflict in the Roman Christian community is between mainly Jewish believers who think it is important to live out the Christian faith in terms of Torah and mainly gentile believers who see no reason to live under Torah.[133] Many Jewish believers were apparently following the pattern set by Daniel and his friends: avoiding meat (14:2; and probably wine—see 14:21) in light of its possible association with paganism and insisting on the observance of Sabbath and other Jewish festivals (14:5). As Paul makes clear, he himself sides with the "strong" who do not view Torah as having continuing authority (14:14; 15:1). But his main concern is not to identify who is right and who is wrong, but to urge that each group "accept" the other (14:1; 15:7), that is, to recognize the right of believers to take varying views on the role of Torah in working out their Christian faith.

I make three observations on the theology stemming from Paul's extensive treatment of this issue. First, we realize that Paul's polemic against the law must be carefully calibrated. He is adamantly opposed to insisting that one can be a member of the new-covenant people of God only by putting oneself under Torah (Galatians). This passage also makes clear that he opposes any attempt to make Torah adherence necessary for what we might call sanctification. However, it is also clear from this passage that Paul gave the right to Jewish believers to choose to continue to follow Torah guidelines as Christians (see also 1 Cor 9:19–21). These points must be integrated into the complicated and debated question of Paul's teaching about the law and Jewish identity (see pp. 572–73).

Second, we also recognize in Paul's polemic here his deep concern for the unity of the Christian community. While differing on "nonessentials," Jewish and gentile Christians in Rome need to embrace one another because only then will they be able "with one mind and one voice" to "glorify the God and Father of our Lord Jesus Christ" (15:6). The bottom line for Paul is expressed clearly in 15:7: these Christians, with their various views about Torah, are to "accept one another" because "Christ accepted you." Believers have no right to reject from their fellowship those whom God in Christ has accepted. The key to this unity, Paul suggests, is a sense of what is truly important: "For the kingdom of God is not a matter of eating and drinking, but of righteousness, peace and joy in the Holy Spirit" (14:17).

Third, as Paul has been making clear for some time (see esp. 11:20, 25; 12:3, 16; 13:8–10), believers should prioritize the good of "the other" rather than focusing on their own "rights" or pleasure (14:15, 19–22; 15:2–3).

---

133. See, e.g., Schreiner, *Romans*, 684–89; Watson, *Paul, Judaism and the Gentiles*, 175–82; Carl N. Toney, *Paul's Inclusive Ethic:* *Resolving Community Conflicts and Promoting Mission in Romans 14–15*, WUNT 2/252 (Tübingen: Mohr Siebeck, 2008), 56–90.

3 THE LETTER CLOSING (15:14–16:27)

The letter closing of Romans, while significantly longer than any of Paul's others, includes the usual elements of his closing sections:

Travel Plans	15:14–29
Request for Prayer	15:30–32
Prayer-Wish for Peace	15:33
Paul's Associates	16:1–2
Exhortation to Greet One Another	16:3–15
The "Holy Kiss"	16:16a
Warning/Exhortation	16:17–19
Eschatological Wish/Promise	16:20a
Concluding "Grace"	16:20b
Greetings from Paul's Associates	16:16b, 21–23
Doxology	16:25–27

The only unusual elements are the warning about false teachers in 16:17–19 and the doxology at the end of chapter 16.[134]

While this section is focused on specifics of Paul's ancient letter-writing, there are nonetheless theological implications that are worth briefly noting.

First, we learn about Paul's own conception of ministry. As he did at the beginning of the letter (1:6–7), he again stresses his particular calling to minister among gentiles (15:16). In the same context, he employs priestly language to characterize his ministerial work. He has a "priestly duty" that will result, he trusts, in the gentiles themselves becoming "an offering acceptable to God."[135] Paul also expresses what was apparently a fundamental sense of ministry calling by speaking of having "fully proclaimed [or 'fulfilled'; the Gk. verb is *plēroō*]" the gospel "from Jerusalem all the way around to Illyricum" (15:19), meaning that "there is no more place for me to work in these regions" (15:23). Paul is convinced he was called by God to be a pioneer church planter. To have "fully proclaimed the gospel," then, means that he has planted vital and healthy churches throughout this region, leaving to the believers in those churches the further job of evangelizing and discipling. Finally, Paul's reference to the "service of the Lord's

---

134. While many interpreters think that the doxology was not a part of Paul's letter (because it is found in different places in some MSS), I think it is authentic.

135. Taking the genitive construction *hē prosphora tōn ethnōn* as indicating apposition (with the NIV and most versions). It could also indicate that the gentiles are offering a sacrifice.

people" in Jerusalem (15:25; see vv. 25–32) reminds us of one of the great projects of his third missionary journey: the "collection" for the Christians in Judea. Mentioned in each of his third-missionary-journey letters (see also 1 Cor 16:1–4; 2 Cor 8–9), the collection had a dual thrust. On the one hand, it exemplified the importance of believers serving one another in specific material ways. Concern for the soul clearly did not displace concern for the body in Paul's churches. Second, Paul saw the collection as one means of mending the growing rift between Paul's diaspora, mainly gentile, churches, and the mainly, if not exclusively, Jewish churches in Judea. If he could get his gentile converts to send money to Jerusalem, and if he could get Jewish Christians to accept it (something that his request for prayer in 15:30–32 suggests was a real concern), he would go some way toward bringing a greater sense of unity to the church of his day.

Second, we learn a bit about the diversity of the early Christian communities. Paul greets twenty-six individuals, two families, and three house churches in 16:3–16. Studies of the names of the people mentioned reveal that (1) nine are women, some of whom were working in gospel ministry;[136] (2) a majority of the names are gentile (confirming the mainly gentile makeup of the church at Rome); and (3) the majority of the names are those of slaves and "freedmen" (slaves who had been given their freedom), or the descendants of slaves or freedmen.[137]

If, as I think, the doxology in 16:25–27 is authentic, it makes indeed an "apt conclusion" for the letter.[138] The "gospel" is again here prominent, a gospel that Paul ties firmly to Jesus Christ (see 1:3). The salvation-historical context of that gospel is a theme that undergirds all of Romans. As Paul says here, the gospel is "in keeping with the revelation of the mystery hidden for long ages past" and "now revealed and made known through the prophetic writings." A special concern with gentile inclusion in this new stage of salvation history is also in keeping with the letter as a whole. As in 1:5, and as spelled out throughout the letter, Paul is at pains to show how the gospel brings both faith and obedience to those who embrace it (v. 26). And, finally, all this is due to "the only wise God" who has acted decisively in Jesus Christ.

136. Paul's mention of Junia (v. 7) has generated discussion, since Paul appears to identify her as an "apostle" (the Greek form of the name, *Iounian*, could come from a masculine name, Junianus, but almost certainly comes from the feminine name Junia). Some interpreters claim that this text recognizes a female as an authoritative apostle (e.g., Jewett, *Romans*, 961–64). However, since we never hear of either Junia or her husband (probably), Andronicus, elsewhere, it is more likely that *apostolos* here has the broader sense of "messenger" or "accredited missionary" (as in 2 Cor 8:23; Phil 2:25; see, e.g., Susan Mathew, *Women in the Greetings of Romans 16.1–16: A Study of Mutuality and Women's Ministry in the Letter to the Romans*, LNTS 471 [London: Bloomsbury T&T Clark, 2013], 101–5).

137. Peter Lampe, *Die stadtrömischen Christen in den ersten beiden Jahrhunderten: Untersuchungen zur Sozialgeschichte*, WUNT 2/18 (Tübingen: Mohr Siebeck, 1987), 135–53; see also idem, "The Roman Christians of Romans 16," in Donfried, *Romans Debate*, 216–30; idem, *From Paul to Valentinus: Christians at Rome in the First Two Centuries* (Minneapolis: Fortress, 2003), 164–83. The most important earlier study is Lightfoot's appendix on "Caesar's Household" in *Saint Paul's Epistle to the Philippians* (London: Macmillan, 1888), 174–77.

138. I borrow the language from I. Howard Marshall's defense of the originality of the doxology: "Romans 16:25–27: An Apt Conclusion," in Soderlund and Wright, *Romans and the People of God*, 170–84.

Chapter 10

COLOSSIANS

ALTHOUGH COMPARATIVELY BRIEF, Paul's letter to the Colossians has had a strong impact on Christian theology and practice.[1] One thinks immediately of its teaching about Jesus's role in creation and his preeminence over the church—teaching that has strongly influenced the development of christological doctrine. Colossians, along with Ephesians, its close relative, develop the notion of the church as "the body," with Christ as its head.[2] From a more practical perspective, Paul's rebuke of false teachers who tie spiritual growth to the following of rules (2:16–23) reminds us that true growth comes only by remaining firmly tied to Christ. Paul's exhortations in 3:1–4:6, again, though brief, summarize and illustrate the basic ethical principles that have provided significant guidance for believers seeking to translate their commitment to the Lord Jesus into practice.

LOCATING THE LETTER

The city of Colossae was located in the Lycus River valley of west-central Asia Minor. Although Colossae was an important city in the region in the fourth- and third-centuries BC, it had declined considerably by Paul's time, smaller and less important than the neighboring cities of Laodicea (cf. 2:1; 4:16) and Hierapolis (4:13). The diversity of population and exposure to the latest ideas via travelers on its major highway meant that Colossae was a place where many different religious and philosophical viewpoints thrived and probably mixed together. These circumstances may help explain the false teaching, which was the basic stimulus for the letter (see "Isolating the Issues" below). Probably most Colossian Christians were gentile, but the community likely also included some Jews. Paul learns about the threat posed by false teachers from Epaphras, probably a convert of Paul's from his three-year stay in Ephesus (Acts 19). Epaphras was the founder of the Christian community in Colossae (only a hundred miles from Ephesus; see 1:7–8; 4:12–13).

---

1. Concepts and occasionally wording in this chapter and the next are taken from Douglas J. Moo, *The Letters to the Colossians and to Philemon*, PNTC (Grand Rapids: Eerdmans, 2008). Used with permission.

2. This focus is often seen as an indication of a post-Pauline author. However, as Stuhlmacher notes, the idea of the church as "body" has roots deep in Paul's teaching in 1 Corinthians (*Biblical Theology of the New Testament*, 462).

Our "location" of the letter assumes that Paul wrote it. Pauline authorship is doubted by many scholars: 60 percent (in Raymond Brown's estimation) of all scholars think the letter is pseudonymous, written by someone in Paul's name.[3] However, not only does the letter claim to have been written by Paul (1:1; 4:18), it includes many personal references and allusions to travels and fellow workers. As John M. G. Barclay notes, "If Colossians is by a later Paulinist, it is unparalleled in its sophisticated adaptation of incidental details to camouflage its inauthenticity."[4] When we combine these factors specific to Colossians with the general problems attending the idea of a pseudonymous *letter* (see pp. 49–51), we can confidently read this letter as written by the apostle Paul.

Paul is in prison as he writes (4:3, 18). Colossians, therefore, is classified with Ephesians, Philippians, and Philemon as a "prison epistle" (2 Timothy, while also written from prison, is included with the "Pastoral Epistles"). Ephesians and Philemon are closely related to Colossians. Colossians and Ephesians share a lot of vocabulary and theology, and all three are written to the same geographic area and mention some of the same coworkers. Identifying the imprisonment from which Paul wrote these letters is not easy. The book of Acts refers explicitly to three imprisonments of Paul: overnight in Philippi (16:19–34); for two years in Caesarea (23:23–26:32; cf. 24:27); and for two years in Rome (28:11–31; cf. v. 30). But Paul's claim that he had "been in prisons" very frequently (2 Cor 11:23) implies that he was imprisoned more often than on these three occasions. Many scholars think that Paul was imprisoned during his three-year stay in Ephesus, although the evidence for this is not strong.[5] Since the overnight stay in Philippi is obviously excluded from consideration, we have, therefore, three viable candidates for the location from which Paul wrote Colossians, along with Ephesians and Philemon: Ephesus (ca. AD 52–55); Caesarea (ca. AD 57–59); or Rome (ca. AD 60–62).

Caesarea is neither a popular nor a likely option. Many scholars opt for Ephesus.[6]

---

3. Brown, *Introduction to the New Testament*, 610.

4. John M. G. Barclay, *Colossians and Philemon*, NTG (Sheffield: Sheffield Academic, 1997), 24. For Pauline authorship, see esp. Ernst Percy, *Die Probleme der Kolosser- und Epheserbriefe* (Lund: Gleerup, 1946), 16–136; and also, e.g., F. F. Bruce, *The Epistles to the Colossians, to Philemon, and to the Ephesians*, NICNT (Grand Rapids: Eerdmans, 1984), 28–33; C. F. D. Moule, *The Epistles of Paul the Apostle to the Colossians and to Philemon*, CGTC (Cambridge: Cambridge University Press, 1968), 13–14; N. T. Wright, *The Epistles of Paul to the Colossians and to Philemon: An Introduction and Commentary*, TNTC 12 (Grand Rapids: Eerdmans, 1986), 31–34; Peter T. O'Brien, *Colossians, Philemon*, WBC 44 (Waco, TX: Word, 1982), xli–xlix; Murray J. Harris, *Colossians & Philemon*, EGGNT (Grand Rapids: Eerdmans, 1991), 3–4; Markus Barth and Helmut Blanke, *Colossians*, AB 34B (New York: Doubleday, 1994), 114–26; Gregory S. Magee, *Portrait of an Apostle: A Case for Paul's Authorship of Colossians and Ephesians* (Eugene, OR: Pickwick, 2013).

5. Ben Witherington has recently questioned the hypothesis of a Pauline Ephesian imprisonment ("The Case of the Imprisonment That Did Not Happen: Paul at Ephesus," *JETS* 60 [2017]: 525–32).

6. E.g., Jean-François Collange, *L'épître de Saint Paul à Philémon*, CNT 11C (Geneva: Labor et Fides, 1987), 21–23; Eduard Lohse, *Colossians and Philemon*, Hermeneia (Philadelphia: Fortress, 1971), 188; Eduard Schweizer, *The Letter to the Colossians: A Commentary* (Minneapolis: Augsburg, 1982), 24–26; Joseph A. Fitzmyer, *The Letter to Philemon: A New Translation with Introduction and Commentary*, AB 34C (New York: Doubleday, 2000), 9–11; Peter Stuhlmacher, *Der Brief an Philemon*, EKKNT 18 (Neukirchen-Vluyn: Neukirchener, 2004), 21; Wright, *Colossians and Philemon*, 34–37; Murphy-O'Connor, *Paul*, 175; Scot McKnight, *The Letter to the Colossians*, NICNT (Grand Rapids: Eerdmans, 2018), 34–39.

But, especially if Paul wrote the letter, Rome, which is the traditional location, is the most likely.[7] If so, we should probably locate Colossians in the earlier part of Paul's two-year imprisonment, in AD 60–61.

ISOLATING THE ISSUES

The key issue in evaluating the theology of Colossians is the nature of the false teaching that Paul opposes.[8] Unfortunately, any precise identification of this teaching eludes us. All our evidence is general and indirect, as we try to reconstruct that teaching on the basis of what Paul says in response to it against the background of the first-century world of Colossae.

The letter itself suggests that there were three main "planks" in the false teachers' platform. First, the false teachers were using the language of "fullness" (cf. 1:19; 2:9, 10). Second, the false teachers were advocating some degree of Jewish-like views (2:16–17) and were perhaps advocating circumcision (v. 11; cf. v. 13; 3:11).[9] Third, they denigrated Christ (e.g., 1:15–20; 2:9, 10, 15, 17, 19). Scholars have proposed several options,[10] but two deserve particular mention. One view is that the teachers were propagating a form of Jewish mysticism, celebrating visions in which they participated with angels in worship (taking "worship of angels" to mean "worship engaged in by angels"; cf. 2:18).[11] Another view, advocated by a majority of scholars, is that the teaching was a mix of two or more religious and/or philosophical traditions. The best-argued and most persuasive of these syncretistic options has been presented by Clinton E. Arnold. Arnold argues that "the Colossian 'philosophy' . . . represents a combination of Phrygian folk belief, local folk Judaism, and Christianity. The local folk belief has some distinctive

---

7. Most of the early commentators place these letters in Rome. The "Marcionite Prologue" identifies Ephesus as the place where Colossians was written, but this same document places Philemon in Rome. Modern defenders of the Roman provenance include Bruce, *Colossians, Philemon, and Ephesians*, 193–96; Moule, *Colossians and Philemon*, 21–25; O'Brien, *Colossians, Philemon*, xlix–liii; Markus Barth and Helmut Blanke, *The Letter to Philemon*, ECC (Grand Rapids: Eerdmans, 2000), 121–26; Harris, *Colossians and Philemon*, 4; David E. Garland, *Colossians and Philemon*, NIVAC (Grand Rapids: Zondervan, 1998), 307–8; Donald Guthrie, *New Testament Introduction*, 3rd ed. (Downers Grove, IL: InterVarsity Press, 1970), 577–80; Carson and Moo, *Introduction to the New Testament*, 521–22.

8. To be sure, a few scholars have questioned the existence of a particular false teaching. See Morna D. Hooker, "Were There False Teachers in Colossae?" in *Christ and Spirit in the New Testament: Studies in Honour of Charles Francis Digby Moule*, ed. Barnabas Lindars and Stephen S. Smalley (Cambridge: Cambridge University Press, 1973), 315–31.

9. This is the least clearly established of the three. Paul mentions circumcision so casually that it is possible he himself is responsible for the language.

10. For a good survey of options, see esp. Allan R. Bevere, *Sharing in the Inheritance: Identity and the Moral Life in Colossians*, JSNTSup 226 (Sheffield: Sheffield Academic, 2003), 13–46.

11. Fred O. Francis, "Humility and Angel Worship in Col. 2:18," *ST* 16 (1962): 109–34 (the article has been re-published with a series of other essays on the Colossian false teaching in Fred O. Francis and Wayne A. Meeks, eds., *Conflict at Colossae: A Problem in the Interpretation of Early Christianity Illustrated by Selected Modern Studies*, Sources for Biblical Study 4 [Atlanta: SBL, 1975], 163–95). Ian K. Smith provides perhaps the fullest analysis of Colossians along these lines: *Heavenly Perspective: A Study of the Apostle Paul's Response to a Jewish Mystical Movement at Colossae*, LNTS 346 (Edinburgh: T&T Clark, 2006). See also O'Brien, *Colossians, Philemon*, xxxvii–xxxviii; Thomas J. Sappington, *Revelation and Redemption at Colossae*, JSNTSup 53 (Sheffield: JSOT, 1991); McKnight, *Colossians*, 25–34.

Phrygian qualities, but it also has much in common with what we could also describe as magic or ritual power."[12] The false teachers were probably people from within the Colossian Christian community who were bragging about their ability to find ultimate spiritual "fulfillment" via their own program of visions and asceticism. This program was drawn partly from Judaism, particularly in its focus on rules about eating and observing certain days. They were preoccupied with spiritual beings, probably because they viewed them as powerful figures capable of having a significant influence on their lives. However, because this identification is open to debate, we must avoid reading Paul's letter too strictly against any particular background.

ANALYZING THE ARGUMENT

The basic argument of the letter is summarized in Colossians 2:6: "So then, just as you received Christ Jesus as Lord, continue to live your lives in him." The first part, then, focuses on the Colossians' acceptance of the gospel of God's Son, and the second on their need to continue to accept and live out this gospel.

1 THE LETTER OPENING: "JUST AS YOU RECEIVED CHRIST JESUS AS LORD" (1:1–2:5)

1.1 The Powerful Gospel of God's Son (1:1–23)

After Paul's usual prescript, in which he mentions Timothy as "cosender" (1:1–2; see the discussion on pp. 52–53), he begins the letter body with a focus on the Colossians' reception of the gospel. This motif frames 1:3–23. Paul begins by thanking God for the Colossians' faith in Christ and love for all God's people, and he claims that these are rooted in the hope stored up for them in heaven and about which they have heard in "the true message of the gospel" (1:4–5). He ends by warning the Colossians that their expectation of being presented before God "without blemish" in the judgment depends on their holding firmly to their faith and not moving from "the hope held out in the gospel" (1:22–23). This passage, then, is about the power of the gospel, the gospel that has at its heart the Son of God, supreme in creation and the church (vv. 15–20). The false teaching will hold no attraction for the Colossians if they truly come to know and understand that they have already received the true word of God and that they have been transferred by God's own power into the new realm of God's own Son.

The elaborate thanksgiving section is framed by the verb "give thanks" (*eucharisteō*)

---

12. Clinton E. Arnold, *The Colossian Syncretism: The Interface between Christianity and Folk Belief in Colossae*, WUNT 2/77 (Tübingen: Mohr Siebeck, 1995; repr., Grand Rapids: Baker, 1996), 243; see, recently, along the same lines, Paul Foster, *Colossians*, BNTC (London: Bloomsbury, 2016), 105–12. David Pao argues for a syncretism within a Jewish framework (*Colossians & Philemon*, ZECNT [Grand Rapids: Zondervan, 2012], 25–310).

in verses 3 ("thank") and 12 ("giving . . . thanks"). Paul is thankful for the Colossians' "faith in Christ Jesus" and "love you have for all God's people" (v. 4)—the combination of the two being a frequent emphasis in Paul, for whom true faith always produces love for others. Almost as common, of course, is the mention of "hope," which here Paul unusually introduces as the basis for faith and love (v. 5).[13] Paul therefore stresses the security that Christ provides, a point he accentuates by asserting that this hope is "stored up for you in heaven." While not yet something the Colossians have experienced, their ultimate salvation already exists, "reserved" for them in heaven.

Introducing a theme that will be important in the letter, Paul now reminds the Colossians that they first heard about the hope stored up in heaven for them through "the true message of the gospel" (v. 5) or, perhaps better, "the message that is [or contains, or reveals] the truth, the message, that is, of the gospel" (*tō logō tēs alētheias tou euangeliou*, a typically Pauline genitive chain). Even as thanksgiving frames verses 3–14, so this focus on the hope that the proclamation of the gospel has brought to the Colossians frames the larger section of verses 3–23 (see v. 23: "the hope held out in the gospel"). In verse 6 Paul further describes the Colossians' experience of the gospel, reflecting on the circumstances in which they first heard it (vv. 7–8) and on its power to transform people not only among the Colossians but also in "the whole world" (v. 6). This last point is the center of verses 3–8. The gospel has come to the Colossians just as it has to other people, and the gospel is transforming people and communities in Colossae just as it has in other parts of the world. The false teachers have urged the Colossians to look beyond the gospel to find true fulfillment; Paul responds by insisting that the gospel has the power to satisfy every spiritual need.

The language "bearing fruit and growing" is applied to the gospel itself in verse 6 and to the Colossians in verse 10. These two verbs remind us of the Genesis creation story, where God commands human beings to "be fruitful and increase in number" (Gen 1:28; see also 1:22). The mandate is reiterated after the flood (Gen 8:17; 9:1, 7), and similar language is also found in God's promises to Abraham and the patriarchs (e.g., Gen 17:20; 28:3; 35:11). A preliminary fulfillment of this "increase" comes as the nation of Israel flourishes in Egypt and, later, in the promised land (Exod 1:7; Lev 26:9). After the dispersal of Israel in the exile, the formula appears again in God's promises to regather his people (Jer 3:16; 23:3). Paul, then, suggests that the ultimate fulfillment of this "bearing fruit and growing" comes in the worldwide transformation of people into

13. "Because of the hope" (*dia tēn elpida*) probably grounds the faith and love (e.g., J. B. Lightfoot, *Saint Paul's Epistles to the Colossians and to Philemon* [London: MacMillan, 1897; repr., Grand Rapids: Zondervan, 1971]), 134; Petr Pokorný, *Colossians: A Commentary* [Peabody, MA: Hendrickson, 1991], 40) rather than being dependent on "give thanks" (T. K. Abbott, *A Critical and Exegetical Commentary on the Epistles to the Ephesians and to the Colossians*, ICC [Edinburgh: T&T Clark, 1897], 196; Charles Masson, *L'Épître de Saint Paul aux Philippiens; L'Épître de Saint Paul aux Colossiens*, CNT 10 [Neuchâtel: Delachaux & Niestle, 1950], 91) or generally what has been said in vv. 3–4 (Lohse, *Colossians and Philemon*, 17).

the image of God by means of their incorporation into Christ, *the* "image of God."[14] In a letter that calls on believers to distinguish the "true" gospel from the false, it is not surprising to find also an emphasis on knowledge: "We continually ask God to fill you with the knowledge of his will through all the wisdom and understanding that the Spirit gives" (v. 9). In a typical connection, Paul notes that right thinking will lead to right living: "So that you may live a life worthy of the Lord and please him in every way" (v. 10). Such a life is empowered by God—"strengthened with all power" (v. 11)—and characterized by joyful dependence on God—"giving joyful thanks to the Father" (v. 12).

Paul's thanks for the Colossians' growth and prayer for their continual advance in the gospel is rooted in God's work for them (vv. 12b–14). The Colossians by God's grace "share in the inheritance" (*tēn merida tou klērou*), language that alludes to the Old Testament promise of land to Israel (e.g., Deut 10:9). In a move typical of the New Testament "christifying" of the Old Testament "land" theme,[15] Paul applies this language to the spiritual privilege enjoyed by God's new-covenant people. Verse 13 elaborates verse 12b. The inheritance believers enjoy is the product of a rescue and transfer (vv. 13–14). The combination of words—"rescue" (*rhyomai*), "redemption" (*apolytrōsis*), and "inheritance" (*klēros*)—alludes to the foundational salvific event of the exodus (see esp. Exod 6:6–8). However, the language may allude even more clearly to the deliverance Israel experienced when God brought his people back from exile.[16] The true and ultimate rescue from exile comes not in (physical) return to the land but in (spiritual) redemption from sin through Christ.[17]

The rescue culminates in a transfer: from "the dominion of darkness" into "the kingdom of the Son he loves" (v. 13). "Kingdom" language is, of course, ubiquitous in the Gospels, but Paul uses it more rarely (only fourteen times). While some scholars think that the kingdom in Paul is basically future, in fact he uses it both to describe the future kingdom (1 Cor 6:9, 10; 15:50; Gal 5:21) and the present, inaugurated rule of God (Rom 14:17; 1 Cor 4:20, 15:24; 1 Thess 2:12 is unclear).

The mention of the "Son" in verse 13 opens the way for verses 15–20, one of the christological high points of the New Testament. As G. H. P. Thompson has put it, "One of the distinctive contributions—if not the distinctive contribution—of

14. See especially Beetham, *Echoes of Scripture*, 51–74; Beale, *Temple and the Church's Mission*, 263–67; Wright, *Colossians and Philemon*, 53–54.

15. See esp. W. D. Davies, *The Gospel and the Land: Early Christianity and Jewish Territorial Doctrine* (Berkeley, CA: University of California Press, 1974).

16. Psalm 107 [106 LXX] celebrates this "redemption" (*lytroō* occurs twice in v. 2; cf. *apolytrōsis* in Col 1:14), using the language of "rescue" (*rhyomai*; vv. 6, 20) and speaking of the way the Lord

brought the exiles "out of darkness, the utter darkness" (v. 14). Isaiah, who had so much influence on Paul, often depicts the exile as a "redemption" and uses "darkness" to describe the exilic condition and "light" the new state into which the Lord brings his people (e.g., 42:7, 16; 49:9).

17. N. T. Wright has especially emphasized this "ultimate return from exile" motif in the NT (e.g., *New Testament and the People of God*, 268–71, passim).

Colossians is its comprehensive vision of reality with the focal point of Christology."[18] The passage stands out from its surrounding context by virtue of both vocabulary and syntax, justifying the usual view that Paul is probably quoting a preformed "hymn" or "creed."[19] The Christology serves the greater purpose of the letter by setting forth Christ as the exclusive instrument through whom God created the universe (vv. 15–17) and through whom he is in the process of pacifying the universe (vv. 18–20). The word *pas* (variously translated "all," "every," "each"), occurring eight times in these verses, is the thread that binds the verses together. Whatever precise form the false teaching at Colossae took, it is at least clear that it was tending to question Christ's exclusive role in providing spiritual growth and security and, thereby, his exclusive role in the universe at large (see, e.g., 2:9–10, 19). The false teachers may have been basing their view of spirituality on cosmology. Christians needed to pay attention to the "powers" because one could achieve spiritual fullness only by taking them all into account (see esp. Paul's counterargument in 2:14–15). The hymn therefore makes mention of the powers in terms of both Christ's work in creation (v. 16) and redemption (v. 20). At the same time, the high Christology of verses 15–20 is not only negative, contesting the false teaching. It also has a positive purpose, as Paul argues that our "rescue" from the "dominion of darkness" (v. 13) is certain and lasting because God accomplished it through none other than the one who is Lord of the universe. As a christological high point here, then, Paul uses language that associates Christ intimately with God the Father himself. As Richard Bauckham has put it, "What the passage does is to include Jesus Christ in God's unique relationship to the whole of created reality and thereby to include Jesus in the unique identity of God as Jewish monotheism understood it."[20]

Several ways of structuring the "hymn" are proposed. But perhaps the best is to identify two main stanzas (vv. 15–16, vv. 18b–20), with a transitional stanza between the two (vv. 17–18a).[21]

18. G. H. P. Thompson, *The Letters of Paul to the Ephesians, to the Colossians, and to Philemon*, CBC (Cambridge: Cambridge University Press, 1967), 155.

19. The traditional character of the passage was first extensively argued by Eduard Norden, *Agnostos Theos: Untersuchungen zur Formengeschichte religiöser Rede*, 4th ed. (Darmstadt: Wissenschaftliche Buchgesellschaft, 1956), 250–54. For a thorough analysis of the passage, with consideration of various hypotheses, see esp. Hans Jakob Gabathuler, *Jesus Christus: Haupt der Kirche, Haupt der Welt—Der Christushymnus Colosser 1,15–20 in der theologischen Forschung der letzten 130 Jahre*, ATANT 45 (Zurich: Zwingli, 1965); Christoph Burger, *Schöpfung und Versöhnung: Studien zum Liturgischen Gut im Kolosser- und Epheserbrief*, WMANT 46 (Neukirchener-Vluyn: Neukirchener, 1975), 3–53; Jean-Noël Aletti, *Colossiens 1,15–20: Genre et Exégèse du texte—function de la thématique sapientielle*, AnBib 91 (Rome: Pontifical Biblical Institute, 1981); and esp. Christian Stettler, *Der Kolosserhymnus: Untersuchungen zu Form, traditionsgeschichtlichen Hintergrund und Aussage von Kol 1,15–20*, WUNT 2/131 (Tübingen: Mohr Siebeck, 2000). It should be noted that some scholars are not convinced that Paul quotes a preexisting hymn, arguing that Paul himself may have composed it. See, e.g., Steven M. Baugh, "The Poetic Form of Col 1:15–20," *WTJ* 47 (1985): 228; O'Brien, *Colossians, Philemon*, 40–42; Moule, *Colossians and Philemon*, 60–62; Barth and Blanke, *Colossians*, 234–36; G. K. Beale, *Colossians and Philemon*, BECNT (Grand Rapids: Baker Academic, 2019), 78.

20. Richard Bauckham, "Where Is Wisdom to Be Found? Colossians 1.15–20 (2)," in *Reading Texts, Seeking Wisdom: Scripture and Theology*, ed. David F. Ford and Graham Stanton (Grand Rapids: Eerdmans, 2003), 133.

21. This is the general preference among recent interpreters. See, e.g., Luis Carlos Reyes, "The Structure and Rhetoric

Paul begins by claiming that the Son is "the image of the invisible God." In both texts where Paul asserts this about Christ (here and in 2 Cor 4:4), the focus is on Christ's revelation of God. Paul may here be alluding to Jewish tradition that associated the "image of God" with God's "wisdom" or "word." In contrast to this tradition, Paul claims that the original image is found in God's Son.[22] Christ is also "the firstborn over all creation." The word *prōtotokos* ("firstborn"), can, of course, have a temporal sense, but it also can have the sense of preeminince. Using the word in this sense, the Old Testament proclaims that Israel is God's "firstborn" (Exod 4:22) and says of David in Psalm 89:27 that "I will appoint him to be my firstborn, the most exalted of the kings of the earth." This latter text is probably especially important for Colossians 1:15, since Psalm 89 rings with messianic allusions, and Paul has just been describing Christ in messianic/kingly terms (vv. 12–14). The NIV "firstborn *over* all creation" (*prōtotokos pasēs ktiseōs*) captures this sense.

In verse 16, Christ's supreme role in creation is cited as evidence ("for," *hoti*) that he does, indeed, have this supremacy over creation. Paul stresses the extent of this supremacy by citing three specific ways in which Christ and the creation are related: "in [*en*] him all things were created," "all things have been created through [*dia*] him," and "[all things were created] for [*eis*] him." The sequence of these three prepositions is echoed in the second main strophe of the hymn (vv. 19–20a). Christ's role in creation probably again alludes to the widespread teaching about God's "wisdom" or "word." Note, for example, Psalm 104:24: "How many are your works, Lord! In wisdom have you made them all; the earth is full of your creatures"; Proverbs 3:19: "By wisdom the Lord laid the earth's foundations"; Wisdom 9:1–2: "O God of my ancestors and Lord of mercy, who have made all things by your word, and by your wisdom have formed humankind to have dominion over the creatures you have made" (NRSV); and see Wisdom 8:5, which states that "wisdom" is "the active cause of all things" (NRSV).

Verses 17–18a, I have suggested, are an intermediary strophe between the two main strophes of the "hymn." This strophe is framed by "and he is" (my translation; *kai autos estin*). The first line of this strophe makes explicit the preexistence of Christ (taking *pro* in a temporal sense: "before"), the second asserts Christ's significance in holding the universe together, while the third proclaims Christ to be the "head of the body, the church." As the opening line of the strophe points back to the first strophe, so this third line points forward to the strophe that follows. The description of the church

---

of Colossians 1:15–20," *Filologia neotestamentaria* 12 (1999): 140–46; Bruce, *Colossians, Philemon, and Ephesians*, 55–56. Somewhat related to this three-stanza structure is the proposal of N. T. Wright, who finds four parts, chiastically arranged (vv. 15–16, v. 17, v. 18a, vv. 18b–20; see "Poetry and Theology in Colossians 1.15–20," in Wright, *Climax of the Covenant*, 101).

22. For an emphasis on the Genesis 1 "image of God" background here, see Sean M. McDonough, *Christ as Creator: Origins of a New Testament Doctrine* (Oxford: Oxford University Press, 2009), 176–83.

as "the body" picks up a metaphor particularly important in Colossians (1:24; 2:19; 3:15) and Ephesians (1:23; 4:4, 12, 16; 5:23, 30). The word *ekklēsia* refers here to the "universal church," embracing all who acknowledge Christ as Lord. But our passage takes a further step in the evolution of the metaphor. Christ is not pictured as the body *per se* but as the "head" (*kephalē*) of the body (cf. also 2:10, 19; Eph 1:22; 4:15; 5:23). In the ancient world, the head was conceived to be the governing member of the body, that which both controlled it and provided for its life and sustenance.[23]

With the second line of verse 18, we move into the second main strophe (anticipated in v. 18a), which elaborates Christ's preeminence in the new creation. This line echoes the first line of the first strophe—*hos estin*, "who is"—and uses again the key word "firstborn" (*prōtotokos*). Christ is the "beginning" or "founder" (*archē*: see Gen 49:3; Deut 21:17) of the church, a role his resurrection manifests. The resurrection of Christ is the first stage and guarantee of the expected resurrection of God's people in the last day (1 Cor 15:20; cf. Matt 27:52–53; Acts 26:23).

Verses 19–20 follow a syntactical pattern more typical of Paul's normal style and may signal that the "hymn" ends at verse 18 or that Paul has more radically modified a possible earlier hymn in these verses. The structure of this sentence is unclear, but perhaps it is best to follow the NRSV: "All the fullness was pleased to dwell . . . and to reconcile."[24] "*All* the fullness" reflects the exclusive emphasis that is the essence of Paul's response to the Colossian false teachers: *only* in Christ can "fullness" be found. Christ is not only supreme; he is all-sufficient. "Fullness" (*plērōma*), as Colossians 2:9 makes clear, means "fullness of God," or "God in his fullness." The claim that all the fullness "was pleased to dwell in him" probably echoes Old Testament descriptions of God "dwelling" in the temple (e.g., Ps 68:16). It was "through" this one who is the fullness that God works to "reconcile to himself all things" (v. 20). What is the nature of this reconciliation? When Paul uses "reconcile"/"reconciliation" language elsewhere (v. 22; Rom 5:10, 11; 11:15; 1 Cor 7:11; 2 Cor 5:18, 19, 20; Eph 2:16), he refers to the restoration of fellowship between God and sinners. Some therefore argue that the reconciliation in this verse is restricted to human beings who respond to the invitation to be reconciled—an interpretation that verses 21–22 could reinforce.[25] But the context makes any limitation on the scope of reconciliation very problematic. The "all things" (*panta*) of verse 20 occurs five other times in the context, and in each case the referent

---

23. See especially Clinton E. Arnold, "Jesus Christ: 'Head' of the Church (Colossians and Ephesians)," in *Jesus of Nazareth, Lord and Christ: Essays on the Historical Jesus and New Testament Christology*, ed. Joel B. Green and Max Turner (Grand Rapids: Eerdmans, 1994), 350–55. See, e.g., Philo, *Rewards* 125: "The virtuous one, whether single man or people, will be the head [*kephalē*] of the human race and all the others will be like the parts of the body which are animated by the powers in and above the head."

24. Most commentators prefer this option; see esp. Moule, *Colossians and Philemon*, 70–71; O'Brien, *Colossians, Philemon*, 51.

25. I. Howard Marshall, "The Meaning of 'Reconciliation'," in *Unity and Diversity in New Testament Theology: Essays in Honor of George E. Ladd*, ed. Robert A. Guelich (Grand Rapids: Eerdmans, 1978), 126–27.

is the created universe. Paul goes out of his way in this context to confirm the universal extent of the word by unpacking "all things" to mean "things on earth or things in heaven." An important clue to the meaning of this universal reconciliation is provided in the follow-up participial clause, "by making peace through his blood, shed on the cross." Paul here suggests that Christ's work of reconciliation fulfills the Old Testament expectation that in the last days God would establish universal *shalom*, "peace," or "well-being."[26] The Old Testament suggests that the wider creation in general suffers from the effects of humanity's fall into sin and is in need of restoration. Paul picks up this point in Romans 8:19–22. In a manner typical of New Testament fulfillment, then, Paul proclaims that this peace has now been established in Christ. Colossians 1:20 teaches, then, not "cosmic salvation" or even "cosmic redemption" but "cosmic restoration" or "renewal."[27] Through the work of Christ on the cross, God has brought his entire rebellious creation back under the rule of his sovereign power. Of course, this "peace," while initially offered to believers and to the community to which they belong, awaits its culmination in a future act of God. However, God's people should now be striving to manifest this shalom won at the cross in our relationships with one another and in our relationships with the created world itself.

Paul rounds off this first stage of his letter body by returning to themes he touched on earlier: the Colossians' reception of the gospel (v. 23; cf. 1:3–8) and their transfer from one spiritual realm to another (vv. 21–22; cf. 1:12–14). At the heart of this paragraph is a favorite literary device of Paul's—a contrast between "once" and "now." "Once" the Colossians were estranged from God because of their evil thoughts and deeds (v. 21). "But now" they are reconciled to God through Christ's death and with the hope of being presented before God as blameless (v. 22). Reconciliation here has its usual Pauline theological reference to the new saving relationship sinners can enjoy with God through Christ—a particularly important instantiation of the broader work of reconciliation Paul refers to in verse 20. The Colossians' hope of being found blameless before God is contingent on their continuing in the faith, as Paul adds in a concluding warning statement (v. 23). Here he alludes to his central concern in the letter: to keep the Colossians on the good spiritual track they have started on and to prevent their succumbing to the false teaching.

1.2 The Mystery of Christ in Paul's Ministry and Christian Experience (1:24–2:5)

These verses are dominated by the first-person singular (1:24–25, 29; 2:1, 4–5; the shift to the first-person plural in 1:28 is probably just a stylistic variation). Paul reflects

---

26. See esp. Isa 52:6–10; and also, inter alios, Isa 9:7; 26:3, 12; 27:5; 52:7; 55:12; 66:12; Jer 29:11; 30:10; 33:6, 9; 46:27; Ezek 34:29; 37:26; Mic 5:5; Hag 2:9; Zech 9:10. See, e.g., Pokorný, *Colossians*, 89; Arnold, *Colossian Syncretism*, 265–69.

27. For this view, often called "pacification," see, e.g., Bruce, *Colossians, Philemon, and Ephesians*, 74–76; O'Brien, *Colossians, Philemon*, 52–57; Aletti, *Colossiens 1,15–20*, 112–13; Arnold, *Colossian Syncretism*, 269.

on his ministry and its significance for the Colossians, elaborating his brief reference to himself as a "servant" of the gospel at the end of verse 23. I draw attention to four themes in particular. First, Paul characterizes his message in terms of "mystery" (*mystērion*; 1:26, 27; 2:2). This language is particularly prominent in Ephesians and Colossians, where ten of the twenty-one Pauline occurrences are found (in Colossians, see also 4:3). While scholars in past years sometimes thought that Paul picked up the word from the Hellenistic "mystery" religions, most now agree that it is the Old Testament and Judaism (especially Qumran) that provide the background. The occurrences of the word in Daniel 2 (translating Aramaic *raz*) are especially interesting, where it refers to the "mystery" of King Nebuchadnezzar's dream—a mystery that God reveals to Daniel. Paul, like Daniel, is also the recipient of divine revelation, as God makes known to him the "mystery" of the nature and extent of the benefits that are available in Christ.[28] The christological focus of Colossians is seen here again, as Paul defines this mystery as "Christ in you" (1:27; cf. "Christ" in 2:2). A second significant theme in these verses is the suffering (1:24) and struggle (1:29; 2:1) that accompany Paul's proclamation of the gospel.[29] The example of Paul's sacrificial ministry should stimulate the Colossians to "stay the course" in the face of temptations to pursue other routes to spiritual fulfillment. Finally, third, we see here again in these verses an emphasis on the theme of "knowledge" (cf. 1:9): "make known" (v. 27); "wisdom" (v. 28); "complete understanding" (2:2); "know" (2:2); "wisdom" (2:3); "knowledge" (2:3). It is possible that this language is also a thrust against the false teachers, who may have been claiming to be purveyors of esoteric knowledge. Once again, Paul responds with a christological emphasis: "*All* the treasures of wisdom and knowledge" are found in Christ (2:3). This last reference alludes to the fourth key theme in this section: the universality of the gospel and the exclusiveness of Christ. Paul preaches the word "in its *fullness*" (1:25); he proclaims Christ with "*all* wisdom," seeking to present "*everyone*" mature in Christ (1:28); he strives for "*all* who have not met me personally" (2:1), hoping that they would have "the *full* riches of *complete* understanding" (2:2). In Christ, and nowhere else, is available the "fullness."[30]

---

28. For the background of the word, see esp. Raymond E. Brown, *The Semitic Background of the Term "Mystery" in the New Testament* (Philadelphia: Fortress, 1968); on Paul's use, Markus N. A. Bockmuehl, *Revelation and Mystery in Ancient Judaism and Pauline Christianity*, WUNT 2/36 (Tübingen: Mohr Siebeck, 1990); Carson, "Mystery and Fulfillment," 390–436.

29. Paul's "filling up" of Christ's sufferings in v. 24 may refer to the widespread idea of "messianic woes," tribulation associated with Messiah's coming (see esp. O'Brien, *Colossians, Philemon*, 79–80). However, it might be better to see here an allusion to Paul's special eschatological significance as the one who is

proclaiming the "mystery" (see esp. B. Clark, *Completing Christ's Afflictions*; and also, e.g., Masson, *Philippiens, Colossiens*, 110–11; Richard Bauckham, "Colossians 1:24 Again: The Apocalyptic Motif," *EvQ* 47 [1975]: 168–70; Hanna Stettler, "An Interpretation of Colossians 1:24 in the Framework of Paul's Mission Theology," in *Mission of the Early Church to Jews and Gentiles*, ed. Jostein Adna and Hans Kvalbein, WUNT 2/127 [Tübingen: Mohr Siebeck, 2000], 192–208).

30. Johannes Lähnemann, *Der Kolosserbrief: Komposition, Situation und Argumentation*, SNT 3 (Gütersloh: Gütersloher, 1971), 45–46.

2 THE LETTER BODY: "CONTINUE TO LIVE YOUR LIVES IN HIM" (2:6–4:6)

I acknowledge that it would be very unusual for an ancient letter-writer to delay for so long getting to the body of the letter, and I would not want to argue too strongly for this literary structure. Yet it also seems to me that it is with 2:6 that Paul turns to his central concern in the letter: exhorting the Colossian Christians to continue on the good spiritual path they have been walking along ever since Epaphras brought the gospel to them. Chapter 2:6–7, then, states the overarching point of the whole letter body. Negatively, the need to "continue to live your lives in him" means that the Colossians need to reject the false teachers and their message (2:8–23). Positively, the Colossians need to continue their spiritual journey by adopting a thoroughly Christian mindset and pattern of living (3:1–4:6).

2.1 Fullness in Christ (2:6–23)

As verse 6a—"just as you received Christ Jesus as Lord"—summarizes Paul's basic point in the letter opening, so 6b summarizes what follows in the letter body: "Continue to live your lives in him." As the Colossians have begun, so they must continue, looking to Christ and Christ alone for all their spiritual needs. The imperative in verse 6b (which could also be translated "walk [*peripateite*] in him") is elaborated in a series of four participles in verse 7. Interestingly, the series climaxes with "overflowing with thankfulness," a note that plays a surprisingly prominent role in Colossians.[31]

The first step in Paul's strategy of weaning the Colossians away from the false teachers is to encourage positive growth in Christ (vv. 6–7). But, as verses 8–23 reveal, Paul recognizes that specific warnings about this teaching are also needed. Three roughly parallel warnings shape this section:

v. 8: "See to it that no one takes you captive through hollow and deceptive philosophy"
v. 16: "Therefore do not let anyone judge you"
v. 18: "Do not let anyone who delights in false humility and the worship of angels disqualify you"

The "hollow and deceptive philosophy" Paul warns about in verse 8 refers to the false teaching and other such deviations from Christian truth. The issue is that it "depends

---

31. David W. Pao, *Thanksgiving: An Investigation of a Pauline Theme*, NSBT 13 (Downers Grove, IL: InterVarsity Press, 2002), 89–90.

on human tradition and the elemental spiritual forces of this world." "Elemental spiritual forces" (NIV) translates a phrase whose meaning is debated (*ta stoicheia tou kosmou*; see also v. 20; Gal 4:3, 9). The NIV appears to adopt one popular view: that the phrase refers to spiritual powers.[32] Others, however, think the phrase might refer to "elementary teachings" (*stoicheia* has this sense in Heb 5:12; see, e.g., KJV, NASB)[33] or to the "elements" or basic components of the universe (see 2 Pet 3:10, 12). This last meaning fits the lexical data best, and makes good sense in this context. The false teachers were apparently fixated on material issues (see, e.g., 2:16, 21), and the material elements of the world were often associated with pagan gods and false worship.[34] But the root issue is christological; the teaching does not depend "on Christ."

This christological focus, so typical of Colossians, continues in verses 9–15. "In" Christ occurs three times and "with" Christ three times (see also "circumcision of Christ" [ESV] in v. 11). With a beautiful play on words, Paul in verses 9–10 gets to the heart of this matter: "*In Christ* all the *fullness* of Deity lives in bodily form" and "*in Christ* you have been brought to *fullness*." Verses 11–15 describe how believers have come to experience this complete spiritual fullness in Christ. First, in what is perhaps a polemical thrust at the false teachers (who may have been advocating circumcision), Paul insists that believers have already experienced the most important circumcision: one "not performed with human hands"—that is, one that is heavenly or divine (v. 11). What is this circumcision? At the end of the verse, Paul refers to "the circumcision of Christ" (see ESV; *tē peritomē tou Christou*). This is sometimes taken to refer to Christ's own circumcision, when he stripped off his body of flesh (a possessive or objective genitive).[35] But it more likely refers to the stripping off of the disastrous power of our own flesh, an act accomplished by Christ: "In the circumcision accomplished by Christ" (subjective genitive).[36]

---

32. See, e.g., Percy, *Kolosser- und Epheserbriefe*, 156–67; Harris, *Colossians and Philemon*, 93; O'Brien, *Colossians, Philemon*, 129–32.

33. Lightfoot, *Colossians and Philemon*, 180; Moule, *Colossians and Philemon*, 90–92; Marianne Meye Thompson, *Colossians, and Philemon*, Two Horizons New Testament Commentary (Grand Rapids: Eerdmans, 2005), 53; Sappington, *Revelation and Redemption*, 164–70.

34. For this view in general, see esp. Michael Wolter, *Der Brief an die Kolosser. Der Brief an Philemon*, ÖTK 12 (Gütersloh: Gerd Mohn, 1993), 122–24; Ulrich Luz, "Der Brief an die Kolosser," in Jürgen Becker and Ulrich Luz, *Die Briefe an die Galater, Epheser, und Kolosser*, NTD 8.1 (Göttingen: Vandenhoeck & Ruprecht, 1998), 220; Margaret Y. MacDonald, *Colossians and Ephesians*, SP 17 (Collegeville: Liturgical, 2000), 97–98; Joseph Blinzler, "Lexikalisches zu dem τὰ στοιχεῖα τοῦ κόσμου bei Paulus," in *Studiorum Paulinorum Congressus Internationalis Catholicus 1961*,

2 vols., AnBib 17–18 (Rome: Pontifical Biblical Institute, 1963), 2:429–43; Rusam, "Neue Belege zu den *Stoicheia tou Kosmou*," 119–25.

35. E.g., O'Brien, *Colossians, Philemon*, 117–18; Beale, *Colossians and Philemon*, 189; James D. G. Dunn, *The Epistles to the Colossians and to Philemon*, NIGTC (Grand Rapids: Eerdmans, 1996), 157–58; Robert McL. Wilson, *A Critical and Exegetical Commentary on Colossians and Philemon*, ICC (Edinburgh: T&T Clark, 2005), 201–4; Robert C. Tannehill, *Dying and Rising With Christ: A Study in Pauline Theology*, BZNW 32 (Berlin: Töpelmann, 1966), 49–50; Beasley-Murray, *Baptism in the New Testament*, 152–53; Robert H. Gundry, *Sōma in Biblical Theology: With Special Emphasis on Pauline Anthropology*, SNTSMS 29 (Cambridge: Cambridge University Press, 1976), 41–42.

36. Lightfoot, *Colossians and Philemon*, 183–84; Harris, *Colossians and Philemon*, 102–3; Arnold, *Colossian Syncretism*, 296–97.

As Paul does elsewhere, he grounds our new spiritual status in our participation with Christ in the foundational redemptive events. Jesus's death, burial, and resurrection are the heart of the gospel (1 Cor 15:1–3), and believers participated in those events (see Rom 6:3–10). Here Paul focuses on burial "with him" and our being "raised with him" (Col 2:12). Our dying with Christ, while not explicitly mentioned, is probably implied in verse 11. Unlike Romans 6, where resurrection with Christ is (probably) future, it is here a past experience: we *were . . . raised with [Christ]*" (*synēgerthēte*, an aorist). It is common to claim that this present resurrection status is a departure from the "authentic Paul," but in fact the notion is clearly hinted at already in Romans 6. As he does in this passage, Paul ties our participation with Christ to baptism—probably in the sense that water baptism can represent, synecdochically, the entire conversion experience (see pp. 220–23 on Rom 6; and pp. 588–90).

In verse 13, Paul starts again, fleshing out further the way in which we experience "fullness" in Christ: we are "made . . . alive," and our sins are forgiven. Our sins, Paul implies in verse 14, have created a state of "indebtedness," resulting from our failure to obey God's law (the "decrees," *tois dogmasin*).[37] God has completely overcome this indebtedness by means of Christ's sacrifice on the cross. Finally, returning to a key issue in the false teaching, Paul celebrates the victory of Christ over spiritual powers (v. 15). Indeed, alluding to the Roman custom of the triumphal procession, in which victorious generals paraded their captives behind them, these powers have been publicly humiliated (see also 2 Cor 2:14 and my notes on that verse). Especially if the antecedent of the pronoun (*autō*) at the end of this verse is "the cross" (e.g., NIV; NRSV), this verse provides key support to the idea of the cross as involving a triumph over evil powers.[38]

The false teaching can be successfully defeated when believers appreciate fully all they are given in Christ. Why look elsewhere when one is already "filled" (vv. 8–15)? However, it is also necessary to be more specific about the weaknesses and deviations of the false teaching. Paul turns to this negative focus in verses 16–23.

The false teachers were apparently insisting on the avoidance of certain foods and the observance of certain religious days. The Colossians are not to worry about the false teachers trying to judge them about such matters, for they are only a shadow of the reality that we have in Christ (vv. 16–17). The false teachers are also, apparently, claiming a superior spiritual experience and "disqualifying" the Colossians for falling short on this matter. Just what was involved in the false teachers' "worship of angels" (v. 18) is unclear. The interpretation of this phrase is an important influence on identifying this teaching. The phrase might indicate that the false teachers were,

37. For the identification of "the decrees" with the law of Moses, see, e.g., Luz, "Der Brief an die Kolosser," 223. See the parallel in Eph 2:15.

38. Other translations think the antecedent might be "Christ" (see, e.g., O'Brien, *Colossians, Philemon*, 128).

via their visions, engaging in the worship that the angels are offering to God (subjective genitive).[39] However, it is perhaps more likely that the reference is to "worship offered to angels" (objective genitive; see "Isolating the Issues" above).[40] In any case, the false teachers are engaging in some kind of mystical experience, leading them to be arrogant ("puffed up"). The central problem, again, is the failure to grasp the utter sufficiency of Christ. He is the "head" from which, and only from which, true spiritual nourishment proceeds (v. 19). Following rules and getting hung up on visions, Paul suggests, involves engagement with the "[material] elements of the world," from which believers with Christ have been decisively separated (v. 20). These kinds of rules are not derived from Christ but reflect a narrowly human orientation (vv. 21–22). They cannot provide for true spiritual progress (v. 23).

2.2 Living a Christocentric Life (3:1–4:1)

Paul's negative focus in 2:16–23 turns back here to the positive (see 2:9–15). He urges the Colossians to live by a new mindset focused on Christ (3:1–4), a mindset that will mean "putting off" certain attitudes and actions (3:5–11), "putting on" others (3:12–17), and living in our households with God-pleasing conduct (3:18–4:1).

The opening and basic exhortation picks up the christological connection that is fundamental to 2:9–15. Christians are people who have been "raised with Christ" (3:1; see 2:12), who have "died" (v. 3), and who will one day "appear with him in glory" (v. 4). In the meantime, our lives are "hidden with Christ in God" (v. 3). Our thinking or mindset (*phroneō*, v. 2) is to reflect our fundamental heavenly identity. We are to "seek the things above" (*ta anō zēteite*, my translation). As Lincoln puts it, Paul

> by no means completely disparages his readers' concern with the heavenly realm. Instead, he attempts to redirect it. In the process it emerges that two antithetical positions about participation in the heavenly realm are in confrontation. The philosophy's advocates take the earthly situation as their starting point, from which by their own efforts and techniques they will move beyond the body, gain visionary experience, and ascend into heavenly spheres. The writer moves in the reverse direction, seeing the starting point and source of the believer's life in the resurrected Christ in heaven, from there it works itself out in earthly life.[41]

This heavenly mindset means that we must turn away from certain kinds of behavior. Verses 5–11 feature two parallel exhortations, "put to death" (v. 5) and "rid

---

39. See esp. Francis, "Humility and Angelic Worship"; and also O'Brien, *Colossians, Philemon*, 142–43; Dunn, *Colossians*, 180–81; Sappington, *Revelation and Redemption*, 158–59; Craig A. Evans, "The Colossian Mystics," *Bib* 63 (1982): 197–201.

40. Harris, *Colossians and Philemon*, 121; Wolter, *Der Brief an die Kolosser*, 146; Beale, *Colossians and Philemon*, 226.

41. Andrew T. Lincoln, "The Letter to the Colossians," in *NIB* 11:638.

yourselves of" (v. 8), each of which is followed by a general class of sins—"whatever belongs to your earthly nature" (v. 5), "all such things as these" (v. 8)—and by a list of five specific sins (v. 5b, v. 8b).[42] Such behavior, Paul warns, is leading to God's wrath (v. 6) and marks our past life apart from Christ (v. 7). These imperatives are embedded in a paragraph that opens (vv. 1–4) and closes (vv. 9b–11) with the "indicative." Actions such as those Paul lists in verses 8–9a are to be put off because we have exchanged the "old self" (*ton palaion anthrōpon*) for the "new self" (*ton neon [anthrōpon]*). By claiming that this "new self" or "new man" is characterized by having "no Gentile or Jew, circumcised or uncircumcised, barbarian, Scythian, slave or free" (v. 11), Paul makes clear he is referring not to a particular nature that the Christian possesses nor even to the Christian as such. Paul's "old man" versus "new man" contrast is rooted in his fundamental Adam/Second Adam theology. As Adam is the "old man," who governs existence in the old realm, so Christ is the "new man," who determines our status and should determine our behavior as Christians (see also Rom 6:6; Eph 2:15; 4:13, 22–24; and see also my notes on these passages and p. 492).[43] We have no evidence that the false teachers were trying to erect ethnic or sociological distinctions within the body of Christ. Paul's assertion that such distinctions are removed in Christ rather reflects his typical teaching about the nature of the new body created in Christ (see also 1 Cor 12:13; Gal 3:28).

As our heavenly mindset requires that we "put off" (*apothesthe*, v. 8) certain activities, so, positively, it also requires that we "put on" (*endysasthe*) others (v. 12; NIV: "clothe yourselves"). Echoing the earlier "vice" lists, Paul now lists five "virtues" that should mark Christian conduct (v. 12). He then singles out for special mention the importance of forgiving others (v. 13) and, as he often does, highlights the fundamental importance of love (v. 14). He is commending behavior that fosters Christian community, an idea that becomes explicit in verse 15. With this verse, the second-person plural imperatives of verses 12–14 give way to two parallel, third-person, passive imperatives: "Let the peace of Christ rule in your hearts" (v. 15) and "let the message of Christ dwell among you richly" (v. 16). I draw attention to the NIV translation "dwell *among* you." The Greek (*en hymin*) could also be translated "*in* [each one of] you." Each is legitimate, but the context favors a reference to the corporate experience of the community—a focus often neglected in Western churches plagued by individualism. Paul does not explicitly mention disunity as a problem in Colossae, but it may have been that debates over the claims of the false teachers were dividing the Colossians.

---

42. These lists of sins, which imitate a popular Hellenistic literary form, are often labeled "vice lists." See, e.g., A. Vögtle, *Die Tugend- und Lasterkataloge im Neuen Testament, exegetisch, religions- und formgeschichtlich untersucht*, NTAbh 16 (Münster: Aschendorff, 1936); and my discussion on p. 629.

43. On this text, see also Darrell L. Bock, "'The New Man' As Community in Colossians and Ephesians," in *Integrity of Heart, Skillfulness of Hands: Biblical and Leadership Studies in Honor of Donald K. Campbell*, ed. C. Dyer and R. B. Zuck (Grand Rapids: Baker, 1994), 158–60.

Paul's vision for the spiritual family in 3:1–17 is now met by his vision for the physical family in 3:18–4:1. Being "heavenly minded" does not mean neglecting our earthly relationships or our responsibilities to others within that family. Indeed, inclusion of this specific matter fits the tone of the letter as a whole. As John M. G. Barclay puts it, these rules for the "household" are "thus entirely consistent with the universalizing thrust of the letter as a whole, in which the tendrils of the Christ-event spread out, as it were, to cover the whole surface of life."[44] The "household" of Paul's day was typically formed in terms of three sets of relationships: husband and wife, parents and children, slaves and masters. A certain form, or set of instructions, had become standard in the world of Paul's day, and Christian authors adopted this form, often called a "household code," for use in Christian exhortation (see esp. Eph 5:21–6:9; also 1 Pet 2:18–3:7).[45] Paul issues similar instructions for these three pairs of relationships: one party—the wife, the children, the slaves—are to "submit" or "obey," while the other party—the husband, the parents (the probable translation of *pateres* here), and the masters—are to exhibit a love and concern rooted in the claims of Christ on us. The requirement that women submit to their husbands has especially drawn attention among contemporary Christians. Some think that this particular motif is an unfortunate carryover from the culture and seek in various ways to marginalize these passages. But they are better seen as a response to an unbalanced appropriation of the "all one in Christ" principle. This principle does not, in this world at least, obliterate distinctions (see my further discussion on pp. 629–36). Household codes in Paul's day were sometimes used to strictly maintain a hierarchical structure that would serve to undergird the stability of the state. But they were not always so used; and certainly, there is no reason to suspect that Paul's adaption of the code has any such larger purpose.[46] Indeed, Paul's requirement that husbands love their wives, that fathers not "embitter" their children, and that masters "provide your slaves with what is right and fair" reveals a reciprocal focus in household relationships that is distinctive to the New Testament. (I tackle the slavery issue on pp. 643–45; and see also my comments on Philemon.) God has instituted the family for our good in this life, and certain ways of relating to each other in that family are expected. For the Christian, however, family relationships are not simply a matter of accomodating to the culture. Rather, these relationships are to reflect our commitment to Christ—the lordship of Christ is mentioned no fewer than seven times in these nine verses.

---

44. John M. G. Barclay, "Ordinary but Different: Colossians and Hidden Moral Identity," *ABR* 49 (2001): 44.

45. See, e.g., Aristotle, *Politics* 1.2.1–23 and 1.5.1–12. And see David L. Balch, "Household Codes," in *Greco-Roman Literature and the New Testament: Selected Forms and Genres*, ed. David Aune (Atlanta: Scholars Press, 1988), 25–35, who also provides a useful overview of theories and scholars.

46. See Daniel K. Darko, *No Longer Living as the Gentiles: Differentiation and Shared Ethical Values in Ephesians 4:17–6:9*, LNTS 375 (London: T&T Clark, 2008).

2.3 Exhortation to Prayer and Christian Witness (4:2–6)

This brief paragraph brings to a close the letter body and at the same time concludes the general series of exhortations about the way the lordship of Christ is to be lived out in daily life (3:5–4:1). The movement of the paragraph is easy to follow: a general encouragement to pray (v. 2), leads to a request to pray for Paul's evangelistic ministry (vv. 3–4), and concludes with exhortations regarding the Colossians' evangelistic ministry (vv. 5–6). As is so often the case, Ephesians provides the closest parallel (Eph 6:18–20).

3 THE LETTER CLOSING: GREETINGS, PLANS, AND INSTRUCTIONS (4:7–18)

This letter closing is typical of Paul's letters, moving rapidly from one topic to another. I follow the NIV divisions, which feature five parts. In verses 7–9, the letter carriers are commended: Tychicus (see also Acts 20:4; Eph 6:21; 2 Tim 4:12; Titus 3:12) and Onesimus (see Philemon). Paul then conveys greetings from a series of people, including, interestingly, Mark and Luke, and conveys his own greetings to "Nympha and the church in her house" (vv. 10–15). The third part of the closing has a unique feature: the request that letters to two churches be exchanged (v. 16). The "letter to the Laodiceans" has occasionally been identified with a known Pauline letter,[47] but it is almost certainly a letter of Paul lost to us. The letter closing ends with an exhortation to Archippus, probably related to his ministry (v. 17), and a final "signature," with a brief prayer request and grace wish (v. 18).

---

47. E.g., John Knox thought it was the letter to Philemon (*Philemon among the Letters of Paul* [London: Collins, 1960], 38–40), while others identify it with Ephesians (e.g., Lightfoot, *Colossians and Philemon*, 244; Abbott, *Ephesians and Colossians*, 305–6; Wright, *Colossians and Philemon*, 160–61[?]).

Chapter 11

PHILEMON

LOCATING THE LETTER

This brief letter is addressed to "Philemon our dear friend and fellow worker—also to Apphia our sister and Archippus our fellow soldier—and to the church that meets in your home" (vv. 1a–2), although as the second-person singular address throughout indicates, Philemon is the primary recipient. The letter is closely tied to Colossians: Onesimus, the subject of this letter, lives in Colossae (see Col 4:9), many of the same individuals are mentioned in both letters (compare vv. 23–24 with Col 4:10–14), and Archippus is prominent in both (v. 2; cf. Col 4:17). This brief note to Philemon must have been written while Paul was in prison (see vv. 1, 9, 13) from the same place (Rome, I have argued) and at the same time (AD 60–61) as Colossians.

ISOLATING THE ISSUES

A single issue dominates the letter: the status and disposition of one of Philemon's slaves named Onesimus (v. 10). Onesimus has become a Christian through Paul (v. 10). He is very dear to Paul and has been useful to him in his imprisonment (vv. 10–13, 16). Onesimus has apparently wronged Philemon in some way (v. 18), but Paul nonetheless wants Philemon to welcome him back (v. 17) "no longer as a slave, but better than a slave" (v. 16). Paul is confident that Philemon will do as Paul asks, indeed "even more than I ask" (v. 21). The issue that Paul addresses is obviously a delicate one, and he avoids coming right out and saying what he wants Philemon to do. Contributing to our difficulty in understanding the letter is the fact that Philemon knows the situation, and so Paul feels no need to go into detail about it. All this means that interpreters struggle to pin down exactly what the issue might have been or what Paul wants Philemon to do about it. Two scenarios are the most likely.

First, Onesimus may have been a runaway slave. He has encountered Paul in Rome, Paul converts him, and Paul now feels duty-bound to send him back to his friend and fellow Christian, Philemon. Paul asks that Philemon receive him back, treat him well as a brother in Christ, and perhaps even give him his freedom. This is the traditional view.[1] The problems with this scenario are: (1) Paul never mentions any remorse on the part of Onesimus; and (2) it beggars belief to think that it would just happen that the runaway slave of a man Paul knows will encounter him in faraway Rome.

Thus, second, many interpreters have recently argued for an alternate scenario. Onesimus has deliberately sought out Paul to enlist the apostle's services as a mediator in a dispute between his master and himself.[2]

A decision between these options is difficult, but I slightly favor the former. I would have expected Paul to have been more explicit had there been a dispute between Philemon and Onesimus, and if Onesimus were a runaway slave, it would better explain Paul's sense of compulsion about sending him back.

ANALYZING THE ARGUMENT

This brief personal note contributes to the theology of Paul in two particular ways. First, Paul's desire that Philemon receive his slave Onesimus back as a brother in Christ has obvious implications for slavery. As is well known, the New Testament in general has little to say about social and institutional evil. Paul's focus, here and elsewhere, is on relations among believers rather than on believers' relations with social and political institutions. Paul's focus is on the relationship between Philemon and Onesimus. Whether this new relationship would transform Onesimus's existing "worldly" relationship to Philemon was not the most important thing. As M. M. Thompson puts it, "If a Christian owned a slave, the highest duty to which that master could be called was not to set the other free but to love the slave with the self-giving love of Christ."[3] Certainly this is the perspective found in the New Testament "household codes," which do not call on Christian masters to liberate their slaves but to treat them fairly and justly (Eph 6:9; Col 4:1; 1 Tim 6:2). There were, of course, good reasons for such caution. Slavery was deeply embedded in the Greco-Roman world, and the fledgling Christian movement was hardly in a position to launch a broadside against such an institution. However, it is also true, as Lightfoot has classically expressed it, that "a principle is boldly enunciated, which must in the end prove fatal to slavery."[4]

---

1. See, e.g., Lightfoot, *Colossians and Philemon*, 310–16; Garland, *Colossians and Philemon*, 294–300.

2. See esp. Peter Lampe, "Keine 'Sklavenflucht' des Onesimus," *ZNW* 76 (1985): 135–37; Brian M. Rapske, "The Prisoner Paul in the Eyes of Onesimus," *NTS* 37 (1991): 187–203; and also, e.g., Barclay, *Colossians and Philemon*, 98–102; Wolter, *Der Brief an die Kolosser. Der Brief an Philemon*, 227–35; Fitzmyer, *Philemon*, 17–23; Peter Arzt-Grabner, "Onesimus Erro: Zur Vorgeschichte des Philemonbriefes," *ZNW* 95 (2004): 131–43;

I. Howard Marshall, "The Theology of Philemon," in Donfried and Marshall, *Theology of the Shorter Pauline Letters*, 177–78 (hesitantly); Murphy-O'Connor, *Paul*, 176–78.

3. Thompson, *Colossians, and Philemon*, 266. See also James Tunstead Burtchaell, *Philemon's Problem: A Theology of Grace* (Grand Rapids: Eerdmans, 1998), 20–34.

4. Lightfoot, *Colossians and Philemon*, 325. This sentiment has been echoed again and again; see, e.g., Bruce, *Colossians, Philemon, and Ephesians*, 197–98 (Philemon creates "an atmosphere

I have hinted at the second theological contribution of Philemon: its practice-oriented vision of the requirements of Christian fellowship. N. T. Wright insists that this is the central theme of the letter.[5] The word "fellowship" (*koinōnia*) is featured in verse 6, where Paul lays the foundation for his appeal, and he picks it up in another form (*koinōnos*) as he transitions to his central appeal (v. 17; "partner" in NIV). In this letter, as Norman R. Peterson has especially emphasized, the existing social relationships among the three key figures—Paul, Philemon, and Onesimus—are reconfigured in light of the responsibilities of Christian fellowship.[6]

Verses 1–7 exhibit the usual elements of the beginning of Paul's letters: identification of author (v. 1a: Paul and Timothy), address (vv. 1b–2), a wish for grace and peace (v. 3), and a thanksgiving (vv. 4–7). The thanksgiving, as we would expect, focuses on Philemon. In chiastic order, Paul gives thanks for his love (v. 5a, v. 7) and faith (v. 5b, v. 6). As I noted above, Philemon's "fellowship based on, or produced by faith" (*hē koinōnia tēs pisteōs*; my own translation of a debated phrase) is a key moment in the letter.[7] Philemon's faith, Paul is suggesting, leads to a fellowship with other believers—including in this particular situation, Paul and Onesimus.

The letter body, in verses 8–20, elaborates the nature of this fellowship among the three. Paul "could be bold and order you to do what you ought to do" (v. 8) but prefers to appeal to him on the basis of the personal relationships bound up with Christian love. This includes Paul's relationship to Philemon (v. 19: he has been instrumental in his conversion); Paul's relationship to Onesimus ("my very heart," v. 12; see also vv. 10, 11, 13, 16); and Philemon's relationship to Onesimus (while "useless" in the past, he is now "useful" to both Paul and Philemon [v. 11]; and Onesimus is a "brother in the Lord" [v. 16]).

In the first part of this letter body (vv. 8–14), Paul focuses on these relationships, hinting at the circumstances that lie behind the letter. In the second part (vv. 15–16), Paul suggests that these circumstances might have been providential: "The reason he was separated from you for a little while" (v. 15). Onesimus's separation from Philemon

---

where it [slavery] could only wilt and die"); Moule, *Colossians and Philemon*, 11 (Paul "applies an explosive charge to the whole institution"); Murray J. Harris, *Slave of Christ: A New Testament Metaphor for Total Devotion to Christ*, NSBT 8 (Downers Grove, IL: InterVarsity Press, 1999), 59. There is debate over the degree of influence that Christianity had on the amelioration of slavery in the later Roman Empire (e.g., William Linn Westermann, *The Slave Systems of Greek and Roman Antiquity*, Memoirs of the American Philosophical Society 40 [Philadelphia: American Philosophical Society, 1955], 159–62). And it is also pointedly asked why, if the principle were so clear, it took so long for slavery to be eradicated (and against the arguments of some of the most biblically oriented Christians of the time; see Wayne A. Meeks,

"The 'Haustafeln' and American Slavery: A Hermeneutical Challenge," in *Theology and Ethics in Paul and His Interpreters: Essays in Honor of Victor Paul Furnish*, ed. Eugene H. Lovering Jr. and Jerry L. Sumney [Nashville: Abingdon, 1996], 249–50).

5. Wright, *Colossians and Philemon*, 170, 183–87.

6. Norman R. Peterson, *Rediscovering Paul: Philemon and the Sociology of Paul's Narrative World* (Philadelphia: Fortress, 1985); see also Wolter, *Der Brief an die Kolosser. Der Brief an Philemon*, 256–57.

7. I think this construal of the Greek is more likely than the alternative, as seen in the ESV: "The sharing of your faith" (giving *koinōnia* an active meaning and taking *tēs pisteōs* as an objective genitive).

has led to his conversion; Philemon may now have his slave back as a "dear brother." Finally (vv. 17–20), Paul explicitly tells Philemon what he wants him to do: "welcome" Onesimus back (v. 17).

Paul closes the letter with a final appeal to Philemon (v. 21) along with his usual information about travel plans (v. 22), greetings from fellow workers (vv. 23–24), and a grace benediction (v. 25).

Chapter 12

EPHESIANS

W HEN PEOPLE THINK of a letter that comes closest to a "pure" Pauline theology, they often point to Romans. However, as important as Romans is, its presentation of Paul's teaching is tied to the particular circumstances of the letter—as, of course, is the case with all of Paul's letters. The same principle applies to Ephesians. However, together with Romans, Ephesians is the letter of Paul that seems least tied to particular issues. It is for this reason that it has been called "the quintessence of Paulinism."[1] One of the striking aspects of this summary of Paul's teaching is its quite different tone and features from what we find in Romans. "Righteousness"/"justify" language occurs forty-nine times in Romans; three times in Ephesians. The law is mentioned sixty-seven times in Romans; once in Ephesians. The Old Testament is quoted around fifty times in Romans; twice in Ephesians. Moreover, the concept of the church, which appears only fleetingly in Romans, is central to Ephesians. These differences, of course, are often taken to indicate that a different author is at work. Nevertheless, I think Paul wrote Ephesians (see below). Moreover, differences in wording do not always indicate differences in concept; one can argue that 2:1–10 contains the concept of justification,[2] while the letter is peppered with Old Testament allusions. Nevertheless, these differences remind us of just how broad and complex Paul's theology is.

Ephesians is especially impressive for the broad canvas on which Paul paints. Paul locates the Christ event in the eternal plan of God and sets it in a cosmic context. God's eternal plan is that the entire cosmos should be summed up in Christ (1:10).[3] The "heavenly realms" (*epouranoi*) is a recurring word, linking together most of the key themes of the letter: our spiritual blessings are there (v. 3); Christ is "seated" there (v. 20); we are therefore "seated" there with him (2:6); the wisdom of God is made known to "rulers and authorities" there (3:10); we carry on our warfare there (6:12).[4]

---

1. Bruce, *Paul*, 424. As Bruce notes, the language was first used by A. S. Peake ("The Quintessence of Paulinism," *BJRL* 4 [1917–18]: 285–311).

2. E.g., Stuhlmacher, *Biblical Theology of the New Testament*, 444.

3. Some interpreters think this is the central theme of the letter (e.g., Peter T. O'Brien, *The Letter to the Ephesians*, PNTC [Grand Rapids: Eerdmans, 1999], 112–13; Max Turner, "Mission and Meaning in Terms of 'Unity' in Ephesians," in *Mission and Meaning: Essays Presented to Peter Cotterell*, ed. Antony Billington, Tony Lane, and Max Turner [Carlisle: Paternoster, 1995], 139–40).

4. The word also occurs in the NT in John 3:12; 1 Cor 15:40 [2x], 48 [2x], 49; Phil 2:10; 2 Tim 4:18; Heb 3:1; 6:4; 8:5; 9:23; 11:16; 12:22.

As Lincoln notes, it is in this letter that "the heavenly dimension is most pervasive."[5] The "heavenly realms" (*epouranioi*) are not equivalent to our usual use of "heaven," since evil spiritual powers are located in these heavenly realms (3:10) and our spiritual battle is being fought there (6:12). The word appears to denote broadly the spiritual realm—that realm where the truth about our world is fully and truly disclosed.[6] Some interpreters argue that this cosmic focus in Ephesians stands in contrast to Paul's typical salvation-historical perspective.[7] But Ephesians does not abandon salvation history for the sake of cosmology: "The cosmic horizon is set forth in Ephesians in terms of salvation history."[8] As in Colossians, the spiritual "powers" are again prominent, as they engage in battle with God and his people.[9]

The church, as I noted above, is a key theological focus of the letter. Ephesians famously stresses the "universal church," the single worldwide believing community where both Jews and gentiles find a home.[10] This theme, as recent scholars have rightly noted, is important for current issues of racial and ethnic tension.[11] Finally, as is usually the case in Paul, being "in Christ" is a key theological refrain, Ephesians having a greater proportion of such references than any other Pauline letter.[12] As Michael Horton notes, "Union with Christ (soteriology) and communion with his body (ecclesiology) form an integral pattern throughout this epistle."[13]

LOCATING THE LETTER

We cannot locate Ephesians in the context of Paul's ministry without dealing with a fundamental question: Did Paul write this letter? For many decades now, mainstream Pauline scholarship has viewed the letter as a pseudepigraphon, composed by a late first-century follower of Paul in the apostle's name.[14] This is not the place to rehearse

---

5. Lincoln, *Paradise Now and Not Yet*, 135.

6. Brannon surveys the history of interpretation of this concept (pp. 11–37) and provides a good overview of its use in Greek generally (pp. 38–72) and the NT specifically (pp. 73–103). He concludes that *epouranioi* does not differ in meaning from the simple *ouranoi*, its semitechnical sense in Ephesians owing to the way the word is used rather than to the word itself (M. J. Brannon, *The Heavenlies in Ephesians: A Lexical, Exegetical, and Conceptual Analysis*, LNTS 447 [London: T&T Clark, 2011]).

7. E.g., Hahn, *Theologie des Neuen Testaments*, 1:344–45.

8. "Dieser kosmische Horizont wird im Epheserbrief heilsgeschichtlich konkretisiert" (Wilckens, *Die Briefe des Urchristentums*, 283).

9. Gombis argues that spiritual warfare is the conceptual framework of the letter (*Drama of Ephesians*, 30–31).

10. Gnilka speaks for many other scholars when he makes the church the central theological focus of the letter (Joachim

Gnilka, *Der Epheserbrief*, 4th ed., HThKNT 10.2 [Freiburg: Herder, 1990], 30).

11. See, e.g., Jarvis J. Williams, *One New Man: The Cross and Racial Reconciliation in Pauline Theology* (Nashville: B&H Academic, 2010), 112–31.

12. Thirty-five of the 160 Pauline occurrences come in Ephesians. See, e.g., John R. W. Stott, *The Message of Ephesians: God's New Society*, The Bible Speaks Today (Downers Grove, IL: InterVarsity Press, 1979), 25.

13. Michael S. Horton, *The Christian Faith: A Systematic Theology for Pilgrims on the Way* (Grand Rapids: Zondervan, 2011), 735.

14. A good recent summary of this view is Ernest Best, *A Critical and Exegetical Commentary on Ephesians*, ICC (Edinburgh: T&T Clark, 1998), 6–45. Brown estimates that 70–80% of "critical scholarship" rejects Pauline authorship of Ephesians (*Introduction to the New Testament*, 629).

the arguments pro and con for this conclusion. I can only point to some careful analyses that, in my view, establish a convincing case for Pauline authorship.[15]

As I noted above (see "Locating the Letter" on Colossians), Ephesians is closely related to Colossians and Philemon. All three are directed to the same general area, they allude to some of the same ministry associates, and Ephesians and Colossians share vocabulary and theological emphases. Paul is in prison as he writes (Eph 3:1, 13; 4:1; 6:20), and I argued above that this imprisonment is probably his Roman confinement narrated at the end of Acts (Acts 28:30–31), suggesting a date of around AD 60–61.

The obviously close relationship between Colossians and Ephesians, exhibited in both vocabulary and theology, raises the question of their relationship. If one or both of these letters was written by a follower of Paul, in his name, these similarities might be due to literary borrowing.[16] Indeed, a number of scholars think that Ephesians is a pastiche, put together with a large borrowing from Colossians and more minor borrowings from other Pauline letters.[17] However, if, as I think, Paul wrote both letters, the parallels are probably due simply to the fact that one person is writing both letters at about the same time to the same part of the world where, apparently, some of the same theological issues were surfacing.[18] Ephesians is not directed to a specific outbreak of false teaching as Colossians is, but we can surmise that Paul is aware that other churches in Asia Minor were exposed to a similar heretical movement.

But which churches? The title "To the Ephesians" found in our Bibles reflects Ephesians 1:1, as found, for instance, in the NIV: "Paul, an apostle of Christ Jesus by the will of God, to God's holy people in Ephesus, the faithful in Christ Jesus." However, as the NIV footnote reveals, "in Ephesus" is missing in a number of good manuscripts.[19] The textual issue is difficult, with strong arguments advanced on each side.[20] Indeed,

---

15. See esp. Harold W. Hoehner, *Ephesians: An Exegetical Commentary* (Grand Rapids: Baker Academic, 2002), 2–61; O'Brien, *Ephesians*, 4–47; Markus Barth, *Ephesians: Introduction, Translation, and Commentary on Chapters 1–3*, AB 34 (Garden City: Doubleday, 1974), 36–50; Carson and Moo, *Introduction to the New Testament*, 480–86; A. van Roon, *The Authenticity of Ephesians*, NovTSup 39 (Leiden: Brill, 1974); Percy, *Kolosser- und Epheserbriefe.*

16. Andrew T. Lincoln (*Ephesians*, WBC 42 [Nashville: Thomas Nelson, 1990], xlvii–lvi) argues the majority view: that Ephesians borrows from Colossians.

17. E.g., Michael Gese, *Das Vermächtnis des Apostels: die Rezeption der paulinischen Theologie im Epheserbrief*, WUNT 2/99 (Tübingen: Mohr Siebeck, 1997), 28–107; Lincoln, *Ephesians*, xlvii–lviii. Edgar J. Goodspeed thought that Ephesians was composed (perhaps by Onesimus [cf. Philemon]) in the 90s on the basis of other letters of Paul (but especially Colossians) as kind of summary and introduction to Paul's letters and thought (*The Key to Ephesians* [Chicago: University of Chicago Press, 1956]).

18. The direction of dependence is not clear (see, e.g., O'Brien, *Ephesians*, 14–21; Best, *Ephesians*, 20–25).

19. Specifically, three of the best early MSS of the Pauline letters: $\mathfrak{P}^{46}$, ℵ, B.

20. On the one hand, the omission of *en Ephesō*, leaving *tois ousin* (a substantive participle construction meaning "the ones who are") without an obvious predicate, is the "more difficult reading" and, when that omission occurs in such early and good manuscripts, a strong case for this omission can be made (e.g., O'Brien, *Ephesians*, 47–49; Best, *Ephesians*, 98–100). On the other hand, it is argued that the omission of the phrase is "too difficult" and that there were good reasons why early scribes may have omitted the phrase (e.g., Frank S. Thielman, *Ephesians*, BECNT [Grand Rapids: Baker, 2010], 11–16; Hoehner, *Ephesians*, 78, 144–48; Clinton E. Arnold, *Ephesians*, ZECNT [Grand Rapids: Zondervan, 2010], 23–29; Lynn H. Cohick, *The Letter to the Ephesians*, NICNT [Grand Rapids: Eerdmans, 2020], 30). The UBS committee included the words, but in brackets (see Bruce M. Metzger, *A Textual Commentary on the Greek New Testament:*

the pros and cons on each side are so finely balanced that even a probable decision is impossible to make. Whether the words are read or not, however, it is possible that our "Ephesians" was in fact a circular letter, addressed both to the Ephesian Christians and Christians living in other nearby cities (e.g., the seven churches of the Revelation [Rev 1–3]).[21] There are no references to Ephesus anywhere else in the letter; indeed, the letter lacks references to specific people or circumstances, its theological teaching apparently not stimulated by particular, local issues. Even if "in Ephesus" is included in 1:1, then, it may be because it is the central church in the district or because our surviving copy was the one sent (or read out to) that church.[22] I tentatively adopt this circular-letter theory, although it will not have much bearing on the exegesis of the text.

ISOLATING THE ISSUES

Uncertainty about the letter's destination along with the lack of specific application in its contents renders it difficult to determine the issues that may have given rise to its teaching. We have no specifics beyond the argument of the letter itself to build on, leaving no option but the inevitably quite subjective "mirror reading" for information. In contrast to Colossians, we have no indication in Ephesians that Paul is responding to false teaching. Nor is there any indication of a particular crisis. Paul does carry over his concern about Christ's (and believers') relationship to spiritual powers from Colossians into Ephesians—suggesting a kind of basic worldview issue that was affecting churches in Asia Minor. He also reflects quite a lot on the inclusion of gentiles within the people of God. But his tone does not suggest the existence of a particular "Judaizing" movement. Other interpreters suggest that an interval of time has led to a flagging of enthusiasm among the readers. This suggestion works better if the letter is written after Paul's time. But it does not take long for this problem to set in: the time between his last contact with the church in about AD 57 (addressing its leaders in Miletus; see Acts 20:17–38) and the time of writing is sufficient for this problem to have arisen.[23] Other scenarios are too specific to have a clear basis in the text.[24] O'Brien suggests the broad concept of "identity formation" may be the best we can do. He elaborates:

A Companion Volume to the United Bible Societies' Greek New Testament (Fourth Revised Edition), 2nd ed. [Stuttgart: United Bible Societies, 1994], 532). Some scholars think that some other destination may have been originally found here: e.g., Lincoln (*Ephesians*, lxxxii) thinks the letter may have been originally addressed to Laodicea and Hierapolis (see Col 4:13, 16). This general idea goes back as far as Marcion, who theorized that our Ephesians may have been the "letter to Laodicea" (see also John Muddiman, *A Commentary on the Epistle to the Ephesians*, BNTC [London: Continuum, 2001], 2–34). However, early Christian evidence strongly supports Ephesus as at least one destination:

fathers who had a text without "in Ephesus" still argued for or assumed an Ephesian destination.

21. O'Brien, *Ephesians*, 47–49; Best, *Ephesians*, 98–100.

22. J. B. Lightfoot, "The Destination of the Epistle to the Ephesians," in *Biblical Essays* (London: Macmillan, 1893), 392; Hoehner, *Ephesians*, 78–79; Arnold, *Ephesians*, 23–29.

23. Thielman, *Ephesians*, 20–27.

24. E.g., I am not convinced that the growth and influence of the emperor cult are serious factors (contra Thielman, *Ephesians*, 21–24).

Having addressed a specific problem in Colossians, Paul has remodeled his letter for a more general Christian readership. He writes Ephesians to his mainly Gentile Christian readers, for whom he has apostolic responsibilities, with the intention of informing, strengthening, and encouraging them by assuring them of their place within the gracious, saving purpose of God, and urging them to bring their lives into conformity with this divine plan of summing up all things in Christ (1:10).[25]

Arnold agrees, though he rightly suggests that this summary can be fleshed out a bit with four specific themes:

1. The threat of spiritual powers overcome by the power of God among his people;
2. Overcoming animosity among gentiles and Jews;
3. The importance of holiness among gentile believers;
4. The need for believers to be established in their identity and relationship to each other.[26]

Best follows a similar line of argument, noting that converted pagans would require a new sense of identity, which Paul provides by arguing that they have "both an eternal setting and, since they are Gentiles, a setting in relation to Israel."[27]

ANALYZING THE ARGUMENT

Along with Colossians, Ephesians exhibits a rather clear two-part structure. Chapters 1–3 are focused more on theory, or "theology proper," while chapters 4–6 focus on the application of that theology.

1 THE BENEFITS OF BEING "IN CHRIST" (1:1–3:21)

1.1 Innumerable Spiritual Blessings (1:1–14)

The letter opens with the usual epistolary features: sender, addressees, and a wish for "grace and peace" (vv. 1–2). In place of the usual thanksgiving, however, Ephesians next features a "blessing," or *berakah* (from the Hebrew for "blessing"—NIV translates "praise"). Paul delays his usual thanksgiving for the *believers'* faith and love (see vv. 15–23) and instead launches into a celebration of *God's* rich provision for his peoples' spiritual needs.

---

25. O'Brien, *Ephesians*, 56–57.

26. Arnold, *Ephesians*, 42–45; cf. similarly Fee, *God's Empowering Presence*, 661.

27. Best, *Ephesians*, 74–75.

The *berakah* unfolds in one long sevntence in Greek, with subordinate clauses of various kinds adding blessing upon blessing—"a kaleidoscope of dazzling lights and shifting colors."[28] In the course of its winding path, this sentence touches on many of Paul's key theological ideas:

Election and Predestination (vv. 4–5, 11)
Adoption to Sonship (v. 5)
Powerful Grace (vv. 6, 7–8)
Redemption (vv. 7, 14)
Forgiveness of Sins (v. 7)
Revelation of the Mystery (v. 9)
Fullness of Time (v. 10)
Summing Up All Things (v. 10)
Gospel (v. 13)
Salvation (v. 13)
Holy Spirit (v. 13)
Inheritance (v. 14)

An impressive number of these theological benefits are found also in Romans 8 (and often with the same language).

The syntactical complexity of the sentence invites several different dividing schemes,[29] but it is easiest to take our cue from the Nestle-Aland Greek text, which puts minor breaks at the three *en hō* ("in whom") clauses:

Praise be to God, who has blessed us . . .
In whom we have redemption (v. 7) . . .
In whom we were chosen (v. 11) . . .
In whom we were also . . . sealed (v. 13)[30]

Note also how three of these units end with the refrain "to the praise of his glory" (see vv. 6, 12, and 14). Perhaps, however, a more useful analysis isolates its three recurring themes: union with Christ as the "place" where we enjoy all our blessings ("in Christ/ him" occurs ten times); God's eternal purpose as the basis for these blessings (vv. 3, 5, 9, 11); and the goal of these blessings in praise to God (vv. 5, 6, 12, 14). The passage

---

28. J. Armitage Robinson, *St. Paul's Epistle to the Ephesians*, 2nd ed. (London: Macmillan, 1907), 19.

29. See the helpful chart of options in Hoehner, *Ephesians*, 160–61.

30. See, e.g., Thielman, *Ephesians*, 43.

also displays a Trinitarian focus. If Christ is the "place" where we experience blessing, and God is both the initiator and goal, the Spirit is also instrumental in securing our blessings (vv. 3, 13–14—creating a bit of an *inclusio*).

Paul proclaims that God is "blessed" (*eulogetos*) because he has "blessed" (*eulogesas*) his people with "every spiritual blessing" (*eulogia*). The "every" stresses the number and variety of blessings, while "spiritual" probably refers to the Holy Spirit.[31] Our blessings are "in the heavenly realms." As I noted above, this concept (Gk. *epouranioi*) is a central motif in Ephesians, referring to the spiritual realm in general. It is via our participation in this realm that our blessings become available to us. Paul introduces another key motif of the letter by asserting that God blesses us "in Christ."

The first specific blessing Paul enumerates is our election, again "in Christ," "before the creation of the world" (v. 4). Paul is certainly not suggesting that those whom God calls are preexistent, and it is unlikely that he is referring here to Christ's preexistence.[32] Rather, God's choosing, which is "before" our time, comes to fruition "in Christ"[33]—the "sphere where God acts with respect to everything, from his fixed point of reference."[34] While some have argued that election here is corporate, focusing on "us," or the church, it is more likely that it is individuals who are chosen by God.[35] Locating this choosing "before the creation of the world" indicates that "God's choice was due to his own free decision and love, which were not dependent on temporal circumstances or human merit" (see also Rom 8:29: "foreknew").[36] This passage therefore supports the traditional idea that God calls individual humans into relationship with himself apart from any consideration of their own actions or merits.[37] Verse 5 continues this theological theme, with "predestined" (from *proorizo*) essentially equivalent here to "chose" in verse 4.[38] In both verses Paul stresses that God's election has a goal: that we might "be holy and blameless" (v. 4), and that we might become God's own sons (v. 5). "Adoption to sonship" translates *huiothesia*, which resonates with two "worlds" in Paul's day: the Old Testament, which pictures Israel, God's "chosen one," as God's son (e.g., Exod 4:22; Deut 14:1; Jer 3:19; Hos 11:1), and Roman law, which made provision for the adoption of men to full legal status. In Christ, *the* Son, God adopts both men and women as his "sons," conveying to them all the rights and privileges of that status (see especially the constellation of similar themes in Rom 8:14–17; 28–30).

31. E.g., O'Brien, *Ephesians*, 95; Rudolf Schnackenburg, *Ephesians: A Commentary* (Edinburgh: T&T Clark, 1991), 50; Fee, *God's Empowering Presence*, 666–68.

32. Contra, e.g., Schnackenburg, *Ephesians*, 53.

33. Thielman, *Ephesians*, 48; Hans Hübner, *An Philemon, an die Kolosser, an die Epheser*, HNT 12 (Tübingen: Mohr Siebeck, 1997), 133.

34. Chrys C. Caragounis, *The Ephesian Mysterion: Meaning and Content*, ConBNT 8 (Lund: Gleerup, 1977), 37.

35. See, e.g., Thielman, *Ephesians*, 99–100.

36. O'Brien, *Ephesians*, 100.

37. See on this issue the useful response of Hoehner (*Ephesians*, 188–93) to M. Barth's rather intemperate and misguided criticism of the doctrine (*Ephesians 1–3*, 105–9).

38. The verb *proorizo* occurs elsewhere in Acts 4:28; Rom 8:29, 30; 1 Cor 2:7; Eph 1:5, 11.

This predestining takes place in, and as a result of, God's love, another key theme in Ephesians.[39] What God does in choosing/predestining us is rooted in God's "pleasure and will"[40] and has the purpose of bringing praise to him for his "glorious grace" (NIV) or "the glory that is displayed by his grace" (v. 6).[41]

Without breaking off his sentence, Paul pauses for breath by introducing the relative phrase "in whom" (NIV "in him"; v. 7). Coming at the beginning of this next sequence, the phrase bears some emphasis, calling attention again to the way in which union with Christ undergirds everything in this passage. "Redemption" (*apolytrōsis*) is another important theological word whose meaning is grounded in both the Old Testament and the Greco-Roman world. In the former, this word and the word group to which it belongs refer to God's great acts of deliverance for Israel, particularly in the exodus and the return from exile. But this word group was also used by Paul's contemporaries to denote the transaction whereby a slave could purchase his or her freedom (see pp. 497–98). God's climactic act of deliverance involves the "payment" of Christ's own blood as the means by which people can have their sins forgiven—all, again, a product of God's grace (v. 7). Paul adds that God has made known to us "the mystery of his will" (v. 9).[42] "Mystery" (*mystērion*) introduces yet another key Pauline theological word, which figures importantly in chapter 3 (vv. 3, 4, 9) and occurs again at the end of the letter in a kind of *inclusio* (6:19; cf. also 5:32). Basically, a "mystery" is a previously hidden, now revealed, truth about the plan of God (see the notes on Col 1:24–2:5). This plan will reach its climax "when the times reach their fulfillment" (*tou plērōmatos tōn kairōn*, "the fullness of times"; v. 10)—a phrase that recalls a similar salvation-historical perspective about the culmination of God's unfolding plan in Galatians 4:4 ("the fullness of time [*to plērōma tou chronou*]," my translation).[43] Paul summarizes that climax here as *anakephalaiōsasthai ta panta en tō Christō*—"to sum up everything in Christ" (my translation). The verb here has the sense of summarizing and bringing into order previous material (as in the conclusion of a speech; cf. Rom 13:9). God's ultimate purpose is universal ("all things") in scope, including not only the earth but the cosmos

---

39. I take *en agapē* at the end of v. 4 with the following verb in v. 5 (NIV; ESV; cf. Arnold, *Ephesians*, 82) rather than with the previous "holy and blameless" (NET; NRSV; cf. Hoehner, *Ephesians*, 182–83; Thielman, *Ephesians*, 50).

40. The rather liturgical style of these verses features repetition and redundancy (Lincoln, *Ephesians*, 12); it is unlikely, therefore, that there is any substantive difference between "pleasure" (*eudokia*) and "will" (*thelēma*).

41. The Gk. is *doxēs tēs charitos*, which most English versions take to be an "attributed genitive" (the ruling noun being the modifier). However, it is also possible (indeed, in my view probable) that the genitive indicates source: God's lavishly bestowed grace is the cause of greater glory to God.

42. It is not clear whether it is God's "wisdom and understanding" that Paul refers to in v. 8 (as the mode in which either he lavishes grace or makes known the mystery) or our "wisdom and understanding" (which God gives along with his grace and/or the knowledge of the mystery). The partial parallel in Col 1:9 could suggest the latter (see NLT).

43. Contra, e.g., Andreas Lindemann, who thinks Ephesians in general, and this text in particular, implies a kind of "abolition" of time in favor of a nontemporal conception of Christ's work (*Die Aufhebung der Zeit: Geschichtsverständnis und Eschatologie im Epheserbrief*, SNT 12 [Gütersloh: Gütersloh Mohn, 1975], cf. 95).

as well—with particular reference probably to spiritual powers ("things in heaven"; cf. v. 21 and Col 1:20).[44] This summing up will happen, of course, "in Christ" (see Col 1:16–17). A number of interpreters think this vision of the entire universe being brought back into harmony in accordance with God's purposes for it (see, again, Col 1:20) comes as close as any text in Ephesians to expressing the main point of the letter.[45]

Paul again starts over, returning now to where he started in verses 4 and 5: "In him we were also chosen" (v. 11). "Chosen" translates a word that means "appoint or choose by lot" (*klēroō*), but, more important for its theological sense here, it comes from a root from which we get the biblical language of "inheritance" (*klēronomia*). Since "inheritance" occurs in this context (v. 14), the verb in verse 11 probably has the nuance "select for an inheritance." God's "inheritance," which originally focused on Israel (e.g., Deut 32:8–9), is now the possession of the church. In two notes typical of this passage, Paul again traces this inheritance to the predestining will of God (v. 11b) and sees it having the ultimate purpose of bringing glory to God (v. 12). The latter part of verse 12 describes "us" (*hēmas*) who receive this inheritance as those "who were first to put our hope in Christ." This translation implies a temporal contrast with others, presumably those named in verse 13: "you also." In this case, it is possible that those who first hoped refers to Jewish Christians, while "you also" refers to gentile Christians—thereby anticipating the important discussion of Jew and gentile in 2:11–22 (see, explicitly, NLT).[46] However, we should not make too much of Paul's shift in pronouns, since he is notoriously casual in moving from first ("we") to second ("you") person. More to the point, it is possible that the prefix to the verb translated in the NIV "first to hope" may have lost any temporal force, being used simply to intensify the verbal idea: "those of us who fully hope."[47] Others think that, even if the prefix has a temporal sense, it might mean simply "hope beforehand," that is, put hope in God before the parousia.[48] A decision here is difficult, but perhaps it would be foreign to this context for Paul to set up any differentiation in the recipients of the blessings he enumerates.

The last two verses (again introduced with "in him," obscured a bit in NIV) shift the focus from God's purpose and plan to believers' experience of the benefits of that plan, with particular reference to the Spirit. As a consequence of their response to the "message of truth, the gospel of your salvation," they have been "marked in him with a

---

44. The word Paul uses is derived not from the noun *kephalē*, head, but the noun *kephalaion*, "main point." The word itself, then, makes no reference to the idea of Christ being the "head" of this restored cosmos. Some, however, in light of, e.g., v. 22, think the idea is probably present here (Hübner, *Philemon, Kolosser, Epheser*, 138; Hoehner, *Ephesians*, 220–21).

45. See, e.g., O'Brien, *Ephesians*, 112–13; Turner, "Mission and Meaning," 139–40. There is debate about whether the prefix *ana* on the verb implies a "return" to an earlier state. Whether this is the case or not, the sense of the verb in terms of "summing up" suggests a bringing together of previously disparate things (see Lincoln, *Ephesians*, 33).

46. E.g., J. A. Robinson, *Ephesians*, 34–35; Abbott, *Ephesians and Colossians*, 21.

47. Lincoln, *Ephesians*, 37; Arnold, *Ephesians*, 90; Hoehner, *Ephesians*, 231–33.

48. Thielman, *Ephesians*, 75–76.

seal, the promised Holy Spirit." The reference is to the initial receiving of the Spirit that marks all who come to Christ (see, e.g., Gal 3:2, 5), a promise that God attaches to the preaching of his word (see Gal 3:14).[49] If the Spirit's work looks back to the moment of conversion, it also looks forward to the culmination of our salvation, our "inheritance" and ultimate "redemption" (see Rom 8:23). The Spirit is our "deposit," our *arrabōn* (see also 2 Cor 1:22; 5:5; and also "firstfruits" in Rom 8:23). This language pictures the Spirit as a bridge, arcing from the "already" of salvation to its "not yet" culmination.

1.2 Thanksgiving and Prayer (1:15–23)

As he often does toward the beginning of his letters, Paul now gives thanks for his readers' spiritual status (vv. 15–16) and prays for them (vv. 17–23). The extent of this prayer is unclear, scholars debating whether it ends at 1:23 or carries into what follows, perhaps even as far as 3:14–21, where Paul prays for his readers again. Paul does little to mark the stages of his argument, 2:1–10 flowing out of 1:17–23, 2:11–22 out of 2:1–10, and 3:1–13 out of 2:11–22.

Paul's thanksgiving is motivated by his readers' "faith in the Lord Jesus" and "love for all God's people" (Col 1:4 and Phlm 5 are parallel). The author has "heard" about the readers, suggesting to many that Paul could not have been the author. But it is quite plausible that Paul is referring to the period of five or six years since he last had direct contact with the Ephesians.

Paul's prayer for the readers flows naturally out of the opening paragraph of the letter: having blessed God for their spiritual blessings, Paul now prays that his readers will be able to appreciate them. Using a biblical metaphor (Ps 13:3; 19:8), Paul prays that "the eyes of [their] heart may be enlightened" so that they might comprehend (1) "the hope to which he has called you"; (2) "the riches of his glorious inheritance in his holy people"; and (3) "his [God's] incomparably great power for us who believe" (vv. 18–19a). The first two pick up points from 1:3–14, but the reference to God's power introduces a new note, one that Paul develops in the rest of the prayer. This power of God is manifested in the resurrection and exaltation of Christ (v. 20). Alluding to Psalm 110:1, a verse that has left its mark throughout the New Testament, Paul celebrates the fact that Christ is "seated . . . at [God's] right hand," and picking up again his characteristic Ephesian word (see 1:3), it is "in the heavenly realms" (*tois epouraniois*) that he has now been elevated. Also characteristic of Ephesians (and resembling Colossians again) is the emphasis on Christ's exaltation over "the powers": "All rule and authority, power and dominion, and every name that is invoked, not only in the present age but also in the

---

49. An allusion to baptism is detected here by many, but Lincoln is right to focus attention on the gift of the Spirit *per se* (*Ephesians*, 40).

one to come" (v. 21). This series of words is a way of saying, in effect, "every spiritual being that you can imagine or worry about." As I noted in commenting on Colossians 1:16, many scholars suggest that Paul uses this language to allude not just to spiritual beings but also to earthly manifestations of those beings: human rulers, societal and governmental structures, etc. A careful middle course might be best here: Paul clearly refers to spiritual beings; but it may be a legitimate hermeneutical move to think that these spiritual beings may indeed influence earthly institutions.[50] Certainly, however, the "all things" (*panta*) at the beginning of verse 22 encompasses these: Christ's rule is universal, leaving nothing outside the sphere of his lordship. Paul makes this point with allusion to another favorite Old Testament verse, Psalm 8:6 (8:7 LXX): "You made them [human beings] rulers over the works of your hands; you put everything under their feet" (see also 1 Cor 15:25–27; Heb 2:8). Paul probably moved to this text from his allusion to Psalm 110:1 because both use the language of "under the feet" to express the idea of rule. Christ, perhaps as "Son of Man" (see Ps 8:4 [8:5 LXX]; cf. ESV), is the ultimate expression and representation of human beings: their rule over all things comes to fulfillment in his rule.

In verse 22b, Paul touches on a key focus in the theology he develops in Ephesians, namely, the connection between the cosmic sphere of God's power in Christ and the church: God has "appointed him [Christ] to be head over everything for the church." The metaphor of "head" (*kephalē*), while it can express different ideas in different contexts, clearly here has the sense of "authority over."[51] The universal reign of Christ is especially "for," or "on behalf of" the church: God's people need not fear the "powers" because Christ rules over them on their behalf. Also typical of Ephesians is the use of *ekklēsia* to refer to the universal church. This way of referring to all believers everywhere is characteristic of Ephesians and Colossians, though it has some precedent in the earlier letters of Paul (see 1 Cor 10:32; 12:28; Gal 1:13). But there is no doubt this represents something of an advance on Paul's thinking, perhaps stimulated by currents of thought in Asia Minor.

Verse 23 further describes this universal church as "his [Christ's] body" and "the fullness of him who fills everything in every way." As we noted in my comments on 1 Corinthians 12, the use of "body" (*sōma*) as a metaphor for the church may have its background in the widepread use of this word to characterize society, "the body politic" (see also pp. 581–87). At the least, this metaphor makes very clear that the essence of the church is its intimate relationship with Christ. The last phrase of verse 23 is difficult to translate. The word "fullness" (*plērōma*) can have either an active—that which is filling—or passive—that which is filled—sense. A few interpreters take the word in the

---

50. Thielman, *Ephesians*, 108.
51. See, e.g., Arnold, *Ephesians*, 115. This metaphorical sense is probably especially drawn from places in the LXX where the translators render Hebrew *rosh* in this sense by *kephalē*.

former sense, but it is difficult to think of the church "filling" Christ.[52] Probably, then, the word is passive, picking up the common Old Testament teaching about the temple being "filled" with God's glory (e.g., 2 Chr 7:1; Isa 6:1; Ezek 44:4). The second word with a "filling" connotation in this verse is the object of the same debate. The participle at the end of the verse could be active or passive in meaning.[53] If passive, Paul would be saying that Christ is "the one who is filled by everything" (see NJB: "The fullness of him who is filled, all in all"). Paul would be saying, in effect, "the church is the one filled by one who is filled."[54] But most English versions and commentators think an active sense is more likely, in which case Paul is stressing that the church can have utter confidence in Christ's "filling it" with his own power and authority, since he is the one who "fills" all things in this way. Cosmic rule implies and includes ecclesiastical rule.[55]

1.3 From Death to Life in Christ (2:1–10)

In chapter 1, Paul has sketched the far-reaching plan of God, summed up in Christ (v. 10) and put into effect through his resurrection and exaltation (vv. 20–23) for the benefit of his church. Now he personalizes, showing how individual believers participate in that resurrection and exaltation (v. 6) and are by that means rescued from death and wrath (vv. 1–3) in order to enjoy life (v. 6) and salvation (vv. 5, 8). These benefits are the product of God's love, manifested in his mercy and grace (vv. 4, 5, 7, 8) and are received by faith (v. 8). And the purpose of it all is that God might receive appropriate praise and glory (v. 7). Some interpreters think that the passage is implicitly set in the context of a baptismal experience.[56] But this is not clear.

Verses 1–5 manifest some typically Pauline, mangled syntax, as the flow of his ideas overcomes his grammar. The "you" in verse 1 is in the accusative case (*hymas*), making it the object of a verb. This verb does not show up until verse 5: "He made us alive." So our basic sentence, as Paul apparently originally intended to write it, would have been "God brought you, who are dead in sin, to new life."[57] However, having begun by focusing on his readers—"you"—Paul decides to develop at some length the plight his readers find themselves in so that the intervention of God on their behalf could be seen in its true significance. Expressing common ideas about humans apart from Christ, then, Paul says we were "dead" because of our sins (vv. 1, 5), "by nature deserving of wrath" (v. 3). This "death" is mainly spiritual: the separation from God that took place when our first parents fell into sin (Gen 2:17: "But you must not eat from the tree of the

---

52. Contra, e.g., J. A. Robinson, *Ephesians*, 42–43.

53. The form is *plēroumenou*, which in form is either middle or passive. If the former, it could have a basically active sense; if the latter, it is, of course, passive in sense.

54. Thielman, *Ephesians*, 114–15; Hoehner, *Ephesians*, 294–301.

55. Lincoln, *Ephesians*, 72–77; Schnackenburg, *Ephesians*, 82; O'Brien, *Ephesians*, 151–52.

56. E.g., Hahn, *Theologie des Neuen Testaments*, 1:363–64.

57. Hübner thinks the "you" refers to gentile Christians (*Philemon, Kolosser, Epheser*, 155), but it more likely refers to Christians in general.

knowledge of good and evil, for when you eat from it you will certainly die"). This is what Paul means by asserting that we are "by nature" under God's wrath: All humans inherit a "fallen nature" from Adam that renders them guilty before God and prevents them from following God's laws and ways (see Rom 5:12–21). It is typical of Ephesians that Paul would also present this dilemma in terms of spiritual powers (v. 2). As we have seen, Paul's main point comes in verse 6, where, echoing 1:20, he indicates that our rescue from this plight comes via our identification with Christ in his resurrection and exaltation. This being "raised" with Christ and "seated" in the heavenlies with him picks up Paul's important union with Christ, or participation, motif (see also, e.g., Rom 6:1–11; Col 2:6–15; 3:1). We were in some sense truly "with" Christ when he died, was buried, was raised, and was exalted—God sees us as "in him," and from that union flows our spiritual blessings. The grace of God in so identifying us with Christ is activated by our response of faith (v. 8).[58] It is this whole process of being "saved" by union with Christ through faith that is "the gift of God."[59] This grace, as John M. G. Barclay has emphasized, while "unconditioned"—stimulated by nothing apart from God himself—is nevertheless "conditional"—in the sense that it demands a response in life, so that we would do the good works that God has intended for us (v. 10).[60]

1.4 From Alienation to Reconciliation in Christ (2:11–22)

Paul's overall purpose in chapter 2 is to encourage his readers to recognize who they are in Christ. "In him" (vv. 6, 10), individuals have been brought from death to life, raised and seated with Christ "in the heavenly realms." And "in" him (vv. 13, 21, 22) gentiles have been brought from a state of alienation to a state of belonging, "fellow citizens with God's people" (v. 19). "Vertical" reconciliation is matched by "horizontal" reconciliation. The "in Christ" conception is unpacked in verses 1–10 in terms of Christ's resurrection and exaltation. In verses 11–22, it is unpacked in terms of his death (v. 13). Obviously, however, the whole of Christ's work is foundational for both overcoming God's wrath and overcoming alienation from God's people. The manner in which Paul presents the inclusion of gentiles in the people of God differs significantly from his polemical tone in letters such as Galatians, Romans, and Philippians. Nothing in this passage, or in Ephesians generally, suggests that the entry of gentiles into the people of God, or the means of that entry (law versus Christ), were being debated.[61] Yet it remained important, positively, to assure gentile believers of their status by reminding

---

58. It is unlikely that "faith" refers to the faith, or faithfulness of Christ (contra O'Brien, *Ephesians*, 175).

59. The "this" (*touto*) in v. 8b is sometimes connected with "faith"—and this is a grammatical possibility, if the neuter *touto* is picking up the idea of "faith" (*pistis*, which is feminine; see, e.g., Chrysostom, "Homily IV on Ephesians" [*NPNF¹* 13:67]).

But the *touto* is probably more likely to refer back to the whole "idea" or "process" in the preceding verses. See, e.g., Stephen E. Fowl, *Ephesians: A Commentary*, NTL (Louisville: Westminster John Knox, 2012), 78.

60. *Paul and the Gift*, 498–500, passim.

61. Lincoln, *Ephesians*, 133.

them of God's reconciling work on their behalf.[62] While often taken to indicate a date after Paul's lifetime, this apparently settled situation could simply be the result of local circumstances.

The paragraph displays an obvious A-B-A structure, with verses 11–13 and 19–22 celebrating the gentiles' inclusion in the new people of God, while verses 14–18 describe the means through which this new situation has come about.[63] The paragraph as a whole, of course, accentuates the concern with the church that is so much a characteristic of Ephesians and contributes significantly to Paul's theology of the new people of God in Christ—especially his vision of the cosmic breadth and unity of the church. As Johnson puts it, "This is the most sweeping and breathtaking statement of human unity and universality enunciated in antiquity."[64]

As he did with respect to individual humans in verses 1–3, Paul begins by describing the plight of gentiles qua gentiles (vv. 11–12). They are "uncircumcised," lacking the sign of God's covenant, excluded from membership in Israel, the covenant people, and "foreigners to the covenants of the promise." Put in other terms, they are "separate from Christ," "without hope and without God in the world." This characterization summarized the way Jews in Paul's day regarded gentiles, but it also, of course, has some basis in the Old Testament itself, which focuses on Israel as the recipients of God's blessing and care. "In Christ Jesus," however, this situation has been dramatically changed: those "who once were far away have been brought near" (v. 13). This language, which is repeated in verse 17, echoes Isaiah 57:18–19: "'I have seen their ways, but I will heal them; I will guide them and restore comfort to Israel's mourners, creating praise on their lips. Peace, peace, to those far and near,' says the LORD. 'And I will heal them.'" Gentiles are brought near "by the blood of Christ," a characteristic way of alluding to Jesus's sacrificial death (see Eph 1:7; cf. Rom 3:25; 5:9; 1 Cor 10:16; 11:25, 27; Col 1:20).

Paul elaborates on the means by which God removed the gentiles' alienation in verses 14–18. Alluding both to the Isaiah text that Paul has used in verse 13 and picking up another characteristic Pauline theme, the apostle asserts that Jesus has become "our peace" (see Isa 57:18, quoted above; cf. Rom 5:1; Col 1:20). Paul elaborates in verses 14b–15a, using the metaphor of a "dividing wall" to describe the barrier that prevented gentiles from having access to God's blessings. It is difficult to know what Paul is referring to, an issue complicated by uncertainties about the relationship among the key phrases. English versions, understandably, in order to make sense of what Paul is saying, paraphrase a bit. In the Greek, however, it makes best sense to pair the

62. Best, *Ephesians*, 235.

63. E.g., Gnilka, *Epheserbrief*, 132–33.

64. Luke Timothy Johnson, *Interpreting Paul*, vol. 2 of *The Canonical Paul* (Grand Rapids: Eerdmans, 2021), 345. For reflection on this text and application to the African church, see Fabrice S. Katembo, *The Mystery of the Church: Applying Paul's Ecclesiology in Africa* (Carlisle: Langham, 2020).

first clause and the last in this series, since both refer to "destroying" or "annulling": "destroying the barrier"/"annulling the law, which consists of commandments taking the form of decrees."[65] On this reading, it is possible that the barrier, or "dividing wall" (*mesotoichon*), alludes to the balustrade in the Jerusalem Temple that separated the "court of the gentiles" from the "court of Israel," thus serving, in effect, to keep gentiles apart from the special privilege of access to God enjoyed by God's people Israel.[66] We know from contemporary Jewish sources that Israel often viewed God's law, or Torah, in this way: as a "hedge" to protect Israel, on the one hand, and to keep gentiles out, on the other.[67] Yet it is not only a part of the law, or a function of the law, that is "annulled," but the law as a whole.[68] Here is where it is imperative to be careful of our language. Paul does not claim that the law is "destroyed" but that it is "rendered powerless" (the Gk. verb *katargeō*). The Old Testament law still bears its authority as "Scripture," and we profit from reading it. But its commands no longer have direct authority for new-covenant believers (see pp. 614–22).

The word "enmity" (*echthra*) is inserted between these clauses to summarize the effect of the law as a barrier to gentiles: it meant hostility between Jew and gentile. Yet the purpose of the law was not only to isolate Israel but to express the will of God, and the breaking of that law therefore meant "hostility" between God and humans also.[69] Both dimensions of hostility are probably intended here. It was specifically the cross through which God "put to death" this hostility (v. 16b).[70] By dying a sacrificial death on the cross, Christ made it possible for sinful humans, "by nature deserving of wrath" (v. 3), to be reconciled to God and, what is especially prominent in this text, for gentiles to be brought together with Jews into "one new humanity." This last phrase could also be translated "one new man" (*hena kainon anthrōpon*), a phrase that alludes to Christ himself, the second Adam, as a corporate figure. Reconciliation is a theological concept that is more important in Paul than its comparatively few references would suggest (see also Rom 5:10–11; 11:15; 2 Cor 5:18–20; Col 1:20–23). And, as he does elsewhere (cf. Rom 5:1, 10–11; Col 1:20), Paul interprets reconciliation in terms of "making peace" (Eph 2:15): "He came and preached peace to you who were far away [the gentiles] and peace to those who were near [Jews]." Paul here alludes again to Isaiah 57:18–19. Paul combines this further allusion to Isaiah 57:18–19 with one to Isaiah 52:7: "How

---

65. See Thielman, *Ephesians*, 169, for this interpretation of the last clause (*ton nomon tōn entolōn en dogmasin*). In Colossians, Paul similarly refers to the "charge of our legal indebtedness" (*cheirographon*) that consisted in decrees (*en dogmasin*; Col 2:14).

66. Josephus uses the Greek word here (*mesotoichon*) to refer to this Temple balustrade (*Ant.* 8.71). Interpreters are curiously reluctant to admit this association with the temple, but granted the temple references later in this passage, it seems to be a natural connection. See esp. Arnold, *Ephesians*, 159. See O'Brien, *Ephesians*, 195–99, for other options.

67. See, e.g., Let. Aris. 139.

68. E.g., Hoehner, *Ephesians*, 374–77; Lincoln, *Ephesians*, 142; contra, e.g., Cohick, *Ephesians*, 186.

69. Thielman, *Ephesians*, 172.

70. "One body" in the phrase "in one body" in v. 16a could also refer to Christ's body as the means of sacrifice. But the emphasis on "one" suggests, rather, that it refers to the church (Aletti, *Essai sur l'écclesiologie*, 149–50).

beautiful on the mountains are the feet of those who bring good news, who proclaim peace, who bring good tidings, who proclaim salvation, who say to Zion, 'Your God reigns!'" This text, which Paul quotes in Romans 10:18, brings together several key Pauline theological concepts: proclaiming good news (*euēngelisato*), peace, salvation, and the reign of God.[71] One aspect of peace that Paul highlights in this context, of course, is the peace God creates between Jew and gentile in the "one new man" (v. 18).

"Consequently" (*ara oun*) in verse 19 brings us back to where Paul started in this section, celebrating the status of gentile believers that has been made possible by Christ's peace-making work on the cross. The status of gentiles before Christ (vv. 11–12) has been reversed: no longer are they "foreigners and strangers" but are "fellow citizens with God's people." But more than this "official" status, gentile believers are also "members of [God's] household" (*oikeioi tou theou*). Paul climaxes his description of the new people of God by employing the language of the temple. God no longer dwells in a building; his new dwelling place is the people of God, composed of believers in Christ from both Jewish and gentile backgrounds (vv. 20–22).[72] This temple, while solidly founded in the ministry of the apostles and prophets and crowned by Christ himself (v. 20), is still growing, focused on attaining the holiness appropriate to God's dwelling place (v. 21).

Paul's vision of the new community that God is creating through the work of Christ comes to clear expression in this paragraph: no less than a new dwelling place for God, created by bringing together believing Jews and believing gentiles. In Christ, *the* "new man," a new community takes shape—one that is no longer "Israel" in the traditional sense because gentiles are included as full and equal members with Jews. As Paul makes clear in Galatians and elsewhere, gentiles are welcomed into the people of God *as gentiles* without having to become Jews in the process. Equally, as this passage makes clear, Jews, as much as they might boast in their status as God's covenant people, need to be "brought near," just as the gentiles.[73] The early Christian language of a "third race" seems entirely appropriate as a designation of this new people.[74] Some interpreters find this emphasis on a "new man" difficult to reconcile with those texts in Paul that stress the continuing significance of Israel and the importance of her history for Christian identity (esp. Rom 11:11–32).[75] But it is not inconsistent for Paul to make these two claims: (1) the new people of God is the continuation in the new age of the people of God he has been forming for centuries (and the church can therefore be labeled "Israel" [Gal 6:16]); and (2) the new people of God transcends the boundaries of Israel as traditionally conceived and can therefore be labeled "a new man."

71. As Beale points out, Paul's application of texts about Israel in Isaiah to the church suggests that he sees the church as the "new Israel" (*New Testament Biblical Theology*, 724–27).

72. On this idea, and its development, see esp. Beale, *Temple and the Church's Mission*, 259–63.

73. O'Brien, *Ephesians*, 202–4.

74. "Third race" is an expression by a number of early Christian writers, as early as the beginning of the second century (Aristides, *Apology* 2.1); cf. also Turner, "Mission and Meaning," 144. See pp. 573–75.

75. E.g., Lincoln, *Ephesians*, 134.

1.5 Proclaiming the Mystery (3:1–13)

As in chapter 1, where Paul recounts believers' spiritual blessings (vv. 3–14) and then prays that his readers would respond appropriately (vv. 15–23), so now also, after celebrating the creation of a new people out of believing Jews and gentiles (2:11–22), he again turns to prayer for his readers ("for this reason" [3:1]). As he introduces his prayer, however, Paul reminds his readers that he is "the prisoner of Christ Jesus for the sake of you Gentiles" (v. 1). He is apparently concerned that his readers will consider his condition as a reason to doubt that God's sovereign plan is really coming to fruition.[76] He therefore exhorts them not to be "discouraged" because of his sufferings (v. 13). For these sufferings are the result of Paul's relentless pursuit of his calling to be a servant of the gospel, with particular focus on the extension of the good news to gentiles. In verses 2–12, then, Paul describes the administration of the "mystery" (see v. 3) that was given to him (vv. 2–6) and how he has "administered" that mystery in his faithful preaching of the good news to gentiles (vv. 7–12; the text has a close parallel in Col 1:24–29). This mystery is the now-revealed purpose of God to bring gentiles together with Jews in one body (see v. 6). In this passage, then, Paul reiterates the "one new people" teaching of 2:11–22 in terms of his own ministry.[77]

The word "mystery" (*mystērion*) is the key word in this passage (see vv. 3, 4, 9). Paul uses this word twenty-one times, with almost half (ten) coming in Colossians (1:26, 27; 2:2; 4:3) and Ephesians (see also 1:9; 5:32; 6:19). It typically refers to an aspect of God's plan of salvation that had previously been "hidden" but that has now been "revealed" in Christ (the contrast of "hidden"/"revealed" is common with this word in Paul [Rom 16:25; 1 Cor 2:7; Eph 3:9; Col 1:26]). So here this mystery "was not made known to people in other generations" but has now been "revealed by the Spirit to God's holy apostles and prophets" (v. 5). It was made known to Paul himself "by revelation" (*kata apokalypsin*, v. 3)—probably referring to his vision of the risen Christ on the Damascus Road. While scholars have traced this concept to several different religious or philosophical sources, it is now generally agreed that Paul has probably taken it from the book of Daniel, which describes dreams and visions as "mysteries," whose meanings are revealed by God to Daniel (Dan 2:18, 19, 27, 28, 29, 30, 47; 4:9).[78] Paul expands the notion, suggesting that many elements of OT revelation were, in fact, part of the "mystery." Paul claims to be the recipient of revelation that makes clear for the first time aspects of God's plan that were not—and could not be—previously recognized. In this passage the "mystery" is that "Gentiles are heirs together with Israel, members together of one body" (v. 6).[79] The Old Testament, of course, anticipates that gentiles

---

76. Gombis, *Drama of Ephesians*, 109–10; Arnold, *Ephesians*, 179.

77. O'Brien, *Ephesians*, 224.

78. See esp. Brown, *Semitic Background*.

79. Paul here uses three words compounded with Gk. *syn*, "with," for emphasis: Gentiles are *synklēronoma*, "heirs with Israel," *syssōma*, "members of a body with Israel," and *symmetocha*, "sharers with Israel." Some interpreters avoid the implication that

would one day worship the God of Israel, but it did not make clear that they would be intimately joined with Israel in "one body."

As we have seen, in verses 2–6 Paul describes himself as one entrusted with the "stewardship" (*oikonomia*, v. 2) of this mystery. In verses 7–12, he elaborates on the way he has engaged in "stewarding" (*oikonomia*, v. 9) this mystery. As he does throughout this passage, Paul stresses that his ministry is based on, and focuses on, "grace" (vv. 2, 7, 8).[80] The cosmic focus in Ephesians comes to the surface again in Paul's claim that the church is the means by which "the manifold wisdom of God should be made known to the rulers and authorities in the heavenly realms" (v. 10). It is difficult to know whether Paul is referring to spiritual beings in general[81] or to evil spiritual beings only.[82] In either case, the point is not that the church is actively engaged in preaching to these powers.[83] Rather, as M. Barth puts it, "By its very existence the church is called and equipped to be the 'theater of God's works.'"[84] In this sense, the existence of the church, in its incorporation of both Jews and gentiles in one body, is the beginning of the fulfillment of the summing up of all things in Christ (1:9–10).[85]

1.6 Prayer for Appreciation of God's Many Blessings (3:14–21)

Using the same transitional phrase that occurs in verse 1—"for this reason" (*toutou charin*)—Paul now finally gets to the prayer that he was going to begin earlier. This prayer to some degree returns to where this section begins, as Paul prays that his audience might fully appropriate and appreciate God's many spiritual blessings (1:3–14). Praying to God as Father is typical, of course, but not typical is the breadth of that fatherhood: every "social grouping" (perhaps the best rendering of the word)[86] derives its name—*patria*—from *the* Father (*patros*) (v. 15). Paul's prayer picks up many of the themes from his prayer in 1:17–23. He prays that his readers might have spiritual strength (3:16–17) and the ability fully to grasp "what is the breadth and length and height and depth" (v. 18 ESV). Some English versions assimilate this series to the reference to "the love of Christ" in verse 19 (e.g., NIV; NLT), and this represents the majority view among commentators.[87] But the reference could also be to God's wisdom[88] or power.[89] Again, as in 1:17–23, the intercession concludes with reference to

the inclusion of gentiles with Israel in a new body was not revealed in the OT by giving *hōs* the sense "it was not known *as much* then as it is now." But this is unlikely (e.g., Lincoln, *Ephesians*, 177).

80. Thielman (*Ephesians*, 89), therefore, rightly notes that "grace" is an important subtheme in this paragraph.

81. Hoehner, *Ephesians*, 462; O'Brien, *Ephesians*, 246; Turner, "Mission and Meaning," 146–47.

82. Clinton E. Arnold, *Ephesians: Power and Magic: The Concept of Power in Ephesians and Its Historical Setting* (Baker: Grand Rapids, 1992), 55–56; Lincoln, *Ephesians*, 185; Best, *Ephesians*, 322.

83. Contra Walter Wink, *Naming the Powers: The Language of Power in the New Testament* (Philadelphia: Fortress, 1984), 89.

84. Barth, *Ephesians 1–3*, 364.

85. Best, *Ephesians*, 313.

86. See Best, *Ephesians*, 338. Lincoln (*Ephesians*, 202) paraphrases "family groupings or classes of angels."

87. See esp. the full discussion in Lincoln, *Ephesians*, 208–13.

88. Lincoln (*Ephesians*, 211) thinks this could be a secondary emphasis.

89. E.g., Arnold, *Ephesians*, 214–17.

"fullness" (*plērōma*) and "filling" (*plēroō*): "That you might be filled to the measure of all the fullness of God" (3:19). Paul ends the paragraph, and the first part of the letter as a whole, with a well-known doxology (vv. 20–21).

2 LIVING IN CHRIST (4:1–6:24)

2.1 The One Church and Its Mission (4:1–16)

Paul uses the verb *parakaleō*, "I exhort" (my translation; NIV: "I urge") to introduce the part of the letter that focuses particularly on the application of his theology (the closest parallel to this transition, as many have noted, is Rom 12:1). Living "a life worthy of the calling you have received" (v. 1) stands as an introductory summary to all that follows. In verses 2–3, Paul begins by urging his readers to act toward one another in humility (v. 2) and to "keep the unity of the Spirit" (v. 3; Col 3:12–14 is similar). In verse 4, however, rather than continuing to exhort his readers, he reinforces his appeal to unity in verse 3 by stressing the "oneness" of the church (vv. 4–6). In a sequence typical of Paul's thinking about the church, the unity of the body leads him to reflect on the diversity within it. In verses 7–16, then, Paul celebrates the diverse gifts the ascended Christ has given the body to attain the destiny that God has for it—to be united and mature.

"One" is the drumbeat in verses 4–6, as Paul uses this word to characterize seven facets of Christian existence: "one body," "one Spirit," "one hope," "one Lord," "one faith," "one baptism," "one God and Father of all." Only two of these require comment. "Faith" might refer to the act of believing, but it is probably rather here the content of what is believed.[90] "Baptism" (*baptisma*) has, of course, the root notion of "immersion," and some interpreters think it here may refer to the believer's "immersion" into Christ's death.[91] However, sixteen of the nineteen New Testament occurrences of this noun refer to the rite of immersion in water. Almost certainly, then, Paul refers here to this Christian rite of initiation—although there is a lot to be said for thinking that water baptism is viewed as part of a larger "conversion-initiation" process.[92]

Ephesians 4:7–16 is framed with references to the role each believer plays in preserving the unity and building up the church: "to each one of us grace has been given" (v. 7)/"as each part does its work" (v. 16). This "grace" (*charis*) takes the form of specific "gifts" (*domata* in v. 8; Paul's usual word for "gift" in this sense—*charisma*—is not used in this passage). As Paul does in 1 Corinthians 12:12–31 and Romans 12:6–8, he moves from the unity of the body of Christ to the diversity of gifts and gifted people

---

90. O'Brien, *Ephesians*, 283.
91. E.g., Hoehner, *Ephesians*, 517–18.
92. See here Thielman, *Ephesians*, 258–59. The three texts in which *baptisma* probably does not refer directly to water immersion are Mark 10:38–39 (2x); Luke 12:50. See my comments elsewhere on Rom 6:4; and on baptism in general, pp. 588–90.

that make up that body. Paul describes the giving of gifts by Christ to his people in Ephesians 4:8 with words taken from Psalm 68:18 (67:19 LXX): "When he ascended on high, he took many captives and gave gifts to his people." However, a quick glance at Psalm 68:18 in our English Bibles reveals a problem; the psalmist says not that God "gave" gifts to people but that he "received" them from people. This change in text raises questions about the nature and integrity of Paul's hermeneutical procedure. It is possible that Paul's quotation reflects a form of the text current in his day and known to his readers.[93] It is also possible that the psalm verse deliberately picks up language about the Levites from earlier in the Old Testament (e.g., Num 8:16, 18–19; and 18:6). As God therefore "received" the Levites in order, in turn, to "give" them as servants to his people Israel, so Psalm 68:18 might be implying both God's "receiving" of gifts and his distribution of them.[94] Perhaps the best option, however, is to think that Paul is reading the psalm, as other Jews in his day were doing, in terms of the celebration of Pentecost. As it was used in this context, Jews viewed the psalm as a reference to Moses ascending Sinai. Paul, in light of the climax of redemptive history in Christ, now reads it as the ascent of Christ who, in virtue of that victory and subsequent descent in the Spirit on the Christian Pentecost, gives gifts to his church.[95] Nothing even approaching a consensus has been reached on this matter, however, meaning that we must leave our options open.[96] What is clear is that Paul again emphasizes the ascended Christ's power (he has "taken many captives") that is now manifested on behalf of his people.[97]

In verses 9–10, Paul adds a parenthetical comment on the language of "ascended" in his quotation. The main point is to stress that Christ, who has "descended," is the same one who has now "ascended higher than all the heavens, in order to fill the whole universe." Paul again encourages his readers by reminding them that their Lord is ruler of all, with the power to supply all their needs and overcome all their enemies. He speaks of Christ's descent as being "to the lower parts of the earth" (*ta katōtera merē tēs gēs*).[98] This English translation (my own) would probably mean to most people that Christ descended to some place that is lower than the earth as we know it (*tēs gēs* would then be a comparative genitive)—probably something like the Greek notion of Hades. Granted Paul's use of "lower parts" (why use it if he meant simply "the earth"?)

---

93. The Aramaic targum preserves such a reading, and while it is considerably later than the NT period, it may reflect a Jewish traditional exegesis that goes back much earlier.

94. See esp. Gary V. Smith, "Paul's Use of Psalm 68:18 in Ephesians 4:8," *JETS* 18 (1975): 181–89; O'Brien, *Ephesians*, 289–93.

95. See esp. W. Hall Harris III, *Descent of Christ: Ephesians 4:7–11 and Traditional Hebrew Imagery*, AGJU 32 (Leiden: Brill, 1996); and also Horton, *Rediscovering the Holy Spirit*, 226–30; Lincoln, *Ephesians*, 156–61; Thorsten Moritz, *A Profound Mystery:*

The Use of the Old Testament in Ephesians, NovTSup 85 (Leiden: Brill, 1996), 58–86.

96. For a recent survey of options and analysis, see Grant R. Osborne, "Hermeneutics and Paul: Psalm 68:18 in Ephesians 4:7–10 as a Test Case," in Harmon and Smith, *Studies in the Pauline Epistles*, 159–77.

97. Arnold (*Ephesians*, 250–52) especially emphasizes this theme.

98. The word *merē* is textually uncertain, but the meaning is much the same whether it is read or not.

and the widespread tradition about descents to Hades in Paul's environment, this interpretation has much to be said for it.[99] However, Paul's point here is to argue from a descent, which would appear to be well known, to his ascent again to heaven. The descent might, then, refer to Christ's "coming down from heaven" to the earth itself (*tēs gēs* then being epexegetic; Christ descended to the lower parts, that is, the earth).[100] A decision is difficult, but I slightly prefer the second interpretation.

In verse 11, Paul resumes the main lines of his argument. The sentence that begins here continues all the way through verse 16 in Greek, as Paul, much like he has done in 1:3–14, piles up subordinate clauses and prepositional phrases. Paul, of course, lists some of the gifts God has given his people in Romans 12:6–8 and 1 Corinthians 12:7–10, 28. Here, to speak more precisely, he has given gifted people. "Apostles," listed first also in 1 Corinthians 12:28, are, of course, the specially chosen men who had seen Christ and who had the authority to establish new-covenant norms. "Prophets," mentioned first in the Romans list, could be simply any person who exhorts and encourages, but may more restrictively refer to those given the ability to decipher special revelations from God.[101] In Ephesians, significantly, Paul elsewhere groups together apostles and prophets as those who provide the foundation for the church (2:20; cf. also 3:5). Only in this list here in Ephesians are "evangelists" and "pastors" (or "shepherds" [*poimenas*]) mentioned. The significance of "evangelist" is clear enough, but we should note that "pastor" or "shepherd" (*poimēn*) in the Old Testament and in Paul's day often referred to a leader or ruler. Jesus is called the "great Shepherd" (Heb 13:20; cf. 1 Pet 2:25; and also Rev 2:27; 7:17; 12:5; 19:15), and Peter calls on elders to "shepherd" (*poimainō*) their flocks (1 Pet 5:2; see also Acts 20:28; Jude 12). The imagery suggests that pastoring involves a particular kind of "leading": exercising loving care of the flock God has entrusted to them. The list ends with "teachers," which comes third in Romans 12:6–8. As has often been noted, Paul shifts his syntax as he comes to these last two gifted people, using a single article to cover both nouns. Some have thought that Paul may be suggesting that the same person performed both these ministries ("pastor-teachers").[102] This is certainly possible, but it might be overinterpreting the syntactical shift. All that the Greek suggests is that these last two can be considered together for some reason. Others therefore think that these two ministered in local churches, whereas apostles, prophets, and evangelists were not confined to one location.[103] Perhaps it is best to think that pastoring and teaching were ministries with significant overlap.[104]

99. E.g., Thielman, *Ephesians*, 269–72; Arnold, *Ephesians*, 253–54.

100. E.g., O'Brien, *Ephesians*, 294–96; Best, *Ephesians*, 384–86; Markus Barth, *Ephesians: Translation and Commentary on Chapters 4–6*, AB 34A (Garden City: Doubleday, 1974), 434. A few interpreters think the reference could be to Pentecost (e.g., Lincoln, *Ephesians*, 247).

101. For further discussion, see pp. 594–95.

102. E.g., Bruce, *Colossians, Philemon, and Ephesians*, 348; Barth, *Ephesians 4–6*, 438.

103. Chrysostom (see *NPNF¹* 13:104); Abbott, *Ephesians and Colossians*, 118.

104. My uncertainty about some of these functions is revealed in conflicting views as to whether pastor or teacher is the wider

The remainder of Paul's run-on sentence is concerned with the purpose for which God has given gifted people to the church (vv. 12–16). This purpose is that the people of God might be united and mature. The latter point is made by means of imagery drawn from human development, Paul contrasting spiritual "infants" (v. 14) with those who are "mature" (v. 15). Paul reinforces this point in verse 13 by claiming that building up the body will lead to it becoming "a mature male" (*andra teleion*; NIV tries to get the idea by translating "become mature"; cf. ESV "mature manhood"). Lurking in the background here is a reference to Christ himself, the "new man" (see 2:15; NIV: "new humanity"). Paul probably shifts from *anthrōpos* (2:15) to *anēr* because the latter often is used to denote "adult males" as opposed to young or immature males.

The maturity of Christ's body, the church, is grounded in the faithful ministry of God's gifted people (vv. 11–12). But the way Paul puts this in verse 12 has created some controversy. He uses three prepositional phrases: (1) "to equip his people"; (2) "for works of service"; (3) "to build up the body of Christ." The three could be parallel and depend on God's giving of gifted people in verse 11. In this case, it would be these gifted people, or, we might say, "ministers," who accomplish these things.[105] On the other hand, the second phrase could depend on the first and the third on the second—which is the way the NIV and most English versions understand the syntax: Christ gave gifted people (v. 11) "to equip his people for works of service, so that the body of Christ may be built up." On this reading, gifted people train Christians in general, who then, through their works of service, build up Christ's body.[106] The controversy arises because these two readings suggest somewhat different conceptions of "ministry." The former stresses the role of appointed ministers; the latter "democratizes" ministry, making the body as a whole responsible for the maturing of the church. Without taking anything away from the significant role particular gifted people play in Paul's conception of the church, I think the context favors the second reading (note v. 7: "To *each* one of us grace has been given"; see also v. 16: "As *each* part does its work").

2.2 The Contrast Between the Old Life and the New (4:17–32)

Paul began this larger section with an exhortation to "live a life worthy of the calling you have received" (v. 1). In verses 12–16, Paul has summarized this calling in general terms. Now he returns to a paraenetic mode, first summarizing "a life worthy of the calling you received" again in general terms (4:17–24) and then turning to specifics (4:25–32; 5:1–7, 8–14, 15–20). The verb *peripateō*, "walk" (translated "live"

---

category. Do all pastors teach, but not all teachers pastor (e.g., O'Brien, *Ephesians*, 300)? Or do all teachers pastor but not all pastors teach (Arnold, *Ephesians*, 260)?

105. E.g., Michael S. Horton, *People and Place: A Covenant Ecclesiology* (Louisville: Westminster John Knox, 2008), 236.

106. Hoehner, *Ephesians*, 398; Thielman, *Ephesians*, 277–79. See Arnold, *Ephesians*, 262, for a clear laying out of the options.

in the NIV), marks out these sections (see 4:17; 5:2, 8, 15). As is typical of the tone of Ephesians, Paul does not point to any particular situation or crisis that sparks these exhortations; they seem to be motivated by a more general concern for spiritual stagnation. As Best notes, the "peril facing Gentile believers is neither persecution brought on by their new attitude to paganism nor the influence of heretical intellectual ideas but a relapse into their former pre-Christian ways."[107]

Paul begins by contrasting his readers' former way of life with the new way of life, the emphasis in these verses (vv. 17–24) falling on characterization of that former life. Strikingly, Paul, writing to gentiles, refers to that former way of life as living "as the Gentiles do." This way of speaking (see also 1 Cor 5:1; 12:2; 1 Thess 4:5; cf. 1 Pet 2:12; 4:3) might simply be a reflection of the typical Jewish view of gentiles. But it is also possible that it suggests again their new identity, one that transcends the old divisions of gentile and Jew (2:15). Paul briefly characterizes this way of life in 4:17b–19. That life, rooted in foolish thinking and hard hearts and manifested in all kinds of sinful behavior, stands in stark contrast to the new life they are called to lead in Christ (vv. 20–24). Paul summarizes with a simple but evocative image: "You did not learn Christ this way" (v. 20; my translation). This might mean nothing more than that believers have "learned about Christ" (cf. NLT: "This isn't what you learned about Christ"). But Paul's unusual wording may make the point that the new life believers learn "about" is nothing less than conformity to the person of Christ. As M. Barth puts it, believers have gone to "the school of the Messiah," where "the medium is the message."[108] In verses 22–24, Paul elaborates the content of this new message. The main verb is "you were taught" in verse 22a, with two infinitives dependent on it: "to put off your old self" in verse 22b, and "to put on the new self" in verse 24. Some interpreters think that this combination has a basic indicative force: "You were taught that you have put off the old self and have put on the new self."[109] But the infinitives are more likely to have an imperative thrust: "You were taught that you should put off the old self and put on the new self."[110] "Old self"/"new self" translates phrases that could also be translated "old man"/"new man" (see NET; *anthrōpos* is the Gk. term). Paul uses similar language in Romans 6:6 and Colossians 3:10–11. As Ephesians 2:15, with its reference to the "one new man" (*hena kainon anthrōpon*) suggests, the "new man" is Christ himself, while the "old man" will then be Adam. The language of "put off" and "put on" (*apothesthai* in v. 22 and *endysasthai* in v. 24) is a metaphor drawn from the taking off and putting on of clothing. Paul's point here, then, is that believers must rid themselves of the enveloping influence of Adam and the sinful values he represents and cover themselves with Christ and the kingdom values he represents. In Romans 6:6 and

---

107. Best, *Ephesians*, 415.
108. Barth, *Ephesians 4–6*, 529.
109. Hoehner, *Ephesians*, 600.
110. Arnold, *Ephesians*, 286; O'Brien, *Ephesians*, 327.

Colossians 3:10–11, Paul implies that this "change of clothing" is something believers have already experienced; here, as I have argued, Paul commands believers to put off the old self and to put on the new. We can reconcile these texts if we recognize that Paul is thinking fundamentally of relationships. In Christ, our tie to Adam is decisively broken; the sin and death he introduced into the world no longer determine our destiny. Yet the influence of Adam remains as long as we live in these mortal bodies, requiring believers continually to fight against that influence.[111] This battle against the old way of thinking can be successful when believers renew their minds (v. 23).[112] Paul suggests that this fundamental reorientation in the believer's way of thinking, or value system, is key to becoming mature and faithful followers of Christ (see also Rom 12:2).[113]

In verse 25, Paul picks up the verb "put off" from his initial general exhortation (v. 22) to introduce a series of exhortations relating to specific forms of behavior (vv. 25–32). The focus is on the negative, as we would expect after the imperative "put off." The series focuses on anger and sinful speech, which are often related to each other in Scripture (vv. 25–26, 29, 31). Amid these specific prohibitions, Paul interjects the general warning about grieving the Holy Spirit (v. 30) and concludes with the positive counterpart of anger and abusive speech—showing kindness and compassion to one another, "forgiving each other, just as in Christ God forgave you" (v. 32; see also Col 3:13; indeed, this paragraph has many parallels with Col 3:8–9, 12–14).

2.3 The Shape of the New Life (5:1–20)

Most commentators think that 5:1–2 concludes the series of exhortations in 4:25–32. However, it might be better to put a minor break between 4:32 and 5:1, with the call to "therefore . . . walk" (*oun . . . peripateite*) marking the new beginning. We find similar wording in 4:1, 17; 5:8, 15—all, arguably, at transition points.[114] The present section, then, would fall into three parts: 5:1–7, 8–14, and 15–20.

The first paragraph is framed by the exhortation to imitate God (NIV "follow God's example") in verse 1 and the warning about being "partners" with disobedient people in verse 7. Imitation as a basis for ethical behavior is sometimes viewed with suspicion, but it plays a clear role in Paul's paraenesis. He calls on believers to imitate him (1 Cor 4:16; 11:1; Phil 3:17; 1 Thess 3:9; cf. 1 Thess 1:6), other believers (Phil 3:17; cf. 1 Thess 2:14), Christ (cf. 1 Thess 1:6), and God (here at Eph 5:1). As he often does, Paul singles out love as a central focus of how Christians should live, and cites Christ's giving of

---

111. See, on this whole idea, pp. 221–22 (on Rom 6:6) and p. 492.

112. In the Greek of vv. 22–24, "renewing the mind" is parallel to "putting on the new man" (infinitives linked by *kai*; cf. NIV: "You were taught . . . to be made new in the attitude of your minds; and to put on the new self"). But the infinitive in v. 23 is logically subordinate.

113. The focus on deeply rooted habits of thinking is suggested here by Paul's wording: "be made new in the spirit of your mind" (my translation; *ananeousthai de tō pneumati tou noos hymōn*).

114. Hoehner, *Ephesians*, 643; cf. also Barth, *Ephesians 4–6*, 555.

himself in sacrificial death as a model of the kind of love we should exhibit (v. 2). Paul then turns to the negative, warning his readers to avoid sexual immorality, impurity, greed, and profane speech (vv. 3–4). He reinforces his exhortation with a warning in verses 5–6 that people who are marked by such sins will not inherit the kingdom of God (see 1 Cor 6:9–10) but will, rather, suffer God's wrath (see Col 3:6).

The motif of light binds verses 8–14 together. The contrast of light and darkness is a natural metaphor for the contrast of good and evil behavior and was widely used in the ancient world. We should not, therefore, think that Paul has drawn the contrast from any particular source.[115] Strikingly, Paul begins by claiming not that believers once lived "in" darkness and now live "in light," but that they *were* "darkness" and *are now* "light." He therefore suggests that these qualities manifest "the core of their being."[116] As people who are "in Christ" and have the Spirit within them and thus *are* light, they must therefore "live" (or "walk"—*peripateite*) "in the light" and discern "what pleases the Lord." People who are light will naturally produce "fruit" typical of the light (v. 9), in contrast to "the fruitless deeds of darkness" (v. 11). Believers are to "expose" (*elenchō*) those evil deeds. The verb "expose" elsewhere refers to rebuking believers (or apparent believers) who are sinning or teaching falsely (1 Tim 5:20; 2 Tim 4:2; Titus 1:9; 2:15). Here, therefore, "the disobedient" whose deeds of darkness are exposed may be people within the Christian community.[117] However, the strength of the language and the context, in which Paul repeatedly contrasts Christian conduct with non-Christian behavior, favor a reference to unbelievers (see 1 Cor 14:24).[118] This suggests that being "exposed by the light" in verse 13 refers to conversion. Likewise, then, verse 14, which appears to be a quotation of an early Christian hymn, will also refer to conversion.[119]

Verses 15–20 cap off this section with a general call to "live a life worthy of the calling you have received" (cf. 4:1). This calling means living as "wise" people—those who know and do the will of God (see v. 17). Wise people will make "the most of every opportunity" (v. 16)—that is, they are to "buy up" the time, the "day of salvation" (2 Cor 6:1), with its opportunities to witness to Christ by the way they live.[120] Two contrasting imperatives in verse 18 introduce the next sequence: "Do not get drunk on wine . . . be filled with the Spirit." The NIV translation echoes most English versions in using "with" in the last clause. On this reading, many think that Paul is contrasting two different kinds of "filling": the negative filling ourselves with wine and the positive filling of the Spirit.[121] However, the preposition translated "with" (*en*) could also

115. Fowl, *Ephesians*, 169.

116. Arnold, *Ephesians*, 328.

117. Barth, *Ephesians 4–6*, 597–98; Arnold, *Ephesians*, 331.

118. O'Brien, *Ephesians*, 372–73; Thielman, *Ephesians*, 345; Andreas Lindemann, *Der Epheserbrief*, ZBK 8 (Zurich: TVZ, 1985), 95; Fowl, *Ephesians*, 170–71.

119. Since these words are not found in any OT or early Jewish source, it is likely they come from an early Christian hymn, perhaps one that depends on Isa 26:19; 60:1 (see, e.g., Moritz, *Profound Mystery*, 97–116).

120. The Greek uses the verb *exagorazō*, which has the sense of "buy up." See my comments on the parallel in Col 4:5.

121. E.g., Arnold, *Ephesians*, 349–51; Gnilka, *Epheserbrief*, 269–70.

indicate means or agent: "be filled by the Spirit." On this reading, Paul is calling on believers to seek "fullness" by means of the work of the Spirit. What is this "fullness"? Paul may be referring back to 3:19, where he prays that "you may be filled [*plērōthēte*] to the measure of all the fullness of God." This latter interpretation is probably to be preferred.[122] Paul spells out what this being filled by the Spirit looks like with a series of participles:

"speaking to one another with psalms, hymns, and songs from the Spirit" (v. 19a)
"singing and making music from your hearts to the Lord" (v. 19b; my translation)
"always giving thanks to God the Father for everything, in the name of our Lord Jesus Christ" (v. 20)
"submitting to one another out of reverence for Christ" (v. 21 ESV)

The communal focus, with "one another" framing these exhortations, is clear.

2.4 Instructions for the Christian Household (5:21–6:9)

Paul now gives instructions for relationships between wives and husbands (5:22–33), children and parents (6:1–4), and slaves and masters (6:5–9). He therefore treats the three basic relationships that characterized the ancient household. This series of instructions, with its call for wives, children, and slaves to "submit" (5:22, 24) or "obey" (6:1, 5), follows a pattern well known in Paul's day, labeled by modern scholars as a "household code" (Ger. *Haustafeln*; see the notes on Col 3:18–4:1). In calling for submission/obedience, Paul is following the pattern of those codes, which often sought to enforce order on the household by encouraging members to "find their place." But Paul significantly breaks the pattern, both by treating wives as willing participants in the household and by calling on the "superior" member of each relationship to treat the "other" with love and respect.

The connection of this code with what precedes it is forged with the call for "mutual submission" in verse 21. As I noted above, the verb in this verse, *hypotassomenoi*, is a participle that appears to be parallel to the ones in verses 19–20. The syntax, therefore, provides a good basis to include verse 21 with verses 18–20, with a break put between verses 21 and 22 (e.g., ESV).[123] However, the verb *hypotassō*, "submit," also introduces the focus of the household code; in fact, verse 22 has no verb in the Greek, it being supplied from the verb in verse 21. This lexical shift constitutes solid grounds for including verse 21 with what follows, in which case we would put a break between verses

---

122. See esp. Wendall Hollis, "Become Full in the Spirit: A Linguistic, Contextual, and Theological Study of ΠΛΗΡΟΥΣΘΕ 'ΕΝ ΠΝΕΥΜΑΤΙ" (PhD diss., Trinity International University, 2001); also, e.g., O'Brien, *Ephesians*, 390–92; Hoehner, *Ephesians*,

703–4. The *en* phrase could also refer to being in the realm of the Spirit (Thielman, *Ephesians*, 360).

123. Arnold, *Ephesians*, 356–57; O'Brien, *Ephesians*, 398–99; Hoehner, *Ephesians*, 716.

20 and 21 (e.g., NIV).[124] In fact, as is universally recognized, verse 21 is transitional, continuing verses 18–20 and introducing verses 22–33. If we put a break in the text, however, I think it should probably be between verse 20 and verse 21.

While superficially a minor matter of paragraphing, the decision about verse 21 is, of course, embroiled in the large and often nasty debate about the roles of women according to New Testament teaching. Verses 22–24, with their exhortation for wives to "submit" (vv. 22, 24), is the focus of controversy here. The verb "submit" suggests the idea of "ordering under." A wife is called to willingly recognize that God has ordained her husband to be her "leader." This, at least, is how we might translate *kephalē* here (NIV: "head"). This word has also been the object of endless debate. As I note elsewhere (see notes on 1 Cor 11:3), this word can, as a metaphor, connote either leadership or provision. In this context, the parallel between wives submitting to their husbands and believers submitting to Christ makes it clear that leadership is the connotation.[125] Two opposing tendencies, moving toward extremes, need to be avoided as we think about "submission" here.[126] On the one hand are those who reject any idea of true reciprocity in verse 21 by treating it as a kind of heading for what follows. On this reading, the verse introduces the topic of subordination, with the three instances following spelling out the relationships in which one "submits" to another.[127] On the other hand are those who put so much emphasis on "mutual submission" in verse 21 that any genuine submission in the marriage relationship is excluded.[128] Both kinds, or instances, of submission are taught here. I think it is clear that verse 21 calls for "mutual submission," along the lines of similar encouragements for Christians to defer to one another; see, for example, Philippians 2:3–4: "Do nothing out of selfish ambition or vain conceit. Rather, in humility value others above yourselves, not looking to your own interests but each of you to the interests of the others." Paul deliberately subverts the normal usage, calling for believers to exhibit a "countercultural attitude."[129] But I also think it is clear that Paul calls on Christian wives in verses 22–24 to exercise genuine submission to their husbands. Of course, this submission is not blind obedience; this text does not warrant the conclusion that a wife must do whatever her husband asks (and it might therefore be significant that "obey," used in 6:1, 5, is not used here).

In verses 25–30, Paul emphasizes the responsibilities of Christian husbands.

---

124. Thielman, *Ephesians*, 365.

125. E.g., Gregory W. Dawes, *The Body in Question: Metaphor and Meaning in the Interpretation of Ephesians 5:21–33*, BibInt 30 (Leiden: Brill, 1998), 134–37.

126. Lincoln, *Ephesians*, 366; George W. Knight III, "Husbands and Wives as Analogues of Christ and the Church: Ephesians 5:21–33 and Colossians 3:18–19," in *Recovering Biblical Manhood and Womanhood: A Response to Evangelical Feminism*, ed. John Piper and Wayne Grudem (Wheaton, IL: Crossway, 1991), 167–68.

127. See esp. Stephen B. Clark, *Man and Woman in Christ: An Examination of the Roles of Men and Women in Light of Scripture and the Social Sciences* (Edinburgh: T&T Clark, 1980), 76; also O'Brien, *Ephesians*, 400–404; Hoehner, *Ephesians*, 717.

128. Tending toward this extreme are Keener, *Paul, Women and Wives*, 133–224; Payne, *Man and Woman*, 279–83.

129. Arnold, *Ephesians*, 356; see also Best, *Ephesians*, 516–17; Thielman, *Ephesians*, 372–74.

They are to love their wives as Christ himself loves the church (v. 25) and as husbands love and care for their own bodies (v. 28). As Paul has noted in verse 23, Christ is not only the "head" of the church; he is also its "Savior." That salvation is secured only by means of Christ's giving himself up for the church (v. 25), by which means he has made "her holy, cleansing her by the washing with water through the word" (v. 26). The relationship between "make her holy" (*hagiasē*) and "cleansing" (*katharisas*, a participle) is debated. They might be coincidental, "making holy" and "cleansing" describing the same thing from two different angles.[130] But Old Testament precedents might rather favor taking the "cleansing" as the first, causative, step toward "making holy" (see ESV: "That he might sanctify her, having cleansed her").[131] Also debated in this verse is whether "washing with water" refers to baptism[132] or is a simple metaphor for spiritual cleansing.[133]

At the end of this passage, Paul shifts ground a bit from a comparison between wife and husband on the one hand and the church and Christ on the other to an assertion about the church: "We are members of his body" (v. 30). He then adds a quotation from Genesis 2:24 about the "original marriage": "For this reason a man will leave his father and mother and be united to his wife, and the two will become one flesh" (v. 31). "This," Paul then says, "is a profound mystery—but I am talking about Christ and the church" (v. 32). Some people think that the "mystery" refers to marriage, the word being taken to mean "sacrament." Others think that Paul is here using "mystery" in a hermeneutical sense: the meaning of Genesis 2:24, hidden until now, is revealed—the passage refers to Christ and the church. But Paul's own comment in verse 32 suggests that his focus is on the "mystical union" of Christ with his people. Verse 30 clearly signals a shift to this emphasis. Probably, then, "mystery" refers to this union, and Paul is using the quotation from Genesis 2:24 as an analogy; as husband and wife become "one flesh," so Christ and his people become "one body."[134]

Reciprocal relationships are also to characterize children and parents: children are to obey (6:1); "parents" (CEB) or "fathers" (most versions) are to avoid exasperating their children—apparently by overly harsh discipline (v. 4).[135] The command to children is grounded in a quotation of the fifth commandment from the Decalogue (Exod 20:12). Paul's application of a command from the Mosaic law to Christians raises questions about the meaning of, and extent to which, Christ has truly "annulled" the law (Eph 2:14). Some conclude that the verse requires us to qualify that kind of claim, and that Paul

---

130. O'Brien, *Ephesians*, 422.

131. Thielman, *Ephesians*, 383.

132. E.g., Best, *Ephesians*, 543.

133. Thielman, *Ephesians*, 384; Hoehner, *Ephesians*, 753 (who notes that Paul might also be alluding to the ancient ritual of the "bridal bath").

134. See esp. Andreas J. Köstenberger, "The Mystery of Christ and the Church: Head and Body, 'One Flesh,'" *TrinJ* 12 (1991): 79–94, esp. 91–92; also Arnold, *Ephesians*, 394–95.

135. The Greek *pateres* here usually means "fathers," but it can mean "parents" (BDAG; see Heb 11:23).

thinks at least the Decalogue continues to be authoritative for believers as part of the "moral law." However, we do better justice to Paul's claims about the law elsewhere if we recognize that Paul can quote Old Testament commands in this way because he views them as "absorbed into the ethical teaching for the newly formed people of God" (see also pp. 614–22).[136] Paul adds that this commandment is "the first with a promise." If, as Lincoln argues, God's "showing love" to those who keep the commandments (after the second commandment; Exod 20:6) is a declaration about God rather than a promise, then this claim is strictly true.[137] Why Paul adds it here, however, is difficult to know. Also difficult to know is what the promise, in a new-covenant context, might mean. For Israel, to "enjoy long life on the earth" means to flourish in the land of Israel. Following a pattern of "spiritualizing" that some see as basic to the New Testament interpretation of the Old Testament, the reference could be to spiritual life or the kingdom of God (for the latter, see, e.g., 1 Cor 6:9; Gal 5:21).[138] However, "living long" is difficult to map as a spiritual benefit. Probably what Paul is promising is quite simply that obedient children will live a long and good life. The promise, as with all proverbial promises of this kind, speaks of what is generally true, not of what will be true in every situation. Paul is working from the same universalizing hermeneutic that we saw at work in Romans 4:13. The "land" promised to the people of God, focused on (but was never confined to!) Palestine, has in the last days been extended to the universal dimensions intended by God all along. This long life may refer to this present world. However, it is also possible that Paul is promising a long life in the "new heavens and new earth."[139] Obedient children, like all faithful believers, can look forward to a "long life"—indeed, an "eternal" life!—in a renewed and transformed world.

Slaves were considered part of the Greco-Roman household, so it is natural that Paul also addresses the relationship of slaves and masters (as he does in the same series in Col 3:18–4:1). Paul again begins with the "subordinate" member, urging Christian slaves to obey their masters, but, more importantly, to obey sincerely, just as if they were serving Christ (6:5–7). Masters, on the other hand, are to treat their slaves "in the same way" (v. 9), that is, recognizing that they too have a "Master" (*kyrios*)—a heavenly one. And this Master is one who will scrutinize the actions of every believer (v. 8).

2.5 Spiritual Warfare and Letter Closing (6:10–20)

Paul brings his exhortations to a climax with his famous "armor of God" passage. The cosmic focus of the letter and its concern with the "powers" emerges here again.

---

136. Thielman, *Ephesians*, 400.

137. Lincoln, *Ephesians*, 404.

138. The Jewish philosopher and theologian Philo, a near contemporary of Paul's, interprets the OT "live long in the land" as immortality (*Special Laws* 2.262).

139. See Beale, *New Testament Biblical Theology*, 214; and on this text, see also D. Moo and J. Moo, *Creation Care*, 134–36.

Our struggle is not against simply human forces but supernatural ones—"the rulers," "the authorities," "the powers of this dark world," the "spiritual forces of evil" (v. 12).[140] Moreover, this struggle will be taking place "when the day of evil comes" (v. 13). This rendering (the NIV) suggests that Paul is thinking of a future "day," perhaps a time of severe testing. But the Greek could also refer to a present "day of evil" (ESV, "in the evil day"). Paul, then, might be referring to the entire period of time between Christ's first coming and his second, a time when tribulation will be the constant threat to Christian faithfulness.[141] Echoing another important theme in the letter, Paul "locates" these powers "in the heavenly realms" (v. 12).

Faced with such opponents, no ordinary weapons are adequate; we need "the full armor of God" (v. 11). This phrase might mean "the full armor that God supplies us with."[142] But Paul's description of the several pieces of armor in verses 14–17 depends heavily on Old Testament passages that depict God, as "the holy warrior," donning these pieces of armor himself (see esp. Isa 59:15b–17). The phrase, then, more likely, has a dual sense: "The armor that is God's own and that he gives to his people."[143] In addition to the Old Testament, Paul probably also describes the armor with allusion to the equipment of Roman soldiers in his day. Paul, of course, compares these various pieces of armor with spiritual qualities: truth, righteousness, preparedness to preach the gospel, faith, salvation, the Spirit, the Word of God. It is unlikely that Paul has thought very carefully about just which pieces of armor to include or about how these spiritual matters fit with the specific pieces of armor he matches them with. His concern is not with the details but with the overall picture: believers fully prepared by God himself to face any threat that might come their way. By locating the powers we fight "in the heavenly realms" and labeling them as spiritual powers, Paul does not want to suggest that our battle is purely in the spiritual realm. Our enemies often take a very human and earthly form.[144]

Paul concludes this section with an exhortation to take up one of our strongest weapons: prayer (v. 18). He concludes the letter with request for prayer for himself (vv. 19–20) and brief closing remarks (vv. 21–23).

140. In keeping with his overall thesis, Arnold thinks there might be reference especially to the magical practices for which Ephesus was famous (*Ephesians: Power and Magic*, 103–22).

141. See esp. Beale, *New Testament Biblical Theology*, 187–224; p. 214 on this text; also Thielman, *Ephesians*, 423.

142. Arnold, *Ephesians*, 444.

143. O'Brien, *Ephesians*, 457, 463.

144. See Horton, *People and Place*, 280, on this point.

Chapter 13

PHILIPPIANS

LOCATING THE LETTER

Philippians is one of the more challenging letters of Paul to locate. The letter makes clear that Paul is in prison (1:13–14)—but where? A few interpreters have answered "Caesarea," where Paul spent two years under Roman confinement (cf. Acts 23:31–26:32; cf. 24:27).[1] But most scholars agree that the two serious options are Ephesus and Rome. As I noted in the "Locating the Letter" section on Colossians, many scholars think it likely that Paul spent some time in prison in Ephesus, despite the silence of Acts on this matter. Ephesus, it is argued, is a reasonable provenance for Philippians, since the letter assumes at least four trips back and forth between Philippi and the place of writing.[2] Ephesus, like Rome, would have had a contingent of the praetorium guard (1:13; "palace guard" in NIV) and administrative servants of the emperor ("Caesar's household" in 4:22). Moreover, certain passages appear to resemble texts Paul wrote on the third missionary journey: the strong warning against Judaizers in chapter 3 sounds a lot like Galatians (whose date, of course, is uncertain); and the attack on "libertines" in 3:17–19 is similar to issues that are prominent in 1 Corinthians.[3] If Paul writes from Ephesus, we would date Philippians to about AD 54–56.

On the whole, however, I prefer the traditional view that locates Philippians during the time of Paul's two-year imprisonment in Rome described in the last verses of Acts. If Paul writes, as I think likely, toward the end of his two-year Roman imprisonment, there would have been plenty of time for the journeys envisaged.[4] Paul makes clear

---

1. E.g., Gerald F. Hawthorne, *Philippians*, WBC 43 (Waco, TX: Word, 1983), xxxvi–xliv (a view discarded in the revised commentary with Ralph P. Martin [see below]; Gerald F. Hawthorne and Ralph P. Martin, *Philippians*, rev. ed., WBC 43 (Nashville: Nelson, 2004).

2. The Philippians hear of Paul's imprisonment; they send Epaphroditus with help for Paul; they learn that Epaphroditus has been ill; Paul learns that they have been concerned for him because of this (see esp. 2:15–30).

3. See, e.g., G. Walter Hansen, *The Letter to the Philippians*, PNTC (Grand Rapids: Eerdmans, 2009), 19–25; others who favor an Ephesian provenance include John Reumann, *Philippians*, AB

33B (New Haven: Yale University Press, 2008), 13–14; Heiko Wojtkowiak, *Christologie und Ethik im Philipperbrief: Studien zur Handlungsorientierung einer frühchristlichen Gemeinde in paganer Umwelt*, FRLANT 243 (Göttingen: Vandenhoeck & Ruprecht, 2012); Jörg Frey, "Der Philipperbrief im Rahmen der Paulusforschung," in *Der Philipperbrief des Paulus in der hellenistisch-römischen Welt*, ed. Jörg Frey and Benjamin Schliesser (Tübingen: Mohr Siebeck, 2015), 5–9; Hawthorne and Martin, *Philippians*, xxxix–l.

4. Moreover, the first two (the Philippians hear of Paul's imprisonment; they send Epaphroditus) may have been at least initiated before Paul arrived in Rome.

in chapter 1 that his death is a possible outcome of his imprisonment, and as Donald Guthrie notes, "It is difficult to believe that any provincial court would have produced in Paul the sense of approaching finality of decision which the Philippian letter implies."[5] If Paul writes from Rome, the many differences between this letter and the three other "prison epistles" probably written from Rome—Ephesians, Colossians, Philemon—suggest that it was not written at the same time. It makes sense, then, to put the other three prison epistles rather early in the Roman imprisonment (perhaps AD 60–61) and Philippians later (AD 61–62).

ISOLATING THE ISSUES

The difficulties of Paul's imprisonment are one reason that Paul writes to the Philippians. The apostle focuses on his own circumstances at both the beginning and the end of the letter. In 1:12–26, he assures the Philippians that his imprisonment has served to advance the gospel and that he is confident about his own future. In 4:10–20, he expresses (muted!) appreciation for material support that the Philippians have given him. The need to thank the Philippians for their gift and to reassure them about his own circumstances is one main reason why Paul writes. But he also writes to exhort the Philippians to remain united and steadfast in the face of the opposition of unbelievers and the threat posed by false teachers who are at least claiming a relationship to Christ.

The opposition the Philippians are facing is varied. Paul refers to opponents in four different texts. In 1:15–17, he mentions some in Rome who are preaching Christ for selfish motives. "Those who oppose you" (1:28) are probably pagans in Philippi. Philippi enjoyed the special status of being a Roman colony. The influence of Roman culture, institutions, and values was therefore particularly strong, undoubtedly leading to conflict between the Christ followers and their pagan neighbors.[6] The "dogs" Paul warns about in 3:2 are Jews or Jewish Christians, as Paul's rehearsal of his own conversion from Judaism to Christ faith in verses 3–11 makes clear. The identity of the "enemies of the cross" in 3:17–19 is harder to determine. They may be the same "Judaizing" group mentioned earlier in the chapter, or perhaps more likely, they are yet another group, marked by a focus on self and pleasure in contrast to devotion to Christ.[7] However we finally identify this last group, it is clear the Philippians are confronted with significant opposition, and this circumstance was a stimulus to the writing of the letter.

---

5. Guthrie, *New Testament Introduction*, 528. Among those who favor a Roman provenance are Peter T. O'Brien, *The Epistle to the Philippians: A Commentary on the Greek Text*, NIGTC (Grand Rapids: Eerdmans, 1991), 19–26; Gordon D. Fee, *Paul's Letter to the Philippians*, NICNT (Grand Rapids: Eerdmans, 1995), 34–37; Silva, *Philippians*, 5–7; Dunn, *Beginning from Jerusalem*, 1009–11; Schnelle, *Apostle Paul*, 366–69.

6. Peter Oakes, *Philippians: From People to Letter*, SNTSMS 110 (Cambridge: Cambridge University Press, 2001).

7. See Robert Jewett, "Conflicting Movements in the Early Church as Revealed in Philippians," *NovT* 12 (1970): 362–90. See O'Brien, *Philippians*, 28–34, for a good survey of views.

Several somewhat abrupt transitions in Philippians have led many scholars to conclude that our canonical letter is, in fact, a composite of two or three originally separate letters. Paul commends fellow workers in 2:19–30 rather than, according to Paul's usual practice, at the end of the letter; "finally" in 3:1 is followed by two chapters of material; and the strong denunciation of false teachers in 3:2 seems to come out of nowhere.[8] I will deal with each of these in the course of analyzing the argument. Here I will only say that imagining a scenario in which separate letters were combined into one, with an appropriate letter opening and closing added, is harder than providing reasonable explanations for the sequence of topics in a single composition.[9]

ANALYZING THE ARGUMENT

Most scholars now agree that, in genre, Philippians is a "letter of friendship." It is marked by a warm tone suggestive of close and positive relationships, by a strong sense of close fellowship in the gospel, and by reciprocity in relationships.[10] The message of the letter focuses on the gospel of Christ and its implications especially for Christian community.[11] As Fee points out, gospel language occurs proportionately more often in Philippians than in any other letter of Paul; and "every significant theological moment in the letter reflects this central core in some way or another, sometimes with emphases unique to the 'contingencies' of Philippians, but at all times expressed in 'coherence' with what Paul says elsewhere in his letters."[12] The believers in Philippi need to appropriate the gospel in their relations with one another so that they can, united "in one spirit," withstand the opposition they are facing.[13] The high and deeply significant Christology of 2:6–11 is, of course, designed to support this point by presenting our Lord's self-abnegation as an example for his people to follow.

Paul plays on the pride the Philippians had in their Roman identity by arguing that their true identity is determined by the gospel (1:27) and has its home and source in heaven (3:20). The obvious references to Roman institutions in the letter have led many in recent years to find in the letter a veiled anti-imperial thrust, according to which Christ as Savior and Lord is implicitly contrasted with the claims of Caesar to be "Savior" and "Lord."[14] But a specifically anti-imperial motif is difficult to identify

8. For a useful survey of views and analysis, see Frey, "Der Philipperbrief"; also Hawthorne and Martin, *Philippians*, xxxii–xxxiv.

9. See David E. Garland, "The Composition and Unity of Philippians: Some Neglected Literary Factors," *NovT* 27 (1985): 141–73, for a strong defense of unity on literary grounds. As Fee notes, there is ultimately only one argument for partition: "The 'argument' of Philippians is not as tidy as we could wish it to be" (*Philippians*, 21).

10. Stanley K. Stowers, "Friends and Enemies in the Politics of Heaven: Reading Theology in Philippians," in Bassler, *Pauline Theology*, 107–17; Silva, *Philippians*, 1–14; Fee, *Philippians*, 29.

11. Hansen, *Philippians*, 30.

12. Fee, *Philippians*, 46–53 (47).

13. Engberg-Pedersen characterizes Philippians as an exercise in community formation (*Paul and the Stoics*, 128).

14. See, e.g., Oakes, *Philippians*.

in the letter.[15] "Joy" is often singled out as the key word, or concept, in the letter; and it is prominent.[16] But even more prominent and arguably integrated more deeply into the argument of the letter is the word *phroneō*, which can be translated "think" or "have a certain mindset."[17] Paul uses this verb to describe his strong feelings for the Philippians (1:7)—feelings that the Philippians reciprocate in the form of their gift to him (4:10). He uses this verb to describe the way gospel-oriented believers should "think" (2:2; 3:15; 4:2) and supremely of the way Christ "thinks" as a pattern for his people to follow (2:5).

As I noted above, the letter body is framed by references to Paul's circumstances (1:12–26 and 4:10–20). The central section is introduced by the general commands in 1:27–30 and unfolds in several stages as Paul mixes admonition (2:1–4, 12–18; 3:12–16; 4:2–9) with warnings about opposition (3:2–11, 17–19), reminders of key theological perspectives (3:20–21), and examples for the Philippians to emulate (2:5–11, 19–30; cf. 3:17).

1 PAUL, THE PHILIPPIANS, AND THE GOSPEL (1:1–26)

1.1 Fellowship in the Gospel (1:1–11)

While set in the usual Pauline form, the salutation is notable for an absence and for an inclusion. It is unusual for Paul not to mention his apostolic status (missing only elsewhere in 1 and 2 Thessalonians and Philemon). Even more unusual is his mention of church "officials"—"overseers" (*episkopois*) and "deacons" (*diakonois*). Perhaps they are singled out here because of their administration of the gift the Philippians have sent. Theologically, it is interesting to see here the assumption of a church-leadership structure that becomes more evident in the Pastoral Epistles ("overseers" in 1 Tim 3:1–2; Titus 1:7; "deacons" in 1 Tim 3:8–12).

At the center of Paul's thanksgiving and prayer for the Philippians (vv. 3–11) is his celebration of their "partnership [or 'fellowship'; *koinōnia*] in the gospel from the first day until now" (v. 5). Paul and the Philippians have enjoyed a particularly close bond since he first preached the gospel in Philippi (probably about twelve years earlier, Acts 16:12–40). Paul accordingly gives thanks "every time I remember you" (v. 3)[18] and is confident that this relationship will continue because the one "who began a good work in you will carry it on to completion until the day of Christ Jesus" (v. 6). "In you"

---

15. See, e.g., Dorothea H. Bertschmann, *Bowing before Christ—Nodding to the State? Reading Paul Politically with Oliver O'Donovan and John Howard Yoder*, LNTS 502 (London: Bloomsbury, 2014), 79–125; Lynn H. Cohick, "Philippians and Empire: Paul's Engagement with Imperialism and the Imperial Cult," in *Jesus Is Lord, Caesar Is Not: Evaluating Empire in New Testament Studies*, ed. Scot McKnight and Joseph B. Modica (Downers Grove, IL: InterVarsity Press, 2013), 166–82.

16. E.g., Ulrich B. Müller, *Der Brief des Paulus an die Philipper*, THKNT 11/1 (Leipzig: Evangelische, 1993), 28–29.

17. See also Silva, *Philippians*, 21.

18. This translation is far more likely than the alternative "every time you remember me" (understanding *hymōn* as a subjective genitive). Paul might in this case be referring to the gift the Philippians sent him. See, for this view, O'Brien, *Philippians*, 58–61; Reumann, *Philippians*, 149.

(*en hymin*) could also be translated "among you," and the "good work" might refer to their corporate health.[19] However, while acknowledging the need to be vigilant about smuggling into the New Testament a Western individualistic focus, a "work" that looks to the future day of the Lord is more likely to be God's work of grace in each of the Philippian believers (cf. v. 10).[20] Paul concludes his thanksgiving with another reference to his strong feelings for the Philippians; he has them in his heart (v. 7)[21] and longs to see them (v. 8).

In keeping with a key motif in the letter, Paul's prayer that the Philippian believers might be "pure and blameless for the day of Christ" (v. 10) hints at the responsibility of believers, to be compared with his assertion of divine sovereignty in the completion of that work (v. 6). On that day, believers will be filled with "the fruit of righteousness" (v. 11), a phrase that might mean either "ethical fruit that is based in forensic righteousness" or, more likely, "fruit which is ethical righteousness" (see Amos 6:12).[22]

1.2 The Advance of the Gospel (1:12–26)

This paragraph is framed by references to "advance"/"progress" (both translating *prokopē*): the "advance of the gospel" (v. 12) and the "progress" of the Philippians in their faith (v. 25). Both references are set in relation to Paul's own circumstances, which dominate this paragraph. It is unusual for Paul to speak of himself this way so early in a letter, but the occasion of Philippians makes it natural for him to put this matter up front. The passage falls into two parts, signaled by the references to "advance"/"progress." In verses 12–18a, Paul rejoices (v. 18a) because his imprisonment has not, as the Philippians might have expected, led to a reduction in gospel preaching but has, rather, "served to advance the gospel" (v. 12). Paul's Roman guards and other Roman officials have come to understand that Paul is under arrest because of his commitment to Christ (v. 13). And other believers in Rome have been stimulated by Paul's circumstances to preach Christ more boldly. Some are motivated by goodwill toward Paul, inspired, perhaps, by his commitment to preach Christ whatever the cost (vv. 15b–16). Others, however, have been emboldened to preach out of "selfish ambition," setting themselves up as rivals of Paul (vv. 15a, 17).[23] Paul's joy, arising from his conviction that, in both

---

19. E.g., Reumann, *Philippians*, 112.

20. E.g., O'Brien, *Philippians*, 64; Matthew S. Harmon, *Philippians*, Mentor Commentary (Fearn, Ross-shire: Mentor, 2015), 86.

21. As in v. 3, some interpreters reverse the usual understanding of the grammar, taking *me* as the object of the infinitive *echein* and *hymas* as its subject: thus "because you have me in your heart" (e.g., Hawthorne and Martin, *Philippians*, 26).

22. In the former case, the genitive *dikaiosynēs* indicates source; in the latter it is a genitive of apposition. The majority

favor the latter (e.g., Hansen, *Philippians*, 63; Silva, *Philippians*, 52; Fee, *Philippians*, 103–4; Joachim Gnilka, *Der Philipperbrief*, 4th ed., HThKNT [Freiburg: Herder, 1987], 53), and probably on good grounds—even though, as Harmon points out, the use of *dikaiosynē* in a forensic sense in 3:9 might favor the former view (Harmon, *Philippians*, 104–5; cf. also O'Brien, *Philippians*, 80; Müller, *An die Philipper*, 46).

23. These verses exhibit a chiastic structure, with insincere preachers the focus in vv. 15a and 17 and sincere preachers in vv. 15b–16.

cases, "Christ is preached" (v. 18a), makes clear that Paul's rival preachers, while personally at odds with him, are proclaiming the true gospel of God.[24]

In the second half of the passage (vv. 18b–26), Paul focuses on the impact his current circumstances might have on the Philippians' own "progress" in the faith. Paul makes clear in these verses that his current imprisonment might end in his execution. Paul is confident, however, that "what has happened to me will turn out for my deliverance" (v. 19). The translation "deliverance," found in the NIV and most other versions as well, might suggest that Paul is confident about being released from prison.[25] But the Greek word here is *sōtēria*, and Paul uses this word and the word group it is from everywhere else to refer to "eternal salvation," usually with a focus on the final destiny of the believer. Rather than referring, then, to physical deliverance (a meaning the word certainly has often in secular Greek), Paul is probably expressing confidence that he will be vindicated by God on the final day of judgment.[26] Some might argue that ultimate salvation could not be contingent on the prayers of other believers, as *sōtēria* is here—see "through your prayers." But Paul also says his salvation comes through "God's provision of the Spirit of Jesus Christ." Assigning both a human and a divine instrument to ultimate salvation is, in fact, quite in keeping with Philippians and fits comfortably into Paul's general scheme of soteriology (see pp. 530–31).

While Paul, then, is confident that he will be vindicated by God (whatever the "lower" court here on earth might decide) and that Christ will be "exalted" in his body (v. 20), he is less certain about the outcome of his trial. Indeed, he is not even sure which outcome to prefer, since his death would mean being "with Christ" (v. 23). Paul here hints at an important aspect of his eschatology, namely, that believers, at death, go to be "with Christ." There is no reason to think (as some have argued) that this hope in any way detracts from, or signals a shift from, his strong conviction that the resurrection of the body at the time of Christ's return is the focus of Christian hope (see, e.g., 1 Cor 15; 1 Thess 4:13–18). Nor does it suggest that Paul has abandoned a sense of imminent expectation for a belief that Christ's coming might be indefinitely delayed. As I argue on pages 541–45, the widespread view that Paul at some point abandoned the belief he held early in his ministry that he would survive until Christ's return does not hold up to scrutiny. Paul's teaching about individual eschatology is

---

24. Reumann, *Philippians*, 203–7, provides a complete survey of options about these teachers. Fee (*Philippians*, 121–22) speculates that the rivalry may reflect a continuation of the tensions that Paul addresses in Romans.

25. E.g., Reumann, *Philippians*, 243.

26. See esp. Paul Cable, "'We Await a Savior': 'Salvation' in Philippians" (PhD diss., Wheaton College, 2017), 109–70; and also most commentators (e.g., Fee, *Philippians*, 131–32; O'Brien, *Philippians*, 109–10; Hansen, *Philippians*, 78–79; Markus N. A.

Bockmuehl, *A Commentary on the Epistle to the Philippians*, BNTC [Peabody, MA: Hendrickson, 1998], 83). Paul probably alludes here to Job 13:16—"I know I will be vindicated" (LXX *touto moi apobēsetai eis sōtērian*, which Paul's wording exactly duplicates). This allusion also favors a reference to eternal salvation, since Job also is referring to his eternal destiny (Silva, *Philippians*, 70). See esp. Hays, *Echoes*, 21–24, on this allusion. Not being "ashamed" here probably has an objective sense, i.e., not receiving a negative verdict in the judgment (see Rom 5:5; and Müller, *An die Philipper*, 58).

consistent, but its application and emphases differ with the issues he addresses and the circumstances he considers. Here, when the issue is the prospect of imminent death, it is natural that Paul focuses on his destiny at the point of death (and, as 3:10–11, 21 reveal, Paul has certainly not jettisoned his belief in resurrection). Moreover, as Bockmuehl notes, "The same co-existence of belief in future blessedness at death leading eventually to eschatological resurrection is also found in Jewish apocalyptic sources."[27] Paul, of course, is quite vague: What does it mean to be "with Christ"? In light of 2 Corinthians 5:1–10 (see my notes there), he might refer to enjoying the blessing of Christ's presence while he waits for the resurrection body.

In any case, Paul, at the end of the day, thinks it more likely that he will be released from his Roman captivity and be able to return to Philippi to continue his work among them, "for your progress and joy in the faith" (v. 25).

2 LIVING GOSPEL-FOCUSED LIVES (1:27–4:1)

2.1 Unity and Humility in the Face of Opposition (1:27–2:4)

The agenda-setting role of 1:27–30 in the letter is widely recognized. This paragraph introduces and summarizes Paul's exhortations to the Philippians. Many interpreters think the next major break occurs after 2:18, where Paul moves from exhortation to commendation of fellow workers.[28] However, it might be more satisfactory to put the break at 4:2, viewing 4:1 as a concluding general exhortation that matches 1:27–30, "stand firm [stēkete] in the Lord" (4:1) harking back to "stand firm [stēkete] in the one Spirit" (1:27).

The gospel is again central in 1:27–30, Paul enjoining his readers to "conduct yourselves in a manner worthy" of that gospel. The verb translated "conduct yourselves" (politeuomai) may have this rather colorless meaning, but it can also mean "live as a citizen." Granted Paul's return to this language in 3:20—"our citizenship [politeuma] is in heaven"—and granted the special status of Philippi as a Roman colony, this "political" nuance is hard to resist.[29] Furthermore, considering the cultural distance between the believers and their environment that this passage assumes (v. 28), it is difficult to think Paul is simply asking the Philippians to be "good citizens." Rather, he is assuming the perspective that becomes explicit in 3:20, calling on them to live as "citizens of heaven" (NLT). Paul will touch on various aspects of this general exhortation in what follows. But he begins with what was clearly a critical need among the Philippians: unity in the face of opposition (1:27b–30). They need to "stand firm in

---

27. Bockmuehl, *Philippians*, 92; on this issue, see esp. the excursus in Gnilka, *Philipperbrief,* 81–88.

28. E.g., Müller, *An die Philipper,* 71.

29. E.g., Lightfoot, *Philippians,* 105; Fee, *Philippians,*

161–62; Silva, *Philippians,* 80, 88; and esp. Winter, *Seek the Welfare,* 82–104. The verb is not used in the LXX and occurs in the NT elsewhere only in Acts 23:1.

the one Spirit [or spirit]"[30] and not be frightened by their opponents. These opponents are probably their pagan neighbors in Philippi. Steadfast and united resistance signals that the Philippian believers are indeed the true people of God, destined for salvation (v. 28, *sōtēria*; cf. v. 19), while their opponents are headed for destruction (v. 28, *apōleia*; see the similar contrast in 2 Cor 2:15 between those who are "being saved" [*sōzomenois*] and those "being destroyed" [*apollymenois*; my translation]). Nor should the Philippians be surprised at the opposition they are facing: "It has been granted to you on behalf of Christ not only to believe in him, but also to suffer for him" (v. 29). Suffering, Paul strikingly claims, is a gracious gift (the verb is *charizomai*, sharing a root with *charis*, "grace"). Believers enjoy the faith that brings them into union with Christ, but that union, as Paul elaborates in 3:10, involves conformity not only to "the power of his resurrection" but also "participation in his sufferings."

In the next paragraph (2:1–4), Paul repeats his call to unity (vv. 1–2), using the language of "thinking" or "having a mindset" (*phroneō*, used twice in v. 2) that reflects a central thread of teaching in the letter. In verses 3–4, Paul then adds an exhortation to humility. (Corporate) unity and (individual) humility are, of course, closely related; we can be united when each of us is willing to subordinate our own interests to the interests of others. The concern for the "other" in this passage—"value others above yourselves" (v. 3), "looking . . . to the interests of the others" (v. 4)—is one of Paul's foundational ethical values, expressing in more concrete terms what it means to "love one another."

2.2 The Gospel Story and Its Significance (2:5–11)

With this passage, we come to the "Mt. Everest of Philippians study."[31] The high Christology of this passage serves a particular rhetorical purpose. But what that purpose is has been debated. It is clear, in general, that Paul introduces the story of Christ's humility (vv. 6–8) and subsequent exaltation (vv. 9–11) to support his call for humility and unity in verses 1–4. But precisely how the passage functions to support these points is disputed. The majority (and traditional) view is that Paul introduces Christ as an example of the humility to which he calls the Philippians. But a vocal minority argues that the passage outlines the fundamental salvation-historical events that ground all Christian conduct (including, of course, humility). In reality, however, we do not need to choose between these options. The "career" of the Messiah that Paul briefly outlines is the heart of the "good news" that Paul preaches and that sustains and empowers the Philippians in their pursuit of gospel living (1:27). However, I also think that Paul

---

30. It is hard to know if *pneuma* refers to the Holy Spirit (NIV; see esp. Fee, *Philippians*, 165–66) or to a general shared attitude (all other versions and most commentators). The latter may be more likely (Fee's appeal to Eph 2:18, where Paul says "we both have access to the Father by one Spirit," is not altogether persuasive, due to the difference in logic).

31. Reumann, *Philippians*, 333.

indicates in verse 5 that elements of this story also provide an ethical ideal that the Philippians are to emulate.[32]

As the formatting in the NIV indicates, verses 6–11 are made up of short lines that lend themselves to a poetic arrangement. Most scholars are convinced that Paul is quoting a hymn composed by someone else and that he has perhaps edited.[33] This is certainly possible, but (1) we should perhaps not speak specifically of a "hymn" but of a passage of "exalted prose" or a "poetic style";[34] and (2) composition by Paul himself as he writes Philippians is certainly not impossible.[35] We just cannot know. Scholars further debate the structure of this hymn or poetic passage. A break between verses 8 and 9 is obvious, and a division within each section of three subsections of three lines each is the most natural arrangement. Verse 8d, "even death on a cross" becomes on this arrangement an emphatic transitional comment (NIV modified to imitate the Greek order):[36]

Who, being in very nature God,
not an advantage considered
his being equal with God

rather, he made himself nothing
by taking the very nature of a servant,
being made in human likeness.

And being found in appearance as a man,
he humbled himself
becoming obedient to death

even death on a cross!

32. As Schnelle (*Apostle Paul*, 372) remarks, Christ here is both "Urbild," the prototype who makes new existence possible, and "Vorbild," an exemplary model to be imitated.

33. Originally argued in detail by Ernst Lohmeyer, *Kyrios Jesus: Eine Untersuchung zu Phil. 2, 5–11*, Sitzungsberichte der Heidelberger Akademie der Wissenschaften, Philosophisch-historische Klasse, Jahrgang 1927/8.4 (Heidelberg: Winter, 1961). Ralph P. Martin surveys the history of interpretation on this matter up to 1967 in *Carmen Christi: Philippians ii.5–11 in Recent Interpretation and In the Setting of Early Christian Worship*, SNTSMS 4 (Cambridge: Cambridge University Press, 1967; repr., *A Hymn of Christ: Philippians 2:5–11 in Recent Interpretation and In the Setting of Early Christian Worship* [Downers Grove, IL: InterVarsity Press, 1997], 24–96); see also Hansen, *Philippians*, 122–33; Morna D. Hooker, "Philippians 2.6–11," in *From Adam to Christ: Essays on Paul*, by Morna D. Hooker (Cambridge: Cambridge University Press, 1990), 89–96; Gnilka, *Philipperbrief*, 108–10.

34. Edsall and Strawbridge, "Songs We Used to Sing," 290–311; Fee, *Philippians*, 192–93; Bockmuehl, *Philippians*, 116–17.

35. Oakes, *Philippians*, 188–210; Robert H. Gundry, "Style and Substance in Philippians 2:6–11," in *The Old is Better: New Testament Essays in Support of Traditional Interpretations*, by Robert H. Gundry, WUNT 2/178 (Tübingen: Mohr Siebeck, 2005), 286; O'Brien, *Philippians*, 198–202.

36. See, e.g., Bockmuehl, *Philippians*, 125; Silva, *Philippians*, 93–94 (this general arrangement goes back to the early and influential work of Ernst Lohmeyer (*Christuskult und Kaiserkult* [Tübingen: Mohr Siebeck, 1919]). And see the good survey of options in Gnilka, *Philipperbrief*, 131–38.

Therefore God exalted him to the highest place
and gave him the name
that is above every name,

that at the name of Jesus
every knee should bow,
in heaven and on earth and under the earth,

and every tongue acknowledge
that Jesus Christ is Lord,
to the glory of God the Father.

The religious, philosophical, or literary background of this passage has been thoroughly debated, with scholars suggesting all kinds of options, some of them, assuming that Paul quotes a preformed hymn, quite improbable. For our purposes, the question of Old Testament influences is pertinent. Paul's claim that Christ took "the very nature of a servant" naturally suggests an allusion to the fourth Servant Song, which, like this passage, connects exaltation ("I will give him a portion among the great," Isa 53:12a) with the servant's humble state ("he poured out his life unto death"; Isa 53:12b). It is unlikely that this last clause is echoed in Philippians 2:7a ("he made himself nothing"), as some argue, because the latter refers to Jesus's incarnation (in my view, at least), while the former refers to the servant's sacrificial death. Actual linguistic connections between Philippians 2:6–11 and the Servant Song are lacking; even "servant" in the LXX is *pais* rather than (as in Phil 2) *doulos*. Still, the two words are often interchangeable, and Paul might be influenced by the Hebrew.[37]

The argument that Philippians 2 alludes to Genesis 1–3 falls into the same category. Linguistic connections are lacking. For instance, while Genesis refers to Adam (and humans generally, of course) as being in the "image" (*eikōn*) of God, Philippians refers to Christ as being in the "form" (*morphē*) of God (v. 6). Many scholars therefore deny any connection.[38] Others, however, note that Paul brings the language of Christ as the *eikōn* of God into conjunction with other words from the *morphē* root.[39] Paul may use *morphē* here because, as the verses cited in the footnote reveal, this word group is amenable to the idea that Christ provides an example to whom believers are to be

---

37. See esp. Joachim Jeremias, "Παις θεου," *TDNT* 5:711–12; Haüsser, *Christusbekenntnis und Jesusüberlieferung bei Paulus*, 219–300; and note the helpful chart in Harmon, *Philippians*, 201–3. Allusion to Isaiah 53 is disputed by many (e.g., Gnilka, *Philipperbrief*, 140–41).

38. E.g., O'Brien, *Philippians*, 196–97; 263–68; Witherington, *Jesus the Sage*, 257–66.

39. See 2 Cor 3:18—"And we all, who with unveiled faces contemplate the Lord's glory, are being transformed [*metamorphoumetha*] into his image [*eikona*] with ever-increasing glory, which comes from the Lord, who is the Spirit"—and Rom 8:29—"For those God foreknew he also predestined to be conformed [*symmorphous*] to the image [*eikonos*] of his Son, that he might be the firstborn among many brothers and sisters" (see, e.g., Ridderbos, *Paul*, 74).

conformed. And a conceptual contrastive parallel can certainly be detected. Adam, tempted to become "like God" (Gen 3:5), was disobedient to God and was plunged into degradation. Christ, who could have used his divine identity for his own purposes, chose rather to humble himself and become obedient.[40] Recognizing the danger here of a circular argument, the importance of the Adam-Christ typology in Paul's theology also favors the possibility of an allusion here.[41] I think therefore that a reference to Adam is likely. However, the allusion is not clear enough to justify basing exegetical and theological conclusions about Philippians 2 on the Adam-Christ parallel.[42]

Michael Gorman has labeled this passage "Paul's master story" and argues that its vision of a God who humbles himself and goes to the cross provides a model of cruciformity that permeates his letters.[43] While not agreeing in all details, I think Gorman's case for the fundamental and formative nature of the theology of this passage is a convincing one. Nowhere else does Paul (with the possible exception of Col 1:15–20) paint his Christology on so broad a canvas, tracing the history of the Messiah from eternity past ("in the form of God") to eternity future (every knee bowing and every tongue confessing) and including in its middle stages incarnation, his obedient life, and the cross.

The rhetorical function of this great christological passage is suggested by the introductory verse 5. For most of Christian history, the verse was interpreted as a call for believers to adopt the same way of thinking that Christ adopted in his incarnation: "In your relationships with one another, have the same mindset [*phroneite*] as Christ Jesus."[44] However, this translation—and every other one—adds words in English to fill out the elliptical Greek. Thus another main alternative translation would be "have the mindset in your relationships with each other that you have as people who are in Christ Jesus."[45] On this reading of the Greek, Paul is calling on the Philippians not to imitate Christ but to introduce into their mutual relationships the mindset that they possess as Christians. The christological text that follows would then remind the Philippians of the basis for this mindset.[46] The Christology of verses 6–11 obviously goes beyond a simple reference to Christ's mindset as something to imitate, and so there is some

40. See esp. Dunn, *Theology of Paul*, 281–86; idem, *Beginning from Jerusalem*, 1024; N. T. Wright, "Jesus Christ Is Lord: Philippians 2.5–11," in Wright, *Climax of the Covenant*, 57–61; Joseph H. Hellerman, *Philippians*, EGGNT (Nashville: Broadman & Holman, 2015), 282–88. Susan Grove Eastman thinks allusion to Adam is present only in vv. 7–8, where Christ, in becoming human, takes on Adam's form (*Paul and the Person: Reframing Paul's Anthropology* [Grand Rapids: Eerdmans, 2017], 135–40).

41. See esp. Ridderbos, *Paul*, 68–78, for the structural importance of the typology in Paul.

42. Bockmuehl, *Philippians*, 133; Ridderbos, *Paul*, 68–78; see also Silva, *Philippians*, 102: "An undeniable network of associations between Phil 2 and Gen 1–3."

43. Gorman, *Inhabiting the Cruciform God*, 12, 23–28.

44. Advocates of this interpretation argue that it is natural to supply the verb "to be" in the second clause: "Think [*phroneite*] among yourselves which [thought] was [*ēn*] Christ Jesus."

45. On this reading of the syntax, the same verb is supplied in the second clause as is used in the first: "Think [*phroneite*] among yourselves as you think [*phroneite*] in Christ Jesus."

46. This interpretation was strongly advocated by Ernst Käsemann ("Kritische Analyse von Phil. 2,5–11," *ZTK* 47 [1950]: 313–60) and Martin (*Hymn of Christ*). See also Hawthorne and Martin, *Philippians*, 104–9; Hansen, *Philippians*, 120–21.

truth in this latter salvation-historical reading. However, this reading of verse 5 also posits an unlikely gap between thinking "in Christ" and thinking in relationship to each other. While the argument about the syntax of the verse is something of a wash, then, the "imitation" reading, according to which the verse calls on the Philippians to "think as Christ thought," is more likely.[47] As I noted in the introduction to the book, the word *phroneō*, used again here, is a key word in the letter, indicating, as Martin puts it, "the outworking of thought as it determines motives, and through motives the conduct of the person involved."[48]

The opening two verses (vv. 6–7) describe a movement from Christ existing (*hyparchōn*) "in very nature God" (*en morphē theou*) to his taking "the very nature of a servant" (*morphēn doulou labōn*). The word *morphē*, translated "very nature" in the NIV, more often translated "form" (e.g., ESV), is a key word in the passage. It often refers to the outward appearance of something or someone. But this meaning does not fit the present context, and there is evidence the word can also connote a "form which truly and fully expresses the being which underlies it."[49] On this reading, it is likely that "form of God" and "equality with God" describe the same state of being; Christ, who existed in the form of God was also equal with God. To be sure, some interpreters have understood the Greek in verse 6b to express the idea of Christ not "grasping for" equality.[50] But the particular combination of Greek words Paul uses here have the sense "not regarding [something] as to be used for one's own selfish interests."[51] Christ possessed equality with God, but chose not to regard it as a status to be used for his own advantage (see NIV). This reading also assumes that Paul is reflecting on the incarnation, a view most scholars hold.[52]

The verb "being" in verse 6 translates a Greek participle (*hyparchōn*) that is often given a concessive sense: "Though he was in the form of God" (NRSV; cf. also ESV; CEB; NAB; NASB). However, Gorman has recently made a strong appeal to give the participle a causal force; Christ's condescension in becoming human and taking the

47. See esp. C. F. D. Moule, "Further Reflections on Philippians 2:5–11," in *Apostolic History and the Gospel: Biblical and Historical Essays Presented to F. F. Bruce on His 60th Birthday*, ed. W. Ward Gasque and Ralph P. Martin (Grand Rapids: Eerdmans, 1970), 264–76; Fee, *Philippians*, 200–201; O'Brien, *Philippians*, 253–62.

48. Martin, *Hymn of Christ*, 62.

49. O'Brien, *Philippians*, 210, citing Moulton-Milligan. Lightfoot argued for a meaning like this based on the use of the word in Greek philosophy (*Philippians*, 127–33). While most modern scholars would question influence from Greek philosophy, many would agree with Lightfoot's basic conclusion (e.g., Silva, *Philippians*, 101; Hansen, *Philippians*, 136–37; Hawthorne and Martin, *Philippians*, 114; Fee, *Pauline Christology*, 378).

50. See Adela Yarbro Collins, "Jesus as Messiah and Son of God in the Letters of Paul," in *King and Messiah as Son of God:*

Divine, Human, and Angelic Messianic Figures in Biblical and Related Literature, ed. John J. Collins and Adela Yarbro Collins (Grand Rapids: Eerdmans, 2008), 114–15.

51. See the classic study of Roy W. Hoover, "The HARPAGMOS Enigma: A Philological Solution," *HTR* 64 (1971): 95–119. While Hoover's results have been contested (e.g., Samuel Vollenweider, "Der 'Raub' der Gottgleichheit: Ein religionsgeschichtlicher Vorschlag zu Phil 2.6[–11]," *NTS* 45 [1999]: 413–33), his basic conclusion stands (e.g., Andrew Ter Ern Loke, *The Origin of Divine Christology*, SNTSMS 169 (Cambridge: Cambridge University Press, 2017], 36–41) and is adopted by most commentators.

52. A notable exception is Dunn, who thinks that Paul is referring to Christ's earthly life (see, e.g., *Theology of Paul*, 281–86; idem, *Christology in the Making*, 114–21). For a clear refutation, see Fee, *Pauline Christology*, 390–93.

form of a slave was an attitude that expressed the very nature of God.[53] Nevertheless, the logic of what Paul is arguing suggests it is more natural that here, at least, he accentuates the condescension of Christ by contrasting his humble state with the high position from which Christ started.[54]

Rather than viewing his exalted preincarnate position as something to be used for his own advantage, Christ "made himself nothing." The Greek verb lying behind the NIV is *ekenōsen*, often translated "emptied" and thus giving rise to the obvious question: What did Christ "empty" himself of? Certain relative attributes of deity (dubbed on the basis of this verse, "kenotic Christology")? In fact, however, as the NIV rendering suggests, this verb need not mean "empty" but can mean simply "to cause to be without result or effect."[55] It is especially telling that Paul qualifies this action not in terms of "emptying" or "putting aside" but of "taking"—"taking the very nature of a servant" (or "slave," *doulos*). As I noted above, many interpreters think that Paul is here reflecting the language of the fourth Servant Song, specifically verse 12: "He poured out his life unto death."[56] This is possible, although Paul's Greek does not reflect the LXX (nor is it a very natural rendering of the Hebrew).[57] The last line of verse 7—"being made in human likeness"—reinforces the focus on incarnation. In that incarnate state, Paul goes on, Christ "humbled himself," a fundamental attitude/action that led to his becoming "obedient to death"—a choice no one but one who is truly God has! As I noted earlier, the last line of verse 8 stands apart from the structure of the passage, making a transition; it is an "arresting musical syncopation, marking the end of the downward narrative but leaving one on the edge of one's seat for what comes next."[58]

As a result of Jesus's humility and obedience, God has "exalted" Christ (note the parallel with Jesus's own teaching: "Those who humble themselves will be exalted" [Matt 23:12b]). This exaltation takes the form of Jesus being given "the name that is above every name"—almost certainly, in this context, the divine name "Lord" (*kyrios*; see v. 11). The whole universe responds to the exalted Christ in worship and acclamation: "every knee" bows (v. 10); "every tongue" acknowledges that "Jesus Christ is Lord." The language of verses 10–11 alludes to Isaiah 45:23, and it is important to set this verse in its context to appreciate Paul's point:

Turn to me and be saved,
    all you ends of the earth;

53. Gorman, *Inhabiting the Cruciform God*, 26–28; see also Bockmuehl, *Philippians*, 133–34; and Fee, who says, "Christ Jesus has revealed the character of God himself" (*Philippians*, 197).
54. Harmon, *Philippians*, 205–6.
55. The meaning given in the standard NT Greek lexicon (BDAG); see also Silva, *Philippians*, 104.
56. E.g., Hawthorne and Martin, *Philippians*, 119.
57. See the caution expressed by Moisés Silva, "Philippians," in Beale and Carson, *Commentary on the New Testament Use of the Old Testament*, 837.
58. Bockmuehl, *Philippians*, 139.

for I am God, and there is no other.
By myself I have sworn,
    my mouth has uttered in all integrity
    a word that will not be revoked:
Before me every knee will bow;
    by me every tongue will swear.
They will say of me, "In the LORD alone
    are deliverance and strength."
All who have raged against him
    will come to him and be put to shame. (Isa 45:22–24)

As Capes notes, Isaiah 45 contains "the most stridently monotheistic language in all the Hebrew Bible," and "the covenant name YHWH/*kyrios* is at the heart of it."[59] Paul's application of this text to Christ speaks volumes about his exceedingly "high" view of Christ. As recent scholars have argued, Paul is here implicitly including Jesus within the divine identity.[60]

2.3 Renewed Call to Gospel Living (2:12–18)

After the theological interlude in 2:5–11, Paul continues to exhort the Philippians. These exhortations are general in nature, giving the paragraph the sense of a conclusion. Many interpreters therefore identify this paragraph as the end of a section that begins in 1:27.

A minor link with the previous paragraph is forged by the reference to the Philippians' obedience in verse 12 (see v. 8). Most English versions connect Paul's reference to his presence and absence to the Philippians' habit of obedience. However, the syntax might suggest that Paul intends to connect this reference to the main imperative of the verse: "Not only in my presence but much more in my absence work out your salvation with fear and trembling."[61] The standard English translation "work out" is a bit misleading. To be sure, "work out" forges a nice combination with the God who works "in us" in verse 13; as it is often put, "work out what God has worked in." This rendering suggests that Paul is calling on believers to manifest or put into practice the salvation

---

59. Capes, *Divine Christ*, 147.

60. See esp. Bauckham, *Jesus and the God of Israel*, 206–9; Wright, *Paul and the Faithfulness of God*, 2:680–88; Larry W. Hurtado, *One God, One Lord: Early Christian Devotion and Ancient Jewish Monotheism* (London: Bloomsbury T&T Clark, 2015), 100–101. Some scholars have recently claimed that Paul is here making an implicitly counterimperial point (e.g., Oakes, *Philippians*, 188–210; Bockmuehl, *Philippians*, 143–44). However, any such rhetoric is indirect at best (Bertschmann, *Bowing before Christ*, 79–99).

61. The phrase about Paul's presence and absence is introduced by the particle *mē*, which usually goes not with an indicative verb (here *hypēkousate*, "obeyed") but with verbs in other moods (here the imperative *katergazesthe*, "work out"). See Verlyn D. Verbrugge, "Greek Grammar and the Translation of Philippians 2:12," in Harmon and Smith, *Studies in the Pauline Epistles*, 113–26; Hellerman, *Philippians*, 129.

they already enjoy. But the verb Paul uses (*katergazomai*) means simply "produce," and "salvation" here probably, as usually in Paul, refers to ultimate deliverance or vindication.[62] Probably, then, Paul is simply calling on the Philippians to commit themselves to live in such a way that they will attain this final salvation. Paul is certainly clear that salvation, from beginning to end, is God's work (v. 13 again) and that it is never based on our work. But he is also very clear in insisting that a person cannot be saved without their own works (see also, e.g., Rom 8:12–13).[63]

In verses 14–16a, Paul adds a warning about grumbling and arguing with one another, reinforcing his concern for unity in the Philippian church (1:27; 2:1–2; cf. 4:2–3). Borrowing language from Deuteronomy 32:5 but reapplying it, Paul ties their own unity to the impression they could make on "a warped and crooked generation"—again reflecting an earlier point (see 1:28).[64] Believers will shine like "stars in the sky,"[65] as they "hold firmly" to the word of life ("the message that promises and communicates life").[66] The personal and reciprocal focus of the letter comes to expression again in verses 16b–18, as Paul links the Philippians' faithful Christian living to his own ministry work and joy.

2.4 Examples of Gospel Faithfulness (2:19–30)

It is unusual for Paul to refer to fellow workers so early in his letter; normally, they are mentioned only at the end. Rather than suggesting that an original letter of Paul was about to come to an end here, I prefer to explain this unusual placement as arising from the particular occasion of Philippians. The Philippians have communicated to Paul their concern for him and, as this passage reveals, their concern for Epaphroditus, the messenger they sent to Paul. They have heard that he has fallen seriously ill (vv. 26–27). While Paul continues to hope that he will be released and go back to Philippi (v. 24), he is concerned to assure the Philippians about his well-being and that of Epaphroditus (vv. 25–30). These circumstances do not entirely account for Paul's commendation here of Timothy (vv. 19–24). It is likely, then, that while Paul is not explicit about the matter, he sets forth Timothy and Epaphroditus as examples of the faithful gospel living to which he calls the Philippians in verses 12–18. Paul is explicit in this letter about the importance of examples (3:17), and the letter reveals a pattern of oscillation between exhortation and citing of others as examples to follow (1:27–2:4 and 2:5–11;

---

62. Many interpreters have suggested that "salvation" might here refer to corporate deliverance (e.g., Hawthorne and Martin, *Philippians*, 139; Hansen, *Philippians*, 172–73; Reumann, *Philippians*, 409; Hellerman, *Philippians*, 131; Gnilka, *Philipperbrief*, 149). Fee (*Philippians*, 234–35) and Bockmuehl (*Philippians*, 151–52) think both individual and corporate experiences are intended. But this would give the word a meaning it has nowhere else in Paul.

63. See esp. Cable, "'We Await a Savior,'" 268–82.

64. The language in Deuteronomy refers to disobedient Israel, while Paul, of course, applies it to community outsiders.

65. Paul again alludes to Scripture; see Dan 12:3: "Those who are wise will shine like the brightness of the heavens, and those who lead many to righteousness, like the stars for ever and ever."

66. The verb Paul uses here could be translated "hold out," which would make some sense in the context (see KJV; NJB; Lightfoot, *Philippians*, 118). But almost all English versions and the great majority of commentators prefer, probably rightly, "hold fast" (the verb is used four other times in the NT, but none in a similar way as here).

2:12–18 and 2:19–30; 3:2–3 and 3:4–11; 3:15–16 and 3:17–19). Note also specific connections between Paul's commendation of these two brothers and his exhortations to the Philippians. Timothy is unlike many others, who "look[s] out for their own interests, not those of Jesus Christ" (v. 21; see 2:3–4); Epaphroditus, in his self-sacrificing ministry, is an example of the kind of people that deserve honor (v. 29; see 2:14–16).

2.5 A Serious Challenge to Gospel Truth (3:1–14)

After a transitional verse (v. 1), Paul warns the Philippians about false teachers (vv. 2–3) and grounds his warning in a passionate recounting of his own "exchange" of previous religious status and accomplishments for Christ (vv. 4–11).

As elsewhere in the letter, a call to "rejoice" serves as a transitional moment (v. 1; cf. 1:18; 2:18; 4:4). The common translation "finally" in 3:1 suggests that Paul is concluding his letter—adding fuel to the fire of speculation about our current Philippians being a composite of two or more letters (see "Isolating the Issues" above). In fact, however, the Greek phrase *to loipon* is often used simply to mark a transition: "further" (NIV) or "whatever happens" (NLT) are better translations here.[67] Paul has warned the Philippians before about false teaching, but thinks it necessary to warn them yet again.[68] The most natural reason for the repetition of this warning was that the false teachers had recently emerged in Philippi and constituted a threat to the community.[69] Paul describes them in harsh but general terms in verse 2. But the tenor of his argument in verses 3–11 makes clear that these teachers were espousing a "Judaizing" theology. It was perhaps similar to that advocated by the agitators in Galatia, with their claim that belonging to God's people required believers, both Jewish and gentile, to be circumcised and to be observant of Torah.[70]

In response to these teachers, Paul boldly appropriates the language of "circumcision" to describe the Christian community (v. 3). Many seek to minimize this claim, arguing that using this language of Christians does not imply that it can no longer be used of Jews.[71] But, at least in the sense that Paul seems to use the language here, his claim does appear to be exclusive. God's people are now confined to those who "serve God by his Spirit, who boast in Christ Jesus." "Replacement" is not the right word, since Israel "according to the flesh" continues to play a role in God's plan (Rom 9–11). But we should not minimize the way in which the identity of God's people is now inextricably tied to Christ and the distinctive new-covenant gift of the Spirit. An incipient

---

67. See Margaret E. Thrall, *Greek Particles in the New Testament: Linguistic and Exegetical Studies*, NTTS 3 (Leiden: Brill, 1962), 25–30.

68. The "same things" (*ta auta*) in v. 1 probably refers back to Paul's warning about false teachers, perhaps when he was with the Philippians or even to teaching earlier in the letter (1:27–30).

69. E.g., Wilckens thinks the abrupt transition in 3:1–2

indicates that Paul heard about these teachers as he was dictating (*Die Briefe des Urchristentums*, 250). Fee, by contrast, views the passage as a general warning, untethered to any actual outbreak of false teaching (e.g., Fee, *Philippians*, 289–90).

70. Reumann, *Philippians*, 469–70.

71. E.g., Bockmuehl, *Philippians*, 191.

Trinitarianism emerges here; the people of God are those who serve *God* by his *Spirit* and who boast in *Christ Jesus*.[72]

Boasting in Christ has as its opposite putting "confidence in the flesh" (v. 3)—relying on merely human things to gain or maintain our spiritual status. Paul himself, circumcised on the eighth day, born a Jew to committed Jewish parents, of a noble Israelite tribe, had a birthright that, in terms of the Jewish faith, gave him solid grounds for confidence (vv. 4–5a). And not only did Paul have an enviable and impeccable birthright, but he built on that foundation a Jewish life of dedication and accomplishment. He aligned himself with the Pharisees, he exhibited zeal by persecuting the church, and "as for righteousness based on the law," he was "faultless" (vv. 5b–6).[73] This last claim could appear to clash with Paul's clear teaching elsewhere that no human can find "righteousness" with God by observing the law (e.g., Rom 3:20; Gal 2:16). But the "righteousness" (*dikaiosynē*) he refers to here is probably not what we might call "saving" righteousness but the upright status, the covenant membership, that faithful observance of the law confirmed for Jews.[74]

All the "gains" arising from Paul's privileges and achievements he totals up and places in the "loss" column in order that he might know Christ (Paul uses accounting terms here)—indeed, he considers them "garbage" or excrement (*skybala*; vv. 7–8). Paul returns to the language of "righteousness" in verse 9 to elaborate on this exchange, contrasting his Jewish "righteousness of my own that comes from the law" with "[the righteousness] which is through faith in Christ." The addition of "my own" (*emēn*) to Paul's description of law righteousness suggests that he is now thinking of righteousness as more than simply something given him because of his Jewish identity; his own effort is involved in this status. We see here an indication of the synergism that Paul sees in his Jewish past—and, by extension, in Jewish experience generally.[75] As E. P. Sanders has memorably made clear, Jews based their hope for salvation on their identity as Jews, based on God's gracious election of Israel. But it is clear from Jewish sources themselves and from Paul's own polemic that another layer was usually added to this covenant identity—a certain pride and dependence on "doing" the law. It is not just "covenant nomism" that Paul rejects here;[76] it is also a sense of achievement based on one's own efforts—both possession of the law and performance of the law. No longer does Paul think that the law, in any sense, defines or confers "righteousness" (*dikaiosynē*).

72. E.g., Fee, *Philippians*, 302.

73. Paul's zeal is often interpreted specifically in terms of Jewish nationalism (e.g., Bockmuehl, *Philippians*, 198–200; Dunn, *Theology of Paul*, 370). But it more likely refers generally to Paul's radical commitment to God (see esp. Dane C. Ortlund, *Zeal without Knowledge: The Concept of Zeal in Romans 10, Galatians 1, and Philippians 3*, LNTS 472 [London: T&T Clark, 2012], 118–36).

74. See O'Brien: "An exemplary way of life that is in conformity with the OT as interpreted along Pharisaic lines" (*Philippians*, 380).

75. See, e.g., Mark A. Seifrid, "The New Perspective *from* Paul," *The Southern Baptist Journal of Theology* 14 (2010): 20–35 (see esp. p. 25); O'Brien, "Was Paul Converted?," 371–75.

76. Contra, e.g., James D. G. Dunn, "Philippians 3:2–14 and

True saving righteousness comes from God (*ek theou*) and is mediated through "Christ faith" (*pisteōs Christou*). This phrase, of course, is open to several possible meanings, depending on how we take the genitive. Many recent interpreters think the genitive is subjective, the phrase then denoting Christ's own faith, or faithfulness.[77] But, as I argue elsewhere (see pp. 379–82), the traditional objective genitive is the better option—in the NIV translation, "faith in Christ."[78]

In verse 10, Paul returns to the theme of "knowing" Christ that he highlighted in verse 8, presenting this now as the result of his "gaining" Christ and being "found in him" (vv. 8b–9a).[79] Echoing a point he made earlier in the letter (1:28–29), Paul makes clear that to know Christ is to participate not only in the benefits he confers—resurrection—but also in the sufferings he undergoes (3:10–11). The believer, who has been raised with Christ, is empowered for this new life. But the believer has also died with Christ (cf. Rom 6:4–6), and that union continues to shape their life, giving it a cruciform shape—a "participation [or 'fellowship'; *koinōnia*] in his sufferings, becoming like him in his death" (Phil 3:10; see also 2 Cor 4:10).

Verses 12–14 are loosely related to verses 4–11. Paul wants to head off any misunderstanding about his status in Christ. He has not "already obtained all this" (v. 12). While enjoying the many rich benefits of knowing Christ, there is much yet for Paul to strive for. And so Paul presses ahead, straining forward to become what he has been called to be in Christ, looking to the "prize of the upward call of God" (v. 14, my translation). The relationship of these words is debated. One option is to see "the upward call" as defining the prize.[80] Another option is to think that the "upward call" is the initial call to salvation, which functions here as the source of that final prize.[81] In either case, Fee summarizes Paul's point well:

> First, God "called" Paul to himself, which will culminate in glory; second, that call, which began at his conversion, is "heavenward" in terms of its final goal; third, God's call found its historical and experiential locus "in Christ Jesus"; and fourth, at the end of the race Paul will gain the prize, the tangible evidence that the goal of God's call has been reached.[82]

---

the New Perspective on Paul," in Dunn, *New Perspective on Paul*, 469–90; Wright, *Paul and the Faithfulness of God*, 2:984–92.

77. Here, see O'Brien, *Philippians*, 398–400; Bockmuehl, *Philippians*, 210–11.

78. On this verse, see esp. Fee, *Philippians*, 324–26; Karl Friedrich Ulrichs argues against the subjective genitive for this verse (*Christusglaube: Studien zum Syntagma Πίστις Χριστοῦ und zum paulinischen Verständnis von Glaube und Rechtfertigung*, WUNT 2/227 [Tübingen: Mohr Siebeck, 2007], 222–47).

79. On this reading, the infinitive construction "to know"

(*tou gnōnai*) in v. 10 expresses the result of "gaining" (*kerdēsō*) and being "found" (*heurethō*) in Christ (see Hellerman, *Philippians*, 189).

80. A few interpreters think that Paul may be alluding to the prize of being called "upward" that was awarded at Greek athletic contests (Hawthorne and Martin, *Philippians*, 210–11).

81. Hansen writes, "The call of God stands at the beginning, not the end, of the race Paul runs" (*Philippians*, 256); cf. also O'Brien, *Philippians*, 433.

82. Fee, *Philippians*, 349.

2.6 Final Call to Gospel Conformity (3:15–4:1)

Paul closes out the section of exhortations begun in 1:27 by calling on the Philippians to (1) take the same viewpoint (*phroneō* is the verb here again) that he and others who are mature in the faith take (vv. 15–16); (2) follow the example of Paul and others who live faithful Christian lives (v. 17); and (3) avoid the bad example of "enemies of the cross of Christ" (vv. 18–19). These latter people are not easy to identify, since Paul describes them in very general terms. Even what appears at first sight to be a rather specific characterization—"their god is their stomach"—turns out to be language that is used broadly to describe people who have selfish motives.[83] It is likely they are at least claiming to be Christians ("enemies of the cross" suggests this), but whether they are to be identified with the "Judaizers" of 3:2[84] or whether they are a different (perhaps libertine) group[85] is unclear.

In contrast to these enemies, who focus on earthly things, are Christians, who recognize that their "citizenship [or 'commonwealth'] is in heaven" (v. 20).[86] The word for citizenship is *politeuma*, a word that obviously echoes Paul's initial exhortation that the Philippians "live as citizens" (*politeuesthe*; 1:27, my translation). While people in Philippi, a colony of Rome, looked to that great center of the world for their inspiration and values, believers in Philippi were to look to heaven for their inspiration and values. "Paul uses his political vocabulary in order to talk about the church as a distinctive body under Christ's authority."[87] The Philippians can live radically countercultural lives because they are sure of the end God has for them. He will send a Savior from heaven, who will transform their "lowly bodies" to be like Christ's "glorious body" (v. 21). As elsewhere in Philippians (1:19, 28; 2:12), this salvation refers especially to future vindication.

The long middle part of the letter ends where it began: with a call to "stand firm" (*stēkete*) (4:1; see 1:27).

3 FINAL GOSPEL MATTERS (4:2–23)

The letter concludes with paraenesis, directed to two individuals (vv. 2–3) and then to the entire community (vv. 4–9), an expression of thanks for the gift the Philippians sent Paul (vv. 10–20), and a brief closing (vv. 20–23).

---

83. Dunn (*Beginning from Jerusalem*, 1011–14), for instance, cites 3 Macc 7.11, which refers to apostate Jews as people "who for the belly's sake had transgressed the divine commandments" (NRSV; see also T. Mos. 7.9; Philo, *Virtues* 182).

84. E.g., Silva, *Philippians*, 182; Reumann, *Philippians*, 589–90.

85. E.g., Fee, *Philippians*, 375; Bockmuehl, *Philippians*, 231–32.

86. The Greek word *politeuma* usually refers to a "common-wealth"; the meaning "citizenship" is not well attested in the NT period (O'Brien, *Philippians*, 460).

87. Bertschmann, *Bowing before Christ*, 114. A confrontation between Roman and Christian values is therefore clear, and those Roman values would include, of course, the imperial cult with its demand for worship of the emperor. But there is nothing in this text to suggest that this was directly in Paul's purview (120–21).

We have no way of knowing who Euodia and Syntyche were, other than that they served with Paul in some kind of ministry. Nor do we know why they were quarrelling. However, as Hellerman remarks, Paul brings to bear on their problem two of the key emphases of the letter: to have the "same mind" (*phronein*) and the priority of the gospel ("contended at my side in the cause of the gospel").[88]

The call to rejoice (v. 4) again serves to transition into a series of general exhortations (vv. 5–9), focusing on the importance of prayer as the means of relieving anxiety (reflecting the serious opposition the Philippians face?; vv. 5–7) and the need to orient one's "thinking" (*logizomai* here rather than *phroneō*; v. 8). As so often in Philippians, Paul presents himself as an example to be imitated (v. 9).

Paul's "thank you" for the Philippians' gift is famous for its rather indirect and convoluted style. Paul is clearly wanting to say two, somewhat contradictory, things at once: thanks for the gift; I am fully sufficient in Christ. He elaborates on the first point in a way that shows he is grateful for their gift, which has been genuinely helpful to him. But, as Paul often makes clear, he is ever vigilant about his ministry being viewed as an opportunity for him to make money. Granted the importance of patronage in his culture, Paul is probably also wanting to avoid any suggestion that he is a "client" of the Philippians, beholden to them for his position and/or livelihood.[89] His policy was apparently therefore not to accept money from people with whom he was directly involved, while being open to receiving gifts when he was not present. While we must be careful about thinking modern evangelists must follow Paul's example in all these specifics, his practice is at least something to consider. The passage, as Silva remarks, presents a "theology of Christian giving."[90]

---

88. Hellerman, *Philippians*, 229.

89. See esp. Hellerman, *Philippians*, 256–57 and also his monograph, *Reconstructing Honor at Philippi:* Carmen Christi *as* Cursus Pudorum, SNTSMS 132 (Cambridge: Cambridge University Press, 2005).

90. Silva, *Philippians*, 205. I once heard a quite effective and well-balanced sermon on this text from a missionary expressing appreciation for the support he was receiving.

Chapter 14

1 TIMOTHY

LOCATING THE LETTER

"More than perhaps for any book in the NT, exegesis of the PE [Pastoral Epistles] is affected by one's critical assumptions."[1] The truth of Mounce's observation is confirmed by the many commentaries on the Pastoral Epistles that are preoccupied with explaining how their late first-century or early second-century teaching extends or contradicts the teaching found in the seven "authentic" Pauline epistles. These commentators reflect the "critical consensus" that these three letters are pseudepigraphs from several decades after the death of Paul. Scholars who adopt this approach naturally come to different conclusions on aspects of Paul's theology than do those who are working with all thirteen letters. Omitting the Pastoral Epistles from the data we use to construct Paul's theology shifts particularly Paul's teaching on the church and its leadership, the role relationship of Christian men and women, and the shape of the interface between the church and the world.[2]

As I have said several times before, the purpose and the scope of this book mean that I cannot give these kinds of issues the attention they deserve.[3] I can only here register my opinion about where 1 Timothy, along with the closely related Titus and

---

1. William D. Mounce, *The Pastoral Epistles*, WBC 46 (Nashville: Thomas Nelson, 2000), xlvi.

2. Note, for instance, Dunn's treatment of "ministry and authority" in his Pauline theology, which, by failing to integrate the Pastorals (and Acts) in the discussion arguably leads to a skewed conclusion (*Theology of Paul*, 580–86). See, for a particularly forceful argument on the canonical issue, Johnson, *Constructing Paul*, 33–41, 74–92.

3. Luke Timothy Johnson, *The First and Second Letters to Timothy: A New Translation with Introduction and Commentary*, AB 35A (New York: Doubleday, 2001), 20–54, provides a useful history of interpretation. A good defense of the "critical consensus" is found in Michael Wolter, *Die Pastoralbriefe als Paulustradition*, FRLANT 146 (Göttingen: Vandenhoeck & Ruprecht, 1988), 11–24. A thorough and balanced argument focusing on theology that situates the Pastorals between Paul and Ignatius is James W. Aageson, *Paul, the Pastoral Epistles, and the Early Church*,

Library of Pauline Studies (Peabody, MA: Hendrickson, 2008); see also Lloyd K. Pietersen, *The Polemic of the Pastoral Epistles: A Sociological Examination of the Development of Pauline Christianity*, JSNTSup 264 (London: T&T Clark, 2004). Defenders of this general approach differ over how many authors may be involved; William A. Richards, *Difference and Distance in Post-Pauline Christianity: An Epistolary Analysis of the Pastorals*, StBibLit 44 (New York: Peter Lang, 2002), thinks each letter was written by a different person. Important defenses of Pauline authorship of at least some of the letters are found in Johnson, *First and Second Timothy*, 55–91; Mounce, *Pastoral Epistles*, xlviii–cxxix. A recent, particularly careful linguistic analysis throws serious doubt on whether the "Pastorals," as a group, stand out in terms of their language from the other Pauline letters (Jermo van Nes, *Pauline Language and the Pastoral Epistles: A Study of Linguistic Variation in the Corpus Paulinium*, Linguistic Biblical Studies 16 [Leiden: Brill, 2018]).

2 Timothy, are to be "located" with respect to the ministry of Paul and point to studies that defend this conclusion.

As Mounce also notes, there is no question that, in vocabulary, tone, and—to some extent—theology, the Pastoral Epistles stand apart within the canonical Pauline corpus. The questions that must be answered are "how did they differ?" and "why?"[4] To be sure, this matter of "difference" must be kept in perspective: *every* letter of Paul differs to some degree from every other letter, as he writes in different circumstances to meet different problems. And, as we will see, we have to be careful not to lump all three "Pastoral Epistles" together, ignoring the distinctive elements of style and theology in each one. Still, plotted on a spectrum of difference, the Pastoral Epistles share certain common features that make them stand out as "more different" than the other ten letters of Paul.

The differences between the Pastoral Epistles, on the one hand, and the other letters of Paul, on the other, must then be frankly acknowledged. Vocabulary and style do differ. However, the supposition that a trusted amanuensis has played a significant role in the composition goes a long way toward explaining these differences. Theological differences, as usually acknowledged, present the greater problem. Here, again, there are differences. Yet the differences should not be magnified, either. Scholars routinely create a chasm at this point by exaggerating certain theological tendencies in the Pastorals, on one side, and the "authentic" Paul, on the other. At the end of the day, the question becomes one of probability. Which is the more likely? That someone thirty-fifty years after Paul's death wrote letters in his name, including numerous autobiographical details, and that these letters were nonetheless received as Scripture by a community highly suspicious of forgeries? Or that Paul, with the assistance of an amanuensis, perhaps toward the end of his life, wrote these letters, developing distinctive theological emphases to meet the particular demands of their time and place? I think the latter is the more probable alternative.

If, as I think, Paul wrote these letters, the remaining question is when. Some scholars think that at least 1 Timothy and Titus could be located within the ministry of Paul covered by Acts—the most likely scenario being that the letters were written on Paul's third missionary journey at some point after leaving Ephesus (see Acts 19).[5] Most date 2 Timothy at the very end of Paul's life, although a few have assigned it to the time of Paul's Caesarean imprisonment.[6] But most scholars who think Paul wrote these letters locate 1 Timothy and Titus during a time of ministry following the imprisonment in

---

4. Mounce, *Pastoral Epistles*, xlvii.

5. E.g., Jakob van Bruggen, *Die geschichtliche Einordnung der Pastoralbriefe* (Wuppertal: Brockhaus, 1982); Bo Reicke, *Re-examining Paul's Letters: The History of the Pauline Correspondence*, ed. David P. Moessner and Ingalisa Reicke (Harrisburg, PA:

Trinity Press International, 2001), 105–20; John A. T. Robinson, *Redating the New Testament* (London: SCM, 1976), 63–79; Johnson, *First and Second Timothy*, 135–37 (on 1 Timothy).

6. See Reicke, *Re-examining Paul's Letters*, 114–15.

Rome described in Acts 28 (ca. AD 62–64) and 2 Timothy during a second Roman imprisonment just before Paul's death (ca. AD 64–66). I prefer this option, partly because it more satisfactorily explains the nature of Paul's theological teaching in these letters (see below).

We must assume that after his release from his first Roman imprisonment (see Acts 28:30–31), pastoral issues in the Ephesian church and perhaps elsewhere forced Paul to change his plans for ministry in Spain (see Rom 15:24) and to return to the eastern Mediterranean. Paul writes 1 Timothy to his trusted ministry associate after the two of them had spent some time together ministering in Ephesus (1 Tim 1:3). Paul's prophecy about "savage wolves" coming in to attack the flock (Acts 20:29–30) had come true, and Paul, after leaving Ephesus for Macedonia, writes Timothy to instruct him about the need to confront these false teachers.

Timothy, of course, whom Paul calls his "true son in the faith" (1:2), was a trusted and beloved ministry colleague. A native of Lystra with a Greek father and Jewish mother, Timothy was enlisted by Paul in his missionary work at the beginning of the second missionary journey (Acts 16:1–3). From then on, Timothy is closely associated with Paul. He is mentioned five further times in Acts and, apart from 1 and 2 Timothy, thirteen times in eight of Paul's letters.

ISOLATING THE ISSUES

All three Pastoral Epistles are written in the shadow of false teaching. Paul begins 1 Timothy by exhorting Timothy to "command certain people not to teach false doctrines any longer" (1:3). Titus, while opening positively with instructions about appointing elders (1:5–9), quickly makes clear that elders are needed because "many rebellious people" have arisen (Titus 1:10). False teaching is not mentioned early in 2 Timothy, but 2:14–3:9 makes clear that Paul's charge to Timothy is fueled by the need to confront false teachers. Our assessment of the theology of these letters must therefore take into consideration this component of false teaching. Unfortunately, we lack the information we would need to identify this teaching. From the letters themselves, we discover the following particulars. The false teaching is:

"demonic" teaching of the "last days" (1 Tim 4:1; cf. 2 Tim 3:1)
a danger from within the church (e.g., 1 Tim 1:6; Titus 1:16)
preoccupied with foolish trivialities (1 Tim 1:6; Titus 1:10; 2 Tim 2:16)
divisive (1 Tim 6:4; Titus 3:9–10)
enamored of (false) "knowledge" (*gnōsis*) (1 Tim 6:20–21; cf. Titus 1:16)
influenced by Judaism (1 Tim 1:7–9; Titus 1:10, 14)
supportive of an ascetic lifestyle (1 Tim 4:3)

While these are not explicitly tied to the false teaching, the false teachers were probably also:

> disparaging authority (1 Tim 2:2; 4:12; 6:2–3; Titus 1:10)
> rejecting "traditional" family and sexual roles (1 Tim 4:3; cf. 5:12–15)
> exclusivistic (cf. 1 Tim 2:4)
> greedy (1 Tim 6:9; Titus 1:11)
> teaching that the resurrection had already happened (cf. 2 Tim 2:17–18)

To be sure, it could be objected that citing evidence from all three letters in this fashion might create a false amalgamation of what may have been two or three distinct movements. However, while it is possible—indeed likely—that the false teaching took different specific forms at Ephesus (1 Timothy) and Crete (Titus), the number of parallels in Paul's guidance to Timothy and Titus point to the existence of a broadly similar movement in both places.[7] Identifying this movement is impossible. Scholars who date the letters in the early second century think Gnosticism may be the culprit.[8] Full-fledged Gnosticism certainly did not exist in the sixties of the first century, when I think the letters were written. However, early gnostic-like ideas may be involved. Similarities between the problems addressed in these letters and in 1 Corinthians might also suggest a common root in "overrealized eschatology" (see esp. the reference to false teachers who claim that "the resurrection has already taken place" [2 Tim 2:17–18]). It is also possible that the churches were influenced by the cultural movement dubbed the "new Roman wife" by Bruce Winter, which was a kind of early "women's liberation movement" that urged women to abandon traditional household duties in favor of independence from their husbands and greater involvement in public life.[9] Beyond these possible general factors, it is useless to speculate further.

False teaching, then, looms large in these letters. Indeed, some interpreters insist that everything Paul teaches is in response to false teaching.[10] This claim is hermeneutically significant because it is often then alleged that some of the controversial teaching of the letters, directed against this false teaching, has local and temporary application only. This is, of course, quite possible; the circumstantial nature of Paul's letters requires that we always assess the ultimate applicability of his teaching in light of these circumstances. But two points important for our discussion below need to be made here.

---

7. Philip H. Towner strikes a good balance between acknowledging the individuality of the letters while also seeing them united by certain themes (*The Letters to Timothy and Titus*, NICNT [Grand Rapids: Eerdmans, 2006], 27–31). Johnson (*First and Second Timothy*, 146) thinks the profile of the false teaching differs between 1 Timothy on the one hand and Titus on the other.

8. See, e.g., Lorenz Oberlinner, *Kommentar zum Titusbrief*, vol. 3 of *Die Pastoralbriefe*, HThKNT 11/2 (Freiburg im Breisgau: Herder, 1996), 52–73.

9. Bruce Winter, *Roman Wives, Roman Widows: The Appearance of New Women and the Pauline Communities* (Grand Rapids: Eerdmans, 2003). See Towner, *Timothy and Titus*, for these last two points.

10. Payne, *Man and Woman*, 296–99.

First, we might question whether some interpreters have exaggerated the influence of the false teaching on what Paul writes. We grant that arming Timothy and Titus to fight this teaching is fundamental. But we might also expect that Paul would move beyond this immediate issue in his teaching of his two ministry associates. Second, we must be cautious about assuming without argument that teaching directed against false teaching is limited in application. We do not assume that justification by faith in Galatians or the high Christology of Colossians are limited in significance because they address false teaching. Neither can we assume without careful argument that Paul's theological response to false teaching in the Pastorals is limited in application.

ANALYZING THE ARGUMENT

The standard critical approach to the Pastoral Epistles tends to view the contribution to the theology of Paul negatively: these letters, written after Paul's death but with appeal to his authority, contradict Paul's own teaching in their advocacy of cultural accommodation, hierarchical gender roles, and an institutional church.[11] On this view, these letters portray a "reactionary" Paul; they are "anti-Paul," characterized by "a taming of Paul, a domestication of Paul's passion."[12] Paul's "religion of conversion" has become a "religion of tradition."[13] If, however, Paul did indeed write these letters himself, the perspective of the Pastorals must be integrated into Paul's theology. The claim that such integration is impossible generally results from a skewed view of "the authentic Paul," on the one hand, and the Paul of the Pastorals, on the other. I look at this matter in more detail in chapter 2. Here I simply note that the particular shape of Paul's theology in these letters arises from the intersection of three factors: (1) the need to counter the particular form that the false teaching has taken; (2) his particular audience, two trusted gospel associates; and (3) the need to begin preparing for the time when his apostolic authority would no longer be available.[14]

Paul focuses on several theological points in light of these factors. Especially prominent is a concern for the accurate teaching and transmission of "sound doctrine" (1 Tim 1:10; 6:3; 2 Tim 1:13; 4:3; Titus 1:9; 2:1, 8). As Mounce notes, Paul sets forth the gospel, both as right belief and right behavior, as the key antidote to heresy.[15]

11. See, e.g., Korinna Zamfir, *Men and Women in the Household of God: A Contextual Approach to Roles and Ministries in the Pastoral Epistles*, NTOA/SNTSU 103 (Göttingen: Vandenhoeck & Ruprecht, 2013); Elizabeth Schüssler Fiorenza, *In Memory of Her: A Feminist Theological Reconstruction of Christian Origins* (New York: Crossroad, 1983), 288–91. Wall, however, while treating the letters as pseudepigraphical, seeks fully to integrate their teaching from a canonical perspective (Robert W. Wall with Richard B. Steele, *1 and 2 Timothy and Titus*, Two Horizons New Testament Commentary [Grand Rapids: Eerdmans, 2012]).

12. Borg and Crossan, *First Paul*, 14–15; see also, e.g., Elliott, *Liberating Paul*, 25–54, 84–90.

13. Michael Wolter, "The Development of Pauline Christianity from a 'Religion of Conversion' to a 'Religion of Tradition,'" in Moessner et al., *Paul and the Heritage of Israel*, 49–69.

14. For a survey of the theology of these letters, see Andreas Köstenberger, *A Commentary on 1–2 Timothy and Titus*, BTCP (Nashville: B&H Academic, 2017), 357–544.

15. Mounce, *Pastoral Epistles*, lxxvi–lxxx. See also Köstenberger, *Commentary on 1–2 Timothy and Titus*, 388–97.

Paul's admonitions to Timothy and Titus to appoint appropriately qualified people to leadership roles (1 Tim 3:1–12; 5:17–25; Titus 1:5–9; cf. 2 Tim 2:2) grow out of this central focus on sound doctrine. It is this development toward an "institutional" church that is especially thought to mark the late post-Pauline origin of the letters. Marshall summarizes the standard view:

> The general consensus is that the PE represent the development of an early catholic view of the church which was occasioned by the rise of heresy and the consequent need to preserve apostolic teaching by an appeal to the "deposit" handed down from Paul, by the development of structures to ensure that teaching was in the hands of trustworthy leaders, and by the development of a discipline to restrain the opponents.[16]

The letters certainly display a great interest in church organization. But such a development, rooted in Paul's earlier practice (Acts 14:23; 20:28),[17] is entirely expected as he contemplates the need to provide for continuity of apostolic teaching in the absence of the apostles themselves. As Marshall says, "The concern of 1 Tim (and of the PE generally) is basically with the gospel and perversions of it rather than purely or primarily with church order and 'bourgeois' ethics. It is the maintenance of the purity of the gospel which matters most of all."[18]

Marshall's allusion to "bourgeois ethics" reflects the famous accusation of Dibelius and others, to the effect that the Pastoral Epistles seek to create peace and security for the church by advising believers to accommodate with existing social structures.[19] Paul's stress on prominent virtues such as "godliness" (*eusebeia*; see 1 Tim 2:2; 3:16; 4:7, 8; 6:3, 5, 6, 11; 2 Tim 3:5; Titus 1:1; the cognate verb is used in 1 Tim 5:4; and the adverb in 2 Tim 3:12; Titus 2:12) and "sobriety" (*sōphrosynē* and cognates; see 1 Tim 2:9, 15; 3:2; 2 Tim 1:7; Titus 1:8; 2:2, 4, 5, 12) are said to reflect this purpose. A concern with the reputation of the church among unbelievers is obvious (e.g., 1 Tim 2:2; 3:7; 5:14; 6:1; Titus 1:6; 2:5, 8, 10), as well as respect for authorities (1 Tim 2:1–2; Titus 3:1). However, these emphases are directed against false teaching that was apparently scorning God's ordination of certain structures in the world to regulate life for the good

---

16. I. Howard Marshall with Philip H. Towner, *A Critical and Exegetical Commentary on the Pastoral Epistles*, ICC (London: T&T Clark, 1999), 516. This consensus is attested clearly in Jürgen Roloff, *Der erste Brief an Timotheus*, EKKNT 15 (Zürich: Benziger, 1988), 169–89, 211–17.

17. Of course, many would claim that these texts simply reveal the status of the church in the late first century.

18. Marshall and Towner, *Pastoral Epistles*, 385.

19. Martin Dibelius, *Die Pastoralbriefe*, 2nd ed., HNT 13 (Tübingen: Mohr Siebeck, 1931), 24–25. On Dibelius's concept of "christlicher Bürgerlichkeit" ("Christian citizenship"), see Reggie M. Kidd, *Wealth and Beneficence in the Pastoral Epistles*, SBLDS 122 (Atlanta: Scholars Press, 1990). For a counter to this view, see Roland Schwarz, *Bürgerliches Christentum im Neuen Testament? Eine Studie zu Ethik, Amt und Recht in den Pastoralbriefen*, ÖBS 4 (Klosterneuburg: Österreichisches Katholisches Bibelwerk, 1983). On the importance of legitimizing the church within the existing culture, see David C. Verner, *The Household of God: The Social World of the Pastoral Epistles*, SBLDS 71 (Chico, CA: Scholars Press, 1983).

of all. Paul is not arguing for conformity to society as such but for recognition of these divinely instituted structures. (Slavery is an obvious exception that I will treat fully on pp. 643–45.) We can detect this same concern behind Paul's exhortations to women to live out their faith in the context of the family (1 Tim 2:9–15; 5:11–15; Titus 2:1–11). And both these concerns for "order" can be related to what most scholars think is the central image of the church in these letters—the "household" (see esp. 1 Tim 3:15).[20] Paul urges believers in general to work out behavior within their location in this spiritual household, and qualifications for leaders often play on the parallel between the social household and the divine one.[21] The theological focus of the Pastorals, while obviously focused on the church and ethics, is not confined to these matters. The fundamental Pauline (and NT) salvation-historical tension created by the two "epiphanies" of Christ is both explicit (Titus 2:11–14) and implicit.[22] God's saving intervention in Christ is often noted, with the title "Savior" (used of both God [1 Tim 1:1; 2:3; 4:10; Titus 1:3; 2:10; 3:4] and Christ [2 Tim 1:10; Titus 1:4; 2:13; 3:6]), a somewhat distinctive feature of the Pastorals (Paul uses "Savior" in only two other texts [Eph 5:23 and Phil 3:20, both referring to Christ]).[23] Also characteristic of the Pastorals is an emphasis on the universal availability of this salvation (1 Tim 2:3–4; 4:10).[24] Finally, as we would expect in "pastoral" epistles, these letters are full of advice on how to administer God's gospel and serve the people of God in ministry.

Paul's instructions to Timothy in 1 Timothy (and to Titus) take the form of "mandates of a ruler" (*mandata principis*), royal correspondence in which "a superior writes to a representative or delegate with instructions concerning the delegate's mission."[25] The letter is not easy to outline, but there is something to be said for finding in it an alternation between advice about the false teaching (1:3–20; 4:1–16; 6:2b–10) and advice about congregational life (2:1–3:16; 5:1–6:2a).[26]

---

20. The natural relationship between the "household" imagery and concern with hierarchy and order is frequently pointed out (e.g., Oberlinner, *Titusbrief*, 81–82).

21. Zamfir (*Men and Women*, 60–97) argues that the author of the Pastorals, in keeping with the early first-century Greco-Roman culture, thinks of the *oikos* as a public space, with the limitations on women's roles that would be appropriate for that situation.

22. Philip H. Towner, *The Goal of Our Instruction: The Structure of Theology and Ethics in the Pastoral Epistles*, JSNTSup 34 (Sheffield: JSOT, 1989), 61–74. On the "epiphany" scheme, see Andrew Y. Lau, *Manifest in Flesh: The Epiphany Christology of the Pastoral Epistles*, WUNT 2/86 (Tübingen: Mohr Siebeck, 1996), 179–259.

23. Towner (*Goal of Our Instruction*, 75–119) notes, as do many, the importance of the "Savior" title in the Christology of Titus (1 Tim uses "Savior" exclusively of God). On the Christology

of the Pastorals, see also Hanna Stettler, *Die Christologie der Pastoralbriefe*, WUNT 2/105 (Tübingen: Mohr Siebeck, 1998); and on the "Savior" theme, George Wieland, *The Significance of Salvation: A Study of Salvation Language in the Pastoral Epistles*, Paternoster Biblical Monographs (Milton Keynes: Paternoster, 2006). Stuhlmacher (*Biblical Theology of the New Testament*, 454) notes that "God and Christ move considerably closer together [in comparison with other Pauline letters]" in the Pastorals.

24. For the importance of salvation in the Pastoral Epistles, see, e.g., Köstenberger, *Commentary on 1–2 Timothy and Titus*, 432–45.

25. Johnson, *First and Second Timothy*, 139 (139–42, 255, etc.); George W. Knight III, *The Pastoral Epistles*, NIGTC (Grand Rapids: Eerdmans, 1992), 70; Towner, *Timothy and Titus*, 34–35.

26. See Ray van Neste, *Cohesion and Structure in the Pastoral Epistles*, JSNTSup 280 (London: T&T Clark, 2004), 143 (summary).

1 DEALING WITH FALSE TEACHERS (1) (1:1–20)

After the letter salutation (vv. 1–2), Paul turns immediately to what is obviously the key issue in the letter, the threat posed by false teachers. Paul urges Timothy to take a strong stance toward them—he is to "command" them to stop teaching "false doctrines" (v. 3). This false teaching promotes "controversial speculations" instead of building up the church (v. 4). The NIV "advancing God's work" obscures the imagery Paul uses here: he speaks of advancing "the household" or "economy" (Gk. *oikonomia*) of God in faith.[27] This imagery sets the tone for the letter, which pictures the church as a spiritual household that must be protected, guided well, and served.[28] As I noted above, we do not find the kind of data we need to identify this false teaching. The context here points to a Jewish influence. The "myths and endless genealogies" mentioned in verse 4 probably involve speculation based on Old Testament passages. The "law" that the false teachers aspire to teach is almost certainly the Torah (v. 7). However, they don't understand how to teach that law (*nomos*) "lawfully" (*nomimōs*; v. 8). The law, Paul says, is not for the "righteous" (*dikaios*) but for sinful people. Reference to the Old Testament law here is confirmed by the way the list of sinful people follows in general the order of the Decalogue (vv. 9b–10).[29] The significance of what he says for his view of the law is debated. Some think that Paul alludes to the restraining influence of the law.[30] But it is more likely that he is referring to the law's function of identifying and condemning sin.[31] The law does not apply in this sense to "the righteous"—meaning probably people who live righteously rather than those who have the status of "righteousness."[32] However, in either case, the implication appears to be that "righteous behavior" is not rooted in the law but, as Paul teaches elsewhere, in the Spirit and the renewed mind.

Paul's celebration of God's grace and mercy in his own life (vv. 12–17) builds on the last words of verse 11: "the gospel . . . which he entrusted to me." The faithful transmission of the gospel message is at the heart of the Pastorals. The chain of transmission begins with God, who entrusted the message to Paul, who then, in turn, entrusts it to Timothy and Titus, who, in turn, are to pass it on to others. At the same time, Paul's

---

27. Johnson helpfully paraphrases *oikonomian theou tēn en pistei* as "God's way of ordering reality as it is apprehended by faith" (*Interpreting Paul*, 417).

28. See esp. Aageson, *Paul, the Pastoral Epistles*, 20–35; Johnson, *First and Second Timothy*, 148–52.

29. We should note that the list includes "those practicing homosexuality." The Greek word is *arsenokoitēs*, the same word Paul uses in 1 Cor 6:9 (see my comments there about its meaning and significance).

30. Schreiner, *Law and Its Fulfillment*, 86–87.

31. See esp. Rosner, *Paul and the Law*, 73–75, referring to Jewish texts that use the word *nomimōs* with this kind of reference.

32. Contra, e.g., Stephen Westerholm, "The Law and the 'Just Man' (1 Tim 1,3–11)," *ST* 36 (1982): 79–95. While many think *dikaios* refers to believers, "just" by faith, neither of the two other occurrences of this word in the Pastorals (2 Tim 4:8; Titus 1:8) has this sense. Nor does Paul use the cognate *dikaiosynē* to refer to justification or righteous status (1 Tim 6:11; 2 Tim 2:22; 3:16; 4:8; Titus 3:5). One occurrence of *dikaioō* does have this sense, however (Titus 3:7; see also 1 Tim 3:16).

focus on God's grace in his life might suggest that the false teachers were using the law "unlawfully" to secure salvation.

After the somewhat parenthetical verses 12–17, Paul returns to the issue of false teaching in verses 18–20, using the word "command" (*parangelia*) to create an *inclusio* with verse 3 (*parangellō*). As Paul serves as a positive example of "holding on to faith," so others serve as negative examples of the same (vv. 19b–20).

2 CONGREGATIONAL LIFE (1) (2:1–3:16)

2.1 Prayer (2:1–7)

Paul's "first" order of business as he turns to congregational life is the importance of prayer for "all people." Praying for all, Paul suggests, is the appropriate response to God's desire to save "all people" (v. 4) and to the redeeming work of Christ for "all people" (v. 6). In verse 2, Paul calls for prayer specifically for government authorities, with the hope that they will allow believers to live "peaceful and quiet lives." The apparent universal scope of Paul's language in this paragraph raises well-known questions about how he views God's purposes and work in redemption. The "all people" in verses 4 and 6 could suggest that Paul thinks that God, true to his desire to save all, sent Christ to redeem all humans. Since Paul obviously does not think that all people will actually be saved, the "will" of God here would have to be qualified in some way, and the limitation in the scope of redemption would lie with humans who have the choice to believe or not. Others, however, insist that the "all" in this paragraph means not "every person without exception" but "all kinds of people." On this view, God's "will" in verse 4 can be taken in its full sense—God indeed wills (and so it is accomplished) that all kinds of people be saved; and to accomplish that, he sent Christ to die for all kinds of people.[33] This sense of "all" occurs elsewhere in Paul (see Rom 11:32 and my comments on that verse; see also 1 Tim 6:10), but it is not clear that it is intended here, since there has been no focus on different groups of people (though see v. 7). Moreover, it is hard to see how "all" could have this sense in the related 1 Timothy 4:10, which refers to God as "the Savior of all people, and especially of those who believe" (see also Titus 2:11). As he does elsewhere (e.g., Rom 3:29–30), Paul cites the "oneness" of God as the basis of his universal redemptive work (1 Tim 2:5). Paul hints that it is because Jesus himself is fully human that he can mediate between God and humans. His mediation is rendered possible because he offers himself as a "ransom" (*antilytron*) for all. The *lytro-* word

---

33. See, e.g., Thomas R. Schreiner, "'Problematic Texts' for Definite Atonement in the Pastoral and General Epistles," in *From Heaven He Came and Sought Her: Definite Atonement in Historical, Biblical, Theological, and Pastoral Perspective*, ed. David Gibson and Jonathan Gibson (Wheaton, IL: Crossway, 2013), 310–15; Knight, *Pastoral Epistles*, 119; Robert W. Yarbrough, *The Letters to Timothy and Titus*, PNTC (Grand Rapids: Eerdmans, 2018), 152. This interpretation preserves the notion of "limited atonement" that many (though by no means all) Reformed theologians find in Scripture.

group is important in Paul's atonement theology, presenting Christ's work as a "buying out" of slavery, an act similar to the exodus experience of Israel (see my notes on Rom 3:24 and also pp. 398–99). Paul also introduces here a key word that expresses his will for believers in these letters: *eusebeia*, "godliness" (v. 2; see above). This word "brings together both a correct knowledge of God and the behavior that is consistent with that knowledge."[34]

2.2 Men and Women in the Worship Service (2:8–15)

Verse 8 is transitional, returning to the theme of prayer from verses 1–2, while introducing the overall concern of verses 9–15—right conduct in the worship service. Even, then, as men pray "without anger or disputing," so the women in the congregation are to "adorn" themselves in a way that befits women who know God. This adornment consists both of transcultural virtues—"good deeds"—and culturally specific forms of dress that send a signal about the kind of women they are. The specifics of dress mentioned in verse 9b were often in Paul's day associated with immoral women or those seeking to broadcast their independence from their husbands. As Paul does with respect to the veil in 1 Corinthians 11:2–16, then, he urges women to avoid sending the wrong message about who they are in Christ. We may detect here the influence of the movement that Winter points out in his *Roman Wives*.

Paul continues his advice to Timothy about women in the congregation in verses 11–15—one of the more controversial passages in Paul's letters.[35] He begins by urging that women "learn"—an important point in a culture where women were often excluded from religious instruction. But they are to learn "in quietness and full submission." "Quietness" points to a teachable spirit. It is unclear to whom the women are to "submit." It is natural to think that Paul might be thinking of submission to husbands, since he uses the language of "submit" with reference to this relationship elsewhere (1 Cor 14:34; Eph 5:24; Col 3:18; Titus 2:5), and the relationship of women and men is clearly the focus of these verses.[36] However, in this context, it is also possible that he refers to submission to the teaching they are hearing.[37] Having told Timothy what he wants women to do, he next tells him what they are not to do: "Teach or assume authority over a man" (v. 12). Every word in this verse is the object of intense scrutiny, and I only scratch the surface of these debates here. "Teach," especially in the Pastoral Epistles, has the strong sense of communicating Christian doctrine (1 Tim 1:10; 4:1,

---

34. Greg A. Couser, "The Sovereign Savior of 1 and 2 Timothy and Titus," in *Entrusted with the Gospel: Paul's Theology in the Pastoral Epistles*, ed. Andreas J. Köstenberger and Terry L. Wilder (Nashville: B&H, 2010), 118; see also Marshall and Towner, *Pastoral Epistles*, 136–44.

35. I deal with this text in some detail (with interaction with scholarly literature up to that point) in "1 Timothy 2:11–15:

Meaning and Significance," *TrinJ* 1 (1980): 62–83. While I would not today want to endorse every point in this article, I continue to be in substantial agreement with its argument.

36. Knight, *Pastoral Epistles*, 139.

37. Marshall and Towner, *Pastoral Epistles*, 454; Towner, *Timothy and Titus*, 215; Yarbrough, *Timothy and Titus*, 173–74.

6, 11, 13, 16; 5:17; 6:1, 2, 3; 2 Tim 2:2; 3:10, 16; 4:3; Titus 1:9, 11; 2:1, 7, 10). "Assume authority" translates a rare Greek verb that, because of its rarity, is difficult to define. Some think it has the negative sense "domineer" and, with this meaning, is then often combined with the first verb. Paul is thus urging Timothy not to allow women "to teach in a domineering way."[38] However, the verb more likely has a relatively neutral meaning: "have authority," "exercise authority,"[39] perhaps with some focus on initiating that authority; hence NIV "assume authority."[40] Moreover, it is likely that Paul is here forbidding two separate but related activities.[41] It is also important to note that it is teaching *men* and having (or assuming) authority over *men* that Paul prohibits—the role relationship of men and women in the church is clearly his focus.

In conclusion, then, I think verse 12 teaches that, within the context of the church, women are not to authoritatively communicate Christian doctrine to men and not to enter into a position of authority over them. Of course, as is rightly noted, these imperatives are given to Timothy in a particular situation as he deals with false teaching in the first-century church of Ephesus. Many interpreters therefore conclude that this advice is limited to that situation and others like it. The limiting factor might be the general lack of educational opportunities in that culture.[42] Others think that Paul issues this prohibition because the women were involved in the false teaching (see 1 Tim 5:13).[43] Still others think that Paul is simply being culturally sensitive. Submission of women in that culture meant that women were not to have visible and public roles in religious ceremonies, and the church, for the sake of its witness, should go along with those cultural restrictions.[44]

The problem with these scenarios, of course, is that none is explicitly brought into play here. To be sure, New Testament authors will not always cite circumstances such as these that they could assume their readers were well aware of. Still, caution is needed. And this is especially the case when Paul appears to ground the prohibitions of verse 12 (note the *gar*, "for") in creation (v. 13) and the fall (v. 14). These verses also present serious interpretive challenges, but the argument from the order of creation (v. 13), at

38. Westfall, *Paul and Gender*, 290–94, e.g., thinks the verb connotes tyrannous rule.

39. See esp. Al Wolters, "The Meaning of Αὐθεντέω," in *Women in the Church: An Interpretation and Application of 1 Timothy 2:9–15*, 3rd ed., ed. Andreas J. Köstenberger and Thomas R. Schreiner (Wheaton, IL: Crossway, 2016), 65–115. Andreas J. Köstenberger, "A Complex Sentence: The Syntax of 1 Timothy 2:12," in Köstenberger and Schreiner, *Women in the Church*, 117–61, argues that the syntax (using *oude* to distinguish the activities) requires that the two verbs must work in unison, denoting two negative or two positive activities; and, since *didaskein* is positive, so is *authentein*.

40. Cognate Greek words, along with the etymology of the word, suggest a possible focus on initiation. This particular nuance may also explain why Paul uses this rare word in place of the word

exousiazō, which he uses elsewhere to mean "have authority." Payne elaborates "assume authority" as "take for herself authority to teach a man without authorization from the church" (*Man and Woman*, 393). However, "assume authority" need not connote illegitimate taking of authority; when a military figure "assumes command," he is simply entering into a position of authority. This more neutral sense is arguably what the NIV is attempting to convey.

41. Mounce, *Pastoral Epistles*, 130.

42. Keener, *Paul, Women, and Wives*, 101–32.

43. See esp. Payne, *Man and Woman*; Westfall, *Paul and Gender*, 279–312. Zamfir, *Men and Women*, 179–95, questions whether the epistles indicate women were involved in the false teaching.

44. E.g., Towner, *Timothy and Titus*, 233–36; Zamfir, *Men and Women*, 195–217.

least, matches the argument that Paul provides elsewhere for his advice about the role relationship of men and women (see 1 Cor 11:2–16; 14:33b–35). This suggests that more than local circumstances are involved in Paul's rationale.

Paul concludes the paragraph with a positive affirmation: "Women will be saved."[45] Yet he qualifies it: "through childbearing" (*teknogonia*). Some think that this word refers to *the* childbirth, the birth of Messiah, the seed of the woman in Genesis 3.[46] But it is more likely, granted the situation Paul addresses in Ephesus, that he is reminding Christian women that they do not have to neglect their roles as mothers and homemakers (see Titus 2:4–5) in order to experience ultimate salvation.[47] We might detect again here the force of a movement in that culture that encouraged women to abandon their normal domestic responsibilities and become more active in public life. Paul, of course, is not teaching that all Christian women must remain in the home and forgo any life outside the home. His point, rather, is to encourage Christian women to recognize that they can fully enjoy all the spiritual benefits of their relationship to Christ while maintaining the roles of mother and homemaker.

2.3 Overseers and Deacons (3:1–13)

Paul's concern that the church in Ephesus be kept from straying into heresy is his reason for encouraging Timothy to appoint the right kind of people to leadership positions. Verses 1–7 focus on the "position" or "office" of overseer (*episkopē*; see also Acts 1:20).[48] The word used here, along with the cognate "overseer" (*episkopos*) refers, as the English "overseer" suggests, to a person who has the responsibility to lead and guide an organization (it is sometimes translated "bishop," but this word carries too much ecclesiological baggage to be useful). "Overseers" as church leaders are mentioned elsewhere in Acts 20:28; Philippians 1:1, and Titus 1:7. The use of the singular form here and in Titus 1:7 suggests to some that Paul envisages a single overseer holding leadership responsibility for the local church.[49] However, the plural forms in Acts and Philippians are a problem for this view. It is better then, to view the singular here as generic and to assume that each church would have had a plurality of overseers. As we will see (see my notes on 1 Tim 5:17 and Titus 1:5–11), "overseer" was probably an alternative way of denoting the leadership role also denoted by the word "elder."

45. NIV "women" represents a singular construction in the Greek, referring to the "woman" of v. 14 (see ESV, "she will be saved"). But the singular is probably generic, so a plural "women" makes the point.

46. Payne, *Man and Woman*, 417–41.

47. Mounce, *Pastoral Epistles*, 144–46; Towner, *Timothy and Titus*, 233–36.

48. The paragraph is introduced with a formula we find five times in the Pastoral Epistles, in various forms: "Faithful is the saying" (*pistos ho logos*; see also 1 Tim 1:15; 4:9; 2 Tim 2:11; Titus 3:8). Knight's study argues convincingly that the formula both signals a citation and draws attention to the saying that follows (here and in 1 Tim 1:15; 2 Tim 2:11) or precedes (1 Tim 4:9; Titus 3:8) (a few think the formula in the present instance refers to 2:15, but most agree it introduces the discussion of the overseer). On the "faithful sayings" in general, see esp. George W. Knight III, *The Faithful Sayings in the Pastoral Epistles* (Grand Rapids: Baker, 1979); and also Towner, *Timothy and Titus*, 143–45.

49. E.g., Oberlinner, *Titusbrief*, 88–93; cf. Towner, *Timothy and Titus*, 246–47.

Paul, of course, does not say anything here explicitly about the responsibilities of the overseer; Timothy was undoubtedly familiar with the position. Most of the qualifications that are listed in verses 2–7 are basic moral virtues whose meaning is clear enough. But three deserve brief mention. First, the requirement that an overseer be "faithful to his wife" in verse 2 translates a phrase (*mias gynaikos andra*) that could also be rendered "husband of one wife." Some scholars have thought this qualification might be intended to disbar men in a polygamous relationship, men who are divorced and remarried, or even men who have had more than one wife for any reason. But none of these more specific interpretations is likely, and like the comparable expression "wife of one husband" in 5:9 (see ESV), the phrase probably simply stresses marital fidelity: a "one-woman man."[50] Second, overseers need to have the ability to "teach," that is, to faithfully communicate Christian doctrine (3:2). The third qualification to be noted is the requirement that overseers manage their households (*oikos*) well (v. 4). Reinforcing the centrality of the "household" image for the church in these letters, this qualification also suggests that overseers play a role in the spiritual household that they have as the *paterfamilias* in their own households.

"Deacons" (vv. 8–13) are also to be people who manage their households well (v. 12)—suggesting, again, some kind of comparable "managerial" role in the church. However, the other qualifications are too general to allow us to make any inferences about their responsibilities. Indeed, the role of "deacon" in the New Testament as a whole is very difficult to pin down. The Greek behind "deacon" is *diakonos*, which is widely used to refer to any Christian as a "servant" of Christ. The word takes on a more official sense in only three passages: in Romans 16:1 (probably), Philippians 1:1, and here. The usual view that *diakonos* connotes menial service, such as waiting on tables, has recently been contested by John N. Collins, who argues that the word often refers to valuable assistants. On this view, the deacons may be people who assist the overseers in their work in some undefined way.[51] The "women" who are mentioned in the midst of qualifications of deacons (v. 11) might refer to the wives of deacons[52] or to female deacons[53]—the latter, perhaps, being a bit more likely.

2.4 Right Behavior in the Household of God (3:14–16)

Scholars generally agree that this passage is central to the argument of 1 Timothy—indeed, many think it is programmatic for the Pastoral Epistles as a whole.[54] Paul hopes

50. See esp. the discussion in Mounce, *Pastoral Epistles*, 170–73.

51. John N. Collins, *Diakonia: Re-interpreting the Ancient Sources* (Oxford: Oxford University Press, 1990), 237–38.

52. Knight, *Pastoral Epistles*, 171; Mounce, *Pastoral Epistles*, 204; Yarbrough, *Timothy and Titus*, 209–11; Wall and Steele, *1 and 2 Timothy and Titus*, 110.

53. Most recent commentators hold this view; see, e.g., Roloff, *Der erste Brief an Timotheus*, 164; Marshall and Towner, *Pastoral Epistles*, 494.

54. Towner labels the passage "the rhetorical and theological highpoint of the letter" (*Timothy and Titus*, 271); Mounce calls the passage "the heart of the Pastoral corpus" (*Pastoral Epistles*, 214).

to return soon to Ephesus, but, in the meantime, wants Timothy to remember what he needs to teach: that believers live appropriately as members of God's household, "the church of the living God." We see again here the importance of the "household" image for the church. We also see the vital significance of the church as "pillar and foundation of the truth" (v. 15).[55] In the face of false teaching and in prospect of apostolic absence, the church must live up to its role as the bulwark and faithful transmitter of Christian doctrine. However, as the focus on behavior in this verse reveals, true doctrine must be accompanied and "adorned" by the manner of life of those who hold to it. The "church" (*ekklēsia*) in this passage may refer to the local church;[56] but it is perhaps more likely that the universal church is in view.[57]

Verse 16, as most English Bibles make clear by their formatting, is the quotation of a "hymn" or at least a "hymn-like" tradition about "the mystery of godliness" (ESV, *to tēs eusebeias mystērion*). Among other things, this text makes clear that Paul's conception of the church in these letters is firmly rooted in standard, early Christology. The hymn as a whole emphasizes Christ's triumphal position in his exaltation as the empowering force for the nourishing of the church. The structure of the hymn is not clear, but most think a three-couplet arrangement of two lines in each, with an alternating focus on earth and heaven, is the most natural:[58]

I   He appeared in *the flesh*,
        was vindicated by the Spirit,

II   was seen by angels,
        was preached among *the nations*,

III   was believed on in *the world*,
        was taken up in glory.

The first couplet features the common Pauline "flesh" (*sarx*)/"Spirit" contrast, which often denotes two separate power spheres within a salvation-historical scheme. As in

---

55. A few interpreters think this language might refer to the behavior required in the household of God (Johnson, *First and Second Timothy*, 231) or to Timothy himself (Wall and Steele, *1 and 2 Timothy and Titus*, 113). However, the flow of the verse suggests the phrase is in apposition to "church of the living God" (Mounce, *Pastoral Epistles*, 224).

56. E.g., Gottfried Holtz, *Die Pastoralbriefe*, THKNT 13 (Berlin: Evangelische Verlagsanstalt, 1986), 88; Mounce, *Pastoral Epistles*, 221.

57. Marshall and Towner, *Pastoral Epistles*, 509; Towner, *Timothy and Titus*, 274.

58. See, e.g., Lorenz Oberlinner, *Erster Timotheusbrief*, vol. 1 of *Die Pastoralbriefe*, HThKNT 11.2 (Freiburg im Breisgau: Herder, 1994), 163; Roloff, *Der erste Brief an Timotheus*, 192–93; Knight, *Pastoral Epistles*, 183. It is possible that the stanzas, then, focus on, respectively, Christ's revelation (lines 1–2), his proclamation (lines 3–4), and his reception (lines 5–6). Others argue for a two-stanza arrangement (Mounce, *Pastoral Epistles*, 216–17).

Romans 1:3–4, therefore, Christ existed in the realm of the flesh, the human arena, but was ultimately elevated to a new and more powerful status "in the sphere of the Spirit."[59] The contrast is, then, probably between Jesus's incarnation and subsequent life on earth and his resurrection, pictured as his being "justified" (*edikaiōthē*—perhaps best rendered here "vindicated"). "Seen by angels" may refer to Christ's triumph over spiritual beings (see 1 Pet 3:18–22),[60] but more likely simply refers to his appearance in the heavenly realm as a result of his ascension.[61] The second line of the third couplet, in chiastic fashion, probably refers to the same event, while the last line of the second couplet and the first of the third focus on the apostolic proclamation of the good news and the response of those who hear.

3 DEALING WITH FALSE TEACHERS (2) (4:1–16)

After attending to the need positively to foster a congregational life that will maintain the truth of the gospel in the face of false teaching, Paul now turns back again to Timothy's need to confront the false teachers themselves. He begins by briefly sketching the false teaching (vv. 1–5). In typical fashion, Paul views the time that he and Timothy minister in as "the last days" (my translation), a time when it was expected that opposition to the people of God would grow stronger and bolder (see also 2 Tim 3:1–9). It is a time period that will last indefinitely until Christ returns in glory. Paul offers one of the few explicit references to the content of the false teaching here, namely, the forbidding of marriage and abstinence from certain kinds of food (v. 3). This ascetic tendency could be rooted in an "overrealized eschatology," an overly enthusiastic conception of the believer's present spiritual state that leads to escape from and disdain for the world.[62]

The rest of the chapter focuses, positively, on the qualities Timothy needs to cultivate in order effectively to counter this teaching. Paul stresses that Timothy should not get entangled in the "godless myths and old wives' tales" (v. 7) that the false teachers are into (see 1:4). Timothy also needs to cultivate basic Christian virtues (vv. 7–8). Paul draws attention to this point by labeling it as one of his "faithful sayings" (v. 9a).[63] As he did in 2:3–6, Paul again highlights the universal scope of salvation; God is "the Savior of all people, and especially of those who believe" (v. 10). It appears that Paul here refers to two "moments" or aspects of God's saving work. God sends his Son to provide, in principle, salvation for all; but that saving work becomes one's own only

---

59. On this view, the *en* is spatial ("in") rather than instrumental ("by").

60. E.g., Holtz, *Pastoralbriefe*, 91.

61. A few interpreters think that *angeloi* might refer to "messengers" (Johnson, *First and Second Timothy*, 233).

62. Towner, *Timothy and Titus*, 294–95.

63. The formula here almost certainly refers back to v. 8 (Knight, *Faithful Sayings*, 62–63).

when a person responds in faith.[64] Timothy will find strength to resist these teachers as he recalls his "initiation" into ministry, when "the body of elders laid their hands" on him (v. 14). We should probably think of an occasion such as is narrated in Acts 13:1–3, when the church, in response to the prompting of the Spirit, laid their hands on Barnabas and Saul to commission them for their missionary enterprise.

4 CONGREGATIONAL LIFE (2) (5:1–6:2A)

Continuing his back-and-forth between the external threat to the church and its internal life, Paul now returns again to the latter. He instructs Timothy about how generally to treat various groups in the church (5:1–2) and then turns to a lengthy discussion of widows (5:3–16).[65] Interpreters who think 1 Timothy originates in the second century sometimes think that at least part of this passage addresses a formal ministerial group of widows.[66] But nothing in the text suggests an official status for widows.[67] Paul recognizes the value of their prayer ministry (v. 5), but does not imply any kind of formal ministerial status. Rather, picking up the Old Testament focus on caring for widows and other helpless society members (e.g., Ps 146:9; Isa 1:17), Paul instructs Timothy about the need to care for these women, who, in that culture, would often find it very hard to secure a living. But Paul also suggests that some abuses of the church's benevolence toward widows needed correction. Paul therefore begins by urging that recognition be given to widows "who are really in need" (v. 3; e.g., "true widows," *tas ontōs chēras*). Widows with families should find support from their relatives rather than depend on the church (vv. 4, 8). And widows who "live for pleasure," Paul suggests—perhaps squandering their resources—should not depend on the church for help (v. 6). Widows who are "put on the list"—presumably an official roll of widows who would receive support from the church—should be characterized by Christian virtues (vv. 9b–10). Moreover, only widows over the age of sixty should be enrolled (v. 9a); younger widows, Paul points out, may still want to marry (v. 11)—indeed, it is desirable that they do so (v. 14). Again Paul hints at problems among the Christian women in Ephesus. Some are idle, "talking nonsense," and have become followers of Satan (vv. 14–15). It is likely here again that some of the Ephesian women were

---

64. Schreiner, "'Problematic Texts,'" 315–19. Another option is to give *malista* the meaning "that is" rather than "especially." On this view, Paul qualifies "all people" by restricting the reference to believers. However, it is doubtful that *malista* has this meaning. None of the other NT or LXX uses clearly has this sense; BDAG does not list such a meaning, nor does LSJ, though Montanari notes one or two texts where it might mean "precisely, exactly, just" (Franco Montanari, *The Brill Dictionary of Ancient Greek*, ed. Madeleine Goh and Chad Schroeder [Leiden: Brill Academic, 2015], 1275). See esp. Vern Poythress, "The Meaning of μάλιστα

in 2 Timothy 4:13 and Related Verses," *JTS* 53 (2002): 523–32; Yarbrough, *Timothy and Titus*, 289.

65. On this latter text, interpreted in the first-century cultural context, see esp. Winter, *Seek the Welfare*, 62–78.

66. An "order of widows" is mentioned in Irenaeus and may be hinted at in Polycarp's *Letter to the Philippians* (ca. AD 120–140); he refers to them as an "altar of God" (ch. 4).

67. Mounce, *Pastoral Epistles*, 274; see Johnson, *First and Second Timothy*, 277.

falling under the influence of cultural pressure to abandon the normal roles of wives and mothers and to seek "meaning" in the public sphere. Paul's exhortation to these women to "marry, to have children," and "to manage their homes" (v. 14) may sound like an attempt to suppress the natural aspirations of women.[68] Putting these points in the context of the cultural pattern we have observed, along with due recognition of the nature of the culture in Paul's day, warns us about simply taking over these principles in our day. Nevertheless, it is difficult to explain everything Paul says about gender roles as culture-bound. An assumption that women have a particular responsibility for the raising of children and management of the home is hard to avoid.

In 5:1, Paul urges Timothy not to harshly rebuke "an older man" (*presbyteros*). In verse 17, Paul again begins speaking about "older men" (*presbyteroi*; NIV: "elders"; see also v. 19). Some interpreters think the word *presbyteros* here continues to refer simply to older men.[69] But the context suggests the word is now being used to designate a person who holds a recognized position of leadership in the church. We read about "elders" who apparently had some kind of leadership role in the Jerusalem Jewish community (Acts 4:5, 8, 23; 6:12; 23:14; 24:1; 25:15). The reference to "elders" in Acts 11:30 suggests that the early Jerusalem church took over this term for its own leaders (see also Acts 15:2, 4, 6, 22, 23; 16:4; 21:18). Paul, then, perhaps in imitation of this model, appointed "elders" in the churches he established on the first missionary journey (Acts 14:23), and we find Paul addressing the elders of the church in Ephesus later on (20:17). "Elder" is used in this official sense also in Titus 1:5, James 5:14, and 1 Peter 5:1, 5. The New Testament evidence therefore suggests a widespread pattern of leadership in the local church, a plurality of elders in each local church. The relationship between these elders and the "overseer" of 1 Timothy 3:1–7 is not clear. Some think that an overseer was one of the elders who was, in a sense, *primus inter pares*, "first among equals."[70] It is perhaps more likely, however, that "elder" and "overseer" were names for the same office-holder, the former derived from the Jewish world and the latter from the Hellenistic world.[71] This relationship is suggested by the abrupt shift from "elders" to "overseer" in Titus 1:5, 7 and by a similar shift in Acts 20 (compare "elders" in v. 17 with "overseers" in v. 28).[72]

Paul implies in verse 17 that elders "direct the affairs" or "rule" (Gk. *proestōtes*, from *proistēmi*, "rule, direct"[73]) the church. Some of them, however, also engage

68. See the discussion in Johnson, *First and Second Timothy*, 270–71.

69. E.g., Holtz, *Pastoralbriefe*, 124; cf. Wall and Steele, *1 and 2 Timothy and Titus*, 132.

70. E.g., Andrew D. Clarke, *A Pauline Theology of Church Leadership*, T&T Clark Library of Biblical Studies (London: T&T Clark, 2008), 47–60.

71. See, e.g., Benjamin L. Merkle, "Ecclesiology in the Pastoral Epistles," in Köstenberger and Wilder, *Entrusted with the Gospel*, 180–90.

72. Compare also *presbyterous* in 1 Pet 5:1 with *episkopountes* [in many MSS] in v. 2.

73. The verb can also mean "give attention to," "care for" (Titus 3:8, 14; perhaps Rom 12:8; 1 Thess 5:12).

in teaching and preaching.[74] All of them are "worthy of double honor"—perhaps meaning simply recognition but more likely meaning financial support: *both* "honor" and "pay."[75] Some reference to financial support is suggested by the texts Paul cites in verse 18 to support this exhortation. He had already referred to Deuteronomy 25:4 in 1 Corinthians 9:9 to support the appropriateness of Christ's workers to receive a "material harvest" (1 Cor 9:11). The second text appears to cite a word of Jesus, making a similar point, from Luke 10:7. This reference, along with the striking reference to this text as well as Deuteronomy 25:4 as "Scripture" (*graphē*), is often cited as a reason to date 1 Timothy later than the lifetime of Paul. But (1) the saying Paul cites may be from the oral tradition of Jesus's teaching;[76] and (2) Paul's reference to Jesus's teaching alongside Old Testament references elsewhere suggests that at least some pieces of the Jesus tradition were beginning to be placed on the level of "Scripture" in Paul's day.

The rest of the paragraph mixes exhortations about elders (Timothy is not to "entertain an accusation" against an elder without solid evidence [v. 19]; he is not to appoint elders too quickly [v. 22]) with exhortations about Timothy's own conduct.

Paul's instructions to Timothy about his ministry to specific groups in the church concludes with exhortations to slaves to "regard their own masters as worthy of all honor" (6:1 ESV).[77] Paul is particularly concerned that believing slaves with believing masters not take advantage of their spiritual relationship to give them less than full service (v. 2—perhaps, then, the masters in v. 1 are unbelievers[78]). Paul also suggests a reciprocal attitude on the part of masters, who "are devoted to the welfare of their slaves." Note also his reference to masters as "beloved" (*agapētoi*; NIV "dear to them"), implying a wholly countercultural way of thinking about the relationship of slaves and masters.[79] Behind these concerns may again lie Paul's concern that the church not unnecessarily "rock" the status quo. (On the wider issue of slavery in Pauline perspective, see pp. 643–45.)

---

74. A few interpreters think that the verse should be translated "elders who direct the affairs of the church," *that is* (*malista*), "those whose work is preaching and teaching" (Knight, *Pastoral Epistles*, 232; Marshall and Towner, *Pastoral Epistles*, 612). But, as I noted in my comments on 4:13, this is an unlikely meaning of the Greek word.

75. Mounce, *Pastoral Epistles*, 309; Verbrugge and Krell, *Paul and Money*, 44–45.

76. Towner, *Timothy and Titus*, 366–67. It is also possible that we can date Luke-Acts early enough (perhaps around AD 62) for Paul to quote from it here (B. Paul Wolfe, "The Sagacious Use of Scripture," in Köstenberger and Wilder, *Entrusted with the Gospel*, 212–16; Michael J. Kruger, *Canon Revisited: Establishing the Origins and Authority of the New Testament Books* [Wheaton, IL: Crossway, 2012], 204–7; Yarbrough, *Timothy and Titus*, 290). See also L. Timothy Swinson, *What Is Scripture? Paul's Use of* Graphē *in the Letters to Timothy* (Eugene, OR: Wipf & Stock, 2014), who argues that "Scripture" encompasses both the OT and the apostolic tradition in the letter.

77. The concept "honor" (*timē/timaō*) binds together the exhortations in this section; see also 5:3 and 17.

78. Knight, *Pastoral Epistles*, 244.

79. Johnson, *First and Second Timothy*, 290; and see esp. Towner, *Timothy and Titus*, 385–90, who notes that Paul reverses cultural expectations by suggesting that slaves can render "benefaction" (*euergesia*) to their masters.

5 DEALING WITH FALSE TEACHERS (3) (6:2B–21)

Paul returns to where he began (1:3–20),[80] mixing denunciations of and warnings about the false teachers with instructions to Timothy about the attitudes and virtues he needs to counter this teaching. Paul again singles out the false teachers' penchant for meaningless controversies (vv. 4–5; see v. 20) and also rebukes them for following "what is falsely called knowledge" (*gnosis*; v. 20)—which may imply that the false teachers were propagating some form of incipient Gnosticism. Paul also adds for the first time a reference to their greed (vv. 5, 9–10, 17–19). Timothy, by contrast, is to follow the example of Paul himself (cf. Phil 4:11) and learn to be "content" (*autarkeia*; v. 6). Timothy will not be bothered by any lack of material possessions if he keeps his focus on what is truly important: "godliness" (*eusebeia*; mentioned in both vv. 6 and 11, illustrating again its importance in the letter) and concomitant virtues such as "righteousness," "faith," "love," "endurance," and "gentleness" (v. 11). Returning again to a prominent theme in chapter 1 (vv. 3, 18), Paul charges Timothy to "keep this command" (6:14)—probably a general reference to both right doctrine and right behavior. He is also to "guard what has been entrusted to your care," that is, the gospel (v. 20).

---

80. See Towner, *Timothy and Titus*, 390, for this grand *inclusio*.

Chapter 15

TITUS

LOCATING THE LETTER

In the "Locating the Letter" section on 1 Timothy, I have argued that we "locate" Titus, along with the letters to Timothy, late in Paul's ministry, after his release from his "first" Roman imprisonment (Acts 28:30–31; ca. AD 62–64). This letter, specifically, assumes that Paul and Titus have spent some time planting churches on the island of Crete, in the eastern Mediterranean. Paul has now moved on to Nicopolis, on the Adriatic coast of Greece (Titus 3:12). He writes to encourage Titus to complete the ministry by securing leaders for the churches and by putting the churches on a solid doctrinal and ethical footing. Titus, whom Paul calls his "true son in our common faith" (1:4), is not mentioned in Acts, but Paul refers to him in 2 Corinthians (2:13; 7:6, 13, 14; 8:6, 16, 23; 12:18), Galatians (2:1, 3), and 2 Timothy (4:10). The similar issues Paul confronts in this letter and in 1 Timothy suggest that they were written at about the same time. It is impossible to know which came first, and does not really affect our interpretation.

ISOLATING THE ISSUES

The key issue Paul confronts is false teaching, which is apparently similar to the false teaching affecting the church at Ephesus at about the same time (see "Isolating the Issues" in my discussion of 1 Timothy).

ANALYZING THE ARGUMENT

The similarities between 1 Timothy and Titus—both written to trusted ministry associates at the same time with reference to similar false teaching—means that the main theological teaching of the letters is very similar. See, therefore, the introductory section in "Analyzing the Argument" in my discussion of 1 Timothy for these themes.

1 THE OCCASION: FALSE TEACHING (1:1–16)

Paul's salutation (1:1–4) is more elaborate than usual, introducing some key themes in the letter: the need to firm up the faith of believers by making sure they know the truth, the ultimate goal of "godliness" (*eusebeia*; see my comments on 1 Tim 2:2), the present moment as the time when God's promises are coming to pass, and the message proclaiming these things with which Paul (and, by extension, Titus) has been entrusted.

Following the pattern we see also in 1 Timothy, the body of the letter alternates between a focus on the need to counter false teaching (1:5–16; 3:9–11) and a focus on right belief and behavior within the church that will prepare it to avoid falling prey to this teaching (2:1–3:8). Concern with false teaching therefore acts as a kind of *inclusio*.[1]

Paul, however, does not begin by warning about the false teaching. Rather, he recommends that Titus appoint leaders who will be prepared to counter this teaching. The list of character traits Paul wants to see in the leaders therefore appropriately climaxes with the need for leaders to "encourage others by sound doctrine" and to be able to "refute those who oppose it" (1:9). The churches in Crete are apparently so new that leaders have not yet been appointed. Paul urges Titus to remedy this situation; he is to appoint elders in every town (v. 5). It is unlikely that there is more than one church per town at this early date, so the natural reading of this verse is that each church would have a plurality of elders. The "overseer" (*episkopos*) of verse 7 may be a separate leader, perhaps drawn from the elders. But the nature of the connection between this verse and what precedes ("for," *gar*) suggests rather that "overseer" is another name for the leadership position denoted also by elder (the singular therefore being generic).[2] The requirements listed are generally straightforward,[3] the only one forcing us to pause being *tekna echōn pista* (v. 6), which might mean having children who "believe" (NIV) or, perhaps more likely, simply "faithful children" (CEB).[4]

The reason why it is so important to appoint the right people to leadership roles is the threat posed by false teaching (v. 10). The general outline of the false teachers is very similar to what we have found in 1 Timothy. The false teachers are disruptive, greedy, apparently viewing the Jewish law as a basis for speculative myths, and claim to know God but deny him by their false doctrine and sinful behavior.

2 INSTRUCTIONS ABOUT MAINTAINING "SOUND DOCTRINE" (2:1–3:8)

"Teach what is appropriate to sound doctrine" (2:1) could be the heading for the rest of the letter body; indeed, it would not be a bad heading for the teaching of the Pastoral Epistles in general. This general imperative is matched by "these, then, are the things

---

1. See esp. van Neste, *Cohesion and Structure*, 232–84.

2. See my comments on 1 Tim 5:17.

3. For a helpful table setting out the various requirements for leaders in the Pastorals, see Mounce, *Pastoral Epistles*, 155–58.

4. Knight, *Pastoral Epistles*, 290; contra, e.g., Towner, *Timothy*

and Titus, 682. Paul's omission of any reference to "deacons" (contrast 1 Tim 3:1–13) might be, as many speculate, because the churches were so new and small that there simply were not enough qualified believers to supply both "offices."

you should teach" in verse 15, forming, again, an *inclusio* around exhortations having to do with the life of the church.

In verses 2–10 Paul gives Titus guidelines for dealing with four distinct groups in the church: "older men" (v. 2), "older women" (vv. 3–5), "young men" (vv. 6–8), and slaves (vv. 9–10). Indirectly, Paul gives advice for another group as well, as he encourages the older women to teach certain things to the younger women (vv. 4–5). Overall, Paul's advice follows the pattern that is so characteristic of the Pastorals, urging believers to maintain what we might call "traditional" roles: older men are to be "temperate, worthy of respect" (v. 2), older women are to teach younger women to "love their husbands and children," to be "busy at home" and "subject to their husbands" (vv. 4–5); young men are to be "self-controlled" (v. 6); slaves are "to be subject to their masters in everything" (v. 9). As we have noted, this kind of ethical instruction has earned for the Pastorals the reputation of being an unPauline expression of "conformist" instruction. However, two things need to be said in response here. First, Paul is explicit about his motivation. He does not want people to view the Christian message as subversive or revolutionary, as if it incites its followers to antisocial behavior (vv. 5, 8). In other words, Paul's advice is to some extent prudential and geared to his own culture's expectations. Second, however, Paul's advice may be an attempt to right what has become an imbalance with respect especially to women's roles. As at Ephesus, we can suspect that the influence of the emancipatory "new Roman wife" movement is being felt on Crete.[5] Paul, then, is not just reinforcing culture-bound roles; he is also reasserting biblical expectations. The precise balance between these two concerns—conformity to society because of the culture of Paul's day, restatement of biblical teaching—is difficult to maintain, and the different points of equilibrium interpreters choose go a long way to explain the intense conflict over these matters in our day.

As grounding for this series of exhortations, Paul in verses 11–14 provides a beautiful condensed outline of the good news. The fundamental Pauline (and NT) pattern surfaces here again, as Paul roots the "imperative" in the "indicative," relating expectations for Christian conduct to the truth of Christian doctrine. The frame of the passage is provided by two "appearances"—the grace of God, connoting here the climactic expression of God's grace in the first coming of Christ (v. 11), and the "glory of our great God and Savior, Jesus Christ," referring, of course, to Christ's second coming (v. 13).[6] The translation of this last phrase is debated. It could also be rendered "the appearance of the glory of our great God and our Savior Jesus Christ" or "the appearance of the glory, that is, our great God and our Savior Jesus Christ." If we opt for one of these last

5. Winter, *Roman Wives, Roman Widows*, 147–69.
6. Paul uses the verb *epiphainō* in v. 11 and the cognate noun *epiphaneia* in v. 13. This language, used with respect to

Christology, is central in the Pastorals (see also 1 Tim 6:14; Titus 3:4; 2 Tim 1:10; 4:1, 8; on this theme, see Towner, *Timothy and Titus*, 435–38).

two renderings, Paul refers to two persons, God the Father and Jesus Christ. On the first option, we have one person: the great God, who is our Savior Jesus Christ. There are strong reasons to adopt this option, meaning this is another verse (see Rom 9:5 and my comments there) in which Paul explicitly calls Jesus God.[7] Paul attaches to his description of this second appearance a concise summary of the way in which Christ has become "our Savior"—by offering himself as a redemptive sacrifice and thereby purifying for himself a people dedicated to him (v. 14). Paul presses into service here one of his common ways of conceptualizing Christ's saving work: the offering of a "ransom," a price paid for release from slavery—slavery from sin, in remembrance of the great ransom from slavery in Egypt experienced by Israel.[8] One of the noteworthy aspects of this passage is its ethical concern. Not only does Christ's redemptive work have the purpose of purifying "a people that are his very own, eager to do what is good" (v. 14); God's grace also "teaches us to say 'No' to ungodliness and worldly passions, and to live self-controlled [*sōphronōs*], upright and godly [*eusebōs*] lives" (v. 12). Perhaps nowhere else in Paul is the tight connection between doctrine and ethics so clear.

"These things" (*tauta*) that Titus is to teach in verse 15 probably both refer back to 2:2–14 and ahead to 3:1–2. The focus in these verses is on outsiders, as Titus is urged to teach the new converts in Crete to be subject to rulers and authorities and to do good to those outside the community. Paul grounds these exhortations in the transformed life of the believers. Amid a life enslaved to evil, "the kindness and love of God our Savior appeared" (v. 4).[9] We find here another use of the "appearance" motif (*epiphainō*; see 2:11, 13) as well as the title of both God and Christ so characteristic of the Pastorals, "Savior" (*sōtēr*). In verses 5–7, Paul employs language and concepts typical of his teaching in other letters but rare in these Pastoral Epistles—being "justified" (*dikaiōthentes*), not by our own works, but by God's grace and mercy, so that we might become "heirs having the hope of eternal life." This transformation is also called a rebirth and renewal accomplished by means of God's Spirit and secured for us through a "washing" or "bath" (*loutrou*; see also Eph 5:26). The language may be purely metaphorical, washing with water being a common way to characterize cleansing from sin.[10] However, it is also possible that the language of washing alludes to water baptism[11]—the decision on this matter becoming almost inevitably ensnared in a circular argument. On the one side, water baptism plays a prominent role in Paul's view of conversion, therefore it is likely this is a reference to it, and we know water baptism is prominent in Paul because

---

7. See esp. Harris, *Jesus as "God,"* 173–85. The syntax, with a single article governing both *megalou theou* and *sōtēros hēmōn Iēsou Christou*, is one reason to favor this reading.

8. The verb *lytroō* is used here; Paul uses the cognate noun *antilytron* in 1 Tim 2:6, and see also Rom 3:24, and my comments there.

9. Mounce (*Pastoral Epistles*, 438) argues that this appearance refers to Christ's appearance and not to the "appearance" of grace in a person's life.

10. Mounce (*Pastoral Epistles*, 439) doubts any reference to baptism.

11. Both Marshall and Towner (*Pastoral Epistles*, 318) and Yarbrough (*Timothy and Titus*, 546) think the reference is to spiritual cleansing and to baptism, as a sign of that cleansing.

this verse and others refer to it. The mirror image of this argument then is employed to support the other side. Paul concludes this paragraph by identifying the previous verses (probably 4–7) as a "faithful saying,"[12] suggesting to some that Paul is quoting a preformed creed here.[13]

3 FALSE TEACHERS AND LOGISTICS (3:9–15)

The last part of the letter body returns to where it began, with focus on the false teachers (vv. 9–11). As Paul does repeatedly in his pastoral advice to Timothy and Titus, he warns Titus about becoming ensnared in foolish and unprofitable controversies and urges him to avoid these divisive people if they do not repent.

The letter ends with the usual references to fellow workers, greetings, and a grace wish (vv. 12–15).

---

12. Knight, *Faithful Sayings*, 80–86.   13. Note the poetic scansion in NA[28].

Chapter 16

2 TIMOTHY

LOCATING THE LETTER

Paul writes his second letter to Timothy under sentence of death: "For I am already being poured out like a drink offering, and the time for my departure is near" (4:6). He is imprisoned (again) in Rome (1:17) after a time of ministry during which he wrote 1 Timothy and Titus (see "Locating the Letter" in my discussion of 1 Timothy for details).[1]

ISOLATING THE ISSUES

As in 1 Timothy and Titus, false teaching continues to be an issue—and the basic profile of that teaching appears to be much the same. However, the balance in 2 Timothy shifts, from teaching about what to teach others to more of a focus on the character and ministry of Timothy himself. Paul is aware that this is his last opportunity to speak into the life of his close friend and colleague (his "dear son"; 1:2), as he seeks to form him in his own faith and character as a faithful minister of the gospel. As Wall puts it, 2 Timothy is "a letter of succession that sets out a Pauline pattern of instruction with the firm exhortation for Timothy to recall what he 'has heard' from Paul (v. 13) so as to pass it on to others (cf. 2:2)."[2] This concern, of course, is not simply about Timothy. Paul exhorts Timothy to faithfulness for the sake of the church. His impending death means that he will not be around to teach believers, plant churches, and preserve true doctrine. That task will now fall to others, like Timothy and those he in turn will teach—and those, in turn, who, having been taught, will teach . . . .

ANALYZING THE ARGUMENT

Paul's awareness of his approaching end and his close relationship with Timothy means that this letter is intensely personal. As L. T. Johnson says, "The most fascinating

---

1. I note that some authors find significant differences in tone between 2 Timothy, on the one hand, and 1 Timothy and Titus, on the other (see, e.g., Aageson, *Paul, the Pastoral Epistles*, 86–89). These differences suggest to some that, while 1 Timothy and

Titus are pseudonymous, 2 Timothy may be substantially from Paul himself (e.g., Gorman, *Apostle of the Crucified Lord*, 612–15).
2. Wall and Steele, *1 and 2 Timothy and Titus*, 227.

dimension of 2 Timothy theologically is the way it pays attention to the character of the individual in a manner unparalleled in Paul's other letters."[3] Paul frequently refers to circumstances in his own life as well as in Timothy's life. He is clearly aware of the imperative need to "pass on" the tradition. This focus leads many interpreters to label the letter a "testament," a literary genre in which a revered person, on the verge of death, passes on to his children and/or heirs basic moral teaching.[4] But it is not clear that 2 Timothy fits this genre.[5]

The general structure of the letter follows the scheme we have found in the other two Pastoral Epistles, with a focus on responding to false teachers (2:14–3:9) sandwiched between passages that more generally use the relationship between Paul and Timothy as the basis for exhortation (1:3–2:13; 3:10–4:8).[6]

1 TIMOTHY AND PAUL (1) (1:1–2:13)

After the typical letter salutation (1:1–2), Paul, as he usually does, gives thanks for the recipient(s) of the letter (1:3–5). Typical of this letter are the personal details, as Paul traces Timothy's "sincere faith" back to his mother and grandmother.

Timothy's coming to faith, however, was accompanied also by a gift (*charisma*), which was conveyed to him by the Spirit when Paul laid his hands on him (v. 6). This probably took place when Paul recruited Timothy to join him in his apostolic mission (Acts 16:1–2). Paul's exhortation to Timothy to make full use of the power conveyed to him as a result of this gift is the central point of verses 6–14. Many interpreters think that Paul exhorts Timothy in this way because he has been failing to use his gift to the full extent. They point to the verb *anazōpyreō*, which could mean "rekindle" (v. 6) and to the reminder in verse 7 that the Spirit God gives "does not make us timid." But this way of reading these verses may be guilty of inappropriate "mirror reading."[7] The verb in verse 6 need not mean *re*kindle (cf. NIV: "fan into flame").[8] And the reference to "timidity" or "cowardice" (*deilia*) in verse 7 could simply be a rhetorical move to highlight the true nature of the Spirit, who is characterized by "power, love and self-discipline." Paul's concern, then, is not so much that Timothy has become "timid" and is failing effectively to minister anymore, but that Paul's

3. Johnson, *First and Second Timothy*, 336.

4. In the OT, Jacob's address to his children in Gen 49 is often labeled a "testament." The genre becomes quite popular in the late Second Temple period (e.g., Testament of the Twelve Patriarchs, Testament of Moses). Among those who label 2 Timothy as a "testament" are Lorenz Oberlinner, *Zweiter Timotheusbrief*, vol. 2 of *Die Pastoralbriefe*, HThKNT 11.2 (Freiburg im Breisgau: Herder, 1995), 1–5; Alfons Weiser, *Der zweite Brief an Timotheus*, EKKNT 16/1 (Düsseldorf: Benziger, 2003), 34–40.

5. Johnson, *First and Second Timothy*, 320–24; Craig A.

Smith, *Timothy's Task and Paul's Prospect: A New Reading of 2 Timothy*, NT Monographs 12 (Sheffield: Sheffield Phoenix, 2006), 67–147; Cynthia Long Westfall, "A Moral Dilemma? The Epistolary Body of 2 Timothy," in Porter and Adams, *Paul and the Ancient Letter Form*, 213–52.

6. See van Neste, *Cohesion and Structure*, 146–233.

7. E.g., Smith, *Timothy's Task*, 216–25.

8. Mounce, *Pastoral Epistles*, 476; Marshall and Towner, *Pastoral Epistles*, 696.

current circumstances—imprisoned, apparently under sentence of death—could have a chilling effect on Timothy's ardor and boldness in ministry. This is revealed by verses 8–14, which highlight Paul's suffering (vv. 8, 12). However, in the very context of this suffering, Paul affirms his unshakable commitment to his Lord—a commitment that grows out of and is sustained by God's powerful grace and by Paul's confidence that that grace will sustain him "until that day" (vv. 9–12). God is fully able, Paul affirms, to "guard my deposit" (v. 12, my translation). It is not clear whether this means "what I have entrusted to [God]" (NIV) or "what has been entrusted to me" (CSB).[9] The immediate context could suggest that Paul is confident about having entrusted his life to God.[10] But the other occurrences of "deposit" (*parathēkē*) in the Pastorals suggest rather that the reference is to the gospel message (1 Tim 6:20; 2 Tim 1:14). In this case, Paul could be thinking of his entrusting this message to others, such as Timothy,[11] or to that message as it has been entrusted to him by God.[12] In any case, it is this "deposit" that Timothy is to guard through the power of God's Spirit (v. 14).

Paul reinforces his appeal to Timothy that he not lose courage for ministry because of Paul's circumstances by noting contrasting examples of reactions to those circumstances. On the one hand, there are those in the province of Asia who have deserted him (v. 15). But, on the other hand, there is Onesiphorus, who searched until he found Paul in Rome (vv. 16–18).[13]

At the beginning of chapter 2, Paul renews his charge to Timothy with a further reference to God's grace and commands him to initiate a chain of faithful teachers who would be able to preserve true Christian doctrine (v. 2). This concern to establish an orderly way of passing on Christian truth is a natural one for someone in Paul's circumstances. Paul reinforces his charge to Timothy with three illustrations in verses 3–7: the soldier who stays focused on his mission in order to please his commander, the athlete who receives the victor's crown because he competes according to the rules, and the farmer, whose hard work means he is the first to receive "a share of the crops." All three images suggest discipline in the context of challenging or difficult circumstances. It should be noted, then, that these images are introduced with Paul's appeal to "join with me in suffering" (v. 3). As Mounce notes, "The theme of suffering ties almost all of the epistle together."[14]

---

9. The issue is the force of the pronoun in the phrase *tēn parathēkēn mou*. Is it subjective—what has been entrusted *by* me—or objective—what has been entrusted *to* me?

10. Mounce, *Pastoral Epistles*, 487–88.

11. Knight, *Pastoral Epistles*, 380; Marshall and Towner, *Pastoral Epistles*, 710–11.

12. Yarbrough, *Timothy and Titus*, 363.

13. Paul's hope that God would have mercy on Onesiphorus's household (v. 16) suggests to many interpreters that he is now dead, in which case v. 18 would provide some biblical warrant to prayers for the dead (see, e.g., Holtz, *Pastoralbriefe*, 163; for a history of interpretation of this issue, see Weiser, *Der Brief an Timotheus*, 142–46). However, it is not clear that Onesiphorus had died; he may simply be separated from his household (Knight, *Pastoral Epistles*, 386).

14. Mounce, *Pastoral Epistles*, 474–75.

As he has done in chapter 1, Paul now grounds his call to faithfulness amid difficult circumstances by reminding Timothy of the utter faithfulness of God to his servants. Jesus, though fully human ("descended from David") has been raised from the dead, from which position of power he empowers his gospel (vv. 8–9) and intervenes powerfully for his servants (vv. 11–13). Paul may be chained, but the gospel for which he suffers is not (v. 9). The "faithful saying" that Paul cites in verses 11b–13 is probably a creed that may have been known to his readers. Paul's powerful notion of the believer's union with Christ governs verses 11b–12a. As he does in Romans 6:3–8 and Colossians 2:9–15, he grounds the believer's status in his or her identification with Christ in both death and resurrection. However, his rhetorical concern is evident in the addition of conditions—it is those who endure who will reign with him, while those who disown Christ will be disowned by him (v. 12b). But the creed ends with a reaffirmation of Christ's commitment to his people, even if they are "faithless." The juxtaposition of warning and assurances here typifies the tension between divine sovereignty and human responsibility that marks Paul's teaching on this issue.

2 TIMOTHY AND THE FALSE TEACHERS (2:14–3:9)

As Paul continues to instruct and encourage Timothy, his focus shifts from his own relationship with and example to Timothy to the manner in which Timothy needs to confront false teachers. This false teaching sounds a lot like the heresy that stimulated the writing of Paul's first letter to Timothy. This kind of teaching, Paul claims, will characterize the "last days" in which the church has its existence (3:1; cf. 1 Tim 4:1). Its adherents indulge in meaningless speculation and useless arguments (2:16, 23; and see also the reference to "myths" in 4:4; cf. 1 Tim 1:6; 4:7; 6:4–5). They have an "overrealized eschatology," claiming that "the resurrection has already taken place" (2:18—the view that probably lies behind the asceticism condemned in 1 Tim 4:2–4). They are greedy (3:2; cf. 1 Tim 6:5–10). They apparently are especially influential over the women (3:6–7; cf. 1 Tim 5:11–15). They may engage in various magical practices, as the comparison with the Egyptian magicians Jannes and Jambres might imply (3:8).[15] Of course, if we assume that Timothy is, as in 1 Timothy, still in Ephesus, we can understand this similarity. Whatever Timothy has done in obedience to Paul after the first letter has not yet stifled these teachers. In this letter, however, Paul goes further in his portrayal of the false teachers' personal faults and sins (see esp. 3:2–9).

Paul's suggested antidote to this false teaching is instructive. He obviously wants Timothy to confront these teachers, but he wants him to do it gently, with the hope that

---

15. Jannes and Jambres are the names given to the magicians who oppose Moses (Exod 7:11–12) in Jewish tradition.

God might grant them repentance (2:25–26). Timothy is not simply to score points in a theological debate; he is to teach his opponents in a way that will both expose their error and lead them to see it for what it is. Paul also knows that the best antidote to false teaching is good teaching; so he wants Timothy to "keep reminding" God's people of gospel truth (2:14). And so he needs to "cut a straight path for the word of truth" (v. 15, my translation), implying that Timothy both knows the truth and will be constant in teaching it. But Paul also stresses the personal virtues and character traits Timothy must have if he is to be successful in confronting this heresy and keeping the church on the path of truth. He is to "flee the evil desires of youth and pursue righteousness, faith, love, and peace" (v. 22). He is to have the wisdom to know which fights to get involved in and which simply to avoid (v. 23). This entire passage, then, is a valuable reminder of those qualities that make for a good pastor: well-trained in the truth, able and committed to teaching it, willing to confront false teaching—but doing all these things with love, patience, and a self-effacing concern for the person being taught.

3 TIMOTHY AND PAUL (2) (3:10–4:22)

In the last part of the letter body, Paul returns to a focus on his own life as a pattern for Timothy. Once more, suffering, which of course Paul is experiencing as he writes, looms large—the passage is bracketed by texts describing Paul's own tribulations (3:11–12; 4:6–8). Indeed, Paul reminds Timothy, such suffering is unsurprising—it is to be expected. In a text apparently not found in the Bibles of prosperity-gospel preachers, Paul says that "everyone who wants to live a godly life in Christ Jesus will be persecuted" (3:12). He has not left concern for the false teachers behind; the descriptions of "evildoers" in 3:13 and those "who will not put up with sound doctrine" in 4:3–4 pretty obviously have them in view. In the face of false teaching and the pressure of persecution, Timothy needs to "stay the course," deepening his conviction about the things he has learned (3:14). This instruction in truth is rooted especially in "the Holy Scriptures, which are able to make you wise for salvation through faith in Christ Jesus" (v. 15). Paul follows this up with an important text about the inspiration of Scripture (v. 16). The meaning and referent of key words and their relationships to each other in this verse are debated. Most English Bibles have as the subject of the verse the phrase "all Scripture." However, some argue that the Greek here—*pasa graphē*, with no article—more naturally would mean "every Scripture" (see NET), presumably in the sense of "every text of Scripture." Paul usually uses the singular *graphē* to refer to a single passage of the Old Testament (e.g., 1 Tim 5:18), so this translation is certainly possible.[16] However, Paul

---

16. E.g., Towner, *Timothy and Titus*, 585–89; Wall and Steele, *1 and 2 Timothy and Titus*, 270.

also uses the singular of *graphē* at least once to refer more broadly to the Old Testament (Gal 3:22), and the lack of article in the phrase is not decisive.[17] At the end of the day, it is very hard to decide between the two options and may not matter all that much. In either case, Paul has in view everything that can be labeled "Scripture." Granted Paul's place in salvation history, with no New Testament yet in view, it would seem likely that "Scripture" here means, basically, the Old Testament—and these are certainly "the holy writings" (*hiera grammata*; my translation) that Timothy learned from infancy (v. 15).[18] However, there is evidence that Paul and others were beginning to view Jesus's teaching and perhaps apostolic writings as on a par with the Old Testament (see, e.g., 1 Tim 5:18; 2 Pet 3:15–16). So it is possible that "Scripture" has a broader reference.[19] My own view is that Paul is making a claim here about the *category* "Scripture" without clear focus on the content or identity of that Scripture. Everything that falls into the category "Scripture," Paul is saying, has the qualities he goes on to list. Paul is not, then, giving us guidance about what is rightly called "Scripture" and what is not. The books to be included in this category are a matter extraneous to this text.

Scholars generally agree today that the first quality Paul ascribes to Scripture is that it is "inspired" or "God-breathed" (*theopneustos*). The alternate translation, "breathing God," for example, "inspiring," is only rarely supported anymore.[20] There is more discussion about whether this word is attributive—"all/every inspired Scripture is profitable"—or predicative—"all/every Scripture is inspired and profitable." However, the syntax favors this second option, and all our English translations adopt this rendering.[21] Even if we were to adopt the attributive interpretation, it would be unlikely to think that Paul intends to single out "inspired Scripture" in contrast to uninspired Scripture.[22] Of course Paul is especially concerned in this passage to highlight the usefulness of Scripture in both—positively—teaching God's people ("teaching," "training in righteousness," "thoroughly equipp[ing]" "the servant [or 'man'] of God") and—negatively—confronting false teaching ("rebuking," "correcting"). But he also wants to remind Timothy of the innate quality of Scripture as the essential basis for this ministry of the word.

Paul climaxes his exhortations to Timothy about pastoral ministry with the famous solemn charge at the beginning of chapter 4: "In the presence of God and of Christ Jesus,

17. The rule that *pas* plus the article means "the whole of" and *pas* without the article means "each" or "every" is not always followed by Paul; see, e.g., "all Israel" (*pas Israēl*) in Rom 11:26. See Moule, *Idiom Book*, 65.

18. Mounce, *Pastoral Epistles*, 566–68.

19. See esp. Swinson, *What Is Scripture*, 150–54.

20. The classic study of Benjamin B. Warfield was critical in settling this issue (*Revelation and Inspiration* [Oxford: Oxford University Press, 1927], 229–59).

21. On the syntax, see esp. Daniel Wallace's summary at "The Relation of θεόπνευστος το γραφή in 2 Timothy 3:16," *Bible.org*, 14 July 2019, https://bible.org/article/relation-font-facegreek qeovpneusto-grafhv-font-2-timothy-316; also, idem, *Greek Grammar Beyond the Basics: An Exegetical Syntax of the New Testament* (Grand Rapids: Zondervan, 1996), 313–14.

22. Stuhlmacher, *Biblical Theology of the New Testament*, 467–68.

who will judge the living and the dead, and in view of his appearing and his kingdom, I give you this charge: Preach the word; be prepared in season and out of season; correct, rebuke and encourage—with great patience and careful instruction" (vv. 1–2). He again sets the importance of faithful preaching of the word in the context of false teaching (vv. 3–4) and adds strong emotional impetus to his charge by a moving reminder of his own faithfulness amid terrible persecution and in the face of his own death (vv. 6–8).

The letter ends with a series of references to coworkers, a final warning about an opponent of Paul's, and a renewed affirmation of God's amazing faithfulness to Paul in all his circumstances (vv. 9–22).

Part 3

THE THEOLOGY
OF PAUL

Chapter 17

THE CENTER OF THE NEW REALM

For the grace of God has appeared that offers salvation to all people. It teaches us to say "No" to ungodliness and worldly passions, and to live self-controlled, upright and godly lives in this present age, while we wait for the blessed hope—the appearing of the glory of *our great God and Savior, Jesus Christ*, who gave himself for us to redeem us from all wickedness and to purify for himself a people that are his very own, eager to do what is good.

—TITUS 2:11–14[1]

THE GOOD NEWS about Jesus Christ is the center of the new realm that Paul celebrates and proclaims. As I argued earlier, being "in Christ" constitutes the web that binds Paul's various theological points together. At the center of that web is the person of Jesus. And closely related in Paul's theology is the language of "gospel."

1 THE GOSPEL[2]

1.1 Background

Paul is very fond of the language of "gospel," or "good news." He uses the verb *euangelizō*, "preach the gospel," twenty-one times (out of fifty-four NT occurrences) and the noun *euangelion*, "gospel," sixty times (out of seventy-six NT occurrences). As is so often the case with Paul's theological vocabulary, his "gospel" language has roots in the Greek Old Testament, where the *euang-* root translates the Hebrew root *b-s-r*.[3] The Hebrew verb can denote "bring news" of any kind; so, for example, in 1 Samuel 4:17 it refers to bringing bad news. Typically, however, it means "bring good news," and the corresponding Greek words always have this sense in the Greek Old Testament.

---

1. I preface each chapter in this part of the book with this quotation from Titus, which perhaps comes as close to touching on Paul's key theological ideas as any other. (I am fully aware of the irony in using a text usually thought not to be written by Paul to summarize his theology.) I highlight particular words in the text that are especially relevant to the chapter contents that follow.

2. The discussion of the gospel that follows borrows from my excursus in *Romans* (NICNT), 54–58. Used with permission.

3. E.g., Dunn, *Theology of Paul*, 167–69.

Second Samuel 18:19 is typical: "Now Ahimaaz son of Zadok said, 'Let me run and take the news [Heb. *basar*; Gk. *euangelizō*] to the king that the LORD has vindicated him by delivering him from the hand of his enemies.'" The most significant occurrences of the language for Paul come in the prophets, where "good news" language is used to herald the eschatological victory of Yahweh. Isaiah 52:7 is particularly pertinent, since Paul quotes this text in Romans 10:15: "How beautiful on the mountains are the feet of those who bring good news [Heb. *mebasser*; Gk. *euangelizomenou*], who proclaim peace, who bring good tidings [Heb. *mebasser*; Gk. *euangelizomenos*], who proclaim salvation, who say to Zion, 'Your God reigns!'"[4] (See also Isa 40:9; 60:6; 61:1 [Luke 4:18]; Joel 2:32 [3:5 MT, LXX]; Nah 1:15 [2:1 MT, LXX].)[5]

While the Greek Old Testament is the most important influence on Paul's use of gospel language, we should not overlook another context in which gospel language was being used in Paul's day: the larger Greco-Roman world. Especially pertinent to Paul's usage is the use of "gospel" language to refer to the emperor.[6] The most famous example occurs in a calendar inscription found in Priene (but which may have been widespread),[7] which hails "the birthday of the god Augustus" as "the beginning of the good tidings [*euangeliōn*] for the world." Based on these kinds of occurrences of the language and taking into consideration the increasing prominence and power of the imperial cult in Paul's day, many scholars have seen in Paul's deployment of "good news" language an implicit anti-imperial claim. True "good news" comes from God's work in Christ, not from any bogus claim the Roman emperor might be making.[8] As Graham Stanton has summarized the matter, "In the Greco-Roman world of Paul's day, 'glad tidings' were associated regularly with the new hope, the dawn of a new era, the 'good news' brought about by the birth, the accession, or the return to health of a Roman emperor."[9] To be sure, the linguistic basis for this claim is not terribly strong. A survey of fifty-eight occurrences of the relevant words in secular Greek sources of the first-century BC and first-century AD reveals that only a handful have any reference to the emperor.[10] Moreover, Paul's use of the language stands apart from Greco-Roman (and Greek OT) usage. The Greco-Roman texts overwhelmingly prefer the verb over the noun and the plural form of the noun over the singular. Paul's pattern in his usage of the terms, however, is different: He prefers the noun to the verb and always uses the noun

4. This passage from Isaiah is quoted in 11QMelch with reference to an eschatological "messenger" or one "anointed of the Spirit" (11QMelch 15–18); see *The Dead Sea Scrolls Reader, Part 2: Exegetical Texts*, ed. Donald W. Parry and Emanuel Tov (Leiden: Brill, 2004), 27.

5. See esp. Peter Stuhlmacher, *Das paulinische Evangelium. I: Vorgeschichte*, FRLANT 95 (Göttingen: Vandenhoeck & Ruprecht, 1968), 152–53, 177–79, 204–6.

6. *NewDocs* 3:10–15.

7. Winter, *Divine Honours for the Caesars*, 24–40.

8. On gospel language in particular, see N. T. Wright, *Paul in Fresh Perspective* (Minneapolis: Fortress, 2005), 59–78.

9. Graham N. Stanton, *Jesus and Gospel* (Cambridge: Cambridge University Press, 2004), 34.

10. See also, for similar reservations, James D. G. Dunn, "The Gospel according to Paul," in Westerholm, *Blackwell Companion to Paul*, 139–40; Michael Wolter, *Paul: An Outline of His Theology* (Waco, TX: Baylor University Press, 2015), 52–53.

in the singular. Beyond the word-usage issue, we must also consider the wider issue of anti-imperial language in Paul. I treat this general issue in more detail on pp. 642–43. Here, however, I note briefly that Paul never explicitly counters imperial claims and that his rhetoric tends to be directed more against the ultimate powers of sin, death, and evil spiritual beings than against any worldly powers. These caveats, while encouraging caution about reading too much anti-imperial rhetoric in Paul, do not necessarily negate the case for some allusion to imperial claims in Paul's use of gospel language. Bruce Winter has shown how deeply imperial pretensions had penetrated society in Paul's day, making it reasonable to think that gospel language, while not all that often connected with the emperor, occurs enough to create a connection in the minds of first-century Christians. As Bernhard Heininger has put it, "The worship of the emperor is for Paul and his missionary preaching a social reality."[11] Hearing the claim that "Jesus brings good news," they could very well at the same time hear the faint counterpart: "and Caesar does not."[12]

1.2 Paul

With the background of Paul's usage in place, we can turn directly to his use of gospel language. As I noted above, Paul, in contrast to both the Greek Old Testament and his environment, prefers the singular noun. In fact, Paul never uses the plural form of the noun, while the Greek Old Testament, for instance, uses the singular only once. At the risk of overinterpreting what might be a happenstance linguistic tendency, it may be that Paul is implicitly stressing the uniqueness of the good news. While false teachers may proclaim what they consider to be a "gospel," there is, in fact, only one gospel (Gal 1:6–9; cf. 2 Cor 11:4). To be sure, Paul can qualify "gospel" in various ways; for example, "gospel of God" (e.g., Rom 1:1; 15:16; 1 Thess 2:9), "gospel of Christ" (e.g., Rom 15:19; 1 Cor 9:12; 2 Cor 9:13), "gospel of our Lord Jesus" (2 Thess 1:8), "our gospel" (1 Thess 1:5; 2 Thess 2:14), "my gospel" (e.g., Rom 2:16; 16:25; 2 Tim 2:8). But these are all ways of referring to the one message of good news. By referring to it as "my" gospel or "our" gospel, Paul does not intend to denote a different message; it simply highlights Paul's and his associates' preaching of that one message.[13]

Gospel language has a broad range of significance in Paul. It is, of course, the instrument that God uses to bring people into the new realm. But it is also the instrument that God uses to produce growth in those who already know Christ. The gospel, Paul says in Colossians, "is bearing fruit and growing throughout the whole world—just as

11. Bernhard Heininger, "Contemporary Religions and Philosophical Schools," in *Paul: Life, Setting, Work, Letters*, ed. Oda Wischmeyer (London: T&T Clark, 2012), 43.

12. To paraphrase the aphorism popular among scholars,

"Jesus is Lord, Caesar is not" (McKnight and Modica, *Jesus is Lord, Caesar is Not*).

13. Wolter, *Paul*, 53–54.

it has been doing among you since the day you heard it and truly understood God's grace" (Col 1:6). Similarly, Paul can talk about preaching the gospel to *Christians* in Rome (Rom 1:15). The expansive reach of the gospel in Paul's theology can be seen in another way. Gospel refers to the message about Christ (1 Cor 15:1; Gal 1:11; 2:2) and, by extension, to the act of preaching that message (Rom 1:9; 1 Cor 9:14 [second occurrence]; 2 Cor 2:12; 8:18; Phil 1:5[?]; 4:3[?]). At places, indeed, Paul appears to use "gospel" to describe the acts by which God inaugurated the good news. See, for example, 2 Timothy 1:9–10:

> He has saved us and called us to a holy life—not because of anything we have done but because of his own purpose and grace. This grace was given us in Christ Jesus before the beginning of time, but it has now been revealed through the appearing of our Savior, Christ Jesus, who has destroyed death and has brought life and immortality to light through the gospel. (See also Eph 3:6.)

The breadth of application of gospel language in Paul reveals the degree to which it becomes almost a technical term. It can denote the events that constitute good news, the message about those acts with special focus on their benefit to humans, and the content of the message. In the Old Testament, the good news the messenger proclaims is "a condition where all things are in their proper relation to each other, with nothing left hanging, incomplete, or unfulfilled (*peace, shalom*); it entails a condition where creation purposes are realized (*good, tob*; cf. Gen 1:4, 10, etc.); it entails a condition of freedom from every bondage, but particularly the bondage resultant from sin (*salvation, yeshua*)."[14] The text in Isaiah that Paul quotes announces to the oppressed people of Israel that, with the coming of good news, "Your God reigns" (Isa 52:7; cf. Rom 10:15). This text in turn echoes an earlier passage in Isaiah that announces to Israel in exile the "good news" that the Lord is coming with power to exercise his rule and to comfort his people (40:9–11). Paul, with the rest of the New Testament, proclaims that the eschatological reign of God has been inaugurated through Jesus's death and resurrection, resulting in his elevation to Lord of all—good news, indeed![15] Only an expansive notion of gospel that covers all that God has done in Christ can explain the

---

14. John Oswalt, *The Book of Isaiah*, 2 vols., NICOT (Grand Rapids: Eerdmans, 1986), 2:368. He is commenting on Isa 52:7, quoted above.

15. For this emphasis, see esp. N. T. Wright, who argues that "the 'gospel' is, strictly speaking, the narrative proclamation of King Jesus" (*not* "a system of how people get saved"; *What Saint Paul Really Said: Was Paul of Tarsus the Real Founder of Christianity?* [Grand Rapids: Eerdmans, 1997], 45; also, e.g., "'The gospel' is not itself 'how to be saved' or 'how to be justified.' 'The

gospel' is God's good news, promised long ago, about his dying and rising son, the Messiah, the lord of the world" [*Paul and the Faithfulness of God*, 2:916]). Michael S. Horton argues that this broad construal of gospel is found in the Reformers also: "For the Reformers, the gospel is not about what happens within us or to us; it is an announcement about who Christ is and what he has accomplished" (*Justification*, 2 vols., New Studies in Dogmatics [Grand Rapids: Zondervan, 2018], 1:181).

breadth of the language in Paul. Thus, for instance, in Romans 1:15, Paul speaks of coming to Rome and preaching the gospel—among the Christians in Rome. And in Romans 2:16, he reminds the Romans that God's determination to judge all people through Jesus Christ is in accordance with his gospel.

However, without taking away anything from this point, it is also important to see that the bulk of Paul's references to gospel focus on the offer of salvation to humans. In a manner typical of the move from Old Testament to New Testament, gospel language in Paul has a less cosmic and more anthropological focus. The good news often connotes the opportunity for sinful humans to find a new saving relationship with a holy and righteous God. Ephesians 1:13 is typical of a broad range of passages: "And you also were included in Christ when you heard the message of truth, the gospel of your salvation" (see also esp. 1 Cor 15:1; Gal 2:2, 5, 14; Eph 3:16; Col 1:5, 23; 2 Thess 2:14; 2 Tim 1:10). The reign of the emperor (see above) was "good news" not simply in itself but in terms of the benefits he offered to his subjects. So also Paul typically uses gospel language to connote the offer of new life that God provides all people in Christ. That Christ died and was raised is, indeed, fundamental—but it is particularly that he died and was raised for *us* that is good news.[16] Therefore while the wider view of gospel is certainly justified, it is also important to retain this cutting edge of Paul's use of the language. As Richard Gaffin Jr. puts it, "To punctuate the gospel, particularly its proclamation, with a full stop after Christ's death, resurrection and ascension, allowing for his future return, does not do the gospel full justice as 'the power of God for the salvation of everyone who believes' and as that gospel involves the revelation of the righteousness of God 'from faith to faith' (Rom 1:16–17)."[17] The famous summary of the gospel in 1 Corinthians 15:1–5 captures this balance well: The "good news" is that Jesus has died, been buried, and been raised from the dead—events that affect the entire cosmos. Yet Jesus's death is particularly "for our sins" (v. 3). We might picture Paul's gospel as a series of concentric circles. The inner circle embraces Christ's death and resurrection as the means of saving sinful humans. Moving further out, the next circle includes the broad scope of God's work in Christ for us, from preexistence and incarnation at one end to Christ's return in glory at the other. Finally, at the outer limits of the gospel trajectory we find the unlimited implications of Christ's installation as Lord for society and the entire created world.[18]

---

16. See, e.g., Peter T. O'Brien, "Was Paul a Covenantal Nomist?," in Carson, O'Brien, and Seifrid, *Paradoxes of Paul*, 293–99; John Piper, *The Future of Justification: A Response to N. T. Wright* (Wheaton, IL: Crossway, 2007), 81–91; Seyoon Kim, *Christ and Caesar: The Gospel and the Roman Empire in the Writings of Paul and Luke* (Grand Rapids: Eerdmans, 2008), 3–71.

17. Richard B. Gaffin Jr., *By Faith, Not by Sight: Paul and the Order of Salvation* (Waynesboro, GA: Paternoster, 2006), 278. See also D. A. Carson, "What Is the Gospel—Revisited," in *For the Fame of God's Name: Essays in Honor of John Piper*, ed. S. Storms and J. Taylor (Wheaton, IL: Crossway, 2010), 147–70.

18. Ridderbos (*Paul*, 54–55) suggests something like this.

2 JESUS: SON OF GOD, MESSIAH, LORD

The point is almost too obvious to make: at the center of the new realm is Jesus. Peter Stuhlmacher's claim is echoed in most Pauline theologies: *"Christology forms the center of Pauline theology."*[19] To be sure, most of Paul's letters do not have a passage dedicated to what we would normally call "Christology." We may guess that in many of the Pauline churches, at least, controversy about who Jesus was had not arisen. Yet Christology in another sense pervades Paul's letters. He refers to the person of Christ almost six hundred times (and to God over five hundred forty times), and virtually all that Paul teaches radiates, like the spokes of a wheel, from Jesus Christ. However, read in context, Stuhlmacher's claim about "Christology" includes both what we would sometimes label the "person" and "work" of Christ. These are intimately tied together in Paul. As Ridderbos puts it, Paul's Christology is "a Christology of redemptive facts."[20] Nevertheless, while needing to be careful not to impose later systematic categories on Paul, it is certainly possible, and indeed useful, to distinguish his teaching about *who* Jesus was and *what* he did.[21] Paul's preaching of the gospel focuses on the latter, since it is what God accomplished in Jesus's death and resurrection that constitutes the good news. But the redemptive value of these events is tied to the nature of the person through whom they were carried out. Paul's preaching and pastoral care of congregations therefore requires him to talk about the person as well as the work of Christ.

In this chapter, then, I focus on the way in which Paul depicts Christ; in the next chapter, I will turn to the way in which Paul describes what Jesus does—or, better, what God does in and through Jesus. A time-honored approach to our subject is to describe Jesus via the several titles he is given. I will include discussion of the important titles in this chapter, but, doing justice to Paul's dynamic christological presentation, I will also survey the stages of Christ's existence as Paul presents them, with a view to their theological significance.

2.1 Climax of History
2.1.1 The "Last Adam"

The most basic claim Paul makes about Christ, explicit in many texts, implicit in all, is that his coming marks the climax of God's purposes in history. The coming of Christ is "the center of time" (to use Cullmann's language), the climax of all that God

---

19. Stuhlmacher, *Biblical Theology of the New Testament*, 318 (emphasis original).

20. Ridderbos, *Paul*, 49.

21. Contra, e.g., Cullmann, whose discussion of Christology is marked by the claim that "it is only meaningful to speak of the Son in view of God's revelatory action, not in view of his being" (*Christology*, 293; see also pp. 3–6).

is doing in and for his creation.[22] It is "the appearing of our Savior, Christ Jesus," that unleashes the eschatological saving events (2 Tim 1:10).

Looking first at history in its broadest perspective, Paul makes this point by comparing Christ with Adam. This comparison is explicit in only two texts, Romans 5:12–21 and 1 Corinthians 15:21–22, 45–49, but it arguably provides the underlying framework for a number of other passages (e.g., Phil 2:6–8; see pp. 303–9) and theological teachings (e.g., the "old man" language of Rom 6:6; Eph 4:22; Col 3:9–10). Adam is the "first man" whose sin brings sin and death to all humanity. Christ, as the "last Adam," more than cancels the effects of Adam's sin, offering all humans the opportunity to escape the death Adam introduced and to experience a new life. Each of the "Adams" or "humans" (*adam*) is a corporate figure, whose actions affect all who belong to them. It was fashionable at one time to think that Paul derived this corporate idea from gnostic-type speculations about a heavenly redeemer figure. But it is now generally agreed that the concept has Jewish antecedents. One intriguing possibility is that the appearance of Jesus to Paul on the Damascus Road led him to identify Christ as the "image of God" and therefore as one comparable to the original man, Adam, who was also, of course, created in the image of God.[23] But whatever its origin, Paul's conception of Christ as "the last Adam" identifies him as the climax of human history.

2.1.2 "Seed of Abraham," "Culmination of the Law"

Christ brings human history to its climactic point; he also brings salvation history to its climax. The story of Israel, the centerpiece of Old Testament salvation history, finds its culminating point in Christ. Paul makes this fundamental point in a number of ways, but I focus on two here.

First, Jesus is *the* "seed of Abraham." This claim arises in the context of Paul's overview of salvation history in Galatians 3:15–4:7. He focuses on three key events: (1) God's promise to Abraham (v. 16); (2) the giving of the law at Sinai (v. 17); and (3) the appearance of Christ (v. 19). God's promise to Abraham, he insists, initiated a covenant that the subsequent introduction of the law could not annul. Moreover, that initial covenant, because it expressed the unconditional promise of God, was a matter of grace. Yet the law covenant, requiring, as it does, human obedience for its validity, stands in contrast to the grace of the Abrahamic provision. Where is Christology in all of this? Just here: Jesus brings to an end the era of the law and introduces the fulfillment of the Abrahamic promise of grace. Jesus, Paul claims, is *the* "seed," the ultimate recipient of the promise to Abraham. Of course, the Old Testament promises

---

22. This is the overall point of his book *Christ and Time: The Primitive Christian Conception of Time and History* (Philadelphia: Westminster, 1950).

23. Kim, *Origin of Paul's Gospel*, esp. 162–268.

to Abraham generally use "seed" as a collective singular; Abraham's "seed" refers to his innumerable descendants (Gen 12:7; 13:15; 24:7). Paul understands this collective sense of the word, as his assertion that all who belong to Christ are "Abraham's seed" reveals (Gal 3:29; see also Rom 4:13–18). In Galatians 3, then, Paul's move from the singular—*Christ* is the "seed of Abraham"—to the plural—*Christians* are the "seed of Abraham"—suggests that he views Christ as a corporate figure.[24] In a development hinted at in many other New Testament texts, Paul views Jesus as the embodiment of Israel, God's true people (e.g., Matt 2:15 [Hos 11:1]). All of God's promises find their fulfillment in him, and the entire plan of God comes to its climax in him.

Second, Christ is the "culmination of the law." Paul's famous claim about Christ and the law in Romans 10:4 is usually rendered in English versions as "Christ is the end of the law." This translation suggests, though it does not strictly require, a discontinuous emphasis—Christ brings the law to an end. But, as I note in my comments on this verse (see pp. 203–4), the word translated "end" (*telos*) often has a telic sense. In this verse, the word appears to combine the senses of "end" and "goal," presenting Christ as the "culmination" (NIV) or "climax" of the law, something like the finish line in a race. Christ is what the law was all along anticipating and pointing toward. Now that he has come, the reign of the Mosaic law over the people of God is at an end. As the culmination of the law, Jesus stands at the center of salvation history.

As I noted above, it is possible that we can trace Paul's concept of the corporate Christ back to his own conversion experience. It is even more likely that this encounter was an important stimulus to his understanding of the law's obsolescence. Jesus's death on a Roman cross would, according to the law, have marked him as a man cursed by God (cf. Deut 21:23, which, significantly, Paul quotes in Gal 3:13). On the Damascus Road, however, Paul was suddenly and unexpectedly confronted with the indisputable evidence that Jesus is none other than God's Messiah. And this revelation confronted Paul with the choice between Messiah and the law. For if the law was the final and definitive expression of God's will, then Jesus could not be the Messiah. But if Jesus was, in fact, the Messiah, then the law must not have the central place in the plan of God that Saul the Pharisee had been giving it.

2.2 Stages of Christ's Existence

As the following survey shows, Paul provides a rather comprehensive summary of the stages of Christ's existence. These stages are rarely narrated but introduced as the basis for theological and/or pastoral purposes. Paul will occasionally mention two or more of these stages together. The most comprehensive texts are 1 Corinthians 15:3–8, which enumerates Christ's death, burial, resurrection, and post-resurrection appearances,

---

24. See, further, pp. 72–74 on Galatians 3.

and Philippians 2:6–11, which refers to Christ's preexistence, incarnation, death, and exaltation. Therefore, while we can readily discern a narrative of Christ behind Paul's theologizing, his actual references to it are what we might term, borrowing a word from the literary world, "episodic." Particular moments of Christ's history are cited to develop or reinforce a theological point.

2.2.1 Preexistence and Incarnation

Paul never asserts in so many words that the Christ he preaches existed before Jesus was born into the world, but he clearly implies it in a number of texts. Only if we posit a genuine personal preexistence of Jesus can we explain how Paul can claim he was involved in the creation of the world (1 Cor 8:6; Col 1:15–17). To be sure, James Dunn has countered that these texts fall short of implying *personal* preexistence. Paul, he argues, is presenting Christ as the "climactic manifestation" of wisdom and implies nothing about his preexistence.[25] It is possible that Paul is interpreting Christ in terms of Old Testament/Jewish wisdom texts in both these passages, although the matter is not as certain as some suggest. But, even if this is the case, Paul is referring in both texts to Christ—a person. He may portray this person in terms of wisdom language, but it is still this person he refers to. And this person, he claims, is "before all things" (Col 1:17) and is the one "through whom all things came" (1 Cor 8:6) and through whom "all things were created" (Col 1:16).

Paul implies the preexistence of Christ also in identifying him as "the spiritual rock" from which the Israelites drank in the wilderness (1 Cor 10:4) and whom they tested during that time (v. 9). While not as clear, it is also possible that texts in which Paul claims that believers were chosen (Eph 1:4) and given grace (2 Tim 1:9) "in Christ" "before the creation of the world" or "the beginning of time" imply preexistence. Preexistence and incarnation, of course, imply one another. Paul refers to the act of Christ becoming human in several texts, including those that speak of his being "sent" (Rom 8:3; Gal 4:4; cf. Rom 10:6; 1 Tim 1:15; 3:16). The best-known incarnation text, of course, is Philippian 2:6–7: "Who, being in very nature God, did not consider equality with God something to be used to his own advantage; rather, he made himself nothing by taking the very nature of a servant, being made in human likeness."[26] Very similar is 2 Corinthians 8:9: "Though he was rich, yet for your sake he became poor." These two texts reveal one of the points of theological significance Paul draws

---

25. Dunn, *Christology in the Making*, 190. In his *Theology of Paul*, Dunn is more nuanced, claiming that Christ's preexistence is indeed taught in this passage but that the preexistence involves "the divine fullness whereby God's presence fills the universe and which is now embodied (incarnate?) in Christ" (277; see also 292). The preexistence of Christ *as a person* still appears to

be denied by Dunn. See, in response, Fee, *Pauline Christology*, 521–22; Larry W. Hurtado, *Lord Jesus Christ: Devotion to Jesus in Earliest Christianity* (Grand Rapids: Eerdmans, 2003), 118–26.

26. On other options for interpreting this passage and reasons to find a reference here to incarnation, see my comments on pp. 303–9.

from Christ's preexistence and incarnation—his humility as a model for Christians to imitate. Michael Gorman has especially drawn attention to this point in Paul's theology, arguing that Philippians 2:6–8 is Paul's "master story" that highlights cruciformity as central to Christian life.[27] The other main point of theological significance emerges clearly in Colossians, where Paul's assertion about Christ's pre-existence and role in creation serves to remind the Colossians that the Christ they serve is far superior to any other spiritual beings.

2.2.2 Earthly Life

The various stories of Christ that Paul works with all have at their heart the assumption that the Christ to whom Paul refers is Jesus of Nazareth. "Jesus" (*Iēsous*, also translated "Joshua") is the sixth most common Jewish male name of the period from 330 BC to AD 200,[28] and it occurs over two hundred times in the letters of Paul. Paul's failure to refer very often to the life of Jesus or to his teaching is well-known. Rudolf Bultmann, following the lead of some other theologians of his day, insisted that the paucity of references indicated Paul's negative attitude toward the earthly life of Jesus. Paul's interest was in the resurrected Lord, not the human Jesus. And 2 Corinthians 5:16 was sometimes cited as evidence of Paul's disregard.[29] But this interpretation of the verse is now almost universally rejected. Paul is not disdaining knowledge of the earthly Jesus but a constrained, earth-bound view of Jesus.

In fact, while not abundant, references to Jesus in the letters of Paul allow us to reconstruct a fairly robust picture of his life.[30] He was truly "human" (*anthrōpos* in Rom 5:15; 1 Cor 15:20–22; Phil 2:7–8; 1 Tim 2:5), "born of a woman" (Gal 4:4). He was a descendant of David (Rom 1:3 [cf. 15:12]; 2 Tim 2:8) and the patriarchs of Israel (Rom 9:5) and had brothers (1 Cor 9:5). He, like other humans, was "weak" (Rom 15:3; 2 Cor 13:4; cf. 2 Cor 1:5; 8:9; Phil 3:10), and, as genuinely human, was brought into relationship with sin (Rom 8:3; 2 Cor 5:21). He was "a servant of the Jews" (Rom 15:8) and was humble and gentle (2 Cor 10:1). He suffered (Rom 8:17; Col 1:24; 1 Thess 2:16) and was executed by means of crucifixion (many places; see below, pp. 356–62) —presumably at the time when Pontius Pilate was governor before whom Jesus made the "good confession" (1 Tim 6:13).[31] Paul knows enough about Jesus's life to imitate him (1 Cor 11:1). And, while references to Jesus's teaching are indeed infrequent, they

---

27. Gorman, *Inhabiting the Cruciform God*, 12, 23–28.

28. Richard Bauckham, *Jesus and the Eyewitnesses: The Gospels as Eyewitness Testimony*, 2nd ed. (Grand Rapids: Eerdmans, 2017), 85.

29. Bultmann, *Theology of the New Testament*, 1:238–39; see also Wilhelm Bousset, *Kyrios Christos: A History of the Belief in Christ from the Beginnings of Christianity to Irenaeus* (Nashville: Abingdon, 1970), 154–55. See, also, in milder form, Becker: "The

starting point and the material content of the Pauline ethic are developed without basic reference to the Jesus tradition" (*Paul: Apostle to the Gentiles*, 113; cf. 113–24).

30. See, e.g., Simon Gathercole, "Paul's Christology," in Westerholm, *Blackwell Companion to Paul*, 176–77.

31. Paul's claim to bear the "marks of Jesus" (Gal 6:17) may refer to the marks of crucifixion on Jesus's body.

do occur (see pp. 26–27). Furthermore, Dunn's reminder that Paul's letters "enter into a conversation that is well under way" with teaching about Jesus already known in the communities, must be borne in mind.[32]

The most important theological point Paul derives from Jesus's life is simply the fact of that human life. Leander Keck restates a point that has been central in the church's Christology: "Logically, the Savior must be sufficiently like us to reach us, and sufficiently different to save us."[33] But, as we have seen, Paul can use particular aspects of Christ's life to make theological points and to draw ethical implications.

2.2.3 Death

In 1 Corinthians 2:2, Paul claims that he "resolved to know nothing while I was with you except Jesus Christ and him crucified." What Paul means by this is that the crucifixion of Christ was for him the focal point of all his theology and preaching. He refers to Jesus's death more than to any other stage of his existence—over fifty times (fifteen of them using the language of "crucify" or "cross").[34] The crucified Messiah is, therefore, the center of gravity in Paul's Christology. While considered foolishness to the Greeks and a stumbling block to Jews (1 Cor 1:23), Jesus's death on a Roman cross signals the turn of the ages and is the foundation for the new people, drawn from both Jews and gentiles, that God calls into being. God acted to reconcile the entire world to himself in Christ (2 Cor 5:9). I will develop this theology of the cross in my chapter on "Inauguration of the New Realm" (pp. 374–404).

2.2.4 Burial

Paul includes Jesus's burial in his brief gospel summary in 1 Corinthians 15:3–8 and twice claims that believers were buried "with him" (Rom 6:4; Col 2:12). Paul may include Jesus's burial in his recital of foundational gospel events because it confirmed Jesus's death.

2.2.5 Resurrection

If Jesus's death is the dominant focus in Paul's Christology, Jesus's resurrection is a close second—it is mentioned in over twenty passages.[35] Indeed, the death and resurrection of Jesus are often paired as two intertwined redemptive events (see esp. Rom 4:25; 6:5, 10; 8:34; 14:9; 2 Cor 4:10; 5:15; 13:4; 1 Thess 4:14). Typical is Romans

---

32. Dunn, *Theology*, 183–95 (189).

33. Keck, *Christ's First Theologian*, 112.

34. Rom 3:25; 4:25; 5:6, 8, 10; 6:5, 8, 10; 7:4; 8:32, 34; 10:7; 14:9, 15; 1 Cor 5:7; 6:20(?); 7:23(?); 8:1; 10:16; 11:24–25; 15:3; 2 Cor 4:10; 5:14, 15; Gal 1:4; 2:21; Eph 2:13; 5:2, 25; Col 1:22; 2:20; 1 Thess 2:15; 4:14; 5:10; 1 Tim 2:6; 2 Tim 2:11; Titus 2:14.

Using the language of crucified/cross: Rom 6:6; 1 Cor 1:17, 18, 23; 2 Cor 2:2; Gal 2:20; 3:1, 13; 6:12, 14; Eph 2:16; Phil 2:8; Col 1:20; 2:14, 15.

35. Rom 1:5; 4:24–25; 6:4, 5, 9; 8:11, 34; 10:9; 14:9; 1 Cor 6:14; 15:4, 12–18, 20–22; 2 Cor 5:15; Gal 1:1; Eph 1:20; 2:6; Phil 3:10–11; Col 1:18; 2:12; 1 Thess 1:10; 4:14; 1 Tim 3:16(?).

14:9: "For this very reason, Christ died and returned to life so that he might be the Lord of both the dead and the living." The pairing is, of course, traditional, as the summary of the gospel in 1 Corinthians 15:3–8 again reveals: "Christ died for our sins . . . he was buried . . . he was raised on the third day."

At the risk of introducing a distinction where none exists, I might suggest that Paul tends to present the significance of Jesus's death for believers as backward looking and his resurrection as forward looking. Jesus's sacrificial death rescues human beings from their slavery to sin, while his resurrection initiates a new age of spiritual power and, ultimately, resurrected life (Rom 6:4; 2 Cor 4:11). Resurrection is an eschatological event. Jesus's resurrection, therefore, signals that the final age of fulfillment has dawned. And, as Romans 1:4 suggests, Jesus's resurrection also signals a new stage in his own unique relationship to the Father as Son of God. Those who belong to Christ share in the power of that new existence (Rom 6:4, 10)—even as they long for the day when the body itself will be raised "with Christ." He is the "firstfruits," whose resurrection provides for the resurrection of all those who belong to him (Rom 8:23; 1 Cor 15:20–23, 45–49; cf. 2 Cor 4:14).

2.2.6 Post-Resurrection Appearances

In the gospel summary we have mentioned already, Paul, after mentioning Christ's death, burial, and resurrection, goes on to recount post-resurrection appearances to Cephas, the Twelve, five hundred brothers, James, "all the apostles," and then to Paul himself (1 Cor 15:5–8; see also 9:1). Paul cites these appearances to underscore the reality of Christ's bodily resurrection.

2.2.7 Ascension and Exaltation

As is the case with other episodes in Christ's existence, Paul does not narrate the ascension. And, in fact, in only two texts does he appear to refer to it: Ephesians 4:8–10, where Paul mentions the ascension as the context of Christ's giving of gifted people to his church; and Philippians 2:9, where Paul claims that "God exalted him to the highest place." But he refers fairly often to the present reign of Christ in his exalted state. Paul follows the lead of Jesus and other early Christians in using the language of Psalm 110:1 to describe Jesus's current reign: "The LORD says to my Lord: 'Sit at my right hand until I make your enemies a footstool for your feet'" (see, e.g., Matt 27:41–46; Heb 1:13). Paul picks up the "right hand" language in Romans 8:34, Ephesians 1:20, and Colossians 3:1 and the "under the feet" language in 1 Corinthians 15:25 and Ephesians 1:22. And, again, probably following the lead of Christians before him, Paul combines the language of Psalm 110:1 with the parallel language of Psalm 8:6: "You made them [human beings] rulers over the works of your hands; you put everything under their feet" (1 Cor 15:25–27; Eph 1:20–22;

cf. Heb 1:13 and 2:6–8).[36] Believers can look forward to sharing in Christ's reign (Rom 8:17; Phil 3:20), even as they begin to experience that reign in the present (Eph 2:6; Col 3:1). In addition, while not always clearly referring to exaltation, Paul regularly assumes that he, and other believers, relate to and are given blessings from a living and active Christ. Paul was converted when God was pleased "to reveal his Son in me" (Gal 1:16), and it was therefore through Christ that Paul was given his apostolic ministry (Rom 1:5). Christ "speaks through" Paul (2 Cor 13:3), and when Paul was hauled before a secular court, "the Lord stood at my side and gave me strength" (2 Tim 4:17). The life of the believer is even now "hidden with Christ in God" (Col 3:3), and believers can look forward to being saved "through [or 'in'] his life" (Rom 5:10). This assumption of Christ's "presence" stands in minor tension with other texts in which Paul appears to assume Christ's "absence"; for example, 2 Corinthians 5:6b: we "know that as long as we are at home in the body we are away from the Lord." Christ retains his physical (though now exalted) body and is presumably therefore "located" somewhere (at God's "right hand"). And Paul's talk of Christ "coming" suggests something like this as well. Resolution of this tension is beyond my pay grade, but we might need to distinguish between Christ's bodily absence and his presence in and through the Spirit.[37]

As we might expect, the theological and pastoral conclusion Paul draws from Christ's exaltation is that believers can be assured of God's care in this life and their vindication in the next because they belong to the one who reigns over all things. Christ's reign means that all things "are placed under his feet," including especially those spiritual powers who might appear to be a threat to the believer's security (e.g., Rom 8:35–39; 1 Cor 15:24–25; Eph 1:20–23; Col 1:16–17; 2:8). Our security in God's purposes and love is guaranteed by Christ, who "is at the right hand of God and is also interceding for us" (Rom 8:34). At the same time, the exalted Christ also will sit in judgment on people (Rom 2:16), even believers (2 Cor 5:10).

2.2.8 Parousia

Paul's eschatological perspective, as we have seen, is characterized by the tension between past fulfillment ("already") and future consummation ("not yet"). Paul refers to this time of future fulfillment by adapting the Old Testament "day of the Lord," replacing "Lord" with a reference to Christ (e.g., 2 Cor 1:14; Phil 1:10; 2:16). That "day" is associated with Christ because it is his coming again that is the heart of that day. Paul refers to the return of Christ in several ways, but particularly common are

---

36. Many scholars suspect that Paul's use of Ps 8 in this context reflects an underlying identification of Jesus as Son of Man. However, this is doubtful, since Paul never uses this title of Jesus. The phrase "under his feet" would probably have been sufficient to link Ps 8:6 with 110:1.

37. For an exploration of this tension see Orr, *Christ Absent and Present*.

three terms: *parousia* ("coming" or "presence," 1 Cor 15:23; 1 Thess 2:19; 3:13; 4:15; 5:23; 2 Thess 2:1, 8); *epiphaneia* ("manifestation," 2 Thess 2:8; 1 Tim 6:14; 2 Tim 4:1, 8; Titus 2:13); and *apokalypsis* ("revelation," 1 Cor 1:7; 2 Thess 1:7).[38] "Parousia," of course, has become, in transliteration, a technical term for Christ's return. The word is especially appropriate because it is used in the papyri to designate the special visits of kings. This association has led some interpreters to suggest that Paul uses this at least partly to make a veiled anti-imperial point; it is the coming of King Jesus that believers look to for deliverance, not the arrival of the emperor or some other earthly king. I explore the theology of Jesus's parousia and associated last-day events in chapter 22 (pp. 534–41). Here I note simply that the "day" of Christ's "coming," or "arrival," is the culminating point in the history of the world. It will trigger the "gathering" of God's people (2 Thess 2:1), whether through resurrection (for dead believers) or rapture (for living believers; 1 Cor 15:23; 1 Thess 4:14–16). Christ's coming is the time when humans will receive ultimate scrutiny with respect to their conduct and eschatological destiny (1 Cor 4:5; 1 Thess 3:13; 5:23; 1 Tim 6:14; 2 Tim 4:1), bringing ultimate salvation to believers (it is our "blessed hope"; Titus 2:13; see also 1 Cor 1:7; 1 Thess 2:19; 4:15–16; 2 Thess 1:7) and final judgment to unbelievers (2 Thess 1:6–7; 2:8).

2.2.9 Handing Over the Kingdom to God the Father

As much as Paul highlights Christ as the center of the new realm, he of course never loses sight of God the Father. The ultimate goal of the Son is that "God may be all in all" (1 Cor 15:28).[39]

3 APPELLATIONS

I use the term "appellation" in my title not to appear more academic by using a fancy word but because the usual word "title" might be somewhat inaccurate. There is some question about whether all these descriptive words are truly "titles." "Appellation" is a slightly broader term, meaning, according to Merriam-Webster online, "an identifying name or title." The tendency in modern scholarship is to investigate Paul's Christology by focusing on what Jesus has done rather than on these appellations. And this tendency is to some extent justified. For instance, Paul never uses "servant" as a title to refer to Jesus (though see Rom 15:8). But we should certainly not assume therefore that Paul does not think of Jesus in terms of the Servant figure found in the latter part of Isaiah.

---

38. On the background and meaning of these terms, see Rigaux, *Thessaloniciens*, 196–206; Milligan, *Thessalonians*, 145–51.

39. Paul's claim in this text that "the Son himself will be made subject to him who put everything under him" raises complex Trinitarian questions. Most agree that the submission referred to here is in terms of what is called the "economic" Trinity rather than the "immanent" Trinity (see, e.g., Schreiner, *1 Corinthians*, 315–16; and the essays in Bird and Harrower, *Trinity without Hierarchy*); see also 1 Cor 11:3 and my notes on that text.

For Paul arguably alludes to Servant texts in Isaiah to describe Jesus (e.g., Rom 4:25; 8:32; 1 Cor 15:3; 2 Cor 5:21; Gal 1:4; perhaps Phil 2:6–7).[40] Nevertheless, the appellations Paul uses to depict Jesus are obviously significant and should not be neglected. Of course, we must be wary about importing into them the significance they ultimately took on in early Christian theologizing.[41] At the same time, it is shortsighted to think that Paul would not have thought "ontologically" about Jesus—that is, about the nature and "being" of the one whom he was proclaiming. Indeed, as we will see, Paul's teaching about Christ naturally feeds into those definitive christological formulations.

3.1 Christ (Messiah)

The question whether "title" is the appropriate way to denote the various appellations Paul uses of Jesus arises especially urgently with respect to the ubiquitous "Christ" (*christos*, often translated in modern versions as "Messiah" [see below]). Paul uses this word to describe Jesus 380 times—far more than any other term. It occurs in several different combinations: "Christ" (212 times); "Jesus Christ" (28 times); "Christ Jesus" (79 times); "Lord Jesus Christ" (59 times); "Lord Christ" (2 times).[42] So often does the term occur that many scholars suspect the word has become simply a proper name in Paul: "Jesus Christ" would be basically equivalent to "Doug Moo."[43] Before we can confirm, deny, or modify this claim, we must look at several lines of evidence.

The distribution of the appellation "Christ" across the biblical canon raises interesting questions.

First, in comparison with the very numerous occurrences in Paul, "Christ" is used much less often in the Gospels, a little over forty times. Moreover, Jesus tends to avoid using the word to describe himself; almost all occurrences are found on the lips of others or as comments by the evangelists. Still, the Gospel writers use the appellation often enough to suggest that it was common currency in their churches and that it continued to make some kind of significant claim about Jesus. See, for example, Mark 1:1: "The beginning of the good news about Jesus the Messiah, the Son of God"; Luke 2:11: "Today in the town of David a Savior has been born to you; he is the Messiah, the Lord"; John 20:31: "But these are written that you may believe that Jesus is the Messiah, the Son of God, and that by believing you may have life in his name." The significance of the appellation "Christ," or "Messiah," continues to be seen in Acts: see, for example, 5:42: "Day after day, in the temple courts and from house to house, they never stopped

---

40. See, e.g., Cullmann, *Christology*, 51, 76–78; Longenecker, *Christology*, 108; Bauckham, *Jesus and the God of Israel*, 205–6.

41. A warning sounded by many scholars, sometimes motivated by the questionable attempt to preserve the historical claims of Paul from later christological formulations (e.g., Schnelle, *Apostle Paul*, 395).

42. Variations across the Pauline corpus are interesting. For

instance, "Christ," used absolutely, is the only way Paul refers to Jesus in Rom 9–11, while he never uses this word alone in the Pastoral Epistles.

43. See especially Nils Alstrup Dahl, "The Messiahship of Jesus in Paul," in *The Crucified Messiah* (Minneapolis: Augsburg, 1974), who argues the language is "on its way" from a title to a proper name in Paul.

teaching and proclaiming the good news that Jesus is the Messiah" (see also 9:22). These texts come from the first part of Acts, which focuses on outreach to Jews, and it is interesting that even in the latter chapters of Acts, "Christ," used absolutely, is present in contexts where witness to Jews is the focus (Acts 17:3; 18:5, 28).[44]

Second, and unexpectedly granted the New Testament usage, the word "Christ" only rarely—if ever!—refers to an eschatological redeemer figure in the Old Testament. English "Christ" is a transliteration of Greek *christos*, which means "anointed one"; and *christos* translates Hebrew *mashiach*. See, for example, John 1:41b: "'We have found the Messiah [*messian*]' (that is, the Christ [*christos*])." *Mashiach* occurs thirty-eight times in the Old Testament, referring to both priests and especially to kings. See, for example, Psalm 2:2: "The kings of the earth rise up and the rulers band together against the LORD and against his anointed [*mashiach*]" (note the reference to the king in v. 6). The only texts that may use *mashiach* as a reference to an eschatological redeemer figure are Daniel 9:25, 26:

> Know and understand this: From the time the word goes out to restore and rebuild Jerusalem until the Anointed One, the ruler, comes, there will be seven "sevens," and sixty-two "sevens." It will be rebuilt with streets and a trench, but in times of trouble. After the sixty-two "sevens," the Anointed One will be put to death and will have nothing. The people of the ruler who will come will destroy the city and the sanctuary. The end will come like a flood: War will continue until the end, and desolations have been decreed. He will confirm a covenant with many for one "seven." In the middle of the "seven" he will put an end to sacrifice and offering. And at the temple he will set up an abomination that causes desolation, until the end that is decreed is poured out on him. (9:25–27)

By capitalizing "Anointed One" in its two occurrences, the NIV suggests the reference might be to *the* anointed one—the redeemer to come. But the NIV footnotes each occurrence, giving "an anointed one" as an option—recognizing that many scholars think the reference here is to the "ruler" who opposes the people of God. These verses are, of course, some of the most hotly debated in all the Old Testament. At the least, then, we have to say that we have no unambiguous Old Testament evidence for "anointed" as a reference directly to the eschatological redeemer figure.

Why, then, do we find the language of "anointed" occurring so commonly in the New Testament? The answer probably lies in Second Temple Judaism. As Matthew Novenson says, "There may not be any messiahs in the Hebrew Bible, but some Jewish

---

44. It should be noted that the NIV, quoted here, has decided to use the transliteration of the Hebrew translation of *christos* in all these occurrences, a way of helping English readers recognize the kind of claim the language is making.

authors of the Hellenistic and Roman periods evidently thought there were."[45] While we do not have evidence for an overwhelming use of "messiah" language in Judaism, we have enough to surmise that the language had become a common way of denoting the eschatological redeemer figure to come. Psalms of Solomon (first-century BC) is often cited, where a warrior king in the mode of David is called "messiah." See, for example, 17:32: "Their king shall be the Lord Messiah" (cf. also 18:7); and 18:5: "The appointed day when his Messiah shall reign." The variety of Jewish perspectives on this coming figure is revealed by the Dead Sea Scrolls text in 1QS 9.11, which appears to refer to two messiahs: "Until there come the Prophet, and the Messiahs of Aaron and Israel." Altogether, then, there is some reason for suspecting that the early Jewish church picked up from their environment the appellation "messiah" to denote the figure predicted in a variety of ways in the Old Testament to redeem Israel and usher in the last days. And it is likely that the Greek Old Testament available to the early Christians was already using Greek *christos* as the translation of *mashiach*. What we might therefore label the "messianic idea" had come to be referred to quite frequently with the language of "messiah."[46] This figure took on royal associations, partly because of the prevalence of references to the king in *mashiach* language and partly because of the dominating connection of this figure with David (e.g., Isa 9:7; Jer 23:5; 29:16; 30:9; 33:15, 17, 22; Ezek 34:23, 24; 37:24, 25; Hos 3:5; note esp. Ps 18:50, which brings together "David," God's king, and "his anointed").[47]

To return to Paul: What is the status of "Christ" language in his theology? The sheer number of times Paul uses the language raises questions about how much significance he gave the appellation. Moreover, Paul never draws theological or pastoral points from the word itself. That is, we never find Paul arguing, explicitly or implicitly, that "because Jesus is the Christ, this [theological point] is true or this [way of living] is what God requires of us."[48] In virtually every place where "Christ" occurs in Paul, another

45. Matthew V. Novenson, *Christ among the Messiahs: Christ Language in Paul and Messiah Language in Ancient Judaism* (Oxford: Oxford University Press, 2012), 52–53; see his survey of the Jewish evidence on pp. 51–58; and also, e.g., Andrew Chester, *Messiah and Exaltation: Jewish Messianic and Visionary Traditions and New Testament Christology*, WUNT 2/207 (Tübingen: Mohr Siebeck, 2007), 329–63.

46. This sentence implies the complexity of relating the *concept* Messiah to the *lexeme* Messiah. On the various ways this relationship is untangled, see esp. Chester, *Messiah and Exaltation*, 193–205.

47. See on this point particularly, Joshua W. Jipp, *Christ Is King: Paul's Royal Ideology* (Minneapolis: Fortress, 2015). Novenson points out that Jewish messianic texts often referenced OT passages about a king or ruler (Gen 49:10; Num 24:17; 2 Sam 7:12–13; Isa 11:1–2; Amos 9:11; Dan 7:13–14) (*Christ among the Messiahs*, 57–58). I part company, then, with those who think

"messiah" language has no clear focus (as argued, e.g., by William Scott Green, "Introduction: Messiah in Judaism: Rethinking the Question," in *Judaisms and Their Messiahs at the Turn of the Christian Era*, ed. Jacob Neusner, William Scott Green, and Ernest S. Frerichs [Cambridge: Cambridge University Press, 1987], 1–14; and James H. Charlesworth, "From Messianology to Christology: Problems and Prospects," in *The Messiah: Developments in Earliest Judaism and Christianity*, ed. James H. Charlesworth [Minneapolis: Fortress, 2009], 3–35).

48. Dahl makes several other linguistic arguments against a titular use of "Christ" in Paul ("Messiahship," 37), which have been effectively refuted by Novenson (Matthew V. Novenson, "Can the Messiahship of Jesus Be Read off Paul's Grammar? Nils Dahl's Criteria 50 Years Later," *NTS* 56 [2010]: 396–412). Chester suggests that Paul gave the title little significance because of its potential revolutionary implications (e.g., a "king" to rival Caesar [*Messiah and Exaltation*, 383–88]).

name—"Jesus," "the Lord"—could have been substituted without any obvious loss of meaning. We can understand, then, why some scholars conclude that "Christ" has lost all titular force for Paul. However, looking at the use of the language in Judaism and the evidence of the Gospels and Acts, others insist that "Christ" carried significant theological weight for Paul.[49] The truth lies somewhere in the middle.[50] While "Christ" has usually lost any clear theological significance in Paul, calling Jesus "Christ" serves to remind early Christians, whether Jewish or gentile, that he is the fulfillment of the Old Testament expectation about an eschatological redeemer. Moreover, there are some texts in which Paul appears to invest more significance in the language. The NIV, for example, translates *christos* with "Messiah" in Romans 9:5: "Theirs are the patriarchs, and from them is traced the human ancestry of the Messiah, who is God over all, forever praised! Amen." Other texts that appear to invest significance in the title are Romans 1:3–4; 15:7–12; 1 Corinthians 15:23–28; 2 Corinthians 5:10; and Galatians 3:16.[51] At the same time, the Old Testament king/messiah was viewed as a representative of the people (e.g., 2 Sam 5:1–5; 19:41–20:1). It is possible, then, that Paul might also use "Christ" to connote Jesus's representative significance (e.g., his resurrection includes and guarantees the resurrection of all who belong to him; we die with him, are crucified with him, etc.).[52] Perhaps, then, a mediating view on this issue is warranted. Novenson, for instance, has argued that *christos* in Paul is neither a title or a proper name; rather, it is an "honorific," "a word that can function as a stand-in for a personal name but part of whose function is to retain its supernominal associations." He compares the way the first Roman emperor, whose name was "Octavian," is often known in history as "Augustus." The latter can function as a proper name—as "Christ" does in Paul—but retains some sense of the "honor" associated with such a name.[53]

It is also important that Paul can refer to the "messianic concept" in other ways. Twice he affirms that Jesus was a descendant of David (Rom 1:3; 2 Tim 2:8; cf. "Root of Jesse" in Rom 15:12 [= Isa 11:10]). Connecting Jesus with David picks up an important thread of teaching found elsewhere in the New Testament (e.g., Matt 1:1; 15:22; 22:41–46; Mark 10:48; Luke 1:32; Rev 5:5). Calling Jesus the descendant of David is no mere biological claim; it is a claim that Jesus is the Davidic figure prophesied as the redeemer and world ruler of the last days.

---

49. See esp. N. T. Wright, "ΧΡΙΣΤΟΣ as 'Messiah' in Paul: Philemon 6," in *Climax of the Covenant*, 41–55.

50. See, e.g., Cullmann, *Christology*, 133–34; Dunn, *Theology of Paul*, 197–99.

51. Andrew Chester, "The Christ of Paul," in *Redemption and Resistance: The Messianic Hopes of Jews and Christians in Antiquity*, ed. Markus Bockmuehl and James Carleton Paget (London: T&T Clark, 2007), 111.

52. See esp. N. T. Wright, "Adam, Israel and the Messiah," in *Climax of the Covenant*, 21–35.

53. Novenson, *Christ among the Messiahs*, 134–38; see also Larry W. Hurtado, "Paul's Messianic Christology," in Boccaccini and Segovia, *Paul the Jew*, 108–10.

3.2 Lord

If "Christ" is the least theologically significant appellation for Jesus in Paul, "Lord" is at the other end of the spectrum. Paul uses this appellation only slightly less often than "Christ"—the word "Lord" (Gk. *kyrios*) occurs 274 times in Paul. How many of those refer to Christ is debated, since Paul uses the same word to refer to God the Father.[54] Probably, however, around 240 of these refer to Christ, in various combinations: "Lord" (151 times); "Lord Jesus" (25 times); "Lord Jesus Christ" (59 times); "Lord Christ" (2 times). The confession that "Jesus is Lord" is a fundamental expression of Christian faith (Rom 10:9; 1 Cor 12:3). Paul almost certainly followed other early Christians in applying this appellation to Christ. The evidence of the Gospels must be carefully considered, since the word can simply be a respectful address (e.g., Matt 13:27; 18:25–32)—and, of course, the Gospels were written after Paul's letters. But we have good reason to believe that the evangelists preserve the language that people in Jesus's day were using of him, and "Lord," in a strong sense, occurs frequently (e.g., Matt 22:43–45). The book of Acts suggests that the resurrection confirmed and perhaps inaugurated a new stage in the lordship: "God has made this Jesus, whom you crucified, both Lord and Messiah" (Acts 2:36; see also, e.g., Acts 10:36). First Corinthians 16:22b suggests that the appellation was applied to Christ at an early date. In this text, Paul transliterates into Greek two Aramaic words. Presented as the NA[28] text does, *marana tha*, the words mean "Come, Lord!" (NIV, along with almost all English versions; *tha* on this reading is an imperative). The two words could also be divided *maran atha*, in which case it would mean "the Lord comes" (*atha* as an indicative). The former is more likely.[55] But, in any case, the point is that this text reveals that "Lord" language was being applied to Christ from an early date (more on this below). Paul, therefore, was not the one who brought this title into Christian theology; nor did it appear only when the early Christian movement left its Palestinian and Jewish home to enter the Greek world—a developmental view popular in the older history-of-religions approach to early Christian theology.[56]

Paul uses "Lord" to denote Jesus so often that the appellation is brought into contact with virtually every theological issue in his letters. If we probe further and try to determine the kind of theological implications Paul draws from "Lord" specifically, a general focus on authority emerges. This, of course, should be no surprise, granted the meaning of the word itself. Two aspects, or "moments" in Jesus's authority as Lord are frequently encountered.[57] First, Jesus has been installed as Lord because of his

---

54. Older scholars sometimes suggested that one could use the presence or absence of the article to settle the matter. But, as Fee points out (*Pauline Christology*, 35), the article is not conclusive for the issue.

55. E.g., Cullmann, *Christology*, 209–10. See the brief discussion in Longenecker, *Christology*, 121–24.

56. This view is found in, e.g., Bousset, *Kyrios Christos*.

57. Gathercole, "Paul's Christology," 174.

resurrection (e.g., Rom 1:4), and believers fall under the sphere of that lordship in this life. Believers, rescued from the old realm by his power, live in the new realm under the dominion of that Lord. Paul hints at this relationship by often referring to Jesus as "our Lord." As believers enter that realm acknowledging Jesus as their Lord (Rom 10:9), so they must live under his lordship (Col 2:6). He issues commands that they are to obey (1 Cor 7:10, 12; 14:37). Believers are to serve (Eph 6:7; Col 3:24) and "please" him (Eph 5:10; Col 1:10), accomplishing his will (Eph 5:17, 22), and are answerable to him (1 Cor 4:4; 5:3–4; 2 Cor 8:21; 10:18; 1 Tim 4:8). This Lord sovereignly determines the lives of new-realm members: he appoints them to ministry (1 Cor 3:5), bestows on them something of his own authority (2 Cor 10:8; 13:10; 1 Thess 4:2), and directs his servants in their ministry locations (1 Cor 16:7; 2 Cor 2:12). Believers owe him obedience. Romans 14:4–9 spells out this relationship especially clearly:

> Who are you to judge someone else's servant? To their own master [*kyriō*], servants stand or fall. And they will stand, for the Lord is able to make them stand.
>
> One person considers one day more sacred than another; another considers every day alike. Each of them should be fully convinced in their own mind. Whoever regards one day as special does so to the Lord. Whoever eats meat does so to the Lord, for they give thanks to God; and whoever abstains does so to the Lord and gives thanks to God. For none of us lives for ourselves alone, and none of us dies for ourselves alone. If we live, we live for the Lord; and if we die, we die for the Lord. So, whether we live or die, we belong to the Lord. For this very reason, Christ died and returned to life so that he might be the Lord of both the dead and the living.

The note of authority must, of course, ultimately be balanced with the note of grace. The Lord not only commands and judges his people; he also dispenses grace to them (e.g., 1 Tim 1:14). Most of Paul's letters open with a wish that God the Father and "Jesus Christ [or Christ Jesus] our Lord" bestow grace on his people (Col 1:2 lacks reference to Christ; and 1 Thess 1:1 varies slightly). The second "moment" of the Lord's authority that Paul regularly brings up is the climax of the new realm: the "day of the Lord" (1 Cor 1:8; 5:5; 2 Cor 1:14; see also 1 Cor 4:5; Phil 3:20; 4:5; Col 3:24; 1 Thess 2:19; 3:13; 4:15, 16, 17; 5:2, 23; 2 Thess 1:7; 2:1, 8; 1 Tim 6:14).

Two indirect aspects of Paul's use of "Lord" to describe Christ also need to be registered.

First, like the word "gospel" (see above, pp. 349–51), the title "Lord" was being used in Paul's day to refer to the Roman emperor and other secular rulers. And it is again thought that Paul might therefore be hinting at an anti-imperial claim when he applies the word to Jesus: "Jesus is Lord" implies "Caesar is not." Paul is certainly clear that Christ's lordship extends beyond the boundaries of the new realm. Although there are many "lords," there is "for us" "but one Lord" (1 Cor 8:6); he is the "Lord of all" (Rom 10:12). Nevertheless, Paul never explicitly contrasts Christ as Lord with the emperor, and of course he calls on Christians to honor the legitimate rights of secular rulers (Rom 13:1–7). As I concluded with respect to gospel language, then, it is possible that Paul would have intended his readers to pick up an anti-imperial thrust in his "Lord" language, but if so, it is muted. And for Paul the more important issue is the lordship of Christ over all—including especially the "powers" and the forces of sin and death.

Second, calling Christ "Lord" has bearing on Paul's understanding of the relationship between Father and Son. Paul follows the pattern attested in the Old Greek translations of the Old Testament of rendering the Tetragrammaton, YHWH, or Yahweh,[58] with the word *kyrios* in his quotations of the Old Testament (e.g., Rom 4:8; 9:28, 29; 10:16; 11:3; 15:11; 1 Cor 1:31; 2:16; 3:20; 10:26; 14:21; 2 Cor 6:17, 18; 10:17; 2 Tim 2:19). To be sure, the evidence we possess from the Old Greek in Paul's day does not make this translation equivalent altogether clear. Extant Greek manuscripts from Paul's day usually put the Hebrew letters *yhwh* or transliterated YHWH in the place of the Tetragrammaton. However, it seems clear that Greek-speaking Jews in Paul's day were using *kyrios* to represent the Tetragrammaton,[59] setting the precedent that New Testament authors, including Paul, follow.[60] It is therefore very significant that Paul can quote Old Testament texts about the "Lord" (Yahweh) and apply them to Jesus. See, for instance, Romans 10:13, which quotes Joel 2:32 (3:5 LXX): "Everyone who calls on the name of the Lord will be saved." The context makes clear that this "Lord," whose name people call on, is Christ (vv. 9–12). Paul therefore here, and elsewhere, implies that Jesus belongs to the identity of God.[61]

3.3 Son of God

The third prominent appellation that Paul uses to describe Christ is "Son of God."[62] It is used far less frequently than the other two appellations we have considered, occurring only seventeen times in the letters of Paul (often in the form of "his Son," where

---

58. English versions usually render the Tetragrammaton with lower caps, "Lord."

59. Bauckham is right in saying that *kyrios* is not really a "translation" of the Tetragrammaton (*Jesus and the God of Israel*, 190; cf. Wright, *Paul and the Faithfulness of God*, 2:701).

60. On this issue, see esp. Joseph A. Fitzmyer, "The Semitic Background of the New Testament *Kyrios*-Title," in *A Wandering Aramean: Collected Aramaic Essays*, SBLDS 25 (Missoula, MT: Scholars Press, 1979), 115–42.

61. See esp. Capes, *Divine Christ*; Chris Tilling, *Paul's Divine Christology*, WUNT 2/323 (Tübingen: Mohr Siebeck, 2012), esp. 105–80; Bauckham, *Jesus and the God of Israel*; Larry W. Hurtado, "The Binitarian Shape of Early Christian Worship," in *The*

Jewish Roots of Christological Monotheism, ed. C. C. Newman, J. R. Davila, and G. S. Lewis, Supplements to the Journal for the Study of Judaism 63 (Leiden: Brill, 1999), 191–213; idem, "Jesus' Divine Sonship in Paul's Epistle to the Romans," in Soderlund and Wright, *Romans and the People of God*, 217–33; Fee, *Pauline Christology*, 583–611. Rowe has argued that this identification of Jesus with Yahweh in the NT suggests that Yahweh in the OT must also include Jesus ("Biblical Pressure," 295–312).

62. Other scholars recognizing the special status of these three "titles" are, e.g., Hahn, *Theologie des Neuen Testaments*, 1:204; Lucien Cerfaux, *Christ in the Theology of St. Paul* (New York: Herder and Herder, 1959), 313.

"his" refers to God). However, its appearance at critical points in Paul's arguments gives the appellation a significance that can't be measured by number of occurrences. Since the Old Testament (following ancient Near Eastern precedent) sometimes calls the king a "son [of God]," some interpreters think that "Son of God" is not much more than a variant of "Messiah."[63] However, the contexts in which Paul uses the language strongly point, rather, to Son of God being an appellation Paul uses to connote the close relationship of Jesus to the Father. Thus, for instance, in Romans 8, to accentuate the enormity of God's gift to us, he calls Jesus "[God's] own Son" (vv. 3, 32); in Colossians 1:13, he is "the Son of his love" (my own translation). The title "primarily expresses Jesus's unique standing and intimate favor with God, and God's direct involvement in Jesus's redemptive work."[64] Thus, God's Son, as Romans 1:3 implies, existed before he entered into this world. Preexistence is suggested also by Paul's claim that the Son was "sent" (Rom 8:3; Gal 4:4). As the Son entered into human history, so the Son, as a result of the resurrection, entered into a new stage of "power" (Rom 1:4) through which he could exercise his rule and bestow salvation (v. 16). Paul also often calls Jesus "Son of God" in soteriological passages, thereby making clear that the same eternal Son, in closest relationship to the Father, is the Son who gave himself for our redemption (Rom 5:10; 8:3, 32; Gal 2:20).

4 JESUS AND GOD

Our discussion of "Lord" and "Son of God" leads naturally into a related topic: Jesus as God in Paul. Several lines of evidence need to be considered.

An obvious starting point is the title "God." Many theologians are convinced that Paul was too wedded to Jewish monotheism to ever have called Jesus "God." However, in a careful exegetical study, Murray J. Harris makes a convincing case that two texts in Paul "very probably" describe Jesus as God:

Rom 9:5: "Theirs are the patriarchs, and from them is traced the human ancestry of the Messiah, who is God over all, forever praised! Amen."
Titus 2:13b: "The appearing of the glory of our great God and Savior, Jesus Christ."

The issue in the former text is punctuation. If we follow the NIV and most English translations and place a comma after "Messiah," then "God" refers to Jesus. Placing a period there, however, would mean that "God" implicitly refers to the Father. (See p. 230 for further analysis.) The issue in the latter text is the syntax and how to construe

63. E.g., A. Y. Collins, "Jesus as Messiah and Son of God," 101–22.
64. Hurtado, *Lord Jesus Christ*, 104; see also, e.g., Gathercole, "Paul's Christology," 173–74; Martin Hengel, *The Son of God: The Origin of Christology and the History of Jewish-Hellenistic Religion* (Philadelphia: Fortress, 1976), 63.

a series of genitives. Does "great God" denote a separate person other than "Savior, Jesus Christ" or the same person (as the NIV, quoted above, implies)? (Again, see p. 230.) I follow Harris in concluding that both texts "very probably" use "God" to designate Jesus. But the qualification ("probably") should be noted. Each text has legitimately debated issues; neither is a "slam dunk" prooftext.

A second appellation to consider is "image." Paul claims that Jesus is the "image [Gk. *eikōn*] of God" (2 Cor 4:4; Col 1:15) and that believers are being conformed to Christ's "image" now (Rom 8:29; 2 Cor 3:18; Col 3:10) and in the future resurrection (1 Cor 15:49). Christ is the perfect image bearer, who restores the image in fallen humanity.[65] "Image of God" language naturally draws our attention to Genesis 1:26–27, which narrates God's creation of the first humans "in his image" (LXX *eikōn*; *homoiōsis*, "likeness," is also used in v. 26). Paul explicitly compares Christ with Adam in 1 Corinthians 15:49, and the comparison is probably implicit in Colossians 3:10 (where "old man" probably refers to Adam). Grant Macaskill is justified in arguing that being identified as "the image of God" and being made "according to the image of God" need to be distinguished: Christ, and Christ alone, is *the* image of God.[66] However, I am not as sure as he is that Adamic allusions are therefore negligible in Paul's christological assertions.

The meaning of "image of God" has been a longstanding matter of theological debate. Ancient authors usually identified the "image" with some human capacity—reason, openness to the deity[67]—while modern authors have tended toward a more relational focus, with the idea of rulership or dominion particularly popular recently.[68] But rulership is better seen as a result or purpose of the image, while the image itself has to do with human identity and worth before God.[69] Marc Cortez has recently suggested that the image involves the manifestation of the divine presence.[70] This would fit well with Paul's identification of Christ as the image, since a central purpose of Christ in Paul is to manifest the divine presence (see, e.g., Col 1:15: "image of the invisible God"). Paul's recognition of Christ as the image of God may stem from his own initial encounter with Christ on the Damascus Road, when "a light from heaven flashed around him" (Acts 9:3; cf. 22:6; 26:13). This is somewhat reminiscent of 2 Corinthians 4:4: "The god of this age has blinded the minds of unbelievers, so that they cannot see the light of the gospel that displays the glory of Christ, who is the image of God." "Glory" and "image" are not related in the Old Testament, but are associated

65. Fee, *Pauline Christology*, 184.

66. Macaskill, *Union with Christ*, 134–36, 230–32.

67. See the survey in Anthony A. Hoekema, *Created in God's Image* (Grand Rapids: Eerdmans, 1986), 33–65.

68. See esp. J. Richard Middleton, *The Liberating Image: The Imago Dei in Genesis 1* (Grand Rapids: Baker, 2005).

69. See esp. John F. Kilner, *Dignity and Destiny: Humanity in the Image of God* (Grand Rapids: Eerdmans, 2015); Ryan S. Peterson, *The Imago Dei as Human Identity: A Theological Interpretation*, JTISup 14 (Winona Lake: Eisenbrauns, 2016).

70. Marc Cortez, *ReSourcing Theological Anthropology: A Constructive Account of Humanity in the Light of Christ* (Grand Rapids: Zondervan, 2017), 101–13.

sometimes in Jewish texts. At any rate, this verse is frequently cited as reason to think that Paul saw in Christ a display of divine glory, and that this way of seeing Christ was rooted in the Damascus Road Christophany.[71]

One other appellation may be briefly considered here: "Savior." While Paul uses this word to describe the work of Christ in Ephesians 5:23 and Philippians 3:20, it is only in the Pastoral Epistles that it is used as a title. What is relevant to our present focus is the way Paul uses "Savior" to describe both God (1 Tim 1:1; 2:3; 4:10; Titus 1:3; 2:10; 3:4) and Christ (2 Tim 1:10; Titus 1:4; 2:13; 3:6). Particularly striking is the juxtaposition in Titus 1:3–4: "Which now at his appointed season he has brought to light through the preaching entrusted to me by the command of *God our Savior,* To Titus, my true son in our common faith: Grace and peace from God the Father and *Christ Jesus our Savior.*" This sharing of a title between Father and Son suggests a close relationship between them.

The evidence that Paul considered Jesus to be "God" is more profitably based on the activities of Christ and of Christians in relationship to Christ. Thus:

Jesus is preexistent and active in creation (see above)
Christians pray to Jesus (e.g., 1 Cor 1:2; 16:22; 2 Cor 12:8; 1 Thess 3:11–13; 2 Thess 2:16)
Christians worship Jesus (e.g., 1 Cor 12:3)

In addition, building on my comments on Romans 10:13 above, we should note the several other passages where Paul cites or alludes to Old Testament monotheistic verses, explicitly claiming they have application to Christ. Especially striking is Paul's allusion to Isaiah 45:23 in Philippians 2:10–11. Here Paul claims that one result of Christ's exaltation will be that "every tongue acknowledge that Jesus Christ is Lord." The allusion to Isaiah 45:23 is unmistakable, and the point Paul is implicitly making here becomes all the more clear when we see that this verse from Isaiah comes in a context that stresses monotheism as much as any other in the Old Testament—verse 22b reads, "I am God, and there is no other."[72]

How Paul, who remained a strict monotheist (Rom 3:30; 1 Cor 8:4), became convinced that Jesus was God is debated. One popular option is that the focus on various "intermediary" figures, such as Wisdom, the Word (*logos*), and angels in Second Temple Judaism paved the way for this move.[73] Paul, of course, calls Jesus, God's

71. See esp. Kim, *Origin of Paul's Gospel,* 137–222; Carey C. Newman, *Paul's Glory-Christology: Tradition and Rhetoric,* NovTSup 69 (Leiden: Brill, 1992), 164–212.

72. On this text and others like it, see Bauckham, *Jesus and the God of Israel,* 186–90.

73. Crispin H. T. Fletcher-Louis, "The Worship of Divine Humanity as God's Image and the Worship of Jesus," in Newman, Davila, and Lewis, *Jewish Roots of Christological Monotheism,* 112–28; Chester, *Messiah and Exaltation,* 45–80.

"wisdom" (1 Cor 1:24; see v. 30) and arguably uses Old Testament and Jewish wisdom texts to characterize Christ's person and eternal nature (e.g., Col 1:15–17). However, the influence of Wisdom (and Word) traditions on Paul has been overemphasized.[74] Moreover, figures such as Wisdom and the Word do not become in Second Temple Judaism independent entities that in any way encroach on the nature or person of God. I think Hurtado, Bauckham, and others have convincingly argued that the Judaism of Paul's day retained a "strict" monotheism that would not have had room for any figures beyond the one God. To quote Bauckham:

> The evidence of the literature is clear that the overwhelming tendency in Second Temple Judaism was to depict God as absolutely unique, to differentiate God as completely as possible from all other reality, and to understand the exclusive worship of God as marking, in religious practice, the absolute distinction between God and all creatures.[75]

Figures such as Wisdom, Word, and angels would not have been understood by Paul as opening up monotheism in a way that would facilitate the inclusion of Christ in the being of God.[76]

There is debate about the categories that best help us get a sense of how Paul is thinking about Christ and the Father—"identity," "worship," "relations."[77] But we find a substantial number of recent scholars arguing for what has been called "Early High Christology," meaning that Christians quite early began viewing Jesus as God, in the strict sense of that word—without, of course, giving up monotheism.[78] Here we find the raw materials of later Christology. Wright states, "It is now, I believe, necessary to assert that, although the writers of the New Testament did not themselves formulate the doctrine of the Trinity, they bequeathed to their successors a manner of speaking and writing about God which made it, or something very like it, almost inevitable."[79]

---

74. See Fee, *Pauline Christology*, 595–630, for a vigorous argument on this point.

75. Richard Bauckham, "The Throne of God and the Worship of Jesus," in Newman, Davila, and Lewis, *Jewish Roots of Christological Monotheism*, 48 (see 48–69).

76. See Bauckham, *Jesus and the God of Israel*, 1–20. Bauckham goes further than Hurtado in dismissing the significance of these figures for the development of NT Christology (see Hurtado's comments in the latest edition of his classic work *One God, One Lord*, 153–57).

77. E.g., Tilling, *Paul's Divine Christology*; Hill, *Paul and the Trinity*.

78. Another sometimes overlooked source for this divine Christology, of course, is Jesus himself. See Loke, *Origin of Divine Christology*.

79. Wright, "Poetry and Theology," 117. See also, at greater length, Hill, *Paul and the Trinity*.

Chapter 18

THE INAUGURATION OF THE NEW REALM

For the grace of God has appeared that offers salvation to all people. It teaches us to say "No" to ungodliness and worldly passions, and to live self-controlled, upright and godly lives in this present age, while we wait for the blessed hope—the appearing of the glory of our great God and Savior, Jesus Christ, *who gave himself for us to redeem us from all wickedness and to purify for himself a people* that are his very own, eager to do what is good.

—TITUS 2:11–14

THE DOMINANT and distinctive feature of all New Testament teaching is the way the early believers celebrate their identity as members of the new realm. Paul, of course, adds his voice to the chorus of praise and wonder:

Therefore, if anyone is in Christ, the new creation has come: The old has gone, the new is here! (2 Cor 5:17)

I tell you, now is the time of God's favor, now is the day of salvation. (2 Cor 6:2b)

Praise be to the God and Father of our Lord Jesus Christ, who has blessed us in the heavenly realms with every spiritual blessing in Christ. (Eph 1:3)

. . . giving joyful thanks to the Father, who has qualified you to share in the inheritance of his holy people in the kingdom of light. For he has rescued us from the dominion of darkness and brought us into the kingdom of the Son he loves, in whom we have redemption, the forgiveness of sins. (Col 1:12–14)

Of course, this enthusiasm for the "already" arrival of the new realm is tempered by the reality of the "not yet" culmination yet to come—and keeping these in right balance is critical to understanding and living in the new realm. But we should not mute the note of rejoicing in the present enjoyment of the new realm that permeates the letters of Paul.

In this chapter, I turn to the inauguration of this new realm. I focus on the founding events that brought the new realm into being. As I do so, however, an initial complicating factor looms before us. From the standpoint of salvation history generally, the establishment of the new realm can be "located" in the climactic events of Jesus's death and resurrrection, along with the subsequent pouring out of God's Spirit. Yet the pastoral situations that Paul addresses mean that he is usually focused on the entrance of believers into that new realm. From the believer's perspective, there are two decisive "moments" in the transfer from old realm to new: God's inauguration of the new realm through the work of Christ, and the believer's own entrance into that realm. Cross and conversion, we might say. Or, to use the language of historical theology, we find in Paul both an outline of the *historia salutis* and the *ordo salutis*. Each needs to receive appropriate emphasis. A "history of [the acts of] salvation" without the "order of [the application of] salvation" would make salvation wholly theoretical. But there can be no *ordo salutis* without its basis in the *historia salutis*.[1] The title of John Murray's book makes the point succinctly: *Redemption Accomplished and Applied*.[2]

While Paul often focuses on one of these "moments" or the other, he also combines them in ways that defy neat categorization. For instance, he proclaims that believers have been "redeemed." This redemption was secured on the cross, when Christ bore the curse of the law on our behalf (Gal 3:13). Yet the experience of that redeeming event becomes real to the believer only at conversion. In Colossians 1:13–14, for instance, our "redemption" is linked with God's rescuing us "from the dominion of darkness" and transferring us into "the kingdom of the Son he loves." We see the same complicated, overlapping relation between redemption "accomplished" and "applied" in Paul's teaching about our participation in the founding events of the new realm. Our new life, Paul proclaims, arises from our having been "crucified with Christ" (Rom 6:6; Gal 2:20), "buried with him" (Rom 6:4; Col 2:12), and "raised with him" (Col 2:12; cf. Rom 6:5, 8).

Paul's theology resists, then, any neat and consistent distinction between cross and conversion.[3] Nevertheless, Paul focuses on one or the other often enough to justify treating each of them in turn. In this chapter, I concentrate on the "accomplished" side of this transition from old realm to new realm.

What I am calling "inauguration of the new realm" overlaps considerably with the dogmatic category of "atonement." Contemporary discussions of atonement reveal

---

1. Horton notes, rightly, that, in a reaction against a tendency to focus too much attention on the personal experience of redemption, some scholars are recently focusing almost exclusively on the accomplishment of redemption and inappropriately minimizing its application (*Justification*, 2:38).

2. John Murray, *Redemption Accomplished and Applied* (Grand Rapids: Eerdmans, 1955).

3. Indeed, Becker claims that Paul has no clearly worked out theory of Jesus's death (*Paul: Apostle to the Gentiles*, 405).

uncertainty about just what "atonement" refers to. Traditionally, the word has been used to refer especially to the *means* by which God solves the human sin problem. Recently, however, scholars have criticized this focus because it neglects the New Testament concern with the entire panoply of new-covenant blessings: transformed lives, transformed communities, and a transformed cosmos. Traditional "atonement" theologies, it is argued, have been far too limited to do justice to the New Testament emphases on these matters.[4] An example of this more expansive understanding of atonement is seen in Scot McKnight's definition: "*Atonement* itself is a metaphor for everything and anything God does for us to make us what he wants to make us in light of who we were, who we are, and who we are meant to be."[5]

We confront here, of course, a problem of definition; and appeal to the biblical usage of the word is little help. The word "atonement" occurs in the NIV as a rendering of words from the *k-p-r* root in the Hebrew Old Testament and the corresponding *hilas-* root in the New; thus, for instance, "atonement cover" in Leviticus 16 (vv. 2, 13, 14, 15) and "sacrifice of atonement" in Romans 3:25. And these words tend to focus on means rather than outcome. But this cannot settle the matter. There is some connection, of course, between this biblical usage of the word and its use in theology to denote a doctrinal locus. But the connection is general and imprecise, and, practically, "atonement" is open to whatever meaning a particular exegete or theologian chooses to give it.

My own preference is to use the word in its more traditional, limited sense, to refer to the means of atonement.[6] I worry that the currently popular, more expansive definitions might either lose the distinct doctrinal focus of traditional atonement theories or mix up the issues of means and outcome in a way that will obscure more than it reveals.[7] I acknowledge the failure at times of believers to draw connections between Christ's work for us and Christ's work in us, to celebrate the cross while failing to live out

---

4. Michael J. Gorman, *The Death of the Messiah and the Birth of the New Covenant: A (Not So) New Model of the Atonement* (Eugene, OR: Cascade, 2014), e.g., 209; Thomas Andrew Bennett, *Labor of God: The Agony of the Cross and Birth of the Church* (Waco, TX: Baylor University Press, 2017), 61–62.

5. Scot McKnight, *A Community Called Atonement* (Nashville: Abingdon, 2007), 36. See also, e.g., Adam J. Johnson, *Atonement: A Guide for the Perplexed* (London: Bloomsbury T&T Clark, 2015); Bennett, *Labor of God*. Jeremy Treat notes the conflicting evaluations of Hans Boersma and Henri Blocher; for the former, penal substitution is a subordinate idea because it is only the means to an end; for the latter, it is primary because it is *the* means to an end (Jeremy Treat, *The Crucified King: Atonement and Kingdom of God in Biblical and Systematic Theology* [Grand Rapids: Zondervan, 2014], 222–23). Of course, the different evaluations depend on whether we are focusing on the what or the how of atonement.

6. Treat notes that theologians have traditionally used "atonement" to describe the means, or mechanism, by which God in Christ accomplishes his purposes (*Crucified King*, 45–49).

7. E.g., Jason Hood criticizes McKnight for expanding the idea of atonement to the point that we miss the theological point of the term ("The Cross in the New Testament: Two Theses in Conversation with Recent Literature [2000–2007]," *WTJ* 71 [2009]: 287). Michael S. Horton cites John Webster's evaluation: "The force of Christ's completed work, Webster judges, 'is simply lost' in this inflated talk of the church's redemptive activity" ("Ephesians 4:1–16: The Ascension, the Church, and the Spoils of War," in *Theological Commentary: Evangelical Perspectives*, ed. R. Michael Allen [London: T&T Clark, 2011], 147; cf. John Webster, *Word and Church* [Edinburgh: T&T Clark, 2001], 226).

our calling to a cross-shaped life. However, collapsing atonement into its outcomes risks losing the objectivity of our new-covenant status. The Reformers rightly insisted that justification is "forensic only" and "by faith alone"—vital points for them that protected the *extra nos*—"outside of us"—basis for our assurance. I suggest that we add to that list a means of atonement that is also "outside of us," a change not in us but in the objective, legal standing of sinners before a holy God. As will become clear, I think this general Reformation theology has solid biblical basis in Paul's teaching. Nevertheless, in the spirit of the Reformers themselves, who insisted that the church be "always reforming," I also want to balance the means of atonement with appropriate focus on its outcome as well. While distinguishing the means of atonement from its outcome, we must insist that the various outcomes—transformed people, transformed communities, transformed cosmos—arise inevitably from that initial atoning event.[8]

1 DIVINE INITIATIVE

1.1 Grace

One of Paul's most distinctive and fundamental theological words is "grace." Its prominence in Paul's teaching is due to at least two factors. First, grace is a fundamental character of God himself. This is revealed in the logic of Romans 4:4–5, among other texts. Justification, Paul argues here, cannot be based on works, because that would mean that God, like an employer honoring a contract, would be obliged to justify a person. Paul rules this scenario out because a God who is obligated to his creatures would not be a God of grace. This text reveals that Paul's view of grace has to do especially with God's "wholly other" character. His unique sovereign relationship to the cosmos means that what he does is always a matter of his own free decision. Strikingly, Paul does not here, or anywhere else, argue for grace as a constituent aspect of God—he assumes it, as a kind of theological postulate (for a similar argument, see Rom 11:6). A second reason why Paul features grace so significantly in his teaching is personal. He himself, the violent persecutor of the church who had become a servant of God and an apostle, had radically experienced grace in his own life. "The grace of our Lord was poured out on me abundantly" (1 Tim 1:14; see also Rom 1:5; 12:3; 15:15; 1 Cor 3:10; 15:10; 2 Cor 12:9; Gal 1:15; 2:9; Eph 3:2, 8).

The grace Paul personally experienced is manifested in the events that inaugurate the new realm. Romans 5:6–8 is a classic expression of this point:

---

8. Robert W. Yarbrough's definition captures both sides of atonement in their relation to each other: "God's work on sinners' behalf to reconcile them to himself. It is the divine activity that confronts and resolves the problem of human sin so that people may enjoy full fellowship with God both now and in the age to come" ("Atonement," in Alexander and Rosner, *New Dictionary of Biblical Theology*, 388).

You see, at just the right time, when we were still powerless, Christ died for the ungodly. Very rarely will anyone die for a righteous person, though for a good person someone might possibly dare to die. But God demonstrates his own love for us in this: While we were still sinners, Christ died for us. (See also Eph 1:4, 6; 2:4; 2 Thess 2:16; Titus 3:4)

So basic is grace to the inauguration of the new realm that Paul can use the word "grace" on its own to depict it: "The grace of God has appeared" (Titus 2:11). Romans 5:15–17 highlights the prominence of grace in both "moments" of the experience of the new realm. In contrast to Adam's trespass that inaugurated the old realm is the "grace and the gift that came by the grace of the one man, Jesus Christ" (v. 15). And it is those "who receive God's abundant provision of grace" who will "reign in life through the one man, Jesus Christ" (v. 17). Atonement, as Hans Boersma has emphasized, is the product of the "hospitality God, his welcoming love."[9] The famous long sentence that opens the body of Paul's letter to the Ephesians, 1:3–14, makes this point repeatedly. God predestines his people to adoption "in love" and in accordance with his "pleasure and will" (vv. 4–5); he freely gives his people "his glorious grace" (v. 6); our redemption, secured through Christ's death, is "in accordance with the riches of God's grace" (v. 7), he reveals the mystery of his will "according to his good pleasure" (v. 9); he predestines us "according to the plan of him who works out everything in conformity with the purpose of his will" (v. 11). At the same time, this great "run-on" sentence highlights the supremacy of God at the other end of his redemptive work. As he initiates his new-realm work by his own decision and will, so that new-realm work has as its ultimate purpose to bring glory to God (vv. 12, 14). God's grace is the motivating cause of the inauguration of the new realm, and his glory is its goal.[10]

1.2 The Faithfulness of Christ[11]
1.2.1 "Active Self-Offering"

As we will see, Christ's sacrificial death on the cross is the heart of the events that inaugurated the new realm. Yet focusing too exclusively on this point can give the impression that Christ's role in inaugurating the new realm is essentially passive—he is the victim whom God sends to the cross. In particularly unfortunate caricatures of this view, the notion of a violent God inflicting punishment unfairly and arbitrarily

---

9. Hans Boersma, *Violence, Hospitality, and the Cross: Reappropriating the Atonement Tradition* (Grand Rapids: Baker, 2004).

10. The "spiritual blessings" that this passage celebrates focus on the believer's appropriation of the new realm; but there is clearly significant overlap with the "moment" of inauguration.

11. As Cole notes, "faithfulness" is an appropriate "umbrella" term for this concept, including within it, e.g., obedience (Graham A. Cole, *Christ the Peacemaker: How Atonement Brings Shalom*, NSBT 25 [Downers Grove, IL: InterVarsity Press, 2009], 103–19).

on the Son is read into Paul or into the tradition. This way of thinking about Paul's teaching must be resisted and corrected.

While it is no doubt true that the center of gravity in Paul's atonement teaching is Christ's sacrifice on the cross, that sacrifice, Paul makes clear, is made willingly by Christ. The divine love that motivates the work of atonement is ultimately triune, as Paul hints at by including Christ's own love in the work of atonement (Gal 2:20; Eph 5:2, 25; cf. Rom 8:35, 39).

This point emerges especially in Paul's focus on Christ's obedience. In the famous Philippians 2 christological hymn, Paul describes the "mindset" of Christ that believers are to imitate, a mindset of humility that, in Christ's case, was manifested in "becoming obedient to death—even death on a cross" (Phil 2:8). Romans 5 makes the same point, contrasting the "disobedience" of Adam with the "obedience" of Christ (v. 19). Many interpreters think this obedience in Romans 5 refers only to what is often labeled "passive obedience": Christ's submission to the Father's will in succumbing to the cross. This interpretation is buttressed by the parallel contrast in verse 18 between the "one trespass" (or "trespass of the one") and the "one righteous act" (or "the righteous act of the one"). However, it is also possible that the obedience of Christ here encompasses his entire life of obedience that culminated in his willingness to bear the cross—what Michael Horton calls "*active* self-offering."[12] In chapter 20, I will pursue further this matter of Christ's obedience in terms of its role in securing the believer's justification.

1.2.2 "The Faith of Christ"

Considerably more focus on Christ's active role in the inauguration of the new realm would be present in Paul if his references to "the faith of Christ" are interpreted to mean "Christ's faith/faithfulness." Indeed, one of the reasons many contemporary interpreters are attracted to this view is just for this reason. The combination of "faith" with various forms of the name of Christ in the genitive has generated a great deal of discussion and debate in the last thirty years.[13] This phrase (that is, the noun *pistis* followed by the name of Christ [or some combination of Christ's names] in the genitive), occurs four times in Galatians (2:16 [2x], 20; 3:22), twice in Romans (3:22 and 26), once in Ephesians (3:12), and once in Philippians (3:9).[14] A rather neutral English scan of the phrase would

---

12. Michael S. Horton, *Lord and Servant: A Covenant Christology* (Louisville: Westminster John Knox, 2005), 223 (emphasis original); Richard N. Longenecker, "The Obedience of Christ in the Theology of the Early Church," in *Reconciliation and Hope: New Testament Essays on Atonement and Eschatology Presented to L. L. Morris on his 60th Birthday*, ed. Robert Banks (Grand Rapids: Eerdmans, 1974), 145. I disagree here with my earlier view (*A Commentary on the Letter to the Romans*, 1st ed., NICNT [Grand Rapids: Eerdmans, 1996], 344).

13. A thorough analysis of the issue and of the arguments on both sides is found in Michael F. Bird and Preston M. Sprinkle, eds., *The Faith of Jesus Christ: Exegetical, Biblical, and Theological Studies* (Peabody, MA: Hendrickson, 2009).

14. Several texts outside the Pauline letters have the same, or a similar, construction (Acts 3:16; Jas 2:1; Rev 2:13; 14:12; note also the phrase "faith of God" [Mark 11:22; Rom 3:3]).

be "[Jesus] Christ faith," and the obvious question is how exactly "Christ" qualifies "faith." When we add to this syntactical uncertainty the lexical uncertainty about the meaning of *pistis*—"faith" or "faithfulness," it is claimed, are both options—the situation becomes quite complicated.[15] The traditional view, reflected in most English translations, is that the genitive in these phrases is objective, yielding the sense "faith in Jesus Christ." However, a view that has grown quickly in popularity over the last decades is that the genitive is subjective: "the faith/faithfulness exercised by Christ" (see NET and CEB).[16] Advocates of this view note how this interpretation would result in an attractive balance between the divine and human elements in God's salvific work: it is achieved by means of Christ's own faithfulness and appropriated by human believing ("for all who believe"). A powerful impetus to this way of reading the phrase is the claim that in some of the texts where the phrase occurs, Paul's argument is undergirded by the story of Christ.[17] Within this narrative and participatory framework, "faith" is not so much believing "in" Christ as it is believing "with" Christ, sharing with Christ the kind of faith in God that Abraham also exhibited. "Faith of [Jesus] Christ" then most naturally refers to Christ's own faith. This participatory focus has been picked up and extended to Paul's theology in general by many others in recent years, and it is this larger theological perspective that has given the greatest impetus to the "faith of Christ" interpretation.

Proponents of "the faith/faithfulness of Christ" also argue that it fits better than the alternative the contexts in which it occurs. In Romans 3:21–22, for instance, Paul claims that God has revealed his righteousness "through Christ faith" and "for everyone who believes."

A reference here to Christ's faithfulness would avoid the tautology of Paul referring twice to human faith. The same argument pertains to Galatians 3:22, with the additional point that Paul here refers to this faith as "coming" when Christ was manifested

15. As R. Barry Matlock notes, *pistis* has two basic meanings relevant to this context: "believing, trusting, having faith," on the one hand, and "being trustworthy, dependable, reliable," on the other ("Saving Faith: The Rhetoric and Semantics of πίστις in Paul," in Bird and Sprinkle, *Faith of Jesus Christ*, 74).

16. As I note earlier (pp. 379–82), Longenecker's defense of the subjective-genitive reading in his Romans commentary is particularly good (*Romans*, 408–13). See also Luke Timothy Johnson, "Rom 3:21–26 and the Faith of Jesus," *CBQ* 44 (1982): 77–90; Campbell, *Deliverance*, 610–16; Richard B. Hays, "ΠΙΣΤΙΣ and Pauline Christology: What Is at Stake?," in *Society of Biblical Literature 1991 Seminar Papers*, ed. E. H. Lovering Jr. (Atlanta: Scholars Press, 1991), 714–29; Wallace, *Greek Grammar*, 114–16. See also the interchange between Richard Hays and James D. G. Dunn in the papers of the SBL Pauline Theology Seminar in 1991 mentioned above. While the subjective-genitive interpretation

has grown in popularity recently, it has a relatively long heritage; see, e.g., Thomas F. Torrance, "One Aspect of the Biblical Conception of Faith," *ExpTim* 68 (1956–1957): 111–14 (and the interchange between Torrance and C. F. D. Moule in the same volume, pp. 221–22); Richard N. Longenecker, *Paul, Apostle of Liberty* (repr., Grand Rapids: Eerdmans, 2015), 136–38; G. E. Howard, "'The Faith of Christ,'" *ExpTim* 85 (1973–74): 212–14; D. W. B. Robinson, "'Faith of Jesus Christ'—A New Testament Debate," *RTR* 29 (1970): 71–81. "Christ's faithfulness" is usually attached to his death for us; but, recently, David J. Downs and Benjamin J. Lappenga have argued that the reference might be also, or even primarily, to the risen work of Christ (*The Faithfulness of the Risen Christ: Pistis and the Exalted Lord in the Pauline Letters* [Waco, TX: Baylor University Press, 2019]).

17. See esp. Richard B. Hays's influential monograph on Galatians, *The Faith of Jesus Christ*.

(v. 23).[18] Finally, it is also argued that a subjective-genitive interpretation is the more natural reading of the grammar.[19]

I readily acknowledge that the subjective-genitive interpretation has much to be said for it. It is also important to stress that an objective or subjective genitive are not the only options. We could also understand the relationship in a less defined sense, Paul simply associating faith with Christ in an unspecified way.[20] Nevertheless, I think the objective-genitive understanding of the phrase makes better sense. Many of the lexical, syntactical, historical, and contextual arguments end up in a standoff.[21] What I think is the decisive point is the comparison between the noun + genitive construction that we find here and the constructions using the cognate verb, for in the case of the verb, all uncertainty disappears. Nouns are always clearly subjects or objects. In the case of "faith" language in Paul, then, the situation is fairly clear. Paul often makes believers the subject of the verb "believe" (*pisteuō*), but he never clearly makes Christ the subject of the verb.[22] In Paul, Christians "believe"; but Christ does not (at the linguistic level, of course).[23] This semantic pattern should determine how we should interpret the ambiguous genitive in this construction here and elsewhere.[24] I also think that the relationship in both Romans 3 and Galatians 3 between this "Christ faith" and the faith of Abraham supports an objective-genitive view.

18. For a good summary of the theological appropriateness of this interpretation in Galatians, see Ardel B. Caneday, "The Faithfulness of Jesus Christ as a Theme in Paul's Theology in Galatians," in Bird and Sprinkle, *Faith of Jesus Christ*, 185–205.

19. They note that in cases where *pistis* is followed by the genitive of a noun denoting a person (or persons), the genitive is usually subjective or possessive. For example, *pistis Abraam* in Rom 4:16 (see also 4:12) means "the faith exercised *by* Abraham"; an objective genitive, "faith in Abraham," is obviously impossible. This subjective rendering of the genitive when it follows *pistis* is, it is argued, typical in Greek, and makes it *a priori* likely that *Iēsou Christou* is also a subjective genitive.

20. See esp. Ulrichs, *Christusglaube*; and also Sam K. Williams, "Again *Pistis Christou*," *CBQ* 49 (1987): 431–47; Dennis R. Lindsay, "Works of Law, Hearing of Faith and *Pistis Christou* in Galatians 2:16–3:5," *Stone-Campbell Journal* 3 (2000): 79–88; Benjamin Schliesser, *Abraham's Faith in Romans 4: Paul's Concept of Faith in Light of the History of Reception of Genesis 15:6*, WUNT 2/224 (Tübingen, Mohr Siebeck, 2007), 257–80; Preston M. Sprinkle, "*Pistis Christou* as Eschatological Event," in Bird and Sprinkle, *Faith of Jesus Christ*, 165–84.

21. Thus, for instance, in response to the semantic argument for the subjective genitive (see above), it should be noted that a genitive following *pistis* certainly need not be subjective. Most such genitives in the NT are, indeed, possessive or subjective, usually employing the personal pronoun (e.g., Rom 1:8: *hē pistis hymōn*, "your faith"). One is objective (Mark 11:22); three others,

though debated, are also probably objective (Jas 2:1; Rev 2:13; 14:12), while only a few are purely subjective (Rom 3:3; 4:12, 16). Only context, then, can determine the force of the genitive. Many early Greek interpreters of Paul interpreted the genitive as objective (see esp. Mark W. Elliott, "Πίστις Χριστοῦ in the Church Fathers and Beyond," in Bird and Sprinkle, *Faith of Jesus Christ*, 277–89; see also I. G. Wallis, *The Faith of Jesus Christ in Early Christian Traditions*, SNTSMS 84 [Cambridge: Cambridge University Press, 1995], who recognizes more diversity in the early witnesses).

22. To be sure, Campbell (*Deliverance*, 914–24) has argued that the subject of *episteusa* ("I believed") in 2 Cor 4:13 (quoting Ps 116:10) is Christ—but this is, I think, unlikely.

23. R. Michael Allen has argued that the notion of Christ's faith is dogmatically necessary in terms of a proper understanding of redemption (*The Christ's Faith: A Dogmatic Account*, T&T Clark Studies in Systematic Theology [London: Bloomsbury T&T Clark, 2009]; idem, "'From the Time He Took on the Form of a Servant': The Christ's Pilgrimage of Faith," *International Journal of Systematic Theology* 16 [2014]: 4–24).

24. For these points and others, see esp. Moo, *Galatians*, 38–48. And see esp. Kevin W. McFadden, *Faith in the Son of God: Christ-Oriented Faith in Pauline Theology* (Wheaton, IL: Crossway, 2020). His defense of the "objective genitive" view, at this point the best available, adds a number of other linguistic and theological arguments.

Two common objections to the objective-genitive view are theological and contextual. Some argue that a focus on human faith detracts from a robustly christological element in salvation. But this misses the fact that the faith involved is faith *in Christ*. Paul's faith takes its significance and power from its object, Christ; *sola fide* and *solus Christus* are two sides of the same theological coin.[25] The contextual argument, as I noted above, is that it would be odd for Paul to refer to human faith twice in the same context (Rom 3:22; Gal 3:22). However, there could be good reason for Paul to do so. In Romans 3, Paul makes two closely related points: God's righteousness is available *only* through faith in Christ—"faith in Christ"—and it is available to *anyone* who has faith in Christ—"to all who believe." An explanation for the repetition in Galatians 3:22 is admittedly harder to discover. Yet it is important to consider the wider context of this verse. Central to Paul's argument in this part of the letter is the faith of Abraham (3:6–9). The discussion of Abraham's faith in this paragraph is a janus, pointing both backward and forward. The "hearing of faith" (my translation) of 3:2 and 5 is compared to the faith of Abraham. And the reference to being blessed along with "Abraham, the man of faith" in verse 9 connects with the claim in verse 14 that the "blessing given to Abraham," related in some way to the promised Spirit, is given through faith. "Faith," then, in this crucial middle part of Paul's argument, is unarguably human faith. This, however, makes it unlikely that "faith" has any other significance in Galatians 3:22, which continues this theme.[26] It is likely, then, that Paul repeats "faith" in 3:22 simply to emphasize its importance.

It is important to keep this argument about the phrase "Christ faith" in perspective. While a subjective-genitive interpretation adds to texts in which Paul stresses the active role of Christ in inaugurating the new realm, this theologically important point is clear enough without those texts. Following Jesus himself, who taught that he lays down his life "of my own accord" (John 10:17–18), and the author to the Hebrews, who contrasts Christ's willing sacrifice with old-covenant sacrifices (Heb 10:5–11), Paul locates the initiative for salvation in Christ as well as in God the Father.

2 INITIATING EVENTS OF THE NEW REALM

Our focus is on the founding events of the new realm—God's acting in and through his Son, particularly in his death and resurrection. These events constitute for Paul the heart of the "good news," as the famous summary in 1 Corinthians 15:1–8 makes clear:

---

25. See, e.g., Linebaugh, *God, Grace, and Righteousness,* 157–60; Barclay, *Paul and the Gift,* 379–82. On the other side of the matter, there is concern that, as Dunn has put it, a focus on "Christ's faith/faithfulness" might detract from a key focus in Paul's thought on human believing (James D. G. Dunn, "New Perspective View," in *Justification: Five Views,* ed. James K. Beilby and Paul Rhodes Eddy [Downers Grove, IL: InterVarsity Press, 2011], 197).

26. See esp. James D. G. Dunn, "*Ek Pisteos*: A Key to the Meaning of *Pistis Christou,*" in Wagner, Rowe, and Grieb, *Word Leaps the Gap,* 361–65; Ulrichs, *Christusglaube,* 140–48; Debbie Hunn, "*Pistis Christou* in Galatians 2:16: Clarification from 3:1–6," *TynBul* 57 (2006): 30–33.

Now, brothers and sisters, I want to remind you of the gospel I preached to you, which you received and on which you have taken your stand. By this gospel you are saved, if you hold firmly to the word I preached to you. Otherwise, you have believed in vain.

For what I received I passed on to you as of first importance: that Christ died for our sins according to the Scriptures, that he was buried, that he was raised on the third day according to the Scriptures, and that he appeared to Cephas, and then to the Twelve. After that, he appeared to more than five hundred of the brothers and sisters at the same time, most of whom are still living, though some have fallen asleep. Then he appeared to James, then to all the apostles, and last of all he appeared to me also, as to one abnormally born.

Paul's concern in this context, as the elaboration in verses 5–8 suggests, is with the third point in this summary: "He was raised." But he sets this point in the broader context of the essential elements of the gospel he preaches: Jesus died, was buried,[27] was raised, and (proving this resurrection) "appeared" to many. The language Paul uses to introduce this passage makes clear that he is citing tradition. What he "passes on" (*paradidōmi*) to the Corinthians is something he himself has "received" (*paralambanō*, v. 3; cf. v. 1). It is entirely to be expected that the earliest Christians would have needed to grapple with the significance of these redemptive events. Why did the Messiah have to die? What does the resurrection accomplish? Peter's speech in Acts 2 reveals one early attempt to answer these questions—and, of course, Jesus himself addressed this issue in his own teaching. Paul assures the Corinthians that his teaching is located within this developing Christian tradition. Paul undoubtedly contributes significantly to this tradition. But we should not forget that he is not creating theology on this point but developing and extending a theology that was already in place.

Paul's brief outline of the "gospel I preach" focuses on the end of Jesus's life. The history of theologizing about the atoning value of Jesus's work has, of course, followed suit, with Jesus's death on the cross as the focus of attention. However, we should begin by noting that Paul can attribute soteriological significance in general to the entire "Christ event." In Ephesians 3:11, he refers to "his [God's] eternal purpose that he accomplished in Christ Jesus our Lord." In 2 Timothy 1:9–10, he refers to the "appearing of our Savior, Christ Jesus, who has destroyed death and has brought life and immortality to light through the gospel." And when Paul becomes more specific about this "in Christ," he mentions eight different "moments" in the story of Christ that have some kind of soteriological value (compare this list with the one on pp. 356–62).

---

27. Paul does not ascribe any soteriological value to Jesus's burial *per se*. Paul probably includes it here, and in Rom 6:3–4 and Col 2:11–15, to attest to the reality of Christ's death.

Preexistence. See Ephesians 1:4: "For he chose us in him before the creation of the world to be holy and blameless in his sight."

Incarnation. See, for example, 2 Corinthians 8:9: "For you know the grace of our Lord Jesus Christ, that though he was rich, yet for your sake he became poor, so that you through his poverty might become rich." See also Romans 8:3; Galatians 4:4.

Life. As I noted above, it is possible, maybe probable, that Paul's references to Jesus's obedience (Rom 5:19; Phil 2:8) at least include Jesus's life of faithful submission to the will of his Father, culminating at the cross.

Death. Paul refers to Jesus's death in several ways: cross/crucify; blood; "flesh" (Eph 2:15; see cross in v. 16; cf. also Col 1:22); "handed over" (Rom 4:25; 8:32; Gal 2:20; Eph 5:2, 25 [note 2 Cor 4:11, referring to Paul: "given over to death" {*eis thanaton paradidometha*}]; cf. also "gave himself" in Gal 1:4). References to Jesus's sufferings probably focus mainly on Jesus's death, but may include his "passion" more generally (2 Cor 1:5).

Burial. Christ's burial is one of the elements of the gospel Paul passes on to the Corinthians (1 Cor 15:4); and in Romans 6:4 and Colossians 2:12, he implies that believers benefit from their identification with Christ in his baptism.

Resurrection. See Romans 4:25; 5:10; 7:4; 14:9; 2 Corinthians 4:10–11; 5:15; 13:4; 1 Thessalonians 1:10.

Ascension/Exaltation. See Romans 8:34; Ephesians 4:8; see also 1 Corinthians 1:8; Philippians 1:6.[28]

Coming Again in Glory. See, for example, Philippians 3:20–21; 1 Thessalonians 1:10; 4:16–17.

This list should not deceive us into thinking that Paul is always interested in investing one moment above others with particular significance. These various moments are finally all of one piece, and we should be wary of too neatly distinguishing them. For instance, being "handed over," which we have included above under Christ's death, may include or at least imply his being "sent" into this world and the life of obedience that eventuated in the cross.[29]

I earlier noted that scholars in recent years have criticized traditional atonement theories for being too narrow, in the sense that they have been preoccupied with the

---

28. It is doubtful that Paul distinguishes ascension, exaltation, and session. Through his resurrection, Christ ascends (Eph 4:8) to the highest position, at God's right hand (Rom 8:34; Eph 1:20; Col 3:1). Exaltation therefore is distinguished from resurrection in Paul. As Brannon puts it, "Christ's resurrection proclaims that he lives forever, and his exaltation or enthronement proclaims that he reigns forever" (*Heavenlies in Ephesians*, 121).

29. Günter Röhser, e.g., argues that "giving over" or "handing over" language in Paul refers to Christ's whole existence, not only his death (*Stellvertretung im Neuen Testament*, SBS 195 [Stuttgart: Katholisches, 2002], 95–120).

means of redemption at the expense of the outcome of redemption. Scholars have criticized traditional views for being too narrow in another sense as well: for focusing too exclusively on Christ's death while inappropriately minimizing other aspects of Christ's redemptive work, such as his life, his resurrection, and his exaltation.[30] Certainly, when considering the New Testament as a whole, this criticism may to some extent be justified. The Gospel of John attributes redemptive significance to the great sweep of Christ's coming to earth and being "lifted up" on the cross. The letter to the Hebrews, as has recently been emphasized, highlights the atoning significance of Christ's ascent to and ministry in the heavenly tabernacle.[31] And, while the Gospels clearly present the death of Christ as the culmination of his work, we should not neglect the theological significance of his life and teaching.[32]

However, the claim that we have focused too much attention on Jesus's death has less force when we focus on Paul's letters. Particularly is this so when we zoom in on the issue we are concerned with in this chapter, the inauguration of the new realm. For many of the soteriological benefits associated with various aspects of Christ's life have to do more with the believer's entry into the new realm or ultimate salvation within that realm than with God's inauguration of that realm in Christ. We are reminded here again of the difficulty of neatly separating the work of God in Christ in inaugurating the new realm and our appropriation of that work as we enter that realm. However, if we ask which events Paul cites in the life of Christ as the basis for bringing people into God's new realm, his focus on Christ's death emerges clearly. Paul never explicitly cites Jesus's earthly life as having soteriological value, although, as we have seen, references to Christ's obedience in Romans 5:19 and Philippians 2:8 might include Jesus's life.[33] Paul ties the inauguration of the new realm to Jesus's incarnation once (2 Cor 8:9; cf. Gal 4:4?), to Jesus's resurrection five times (Rom 1:4[?]; 4:25; 5:10; Eph 1:19–23; Col 2:12), and to Jesus's death twenty-eight times. The implication of these statistics is confirmed by explicit references. In the 1 Corinthians 15 text quoted above, for instance, it is only Jesus's death that Paul claims is "for our sins" (1 Cor 15:3). Paul elsewhere summarizes his message in terms of the "message of the cross" (1 Cor 1:18; see also 1:17;

---

30. See, e.g., Peter J. Leithart (*Delivered from the Elements of the World: Atonement, Justification, Mission* [Grand Rapids: Baker, 2016]), who argues that the pattern of the Levitical sacrifices, whose efficacy is based on several distinct "moments," and not on death alone, is reason to think Christ's atoning work likewise includes his life, death, resurrection, and ascension (e.g., 115).

31. See esp. David Moffit, *Atonement and the Logic of Resurrection in the Epistle to the Hebrews*, SupNovT 14 (Leiden: Brill, 2011).

32. For criticism of the tendency to ignore Jesus's life in atonement discussions, see, e.g., N. T. Wright, *The Day the Revolution Began: Reconsidering the Meaning of Jesus' Crucifixion* (New York:

HarperOne, 2016), 170–73, 195–200; Leithart, *Delivered from the Elements of the World*, 115, passim.

33. On one reading of 2 Cor 5:19, God's reconciling activity is the product of his "being in Christ"—probably a reference to the entire life of Christ (Harris, *Second Epistle to the Corinthians*, 442–43). This conclusion assumes the very debated point that the syntax of the verse consists of an independent clause—"God was in Christ"—followed by an adverbial participle—"reconciling the world" (NLT)—rather than a periphrastic construction—"God was reconciling the world to himself in Christ" (NIV; see also ESV; NRSV; CEB; CSB).

Gal 3:1; 6:14; Eph 2:16; Phil 3:18; Col 1:20; 2:14). Of course, there are clear rhetorical reasons for this focus on the cross in some contexts, where Paul is countering a spirit of triumphalism with a reminder of the believer's cruciform existence. And not all these references are connected directly to soteriology. But the focus remains clear enough. Paul's focus is clearly and unarguably on the cross as the decisive event in securing salvation for the people of God, and any atonement theory that lays claim to Paul's witness must account for that focus.

Before moving on to probe the significance of Jesus's death for Paul, I briefly comment on the significance of resurrection for our subject. In general, Paul's references to Christ's resurrection take on seven patterns. Christ's resurrection:

1. is critical to faith (Rom 10:9; 1 Cor 15:14, 17; cf. 2 Tim 2:8–9);
2. is simply paired with death (Rom 4:25; 5:9–10; 6:3–10; 7:4; 8:17, 34; 14:9; 1 Cor 15:3–4; 2 Cor 4:10–12; 5:14–15; 1 Thess 4:14);
3. is contrasted with Jesus's earthly life (Rom 1:3–4; 1 Tim 3:16; 2 Tim 2:8–9);
4. leads to exaltation (Rom 8:34; Eph 1:20; 2:6–7);
5. guarantees the resurrection of believers (Rom 8:11; 1 Cor 6:14; 2 Cor 4:13–14; 1 Thess 4:14);
6. leads to new life and power for the Christian life (Rom 6:4; 7:4; Col 3:1);
7. and confers soteriological benefit (Rom 1:4[?]; 4:25; 5:10).

Several points in this list deserve comment. First, Paul's very common pairing of death and resurrection captures what is for him a fundamental pattern of Christ's life. On the one hand, this pattern provides a template for the lives of his followers, who by identifying with his death are assured of new life and who are called on to lead lives of humiliation, service, and even suffering in order to enjoy new life and ultimate resurrection life. See especially 2 Corinthians 4:10–12: "We always carry around in our body the death of Jesus, so that the life of Jesus may also be revealed in our body. For we who are alive are always being given over to death for Jesus's sake, so that his life may also be revealed in our mortal body. So then, death is at work in us, but life is at work in you." (See also, e.g., Rom 5:9; 8:17; 2 Cor 5:14–15; 13:4; Phil 3:10–11.)

At the same time, the two events in this pattern are often cited as the basis for benefits granted the believer, Christ's death providing the basis for initial entrance into the new realm, with his resurrection providing the basis for faithful living in that realm (see esp. Rom 5:10; 6:3–8; 7:4; 2 Tim 2:11–12). As believers participate in this life and are represented before God by this "living one," they find hope for ultimate vindication in the judgment of God. As we will see later, Paul's concept of justification includes not only a decisive moment of entrance into divine favor at conversion but also a final declaration of "being right with God" in the judgment to come. Christ's resurrected life is important as the means by which this final verdict will be confirmed.

Second, while this pattern might suggest we can neatly link the death of Christ to our entry into the new life and the resurrection to its ultimate confirmation, Paul's theology resists such a neat categorization. Death and resurrection are together fundamental for both aspects of our salvation. Romans 4:25 is especially important, since it claims that Jesus's resurrection contributes to our justification (taking the Gk. preposition *dia* here to mean "for the benefit of").[34] We could perhaps think that Paul is focusing here on the final aspect of justification, but this is unlikely in this context. Perhaps Paul is suggesting that, while Christ's death is the definitive moment of justification, the resurrection was also necessary as the moment when that "justification," in its more positive aspect—a new status of "rightness"—was secured.[35] We may helpfully here compare the (probably traditional) christological claim Paul makes in 1 Timothy 3:16: Christ "was vindicated [*edikaiōthē*, 'was justified'] by the Spirit."[36]

3 THE MEANING OF JESUS'S DEATH

Martin Hengel claims that Jesus's atoning death and resurrection is "the most frequent and most important confessional statement in the Pauline Epistles."[37] This observation is easily confirmed by even a cursory reading of Paul's letters. However, what is somewhat surprising is that, while Paul repeatedly stresses the central importance of Christ's death "for our sins" and his resurrection, he rarely comments directly on the way in which Christ's death and resurrection take care of the human sin problem. We may surmise that this was not an issue in the churches of Paul, and for that reason he had no need to address the matter in any detail.

However, while our evidence is not as abundant or as clearcut as we might like, Paul provides enough data for us to get a good general sense of how he views the significance of Christ's death.

3.1 "On Behalf of" Us/Our Sins

We begin at the most basic level with Paul's frequent claim that Christ died "on behalf of" believers.[38] He makes this point, using the preposition *hyper*, sixteen

---

34. On this text, see p. 215.

35. See, e.g., Horton, *Justification*, 2:257–80.

36. On the soteriological significance of the resurrection, see esp. Gaffin, *Resurrection and Redemption*, and also Marshall, *Aspects of the Atonement*, 68–97. I should note, however, that as the NIV translation "vindicated" suggests, it is also possible that Paul is using *dikaioō* in this verse with a meaning at least not directly related to the *doctrine* of justification.

37. Martin Hengel, *The Atonement: The Origins of the Doctrine in the New Testament* (Philadelphia: Fortress, 1981), 37; see also Simon Gathercole, *Defending Substitution: An Essay on Atonement in Paul* (Grand Rapids: Baker, 2015), 78.

38. Of course, Paul often more generally claims that Christ died for "all" (see esp. 2 Cor 5:14–15; 1 Tim 2:4–6; 4:10; Titus 2:11). Many theologians in the Reformed tradition, nevertheless, argue on logical and theological grounds that Christ effectively

times.[39] Most of the occurrences of the preposition in these texts have a personal object. Romans 5:8 is typical: "God demonstrates his own love for us in this: While we were still sinners, Christ died *for* us" (see also Rom 5:6; 14:15; 2 Cor 5:14, 15; 1 Thess 5:10). Similarly, Paul speaks of Christ being "crucified" for us (1 Cor 1:13), "giving" himself for us (using a form of *paradidōmi*: Rom 8:32; Gal 2:20; Eph 5:2, 25; using *didōmi*: 1 Tim 2:6; Titus 2:14), being made sin for us (2 Cor 5:21), and becoming a curse for us (Gal 3:13). In a departure from normal Greek usage, Paul also speaks of Christ dying (1 Cor 15:3) or "giving himself" "for our sins" (Gal 1:4).[40] Paul's use of both these formulas makes clear that Christ dying "for us" has atoning significance. It is by dealing with our sins that Christ's death benefits us.[41] In dying, Christ takes on himself "the consequences of our sins."[42]

3.2 The Old Testament

If we probe just how Christ's death is "on our behalf," we naturally turn to the Old Testament, which has such a formative influence on Paul's theology. And, indeed, in 1 Corinthians 15:1–8 Paul claims that Christ's death "for our sins" was "according to the Scriptures"—*kata tas graphas* (v. 3). It is probable that this phrase modifies both parts of the previous sentence. It is not only Christ's death that is "according to the Scriptures" but Christ's death for sins.[43] It is unclear just which Old Testament texts Paul might have in view here. Nor does it help to look at Paul's teaching elsewhere. Somewhat surprisingly, he never explicitly cites an Old Testament text to illuminate or explain the death of Christ for us. Most interpreters, however, rightly consider that the figure of the Servant in the fourth "Servant Song" (Isa 52:13–53:12) is a key Old Testament source for Paul's thinking about Jesus's death—and in 1 Corinthians 15:3 also.[44] As is well known, the Servant in Isaiah 53 suffers and is "handed over" (in the LXX) to death because of the sins of the people. See especially:

died only for (or atoned only for) the elect (see, e.g., Jarvis J. Williams, *For Whom Did Christ Die? The Extent of the Atonement in Paul's Theology*, Paternoster Biblical Monographs [Milton Keynes: Paternoster, 2012]; Jonathan Gibson, "The Glorious, Indivisible, Trinitarian Work of God in Christ: Definite Atonement in Paul's Theology of Salvation," in Gibson and Gibson, *From Heaven He Came and Sought Her*, 331–74). I respect this tradition and admit that some of the arguments for it are strong. Nevertheless, I am not convinced that this view can adequately explain some of these universal texts. For a useful discussion of various views, see Adam J. Johnson, ed., *Five Views on the Extent of the Atonement* (Grand Rapids: Zondervan, 2019).

39. Martin Gaukesbrink, *Die Sühnetradition bei Paulus: Rezeption und theologischer Stellenwert*, FB 32 (Würzburg: Echter, 1999), 261.

40. See Reimund Bieringer, "Dying and Being Raised For: Shifts in the Meaning of *Hyper* in 2 Cor 5:14–15," in *Theologizing in the Corinthian Conflict: Studies in the Exegesis and Theology of 2 Corinthians*, ed. M. S. Ibita, D. Kurek-Chomycz, R. Bieringer, and T. Vollmer (Leuven: Peeters, 2013), 167.

41. Contra Cilliers Breytenbach, "'Christus Starb für Uns': Zur Tradition und Paulinischen Rezeption der sogenannten 'Sterbeformeln,'" *NTS* 49 (2003): 447–75.

42. Simon J. Gathercole, "The Cross and Substitutionary Atonement," *Scottish Bulletin of Evangelical Theology* 21 (2003): 160–61; see also Bieringer ("Dying and Being Raised," 167): "For the removal of sins."

43. Schrage, *Der erste Brief an die Korinther*, 4:34.

44. Gathercole (*Defending Substitution*, 64–68) particularly clearly documents the connections between Isa 53 and 1 Cor 15.

V. 5a: "He was pierced for our transgressions, he was crushed for our iniquities";
LXX: "But he was wounded because of our acts of lawlessness and has been
weakened because of our sins [*dia tas hamartias hēmōn*]" (NETS);

V. 8b: "For the transgression of my people he was punished"; LXX: "He was led
to death on account of the acts of lawlessness of my people" (NETS);

V. 12 LXX: "Because his soul was given over to death, and he was reckoned
among the lawless, and he bore the sins of many [*dia tas hamartias autōn
paredothē*]" (NETS).[45]

This is the only passage in the Old Testament in which someone's death is pictured
as "for" or "in place of" others. The general profile of this Servant figure, as one who
dies because of and for the sake of the sins of the people, provides an obvious source for
Paul's elaboration of the meaning of Jesus's death—a connection that had already been
forged in the Christian tradition, going back to Jesus himself, to which Paul alludes
in this context.[46] But there is no reason to think that Isaiah 53 is the only part of the
"Scriptures" that Paul has in view here. The tradition before him, for instance, used
psalms that describe the suffering and vindication of a "righteous person" (often David
himself) to characterize Jesus's death (e.g., Pss 22; 69).[47] The fact that Paul puts words
from one of these psalms on the lips of Jesus in Romans 15:3 (Ps 69:9b) makes clear that
he was familiar with this tradition. Another important Old Testament source for Paul's
interpretation of Jesus's death is the Old Testament sacrificial system. The "Scriptures"
Paul cites in 1 Corinthians 15:3 probably include reference to this tradition. And we must
remember that these passages and concepts do not exist in watertight compartments.
The sin-bearing work of the servant of Isaiah 53 is interpreted in sacrificial terms: "The
LORD makes his life an offering for sin [Heb. *'asham*; LXX *peri hamartias*]" (v. 10). While
it is debated, Paul's use of this same phrase in Romans 8:3 is probably a further allusion
to this sacrifice (see NIV; NLT; NJB; CSB).[48] This "sin offering," also called a "guilt
offering" (most English versions) or a "reparation offering" (NAB; cf. NJB) is prescribed
in Leviticus 5:14–6:7. "Reparation" is argued to be the better rendering because the text
emphasizes that the sin involves a "direct offence against the Lord."[49] The slaughter
and offering of the animal "makes atonement" (Lev 6:7). However, the background for

---

45. Two other passages in Paul may allude to the Servant
figure in connection with Jesus's death: Rom 4:25—"he was delivered over to death for our sins" (*hos paredothē dia ta paraptōmata
hēmōn*); cf. Isa 53:12 (cited above); and Rom 5:19b—"through the
obedience of the one man the many will be made righteous"; cf.
Isa 53:11b: "By his knowledge my righteous servant will justify
many" (see Moo, *Romans* [NICNT], 288, 345).

46. For the view that Isaiah 53 was important in Jesus's own
description of his death, see Moo, *Old Testament*, 79–172.

47. See, again, Moo, *Old Testament*, 225–300.

48. Moo, *Romans* (NICNT), 480.

49. See, e.g., Nobuyoshi Kiuchi, *Leviticus*, AOTC (Downers Grove, IL: InterVarsity Press, 2007), 110–19 (116). Jay Sklar
sees the betrayal of covenant loyalty to be the fundamental issue
with which this sacrifice deals (*Leviticus: An Introduction and
Commentary*, TOTC [Downers Grove, IL: InterVarsity Press,
2014], 118–19).

Paul's sacrificial language should not be confined to one sacrifice. He also compares Christ to "the Passover lamb" (1 Cor 5:7), and as I will argue below, he also refers to the Day of Atonement ritual in Leviticus 16 in Romans 3:25. And the words of institution that Paul quotes in 1 Corinthians 11:24, 25—"this is my body, which is for [*hyper*] you" and "this cup is the new covenant in my blood"—are ultimately allusions to the covenant-inaugurating sacrifice of Exodus 24:8 and, probably, the Passover Lamb also. Finally, Paul also alludes to the Genesis 22 story about Abraham's "sacrifice" of Isaac in Romans 8:32. Compare the first part of this verse—"he who did not spare his own Son, but gave him up for us all" (*hos ge tou idiou huiou ouk epheisato all' hyper hēmōn pantōn paredōken auton*)—with Genesis 22:12: "You have not withheld from me your son, your only son" (LXX: *ouk epheisō tou huiou sou tou agapētou*).

Of course, Paul also ties God's redemptive work in Jesus into the larger biblical story. He utilizes two levels in this story to interpret the work of Christ: the broad human story in which Adam and Christ function as representative heads of humanity, and the story of Israel, with a particular focus on the plight created by her sin and idolatry and the anticipated rescue from that plight in a fresh and spectacular work of God.

While, as so often is the case, the Old Testament and Jewish teaching provide the key background for Paul's theologizing, we should not neglect the larger Greco-Roman world, where the idea of giving one's life for another was fairly widespread. Recent discussion of Jesus's vicarious death has drawn attention, for instance, to the Greek "heroic death" motif, which features a person dying in order to avert a catastrophe.[50]

3.3 Sacrifice and Substitution

The means by which God inaugurates the new realm is the whole work of Christ, but, as we have seen, with particular focus on his death. Paul uses Old Testament texts, concepts, and broad themes to illuminate the meaning of that death—a death that he clearly presents as vicarious—"for us." But that "for us" remains undefined. What does Paul say about *how* that death benefits us? Answering this question is complicated by a matter I raised earlier. Paul does not always distinguish between the inauguration of the new realm in salvation history and the entrance into that realm on the part of individual humans. And the issue is complicated by a further factor I discussed briefly

---

50. A notable example of this tradition is the story of Alcestis, who, in the play of that name by Euripides, gives herself to death in place of her husband Admetus. See, on this tradition, esp. Christina Eschner, *Gestorben und Hingegeben "für" die Sünder: Die griechische Konzeption des Unheil abwendenden Sterbens und deren Paulinische Aufnahme für die Deutung des Todes Jesu Christi*, 2 vols., WMANT 122 (Neukirchen-Vluyn: Neukirchener, 2010). The focus on the Greek world as an explanation of Paul's "on behalf of" (*hyper*) language is found also in Hengel, *Atonement*, 4–32. See also Gathercole, *Defending Substitution*, 85–107 (with particular focus on Rom 5:6–8); Wolter, *Paul*, 101–2.

above: whether we focus on the mechanism, or means, by which Christ's death benefits us or on the benefits themselves (the "outcomes"). I will return to the implications of this distinction below. For now, however, my interest is in probing Paul's teaching about the means by which Jesus's death benefits sinful humans.

Paul describes Christ's death and its benefits in several different ways, and it will be important not to fall prey to a reductionism that minimizes the richness of Paul's teaching. However, I argue that central to Paul's construal of Christ's death is sacrifice. To be sure, the place of sacrificial notions in Paul's interpretation of Christ's death is debated, a number of scholars expressing doubt about their significance for Paul.[51] But the evidence for sacrifice as a key interpretive grid for Paul's view of Jesus's death is compelling.[52] I sketched the picture of sacrifice in Paul briefly above as I looked at the Old Testament roots of his teaching. I need now to fill out that picture.

3.3.1 Sacrifice

I begin by setting forth here those texts I mentioned earlier in which Paul explicitly describes Jesus's death on the cross as a sacrifice. There are, in fact, only five (and three of these are debated):

> Eph 5:1–2: "Follow God's example, therefore, as dearly loved children and walk in the way of love, just as Christ loved us and gave himself up for us as **a fragrant offering and sacrifice** [*prosphoron kai thysian*] to God."
>
> 1 Cor 5:7: "Christ, **our Passover lamb**, has been sacrificed."
>
> Rom 3:24–25: "All are justified freely by his grace through the redemption that came by Christ Jesus. God presented Christ as **a sacrifice of atonement** [*hilastērion*] through the shedding of his blood—to be received by faith."[53]
>
> Rom 8:3: "God . . . [sent] his own Son in the likeness of sinful flesh to be a **sin offering** [*peri hamartias*]."[54]
>
> 2 Cor 5:21: "God made him who had no sin to be sin [NIV fn: **sin offering**] for us, so that in him we might become the righteousness of God."[55]

---

51. E.g., Ernst Käsemann, "Die Heilsbedeutung des Todes Jesu nach Paulus," in *Zur Bedeutung des Todes Jesus. Exegetische Beiträge*, ed. Hans Conzelmann, Ellen Fesseman-van-Leer, and Ernst Haenchen (Gütersloh: Gütersloher, 1967), 11–34.

52. E.g., Dunn, *Theology of Paul*, 212–18; Thomas Knöppler, *Sühne im Neuen Testament: Studien zum urchristlichen Verständnis der Heilsbedeutung des Todes Jesu*, WMANT 88 (Neukirchen-Vluyn: Neukirchener, 2001), 133–34; Stephen Finlan, *The Background and Content of Paul's Cultic Atonement Metaphors*, AcBib 19 (Atlanta: SBL, 2004); Boersma, *Violence, Hospitality, and the Cross*, 212–18.

53. See my discussion of this text below.

54. The Greek *peri hamartias* here often translates a Hebrew word meaning "sin offering" in the LXX (see Moo, *Romans* [NICNT], 502–3).

55. As the NIV suggests, an allusion to sacrifice in this verse is less clear than in the others. Christ "becoming" sin could well refer simply to his entrance into the full human state of sinfulness. Still, the "for us" that follows could suggest a reference to sacrifice. See my discussion on p. 178.

While this evidence might seem rather meager, there are other less explicit allusions to sacrifice in Paul's teaching about Jesus's death that build a much stronger case. See, for example, Ephesians 2:13–16:

> But now in Christ Jesus you who once were far away have been brought near by the blood of Christ. For he himself is our peace, who has made the two groups one and has destroyed the barrier, the dividing wall of hostility, by setting aside in his flesh the law with its commands and regulations. His purpose was to create in himself one new humanity out of the two, thus making peace, and in one body to reconcile both of them to God through the cross, by which he put to death their hostility.

Paul uses four apparently parallel expressions to describe the means by which gentiles have been "brought near" and reconciled with Jews: "the blood of Christ," "flesh," "one body," and "the cross." The parallelism makes clear that the reference in each case is to the death of Christ, and the language of "blood" and "flesh" probably connotes the idea of sacrifice.[56] In a text somewhat parallel to this text in Ephesians, Paul specifies "[in] Christ's physical body through death" ([en] tō sōmati tēs sarkos autou dia tou thanatou) as the means of reconciliation between humans and God—also probably an allusion to sacrifice (Col 1:22). We may add here the six other passages in which Paul refers to Christ's blood as the means of redemption. Crucifixion was a relatively bloodless form of execution, so these references also probably allude to sacrifice (Rom 3:25; 5:9; Eph 1:7; Col 1:20).[57] Particularly significant are the references to "blood" and "body" in Paul's allusions to and quotations of the words of institution from the Last Supper (1 Cor 10:16; 11:25, 27). We may assume that Paul's churches regularly celebrated the Supper and thus had this langauge drilled into them, which (1) focuses on Jesus's death, and (2) interprets that death as a sacrifice. Two other passages use the language of "washing" to depict Christ's work on behalf of humans (Eph 5:26 and Titus 3:5, both using loutron). Words from this root refer often to ritual cleansing in the Old Testament, a cleansing usually accomplished by sacrifice.[58]

Paul's readers would probably also detect sacrificial allusions in his frequent claim that Christ's death provides for "forgiveness of sin" (Rom 3:25; 4:6–8; 2 Cor 5:19; Eph 1:7; Col 1:14; see also Eph 4:32; Col 2:13; 3:13). The "problem" of sins that are counted against people will be matched by an appropriate and fitting "solution." The solution to

---

56. Thielman, *Ephesians*, 168; Knöppler, *Sühne im Neuen*, 133–73.

57. Morris (*Apostolic Preaching*, 108–22) argues that "blood" in these kinds of contexts consistently refers to death in both the LXX and NT.

58. Note, e.g., that *louō*, "wash," occurs twenty-three times in Leviticus (out of forty-four total in the LXX).

the problem of sin in the Old Testament is sacrifice. Indeed, even when the recognition dawns that the sacrifices cannot take care of this sin problem, the ultimate solution is still presented in terms of sacrifice (see my comments on Isa 53 above).

3.3.2 Substitution

Unfortunately, Paul's teaching about Jesus's death as a sacrifice remains relatively undeveloped. However, several lines of evidence suggest that, at the deepest level, Christ's death atones because he suffers and dies in the sinner's place. This "place-taking" is then often elaborated in terms of punishment. "Penal substitution" is the label often attached to this interpretation. This view sees Christ as standing in our place, taking on our sins as our substitute and, on the cross, paying in his death the penalty of divine judgment that our sins had incurred. While this specific label is of relatively recent origin, this general way of conceiving atonement has been part of the church's understanding of the cross from the earliest centuries,[59] and bears at least a family resemblance to the "satisfaction" view put forth by Anselm of Canterbury in his classic work *Cur Deus Homo*. Common to this stream of interpretation is an insistence that the human sin problem cannot be solved unless the righteous judgment of God against sin is somehow dealt with—and the cross was the place where this was done.[60] Penal substitution finds an important place in the Reformation, and many later Protestant theologians elevated it to a place of primacy—a place that my own quite unscientific survey of recent Christian praise music suggests that it still has for many believers. I first survey evidence for finding this conception in Paul and then deal with some important objections to it.

3.3.2.1 Evidence for Substitution

As we have seen, Paul regularly characterizes Jesus's death as "for us," "on our behalf," using the preposition *hyper*. The exact manner in which Christ's death is "for us" varies in Paul. In 2 Corinthians 5:14, for instance, Christ being "for" us takes the form of representation: "For Christ's love compels us, because we are convinced that one died for [*hyper*] all, and therefore all died." The logic of this claim works only if Paul is thinking of Christ as the "second Adam," the head of all humans, whose death is then our death as well. He dies "for [*hyper*] us" in that we all died, in God's sight, in and with him. But the preposition *hyper*, as is widely recognized, sometimes takes on the nuance "in place of"; after all, one often acts for someone by doing something in their place. Winer's comment is widely quoted: "In most cases one who acts in behalf

---

59. Barry D. Smith, *The Meaning of Jesus' Death: Reviewing the New Testament's Interpretations* (London: Bloomsbury, 2017).

60. See, e.g., Fleming Rutledge, *Crucifixion: Understanding the Death of Jesus* (Grand Rapids: Eerdmans, 2015), 144–46.

of another takes his place."[61] "I will pay your debt for you" might mean either "I will take your money to the bank" or "I will use my own money to discharge your debt."[62] Certain occurrences of *hyper* in Paul have this "place taking" idea. In Galatians 3:13, for instance, Paul claims that "Christ redeemed us from the curse of the law by becoming a curse for us, for it is written: 'Cursed is everyone who is hung on a pole.'" Christ becoming a curse "for [*hyper*] us" takes here the specific form of Christ receiving the curse in our place.[63] While debated, other texts arguably use the preposition with this sense (Rom 5:6–8; 9:3; 2 Cor 5:14, 21; Titus 2:14; cf. 1 Cor 15:29; Phlm 13). Paul never uses the preposition that normally conveys a substitutionary sense, *anti*, although it does occur as a prefix on an important soteriological word, *antilytron*, "ransom," in 1 Timothy 2:6.

My reference to "ransom" brings us to a second point. This preposition *anti* is here built on a root, *lytr-*, from which several important New Testament soteriological words are derived. Paul himself uses only two of these words: *lytroō* ("redeem," Titus 2:14) and *apolytrōsis* ("redemption," Rom 3:24; 8:23; 1 Cor 1:30; Eph 1:7, 14; 4:30; Col 1:14).[64] "Redemption," as I noted earlier, is sometimes used generally to depict the new state of affairs believers enjoy in Christ. See, for example, 1 Corinthians 1:30: "It is because of him that you are in Christ Jesus, who has become for us wisdom from God—that is, our righteousness, holiness and redemption." The same broad sense is suggested in two other texts in which Paul refers to "redemption" as something believers possess and associates it with "the forgiveness of sins" (Eph 1:7; Col 1:14). The breadth of the concept is revealed also in the way Paul can use it to describe both past (Rom 3:24; 1 Tim 2:6; Titus 2:14) and future (Rom 8:23; Eph 1:14) acts of deliverance. Our tendency to use "redemption" as a general way of referring to salvation therefore has some basis in Paul, and all this might suggest that we should include redemption in the category of umbrella soteriological terms that I consider in a later chapter.

However, it is also possible that some, most, or even all these occurrences of *lytr-* words in Paul have a more specific connotation that is relevant to our focus on the nature of Jesus's atoning death. Words from this root, usually rendered with a form of "redeem" or "ransom," are used in two contexts that have likely influenced Paul's use of the language. First, these words were used in Paul's day to refer to money used to

61. G. B. Winer, *Grammar of New Testament Greek* (New York: Macmillan, 1889), 382. See also R. E. Davies, "Christ in Our Place—the Contribution of the Prepositions," *TynBul* 21 (1970): 82; Harris, *Prepositions and Theology*, 211–16; Ridderbos, *Paul*, 190.

62. Note also, e.g., John 11:50–52, where Jesus's death "for" (*hyper*) the people means that they will not "perish."

63. Ridderbos, *Paul*, 190. Wright (*Day the Revolution Began*, 82–83) argues that the curse was removed in order to extend

God's promise to the gentiles. This is certainly part of what is being said here ("he redeemed us in order that the blessing given to Abraham might come to the Gentiles"—v. 14a), but it was also so that soteriological benefits could flow to all of "us": "So that by faith we might receive the promise of the Spirit" (v. 14b).

64. The verb *lytroō* occurs also in Luke 24:21; 1 Pet 1:18; *apolytrōsis* in Luke 21:28; Heb 9:15; 11:35. See also *lytron*, "ransom" (Matt 20:28; Mark 10:45), *lytrōsis*, "ransoming" (Luke 1:68; 2:38; Heb 9:12), and *lytrōtēs*, "redeemer" (Acts 7:35).

purchase the freedom of prisoners of war or slaves.[65] One in bondage was "redeemed" out of that situation of bondage by the payment of some kind of equivalent compensation. Second, "redemption" words were widely used in the LXX to refer to a variety of transactions.[66] Closest to the secular Greek usage are texts that refer to a *lytron* being paid for the release of slaves or as compensation for damaged property. See, for instance, Exodus 21:28–30:

> If a bull gores a man or woman to death, the bull is to be stoned to death, and its meat must not be eaten. But the owner of the bull will not be held responsible. If, however, the bull has had the habit of goring and the owner has been warned but has not kept it penned up and it kills a man or woman, the bull is to be stoned and its owner also is to be put to death. However, if payment is demanded, the owner may *redeem* [LXX: *dōsei lytra*, "give ransoming things"] his life by the payment of whatever is demanded.

A theological application of the language grew from this commercial sense. In Psalms, petitioners often ask God to "redeem" them out of a situation of affliction or distress, or praise God for "redeeming" them in this way. "Redeem [*lytrōsai*] Israel, O God, out of all his troubles" (Ps 25:22 ESV [24:22 LXX]). The cause or situation of distress can also be spiritual: Sheol, the realm of the dead, or the "pit" (e.g., Ps 49:15; 103:4) or "sins" (Ps 130:8). The "bondage" from which one is redeemed is often identified with the time of Israel's slavery in Egypt. Language such as we find in Exodus 6:6 is echoed again and again throughout the Old Testament: "Say therefore to the people of Israel, 'I am the LORD, and I will bring you out from under the burdens of the Egyptians, and I will deliver you from slavery to them, and I will redeem [*lytroō*] you with an outstretched arm and with great acts of judgment" (ESV). Indeed, it is fair to say that someone acquainted with the Old Testament in Greek when hearing "redemption" language would probably think first of all of the exodus.[67] As the text in Exodus makes clear, the LXX use of redemption language tends to preserve the idea of liberating from bondage that we find in secular Greek.

These data about redemption language in secular and LXX Greek suggest that Paul would have used this language to connote liberation from slavery: new-covenant believers experience a "liberation" similar to that which old-covenant believers experienced

---

65. See, e.g., Papyrus Oxyrhynchus I.48 for *lytron* used to refer to the "ransom" of a slave. Josephus frequently uses *lytron* to refer to the "ransom" for prisoners of war; see, e.g., *J.W.* 1.274.

66. The LXX uses Paul's favorite word from this root— *apolytrōsis*, "redemption"—only once (Dan 4:34), while *lytroō*, "redeem," occurs very often (108 times). The latter word most often translates two Hebrew words, *ga'al* and *padah*.

67. Although the language is also used often to refer to God's redeeming act in bringing Israel back from her exile (see, e.g., Brant Pitre, *Jesus, the Tribulation, and the End of the Exile: Restoration Eschatology and the Origin of the Atonement* [Grand Rapids: Baker, 2005)], 407).

in the exodus. In Paul, however, the slave master is sin, which holds humans under bondage. Thus, in Romans 3:24 the "redemption" that Paul celebrates is a liberating act that has as its background Paul's claim in 3:9 that all humans are "under the power of sin" (*hyph hamartian*). The debated issue, and the one pertaining especially to our current discussion, is whether "redemption" language in Paul connotes the idea of a "price paid" to secure release or liberation. Leon Morris, in a classic treatment, argued strongly that this notion of "price paid" was inherent in the word group. If this is so, then "redemption" in Paul would connote the idea of God paying a price to secure the freedom of his people from sin and death. That "price paid" would be Jesus's giving of himself in death, and this paying of a price makes sense only if Jesus takes our place, paying the ransom price that we ourselves "owed."[68]

The conclusions of Morris—and, of course, many others—on this matter have been contested. David Hill and others point out that redemption language in the Old Testament, particularly when it is used to depict God's redeeming activity, tends to lose any idea of a "price paid."[69] These latter scholars have a point. LXX references to God's "redemption" do not always include any explicit allusion to a "price paid" for that redemption. However, as I noted above, the language clearly has the notion of "price paid" or "ransom" in legal texts in Leviticus and Numbers; and this notion is not lost in the later LXX; see, for example, Psalm 49:7–9 (48:8–10 LXX): "No one can redeem the life of another or give to God a ransom for them—the ransom for a life is costly, no payment is ever enough—so that they should live on forever and not see decay." See also Isaiah 45:13: "I will raise up Cyrus in my righteousness: I will make all his ways straight. He will rebuild my city and set my exiles free, but not for a price [*lytrōn*] or reward [*dōron*]," says the LORD Almighty."

The question is whether we have adequate grounds to conclude that redemption language, when there is no contextual reference to "price paid," still has that connotation—built into the words themselves, as it were. I think the data from the LXX might suggest that this is the case, and early Christian use of the verb further suggests this; see 1 Peter 1:18–19: "You know that it was not with perishable things such as silver or gold that you were redeemed from the empty way of life handed down to you from your ancestors, but with the precious blood of Christ, a lamb without blemish or defect." Paul's own usage suggests that some notion of a "price paid" is included in the sense of these words. While "redemption" language is not used in the context, Colossians 2:14–15 indicates that Paul associates "forgiveness of sins" with the discharge of a legal debt: the notion of a price paid on the cross—"nailing it to the cross"—seems close at hand. The payment of a price for our liberation from sin is more explicit in Paul's use of "buy" language

---

68. Morris, *Apostolic Preaching*, 9–59; and also, e.g., Finlan, *Background and Content*, 164–68.

69. David Hill, *Greek Words and Hebrew Meanings: Studies in the Semantics of Soteriological Terms*, SNTSMS 5 (Cambridge: Cambridge University Press, 1967), 58–80.

to refer to the work of the cross.[70] See, for instance, Galatians 3:13: "Christ redeemed [*exagorazō* is the verb] us from the curse of the law by becoming a curse for us." The obvious substitutionary notion in the second part of the verse suggests that the verb here does not mean simply "liberate" but "buy out of" (see also Gal 4:5). Paul makes a similar point elsewhere, using the simple form of this verb (*agorazō*): "You were bought at a price" (1 Cor 6:20; see also 7:23).[71] These texts, taken together, provide a solid basis for the conclusion that Paul views liberation from bondage as an important benefit of the new realm, and that this liberation occurs only at the "cost" of the death of Christ.[72]

If at least some occurrences of "redemption" language in Paul include the notion of a "price paid," it is natural to ask a follow-up question: To whom was this "ransom" paid? One response to this question is simply to dismiss it. Since the Bible neither asks this question nor explicitly answers it, we are speculating without any real data to go by, pressing the metaphor beyond the limits of the way it is used in Scripture.[73] Marshall's warning is apropos: too often we get into theological trouble by theorizing without adequate data (as Sherlock Holmes would put it). However, in this case, I think Scripture might at least imply an answer to our question. One popular answer in the early church was that the ransom was paid to Satan so that he would release sinners from his control. This view has possible exegetical basis in Paul; in Colossians 2:13–15, the apostle links the forgiveness of sins with the canceling of "the charge of our legal indebtedness, which stood against us and condemned us" and goes on to celebrate Christ's victory over "the powers and authorities." However, in light of broader biblical teaching, it is likely that the one who demands the debt our sins have accrued is God, the giver of the law, not Satan. And this appears to receive confirmation from Romans 3:25–26.

Romans 3:21–26 is one of the most significant soteriological texts in the New Testament, relating God's justifying act through faith in Christ to redemption, grace, and Christ's work on the cross. The cross, Paul claims in verses 25b and 26a, has the purpose of demonstrating "the righteousness of God" (*tēs dikaiosynēs autou* [referring to God]). As I argue in the exposition above (pp. 210–11), the occurrences of this phrase in verse 25b and 26a probably refer not to God's saving or "communicative" righteousness (as in vv. 21 and 22) but to his intrinsic righteousness. Only if we give the phrase this meaning does it make sense for Paul to assert that God acted in Christ to display his righteousness "because God had not fully punished sins committed beforehand."[74] In the Old Testament period, Paul is suggesting, God did not punish sins

---

70. See, e.g., Dunn, *Theology of Paul*, 228.

71. Ridderbos notes the family resemblance among these terms (*Paul*, 193).

72. I. Howard Marshall introduces what may be a useful distinction between "price" and "cost" ("The Development of the Concept of Redemption in the New Testament," in Banks, *Reconciliation and Hope*, 153).

73. See, e.g., Leon Morris, *The Atonement: Its Meaning and Significance* (Downers Grove, IL: InterVarsity Press, 1983), 129–30.

74. Longenecker, *Romans*, 434.

with the full severity he should have. People who sinned should have suffered spiritual death, because they did not yet have an adequate sacrifice to atone for their sins. But in his mercy God "passed over" their sins. In doing so, however, God acted against his character, which requires that he respond to sin with wrath. In giving himself as a "sacrifice of atonement," Christ paid the price for the sins of all people—both before his time (v. 25b) and after (v. 26a). All this suggests quite strongly that the price involved in the redemptive work of Christ was paid in order to vindicate God's righteousness in forgiving sinners. The reconciliation of God's character as holy and perfectly just, on the one hand, and of his declaring distinctly unholy people as just before him, on the other, is what this paragraph is finally all about—and, arguably, what the gospel is finally all about. As Horton notes, if we have not wrestled with this tension, "we have probably not yet wrestled yet with Paul's doctrine of God."[75] In any case, to return to my main point, the notion of Christ as our substitute, rendering to God the payment that we could not make, seems clear.[76]

One other controversial word from this same context requires brief comment: *hilastērion* (NIV "sacrifice of atonement," v. 25a). The addition of the phrase "through the shedding of his blood" (literally, "in his blood," *en tō autou haimati*) suggests a sacrificial allusion. The particular background here, as most scholars now recognize, is the Leviticus 16 Day of Atonement ritual. The word Paul uses occurs in Leviticus 16 to denote the "mercy seat" or, as the NIV puts it, "atonement cover" (see Lev 16:2 [2x], 13, 14 [2x], 15 [2x]; note also the only other occurrence of this word in the NT [Heb 9:5]). In a beautiful typological picture, Paul presents Christ's cross as the place where God now deals definitively with human sin.[77] However, important for our purposes here is the fact that, while the word *refers* to the Old Testament "atonement cover," the word *means* "propitiation." The word therefore presents Christ's death as the means by which God's wrath is averted. Paul typically thinks of wrath as being inflicted on unbelievers at the time of the judgment. Those who are in Christ can be certain of escaping God's wrath on that day because, in keeping with his usual eschatological perspective, it has been fully absorbed by Christ on the cross (Rom 5:9; 1 Thess 5:9–10).

75. Horton, *Justification*, 2:180.

76. For a more detailed defense of this interpretation, see Moo, *Romans* (NICNT), 257–64.

77. See again Moo, *Romans* (NICNT), 252–57; and pp. 210–11 above. The NIV "sacrifice of atonement" at Rom 3:25 is an attempt to bring out the significance of this word in this context. Old Testament scholars are engaged in a lively debate about the significance of the Day of Atonement. Following the pioneering work of Jacob Milgrom, some scholars claim that the rituals of this day focused (perhaps exclusively) on the purification of the sanctuary (*Leviticus 1–16: A New Translation with Introduction and Commentary*, AB 3 [New Haven, CT: Yale University Press, 1998], 1009–83). However, the text appears to claim a broader signficance of the Day; see, e.g., Lev 16:33–34: "[The priest is to] make atonement for the Most Holy Place, for the tent of meeting and the altar, and for the priests and all the members of the community. This is to be a lasting ordinance for you: Atonement is to be made once a year for all the sins of the Israelites." Moreover, Paul would probably have interpreted the Day as his Jewish contemporaries did, as the time when God provided "forgiveness on a grand scale" (Roy Gane, *Cult and Character: Purification Offerings, Day of Atonement, and Theodicy* [Winona Lake, IN: Eisenbrauns, 2005], 233; see, e.g., 11Q19 (Temple Scroll) 26.9–10; m. Yoma 8:8–9; b. Yoma 86a).

Verse 26b summarizes the dense theology of this paragraph: God, Paul says, is both "just and the one who justifies those who have faith in Jesus" (v. 26b). In the face of human sin and the condemnation under which sinners stand, God has sent Christ to be a full and final sacrifice for sins as a means of "justifying" believers—putting them in a legal state of righteousness—and remains "just" while doing so because Christ is our substitute, bearing the full judgment we deserve.

I conclude this section on the positive case for substitution in Paul with two final minor points. First, Paul's portrayal of Christ's death is often thought to depend on the way in which Jewish martyrs during the Maccabean revolt are depicted in 2 and 4 Maccabees (see p. 211n55). These stories portray the martyrs' deaths as standing in place of the death/judgment Israel deserved. Second, as I noted above, Paul's depiction of Christ's death "for" us sometimes appears to tap into widespread Greek traditions about people dying on behalf of others. And the people who die in these traditions were often viewed as dying "in place of" others.[78]

3.3.2.2 Objections to Substitution

Objections to "penal substitution" have surfaced repeatedly in the history of atonement discussions, and these have been expressed quite forcefully again in recent years. Some of these objections are legitimate protests at the way this view has sometimes been expressed. Others lie beyond the parameters of our task here. Three of them fall within the scope of the present study.

Defenders of penal substitution have often appealed to the Old Testament sacrificial system for the biblical roots of this conception. Yet several scholars have recently argued the notion of sacrifice as a substitute for the sinful Israelite is not well supported. One influential view is that the sacrificial victim does not suffer in place of the sinner but rather, in some sense, absorbs the sinner through identification.[79] This view is one among many in recent Old Testament studies, where the strong tendency is to doubt that the Old Testament sacrifices operated according to a substitutionary logic. However, while the issue falls well outside my own area of expertise, there seems to be some reason to think that "substituition," in some sense, may have been involved in at least some sacrificial rituals. The scapegoat ritual that culminated the Day of Atonement ritual certainly appears to have a substitutionary (even if not "penal") logic:

> He is to lay both hands on the head of the live goat and confess over it all the wickedness and rebellion of the Israelites—all their sins—and put them on the goat's head. He shall send the goat away into the wilderness in the care of someone

---

78. See esp. Gathercole, *Defending Substitution*, 85–107.

79. On this view of the OT cult, see esp. H. Gese, "The Atonement," in *Essays in Biblical Theology* (Minneapolis: Augsburg, 1981), 93–116; and also, e.g., Stuhlmacher, *Biblical Theology of the New Testament*, 325.

appointed for the task. The goat will carry on itself all their sins to a remote place; and the man shall release it in the wilderness. (Lev 16:21–22)[80]

Certainly interpreters and theologians through most of church history were convinced this was the case; and not all their views should be dismissed as a reading of assumed New Testament views back into the Old Testament.[81] On the whole, then, partly because the matter is so debated and partly because we cannot be sure how Paul himself understood the matter, we cannot cite the Old Testament sacrificial logic as a reason to *contest* a substitutionary interpretation of Jesus's death in Paul. And there are elements within the sacrificial system that could provide support for the notion.

A second objection is tied to this first one. The idea that Israelites benefited from sacrifices because they were identified with them fits into a powerful strain of Pauline teaching: the participation of believers in and with Christ. Advocates of this general approach rightly appeal to Paul's ubiquitous focus on believers being "in Christ," with the corresponding idea of our doing things "with" Christ. The word "interchange," popularized by Morna Hooker, is often used to describe this general focus in Paul's theology.[82] Christ identifies with us in such a way that he takes on himself our sins and we take on his righteousness. He becomes what we are that we might become what he is, to cite a very old way of putting the matter. This being the case, it is argued, it is unlikely that Paul thinks of Jesus's sacrificial death in terms of penal substitution.[83] Rather, Jesus's death atones for sins because sinners identify with him and share his own victory over sin and its consequences.[84]

Some scholars introduce confusion into the discussion by giving the label "substitution" to this view: "soft" substitution rather than "hard" substitution.[85] "Soft"

80. See Gathercole, *Defending Substitution*, 37.

81. Modern scholars who find some notion of substitution in the sacrificial system include, e.g., Stephen Hultgren, "*Hilasterion* (Rom. 3:25) and the Union of Divine Justice and Mercy Part I: The Convergence of Temple and Martyrdom Theologies," *JTS* 70 (2019): 69–109; Gordon J. Wenham, "The Theology of Old Testament Sacrifice," in *Sacrifice in the Bible*, ed. Roger T. Beckwith and Martin J. Selman (Carlisle: Paternoster, 1995), 75–87; Richard Averbeck, "Crucial Features of Sin Offering Atonement in Leviticus 4–5 and 16" (unpublished MS).

82. Morna D. Hooker, "Interchange in Christ," *JTS* 22 (1971): 349–61; see also idem, "Interchange and Atonement," in Hooker, *From Adam to Christ*, 24–41.

83. See, e.g., Dunn, *Theology of Paul*, 214–23.

84. See esp. Otfried Hofius, "Sühne und Versöhnung: Zum Paulinischen Verständnis des Kreuzestodes Jesu" in *Paulusstudien*, WUNT 2/51 (Tübingen: Mohr Siebeck, 1994), 33–49; Richard H. Bell, *Deliver Us from Evil: Interpreting the Redemption from the Power of Satan in New Testament Theology*, WUNT 2/216 (Tübingen: Mohr Siebeck, 2007); Joel B. Green and Mark D. Baker, *Recovering the Scandal of the Cross: Atonement in New Testament and Contemporary Contexts* (Downers Grove, IL: InterVarsity Press, 2000); Stephen H. Travis, "Christ as Bearer of Divine Judgment in Paul's Thought about the Atonement," in Green and Turner, *Jesus of Nazareth: Lord and Christ*, 333–45.

85. For a useful analysis of the distinction, see, e.g., Sung-Ho Park, *Stellvertretung Jesu Christi im Gericht: Studien zum Verhältnis von Stellvertretung und Kreuztod Jesu bei Paulus*, WMANT 143 (Neukirchen-Vluyn: Neukirchener, 2015); Bernd Janowski, *Stellvertretung: Alttestamentliche Studien zu einem theologischen Grundbegriff*, SBS 165 (Stuttgart: Katholisches Bibelwerk, 1997); Jörg Frey, "Probleme der Deutung des Todes Jesu in der Neutestamentlichen Wissenschaft: Streiflichter zur exegetischen Diskussion," in *Deutungen des Todes Jesu im Neuen Testament*, ed. Jörg Frey and Jens Schröter (Tübingen: Mohr Siebeck, 2005), 3–50; Jens Schröter, "Sühne, Stellvertretung und Opfer: Zur Verwendung Analytischer Kategorien zur Deutung des Todes Jesu," in Frey and Schröter, *Deutungen des Todes Jesu im Neuen Testament*, 51–71.

substitution or, as it is sometimes called, "inclusive substitution," stresses the sinner's identification with the death of the sacrificial victim.[86] Jesus's sacrifice atones for sins because sinners die with him and are brought to new life in him. However, it is confusing to use the language of substitution to refer to this idea. On this view, Christ represents us, so that what happens to him happens also to us; but he is not, in any normal sense of the English word, our "substitute."[87]

More important than the label, of course, is the question of substance. Many contemporary Pauline theologians think the "interchange" or "participation" motif looms large in Paul's theology—and I agree. However, it is a further step to argue that this "participatory" conception leaves no room for true substitutionary logic. James Dunn, for instance, claims that Paul's teaching is not that Christ dies in place of others so that they need not die; rather "Christ's sharing *their* death makes it possible for them to share *his* death."[88] However, this does not take matters far enough. For Paul speaks also of another kind of "death." As James Denney puts it, "Christ died for our sins. *That death we did not die*" (emphasis original).[89] Paul uses the language of death in different ways, meaning that it is quite logical for him to assert both that "we die [identify with his death on the cross] with Christ" and "Christ dies [suffers the penalty for sin] in our place [so that we don't have to]."[90] We find, in other words, two "levels" of conceptualization: the broad, all-embracing "with Christ" and the more specific "Christ in our place." An appropriate recognition of our participation with Christ does not exclude the substitutionary logic of Christ taking our place. A genuinely substitutionary logic is a key mechanism *within* the interchange model. We can become what Christ is (in a limited sense, of course) because he became what we are—but this "becoming what we are" involves his taking our place: carrying our sin and suffering the just punishment of that sin on our behalf. Paul understands the "logic" of Christ's work for us in terms both of "correspondence"—Christ "confers some things upon us which he himself may be said to enjoy"—and "contrariety"—"Christ wins those benefits for us who had himself no need of them and has himself no part in them."[91] While the participation focus certainly captures a significant aspect of Paul's theology, it does not logically, and should not exegetically, push out all ideas of substitution. Our participation with Christ in inaugurating redemptive events and his dying for sins on our behalf belong together

86. Daniel Bailey uses the language of "place-taking" to capture this idea ("Concepts of *Stellvertretung* in the Interpretation of Isaiah 53," in *Jesus and the Suffering Servant: Isaiah 53 and Christian Origins*, ed. William H. Bellinger Jr. and William R. Farmer [Harrisburg, PA: Trinity Press International, 1998], 223).

87. See also Gathercole, *Defending Substitution*, 118–53; Röhser, *Stellvertretung im Neuen Testament*, 33.

88. Dunn, *Theology of Paul*, 223. See also, e.g., Boersma, *Violence, Hospitality, and the Cross*, 221–23. Paul's frequent reference to believers dying, or being crucified, or being buried, or being

raised, or being vindicated "with Christ" (e.g., Rom 6:5–8; Gal 2:19–20; Col 2:12–13; Eph 2:5–6; Phil 3:21; 1 Thess 4:14) is the primary textual basis for this participatory concept.

89. James Denney, *Studies in Theology*, 4th ed. (London: Hodder & Stoughton, 1895), 126.

90. E.g., Gathercole, *Defending Substitution*, 55.

91. Thiselton, *Hermeneutics of Doctrine*, 339 (he quotes in the last instance from J. K. S. Reid, *Our Life in Christ* [London: SCM, 1963], 90–91).

under the umbrella of Paul's basic "union with Christ" conception.[92] The legitimate focus on participation, then, does not eliminate substitution from Paul's atoning logic.

In addition to the claim that Paul's participation emphasis rules out the idea, a third objection to the substitutionary model is that Paul's teaching about the work of Christ moves in another direction entirely. Paul's fundamental way of thinking about Christ's work is in terms of his liberating activity. The basic human problem on this view is not that people commit *sins* and must be forgiven but that they are slaves to the power of "Sin" and must be set free from it. Paul's common reference to "sin" in the singular and his references to "setting free" and "redemption" show that this way of reading Paul has a basis in his teaching.

However, first, many scholars who take this approach to Paul—labeled the "apocalyptic Paul" movement—isolate this liberative motif at the expense of other emphases. Thus, for instance, Paul's references to sin in the singular cannot be isolated from his references to sin in the plural. Paul often makes clear that the human dilemma is that people are guilty because they commit sins. "Sin" in the singular appears to be Paul's way of vividly picturing the power and devastating effects of human sin in the life of human beings (see pp. 410–41). Second, we must rightly order the genuine focus on liberation in Paul to the clear focus on sacrifice that I have outlined above. These are sometimes placed on the same level and either contrasted with each other as mutually exclusive options or integrated as two parallel ways of thinking about the work of Christ. It might be better, however, to order these on different levels. On this view, liberation is one of the several benefits secured by Christ's sacrificial death. Several texts in Paul suggest this arrangement. "Redemption" in Romans 3:24 appears to be tied to Christ's "sacrifice of atonement" in verse 25. Being set "free from the law of sin and death" in Romans 8:2 is based on Christ's "sin offering" in verse 3. We were "redeemed" by means of Christ becoming a curse for us on the cross (Gal 3:13). Our "redemption," described also as "forgiveness of sins," comes via Christ's "blood" (Eph 1:7). And note the sequence in Galatians 1:4: Christ "gave himself for our sins to rescue us from the present evil age." Rescue from this evil age comes by means of Christ "giving himself" for our sins. As Henri Blocher has argued, liberation, or the related idea of victory, is indeed an important part of biblical teaching about Christ's work. But the issue, as he puts it, is this: "*How* is the battle fought and the victory gained?" And the answer to that

---

92. Marshall, *Aspects of the Atonement*, 91–92; Richard B. Gaffin Jr., "Atonement in the Pauline Corpus: 'The Scandal of the Cross,'" in *The Glory of the Atonement: Biblical, Historical and Practical Perspectives: Essays in Honor of Roger Nicole*, ed. Charles E. Hill and Frank A. James III (Downers Grove, IL: InterVarsity Press, 2004), 144–45. Gaffin writes: "For Paul the participatory or relational involves an inalienable juristic, forensic aspect, and the forensic does not function apart from the relational" (145). See also the distinction in Francis Turretin between Christ as our "surety," involving forensic imputation, the foundation of justification, and Christ as our "head," securing moral and internal infusion—the principle of sanctification (*Institutes of Elenctic Theology*, 3 vols. [Phillipsburg, NJ: P&R, 1997 {1679–1685}], topic 16, Q. 3 part 6).

question is through the sacrificial death of Christ on the cross.[93] Or, as Horton puts it, "Vicarious substitution is not the whole story, but there is no story apart from it."[94]

4 CONCLUSION

I reiterate a key thread in my discussion of the inauguration of the new realm. In my view, we more faithfully summarize Scripture if we distinguish *manifestations* of the new realm and the *means* and *mechanism* by which that new realm is inaugurated. Those means encompass the breadth of Christ's work. Paul, as we have seen, attributes saving significance to Christ's incarnation, life, death, resurrection, and exaltation— thereby creating important biblical-theological bridges with other New Testament authors, who give greater attention to some of these moments than Paul does (e.g., incarnation in John or exaltation in Hebrews). Yet while including the whole gamut of Christ's life in the means of atonement, for Paul, clearly, it is Christ's death that is the decisive moment. Imitating and continuing a central Old Testament narrative thread, Paul views human sin, and the death, judgment, and wrath it incurs, as the fundamental barrier to God's purposes.[95] God is, of course, working to create unified and loving communities and a renewed cosmos. But the means by which he is bringing this about, Paul suggests, comes via the renewal of individuals. And this renewal happens only through the appropriation of the benefits of Christ's death. Jew and gentile are brought together into one body by means of "the blood of Christ" (Eph 2:13); the entire creation will be "liberated from its bondage to decay" when it is brought into "the freedom and glory of the children of God" (Rom 8:21); the reconciliation of all things takes place by means of "his blood, shed on the cross" (Col 1:20). As human sin first derailed God's purposes, bringing a curse on the ground as well as on humans (Gen 3:17), so the cure of human sin opens the way to a new creation. And sin, Paul teaches, is dealt with through the sacrificial death of Jesus, who gave himself for us by taking our place, bearing God's wrath against sin, and therefore removing the great obstacle in the way of God's redeeming work. Here we identify the *mechanism* that God has employed to take care of the human sin problem: substitutionary, sacrificial death. We may, perhaps, think of a series of concentric circles, with the outermost one

---

93. Henri A. G. Blocher, "*Agnus Victor*: The Atonement as Victory and Vicarious Punishment," in *What Does It Mean to Be Saved? Broadening Evangelical Horizons of Salvation*, ed. John G. Stackhouse Jr. (Grand Rapids: Baker Academic, 2002), 78; see also Rutledge, *Crucifixion*, 530–31. Another reason to put substitutionary sacrifice at the center of God's work of atonement is that it answers a question to which the NT demands an answer: Why did God go to the extent of sending his Son to die on a Roman cross to inaugurate the new realm? See, e.g., Kevin J. Vanhoozer,

"The Atonement in Postmodernity: Guilt, Goats, and Gifts," in Hill and James, *Glory of the Atonement*, 389; cf. Horton: "What would a God be like who gave up his Son to death if it were *not* necessary?" (*Lord and Servant*, 195).

94. Horton, *Justification*, 2:235.

95. The juridical imagery of this atonement perspective is identified as central also by, e.g., Henri A. G. Blocher, "Biblical Metaphors and the Doctrine of the Atonement," *JETS* 47 (2004): 645.

enclosing the wide sweep of new-covenant blessings, the next one in enclosing union with Christ, and the inner circle focused on Christ's sacrificial offering on our behalf. The outer circle, encompassing the incredibly broad range of things God is wanting to accomplish, is arguably in some sense the most important. But the innermost circles should be our focus if we are wanting to answer the "how" question. Liberation from our slavery to the powers, victory over Satan, peace with God and with other people, a new "home" characterized by righteousness and holiness (see the next chapter)—all these need to be fundamental themes in our preaching and teaching. But the means to achieve these ends is the sacrificial death of Christ, "for us" and "in our place."[96] Finally, I return to where I began: the *motivation* of this new realm is the love, expressed in grace, of the triune God. Our view of what God has done to inaugurate the new realm goes badly astray without this emphasis on the full involvement of all three persons of the Godhead. Referring to Moltmann's stress on the suffering of *God*—not just the Son—in securing our salvation, Thiselton rightly notes that an appropriate reminder of this truth heads off many of the modern criticisms of traditional atonement teaching.[97]

---

96. Horton, *Lord and Servant*, 252. What atonement theory we privilege will depend, then, to some extent, on what we are talking about. For instance, Michael F. Bird, while not dismissing other atonement perspectives, claims the *Christus Victor* model is the "crucial integrative hub" of atonement theories; "the canopy under which the other modes of atonement gain their currency." But he also affirms that "Jesus' substitutionary death constitutes the basis and center of the divine victory" (*Evangelical Theology: A Biblical and Systematic Introduction* [Grand Rapids: Zondervan, 2013], 414, 418).

97. E.g., the idea that penal substitution involves "divine child abuse." See Thiselton, *Hermeneutics of Doctrine*, 336.

Chapter 19

THE OLD REALM: THE CONTEXT FOR THE GOOD NEWS

> For the grace of God has appeared that offers salvation to all people. It teaches us to say "No" to *ungodliness and worldly passions*, and to live self-controlled, upright and godly lives in this present age, while we wait for the blessed hope—the appearing of the glory of our great God and Savior, Jesus Christ, who gave himself for us to redeem us from all wickedness and to purify for himself a people that are his very own, eager to do what is good.
>
> —TITUS 2:11–14

T HE THEOLOGY PAUL assumes and communicates in his letters is driven by his core conviction that in Christ God had inaugurated a new state of affairs that offered salvation to humanity and renovation of the entire universe. This new state of affairs, what I am calling the new realm, assumes that the world as it exists does not offer any such hope for humans or the world. Paul's proclamation of a new realm therefore presumes the existence of an old realm. As I have made clear elsewhere (pp. 27–34), the "old" and "new" in these designations must be given full range. Paul often conceptualizes matters in a strong "once"/"now" contrast, with the transition coming at the cross. This contrast marks the broader history of salvation as well as the history of the individual. Thus, the "mystery" that Paul administers, he says, "for ages past was kept hidden in God" but has now been "made known to the rulers and authorities in the heavenly realms" (Eph 3:9–10). So also "we" were once "in the realm of the flesh," with sin and the law conspiring to inflict death; "now," however, we "serve in the new way of the Spirit" (Rom 7:5–6). Yet the contrast is not purely temporal. Abraham experienced God's righteousness by faith, and David had his sins forgiven long before the cross (Rom 4:1–8), while people after the cross who do not embrace its saving power remain prisoners of sin and death (e.g., Eph 4:17–19). The old realm has been dealt a death blow, but it continues to exercise power until the day when the new realm is fully in force.

In this chapter, I outline Paul's theology of the old realm. My decision to investigate

Paul's teaching on the old realm *after* describing the way Paul reflects on the inauguration of the new realm requires brief justification.

Especially since E. P. Sanders's *Paul and Palestinian Judaism* in 1977, Pauline scholars have argued that Paul's theological reasoning moved "from solution to plight." In place of the traditional and popular conception of the pre-Christian Paul struggling with a sin problem and finding, in his conversion, the solution to that plight in Christ, these scholars want to reverse the sequence: Paul was a rather self-satisfied Jew who, confronted suddenly and surprisingly with the reality of the resurrected Christ, was forced to reassesses his pre-Christian situation. The reality of Christ was the point from which all his theological reasoning proceeds. Paul's understanding of his plight—and, by extension—the plight of humanity arose from the "solution" he had discovered in the risen Jesus. Once convinced that this solution had as its heart a crucified Messiah, Paul, in fact, viewed his plight in far darker terms than before—after all, a very serious sin problem must be the reason for such a serious means of redemption from that sin.[1] This "solution-to-plight" direction in Paul's theologizing has been widely accepted; as André du Toit puts it, "Paul's personal experience of grace led him to a new hamartiology."[2]

However, other scholars have either rejected or modified this "solution-to-plight" reading of Paul's theology.[3] Certainly, if the picture of an agonized Saul of Tarsus is overdrawn on the one hand, the picture of a smug, satisfied Jew on the other also requires modification. After all, it is hard to believe that Saul, obviously a "religious" man, would not have entertained doubts now and then about his faith and his relationship to his Lord. More important for our purposes, we should not assume that the direction of Paul's *experience* must be the direction of his theological argument. Of course, Paul's letters, being the occasional documents that they are, do not usually furnish us with clear evidence of the sequence of his theological argument. The clues they do contain suggest variety in the sequence of Paul's theological reasoning.[4] Nevertheless, passages such as Philippians 3:2–11 do, indeed, suggest that Paul was a pretty self-satisfied Jew, confident in his standing with God provided by "the righteousness of the law." For him personally, "solution" probably did precede "plight," and I suspect this sequence provides a more natural reading of his theology. It is for this reason that I move in this

---

1. Sanders, *Paul and Palestinian Judaism*, 442–46. Douglas Campbell has pressed the point to an extreme. Following the lead of Barth and the Torrances, he denies any "prospective" logic in Paul's gospel: one cannot work forward from sin to salvation but only back from salvation to sin (e.g., *Deliverance*, 74—this is the recurring theme in his *Pauline Dogmatics*).

2. André du Toit, "The Centrality of Grace in the Theology of Paul," in Breytenbach and du Toit, *Focusing on Paul*, 89.

3. See esp. Frank S. Thielman, *From Plight to Solution: A Jewish Framework to Understanding Paul's View of the Law in Galatians and Romans*, NovTSup 41 (Leiden: Brill, 1989); and also Ines Pollmann, *Gesetzeskritische Motive im Judentum und die Gesetzeskritik des Paulus*, NTOA/SUNT 98 (Göttingen: Vandenhoeck & Ruprecht, 2012), 183–233. N. T. Wright suggests a three-stage process: original plight—solution—reimagined plight (*Paul and Faithfulness of God*, 2:747–50).

4. See, e.g., Pollmann, *Gesetzeskritische Motive im Judentum*, 233–34.

book on Paul's theology from the breaking in of the new realm to an analysis of the old realm.

The chapter falls into three parts, as I (1) describe the fundamental nature of the old realm; (2) flesh out details of the old realm by focusing on two key narratives informing Paul's understanding; and (3) summarize Paul's conception of the human being as one caught up in these narratives.

1 THE FUNDAMENTAL NATURE OF THE OLD REALM

A passage that brings together some of Paul's more fundamental convictions about the old realm is Ephesians 2:1–3:

> As for you, you were dead in your transgressions and sins, in which you used to live when you followed the ways of this world and of the ruler of the kingdom of the air, the spirit who is now at work in those who are disobedient. All of us also lived among them at one time, gratifying the cravings of our flesh and following its desires and thoughts. Like the rest, we were by nature deserving of wrath.

1.1 Sin[5]

In the Ephesians text just quoted, Paul claims that his readers (mainly gentiles) were "dead in your transgressions and sins." "Sin leading to death" is the core reality of the old realm and exerts a powerful influence on all Paul's theology. He undoubtedly deduces this brute fact about his world from his own observation and experience, but the apostle is also deeply influenced by the "fall" narrative of Genesis 3, a text that has a powerful influence on his thinking. I look at death, the divine penalty imposed upon sin, a bit later; here I focus on the language Paul uses to characterize humans outside of Christ.

1.1.1 The Vocabulary of Sin

The word "sin" (*hamartia*) is by far the most common word Paul uses to denote this condition. It occurs sixty-four times in his letters, while two related terms, *hamartanō* ("commit sin") and *hamartōlos* ("sinner") are used, respectively, seventeen times and eight times. At the same time, these Greek words translate the most common words for sin in the Old Testament, the Hebrew verb *khata'* and its corresponding noun, *khatta't*. The often quoted verse, Romans 3:23, illustrates the summarizing and general scope of the word group in Paul: "For all have sinned [*hēmarton*] and fall short of the

---

5. In the following paragraphs, I rely on and quote from my article on this issue, "Sin in Paul," in *Fallen: A Theology of Sin,* ed. Christopher W. Morgan and Robert A. Peterson (Wheaton, IL: Crossway, 2013), 107–30. Used by permission.

glory of God." Before looking further at the nature of sin in Paul, we should briefly note other key words. "Trespass" (*paraptōma*) is another rather colorless word for sin in Paul; note how in Romans 5:12–21 he can interchange "sin" (vv. 12, 13, 20, 21) and "trespass" (vv. 15 [2x], 16, 17, 18, 20). The word "transgression" (*parabasis*) has a more focused sense (it occurs five times in Paul; its cognate *parabatēs* occurs three times). This word denotes a particular kind of sin, an open-eyed violation of a command of God, as when Israel transgressed the law of God (Rom 2:23; cf. 2:25, 27), or when Adam transgressed by disobeying the command given to the first human couple in the garden (Rom 5:14; cf. 1 Tim 2:14). God gave the law (on my reading of the verse) to produce "transgressions" (Gal 3:19; cf. 2:18).[6] This connection between the law and transgression explains the enigmatic claim by Paul in Romans 4:15 that "the law brings wrath." For, as Paul explains in the second part of the verse, only in the presence of "law" of some kind can one speak of "transgression." As we will see in more detail below, then, the giving of the law did not rescue Israel from their sin problem—in one sense at least, the law made it worse by setting forth specific commandments and prohibitions that were "transgressed" by the people of Israel. Paul can also use the language of "desire" or "passion" (*epithymia* and *pathos/pathēma*) to refer to the inner "bent" toward oneself and away from God that is the stimulus for sinful acts. To be sure, "desire" (*epithymia*) can have a neutral meaning in Paul (Phil 1:23), but usually denotes some kind of illicit desire or the "passions" that characterize human beings outside of Christ (the word occurs nineteen times in Paul). See, for example, 2 Timothy 2:22: "Flee the evil desires [*epithymias*] of youth and pursue righteousness, faith, love and peace, along with those who call on the Lord out of a pure heart."

We can flesh out the nature of the old realm in Paul's thinking by considering some of the other words he uses to depict sin. Several of these stress the negative, being formed by a base word with the prefix *a-* added. This Greek alpha functions much like our prefixes "un-" or "dis-" in English. Thus sin can be characterized as "**un**righteousness" (**a**dikia [12x]; cf. also **a**dikos, "**un**righteous" [3x]), "**dis**obedience" (**a**peitheia [4x] and the corresponding verb **a**peitheō [5x]; see also parakoē [2x]), "**un**cleanness" (**a**katharsia [9x]), "lawless" (**a**nomos [6x]), "godlessness" (**a**sebeia [4x]; cf. **a**sebēs, "**un**godly" [3x]), "**un**belief"/"**un**faithfulness" (**a**pistia [5x]; cf. **a**pisteō, "**dis**believe"/"to be **un**faithful" [2x]), "ignorance" (**a**gnoia [1x]). Other words denoting sin in general in Paul are: "error" (plane [4x]), "vanity"/"futility" (mataiotēs [2x]; cf. also "become futile" (mataioō [1x]), "lie" (pseusma [1x]; cf. "liar" [pseustēs, 3x]), "to stumble" (proskoptō [2x]), "to cause to stumble" (skandalizō [3x]). In addition, of course, Paul uses a number of phrases to express the idea of sin; for example, "doing wrong" (Rom 13:4), "deeds of darkness" (Rom 13:12), "do not obey the gospel" (2 Thess 1:8).

---

6. Moo, *Galatians*, 233–34.

1.1.2 The Nature of Sin

The two most fundamental forms of sinful behavior that Paul identifies are "misdirected religion" and a focus on self at the expense of "others."[7] In Paul's famous indictment of all humanity in Romans 1:18–3:20, "misdirected religion" is at the core of the problem. God graciously gave humans some degree of knowledge of the true God, but humans turned away from that knowledge. The well-known passage in Romans 1:18–32 suggests that the rich but sad panoply of human sinning has its roots in the decision to worship idols in place of the living God. The Ephesians text I quoted above singles out the sinful self-focus characteristic of humans by nature by referring to "gratifying the cravings of our flesh and following its desires and thoughts."

It is also important to note that sin involves not just our actions: it is rooted in our very pattern of thinking. As we have seen, the sinful actions that humans commit (or the things that they sinfully fail to do) reveal the fact that humans are "under sin." And this condition, as would be expected, affects the mind. When people turned away from knowledge of God, God "gave them over to a depraved mind" (Rom 1:28). Their "minds were hardened" (2 Cor 3:14 ESV); they were "darkened in their understanding and separated from the life of God because of the ignorance that is in them" (Eph 4:18). They have a pattern of thinking, a "mindset" that is "set on earthly things" (Phil 3:19; see Rom 8:5–7). We should not be surprised, then, when non-Christians have trouble understanding things that seem very logical to us believers. Non-Christians are incapable of thinking rightly about many issues. A critical part of God's new-covenant work, therefore, is the "renewing" of the mind (Rom 12:2; Eph 4:23).

Sin is basically the failure to honor God as God: It is "a rejection of the supremacy of God and his lordship over our lives."[8] In this vein, Paul can also characterize sin as a failure to live up to the fundamental response that people are to make to God, namely, faith. As we noted above, then, Paul can describe sin in terms of a failure to believe. "Not believing" is the root of other sins and of estrangement from God (Rom 3:3; 4:20; 11:20, 23). Especially interesting is the claim that Paul makes in warning the strong in faith not to compel the weak in faith to act against their consciences: "Everything that does not come from faith is sin" (Rom 14:23). Paul suggests here that sin can be relative to the believer's own strength of conscience. Eating meat (14:3, 6) or drinking wine (v. 21) would not be sinful, Paul makes clear, for those whose faith is strong, that is, for those who are convinced in Christ that it is not wrong to eat meat or to drink wine (v. 14). But these acts would be sinful for the Christian who has not yet been convinced that they are free in Christ to do them. The sin in this case would appear

---

7. See Dunn, *Theology of Paul*, 114–24. He identifies misdirected religion, self-indulgence, and sins as the three main consequences of "sin."

8. Schreiner, *Paul*, 103.

to be the disconnect between mind and act. Indirectly, then, Romans 14:23 testifies to the importance of the mind in Paul's conception of sin.

Paul, of course, breaks these fundamental sinful impulses down into specific sinful manifestations. I will briefly mention some of these sinful manifestations in my chapter on "Living in the New Realm."

1.1.3 Sin as Power

A popular recent approach to Paul's theology has been dubbed the "apocalyptic Paul perspective" (see pp. 30–31). This approach emphasizes the way in which Paul presents both the human dilemma and God's response to that dilemma in terms of antithetical powers. Paul's way of conceptualizing sin, especially in his letter to the Romans, is thought to provide one important basis for this view of Paul. Romans is distinctive in its use of "sin" (*hamartia*), both in terms of frequency of usage and in terms of the form of the word. Outside Romans, Paul uses *hamartia* sixteen times, seven times in the singular. Romans uses the word with much greater frequency (forty-eight occurrences) and, moreover, strongly favors the singular form of the word. Forty-five of the forty-eight occurrences are in the singular (and two of the three plurals come in OT quotations: 4:7 [= Ps 32:1]; 11:27 [= Isa 27:9]; see also 7:5). Moreover, Paul attributes quasi-personal powers to "sin." It "reigns" (5:21; cf. 6:13, 14), can be "obeyed" (6:16–17), pays wages (6:23), seizes opportunity (7:8, 11), "deceives," and "kills" (7:11, 13). Sin, to use the vivid language of Beverly Roberts Gaventa, is a "cosmic terrorist."[9] As I have noted before, the way we understand the human condition ("plight") will have significant bearing on our conception of the response required ("solution"). Those who see sin in Paul as mainly a power holding sway over humans will therefore tend to focus on the *Christus victor* model of atonement.

The conception of sin as "power" obviously has basis in Paul's teaching, and in fact it fits quite well into our overall conception of Paul's theology in terms of contrasting "realms." In this view, we can think of the old realm as a place where powers such as sin and death reign, in contrast to the new realm, where righteousness and life reign. This scheme of competing realms, each with its own powers, is a particularly helpful way of explaining the basic teaching of Romans 5–8.

While there is, then, some truth in this picture, it has been overdrawn. We must be careful to recognize just what Paul is trying to claim by speaking of sin in this way— especially critical is the need to allow room for metaphor and rhetoric.[10] For example,

---

9. Beverly Roberts Gaventa, *Our Mother Saint Paul* (Louisville: Westminster John Knox, 2007), 130; see 125–36. See also, e.g., Susan Harding, *Paul's Eschatological Anthropology: The Dynamics of Human Transformation* (Minneapolis: Fortress, 2015). For a series of essays on this topic, see Nijay K. Gupta and John K. Goodrich, eds., *Sin and Its Remedy in Paul* (Eugene, OR: Cascade, 2020).

10. See esp. Günter Röhser, "Paulus und die Herrschaft der Sünd," *ZNW* 103 (2012): 84–110.

the threat of terrorism in a particular country or region may lead media sources to speak in terms of fear "gripping the country" or "stalking the streets," or people "living every day under fear." The purpose is not to suggest that a power called "fear," abstracted from the emotions of individual people, has invaded the region. Similarly with "sin" in Paul. Despite the frequency of the singular form in Paul, he also obviously refers often to "sins" committed by humans.[11] In Romans 3, for instance, the claim that all humans are "under sin" (v. 9) is a conclusion Paul draws from his detailed description of sins committed by gentiles and Jews alike (1:18–2:29), and it is reinforced by a series of Old Testament texts referring to different kinds of sinning (3:10–18). In this light, Paul's claim that "sin entered the world" (5:12) does not mean that the power Sin entered and led to sinning; rather, as the parallel, later verses indicate, sin entered and death began its reign through "the trespass"/"disobedience" of Adam (5:17–19). Paul's portrayal of sin as a power is a way of vividly picturing the power and devastating effects of human sin in the life of human beings. He shows that individual acts of sin constitute a principle, or "network," of sin that is so pervasive and dominant that the person's destiny is determined by those actions. In doing so, he follows Old Testament precedent, which also pictures sin as a power: it is "crouching at your door; it desires to have you" (Gen 4:7).

1.2 The Consequences of Sin

In the Ephesians passage I quoted earlier, Paul, in a way characteristic of his teaching, links sinful behavior with its consequences: people are "dead in transgressions and sins" and are "by nature deserving of wrath." "Death" and "wrath" are two of the many ways Paul denotes the fate of humans apart from Christ. Others are "condemn/condemnation" (*katakrinō, katakrima*); "trouble and distress" (*thlipsis kai stenochōria*); "curse" (*katara*, cf. *anathema*); "punish/punishment" (*ekdikos, ekdikēsis, dikē*); "perish," "destroy/destruction" (usually *apollymi, apōleia*, three times *olethros*, once *phthora*). "Death," however, is the most common way for Paul to designate the fate of humans because of sin (while several texts are in dispute, I think Paul uses the noun *thanatos* twenty-six times in this way; the verb *apothanō* four times). Death, Paul teaches, echoing Genesis 2:17, is the immediate and inevitable consequence of sin (Rom 5:12). The exact meaning of this "death" is not easy to pin down. In the Genesis account, as in Paul's appropriation of it, physical death and "spiritual" death are intertwined in ways that make it difficult to neatly separate them. In fact, Paul appears to use "death" and related words to designate a "physico-spiritual entity"—"total death," the penalty

---

11. A point stressed by Simon Gathercole, "'Sins' in Paul," *NTS* 64 (2018): 144–53. He also notes that some instances of singular *hamartia* in Paul refer to individual sins or to a pattern of life, not to a "power." See also Robert H. Gundry, "The Inferiority of the New Perspective on Paul," in Gundry, *Old Is Better*, 216–18.

incurred for sin.[12] But Paul's focus, as attested, for example, by the variation between "death" and "condemnation" in Romans 5:12–21, is on spiritual death. Perhaps we may view Paul as thinking of physical death in the limited sense as it is bound up with sin.[13] Paul, of course, teaches that all people, including believers, must still experience physical death (e.g., Rom 8:10), the "last enemy" (1 Cor 15:26). But believers have been rescued from spiritual death through their union with Christ (note the past tense in Eph 2:1: "You *were* dead in your transgressions and sins"), and while having to pass through the experience of death, they are assured that they will escape the "eternal death" that unbelievers will suffer.

Wrath is the second consequence of sin according to Ephesians 2:1–3, as Paul asserts that people are "by nature deserving of [or are 'children of,' *tekna*] wrath." "Wrath" is the second most common way Paul refers to the consequences of sin—seventeen occurrences in his letters. "Wrath" translates Greek *orgē*, and Paul follows closely the pattern of usage in the LXX, using the word to refer at times to human anger but more often to denote the reaction of God to sin and to sinful humans (the word occurs over 200 times in the LXX with this sense). Some interpreters argue that the idea of God being angry with sinners is a notion more in keeping with the Greco-Roman gods than with the loving God of the Bible, or that, if we retain the idea, it should be understood in terms of a kind of mechanical cause and effect.[14] But wrath is an aspect of God's person, as is clear from the many Old Testament texts that make the "kindling" of God's wrath the basis for his judgment. God's wrath is necessary to the biblical conception of God. "As long as God is God, He cannot behold with indifference that His creation is destroyed and His holy will trodden underfoot. Therefore He meets sin with His mighty and annihilating reaction."[15] The Old Testament regularly pictures God as responding to sin with wrath;[16] but, particularly in the prophets, the wrath of God is associated with the day of the Lord as a cosmic, climactic outbreak of judgment. Paul's language of

12. See esp. Beker, *Paul the Apostle*, 224; T. Barrosse, "Death and Sin in Saint Paul's Epistle to the Romans," *CBQ* 15 (1953): 449–55; J.-M. Cambier, *L'évangile de la justice et de la grace*, vol. 1 of *L'évangile de Dieu selon l'épître aux Romains: Exégèse et théologie biblique*, StudNeot 3 (Brussels: Desclée de Brouwer, 1967), 227–29.

13. John Polkinghorne suggests that what entered the world with sin was the "bitterness of mortality" (*The God of Hope and the End of the World* [New Haven: Yale University Press, 2002], 126). The meaning of "death" here has significance for debates over the mode and timing of creation. The generally accepted age of the earth makes it impossible to think that physical death, in all its forms, entered the world with Adam's sin (and this is occasionally used as an argument for a seven, 24-hour day creation scenario). I don't think anything in this passage, or elsewhere in Paul, eliminates the possibility (in my view probability) that physical death existed in the world long before Adam.

14. See, e.g., Anthony Tyrrell Hanson, *The Wrath of the Lamb* (London: SPCK, 1957), 84–85; G. H. C. MacGregor, "The Concept of the Wrath of God in the New Testament," *NTS* 7 (1960–61): 101–9. Stephen H. Travis, while more nuanced, also disputes any "retributive" notion in the wrath of God: "God does not impose punishment retributively from outside, but allows people to experience the consequences of their refusal to live in relationship with him" (*Christ and the Judgement of God: The Limits of Divine Retribution in New Testament Thought*, 2nd ed. [Peabody, MA: Hendrickson, 2008], 60–62 [62]).

15. Nygren, *Commentary on Romans*, 98.

16. E.g., when Moses tries to avoid the task God has given him (Exod 4:14); when Pharaoh and the Egyptians refuse to obey his command to let his people go (15:7); when Israel turns to idolatry at Sinai (32:10–12). Often God's wrath strikes in the course of historical events; e.g., in a fire that destroys rebellious Israelites (Num 11:1); in the Babylonian conquest of Jerusalem (Jer 21:3–7).

wrath is also future oriented, as seen in Romans 2:5, where Paul warns Jewish people about "storing up wrath against yourself for the day of God's wrath" (see also, e.g., Rom 5:9; Col 3:6; 1 Thess 1:10). However, Paul can also refer to wrath as a present reality under which people outside of Christ stand (e.g., Rom 1:18; see also 3:5; 4:15; 9:22).

Paul often refers to the devastating effects that sin has on human relationships, urging Christians to overcome their propensity to privilege their own interests above others and so avoid these effects. But it is the eternal consequences of sin—"death," "wrath," "condemnation," "destruction," etc.—that Paul most often mentions and that a person's embrace of the gospel rescues them from.

1.3 The Cosmic Dimension

While not a prominent part of Paul's theology,[17] the apostle recognizes that the old realm is inhabited by, and strongly influenced by, cosmic powers. Again, our key text, Ephesians 2:1–3, alludes to this dimension of the old realm. Before they were Christians, the Ephesians followed "the ruler of the kingdom of the air, the spirit who is now at work in those who are disobedient" (v. 2). Human sin is part of a bigger picture, enmeshed in a nexus of evil.

The "ruler of the kingdom of the air" is undoubtedly to be identified with the spiritual being who is particularly involved in tempting humans to abandon God and follow the way of sin, namely, the "devil"(*diabolos*; cf. Eph 4:27; 6:11; 1 Tim 3:6, 7; 2 Tim 2:26) or "Satan" (*satanas*; cf. Rom 16:20; 1 Cor 5:5; 7:5; 2 Cor 2:11; 11:14; 12:7; 1 Thess 2:18; 2 Thess 2:9; 1 Tim 1:20; 5:15). Following the Old Testament, Paul makes clear just how great is the influence of Satan over this world and the humans who belong to it. He is "the god of this age" (2 Cor 4:4).

Paul refers occasionally to other spiritual beings as well. "Angel" (*angelos*) usually refers to the good angels in Paul (1 Cor 4:9; 6:3; 11:10[?]; 13:1; 2 Cor 11:14; Gal 1:8; 3:19; 4:14; Col 2:18; 2 Thess 1:7; 1 Tim 3:16 [?]; 5:21), but several could refer to evil angels. Paul uses a variety of terms, drawing from his own culture, to refer to other evil spiritual beings: "authorities" (*exousiai*; cf. 1 Cor 15:24; Eph 1:21; 2:2; 3:10; 6:12; Col 1:16; 2:10, 15); "rulers" (*archai*; 1 Cor 15:24; Eph 1:21; 3:10; 6:12; Col 1:18; 2:10, 15); "powers" (*dynameis*; cf. Rom 8:38; 1 Cor 15:24; Eph 1:21); "dominion" (*kyriotētes*; cf. Eph 1:21; Col 1:16); "thrones" (*thronai*; cf. Col 1:16).[18] The existence of spiritual beings of various sorts and their critical impact on the affairs of human beings were fundamental components of the ancient worldview. Translation of this emphasis into

---

17. Dunn rightly notes that Paul does little theologizing about these powers (*Theology of Paul*, 104–10).

18. Determining whether Paul intends to refer to good or evil beings in some of these texts is difficult (e.g., on Col 1:16, see Moo, *Colossians*, 122–23). "The elements of the world" (*ta stoicheiai tou kosmou*; cf. Gal 4:3, 9; Col 2:8, 20) is often taken as a reference to spiritual beings also, but this identification is unlikely: the reference is probably to the material "elements" of the universe, with possible derivative significance for spiritual powers. See Moo, *Colossians*, 187–93; idem, *Galatians*, 260–63.

our culture is contested. On the one hand, the ancient worldview about the significance of spiritual beings for the affairs of this world is, in a fundamental sense at least, the biblical worldview as well. Spiritual powers, while defeated in Christ (Col 2:15), are still active and powerful: "Our struggle is not against flesh and blood, but against the rulers, against the authorities, against the powers of this dark world and against the spiritual forces of evil in the heavenly realms" (Eph 6:12). Human sin, Paul makes clear, can often be traced to the influence of these beings. More contested is whether we are justified in finding reference in these texts to the various structures, persons, and institutions through whom evil "powers" might be working today. On this view, the language of these texts can be applied to "unseen forces working in the world through pagan religion, astrology, or magic, or through the oppressive systems that enslaved or tyrannized human beings."[19] Paul may suggest something of this sort when he suggests that a believer who participates in idolatrous temple meals is, in fact, participating with demons (1 Cor 10:18–21). Nevertheless, it is important that we not simply dismiss Paul's obvious belief in these spiritual beings and the influence they have both on individuals and societal structures.[20]

Another aspect of what we might call the "cosmic context" is the effect that human sin has had on the world in general. Romans 8:19–22 is the relevant text:

> For the creation waits in eager expectation for the children of God to be revealed. For the creation was subjected to frustration, not by its own choice, but by the will of the one who subjected it, in hope that the creation itself will be liberated from its bondage to decay and brought into the freedom and glory of the children of God. We know that the whole creation has been groaning as in the pains of childbirth right up to the present time.

The "creation" (*ktisis*) that Paul has in view here, as most interpreters recognize, is the "subhuman" creation. Following the lead of psalmists and prophets (e.g., Ps 65:12–13; Isa 24:4; Jer 4:28; 12:4), Paul personifies the world of nature in order to portray its "fall" and anticipated glory. This passage makes no direct reference to human sin. But Paul clearly has the story of Genesis 3 in view here; "the one who subjected [creation]" is clearly God, and his subjection must be the curse that he pronounces on "the ground" (Gen 3:17). However, he is also probably reflecting passages such as Isaiah 24, where

19. N. T. Wright, *Colossians and Philemon*, 72. See, for this general way of thinking about the "powers" in the NT, the three-volume project of Walter Wink (*Naming the Powers*; *Unmasking the Powers: The Invisible Forces that Determine Human Existence*; *Engaging the Powers: Discernment and Resistance in a World of Domination* [Philadelphia: Fortress, 1984; 1986; 1992]).

20. See, e.g., Clinton E. Arnold, *Powers of Darkness: Principalities and Powers in Paul's Letters* (Downers Grove, IL: InterVarsity Press, 1992); Robert Ewusie Moses, *Practices of Power: Revisiting the Principalities and Powers in the Pauline Letters* (Minneapolis: Fortress, 2014).

the "groaning" of the earth is traced to continuing human abuse of the world they were given to steward (Isa 24:4–5).[21] Human sin, Paul is affirming, has had an impact on the cosmos. Just what this impact is, is very difficult to pin down. Probably the focus is on a disruption in the relationship between humans and the earth. Human sin has affected the state of nature itself—and will continue to do so until the end of this age.

2 THE STORY OF THE OLD REALM: UNDERLYING NARRATIVES

As I explained earlier, I occupy a middle ground between those who think that narrative is the most important, or one of the most important, entry points into Paul's thinking and those who dismiss narrative as having no significant bearing on Paul's theology (pp. 11–14). While Paul rarely expresses his theology in narrative form, he often clearly presupposes one or more narratives as the jumping-off point of his theological teaching. And, of course, we would expect nothing less, granted the prevalence of narrative in Paul's Scriptures and the basic narrative form of the gospel story itself. Two narratives have a strong bearing on Paul's theology of the old realm: the broad human narrative and the narrative of Israel.[22]

2.1 The Story of Humankind

I may be stretching matters to refer here to "narrative," since what I have in view is really only two "moments" in time: the entrance of sin and death in Adam and the victory over them won through Christ. The significance of Adam in Paul's theology is debated. He refers to Adam only four times (Rom 5:14; 1 Cor 15:22; 1 Cor 15:45; 1 Tim 2:13–14), although several other passages clearly refer to him (Rom 5:12, 15–19; 1 Cor 11:8–9; 15:21, 47–49). But many other texts may imply reference to Adam. In general, we agree that the contrast between Adam and Christ, and, by derivation, creation and new creation, is a fundamental building block of Paul's teaching, undergirding his theological argument at many points.[23] In general, Paul shows no interest in the person of Adam (unlike his Jewish near-contemporary, Philo of Alexandria). Paul's focus is on the comparison between Adam and Christ. Two texts are particularly important for our topic here.

The first Adam-Christ comparison claims simply that through the "man" Adam, death came into world, leading ultimately to the death of all humans (1 Cor 15:21–22). This point is elaborated in Romans 5:12–21, a text that will require careful attention.

---

21. See esp. Jonathan A. Moo, "Romans 8.19–22 and Isaiah's Cosmic Covenant," *NTS* 54 (2008): 74–89; Richard Bauckham, "The Story of the Earth according to Paul: Romans 8:18–23," *RevExp* 108 (2011): 93–94; D. Moo and J. Moo, *Creation Care*, 147–52.

22. Stendahl labels the stories of Adam and Christ on the

one hand and Abraham and Christ on the other as the "spanning arches" in Paul's theology (*Final Account*, 26).

23. E.g., Ridderbos, *Paul*, 283: "Adam was a figure who lay behind a great deal of Paul's theologizing." See also, e.g., Beker, *Paul the Apostle*, 100; Dunn, *Theology of Paul*, 199–204.

Romans 5:12–21 is best seen as setting forth the *basis* for the assurance of ultimate salvation articulated in verses 1–11.[24] Simply put: we "boast in the hope of the glory of God" (v. 2) because we are in Christ and not in Adam. Or, more expansively: "In order to accomplish this [namely, God's promise to save all those who are justified and reconciled through Christ], there exists a life-giving union between Christ and his own that is similar to, but more powerful than, the death-producing union between Adam and all his own." Paul begins by tracing the entrance of sin and death into the world to Adam (v. 12). Both the internal structure of this verse and its function in the discourse of verses 12–21 are debated. When it comes toward the beginning of a sentence, "just as"[25] normally introduces the protasis of a comparative sentence. We would expect, in other words, to find a "so also" clause to complete the sentence. Some scholars have identified such a "so also" clause in this verse or the next, but their identifications are not very plausible.[26] Most scholars therefore conclude that Paul starts a comparison in this verse that he does not (grammatically) finish. English translations mark this break in syntax by inserting a dash after verse 12 (e.g., NRSV; ESV; NAB; NASB; NET; NIV).

The first clause attributes the entrance of sin into the world to "one man." This "man" is, of course, Adam, whose very name in Hebrew means "man" or "human." As I noted earlier, the "sin" that enters the world through Adam cannot be divorced from his own act of disobedience; at the same time, however, sin here is also the bridgehead that paves the way for "sinning" as a condition of humanity.[27] Paul's claim that "sin came into the world through one man" would have been nothing new to anyone who knew their Old Testament or Jewish tradition. Nor would his second assertion in this verse: "And death through sin [came into the world]."[28] The unbreakable connection between sin and death, made clear in Genesis 2–3, was a staple of Jewish theology.[29] "Death" in this paragraph is contrasted with eternal life (v. 21) and appears basically equivalent to "condemnation" in verses 16–18. As I argued earlier, then, "death" here, is a "physico-spiritual entity"—"total death," the penalty incurred for sin.[30] As verse

---

24. For this reading of the sequence of argument in this part of Romans, see Moo, *Romans* (NICNT), 290–95.

25. Greek *hōsper*, repeated in vv. 19 and 21, where it is completed with *houtōs kai*.

26. Since the apodosis of this kind of sentence is often introduced with *houtōs* ("so also"), the most obvious possibility is to make v. 12c–d the apodosis; thus: "(a) just as sin entered the world through one man, (b) and through sin death, (c) *so also* death spread to all people, (d) because all people sinned" (J. T. Kirby, "The Syntax of Romans 5.12: A Rhetorical Approach," *NTS* 33 [1987]: 283–86). But when *houtōs* has this function in the NT, it is either used alone (Matt 13:40; 24:27, 37; Luke 17:24; Rom 6:19) or with *kai* following (John 5:21, 26; Rom 5:19, 21; 6:4; 11:31; 1 Cor 11:12; 15:22; 16:1; Gal 4:29; Jas 2:26). The order found in

v. 12—*kai houtōs*—never occurs to complete a comparison and is a most unnatural way to do so. There are several other options, all of them, in my view, unlikely.

27. Taking *kosmos*, "world," to be the world of humanity (see "all people" in v. 12c and the repeated "many" and "all" in vv. 15–19); see, e.g., Cranfield, *Romans*, 1:274.

28. We must supply "came into the world" (*eis ton kosmon eisēlthen*) from the first clause.

29. See, particularly, A. J. M. Wedderburn, "The Theological Structure of Romans V.12," *NTS* 19 (1972–1973): 339–42.

30. See esp. Beker, *Paul the Apostle*, 224; Barrosse, "Death and Sin," 449–55; Cambier, *L'évangile de la justice et de la grace*, 227–29. For a helpful overview of the options for the meaning of death in this context and their theological implications, see

12b depicts the *entrance* of death as the consequence of sin, verse 12c makes explicit that this death has *spread* to every person. The exact relationship of this clause to its context depends on what the adverb "in this way" (*houtōs*) means. If it is not correlative with "just as" (which I have seen reason to doubt), there are three possibilities. (1) It may pick up verse 12a–b as the general condition in which sin and death spread to all people; Adam having introduced sin into the world, and with it death—it was in these circumstances that death spread and all sinned.[31] But it would be unusual for the word to mean simply "in these circumstances." (2) "In this way" (*houtōs*) might pick up the reference to "the one man"; as one man was responsible for the *entrance* of sin and death (v. 12a), so, "in this [same] way," was one man responsible for the *spread* of death.[32] Defenders of this interpretation point to the emphatic position of "through one man"[33] and to the form of the comparison in verses 18 and 19, where Adam's sin is the cause of the condemnation of all people. But it may be significant that Paul in verse 12—unlike in verses 18–19—speaks not of "the sin of one man" but of "sin" entering through one man. This suggests that Paul's focus is not at this point on the corporate significance of Adam's act but on his role as the instrument through whom sin and death were unleashed into the world. (3) With the majority of commentators, then, I think that "in this way" draws a comparison between the manner in which death came into the world—through sin—and the manner in which death spread to everyone—also through sin.[34] On this view, we may interpret verse 12 chiastically:

A sin (12a) produces
    B death (12b);
    B' all die (12c)
A' because all sin (12d).

Verse 12d, then, explains why death is universal (v. 12c): sin is also universal; "all sinned."[35] Paul asserts that the entrance of death into the world through the sin of Adam has led to death for all people; and all people die, Paul asserts, because all people "sinned." In a sense, then, Paul's concern in this verse, and throughout the passage, is not with "original sin," or better, "originating sin," but with "original death."[36] Nevertheless, the connection of sin with death in a universal perspective is

---

Thomas H. McCall, *Against God and Nature: The Doctrine of Sin*, Foundations of Evangelical Theology (Wheaton, IL: Crossway, 2019), 311–23.

31. Godet, *Romans*, 206.

32. See, e.g., Ridderbos, *Paul*, 96.

33. The phrase *di henos anthrōpou* comes first in its clause.

34. On this view, the point is that, as death *came into* the world through sin, so death *spread* to everyone "in the same way"—by sinning.

35. I assume, with most interpreters and translations, that the opening of this last clause in v. 12 (Gk. *eph hō*) has a causal meaning. See the exposition on p. 218.

36. See, e.g., Dunn, *Romans 1–8*, 273.

a key teaching here. Unfortunately, Paul does not directly tell us how this connection "works." He clearly teaches that there is a causal nexus between sin and death, which, exhibited in the case of Adam, has repeated itself in the case of every human being. No one, Paul makes clear, escapes the reign of death because no one escapes the power of sin. Each of us dies because each of us sins.

But, of course, there is more in this paragraph. Recognizing, perhaps, that he has failed to complete the comparison he began in verse 12, Paul restates the first part of the comparison and then completes it with the second part in verses 18–19. The movement of the argument is again from Adam to Christ, as the apostle continues to reassure believers that they will certainly enjoy the eternal life that their justification has secured for them. Our concern, however, is with the way in which Paul presents Adam's side of the comparison. Repeating the point he made earlier in verse 12, though using a different word, Paul attributes to Adam a "trespass" (*paraptōma*) that has brought "condemnation" (*katakrima*) to all humans. And, just in case we have missed this critical point, Paul reiterates it in verse 19, using the same basic structure as in verse 18 but with different language.

The precise relationship between Adam's sin and the sin of all humans is unclear in this passage. The nub of the issue can be simply put. How do we integrate two of Paul's apparently contradictory claims?

1. Each human being dies because each human being sins (Rom 5:12); and
2. Each human being dies because Adam sinned (Rom 5:18, 19; cf. 1 Cor 15:21).

Among the half dozen or so options that have been suggested, three deserve, in my view, serious consideration.

First, we could be content to posit an unresolved tension between the individual and the corporate emphasis.[37] Paul does not resolve these two perspectives, and we should not force a resolution that Paul himself never made. The exegete in me applauds the concern to let each text have its own say. However, the theologian in me is reluctant to give up too early in the pursuit of an interpretation that integrates Paul's teaching.

Second, then, we might privilege the apparently individual focus of verse 12 and interpret verses 18–19 in light of it. The most likely way to do this is to assume a middle

---

37. See particularly Wedderburn, "Theological Structure," 338–39. Advocates of this view note that contemporary Judaism evidenced a similar tension between individual and Adamic responsibility for sin and death. Note, e.g., how the Syriac Apocalypse of Baruch can assert, on the one hand, "When Adam sinned and death was decreed against those who were to be born" (23.4) and "What did you [Adam] do to all who were born after you?" (48.42), and, on the other hand, "Adam is, therefore, not the cause, except only for himself, but each of us has become our own Adam" (54.19). Similarly, note 54.15: "Although Adam sinned first and has brought death upon all who were not in his own time, yet each of them who has been born from him has prepared for himself the coming torment" (translations from *OTP*). See also LAB 13.8, 9. On the Jewish conception of sin and death, see esp. Davies, *Paul and Rabbinic Judaism*, 17–35.

term in the connection between Adam's sin and the condemnation of all humans. Each person dies because each person sins; but each person necessarily sins because of a sin nature inherited from Adam.[38] Death, then, is due immediately to the sinning of each individual but ultimately to the sin of Adam; for it was Adam's sin that corrupted human nature and made individual sinning an inevitability. This view has much in its favor. It retains the normal meaning of "sin" in verse 12 while explaining at the same time how Paul could assert that Adam's sin brings condemnation upon all (vv. 18–19). It also explains why all people act contrary to the will of God—there is a fatal, God-resisting bent in all people, inherited from Adam. The obvious drawback to this view is its need to add a step in Paul's argument that is not explicit in the context. Moreover, assuming this intermediate step appears to stand in some tension with Paul's persistent focus on the significance of the one act of the one man Adam. "Many died by the trespass of the one man" (v. 15a); "the judgment followed one sin and brought condemnation" (v. 16b); "by the trespass of the one man, death reigned" (v. 17a); "one trespass resulted in condemnation for all people" (v. 18a). On the view we are examining, these statements must be expanded to mean "one man's trespass *resulted in the corruption of human nature, which caused all people to sin, and so* brought condemnation on all people."

Third, then, we might reverse the procedure and interpret verse 12 in light of verses 18–19. Paul can view the sin of all people (v. 12) and the sin of Adam (vv. 18–19) as a single complex in light of Adam's significance as a corporate figure. Drawing from the well-known biblical concept of corporate solidarity,[39] we would then see Adam as the representative head of the human race, whose sin is at the same time the sin of all people.[40] "In Adam all die" (1 Cor 15:22) because in Adam all sinned. This view also requires us to "read something into" the text—in this case the notion of Adam as a corporate, representative figure. However, what is read into the text here is arguably a conception that Paul makes quite determinative in his way of picturing the work of Christ, the "second Adam."[41]

---

38. See, e.g., Harding, who argues that "sin entered the world" in v. 12a refers to ontological sin, which leads to the actual sinning of v. 12d (*Paul's Eschatological Anthropology*, 114–19). See also McCall, *Against God and Nature*, 149–205. Others (e.g., Luther and Calvin) think that "all sinned" in v. 12 means that all people exist "in a state of sin." According to them, Paul is not basing the universal reign of death on individual acts of sin but on sinful human nature. (Note, however, that Calvin's comment on p. 210 of his commentary, and his discussion in the *Institutes* [2.1.5–8] appear to presume original guilt in some sense.) However, there is little evidence that the verb *hamartanō* can denote the possession of a sin nature, and the view is little defended in our day.

39. The classic biblical example is Joshua 7, where a sin committed by one individual, Achan, is also said to be "Israel's sin" (vv. 1, 11) and the reason why God's anger "burns against Israel" (v. 1). H. W. Robinson (*Corporate Personality in Ancient Israel* [repr., Philadelphia: Fortress, 1980]) is one of the key proponents of the importance of solidarity in OT thought. Robinson and others certainly go too far in speaking of corporate *personality* (see J. W. Rogerson, "The Hebrew Conception of Corporate Personality: A Reexamination," *JTS* 21 [1970]: 1–16), but the importance of corporate categories for the OT and Jewish thinking is generally accepted.

40. See, again, the exposition on pp. 218–20.

41. See esp. Ridderbos, *Paul*, 53–64.

On the whole, then, I prefer this third view. As a representative figure, Adam's sin is considered to be the sin of all humans, earning for all the sentence of death/condemnation.[42]

2.2 The Story of Israel

Recent study of Paul has stressed the importance of reading the apostle against the background of his first-century Jewish world. The orientation of Jews living in this world was decisively shaped by their sense of taking part in an ongoing story, focused on God's relationship with his people Israel. God initiates this relationship through his call of Abraham, and it is confirmed by covenant with both Abraham and the patriarchs. God formalizes his special relationship with Israel by giving them his law, a law that, if obeyed, will secure for the people possession of the land God gives them. Because of their stubborn failure to honor God by following his law, Israel is sent into exile. Yet, as anticipated as early as the "second giving of the law" in Deuteronomy, exile would not be the end of the matter. In an act of sheer grace, God promises to rescue his people from exile, establish them in their land again, transform their hearts and minds, and shower blessings on them (Deut 30:1–10).[43] As the Old Testament comes to its end, we find some Israelites back in their land again but without experiencing the blessings promised by the prophets for the time of restoration. Paul, then, like most, or at least many Jewish people in his day, lives in expectation of the day when God would fulfill those prophecies. Unlike most of his fellow Jews, however, Paul is convinced that God has begun to fulfill those prophecies through Jesus of Nazareth, Messiah and Son of God. A central issue in current scholarship arises at just this point. How much difference for Paul's reading of the Israel story did his new conviction about the shape of salvation history make? To focus on the issue I deal with in this chapter: Granted the inauguration of a new realm, how then does the story of Israel shape Paul's understanding of the old realm? Three particular aspects of that story deserve attention: Paul's understanding of Israel's plight, of the role of the law of Moses (Torah), and of the broader human significance of Israel's experience of the law.

2.2.1 Israel's Plight

N. T. Wright has had an enormous influence on our understanding of Paul's theology in the last four decades. Perhaps his key hermeneutical starting point is an

---

42. A strong objection to this view arises from recent scientific discoveries that raise problems for the idea that all humans could be biologically descended from a single human like Adam. While I think it important that biblical scholars take account of scientific findings, I think the jury may still be out on the scientific data on this matter. In any case, I think Paul's argument from Adam's representative significance is difficult to maintain if Adam were not a single historical figure. See Douglas J. Moo, "'The Type of the One to Come': Adam in Paul's Theology," *TrinJ* 40 (2019): 145–64.

43. The basic outline of this story is clear in the OT and acknowledged by virtually all scholars. See a useful and succinct summary in Mark J. Boda, *A Severe Mercy: Sin and Its Remedy in the Old Testament* (Winona Lake, IN: Eisenbrauns, 2009), 515–23.

insistence on reading Paul against the backdrop of the story of Israel—as Wright conceives it. This approach to Paul is evident in his distinctive (though certainly not unique) interpretation of Israel's plight in terms of "exile" and "vocation."

The exile, of course, was the geographic dispersion of the people of Israel as God's punishment for their persistent sin. The prophets warned Israel about exile to come but also predicted that God, in his grace, would restore his people after a period of exile. The end of the Old Testament finds some Israelites back in their land again. However, according to Wright, and others, the physical return to the land of a small number of Israelites after being exiled in Babylon did not truly end the exile. The meager number of Israelites in the land and their subjection under foreign powers were a far cry from the golden age predicted by the prophets for the time of restoration. Nehemiah calls out to God: "But see, we are slaves today, slaves in the land you gave our ancestors so they could eat its fruit and the other good things it produces. Because of our sins, its abundant harvest goes to the kings you have placed over us. They rule over our bodies and our cattle as they please. We are in great distress" (Neh 9:36–37). Such passages suggest that postexilic Israel did not think her exile had ended. Jews in Paul's day, subjected to the gentiles in the form of the Romans, would have had good reason to think of themselves as still in exile. However, while Paul's fellow Jews were looking for national deliverance that would end their exile, Paul saw the spiritual victory won by Christ as the end of Israel's exile.[44]

Wright's "Israel-still-in-exile" scenario rightly draws attention to a key dynamic in the story of redemption, what has been labeled the "S-E-R" pattern: Sin-Exile-Restoration. One sees this pattern as early as Deuteronomy.[45] Moses "reissues" the law to the people, promising them great blessing for their obedience, but warning them that a curse would fall on them if they disobeyed. By the end of Moses's sermon, it becomes clear that the latter scenario would, in fact, be Israel's fate (esp. chs. 27–32). Their sin will lead to exile. But God promises that after exile, he will again extend his grace to Israel, restoring their fortunes and accomplishing his purposes in and through them. Wright's focus on exile therefore taps into a major structural component of salvation history.

However, I also register four concerns about the "Israel-in-exile" template.

First, most basically, Wright shifts the meaning of "exile" from a geographical to a spiritual focus. Exile in his scheme is basically a convenient way of saying that the prophecies of restoration had not yet been fulfilled.[46] In one sense, then, the idea

44. A recent statement of N. T. Wright's view along with critical evaluations is found in James M. Scott, ed., *Exile: A Conversation with N. T. Wright* (Downers Grove, IL: InterVarsity Press, 2017).

45. See, e.g., Paul A. Barker, *The Triumph of Grace in Deuteronomy: Faithless Israel, Faithful Yahweh in Deuteronomy*, Paternoster

Biblical Monographs (Waynesboro, GA: Paternoster, 2004); J. Gordon McConville, *Grace in the End: A Study in Deuteronomic Theology* (Grand Rapids: Zondervan, 1993).

46. Steven M. Bryan, *Jesus and Israel's Traditions of Judgement and Restoration*, SNTSMS 117 (Cambridge: Cambridge University Press, 2002), 12–14.

is uncontroversial. All agree that the great spiritual and material blessings that the prophets predicted would be experienced by the people once they were back in their land had not yet found fulfillment. Yet by calling this situation "exile," a word that Paul never uses, Wright subtly but significantly shapes the way we understand the plight that Paul highlights as the backdrop to the work of Christ.

Second, outlining Paul's theology in terms of "end of exile" may oversimplify a more complex reality—in two ways. On the one hand, as Wright has acknowledged, Jews in Paul's day probably had different views of their condition. Some undoubtedly would have thought of themselves as, indeed, still in exile and longing for deliverance. Others, however, perhaps especially those who were enjoying their status within the nation, probably did not conceive of themselves as still in exile.[47] On the other hand, the coming of Christ, while bringing many restoration promises to fulfillment, would have partially "ended the exile." But Paul is clear that many of these prophecies await fulfillment, especially (at least in my view) prophecies about Israel's final deliverance (e.g., Rom 11:25–28).[48]

Third, and perhaps most relevant to the current issue, privileging exile language as our way of conceiving the old realm presents the issue in terms of the nation of Israel. Yet Paul's discussion of sin is focused basically on the individual. Of course, Paul often ties the situation of the individual to the larger corporate entity of which he or she is a part. But to the degree that Paul does this with respect to sin, the focus is on solidarity with Adam—a *human* problem—rather than solidarity with Israel. Certainly Paul, following an important biblical pattern, suggests that Israel reenacts the story of Adam.[49] But in his concern to bring all humans under condemnation because of sin, Paul uses the Adam solidarity to make his case.[50] The human story, with its tragic beginnings in Adam, appears to be the story that Paul uses to inform his view of the old realm. Exile is the punishment for Israel's covenant unfaithfulness; yet, as we have seen, it is the language of death, wrath, and condemnation that Paul uses to characterize the plight of humans. The language of exile tends to privilege the story of Israel in way that is characteristic of the New Perspective in general but that, like that movement as a whole, tends to shift the center of gravity in Paul's theologizing a bit too far toward the "Israel" side and away from the "human" side (see further below). Exile, after all, is not the fundamental issue; it is a manifestation of a deeper issue, namely, sin.

---

47. Richard B. Hays, "Victory over Violence: The Significance of N. T. Wright's Jesus for New Testament Ethics," in Newman, *Jesus and the Restoration of Israel*, 142–48; Bryan, *Jesus and Israel's Traditions*, 15–16. James C. VanderKam identifies three different narratives about "exile" in Judaism ("Exile in Jewish Apocalyptic Literature," in Scott, *Exile: Old Testament, Jewish, and Christian Conceptions*, 89–109). See also Steve Mason, "N. T. Wright on Paul the Pharisee and Ancient Jews in Exile," *SJT* 69 (2016): 432–52.

48. Mark Seifrid suggests that Paul viewed Jewish rejection of Christ as a "new exile," to be ended with Christ's return (*Christ, Our Righteousness: Paul's Theology of Justification*, NSBT 9 [Downers Grove, IL: InterVarsity Press, 2000], 168). See the response of Hafemann, "Paul and the Exile," 329–71.

49. See esp. Beale, *New Testament Biblical Theology*, 46–58.

50. See Timo Eskola, "How to Write a Synthesis: Wright and the Problem of Continuity in New Testament Theology," in Scott, *Exile*, 243–47.

A second way of conceiving of the human plight against the backdrop of Israel's story has received greater emphasis in some of Wright's more recent books: vocational failure.[51] God created humans to be his image bearers and to steward the world God had created. This vocation fell to Israel, called to be a nation that would spread the knowledge of God to the world. It is Israel's failure in this vocation that Paul singles out in passages such as Romans 2:17–24. Wright is justified in pointing out this theme in Scripture: Israel is called to be "a light for the Gentiles" (Isa 49:6). However, passages that put Israel in the role of stimulating the salvation of the nations are comparatively few. More often, the conversion of the gentiles is attributed to God's work on behalf of Israel. However, Wright expands the idea of "vocation" to include worshiping and serving God—a point that deserves emphasis in our reading of the Old Testament and in current Christian life as well. That being said, the danger of Wright's "vocational" emphasis is that it can detract from what Scripture clearly indicates is the main issue— again, sin. It is the tragic human bent to follow our own path rather than the path that God lays down for us that is the basic problem. Failure to worship rightly and to pursue our vocation are manifestations of this root failure. In dozens of passages, the prophets announce the coming of God's wrath on humans because of sin—often on the nations but on Israel also, as we see, for instance, in Daniel 9. Why is Israel in exile, longing for deliverance? Because "we have sinned and done wrong. We have been wicked and have rebelled; we have turned away from your commands and laws. We have not listened to your servants the prophets, who spoke in your name to our kings, our princes and our ancestors, and to all the people of the land" (Dan 9:5–6). This theme is repeated throughout this chapter and is representative of the prophets' focus in their rebuke of Israel. It is sin/disobedience that occasions God's anger and wrath (see v. 16).

Paul stands in clear continuity with this analysis. In Romans 1–3 he repeatedly cites disobedience of the law as defining Israel's plight, famously bringing the gentiles also under the same indictment (see 2:14–15). Though not having Torah, they also have a form of "law," and they, too, have failed to live up to it. Yes, Paul implies that Israel has been guilty of failing to fulfill their vocation. In 2:20–21 he faults Israel for failing to be "the light to the nations" that God intended the nation to be. But Paul does not then fault Israel for failing in this mission but accuses them of failing to obey the law of which they themselves are so proud.[52] Paul's relentless focus on actual sinning in these chapters is fittingly climaxed in his famous assertion in 3:9: "Jews and Gentiles alike are all under the power of sin."[53] So Paul also warns that humans stand under and are

---

51. See especially Wright, *Day the Revolution Began.*

52. Bultmann's suggestion that even the attempt to obey the law is sinful (constituting an attempt to assert ourselves in the face of God; *Theology of the New Testament*, 1:264–67) is now generally and appropriately dismissed.

53. For the focus on actual sinning in Paul, see also Rom 1:32; 2:1, 12; 3:7, 9–20; 4:25; 5:12–14, 19; 6:1–2; 1 Cor 15:3; Gal 1:4; Eph 1:7; 2:1, 5; Col 2:13, 14; 1 Tim 1:15.

threatened by God's wrath. He does this three times in Romans 1–3 (1:18; 2:5; 3:5) and seven times elsewhere (e.g., "children of wrath" in Eph 2:3).[54]

It is important in its own regard to rightly describe Paul's view of the human plight. But it is also important because our conception of the plight directly impacts our understanding of the solution to that plight (see pp. 405–7).

2.2.2 The Law (Torah)

A central element in Paul's discussion of the old realm is the role of the Old Testament law. We should pause to allow that claim to sink in. The law *of God* as part of the old realm of *sin and death*? Yet Paul is quite adamant about both sides of the matter. The law given to Israel through Moses is, indeed, God's law—a law that is "good" (Rom 7:12, 16), "holy" (v. 12), "righteous" (v. 12), and "spiritual" (v. 14).[55] Yet this same law, Paul affirms in the same letter, "brings wrath" (4:15), increases the trespass (5:20), and arouses sinful passions (7:5). Paul's association of God's law with the old realm is one of the most debated points in his theology.[56]

2.2.2.1 Definition: Law and Torah

Paul uses the word *nomos* 121 times in his letters, although the occurrences are not distributed evenly. The word occurs 74 times in Romans and 32 times in Galatians; yet not at all in 2 Corinthians, Colossians, 1 and 2 Thessalonians, 2 Timothy, Titus, and Philemon. Paul's *nomos* is, of course, tightly connected to the Old Testament use of *torah*, which is usually translated by *nomos* in the LXX. The focus on the Mosaic law in Paul's use of the word is evident throughout his letters. Particularly significant are Galatians 3, where Paul claims that the law came "430 years" after Abraham (v. 17; see also Rom 5:13–14, 20), and Romans 2:12; 3:19; 1 Corinthians 9:20–21, where the difference between having *nomos* and not having it is the difference between Jew and gentile. More than 90 percent of the occurrences of *nomos* in Paul refer to the Mosaic law. Although some have suggested that this translation introduced a harder, more legalistic conception than is fair to the Hebrew word,[57] *nomos* is a fair equivalent for *torah* in its usual Old Testament meaning—the body of commands, with sanctions, given through Moses to Israel at Sinai.[58] Paul, then, associates the law with "doing" and "works." He legitimately finds in Torah itself a witness to this essential meaning of

---

54. See also Rom 4:15; 5:9; 9:22; 1 Thess 1:10; 2:16; 5:9.

55. A few interpreters have thought that Paul in Gal 3:19 implies that the law was given by angels rather than by God (e.g., Hans Hübner, *Law in Paul's Thought: Studies of the New Testament and Its World* [Edinburgh: T&T Clark, 1984], 26–29; Martyn, *Galatians*, 356–57), but this is very improbable.

56. "The most intricate doctrinal issue in [Paul's] theology" (Schoeps, *Paul*, 168).

57. E.g., S. Schechter, *Aspects of Rabbinic Theology* (New York: Schocken, 1961 [orig. ed. 1909]), 117–19; C. H. Dodd, "The Law," in *The Bible and the Greeks* (London: Hodder & Stoughton, 1935), 25–41.

58. See esp. Stephen Westerholm, "*Torah, Nomos,* and Law: A Question of 'Meaning,'" *SR* 15 (1986): 327–36; idem, *Perspectives*, 298–300; Dunn, *Theology of Paul*, 131–32.

the law, quoting Leviticus 18:5, "The person who does these things will live by them" (Rom 10:5; Gal 3:12).[59] "Life" in the Old Testament sense of blessing and peace in the land comes via doing the law. Of course, the Pentateuch makes clear that this call for doing the law is embedded in a bigger story of God's grace. But Paul does not use *nomos* to denote this broader story; for him, "law" is what God commands and is to be met by the human response of obedience.

This is not to ignore, however, that the Hebrew and Greek words each have their own semantic range and that these semantic ranges do not map neatly on to the other. In the case of *nomos*, its semantic range extends beyond our English "law."[60] Because the Mosaic law was, for the Jews, the heart of their Scripture, Paul can use *nomos* to designate the Pentateuch or the Old Testament as a whole (see Rom 3:19a; 1 Cor 9:8, 9; 14:21, 34; Gal 4:21b). In other passages, *nomos*, by synecdoche, designates the Mosaic covenant, or the "law-administration" of the Old Testament (Rom 3:21a; 6:14–15; 7:4, 6[?]).[61] In another extension from its reference to the Mosaic law, it can designate divine "law" generally (Rom 2:14; 8:7[?]) or the "Christian" form of God's law (Gal 6:2 and see *ennomos Christou* in 1 Cor 9:21; and my discussion on pp. 614–22). More debated is the question whether Paul ever uses *nomos* without direct reference to "law" of some kind. Yet there is ample warrant in Hellenistic Greek for using the term to mean "principle," "norm," or "force," and several of Paul's uses fit best here (Rom 3:27; 7:21, 23[?], 25[?]; 8:2).[62]

Another definitional issue arises in light of the history of interpretation, where it has been popular to divide the Mosaic law into three categories—moral, ceremonial, and civil.[63] Of course, it is quite appropriate and useful to categorize the various kinds of Old Testament commandments, and Jesus's reference to the "more important matters of the law" (Matt 23:23) shows that the New Testament can prioritize certain commandments over others. And it is probably not simply by accident that Paul, when he cites examples of Old Testament commandments, tends to focus on Decalogue commandments (Rom 7:7, 13:9). But it is not easy even within the Ten Commandments to distinguish between what is "moral"—and therefore, it is assumed, eternal—and what is not—as the controversy over the Sabbath command reveals. More important, Jews in Paul's day did not divide up the law into categories; on the contrary, there was a strong insistence that the law was a unity and could not be obeyed in parts.[64] Nor, apparently, did Paul,

---

59. See esp. Sprinkle, *Law and Life*, 136–42; cf. Gathercole, "Torah, Life, and Salvation," 126–45; Watson, "Constructing an Antithesis," 101–2.

60. See, e.g., Winger, *By What Law?*

61. See, e.g., Matthew B. Leighton, "'Mosaic Covenant,' as a Possible Referent for *NOMOS* in Paul," *TynBul* 69 (2018): 161–81.

62. On each of these verses, see the relevant discussion in Moo, *Romans* (NICNT).

63. See Walter C. Kaiser Jr., *Toward an Old Testament Theology* (Grand Rapids: Zondervan, 1978), 114–16.

64. While there was some debate among Jews about how much of the law was required to be obeyed by a proselyte, the view that the law was fundamentally a unity was basic. See m. 'Abot 4:2; b. Šabb. 31a; and the discussion in E. E. Urbach, *The Sages: Their Concepts and Beliefs*, 2 vols. (Jerusalem: Magnes, 1979), 1:360–65.

as Galatians 5:3 implies: "I declare to every man who lets himself be circumcised that he is obligated to obey the whole law." This being the case, we would require clear contextual evidence to think that the word *nomos* in certain texts can apply only to one part of the law.

Finally, in terms of the basic meaning of *nomos*, we should note the suggestion that *nomos* in Paul sometimes means "legalism."[65] This specific extension of the semantic range of *nomos* is an attempt to get around the tension I noted earlier. On this view, the "law as God gave it" is good and holy; it is "the law as humans have perverted it" that accounts for the negative assertions about *nomos*. However, while Paul can of course refer to the concept of legalism, the evidence that he uses *nomos* to refer to this notion is not compelling.[66]

2.2.2.2 The Law as Torah: Fundamental Salvation-Historical Perspective

We can best perceive the salvation-historical locus of Paul's view of the law by working through a key text: Galatians 3:15–4:7. This text, coming in the first letter Paul wrote (in my view at least), is a classic passage on this issue. Of course, Galatians hardly presents an even-handed treatment of the law in salvation history. As we have seen (pp. 56–57), Paul in Galatians is responding to "agitators" (Paul's word for them; see 5:12) who are arguing that to belong to God's people, the "seed of Abraham," and consequently receive divine vindication on the day of judgment, requires circumcision and obedience to at least a good chunk of the Mosaic law. Paul writes to refute these agitators and to call the Galatians back to the gospel that he first preached to them—the only true gospel. These circumstances mean that Paul is hardly neutral about the law in this letter. To counter the agitators' overemphasis on the law, he naturally focuses on the problems with the law. He is engaged in a balancing operation, putting all his weight on the negative side of the law in order to bring the Galatians back to an even keel in their theology. This does not mean, of course, as some have alleged, that Paul's teaching about the law in Galatians must be dismissed as a pastorally motivated overreaction in favor of the more neutral stance of Romans. In fact, all the negative points about the law in Galatians are repeated in Romans. The difference is that Romans does not have in view the same polemical issues as Galatians and hence has more positive things to say about the law.

The contrast in 3:10–14 between Abraham, faith, and blessing, on the one hand, and the law and curse, on the other, sets the stage for Paul's salvation-historical argument, as Paul now claims that the Abrahamic blessing can flow to the gentiles through the singular "seed" of Abraham, the Messiah Jesus (3:16), in whom all who believe become,

---

65. E.g., C. E. B. Cranfield, "St. Paul and the Law," *SJT* 17 (1964): 43–68; Fuller, *Gospel and Law*, 87–88.

66. I deal with the issue in my article, "'Law,' 'Works of the Law,' and Legalism in Paul."

in turn, the "seed" of Abraham (3:26–29). This positive argument is then matched by the negative argument that what Christ provides is not what the law is able to provide. Paul's key point is that the law is unable to secure the "inheritance" (3:18), that is, to secure for either Jews or gentiles the blessing that God promised through Abraham. The law cannot alter the gracious and promissory covenant that God established with Abraham (3:15–17); it cannot "impart life" (3:21).

Paul argues from the sequence of salvation history to ground this central point. The law of Moses "was added" (3:19) 430 years after the promise (v. 17) and was intended to be in force only "until the Seed to whom the promise referred had come" (v. 19). God gave the law to Israel not to solve its sin problem but—in a rather stunning claim—to exacerbate the problem. It was given "because of transgressions" (3:19), that is, to show up sin in its true colors as a violation of God's good commandments (see my discussion above on pp. 73–74 concerning "transgression" [*parabasis*], where I refer to the translation problem in this verse). We should note that Paul makes a similar point in Romans 5:20a—"The law was brought in so that the trespass might increase"—and he hints at the same idea in Romans 3:20; 4:15; 7:7–10; and 1 Corinthians 15:56. Chris Vlachos has usefully dubbed this the "catalytic" effect of the law.[67] More positively, Paul affirms that the law exercised a custodianship over Israel—it was the *paidagōgos* (Gal 3:24, "guardian" [NIV; ESV] or "disciplinarian" [NRSV]). This focus on sequence of time in the context strongly suggests, then, that the *eis* in Galatians 3:24 indicates not purpose—"to bring us unto Christ" (KJV)—but termination: "until Christ came" (NIV).[68] The "we" to which Paul refers in these verses probably refers to Paul and his fellow Jews, not Paul and fellow Christians or people in general.[69]

In a variation of this same point, Paul says that Israel was "held in custody under the law" before Christ came (Gal 3:23). Paul uses this phrase "under [the] law" (*hypo nomon*) four other times in Galatians and six times elsewhere (Gal 4:4, 5, 21; 5:18; see also Rom 6:14, 15; 1 Cor 9:20 [4x]). The omission of the article in each instance does not indicate that Paul is thinking of divine "law" in general or of law as a principle (as some older commentators thought); the "law" in question is so well known that there is no need to make the word *nomos* definite. As the context in each case makes clear, the law to which Paul refers is the Mosaic law, the Torah. Reformed interpreters have

---

67. Chris Vlachos, *The Law and the Knowledge of Good and Evil: The Edenic Background of the Catalytic Operation of the Law in Paul* (Eugene, OR: Wipf & Stock, 2009).

68. For both these points, see Moo, *Galatians*, 243–44.

69. To be sure, it is notoriously difficult to pin down the referents in Paul's first-person plural verbs and pronouns, and especially this is true in Galatians. On the basis of 2:15 ("we who are Jews by birth"), many interpreters think that Paul rather consistently uses "we" to denote himself and fellow Jews in the letter (e.g., Longenecker, *Galatians*, 229). But it is difficult to enforce this consistency throughout the letter. Paul's shift of pronouns appears at times to have more to do with rhetorical considerations. Nevertheless, the salvation-historical focus of the argument in this part of Galatians (Abrahamic promise—Mosaic law—Christ) suggests that Paul here is referring not to a general experience of people with "law" but to the specific experience of Israel with *the* law (Torah) that God uniquely gave them (see the discussion on p. 74).

often interpreted the phrase as a reference to the condemnation pronounced by the law.[70] And support could be found for this interpretation in the parallel between being "under sin" in Galatians 3:22 and being "under the law" in verse 23, and in 4:5, which refers to God's redemption of those who were "under the law."[71] But other evidence points in a different direction.

First, the assertion of verse 22 about being under sin is something of an anomaly in the flow of this context, speaking of "Scripture" (rather than "the law") and of the whole world, that is, "everything" (rather than just the Jews). The closer analogy is with the *paidogōgos* in verse 24. And this word, as we have seen, denotes not the cursing effect of the law but its custodianship of the people of Israel during the time of their "minority."

A second reason for preferring this broader interpretation of the phrase is Paul's assertion in 4:4 that Jesus was himself "born under the law." Since Jesus was not born subject to the curse (although he later voluntarily and vicariously took it upon himself; cf. 3:13), the phrase here cannot mean "under the curse of the law." Jesus, Paul is stressing, was a Jew and lived as one who was subject to the requirements of the Mosaic law that had been given to oversee the Jewish people. Like most of the other phrases about bondage in the context, then, "under the law" refers to a status of close supervision and custodial care. As Paul goes on to argue in 4:1–7, this period of time is similar to the minority of a child, held under supervision until the child comes to maturity.[72] Paul's salvation-historical conception can allow him to associate this pre-Christian, objective situation of guardianship and immaturity with subjection to the curse and wrath of God. Hence the phrase can occasionally include within it (as in 4:5) nuances of condemnation. But this is a nuance and not the basic meaning of the phrase. Paul, then, uses the phrase "under the law" to depict the situation of Israel before the coming of Christ, when the Israelites were subject to the authority and supervision of the Mosaic law.

It is in this context that Paul introduces the controversial phrase "the elements of the world" (*ta stoicheia tou kosmou*, 4:3; cf. also v. 9 and Col 2:8, 20). The phrase is often thought to refer to spiritual beings (cf. NIV: "The elemental spirits of the world"). Others think it refers to fundamental principles. But a strong case can be made for taking it as a reference to material elements, in which case Paul is probably thinking of the way that material things often become the vehicle for the worship of false gods. Paul therefore may use the *stoicheia* language in order to associate the situation of the gentile Galatians in their pre-conversion state with that of the Jews before Christ. It is

70. See esp. Schreiner, *Law and Its Fulfillment*, 77–81; Wilson, *Curse of the Law*, 35–36.

71. E.g., Thielman, *From Plight to Solution*, 77–78; In-Gyu Hong, "Being 'Under the Law' in Galatians," *Evangelical Review of Theology* 26 (2002): 354–72.

72. See especially Linda Belleville, "'Under Law': Structural Analysis and the Pauline Concept of Law in Galatians 3:21–4:11," *JSNT* 26 (1986): 53–78; Longenecker, *Galatians*, 145–49.

not that he equates the law with the "elements" or even sees the law as part of those "elements." Rather, he suggests that the state of Jewish people under the law and the gentiles under the "elements" are parallel to some degree.[73]

Galatians 3–4 demonstrates that salvation history plays an important role in Paul's understanding of and critique of the law. As a number of interpreters have put it, the key question Paul sets before the Galatians as a response to the agitators is, "What time is it?" It is now the time, Paul asserts, when the Messiah whom God promised has come and has ended the regime of the law. To place oneself under that law is, then, in effect to go back to an earlier phase of salvation history when sins had not yet been dealt with. However, while this salvation-historical perspective is basic to Paul's presentation of the old realm, this perspective ultimately transcends the "historical" part of this depiction. Abraham and David, who obviously lived in the era before the culmination of salvation history, experienced "righteousness" and "forgiveness" (Gal 3:6; see Rom 4:1–8). While "under the law" in one sense, they nevertheless escaped the condemnation that characterizes the old realm. At the same time, of course, people who live after the coming of Christ and who do not respond in faith to him continue to live in that old realm. Ultimately, then, Paul's salvation history cannot be located in strictly temporal categories.

Paul's well-known claim in Romans 10:4 that Christ is "the end of the law" makes a similar salvation-historical point. The translation "end" found in many English versions suggests that the point of the verse is basically discontinuity: Christ has brought the law to an end. However, the Greek word involved, *telos*, often has, as etymology might suggest, a telic force, indicating a goal or purpose. Recognizing the race imagery that Paul uses in the context ("pursue," "attain," "stumbling" [9:31–32]), this meaning of "goal" in the sense of the finish line of a race, is probably the sense Paul intends. All along the law has been pointing to or moving toward Christ. With that goal having been reached, the "race" of the law comes to an end. Nuances of both "end" and "goal" are part of Paul's meaning here: "culmination" (NIV) or "climax" are good English equivalents.[74] Romans 10:4, therefore, presents elements of both continuity and discontinuity. Christ is that to which the law has been pointing; now that he has come, a whole new situation with respect to the place of the law in the life of the people of God exists.[75]

For many interpreters, as we will see below, this salvation-historical argument pretty much covers the ground in terms of Paul's critique of the law. However, I will argue

---

73. See, on this whole issue, Moo, *Galatians*, 260–63.

74. This does not mean that I am advocating a double meaning for *telos*; rather, I am suggesting we may need to use two English words, or a phrase, to capture the single meaning of this word in this context.

75. See, at greater length, Moo, *Romans* (NICNT), 654–60; and also Wright, "Romans," 656–57.

that Paul identifies another problem with the law, one, indeed, that is more basic than the salvation-historical problem.

2.2.2.3 The Problem with the Law

Recent interpreters of Paul have often focused on the salvation-historical issue we have just surveyed as pretty much exhausting Paul's critique of the law. The problem with the law is that "its day is over." Paul's salvation-historical critique is often, however, thought to include another critique as well. By arguing for the continuing authority of the law, Paul's Jewish-Christian opponents were effectively maintaining the law's effect of excluding gentiles from the exclusive preserve of the (Jewish) people of God. This combined critique is associated especially with proponents of the "New Perspective on Paul." Before considering other aspects of Paul's critique of the law, then, it will be useful to spend some time discussing this influential way of interpreting Paul's interaction with Judaism and the law.

2.2.2.3.1 The New Perspective[76]

The New Perspective on Paul has its roots in a new perspective on Judaism. In 1977 a book was published that was destined to change the landscape of Paul and the law dramatically. E. P. Sanders's *Paul and Palestinian Judaism* marks a watershed in interpretations of Judaism as a backdrop for Paul's theology. What Sanders argued (at least in the main) was not new, but the time was apparently ripe for a sea change in the way New Testament scholars viewed first-century Judaism.[77] Sanders's basic proposal found ready acceptance and has, in many quarters, attained the status of an assumed result of scholarship.

Sanders advances his view of Judaism in the face of the widespread assumption that early Judaism was "legalistic." After a study of Jewish sources likely to give us evidence about first-century Jewish beliefs, Sanders concludes that these sources almost unanimously portray a view of soteriology that he dubs "covenantal nomism." Foundational to the Jewish view of salvation is the covenant that God entered into with the people Israel. God had chosen Israel, and Jews in Paul's day believed that that original gracious choice was the basis for their salvation. Viewed from this perspective, Jews did not have to do the law to be saved; they were already saved. They obeyed the law, rather, to maintain their covenantal status. As Sanders put it, Jews did not do the law to "get in" (which would be legalism) but to "stay in" ("nomism").

---

76. The substance, and much of the wording, in this section and in section 2.2.2.3, is taken from Moo, *Romans* (NICNT), 222–37. Used with permission.

77. Scholars who anticipated the direction of Sanders's argument were Montefiore, *Judaism and St. Paul*, and George Foot Moore, *Judaism in the First Centuries of the Christian Era: The Age of the Tannaim*, 3 vols. (Cambridge, MA: Harvard University Press, 1927).

Sanders's view of Judaism, which quickly found widespread acceptance, had an immediate impact on the study of Paul's theology, as scholars scrambled to relate Paul's varied teaching on these matters to Sanders's depiction of Second Temple soteriology. But so closely entwined is Paul's teaching on Judaism and the law with his major theological emphases in letters such as Romans and Galatians that the Sanders "revolution" inevitably and quickly spawned a series of fresh readings of those letters and their theological emphases. These new interpretations naturally took many different shapes. Sanders's original study focused mainly on Palestinian Judaism but did have a section on Paul as well. Among other points, Sanders argued that Paul rejected covenantal nomism because of his "exclusivist soteriology": since salvation was, by definition, to be found in Christ alone, the law and its underlying covenant could not be a means of salvation. Most scholars, even those who agreed with Sanders's portrayal of first-century Judaism, were not satisfied with this response. One of the early and more radical proposals was that Paul had simply caricatured his Jewish heritage in order to make his preaching of Christ all the more attractive to his listeners.[78]

But the most plausible and ultimately the most popular of the reactions to this new perspective on Judaism was what has come to be known as "the New Perspective on Paul." James Dunn, a leading proponent of this new way of reading Paul, gave the movement its name in a 1983 article, but his ideas were in many ways anticipated by N. T. Wright in a 1978 lecture.[79] These two scholars have written a great deal on this issue and are the best representatives of the New Perspective.[80] However, even a quick perusal of these two leading New Perspective scholars' interpretations of Paul and of Romans reveals significant differences in their approaches and conclusions. Such differences would be multiplied considerably if other scholars generally considered New Perspective in their approach were included.[81] All this makes for a problem of definition. One scholar's New Perspective may be quite different than another's.

What, then, are the defining characteristics of the New Perspective? At its heart, the New Perspective offers a reading of Paul's teaching that aligns what he says with the Judaism that Sanders described. The motivation is good and appropriate. The letters of Paul have to make sense as first-century documents dealing with the issues of that day. Too often, Wright, Dunn, and others complain, the church has read Paul in light of

---

78. See esp. Heikki Räisänen, *Paul and the Law*, WUNT 2/29 (Tübingen: Mohr Siebeck, 1983); idem, "Paul's Theological Difficulties with the Law," in *Studia Biblica 1978*, vol. 3, ed. E. A. Livingston, JSNTSup 2 (Sheffield: JSOT, 1980), 310–20.

79. See, respectively, Dunn, "The New Perspective on Paul," *BJRL* 65 (1983): 95–122 (republished with additional notes in idem, *Jesus, Paul and the Law: Studies in Mark and Galatians* [Louisville: Westminster John Knox, 1990], 183–214); and N. T. Wright, "The Paul of History and the Apostle of Faith," *TynBul* 29 (1978): 61–88.

80. For a convenient summary, see Dunn, *Theology of Paul*, esp. 334–89; see also his more recent "In Search of the Historical Paul," in Spitaler, *Celebrating Paul*, 15–48.

81. See esp. Don B. Garlington, "The New Perspective on Paul: Two Decades On," in *Studies in the New Perspective on Paul: Essays and Reviews*, by Don B. Garlington (Eugene, OR: Wipf & Stock, 2008).

its own issues rather than in light of the issues of Paul's world. Granted "covenant nomism" as the shape of Jewish soteriology, then, it would be difficult to think that Paul would be criticizing Jews for arguing that they could get right with God by obeying the law. Jews, as Sanders had allegedly shown, just did not believe that. What would fit Paul's own Jewish context, however, would be an attack on covenantal nomism itself. This, Dunn and Wright claim, is what we actually find in Paul. His polemic against the law assumes that a new stage of salvation history has dawned, revealing that the Jewish tendency to confine salvation to their own nation was misguided. It is ethnic exclusivism, not personal legalism, that Paul finds wrong with Judaism.

The New Perspective in general, then, rotates Paul's central theological axis away from the vertical—the human and God—and toward the horizontal—Jews and gentiles. New Perspective advocates often fault the interpretive tradition derived especially from the Reformation (and from Luther in particular) for a myopic and anachronistic preoccupation with the individual and his or her status before God—a theme sounded in the influential article of Krister Stendahl, "Paul and the Introspective Conscience of the West."[82] Paul's cultural context, religious background, and theological concerns suggest, rather, that his immediate concern was with the *people* of God (corporate), and especially with the integration of gentiles into the people of God (horizontal). An ethnocentric reading of Paul takes center stage, relegating an anthropocentric reading to a more subordinate role. Paul's gospel is not, at least first of all, the story of the individual's transformation from sinner to saint—or even the story of humankind's restoration. Rather, the gospel proclaims Israel's restoration, a restoration that takes place in and through the ministry of Jesus, Israel's Messiah and representative, and that extends God's grace to the gentiles.[83]

The books that most explicitly reveal this ethnocentric concern—Galatians and Romans—are also the ones that feature significant teaching on the Mosaic law and justification. A reinterpretation of these doctrines both fuels the new paradigm and emerges, in turn, from the paradigm. Most New Perspective advocates agree that Paul attacked a misuse of the law among his fellow Jews. But, contra the Reformers and their heirs, this misuse was not a legalistic attempt to find justification through doing what it required. Rather, Jews were misusing the law by turning it into a charter of national privilege, insisting that it virtually guaranteed the salvation of Israel while at the same time it excluded gentiles.[84] The dichotomy that lies at the heart of Paul's

82. Stendahl's essay first appeared in *HTR* 56 (1963): 199–215; and see also his *Paul among Jews and Gentiles*.

83. N. T. Wright has been especially keen to stress the importance of reading Paul's theology in terms of a continuation of Israel's story (a focus that marks his whole Christian Origins and the Question of God series; see esp. the introductory volume, *The New Testament and the People of God*. See also the series of

essays evaluating N. T. Wright's approach in Newman, *Jesus and the Restoration of Israel*).

84. "In attacking the covenantal nomism of the Judaism of his day Paul was attacking neither the law, nor the covenant . . . , but a covenantal nomism which insisted on treating the law as a boundary marker round Israel, marking off Jew from Gentile, with only those inside as heirs of God's promise to Abraham. In

teaching on the law, then, is not, as the Reformers and their heirs mistakenly thought, human doing ("works" or "works of the law") versus human believing ("faith"), but works of covenant identification (confined by definition to Israel) versus new-covenant faith (open to all without distinction).[85] Since, on this reading, Paul's problem with the law was restricted mainly to this Jewish misunderstanding, New Perspective proponents in general tend to find a more positive role for the law in salvation history than was typical of (especially) the Lutheran stream of Reformation teaching. Freed from its Jewish perversion into a nationalistic document, the law was free to function positively in the new age of universal redemption.

2.2.2.3.2 Beyond the New Perspective

The "New" Perspective is hardly new anymore. And, inevitably, certain approaches have arisen that go well beyond the New Perspective in their view of the law in Paul. The most important of these is now being labeled the "Paul within Judaism" approach.[86] The fundamental tenet of this movement is that Paul opposed the law only with respect to its being imposed on gentiles. Paul himself remained Torah-observant as a messianic believer, and he taught/assumed that Jewish Christians would likewise remain Torah-observant.[87] While agreeing on this basic point, advocates of this movement divide significantly over soteriology. A less radical form of this movement, often given the label "messianic Judaism," maintains that Christ is the only Savior for both Jews and gentiles. Others take a more radical approach, arguing, with advocates of the earlier "bi-covenantalim," that Paul views Jesus Christ as the Savior only of gentiles; Jews are given a path to salvation via their own Torah covenant.

The soteriological aspect of the "Paul within Judaism" movement must be rejected out of hand. Three key points may be briefly made. First, this so-called "bi-covenantal" view, positing a "special way" (*Sonderweg*) of salvation for the Jewish people apart from

---

short, it was the law abused to which Paul objected, not the law itself" (James D. G. Dunn, *The Partings of the Ways: Between Judaism and Christianity and Their Significance for the Character of Christianity* [Philadelphia: Trinity Press International, 1991], 138). As, e.g., Francis Watson has pointed out, it is unclear why Dunn thinks that Jews were wrongly treating the law as "marking off Jew from Gentile," which appears to be precisely what the law was intending to accomplish (*Paul and the Hermeneutics of Faith*, 328–29).

85. Some interpreters shift the latter dichotomy a bit further toward a salvation-historical context by interpreting some of Paul's key references to "faith" as referring to the faith or faithfulness of Christ (esp. Rom 3:22; Gal 2:16; also Rom 1:17; 3:26; Gal 3:22). See discussion on pp. 379–82.

86. For an overview of this movement, see the essays in Nanos and Zetterholm, *Paul within Judaism*. Note also Magnus Zetterholm's criticism of the New Perspective for continuing the traditional critique of Judaism (*Approaches to Paul: A Student's Guide to Recent Scholarship* [Minneapolis: Fortress, 2009], 95–126). Other works advancing this general view are John Gager, *Reinventing Paul* (Oxford: Oxford University Press, 2000); Lloyd Gaston, *Paul and the Torah* (Vancouver: University of British Columbia, 1987); Boccaccini and Segovia, *Paul the Jew*; Elliott, *Liberating Paul*, 66–72; Nanos, *Mystery of Romans*; Eisenbaum, *Paul Was Not a Christian*, 135–53; Kathy Ehrensperger, *That We May Be Mutually Encouraged: Feminism and the New Perspective in Pauline Studies* (London: T&T Clark, 2004), 123–59; Campbell, *Paul and the Creation of Christian Identity*; David Rudolph and Joel Willitts, eds., *Introduction to Messianic Judaism: Its Ecclesial Context and Biblical Foundations* (Grand Rapids: Zondervan, 2013); Thiessen, *Paul and the Gentile Problem*.

87. See, e.g., Paula Fredriksen, *Paul: The Pagan's Apostle* (New Haven: Yale University Press, 2017), 94–130; Mark D. Nanos, "A Jewish View," in Bird, *Four Views of the Apostle Paul*, 159–93.

Christ, pretty clearly (as most of its adherents admit) is not the view Paul everywhere teaches. Its validity, then, depends on privileging certain passages over others. Better to assume consistency in Paul's teaching on this vital point, if a view that maintains such consistency is exegetically responsible—as I think it is. Second, as I note elsewhere, the idea that Paul in Romans 11:26 teaches that Jews can find salvation apart from Christ flies in the face of the massive christological emphasis of the letter as a whole (see esp., in this larger context, 10:5–13; and my comments on pp. 572–73). Third, the assumption that Paul thinks his Jewish compatriots are in a saving relationship with God apart from Christ simply cannot do justice to the depths of Paul's emotion about his fellow Jews in texts such as 9:1–3 (see also 10:1). The Jewish people, Paul affirms, like gentiles, can find salvation only through Christ. Likewise, the salvation of many Jews in the last days (11:26), while its mechanics are not spelled out for us in any detail, also comes through Christ.

The view that Paul remained Torah-observant and expected Jewish Christians to follow suit is not as problematic as the soteriological issue but nonetheless cannot be sustained. Mark Kinzer, advocating this view, appeals to the "Pauline syllogism": Paul encourages believers who are circumcised to remain circumcised (1 Cor 7:17–20); all who are circumcised are obligated to observe Torah; therefore all those born as Jews must live as Jews.[88] The problem with this syllogism arises in its assumption of what circumcision entails. Paul's radical claim in verse 19, that "circumcision is nothing and uncircumcision is nothing," shows that he sees little significance in the rite. Those who are circumcised, in this context, then, are Jewish-Christian males who were marked with the covenant sign as infants but who no longer are to put any stock in the matter. Another problem with this view is its claim that Paul addresses his negative remarks about the law to gentiles only. Thus, for instance, his assertion that "you also died to the law" (Rom 7:4) is directed to gentiles (God-fearers, perhaps); those who are "not under the law" (6:14, 15) are gentile Christians. According to Mark Nanos, Paul opposes only "those rites involved in Christ-following non-Jews becoming Jews."[89] While affirming the necessity for Jews, as Christians, to be Torah-observant, he insists that it not be imposed on gentiles.

But this exegetical move is dubious, to say the least.[90] We are required to adopt strained and unlikely interpretations of many Pauline texts.[91] The most natural reading

---

88. Kinzer, *Post-Missionary Messianic Judaism*, 72–73; see also, e.g., Thiessen, *Paul and the Gentile Problem*; Anders Runesson, "The Question of Terminology: The Architecture of Contemporary Discussions of Paul," in Nanos and Zetterholm, *Paul within Judaism*, 216–17.

89. Mark D. Nanos, "The Question of Conceptualization: Qualifying Paul's Position on Circumcision in Dialogue with Josephus's Advisors to King Izates," in Nanos and Zetterholm, *Paul within Judaism*, 138–40.

90. See esp. Karl Olav Sandnes, *Paul Perceived: An Interactionist Perspective on Paul and the Law*, WUNT 2/412 (Tübingen: Mohr Siebeck, 2018), esp. 27–51.

91. Donald A. Hagner does not exaggerate much when he labels these interpretations "tortuous exegesis" (*How New Is the New Testament?* [Grand Rapids: Baker, 2019], 9).

of, for example, 1 Corinthians 9:19–22, is that Paul and, by implication, his fellow Jews, were no longer bound fundamentally to the authority of the Mosaic law.[92] Galatians, to be sure, is written exclusively to gentile Christians; and while I think it is unlikely, it is possible that Romans is also. But in both letters, Paul advances a theology of the law that takes into account Jews as well as gentiles. In Galatians 3 Paul argues that the law was intended to last only until "the Seed to whom the promise referred had come" (v. 19); the law held Israel in custody only "until Christ came" (v. 24). The coming of Christ means that God's people, whether Jews or gentiles, are no longer "under the law." We find a similar argument in Romans. Following widespread Jewish assumptions, Paul identifies the "law" with Jews, in distinction from gentiles (Rom 2:12–14; 3:19). Those who are "not under the law" (6:14, 15) and who have "died to the law" (7:4) would naturally be assumed to at least include Jews. Christ is the "culmination" of the law (10:4) for *all* who believe. While he was certainly open to Jewish Christians continuing to be Torah observant (the implication of Rom 14:1–15:12), the turn of salvation history that put Christ in place of the law, removing the law as an authority over the people of God, applies fully and equally to Jews and gentiles alike. Indeed, Paul's polemic suggests that it applies especially to Jews. Moreover, while it is surely important that the church not become a place where people must put aside their specific ethnic and cultural identities, the church must also be a place where such specific identities take a back seat to one's more fundamental identity as a Christian. While Torah observance itself was certainly not wrong, insisting on it could be erecting an unnecessary barrier to the unity with which Paul is so concerned (see, further, pp. 433–35).[93]

2.2.2.3.3 *Works of the Law*

The phrase "works of the law" (*[ta] erga [tou] nomou*) has become a critical turning point in the debate about Paul's view of the law—between, if I might speak all too simplistically, the "old perspective" on Paul and the new.[94] A brief discussion of this phrase will help clarify some of the issues and launch us into the criticism phase of my New Perspective discussion.

Paul's problem with the law, for many scholars, is that reliance on the law is fruitless and, indeed, dangerous, because sinful humans are unable to obey it. Theologians throughout the history of the church have argued this anthropological point, but it became especially prominent with the Reformers and their heirs. And key evidence

---

92. Contra, e.g., Rudolph, who, as a vocal proponent of the "messianic Judaism" movement, wrote his dissertation on this text (*Jew to the Jews*).

93. For a particularly clear response to this movement, see esp. Wright, *Paul and the Faithfulness of God*, 1:428–43.

94. Friedrich Wilhelm Horn correctly notes that almost all the issues pertaining to the New Perspective are tied to interpretations of this phrase ("Juden und Heiden: Aspekte der Verhältnisbestimmung in den paulinischen Briefen. Ein Gespräch mit Krister Stendahl," in *Lutherische und Neue Perspektive: Beiträge zu einem Schüsselproblem der gegenwärtigen exegetischen Diskussion*, ed. Michael Bachmann, WUNT 2/182 [Tübingen: Mohr Siebeck, 2005], 29).

for this view is found in Paul's claim that a person cannot be justified "by the works of the law" (Rom 3:20, 28; Gal 2:16 [3x]; 3:2, 5, 10). The phrase is not used in Greek (as far as we know) before Paul's day and has few clear equivalents in other languages.[95] Some interpreters across church history have thought that the phrase might have a restricted sense, referring to the ceremonial aspects of the law of Moses.[96] Some early defenders of the New Perspective on Paul suggested something similar, arguing that the phrase highlighted certain forms of conformity to the law that separated Jews from gentiles.[97] However, most interpreters now agree that the phrase "simply denotes doing what the law requires," the law being the Mosaic law, the Torah.[98] The debate, then, is not so much about the *meaning* of the phrase as about its *significance*.[99] Those who think Paul singled out human inability to fulfill the law as a basic problem argue that the phrase, while *referring* to "what is done in obedience to Torah," *signifies* "what is done," or "works," in general.[100] On this basis Paul's "works of the law" texts refute the idea that a person could gain a right standing with God by anything that that person did.[101] On the other hand, advocates of the New Perspective argue that the *significance* of the phrase should be confined to its *referent*. Paul has no quarrel with "works"; his

95. The most important possible parallels are in the Dead Sea Scrolls (4QFlor [4Q174] 3.7; 1QS 5.21; 6.18; 4QMMT 27 (4Q398 Frgm. 14–17 II 3). These occurrences are debated in form and meaning. See, e.g., Jacqueline C. R. de Roo, *Works of the Law at Qumran and in Paul*, NT Monographs 13 (Sheffield: Sheffield Phoenix, 2007); Craig A. Evans, "Paul and 'Works of the Law' Language in Late Antiquity," in Porter, *Paul and His Opponents*, 201–26. Rough parallels to Paul's "works of the law" may also be found in 2 Bar. 57.2 ("the works of the commandments") and possibly also in the common rabbinic reference to "works" in general (Str-B 3:160–61).

96. Among early theologians who defined the phrase this way were Origen, Jerome, and Pelagius (see M. F. Wiles, *The Divine Apostle: The Interpretation of St. Paul's Epistles in the Early Church* [Cambridge: Cambridge University, 1967], 67–69). Calvin contested the limited meaning (*Institutes* 3.11.19). In anticipation of the current debate, the Reformers, in fact, frequently polemicized against any restriction in the scope of "the works of the law" (see Stephen J. Chester, "It Is No Longer I Who Live: Justification by Faith and Participation in Christ in Martin Luther's Exegesis of Galatians," *NTS* 55 [2009]: 315–37).

97. Dunn's early writings on this topic suggested such a restriction (see, e.g., "New Perspective on Paul," 107–11). In his later work, however, he argues that the phrase refers more broadly to "law obedience" (see below). Note Dunn's admission that his first article might have left the wrong impression ("Additional Note" in the reprint of "New Perspective on Paul," in *Jesus, Paul and the Law*, 210).

98. See, e.g., Dunn, *Beginning from Jerusalem*, 475. The syntax of the phrase is debated, but the genitive *nomou* is probably objective, the phrase meaning "works done in obedience to the

law" (Moo, *Galatians*, 158; contra, e.g., Michael Bachmann, "Keil oder Mikroskop? Zur jüngeren Diskussion um den Ausdruck 'Werke des Gesetzes,'" in Bachmann, *Lutherische und Neue Perspektive*, 72–102).

99. This point is rightly emphasized by Matlock, *Unveiling the Apocalyptic Paul*, 436; A. Andrew Das, "Paul and Works of Obedience in Second Temple Judaism: Romans 4:4–5 as a 'New Perspective' Case Study," *CBQ* 71 (2009): 796.

100. M. J. Thomas has surveyed patristic interpretations of "the works of the law," concluding that the focus tended to be on works particular to the Jewish covenant. Early interpreters also tended to argue that Paul ruled them out because of the inauguration of a new covenant, and law, in Christ (*Paul's "Works of the Law" in the Perspective of Second Century Reception*, WUNT 2/468 [Tübingen: Mohr Siebeck, 2018]).

101. This general view is shared by virtually all the Reformers and became a hallmark of traditional Protestant interpretation. In contrast to the claims of some interpreters, the Reformers did not miss the original historical referent in the phrase. In the preface to his commentary on Galatians, for instance, Calvin notes that the phrase refers to "the ceremonies," but, he argues, more than ceremonies are involved. He claims, "The question could not be settled without assuming the general principle, that we are justified by the free grace of God; and this principle sets aside not only ceremonies, but every other kind of works." Similarly, in his comments on Gal 2:16, he notes that Origen and Jerome take "works of the law" to refer to ceremonies. He agrees but then argues that Paul extends the significance of the phrase to the larger and more consequent issue. Paul deals with works "of the law," then, partly because, since they are demanded by God, they are the highest form of works (Calvin, *Galatians and Ephesians*).

criticism is confined to "works *of the law*," "*Torah* works." "Ethnocentrism" is the matrix within which the phrase must be understood. The Jewish people insisted on "the works of the law" not primarily as a means of establishing a relationship with God (which, in any case, they already enjoyed as members of Israel) but as a means of enforcing their own special status and thereby, in effect, keeping gentiles out.[102] And since the phrase functions in this very specific historical context and since Paul criticizes "works of the law" for this particular reason, it is illegitimate to move from "works of the law" to "good works" in general.[103]

New Perspective advocates are certainly right to argue that traditional interpreters have often neglected the specific historical factors affecting Paul's teaching about the law. But their own matrix for interpreting "works of the law" goes too far in the other direction.

First, while obedience to the law was indeed stressed as a means of erecting a boundary between Judaism and the gentiles, it also had great "intrinsic" significance as the means by which covenant membership, or "righteousness," was to be maintained and secured on the day of judgment. "Works of the law," then, could function in this latter context as well as the former.

Second, I am not persuaded that the possible equivalents of the phrase in Paul's Jewish world suggest the kind of specific sociological function for the phrase that New Perspective advocates suggest.

Third, the interchange between "works of the law" and "works" in Romans suggests that we cannot keep these in separate categories. Paul's claim that "works of the law" cannot justify (3:20, 28) seems to be parallel with his claim that Abraham was not justified by "works" (4:1–8). This general meaning of "works" is clear also in Romans 9:11–12, where Paul specifically unpacks the word in terms of doing "anything good or bad" (see also 11:6).[104] We should therefore view "works of the law" as a subset of (rather than separate from) the general category of "works."

---

102. The view is widespread, but the clearest and fullest case is made by James D. G. Dunn in a series of writings. See, e.g., his paraphrase of its meaning: "Acts of obedience required by the law of all faithful Jews, all members of the people with whom God had made the covenant at Sinai—the self-understanding and obligation accepted by practicing Jews that E. P. Sanders encapsulated quite effectively in the phrase 'covenantal nomism'" (James D. G. Dunn, "Echoes of Intra-Jewish Polemic in Paul's Letter to the Galatians," *JBL* 112 [1993]: 466).

103. While distancing himself in several crucial ways from the New Perspective, Watson makes this point quite vigorously: "The critique of Luther's essentially allegorical interpretation of Paul's critique of works is presented here with all the emphasis I can muster" (*Paul, Judaism, and the Gentiles*, 25; argument on pp. 121–31). See also, for this general point of view, Barclay, "Paul, the Gift and the Battle," 40–42. New Perspective advocates are

not always clear about whether Paul's polemic against "works of the law" has broader theological implications. For instance, in his commentary on Romans (in the *New Interpreter's* series), N. T. Wright insists quite strongly in the "Commentary" section that "works of the law" are signs that one belongs to Israel and that any notions of legalism or "proto-Pelagianism" are simply not present (e.g., 459–61). But in the "Reflections" section he acknowledges other "overtones" in Paul's teaching, including some that are compatible with traditional Reformation teaching (464). N. T. Wright is even clearer about these "old perspective" elements in Paul's teaching in his *Paul and the Faithfulness of God* (e.g., 2:1038–39). Note also Dunn's remarks in his summative essay, "The New Perspective on Paul: Whence, What, Whither?," in Dunn, *New Perspective on Paul*, 27–28.

104. Brendan Byrne, "The Problem of *Nomos* and the Relationship with Judaism in Romans," *CBQ* 62 (2000): 299–300.

Fourth, we would expect "works of the law" in Romans 3:20 and 28 to be something of a summary of the extended discussion of Jewish "doing" in chapter 2. But the context of chapter 2 makes clear that this "doing" is not restricted to any particular kind of works. In fact, Paul makes clear that the problem with Jewish works is essentially the same as the problem with gentile works (see vv. 2–3, 22–23, 25, 27).[105] Again, this makes it unlikely that the problem with "works of the law" is narrowly Jewish. Rather, the inability of "works of the law" to justify appears to be bound up with a fundamental *human* problem: universal, enslaving sinfulness (a broad application that, as we have seen, is probably connoted by Paul's language of "all flesh" [*pasa sarx*; NIV: "no one"] at Rom 3:20). In other words, the "problem" with "works of the law" is not fundamentally that they are "Torah works" that maintained Israel's privileged position. The problem is that they are "works" that humans, under sin's power (3:9), are unable to produce in adequate measure to secure righteous standing with God. To put it another way, the problem is not with the Jews' *possession* of the law but with their failure to *perform* it.

Fifth, while Galatians undoubtedly focuses considerable attention on salvation history, this broader "human" problem also comes to expression in the letter. The interpretation of 3:10 is pivotal to this issue and is one of the reasons the verse has received so much attention in recent years. Here Paul writes, "For all who rely on the works of the law are under a curse, as it is written: 'Cursed is everyone who does not continue to do everything written in the Book of the Law.'" A broadly "New Perspective" approach to the verse interprets the curse in purely salvation-historical terms; Israel, as the exile reveals, fell under God's curse, and anyone who now wants to identify with Israel by Torah observance will fall under that same curse.[106] The "traditional" reading, on the other hand, insists that the logic of the verse reveals that Paul is warning the Galatian Christians directly ("as many as") that reliance on "works of the law" will bring them under the curse because (implicitly) they will not be able to produce sufficient works to avoid the curse. This latter reading, while widely criticized, seems to be, in fact, the only way to make sense of the text.[107] And it finds confirmation in verse 12, where Paul identifies the law with the principle of *doing* (3:12; cf. also 5:3).[108] The point is, then,

---

105. See, e.g., Simon Gathercole, "The Doctrine of Justification in Paul and Beyond: Some Proposals," in *Justification in Perspective: Historical Developments and Contemporary Challenges*, ed. Bruce L. McCormack (Grand Rapids: Baker, 2006), 238–40; David I. Starling, *Not My People: Gentiles as Exiles in Pauline Hermeneutics*, BZNW 184 (Berlin: de Gruyter, 2011), 215.

106. For the "Israel in exile" view, see esp. Wright, "Curse and Covenant," 137–56; Scott, "'For as Many as Are of Works of the Law,'" 187–221. See also above, pp. 420–22.

107. See esp. Thomas R. Schreiner, "Is Perfect Obedience to the Law Possible: A Re-Examination of Galatians 3:10," *JETS* 27 (1984): 151–60; A. Andrew Das, *Paul and the Jews* (Peabody,

MA: Hendrickson, 2003), 36–42; Seyoon Kim, *Paul and the New Perspective: Second Thoughts on the Origin of Paul's Gospel* (Grand Rapids: Eerdmans, 2002), 139–43; Westerholm, *Perspectives*, 375; Timo Laato, "Paul's Anthropological Considerations: Two Problems," in Carson, O'Brien, and Seifrid, *Paradoxes of Paul*, 354–59; Eckstein, *Verheissung*, 123. See also my discussion of this verse in the exposition (pp. 71–72).

108. Sprinkle, on the basis of a careful study of Lev 18:5 in the OT and Judaism and its place in Paul's argument, concludes that the text has clear soteriological implications; it refers to a way of salvation (*Law and Life*, 136–42; see above, pp. 72–73).

that Paul here views reliance on doing the law ("works of the law") as bringing people under the curse, not simply because the law belongs to a past stage of salvation history but because the law is bound up with "doing," and "doing," or "works" in general, are never able to justify a person before God. Paul's polemic against "works of the law" in Galatians, then, rests ultimately on a pessimistic anthropology. Stephen Westerholm puts the point well: "The fundamental question addressed by Galatians thus is not 'What is wrong with Judaism (or the Sinaitic law)?' but 'What is wrong with humanity that Judaism (and the Sinaitic law) cannot remedy?'"[109]

Without, then, dismissing the importance of salvation history and ethnocentrism in Paul's view of the law, anthropology plays a role in Paul's critique also. The inability of *Israel* to obey the Mosaic law, a failure so massively documented in the Old Testament, is emblematic of the inability of *humans* in general to live up to "law" (the standard of behavior that God requires of his creatures).

2.2.2.3.4 The New Perspective Again

The "New" Perspective has been with us, in one form or another, for over forty years. Over those years, as we would expect, the movement has morphed in various ways. One welcome development that we see in the more recent writings of both Dunn and Wright is a tendency to soften their earlier "not-but" rhetoric in favor of a "not only-but also" approach—from New Perspective *in place of* Reformation theology to New Perspective insights *added to* and *qualifying* Reformation theology. Both Dunn and Wright are now clear about wanting to preserve fundamental Reformation teaching on soteriology, viewing their own contributions as adding important nuance to it.[110] Fair assessment of the New Perspective should focus on the current state of the movement.

---

109. Westerholm, *Perspectives*, 381; see his whole argument on 371–84; and see also esp., Silva, "Faith Versus Works of the Law in Galatians," 217–48; Gundry, "Grace, Works, and Staying Saved in Paul," 15–32; Kim, *Paul and the New Perspective*, 61–75; Michael F. Bird, *The Saving Righteousness of God: Studies on Paul, Justification and the New Perspective*, Paternoster Biblical Monographs (Waynesboro, GA: Paternoster, 2007), 123; Longenecker, *Triumph of Abraham's God*, 76–77; Otfried Hofius, "'Werke des Gesetzes': Untersuchungen zu der paulinischen Rede von den ἔργα νόμου," in *Paulus und Johannes: Exegetische Studien zur paulinischen und johanneischen Theologie und Literatur*, ed. D. Sänger and U. Mell, WUNT 2/198 (Tübingen: Mohr Siebeck, 2006), 299–301.

110. See esp. Dunn, "New Perspective on Paul: Whence, What, Whither?," 1–88; idem, "A New Perspective on the New Perspective on Paul," *Early Christianity* 4 (2013): 157; idem, "What's Right about the Old Perspective on Paul," in Harmon and Smith, *Studies in the Pauline Epistles*, 214–29. Wright (*Paul and the Faithfulness of God*, 2:1513–14) is worth quoting at some

length: "In particular, there is no need to perpetuate the battle between things that call themselves the 'new perspective' or the 'old perspective' on Paul. Both were, in any case, misleading in their singularity: there are many 'new perspectives' on the loose by now, and a good many significantly different 'old perspectives' as well. Insofar as the 'New Perspective' ran the risk of collapsing into 'sociology' or 'comparative religion,' it of course needed to be rethought theologically to take account of, and to give the central place to, Paul's emphases on the divine act in the cross of the Messiah and its appropriation by faith. Insofar as the 'old perspective' continued to base itself on a caricature of ancient Jewish beliefs, forcing old Jewish texts as well as Paul himself to give answers to questions they were not asking while ignoring the ones they were faced with, it of course needed to be rethought theologically to take account of, and give a central place to, the Jewish and Pauline emphases on the surprising and freshly revelatory divine act in fulfilling the covenant with Abraham and completing (balancing both meanings of *telos* in Romans 10.4!) the covenant with Moses. But I hope that the discussion in this book has given a quite new

It is unfortunate that reactions to the New Perspective are often binary—one is either for it or against it.[111] In fact, in my view at least, it is a mixed bag. Many of the insights in this movement are welcome; others, not so helpful. The more nuanced view of Judaism presupposed in the New Perspective, while itself somewhat simplistic and imbalanced (see below), is an important corrective to unfortunate stereotypes in Christian interpretations of Judaism. The movement's emphasis on "people" issues in Paul's theological agenda also brings to our attention a matter critical for Paul and his ministry but sometimes neglected in the rush to find enduring theological principles in his letters. To put what follows, then, in perspective, my quarrel with New Perspective advocates is often not so much over what they say but about what they do not say—or, perhaps better, the overall balance that they give to certain issues.

Paul is without doubt deeply concerned with the "people" or "national" question—as Paul puts it in his thematic overview of the letter in Romans 1:16, the good news is "first to the Jew, then to the Gentile." But the phrase immediately preceding this one— "for everyone who believes"—makes clear that the "good news" that Paul proclaims in Romans has first of all to do with God's provision in Christ for all humanity to be restored to peaceful relationship with God.[112] The context of Paul's own ministry and the divisions in the Roman Christian community require Paul to spell out how this provision for all human beings in Christ specifically works its way out in terms of Jews and gentiles. Galatians is even more focused on the "people" question, as Paul argues that being in Christ, without law obedience, is sufficient to bring gentiles into the Abrahamic people of God. New perspective advocates are quite right to draw attention to this critical theme. However, making it the primary theme in Paul creates an imbalance in Paul's overall gospel message.[113]

As I noted above, a fundamental methodological perspective that undergirds New Perspective readings of Romans is an emphasis on the way the story of Israel shapes its teaching and structure. In 1992, N. T. Wright claimed: "Paul presupposes this story [of Israel] even when he does not expound it directly, and it is arguable that we can only understand the more limited narrative worlds of the different letters if we locate

---

set of angles of vision—perspectives, I almost said—on the false either/or of the last generation. Protests are often necessary, even if sometimes overstated. Reactions are sometimes appropriate, even if sometimes shrill or merely nostalgic. Fuller integration, fuller reconciliation, is always the Pauline aim, and I hope we have gone a good way towards achieving it."

111. There are, of course, many exceptions. Two books that argue for a *via media* between "old" and "new" perspectives are Garwood Anderson, *Paul's New Perspective: Charting a Soteriological Journey* (Downers Grove, IL: InterVarsity Press, 2016); and Chester, *Reading Paul with the Reformers.*

112. Contra, e.g., Dunn, who claims that the "surmounting

of ancient hostilities [between gentiles and Jews]" was "*the climactic achievement of the gospel*" (emphasis original; "New Perspective on Paul: Whence, What, Whither?," 31).

113. See also Brendan Byrne: "While applauding many aspects of the New Perspective on Paul—indeed believing myself to stand fundamentally within it—I would hope that it will not lose sight of the more radical vision that previous generations have drawn from Paul's letter to Rome" ("Interpreting Romans Theologically in a Post-'New Perspective' Perspective," *HTR* 94 [2001]: 241); and also Hahn, *Theologie des Neuen Testaments,* 1:232; Gundry, "Inferiority of the New Perspective on Paul," 204–6.

them at their appropriate points within this overall story-world, and indeed within the symbolic universe that accompanies it."[114] And in his 2013 *magnum opus*, he writes:

> This, I suggest, is the deep, underlying point at which we can discern what the so-called "New Perspective on Paul" might really have been all about. It is not so much a matter of whether "Jews believed in grace too," whether Paul was interested in "staying in" rather than "getting in," or whether the "solution" preceded the "plight" or vice versa, important though all those questions are. Rather, it was and is a matter of discerning whether the underlying narrative which we have seen to be so powerful for so many (not all) Jews in Paul's day was taken over, modified or simply abandoned.[115]

Although this narrative approach to Paul's theology is more important for N. T. Wright than for Dunn, it is generally important to New Perspective interpretation.[116] We may grant that Paul locates Jesus's death and resurrection and the good news he proclaims within the great narrative of salvation history. Indeed, it is fair to say that some traditional theological approaches to Paul have focused so much on individual history (how "I" am saved) that they have virtually ignored salvation history (how God's purposes for creation and for Israel are fulfilled in Christ). But a key point of divergence in drawing out the significance of Paul's teaching on the law is how Israel's story figures in Paul's teaching. The New Perspective approach tends to stress continuity in the story of Israel as it has been extended into the messianic era. Hence, for instance, Paul's discussion of the law and the works it calls for have no relevance beyond Israel and her experience. However, a strong case can be made for the idea that Paul, without ignoring ways in which Israel's experience is unique, also sees Israel's experience with the law as paradigmatic. That is, Israel's particular history with Torah has implications and significance for all human beings in their own struggle with "law" and its consequences (see below, pp. 448–50). Paul brings into his theology the narrative of Israel not only to show how God's work in Christ brings that story to its climax but also to draw from it implications for human experience generally. On this basis, then, "works of the law," as I argue above, while *referring* to Israel's doing of the law, also *signifies* the experience of all humans with respect to their own "doing," or works.

As we have seen, the New Perspective on Paul is rooted deeply in the soil of the "New Perspective on Judaism."[117] Dunn, Wright, and other New Perspective advocates affirm (broadly) Sanders's view of Jewish soteriology and are concerned to make sense

---

114. Wright, *New Testament and the People of God*, 405.

115. Wright, *Paul and the Faithfulness of God*, 1:460 (see 1:495–505).

116. N. T. Wright criticizes Dunn for not paying enough attention to story (*Paul and His Recent Interpreters*, 98).

117. Note Dunn's first bullet point in his definition of the New Perspective: it "builds on Sanders' New Perspective on Second Temple Judaism" ("New Perspective on Paul: Whence, What, Whither?," 16).

of Paul in light of that soteriology. It would be going too far to claim that these movements stand or fall together. But certainly any fair response to the New Perspective on Paul cannot avoid dealing with the New Perspective on Judaism.[118] As I have made clear above, there are elements of Sanders's covenantal nomism that I appreciate and underscore. But I am also convinced that his version of Paul's Jewish environment is flawed in certain respects.

Before turning to criticism of Sanders's proposal, we should first acknowledge that elements of Paul's critique of Judaism fit quite well into the basic covenantal structure that Sanders outlines. As he argues, Paul's denial that works of the law can justify may signify simply an attack on the covenant as understood by Jews. Sanders notes that Jews regarded the *intention* to obey the commandments as sufficient to maintain one's covenant status.[119] Paul, however, insists that only what is *actually done* counts (Rom 2:1, 23–24, 25–27; Gal 5:2–3). This argument is an outright attack on the covenantal nomism that Sanders has sketched.[120] The denial of special status to the Jews is an implicit rejection of the election that was the foundation for covenantal nomism,[121] and coheres with the polemic of John the Baptist (Matt 3:7–10) and of Jesus.[122] How does this critical attitude toward the covenant cohere with the Old Testament itself? As we have seen, Paul is close to the prophets in his criticism of those who rely on the covenant as an automatic protection from judgment. And, while he is more explicit, Paul's polemic against the Mosaic covenant is in keeping with the pessimistic attitude expressed toward that covenant in Deuteronomy (see ch. 32) and many of the prophets (e.g., Jer 31:31–34). Paul stresses that the Abrahamic promise, to which one must respond with faith, and which is now fulfilled in Christ, is the true locus of salvation (Rom 4). He therefore does not deny the promise of salvation given in the Scriptures to the Jews but attaches it not to the Mosaic covenant, as did Judaism, but to the Abrahamic.[123] One could, at the least, make a very good case for finding Paul's interpretation of the Old Testament to be more accurate than that of covenantal nomism. "Works of the law"—those things done by Jews in obedience to the law by which they sought to maintain their covenant status—cannot justify because the covenant within which they performed those works was inadequate to bring justification. Jewish works, then, are no different from gentile works, once the larger framework of the covenant—as usually understood in first-century Judaism—is eliminated.

---

118. Note in this regard the warning of J. Christiaan Beker: "We might wonder whether the work of Krister Stendahl and E. P. Sanders influences our treatment of Judaism so heavily these days that their important contributions are unduly exaggerated and—as it were—considered to be dogmatic, unassailable truth" ("Echoes and Intertextuality: On the Role of Scripture in Paul's Theology," in Evans and Sanders, *Paul and the Scriptures of Israel*, 68).

119. Sanders, *Paul and Palestinian Judaism*, 157–82.

120. As Wright ("Paul of History") emphasizes.

121. Sanders, *Paul, the Law and the Jewish People*, 47.

122. Dale C. Allison Jr., "Jesus and the Covenant: A Response to E. P. Sanders," *JSNT* 29 (1987): 61–63.

123. Morna D. Hooker, "Paul and Covenantal Nomism," in *Paul and Paulinism: Essays in Honour of C. K. Barrett*, ed. Morna D. Hooker and Stephen G. Wilson (London: SPCK, 1982), 51.

We have argued, however, that Paul's argument runs more deeply than criticism of the covenant *per se*, encompassing all humans and rooted in human inability to do the law. Tying these general theological points to Paul's claim about the inadequacy of the law requires, ultimately, a different view of the Jewish perspective than Sanders argues for. In what follows, I briefly outline reasons why I am not persuaded that Sanders's covenantal nomism adequately describes Paul's Jewish environment.

First, Sanders's claim of a virtually monolithic view on the basic pattern of Jewish soteriology must be questioned. Subsequent studies have suggested that Jewish soteriology, as we might expect considering the amount of material, the long time periods involved, and the diversity of general perspective, was far more complex than Sanders allowed for. The fullest argument for diversity in first-century Jewish soteriology is made in the first volume of *Justification and Variegated Nomism*.[124] Summarizing the results of careful studies of the diversity of Jewish literature, D. A. Carson concludes that covenantal nomism is reductionistic because it irons out considerable differences in soteriological perspective.[125] Moreover, all scholars acknowledge that first-century Judaism placed great emphasis on obedience to the law. Even if all our extant theological sources taught covenantal nomism (which I question), one might still find significant pockets of legalism among "Jews on the street." The gap between the average believer's theological views and the informed views of religious leaders is often a wide one. Any faith that emphasizes obedience, as Judaism undoubtedly did, is likely to produce some adherents who, perhaps through misunderstanding or lack of education, turn their obedience into a meritorious service that they think God must reward. Christianity, with considerably less emphasis on law, certainly produces such adherents; is it not likely that, as the New Testament suggests, first-century Judaism did also?[126]

---

124. D. A. Carson, Peter T. O'Brien, and Mark A. Seifrid, eds., *The Complexities of Second Temple Judaism*, vol. 1 of *Justification and Variegated Nomism*, WUNT 2/140 (Tübingen: Mohr Siebeck, 2001). See the helpful topical review by Simon Gathercole ("Early Judaism and Covenantal Nomism: A Review Article," *EvQ* 76 [2004]: 153–62).

125. D. A. Carson, "Summaries and Conclusions," in Carson, O'Brien, and Seifrid, *Complexities of Second Temple Judaism*, 543–48. Note also the judgment of Longenecker in his 2016 commentary: "Where I continue to differ with him [Sanders] is principally with respect to his confidence that 'covenantal nomism' dominated the totality of mainline Jewish thought and practice in Paul's day" (*Romans*, 365). Longenecker briefly touches here on an important theme in his *Paul, Apostle of Liberty*.

126. See, e.g., Seifrid, *Justification*, 56–57; Donald A. Hagner, "Paul's Quarrel with Judaism," in *Anti-Semitism and Early Christianity: Issues of Polemic and Faith*, ed. Craig A. Evans and Donald A. Hagner (Minneapolis: Fortress, 1993), 138–39; idem,

"Paul and Judaism: The Jewish Matrix of Early Christianity: Issues in the Current Debate," *BBR* 3 (1993): 118–19; T. F. Best, "The Apostle Paul and E. P. Sanders: The Significance of Paul and Palestinian Judaism," *RestQ* 25 (1982): 72–73; Moises Silva, "The Law and Christianity: Dunn's 'New Synthesis,'" *WTJ* 53 (1991): 349–50. Longenecker's suggestion (*Paul, Apostle of Liberty*, 68–85) that Judaism probably featured at least two kinds of approaches—an "acting legalism" and a "reacting nomism"—has (despite Sanders's criticisms) much to be said for it. Scholars are giving more and more recognition to the diversity of first-century Judaism, to the point of speaking of "Judaisms" (e.g., Jacob Neusner, *Judaic Law from Jesus to the Mishnah*, SFSHJ 84 [Atlanta: Scholars Press, 1993], 49–53; Bruce W. Longenecker, *Eschatology and the Covenant: A Comparison of 4 Ezra and Romans 1–11*, JSNTSup 57 [Sheffield: Sheffield Academic, 1991], 32–33]. Note also the careful criticisms of Sanders in Timo Laato, *Paulus und das Judentum: Anthropologische Erwägungen* (Åbo: Åbo Academy, 1991), 38–82; see also Schreiner, *Law and Its Fulfillment*, 92–121.

While this first point is an important one, it is limited in its ability to help us understand and apply Paul's teaching. For if it is the case that some forms of Judaism departed from covenantal nomism and it is that kind of Judaism that Paul is opposing, then we would have to acknowledge that Paul's rhetoric does not really touch Judaism *per se*. And this is a conclusion that we should be reluctant to draw, not only because it would significantly restrict the application of Paul's teaching but also because it would not seem to fit Paul's evident concern to criticize Judaism itself. So it is important that we turn to other matters that pertain to the essentials of covenantal nomism.

Sanders, as we have seen, argues that Jews relied for their standing with God on his election, by grace, instantiated in his covenant with Israel. A second general line of attack on the adequacy of covenantal nomism as the ruling paradigm for understanding first-century Judaism focuses on the three key words in this description: "covenant," "election," and "grace."

Covenant. While Sanders viewed covenant as an undergirding theological axiom informing virtually all Jewish thinking and teaching about salvation, there is some question whether it was quite so fundamental.[127] Sanders himself admits that some passages, especially in the rabbinic literature, can be read as if salvation is a matter of recompense: Jews earn salvation by doing the law. But he claims that these texts must be read in light of the all-embracing theory of covenant. However, other scholars are not as convinced as Sanders that covenant can simply be read into all these texts. An important study of these texts argues that in fact the two strands of soteriological teaching—salvation by election and salvation by "recompense"—run side by side in rabbinic literature as two alternative schemes.[128] And other scholars have argued that several Jewish writings from the New Testament period lack the undergirding covenantal structure that Sanders claims to be omnipresent.[129] To some extent, Sanders anticipated such criticisms, arguing generally that Jewish texts that appeared to challenge covenantal nomism should be dismissed because either (a) the larger structure of covenant and election must be assumed as the informing theology of the difficult text; or (b) the passages are homiletical in nature. But, to take the latter point first, homiletical passages often provide an important clue to how theology really is understood. To take a contemporary parallel: Which would provide a more accurate reading of the theology of a given pastor—their

127. E.g., Charles H. Talbert, "Paul, Judaism, and the Revisionists," *CBQ* 63 (2001): 7–10; Gundry, "Inferiority of the New Perspective on Paul," 195–200. Jacob Neusner raises a similar question about Sanders's treatment ("The Use of the Later Rabbinic Evidence for the Study of Paul," in *Approaches to Ancient Judaism*, vol. 2, ed. W. S. Green, BJS 9 [Chico, CA: Scholars Press, 1980], 47–52)—and see E. P. Sanders's response in the same volume ("Puzzling Out Rabbinic Judaism," 69–75).

128. Friedrich Avemarie, *Torah und Leben: Untersuchungen zur Heilsbedeutung der Torah in der frühen Rabbischen Literatur*, WUNT 2/92 (Tübingen: Mohr Siebeck, 1996); idem, "Erwählung und Vergeltung: Zur Optionalen Struktur Rabbischer Soteriologie," *NTS* 45 (1999): 108–26; Charles L. Quarles, "The Soteriology of R. Akiba and E. P. Sanders' *Paul and Palestinian Judaism*," *NTS* 42 (1996): 185–95; Stanton, "Law of Moses," 105–6.

129. E.g., Talbert, "Paul, Judaism, and the Revisionists," 7–10.

doctrinal statement or a transcript of one of their sermons? One could claim that the doctrinal statement, a carefully thought-out document, should have precedence. But one could also argue that the sermon expresses more accurately what the preacher *really* believes. At any rate, it is not legitimate to exclude homiletical passages from consideration. Perhaps, however—turning now to the former point—Sanders thinks that homiletical passages should be excluded because they do not, by their very nature, specifically include the theology that lies behind the homily. The point is, in general, well-taken. Certain theological truths can be so taken for granted that we feel no need to make reference to them. But if a homiletical passage assumes a theology that runs counter to the alleged informing theology, questions must be raised about whether that informing theology is, in practice, being honored. In general, then, we might question whether "covenant" had the living and vital theological role in first-century Judaism that Sanders's "covenantal nomism" claims.[130]

Election. The "covenant" in Sanders's covenantal nomism implies God's election of the nation of Israel as the basis for her standing with God. But the proliferation of Jewish sectarian groups in Paul's day calls into question the adequacy of national election to account for the particular claims the different groups were making.[131] The existence of these groups, all arguing vociferously that they were the remnant, the "true Israel," meant that the question of "staying in," if not of "getting in," could not be answered simply in terms of the election of Israel as a people. The Qumran covenanters, for instance, claimed to represent true Israel and anathematized "mainline" Judaism. Clearly God's covenant with Israel—entered into, of course, with all of Israel—could not be the differentiating factor. Both the Qumran covenanters and, for instance, the Pharisees, started out at precisely the same point with respect to the covenant. What, then, led the Qumran covenanters to claim that they were "in" and the Pharisees were "out"? It was adherence to the community through acceptance of its teaching and practices. In effect, therefore, for many Jewish groups in Paul's day, national election had been replaced by a form of individual or at least community election. And one's elect status was determined on the basis of adherence to Torah as interpreted and practiced by the particular community. For such groups, "getting in," while perhaps theoretically acknowledged as a national privilege, recedes in importance with respect to "staying in"—based on faithful adherence to Torah as defined and elaborated by each

---

130. As Henri A. G. Blocher puts it, instead of a sense of "getting in," many Jews in Paul's day may have had a "semi-tacit consciousness of having been born there, of always having been there" ("Justification of the Ungodly [*Sola Fide*]: Theological Reflections," in Carson, O'Brien, and Seifrid, *Paradoxes of Paul*, 489; see also P. Enns, "Expansions of Scripture," in Carson, O'Brien, and Seifrid, *Complexities of Second Temple Judaism*, 98). Watson notes that "commandment" occupies a more prominent

position than "covenant" in many Jewish works—in contrast to Paul's priorities (*Paul and the Hermeneutics of Faith*, 8–11). See also Das, *Paul and the Stories of Israel*, 65–92.

131. Seifrid, *Justification*, 78–133; Ellen Juhl Christiansen, *The Covenant in Judaism and Paul*, AGJU 27 (Leiden: Brill, 1995); and esp. Mark Adam Elliott, *The Survivors of Israel: A Reconsideration of the Theology of Pre-Christian Judaism* (Grand Rapids: Eerdmans, 2000).

particular group. In this sense, the Judaism of Paul's day continued the Old Testament teaching about the "remnant"—those faithful Israelites who were "in" because of their conformity to the demands of God's law. As I. Howard Marshall puts it, reflecting on the different Jewish sects in Paul's day, "For them and for other groups the problem was not one of 'staying in' the covenant people but of regaining entry by fulfilling the appropriate conditions laid down by the particular group."[132]

Grace. Sanders and his followers have emphasized that the traditional tendency to differentiate Judaism and Christianity in terms of grace was misguided. Jews believed firmly in grace, following the teaching of Deuteronomy and other Old Testament books, for God had taken the initiative in calling Israel from among all other nations to be his own people. Yet, as John M. G. Barclay has pointed out, "grace" takes many different forms. Jewish teachers in Paul's day did indeed highlight, or at least assume, grace defined in terms of the priority of God's work in constituting the people of God. Paul, however, while also holding to the priority of God's grace, also stresses its incongruity—that is, that God gives grace to those who have no basis at all to expect it.[133] The grace that characterizes Judaism, then, does not necessarily assume that those who experience grace have done nothing to be worthy of it. Unlike Paul, then, a conviction about God's grace for Judaism did not necessarily imply the exclusion of "works" as a context for the distribution of that grace.

A third consideration that raises questions about the adequacy of covenantal nomism as a satisfactory model to explain Jewish soteriology is the acknowledged importance of obedience to the law ("nomism") in the model. We can readily agree that first-century Judaism in general held to the idea that the grace of God was basic to salvation— although a number of interpreters argue that righteous living was more important as a basis for Israel's standing before God than Sanders allows.[134] But first-century Judaism, on Sanders's own showing, also believed that, if one "got in" by grace, one "stayed in" by obedience. What mattered on the day of judgment, therefore—and what ultimately separated Jew from Jew—was the quality and consistency of obedience to the law. To put it another way, in an undoubtedly overly simple dichotomy, we must distinguish between election (by God's grace) and salvation (by God's grace plus works of obedience to Torah). In practice, then, Jews were saved through a combination of

132. Marshall, "Salvation, Grace and Works in the Later Writings in the Pauline Corpus," *NTS* 42 (1996): 357 (he is referring especially to M. A. Elliott's *Survivors of Israel*); see also Sprinkle, *Law and Life*, 203–4.

133. Barclay, *Paul and the Gift*, see esp. 194–340 on Judaism. See, e.g., p. 316: "On the logic of the congruent gift, God's grace is not the opposite of recompense, but is *simultaneously* gift and reward. . . . Those who deserve gifts are still the recipients of gifts, given voluntarily and without legal requirement. They do not *cause*

the gift to be given (that is always a matter of the benefactor's will), but they prove themselves to be its suitable recipients and thus provide the *condition* for its proper distribution." See also Stephen Westerholm: "Sanders himself gives us reason to doubt that it [Judaism] assigned the *same* importance to grace as the apostle" (*Justification Reconsidered: Rethinking a Pauline Theme* [Grand Rapids: Eerdmans, 2013], 31).

134. See, e.g., Linebaugh, *God, Grace, and Righteousness*, 93–121, on Wisdom of Solomon.

grace and works—what we appropriately can label "synergism."[135] And it is just this synergism that Paul seems to be attacking in a number of passages. Paul is not denying that Jews stressed the foundational importance of God's elective grace for their identity. What he is denying is that obedience to the law is the necessary and adequate means by which that election can be confirmed and remain valid for God's ultimate verdict of justification. This, of course, is just the point he has made at length in Romans 2. Real Jewish covenant privileges (cf. 3:1–2) have no value when the law is not obeyed. As Carson puts it in the conclusion to volume 1 of *Justification and Variegated Nomism*, "The category of covenantal nomism cannot itself accomplish what Sanders wants it to accomplish, viz. serve as an explanatory bulwark against all suggestions that some of this literature embraces works-righteousness and merit theology, precisely because covenantal nomism embraces the same phenomena."[136] The "nomism" in Sanders's famous descriptive phrase must be given greater weight than is usually done.[137]

A fourth and final consideration is the adequacy of Sanders's model to explain the data of the New Testament itself. We can acknowledge that we are always involved in a kind of circle as we study the New Testament—as we must!—against its first-century context. Our interpretation of specific texts will often depend on, or at least be importantly affected by, our understanding of the background assumed by the biblical author. Yet our identification of that background will also rightly be judged by the degree to which it can furnish a natural interpretation of the New Testament texts. Considerable effort has been expended in trying to show how Romans and Galatians can be explained as responses to covenantal nomism. I am not convinced, in general, that these readings of Romans and Galatians satisfactorily account for all the data in these books. Yet, while other New Testament books have not been entirely neglected in the discussion, it is fair to say that they have not been given the attention they deserve. Some of these books appear, indeed, to assume views of Judaism that do not fit at all well with covenantal nomism.[138] In general, then, I am convinced that the teaching of Paul—and of Jesus and

---

135. See esp. Seifrid, *Justification*, 56–57, 71–81 (he finds a clear emphasis on the importance of works for eventual salvation in Psalms of Solomon and 1QS); Laato, *Paulus und das Judentum*, 73–75, 195–211; Byrne, "Interpreting Romans Theologically," 230; Gundry, "Grace, Works, and Staying Saved," 19–20, 35–36; Stephen Westerholm, *Israel's Law and the Church's Faith* (Grand Rapids: Eerdmans, 1988), 143–50; Timo Eskola, *Theodicy and Predestination in Pauline Soteriology*, WUNT 2/100 (Tübingen: Mohr Siebeck, 1998), 27–94; Thurén, *Derhetorizing*, 146–48; Gathercole, *Where Is Boasting?*; Michael F. Bird, "Justification as Forensic Declaration and Covenant Membership: A Via Media between Reformed and Revisionist Readings of Paul," *TynBul* 57.1 (2006): 113. Michael S. Horton has argued that "covenantal nomism" makes the fundamental mistake of "monocovenant-alism," collapsing the biblical distinction between salvation by faith alone in the Abrahamic covenant with the works principle of the (typical) Mosaic covenant (*Covenant and Salvation: Union with Christ* [Louisville: Westminster John Knox, 2007], 11–101).

136. Carson, "Summaries and Conclusion," 545.

137. Dunn himself acknowledges that Sanders's "covenantal nomism" puts too much emphasis on "covenant" and too little on "nomism" ("New Perspective: Whence, What, Whither?," 55–63).

138. See, e.g., Marshall, "Salvation, Grace and Works in the Later Writings of the Pauline Corpus," 339–58. In a more roundabout way, it has also been argued that the polemic regarding "works" in James presupposes a broad meaning of Paul's "works of the law" (Friedrich Avemarie, "Die Werke des Gesetzes im Spiegel des Jakobusbriefs: A Very Old Perspective on Paul," *ZTK* 98 [2001]: 282–309).

Matthew and Luke and Mark and Peter—cannot satisfactorily be explained without the assumption that some Jews, at least, had drifted from a biblical conception of the primacy and sufficiency of God's grace into a belief that accorded their own works, done in obedience to the law, as basic to their justification and final salvation.

2.2.2.3.5 *"What the Law Was Powerless to Do" (Rom 8:3)*

I emphasize again that a wholesale rejection of the insights of the New Perspective would be shortsighted. Advocates of this general view are quite right to insist that traditional interpretation has often failed to recognize the degree to which Paul's concerns with the law had to do with his passion to include gentiles as full members within the people of God. The law of Moses effectively acted as a barrier to gentile inclusion, and it is certainly for that reason that Paul often insists that the coming of Christ introduced a new era in which the law no longer held sway over the people of God. However, while the issue of ethnocentrism was often the presenting problem that Paul was dealing with, I think Paul also questions the law not just because it kept gentiles out but because it kept Jews and gentiles alike "out"—out of favor with God—because of sinful inability to keep it. The law, while God's good and holy law, is "letter," *gramma*, a word Paul uses to denote the external, "written on tablets" nature of the law (Rom 2:27, 29; 7:6; 2 Cor 3:6, 7). Francis Watson has cogently argued that the Pentateuch itself teaches this view of the law.[139] As the prophets recognized, the law did not have the power to change human hearts (e.g., Jer 31:31–34; Ezek 36:24–32). This heart change requires the work of the new-covenant gift of the Spirit, which Paul sets in contrast with "letter" in Romans 7:6 and 2 Corinthians 3:6, 7.

A similar point is made in Romans 7:7–25. Readers are often preoccupied with identifying the "I" in this passage, but the real point of these verses is not about anthropology but about the law. The initial paragraph explains how the law, a good gift from God (v. 12), could nonetheless become allied with "death": sin has coopted the law for its own purposes (vv. 8–11). How could sin do this? Because, while the law is "spiritual," "I am unspiritual [*sarkinos*, 'fleshly']" (v. 14). Human inability means that the law God gives his people Israel can never win the final victory over sin and death. Romans 8:3 neatly summarizes this point: it is "what the law was powerless to do because it was weakened by the flesh."

2.2.2.4 Torah and "Law"

As I noted above (pp. 11–14), scholars have recently often appealed to a "narrative substructure" as the context for Paul's theologizing. And, of course, Paul's interpretation

---

139. Watson, *Paul and the Hermeneutics of Faith*; see esp. his summary of his important book on 275–76.

of the "Christ event" is heavily indebted to a reading of that event in terms of the climax of a long salvation history. However, there is good reason to think that Paul also uses the salvation-historical narrative in what we might call a paradigmatic manner, mining the experience of Israel to shed light on the human condition generally. As Christopher Seitz puts it, "Reflexively, Paul understands the oracles of God as having to do with human nature and destiny as a totality, and he is seeking to work this out, to penetrate a great mystery, or plan of God, as he calls it. The personal revelation to Israel has a purpose that is larger because the God of Israel is the creator of all things, maker of heaven and earth, the seas and all that is in them."[140] The experiences of Israel function as "types" (*typoi*; 1 Cor 10:6). Paul can therefore warn the Corinthians about falling into the same idolatrous patterns as Israel in the wilderness (1 Cor 10:1–11) or compare old and new covenants to the histories of Sarah and Hagar (Gal 4:21–31). Paul's implicit inclusion of gentiles in conditions that, strictly speaking, apply only to Israel suggest that he sees Israel's experience with the law as typical of the experience of humans with "law" of any kind. Thus, for example, Paul can claim that gentiles were "under the law" (Rom 6:14, 15) and therefore need to be released from its bondage (7:4). And note the logic of Romans 3:19, in which Paul moves from the law's condemnation of Israel to the condemnation of all people: "Now we know that whatever the law says, it says to those who are under the law, so that every mouth may be silenced and the whole world held accountable to God." While widely criticized, then, Bultmann's claim that the Jewish person can stand as a representative of the "religious person" in general has some basis in Paul's appeal to the Old Testament.[141] As Horton puts it, "As the story unfolds, it becomes progressively clearer that Israel is like Hamlet's play-within-a-play, a parable of the wider history of humanity."[142]

This wider, "theological" sense of "law" ties into the question of "natural law," that is, divine commandments that are applicable to and, to some extent at least, accessible to all humans. In my view, Paul refers to this general concept, which was widepread in his day, in passages such as Romans 2:14–15: "Indeed, when Gentiles, who do not have the law, do by nature things required by the law, they are a law for themselves, even though they do not have the law. They show that the requirements of the law are written on their hearts, their consciences also bearing witness, and their thoughts sometimes accusing them and at other times even defending them."[143] This universally

---

140. Christopher Seitz, "Jewish Scripture for Gentile Churches: Human Destiny and the Future of the Pauline Correspondence. Part I: Romans," *ProEccl* 23 (2014): 307 (and see 300–307); and also, e.g., Stephen Westerholm, "Canonical Paul and the Law," in *Torah Ethics and Early Christian Identity*, ed. S. J. Wendel and D. M. Miller (Grand Rapids: Eerdmans, 2016), 210–11; Starling, *Not My People*, 203–11; Dietzfelbinger, *Der Sohn*, 73. There is some basis for this application of the law to gentiles in Jewish teaching. See, e.g., LAB 11.2: "I [God] have given an everlasting Law into your [Moses's] hands and by this I will judge the whole world" (*OTP* 2:318; see also 2 Bar. 48.47; 4 Ezra 9.11–12). I am indebted to Terrence L. Donaldson for these references ("Paul, Abraham's Gentile 'Offspring,' and the Torah," in Wendel and Miller, *Torah Ethics and Early Christian Identity*, 146–47).

141. Bultmann, *Theology of the New Testament*, 1:264–65.

142. Horton, *Justification*, 2:70.

143. I offer a brief defense of this interpretation on pp. 205–6. See, at more length, Moo, *Romans* (NICNT), 158–64.

applicable "law" provides an important basis for a fundamental universal ethic that can take shape in, for example, a nation's positive laws.[144]

3 THE NATURE OF HUMAN BEINGS

The old realm is not just a "place" where humans live; it is also a form of life that characterizes the inhabitants of that realm. Paul describes "old-realm" humans with a variety of suggestive terms. Some of the terms he uses, indeed, extend beyond the life of the old realm *per se*, describing humans generally and moving into their new-realm existence. Nevertheless, this seems as good a place as any to consider what we might label Paul's "anthropology."

3.1 Preliminary Points

Paul's thinking about the nature and constitution of persons is manifested especially in the several key words he uses to depict people—"body," "flesh," "soul," etc. But before I glance at these key words, some preliminary points must be made. First, these terms should not be understood as defining different "parts" of the human being. Such an approach tends toward a dualistic view of the human person, in which there is a strong contrast between a person's material part and their spiritual part. This "body-soul" dichotomy was deeply rooted in the Greco-Roman culture of Paul's day and has continued to exercise a strong influence on Christian perceptions of human beings ever since. Paul's view, however, is determined by the Old Testament, which is monistic rather than dualistic. The human being is viewed as essentially a single entity. The various words Paul uses to depict people, then, are not intended to isolate certain parts of a person but to provide a certain perspective on the single, whole person.[145] However, while adopting an essentially monistic approach to Paul's anthropology, we also need to leave room for some small element of dualism. Paul can speak, for instance, of his uncertainty about whether his being "caught up to the third heaven" was "in the body or out of the body" (2 Cor 12:1–3). And, while much debated, one popular understanding of Paul's view of the intermediate state sees him referring to a time between death and Christ's return when the believer is "at home with the Lord" but "away from the body" (2 Cor 5:8; see vv. 1–10). A fundamentally monistic approach

144. For a defense of natural law as rooted in Scripture, see esp. David VanDrunen, *Divine Covenants and Moral Order: A Biblical Theology of Natural Law*, Emory University Studies in Law and Religion (Grand Rapids: Eerdmans, 2014). For a critique, see John Frame, "Review of David VanDrunen's *A Biblical Case for Natural Law*," *The Works of John Frame & Vern Poythress*, May 10, 2012, https://frame-poythress.org/review-of-david-van-drunens-a-biblical-case-for-natural-law.

145. See esp. David Stacey, *The Pauline View of Man: In Relation to Its Judaic and Hellenistic Background* (London: Macmillan, 1956); and, from a broader theological perspective, John W. Cooper, *Body, Soul, and Life Everlasting: Biblical Anthropology and the Monism-Dualism Debate* (Grand Rapids: Eerdmans, 2000). This essentially monistic approach dovetails, though perhaps not perfectly, with the findings of modern neuroscience. See esp. Joel B. Green, *Body, Soul, and Human Life* (Grand Rapids: Baker, 2008).

to Paul's anthropology renders the second preliminary issue less important: Does Paul teach a dichotomist or trichotomist view of the human being? That is, is the human being basically composed of two parts—body and spirit/soul—or three parts—body, spirit, soul? Paul's way of contrasting body with spirit (1 Cor 5:3–4; 7:34; 2 Cor 7:1; Col 2:5) or flesh with spirit (1 Cor 5:5) could imply the former; but 1 Thessalonians 5:23 is regularly cited in favor of the latter: "May your whole spirit, soul and body be kept blameless at the coming of our Lord Jesus Christ." Paul simply does not provide the kind of evidence we need to decide this issue; it must be determined on the basis of broader theological considerations.

Second, it is important to recognize also that Paul's perspective on human beings does not involve the human in the abstract but the human as he or she is embedded in the sweep of salvation history.[146] Paul makes clear that humans are to some extent quite basically defined in terms of their relationship either to Adam or to Christ. As C. Kavin Rowe puts it, "For Paul, anthropology is what the human being has been through its history from the first Adam until the second—and, then, what it can become in light of the Christ-event."[147] The contrast between Adam and Christ is one of the key frameworks for Paul's theology, and it has clear anthropological implications. We can see this in relationship to "image" language, which Paul clearly attaches to the Adam-Christ contrast: "And just as we have borne the image of the earthly man, so shall we bear the image of the heavenly man" (1 Cor 15:49). The association of Adam with "image" is grounded, of course, in Genesis 1:26–27:

> Then God said, "Let us make mankind in our image, in our likeness, so that they may rule over the fish in the sea and the birds in the sky, over the livestock and all the wild animals, and over all the creatures that move along the ground."
>
> So God created mankind in his own image,
>   in the image of God he created them;
>   male and female he created them.

Paul recognizes that humans continue to bear the image of God (1 Cor 11:7).[148] He himself does not unpack just what that "image" might be, though Marc Cortez's argument for "manifestation of the divine presence" is intriguing (see p. 371). If this is so, then, for Paul, Christ is the one in whom God's presence is ultimately manifested (2 Cor 4:4; Col 1:15); and we, conformed to that image, grow in our potential to

---

146. Eastman, *Paul and the Person*.

147. Rowe, *One True Life*, 95. See esp. Cortez, *ReSourcing Theological Anthropology*.

148. In this context, of course, Paul attributes "image" to men in distinction from women. But his purpose is not to deny that both men and women bear God's image but to suggest a specific way men function with respect to women (see p. 142). See also Jas 3:9 (using Gk. *homoiōsis*, "likeness").

manifest God (Rom 8:29; 1 Cor 15:49; 2 Cor 3:18; Col 3:10). At the same time, it is Christ who is the template for true humanity.[149]

The Adam-Christ contrast is basic to another anthropologically related set of terms in Paul: "new man" and "old man" (Rom 6:6; Eph 4:22–24; Col 3:9–11; NIV and other versions render "new/old person" or "new/old self"). These phrases are often thought to refer to people, or to parts of people (e.g., "old nature" versus a "new nature"). But behind the contrast between "old man" and "new man" is the contrast between Adam and Christ, the "first man" and the "last" (1 Cor 15:45; see Rom 5:15, "the one man, Jesus Christ").[150] Those, then, who are "in Adam" belong to and exist as "the old man"; those who are "in Christ" belong to and exist as "the new man." In other words, these phrases denote the solidarity of people with the "heads" of the two contrasting ages of salvation history.[151] The "old man" is what we were "in Adam"—the "man" of the old age, who lives under the tyranny of sin and death.[152]

3.2 Paul's Anthropological Terms
3.2.1 Flesh (sarx)[153]

I begin with the most important term Paul uses to designate the human being as a participant in the old realm: "flesh."

"Flesh" is one the most difficult words in Paul's theological vocabulary. The semantic range and complexity of the word in Paul are reflected in the NIV, where twenty-eight different words or phrases are used to translate *sarx* (and the NIV is no outlier here; every other modern English Bible displays a similar pattern). As Anthony Thiselton has pointed out, *sarx* in Paul is a "polymorphous concept," and its meaning is very much context-dependent.[154] Scholars have, of course, tried to categorize Paul's uses of *sarx*. I prefer to identify five basic senses. The most basic meaning of *sarx*, and the most common in secular Greek is (1) "the material that covers the bones of a human or animal body" (BDAG). Paul occasionally uses the word with this sense. The clearest is 1 Corinthians 15:39: "Not all flesh is the same: People have one kind

---

149. Cortez, *ReSourcing Theological Anthropology*, 116–29; see also Jason Maston, "Christ or Adam: The Ground for Understanding Humanity," *Journal of Theological Interpretation* 11 (2017): 277–93.

150. Ridderbos, *Paul*, 62–64.

151. Paul can therefore use the phrases with a corporate meaning. This seems to be the case in both Col 3:10–11—"the new man" includes Greek and Jew, circumcision and uncircumcision, etc.—and Eph 2:15—Jews and Greeks are united into "one new man."

152. John Murray, *Principles of Conduct* (Grand Rapids: Eerdmans, 1957), 211–19, has a very helpful discussion, although his conception differs slightly from ours. See also Beasley-Murray, *Baptism in the New Testament*, 134; H. Frankemölle, *Das*

Taufverständnis des Paulus: Taufe, Tod und Auferstehung nach Röm 6, SBS 47 (Stuttgart: Katholisches, 1970), 74–76; C. K. Barrett, *From First Adam to Last: A Study in Pauline Theology*, Hewett Lectures 1961 (London: Adam & Charles Black, 1962), 98–99.

153. Material in this section is taken from my article, "'Flesh' in Romans: A Problem for the Translator," in *The Challenge of Bible Translation: Communicating God's Word to the World. Essays in Honor of Ronald F. Youngblood*, ed. Glen S. Scorgie, Mark L. Strauss, and Steven M. Voth (Grand Rapids: Zondervan, 2003), 365–79.

154. Anthony Thiselton, *The Two Horizons: New Testament Hermeneutics and Philosophical Description with Special Reference to Bultmann, Heidegger, Gadamer, and Wittgenstein* (Grand Rapids: Eerdmans, 1979), 408–11.

of flesh, animals have another, birds another and fish another" (see also Eph 2:11; Col 2:13; cf. Gal 6:13). Following precedents in secular Greek, Paul also (2) applies *sarx* to the human body as whole; for example, 2 Corinthians 7:1: "Since we have these promises, dear friends, let us purify ourselves from everything that contaminates body [*sarx*] and spirit, perfecting holiness out of reverence for God" (see also 1 Cor 5:5[?]; 6:16; 2 Cor 12:7; Gal 4:13; Eph 5:31). But more often, Paul (3) uses *sarx* to refer not to the human body narrowly but to the human being generally. First Corinthians 1:28–29 illustrates this use of the word: "God chose the lowly things of this world and the despised things—and the things that are not—to nullify the things that are, so that no one [*sarx*] may boast before him" (see also 1 Cor 1:29; Gal 1:16; 2:16). This sense of the word merges almost imperceptibly into a bit broader concept (4): the human state or condition. While debated, 1 Corinthians 10:18, where Paul refers to Israel *kata sarka* ("according to the flesh"), probably falls into this category. Finally (5), in a usage that is distinctively (though not uniquely) Pauline, *sarx* can designate the human condition in its fallenness. As Timo Laato has neatly put it, the difference between meanings (4) and (5) is the difference between the human being in *distinction* from God and the human being in *contrast* to God.[155] The latter is often called the "ethical" use of *sarx*, in contrast to the "neutral" use of meaning (4).[156] A clear example of the "ethical" use is Galatians 5:16–17: "So I say, walk by the Spirit, and you will not gratify the desires of the flesh [*sarx*]. For the flesh [*sarx*] desires what is contrary to the Spirit, and the Spirit what is contrary to the flesh [*sarx*]. They are in conflict with each other, so that you are not to do whatever you want." This sense of *sarx* is quite common in Paul (anywhere from twenty-five to thirty occurrences, depending on how one interprets several notoriously difficult texts).

The neat dual categorization of "neutral" versus "ethical" has, however, been challenged. James D. G. Dunn, for example, argues that the meanings of *sarx* in Paul occupy a spectrum of meaning. In contrast to scholars who suggest that Paul may have derived his more neutral sense of *sarx* from the Old Testament and Jewish world and the more negative sense from the Greek world, Dunn, along with many others before him, traces the spectrum of Paul's usage to the Hebrew *basar*, with its sense of "human mortality."[157] One implication of this conclusion is that a certain negative nuance often clings to *sarx* even when Paul uses it in apparently neutral senses. Dunn has a point, as several texts make clear. In Romans 1:3, for instance, Paul describes Christ as the Son "who was descended from David according to the flesh [*sarx*]" (ESV). "Flesh" here obviously does not have a negative sense, but it does suggest a less-than-complete perspective on Christ,

---

155. Laato, *Paulus und das Judentum*, 95.
156. See, e.g., Davies, *Paul and Rabbinic Judaism*, 19; D. E. H. Whitely, *The Theology of St. Paul* (Philadelphia: Fortress, 1972), 39.

157. Dunn, *Theology of Paul*, 62–70; cf. also Dunn's "Jesus—Flesh and Spirit: An Exposition of Romans I.3–4," *JTS* 24 (1973): 44–51; Stacey, *Pauline View of Man*, 154–73.

who must also be understood as the one "appointed the Son of God in power" "through the Spirit of holiness" (v. 4; see also Rom 4:1; 9:5, 8; Gal 4:23, 29).

For our purposes, what is especially important is to trace the connection between "flesh" and human sin. The natural human condition is to be "in the flesh," to be fundamentally determined by the perspective of this world, in contrast to the world to come. And sin is the inevitable result of this condition. We are people who, by virtue of our belonging to this world, are governed by the flesh, "gratifying" its cravings and "following its desires and thoughts" (Eph 2:3). The natural person therefore cannot please God (Rom 8:8); he or she sins and dies (7:5), thinking and acting as a person who takes no account of the divine realm (8:4–7). Christians, because they are still in this world, must strive to avoid falling into such patterns of thought and activity (8:12–13; 13:14).

3.2.2 Spirit (pneuma)

Paul's habit of contrasting "flesh" with "spirit" makes it natural to tackle "spirit" next. The word, of course, renders Greek *pneuma*, and the large majority of Paul's uses of this word do not concern us here—they refer to the Spirit of God, the Holy Spirit. Almost all of Paul's contrasts between *sarx* and *pneuma* are therefore putting in opposition the sin-prone human and the powerful new-covenant Spirit of God (e.g., Rom 8:4–13; Gal 5:17–24). Paul also uses *pneuma* to refer to an "attitude" shared by people ("one with him in spirit" in 1 Cor 6:17), to spiritual beings (1 Cor 12:10; Eph 2:2; 2 Thess 2:2 [see ESV]; 1 Tim 4:1), and to create a rhetorical contrast with the Holy Spirit (e.g., 1 Cor 2:12: "What we have received is not the spirit of the world, but the Spirit who is from God"; see also Rom 8:15; 2 Cor 11:4). A little over a dozen times, however, Paul uses *pneuma* to refer to human beings ("spirit"; Rom 1:9; 8:16b; 12:11[?]; 1 Cor 2:11a; 5:3, 4, 5; 7:34; 2 Cor 7:1, 13; Gal 6:18; Col 2:5; 2 Tim 4:22; Phlm 25).[158] First Corinthians 14:14 is typical of the word in this sense: "My spirit prays, but my mind is unfruitful." The word appears, then, to characterize humans in terms of their "godward" side, their openness to the influence of the divine. While all humans can therefore be viewed as "spirit," it is Christians, indwelt by the Holy Spirit, who most clearly display this side of human experience. Indeed, Paul prefers "spirit" to "soul" to depict this aspect of humans particularly for this reason.[159]

3.2.3 Soul (psychē)

As Stacey notes, Paul uses this word less frequently than other people in his environment—there are only thirteen occurrences in his letters. Perhaps, he surmises, this is because Paul prefers a term such as "spirit" that ties his view of humans more

---

158. Fee wants to associate Paul's use of *pneuma* in reference to humans closely with his typical use of the word to refer to the Holy Spirit (*God's Empowering Presence*, 24–26, passim).

159. See Stacey, *Pauline View of Man*, 126–27.

closely to the biblical story line.[160] The dualism that has significantly marked the Western intellectual tradition reveals itself especially clearly in our popular view of this word. We tend to think of the "soul" as some kind of inner part of the human being. To be sure, some of Paul's uses of the word could suggest this idea. For example, Paul can encourage believers to do the will of God "from the soul" (Eph 6:6, my translation). But he also uses the word to refer simply to a person as a whole, as in Philippians 2:30, where Paul says that Epaphroditus "risked his soul" for the work of Christ (my translation). This usage imitates the Old Testament, where *nephesh* (regularly translated with Gk. *psychē*) frequently denotes simply a person. See, for example, Genesis 2:7: "Then the LORD God formed a man from the dust of the ground and breathed into his nostrils the breath of life, and the man became a living being [*nephesh/psychē*]."[161] If, then, we adopt the perspectival approach to Paul's anthropological terms that we argued for above, "soul" should not be viewed as the inner part of the human but as "the whole human being *seen from the point of view of one's inner life*."[162]

3.2.4 Body (sōma)

"Body" is the anthropological term Paul uses most often. The word occurs ninety-one times in his letters, forty-six of these coming in 1 Corinthians, where many theological themes are tied to the word: the importance of honoring God in our "bodies" (chs. 5–6), the need to refrain from any practice that would ignore the importance of Christ's physical body (ch. 10) or his "body," the church (chs. 11, 12), and the need to affirm the reality of the resurrection body (ch. 15).[163] As this brief overview of occurrences in 1 Corinthians reveals, not all Paul's uses of "body" are anthropological, but his various applications of the word all extend from the basic sense of the human as "body." I phrase matters in this way to defer again to a perspectival approach that does not speak of humans "having" a body but in terms of humans "being a body" (to paraphrase Bultmann's well-known comment on this issue[164]). By speaking of a human in terms of "body," Paul connotes something about the nature of the person as a whole. Bultmann stressed the idea of one's relationship with oneself, but Ernst Käsemann is probably closer to the mark in his emphasis on relationship with the world and with others.[165] To refer

---

160. Stacey, *Pauline View of Man*, 121.

161. The full Hebrew phrase in Gen 2:7 is *nephesh khayyah*; for *nephesh* on its own to denote a human, see, e.g., Lev 2:1; 4:2; Josh 10:35.

162. Wright, *Day the Revolution Began*, 283; see also, e.g., Stacey, *Pauline View of Man*, 121–27; Bell, *Deliver Us from Evil*, 189–229. Without suggesting that they are semantically identical, our current English use of "soul" has affinities with this use of *psychē*; one will find newspaper articles stressing the loss of human life in a disaster by referring to, e.g., "Twelve souls perished."

163. Dunn (*Theology of Paul*, 52) remarks on these connections; see also Martin, *Corinthian Body*.

164. "Man does not *have* a *soma*; he *is soma*" (Bultmann, *Theology of the New Testament*, 1:194).

165. See Ernst Käsemann, *Perspectives on Paul* (Philadelphia: Fortress, 1971), 114; followed by Stuhlmacher, *Biblical Theology of the New Testament*, 307. See the discussion in Eastman, *Paul and the Person*, 85–105.

to a person as "body" is to stress the side of the person that engages with the world, "the whole person seen in terms of public, space-time presence."[166] It is important to distinguish the human as "flesh" and the human as "body." The former, as we have seen, often has a negative nuance, depicting humans as fallen and prone to sin. The latter is basically neutral. As John A. T. Robinson puts it, "While *sarx* stands for man, in the solidarity of creation, in his distance from God, *soma* stands for man, in the solidarity of creation, as made for God."[167] To be sure, Paul can sometimes suggest that sin is rooted in our bodily existence (see esp. Rom 6:6; 8:13, 23). But he says this simply to remind us that our bodies in this life, unredeemed as they are, can become the platform for sin. In a point that follows biblical precedents and that differs fundamentally from the typical Greco-Roman viewpoint (and the tendency toward dualism in many forms of thinking since Paul's day), the body, Paul affirms, is destined for resurrection. We will live forever in bodies. Sin in Paul is not, then, tied inescapably to life in the body. He therefore makes clear that ascetic practices—the "denial" of the body and its natural functions—in themselves have no power to conquer our sinful tendencies (Col 2:23).

As I noted above, we may need to modify a purely monistic approach to Paul's anthropology in order to explain the whole spectrum of Paul's use of this word.[168] If we adopt the usual view of the intermediate state, Christians exist without a body for some period of time.

3.2.5 Mind (nous)

Paul refers to the "mind," or *nous*, twenty-one times, a word he uses to connote the "thinking I."[169] In the Greek world, the "mind" was generally considered the highest part or capacity of human beings. Paul's more pessimistic view of humans leads him to downgrade the potential of the mind. God has given humans over to a "depraved mind" (Rom 1:28), so that they are not able to understand truly who God is, who they are in relationship to him, or what the world they live in is really like (see the list of vices following Rom 1:28 in vv. 29–31; and also Eph 4:17; Col 2:18; 1 Tim 6:5; 2 Tim 3:8; Titus 1:15). The mind must be "renewed" if it is to access truth (Rom 12:2; Eph 4:23). Paul elsewhere stresses that the Holy Spirit is the agent who gives humans access to the "wisdom" that truly understands matters of the spiritual realm (1 Cor 2:6–16).

---

166. Wright, *Day the Revolution Began*, 283. See also Harris: "The organ of an individual's communication with the external world on which he acts and which acts on him, be it on earth or in heaven" (*Raised Immortal*, 120).

167. John A. T. Robinson, *The Body: A Study in Pauline Theology* (Philadelphia: Westminster, 1977), 186. See on this point Lorenzo Scornaienchi, *Sarx und Soma Bei Paulus: der Mensch Zwischen Destruktivität und Konstruktivität*, NTOA 67 (Göttingen: Vandenhoeck & Ruprecht, 2008).

168. A point Gundry makes in his monograph (*Sōma in Biblical Theology*).

169. Dunn, *Theology of Paul*, 75.

3.2.6 Heart (kardia)

"Heart" occurs fifty-two times in Paul. It refers not simply to the seat of our emotions (as it does often in modern English) but to the hidden (see 2 Cor 5:12) center of a person's being. What is "in the heart" therefore determines the orientation of a person. If the "heart" is strengthened, a person will be "blameless and holy" (1 Thess 3:13; cf. 2 Thess 2:17; 1 Tim 1:5). It is for this reason that Christ and the Spirit dwell "in the heart" (Rom 5:5; Gal 4:6; Eph 3:17). Paul's use of *kardia* therefore resembles closely, and is probably dependent on, the use of Hebrew *lev/levav* in a similar way in the Old Testament; see, for example, the central demand of the Shema in Deuteronomy 6:5–6: "Love the LORD your God with all your heart and with all your soul and with all your strength. These commandments that I give you today are to be on your hearts."

3.3 Human Incapacity

As a concluding word in this section, I draw attention to what is Paul's most important perspective on humans: their inability to please God. Paul's Jewish contemporaries held a variety of views on the capacity of humans to respond rightly to God, the Essenes of the Qumran community being quite pessimistic about human ability, while the Pharisees were more optimistic. This more optimistic assessment seems to have been the typical stance in the Judaism of Paul's day. As Westerholm notes, "A Judaism for which the Sinaitic covenant provides the framework within which God's favor is enjoyed appears committed to the conviction that human beings (or Jews at least) *can* do the good required by the covenant for participation in its blessings."[170] In response to the modestly optimistic view of human capacity to understand and respond to the divine, Paul focuses on the negative. In addition to the points I have made above, I might also briefly overview the "classic" text on sinfulness in Romans 1:18–3:20. The argument of this passage drives relentlessly to one conclusion: because all humans are "under the power of sin" (3:9), no human can be put right with God by their own exertions (3:20—see above, pp. 208, 435–39, for the validity of this interpretation). Paul gets to this point by accusing both gentiles and Jews of culpably turning away from the knowledge of God they had been given. Gentiles, even though they know [something about] God, turn away from that knowledge to devise gods of their own making (1:19–22). They are therefore "without excuse" (1:20), an accusation that links the predicament of the gentiles with that of the Jews (2:1). For Jews also, and to a greater degree, have knowledge of God. Yet they also have turned from it, failing to honor

---

170. Stephen Westerholm, "Paul's Anthropological 'Pessimism' in Its Jewish Context," in Barclay and Gathercole, *Divine and Human Agency*, 97; see also Timo Laato, *Paul and Judaism: An Anthropological Approach*, SFSHJ 115 (Atlanta: Scholars Press, 1995); Preston M. Sprinkle, *Paul and Judaism Revisited: A Study of Divine and Human Agency in Salvation* (Downers Grove, IL: InterVarsity Press, 2013).

God by observing the law he graciously gave them (ch. 2). While of course Paul is not thinking here of the world's religions, what he says in these chapters certainly applies to them. While preserving to a greater or lesser degree insights into the divine, these religions do not ultimately provide access to God.[171]

We see here again the conjunction in Paul's thought between "solution" and "plight," and we can imagine Paul arguing the point in both directions. Because humans are locked up under sin, only a powerful display of divine grace and power can rescue them. Or, in what was arguably the direction of Paul's own thinking, God has gone to the incredible lengths of sending his own Son to die on a Roman cross, and therefore the plight of humans must be quite desperate—much more desperate than Paul realized in his relatively self-complacent Jewish life.

---

171. See, e.g., Harold A. Netland, *Encountering Religious Pluralism: The Challenge to Christian Faith and Mission* (Downers Grove, IL: InterVarsity Press, 2001); Gerald R. McDermott and Harold A. Netland, *A Trinitarian Theology of Religions: An Evangelical Proposal* (Oxford: Oxford University Press, 2014).

Chapter 20

THE BLESSINGS OF
THE NEW REALM

For the grace of God has appeared that offers *salvation* to all people. It teaches us to say "No" to ungodliness and worldly passions, and to live self-controlled, upright and godly lives in this present age, while we wait for the blessed hope—the appearing of the glory of our great God and Savior, Jesus Christ, who gave himself for us *to redeem us from all wickedness and to purify for himself a people* that are his very own, eager to do what is good.

—TITUS 2:11–14

A S I NOTED in the introduction to chapter 18, we cannot always neatly separate the "accomplishment" of salvation in the events of Jesus's life, death, resurrection, and ascension, on the one hand, from the "application" of that salvation in the life of believers, on the other hand. Some of Paul's key conceptions, such as, for instance, his teaching about what we experience "with Christ," simply cannot be pinned down in terms of this kind of chronology. There is a sense in which God's saving work is a seamless garment that cannot be torn without distortion. I remain convinced, however, that it is still helpful to analyze Paul's key ideas about salvation by focusing either on the initial redemptive events or on the experience of "every spiritual blessing" in the believer's life. See Ephesians 1:3: "Praise be to the God and Father of our Lord Jesus Christ, who has blessed us in the heavenly realms with every spiritual blessing in Christ." The risk of distortion means, however, that we will have to make sure not to separate what Paul wants to keep together.

1 APPROACH AND PERSPECTIVE

We may think of Paul's soteriology in terms of a map that, in its broadest scope, is divided into two territories: the old realm of sin and death and the new realm of Christ and righteousness. When we zero in on the details of Paul's soteriological map, we confront an immediate problem: the map reveals a lot of different roads, leading from one place to another, intersecting with one another, with no markings indicating which is a main interstate (or motorway) and which is a minor, two-lane route. Confronted with this maze, our challenge is to make sense of it all without imposing a structure on Paul's varied teaching that is simply not there. We should not assume that Paul himself thought about Christ's work in discrete categories. Despite the risk, I forge ahead with a tentative attempt to map out Paul's soteriological landscape.

Scholars do not agree on the best terminology to denote the various approaches. "Metaphor" is the most popular, with the suggestion that Paul has appropriated certain forms of discourse from his own world to conceptualize God's work in Christ. Others, while acknowledging that metaphor is probably always involved in speaking of God, think that the language of metaphor runs the risk of turning reality—God really does love us, we really do sin, he really does reconcile us—into arbitrarily chosen ways of speaking.[1] Others, therefore, prefer to speak of "accounts" (Peter Leithart), "models" (Michael Gorman), or "perspectives" (Colin Gunton). In keeping with my overall, spatially oriented "realm" concept, I will bypass this discussion and use the language of "route." Paul portrays the breadth and richness of our new-realm blessings by identifying several different routes, each with its distinctive destination. Those destinations in the new realm are matched with correlative points of departure in the old realm: "solution" and "plight" are naturally related to each other.

2 A FLYOVER OF THE NEW REALM

Before looking at specific features of Paul's new-realm landscape, we should do a flyover at thirty thousand feet to get a sense of its general shape.

The first thing we see, so pervasive that it could not be missed, is Christ. "In Christ" language is everywhere in Paul, and to be "in Christ" is equivalent to being in the new realm. See, for example, 2 Corinthians 5:17: "Therefore, if anyone is in Christ, the new creation has come: The old has gone, the new is here." As I have argued elsewhere (pp. 35–39), union with Christ is as close to the heart of Paul's theology as anything. As we would expect, then, union with Christ is the fundamental and all-encompassing blessing of the new realm. But union with Christ is also the source of all other blessings. Arguing for the sufficiency of Christ in the face of false teachers who are insisting on "adding" to Christ, Paul reminds the Colossians that "in Christ you have been brought to fullness" (Col 2:10). As John Murray puts it, union with Christ "underlies every

---

1. Moreover, as Westerholm points out, the metaphors, if we are to use that term, are not "dead": "Sinners are declared righteous (not reconciled), enemies are reconciled (not declared righteous), and so on" (*Justification Reconsidered*, 11). On metaphors in relationship to atonement, see also Boersma, *Violence,* *Hospitality, and the Cross*, 99–114; Gaffin, "Atonement in the Pauline Corpus," 154–55. The classic study of the role of metaphors in theology is Janet Martin Soskice, *Metaphor and Religious Language* (Oxford: Clarendon, 1985).

step in the application of redemption."[2] The text from Ephesians quoted above ends with the phrase "in Christ," and this phrase, or its equivalent, is the leitmotif of the long sentence this verse introduces (Eph 1:3–14). Union with Christ is the locus of the "great exchange" that denotes a fundamental Pauline (and biblical) soteriological logic: Christ became what we are, so that we might become what he is. Second Corinthians 5:21 is the classic Pauline text: "God made him who had no sin to be sin for us, so that in him we might become the righteousness of God." See also 2 Corinthians 8:9: "For you know the grace of our Lord Jesus Christ, that though he was rich, yet for your sake he became poor, so that you through his poverty might become rich." Calvin, who puts union with Christ and the "great exchange" at the center of his theology, writes:

> This is the wonderful exchange which, out of his measureless benevolence, he has made with us; that, becoming Son of man with us, he has made us sons of God with him; that, by his descent to earth, he has prepared an ascent to heaven for us; that, by taking our mortality, he has conferred his immortality upon us; that, accepting our weakness, he has strengthened us by his power; that, receiving our poverty unto himself, he has transferred his wealth to us; that, taking the weight of our iniquity upon himself (which oppressed us), he has clothed us with his righteousness.[3]

A second characteristic feature of Paul's new-realm teaching is his emphasis on its *inclusiveness*. It is a realm in which all are equally invited to share, on the same basis: being joined with Christ by faith. Of course Paul pursues this theme especially with respect to the inclusion of gentiles, a natural focus granted salvation history and his own role as "apostle to the gentiles." The Old Testament is from the start marked by an inclusive vision. The initial promise to Abraham concludes with "all peoples on earth will be blessed through you" (Gen 12:3).[4] The ultimately universal scope of the blessing conferred on and through Abraham is confirmed several times (Gen 17:3–4; 18:18; 22:18; 26:4). However, intertwined with this universal focus in the promise is a particular focus that ultimately comes to dominate. Abraham will be the father of a great multitude of descendants, who will be given a land of their own, and who will exercise some kind of dominion over the nations (e.g., Gen 12:2; 15; 17:2, 7–8, 19–22; 22:17). This particularistic focus, of course, dominates Old Testament history. Israel is given land and law, but fails to confirm God's gracious covenant and is therefore sent into exile. We should not, however, miss the universalistic notes that continue to sound throughout this history—a note that hits its greatest volume in the second part of the book of Isaiah. Nevertheless, in the Old Testament this universalism is "a peculiarly

---

2. Murray, *Redemption*, 161.

3. *Institutes*, 4.17.2. See Horton, *Justification*, 195–219, on the "great exchange" in the Reformers.

4. In favor of this translation of the debated text, see esp. Chee-Chiew Lee, "*Goyim* in Genesis 35:11 and the Abrahamic Promise of Blessing for the Nations," *JETS* 52 (2009): 467–82.

particularistic universalism, specifically oriented around Israel's self-identity."[5] Only by inclusion in Israel could salvation for gentiles be achieved. If we now continue this extremely generalized overview into the Second Temple period, a concern to maintain the integrity of Israel in the face of both persecution and dispersion is particularly evident. Torah observances that would serve to distinguish Israel from the nations were especially emphasized: circumcision, food laws, and observance of Sabbath and other Jewish holy days.

Paul, called by God to bring the gospel to the gentiles, focuses especially often on the way the coming of Messiah impacts this particularistic history and theology. Without removing Israel from the scope of God's promises (see, e.g., Rom 9–11; see pp. 558–65), Paul's battle with Jews and some Jewish Christians, who wanted to maintain a strong element of particularism, leads him to stress the breaking down of ethnic barriers in the new covenant. Gentiles can become full members of the people of God without becoming Jews.[6] This issue, of course, dominates Galatians, where Paul insists that being in Christ by faith is the only and sufficient requirement for salvation, for Jew and gentile equally. But his focus, dictated by the circumstances he addresses, is on gentile inclusion: he wants to show how "the blessing given to Abraham might come to the Gentiles through [or 'in,' *en*] Christ Jesus" (Gal 3:14).

The theology of Romans, while broadly embracing many different matters, continues to highlight this central issue. Indeed, in distinction from Galatians, Romans combines a continuing, though strictly limited, particularism with its characteristic universalistic focus. We find this balance in the statement of the letter's theme: the gospel promises salvation "first to the Jew, then to the Gentile" (1:16). The "first to the Jew" theme is developed and explained particularly in chapters 9–11, while "to the Gentile" is picked up again and again. Israel's covenant has no ability to shield the people from God's wrath (ch. 2); Jews, as well as gentiles, are "under the power of sin" (3:9). Israel's law, so basic to that covenant, has ultimately had the effect of driving Israel ever deeper into sin (3:20; 4:15; 5:20; 7:7–25). Paul claims Abraham as the "father" of all those who believe, citing Abrahamic promise passages I highlighted above (4:13–22; see Gen 17:5 in v. 17 and 15:5 in v. 18).[7] The combination of a limited,

---

5. Aaron Sherwood, *Paul and the Restoration of Humanity in Light of Ancient Jewish Traditions*, Ancient Judaism and Early Christianity 82 (Boston: Brill, 2013), 131; cf. 29–133.

6. Paul may have been prompted at least partly to make this move through his reading of the "pilgrimage of the gentiles" theme in the OT (and especially Isaiah), which tells of gentiles joining in worship of Israel's God, often in response to God's salvation of his people in the last day. Terence Donaldson doubts the significance of this theme for Paul ("Paul within Judaism: A Critical Evaluation from a 'New Perspective' Perspective," in Nanos and Zetterholm, *Paul within Judaism*, 284–93), but it has likely had some influence (Matthew V. Novenson, "The Jewish Messiahs, the Pauline Christ, and the Gentile Question," *JBL* 128 [2009]: 357–73; Lionel J. Windsor, *Paul and the Vocation of Israel: How Paul's Jewish Identity Informs His Apostolic Ministry, with Special Reference to Romans*, BZNW 205 [Berlin: de Gruyter, 2014], 122–25).

7. For this universalistic interpretation in the Genesis texts, see, e.g., Bruce Waltke, *Genesis* (Grand Rapids: Zondervan, 2001), 260.

continuing benefit for Israel with a focus on gentile inclusion is climactically expressed in Romans 15:7–13. At the same time, Paul clearly ties the blessing of the gentiles to the salvation-historical purposes in and for Israel (11:17–24). Gentile inclusion is not as dominant a theme in the other letters of Paul, but it continues to surface (see, e.g., Eph 2:12–22; 3:1–10; Col 1:27; 1 Thess 2:16–17; 1 Tim 2:7; 2 Tim 4:17).

Inclusion of the gentiles is a theme that New Perspective advocates especially have drawn attention to in the last few decades. This movement is characterized by a rotation of Paul's central theological axis from a vertical to a horizontal orientation. New Perspective advocates often fault the interpretive tradition derived especially from the Reformation (and from Luther in particular) for a myopic and anachronistic preoccupation with the individual and his or her status before God. Paul's cultural context, religious background, and theological interests suggest, rather, that his immediate concern was with the people of God, and especially with the integration of gentiles into the people of God. An ethnocentric reading of Paul takes center stage, displacing an anthropocentric reading to a more subordinate role.[8] Paul's gospel is not, at least, first of all, the story of the individual's transformation from sinner to saint—or even the story of humankind's restoration. Rather, the gospel proclaims Israel's restoration, a restoration that takes place in and through the ministry of Jesus, Israel's Messiah and representative, and that extends God's grace to the gentiles.

I have concerns with the overall emphases in the New Perspective, concerns that I detail in chapter 19 (pp. 430–33, 439–48). To repeat briefly what I say there, I think this movement in general has tipped the scales too far in favor of the "horizontal" aspect of Paul's gospel—inclusion of gentiles—and away from its "vertical" aspect—acceptance before God.[9] However, here I simply want to acknowlege that, while perhaps imbalanced, the New Perspective has rightly drawn attention to the importance of gentile inclusion in Paul's theology—a matter that has sometimes been ignored or downplayed. Indeed, the issue, in its broader parameters, was one of the most important theological challenges faced by the early church. What is the meaning of the Old Testament, with its Israel-focus, for the new-covenant people of God? What role does Torah have in this new era? How may gentiles be admitted into this new realm? Paul, as he proclaimed Christ to the gentiles, was thrown into these issues, and he naturally spends quite a bit of time on them.

I began by describing this basic contour of the new realm as "inclusiveness." I deliberately use a term with broad application because Paul himself moves in this direction.

---

8. See, e.g., Dunn's comment, looking back at the history and development of the New Perspective: "The surmounting of these ancient hostilities [i.e., including gentiles with Jews] was not merely a by-product of the gospel, far less a distraction from the true meaning of the gospel, but the climactic achievement of the gospel, the completion of God's purposes from the beginning of time" (Dunn, "New Perspective on Paul: Whence, What, Whither?," 31).

9. This has been a hallmark of Westerholm's writing on this issue; see, e.g., *Justification Reconsidered*, 12–22. See also, e.g., Lohse, *Der Brief an die Römer*, 25–32.

While his historical context put the issue of *gentile* inclusion in the forefront, he suggests very clearly that gentile inclusion is part of, and a signal for, a larger inclusiveness. This focus surfaces especially in the justly famous Galatians 3:28: "There is neither Jew nor Gentile, neither slave nor free, nor is there male and female, for you are all one in Christ Jesus." Since it appears in slightly different form again in 1 Corinthians 12:13 and Colossians 3:11, this classic assertion of new-realm inclusiveness would appear to have been fundamental in Paul's thinking. These texts, along with other elements of Paul's teaching (see pp. 461–64), provide a secure basis to conclude that the inclusiveness Paul teaches with respect to gentiles extends to every arena of human division: race, nationality, gender, socioeconomic class, etc. The new realm is not *universal—only* those belonging to Christ by faith enter—but it is *inclusive—all* those belonging to Christ by faith enter.

3 Basic Contours of the New Realm

We are now in a position to descend to three thousand feet or so and begin to isolate the general contours of the new realm.[10] When we do this, five basic "umbrella" blessings emerge.

3.1 New Covenant

The first general feature of the new realm is the new covenant. Surprisingly, in light of its importance in the Old Testament and in Paul's Jewish environment, Paul uses the word "covenant" (*diathēkē*) only nine times. "Covenants"—perhaps referring to the several iterations of God's covenant with Israel—signal God's special gifts to Israel (Rom 9:4; see also Eph 2:12, "covenants of the promise"). At the outset of Israel's history stands the promissory covenant that God entered into with Abraham (Gal 3:17; cf. also Rom 11:27, in light of Rom 11:28). The subsequent contrast between covenants in Galatians 4:24 suggests that this Abrahamic covenant finds its fulfillment, or culmination, in a covenant that brings God's people into the new realm of freedom. This contrast between the "old" covenant of Sinai and the new covenant inaugurated in Christ is explicit in 2 Corinthians 3 (see vv. 6, 14).[11] The foundational nature of the new covenant in Paul is implied also by his citation of Christ's "word of institution" over the cup in the Lord's Supper (1 Cor 11:25).

However, I would argue that "new covenant," *as a concept*, is far more important in Paul than the number of explicit references indicate.[12] Paul's regular description of the

---

10. An abbreviated form of the following two sections will be published in *Bibliotheca Sacra* in a forthcoming issue, and these articles, in turn, were based on the Griffith-Thomas lectures that I delivered at Dallas Theological Seminary, Feb. 5–8, 2019.

11. As Horton notes, it is the absorption of the Abrahamic covenant into the Mosaic covenant that Paul contests in Galatians (*Justification*, 2:86).

12. See also esp. Gorman, *Death of the Messiah*.

church as the place where Old Testament prophecies of restoration are being fulfilled confirms the textual evidence I cited above that he has taken over the fundamental "covenant" structure of the prophets. Arguing that the people of Israel had broken the original covenant (Isa 24:5; Jer 11:10; 22:9; 31:32; 34:18; Ezek 16:59; 17:18, 19; 44:7; Hos 6:7; 8:1), they predict that God will enter into a "new covenant" with his people (Jer 31:31; cf. Isa 59:21)—an "everlasting covenant" (Isa 55:3; 61:8; Jer 32:40; 50:5; Ezek 16:60–62; 37:26), or "covenant of peace" (Isa 54:10; Ezek 34:25; 37:26) that the servant of the Lord will inaugurate (Isa 42:6; 49:8). This covenant means that the great promise that God would be his people's God and that his people would be his people will be fulfilled.[13] Paul reflects this fundamental "covenant" structure in frequent claims that Old Testament prophecies about the new covenant are fulfilled in the church of his day (e.g., Hos 1:10 and 2:23 in Rom 9:25–26; Isa 11:10 in Rom 15:12; Isa 49:8 in 2 Cor 6:2; Jer 32:38 and Ezek 37:27 in 2 Cor 6:16).[14] Paul's claim that the church is the place where God's new covenant is being enacted is especially clear in his claim that believers enjoy distinctive new-covenant blessings. Primary among these blessings is the gift of the Spirit.

3.2 The Spirit

The powerful presence of God's Spirit is the most important general contour of the new realm. The Spirit, of course, has been present and active among the people of God since the beginning—although the precise nature of that activity is quite debated.[15] In any case, the prophets predicted that in the last days God would pour out his Spirit on his people (Isa 44:3; 59:21; Ezek 11:19; 36:26–27; 37:14; 39:29; Zech 12:10[?]; Joel 2:28–32). The eschatological gift of the Spirit comes upon God's people for the first time at Pentecost (Acts 2), and becomes the decisive mark of true conversion (Acts 8:15–19; 9:17; 10:44–47 [cf. 11:15–16]; 19:6). For Paul, also, possession of the Spirit is the key identifying mark of belonging to the eschatological people of God. Romans 8:9 is especially clear: "You, however, are not in the realm of the flesh but are in the realm of the Spirit, if indeed the Spirit of God lives in you. And if anyone does not have the Spirit of Christ, they do not belong to Christ" (see also Rom 8:14; 1 Cor 12:13; 2 Cor 1:22; 5:5; 11:4; Gal 4:6; Eph 1:13; 4:30). Likewise, when Paul reminds the Galatians of their entry into salvation, he puts it in terms of receiving the Spirit (Gal 3:2, 3, 5). As James Dunn, who especially highlights this feature of Paul's theology, puts it,

13. See for this particular emphasis Gorman, *Death of the Messiah*, esp. 51–68.

14. This pattern is elaborated especially in Beale, *New Testament Biblical Theology*.

15. Sinclair Ferguson's summary is judicious: "Any biblical theology of the Spirit's work must recognize the progressive and cumulative character of historical revelation. But systematic or logical considerations invite the conclusion that the Spirit's activity in the OT epoch involved personal renewal of a moral and spiritual nature" (*The Holy Spirit* [Downers Grove, IL: InterVarsity Press, 1996], 25).

"Reception of the Spirit was the decisive and determinative element in the crucial transition of conversion" and "the presence of the Spirit in a life was the most distinctive and defining feature of a life thus reclaimed by God."[16] An important distinguishing feature of the Spirit's presence was its tangible nature. It is vitally important that a believer "hear" and take to heart God's word of acceptance: "You are justified, or reconciled, or redeemed." But the Spirit's presence is known firsthand to the believer; he "testifies with [or to] our spirit" (Rom 8:16). This tangible manifestation of God's presence would be even clearer if, as Graham Twelftree has argued, the coming of the Spirit was regularly accompanied by miracles.[17]

Paul compares the Spirit to a seal, suggesting that the presence of the Spirit authenticates God's presence in the believer. See, for example, Ephesians 1:13: "And you also were included in Christ when you heard the message of truth, the gospel of your salvation. When you believed, you were marked in him with a seal, the promised Holy Spirit." However, the Spirit functions not only to authenticate the presence of salvation but also guarantees future salvation (Eph 4:30). In Romans 8, Paul celebrates the presence of the Spirit in the lives of believers but also calls the Spirit "firstfruits," the first stage or "downpayment" on God's continuing work in his people. He makes the same point by labeling the Spirit an *arrabōn*, a "deposit" (NIV) or "first installment/guarantee" (NRSV; 2 Cor 1:22; 5:5; Eph 1:14). Romans 8:9, cited above, makes clear that a full appreciation of the Spirit's work requires that we focus not only on our position "in" the Spirit but also on the Spirit's dwelling "in" us. This interchange, which we find also with respect to Christ—we are "in Christ," but "Christ lives in me" (Gal 2:20)—warns us about not locking ourselves into any single "grammar" of salvation. As we will see later, Paul often uses the language of the Spirit's presence "in" us to connote the transforming work of God in our lives.

3.3 New Creation[18]

As a Jew whose worldview is formed by the Hebrew Scriptures, Paul naturally appropriates the template of covenant to depict the blessings of the new realm (see 3.1 above). But Paul's horizon is ultimately broader than this. He announces not only the culmination of God's program to redeem a people but also the culmination of God's creation project. Our starting point in looking at this contour of the new realm is, of course, the phrase "new creation." Paul uses this phrase only twice, and it appears nowhere else in the Old Testament or New Testament (2 Cor 5:17; Gal 6:15). To be sure, there is lively debate about the referent of the phrase. The Greek word *ktisis* can mean "creature," and while no modern translation follows the KJV in adopting this

---

16. Dunn, *Theology of Paul*, 425; see 413–41.

17. Graham H. Twelftree, *Paul and the Miraculous: A Historical Reconstruction* (Grand Rapids: Baker, 2013), 179–205.

18. For more detail on all the following points, see esp. Moo, "Creation and New Creation," 39–60.

translation,[19] many of them suggest that Paul has in view in both key texts the individual believer. See, for example, the ESV translation of 2 Corinthians 5:17a: "Therefore, if anyone is in Christ, he is a new creation." Many scholars agree.[20] Another option is that the phrase, especially in Galatians, refers to the new community. However, the phrase probably echoes Isaiah's expansive vision of God's redemptive work extending to the entire cosmos, encompassing "new heavens and a new earth" (Isa 65:17; see 66:22). Jewish authors sometimes used "new creation" in this sense (e.g., Jub. 1.29; 4.26, 1 En. 72.1, 1QS 4.25, and 2 Bar. 44.12).[21] "New creation" is Paul's shorthand for the entirety of God's redemptive work, the new state of affairs inaugurated by Christ, including individual renewal, community restoration, and cosmic redemption.[22] The phrase therefore is a reminder of two important points. First, as Horton puts it,

> The *historia salutis* not only comes before the *ordo salutis*; the former is the canvas on which the particular figures are painted. . . . The individual is part of the new creation because there is a decisive, epochal and cosmic new creation in the first place with Christ's uniquely redemptive work as its achievement and "firstfruits."[23]

Second, this language reminds us that, while Paul's theology often focuses on the individual, the new realm he envisages embraces the entire universe.

3.4 Salvation

Fourth, and continuing our focus on blessings given to believers, is salvation.[24] Paul uses words referring to this concept over sixty times. And, while a few instances are debated, it is likely that every occurrence of the word group in Paul refers to deliverance in a theological sense.[25] As so often the case, Paul's use of salvation language is strongly influenced by the Old Testament. In this case, two contexts are important. First, "salvation" language occurs in the well-known sequence of sin—divine anger—distress—deliverance that marks the history of the judges. The verb *sōzō*, "save, deliver," occurs nineteen times in Judges in this sense; see, for example, Judges 2:16–18:

---

19. There is good lexical ground for rendering *ktisis* as "creation." To be sure, the word sometimes refers to a single "created thing" (Rom 1:25; 8:39; Heb 4:13). The word may also have this meaning in Col 1:23 ("every creature under heaven"; see NRSV; NIV; NAB), but it more likely refers to "the whole creation under heaven" (ESV; NASB; NET). In 1 Pet 2:13, the word refers to an "[established] authority." All the other NT occurrences of *ktisis* mean "creation" in a general sense (see Mark 10:6; 13:19; Heb 9:11; 2 Pet 3:4; Rev 3:14).

20. See, e.g., Hubbard, *New Creation*.

21. The most thorough analysis of the background of the phrase is found in Mell, *Neue Schöpfung*.

22. See, e.g., T. Ryan Jackson, *New Creation in Paul's Letters:*

A Study of the Historical and Social Setting of a Pauline Concept, WUNT 2/272 (Tübingen: Mohr Siebeck, 2010). See esp. my fuller development of the idea of "new creation" in ch. 24 (pp. 645–47).

23. Horton, *Rediscovering the Holy Spirit*, 178.

24. For salvation as a broad category in Paul, see, e.g., Anderson, *Paul's New Perspective*, 298–308.

25. The most debated occurrence is *sōtērian* in Phil 1:19, which most English versions translate as "deliverance" (e.g., NRSV; NIV; ESV; note "release" [from prison] in CEB). A compelling argument for interpreting the word here (and all other cognate words in Philippians) as a reference to eternal "salvation" is found in Cable, "'We Await a Savior.'"

Then the LORD raised up judges, who delivered [sōzō] them out of the power of those who plundered them. Yet they did not listen even to their judges; for they lusted after other gods and bowed down to them. They soon turned aside from the way in which their ancestors had walked, who had obeyed the commandments of the LORD; they did not follow their example. Whenever the LORD raised up judges for them, the LORD was with the judge, and he delivered [sōzō] them from the hand of their enemies all the days of the judge; for the LORD would be moved to pity by their groaning because of those who persecuted and oppressed them. (NRSV)

Israel's temporary deliverance at the hands of these "judges" or "leaders" finds its typological fulfillment in the permanent deliverance that Christ wins for his people. The second Old Testament source for Paul's salvation language is, as so often, Isaiah, who mediates God's promise to deliver his people Israel and restore them to their inheritance.[26]

"Salvation" is an umbrella soteriological concept in Paul.[27] "By this gospel you are saved" is Paul's introduction to his famous summary of the gospel in 1 Corinthians 15:3–8. Christ followers can be described generally as "those who are being saved" (1 Cor 1:18; 2 Cor 2:15); the Christian message is "the gospel of your salvation" (Eph 1:13). These texts make clear that salvation covers the entirety of Christian experience. As many interpreters have put it, salvation can be spoken of in three tenses: past—"I have been saved" (e.g., Rom 8:24)—present—"I am being saved" (e.g., 2 Cor 2:15)—and future, "I will be saved." But it is this last "tense" that Paul most often uses in his language of salvation, focusing on the believer's ultimate deliverance. Our salvation, Paul writes to the Roman Christians, is "nearer now than when we first believed" (Rom 13:11). Paul typically uses salvation absolutely. But he occasionally also specifies what believers are saved *from*—the final outpouring of wrath (Rom 5:9; cf. 1 Thess 5:9; cf. 1 Cor 3:15, with its comparison between being "saved" and "escaping through the flames"), and, once, what they are saved *for*—"his heavenly kingdom" (2 Tim 4:18 NRSV).[28]

3.5 Life

A fifth umbrella conception is "life." "Life," as we would expect, is often contrasted with "death." With Genesis 3 in view, Paul uses death at times to refer to the judgment under which all people fall because of sin. "Life," as its opposite, then, often has a

---

26. See 2 Cor 6:2, quoting from Isa 49:8: "In the time of my favor I heard you, and in the day of salvation [sōtērias] I helped you." See also the quotation from Isa 59:20 in connection with the "salvation" of "all Israel" (Rom 11:26).

27. The noun "salvation" (sōtēria) occurs eighteen times in Paul; the verb "save" (sōzō) twenty-nine times; the title "Savior" (sōtēr) twelve times; and the adjective "saving" (sōtērios) twice. Ten of Paul's uses of sōtēr, "Savior," occur in the Pastoral Epistles,

where Paul uses the title for both God and Christ (see, e.g., Titus 1:3–4). See also Eph 5:23 and Phil 3:20. Also relevant is the verb *rhyomai*, which Paul usually uses for deliverance from this-worldly dangers, but which he uses four times to refer to spiritual deliverance (Rom 7:24; 11:26 [= Isa 59:20]; Col 1:13; 1 Thess 1:10).

28. See also 2 Tim 1:10, which claims that "our Savior, Christ Jesus," "has destroyed death and has brought life and immortality to light through the gospel."

forensic flavor as well (note, e.g., its contrast with "wrath" in Rom 2:8, and with "condemnation" in Rom 5:18). However, Paul ultimately uses the language so widely that it should also be seen as a general way of connoting the blessings of the new realm. See, for example, 2 Corinthians 2:15–16: "For we are to God the pleasing aroma of Christ among those who are being saved and those who are perishing. To the one we are an aroma that brings death; to the other, an aroma that brings life. And who is equal to such a task?" Paul often qualifies "life" as "eternal" (*aiōnios*; see Rom 2:7; 5:21; 6:22, 23; Gal 6:8; 1 Tim 1:16; 6:12; Titus 1:2; 3:7). More so than "salvation," "life" refers approximately equally in Paul to the life believers already enjoy and to the life they will finally enjoy in the consummated kingdom.[29] When life refers to this "not yet" side of our experience, it often refers to, or is associated with, resurrection (e.g., 1 Cor 15:42, 45).

4 SPECIFIC LANDFORMS OF THE NEW REALM

Our flyover has enabled us to get a sense of the new realm as a whole. Our three thousand foot overview has enabled us to identify some general contours of that realm. We now descend a bit further, flying our drone over the landscape of the new realm so that we can isolate some of its more detailed landforms. It will be helpful to think of these landforms as destinations of various roads that lead from old realm to new.

4.1 From Condemnation to Vindication: Justification
4.1.1 Preliminary Remarks

The first route I trace runs from the condemnation under which humans suffer in the old realm to the verdict of justification enjoyed in the new realm. Paul's teaching about justification has, of course, been singled out as one of his most important contributions to Christian theology. The Reformers' "rediscovery" of the gospel, especially in its Lutheran trajectory, had at its heart the claim that sinners were declared right with God (in a forensic, or judicial sense) by grace alone and by faith alone, and that this verdict of "justified" preceded (logically, at least) any movement toward moral righteousness. This "forensic only" view of justification has been fundamental in most Protestant theology ever since. However, the doctrine has always had its detractors, and these critics have grown even more vocal lately. Three developments have fueled this criticism. First, the reevaluation of the apostle Paul's appropriation of his Jewish heritage that has followed the "Sanders revolution," and which is at the heart of the New Perspective, has inevitably turned scholarly attention to the Pauline teaching on

---

29. By my count, eleven references to life focus on the present, nine on the future. Many occurrences have no clear temporal focus.

justification, since it is so thoroughly interwoven with his response to Judaism. Second, the strong current toward ecumenical rapprochement has stimulated both Protestant and Roman Catholic theologians to look afresh at their respective teachings on justification and to wonder whether this historically divisive doctrine need any longer be a cause of separation between the two movements. And, third, the perennial concern that "justification-by-faith-alone" might be partly responsible for the widespread failure of Christians to take seriously the demands of discipleship has fostered a fresh batch of articles and books proposing various revisions to the traditional teaching. These three powerful currents—the academic, the ecclesiological, and the practical—have flowed together to produce a flood of articles and books on justification.

I cannot enter into all these debates. However, if I spend more time here than on some other landforms in Paul's new realm landscape, it is because the intensity and breadth of discussion require careful response. At the end of the day, while I understand and even sympathize with some of the concerns that revisionist interpreters have raised, I think the basic Reformation view of justification is well grounded in Paul's teaching.

4.1.2 The Status of Justification in Paul's Theology

By beginning our survey of Paul's teaching about the benefits of Christ's death and resurrection with justification, I do not necessarily endorse the widespread view within certain Protestant (especially Lutheran) contexts that justification has a privileged position at the very center of Paul's theology. This traditional focus on justification was severely criticized a century ago by W. Wrede and A. Schweitzer, who argued that Paul only deployed justification teaching to counter Jewish theology.[30] They have been followed, at least in part, by many contemporary scholars, who judge participation with Christ to be far more important and basic than justification to Paul's theological thinking.[31] To use the imagery that Schweitzer used, justification by faith is a "subsidiary crater" in terms of its impact on Paul's theology. It is not basic to his own theological outlook. Rather, justification is a "battle doctrine" that arose from the need to confront Judaism. These critics have a point. Traditional "justification" language is absent entirely from many of Paul's letters. And it is also true that the texts in which the language is used (Galatians, Romans, Philippians 3) involve dialogue with Jewish viewpoints and disputes over Torah. Paul does, then, deploy the doctrine for polemical purposes. But Paul's teaching on justification is more than an occasional strategy to deal with Jewish opponents. The concept of "righteousness," which, as I will argue, is judicial or forensic in focus, picks up a central element of the Old Testament story.

---

30. Schweitzer, *Mysticism of Paul the Apostle*, 205–6, esp. 219–26; Wrede, *Paul*, 122–37.

31. See esp. Sanders (*Paul and Palestinian Judaism*, 434–42;

501–8); and also, e.g., Philip Esler, *Galatians* (London: Routledge, 1998), 153–59; Gorman, *Inhabiting the Cruciform God*, and, in more polemical form, Campbell, *Quest for Paul's Gospel*; idem, *Deliverance*.

Israel, condemned for her failure to obey God's covenant law, is sent into exile. But in that exile, the prophets announce a new work of God according to which, in his grace, he manifests his righteousness by vindicating his people. In a typical maneuver, Paul now finds that promised righteousness revealed in the gospel (Rom 1:17; see 3:21), but revealed now not for Israel *per se* but to every person who responds to the good news in faith. It is not, then, controversy with Jews only that sparks Paul's justification teaching. That teaching, more basically, is Paul's continuation, in modified form, of a key story line from the Old Testament, showing how the condemnation pronounced by the law is overcome by the gospel. The prominence of the law in passages where Paul uses justification language may be more relevant than reference to Jewish issues *per se*.[32]

Moreover, the doctrine of justification guards Paul's theology at a vital point. Justification by faith is the anthropological reflex of Paul's basic conviction that what God has done in Christ for sinful human beings is entirely a matter of grace (see especially Rom 3:24; 4:1–8, 16).[33] Justification, as Michael Allen has put it, is "the forensic entryway of the gospel"—or, to put it in our categories, the forensic point of entry into the new realm.[34]

We should also note that, while Paul is no doubt responsible for giving justification a prominent role in early Christian soteriology, he himself probably derived the doctrine from tradition before him. As James Dunn notes, Paul's appeal to Peter in Galatians 2:15–16 implies as much:

> We who are Jews by birth and not sinful Gentiles know that a person is not justified by the works of the law, but by faith in Jesus Christ. So we, too, have put our faith in Christ Jesus that we may be justified by faith in Christ and not by the works of the law, because by the works of the law no one will be justified.[35]

Balance here is difficult to find. I don't think justification is at the center of Paul's theology; as I argue above (pp. 35–39), our union with Christ is a better candidate for this honor. At the same time, I share the concern of scholars and theologians, both ancient and modern, who worry that undue attention to justification can warp the shape of Paul's thought, diminishing his obvious concern with producing transformed individuals living in transformed communities. However, on the other hand, a rush to transformation can bypass the need for humans to be given a new "objective" status

---

32. Watson, *Paul and the Hermeneutics of Faith*, 36–38; Wright, *Paul and the Faithfulness of God*, 2:1039; Beker, *Paul the Apostle*, 260. Schnelle accuses Schweitzer and Wrede of confusing the origin of Paul's view with its importance (*Apostle Paul*, 471).

33. See Schnelle, *Theology of the New Testament*, 214; Wolter, *Paul*, 385.

34. R. Michael Allen, *Justification and the Gospel: Understanding the Contexts and Controversies* (Grand Rapids: Baker, 2013), 53.

35. Dunn, *Beginning from Jerusalem*, 484.

before God that is the necessary first step toward that transformation. That status is characteristically denoted by Paul with the language of justification. Justification, we might say, is *primus inter pares*, "first among equals," in Paul's list of new-realm blessings. If, then, justification by faith is not the center of Romans or of Paul's thought in the logical sense, in another sense it expresses a central, driving force in Paul's thought.[36] In this respect, the Reformers were not far wrong in giving to justification by faith the attention they did. For this reason and in order to deal adequately with the avalanche of new literature on the subject, I give justification a bit more space here than other new-realm blessings.

4.1.3 Methodology

In my brief discussion of the importance of justification in Paul, I have bracketed a basic question: What do we mean by "justification"? Different definitions naturally effect the question about the prominence of justification in Paul. Many theologians, especially in the Lutheran tradition, use "justification" to refer to the entire spectrum of soteriology; they naturally think it is basic and ubiquitous. Other theologians and scholars, however, work with a much narrower definition, sometimes assuming justification relates only to (selected) words from the *dikaio-* root; these interpreters think "justification" pops up only sporadically. Of course, a number of mediating options between these two poles are defended. Some interpreters, for instance, use "justification" as a catchall word for the objective, status-oriented aspect of Paul's soteriology.

Since neither Paul nor any other New Testament author defines for us the *concept* of justification, interpreters and theologians must inevitably make a somewhat arbitrary decision on this matter. In my view, a tight definition based on (but not necessarily restricted to) significant occurrences of Paul's *dikaio-* language is the best way to go. Too broad a definition loses the particular contribution that this language makes to our understanding of Paul's soteriology.[37] This is not to lapse into a methodologically questionable definition of a *concept* in terms of a certain *lexeme*—it is simply that, in this case, concept is closely related to a particular lexeme. Nor are we excluding other language in Paul that can plausibly be tied to the concept we derive from these key instances of *dikaio-* words.

This matter of definition has considerable significance for interpretations of justification. Unfortunately, confusion arises because our methodology is inescapably

---

36. See esp. Allen, *Justification and the Gospel*, 3–19 ("While justification does not say everything, it does say certain essential things," 15).

37. Allen and Treier point out this methodological issue in their review of Peter Leithart's proposal for a broader meaning of

justification (R. Michael Allen and Daniel J. Treier, "Dogmatic Theology and Biblical Perspectives on Justification: A Reply to Leithart," *WTJ* 70 [2008]: 105–10). See also the pertinent remarks in Wright, *Paul and the Faithfulness of God*, 2:913–14.

subjective. The key question is: Which are the *key*, or *significant*, occurrences of *dikaio-* language that we should use to define the concept? There is great danger here of falling into a viciously circular argument. We identify "key" occurrences of the language based on a concept of justification we have already established; then we use those occurrences to determine the concept. As we will see below, contemporary disputes about the meaning of justification in Paul come down on very different sides of this methodological issue. For now, I would simply argue that key occurrences of the *dikaio-* root stand out at several points in Paul's letters; that these words have historically provided the basis for constructing a concept of justification; and that it is methodologically sensible to begin with these occurrences to establish a concept and then, if necessary, work outward to see what other words or texts should be included.[38]

4.1.4 "Righteousness" Language[39]

If, as I contend, the *concept* of justification is closely aligned with *dikaio-* language, an obvious first step is to analyze key words from the Greek *dikaio-* root. The three key words are the noun *dikaiosynē* ("righteousness"), which Paul uses fifty-seven or fifty-eight times,[40] the verb *dikaioō* ("justify"), which occurs twenty-seven times in Paul, and the adjective *dikaios* ("righteous," "just"), eighteen times.[41] This vocabulary is not spread evenly across the Pauline corpus, being clustered in Romans, Galatians, and Philippians 3. And, as we will see, not all these words contribute to the concept of justification.

4.1.4.1 The Old Testament

Righteousness language occurs in all forms of ancient Greek,[42] but the widespread and theologically significant use of the terminology in the LXX, along with Paul's frequent appeal to the Old Testament in discussing the words, shows that the Old Testament and Jewish background is decisive. Words from the *dikaio-* root consistently (though not universally) translate words from the Hebrew *ts-d-q* root: the noun *dikaiosynē* ("righteousness") normally translates *tsedeq* and *tsedaqah* (which probably have the same basic meaning); *dikaioō* ("justify") usually translates *tsadaq*; and *dikaios* ("righteous," "just") typically translates *tsaddiq*.[43] This considerable linguistic overlap

---

38. My approach is similar to that of Wolter, *Paul*, 334–40.

39. Portions of the following discussion are drawn from or adapted from my *Romans* (NICNT), 82–100.

40. The exact number depends on a textual variant in Rom 10:3.

41. Readers of Scripture in English are disadvantaged here, because the single Greek root that is common to all these words is represented in at least two different roots in English (just- and right-). Attempts to avoid this English problem have not been

successful (e.g., by coining a verb, "righteousing," or using "rectify"/"rectification" language).

42. See the survey in Schrenk, *TDNT* 2:178–225; and also Mark A. Seifrid, "Paul's Use of Righteousness Language Against Its Hellenistic Background," in Carson, O'Brien, and Seifrid, *Paradoxes of Paul*, 39–74.

43. Ziesler, *Meaning of Righteousness*, 22–67, gives a full survey of the OT data.

suggests that the meaning of *dikaio-* words for Greek-speaking Jews like Paul would have been decisively influenced by the meaning of *ts-d-q* words.

Scholars have long debated the basic sense of this word group. While heeding Seifrid's warning about not imposing on the rich vocabulary of righteousness in the Old Testament a single "basic concept,"[44] I suggest that these words often, and perhaps even basically, allude to the notion of doing, or being, "right," the "rightness" being determined by the particular situation in which one is placed.[45] "Rightness" is, of course, determined by God, allowing us to bypass the longstanding debate about whether the language indicates conformity to a norm[46] or "mutual fulfillment of claims arising from a particular relationship."[47] It is both. Many instances of "righteousness" language reveal that the norm or relationship that lies behind the word is God's own character or his commitment to do "right" with respect to his creation. At the same time, then, God's decision to bind himself to Israel in a covenant relationship means that many instances of the *ts-d-q* root assume that this "rightness" is defined (though certainly not exhausted) in terms of this covenant structure (see below). On the other hand, "righteousness" language will, by a simple extension, often connote the status of a person who has conformed to the expected norm. "Righteousness" in this sense can describe the state of the person who has fulfilled the expectations placed upon them by their divinely created status and/or their covenant relation—including behavior but penetrating also to the heart attitude.[48] This is the sense the word appears to have in the frequent refrain in the Psalms, "according to my righteousness." See, for example, Psalm 7:8 (7:9 LXX): "Let the LORD judge the peoples. Vindicate me, LORD, *according to my righteousness, according to my integrity*." See also, for example, Ezekiel 33:12–13:

> Therefore, son of man, say to your people, "If someone who is righteous disobeys, that person's former righteousness will count for nothing. And if someone who is wicked repents, that person's former wickedness will not bring condemnation. The righteous person who sins will not be allowed to live even though they were formerly righteous." If I tell a righteous person that they will surely live, but then they trust in their righteousness and do evil, none of the righteous things that person has done will be remembered; they will die for the evil they have done.

---

44. Mark A. Seifrid, "Righteousness Language in the Hebrew Scriptures and Early Judaism," in Carson, O'Brien, and Seifrid, *Complexities of Second Temple Judaism*, 418.

45. For similar views, see, e.g., Seifrid, "Righteousness Language"; Westerholm, *Perspectives*, 267–78; Thomas R. Schreiner, *Faith Alone: The Doctrine of Justification* (Grand Rapids: Zondervan, 2015), 216–29; Irons, *Righteousness of God*, 131–77.

46. For a concise survey, see Piper, *Justification of God*, 82–83; Seifrid, "Righteousness Language," 419–22.

47. See esp. Hermann Cremer and Ernst Kappeler, *Die Paulinische Rechtfertigungslehre im Zusammenhange ihrer geschichtlichen Voraussetzungen* (Gütersloh: C. Bertelsmann, 1900). This basic approach to the language has been followed by a large number of modern OT (and NT) scholars.

48. See Moo, "Genesis 15:6."

The "righteous" person in this passage is someone who consistently *does* what is "right" before God, and such a person can be said to be in a *state* of "righteousness." As Seifrid notes, "An absolute distinction between 'status' and 'behavior' is illegitimate."[49] Or, to put it another way, people who have the status of "rightness" before God express that reality by their "righteous" actions.

The single most important word in the family of "righteousness" words for Paul's teaching on justification is the verb "justify," translating *tsadaq*. The nine times *dikaioō* translates the hiphil of this verb are particularly significant. This form of the verb almost always has a judicial or forensic connotation.[50] Sometimes the judge who "pronounces righteous," or acquits, is human (Deut 25:1; Isa 5:23), and at other times divine (Exod 23:7; 1 Kgs 8:32; 2 Chr 6:23; Ps 82:3; Isa 50:8). Even when the term is not used with explicit reference to the law court, forensic connotations remain (see Gen 38:26; 44:16; Jer 3:11; Ezek 16:51–52). This legal justification is a recognition of the reality that the person being "justified" is, in fact, "just": Israelite judges are to "justify the just and condemn the ungodly" (Deut 25:1, my translation; see 1 Kgs 8:32; 2 Chr 6:23). A key symptom of injustice is the "justifying" of the guilty (Isa 5:23), in contrast to the strict and accurate judicial assessment of the Lord, who "will not justify the guilty" (Exod 23:7, my translation). Old Testament "justification" thus takes the form of a legal recognition of an already existing righteousness.[51]

The noun *dikaiosynē* also sometimes has a judicial flavor. "Justice" and *dikaiosynē* are often related to each other or even put in parallel with each other. See, for example, 1 Kings 10:9, where the king is to "do judgment in righteousness" (NETS). Texts that use "righteousness" to depict God's eschatological salvation of Israel probably pick up this judicial flavor. In these passages, English versions (e.g., NRSV, NETS) often translate the word as "vindication." See, for example, Psalm 37:6 (36:6 LXX): "He will make your vindication [NRSV and NETS; *dikaiosynēn*] shine like the light, and the justice of your cause like the noonday" (see also, e.g., Ps 35:27 [34:27 LXX]; Isa 58:8; 62:1, 2; 63:1; Mic 7:9).

4.1.4.2 Paul

Paul, as we have seen, uses the noun *dikaiosynē* fifty-seven (or fifty-eight) times, with a particularly high concentration in Romans. It occurs with several meanings in the New Testament (see, e.g., BDAG), but two are relevant to our concern here: "juridical correctness" and "upright behavior" (to quote BDAG). John Ziesler, in what remains the most substantial lexical/theological study of the language of righteousness in Paul, argues that the verb *dikaioō* means "justify" in a forensic sense but that the

---

49. Seifrid, "Righteousness Language," 422.
50. See Ziesler, *Meaning of Righteousness*, 18–22.

51. See, e.g., Westerholm, *Perspectives*, 263–64.

noun *dikaiosynē* refers to a combination of forensic and moral righteousness.[52] This neat distinction has, however, drawn few followers. And rightly so.[53] In both Galatians and Romans, the verb and the noun overlap significantly, with key occurrences of each so closely related that a difference in meaning is unlikely (see, e.g., Rom 3:20, 21, 22, 24, 25, 26; 4:2, 3, 5; Gal 2:16, 21; 3:6, 8, 21, 24; 5:4, 5). The connections in Galatians are particularly tight, suggesting that the verb and the noun occupy the same basic semantic space; and here the focus is on status before God, not on behavior. "Righteousness" is not a status or mode of being that a person earns or achieves by his or her own efforts but is a status "reckoned" to them (Rom 4:3, 6, 9, 11, 22; Gal 3:6[54]). It is a "gift" (Rom 5:17), not something that a person can claim for one's own (Rom 10:3–6; Phil 3:9; Titus 3:5). Most of the occurrences of *dikaiosynē* in Paul fall into this semantic range, providing a strong basis for the forensic focus of justification in Paul.[55] "Righteousness" in this sense denotes a judicial status given by God to sinful humans. And it is given, as many of the texts cited above make clear, "by faith."

Nevertheless, Paul also uses *dikaiosynē* in the Old Testament sense of a person's "rightness" as a reflection of their behavior or as a way of denoting that behavior itself. Clear occurrences of the word in this sense are found in Romans 6:13, 16, 18, 19, 20; 2 Corinthians 6:14 (opposite *anomia*); Ephesians 5:9; 1 Timothy 6:11; and 2 Timothy 2:22; 3:16 (other possible examples include Rom 14:17; 2 Cor 6:7; 9:9, 10; 11:15; Eph 6:14; Phil 1:11; 2 Tim 4:8; Titus 3:5; see also Matt 5:20; Luke 1:75; Acts 10:35; Jas 1:20). Some argue that these occurrences should also be integrated into Paul's concept of justification. I think, however, there are good reasons to exclude them. I will return to this matter below (pp. 483–85).

While not directly referring to justification, the phrase "the righteousness *of God*" (*[hē] dikaiosynē [tou] theou*) is related and deserves a brief discussion. This phrase is especially important to the argument of Romans, since, of Paul's nine uses of the phrase, eight occur in this letter (1:17; 3:5, 21, 22, 25, 26; 10:3 [twice]; the other occurrence is in 2 Cor 5:21). Romans 3:21–24 in particular reveals the close connection between "God's righteousness" and "justification": the "righteousness [*dikaiosynē*] of God" in verses 21 and 22 is picked up by the verb "justify" (*dikaioumenoi*) in verse 24.

---

52. Ziesler, *Meaning of Righteousness*, e.g., 162–63. This distinction has been followed by Longenecker in his commentary on Galatians (*Galatians*, e.g., 95 [with ref. to 2:21]).

53. For brief critiques of Ziesler on this point, see Seifrid, "Righteousness Language," 442; John Reumann, *"Righteousness" in the New Testament* (Philadelphia: Fortress, 1982), 56–59.

54. The "reckoning" or "crediting" language in these verses is, of course, taken from Gen 15:6: "Abram believed the LORD, and he credited it to him as righteousness." This text is quite debated, some interpreters insisting it refers to relational righteousness only, others that it is equivalent to Paul's "justification." However, while

a relationship to justification in the Pauline sense is required by the way Paul integrates the text into his teaching, it may be better to think that "righteousness" in this verse refers more broadly to the total "right" response to God that he demands of his people, a response that involves, as Keil and Delitzsch put it, "correspondence to the will of God both in character and conduct" (C. F. Keil and F. Delitzsch, *Commentary on the Old Testament: The Pentateuch* [Grand Rapids: Eerdmans, 1969], 213; and see Moo, "Genesis 15:6").

55. Wright, *Paul and the Faithfulness of God*, 2:945–46.

There is considerable debate about the meaning of the phrase, involving both lexical and syntactical matters. What does the word *dikaiosynē* mean in the phrase, and what is the connection between this word and "God" (indicated with a genitive construction in Greek)?[56]

In secular Greek, a god's *dikaiosynē* is usually a divine attribute, and biblical texts also ascribe "righteousness" to God. Taking as our starting point key passages in Isaiah 40–66, we read that "in the LORD alone are righteousness and strength" (45:24; NIV adapted); the Lord is "a righteous God and a Savior" (45:21); and God's Servant is also "righteous" (53:11). "Attribute" is a bit too static and ontological to capture the sense of the word in passages like these; "God's righteousness" is an experienced aspect of God's character. The relational sense of the word is seen in the many texts where God is said to act "in righteousness." This idea brackets Psalm 143 (to which Paul alludes in Rom 3:20): "In your faithfulness and righteousness come to my relief" (v. 1b); "in your righteousness, bring me out of trouble" (v. 11b).[57] As Psalm 143:1 reveals, "righteousness" and "faithfulness" are closely related in some of these passages, and some interpreters think that "God's righteousness" then might mean essentially "God's faithfulness" or, more specifically, God's "covenant faithfulness."[58] But there are problems with this view.[59] "Faithfulness" moves too far from the focus on the juridical that appears to be basic to the lexeme. The "covenant faithfulness" view, popularized by N. T. Wright, has a further series of problems. Righteousness language and covenant language are rarely found together (although, in fairness, if covenant is a basic enough category, this is not altogether surprising).[60] A more serious objection is that the "standard" by which God is judged to do "right" goes beyond (and behind) the terms of the covenant. Note, for example, Psalm 96:13: "Let all creation rejoice before the LORD, for he comes, he comes to judge the earth. He will judge the world *in righteousness* [*dikaiosynē*] and the peoples in his faithfulness." God's righteousness, then, while finding particular historical expression in his faithfulness in maintaining the "right" of his covenant people, is finally rooted more deeply in his own character as God. As Linebaugh says, "A covenantal context does not dilute the notion of normativity which *dikaiosyne* conveys . . . ; it locates and particularises the norm."[61]

"The righteousness of God" in this sense—his commitment to act according to his

---

56. For a survey of historical views, see Irons, *Righteousness of God*, 9–60.

57. See also, e.g., Ps 36:6; 71:2; 89:16; 145:7; Isa 41:2; 42:6; 45:13.

58. See esp. Sam K. Williams, "The 'Righteousness of God' in Romans," *JBL* 99 (1980): 241–90; N. T. Wright, *Justification: God's Plan and Paul's Vision* (Downers Grove, IL: InterVarsity Press, 2009), 55–78; idem, *Paul and the Faithfulness of God*, 2:1055–71.

59. The most important critique of the "covenant faithfulness" view is Irons, *Righteousness of God*.

60. Seifrid, "Righteousness Language," 423–24.

61. Linebaugh, *God, Grace, and Righteousness*, 131. See also Seifrid: "All 'covenant-keeping' is righteous behavior, but not all righteous behavior is 'covenant-keeping'" ("Righteousness Language," 424).

own character—is what pretty clearly is intended by Paul in Romans 3:5 and, arguably, also in 3:25 and 26 (see p. 211). The other occurrences of the phrase in Paul have a more positive sense, being related to the gospel or to salvation. Here again, Paul reflects an important strain in the Old Testament occurrences of this phrase, where righteousness is linked with salvation. See, for example, Psalm 98:2, "The LORD has made his salvation known and revealed his righteousness to the nations," and Isaiah 51:5, where God promises Israel in exile that "my righteousness draws near speedily, my salvation is on the way" (cf. v. 8). Some argue that "righteousness" *means* "salvation" in such passages, but this ignores the particular semantic contribution of "righteousness" in these texts. Rather, God's saving intervention on behalf of his exiled nation is characterized as a "right" or "just" act. This act relates to both God and Israel; God's salvation is an act of "establishing right" as well as an act that results in a vindication of Israel's "rightness" (they really are the people whom the only true God loves and cares for).[62] Paul refers to both sides of this activity, sometimes focusing on God's initiative in "revealing" his righteousness (Rom 1:17; 3:21–22), and at other times focusing on the resulting status of rightness conferred on humans (Rom 10:3; 2 Cor 5:21 [probably; see p. 178]). Understood in this way, "God's righteousness" denotes the eschatological intervention of God, manifesting his "right-doing" on behalf of his people, a manifestation that brings to them the status of "right standing" before him. In this sense, then, "the righteousness of God" has as its end point the granting of the status of "justification" to those who trust Christ by faith. The action of "justifying" results in the status of "righteousness," a process that manifests God's own "righteousness." "Righteousness of God," then, is a multivalent concept in Paul.[63]

One final aspect of Paul's proclamation of the "revelation of God's righteousness" is especially important for the concept of justification. As we have seen, Isaiah and other prophets predict that God will act in his righteousness on behalf of his people Israel. While there are places where God's deliverance is related to people's obedience or righteousness, references to faith in terms of God's righteousness are virtually

---

62. See, e.g., Irons: "God's righteousness is conceived of as coming from God and being bestowed on the righteous oppressed" (*Righteousness of God*, 205).

63. Several scholars have captured this breadth of meaning. See, e.g., J. H. Ropes, "'Righteousness' and 'The Righteousness of God' in the Old Testament and in St. Paul," *JBL* 22 (1903): 211–27; Wright, *Paul and the Faithfulness of God*, 2:796–804; Irons, *Righteousness of God*, 205. See also Stuhlmacher, who argues that "righteousness of God" in Paul includes "both poles of the event of justification. . . . The gracious activity of God himself and the end result of the divine work in the form of the righteousness granted to the sinner" ("Theme of Romans," in Donfried, *Romans Debate*, 339). See also Bird, *Romans*, 111: "God's righteousness is

chiefly a way of designating his saving action as it is expressed in his feats of deliverance for his people. The righteousness of God then is the character of God embodied and enacted in his saving works." Thielman, who defends a view very close to my own (though he stresses the idea of "fairness"), refers to a "property" of God (Frank S. Thielman, "God's Righteousness as God's Fairness in Romans 1:17: An Ancient Perspective on a Significant Phrase," *JETS* 54 [2011]: 38). With respect to the issue of "righteousness of God," I am especially indebted in my thinking to Matthew Monkemeier ("'A Righteous God and Savior': Romans 1:17 and the Old Testament Concept of God's Righteousness" [PhD diss., Wheaton College, 2020]).

nonexistent. It would fall to Paul to appropriate other Old Testament texts (Gen 15:6; Hab 2:4) that connect "righteousness" and faith to make this connection. And, in a key point highlighted usefully by the New Perspective, this focus on faith functions to break down the difference between Jew and gentile. God's righteousness is displayed in Christ, and all—Jew and gentile alike—are invited to enter into union with Christ by faith. Thus it is only those—but also, of course, *all* those—who believe who benefit from the eschatological revelation of God's righteousness. As Stuhlmacher puts it, "For Paul the righteousness of God is essentially a righteousness that comes by faith."[64]

4.1.5 Justification as Forensic

The Protestant Reformers insisted that God's justifying work is a purely judicial action; we might even add "forensic alone" to the list of well-known Reformation *solas* (e.g., "faith alone," "grace alone").[65] The Reformers' insistence on the point set them at odds with the bulk of the Roman Catholic tradition, a point reiterated at the Council of Trent, held in twenty-five intermittent sessions between 1545 and 1563, where the claim was made that justification is "not the remission of sins merely, but also the sanctification and renewal of the inward man."[66] The theological landscape is much more complex these days, with some Roman Catholics giving greater attention to the forensic element and some Protestants distancing themselves from a "forensic-only" view. I will analyze some of the reasons for this shift below. But I begin by briefly sketching the reasons why I think a forensic view of justification is correct.

First, as we have seen, Paul's use of the verb *dikaioō* takes up the use of the hiphil form of *tsadaq* in the Old Testament. And this verb means "*declare* righteous," not "*make* righteous." Its forensic flavor is undeniable.

Second, several contexts in which Paul uses the verb make clear that he retains this forensic focus of the verb. In Romans 2:12–13, for instance, *dikaioō*, "justify," as well as the adjective *dikaios*, "righteous," are antonyms of "judge," "condemn" (*krinō* and *apollymi*): "All who sin apart from the law will also *perish* apart from the law, and all who sin under the law will be *judged* by the law. For it is not those who hear the law who are *righteous* in God's sight, but it is those who obey the law who will be *declared righteous*." Similarly, in Romans 8:33–34, *dikaioō*, "justify," is the opposite of *katakrinō*, "condemn": "Who will bring any charge against those whom God has chosen? It is God

---

64. Peter Stuhlmacher, "The Apostle Paul's View of Righteousness," in *Reconciliation, Law, and Righteousness: Essays in Biblical Theology* (Philadelphia: Fortress, 1986), 80.

65. Indeed, Alistair McGrath argues that it was this "deliberate and systematic distinction . . . between justification and regeneration" that distinguished Protestant from medieval Roman Catholic theology (*Iustitia Dei: A History of the Christian Doctrine of Justification*, 2 vols. [Cambridge: Cambridge University Press, 1998], 1:183–86). We should not ignore, however, clear anticipations of a "forensic only" view in the church fathers (see, e.g., Thomas C. Oden, *The Justification Reader* [Grand Rapids: Eerdmans, 2002]).

66. Council of Trent, 6th Session, ch. 7 (www.ewtn.com /catholicism/library/decree -concerning-justification--decree -concerning-reform-1496).

who *justifies*. Who then is the one who *condemns*? No one. Christ Jesus who died—more than that, who was raised to life—is at the right hand of God and is also interceding for us." We might add here the many texts in which Paul depicts the end of those who do not know Christ in terms of being "judged" or "condemned" (e.g., 1 Cor 11:32, 34; 2 Thess 2:12). These texts suggest that the issue of judicial verdict loomed large in Paul's conceptualization of salvation. And "justification" is the language that appears to stand against these warnings in a positive sense.[67]

Paul's insistence that justification is "before God" also lends a judicial flavor to the word (Rom 3:20 [NIV "in God's sight"]; Gal 3:11). Paul links justification with the forgiveness of sins (Rom 4:5–8). He views justification in parallel with reconciliation, which is a matter of restored relationship rather than transformation (Rom 5:9–10; cf. 2 Cor 5:14–21). Also significant are contexts where Paul does not use *dikaioō* with reference to justification *per se* but where the word clearly has a judicial flavor (1 Cor 4:4; 1 Tim 3:16). Paul cites two Old Testament texts to buttress his teaching about justification (Gen 15:6 and Hab 2:4), and while there is controversy over both texts, they arguably use *dik-* words in the sense of standing with God. Paul uses a number of "minor" words from the *dik-* root; and these also have a distinctly forensic flavor.[68] Finally, I add an argument from silence (which by its nature cannot be overly compelling). It is striking that, after having developed a clear teaching about justification in Romans 1–5, Paul in Romans 6 asks whether the grace found in justification opens the way to cavalier sinning. Paul's response is *not* to say, "Well, of course you should not sin because you have enjoyed the grace of justification; justification itself has transformed you." Rather, he argues from the believer's participation in Christ's death—we die to sin's power *with* the one who died *for* us to justify us. Justification leads to, but does not itself include, rescue from sin's power.

Based on this fundamental meaning of *dikaio-* language, and particularly the verb *dikaioō*, I conclude that justification is God's judicial decision to consider a sinful human being to be "right" before him—entailing both a declaration of innocence in the divine law court and also the conferral of a righteous status. Thiselton rightly stresses that God's word "justified" is "an illocutionary speech-act of declaration and verdict." He elaborates: "The word *declares* (versus *states*) not the standing which he receives *causally* from his own acts *in history*, but the standing which he *receives eschatologically* at the *last judgment*, as the verdict 'everything put right' is *anticipated in the hiddenness*

---

67. The particular forensic significance of the language (which is a matter of dispute; see below) is the focus of James B. Prothro, *Both Judge and Justifier: Biblical Legal Language and the Act of Justifying in Paul*, WUNT 2/461 (Tübingen: Mohr Siebeck, 2018).

68. See *dikaiōma* ("righteous decree"; see Rom 1:32; 2:26; 5:16, 18; 8:4); *dikaiōsis* ("justifying" or "justification" [NIV]; see 4:25; 5:18); *dikaiokrisia* ("righteous judgment"; see 2:5); *endikos* ("just"; see 3:8). The words *adikia* ("unrighteousness") and *adikos* ("unrighteous"), with the alpha-privative prefix (much like our "un-"), refer, as one would expect, to behavior that God condemns (1:18 [2x], 29; 2:8; 3:5 [both words]; 6:13), but can also refer to an alleged failure to "act rightly" on God's part (9:14).

of the present by faith on the basis of the gift from God and union with Christ."[69] While not as closely tied to legal metaphors as might be desirable, "vindication" (which we have noted is important for this word group in the OT) might be another way of expressing the idea.[70]

With this basic concept in view, we can then integrate a few other expressions and ideas into the concept of justification. Negatively, this would include the forgiveness of sins, the "not counting" of sins against a person. The connection between justification and forgiveness is particularly clear in Romans 4:5–8:

> However, to the one who does not work but trusts God who justifies the ungodly, their faith is credited as righteousness. David says the same thing when he speaks of the blessedness of the one to whom God credits righteousness apart from works:
>
> > "Blessed are those
> >   whose transgressions are forgiven,
> >   whose sins are covered.
> > Blessed is the one
> >   whose sin the Lord will never count against them."

On the whole, forgiveness does not, at least explicitly, play a major role in Paul (see also 2 Cor 5:19; Eph 1:7; 5:32; Col 1:14; 2:13; 3:13).[71] But the idea certainly lurks behind conceptions such as justification. As the Old Testament massively makes clear, sinning is the basic obstacle to fellowship between humans and God. Forgiveness based on God's mercy and actuated through the appropriate sacrifices was the remedy for this problem. Forgiveness of sins is therefore probably assumed in many of the new-realm blessings that Paul celebrates.

A second set of words to be integrated into the Pauline concept of justification involves the idea of being found "blameless" in the judgment. To be sure, it is not always clear whether Paul is focusing on what we might call ethical blamelessness or judicial blamelessness. But the contrast in Colossians 1:22, for instance, shows that the focus is at least sometimes on the latter: "But now he has reconciled you by Christ's physical body through death to present you holy in his sight, without blemish and free from accusation" (see also, perhaps, 1 Cor 1:8; Eph 1:4; 5:27; and see also pp. 623–25 on the implications for holiness).

---

69. Thiselton, *First Epistle to the Corinthians*, 455, 457 (emphases original).

70. Don B. Garlington goes so far as to claim that *dikaioō* means "to vindicate as the people of God" ("Even We Have Believed": Galatians 2:15–16 Revisited," *CTR* 7 [2009]: 12, perhaps tilting a bit too far toward N. T. Wright's view). Bird also emphasizes the concept of vindication in his view of justification ("Justification as Forensic Declaration," 122).

71. As Morris notes, Paul prefers to present Christ's work with more positive terms (Leon Morris, "Forgiveness," in *Dictionary of Paul and His Letters*, ed. Gerald F. Hawthorne and Ralph P. Martin [Downers Grove, IL: InterVarsity Press, 1993], 311).

Another idea sometimes associated with justification is covenant membership. N. T. Wright, while endorsing a "forensic-only" view of justification, interprets the legal verdict against the background of the covenant. To be justified, in his view, is not only to be declared to be "in the right" but also to be recognized as one who is "in" the covenant—a member of the people of God.[72] Moreover, he also suggests that justification involves the recognition of an already existing reality: it is God's "call" that transfers people into the covenant, while justification enables us to know who is in and who is out.[73] And this recognition has particular focus on the gentiles, now "marked out" by their faith as members of God's people. Our response to Wright on this point will depend, as is often the case, on how seriously we take some of his stronger assertions on this issue. However, we should at least register some doubts about the "membership in the people of God" aspect of Wright's view. The use of the verb in the Old Testament and in Paul offers little basis for the notion that the word *means* "to be included in God's people."[74] As I noted above, "righteousness" denotes God's vindication of people already in covenant relationship with him. In other texts, justification language denotes God's initial acceptance of a person, an acceptance that at the same time normally implies that one "enters" the people of God. But that the language does not *denote* entrance into the people of God is clear, for instance, in the key text of Genesis 15:6 (cf. Gal 3:6): there is no "people of God" for Abraham to join at this point; his "justification" is foundational to the process by which that people is being created.[75] To be justified, of course, entails that one becomes a member of God's people, but the word itself simply does not mean this. As Simon Gathercole insists, "The *content* of the doctrine of justification by faith should be distinguished from its *scope*."[76] It is also doubtful that being justified in Paul ever has the sense of a recognition of an existing reality. Passages such as Romans 4:5; 5:1, 9 make clear that justification is God's powerful word, creating a new status that did not exist before.[77]

---

72. N. T. Wright sometimes speaks as if this latter idea is what justification is all about. See, e.g., *What Saint Paul Really Said*, 119: "Justification . . . is not a matter of *how someone enters the community of the true people of God*, but of *how you tell who belongs to that community*" [emphasis original]. In other writings, however, Wright balances this perspective with the typical notion of "being in the right," which he explains, e.g., as "his or her sins having been forgiven through the death of Jesus" ("New Perspectives on Paul," in McCormack, *Justification in Perspective*, 258).

73. See, e.g., Wright, "Romans," 468; cf. also 466, 481; idem, *What Saint Paul Really Said*, 113–33; idem, *Paul in Fresh Perspective*, 111–13. Of course, this way of describing justification has some parallel with the Reformation tradition, which often conceptualizes the matter in just this general manner; justification is God's recognition of a person's "rightness" based on their identification with Christ and his own righteousness.

74. Westerholm is quite blunt: "So 'righteousness' does not mean, and by its very nature *cannot* mean, membership in a covenant" (*Justification Reconsidered*, 63). See also Horton, *Justification*, 2:294: "The tendency in new perspective scholarship is to pour connotations into denotations, entailments into definitions, implications of a meaning into the meaning of the term itself."

75. N. T. Wright tries to rescue his interpretation by suggesting that the text speaks of "membership in . . . the covenant family which God was creating" (*Justification*, 134). But this seems to be an attempt to force a text to fit a preordained mold. See, on this point, Piper, *Future of Justification*, 42–44.

76. Simon J. Gathercole, "Justified by Faith, Justified by His Blood: The Evidence of Romans 3:21–4:25," in Carson, O'Brien, and Seifrid, *Paradoxes of Paul*, 156. For more detail on Wright's view and reactions to it, see Moo, *Galatians*, 54–56.

77. See on this point, e.g., Piper, *Future of Justification*,

Another recent redefinition of the forensic meaning of justification has been put forward by Douglas Campbell. Working out of the "apocalyptic Paul" way of conceptualizing Paul's thought, which stresses power structures (see pp. 30–31), Campbell argues that "God's righteousness" is a wholly liberative activity, his sovereign intervention to right wrongs. This focus on liberation, or "deliverance," fits the Old Testament conception of the duties of the king, whose "forensic" activity takes the form of decisive action on behalf of the downtrodden rather than the even-handed weighing of evidence by the judge in a court of law.[78] However, as we have seen, the Old Testament conception of "righteousness" is fundamentally bound up with "rightness," not simply the exercise of power. Moreover, Campbell is able to sustain this revised forensic reading of Paul only by ignoring or radically reinterpreting key Pauline texts.[79]

4.1.6 Forensic Only?

I noted above that Roman Catholic theologians have traditionally contested the "forensic only" sense of the word, arguing that it denotes not just a legal but also a "real" or "effectual" "making right." A significant number of recent interpreters from a variety of theological traditions have argued much the same, expanding the scope of justification to include a transformative element.[80] For instance, here is Michael Gorman's definition:

> Justification is the establishment of right covenant relations—fidelity to God and love for neighbor—by means of God's liberating grace in Christ's faithful and loving death and our co-crucifixion with him. Justification therefore means co-resurrection with Christ to a new life of faithfulness toward God and love toward

---

39–44; Gathercole, "Doctrine of Justification," 228–31. For a broader criticism of N. T. Wright's view on justification, see esp. Gathercole, "Doctrine of Justification," 219–41, 228–40; Bird, "Justification as Forensic Declaration," 109–30, 115–16; idem, *Saving Righteousness of God*, 113–54; Piper, *Future of Justification*; Schreiner, *Faith Alone*, 244–61.

78. Campbell, *Deliverance*, 675–702.

79. See, in greater detail, D. J. Moo, review of *The Deliverance of God: An Apocalyptic Rereading of Justification in Paul*, by Douglas A. Campbell," *JETS* 53 (2010): 143–50; for a series of essays in which Campbell elaborates his view and others evaluate/criticize it, see Tilling, *Beyond Old and New Perspectives on Paul*.

80. The transformative power of justification is an important part of Käsemann's influential definition of "God's righteousness" in terms of both gift and power (see, e.g., "Righteousness of God in Paul," 168–82) and has been taken up by his followers; see, e.g., Stuhlmacher: "The justification of which he speaks is a process of becoming new that spans the earthly life of a believer, a path from faith's beginning to its end" ("Apostle Paul's View of

Righteousness," 72; see also idem, *Grundlegung*, 332–34). A broad understanding of justification as including both forensic and transformative aspects was widespread before the Reformation, rooted ultimately in Augustine. Such a view was hinted at in the work of Adolf Schlatter (e.g., *The Theology of the Apostles*, trans. Andreas J. Köstenberger [Grand Rapids: Baker, 1999], 248–50) and is becoming widespread in current scholarship (e.g., Eberhard Jüngel, *Justification: The Heart of the Christian Faith. A Theological Study with Ecumenical Purpose* [Edinburgh: T&T Clark, 2001], 208–11; Don B. Garlington, *Faith, Obedience, and Perseverance: Aspects of Paul's Letter to the Romans*, WUNT 2/79 [Tübingen: Mohr Siebeck, 1994], 155–61; Dunn, "New Perspective on Paul: Whence, What, Whither?," esp. 80–86; Gorman, *Inhabiting the Cruciform God*, 48–57; idem, *Becoming the Gospel*, 218–57; Jean Noël Aletti, *Justification by Faith in the Letters of Saint Paul: Keys to Interpretation*, trans. Peggy Manning Meyer, AnBib Studia 5 [Rome: Gregorian & Biblical Press, 2015]; Leithart, *Delivered from the Elements of the World*, 179–214; Pitre, Barber, and Kincaid, *Paul, a New Covenant Jew*, 162–210).

others, expressed concretely as biblical justice, within the Spirit-empowered people of God, with the certain hope of God's welcome, on the day of judgment, into the fullness of resurrection life.[81]

The case for a "more-than-forensic" meaning of justification in Paul rests on three main arguments.

First, it is argued that a "forensic-only" view can be maintained only if we arbitrarily ignore many occurrences of the relevant words in Paul. For instance, in Romans 6:7 Paul grounds his claim that Christians are no longer slaves to sin on the fact that Christians, when they die with Christ, "are justified [*dedikaiōtai*] from sin." Translations such as the NIV, which render this as "set free from sin" simply mask the fact that "justification" language occurs here, and that being "justified" involves rescue from sin's power as well as its penalty. As Scott Hafemann puts it, what is involved in Romans 6:7 is an "indicative-performative speech act" that means freedom from "the claims and consequences of sin both personally and forensically."[82] Gorman has forcefully made a similar point, arguing that Paul in several contexts interprets justification in transformative terms. For instance, in Galatians 2:15–21, Paul moves from justification (vv. 16–17) to the transformational idea of co-crucifixion with Christ (vv. 19–20). In 1 Corinthians 6, Paul cites "justification" (v. 11) to make a claim about "righteous" conduct.[83]

However, to take the last of these points first, association does not mean identification. It has always been acknowledged by the best defenders of a "forensic-only" view of justification that being justified necessarily means that one is also "sanctified," "transformed," turned into an obedient child of God. But the texts Gorman cites do not indicate that justification must itself *include* these transformative elements. Indeed, the fact that, for instance, in 1 Corinthians 6:11 Paul refers both to justification and sanctification suggest that these two concepts are distinct from one another.

The argument regarding Romans 6:7 brings us back to the methodological point we made earlier: Which occurrences of *dik-* language should "count" in constructing our doctrine of justification?[84] Gorman argues that all occurrences of *dik-* language in Paul should be considered in building our doctrine of justification unless there is strong reason not to do so.[85] The point may, in somewhat milder form, be granted. Are there, then, sufficient reasons to doubt that Paul is using *dik-* in the sense he has used the verb earlier in the letter? I think so. First, it should be noted that Paul here

---

81. Gorman, *Becoming the Gospel*, 228.

82. Hafemann, "Reading Paul's ΔIKAIO-Language," 225–26. Campbell also insists the verse contributes to Paul's doctrine of justification, with the idea here of liberation setting the agenda for his other uses of the language (Douglas A. Campbell, "Rereading Paul's ΔIKAIO-Language," in Tilling, *Beyond Old and New Perspectives on Paul*, 207–13).

83. See again here Gorman, *Inhabiting the Cruciform God*, 63–72; idem, *Becoming the Gospel*, 234–40 (on 1 Cor 6).

84. A second issue in Rom 6:7 is the referent of "the one who dies." Some think Paul refers to Christ (e.g., Prothro, *Both Judge and Justifier*, 186–97).

85. Gorman, *Becoming the Gospel*, 223.

uses a combination of verb—*dikaioō*—and preposition—*apo*—that he uses nowhere else.[86] Since words take their meaning from their association with other words, this unusual collocation may suggest that Paul is giving *dikaioō* a distinctive meaning here. Moreover, this occurrence of the verb occurs in a context that features several instances of the noun *dikaiosynē*. The noun in these verses is contrasted with "wickedness" (v. 13), "sin" (vv. 18, 20), and "impurity" (v. 19).[87] As we have seen, Paul operates with two semantic categories of *dik-* language—for the sake of brevity, the "moral" and the "forensic." I do not think it is helpful simply to merge these in order to support a broader concept of justification. Paul usually indicates pretty clearly, by word oppositions and context, which meaning of the word he is using. We have good reason, then, to conclude that the occurrences of *dik-* language in Romans 6 are being used by Paul in a new, ethically oriented "language game," and that this new conceptual context affects the meaning of these key words we find in it.[88]

Another very common criticism of the forensic-only view of justification is that it fails to do justice to the powerful effects of God's justifying word. As the criticism is often put, it turns justification into a "legal fiction." However, this claim rests on a fundamental logical and semantic error. God's justifying word is indeed powerful, accomplishing always and perfectly what he intends to accomplish. But the point here is that the action so accomplished is the action denoted by the verb *in its forensic sense*. God's "word" of "justified" is a powerful, effective speech act that creates a new reality—but, as the meaning of the word suggests, a *forensic* reality.[89] And this reality has incredible consequences for the sinner, bound in death, now released from that sentence in order to enjoy a new relationship with the God of the universe. Only if we assume at the outset that "justify" must indicate transformed behavior is the charge of "legal fiction" appropriate.

Finally, in general, I entirely endorse the importance of connecting justification with transformation.[90] But we can make this connection without trying to smuggle a transformative element into justification, a move that violates the forensic sense of the

---

86. The combination occurs twice in the LXX, but neither verse (Isa 45:25 and Jer 3:11) is at all similar to Rom 6:7.

87. The contrast between *dikaiosynē* and *anomia* is fairly common in the LXX (Ps 45:7; Isa 5:7; 33:15; 64:5; Ezek 18:21, 24, 27; 33:12, 13, 18, 19). The apparent parallel between *dikaiosynē* and *thanatos* ("death") in Rom 6:16 could suggest that "righteousness" here denotes the status of being right with God as opposed to the state of (spiritual) death. But Paul does not follow a neat parallelism in the verse, so this point is not decisive.

88. Motyer argues that Paul's choice to use *dikaio-* language both forensically and ethically suggests an "inner theological connection" between the two (Stephen Motyer, "Righteousness by Faith in the New Testament," in *Here We Stand*: Justification by Faith Today, ed. J. I. Packer [London: Hodder & Stoughton, 1986], 55). But it is just the nature of the connection that is at

issue; and it is questionable semantics to suggest the connection must reside in the lexeme.

89. As Blocher puts it, "The judge's verdict does change the real situation—in the forensic sphere" ("Justification of the Ungodly," 494). See also, e.g., Thiselton, *First Epistle to the Corinthians*, 455. Bultmann made this point some time ago, noting that the criticism rests on the (mistaken) assumption that the righteousness Paul refers to is ethical (*Theology of the New Testament*, 1:267).

90. As Garcia notes, "The less capable we are of accounting for the positive, biblical role of obedience and perseverance in salvation within a Reformed theological model, the more attractive the alternative positions of the New Perspective, Rome, and Constantinople will appear" (Mark A. Garcia, "Debating Justification Productively: A Review," *Scottish Bulletin of Evangelical Theology* 31 [2013]: 224).

language.[91] Rather, we must insist on maintaining the inextricable connection Paul makes between justification and transformation—both inevitable products of being "in Christ." Calvin is particularly clear on this point.[92] We should, additionally, note the importance of God's Spirit in bridging what some might see as a gap between the forensic verdict of "justified" and the transformed life of the believer. Galatians makes this point clearly. Since Christ is *the* "seed of Abraham" (Gal 3:16), it is only in and through Christ that a person can receive the promised "blessing of Abraham"—and, Paul says, "the promise of the Spirit" (v. 14). The promised Spirit links the first part of Galatians, with its focus on justification, to the last part, with its focus on the new life of the believer. With the "blessing of Abraham" (in context, justification), God also gives the Spirit—which becomes the controlling power in the believer's life.[93]

4.1.7 Justification "in Christ"

As is the case with all the spiritual blessings of the new realm, justification is "in Christ" (see, e.g., Gal 2:17). I need not here pursue the debate over whether it is theologically more appropriate to think of our union with Christ as leading to justification or of justification as initiating that union.[94] Paul usually singles out our participation in Christ's death as the basis for justification, but at least two texts suggest that the resurrection was also involved. In Romans 4:25, perhaps citing an existing creed, Paul says that "[Christ] was delivered over to death for our sins and was raised to life for our justification." As I note in my comments on the text (p. 215), it is possible that the first half of the verse refers to present justification—based on Christ's death—while the second part refers to future justification. However, both parts of the verse more likely refer to present justification. If so, the most likely interpretation is that we must read the text with an unexpressed assumption, namely, that Jesus's resurrection was our own justification/vindication (see 1 Tim 3:16).[95] In our union with Christ, then, his justification becomes ours.[96]

---

91. See the pertinent remarks on this issue by James D. G. Dunn, "New Perspective Response" (to the "deification view"), in Beilby and Eddy, *Justification: Five Views*, 256.

92. William B. Evans has recently surveyed some of the ways that union with Christ and justification are related in historical and contemporary Reformed theology ("Déjà Vu All over Again? The Contemporary Reformed Soteriological Controversy in Historical Perspective," *WTJ* 72 [2010]: 135–51).

93. See Chee-Chiew Lee, *The Blessing of Abraham, the Spirit, and Justification in Galatians: Their Relationship and Significance for Paul's Theology* (Eugene, OR: Pickwick, 2013), 193–98.

94. Horton, e.g., argues that the forensic verdict must (logically) precede union (*Covenant and Salvation*, 147; idem, *Justification*, 1:469–71). However, Blocher attractively suggests a *via media*: within the single work of God, we may posit two stages of

"justification" (using the term here very broadly), one involving Christ's payment of our legal debt—the basis for our regeneration—and the second our actual justification—stemming from our union with Christ (see Blocher, "Justification of the Ungodly," 497–98).

95. Possibly quoting a hymn, Paul in 1 Tim 3:16 claims that Jesus "was justified [NIV "vindicated"] by the Spirit." The verb *dikaioō* is used here, so the verse might be referring to Jesus's resurrection as his "justification." However, the verb *dikaioō* has a range of meaning (see above), and not all occurrences of the verb in Paul refer to the concept of justification. So we must, perhaps, be more cautious than many are in citing this text as grounds for Jesus's "justification."

96. See especially Gaffin, *Resurrection and Redemption*; also Marshall, *Aspects of the Atonement*, 68–97; Horton, *Justification*, 2:257–80.

If, then, justification occurs "in Christ," we might explore a bit more just what this means. One popular way of unpacking this concept is to appeal to a widespread motif in Paul that has been dubbed "interchange." Christ and the sinners he represents swap roles and status. He becomes what we are in order that we might become what he is. I alluded to this time-honored idea of the "great exchange" as basic to all the blessings we enjoy in the new realm (pp. 460–61). Particularly pertinent to our present topic is 2 Corinthians 5:21: "God made him who had no sin to be sin for us, so that in him we might become the righteousness of God." The meaning of both parts of this verse are debated, but I think it likely that the second part means, in effect, "so that we in Christ might have the status of righteousness before God" (see p. 178). If this is the case, then we have here a reference to interchange as the mechanism by which people become justified in Christ. But we can be more specific about the nature of this "interchange." Christ "being made sin" cannot mean that Christ became a sinner but that sin was "credited to" Christ; God sent his Son "in the likeness of sinful flesh" (Rom 8:3). In a similar manner, then, sinners "become" the righteousness of God by having righteousness credited to them. The conceptual framework is thoroughly forensic.

Some theologians and scholars argue that the logic of this forensic situation requires yet a further step. The Old Testament makes clear that the forensic verdict of "justified" must be based on the actual facts of the situation (e.g., Exod 23:7; Prov 17:15; Isa 5:23). Yet, in a justly famous text expressing the essence of his teaching about justification, Paul claims that God is one who, in Christ, "justifies the ungodly" (Rom 4:5). Since the context refers explicitly to faith being credited as righteousness (citing Gen 15:6), it might be simply that the believer's faith is counted as sufficient basis for the declaration of righteousness.[97] For others, however, faith itself does not meet the standard of obedience that God has set for his judicial vindication. They argue that it is the righteousness of Christ that provides the basis for God's justifying verdict. Sinners who take refuge by faith "in Christ" have accredited to them the righteousness that Christ has won by means of his obedience in both life and death (respectively, his active and passive obedience).[98] This notion, which has been especially prominent in the Reformed theological tradition, falls short of demonstration on a narrowly exegetical basis. But there is a certain logic in this formulation that appears to explain larger patterns of biblical teaching about righteousness and justification.[99]

---

97. E.g., Robert H. Gundry, "The Nonimputation of Christ's Righteousness," in Gundry, *Old Is Better*, 225–51. Others who deny the idea of imputation include, e.g., Wright, *Justification*, 68–69, 213, 232; Mark W. Elliott, "Judaism, Reformation Theology, and Justification," in Elliott et al., *Galatians and Christian Theology*, 155–58.

98. The basis of our justification in the "alien righteousness" of Christ is shared in most Reformation traditions. The more specific focus on Christ's active and passive obedience as the essence of this righteousness is typical of the Reformed tradition (see, e.g., Heppe, *Reformed Dogmatics*, 546–51).

99. See, e.g., D. A. Carson, "The Vindication of Imputation: On Fields of Discourse and, of Course, Semantic Fields," in *Justification: What's at Stake in the Current Debates?*, ed. M. A. Husbands and D. J. Treier (Downers Grove, IL: InterVarsity Press, 2004), 58–66; Vickers, *Jesus' Blood and Righteousness*, 73–86;

4.1.8 Justification by Faith Alone

While I will treat "faith" more fully below, I should here at least reiterate a point I made earlier: justification is by faith. In the Old Testament, after the inauguration of the Mosaic covenant, the "righteousness" that God looks for in his people is defined in terms of conformity to the law. In one of his best known and most distinctive emphases, however, Paul insists that God justifies people by faith and not by "works" (Rom 4:2), or "the works of the law" (3:20, 28; see Gal 2:16). This contrast, as I argue elsewhere (see pp. 435–39), justifies the typical Reformation slogan that justification is "by faith alone" (*sola fide*). This emphasis has both intensive and extensive significance. On the one hand, faith is tied to grace and gospel as the means by which God breaks through the thoroughly hopeless condition of sinful humans. On the other hand, faith, not being tied to any ethnic identity, can be exercised by both Jews and gentiles alike. Justification is by faith, not (human) works; and by faith and not by (Jewish) works of the law.

4.1.9 Justification as "Already" and "Not Yet"; Judgment according to Works

Paul sends somewhat conflicting signals about the time of God's justifying verdict. On the one hand, texts such as Romans 5:9 suggest that justification takes place at the moment of conversion: "Since we have now been justified by his blood, how much more shall we be saved from God's wrath through him!" (see also 5:1). This being the case, it is natural to think that justification in Paul belongs exclusively to the "already" end of the "already-not yet" spectrum of fulfillment.[100] However, other texts suggest that Paul might also think of justification in some sense to be a future, "end-time" phenomenon. Several texts in Romans might have such a reference (see, e.g., Rom 2:13; 5:19; 8:33; see also 3:20, 28),[101] but it is especially in Galatians that we find evidence of a future aspect of justification. Galatians 5:5 is particularly significant: "For we by the Spirit by faith await the hope of righteousness" (my translation). The issue is how to relate the words "hope" and "righteousness" near the end of the verse (a genitive construction in Greek). As I argue above on p. 80, it is likely that the phrase should be rendered "the hope of

Piper, *Counted Righteous in Christ*; Beale, *New Testament Biblical Theology*, 469–80. Bird's view is similar, though he prefers to speak of "incorporated righteousness" ("Justification as Forensic Declaration," 114–15). A particularly attractive way of conceiving this traditional concept of imputation is Mark Garcia's analogy with the "attribution" of the two natures in Christ. He writes: "The distinctive righteousness of Christ, which is proper to him alone, is 'attributed' to believers only within and because of the reality of their union with him. This 'attributed' righteousness, proper to Christ alone, is ours 'improperly' but truly because of the reality of the union" ("Imputation and the Christology of Union

with Christ: Calvin, Osiander, and the Contemporary Quest for a Reformed Model," *WTJ* 68 [2006]: 246; see also Beale, *New Testament Biblical Theology*, 469–80).

100. This is probably the standard view in Reformation circles. Horton's claim is representative: "There is no future aspect to justification itself. In justification, the believer has already heard the verdict of the last judgment" (*Christian Faith*, 705).

101. For these latter two texts, see Dunn ("Jesus the Judge: Further Thoughts of Paul's Christology and Soteriology," in Dunn, *New Perspective on Paul*, 401–2).

[attaining] righteousness" (see NIV, "the righteousness for which we hope"). Moving from this key verse, then, we find other indications that justification in Galatians is not bound only to the entry point.[102] This future-oriented focus makes good sense in light of the rhetorical situation of the letter. Paul argues *from* the good start that the Galatians have made *to* the need to continue as they began (3:1–5). A definitive act of justification at the beginning of the Christian life is presumed, as the parallel Paul draws between Abraham's experience and the Galatians' makes clear. And Romans, as we have seen, written in a different (and arguably less polemical) situation, affirms such a definitive initial justification unmistakably. But the situation in Galatia requires that Paul emphasize how the Galatians are to *maintain* their status of righteousness and, especially, how they can expect to be found to be in the "right" in the judgment.[103] This last point deserves particular attention. Without denying that first-century Judaism viewed God's election as the ultimate basis for their place in the covenant, I think it is also the case that, in practice, many Jews operated with a "a semi-tacit consciousness of having been born there, of always having been there," as Henri Blocher puts it.[104] In this scenario, the question becomes not simply how one "gets in" initially or how one "stays in" but how one can hope to "get in" the eternal kingdom on the day of judgment.[105] This seems to be exactly the issue that Galatians is addressing.[106] A final aspect of justification appears to be well established in Paul.[107]

---

102. See Douglas J. Moo, "Justification in Galatians," in *Understanding the Times: New Testament Studies in the 21st Century. Essays in Honor of D. A. Carson on the Occasion of His 65th Birthday*, ed. Andreas J. Köstenberger and Robert W. Yarbrough (Wheaton, IL: Crossway, 2011), 160–95; and also Gaffin, *"By Faith, Not by Sight,"* 98; A. Andrew Das, "Oneness in Christ: The *Nexus Indivulsus* between Justification and Sanctification in Paul's Letter to the Galatians," *Concordia Journal* 21 (1995): 173–86. Yon-Gyong Kwon argues that justification in Galatians is exclusively future (*Eschatology in Galatians: Rethinking Paul's Response to the Crisis in Galatia*, WUNT 2/183 [Tübingen: Mohr Siebeck, 2004], 51–76).

103. Moo, *Galatians*, 60–62. The contrast between Galatians and Romans on this point relates to their situations. In contrast to Galatians, where the agitators make it necessary for Paul to focus on warning about continuance in righteousness and ultimate vindication—the "not yet," Romans focuses on the definitive act of justification in the present—the "already," as the basis for assurance. The "already" and "not yet" aspects of justification overlap significantly with the "justified by faith"/"judged according to works" tension. For a survey of options, most of which apply also to the justification debate, see Dane C. Ortlund, "Justified by Faith, Judged according to Works: Another Look at a Pauline Paradox," *JETS* 52 (2009): 323–39.

104. Blocher, "Justification of the Ungodly," 488–89. See also Watson, *Paul and the Hermeneutics of Faith*, 8–11.

105. Gathercole has drawn attention to the importance of this future "getting in" in Jewish literature and its comparative neglect in the debate (*Where Is Boasting?*, 113–19).

106. Others who advocate a future aspect of justification are Stuhlmacher, "Apostle Paul's View of Righteousness," 72 ("Justification designates in Paul both the sharing in God's grace that has already been given by faith and acquittal before God in the last judgment"); Charles H. Cosgrove, "Justification in Paul: A Linguistic and Theological Reflection," *JBL* 106 (1987): 652–54; Peter T. O'Brien, "Justification in Paul and Some Crucial Issues of the Last Two Decades," in *Right with God: Justification in the Bible and the World*, ed. D. A. Carson (Grand Rapids: Baker, 1992), 90; Paul A. Rainbow, *The Way of Salvation: The Role of Christian Obedience in Justification* (Milton Keynes: Paternoster, 2005), 155–74; Gaffin, *"By Faith, Not by Sight,"* 95–97; Beale, *New Testament Biblical Theology*, 497–524; Bradley G. Green, *Covenant and Commandment: Works, Obedience and Faithfulness in the Christian Life*, NSBT 33 (Downers Grove, IL: InterVarsity Press, 2014), 105–45; Schreiner, *Faith Alone*, 231–38. See also Gathercole, who argues that "salvation should be viewed as a unity, with justification referring to the whole while highlighting a certain aspect" ("Doctrine of Justification," 230).

107. N. T. Wright has especially stressed this final aspect of justification. And while he suggests that the ultimate verdict will be based on "the whole life lived," he also affirms that the initial and final verdicts will perfectly match: "The law court

As this last paragraph makes clear, Paul's teaching about a final aspect of justification is tied to his teaching about the judgment. The revelation of God's grace in the gospel has not led Paul to remove the standard Jewish idea of a final judgment from his teaching. See, for example, Romans 2:16, where Paul refers to "the day when God judges people's secrets through Jesus Christ, as my gospel declares" (see also Rom 2:5, 7–10; 1 Cor 4:5; 2 Cor 5:10; 2 Thess 1:5–10).[108] A judgment that involves ultimate condemnation for unbelievers and the wicked is not hard to integrate into Paul's larger teaching. However, Paul also makes clear that believers must face this day of judgment as well (see Rom 14:10; 1 Cor 4:5; 2 Cor 5:10). Those who belong to Christ, Paul affirms, can have confidence as they look to that day. The one who justifies the person who trusts in Christ can be counted on to spare believers from condemnation (Rom 8:33–34; see also 1 Cor 1:8; Eph 1:14; Phil 1:6).[109] Yet Paul can also cite the day of judgment as a basis for his exhortation to believers, warning them of the consequences for them on that day should their lives not measure up to God's expectations of them (Rom 8:12–13; 1 Cor 3:10–15[?]; 10:5–10; 2 Cor 5:10; Gal 6:7–9). These texts are controversial. Some interpreters think that they can be integrated successfully into Paul's fundamental teaching about the decisive nature of initial justification if this judgment has to do only with the degree of reward believers will be granted on that day.[110] As Paul puts it in 1 Corinthians 3, "the Day" will reveal the quality of every believer's work, with a "reward" granted to those who build well. Yet even if what the believer has built is "burned up," the believer himself or herself "will be saved—even though as one escaping through the flames" (vv. 12–15). However, as I noted in my comments on this text, its meaning and theological significance are not clear. Moreover, the language of "life" and "death"/"destruction" that Paul uses in Romans 8:12–13 and Galatians 6:7–9 points to the judgment as involving ultimate matters of salvation versus condemnation. Paul retains from his Old Testament and Jewish heritage the idea of a day of judgment on which ultimate issues of salvation are determined for all humans. He is also clear that this judgment will involve human works—a particularly controversial claim that I will examine in more detail in the next chapter.

Paul's teaching about a future judgment for all humans clearly fits with the future aspect of justification that I have defended above. However, I do not want to undercut

---

verdict, implementing God's covenant plan, and all based on Jesus Christ himself, is announced both in the *present*, with the verdict issued on the basis of faith and faith alone, and also in the *future*, on the day when God raises from the dead all those who are already indwelt by the Spirit. The present verdict gives the *assurance that* the future verdict will match it; the Spirit gives the *power through which* that future verdict, when given, will be seen to be in accordance with the life that the believer has then lived" (*Justification*, 251).

108. See esp. Kent L. Yinger, *Paul, Judaism, and Judgment according to Deeds*, SNTSMS 105 (Cambridge: Cambridge University Press, 1999); see also, e.g., Chris VanLandingham, *Judgment and Justification in Early Judaism and the Apostle Paul* (Peabody, MA: Hendrickson, 2006), 18–240.

109. On the theme of confidence for believers in the judgment, see Park, *Stellvertretung Jesu Christi im Gerich*, 228–335.

110. See esp. Mattern, *Das Verständnis des Gerichtes bei Paulus*; also McFadden, *Judgment according to Works*.

what seems to be a clear emphasis on the definitive nature of initial justification. What Jewish theology usually relegated to the final judgment, Paul, with his typical inaugurated eschatological emphasis, locates at the moment of conversion.[111] When a person is joined to Christ "by faith alone," a definitive verdict of "justified" is pronounced over that person.[112] Affirming a future aspect of justification undeniably sits uneasily with this emphasis, raising the imperative question about just what this final aspect of justification entails. Perhaps, as some have argued, it involves the public proclamation of what has already been decided.[113] In any case, Paul is clear in affirming that justification, whatever temporal aspect we are talking about, is secured only by faith.[114]

4.2 From Enmity to Peace: Reconciliation

The road from condemnation to justification is one of the main thoroughfares leading from the old realm to the new. However, to reiterate what I said earlier, the critical significance of justification should not be allowed to overshadow other important "spiritual blessings" that we who inhabit the new realm are given. One of the more prominent of these is reconciliation.

To be sure, the language of reconciliation is not all that common in Paul. The noun *katallagē*, "reconciliation," occurs four times (Rom 5:11; 11:15; 2 Cor 5:18, 19) and the verb *katallassō*, "reconcile," nine times (the simple *katallassō* in Rom 5:10 [twice]; 1 Cor 7:11 [but not here in a soteriological sense]; 2 Cor 5:18, 19, 20; the compound *apokatallassō* in Eph 2:16; Col 1:20, 22). However, to consider reconciliation a minor theme in Paul would be to make the error of defining the *concept* "reconciliation" narrowly in terms of the *lexeme* "reconcile." To get a full picture of this concept in Paul requires that we consider also the lexeme "peace."

---

111. As Linebaugh therefore suggests, the relationship of the "already" and "not yet" of justification is the reverse of what N. T. Wright (and many others) claim it to be: "Present justification is not an accurate 'anticipation of the future verdict' . . . ; the future word of justification is an echo and effect of the justifying judgment enacted in the cross" (*God, Grace, and Righteousness*, 146).

112. One can avoid the tension by denying that justification is a purely forensic declaration (see, e.g., Travis, who argues that "the problem of the relation between justification and final judgement is a problem only when justification is seen in purely forensic terms" [*Christ and the Judgement of God*, 96]).

113. See, e.g., Turretin: the sentence of justification pronounced on the last day "will not be so much a new justification, as the solemn and public proclamation of a sentence once passed and its execution by the assignment of the life promised with respect to an innocent person from the preceding justification" (*Institutes of Elenctic Theology*, 16th topic, Q. X, part VIII). The seventeenth-century theologian William Ames suggested glorification might be viewed as the "carrying out of the sentence of justfication" (*The*

Marrow of Theology [repr., Durham, NC: Labyrinth, 1983], 172; quoted by Michael S. Horton, "Traditional Reformed Response" [to the "deification view"], in Beilby and Eddy, *Justification: Five Views*, 247). See also Beale, *New Testament Biblical Theology*, 497; Schreiner, *Faith Alone*, 257–69.

114. I therefore part ways at this point with N. T. Wright. I agree with him that a final aspect of justification is taught in Paul, but I disagree with his claim that the final verdict is "based on the whole life lived" (e.g., *Paul in Fresh Perspective*, 111–13). He has reaffirmed this view in a 2011 article, arguing also that traditional distinctions among different kinds of causality (e.g., works being only evidential) have no basis in Paul (N. T. Wright, "Justification: Yesterday, Today, and Forever," *JETS* 54 [2011]: 60–61). For others who suggest that works play some kind of instrumental role in ultimate justification, see Dunn, "New Perspective on Paul: Whence, What, Whither?," 80–89; idem, "Jesus the Judge," 407; Yinger, *Paul, Judaism, and Judgment*, 288; J. R. Daniel Kirk, *Unlocking Romans: Resurrection and the Justification of God* (Grand Rapids: Eerdmans, 2008), 223–27.

The close relationship between "reconciliation" and "peace" is clear in Romans 5:1–11, a paragraph bookended by "peace" at the beginning (v. 1) and "reconciliation" at the end (v. 11; see also v. 10). Similarly, in Colossians 1:20 Paul teaches that God's "reconciling" all things takes place as he makes "peace through his [Christ's] blood, shed on the cross." Paul appears to treat "reconciliation" and "peace" as overlapping or even roughly equivalent ideas. And "peace" appears much more frequently in Paul, with broad reference to the experience of, and living out of, salvation. The noun *eirēnē*, "peace," occurs forty-three times in Paul; the verb *eirēneuō*, "live in peace," three times (Rom 12:18; 2 Cor 13:11; 1 Thess 5:13), and the verb *eirēnopoieō*, "make peace," once (Col 1:20). Classifying occurrences of the noun is difficult because Paul tends to use the term broadly to designate the new state of affairs inaugurated by Christ. Paul speaks in this sense of "the peace of God" (Phil 4:7), "the peace of Christ" (Col 3:15), and "the gospel of peace" (Eph 6:15). He refers to God as "the God of peace" (Rom 15:33; 16:20; Phil 4:9; 1 Thess 5:23; see also 2 Cor 13:11) and to Christ as the "Lord of peace" (2 Thess 3:16). Christians are to send emissaries on "in peace" (1 Cor 16:11). Nor should we neglect the opening prayer wishes in Paul's letters, in each one of which he prays that his readers might experience "peace" (Rom 1:7; 1 Cor 1:3; 2 Cor 1:2; Gal 1:3; Eph 1:2; Phil 1:2; Col 1:2; 1 Thess 1:1; 2 Thess 1:2; 1 Tim 1:2; 2 Tim 1:2; Titus 1:4; Phlm 3; see also the prayer wishes in Rom 15:13; Gal 6:16; Eph 6:23). "Peace" also refers to harmonious relationships among believers (Rom 14:19; 1 Cor 7:15; 14:33; 2 Cor 13:11; Gal 5:22[?]; Eph 4:3; Phil 4:7[?]; 1 Thess 5:13; 2 Tim 2:22; see also Eph 2:14, 15)—a peace that believers are to extend, as much as possible, to unbelievers (Rom 12:18). Especially important for our purposes are places where Paul uses "peace" in a more directly soteriological sense (Rom 2:10; 5:1; 8:6; 14:17[?]; Eph 2:17 [2x]; 6:15; Col 3:15; cf. "making peace" in Col 1:20). In Christ a state of "peace" between believers and God has been established, peace that will be consummated on the last day (Rom 2:10).

The breadth of the language in Paul reflects the use of *eirēnē* as the translation of *shalom* in the Old Testament (*eirēnē* occurs over 200 times in the LXX). "Peace" is a general state of affairs that marks the life of the godly. See, for example, the "Aaronic blessing" from Numbers 6:24–26: "The LORD bless you and keep you; the LORD make his face shine on you and be gracious to you; the LORD turn his face toward you and give you peace"; and Psalm 119:165: "Great peace have those who love your law, and nothing can make them stumble." The word therefore moves significantly away from the usual semantic range of "peace" in English; it is often rendered in translation by other words, such as "prosperity" (Ps 72:3 NIV; ESV; NLT), "welfare" (Jer 15:5; 29:11 ESV), "securely" (Ezek 38:8 ESV), and "health" (Ps 38:3 NLT). Paul's use of the word reflects particularly its use in key prophecies about the restored state of the people of Israel:

For a child has been born for us,
    a son given to us;
authority rests upon his shoulders;
    and he is named
Wonderful Counselor, Mighty God,
    Everlasting Father, Prince of Peace.
His authority shall grow continually,
    and there shall be endless peace
for the throne of David and his kingdom. (Isa 9:6–7 NRSV)

How beautiful upon the mountains
    are the feet of the messenger who announces peace,
who brings good news,
    who announces salvation,
    who says to Zion, "Your God reigns." (Isa 52:7 NRSV)

But he was wounded for our transgressions,
    crushed for our iniquities;
upon him was the punishment that made us whole
        [LXX: "chastisement of our peace," *paideia eirēnēs*],
    and by his bruises we are healed. (Isa 53:5 NRSV)

I have seen their ways, but I will heal them;
    I will lead them and repay them with comfort,
    creating for their mourners the fruit of the lips.
Peace, peace, to the far and the near, says the LORD;
    and I will heal them. (Isa 57:18–19 NRSV)[115]

Paul's dependence on these prophetic announcements is clear; he quotes Isaiah 52:7 in Romans 10:15, and he clearly alludes to Isaiah 57:18–19 in Ephesians 2:14–17. A related Old Testament theme might also have an impact on Paul's teaching about reconciliation: the comparison of Yahweh's relationship with Israel to a marriage. God, as the bridegroom, takes Israel as his wife. Yet Israel is an unfaithful spouse, spurning her true husband despite all his goodness and faithfulness to her (Isa 62:5; Jer 2:2; 3:1; Ezek 16:32; and, of course, Hos 1–3). And, while the language of peace and reconciliation is not generally found in these texts, God's gracious willingness to take back his wayward partner embodies the concept pretty clearly.

---

115. See also, e.g., Isa 55:12; 66:12; Jer 30:10; 33:6; Ezek 37:26; Zech 9:10.

The "peace" word group, therefore, has a clear basis in the LXX. This is not the case, however, with the word group "reconcile." The words occur only six times in the LXX, and only four of the occurrences (in 2 Maccabees) are relevant to the concept of reconciliation.[116] The appearance of this word group denoting reconciliation only in late LXX and Greek-oriented material suggests that the word may have its home in the Greco-Roman environment. Cilliers Breytenbach has drawn attention to the use of "reconciliation" language in Greek diplomatic correspondence.[117] It is doubtful, however, that we have enough data to trace Paul's use of the language to a particular context such as this—and it might not be all that important that we do so.[118] The overlap of "reconciliation" and "peace" suggests that the two are alternative ways of referring to the same concept—one, as we have seen, that is derived from the Old Testament.[119]

As my survey of "peace" language in Paul above suggests, the concept denoted by this word group in Paul is very broad. Of course, it refers specifically to the establishment of harmonious relations between God and humans ("peace with God," e.g., Rom 5:1). But it also denotes the new relationship between Jews and gentiles that the work of Christ has inaugurated. The "peace" (with God) that Jewish and gentile believers alike enjoy (Eph 2:17) means that they are also at peace with each other (Eph 2:14, 15; see also Rom 15:13 in context). A state of "peace" is to characterize the thinking and attitude of God's people; we are to live in "peace" with one another (2 Cor 13:11; Col 3:15) and, as much as possible, with those outside the body as well (Rom 12:18). Indeed, God's work of reconciling extends to the cosmos itself: God, through Christ, is working "to reconcile to himself all things, whether things on earth or things in heaven, by making peace through his blood, shed on the cross" (Col 1:20).[120] It is tempting to find this same idea in 2 Corinthians 5:19a, which shares some important conceptual ideas with the Colossian text: "God was reconciling the world to himself in Christ, not counting people's sins against them." The "world" here, in other words,

116. The noun *katallagē* occurs in Isa 9:4; 2 Macc 5:20; the verb *katallassō* in Jer 31:39; 2 Macc 1:5; 7:33; 8:29. Only the 2 Maccabees texts refer to "reconciliation" in the sense relevant for this discussion. Stanley E. Porter argues that Paul's use of the language in 2 Cor 5:18–21 has no parallel in Greek literature ("Reconciliation and 2 Cor 5:18–21," in Bieringer, *Corinthian Correspondence*, 693).

117. Cilliers Breytenbach, *Versöhnung: Eine Studie zur Paulinischen Soteriologie*, WMANT 60 (Neukirchen-Vluyn: Neukirchener, 1989). For a criticism, see Stuhlmacher, *Grundlegung*, 318–19.

118. See also Porter, "Reconciliation and 2 Cor 5:18–21."

119. As so often in Paul's theology, Isaiah 40–66 appears to have strongly influenced Paul's "peace" teaching (Otfried Hofius, "Erwägungen zur Gestalt und Herkunft des paulinischen Versöh-

nungsgedankens," in *Paulusstudien*, 11–14; Kim, *Paul and the New Perspective*, 218–20; Michael J. Gorman, "The Lord of Peace: Christ our Peace in Pauline Theology," *JSPL* 3 [2013]: 226–31).

120. Noting that Paul applies reconciliation language to the Colossian Christians in Col 1:21–23 and that Paul elsewhere uses the word group with reference to believers, some interpreters argue that reconciliation in Col 1:20 also applies only to humans (Marshall, "Meaning of 'Reconciliation,'" 126–27). But the context makes this kind of limitation on the scope of reconciliation very problematic. The "all things" of v. 20 occurs five other times in the context, and in each case the referent is the created universe. And, of course, in this context, Paul goes on to specify that the scope of "all things" includes *things on earth or things in heaven*. The neuter form (Gk. *ta . . . ta*) and the parallelism with v. 16 make clear that all created things are included (see Moo, *Colossians*, 134–35).

might refer to the cosmos.[121] This, however, is not altogether clear, since "not counting people's sins" in the last part of the verse might suggest that the "world" here is the world of human beings.

However we interpret 2 Corinthians 5:17, Colossians 1:20 makes clear that reconciliation has a cosmic dimension. Reconciliation also, as we have seen, refers to the restoration of relationships between humans and God and among humans. In addition, "peace"/"reconciliation" occurs throughout Paul's letters (unlike, e.g., justification). These factors suggest that reconciliation is one of the more important blessings given to those who inhabit the new realm. Indeed, some interpreters argue that reconciliation lies at the very heart of Paul's theology.[122]

Justification is an image of our new-realm standing that is rooted in the judicial sphere. Reconciliation/peace, on the other hand, reflects the context of relationship. Some interpreters, noting the parallelism between justification and reconciliation in texts such as Romans 5:9–10, suggest that we should interpret one of these concepts in light of the other. It is especially often suggested that justification should be interpreted as more than forensic in light of this parallel. However, the fact that these two concepts are placed in similar contexts does not mean they overlap in meaning with each other. The parallel between them is structural, not semantic.[123] Justification and reconciliation denote two distinct ways of describing the believer's new-realm status.

Reconciliation presumes that the relationship between God and humans—and also between humans, between ethnic groups (Jews and gentiles), and indeed of humans with the cosmos—has been disrupted, creating the need for this act of reconciliation. It is, of course, sin that is the ultimate reason for the disruption, as 2 Corinthians 5:19 suggests. God's reconciling of the world to himself involves, negatively, "not counting people's sins against them." Sin has brought a state of enmity between God and humans; we are alienated from him (Rom 5:10; 11:28; Col 1:21). Some interpreters insist that this enmity is entirely on the human side.[124] However, Paul implies that the enmity is two-sided. Humans are "enemies" of God because they sin against him; God is an "enemy" of humans because their sin evokes his wrath and judgment against

---

121. See my notes on 2 Cor 5:19 on p. 177. Other texts in Paul may indirectly suggest this cosmic focus in his teaching about reconciliation/peace. Gorman has suggested that Paul's quotation of Isa 11:10 in Rom 15:12 may be intended to evoke all of Isa 11:1–10, a passage that portrays the eschaton as a "peaceable kingdom" in which the world of nature is "put right" (*Death of the Messiah*, 158).

122. See esp. Martin, *Reconciliation*; Gorman, "Lord of Peace," 219–53; idem, *Becoming the Gospel*, 142–80; Willard M. Swartley, *Covenant of Peace: The Missing Peace in New Testament Theology and Ethics* (Grand Rapids: Eerdmans, 2006);

Marshall, *Aspects of the Atonement*, 98–137; Jacques Dupont, *La Réconciliation dans le Théologie de Saint Paul*, ALBO 2.32 (Bruges/Paris: Desclée, 1953), 50–52. Some of these authors are reacting against Ernst Käsemann, who downgraded reconciliation in favor of justification ("Some Thoughts on the Theme 'The Doctrine of Reconciliation in the New Testament,'" in *The Future of Our Religious Past: Essays in Honor of Rudolf Bultmann*, ed. James M. Robinson [London: SCM, 1971], 51–64).

123. Anderson, *Paul's New Perspective*, 312.

124. E.g., Hofius, "Erwägungen zur Gestalt und Herkunft des Versöhnungsgedankens," 4.

them.[125] Our being "God's enemies" in Romans 5:10 follows immediately on a reference to God's wrath (5:9), and in Romans 11:28 the language of "enemies" applied to the Jewish people is paralleled by "loved," clearly denoting God's love. Colossians 1:21, on the other hand, focuses on human enmity against God: "Once you were alienated from God and were enemies in your minds because of your evil behavior."

The specific means by which we get from enmity to peace again involves Jesus's death as a sacrifice, as Colossians 1:19–22 makes clear:

> For God was pleased to have all his fullness dwell in him, and through him to reconcile to himself all things, whether things on earth or things in heaven, by making peace through his blood, shed on the cross. Once you were alienated from God and were enemies in your minds because of your evil behavior. But now he has reconciled you by Christ's physical body through death to present you holy in his sight, without blemish and free from accusation.

The Colossians were reconciled "by Christ's physical body through death," the language of "body" almost certainly focusing on Christ as a sacrificial victim. The reconciliation of all things, likewise, takes place as God makes peace "through [Christ's] blood, shed on the cross." Ephesians 2:14–16 is equally clear. Reconciliation between Jews and gentiles is accomplished by Christ's "cross" (v. 16) and "in his flesh" (v. 15), and these phrases are governed by God's means of "bringing near" those who were far off: "By the blood of Christ" (v. 13).

Reconciliation, then, takes place at the cross. It is an objective state brought about by Christ's sacrificial death.[126] His death has inaugurated a state, or realm, of "peace," a state awaiting its consummation in the future ("already" and "not yet"). Thus, for instance, the reconciliation of the cosmos, including evil spiritual powers (Col 1:20; "things in heaven"), clearly has not yet been effected. Yet reconciliation must be appropriated. Second Corinthians 5:18–20 clearly expresses both the objective and subjective side of reconciliation:

> All this is from God, who reconciled us to himself through Christ and gave us the ministry of reconciliation: that God was reconciling the world to himself in Christ, not counting people's sins against them. And he has committed to us the message of

---

125. See, e.g., Ridderbos, *Paul*, 183–85; Morris, *Apostolic Preaching*, 199. Paul uses *echthros* ("enemy") nine times. Six are active (denoting the hostility of the subject toward others—see Rom 12:20; 1 Cor 15:25, 26; Gal 4:16; Phil 3:18; Col 1:21), one is passive (2 Thess 3:15), and two (Rom 5:10; 11:28) probably work both ways.

126. The objective side of reconciliation is fundamental for Paul's teaching. See, e.g., Denney, *Death of Christ*, 145–46; Bell, "Sacrifice and Christology," 12–13; Morris, *Apostolic Preaching*, 198–99; Ladd, *Theology of the New Testament*, 493–94; Murray, *Redemption*, 41–42.

reconciliation. We are therefore Christ's ambassadors, as though God were making his appeal through us. We implore you on Christ's behalf: Be reconciled to God.

God "reconciled" believers (and the cosmos?) to himself in Christ; yet Paul can also plead that people "be reconciled to God."[127] I. Howard Marshall puts it well: "God acts in Christ to overlook the sins of mankind, so that on his side there is no barrier to the restoration of friendly relations. The message of the Christian preacher is a declaration of this fact."[128] Reconciliation reveals the difficulty I noted above in neatly separating out means and outcome. Our distinction between the two "moments" of reconciliation is a valid inference from Paul's teaching. Yet God's reconciling activity is ultimately one act, and many of Paul's references probably allude to both together.

4.3 From Slavery to Freedom: Redemption and Victory

A third route in Paul's soteriological landscape runs from slavery to freedom. Pauline scholars have focused attention on this concept in recent years as a central element of the so-called "apocalyptic Paul" movement. Advocates of this approach think that Paul presents God as responding to the human predicament by a sovereign liberating act.[129] The fundamental human problem is imprisonment under powers—especially the powers of sin and death. God's response to that problem is, then, appropriately, to liberate humans by an exercise of his power in Christ. Leaving aside for now the meaning and appropriateness of the term "apocalyptic," I simply note here that the movement both reflects and fuels the renewed popularity of the *Christus Victor* model of the atonement. This view of God's work in Christ, elevated to the "classic" view by some, views the atonement as consisting in the victory of God in Christ over Satan and evil spiritual forces.[130]

Several vocabulary combinations contribute to this theme. The most obvious is Paul's contrast between slavery and freedom to denote the nature of old-realm life versus life in the new realm. The old realm is dominated by sin, death, and the law. People are helpless captives of these powers, as their inevitable sinning, in and because of Adam, means that they suffer under penalty of death (Rom 5:12–21). The law, the Torah that God gave Israel, may have been supposed to change or ameliorate this situation, but it has, rather, made the situation worse. Sin uses God's good law to bring and confirm people in death (Rom 7:7–25; see also 5:20; Gal 3:19). Believers therefore are "put to

---

127. Paul's exhortation "be reconciled to God" is variously interpreted as a quotation from his typical evangelistic preaching (Porter, Καταλλάσσω, 139–40; Harris, *Second Epistle to the Corinthians*, 447–48) or as a plea directed to the Corinthian Christians (Breytenbach, *Versöhnung*, 178–79; Guthrie, *Second Corinthians*, 312). The latter is more likely in light of the follow-up in 6:1–2.

128. Marshall, "Meaning of 'Reconciliation,'" 123.

129. See esp. Campbell, *Deliverance*.

130. The classic defense of this atonement theory is Gustav Aulén, *Christus Victor: An Historical Study of the Three Main Types of the Idea of Atonement* (New York: Macmillan, 1931).

death" to the law (Rom 7:4, my translation), even as they "die to sin" (6:2). As Paul makes clear in these contexts, "dying to" is language for transfer out of the realm of slavery (cf. Rom 6:2 with 6:6, 14). In contrast, then, the new realm is dominated by freedom: "For freedom Christ has set you free" (Gal 5:1; cf. 2:4; 1 Cor 7:22).

Another set of terms that point to this "power" oriented conception of Christ's work are those that are drawn from the *lytr-* root. In chapter 18, I surveyed Paul's use of this language to denote God's work to inaugurate the new realm. As I noted there, redemption is hard to "locate" on the salvation-historical spectrum. It can refer to the point of inauguration or the point of appropriation—or, indeed, both taken together. Paul elaborates redemption in terms of the "forgiveness of sins" (Eph 1:7; Col 1:14), and it refers both to past (Rom 3:24; 1 Tim 2:6; Titus 2:14) and future (Rom 8:23; Eph 1:14) acts of deliverance. Our tendency to use "redemption" as a general way of referring to salvation therefore has some basis in Paul, and all this might suggest that we should include redemption in the category of umbrella soteriological terms we considered above. However, we include the concept here because the basic meaning of the word group has to do with liberation, as we have seen in its Old Testament usage (see again, ch. 18).

An act of liberation usually, of course, involves a victory over those forces holding people captive. It is therefore natural to include Paul's teaching about Christ's work as a victory over evil powers within this general conceptual category. While "liberation from" is Paul's typical way of expressing the believer's new-realm status vis-à-vis the law, sin, and death, he can also occasionally use the language of "victory over" (1 Cor 15:54, 55, 57). The key text is Colossians 2:13–15 (with a partial parallel in 2 Cor 2:14):

> When you were dead in your sins and in the uncircumcision of your flesh, God made you alive with Christ. He forgave us all our sins, having canceled the charge of our legal indebtedness, which stood against us and condemned us; he has taken it away, nailing it to the cross. And having disarmed the powers and authorities, he made a public spectacle of them, triumphing over them by the cross.

The role of Christ's death in this triumph over the powers is not entirely clear, since the last word of this quotation in the NIV, "cross," translates a Greek pronoun that could refer to Christ (e.g., ESV, CSB). However, the prominence of the cross in a somewhat parallel verse earlier in the letter (1:20) suggests that Paul might here also be referring to the cross. Believers' freedom from the oppression of spiritual powers is an important theme in Colossians (see esp. 2:10; cf. 1:16; perhaps 2:8, 20 [if *stoicheia tou kosmou*, as many think, refers to spiritual powers]). While I will develop this point later, it is worth noting here that the means by which this victory is accomplished is the removal of "the charge of our legal indebtedness": the victory is won through the removal of condemnation by means of Christ's death.

4.4 From "Not My People" to "God's Own People": Holiness

The language of my title for this section is adapted from Paul's quotation of Hosea 2:23 in Romans 9:25. I use this language because it gets to the heart of the key Pauline language to depict the destination of this fourth route from old realm to new: "holiness," a concept denoted particularly by words from the *hag-* root. Our English Bibles obscure (inevitably) the connections among these words by using some form of both "holy" and "saint"/"sanctify" to render these words:

"sanctify" (*hagiazō*)—nine occurrences

"sanctification"/"holiness" (*hagiasmos*/*hagiōsynē*)—eight/three occurrences, respectively[131]

"saint"/"holy one[s]"/"God's people" (*hagios*)—seventy-six occurrences

"holy"/"pure"/"innocent" (*hagnos*)—five occurrences

Of course, not every occurrence of these terms relates to our present topic and, in turn, Paul uses several other words that arguably contribute to this concept: "clean" (*katharos*, eight occurrences); "purify" (*katharizō*, three occurrences); "without blemish," "blameless" (*amōmos*, four occurrences); "blameless" (*anenklētos*, five occurrences; and *amemptos*, three occurrences).

Paul's "holiness" language is taken from the Greek Old Testament, where the *hag-* root translates the Hebrew *q-d-sh* root. This language is very common in the Old Testament, where it occurs over eight hundred times to describe God and, by derivation, the people of God. Israel was called to imitate their "holy" God by being a "holy" people (e.g., Lev 11:44, 45; 19:2; cf. 1 Pet 1:16). The basic sense of "holiness" as applied to the people is "separation to and for Yahweh."[132] Ferguson writes that in sanctification "God repossesses persons and things that have been devoted to other uses, and have been possessed for purposes other than his glory, and takes them into his own possession in order that they may reflect his own glory."[133]

Paul uses the language along these lines. As Ridderbos puts it, to be "holy" in Paul involves "being appropriated and dedicated to God."[134] This basic sense of the language is clear from texts in which he labels as "holy" the Scriptures (Rom 1:2), the law (Rom 7:12), the kiss as a form of Christian greeting (Rom 16:16; 1 Cor 16:20; 2 Cor 13:12; 1 Thess 5:26), or the apostles and prophets (Eph 3:5). "Holiness" as a cultic category is prominent in Hebrews, but less so in Paul.[135] Yet the imagery of the cult clearly

---

131. The related noun *hagiotēs* is a textual variant in 2 Cor 1:12.

132. William J. Dumbrell, *The Faith of Israel: A Theological Survey of the Old Testament*, 2nd ed. (Grand Rapids: Baker, 2002), 45.

133. Ferguson, *Holy Spirit*, 140.

134. Ridderbos, *Paul*, 291.

135. However, his contrast between "holiness" and "uncleanness" (*akathartos*, 1 Cor 7:14; *akatharsia*, 1 Thess 4:7) and "common" (*koinos*, Rom 14:14) reveals that this nuance is not entirely absent in Paul.

lies behind some of Paul's uses of the language. In 2 Corinthians 6:17 Paul issues a command to the church, citing Isaiah 52:11 (Ezek 20:34, 41): "Come out from them and be separate, says the Lord. Touch no unclean thing, and I will receive you." He then follows this up with a concluding exhortation in 7:1: "Therefore, since we have these promises, dear friends, let us purify ourselves from everything that contaminates body and spirit, perfecting holiness out of reverence for God." The language Paul uses here—"purify" (*katharizō*), "contaminates" (*molysmos*)—is often applied to sacrifices in the Old Testament. Believers no longer offer animal sacrifice, but Paul calls on them to offer themselves as a "living sacrifice, holy [*hagian*] and pleasing to God" (Rom 12:1; see also Rom 15:16; Eph 5:27).

The pre-Christian Paul would, of course, have attributed this holiness to Israel, separate for God and from the gentiles. The apostle Paul redraws the boundaries, with holiness now encompassing all who are in Christ.[136] Indeed, *hagioi*, "holy ones," is the word Paul most often uses (forty-three times) to denote Christ followers. First Corinthians 1:2 is typical: "To the church of God in Corinth, to those sanctified [*hēgiasmenois*] in Christ Jesus and called to be his holy people [*hagiois*], together with all those everywhere who call on the name of our Lord Jesus Christ—their Lord and ours." See also 1 Corinthians 6:11b: "But you were washed, you were sanctified [*hēgiasthēte*], you were justified in the name of the Lord Jesus Christ and by the Spirit of our God." The word does not therefore have first of all a moral sense. It says nothing about the actual way in which those called "holy" are living, but denotes their status as the people of God (hence the NIV decision to translate *hagioi* often as "God's people" or "the Lord's people").[137] However, Paul is also clear that those who have the status of "holy" are expected to confirm that status with a holy lifestyle, appropriating "the moral condition answering to the fact of having been appropriated to the Lord."[138] "For God did not call us to be impure, but to live a holy life" (1 Thess 4:7). This call to holiness is inherent in God's calling people to himself (Eph 1:4; 5:27; Col 1:22; 1 Tim 1:9). Yet, in a typical combination for Paul's theology, he also reminds us that God, in his *Holy* Spirit, supplies the means by which this holiness can be attained (Rom 15:16; 2 Thess 2:13).

Paul's use of the plural *hagioi* in his address to the churches suggests that he is mainly referring to the individual believers who make up the church to which he writes. But Paul also thinks of the community as a whole as "holy": "Christ loved the church and gave himself up for her to make her holy" (Eph 5:25b–26a). This conception comes to the fore especially in Paul's use of temple language to denote the community. The last

---

136. See Wolter, *Paul*, 17–18.

137. This "positional" sense of the language in Paul has been stressed especially by Peterson, *Possessed by God*.

138. Ridderbos, *Paul*, 263.

few decades have seen a renewal of interest in the temple idea, to some degree a product of renewed focus among Old Testament theologians on the significance of sacred space. To be sure, Paul can describe the individual believer as a "temple of God" (1 Cor 6:19), but more often he compares the entire Christian community to a temple (1 Cor 3:16–17; 2 Cor 6:16; Eph 2:21; note that "holy" is used in two of these texts). By doing so, Paul suggests that the presence of God, manifest especially in the Old Testament sanctuary and temple, is now located in the new-covenant people of God. The status of this people as "holy" naturally entails the expression of that holiness in their relations with one another and with the world outside the church.

4.5 From Homelessness to Belonging: Adoption

Yet another route from old realm to new realm embraces several rather diverse sets of contrasts and concepts that can generally be lumped under the category of "new relational identity." We might summarize by grouping the relevant data into two basic conceptions.

First, life in the new realm involves living as "sons of God." I retain the masculine language in order to convey the full force of the imagery. Paul speaks of believers as "sons" of God in several passages.[139] A more technical word referring to the same concept is *huiothesia*, "adoption" (Rom 8:15, 23; 9:4; Gal 4:5; Eph 1:5).[140] Adoption was a feature of Paul's Greco-Roman environment. In that culture, when a male was adopted, that male became legally entitled to all the rights and privileges pertaining to that new status.[141] Paul celebrates the fact that, in Christ, men and women equally can become "sons" in this sense. While Paul does not often use the language of "adoption," the concept is a significant one in Paul's portrayal of new-realm blessings. For one thing, the concept embraces both the believer's "already" and "not yet": we now have the Spirit of adoption, leading us to cry "Abba, Father" (Rom 8:15), but we also await the day we receive our full adoption when our bodies are redeemed (v. 23). In both Galatians 4 and Romans 8, Paul transitions from our present to our future via the idea of inheritance. A son is, by definition, an heir; and an heir, by definition, while legally assured of his or her inheritance, does not yet possess it. So, Paul makes clear, as God's sons we rejoice in what we now have and long for what is still to come.

---

139. Using *huios*: Rom 8:14, 19; 9:26 [Hos 1:10]; 2 Cor 6:18 [with *thygateras*, "daughters"]; Gal 3:7, 26; 4:6, 7 [cf. 1 Thess 5:5]; using *teknon*: Rom 8:16, 17, 21; Eph 5:1; Phil 2:15 [cf. Gal 4:28; Eph 5:8]. As the shift between words in Rom 8:14–17 suggests, the words in these contexts have the same meaning.

140. The word is probably best translated "adoption (to sonship)," rather than "sonship." See J. M. Scott, *Adoption as Sons*; Erin M. Heim, *Adoption in Galatians and Romans: Contemporary Metaphor Theories and the Pauline Huiothesia*, BibInt 153 (Leiden: Brill, 2017), esp. 117–24; contra Byrne, *"Sons of God."* Burke argues that both act (adoption) and status (sonship) are included (*Adopted into God's Family*, 149–51).

141. For the background of the term, see David B. Garner, *Sons in the Son: The Riches and Reach of Adoption in Christ* (Phillipsburg, NJ: P&R, 2017).

This conception also ties into an Old Testament theme. For, in addition to the influence from the Roman legal institution of adoption, Paul undoubtedly intends us to draw a comparison with Israel as God's "son" (see, e.g., Exod 4:22; Jer 3:19; 31:9; Hos 11:1). Finally, as Paul makes clear in both Galatians 4 and Romans 8, our sonship is tied to Christ's own sonship; like him, we cry "Abba, Father" (Rom 8:15; Gal 4:6). We are sons because God sent "his Son" (Gal 4:4); we are sons in him, who is the Son (note the references to God's Son in Rom 8:3, 29, 32). Perhaps we can discern here a secondary connection also. In Romans 8:29 Paul claims that we are "predestined to be conformed to the image of his Son." As sons, God's goal for us is that we increasingly become like the Son. The Son is himself *the* image of God" (2 Cor 4:4; Col 1:15), and our destiny is to share, derivatively and partially, in that image. And this conception also picks up a key biblical-theological theme. In Christ, God is restoring humans to that "image of God" in which he first created us, an image that, while never lost, has been sadly defaced by sin. As Blocher puts it, "In the Son we become sons, an act of grace which fulfills and transcends our primeval quasi-sonship."[142] And, at the risk of extending this chain of references to the breaking point, perhaps here we could also bring into conversation the concept of "glory," since Paul implies some degree of relationship between the concepts of "image" and "glory" (see Rom 1:23; 1 Cor 11:7; 2 Cor 3:18; 4:4). "Glory" denotes first of all—continuing a central Old Testament theme—the "weighty presence" of God himself (Rom 3:7, 23; 6:4). In a move typical of Paul's high Christology, Christ is then said also to possess, or share, this glory (Rom 8:17; 1 Cor 2:8; 2 Cor 3:18; 4:4; 2 Thess 2:14; Titus 2:13). Within the soteriological realm, Paul usually uses "glory" to refer to the ultimate state of our new-realm existence (Rom 5:2; 8:17, 18, 21; 9:23; 1 Cor 2:7[?]; 15:43; 2 Cor 4:17; Col 1:27; 3:4; 1 Thess 2:12[?]; 2 Thess 2:14[?]; 2 Tim 2:10; cf. Rom 2:7), but he can also claim that we are even now "being transformed into his image with ever-increasing glory" (2 Cor 3:18). Here again there comes to expression the underlying logic of participation. We are joined to Christ, the Son, the image of God, the "Lord of glory," and because of that union we are sons, being created in his image and destined for glory.

One final word about the adoption concept. Adoption language very helpfully brings together in one image the legal and the relational—two perspectives on new-realm life that, as important as they each are in their own right, need finally to be deeply connected to each other.[143] When we are adopted as God's sons, we are given a new legal standing at the same time as we are integrated into a new family: we are "members of [God's] household" (Eph 2:19).

---

142. Blocher, *In the Beginning*, 90.

143. Kevin J. Vanhoozer, "Wrighting the Wrongs of the Reformation? The State of the Union with Christ in St. Paul and Protestant Soteriology," in *Jesus, Paul and the People of God:*

A Theological Dialogue with N. T. Wright, ed. Nicholas Perrin and Richard B. Hays (Downers Grove, IL: InterVarsity Press, 2011), 235–59; Macaskill, *Union with Christ*, 242–43, passim.

The second concept to consider here is the idea of being God's people. I will delve into this concept later when I talk about the new-realm people of God (pp. 569–73). Here, briefly, I note simply that being the people of God is a central theme of the Old Testament depiction of Israel, both in terms of her destiny and in terms of her call. In the midst of the exile, God continued to promise Israel that he would be their God and they would be his people (e.g., Jer 32:38; Ezek 14:11; 37:23). Paul quotes this language and sees it fulfilled in the experience of the Christians of his day (2 Cor 6:16). Another dimension of the "people" language is its application to gentiles. In Romans 9:25–26 Paul quotes language from Hosea 1 and 2, applying to gentile Christians its promise that the northern tribes of Israel would be moved from the status of "not my people" to "children of the living God." In a motif to which many recent scholars have rightly drawn attention in Paul, the apostle is deeply concerned to stress the full integration of gentiles into the new-covenant people of God. Perhaps this "people" conception is also where we might integrate Paul's teaching that Christians receive an "inheritance." In the Old Testament, this "inheritance" is especially the land (e.g., Deut 31:7; Josh 11:23; Ps 105:11; Jer 3:18; Ezek 47:13). Claiming that Christians have an inheritance (Gal 3:18; 4:30; Eph 1:14, 18; 5:5; Col 1:12; 3:24; cf. "inherit" in 1 Cor 6:9, 10; 15:50 [2x]; Gal 5:21), then, probably implicitly claims that believers, both Jew and gentile (note Eph 3:6), are the recipients of this promise of God—not in the form of a single piece of geography but in the form of the whole cosmos (see Rom 4:13).

4.6 From the Image of the Earthly Man to the Image of the Heavenly Man: Transformation

My heading adapts language from 1 Corinthians 15:44b–49, which contrasts Adam and Christ as the two "realm rulers" whose acts and character determine all who belong to those realms. People who have been transferred into the new realm will be conformed to the "heavenly man," Christ: "And just as we have borne the image of the earthly man, so shall we bear the image of the heavenly man" (v. 49). In the context, of course, Paul is referring specifically to the nature of the resurrection body. But the point has broader application. Conformity to Christ's image in a general sense is a blessing of the new realm.

Being conformed to Christ belongs to the general idea of transformation. As I pointed out in my introduction to this chapter, the idea of transfer from one realm to another is probably the most basic way Paul conceives of Christian experience. But I also noted that it is vitally important to add to this "positional" focus, a focus on internal transformation as well. I dealt earlier with the common objection that a strictly forensic justification leaves believers unchanged in terms of their day-to-day lives. This objection has some force when the balance in our presentation of Paul's theology falls too heavily on the forensic or "positional" side of things. Paul, at least, would certainly not want us to make this mistake. The apostle would thoroughly endorse Horton's point: "What God is after in redemptive history is not merely the forgiveness of humanity and restoration to an original state but the fulfilment of the original commission for humanity and, through a successful outcome to its trial, entrance into God's glory."[144] The solution to this imbalance, however, is not to smuggle transformative notions into justification, but to robustly assert transformation emphases along with the strictly positional perspective.

Several of the blessings we have already considered contribute significantly to this transformation focus in Paul: the work of the Spirit, "new creation," new covenant, and holiness. Here I want to add several other perspectives that contribute to this theme. The most basic, of course, is the language of "transformation" itself, although occurrences are sparse in Paul. He uses the synonymous verbs *metamorphoō* and *symmorphizō* (both "transform") three times (the former in Rom 12:2; 2 Cor 3:18, and the latter in Phil 3:10) and the adjective *symmorphos* twice (Rom 8:29; Phil 3:21). Romans 12:2 is the best known: "Do not conform [*syschēmatizesthe*] to the pattern of this world, but be transformed [*metamorphousthe*] by the renewing of your mind. Then you will be able to test and approve what God's will is—his good, pleasing and perfect will." This call to be transformed comes at a pivotal point in the argument of Romans, as Paul moves from his exposition and celebration of the many "mercies" of God (12:1) to his call to lead lives appropriately conformed to those blessings. A transformed life will have a cruciform shape, as believers identify with and imitate their crucified Lord. They, like Paul, are "becoming like [*symmorphizomenos*] him in his death" (Phil 3:10; see 2:5–8) so that they might likewise share in his resurrection power (see also Phil 3:21). The two other transformation texts introduce other basic perspectives.

In Romans 8:29, Paul identifies as the purpose of God's predestination of believers is "to be conformed [*symmorphous*] to the image of his Son." The "conformity" Paul is thinking of here could be the believer's ultimate sharing in the glory of Christ (see the end of v. 30 and 1 Cor 15:49 above),[145] but it perhaps more likely refers to the final end of a process of conformity in lifestyle to the example of Christ (see Eph 1:4, where God's election has the purpose that we might be "holy and blameless in his sight"). "Image" language in these texts should also be noted. As mentioned above, Christ is *the* image of God (2 Cor 4:4; Col 1:15), and those who are in Christ therefore are being transformed into that image themselves (Rom 8:29, see 2 Cor 3:18; Col 3:10 [using *eikōn*, "image"]). And since Christ does image God fully, being conformed to Christ's likeness involves also becoming "like God" (*kata theon*; Eph 4:24). This imaging of Christ and God brings us back to the beginning of this chapter, where I identified

---

144. Horton, *Lord and Servant*, 220; see also Dunn: transformation is "Paul's most basic conception of the salvation process" (*Theology of Paul*, 468).

145. This is the view I argue in my *Romans* (NICNT), 556.

a fundamental plank in Paul's view of new-realm blessings: his version of the "great exchange." Christ becoming like humans that we might become like him. This way of thinking about God's work on behalf of the believer has been critical in the Eastern church, where it has been labeled "theosis." Some recent Pauline theologians have used this term to describe the basic train of thought I have identified in this paragraph.[146] However, the term itself may carry too much baggage from the larger conceptual world of Eastern theology to be useful in characterizing Paul's thought.[147] "Deification" and "Christosis" are other labels that have been applied to the Pauline teaching.[148] Whatever term we use, it is obviously important to recognize the limits of our becoming "like Christ" or "like God."

A second concept that surfaces in a key transformation text is "glory" (*doxa*): "And we all, who with unveiled faces contemplate the Lord's glory, are being transformed into his image with ever-increasing glory, which comes from the Lord, who is the Spirit" (2 Cor 3:18). As we noted in my comments on this verse (pp. 171–72), Paul here betrays his high Christology, attributing to Christ the Lord the glory that is intrinsic to God. The new-covenant people of God, who are being transformed into Christ's image, enjoy an increasing measure of glory. The glory that humans fall short of because of sin (Rom 3:23) is something that we are promised in Christ. We boast in the "hope of the glory of God" (5:2), that is, we boast that we will one day share in that glory (a topic to which Paul returns in Rom 8; see esp. the "bookends" of vv. 18 and 30). As in these Romans texts, "glory" is often a future eschatological blessing in Paul (see also, e.g., Phil 3:21; Col 3:4).[149] However, 2 Corinthians 3:18 makes clear that we must think of "glory" in terms of the typical tension of the "already" and the "not yet." While glory in a final sense is future, believers even now begin to experience that glory. But what is that "glory"? It is usual to think of the Old Testament "glory" (*kavod*) as fundamentally denoting the "weighty" presence of God, especially as that presence is displayed in splendor. The present and future "glorification" of the believer may then simply be another way of referring to becoming like God.[150] Others, however, have argued that

---

146. See esp. Gorman, who offers this definition: "Theosis is transformative participation in the kenotic, cruciform character and life of God through Spirit-enabled conformity to the incarnate, crucified, and resurrected/glorified Christ, who is the image of God" (*Inhabiting the Cruciform God*, 125).

147. Eastern theologians operate with an important distinction between God's "essence" and his "energies"; theosis involves becoming like God in his energies. On theosis, see, e.g., Andrew Louth, "The Place of *Theosis* in Orthodox Theology," in *Partakers of the Divine Nature: The History and Development of Deification in the Christian Tradition*, ed. Michael J. Christensen and Jeffery A. Wittung (Grand Rapids: Baker, 2007), 32–44; Russell, *Doctrine of Deification*; Macaskill, *Union with Christ*, 44–76; Hallonsten, "Theosis in Recent Research," 281–93; James R. Payton Jr., *The*

Victory of the Cross: Salvation in Eastern Orthodoxy (Downers Grove, IL: InterVarsity Press, 2019), 12–40. For a succinct explanation of why the language may not be entirely helpful, see esp. McDonough, *Creation and New Creation*, 195–202.

148. For the former, see, e.g., Veli-Matti Kärkkäinen, *Salvation as Deification and Justification* (Collegeville, MN: Liturgical, 2004); for the latter, see Ben C. Blackwell, *Christosis: Pauline Soteriology in Light of Deification in Irenaeus and Cyril of Alexandria*, WUNT 2/314 (Tübingen: Mohr Siebeck, 2011).

149. As Wolter describes it, "a comprehensive designation for the eschatological salvation that was expected" (*Paul*, 187).

150. Horton notes that glorification and deification are closely related in Reformation thinking (*Rediscovering the Holy Spirit*, 285).

"glory" belongs to a complex of ideas related to "image" (see Rom 8:29–30; 2 Cor 3:18) and that these words connote especially the idea of rule. Believers who are being "glorified" therefore are being transformed into people who can "image" God by ruling the world faithfully on his behalf.[151] This idea has a good basis in Genesis 1, where the creation of humans in God's "image" probably has some allusion to rule.[152] And it appropriately notes the way Christ's sonship, our sonship "in him," image, and glory are all juxtaposed in Romans 8. However, while perhaps an aspect of glory, rulership probably should not be seen as *the* reference in the word. Paul's general usage suggests the broader notion of becoming like God and Christ.[153]

5 CONCLUSION

Having surveyed the "spiritual blessings" that Paul associates with the new realm, I reiterate again a point I made at the beginning: my attempt to chart Paul's soteriology by dividing what he says into particular categories will inevitably distort his teaching in some way. I am sure that my map of six routes from old realm to new realm that I have constructed falls prey to this criticism. And to repeat a second point, the routes I have mapped are not like walled-off roads neatly separated from each other. They intersect with one another, overlap at times, and join at odd angles. The diversity of images means that teachers and preachers can choose which image might communicate best to a particular audience. Scot McKnight compares it to a golfer who chooses a particular club for a particular purpose. Yet if we are attempting to describe Paul's theology as a whole, a more apt comparison might be the latte, which will taste right only if the various ingredients are measured and mixed the right way.[154] As Anthony Thiselton puts it, the "pluriformity of models" "function conjointly to qualify single models, or to cancel off certain unwanted overtones in other models. Isolated models that appear to claim comprehensiveness risk pressing one aspect of interpretation at the cost of underplaying others."[155]

We thus find in Paul a picture of the new realm that is rich and diverse: we enjoy "every spiritual blessing" in Christ (Eph 1:3). And, while the problem is not nearly

---

151. Silvia C. Keesmaat, *Paul and His Story: (Re)Interpreting the Exodus Tradition*, JSNTSup 181 (Sheffield: Sheffield Academic Press, 1999), 84–120; and esp. Haley Goranson Jacob, *Conformed to the Image of His Son: Reconsidering Paul's Theology of Glory in Romans* (Downers Grove, IL: InterVarsity Press, 2018).

152. See esp. Middleton, *Liberating Image*.

153. See esp. Sigurd Grindheim, "A Theology of Glory: Paul's Use of Δόξα Terminology in Romans," *JBL* 136 (2017): 451–65.

154. Trevor Hart comments, "The plurality of biblical imagery does not seem to be intended purely or even primarily as a selection box from which we may draw what we will according to our needs and the pre-understanding of our community. . . . The metaphors are not to be understood as exchangeable, as if one might simply be substituted for another without net gain or loss, but complementary, directing us to distinct elements in and consequences of the fullness of God's saving action in Christ and the Spirit" ("Redemption and Fall," in *The Cambridge Companion to Christian Doctrine*, ed. Colin E. Gunton [Cambridge: Cambridge University Press, 1997], 190). See also Gaffin, "Atonement in the Pauline Corpus," 154–56.

155. Thiselton, *Hermeneutics of Doctrine*, 331.

as widespread or acute as some have made it out to be, there is no doubt that we have sometimes failed to appreciate the breadth of our new-realm blessings. We have sometimes focused too exclusively on the individual believer while neglecting the very important focus on the community and the healing of rifts between ethnic, social, and economic groups within that community. Our preoccupation with the individual has often gotten in the way of appreciating the cosmic scope of God's purposes. We have limited new-realm blessings to forgiveness and a new state of righteousness while not adequately emphasizing the life of righteousness to which we are called. Our survey of new-realm soteriological blessings has, I hope, both reasserted the importance of the objective/forensic basis for our new-realm life at the same time as it has sought to bring into the picture other significant contours of that landscape.

Chapter 21

ENTERING THE NEW REALM

For *the grace of God has appeared* that offers salvation to all people. It teaches us to say "No" to ungodliness and worldly passions, and to live self-controlled, upright and godly lives in this present age, while we wait for the blessed hope—the appearing of the glory of our great God and Savior, Jesus Christ, who gave himself for us to redeem us from all wickedness and to purify for himself a people that are his very own, eager to do what is good.

—TITUS 2:11–14

CENTRAL TO PAUL'S THEOLOGY is his conviction that God has acted in Christ to inaugurate a new realm of righteousness and life as an alternative to the old realm of sin and death. Sadly, however, the coming of the new realm, with all its benefits, has not obliterated the old realm. While destined to win the day, the new realm in this age exists side-by-side with the old realm, which is decisively defeated but not yet destroyed. All humans begin their existence in the old realm, bound to the "old man" and the sin and death he has introduced as the dominant powers in that realm. A person can participate in the new realm only by means of a transfer from the old realm to the new. As Paul puts it in Colossians 1:13: "For he has rescued us from the dominion of darkness and brought us into the kingdom of the Son he loves."

In this chapter, therefore, I survey the ways Paul talks about sinful humans entering the new realm. Basic to Paul's teaching on this issue is a careful balance between the initiative of God and the response of human beings. God's grace and the election to new-realm status that is the result of that grace are fundamental. Yet the human decision to respond to God's grace in faith is both real and necessary as well.

Paul uses a rich series of images to describe the transfer from old realm to new, as the following overview reveals:

"You have been set free from sin and have become slaves to righteousness" (Rom 6:18)/"slaves of God" (v. 22)

"You also died to the law through the body of Christ, that you might belong to another" (Rom 7:4)

"You, however, are not in the realm of the flesh but are in the realm of the Spirit"
  (Rom 8:9)

"You, though a wild olive shoot, have been grafted in among the others and now
  share in the nourishing sap from the olive root" (Rom 11:17; see also vv. 19, 24)

"God is faithful, who has called you into fellowship with his Son, Jesus Christ
  our Lord" (1 Cor 1:9) (and many other verses; see below)

"God was pleased through the foolishness of what was preached to save those
  who believe" (1 Cor 1:21; and see v. 23: "We preach Christ crucified")

"My message and my preaching were not with wise and persuasive words, but
  with a demonstration of the Spirit's power, so that your faith might not rest
  on human wisdom, but on God's power" (1 Cor 2:4–5)

"[Paul and Apollos], servants, through whom you came to believe" (1 Cor 3:5)

"I became your father through the gospel" (1 Cor 4:15)

"But whoever loves God is known by God" (1 Cor 8:3)

"Are you not the result of my work in the Lord?" (1 Cor 9:1)

"I have made myself a slave to everyone, to win as many as possible" (1 Cor 9:19)

"For we were all baptized by one Spirit so as to form one body—whether Jews
  or Gentiles, slave or free—and we were all given the one Spirit to drink"
  (1 Cor 12:13)

"By this gospel you are saved" (1 Cor 15:2)

"He anointed us, set his seal of ownership on us, and put his Spirit in our hearts
  as a deposit, guaranteeing what is to come" (2 Cor 1:21b–22)

"To the one we are an aroma that brings death; to the other, an aroma that
  brings life" (2 Cor 2:16)

"You are a letter from Christ, the result of our ministry, written not with ink
  but with the Spirit of the living God, not on tablets of stone but on tablets of
  human hearts" (2 Cor 3:3)

"Ministers of a new covenant . . . of the Spirit" (2 Cor 3:6)

"The ministry that brings righteousness" (2 Cor 3:9)

"We, who were the first to put our hope in Christ" (Eph 1:12)

"You also were included in Christ when you heard the message of truth, the gospel
  of your salvation" (Eph 1:13)

"[God] made us alive with Christ" (Eph 2:5)

"Brought near by the blood of Christ" (Eph 2:13)

"You were once darkness, but now you are light in the Lord" (Eph 5:8)

"Just as you received Christ Jesus as Lord" (Col 2:6)

"In him you were also circumcised with a circumcision not performed by
  human hands. Your whole self ruled by the flesh was put off when you were
  circumcised by Christ" (Col 2:11)

"God made you alive with Christ" (Col 2:13)

"For we know, brothers and sisters loved by God, that he has chosen you, because our gospel came to you not simply with words but also with power, with the Holy Spirit and deep conviction. You know how we lived among you for your sake. You became imitators of us and of the Lord, for you welcomed the message in the midst of severe suffering with the joy given by the Holy Spirit" (1 Thess 1:4–6)

"You turned to God from idols to serve the living and true God" (1 Thess 1:9)

"And we also thank God continually because, when you received the word of God, which you heard from us, you accepted it not as a human word, but as it actually is, the word of God, which is indeed at work in you who believe" (1 Thess 2:13)

"Christ Jesus might display his immense patience as an example for those who would believe in him and receive eternal life" (1 Tim 1:16)

"Onesimus, who became my son while I was in chains" (Phlm 10)

The diversity of language Paul uses to depict the transfer from old realm to new is obvious, but there are also four rather constant themes worth noting. First, as we would expect, Paul regularly puts Christ at the center of this transfer. He is the one "in whom" or "with whom" or "for whom" conversion takes place. Second, Paul regularly refers to the work of the Holy Spirit as instrumental in bringing people into the new realm. Third, there is frequent mention of human instruments, such as Paul or other servants of Christ. And there is, fourth, yet another instrument of transfer often featured: the word of God, or the gospel. As 2 Corinthians 2:14–4:6 reveals, these means of conversion are related to one another as aspects of new-covenant ministry. This passage is framed by references to the word of God/the gospel: "We do not peddle the word of God for profit" (2:17); "nor do we distort the word of God. On the contrary, by setting forth the truth plainly we commend ourselves to everyone's conscience in the sight of God. And even if our gospel is veiled, it is veiled to those who are perishing" (4:2b–3). The immediate and larger context of this passage focuses on the ministry of Paul and other preachers of God's word. And so it is not surprising that this topic is central in this passage. Paul and other preachers have "competence" in ministry, the power to change people's hearts, not because they are particularly eloquent but because they are "ministers of a new covenant" (3:4–6). And central to the new covenant is the work of the Spirit, now "poured out" on believers (see, e.g., Rom 5:5–6). Overcoming the hardness of human hearts, the Spirit has the power to "give life" (3:6), to confer "righteousness" (v. 9), and to transform idolatrous humans into Christ's own image (v. 18). In summary, gospel ministers transform humans by proclaiming God's word in the power of the Spirit.

Paul's longest reflection on conversion, 1 Thessalonians 1:2–2:12, reinforces these points. First Thessalonians 1:9b is perhaps the clearest description of conversion in Paul's letters: "You turned to God from idols to serve the living and true God" (1:9b). Yet the Thessalonians have reason to question the wisdom of their decision to convert. Not only are they facing trials (3:3–4), but the apostle who evangelized them has himself fled the persecution. Out of his concern over the stability of the faith of these new believers, Paul writes to remind them of his deep love and sacrificial work among them (2:1–12) and of the true instrument of their conversion: "For we know, brothers and sisters loved by God, that he has chosen you, because our gospel came to you not simply with words but also with power, with the Holy Spirit and deep conviction" (1:4–5a). Preaching of the gospel, accompanied by the power of the Spirit, is what led the Thessalonians to turn to the living God.

1 GOD'S INITIATIVE: CALLING AND ELECTION

One does not read very far in the Pauline letters before realizing that the apostle views entrance into the new realm as a work of the triune God. The Father sends the Son, whose death and resurrection open the doors to that realm, while the Spirit empowers the proclamation of the gospel so that it has the effect that God intends. Paul's realistic and negative appraisal of the old realm underlies this conviction about God's initiative. In that old realm, sin reigns (Rom 5:21), and people are therefore slaves to it (6:17, 18, 19, 20, 21). Satan has blinded people so that they cannot see and appreciate the riches of the new realm (2 Cor 4:4). As Paul says of Israel, "Even to this day when Moses is read, a veil covers their hearts" (3:15). It is only when a person "turns to the Lord" that the "veil is taken away" (v. 16). God must "shine his light in our hearts" to enable people to turn to Christ (4:6). Turning to the Lord is actuated, as we saw above, by the preaching of the gospel. God himself prepares the way for Paul's preaching, "opening doors" for the gospel (2:12; Col 4:3). As they preach, the apostles "spread the aroma of the knowledge of [God]," bringing death to some and life to others (2 Cor 2:14–16).

At the same time, God's work in bringing sinners into the new realm in no way cancels out the importance of human response in the process. Note, in the quote from 2 Corinthians 3:16, the reference to turning to the Lord. Again and again Paul refers to faith as the essential human response that transfers a person from old realm to new. How to configure the relationship between God's agency and human agency in this transfer has been a long-standing theological controversy, to which I will return at the end of the chapter. For now, however, I signal the direction of my treatment by noting the relative emphasis on these two agencies in Galatians 4:9: "But now that you know God—or rather are known by God."

We begin with two specific concepts that focus on this ultimate matter of "being known by God": calling and election.

Theologians typically distinguish election and calling. And one of the clearest textual bases for such a distinction is the well-known Romans 8:29–30: "For those God *foreknew* he also *predestined* to be conformed to the image of his Son, that he might be the firstborn among many brothers and sisters. And those he *predestined*, he also *called* [*kaleō*]; those he called [*kaleō*], he also justified; those he justified, he also glorified." Predestinating and—probably, see below—foreknowing refer to election, and these two terms are obviously logically prior to calling. However, this whole passage is governed and perhaps summarized by "calling" in verse 28: "And we know that in all things God works for the good of those who love him, who have been *called* [*klētos*] according to his purpose." Other passages suggest a close relationship between election and calling. For instance, in Romans 9:11–12, Paul teaches: "Yet, before the twins [Jacob and Esau] were born or had done anything good or bad—in order that God's purpose in election [*hē kat eklogēn prothesis*] might stand: not by works but by him who calls [*kaleō*]—she was told, 'The older will serve the younger'" (note also *kaleō* in 9:24–26). Similarly, 2 Thessalonians 2:13–14: "But we ought always to thank God for you, brothers and sisters loved by the Lord, because God *chose* [*haireō*] you as firstfruits [or 'from the beginning'] to be saved through the sanctifying work of the Spirit and through belief in the truth. He called [*kaleō*] you to this through our gospel, that you might share in the glory of our Lord Jesus Christ." And, in 1 Corinthians 1:24–28, Paul denotes the Corinthians' entry into the people of God with both the language of "calling" (vv. 24 and 26) and of "choosing" or electing (vv. 27 and 28).

Election and calling in Paul therefore are closely related yet also distinct. They refer to two stages in what is ultimately a single process by which God brings sinful humans into relationship with himself. Election usually has in view the eternal decision of God to bestow his favor on certain people (see below), while calling usually refers to the actuation of that decision in history. As Ridderbos puts it, the latter is "the effectual calling by the gospel through which God's electing grace is realized."[1] Yet Paul can also use language of either election or calling to refer to the whole process.

The importance of concepts in a given author's writings is often best determined not by the number or length of direct descriptions but by the frequency of casual or indirect references to it. By this measure, "calling" is a basic idea in Paul's theology. First Corinthians 7:17–24 illustrates this point well:

> Nevertheless, each person should live as a believer in whatever situation the Lord has assigned to them, just as God has **called** them. This is the rule I lay down in

---

1. Ridderbos, *Paul*, 235.

all the churches. Was a man already circumcised when he was *called*? He should not become uncircumcised. Was a man uncircumcised when he was *called*? He should not be circumcised. Circumcision is nothing and uncircumcision is nothing. Keeping God's commands is what counts. Each person should remain in the situation they were in when God *called* them.

Were you a slave when you were *called*? Don't let it trouble you—although if you can gain your freedom, do so. For the one who was a slave when *called* to faith in the Lord is the Lord's freed person; similarly, the one who was free when *called* is Christ's slave. You were bought at a price; do not become slaves of human beings. Brothers and sisters, each person, as responsible to God, should remain in the situation they were in when God *called* them.

Paul is not, of course, discussing "calling" in this passage. His concern is with believers who think their new spiritual identity requires that they change their marital status (7:1–16; see also 7:25–40). God's "calling" in this paragraph is clearly Paul's shorthand for the moment that we might characterize as "became a Christian," "was converted," "came to know Christ," etc. Nor have I cherry-picked a passage featuring "call" language that is an outlier in Paul. True, no other passage has quite the density of references to calling as this one. But throughout his letters, Paul consistently uses "call" in a similar way to mark the moment of conversion (Rom 4:17[?]; 8:30; 9:7 [Gk. *kaleō* translated as "will be reckoned" by NIV], 12, 24, 25, 26; 1 Cor 1:9; Gal 1:6, 15; 5:8, 13; Eph 4:1, 4; Col 3:15; 1 Thess 2:12; 4:7; 5:24; 2 Thess 2:14; 1 Tim 6:12; 2 Tim 1:9). Calling in Paul is "effectual," to use the language of systematic theology. That is, God's "call" in Paul is not simply an invitation to be saved but infallibly accomplishes the transfer of a person from old realm to new.[2] This understanding of calling is, to be sure, based mainly on negative evidence. Paul never suggests that any second step or response from an individual is needed to complete the act of calling. Yet this failure ever to mention the need of human response to make God's calling effective is surely telling. N. T. Wright has a point, therefore, when he points to "calling" as the standard Pauline way of denoting the transfer of humans into the new realm.[3]

Paul refers to the concept of election with several words. The Greek word translated "election," *eklogē*, occurs five times (Rom 9:11; 11:5, 7, 28; 1 Thess 1:4). Several other cognate words are also to be considered: *eklegomai*, "choose" (1 Cor 1:27 [2x], 28; Eph 1:4); *klēsis*, "calling" (Rom 11:29; 1 Cor 1:26; 7:20; Eph 1:18; 4:1, 4; Phil 3:14; 2 Thess 1:11; 2 Tim 1:9); *eklektos*, "elect" (Rom 8:33; 16:13; Col 3:12; 2 Tim 2:10; Titus 1:1

2. For a recent systematic treatment, see Jonathan Hoglund, *Called by Triune Grace: Divine Rhetoric and the Effectual Call* (Downers Grove, IL: InterVarsity Press, 2016).

3. See, e.g., N. T. Wright, *Paul in Fresh Perspective*, 111–13.

I am not so sure that I would endorse the implication that Wright draws from this, namely, that justification therefore does *not* denote the moment of transfer.

[1 Tim 5:21 with reference to angels]); and *klētos*, "called" (Rom 1:1, 6, 7; 8:28; 1 Cor 1:1, 2, 24). Finally, several other words or word groups also probably refer to the same theological concept: "predestine," *proorizō* (Rom 8:29, 30; Eph 1:5, 11 [1 Cor 2:7 with reference to Christ]); "purpose," *prothesis* (Rom 8:28; 9:11; Eph 1:11; 3:11; 2 Tim 1:9; 3:10); "choose [by lot]"/"inheritance," *klēroō/klēros* (Eph 1:11; Col 1:12); "appoint [*etheto*] . . . to receive salvation" (1 Thess 5:9); and "foreknow," *proginōskō* (Rom 8:29; 11:2). The over sixty references to election/calling suggest that the divine initiative in salvation is fundamentally important in Paul.

Election, of course, is a concept Paul derives from the Old Testament. Fundamental to Israel's identity is their having been chosen by God. Deuteronomy 7:6 is a classic text: "For you are a people holy to the LORD your God. The LORD your God has chosen [LXX *proaireō*] you out of all the peoples on the face of the earth to be his people, his treasured possession." See also, for example, Isaiah 41:8–9: "But you, Israel, my servant, Jacob, whom I have chosen [LXX *eklegō*], you descendants of Abraham my friend, I took you from the ends of the earth, from its farthest corners I called you. I said, 'You are my servant'; I have chosen you and have not rejected you." As these texts suggest, election is almost exclusively corporate in the Old Testament; God chooses a people, Israel.[4] The consciousness of being a special people, chosen by God himself, was built into the DNA of the Jewish people. Indeed, this sense of being a special, set-apart people was so strong that it became a stumbling block, leading many Jews to ignore their covenant obligations out of a false sense of security. This attitude was regularly decried by the prophets (see, e.g., Jeremiah's famous "temple sermon" [Jer 7]), and Paul continues this critique in passages such as Romans 2. But Paul goes much further than the prophets (though there are clear indications of this direction in passages such as Isa 40–66) in claiming that gentiles are being chosen and called to belong to the new realm alongside Jews (e.g., Rom 9:24–26). This extension of God's electing grace to gentiles necessarily forces a modification in the corporate structure of election. "Gentiles" do not compose a delimited group that might naturally be the object of God's calling. A movement away from a strictly corporate focus was underway already in the Old Testament. The development of the remnant idea in the latter stages of the Old Testament makes clear that there are important distinctions within Israel; to use Paul's words, "not all who are descended from Israel are Israel" (Rom 9:6). The Old Testament does not explicitly attach election language to this differentiation, but we may at least find here the seeds of a possible move to a more individual focus in election. The debate about who might be the "true Israel" in the Second Temple period would likely have further stimulated such a development.[5]

---

4. Some, however, would argue that God's dealings with Abraham and Jacob constitute examples of individual election (e.g., Robert A. Peterson, *Election and Free Will: God's Choice and Our Responsibility* [Wheaton, IL: Crossway, 2007], 38–41).

5. Seifrid, *Justification*, 85–89; Elliott, *Survivors of Israel*.

With the Old Testament evidence in view, it is not surprising that many interpreters think that Paul's election is also corporate. One popular form of this view has been put on the map by Barth, who viewed Christ, the "new Israel," as *the* elect one (see, e.g., Luke 9:35). Individual humans become elect, then, by being incorporated into Christ.[6] Advocates of this view, in addition to the admittedly strong evidence from the Old Testament and Second Temple Jewish literature, typically appeal especially to the plural forms in Romans 8:29–30—"*those* God foreknew he also predestined"—and to Ephesians 1:4, which also uses a plural pronoun and connects election with being "in Christ": "He chose us in him before the creation of the world." However, these texts are by no means decisive. Plural forms, while often seized on as clear evidence of a corporate focus in Paul, do not, in themselves, prove anything. The question is whether the forms are "corporate" or "distributive"—that is, whether Paul means to say "God chose our group" or "God chose each one of us." And everyone agrees that election, as just about everything else in Paul, is "in Christ." The issue again is whether Paul means "God chose us as/because we are incorporated into Christ" or "God's choosing of us takes place in Christ."[7] Romans 8:29 is ambiguous in the same way, though I think an individual focus makes better sense in this context. Not only is nothing said here about "in Christ" or the church, but the purpose of Paul is to assure individual believers—not the church as a whole—that God is working for *their* "good" and will glorify *each of them*.

The classic debated text of Pauline election is Romans 9:6–29. I refer to my exegesis of this text earlier in this volume (pp. 230–32). Here, I may simply reiterate my three reasons for thinking that this text refers to the salvation of individuals: (1) key vocabulary is characteristic of Paul's salvation teaching; (2) the rhetorical focus in the context requires a reference to individuals and their salvation; and (3) Paul's own rhetorical questions in verses 14 and 19 make best sense if the salvation of individuals is his ultimate reference. The evidence of the related language of "calling" that I surveyed above further supports the view that Paul's teaching about election focuses on the salvation of individuals. As the lengthy text from 1 Corinthians 7 that I quoted earlier makes clear, God's calling affects individuals; for example, verse 20: "*Each person* should remain in the situation they were in when God called them."

2 GRACE

Paul's reflex tendency to describe entrance into the new realm in terms of God's initiative is closely parallel to his focus on grace (as I suggested above). "Grace" (Gk. *charis*)

---

6. Barth, *CD* II/2. See also, e.g., William W. Klein, *The New Chosen People: A Corporate View of Election* (Eugene, OR: Wipf & Stock, 2015); Thornhill, *Chosen People*.

7. See, e.g., O'Brien, *Ephesians*, 99.

is one of the most important words in Paul's theological vocabulary. Dunn writes, "*Charis* joins *agape* at the very centre of Paul's gospel. More clearly than any other, these two words, 'grace' and 'love,' together sum up and most clearly characterize his whole theology."[8] The prominence of the concept of grace in Paul's teaching is due to at least two factors. First, grace is a fundamental character of God himself. This is revealed in the logic of Romans 4:4–5, among other texts. Justification, Paul argues here, cannot be based on works because that would mean that God, like an employer honoring a contract, would be obliged to justify a person. Paul rules this scenario out because a God who is obligated to his creatures would not be a God of grace. This text reveals that Paul's view of grace has to do especially with God's "wholly other" character. His unique, sovereign relationship to the cosmos means that what he does is always a matter of his own free decision. Strikingly, Paul does not here, or anywhere else, argue for grace as a constituent aspect of God—he assumes it, as kind of a theological postulate (for a similar argument, see Rom 11:6). A second reason why Paul features grace so significantly in his teaching is personal. He himself, the violent persecutor of the church who has become an apostle and servant of God, has radically experienced grace in his own life. "The grace of our Lord was poured out on me abundantly" (1 Tim 1:14; see also Rom 1:5; 12:3; 15:15; 1 Cor 3:10; 15:10; 2 Cor 12:9; Gal 1:15; 2:9; Eph 3:2, 8).

I noted in chapter 18 the fundamental role of grace in inaugurating the new realm. Yet God's grace is also needed to enable sinful humans to enter and flourish in the new realm. Indeed, Paul uses grace language especially often to characterize this moment of entrance; hence I discuss the concept here.

Paul refers to the concept of grace with several different words. But by far the most important is *charis*. The word occurs one hundred times in Paul's letters, with a range of meanings and nuances (the broad semantic domain of the word is attested in the long and complex entry in BDAG). However, particularly important in Paul is what we might call the arc of "giving"; as John M. G. Barclay summarizes, the word *charis* connotes "the graciousness of the giver, the grace conveyed, and the gratitude returned."[9]

At the heart of this semantic domain is the notion of "favor" or "gift." This sense is obvious when Paul uses the word to describe his collection of money for the Jerusalem believers (1 Cor 16:3; 2 Cor 8:1, 4, 6, 7, 19; 9:8). Similarly, he refers to his own apostolic ministry, and the ministry of others, as a *charis* from God (Rom 1:5; 12:3; 15:15; 1 Cor 3:10; Gal 2:9; Eph 3:7, 8; cf. Rom 12:6; Eph 4:7). At the end of the arc of giving, *charis* refers to the response of those who receive gifts, in the sense of gratitude or "thanks" (Rom 6:17; 7:25; 1 Cor 10:30; 15:57; 2 Cor 2:14; 8:16; Col 3:16; 1 Tim 1:12; 2 Tim 1:3). But Paul's most characteristic use of the word, and its most theologically significant,

---

8. Dunn, *Theology of Paul*, 320; see also du Toit, "Centrality of Grace," 85–89.

9. Barclay, *Paul and the Gift*, 582.

is its application to the manner in which God inaugurates, sustains, and calls people to enter his new realm in Christ. "Grace" is rooted in the nature of God, who is always free to do as he chooses in his interactions with his creatures.[10] As Romans 4:4–5 suggests, then, "grace" from God's side correlates with "faith" from the human side, while it stands in contrast to human "works." Titus 3:5–7 is another text that makes this point rather clearly: "He saved us, not because of righteous things we had done, but because of his mercy. He saved us through the washing of rebirth and renewal by the Holy Spirit, whom he poured out on us generously through Jesus Christ our Savior, so that, having been justified by his grace, we might become heirs having the hope of eternal life" (see also Rom 11:5–7). See also, for example, 2 Timothy 1:9: "He has saved us and called us to a holy life—not because of anything we have done but because of his own purpose and grace. This grace was given us in Christ Jesus before the beginning of time."

Of course, the *concept* of grace in Paul is signaled by additional words as well. The cognate verb *charizomai*, which Paul uses five times with the meaning "give freely," should also be considered. See, for example, Romans 8:32: "He who did not spare his own Son, but gave him up for us all—how will he not also, along with him, graciously give [NIV uses these two words for *charizomai*] us all things?" Ephesians 2:4–5 introduces two other key words into the mix: "But because of his great love [*agapēn*] for us, God, who is rich in mercy [*eleei*], made us alive with Christ even when we were dead in transgressions—it is by grace [*chariti*] you have been saved."

Paul refers to God's "mercy" over twenty times (the noun *eleos* occurs in Rom 9:23; 11:31; 15:9; Gal 6:16; Eph 2:4; 1 Tim 1:2; 2 Tim 1:2, 16, 18; Titus 3:5; the verb *eleeō* in Rom 9:15 [twice], 18; 11:30, 31, 32; 1 Cor 7:25; 2 Cor 4:1; Phil 2:27; 1 Tim 1:13, 16).[11] Scholars often distinguish God's "mercy" from his "grace" by suggesting that the former focuses on people as helpless and needy while "grace" focuses on them as guilty and undeserving.[12] There may be something to this, but, as the Ephesians text suggests, Paul can shift from one to the other without indication of much difference in meaning. We see the same interchange in 1 Timothy 1:13–16, where Paul accredits for his conversion both God's "mercy" (vv. 13, 16) and his grace (v. 14). God's love for his world and especially for sinful humans is a well-known feature of Paul's, and New Testament, teaching. God's love in Christ frames the great argument of Romans 5–8. His love initiates his intervention through Christ (5:8; cf. v. 5), and the believer therefore lives in the sphere of that undeserved and richly bestowed love (8:35, 37, 39; see also Rom 9:13, 25; 15:30[?]; 2 Cor 9:7; 13:14; Gal 2:20; Eph 1:4, 6 [God's love for

---

10. See also Wolter, *Paul*, 385.

11. See also the cognate words *oiktirmos* (Rom 12:1; 2 Cor 1:3; Phil 2:1; Col 3:12) and *oiktirō* (Rom 9:15 [twice]), often translated "compassion" or "have compassion."

12. E.g., Sam Storms, *Chosen for Life: The Case for Divine Election* (Wheaton, IL: Crossway, 2007), 78–79.

Christ]; 2:4; 3:18; 5:2, 25; 6:23; Phil 2:1[?]; Col 1:13 [love of God for Christ]; 3:12; 1 Thess 1:4; 2 Thess 2:13, 16; 3:5; 1 Tim 1:14). A final, related word group to be added to the concept of grace is "kindness" or "goodness" (*chrēstotēs*; see Rom 2:4; 11:22 [three times]; Eph 2:7; Titus 3:4; and note also *chrēstos*, "kind," in Rom 2:4). At the risk of introducing distinctions that are not clear in Paul, we might suggest that God's "love" and "kindness" are closer to what we might call divine "attributes," while "mercy" and "grace" are the outworking of these attributes as he interacts with his created world.[13]

The free and utterly undeserved activity of God in inaugurating, sustaining, and calling people to enjoy the benefits of the new realm is at the very heart of Paul's theology. That being the case, it is natural that Paul often "locates" God's grace in Christ, as, for example, in Romans 5:15, where the "trespass" of Adam is contrasted with "God's grace and the gift that came by the grace of the one man, Jesus Christ" (see also v. 17). As Michael Gorman puts it, "The interweaving of God's grace/love and initiative (a theological claim properly speaking) and Christ's grace/love and self-gift (a christological claim) is certainly one of the richest and most profound contributions of Paul to Christian theology."[14] So basic is God's grace to his new realm that that realm can be characterized simply by the word "grace." God's grace "reigns" in the new realm (Rom 5:20, 21). Paul can characterize his apostolic work as an "administration of God's grace" (Eph 3:2). The inauguration of the new realm can be characterized as the "appearance" of grace (Titus 2:11; see also Phil 1:7; Col 1:6). Nor is grace related only to the entrance into the new realm. It is, rather, constitutive of the new realm in all its aspects; believers "stand in grace" (Rom 5:2) and are "located" "under grace" (Rom 6:14, 15)—as Beker put it, "the domain of our life in Christ."[15] In his most common use of the word, at both the beginning and end of most of his letters, Paul expresses his wish that the people of God experience that grace (Rom 1:7; 16:20; 1 Cor 1:3; 2 Cor 1:2; 13:13; Gal 1:3; 6:18; Eph 1:2; 6:24; Phil 1:2; 4:23; Col 1:2; 4:18; 1 Thess 1:1; 5:28; 2 Thess 1:2; 3:18; 1 Tim 1:2; 6:21; 2 Tim 1:2; 4:22; Titus 1:4; 3:15; Phlm 3, 25).

The word *charis* appears over 150 times in the Greek Old Testament, usually in the sense of "favor" (most often translating Hebrew *khen*, "favor"). Dunn suggests that Paul chose the word *charis* to combine nuances of both *khen* and the more theologically significant *khesed* (variously translated as "mercy," "covenant loyalty," "faithfulness") for "the unilateralness of *chen* and the lasting commitment of *chesed*."[16] While these lexical connections should not be ignored, Paul's use of the word owes just as much to the general teaching about God's initiative in his relationship with Israel. Deuteronomy 9:4–6 is a classic text:

---

13. See, e.g., Louis Berkhof, *Systematic Theology* (Grand Rapids: Eerdmans, 1938), 70–72.

14. Gorman, *Death of the Messiah*, 173.

15. Beker, *Paul the Apostle*, 265.

16. Dunn, *Theology of Paul*, 320–21. The word *khesed* is translated with a number of Greek words, but *eleos* ("mercy") is the most common.

After the LORD your God has driven them out before you, do not say to yourself, "The LORD has brought me here to take possession of this land because of my righteousness." No, it is on account of the wickedness of these nations that the LORD is going to drive them out before you. It is not because of your righteousness or your integrity that you are going in to take possession of their land; but on account of the wickedness of these nations, the LORD your God will drive them out before you, to accomplish what he swore to your fathers, to Abraham, Isaac and Jacob. Understand, then, that it is not because of your righteousness that the LORD your God is giving you this good land to possess, for you are a stiff-necked people.

While the Old Testament story of God's interactions with Israel provides the basis for Paul's teaching about grace, his own environment, both Judaism and Greco-Roman culture, is also important. In a significant monograph, John M. G. Barclay argues that Paul's teaching on grace needs to be situated within the larger issue of "gift."[17] The exchange of gifts was an important thread in the social fabric of Paul's culture, used to cement relationships, especially between patrons and their dependents. One often gave a gift, then, to those who already had some claim on a person. And they were often given with the expectation, or hope, of a return of the favor—that is, to use Barclay's terminology, the gift was "circular." In the Old Testament, as I noted above, God's gift of election to Israel is "incongruous"—that is, it is given "without regard to the worth of the recipient."[18] However, in both the Jewish world of Paul's day and in the wider culture, gifts were often viewed as being given to those who had some claim on the one giving the gift. In contrast, Paul's understanding of the gift of God's grace is that it is given without any regard for the recipient. As I noted in chapter 18, Barclay's claim that "gift" or "grace" took different forms enables us to fine-tune the contrast between Paul and his Jewish world. Both certainly believed in "grace," but they defined it differently.

For our purposes here, four aspects of Paul's teaching on grace as Barclay identifies them are particularly worth emphasizing. First, as I noted above, in contrast to most of his contemporaries, Paul viewed grace as incongruous. This view of grace, of course, is the usual way it has been understood in Paul, but it deserves mentioning again. God inaugurates the new realm and calls individuals to participate in it who, by virtue of sin, have absolutely no claim on God's favor. Second, God's grace is *efficacious*: it infallibly accomplishes what God intends it to accomplish.[19] Third, while God's grace is

---

17. Barclay, *Paul and the Gift.* For the Greco-Roman context of Paul's teaching, and agreeing with many of Barclay's conclusions, see also James R. Harrison, *Paul's Language of Grace in Its Graeco-Roman Context*, WUNT 2/172 (Tübingen: Mohr Siebeck, 2003).

18. Barclay, *Paul and the Gift*, 73.

19. This has often been labeled "irresistible grace." However, the word "irresistible" may connote that God imposes his will on people in a way that does not accord with genuine human responsibility (see, e.g., Michael Allen, *Sanctification*, New Studies in Dogmatics [Grand Rapids: Zondervan Academic, 2017], 244–46).

unconditioned, it is not *unconditional*. That is, God's grace is not given after the fulfillment of prior conditions, but it is given in expectation of a response. Indeed, Paul teaches that response is absolutely necessary, since the salvific goal of God in giving the gift is not attained without appropriate human response. Barclay here reminds us that no one in the ancient world would have expected a gift to be given without thought of subsequent obligation. Fourth, incongruous grace is fundamental to Paul's own experience and to his preaching and theology. "It is the incongruous grace that Paul traces in the Christ-event and experiences in the Gentile mission that is the explosive force that demolishes old criteria of worth and clears space for innovative communities that inaugurate new patterns of social existence."[20] It was not, then, the gentile mission that generated Paul's distinctive theology. "Paul's radical policy in his Gentile mission is not a protest against 'nationalism': it is the disruptive aftershock of the incongruous gift of Christ."[21]

3 HUMAN RESPONSE: FAITH

As I noted in the introduction to this chapter, Paul's emphasis on God's role in bringing people into the new realm by no means excludes the meaningful role of humans. Paul refers to this human agency in a variety of ways. People "call on the name of our Lord Jesus" (1 Cor 1:2; cf. Rom 10:13, 14), accept the good news (Rom 10:16), "find" God (Rom 10:20 [=Isa 65:1]), "hear" the gospel (Eph 1:13; Col 1:6; see Gal 3:3, 5), "put [their] hope in Christ" (Eph 1:12), "welcome" the message (1 Thess 1:6), and turn "from idols to serve the living and true God" (1 Thess 1:9). Repentance, which has a strong presence in the Christian theological tradition, has only a small role in Paul. He uses the noun (*metanoia*) four times (Rom 2:24; 2 Cor 7:9, 10; 2 Tim 2:25) and the verb (*metanoeō*) once (2 Cor 12:21; see also *metamelomai* in 2 Cor 7:8 [twice]). It is possible that Paul did not think "repentance" language was strong enough to denote the epochal transfer from old realm to new.[22] Another aspect of human response is baptism. As I will argue below (pp. 588–90), Paul views baptism in water as one aspect of "conversion-initiation." It does not itself effect conversion but puts a seal on conversion and marks a person's entry into the new realm.

By far the most important language for the human role in entering the new realm is faith. Benjamin Schliesser rightly identifies "an explosive increase in talk of faith in early Christianity,"[23] and Paul certainly contributes to this explosion. He uses the noun

---

20. Barclay, *Paul and the Gift*, 498–99.

21. Barclay, *Paul and the Gift*, 361. This being the case, then, Paul sees grace as important not only in enabling gentiles to join the people of God; it is necessary for Jews also (Starling, *Not My People*, 215). See my review of Barclay's book for more detail on these points (Douglas J. Moo, "John Barclay's *Paul and the Gift*

and the New Perspective on Paul," *Themelios* 41.2 [Aug 2016]: 279–88, http://themelios.thegospelcoalition.org/article/john-barclays-paul-and-the-gift-and-the-new-perspective-on-paul).

22. Dunn, *Theology of Paul*, 326–29.

23. Benjamin Schliesser, "Faith in Early Christianity: An Encyclopedic and Bibliographical Outline," in *Glaube: Das*

"faith," *pistis*, 142 times, the verb "believe" or "have faith," *pisteuō*, 54 times, and the adjective "faithful," *pistos*, 33 times. Paul ties the language of faith so often to Christian experience that he can use "faith" as shorthand for the new realm and its central concerns and teaching. Thus he summarizes his preaching as "the message concerning faith" (Rom 10:8), he characterizes the inauguration of the new realm in terms of the "coming" of faith (Gal 3:23, 25),[24] and uses faith language to denote Christians (e.g., 1 Thess 1:3, 7, 8; 2:10, 13; 3:2, 5, 6, 7, 10), even as "unfaith" language—Greek *a-pistos*—denotes those outside the new realm (1 Cor 6:6; 7:12, 13, 14 [2x], 15; 10:27; 14:22 [2x], 23, 24; 2 Cor 4:4; 6:14; 1 Tim 5:8; Titus 1:15). As Michael Wolter notes, "faith" in Paul functions both as "identity marker"—unifying the church—and "boundary marker"—setting off the church from its culture.[25] Paul's tendency to use "faith" with this broad application climaxes in places where he uses "*the* faith" to refer to what we might today call "Christianity."

This application of the language of faith is particularly common in the Pastoral Epistles. Timothy and Titus are both called Paul's "[true] son in the faith" (1 Tim 1:2; Titus 1:4), Timothy is to be nourished on "the truths of the faith" (1 Tim 4:6), and older men are to be "sound in faith" (Titus 2:2). Conversely, Paul warns about people who have "denied the faith" (1 Tim 5:8), or "wandered from the faith" (1 Tim 6:10), or "departed from the faith" (1 Tim 6:21), or "as far as faith is concerned are rejected" (2 Tim 3:8). This use of "faith" language in the Pastorals is often singled out as one of the reasons to think that the letters were written in Paul's name after his life by a follower who had a more "static" and "creedal" view of the faith. However, similar language occurs in other Pauline letters (see "unity in the faith" in Eph 4:13 and "strengthened in the faith" in Col 2:7),[26] including what is probably his earliest letter (Gal 1:23).[27] This use of "faith" in Paul is sometimes characterized as "the faith that one believes" (Latin *fides quae creditur*) as opposed to the "faith that believes" (*fides qua creditur*), but this may drive an unnecessary wedge between these two notions. Paul's "*the* faith" is not the object of belief but a semantic extension of the central Christian identity marker of "believing" into an abstract characterization of the movement.

In any case, the distinctive and theologically central usage of faith language in Paul is to describe the disposition toward Christ and the gospel that God requires of his people. Faith in the intellectual sense of believing that something is true is part of this

Verständnis des Glaubens im frühen Christentum und in seiner jüdischen und Hellenistisch-Römischen Umwelt, ed. Jörg Frey, Benjamin Schliesser, and Nadine Ueberschaer, WUNT 2/373 (Tübingen: Mohr Siebeck, 2017), 3.

24. I argue elsewhere that "faith" in these verses refers to the new christological focus of human believing in the new realm (pp. 71–74).

25. Wolter, *Paul*, 253–54.

26. This verse might refer to being "established by means of [one's] faith [*tē pistei*]," but perhaps more likely means "established in the sphere of *the* faith" (Moo, *Colossians*, 181–82). There are several other possible instances of this use of *pistis* in the earlier Pauline letters: Rom 12:6; 1 Cor 16:13; 2 Cor 13:5; Phil 1:27; Col 1:23.

27. Moo, *Galatians*, 114.

disposition, as, for example, 1 Thessalonians 4:14 reveals: "For we believe that Jesus died and rose again, and so we believe that God will bring with Jesus those who have fallen asleep in him" (see also Rom 10:9). But Pauline faith goes much further, involving a deep-seated attitude of trust and commitment to Christ and the message about him. Pauline faith, as theologians throughout the history of the church have emphasized, is not mere mental assent but a powerful movement of the will.[28]

A better appreciation of Pauline faith can be gained by taking account of its positive and negative accompaniments.

Positively, as I noted above, faith is correlated with grace (see my comments on Rom 4:4–5). Grace as the content and mode of God's giving somehow requires that the only appropriate human response to such giving is faith. Since grace, as we have seen, connotes God's unconstrained freedom to act as he chooses, faith must be of such a nature that it imposes no constraint on God. This particular characteristic of human faith becomes clearer when we turn to the negative accompaniment. We see again in Romans 4:4–5 that faith is contrasted with "works."

The contrast between faith and "works" or "works of the law," is, of course, a prominent theme in Paul (see especially 435–39). As I noted earlier, many interpreters, especially those who adopt some form of the New Perspective on Paul, argue that the former should be folded into the latter: "works" is simply an abbreviation of "works of the law." The contrast, then, is limited to faith versus the Mosaic law or the Torah. Paul is not polemicizing against general human works but only against Torah adherence. Without repeating those arguments here, I simply remind the reader that it is far more likely that "works of the law" should be seen as a specific form of "works." The antithesis between works and faith that was so important for Reformation theology has been chipped away at from the other side as well, by arguing that faith in Paul is basically Christ's own faith. However, even if the phrase "faith of Christ" has this sense (which I doubt; see 379–82), Paul often clearly refers to human "believing." Both faith and works in Paul therefore often, if not always, refer to an anthropological contrast between "believing" and "doing." The Reformers were completely justified in finding in Paul a fundamental opposition between human doing and human believing.

"Believing" in Paul, then, is not something that a person "does"—it is "fundamentally receptive."[29] Luther compared faith to holding out "open hands"—willingly receiving the gift that God through the gospel seeks to give people.[30] This opening

---

28. Jeanette Hagen Pifer helpfully summarizes faith in Paul as involving a turning from oneself and a "positioning of oneself in a dependent relationship to Christ by the Spirit"—"not I but Christ" (Gal 2:19–21) (*Faith as Participation: An Exegetical Study of Some Key Pauline Texts*, WUNT 2/486 [Tübingen: Mohr Siebeck, 2019], e.g., 219–20).

29. Schreiner, *Paul*, 248.

30. Martin Luther, *Lectures on Galatians 1535, Chapters 1–4*, vol. 26 of *Luther's Works*, ed. Jaroslav Pelikan (St. Louis: Concordia, 1963), 208–9. Calvin makes the same point with a different metaphor: "We compare faith to a kind of vessel; for unless we come empty and with the mouth of our soul open

of the hands is itself activated by God's Spirit in the preaching of the gospel. In two texts, in fact, Paul may specifically label faith a "gift" from God. In the well-known Ephesians 2:8–9, Paul says: "For it is by grace you have been saved, through faith—and this is not from yourselves, it is the gift of God—not by works, so that no one can boast." Yet because the Greek word for "this" (*touto*, neuter) does not "agree" with the Greek word for "faith" (*pistis*, feminine), the connection between them is not clear. Contrary to some, "this" could refer to "faith," since neuter pronouns sometimes refer back to the concept denoted by a Greek word; for example, "this concept of faith . . . is the gift of God." However, it may be more likely that the "this" refers to the whole process of being "saved" by union with Christ through faith (see p. 278). Philippians 1:29 is clearer: "For it has been granted to you on behalf of Christ not only to believe in him, but also to suffer for him." Some interpreters dismiss the significance of this text because its focus is on suffering.[31] However, this does not detract from the fact that Paul here teaches, or assumes, that faith, like suffering, is a gracious gift from God.[32] Whatever we conclude from these two verses, believing, in Paul, is not a purely human "decision"; it is a response that the gospel itself triggers. "Faith comes from hearing the message," Paul claims (Rom 10:17).[33] Paul is concerned that his hearers' faith be securely grounded in the Spirit's work through his preaching (1 Cor 2:4–5). At the same time, it is important not to go as far as some theologians, who virtually view believing as something that God does through us. Humans believe. Faith is an act that, while empowered by the Spirit and the gospel, humans are responsible for. It is especially important, finally, to emphasize the christological focus of faith in Paul. The verb *pisteuō* and the noun *pistis* often have Christ as their object. As I stressed earlier, then, faith possesses the power to justify not in itself but as the agency by which we are joined to Christ. Likewise, faith enables the believer to be sustained and to grow in his or her Christian experience because it keeps us in intimate relationship with Christ, who supplies all believers need for spiritual growth and ultimate salvation.

The general conception of faith I have sketched in the last paragraph stands in continuity with the general Reformation teaching, where "faith" versus "works" was a fundamental soteriological contrast. This conception of faith is, however, often criticized as opening the door to a lackadaisical attitude to Christian discipleship. As a

---

to seek Christ's grace, we are not capable of receiving Christ" (*Institutes* 3.11.7).

31. E.g., Ridderbos, *Paul*, 234.

32. E.g., Schnelle, *Theology of the New Testament*, 307–9; Francis Watson, "The Triune Divine Identity: Reflections on Pauline God-Language, in Disagreement with J. D. G. Dunn," *JSNT* 80 (2000): 99–124. Mark Seifrid (over-?) emphasizes this

point, commenting on Melanchthon's interpretation of Romans (Mark Seifrid, "The Text of Romans and the Theology of Melanchthon," in *Reformation Readings of Paul: Explorations in History and Exegesis*, ed. R. Michael Allen and Jonathan A. Linebaugh [Downers Grove, IL: InterVarsity Press, 2015], 97–122).

33. For this construal of the debated phrase *to rhēma tēs pisteōs*, see, e.g., Moo, *Romans* (NICNT), 684.

way of guarding against this all-too-common problem, many contemporary interpreters suggest that we expand our view of faith to include, in some form, obedience.[34] Advocates of this redefinition, negatively, dismiss the faith-versus-works contrast by interpreting the latter narrowly in terms of "works of the law." Paul can certainly use *pist-* words to refer to being "faithful" (see *pistis* in Rom 3:5; Gal 5:22[?]; 1 Tim 2:7; 2 Tim 2:22; 3:10; Titus 2:10; *pisteuō* in 1 Cor 9:7) or with the meaning "entrust" (see the passive of *pisteuō* in Rom 3:2; Gal 2:7; 1 Thess 2:4; 1 Tim 1:11; Titus 1:3). Further evidence of a semantic overlap between faith and obedience is the way Paul can use them in similar contexts. Thus, while Paul often refers to "faith" as the means of entry into the new realm, he can also speak of "obeying" the gospel (Rom 10:16; the verb is *hypakouō*, which NIV translates as "accepted"; see also 2 Thess 1:8; and cf. Rom 15:18). The phrase that brackets the whole letter to the Romans, "the obedience of faith" (1:5; 16:26; my translation), is then cited as a clear enunciation of the overlapping nature of these two ideas in Paul.

An expansive notion of *pistis* that includes both "faith" and "faithfulness" in Paul is, it is argued, a natural conclusion from the Old Testament use of "faith" language: the noun *'emunah* and the cognate verb *'aman*. The former, as the lexica indicate, almost always means "faithfulness," "trustworthiness," or "steadfastness." Typical is Deuteronomy 32:4, where Moses confesses that the Lord is "a faithful God." It is often argued that the verb also focuses mainly or exclusively on the idea of being faithful. However, this is not clear. To be sure, the verb often has this sense: Samuel is considered a "trustworthy prophet of the LORD" (1 Sam 3:20 NRSV; see also, e.g., 1 Sam 22:14; Isa 1:21, 26—this meaning is especially common when the verb is in the niphal).[35] But the verb can sometimes refer to factual, or intellectual conviction, as, for example, in 1 Kings 10:7: the Queen of Sheba "did not believe the reports until I came and my own eyes had seen it" (NRSV). However, in several key texts this verb refers to a person's fundamental posture or disposition toward God—the basic response to God that leads to, but does not clearly include, faithfulness. Note the following verses:

---

34. See, e.g., Matthew W. Bates, *Salvation by Allegiance Alone* (Grand Rapids: Baker, 2017); Gorman, *Becoming the Gospel*, 23, 90–91; Garlington, *Faith, Obedience, and Perseverance*, 146, 163; Timothy G. Gombis, *Paul: A Guide for the Perplexed* (London: T&T Clark, 2010), 101–6. The treatment of faith in Mundle also moves in this direction (Wilhelm Mundle, *Der Glaubensbegriff des Paulus: Eine Untersuchung zur Dogmengeschichte des ältesten Christentums* [Darmstadt: Wissenschaftliche Buchgesellschaft, 1977]). Nijay K. Gupta, while recognizing a spectrum of usage in Paul, stresses the concept of trust and denies that Paul pits faith versus works (*Paul and the Language of Faith* [Grand Rapids: Eerdmans, 2020], see, e.g., 177–90).

35. For surveys of the OT and Jewish use of the language, see, e.g., William Henry Paine Hatch, *The Pauline Idea of Faith in Its Relation to Jewish and Hellenistic Religion* (Cambridge: Harvard University Press, 1917), 1–29; Dennis R. Lindsay, *Josephus and Faith: Pistis and Pisteuein as Faith Terminology in the Writings of Flavius Josephus and in the New Testament*, AGJU 19 (Leiden: Brill, 1993), 21–73. Schliesser notes that the Latin *fides* often refers to "trustworthiness," with the corresponding idea of mutual trust within a relationship ("Faith in Early Christianity").

And when the LORD sent you from Kadesh-barnea, saying, "Go up and occupy the land that I have given you," you rebelled against the command of the LORD your God, neither *trusting* him nor obeying him. (Deut 9:23 NRSV)

> If you do not *stand firm in faith*,
>   you shall not stand at all. (Isa 7:9 NRSV)

And when the Israelites saw the mighty hand of the LORD displayed against the Egyptians, the people feared the LORD and *put their trust* in him and in Moses his servant. (Exod 14:31)

In spite of this, you did not *trust* in the LORD your God. (Deut 1:32)

You found his heart *faithful* to you, and you made a covenant with him to give to his descendants the land of the Canaanites, Hittites, Amorites, Perizzites, Jebusites and Girgashites. You have kept your promise because you are righteous. (Neh 9:8)

> Their hearts were not *loyal* to him,
>   they were not faithful to his covenant. (Ps 78:37)

So this is what the Sovereign LORD says:

> "See, I lay a stone in Zion, a tested stone,
>   a precious cornerstone for a sure foundation;
> the one who *relies* on it
>   will never be stricken with panic." (Isa 28:16)

> "You are my witnesses," declares the LORD,
>   "and my servant whom I have chosen,
> so that you may know and *believe* me
>   and understand that I am he.
> Before me no god was formed,
>   nor will there be one after me." (Isa 43:10)

The Ninevites *believed* God. A fast was proclaimed, and all of them, from the greatest to the least, put on sackcloth. (Jonah 3:5)

In all these texts, the language of "believing" refers to a fundamental attitude of trust in and dependence on God—a meaning that it is quite close to the typical

Pauline use of *pist-* language. To be sure, as we have seen, this sense is not clearly found in the Hebrew noun and therefore not typically in the noun *pistis*, which is the usual translation of the Hebrew word in the LXX. However, rather than thinking that the verb *pisteuō* in Paul takes on the sense of "faithful" that is otherwise unattested for this verb, it makes better sense to think that *pistis* in Paul is accommodated to its cognate verb, focusing on the specific kind of "faithfulness" that the gospel calls for—humble acceptance and commitment to the Christ the gospel proclaims.

While the *words* "faith" (*pistis*) and "believe" (*pisteuō*) are the overwhelmingly most important means by which Paul denotes the human response to God's gracious gospel message, we must of course remember that it is ultimately the *concept* that is important. And two other words deserve at least brief mention in this regard. I start with the Old Testament, where the Hebrew verb *batakh* often occurs in the sense of "rely on" or "trust in." A good example is the taunt directed at the Israelite leaders by the spokesperson of the Assyrian king, who warns them not to "depend on" the God of Israel to deliver them (Isa 36:4–9). Hezekiah, of course, responds by putting his trust in the Lord, displaying the quality for which he is praised in the introduction to his reign in 2 Kings: "Hezekiah trusted in [*batakh*] the Lord, the God of Israel. There was no one like him among all the kings of Judah, either before him or after him" (2 Kgs 18:5). Two other texts illustrating this use of the word are:

> "Trust in the Lord forever, for the Lord, the Lord himself, is the Rock eternal" (Isa 26:4)
> "But blessed is the one who trusts [LXX: *peithō*] in the Lord, whose confidence is in him" (Jer 17:7)

These texts are not directly relevant to Paul's use of the words "faith"/"believe," since the LXX never translates the Hebrew verb in these texts (*batakh*) with the *pist-* root. But these passages might be relevant to the concept of faith in Paul. Note, for instance, Psalm 78:22 [77:22 LXX], where the parallelism suggests that "believe" (Heb. *'aman*/ LXX *pisteuō*) and "trust" (Heb. *batakh*/LXX *elpizō*) interpret each other: "For they did not *believe* in God or *trust* in his deliverance." Moreover, Paul uses two of the Greek words that regularly translate this Hebrew word several times in a way that echoes these Old Testament texts and that contributes to our appreciation of the concept of faith.[36] See, for example:

---

36. Two Gk. words consistently translate *batakh*: *elpizō*, "hope," and *peithō*, "depend on," "trust in" (in its 2nd perfect form).

"If only for this life we *have hope* in Christ, we are of all people most to be pitied"
    (1 Cor 15:19)
"He has delivered us from such a deadly peril, and he will deliver us again.
    On him we have *set our hope* that he will continue to deliver us" (2 Cor 1:10)
"That is why we labor and strive, because we have *put our hope* in the living
    God, who is the Savior of all people, and especially of those who believe"
    (1 Tim 4:10)
"The widow who is really in need and left all alone *puts her hope* in God and
    continues night and day to pray and to ask God for help" (1 Tim 5:5)
"Command those who are rich in this present world not to be arrogant nor to put
    their hope in wealth, which is so uncertain, but to *put their hope* in God, who
    richly provides us with everything for our enjoyment" (1 Tim 6:17)
"Indeed, we felt we had received the sentence of death. But this happened that we
    might not *rely on* ourselves but on God, who raises the dead" (2 Cor 1:9)

In these texts, Paul uses "hope" (*elpizō*; in the first five verses) and "depend on"
(*peithō*; in the last verse), similarly as in the Old Testament texts cited above, to refer to
a basic stance of trust in or reliance on God or Christ. These texts enrich and elaborate
the concept of faith in Paul.

Of course, the two Old Testament texts that shed the greatest light on the Pauline
notion of faith are those that he explicitly cites with reference to faith: Genesis 15:6
and Habakkuk 2:4. While the meaning of both texts is debated, a good case can be
made that *'aman* in both refers to this same fundamental disposition toward God.[37]
Genesis 15:6, of course, is the key text in Paul's long discussion of Abraham's faith
in Romans 4 (see also Gal 3:6). While not perhaps the first time Abraham exercised
faith, his faith in response to the promise of God in Genesis 15 is the first time it is
mentioned. Paul's overall purpose in this chapter is to marshal scriptural support for
his claim that justification is given by faith rather than by works, and to show also how
Abraham foreshadows the inclusion of Jews and gentiles together in the people of God.
Yet Paul indirectly elaborates here also his notion of faith. In a startling juxtaposition,
Paul claims that Abraham's faith was "against all hope" and yet "in hope" (Rom 4:18).
That is, he believed God's promise about his numerous descendants "against" the
physical evidence (his advanced age and Sarah's infertility [v. 19]), but he did so in the
hopeful confidence that the God he serves is "the God who gives life to the dead and
calls into being things that were not" (v. 17). Paul also makes clear that Abraham's faith
became his settled disposition toward God, meaning that later in his life, Abraham

37. See, e.g, Moo, "Genesis 15:6"; idem, *Galatians*, 207; idem,
Romans (NICNT), 81.

"did not waver through unbelief . . . but was strengthened in his faith" (v. 20). Paul's brief citation of Habakkuk 2:4 in two places (Rom 1:17 and Gal 3:11) reveals much less about faith. The issue here, indeed, is complicated by the widespread view that *'emunah* in this verse should be translated "faithfulness" rather than "faith" (see, e.g., NIV). However, a case can be made here also for viewing the word as indicating the basic stance toward God that the difficult circumstances of Habakkuk's day require—a trust or reliance on God and his promise (e.g., the vision) that is not far from the Pauline idea of faith.[38] Such a stance of trust in God is necessary in Paul's day also, when the unexpected turn in salvation history (gentiles streaming into the kingdom of God) has perhaps given some reason for wondering just what God is about.

Paul undoubtedly forges an important connection between faith and obedience. However, it is the nature of that connection that must be explored. For instance, it is interesting that Paul's language of "obeying the gospel" (see ESV, NRSV) in Romans 10:16 has no exact parallel in terms of "faith" language. Paul never makes the gospel, or the message, the object of believing.[39] "The obedience of faith" in Romans 1:5 and 16:26 is much debated, but I would argue that it refers to the obedience that arises from faith (see p. 199). The two, in other words, are intimately connected but nevertheless distinct.[40] Moreover, if "faith," as some argue, includes the notion of obedience, it is difficult to see why Paul would have had to add "obedience" to the word. While, then, Paul can use *pist-* language to denote faithfulness, it is unlikely that he combines the meanings faith and faithfulness in any given occurrence of the language.[41]

Of course, an insistence that faith not be expanded to *include* works or obedience does not mean that we are restricting Pauline faith to a fruitless intellectual act such as James decries (Jas 2:14–26). If we insist on not *mixing* faith and works, it is also vital not to *separate* them.[42] The more we stress the need to wall off faith from works in terms of their semantic ranges, the more we need to define faith in such a way that a natural—indeed, inevitable—path from the one to the other is ensured. Faith is distinct from works, but for Paul faith is also always a "faith working through love" (Gal 5:6, my translation). Faith in Paul includes a 180-degree turn of the compass travel arrow,

---

38. Watson suggests, indeed, that both are implied here: "'Faithfulness' speaks more adequately of the way of life that corresponds to the vision, whereas 'faith' speaks of the fundamental orientation towards the vision presupposed in this way of life; but each clearly entails the other" (*Paul and the Hermeneutics of Faith*, 148). I would merely comment that, while both may be entailed, the focus here appears to be on the latter idea.

39. There are three possible exceptions, but none is clear. The phrase *akoēs pisteōs* in Gal 3:2, 5 might mean "believing what you heard" (NIV), but against this, see Moo, *Galatians*, 182–83. The phrase *tē pistei tou euangeliou* in Phil 1:27 might mean "faith directed toward the gospel," but probably means "faith that has to

do with the gospel." Likewise, the genitive phrase *pistei alētheias* in 2 Thess 2:13 might mean "belief in the truth" (NIV), but might more likely mean "true faith."

40. Brown, "'Obedience of Faith' in Romans."

41. Kevin W. McFadden, "Does Πίστις Mean 'Faith(Fulness)' in Paul?," *TynBul* 66 (2015): 251–70. For criticisms of the expansive meaning of "faith," see, e.g., Will N. Timmins, "A Faith Unlike Abraham's: Matthew Bates on Salvation by Allegiance Alone," *JETS* 61 (2018): 595–615; Horton, *Justification*, 2:411–15.

42. Du Toit decries the tendency to underplay the importance of obedience in Paul's theology ("Faith and Obedience in Paul," in Breytenbach and du Toit, *Focusing on Paul*, 117–27).

the arrow that sets the course for our lives. In our sinful condition, our travel arrow is pointed to self and world. Integral to Pauline faith is the new orientation of that travel arrow—pointing now to Christ and others. I have used the language of "disposition" to describe faith throughout this chapter. I want now to highlight the usefulness of this language to chart a secure path from faith to works. Jonathan Edwards is one of many theologians who have found this language appropriate to characterize biblical faith:

> As the whole soul in all its faculties is the proper subject and agent of faith, so undoubtedly there are two things in saving faith, viz., belief of the truth and an answerable disposition of heart. And therefore faith may be defined, a thorough believing of what the gospel reveals of a Saviour of sinners, as true and perfectly good, with the exercises of an answerable disposition towards him.[43]

The language of disposition leads to another important point about Pauline faith. While we are considering the concept in a chapter on "entering" the new realm, it is vital to recognize that Paul views faith as fundamental to the Christian life from beginning to end: "Coming to faith brings salvation, and holding on to faith assures it."[44] Paul often thanks God for the continuing faith of the believers to whom he writes (Eph 1:15; Col 1:4; 1 Thess 1:3, 8; 2 Thess 1:3, 4; 2 Tim 1:5; Phlm 5), he exhorts believers to stand firm "by faith" (2 Cor 1:24), and assumes that the faith of believers will "continue to grow" (2 Cor 10:15). (Faith throughout the Christian life is also clear in Gal 2:20; Eph 6:16; Phil 1:27; 2:17; Col 2:5, 7; 1 Thess 3:2, 6, 8, 10; 5:8; 1 Tim 1:4; 2:15; 6:11; 2 Tim 1:13; 4:7; Titus 2:2.)

Finally, we should also note that faith in Paul serves to bind believers together; we are all part of the "household of faith" (Gal 6:9 ESV).[45] The "identity marker" of Torah that characterized the people of God in the past has now been replaced by the identity marker of faith. An important application of this principle in Paul, rightly highlighted by New Perspective advocates, is its inclusiveness. As Paul frequently emphasizes in

---

43. "Observations concerning Faith," §§40–50 ("Sin in Paul," in *Fallen: A Theology of Sin*, ed. Christopher W. Morgan and Robert A. Peterson [Wheaton, IL: Crossway, 2013], 107–30). Some authors think that Edwards therefore views faith as incorporating obedience (William B. Evans, *Imputation and Impartation: Union with Christ in American Reformed Theology*, Studies in Christian History and Thought [Eugene, OR: Wipf & Stock, 2008], 96, 108), but I do not read Edwards as going this far. For remarks that go in the same direction as Edwards, see also, e.g., Kyle B. Wells, *Grace and Agency in Paul and Second Temple Judaism: Interpreting the Transformation of the Heart*, NovTSup 157 (Leiden: Brill, 2015), 306–7; Thiselton, *Hermeneutics of Doctrine*, 349–52; Barclay, *Paul and the Gift*, 506–8.

44. Wolter, *Paul*, 80. Barclay pertinently notes that a disposition both dictates actions and is formed by those actions (*Paul and the Gift*, 508).

45. Dunson rightly notes that "faith" in Romans is exercised by individuals, but that it also functions to unify and build up the people of God (Ben C. Dunson, "Faith in Romans: The Salvation of the Individual or Life in Community?," *JSNT* 34 [2011]: 19–46). The social focus of "faith" language is emphasized by Morgan, *Roman Faith and Christian Faith*. For assessment of her book, see *NTS* 64 (2018): 243–61.

Romans, God's grace and righteousness are now available to all who believe (Rom 1:16; 3:22; 4:11, 16; 10:4, 11, 13). No longer does the Torah, a special possession of Israel, mark out the people of God. Faith, a response potentially open to all humans, is now that marker.

4 THE INTERPLAY OF DIVINE AND HUMAN AGENCIES

Paul, then, is clear that people enter the new realm by responding in faith to the gospel message. The "decision" to respond in belief to the proclamation of God's good news in Christ, while sometimes given too prominent a place in contemporary evangelicalism, has a secure place in Paul's theology. He is equally clear that people are drawn into the new realm by God's sovereign power. The relationship between these two clear teachings is fraught and is one aspect of the larger theological and philosophical question of the relation between divine and human agency in Scripture.[46]

On the one hand are those who try to honor Paul's emphasis on human agency by arguing that God's election and calling are based on the foreseen faith of humans. This way of thinking about election in Paul is often grounded exegetically in Romans 8:29: "For those God foreknew he also predestined to be conformed to the image of his Son." Predestination, or election, is based on God's foreknowledge, interpreted to mean his knowing [something] ahead of time, the "something" being assumed to be faith. However, as we have seen in my exegesis of this passage (pp. 228–29), the verb "foreknow" (*proginōskō*) probably means "choose ahead of time." Moreover, any human virtue, activity, or disposition is very hard to read into the strong focus on God's sovereignty that marks Paul's treatment of election in Romans 9:6–29. Everything depends, Paul affirms, on the God "who calls" (v. 12).[47] At stake in all this, as Paul makes clear in 11:5–7, a text that takes up the argument of these verses, is the grace of God. Paul rules

---

46. Several authors suggest that two patterns can be observed in the OT. One, seen in Deuteronomy, focuses on human response as key to ultimate restoration; and another, attested in some of the prophets (Isaiah 40–55; Jeremiah, Ezekiel), focuses on God's unilateral action. See, e.g., Sprinkle, *Paul and Judaism Revisited*, 38–57; see also J. Maston, *Divine and Human Agency in Second Temple Judaism and Paul: A Comparative Study*, WUNT 2/297 (Tübingen: Mohr Siebeck, 2010); Wells, *Grace and Agency*, 25–62. It might be better, however, to think of two emphases within a focus on God's grace; Deuteronomy itself appears ultimately to see Israel's restoration as a matter of grace (e.g., McConville, *Grace in the End*).

47. In light of the somewhat parallel language in Rom 9:14–23, many theologians in the Calvinist tradition have asserted "double predestination": as God positively elects some for salvation, so also he positively damns others. One critical issue here,

which has been a matter of considerable debate among Reformed theologians, is whether God's choosing has regard for humans in their originally created state "before the fall" (supralapsarianism) or in their fallen state (infralapsarianism). (For a brief discussion of this issue, see Berkhof, *Systematic Theology*.) This admittedly somewhat speculative issue is one that Paul does not directly address, though I think his soteriology more naturally fits the latter than the former. The point of this, then, is to recognize that God's election to salvation—creating "righteous" people who are by nature very unrighteous—has quite a different shape than God's damnation—simply confirming, or leaving, people in the sinful state they were already in. The lack of symmetry in Rom 9:22–23 might suggest this difference. God actively "prepared in advance" glory for "the objects of his mercy," but "the objects of his wrath" were "prepared for destruction." See, on this whole issue, the perceptive treatment of Williams, *Election of Grace*, 108–52.

out any human claim on God as a violation of his grace. Perhaps, as my Arminian friends and colleagues insist, foreseen faith, as the product of "prevenient" grace, need be no threat to God's freedom and grace. But by making the human decision to believe the crucial point of distinction between those who are saved and those who are not and thus making God's election a response to human choice, this perspective seems to me to minimize Paul's insistence that election to salvation is itself an act of God's grace (see 11:5)—a decision he makes freely and without the compulsion of any influence outside himself.

A better option, then, is to view God's agency as primary. Augustine had it right: "God does not choose us because we believe, but that we may believe."[48] At the same time, this sovereign and unconstrained exercise of God's power does not erase or erode genuine human agency. As Calvin argued, agency is not a zero-sum game: both a robust divine agency and true human agency can be accommodated.[49] This way of viewing the matter is suggested by many texts in Paul and in Scripture generally that put divine agency and human agency with respect to the same matter side by side.[50] One example in Paul is 1 Corinthians 15:10: "But by the grace of God I am what I am, and his grace to me was not without effect. No, I worked harder than all of them—yet not I, but the grace of God that was with me." God's grace is the prime mover in Paul's fruitful apostolic ministry. Yet, at the same time, Paul's own hard work is also key to his success. We need, perhaps, to be more cautious in our formulations and to insist on the absolute cruciality and meaningfulness of human agency at the same time as we rightly make God's agency ultimately basic. Such a double emphasis may strain the boundaries of logic (it does not, I trust, break them!) or remain unsatisfyingly complex, but it may have the virtue of reflecting Scripture's own balanced perspective.[51]

---

48. *Predestination of the Saints* 17.34 (www.newadvent.org /fathers/15121.htm). See especially the thoughtful and judicious discussion of election in Williams, *Election of Grace*; and also Wells, *Grace and Agency*, 207–306; Maston, *Divine and Human Agency*, 167–78.

49. See, e.g., Barclay, *Paul and the Gift*, 126–29 (on Calvin), 441–42. He coins the term "energism" to describe this interplay.

50. For a selection of texts and discussion, see Allen, *Sanctification*, 227–44.

51. For the understanding of the relationship between God's sovereignty and human responsibility that underlies this approach, see J. Feinberg, "God Ordains All Things," in *Predestination and Free Will: Four Views of Divine Sovereignty and Human Freedom*, ed. David Basinger and Randall Basinger, Spectrum Multiview Series (Downers Grove, IL: InterVarsity Press, 1986), 17–43; D. A. Carson, *Divine Sovereignty and Human Responsibility: Biblical Perspectives in Tension* (Grand Rapids: Baker, 1994), e.g., 201–22.

Chapter 22

THE CONSUMMATION OF THE NEW REALM

For the grace of God has appeared that offers salvation to all people. It teaches us to say "No" to ungodliness and worldly passions, and to live self-controlled, upright and godly lives in this present age, *while we wait for the blessed hope—the appearing of the glory of our great God and Savior, Jesus Christ,* who gave himself for us to redeem us from all wickedness and to purify for himself a people that are his very own, eager to do what is good.

—TITUS 2:11–14

PAUL'S ATTEMPT TO CONVINCE the Corinthians that resurrection (both of Christ and of believers) is integral to the gospel includes an overview of the eschatological agenda:

But Christ has indeed <u>been raised</u> from the dead, <u>the firstfruits</u> of those who have fallen asleep. For since death came through a man, the resurrection of the dead comes also through a man. For as in Adam all die, so in Christ **all will be made alive.** But each in turn: <u>Christ, the firstfruits</u>; **then, when he comes ["at his coming"—parousia], those who belong to him. Then the end will come, when he hands over the kingdom to God the Father after he has destroyed all dominion, authority and power.** For <u>he must reign</u> **until he has put all his enemies under his feet.** The last enemy to be destroyed is death. For he "has put everything under his feet." Now when it says that "everything" has been put under him, it is clear that this does not include God himself, who put everything under Christ. When he has done this, then **the Son himself will be made subject to him who put everything under him, so that God may be all in all.** (1 Cor 15:20–28)

This paragraph reveals the fundamental "already"/"not yet" tension that characterizes New Testament eschatology. "Already" God has inaugurated his end-time redemption program by raising his Son from the dead (v. 20). The "reign" of the messianic Son has begun (v. 25), and the kingdom of God has been established (v. 24). At the same time, God's enemies—notably, "death"—have not yet been vanquished (vv. 25–26). It is only at Christ's "coming" (Gk. *parousia*) that this will happen, when the Son hands the kingdom to the Father and God becomes "all in all" (vv. 24, 28). Bridging the "already" and the "not yet" in this paragraph is Christ, the resurrected one, as "firstfruits." The image captures well the logic of the "already"/"not yet." A decisive start in God's eschatological program has begun. Yet it is only a start. The full crop has not yet been gathered in. At the same time, an organic connection between the beginning and the end is clear. What believers experience when their bodies are raised in the end is part of the same resurrection Christ experienced.

Hope, therefore, as Paul suggests in Romans 8:24, is built into the DNA of the Christian life: "In this hope we were saved" (see also Eph 4:4). He famously singles out hope, along with faith and love, as that which "remains" (1 Cor 13:13). Unbelievers, by contrast, "have no hope" (1 Thess 4:13; see Eph 2:12). In this last sense, "hope" (*elpis*) has a subjective sense, referring to a person's attitude; see, for example, 2 Corinthians 1:7: "And our hope [*elpis*] for you is firm, because we know that just as you share in our sufferings, so also you share in our comfort" (of course, the cognate verb, *elpizō* is often used in this way).[1] But Paul also uses "hope" to refer to the content of what a believer hopes for, as in, for example, Galatians 5:5: "For through the Spirit we eagerly await by faith what we hope for, namely righteousness" (my translation)[2]; our "hope" also consists of "the glory of God" (Rom 5:2; see Col 1:27), "salvation" (1 Thess 5:8), "eternal life" (Titus 1:2; 3:7), "the appearing of the glory of our great God and Savior, Jesus Christ" (Titus 2:13).

We have seen how Paul, with other early Christians, was overwhelmed by the realization that they were living in "the last days." However, without detracting in the least from this "already" perspective, it is important not to lose sight of the significance of the "not yet" in Paul's understanding of salvation history.[3] The presence of "the last days" does not remove the reality of "*the* last day" that is still impending. As Beker puts it, "A D-Day without an impending V-Day loses its character as D-Day. Likewise a D-Day that is celebrated as if it were V-Day loses sight of the reality of things."[4] Many of the false teachings addressed by New Testament authors appear to have been at least

---

1. See also Rom 12:12; 15:4, 13; 1 Cor 9:10; 2 Cor 1:7; 3:12; 10:15; Phil 1:20; 1 Thess 1:3; 2 Thess 2:16. Paul also uses other words to denote the believer's act of hoping: *apekdechomai* ("await eagerly": Rom 8:19, 23, 25; 1 Cor 1:7; Gal 5:5; Phil 3:20); *apokaradokia* ("eager expectation": Rom 8:19; Phil 1:20); *anamenō* ("await"; 1 Thess 1:10). See especially the survey of texts in Gottfried Nebe, *"Hoffnung" bei Paulus: Elpis und ihre Synonyme im Zusammenhang der Eschatologie*, SUNT 16 (Göttingen: Vandenhoeck & Ruprecht, 1983), 19–32.

2. For this understanding of the genitive phrase *elpida dikaiosynēs*, see p. 80.

3. A strong futuristic focus in Paul's conception of salvation history is a feature of Beker's understanding of Paul's "apocalyptic" theology (*Paul the Apostle*, 135–81).

4. Beker, *Paul the Apostle*, 177.

partly rooted in an imbalance in emphasis between these two eschatological moments. This variety of emphasis goes some way to explaining the diversity in Paul's own teaching about the future. Some of his letters focus extensively on future eschatology (e.g., 1 and 2 Thessalonians), while others have very little such teaching (e.g., Ephesians and Colossians). Indeed, not only do some letters lack material on future eschatology, but they appear to shift events from the future to the present.[5] The resurrection is the classic case in point. In the earlier letters, Paul locates believers' resurrection at the time of Christ's parousia (e.g., 1 Cor 15:20–28 [quoted above]; 1 Thess 4:13–18). In Ephesians and Colossians, however, Paul teaches that believers have already "been raised with Christ" (Eph 2:6; Col 3:1). Moreover, Paul's "mode" of doing eschatology appears to change also. As Dunn puts it, 2 Thessalonians is distinct because, unlike his other letters, Paul here speaks as "an apocalyptic visionary."[6] These differences are thought by some scholars to be so serious that the same author could not have written all these letters. Partly (or even mainly) on this basis, 2 Thessalonians, Ephesians, and Colossians, for instance, are often attributed to a writer after Paul's time. I deal with the general issue of authorship elsewhere (pp. 49–51). Here I simply reiterate with respect to these eschatological issues a point about the larger question of authorship. The varied teaching in the letters is better seen as reflecting the different circumstances Paul is addressing than as the perspectives of different authors. True, there are undeniable tensions in what Paul says on some eschatological issues, and these I will address below. Some of these tensions may reflect development in Paul's thinking. However, these developments involve organic movement rather than the replacement of one view with a different one.

My discussion of Paul's future eschatology will move from the general to the specific: from the "day of Christ" as the broad Old Testament-based characterization of the end times to Christ's "coming" as a more specific way of denoting that time, to the respective impact of that coming on believers and unbelievers.

1 THE DAY OF THE LORD CHRIST

Paul's most general way of referring to the consummation is by means of the language of the "day." He picks up this designation from the Old Testament, where "the day of the Lord" refers to the anticipated time of God's intervention to set things right. This intervention is usually pictured in terms of God's judgment on his enemies. In Joel 1:15, for instance, the prophet warns the people: "Alas for that day! For the day of the LORD is near; it will come like destruction from the Almighty." Joel goes on to describe this "day" as "a day of darkness and gloom" (2:1–2), "dreadful" (v. 11), "the great and

---

5. See, e.g., Sanders, *Paul: The Apostle's Life*, 408–32.   6. Dunn, *Theology of Paul*, 307–10.

dreadful day of the LORD" (v. 31). Yet the prophet also suggests that the "day of the LORD" will bring salvation to Israel: "Everyone who calls on the name of the LORD will be saved" (2:32; see 3:14–16 and Obad 15–17). This positive outcome for the righteous is more explicit in abbreviated references to the "day of the LORD" as "that day" (e.g., Jer 30:8–9; Hos 2:16–23; Amos 9:11). Some of the prophets (see esp. Zephaniah) make clear that Israel will not be exempt from the judgment of this "day."[7]

In a move typical of Paul's christological focus, the Old Testament "day of the LORD" becomes "the day of the Lord Jesus" (2 Cor 1:14). In fact, Paul refers to this day with ten slightly different formulations:

1. "The day": Rom 13:12, 13(?); 1 Cor 3:13; 1 Thess 5:4 (NIV: "this day," *hē hēmera*)
2. "That day": 2 Thess 1:10; 2 Tim 1:12, 18; 4:8
3. "The day of God's wrath": Rom 2:5
4. "The day when God judges": Rom 2:16
5. "The day of redemption": Eph 4:30
6. "The day of the Lord": 1 Cor 5:5; 1 Thess 5:2; 2 Thess 2:2
7. "The day of Christ": Phil 1:10; 2:16
8. "The day of the Lord Jesus": 2 Cor 1:14
9. "The day of Christ Jesus": Phil 1:6
10. "The day of our Lord Jesus Christ": 1 Cor 1:8[8]

While Paul hints that this "day" has already dawned (Rom 13:11–14), all the explicit occurrences of the language in the list above portray it as future, closely associated with Christ's return in glory. Paul imitates the Old Testament pattern of picturing "the day" as involving both judgment and salvation. See, for example, 2 Thessalonians 1:8b–10:

> Those who do not know God and do not obey the gospel of our Lord Jesus . . . will be punished with everlasting destruction and shut out from the presence of the Lord and from the glory of his might on the day he comes to be glorified in his holy people and to be marveled at among all those who have believed.

Other passages highlight one of these sides or the other, either ultimate salvation for believers (Eph 4:30) or judgment of unbelievers (Rom 2:5; 1 Thess 5:2, 4). More often, however, Paul pictures the day as the time when believers appear before Christ for ultimate assessment. Typical is 1 Corinthians 5, where Paul expresses his hope that

---

7. See, e.g., G. von Rad, *TDNT* 2:944–47; Rowley, *Faith of Israel*, 178–200.

8. See also "the day of evil" in Eph 6:13, which might refer to the last day but perhaps more likely refers to the entire church age (see p. 295). And see also L. Joseph Kreitzer, *Jesus and God in Paul's Eschatology*, JSNTSup 19 (Sheffield: JSOT, 1987), 112–28.

the man within the Christian community who is "sleeping with his father's wife" (v. 1) might "be saved on the day of the Lord" (v. 5). Paul here appears to presuppose that the "day of the Lord" has the potential, for those within the Christian community, to result in either salvation or judgment. The goal for believers is that they might appear "pure and blameless" (Phil 1:10), a goal that Paul is confident he and other believers will reach: "He will also keep you firm to the end, so that you will be blameless on the day of our Lord Jesus Christ. God is faithful, who has called you into fellowship with his Son, Jesus Christ our Lord" (1 Cor 1:8–9; see also Phil 1:6; 2 Tim 1:12). Herman Ridderbos defines the "day" as "the great future that dawns with Christ's coming," suggesting that the "day" refers to an extended period of time.[9] This may be so, but it appears that most of Paul's references to the "day" suggest a concentrated moment of time.

Before looking at the specific content of this "day," I briefly survey three other general designations of the end events in Paul. In comparison with the Gospels, where it is ubiquitous, "kingdom" language is relatively rare in Paul (only fourteen times). Paul usually refers to the "kingdom of God" (nine times) but also refers to "the kingdom of the Son he loves" (Col 1:13) and "the kingdom of Christ and of God" (Eph 5:5). Paul can use "kingdom" (*basileia*) to refer to the inaugurated state of God's redemptive work (Rom 14:17; 1 Cor 4:20; 15:24; Col 1:13; 4:11), but more often refers to the final instantiation of God's realm (1 Cor 6:9, 10; 15:50; Gal 5:21; Eph 5:5; 1 Thess 2:12; 2 Thess 1:5; 2 Tim 4:1, 18).[10]

"Glory" (*doxa*) is a second general way of referring to the consummation. It refers to this final state at least eleven times in Paul (Rom 2:7[?], 10[?]; 5:2; 8:18, 21; 1 Cor 15:43 [qualifying our resurrection body]; 2 Cor 4:17; Phil 3:21 [qualifying Christ's resurrection body]; Col 1:27 ["hope of glory"]; 3:4; 1 Thess 2:12; 2 Thess 1:9; 2:14). However, Paul also applies the word to the inaugurated stage of God's redemptive plan (e.g., Col 1:27a: "God has chosen to make known among the Gentiles the riches that consist of the glory that belongs to the mystery"),[11] and 2 Corinthians 3:18 is especially clear in bringing out the "already"/"not yet" character of glory in Paul: as we "contemplate the Lord's glory," we "are being transformed into his image with ever-increasing glory." In secular Greek, the word *doxa* means "opinion," "judgment," "estimation."[12] But the LXX translators used it for the Hebrew *kavod*, and it is through this correspondence that its typical New Testament sense develops.[13] From its basic meaning "be weighty,"

---

9. Ridderbos, *Paul*, 530–31.

10. I use "realm" in agreement with those who argue that the popular language of "reign" unduly minimizes the materiality—the "placeness"—of the kingdom in the NT.

11. My own cumbersome translation, in which I try to suggest the significance of the series of genitives (*to ploutos tēs doxēs tou mystēriou*). Most translations, such as the NIV, here and elsewhere interpret the genitive *doxēs* as a qualitative genitive ("the glorious riches"). This, in my view, detracts from the theological importance of this word.

12. See LSJ.

13. Newman, *Paul's Glory-Christology*, 134–53.

kavod came to denote the "honor" or "importance" or "prestige" of people (e.g., Ps 49:16; Isa 16:14; see Matt 4:8) and, when applied to God, his "weighty" and magnificent presence—as revealed in nature (Ps 97:1–6), the tabernacle (Exod 40:34), and at the climax of history, to all peoples (Isa 40:5; 66:18).[14] This last usage may be the source of Paul's application of the language to the end events.[15]

A third general description of the eschatological future employs the language of inheritance. In the Old Testament, "inheritance" often refers to the territories allotted to Israel's tribes in the land of Israel (e.g., Jer 3:19a: "I myself said, 'How gladly would I treat you like my children and give you a pleasant land, the most beautiful inheritance of any nation'"), but could also denote the people themselves (e.g., Deut 32:9; cf. also Joel 4:2). In a move typical of the New Testament "Christifying" of the Old Testament land theme,[16] Paul applies this language to the spiritual privilege enjoyed by God's new-covenant people. Also typical is Paul's insistence that the privilege of this inheritance is now extended to gentiles (Eph 3:6). Paul's inaugurated eschatological viewpoint emerges here again: the "inheritance" (*klēronomia*) is both something believers already possess (Eph 1:14, 18) and something they hope for (Eph 5:5; Col 3:24; see also *klēros* in Col 1:12). Of course, in this case, the word itself captures this tension; an "inheritance" is by definition something promised but not yet possessed. Paul makes this point explicitly with the cognate *klēronomos*, "heir": "Now if we are children, then we are heirs—heirs of God and co-heirs with Christ, if indeed we share in his sufferings in order that we may also share in his glory" (Rom 8:17; see also Rom 4:13; Gal 3:29; 4:7; Eph 3:6; Titus 2:7). Paul, then, shifts the focus from the inheritance of a specific piece of real estate (the promised land) to the world (see my discussion below, pp. 645–47).

These three terms overlap with each other. Paul refers to "inheriting [using *klēronomeō*] the kingdom of God" (1 Cor 6:9, 10; 15:50; Gal 5:21); the future glory consists in "the inheritance" (Eph 1:18)[17]; and "glory" and "kingdom" parallel one another in reference to the end state (1 Thess 2:12).

2 THE PAROUSIA

Christ is the Lord of the "day of the Lord," especially in his role as the "coming one." Paul often parallels the language of the "day" and the coming of Christ: in his prayers that believers might be "blameless" (1 Cor 1:8; Phil 1:10; 1 Thess 3:13; 5:23), in his boasting about his churches (Phil 2:16; 1 Thess 2:19), and in his hope for salvation

---

14. See G. von Rad, *TDNT* 2:238–42.

15. It is also possible that "glory" carries connotations of rulership. See my discussion on p. 502.

16. See esp. Davies, *Gospel and the Land*.

17. Again, I disagree with most translations, which interpret *doxēs* as a descriptive genitive, modifying "inheritance" (e.g., NIV, ESV, NLT) or "riches" (CSB).

(1 Cor 5:5; 15:23).[18] The best-known term for this "coming" is *parousia*. Paul uses it seven times to refer to this event, six of them in the Thessalonian correspondence (1 Thess 2:19; 3:13; 4:15; 5:23; 2 Thess 2:1, 8; see also 1 Cor 15:23).[19] Usually translated "coming," the word in fact focuses not on movement but on the results of that movement, "arrival" or "presence." The word is not, however, a technical theological term. Paul uses it seven other times to refer to the "coming, arrival" or "presence" of other people. Two particular uses of the word in his day may have influenced Paul's choice of this word. First, the word referred to the "coming of a hidden divinity, who makes his presence felt by a revelation of his power."[20] Second, *parousia* also sometimes referred to the official "arrival" of a person of high honor, including the arrival of the emperor.[21] The former application of the word would have obvious relevance for Paul's usage, although there is some question about how widespread this usage may have been. A number of scholars have seized on the second use of the word to buttress the claim that Paul applied certain terms to Christ in order to counter imperial propaganda surrounding the increasingly important emperor cult. It is not the "arrival" of the king of Rome that believers should anticipate but the "arrival" of King Jesus. It is possible that Paul may intend such an allusion, although here again caution is needed. In addition to the noun *parousia*, Paul also uses verbs of motion to describe Christ's climactic work: "come" (*erchomai*; 1 Cor 4:5; 11:26; 2 Thess 1:10), "come in" (*hēkō*; Rom 11:26[?]), "come down" (*katabainō*; 1 Thess 4:16), and see also the Aramaic *marana tha* ("Come, Lord!") in 1 Corinthians 16:22. In popular accounts of Paul's eschatology, these verbs of movement are often given a lot of attention. And it is hard to remove all sense of physical movement from the "come down" of 1 Thessalonians 4:16. Otherwise, however, the focus is not on movement but on the appearance or arrival of Christ (as the word *parousia* stresses).

The focus on arrival or presence in Christ's "coming" is highlighted by three other words Paul uses to describe the event: "revelation" (*apokalypsis*; 1 Cor 1:7; 2 Thess 1:7), "appearance" (*epiphaneia*; 2 Thess 2:8; 1 Tim 6:14; 2 Tim 4:1, 8),[22] and "appear, reveal" (*phaneroō*; Col 3:4). All three words focus on the parousia as the time when the

---

18. See on this point Nicholl, *From Hope to Despair*, 51; Kreitzer, *Jesus and God*, 112–29.

19. N. T. Wright speculates that Paul may have been the first to apply the word to Christ's return, perhaps in conscious opposition to the word's application to Caesar's "arrival" (*Resurrection*, 231).

20. BDAG.

21. See, e.g., 3 Macc 3:17, where King Ptolemy Philopator speaks of his reception among Jews in Alexandria: "They accepted our presence [*parousian*] by word, but insincerely by deed, because when we proposed to enter their inner temple and honor it with magnificent and most beautiful offerings, they were carried away

by their traditional arrogance." The Emperor Nero had coins struck in memory of his visit to Patras and Corinth that carried the inscription *Adventus Augusti Corinth*. The Latin *adventus* is naturally rendered *parousia* in Greek (*TDNT*). See also, e.g., Moulton-Milligan. On the relevance of both these backgrounds, see, e.g., N. T. Wright, *Surprised by Hope: Rethinking Heaven, the Resurrection, and the Mission of the Church* (New York: Harper One, 2008), 128–33.

22. N. T. Wright, however, might err on the side of minimizing the idea of movement when he claims that Christ's *epiphaneia* means "appearing where he already is" (*Surprised by Hope*, 135).

veil concealing the glory of Christ is torn away, resulting in believers being comforted and vindicated in the eyes of the world and in unbelievers being faced with the reality that the one they had rejected is, in fact, the Lord of the universe. At the same time, these words highlight the "already"/"not yet" character of Paul's eschatology. God "revealed [*apokalyptō*] his Son" to Paul on the Damascus Road (Gal 1:16; cf. v. 12); Christians "eagerly wait for our Lord Jesus Christ to be revealed [*apokalypsis*]" (1 Cor 1:7). Christians celebrate "the appearing [*epiphaneia*] of our Savior, Christ Jesus" to bring life to people through the gospel (2 Tim 1:10); we now have as our "blessed hope" "the appearing [*epiphaneia*] of the glory of our great God and Savior, Jesus Christ" (Titus 2:13).[23] Christ "appeared [*phaneroō*]" to the world in his incarnation (cf. 1 Tim 3:16); he, who is "our life," will "appear [*phaneroō*]" again in glory (Col 3:4). The current stage of salvation history is bracketed by these two "appearances."

3 RESURRECTION AND RAPTURE

Jesus's ultimate "appearance" or "coming" is the specific event associated with the day of the Lord. Paul's focus, however, is not so much on that appearance or coming itself but on its effect on both believers and unbelievers. For believers, Christ's coming unleashes their ultimate transformation:

> I declare to you, brothers and sisters, that flesh and blood cannot inherit the king-dom of God, nor does the perishable inherit the imperishable. Listen, I tell you a mystery: We will not all sleep, but we will all be changed—in a flash, in the twinkling of an eye, at the last trumpet. For the trumpet will sound, the dead will be raised imperishable, and we will be changed. (1 Cor 15:50–52)

These verses culminate Paul's defense and explanation of the resurrection. In a sense, Paul here provides the ultimate reason why resurrection is necessary. Since human beings cannot enter the final state of God's kingdom in our current flesh-and-blood bodies, we must be "changed." For believers who have died, this change, or transformation, will take place by means of resurrection. Paul begins his treatment of resurrection in this chapter by asserting its indispensable role in the new realm. Only if Christ has been raised can there be any good news; only if he is raised does our faith make any sense at all (vv. 1–19). As I noted above, Paul then argues that Christ's resurrection, the "firstfruits," both initiates and guarantees our own resurrection; as Horton puts it, Christ's resurrection and ours "*belong to the same event*."[24] In verses 29–34, Paul argues

---

23. Like *parousia*, *epiphaneia* was also sometimes used to refer to the "appearance" of a deity (see, e.g., H. Conzelmann, *TDNT* 9:315–16).

24. Horton, *Rediscovering the Holy Spirit*, 189 (emphasis original).

for resurrection as the logical implication of other Christian teaching. Then, in the verses immediately preceding verses 50–52, he deals with one last potent objection to the notion of resurrection: How can we envisage the nature of a body that will suit eternal life? Paul asserts that God is quite capable of providing just such a body. Our present bodies are built for this life; they are "natural" (*psychikos*) and destined to perish (vv. 42–44). The resurrection body, by contrast, is "spiritual" (*pneumatikos*). Paul's whole discussion is predicated on the materiality of the resurrection body, so this clearly cannot mean that the body is composed of "spirit." Rather, he means that the resurrection body is a body suited for life in the Spirit.[25]

While Paul does not refer specifically in 1 Corinthians 15 to the parousia, parallels with other texts that do focus on the parousia (1 Thess 4:13–18, especially) make clear that this transformation by resurrection occurs at the time of Christ's final appearance. The same is true in Philippians 3:20–21.[26] As people whose "citizenship is in heaven," Christians naturally "eagerly await a Savior from there" who will prepare us for our heavenly existence by transforming "our lowly bodies so that they will be like his glorious body." The language of "transform" (*metaschēmatizō*) in this text suggests a continuity between the earthly and the heavenly body that is not entirely clear in 1 Corinthians 15. The issue is complicated by 2 Corinthians 5:1–10. This passage extends Paul's claim in 4:16 that "though outwardly we are wasting away, yet inwardly we are being renewed day by day." Not only do Christians in this life enjoy inward renewal; we can also be confident that when our "outward" parts, our bodies, are "destroyed," we will be given a new body, a body that Paul says will "clothe over" (*ependyomai*) our earthly bodies (5:1–2). This language could suggest that believers exchange one body for another, and that this exchange takes place when we die (when the "earthly tent . . . is destroyed," v. 1; see also 1 Cor 15:53: "The perishable must clothe itself [*endysasthai*] with the imperishable").[27] However, Paul sends different signals about this issue in this passage, for he appears to envisage a time when believers are without a body in verses 4–9. The matter of timing appears to be settled by yet another passage, 1 Thessalonians 4:13–18.

As we have seen, the issue that stimulates Paul to reassure the Thessalonians in this passage is unclear (pp. 88–89). What is clear is Paul's overall focus on the timing of the resurrection. In response to the Thessalonians' fear that brothers and sisters who have died may somehow be disadvantaged at Christ's parousia, Paul claims that, in fact, the dead will be the first to be joined, via resurrection, with Christ. This text appears

25. On the materiality of the resurrection body, see esp. Wright, *Resurrection*.

26. See, e.g., Joseph Plevnik, *Paul and the Parousia: An Exegetical and Theological Investigation* (Peabody, MA: Hendrickson, 1997; repr., Eugene, OR: Wipf & Stock, 2014), 179–80.

27. See especially Harris, *Second Epistle to the Corinthians*, 378–80 (though he qualifies the possession of the body as "ideal").

to settle the issue of the time of the resurrection. We should probably, then, because of its clarity on the matter, give it precedence and interpret Paul's other resurrection texts in light of it.

4 THE QUESTION OF TIMING: "IMMINENCE"

If, then, believers' bodies are raised at the parousia, with the result that they will be "with the Lord forever" (1 Thess 4:17), what is the situation of believers who die before the Lord returns? As this passage and 1 Corinthians 15:50–58 make clear, Paul identifies the resurrection of the body as the moment when death is "swallowed up in victory" (1 Cor 15:54). The prominence of resurrection in Paul's hope for the future is a natural corollary to the biblical view of human beings. As we have seen (pp. 455–56), biblical authors, in contrast to many in the Greco-Roman world (including probably the Corinthians Paul has in view in 1 Cor 15), view the body as a basic component of the human person. Paul reflects this perspective when he indicates his hope, at death, not to be "unclothed" (that is, without a body; see 2 Cor 5:4). The Christian church has often been deeply influenced by a spiritual/material dualism going back to the philosophy of Plato and the neo-Platonists that tends to view the Christian hope in terms of the immortality of the soul and an ethereal, nonmaterial "heaven." Paul's view is in stark contrast to this. As we will see below, he implies that the eternal home of the believer is not heaven but a renewed heaven and earth. Recent authors are quite justified, then, when they reassert this biblical—and Pauline—focus on resurrection of the body as central to our Christian hope.[28]

Nevertheless, the question about the status of the believer between death and resurrection (at the parousia) needs to be asked. One popular answer to this question is that Paul has little to say about the matter because, at least in his early letters, he was certain that the parousia was "imminent," certainly to happen within his lifetime. On this view, the Paul of the Thessalonian letters and 1 Corinthians held to an "any-moment" parousia; it is only in 2 Corinthians 5, perhaps, that Paul explicitly deals with the state of believers between death and the parousia. I touch here on a significant broader issue pertaining to theories of the development of New Testament theology as a whole. It has been widely argued that the early church experienced a waning of eschatological fervor that affected the shape and material of New Testament teaching. An initial belief in the immediate coming of Christ and end of history gave way to a realization that the parousia might be "delayed."

However, the essential premise of this influential way of reading the New Testament

---

28. See esp. N. T. Wright and his works *Resurrection*; *Surprised by Hope*; and *Day the Revolution Began*.

needs to be questioned. Here, of course, I will look at the Pauline evidence. And when we do, we find that the evidence for the idea that the parousia would certainly occur within a few years is not very compelling. Paul's use of the first-person plural form in 1 Thessalonians 4:15—"*we* who are still alive, who are left until the coming of the Lord"—need not mean that Paul was certain he would be alive until the parousia. He simply supposes for the sake of his argument that he would be. We might paraphrase "those of us who are alive" (see p. 99). Nor does Paul's claim in 1 Corinthians 7:29 that "the time is short" (see v. 26, "the present crisis") necessarily indicates a belief that the coming of the Lord would take place within a few short years. For Paul and other early Christians—and, indeed, for all Christians—the time is always short, in the sense that Christ's coming is impending.[29] Paul could certainly suppose that he *might* live until the parousia, for its timing is unknown and incalculable. Moreover, it is entirely possible that Paul grew less hopeful that he would live to experience the parousia as time went by. But there is no good evidence that he ever held or taught the idea of an "immediate" parousia.[30]

But what, then, does Paul say about the state of believers between death and the parousia? In a phrase, "not much." Paul responds to concerns about believers who have died in 1 Thess 4:13–18, but he speaks only to their eventual status at the parousia and not to their current situation. Second Corinthians 5:1–10 is more helpful, since Paul here appears to teach that believers, even when "away from the body" are "at home with the Lord" (v. 8).[31] But the clearest, and best known, text is Philippians 1:23, where Paul, reflecting on the uncertainty of his situation as a Roman prisoner, asserts his desire "to depart [i.e., die] and be with Christ."[32] Paul therefore pretty clearly teaches that believers who die are "with the Lord."[33] Yet because they are "unclothed," without a body, until the parousia, the assumption is that believers after death "go" to be with Christ as bodiless "souls," waiting to be "clothed" again with a (resurrection) body. This view of

---

29. Plevnik argues that several textual variants in the paragraph of 1 Cor 15:50–58 reveal the efforts of scribes to avoid the notion of an immediate parousia (*Paul and the Parousia*, 159–60). But nothing in the established text suggests the notion of an "immediate" parousia. Indeed, "we will not all sleep" (v. 51) opens the door to the possibility that Paul identifies himself with those who might die before the parousia.

30. See, e.g., Moore, *Parousia in the New Testament*, 108–25; Campbell, *Paul and the Hope of Glory*, 367–71. See also Beker, who comments, "Paul is simply not an apocalyptic fanatic who runs breathlessly through the Roman Empire because the end of the world is imminent" (*Paul the Apostle*, 178). Dunn (*Theology of Paul*, 310–11) rightly doubts that the so-called "delay of the parousia" had a formative effect on Paul's theology. Plevnik (*Paul and the Parousia*, 272–80) also questions whether Paul's teaching about the time of the end shifted over time; but he argues that Paul's consistent teaching was of an "any-moment" parousia.

31. It must be admitted, however, that the many exegetical issues in this passage mean its contribution to this issue is not entirely clear. Paul Hoffmann, e.g., doubts that it speaks of an "intermediate state" at all (*Die Toten in Christus. Eine Religionsgeschichtliche und Exegetische Untersuchung zur Paulinischen Eschatologie*, NTAbh 2 [Münster: Aschendorff, 1966], 253–85).

32. See again Hoffmann (*Toten in Christus*), who argues this is the only clear text relating to the intermediate state in Paul's letters.

33. This being the case, it also makes clear that one can legitimately speak of Christian hope in terms of "going to heaven" when one dies, for "heaven" is where Christ is currently located. N. T. Wright, then, is justified in protesting about the use of this language when it becomes the expression of the believer's ultimate hope (*Day the Revolution Began*, 214, passim), but he goes too far when he implies it always betrays a less-than-biblical viewpoint.

what is called the "intermediate state" has been the mainstream teaching of orthodox Christians. Yet we might entertain a tweak to this perspective. As we have seen, Paul appears to suggest at places that believers at death discard one body only to immediately possess another. Yet he is also clear that believers only inherit the resurrection body at the parousia. Several interpreters have suggested that these might be reconciled if we think of these two sets of texts as looking at matters from two different viewpoints: that of the "participant" and that of the "onlooker." The participant, the one who dies before the parousia, experiences an immediate transition from the old body to the new. But from the standpoint of the onlooker, this transition is, in fact, separated by an indefinite period of time.[34] This view is different than the traditional "soul-sleep" view in that it posits a different influence of the concept of "time" between this world and the next.

But the Thessalonians passage highlights another effect of the parousia: the "rapture." The word "rapture" is, of course, not a New Testament word. The English word comes from the Latin verb *rapio* ("seize" or "carry away"), which was used in the Vulgate to translate the Greek word *harpagēsometha*, we "will be caught up [. . . to meet the Lord in the air]" in 1 Thessalonians 4:17. In popular circles, the "rapture" (in accordance with its verbal sense) is often thought of in terms of physical movement—believers are physically moved off the earth into heaven by the Lord. Moreover, this physical "taking away" is also usually thought to be necessary in order to rescue believers from harm. But neither of these notions gets at the heart of the matter. To be sure, physical movement is pretty clearly implied in the 1 Thessalonians text—and perhaps in others. But, as I argue above, the more important aspect of "rapture" is bodily transformation. Theologically, "rapture" is best seen as a parallel to resurrection. When the Lord returns, dead saints are raised from the dead; living saints are "raptured." This passage, then, gives more specificity to Paul's teaching in 1 Corinthians 15 that "we will all be changed" (v. 51). It should also be emphasized that the physical movement that may be found in this passage is not a movement to escape *from* something but a movement to be joined *to* something. Believers are "caught up" in order to "meet the Lord." The word translated "meet" (*apantēsis*) fits and makes more likely the associations of parousia with the visit of a dignitary. For the word sometimes refers to the "meeting" that takes place when a delegation from a town goes out to greet the dignitary and accompanies the dignitary back to town.[35] The two other occurrences of this term in the New Testament seem

---

34. See esp. Thiselton, *Life after Death*, 68–75; John Polkinghorne, "Eschatology: Some Questions and Some Insights from Science," in *The End of the World and the Ends of God: Science and Theology on Eschatology*, ed. John Polkinghorne and Michael Welker (Harrisburg, PA: Trinity Press International, 2000), 31–40; Harris, *Raised Immortal*, 133–42; Thomas F. Torrance, *Space, Time and Resurrection* (Edinburgh: T&T Clark, 1976), 98–105; James T. Turner, *On the Resurrection of the Dead: A New Metaphysics of Afterlife for Christian Thought*, Routledge New Critical Thinking in Religion, Theology and Biblical Studies (New York: Routledge, 2019), 183–216. As Turner's book especially reveals, this issue is complicated by differing views of the nature of "time"—a philosophical/theological issue far beyond my competence to judge.

35. See esp. Green, *Thessalonians*, 226–28; Wright, *Resurrection*, 217–18; Nicholl, *From Hope to Despair*, 43–45.

to bear this meaning (Matt 15:6; Acts 28:15). This would suggest that the saints, after meeting the Lord in the air, accompany him back to earth.

These passages, taken together, paint a pretty clear picture. When Christ appears, his people will gather to meet him. In order to prepare them for eternal life in the ultimate form of the kingdom, their bodies will be transformed, either through resurrection or "rapture." To be sure, some interpreters have argued that this scenario is too simple—that in order to satisfy all the biblical evidence, we must posit a two-stage "coming" of Christ, one to redeem the people of God and another to judge the wicked. The most popular form of this teaching, which has been especially popular in North American evangelicalism and among Christians influenced by that strand of evangelicalism, is "pretribulationism," so called because it holds that the rapture of living believers takes place "before" a final intense period of tribulation for the world.[36] It is, of course, possible that, as the coming of Messiah initially is seen in retrospect to be divided into two distinct moments, so will be the final coming of Messiah.[37] However, 2 Thessalonians 2:1–12 throws up real difficulties for this view. Paul writes shortly after 1 Thessalonians 4–5 in response to continuing uncertainty and even alarm about the day of the Lord (2 Thess 2:2). While, as noted earlier (pp. 106–9), this text bristles with exegetical problems, it is pretty clear that Paul's main point is to disabuse the Thessalonians of the idea that "the day of the Lord has already come" (v. 2). That day cannot come, Paul asserts, until certain things happen—the "rebellion" and the revelation of "the man of lawlessness" (v. 3). What Paul means by these references is disputed, but, as I argued earlier (see pp. 106–9), it is likely they denote events immediately preceding the parousia. Paul's claim that these events must come first, and his complete silence about any idea of being "raptured" before they occur, strongly suggest that these believers will be present during those events.

It is important to keep this issue in perspective. While, as I noted above, some evangelicals have elevated the notion of a pretribulational rapture to the status of a key doctrine, no text in Paul—or elsewhere in the New Testament—is clear about the matter. Moreover, we must maintain an appropriately Pauline view of suffering and tribulation. While some passages outside of Paul *may* suggest the idea of an unprecedented period of tribulation for God's people immediately before the parousia, Paul never suggests the idea.[38] He uniformly expects that the believers to whom he writes

36. There are, of course, other views on this matter. Some scholars have posited a "mid-tribulational rapture" (e.g., Gleason L. Archer, "The Case for the Mid-Seventieth-Week Rapture Position," in Richard R. Reiter, Paul D. Feinberg, Gleason L. Archer, and Douglas J. Moo, *Three Views on the Rapture: Pre-, Mid-, or Post-Tribulation* [repr., Grand Rapids: Zondervan, 1994], 113–46); others, more recently, advocate what they call a "prewrath" rapture (e.g., Alan Hultberg, "The Case for a Prewrath Rapture," in Hultberg, *Three Views on the Rapture*, 109–54).

37. The strongest of the "pretribulational" arguments is that only a two-stage parousia can explain how the parousia is sometimes presented as happening unexpectedly and at other times as an event that will be preceded by signs.

38. I am, in fact, unpersuaded that any passage has this sense; texts often cited for the idea (Matt 24:9, 21, 29; Mark 13:19, 24; Rev 2:10; 3:10; 7:14) probably refer to tribulations that believers suffer throughout this stage of salvation history. For an emphasis on the entire church age as a time of eschatological "tribulation,"

will experience tribulation—as he himself did (e.g., 2 Cor 11:23–28). His perspective is summarized well in the warning that Luke reports Paul and Barnabas uttered at the end of the first missionary journey: "We must go through many hardships [*thlipseōn*, 'tribulations'] to enter the kingdom of God" (Acts 14:22). See also 2 Timothy 3:12: "Everyone who wants to live a godly life in Christ Jesus will be persecuted." In every place and every era—albeit in quite different degrees—God's people suffer, both from the general effects of a fallen world and from the specific hostility of Satan and those who oppose the gospel. There is no escape from "tribulation" before we are ushered into God's eternal kingdom.[39]

5 JUDGMENT

5.1 Unbelievers

We have seen that Paul, following the Old Testament, presents the day of the Lord as a time of both salvation and judgment. The former tends to prevail in Paul, partly because he is, of course, writing to believers. But he also refers quite often to the judgment aspect of the day. He does so in order both to comfort believers by reminding them of the way that God will ultimately right all wrongs and to warn them not to fall into a way of life that would subject them to this judgment. Both purposes are evident in the Thessalonian correspondence:

> But you, brothers and sisters, are not in darkness so that this day should surprise you like a thief. You are all children of the light and children of the day. We do not belong to the night or to the darkness. So then, let us not be like others, who are asleep, but let us be awake and sober. For those who sleep, sleep at night, and those who get drunk, get drunk at night. But since we belong to the day, let us be sober, putting on faith and love as a breastplate, and the hope of salvation as a helmet. For God did not appoint us to suffer wrath but to receive salvation through our Lord Jesus Christ. (1 Thess 5:4–9)

> God is just: He will pay back trouble to those who trouble you and give relief to you who are troubled, and to us as well. This will happen when the Lord Jesus is revealed from heaven in blazing fire with his powerful angels. He will punish those who do not know God and do not obey the gospel of our Lord Jesus. They will be punished with everlasting destruction and shut out from the presence of the Lord and from

---

see Beale, *New Testament Biblical Theology*, 199–203. See also, along similar lines, C. Marvin Pate and Douglas W. Kennard, *Deliverance Now and Not Yet: The New Testament and the Great Tribulation*, StBibLit 54 (New York: Peter Lang, 2003).

39. I defend this view at greater length in "The Case for the Posttribulation Rapture," in Hultberg, *Three Views on the Rapture*, 185–241.

the glory of his might on the day he comes to be glorified in his holy people and to be marveled at among all those who have believed. (2 Thess 1:6–10a)

As the beginning of the 2 Thessalonians text reveals, God's judgment of unbelievers is a manifestation of his innate "justice"; it is a "just judgment" (v. 5, *dikaias kriseōs*). Paul follows the Old Testament and Second Temple Judaism in basing God's judgment of humans on what they have done. As he says in Romans 2:6, quoting Psalm 62:12 (see also Prov 24:12), God "will repay each person according to what they have done." He elaborates the two possible outcomes of this "repayment" in verses 7–11: those who "do good" will be rewarded with "glory, honor and peace" (v. 10), while the one who "does evil" will be punished with "trouble and distress" (v. 9). Yet in this passage Paul also suggests that more than works *per se* are involved. Those who do good are also described as "those who by persistence in doing good seek glory, honor and immortality" (v. 7), while those who do evil are also those who "reject the truth" (v. 8).[40] Paul also stresses the universalism of this final assessment: it is "first for the Jew, then for the Gentile" (vv. 9, 10). The "first for the Jew" reflects Paul's larger concern in Romans 2 to puncture the assumption that God's covenant with Israel will shield Jewish people from a negative verdict in the judgment. The focus on a twofold criterion for judgment emerges in other texts also. Note, for example, 2 Thessalonians 2:12: "All will be condemned who have not believed the truth but have delighted in wickedness." While, then, what people *do* is obviously a basic criterion of judgment in Paul, what people *believe* is also fundamental. In 2 Thessalonians 1:8, cited above, unbelievers are "punished" because they "do not know God and do not obey the gospel of our Lord Jesus."[41] Something of this same may be implied in Romans 2:16, where Paul claims that on the last day God "judges people's secrets through Jesus Christ, as my gospel declares."[42]

Paul describes the negative verdict in the judgment and the ultimate destiny of those who are so judged in a number of ways:[43]

> "Death." In one verse, Paul uses this language ("die," *apothnēskō*) to refer to the negative verdict in the judgment: "For if you live according to the flesh, you will die" (Rom 8:13).

---

40. For the view that this debated text describes the criteria of judgment, see pp. 204–5.

41. To be sure, the Greek here, which repeats the article before "those who do not obey," might suggest that Paul refers to two separate groups (see ESV; and Marshall, *1 and 2 Thessalonians*, 177–78). But it is more likely that the reference is to a single group described in two ways (so most commentators; see, e.g., Best, *Thessalonians*, 260).

42. It is possible that Rom 2:2 also links judgment to the gospel, if "based on truth [*kata alētheian*]" refers to a judgment "based on *the Truth*" rather than a "truthful judgment" (ESV "the judgment of God rightly falls").

43. "Hell," which occurs thirteen times in the NIV (translating *gehenna*, *hades*, and *tartarus*), does not occur in Paul. The content of this section is an updated version of my article, "What Does Paul Teach about Hell?," in *Hell under Fire: Modern Scholarship Reinvents Eternal Punishment*, ed. Christopher W. Morgan and Robert A. Peterson (Grand Rapids: Zondervan, 2004), 91–109.

"Judge." The Greek word *krinō* often has a neutral sense ("assess"; see, e.g., Rom 2:16; 3:6; 2 Tim 4:1), but it can also denote a negative verdict in the judgment (Rom 2:12; 2 Thess 2:12). The compound form of this verb—*katakrinō*, "condemn," and its noun form *katakrima*, "condemnation"—obviously has a negative sense. While stating a general circumstance, Romans 8:1—"there is now no condemnation"—certainly has the future at least in view.

"Wrath" (usually Gk. *orgē*, once *thymos*; see Rom 2:5, 8; 3:5; 5:9; 9:22 [twice]; 12:19; 13:4[?], 5[?]; Eph 2:3[?]; 5:6; Col 3:6; 1 Thess 1:10; 2:16; 5:9). Typical is Ephesians 5:6: "Let no one deceive you with empty words, for because of such things God's wrath comes on those who are disobedient."

"Perish," "destroy," "destruction" (usually Gk. *apollymi*, *apōleia*, three times *olethros*, once *phthora*; see Rom 2:12; 9:22; 14:15[?], 20[?]; 1 Cor 1:18; 15:18; 2 Cor 2:15; 4:3; Gal 6:8; Phil 1:28; 3:19; 1 Thess 5:3; 2 Thess 1:9; 2:10; 1 Tim 6:9). Galatians 6:8 is a good example of this use: "Whoever sows to please their flesh, from the flesh will reap destruction [*phthora*]; whoever sows to please the Spirit, from the Spirit will reap eternal life."

"Punish" (Gk. *ekdikos*, *ekdikēsis*, *dikē*; see Rom 12:19; 13:4; 1 Thess 4:6; 2 Thess 1:8, 9). Second Thessalonians 1:8: "He [God] will punish those who do not know God and do not obey the gospel of our Lord Jesus."

"Trouble" (*thlipsis*; 2 Thess 1:6); "trouble and distress" (Gk. *thlipsis kai stenochōria*, Rom 2:9: "There will be trouble and distress for every human being who does evil: first for the Jew, then for the Gentile").

"Shut out." Unbelievers will be "shut out" from the "presence of the Lord and from the glory of his might" (2 Thess 1:9).

These words all describe the same reality, as their overlap indicates: "perish" and "condemn" (2 Thess 2:9–10); "punish," "destroy," and "shut out from the presence of the Lord and from the glory of his might" (1:8–10); "perish" and "judge" (Rom 2:12). This reality, of course, is what we term "hell," a word Paul never uses, but a concept these verses clearly have in view. Traditionally, it has been thought that Paul, and other biblical authors, teach that unbelievers will suffer the punishment of conscious eternal torment; for eighteen centuries, "almost all Christian theologians taught the reality of eternal torment in Hell."[44] This doctrine has understandably been controversial, and is especially so in the context of a tolerant postmodernity. Two alternatives, significantly based on Paul's teaching, have become particularly popular: annihilationism and universalism.

---

44. Richard Bauckham, "Universalism: A Historical Survey," *Them* 4.2 (1979): 48 (quoted in Trevor Hart, "Eschatology," in *The Oxford Handbook of Evangelical Theology*, ed. Gerald R. McDermott [Oxford: Oxford University Press, 2010], 270). Hart notes language in the Athanasian Creed and the Westminster Confession and theologians such as Tertullian, Augustine, the Reformers, and Edwards (273).

5.1.1 Eternal Destruction?

Annihilationists teach that unbelievers, perhaps after a time of punishment after death, will simply cease to exist. Most forms of this view assume that humans were not created immortal; "immortality" is conferred only on believers when their bodies are raised from the dead. The bodies of unbelievers are also raised, but they are not given the gift of immortality. Lacking that gift from God, therefore, they naturally at some point cease to exist. In this sense, God need not "annihilate" them; his withholding from them the gift of immortality ensures their eventual extinction.[45] Paul gives little guidance to us on this matter of immortality. The idea of a general resurrection, while clearly taught by other biblical authors (e.g., John 5:28–29), is not explicit in Paul.[46] The "all" who are made alive in 1 Corinthians 15:22 are almost certainly believers; nor does verse 24, as some have argued, refer to a resurrection of the unrighteous.[47] Nevertheless, a resurrection of the unrighteous is probably presupposed in Paul. Considerable development in the notion of life after death took place in the Second Temple period. There was an increasing emphasis on resurrection as the point of entry into a far more extensive system of reward and punishment. Jewish theologians who taught a resurrection of the body differed on who would experience that resurrection. Most taught that only the righteous would be raised; some extended the privilege to all Israel; and some to both the particularly righteous and the most notorious sinners. But several Jewish works also attest to the idea of a general resurrection as the prelude to reward and punishment (e.g., T. Ben. 10.8; 4 Ezra 7.32, 37; 2 Bar. 30.2–5; 42.8; 49.1–51.10).[48] The Pharisees held this last view.[49] Paul, of course, was a Pharisee (e.g., Acts 23:6; 26:5; Phil 3:5) and, according to Luke, expresses his agreement with the notion of a resurrection of both the righteous and the unrighteous (Acts 24:15).

However, it is still the case that Paul attaches the idea of "immortality" to the resurrection bodies of the righteous. In 1 Corinthians 15:52 he writes, "The dead will be raised imperishable" (*aphthartoi*, "immortal"). And he contrasts this "imperishable" or "immortal" body with the "perishable" body all humans have apart from Christ (v. 42; cf. also Rom 2:7; 2 Tim 1:10). Murray Harris has shown that Paul uses "immortality"

45. For this view, see, e.g., Fudge, *Fire That Consumes*, 263–64, et al.; LeRoy Edwin Froom, *The Conditionalist Faith of our Fathers*, 2 vols. (Washington: Review and Herald, 1966); J. W. Wenham, "The Case for Conditional Immortality," in *Universalism and the Doctrine of Hell*, ed. Nigel M. de S. Cameron (Grand Rapids: Baker, 1992), 161–91; Philip Edgcumbe Hughes, *The True Image: The Origin and Destiny of Man in Christ* (Grand Rapids: Eerdmans, 1989), 398–407.

46. Wolter, e.g., doubts that Paul teaches a general resurrection of the dead (*Paul*, 209).

47. The claim is that "then the end" (*eita to telos*) marks a third stage in resurrection, after Christ's and believers' (v. 23).

But this is unlikely; see, e.g., Thiselton, *First Epistle to the Corinthians*, 1231.

48. See the survey in Murray J. Harris, *From Grave to Glory: Resurrection in the New Testament* (Grand Rapids: Zondervan, 1990), 69–79.

49. See esp. Josephus, *J.W.* 2.164. Josephus certainly accommodates the Jewish views of his day to standard Greek conceptions, but his reliability on this point is confirmed by other sources. See also the conclusion of E. P. Sanders: most Jews in Paul's day probably believed in an afterlife of reward and punishment (*Judaism: Practice and Belief, 63 BCE–66 CE* [Philadelphia: Trinity Press International, 1992], 303).

to mean "the immunity from death and decay that results from having or sharing the eternal divine life."[50] Yet this is not quite what theologians mean when they speak of "immortality." Paul does not provide us with the data we need to decide his view on this, although, as we will see, his claim about "eternal" destruction might presuppose the idea.[51]

Second Thessalonians 1:6–9, where Paul comforts the Thessalonians amid severe persecution, is the clearest text on this issue in Paul. "On the day [the Lord] comes to be glorified" (v. 10), unbelievers will "be punished" (dikēn tisousin) consisting of "eternal destruction" (olethron aiōnion) and be "shut out from the presence of the Lord and from the glory of his might" (v. 9). Just what Paul means here is much debated. First, there is the question of what "destruction" means. As the list above reveals, this language is Paul's most common way of depicting the fate of unbelievers. The English could certainly point toward an ultimate annihilation of the unrighteous. However, it is not clear that these words mean "destruction" in the sense of "extinction." In fact, leaving aside for the moment judgment texts, none of the key terms usually has this meaning in the Old Testament (in the LXX) or in the New.[52] Rather, they usually refer to the situation of a person or object that has lost the essence of its nature or function.[53] The English "destroy"/"destruction," then, can give a false impression of the strength of these words.

A further consideration that militates against taking Paul's language to refer to annihilation is the characterization of this "description" as "eternal." It is hard to see how an act such as being annihilated could be "eternal." In response to this point, it is argued that the word translated "eternal" (aiōnios) has a qualitative rather than temporal sense: It refers to destruction that lasts "for an age" (aiōn, "age," is the root of the word). However, most scholars today agree that the word has a mainly temporal significance in our literature.[54] Moreover, even if it had a qualitative sense here, the "age" in question is the age to come, an age that has no end.[55] A more promising way of squaring aiōnios

50. Harris, Raised Immortal, 189.

51. See, e.g., Robert A. Peterson, Hell on Trial: The Case for Eternal Punishment (Phillipsburg, NJ: P&R, 1995), 176–78. And on the larger question of immortality in the Bible, see Cooper, Body, Soul, and Everlasting Life, esp. 215–17.

52. Indeed, Best claims that olethros never has the meaning "annihilation" in the LXX (Thessalonians, 261–62, though he admits Wis 1:14 might be an exception).

53. The key words for "destroy" and "destruction" can also refer to land that has lost its fruitfulness (olethros in Ezek 6:14; 14:16); to ointment that is poured out wastefully and to no apparent purpose (apōleia in Matt 26:8; Mark 14:4); to wineskins that can no longer function because they have holes in them (apollymi in Matt 9:17; Mark 2:22; Luke 5:37); to a coin that is useless because it is "lost" (apollymi in Luke 15:9); or to the entire world

that "perishes," as an inhabited world, in the flood (2 Pet 3:6). In none of these cases do the objects cease to exist; they cease to be useful or to exist in their original, intended state. One text that is not as clear on this point is 1 Cor 10:9, 10, where Paul uses apollymi to refer to the death of idolaters. However, what is "destroyed" is "life as we know it in this world." Whether this implies extinction is not at all clear and can be decided only after the broader teaching about life after death has been decided. But note that most evangelical annihilationists posit that unbelievers exist for some time after death, so clearly they cannot argue that the language of destruction when applied to physical death must mean extinction.

54. See, e.g., H. Saase, TDNT 1:197–209; Harris, Raised Immortal, 182–83.

55. See, e.g., Morris, Thessalonians, 205.

with annihilationism, therefore, is to argue that the word refers not to the action itself but to the results of the action.[56] The "destruction" has "eternal" consequences. There is some point to this claim. In other New Testament passages where "eternal" describes a noun of action, it is sometimes the results of the action that are indicated. The "eternal sin" of Mark 3:29, for instance, means "a sin whose consequences last forever" (see also Heb 5:9; 6:2; 9:12; Jude 7). Nevertheless, even if this is the sense of the word here, one must still ask how a destruction whose consequences last forever can be squared with annihilationism. For eternal consequences appear to demand an eternal existence in some form.

Another factor to consider in this text is the possible connection between "destruction" and the rest of 2 Thessalonians 1:9: "Shut out from the presence of the Lord and from the glory of his might."[57] The NIV inserts an "and" to help the English reader make sense of the verse: "punished with everlasting destruction *and* shut out from . . ." In fact, however, "from the presence of the Lord" in the Greek is connected directly to "destruction"; see, for example, the CSB: "Eternal destruction from the Lord's presence." This may suggest that "destruction" is not so much an act of annihilation but a state of deprivation, a "ruin" that consists especially in eternal separation from God.

Finally, it appears that whatever Paul refers to here must be a state that could also exist during this life. The "destruction" threatened on the last day is a continuation of the "destruction" that people apart from Christ already experience. The vocabulary is the same: unbelievers doomed to "destruction" are already "perishing" (or "in the process of being destroyed"; 1 Cor 1:18; 2 Cor 2:15; 4:3; 2 Thess 2:10). Several of Paul's other key words for the final state work the same way. The "death" and "condemnation" pronounced on the wicked on the last day are already in effect for humans apart from Christ; "wrath," usually associated with the last day, is already in some sense operative (Rom 1:18; 3:5[?]; 4:15; 1 Thess 2:16). Matching Paul's inaugurated eschatology of life is an inaugurated eschatology of death. The judgment of hell is not, for Paul, the imposition of a new state. This condition is fixed forever for those who do not respond to God's grace in Christ and the work of his Spirit. This continuity also makes it difficult to interpret "destruction" in the sense of annihilation.

If, then, annihilation is not what Paul envisages for the destiny of unbelievers, what is? As the list above indicates, Paul's descriptions of what awaits unbelievers on the "day" are general and vague. True, he refers to fire and flames in two judgment texts (1 Cor 3:13–15; 2 Thess 1:7–8), but (as elsewhere in Scripture where this kind of language appears) it is likely the language is metaphorical rather than realistic. It would be bad interpretation to think he is directly describing the nature of hell. Paul, then, does not

---

56. E.g., Fudge, *Fire That Consumes*, 37–50.
57. In defense of this translation, pertaining to the force of *apo* ("shut out from"), see p. 106.

give us adequate data on which to build a clear idea of the afterlife for unbelievers. However, three points appear to be relatively secure: unbelievers will experience a positive infliction of punishment from God,[58] this punishment is eternal, and at the heart of this punishment is an eternal separation from God, a separation that continues and finalizes a separation that has been the effect of sin on humans ever since Adam.[59]

5.1.2 God "All in All"?

Few interpreters deny that Paul in some passages teaches the reality of a punishment for the wicked in the afterlife. But a significant number of contemporary scholars minimize this evidence, arguing either that the punishment will be only temporary, followed by restoration to fellowship with God, or that warnings about final punishment serve a rhetorical purpose and do not represent the true heart of Paul's theology.[60] Particularly important in this regard are several Pauline texts that are alleged to teach salvific universalism. We have discussed each of these in the exegesis above, so a brief overview is all that is needed here.

1 Corinthians 15:20–28. In the passage we quoted at the beginning of this chapter, Paul claims that "in Christ all will be made alive" (v. 22) and that everything will ultimately be subjected to God, so that he might be "all in all" (v. 28). Here, according to some interpreters, Paul expresses optimism about the ultimate fate of the world. Borrowing from Jewish apocalyptic, he teaches a future universal extent of God's life-giving power. For God to reclaim his sovereignty over creation, he must bestow on all human beings a new resurrection life, a life that conquers death itself.[61] Paul's claim in verse 22 that "in Christ all will be made alive" could refer to a general resurrection of the dead, a view, as we have seen above, that the Pharisee Paul may have been assumed to hold.[62] But even if this is Paul's reference, universalism does not follow, for a universal resurrection does not entail universal salvation. More importantly, however,

---

58. Stephen Travis questions that God will positively punish sinners in this way, arguing that "retribution" is not taught in Scripture. Rather, "the consequences of sin follow by inner necessity" (*Christ and the Judgement of God*, 84). However, his exegesis is not always convincing, and Garry Williams criticizes Travis for defining retribution as a purely external reaction ("Penal Substitution: A Response to Recent Criticisms," in *The Atonement Debate: Papers from the London Symposium on the Theology of the Atonement*, ed. David Hilborn, Justin Thacker, and Derek Tidball [Grand Rapids: Zondervan, 2008], 174–78).

59. An option that avoids some of the theological concerns with the traditional view (especially the eternal duration of sin) is that hell is a state in which the condemned are reconciled to God (but not saved!) as they acknowledge the justice of God's judgment of them (see, e.g., Henri A. Blocher, "Everlasting Punishment and the Problem of Evil," in Cameron, *Universalism and the Doctrine of Hell*; and, for a wider description of the view, Stephen N.

Williams, "The Question of Hell and Salvation: Is There a Fourth View?," *TynBul* 57 [2006]: 263–83).

60. See the survey and outline of the alleged two different perspectives in Paul in Sven Hillbert, *Limited and Universal Salvation: A Text-Oriented and Hermeneutical Study of Two Perspectives in Paul*, ConBNT 31 (Stockholm: Almqvist & Wiksell, 1999); see also, along the same lines, M. Eugene Boring, who concludes that these two perspectives cannot be reconciled ("The Language of Universal Salvation in Paul," *JBL* 105 [1986]: 269–92). An argument for universalism from an "evangelical" perspective is offered by Gregory McDonald in *The Evangelical Universalist* (Eugene, OR: Cascade, 2006). See also Campbell, *Pauline Dogmatics*, 429–37.

61. See, e.g., Hultgren, *Paul's Gospel and Mission*, 104.

62. E.g., Robert D. Culver, "A Neglected Millennial Passage from St. Paul," *BSac* 113 (1956): 141–52.

it is unlikely that verse 22 refers to a universal resurrection. "In Christ all will be made alive" is interpreted in verse 23: "But each in turn: Christ, the firstfruits; then, when he comes, those who belong to him." Paul is thinking in this verse of the resurrection of Christians. As all those who belong to Adam die, so all those who belong to Christ will be raised from the dead.[63] Nor is it necessary, for God to be "all in all," for every creature to enter finally into a saving relationship with him. Paul affirms that God's nature and purposes demand that all creatures be finally subject to his authority, but the nature of that submission is not spelled out.

Romans 5:18. The similarity between Adam and Christ that is at the heart of Romans 5:12–21 extends, it appears, to the universal scope of those who are affected by their actions. Adam brings condemnation on "all people"; Christ brings "justification and life for all." The extent of eternal life will match the extent of death and condemnation.[64] However, as I have pointed out above, Paul qualifies the "universalism" on Christ's side (in a way he does not with respect to Adam's act) in the immediate context. Only those who "*receive*" God's gift of grace will reign in life (v. 17). The universalism of this text, then, might be restricted, as in 1 Corinthians 15:22, to believers: "the all" who are justified are the "all in Christ."[65] Or what is universal is not the attainment of justification but the offer of justification.[66]

Romans 11:32. Paul's long and convoluted survey of salvation history culminates in an apparently universal promise: God has "bound everyone over to disobedience so that he may have mercy on them all." Again, it is argued that this text teaches salvific universalism, and God will have mercy on—save—every single person.[67] The problem again with this view is that it contradicts Paul's teaching elsewhere. Paul may, then, mean simply that God's mercy is potentially available to all.[68] But a reference to an offer of mercy here does not square well with Paul's emphasis throughout Romans 9–11 on the God who is sovereignly working in salvation history to accomplish his purposes—and not least in the showing of mercy (see 9:15–16). When we put this verse

63. See esp. W. V. Crockett, "The Ultimate Restoration of All Mankind: 1 Corinthians 15:22," in *Studia Biblica 1978: Papers on Paul and Other New Testament Authors*, ed. E. A. Livingstone (Sheffield: Academic, 1980), 83–87. Hultgren objects to this interpretation by arguing that the phrase "in Christ" must be adverbial, modifying "will be made alive," rather than adjectival, modifying "all" (*Paul's Gospel and Mission*, 104). But my interpretation does not require that "in Christ" be adjectival; it simply insists that the word "all" be defined—as it always must be—by the context.

64. See, again, Hultgren, *Paul's Gospel and Mission*, 82–124; and also C. K. Barrett, *The Epistle to the Romans*, HNTC (New York: Harper & Row, 1958), 116–17.

65. E.g., Augustine, *On Nature and Grace* 41.48 (see *NPNF¹* 5:137–38).

66. Rapinchuk, "Universal Sin and Salvation," 427–41.

67. Origen was an early advocate of such a view, holding that there would in the end be an *apokatastasis* ("restoration") of all things. He was opposed, however, among others, by Augustine (see *City of God* 21.24). Modern advocates of the universalistic interpretation of this verse include Jewett, *Romans*, 711–12; and T. Nicklas, "Paulus und die Errettung Israels: Röm 11,25–36 in der exegetischen Diskussion und im jüdisch-christlichen Dialog," *Early Christianity* 2 (2011): 173–97.

68. Henry Alford, *The Greek Testament*, rev. ed., 8 vols. (Chicago: Moody, 1958), 2:437.

in its context, we get a very different result. Paul is commenting on the process that he has outlined in verses 30–31 (and several other times in this chapter). That being the case, "all" might refer to the unbelieving Jews about whom he has been speaking in verse 31.[69] But we can hardly eliminate from Paul's reference the gentiles in the church at Rome whom Paul has been addressing throughout this section. Considering the corporate perspective that is basic to chapter 11, then, it seems best to think that "all" refers to "all the groups" about which Paul has been speaking: Jews and gentiles.[70] Paul is not saying that all human beings will be saved. Rather, he is saying that God has imprisoned in disobedience first gentiles and now Jews so that he might bestow mercy on each of these groups of humanity. How many from each of these groups will ultimately be saved, Paul does not say.

Colossians 1:20. The climax of the "Christ hymn" in Colossians 1:15–20 is that God's purpose through the cross of Christ is to "reconcile to himself all things, whether things on earth or things in heaven." This text, is, of course, a well-known basis for the doctrine of *apokatastasis*, or "restoration," in a universalistic sense. And the context, where "all" or "every" (Gk. *pas*) is a key word, certainly points to universality. However, the universalism is not restricted to humans; the entire universe is included. As Peter O'Brien points out, hostile spiritual powers "are shown as submitting against their will to a power they cannot resist. They are reconciled through subjugation."[71] "Salvific" universalism cannot, then, be the direct teaching. Rather, since Paul elaborates "reconcile" with "making peace," the text is probably referring to the establishment of worldwide *shalom*, a universal pacification according to which God exerts his sovereignty over all things.

1 Timothy 2:4. The final text sometimes used to support universalism in Paul is 1 Timothy 2:4, with its famous claim that God "wants all people to be saved and to come to a knowledge of the truth." Universalists argue that an omnipotent God will surely accomplish what he "wishes." If God wants all people to be saved, then all people will be saved—whether through faith in this life, through an encounter with Christ after death, or by some other means.[72] The problem with this interpretation is that Paul teaches quite explicitly in this very letter that faith, which Paul confines to this life and limits only to some people, is necessary for salvation (1:16; 2:15; 3:16; 4:10). Moreover, it is not at all clear on logical or theological grounds that whatever God "desires" he accomplishes. Theologians since the early days of the church have

---

69. F. Refoulé, ". . . *Et ainsi tout Israël sera sauvé*": *Romains 11,25–32*, LD 117 (Paris: Cerf, 1984), 233–35.

70. See, e.g., Calvin, *Romans*, 442–43; Murray, *Romans*, 2:102–3. The Greek is *tous pantas*, the article perhaps emphasizing the collective, or corporate, aspect. On universal texts in Romans generally, see esp. Stephen Pegler, "The Nature of Paul's Universal

Salvation Language in Romans" (PhD diss., Trinity Evangelical Divinity School, 2002).

71. O'Brien, *Colossians, Philemon*, 56.

72. See, e.g., John Hick, *Evil and the God of Love* (London: Macmillan, 1966), 378–80.

recognized the need to distinguish between God's "general" will—his "desires," as it were—and his effective will. One must analyze carefully biblical expressions about God's "will" before deciding in which category to place them. What, then, does Paul mean in this verse? Two interpretations deserve mention. First, since Paul seems to be combating in the Pastoral Epistles a heresy that confined salvation to a select few, the point of verse 4 might be that God extends a gracious offer of salvation to all human beings. Only some, however, will accept.[73] Second, Paul might be emphasizing that God's will for salvation extends to "all kinds of people." We have seen that Paul uses universal language in this sense elsewhere (Rom 11:32); and verse 1, with its call for prayers to be offered for "everyone" (*pantōn anthrōpōn*, the same Greek words occur in v. 4), supports this nuance.[74]

If we restrict our focus to the immediate context of each of these texts, they could be interpreted in a universalistic sense. But when we expand our vision to include all the Pauline material (to say nothing of the rest of the NT), universalist interpretations become fraught with issues. This conclusion, of course, follows only if we are committed to take seriously all the Pauline data. The viability of a salvific universalistic viewpoint is determined, then, by one's presuppositions about the nature of Scripture and the hermeneutical implications that flow from those presuppositions. If, as I do, we rule out any view that requires us to dismiss some texts or to engage in patently problematic exegesis, universalism is not an option. For it is much easier to explain the texts we have looked at above in a non-universalist way than to suppose that a dozen or so other texts that refer to the reality and enduring nature of hell can be explained in other ways.[75]

5.2 Believers and the Judgment

Granted Old Testament and Jewish teaching, as well as familiar Christian doctrine, we are not surprised that Paul teaches that the unrighteous would face the judgment of God. Paul's clear teaching that God will also judge believers is a bit more unexpected. Yet the evidence for this teaching in Paul is abundant.[76] We have already noted texts that indicate that God's judgment is universal, encompassing all humans (e.g., Rom 2:7–10, 16). Several other texts focus on judgment for Christians in particular:

---

73. See, for a recent defense of this view, Marshall and Towner, *Pastoral Epistles*, 426–27.

74. E.g., Knight, *Pastoral Epistles*, 307.

75. It is worth noting that a universalistic interpretation of Paul does not fit well with the Jewish background. As A. Oepke notes, the idea of a final restoration of all sinners is foreign to Paul's Jewish heritage (*TDNT* 1:392). Had he diverged from this view, we would have expected him to be much clearer about it.

76. Christian Stettler draws attention to the prominence of judgment in Paul's soteriology (*Das Endgericht bei Paulus: Framesemantische und Exegetische Studien zur paulinischen Eschatologie und Soteriologie*, WUNT 2/317 [Tübingen: Mohr Siebeck, 2017], esp. 49–71).

You, then, why do you judge your brother or sister? Or why do you treat them with contempt? For we will all stand before God's judgment seat. It is written: "As surely as I live," says the Lord, "every knee will bow before me; every tongue will acknowledge God." So then, each of us will give an account of ourselves to God. (Rom 14:10–12)

Therefore judge nothing before the appointed time; wait until the Lord comes. He will bring to light what is hidden in darkness and will expose the motives of the heart. At that time each will receive their praise from God. (1 Cor 4:5)

For we must all appear before the judgment seat of Christ, so that each of us may receive what is due us for the things done while in the body, whether good or bad. (2 Cor 5:10)

You know that you will receive an inheritance from the Lord as a reward. It is the Lord Christ you are serving. Anyone who does wrong will be repaid for their wrongs, and there is no favoritism. (Col 3:24–25)

Related to these warnings about judgment to come are texts in which the ultimate fate of believers appears to be a matter to be determined in the future:

For if you live according to the flesh, you will die; but if by the Spirit you put to death the misdeeds of the body, you will live. (Rom 8:13)

But they were broken off because of unbelief, and you stand by faith. Do not be arrogant, but tremble. For if God did not spare the natural branches, he will not spare you either. Consider therefore the kindness and sternness of God: sternness to those who fell, but kindness to you, provided that you continue in his kindness. Otherwise, you also will be cut off. (Rom 11:20–22)

Do you not know that in a race all the runners run, but only one gets the prize? Run in such a way as to get the prize. Everyone who competes in the games goes into strict training. They do it to get a crown that will not last, but we do it to get a crown that will last forever. Therefore I do not run like someone running aimlessly; I do not fight like a boxer beating the air. No, I strike a blow to my body and make it my slave so that after I have preached to others, I myself will not be disqualified for the prize. (1 Cor 9:24–27)

Nevertheless, God was not pleased with most of them; their bodies were scattered in the wilderness. Now these things occurred as examples to keep us from setting our hearts on evil things as they did. Do not be idolaters, as some of them were; as it is written: 'The people sat down to eat and drink and got up to indulge in revelry.' We should not commit sexual immorality, as some of them did—and in one day twenty-three thousand of them died. We should not test Christ, as some of them did—and were killed by snakes. And do not grumble, as some of them did—and were killed by the destroying angel. (1 Cor 10:5–10)

Do not be deceived: God cannot be mocked. A man reaps what he sows. Whoever sows to please their flesh, from the flesh will reap destruction; whoever sows to please the Spirit, from the Spirit will reap eternal life. (Gal 6:7–9)

By the grace God has given me, I laid a foundation as a wise builder, and someone else is building on it. But each one should build with care. For no one can lay any foundation other than the one already laid, which is Jesus Christ. If anyone builds on this foundation using gold, silver, costly stones, wood, hay or straw, their work will be shown for what it is, because the Day will bring it to light. It will be revealed with fire, and the fire will test the quality of each person's work. If what has been built survives, the builder will receive a reward. If it is burned up, the builder will suffer loss but yet will be saved—even though only as one escaping through the flames. (1 Cor 3:10–15)

But now he has reconciled you by Christ's physical body through death to present you holy in his sight, without blemish and free from accusation—if you continue in your faith, established and firm, and do not move from the hope held out in the gospel. (Col 1:22–23a)

Watch your life and doctrine closely. Persevere in them, because if you do, you will save both yourself and your hearers. (1 Tim 4:16)

Command them to do good, to be rich in good deeds, and to be generous and willing to share. In this way they will lay up treasure for themselves as a firm foundation for the coming age, so that they may take hold of the life that is truly life. (1 Tim 6:18–19)

Taken together, these passages suggest that believers will face judgment (1) that has two possible outcomes—eternal life or eternal death (Rom 8:13; Gal 6:7–9); and (2) whose outcome depends on what believers have "done" (1 Tim 6:18–19). However, these texts must be juxtaposed with another series of texts that assure believers by asserting that their current state of salvation will infallibly be confirmed at the time of the judgment. I have identified some of these passages above in my discussion of the day of the Lord (1 Cor 1:8–9; Phil 1:6; 2 Tim 1:12; see also Rom 8:31–39; Eph 1:14).

Resolution of these two strands of teaching is not easy and has been a matter of long, and sometimes rancorous, debate.[77] I have already tackled some aspects of this issue in my discussion of justification (pp. 488–91). As I noted in that earlier discussion, many interpreters argue that these two strands of teaching may be reconciled if we view the coming judgment of believers as confined to the question of degree of reward. Paul certainly teaches that believers will receive a "reward" at the judgment. See, for example, 2 Timothy 4:8: "Now there is in store for me the crown of righteousness, which the Lord, the righteous Judge, will award to me on that day—and not only to me, but also to all who have longed for his appearing" (see also 1 Cor 9:25; "praise from God" in 1 Cor 4:5). However, the reward in this verse is "righteousness," the final confirmation of the right standing with God given to every believer. Elsewhere, Paul suggests that the spiritual flourishing of believers is his "reward" (1 Thess 2:19; see also, probably 1 Cor 3:10–15). While, then, Paul clearly envisages the parousia as a time when believers will receive a "reward," it is not clear that he thinks in terms of *degrees* of reward. Rather, he suggests that judgment for believers is binary. As several of the texts listed above make clear, the issue for believers is whether they receive a reward, on the one hand, or are condemned, on the other (see esp. Rom 8:13 and Gal 6:7–9). I reiterate here also my conviction that Paul does teach that initial justification is, in fact, a final and unchangeable verdict; that true believers are assured of infallibly attaining final salvation. I am drawn to this conclusion especially by the logic of texts such as Romans 5:9–10, where Paul claims that people who are "justified" and "reconciled" will be "saved" on the last day. Here, it seems to me, we glimpse a core Pauline theological conviction that deserves to have a certain priority in our assessment of various texts. At the same time, we should not dismiss too quickly the illocutionary force of Paul's warning passages. These warnings are intended to accomplish something in the lives of believers. Without lapsing into an irrational "both/and," we should still seek to honor Paul's rhetorical purposes in both his warning texts and his assurance texts. As it has been put, Paul seeks, on the one hand, to "comfort the afflicted" and, on the other, to "afflict the comfortable."[78]

---

77. On one side are those who think the warning passages clearly imply that genuine believers might forfeit their salvation in the judgment: e.g., B. J. Oropeza, *Paul and Apostasy: Eschatology, Perseverance, and Falling Away in the Corinthian Congregation*, WUNT 2/115 (Tübingen: Mohr Siebeck, 2000); idem, *Jews, Gentiles, and the Opponents of Paul*; Williams, *Election of Grace*, 153–65; Dunn, *Theology of Paul*, 497–98. On the other side are those who insist that those who are truly converted will infallibly attain eternal salvation: e.g., Judith M. Gundry Volf, *Paul and* *Perseverance: Staying in and Falling Away* (Louisville: Westminster John Knox, 1990).

78. See on this point esp. Laurie Norris, "The Function of New Testament Warning Passages: A Speech Act Theory Approach" (PhD diss., Wheaton College, 2011). Schreiner and Caneday follow a generally similar line of argument (Thomas R. Schreiner and Ardel B. Caneday, *The Race Set before Us: A Biblical Theology of Perseverance and Assurance* [Downers Grove, IL: InterVarsity Press, 2001]); as does Wilson (*Warning-Assurance Relationship*).

6 ISRAEL

Paul, with other New Testament writers, was convinced that the promises God made to his people Israel in the Old Testament were finding their fulfillment in Christ and the new-covenant people of God. "For no matter how many promises God has made, they are 'Yes' in Christ" (2 Cor 1:20). Abundant evidence for this appropriation of the Old Testament is provided in Romans 1–8. Christ is the promised "seed of David" (1:3); the revelation of the righteousness of God that would vindicate God's people has occurred, valid for all who believe, Jew and gentile alike (v. 17; cf. 3:21–26). At the same time, Paul applies to the church various descriptions first applied to Israel. Believers, whether Jew or gentile, are children of their "father" Abraham (ch. 4); theirs is the "hope of glory" (5:2); they are recipients of the eschatological ministry of the Spirit (8:1–11); they are the adopted children of God and thereby God's heirs (vv. 14–17). These clear and repeated implicit claims about the church as the "place" where promises and blessings originally attached to Israel are now being experienced is one of the stimuli for Paul's long and complex discussion of Israel in chapters 9–11. As I note in my exegesis (pp. 229–30), Paul in these chapters tackles from different angles the tension created by the conflict between Israel's "privileges," recorded in the Old Testament, and its "predicament"—estranged from God because of their rejection of Christ. I deal elsewhere with the implications of this passage for the current situation of Israel vis-à-vis the church (pp. 558–65). Here, appropriate to an overview of the "consummation of the new realm," I ask whether Paul sees a future for ethnic Israel.

The trend of teaching in Romans 1–8, reinforced by the apparent "universalizing" of God's election in 9:6–29, would strongly suggest a negative answer to this question. There is no future for ethnic Israel apart from the continuing conversion of individual Jewish persons who respond to Christ and become integrated into the church, the people of God of this era. I admit that this view has, at least at first sight, a claim to fit better into Paul's overall theology of New Testament fulfillment and the shift he repeatedly documents from Israel to the church. However, my exegesis compels me to a different view. Paul does, indeed, teach that there is a future for ethnic Israel.

The crucial text is, of course, Romans 11:25–27:

I do not want you to be ignorant of this mystery, brothers and sisters, so that you may not be conceited: Israel has experienced a hardening in part until the full number of the Gentiles has come in, and in this way all Israel will be saved. As it is written:

"The deliverer will come from Zion;
  he will turn godlessness away from Jacob.

And this is my covenant with them
  when I take away their sins."

In the first part of this book, I conclude that "the most natural reading of this sequence sees all Israel being saved as a new stage in salvation history that comes after all elect Gentiles have come into the kingdom."[79] Here I expand on my reasons for drawing this conclusion.[80]

Paul signals the importance of this text by introducing it as a "mystery" (*mystērion*). The word often in Paul is applied to the relationship of Jews and gentiles in the new-covenant people of God (e.g., Eph 3:3–6), so it is no surprise that he uses it here. In this text, it might refer specifically to hardening that Israel is experiencing.[81] Or it might refer to the promise that "all Israel will be saved" (v. 26).[82] But probably it refers to the sequence of salvation history that is the basic scaffolding of verses 11–32:[83]

v. 11: Israel's "transgression → salvation comes to the Gentiles
    → to make Israel envious
v. 12: Israel's "transgression" → riches for the world
    Israel's "loss" → riches for the Gentiles
    Israel's full inclusion → greater riches
v. 15: Israel's "rejection" → reconciliation [of] the world
    Israel's "acceptance" → life from the dead[84]
vv. 17–23: "natural" branches broken off → wild olive shoots grafted in
    → God is able to graft them in again
vv. 25–26: Israel's hardening "in part" → full number of the gentiles comes in
    → "in this way all Israel will be saved"
vv. 30–31: Israel's disobedience → mercy for gentiles → mercy "now" for Israel

It is this sequence that Paul succinctly states in verses 25b–26a. The hardening of Israel "in part" (v. 25) describes the initial "transgression" or "loss" of Israel—the breaking

79. I defend this view in greater detail in my *Romans* (NICNT), 734–44.

80. The content and some of the wording of what follows is adapted from Douglas J. Moo, *Encountering the Book of Romans: A Theological Survey*, 2nd ed. (Grand Rapids: Baker, 2014), 156–58. Used by permission.

81. E.g., Ferdinand Hahn, "Zum Verständnis von Römer 11.26a: '. . . und so wird ganz Israel gerettet werden,'" in Hooker and Wilson, *Paul and Paulinism*, 224.

82. E.g., Cranfield, *Romans*, 2:573–74.

83. E.g., Schreiner, *Romans*, 595–96; Beker, *Paul the Apostle*, 333–35.

84. This phrase is a bit of a linchpin in interpretations of the passage. If it refers to the eschatological resurrection of the dead, it favors the view that Israel's salvation occurs in the future (e.g., Munck, *Christ and Israel*, 126–27; William D. Davies, "Paul and the Gentiles: A Suggestion concerning Romans 11.13–24," in *Jewish and Pauline Studies* [Philadelphia: Fortress, 1984], 132; Beker, *Paul the Apostle*, 153). However, if it means new spiritual life, it could apply to any point in time (e.g., N. T. Wright, "Christ, the Law and the People of God: The Problem of Romans 9–11," in *Climax of the Covenant*, 248; D. Judant, *Les deux Israël: Essai sur le mystère du salut d'Israël selon l'économie des deux Testaments* [Paris: Cerf, 1960], 182–91).

off of natural branches. This matches the situation in Paul's day, when, surprisingly and distressingly, so many of his kinspeople have rejected the good news of Christ. The "full number[85] of the Gentiles" would, then, appear to describe the extension of God's saving grace to gentiles (their "riches," the wild shoots grafted in)—also something that has taken place in Paul's time (and partly through his own ministry). But what does the third step in verses 25b–26, "all Israel will be saved," describe?[86] One view, with a long and distinguished pedigree in the interpretation of the church, is that Paul here summarizes the whole process: It is through this oscillation between Jew and gentile that God brings all the elect ("the church") to salvation. However, the addition of the "all" before "Israel" changes the extent of the word but not its meaning, and "Israel" consistently refers to ethnic Israel in this context (e.g., v. 25).[87] Probably, then, "all Israel will be saved" refers to the third step in the sequence, when Israel is made envious, "greater riches" appear, Israel is "accepted," natural branches are grafted in again, and Israel receives mercy. The question then becomes, "When does this happen?" Some interpreters insist that consistency with Paul's theology elsewhere demands that we see this as an ongoing process operative throughout salvation history.[88] However, I think it more likely that this step in the sequence is one that is still future from Paul's perspective—and from ours. An important indicator that this step is a future one is the "until" in verse 25, which naturally means that the hardening of Israel will one day be removed, allowing the salvation of "all Israel." "All Israel," as I note in my exposition (pp. 235–37), does not mean "every single Israelite" but, having a corporate sense seen in the Old Testament, a great many Israelites (similar to our claim, e.g., that "all America was watching the events in Washington").

On this view, verses 26b–27 refer to the coming of Christ as the time when this salvation of Israel takes place. In these verses, Paul quotes Isaiah 59:20–21 and 27:9 (with a possible allusion to Jer 31:31–34). The main text, Isaiah 59:20–21, speaks of the deliverer coming "to" or "for the sake" of Zion. Paul, however, quotes the text as saying that "the deliverer will come *from* Zion." Paul has probably deliberately changed the text in order to fit the new shape of salvation history. The deliverer cannot come "to Zion" to rescue Israel because Israel is not located in "Zion"; the people of Israel have rejected the deliverer who has already come, sending them into a new, spiritual exile. Following up on this spatial metaphor then, Paul pictures the Israel of his day as located outside

---

85. "Full number" translates *plērōma*, a word that usually has a qualitative meaning, "fullness." But since the "fullness" in this case is achieved by numerical addition, the NIV's "full number" is accurate.

86. There is some debate about the *means* of this salvation, some arguing that Israel is saved through its own Torah covenant. I argue against this option on pp. 235–36.

87. Romans 9:6 might be an exception (see p. 231), but, of course, it is pretty far away from 11:26.

88. Evidence supporting this view is found in v. 32, where the probable reading of the text indicates that Israel is receiving mercy "now" (*nyn*). NA[28] and UBS[5] tentatively include this *nyn*, following the potent combination of the primary Alexandrian uncials א and B and a part of the Western tradition (the original hand and third corrector of D). In this they are followed by most of the commentators.

the holy land, thus requiring that the "deliverer" come *from* Zion. God has already established his Messiah in "Zion" (Rom 9:33, quoting Isa 28:16).[89] It is therefore "from" there that Messiah will come again to rescue the hardened and unbelieving Israel from her renewed exile. While, therefore, the "redeemer" in Isaiah 59:20 is Yahweh himself, Paul probably intends to identify Christ as the Redeemer.[90] The coming of the deliverer will "turn godlessness away from Jacob" in accordance with God's covenant. In the context (see v. 28), the covenant is probably the promise-covenant that God entered into with Abraham and his descendants. The covenant has, of course, had an initial and definitive fulfillment in the first coming of Christ.[91] But, in a pattern typical of the New Testament, Paul suggests that this covenant with Abraham awaits its final consummation—a consummation that will affect Israel in particular.

It is true that Paul's teaching about a final ingathering of Jewish people has no parallel elsewhere in his writings. But this may be explained by the contingent character of all that Paul wrote. In most of the situations where Paul taught about Israel or the Jews, he was concerned to establish the right of gentiles to enter fully into the people of God—usually against a Jewish-oriented attempt to exclude them or to impose inappropriate restrictions on them (e.g., Rom 3–4; Galatians; Phil 3). Only in Romans 11, apparently, did Paul face a situation in which he needed to remind gentile Christians of the continuing significance of Israel's election.[92]

We must now assess some of the wider theological implications of the view of Romans 11:25–27 that I have argued for. First, there is the apparent tension between Paul's removal of a "most-favored nation" status for Israel—even in a text as near as chapter 9—and his claim here that Israel will enjoy a certain privilege at the parousia. The tension is real, but arguably matches the tricky balance between universalism and particularity that marks Paul's theology. Paul asserts *both* that the new stage of salvation history "levels the playing field"—salvation is "to *everyone* who believes" (Rom 1:16)—but at the same time maintains some kind of priority for Jews—"first to the Jew." Nor does Paul's teaching about the freedom of God to elect whomever he chooses (ch. 9) mean that God cannot take into consideration ethnic identity; only that ethnic identity is never the *basis* for God's choice. There is, therefore, nothing contradictory to chapter 9, if Paul, in chapter 11, affirms that God, in faithfulness to his own pledged

89. Other texts that may have influenced Paul to use Zion this way are Isa 2:2–4; Ps 14:7; 110:2; Mic 4:2. For this general approach, see esp. Elisee Ouoba, "Paul's Use of Isaiah 27:9 and 59:20–21 in Romans 11:25–27" (PhD diss., Wheaton College, 2010); and also, e.g., Bruce W. Longenecker, "Different Answers to Different Issues: Israel, the Gentiles and Salvation History in Romans 9–11," *JSNT* 36 (1989): 117n21.

90. See the similar language in 1 Thess 1:10: "Jesus, the one who delivers us from the wrath to come."

91. Thus many scholars think this reference to covenant points to a present fulfillment of Israel's salvation; e.g., Wright, "Christ, the Law and the People of God," 250–51; Dieter Zeller, "Israel unter dem Ruf Gottes (Röm 9–11)," *IKZ* 2 (1973): 296.

92. Paul's claim that "the wrath of God has come upon them at last" (1 Thess 2:16) appears at first sight to contradict the view I have argued for here. However, I argue for an interpretation of this difficult verse that can reconcile the two (pp. 93–94).

word, will choose to save a great number of Jews in the last days. Paul's reassertion of this traditional hope contradicts his teaching in Romans 9 only if that chapter claims that the election of Israel is exhaustively fulfilled in the remnant of Paul's day or if it teaches that God cannot take ethnic identity into account in his decision about whom to save. But Paul affirms neither of these there.

A second theological issue that Paul's affirmation of a future for Israel raises is the extent of this future.[93] A particular piece of geography was one of the basic components of God's original promise to Abraham (Gen 12:1–3) and, of course, has a prominent role in the subsequent development of God's redemptive plan. After their deliverance from Egypt and their testing in the wilderness, the people of Israel ultimately possess the land God promised them. Yet their possession of the land was always contingent on their faithful adherence to the covenant (Deut 29–32). As early as the latter chapters of Deuteronomy, it becomes clear that Israel would indeed fail to maintain her covenant obligation and forfeit their possession of the land. Yet even amid these dire warnings and pessimistic predictions, a clear note of grace and God's continuing faithfulness is sounded. After the people's exile, God would bring his people back to their land again. This sequence outlined in Deuteronomy becomes a template for the history of Israel and the land. The people fail to obey the law they were given; God expels them from their land because of their rebellion; and God promises that he will bring his people back from exile and settle them again in their land. It might appear that the Old Testament ends with these promises fulfilled—under the leadership of Ezra and Nehemiah, the people of Israel return to their land, rebuild their temple, and establish a degree of political autonomy. However, the situation of Israel in the land at the end of the Old Testament is a far cry from the picture the prophets predict. Only a minority of Jews are back in their land; the repeated wars and occupations by foreign powers make a mockery of the prophets' predictions of peace and security; and the people fail to display the spiritual vitality and faithfulness to God that was to characterize the Israel of the "last days."

Paul never directly addresses the question about the way the Old Testament land promise is fulfilled in "the last days." This silence has opened the way for very different answers to the question. One trajectory stresses the need for continuity between Old Testament promise and New Testament fulfillment, insisting that the promise of a specific land to the people of Israel remains in force. This geographic aspect of fulfillment should, then, be assumed to be included in Paul's prediction of a future culmination of God's covenant promise to Israel.[94] Other interpreters, however, noting the pattern of Old Testament promises being fulfilled in the present stage of salvation history, argue for a "spiritualized" fulfillment of the land promise. Christ himself

93. The following discussion is adapted from D. Moo and J. Moo, *Creation Care*, 131–36.

94. See, e.g., Michael J. Vlach, *Has the Church Replaced Israel? A Theological Evaluation* (Nashville: B&H Academic, 2010); Mark

embodies the fulfillment of the land promise. As W. D. Davies puts it in an influential study, "In sum, for the holiness of place, Christianity has fundamentally, though not consistently, substituted the holiness of a Person; it has Christified holy space."[95] The believer's "inheritance" is no longer a piece of real estate, but Christ and his promises (e.g., Rom 8:17; Eph 1:14).

I think this last approach captures some basic aspects of Paul's teaching. However, I do not think either approach does justice to the full spectrum of Paul's teaching on the issue. It is perhaps fair to say that a degree of *Christifying* or *spiritualizing* the Old Testament land promise occurs in Paul. At the same time, however, Paul suggests that the land promise has also been *universalized*. The text that most clearly suggests this is Romans 4:13: "It was not through the law that Abraham and his offspring received the promise that he would be heir of the world, but through the righteousness that comes by faith." Paul's reference in this verse to the "world" (Gk. *kosmos*) is therefore noteworthy. "Inheriting the world" is Paul's shorthand way of summarizing the three elements of the promise God made to Abraham: that he would have an immense number of descendants, embracing many nations (Gen 12:2; 13:16; 15:5; 17:4–6, 16–20; 22:17); that he would possess the land (13:15–17; 15:12–21; 17:8); and that he would be the means of blessing to all the peoples of the earth (Gen 12:3; 18:18; 22:18). Of course, the context of Romans 4 makes clear that Paul's focus is on the first of these aspects of the promise. Inclusion of gentiles within the spiritual family of Abraham is what this part of Romans 4 is all about. But Paul would never have chosen the combination of "inherit" and "world" if he wanted to say only this. Reference to the geographical element of the promise is unmistakable. As Mark Forman pertinently notes, Paul's concept of inheritance is "non-territorial," but it is not "non-material."[96] And by speaking of the "world" rather than the "land," Paul implies a universalizing of the geographical promise.[97] The Old Testament itself plainly hints at an expansive "seed" of Abraham, requiring an expansive place for them to live. God's promise to Abraham ultimately has in view not just one nation living in one area but "many nations" (Rom 4:18) inhabiting

---

Reasoner, "The Salvation of Israel in Romans 9–11," in *The Call of Abraham: Essays on the Election of Israel in Honor of John D. Levinson*, ed. Gary A. Anderson and Joel S. Kaminsky (Notre Dame: University of Notre Dame Press, 2013), 256–79.

95. Davies, *Gospel and the Land*, 385. See also, e.g., Elmer A. Martens, *Plot and Purpose in the Old Testament* (Downers Grove, IL: InterVarsity Press, 1981), 247–48.

96. Mark Forman, *The Politics of Inheritance in Romans*, SNTSMS 148 (Cambridge: Cambridge University Press, 2011), 6.

97. The claim about God's promises (including land) being fulfilled in "the seed," namely, Christ (Gal 3:16) would also make this point (Jason S. DeRouchie, "Father of a Multitude of Nations: New Covenant Ecclesiology in OT Perspective," in *Progressive Covenantalism: Charting a Course between Dispensational and Covenant Theology*, ed. Stephen J. Wellum and Brent E. Parker [Nashville: B&H Academic, 2016], 32–33).

Paul reflects certain tendencies in the Judaism of his day. For instance, the author of the intertestamental Jewish book *Jubilees* attributes these words to God, renewing the promise to Jacob when his name was changed to "Israel": "'I am the LORD who created heaven and earth, and I shall increase you and multiply you very much. And there will be kings from you; they will rule everywhere that the tracks of mankind have been trod. And I shall give to your seed all of the land under heaven and they will rule in all nations as they have desired. And after this all of the earth will be gathered together and they will inherit it forever'" (32:18–19).

the whole world. For our purposes, then, it is especially important to note that Paul sees the fulfillment of the promise as including the whole of creation. One might object that we should not make too much of this reference since Paul is not really talking about the created world in this context. But we argue that this makes his reference all the more telling. For it suggests that early Christians were naturally including the created world as participating in the fulfillment of God's redemptive plan in Christ. Reference to the "new creation" (2 Cor 5:17; Gal 6:15) reinforces and carries further this focus on the created world in the redemptive work of God.

I suggest, much more cautiously, that Ephesians 6:2–3 might reflect a similar universalizing of the land promise: "'Honor your father and mother'—which is the first commandment with a promise—'so that it may go well with you and that you may enjoy long life on the earth [*gēs*; ESV 'land'].'" "Long life on the land," the Old Testament form of blessing for covenant obedience, would have something else as its New Testament counterpart. If we adopt the popular "spiritualizing" hermeneutic, the reference could be to spiritual life or the kingdom of God (for the latter, see, e.g., 1 Cor 6:9; Gal 5:21).[98] Some think that Paul's use of "inheritance" (a word, as we have seen, related to the land) in Ephesians supports this interpretation. However, the word is actually used in Ephesians as a very general way of depicting all that God has promised his people in Christ (1:14, 18; 5:5), so insisting that 6:3 must have a spiritual meaning because these earlier texts do can end up being a case of circular reasoning. It is in any case necessary to remember that one important blessing God has promised his people is quite physical indeed—a resurrection body. However, the main problem with a "spiritual" interpretation of 6:3 is that the reference to "living long" is simply not a concept that is easily translated into a so-called "spiritual" benefit. Probably what Paul is promising is quite simply that obedient children will live a long and good life. The promise, as with all proverbial promises of this kind, speaks of what is generally true, not of what will be true in every situation. In any case, the NIV is probably correct to translate *gē* as "earth" here, since this is how Paul uses the word elsewhere.[99] Paul may, then, be working from the same universalizing hermeneutic that we saw at work in Romans 4:13. The "land" promised to the people of God, focused on (but never confined to) Palestine, has in the last days been extended to the universal dimensions intended by God all along. As believers share with Abraham the inheritance of the "world," so obedient children are promised long life on the "earth." And, of course, this conception has explicit antecedent in the teaching of Jesus, who promised that the "meek" would "inherit the earth" (Matt 5:5).

---

98. The Jewish philosopher and theologian Philo interprets the OT "live long in the land" as immortality (*Special Laws* 2.262).

99. The word *gē* occurs fourteen times in Paul's letters. One refers to the earth in terms of its physical makeup ("dirt," 1 Cor 15:47), but the others all clearly mean "earth," not "land."

I tentatively suggest, then, that Paul understands the promise accompanying the commandment about obedient children to involve living for a long time on the earth, interpreted as a physical reality. One important question remains: When does Paul think this promise will be fulfilled? Most interpreters think Paul reflects the widespread Old Testament teaching, found especially in Proverbs, that promises blessings to God's faithful people in this life. Obedient children will do "well" and enjoy a long life in this present world. However, it is also possible that Paul is promising a long life, not necessarily their present life on earth, but in the "new heaven and new earth." Obedient children, like all faithful believers, can look forward to a "long life"—indeed, an eternal life!—in a renewed and transformed world. Which of these options we should choose is unclear, but the ambiguity reminds us that, for Paul, we live in the overlap of the ages, in the tension of the "already" and the "not yet."

What does seem to be clear is that Paul, with other New Testament writers, has not abandoned the resolute Old Testament emphasis on a material aspect of God's redemptive work. Recent interpreters, from a number of angles, have rightly stressed the importance of "place" in human history and in biblical theology. As Walter Brueggemann puts it in his insightful book on the land, "We cannot therefore deny the central and enduring referent, which is land, unless we are to succumb to an otherworldly hermeneutic."[100]

I have strayed a long way from Romans 11. Drawing the threads of this discussion together, I conclude that Paul predicts that the consummation of the new realm will include a spiritual revival in Israel, leading many Jewish people at that time to turn to Christ for salvation. At the same time, I see no basis in Paul to extend this future blessing beyond the spiritual. The land promise no longer involves a particular territory for Israel; that promise has been transmuted into a promise that the people of God, Jew and gentile alike, will enjoy the "geography" of a new heaven and new earth.[101] And this universalizing of land is rooted in the original terms of the Abrahamic promise, which included both a narrow and broad "territorial" aspect, with hints that the former would finally give way to the latter.[102]

---

100. Walter Brueggemann, *The Land: Place as Gift, Promise, and Challenge in Biblical Faith*, 2nd ed. (Minneapolis: Fortress, 2002), 167. See, e.g., Volker Gäckle, "Die Relevanz des Landes Israel Bei Paulus," *ZTK* 112 (2015): 141–63; Craig G. Bartholomew, *Where Mortals Dwell: A Christian View of Place for Today* (Grand Rapids: Baker, 2011); Oren R. Martin, *Bound for the Promised Land: The Land Promise in God's Redemptive Plan*, NSBT 34 (Downers Grove, IL: InterVarsity Press, 2015), esp. 112–37; Christopher J. H. Wright, *Old Testament Ethics for the People of God* (Leicester: Inter-Varsity, 2004), 89–99; Beale, *New Testament Biblical Theology*, 751; Geoffrey A. Lilburne, *A Sense*

of Place: A Christian Theology of the Land (Nashville: Abingdon, 1989), esp. 105–10.

101. See esp. Bruce K. Waltke with Charles Yu, *An Old Testament Theology: An Exegetical, Canonical, and Thematic Approach* (Grand Rapids: Zondervan, 2007), 558–87; Gary M. Burge, *Jesus and the Land: The New Testament Challenge to "Holy Land" Theology* (Grand Rapids: Baker, 2010).

102. Paul R. Williamson, "Promise and Fulfillment: The Territorial Inheritance," in *The Land of Promise: Biblical, Theological and Contemporary Perspectives*, ed. Philip Johnston and Peter Walker (Downers Grove, IL: InterVarsity Press, 2000), 17–32.

7 BEYOND THE PAROUSIA?

The parousia is the climactic moment in Paul's future eschatology. He never refers to any event beyond this moment, although it does usher in the time when God is "all in all" (1 Cor 15:28). And his reference to "everlasting destruction" of the ungodly makes clear that "hell," in some form, endures after the parousia (2 Thess 1:9). Many scholars argue that Paul's scenario of end events leaves no room for any further historical or earthly eschatological occurrence.[103] On this view, the idea that Christ's parousia might usher in a time of earthly blessing before the final judgment, the "millennium," is seen as incompatible with Paul's eschatological teaching. I am not so sure of this. Much depends on whether "then the end will come" (1 Cor 15:24) means that the parousia (v. 23) *is* the end or whether it means that the parousia ushers in the end. The latter interpretation would allow for intervening events before that end comes. If, then, one finds some basis for a post-parousia millennium in Revelation 20:4–6 (as I cautiously think might be the case), then there is nothing in Paul that contradicts this scenario.[104] In terms of Paul's theology, however, it must be said that the new creation more than satisfies the material fulfillment that is the theological rationale of a future millennium.[105]

8 NEW CREATION

"New creation," as I argued above (pp. 466–67), is one of Paul's basic ways of characterizing the new realm inaugurated by God in Christ. While the phrase itself appears only twice in his letters (1 Cor 5:17; Gal 6:15), the concept connoted by the phrase is important in reminding us that God's purposes extend beyond humans to encompass his entire creation. As I conclude my overview of Paul's future eschatology, it is very important, after all my attention to the destiny of humans, that we make sure to recognize the breadth of Paul's vision. To be sure, Paul seldom mentions the wider creation in his letters, so I can understand to some degree why it does not appear in many treatments of his theology. However, a hope for creation as a whole appears often enough to demand that we integrate this into Paul's view of the future.

The single most important passage is Romans 8:19–23. As I have noted in my exegesis (pp. 227–28), Paul here discusses the place of the nonhuman created world

---

103. E.g., Davies, *Paul and Rabbinic Judaism*, 291–98.

104. Kreitzer cautiously thinks a "messianic age to come" might be indicated, predating "the eternal age to come" (*Jesus and God*, 134–54; see also Wilber Wallis, "The Problem of an Intermediate Kingdom in 1 Corinthians 15:20–28," *JETS* 18 [1975]: 229–40).

105. Richard Bauckham, "The Millennium," in *God Will Be All in All: The Eschatology of Jürgen Moltmann*, ed. Richard Bauckham (Minneapolis: Fortress, 2001), 123–48.

in God's wider plan. As a consequence of human sin, originated and concentrated in Adam, the creation has been "subjected to frustration" (v. 20). Paul refers to this as the "groaning" of creation (v. 22), an apt and poignant description of the state of the created world—our degraded "environment"—in our own day. Yet, as is the case for believers also (v. 23), this groaning is hopeful—leading to eventual redemption. When the children of God are revealed, creation's groaning will be ended: it will be "liberated from its bondage to decay" (v. 21). This "decay" (*phthora*) is difficult to identify, since the word can be translated "corruption" (e.g., ESV; cf. Eph 4:22) or "ruin," "destruction" (cf. Gal 6:8). In general, however, we may say that the "decay" of creation includes that it is used and abused in ways God never intended, preventing it from being what it was designed to be and thereby hindering its ability to fully glorify God. That will change when Christians are finally redeemed. Creation itself will share in the freedom that accompanies the glory that believers will experience. If, as Haley Goranson Jacob has argued, the "glory" in view here is linked to the glory associated with God's rulers, it might be said that creation finds its freedom precisely when God's human creatures rule within creation as they were created to.[106]

The overall point to make about Romans 8:19–22 is that it clearly presumes a role for the created world in eternity. And we may add to this point the evidence we have adduced above for a promise of "land" that incorporates the whole world. Creation is destined not for destruction but for renewal.[107] Colossians 1:20, which refers to the "reconciliation" of all things, fits this same scenario. A similar focus on the breadth of reconciliation might be found in 2 Corinthians 5:19: "God was reconciling the world [*kosmos*] to himself in Christ."[108]

These passages are sufficient to warn us against an inappropriately anthropocentric view of God's ultimate purposes. They also suggest that Paul's vision for the human future is not of a disembodied existence in "heaven" but of resurrected bodies enjoying a "new heavens and new earth" (e.g., Rev 21:1).

---

106. Jacob, *Conformed to the Image of His Son.*

107. Other texts appear to suggest more discontinuity between this creation and the next (e.g., 2 Pet 3:6–13). However, it is far easier to reconcile that passage with the more continuous scenario of Romans 8 than the reverse (see, e.g., Rev 21:1–4). See D. Moo and J. Moo, *Creation Care,* 153–61.

108. On the wider issue of eschatology and the created world, see esp. Moo, "Nature in the New Creation," 449–88; and D. Moo and J. Moo, *Creation Care.*

Chapter 23

THE PEOPLE OF THE NEW REALM

> For the grace of God has appeared that offers salvation to all people. It teaches us to say "No" to ungodliness and worldly passions, and to live self-controlled, upright and godly lives in this present age, while we wait for the blessed hope—the appearing of the glory of our great God and Savior, Jesus Christ, who gave himself for us to redeem us from all wickedness and to purify for himself *a people that are his very own*, eager to do what is good.

> —TITUS 2:11–14

PAUL'S WORLDVIEW had as its central symbol the unity and holiness of the *ekklēsia* [church] itself."[1] So claims N. T. Wright, and his focus on the church is echoed by many contemporary exegetes and theologians.[2] This emphasis on the corporate experience of believers is often linked to criticisms of an excessive individualism, laid at the doorstep of the Western intellectual tradition. There is some point to this criticism. Christians, both academic and lay, have often isolated the individual from his or her community and relationships in a way that is true neither of Scripture nor of reality. As I have argued elsewhere, however (pp. 31–34), some recent scholars have tilted the balance too far toward the corporate side. Paul may not have worked from the paradigm memorably described by Krister Stendahl as "the introspective conscience of the West." But he has a lot to say about the individual person, locked up under sin, redeemed by Christ's atoning work, invited to believe and so be saved, destined for scrutiny on the day of Christ. Nevertheless, Wright and others are quite justified in drawing attention to the corporate dimension of Christian experience in Paul. The person saved by faith is immediately and determinedly joined to other believers in a new community, the church. And Wright is probably correct to suggest that when people asked to see evidence of God's new-realm work, Paul would have pointed not only to individuals but to the community. At the same time, it is important to stress

---

1. Wright, *Paul and the Faithfulness of God*, 1:563.
2. See, e.g., Johnson, *Interpreting Paul*, 231: "The central concern in Paul's letters is the stability and integrity of his churches."

that the essence and origin of the community of Christ is the same as the individual in Christ: God's grace, displayed in the crucified Christ, with all the implications of this fundamental reality in the cruciform nature of both individual and community.[3]

I maintain the imagery I have used throughout the book by labeling this community "the people of the new realm." To be sure, Paul himself does not often use "people" (Gk. *laos*). The word occurs only twelve times in his letters, and nine of these are in OT quotations.[4] However, the term has a secure place in his own theology, as, for example, Titus 2:14 makes clear: "[Christ] gave himself for us to redeem us from all wickedness and to purify for himself a people that are his very own, eager to do what is good." The density of references to "people" in Old Testament quotations and in Romans 9–11 suggests an important reason for Paul to use this language: it makes a solid connection with the Old Testament, where "people" (usually Heb. *'am*) is used hundreds of times to denote Israel. The language of Deuteronomy 7:6 is typical: "For you are a *people* holy to the LORD your God. The LORD your God has chosen you out of all the peoples on the face of the earth to be *his people*, his treasured possession." Paul is obviously acquainted with the language, as his quotation in 2 Corinthians 6:16 makes clear: "For we are the temple of the living God. As God has said: 'I will live with them and walk among them, and I will be their God, and they will be my people.'" This quotation also urgently raises a basic question in Paul's theology of the new-realm people: How are the people of the new realm related to the people of the old realm? Or, to put it in more familiar terms: How does Paul conceive of the relationship between Israel and the church?

1 "THE ISRAEL OF GOD"

The title of this section is a phrase from the end of Paul's letter to the Galatians, where he says, "Peace and mercy to all who follow this rule—to the Israel of God" (6:16). The NIV reflects the interpretation I argued for on pp. 86–87 that "the Israel of God" describes "all who follow this rule"—in the context, both Jewish and gentile believers. This is the "Israel according to the Spirit" that Paul implies by labeling ethnic Israel "the Israel according to the flesh" (1 Cor 10:18; my translation).[5] This interpretation can find support in the syntax of the verse. But it must be said that one's decision about this text is considerably affected by the way one reads Paul's teaching elsewhere about the relationship of the church and Israel. My view of Galatians 6:16, then, both reflects

---

3. Walter Klaiber, *Rechtfertigung und Gemeinde: Eine Untersuchung zum paulinischen Kirchenverständnis*, FRLANT 127 (Göttingen: Vandenhoeck & Ruprecht, 1982), 83–85.

4. Rom 9:25 (2x; Hos 2:23), 26 (Hos 1:10); 10:21 (Isa 65:2); 11:1, 2; 15:10 (Deut 32:43), 11 (Ps 117:1); 1 Cor 10:7 (Exod 32:6); 14:21 (Isa 28:11–12); 2 Cor 6:16 (Lev 26:12; Jer 32:38; Ezek 37:27); Titus 2:14.

5. As I indicate in my exegesis, I am less certain that "Israel" is used to describe the church in Rom 9:6.

and impacts my overall reading of Paul who, in my view, consistently applies language about Israel from the Old Testament to the new-realm people of God and repeatedly stresses that prophecies about the end-time redemption of Israel are now being fulfilled in the creation of, existence of, and culmination of that people.

I have argued that Paul applies Israel language to the church in two passages. Second Corinthians 6:16 claims that the church is the temple of God and God's people. And in Titus 2:14, Paul appropriates typical Old Testament language about Israel when he describes the new-realm people of God as "a people that are his very own." In the only places the equivalent Greek phrase (*laos periousios*) is used in the Old Testament (five times), it is used to describe Israel—including in the Deuteronomy 7:6 passage quoted above ("his people, his treasured possession"; see also Exod 19:5; 23:22; Deut 14:2; 26:18). Paul could hardly be more explicit. What Israel was in the Old Testament, the church is now in the New Testament. Paul makes this same point in subtler ways. In Romans, for instance, Paul applies titles and characterizations typical of Old Testament Israel to the new-covenant people of God, composed of both Jews and gentiles. "The righteousness of God" that the prophets promised would vindicate Israel has now vindicated "all who believe" (1:17; 3:21–22). Abraham is not only the "father" of Israel but of "all who believe" (Rom 4:11). The "glory" that would characterize Israel is now given to believers (Rom 5:2; 8:18, 30). Israel is called God's son (Exod 4:22); now, however, it is Christ who is *the* Son (Rom 8:3, 32), and those who belong to him are "sons" of God (Rom 8:14–17). Moreover, I have argued above (pp. 562–63) that the promise of land, a key component of God's blessing of Israel, has now been "Christified" and universalized. The inheritance is Christ himself and, ultimately, the new heaven and earth. Paul, in a word, sees Christ as the new and true Israel, the one in whom all God's promises are coming to fruition; and believers, Jew and gentile alike, inherit those promises as the "new Israel" in him.[6]

It might be objected (and, in fact, often is) that the church's appropriation of these blessings runs roughshod over the inescapable fact that they were originally promised to the nation of Israel. Traditional dispensationalism therefore insists that God's integrity demands that what was promised to Israel be fulfilled in Israel—in a reconstituted nation, back in its own land, perhaps during the millennium.[7] However, the evidence for the hermeneutic of fulfillment of Old Testament promises in the life of the church

---

6. For a good discussion of this viewpoint, with a lot more evidence from throughout the NT, see esp. Beale, *New Testament Biblical Theology*, 651–749.

7. "Literal" interpretation is a hallmark of traditional dispensationalism; see, e.g., Charles Ryrie in his classic *Dispensationalism Today.* He writes, "Consistently literal or plain interpretation is indicative of a dispensational approach to the interpretation of the

Scriptures" ([Chicago: Moody, 1965], 46). Of course, "literal" is open to several interpretations, and recent, "progressive," forms of dispensationalism have backed off this claim a bit (see, e.g., Craig A. Blaising and Darryl L. Bock, eds., *Dispensationalism, Israel and the Church: The Search for Definition* [Grand Rapids: Zondervan, 1992]).

is, in my view, overwhelming. Perhaps, then, the integrity issue can be handled if we distinguish carefully between prophecies directed to Israel *as a nation* (and which must be fulfilled in a national Israel) and prophecies directed to Israel as *the people of God* (which can be fulfilled in the people of God—*a people that includes the church*). It should be noted that such an approach is not allegorical or nonliteral; it simply calls upon the interpreter to recognize the intended scope of any specific prophecy. This distinction is, admittedly, not easy to make, and in practice it will be the New Testament evidence that will be decisive in making the distinction. Another factor to consider is the intensely christological focus of the biblical story line: Israel is climactically narrowed down to one faithful Israelite, Jesus Christ. All God's promises to Israel therefore appropriately are fulfilled in him—and in those who by faith are "in him."[8] In that light, then, I have argued that Romans 11 is best interpreted as indicating a continuing significance for ethnic Israel in God's plan. God's promises to the patriarchs (11:28) point to a future for ethnic Israel. I find no evidence in Paul, however, that this significance extends to anything beyond the spiritual—namely, a conversion to Christ of many Jews at the time of the parousia.[9]

The broad outlines of the hermeneutic I have described above have characterized much of the Christian tradition (even the matter of a future for ethnic Israel has more purchase in the tradition than is sometimes realized).[10] Of course, as I have noted, dispensationalists have for a long time criticized this hermeneutic. In response, they insist that God will "literally" fulfill his Old Testament promises to Israel—but in the *future*. While not being identified with "Israel," the church is the complete expression of God's people in this era. A number of recent interpreters, however, go much further, arguing that at least certain texts in Paul point to a recognition of the continuing theological significance of Israel in the *present*. The "Messianic Jewish" movement claims that Paul himself remained Torah-observant and expected other Jewish converts to Christ to do the same. The "Paul within Judaism" movement tends to be more radical, its adherents often insisting that the Torah covenant remains the vehicle of salvation for Jewish people. I have dealt with aspects of these movements in other places (see pp. 433–35). Here I will focus briefly on the issues these movements raise for Paul's concept of the church.

---

8. See, e.g., I. M. Duguid, "Israel," in *Dictionary of the Old Testament Prophets*, ed. Mark J. Boda and J. Gordon McConville (Downers Grove, IL: InterVarsity Press, 2012), 395–96. This is an important thesis of Brent E. Parker, "The Israel-Christ-Church Relationship," in Wellum and Parker, *Progressive Covenantalism*, 39–68.

9. Contra those who argue that the political side of Israel's existence has not come to an end (e.g., Douglas Harink, ed., *Paul, Philosophy, and the Theopolitical Vision: Critical Engagements with Agamben, Badiou, Zizek, and Others*, Theopolitical Visions 7 [Eugene, OR: Cascade, 2010], 274–79).

10. In addition to Beale (see fn. 6 above), an excellent defense of this general approach is found in Eckhard J. Schnabel, "Die Gemeinde des Neuen Bundes in Kontinuität mit Diskontinuität zur Gemeinde des Alten Bundes," in *Israel in Geschichte und Gegenwart: Beiträge zur Geschichte Israels und zum Jüdisch-Christlichen Dialog*, ed. Gerhard Maier (Wuppertal: Theologische, 1996), 145–213.

Critics of what we might call the "traditional" view often apply to it the label of "supersessionism." "Supersede," according to the dictionaries, means "1. To take the place of; replace; 2. To cause to be set aside, especially to displace as inferior or anti-quated."[11] Supersessionism, then, views the church as the *replacement* of Israel.[12] This model, it is argued, cannot accommodate the breadth of Paul's teaching and falls prey to the anti-Semitism that has so often plagued the Christian tradition. To respond first to the latter point. There is no doubt that, sadly, anti-Semitism, in various forms, has too often characterized the Christian church and that "supersessionism" has provided a theological basis for it. However, to decry a certain inference drawn by some from a theological position does not, of course, logically negate the view—unless, indeed, the inference is so obviously wrong and so intimately tied to the theology that the theological position cannot stand. I question in this case whether this is so. Moreover, "anti-Semitism" is a label that must be carefully defined. To claim, for instance, that Christ is the only way for humans to be saved and that, by inference, the Torah cov-enant of Israel is no longer in force is, in one sense, "anti-Judaism" (questioning the saving value of the Jewish religion) but not "anti-Semitic" (expressing hostility to a certain class of people). More important for our purposes here is the question whether "supersessionism" is an accurate way to describe Paul's theology. On this matter, a nuanced answer is necessary. While there is a sense in which it is accurate, the word by itself is inadequate to capture Paul's view.

The closest Paul comes to defining the relationship between Israel and the church is in his famous olive-tree analogy (Rom 11:17–24). The olive tree, representing the people of God across the span of salvation history, is rooted in God's promises to the patriarchs.[13] From those roots grows only one tree: there is only one people of God. Gentiles who come to faith in Christ are joined to that tree—they do not constitute a new tree. In this limited sense, we might label not Paul, but the arrogant gentiles that Paul has in view here (vv. 13–14, 18, 25), as "supersessionist." And, an important point we should not miss is that Jews also must be joined to that tree by faith—they are cut off if they do not believe. In the context, it is then clear that this single people of God is defined christologically: the "faith" required of both Jew and gentile is "faith in Christ" (see esp. 10:8–13). I draw two important conclusions from this text. First, the notion of "replacement" implied in "supersessionism" ignores the organic link between the

11. *American Heritage Dictionary of the English Language*, 4th ed. (Boston: Houghton Mifflin Harcourt, 2009).

12. A replacement view, in some form, has been popular in Reformed and covenant theology; e.g., Bavinck: "The community of believers has in all respects replaced carnal, national Israel" (Herman Bavinck, *Reformed Dogmatics*, 4 vols. [Grand Rapids: Baker, 2008], 4:667).

13. As Pablo Gablenz points out, then, gentiles are integrated into the people of God, not into Israel *per se* (*Called from the Jews and from the Gentiles: Pauline Ecclesiology in Romans 9–11*, WUNT 2/267 [Tübingen: Mohr Siebeck, 2009], 269–71). See also Love L. Sechrest, *A Former Jew: Paul and the Dialectics of Race*, LNTS 410 (London: T&T Clark, 2009); Sandnes, *Paul Perceived*; Windsor, *Paul and the Vocation of Israel*, 45–61, passim.

Old Testament and New Testament forms of the people of God. The church does not "take the place" of Israel but grows out of Israel. Donald Hagner, representing a widely held view, refers to "Paul's Christianity" as "fulfilled Judaism."[14] Second, however, it is also clear that this organic growth means that certain forms, or administrations, of God's plan, have fallen away. God's people are no longer defined in terms of the Torah covenant (and, of course, the OT itself makes clear that God's people always extended beyond the confines of Israel). Paul went to great lengths to make just this point in the face of Jews and Jewish-Christians who insisted on more continuity between Torah and Christ. In terms, then, of the context in which Paul was ministering, there is *a limited sense* in which Paul was indeed "supersessionist." The church "takes the place" of Israel, which is displaced as "antiquated." "We . . . are the circumcision," Paul claims in Philippians 3:3, and in the context it is clear that the claim is an exclusive one. Followers of Jesus, and only followers of Jesus, constitute the people of God.[15] The church, according to Paul, displays what Daniel Boyarin has labeled a "particularist universalism": it is open to all, but restricted to those who belong to Christ.[16]

2 A "THIRD RACE"

The early Christian leaders who called the church a "third race" (*tertium genus*) accurately captured Paul's vision of the church: neither gentile or Greco-Roman (the "first race") nor Jewish (the "second race").[17] Paul implicitly works with this threefold division, as 1 Corinthians 10:32 reveals: "Do not cause anyone to stumble, whether Jews, Greeks or the church of God." Jews and gentiles are brought together through and in Christ to become "one new man" (Eph 2:15; my translation [*hena kainon anthrōpon*]; see also 4:13). Paul expands on this vision of unity in several texts, whose similarities suggest that he quotes a fundamental tenet of this "one new man":

All of you who were baptized into Christ have clothed yourselves with Christ. There is neither Jew nor Gentile, neither slave nor free, nor is there male and female, for you are all one in Christ Jesus. (Gal 3:27–28)

For we were all baptized by one Spirit so as to form one body—whether Jews or Gentiles, slave or free—and we were all given the one Spirit to drink. (1 Cor 12:13)

---

14. Hagner, *How New Is the New Testament?*, 11; see also 20, 171.

15. The dual focus in Paul's teaching—the church is the continuation in salvation history of the people of God/the church is the true Israel—is noted by, e.g., Rudolf Schnackenburg, *The Church in the New Testament* (New York: Seabury, 1965), 155.

16. Daniel Boyarin, *A Radical Jew: Paul and the Politics of Identity* (Berkeley, CA: University of California Press, 1994).

17. Wolter, *Paul*, 33–50, 433–39. For "new race" or "third race" applied to the church, see, e.g., *Diognetus* 1; Tertullian, *Ad nationes* 1.8.

. . . the new self, which is being renewed in knowledge in the image of its Creator. Here there is no Gentile or Jew, circumcised or uncircumcised, barbarian, Scythian, slave or free, but Christ is all, and is in all. (Col 3:10b–11)[18]

The differences among people that matter so much in our world are left at the door of the church. Paul's own ministry, as well as the salvation-historical context he found himself in, meant that he focused especially on the ethnic issue of Jew and gentile. But these passages reveal that he extended this erasure of distinction to the social realm as well as to matters of gender—and, indeed, beyond. The particular relationships Paul mentions are examples of a larger principle that applies to all "worldly" distinctions. However, this lack of "distinction" does not mean that differences among people are erased. As Paul makes clear in a number of ways, Jews who become Christians remain Jewish, slaves who "put on Christ" (often) remain slaves, and, of course, men and women do not discard their gender identity.[19] Thus, for instance, in Paul's exhortations to the strong and the weak in Romans 14:1–15:13, he recognizes that Jewish believers have the freedom to work out their new spiritual identity in terms defined by Torah. The inauguration of the new realm does not mean the erasure of all aspects of human identity. Belonging to Christ and to his people establishes a "meta-identity" that does not erase but trumps worldly identities.[20] Paul claims that these "earthly" identities are subsumed and subordinated to the more basic identity of "Christian." The "strong in faith" are not to stand in judgment over those weak in faith who choose to observe Sabbath (Rom 14:5). But this tolerance operates within "an intolerance that insists on Christ alone as the basis for community solidarity, a basis which also implies a proscription of actions deemed to threaten this union."[21] This latter point needs to be stressed in response to the "Messianic Judaism" movement. Advocates of this view, who insist that Jews who become Christians should remain Torah-observant, do not give adequate emphasis to this concern for unity in Paul's vision of the church. Insistence on strict observance of the Torah (which, in my view, does not express Paul's view) tends to drive a wedge between Jewish and gentile believers.[22]

To use the current terminology, then, the particular identity Paul ascribes to the new community gathered around Jesus the Messiah suggests that the "parting of the

---

18. See, on these texts, Bruce Hansen, *All of You Are One: The Social Vision of Galatians 3.28, 1 Corinthians 12.13 and Colossians 3.11*, LNTS 409 (London: T&T Clark, 2010).

19. Campbell has stressed this point in *Paul and the Creation of Christian Identity*; see also Justin K. Hardin, *Galatians and the Imperial Cult: A Critical Analysis of the First-Century Social Context of Paul's Letter*, WUNT 2/237 (Tübingen: Mohr Siebeck, 2008), 225–31.

20. Bird, *Anomalous Jew*, 80. See also David G. Horrell,

"Ethnicisation, Marriage and Early Christian Identity: Critical Reflections on 1 Corinthians 7, 1 Peter 3 and Modern New Testament Scholarship," *NTS* 62 (2016): 439–60; Miroslav Volf, *Exclusion and Embrace: A Theological Exploration of Identity, Otherness, and Reconciliation* (Nashville: Abingdon, 1996), 49–53.

21. David G. Horrell, *Solidarity and Difference: A Contemporary Reading of Paul's Ethics*, 2nd ed. (London: T&T Clark, 2015), 195.

22. See also my remarks on this movement on pp. 433–35.

ways" (between Judaism and Christianity) was well under way.[23] While it is no easy matter to define "Judaism," considering the variety of Jewish views in the first century, one can identify a "common Judaism," unified and distinguished from other religions by four tenets: (1) worship of God in the temple; (2) election of Israel, solidified in the covenant; (3) Torah observance; and (4) monotheism.[24] As Paul's letters make clear, all four of these were radically redefined by early Christians. Worship of God now takes place in the community of believers, the "new temple." Election is no longer confined to Israel but extended to "all who believe." Torah witnesses to God's work in Christ and is a source of wisdom in guiding the church, but its observance no longer delimits the people of God. And monotheism, while stoutly maintained, is now a "christological monotheism." Those who cite these "common" beliefs to argue for strong continuity between Paul's view and Judaism must give these key identity markers uselessly elastic definitions to justify that commonality.[25]

3 THE NATURE OF THE CHURCH

3.1 *Ekklēsia*

Paul's most common designation of the new-realm people of God is, of course, "church" (*ekklēsia*). Paul uses the word sixty-two times (out of 114 total NT occurrences), all of them referring to the people of the new realm. Scholars and, more often, pastors have suggested that the etymology of the word might furnish an important clue to its application to the church: *ekklēsia* comes from *ek kaleō*, "call out"—the church is made up of people called out from their culture. However, etymology is always an uncertain guide to the origin and meaning of a word, and in this case there is no evidence that this etymology plays a role in Paul's theology of the church. As is usually the case, the better guide to meaning is the usage of the word. Here we must consider the way it is used both in the Greco-Roman world and in the Greek Old Testament.[26]

The word *ekklēsia* was used in the Greco-Roman world of Paul's day to denote several kinds of "gathering."[27] A New Testament example of this "secular" usage comes in Acts 19, where Luke chooses to denote the gathering in the Ephesian theater to protest the preaching of Paul and his associates as an *ekklēsia* (Acts 19:32, 41; NIV "assembly"). The word had long been used to denote official "assemblies" of people (usually men only) in cities such as Athens for the purpose of directing the community.[28] It also

23. See, e.g., Hagner, *How New Is the New Testament?*

24. For these four defining characteristics of "common Judaism," see Dunn, *Partings of the Ways*, 18; for "common Judaism," see Sanders, *Judaism: Practice and Belief*, e.g., 256–57, passim.

25. See esp. Richard Bauckham, "The Parting of the Ways: What Happened and Why?," *ST* 47 (1993): 135–51.

26. See, for a survey of this background, Aletti, *Essai sur l'ecclesiologie*, 13–23.

27. See the recent survey of evidence in Ralph J. Korner, *The Origin and Meaning of Ekklesia in the Early Jesus Movement*, Ancient Judaism and Early Christianity 98 (Leiden: Brill, 2017), 22–80.

28. *TDNT* 3:513–17.

denoted voluntary associations, gatherings of like-minded people for fellowship or other purposes (perhaps something like our business groups, like Rotary Club in the United States). These purposes were sometimes academic in focus, so that the word could refer to scholastic societies.[29] There is also evidence that *ekklēsia* could denote gatherings of Jews in association with the synagogue.[30] It is probably safest to avoid claiming any one of these ancient specific applications of the language of *ekklēsia* as *the* background for Paul's use of the term.[31] Suffice to conclude that the word was being widely used in Paul's day to refer to the kind of assembly that characterized the early church.

However, another probable influence on Paul's use of *ekklēsia* is the Greek Old Testament.[32] The word occurs over a hundred times in the LXX, almost always translating Hebrew *qahal*, and it often denotes a gathering of the people of Israel. First Chronicles 28:8 is typical: "So now I charge you in the sight of all Israel and of the assembly [*qahal*; *ekklēsia*] of the LORD, and in the hearing of our God: Be careful to follow all the commands of the LORD your God, that you may possess this good land and pass it on as an inheritance to your descendants forever" (see also, e.g., Deut 18:16; 31:30; Ps 149:1; Mic 2:5; and in the NT, see Acts 7:38).[33] This matter of the background for Paul's use of *ekklēsia* is best settled in terms of a "both/and" rather than an "either/or." For the two backgrounds together—the Greco-Roman and the Old Testament—help explain Paul's varied use of the term. On the one hand, Paul typically uses *ekklēsia* to denote a local gathering. Contrary to popular Christian lingo, Paul never uses the word to refer to a building—in fact, there is no evidence from the New Testament era that believers worshiped in buildings dedicated to that purpose. Rather, believers gathered in private homes and perhaps in work spaces owned or used by believers. Thus, for instance, referring to Priscilla and Aquila, Paul can refer to "the church that meets at their house" (or "the assembly at their house"; Rom 16:5; 1 Cor 16:19). The *ekklēsia* is not the place where Christians gathered but is the actual gathering itself. See, for example, 1 Corinthians 11:18: "In the first place, I hear that when you come together as a church, there are divisions among you, and to some extent I believe it." However, alongside this "local" application of *ekklēsia*, we find also in Paul a broader conception. He hints at this larger entity by referring to "all the churches" (Rom 16:16;

29. See esp. Claire S. Smith, *Pauline Communities as "Scholastic Communities,"* WUNT 2/335 (Tübingen: Mohr Siebeck, 2012), who develops a suggestion of Edwin Judge.

30. Ralph J. Korner, "*Ekklēsia* as a Jewish Synagogue Term: Some Implications for Paul's Socio-Religious Location," *Journal of the Jesus Movement in Its Jewish Setting* 2 (2015): 53–78. Paul never uses "synagogue" to describe a Christian gathering; see, however, Jas 2:2.

31. This is Wayne A. Meeks's conclusion after surveying the evidence (*The First Urban Christians: The Social World of the Apostle Paul* [New Haven: Yale University Press, 1983], 84).

George van Kooten argues that Paul's language comes from the civic assemblies in Paul's world ("Ἐκκλησία τοῦ θεοῦ: The 'Church of God' and the Civic Assemblies [ἐκκλησίαι] of the Greek Cities in the Roman Empire. A Response to Paul Trebilco and Richard A. Horsley," *NTS* 58 [2012]: 522–48).

32. See esp. G. K. Beale, "The Background of Ἐκκλησία Revisited," *JSNT* 38 (2015): 151–68.

33. Thompson speculates that Paul's preference for "church of God" in place of the LXX tendency to use "church of the Lord" might reflect apocalyptic Judaism (*Church according to Paul*, 30–31).

1 Cor 7:17; 2 Cor 8:18; 11:28; cf. 1 Cor 11:16).[34] Paul's instructions about the collection for the Jerusalem Christians in 2 Corinthians 8–9 presume some degree of relationship among churches in a particular area. These texts do not yet use the word for something beyond a local assembly. But Paul clearly takes this step in other passages.[35] He refers to himself, for instance, as one who "persecuted the church" (1 Cor 15:9; Gal 1:13; Phil 3:6), where "church" does not seem to designate a local, physical gathering but rather what we might call a theological entity. Other texts that move in this direction are, for example, 1 Corinthians 10:32, where "church of God" is set alongside "Jews" and "Greeks," and 1 Corinthians 12:28: "And God has placed in the church first of all apostles, second prophets, third teachers, then miracles, then gifts of healing, of helping, of guidance, and of different kinds of tongues" (the ministry of apostles and prophets was not confined to a local church). It is also possible, as many argue, that Paul's typical address, such as "to the church of God in Corinth," means something like "to the church of God in its Corinthian manifestation."[36] The dual background we have sketched above, then, might help explain these two directions in Paul's use of the language: a local, physical application drawn from his Greco-Roman context, and a broader, more theologically oriented application indebted to the Old Testament "assembly of the Lord."[37]

The evidence for this broader extent of *ekklēsia*—whether encompassing a number of house churches in a certain location or referring to the new-realm people of God generally—is more fundamental in Paul than has often been recognized.[38] In this light, the development we find in Ephesians and Colossians is unsurprising. If in the earlier letters of Paul, "church" occasionally denotes a universal entity, in Colossians and Ephesians it usually does so. Moreover, the "church" is given a cosmic or heavenly dimension that it does not have in the earlier letters and is equated with Christ's own body. See, for example, Ephesians 1:22–23: "And God placed all things under his feet and appointed him to be head over everything for the church, which is his body, the fullness of him who fills everything in every way." Many scholars allege that the more "mystical" sense of *ekklēsia* in these letters indicates that Paul could not have written them. However, while these letters certainly focus on the universal church and its cosmic significance in a way that Paul's earlier letters do not,[39] it is easy to see this as

---

34. Meeks suggests that the preposition *kata* Paul uses when he refers to "house churches"—e.g., *tē kat' oikon sou ekklēsia*, "the church *kata* your [Philemon's] house" (Phlm 2; cf. also Rom 16:5; 1 Cor 16:19; Col 4:15)—might suggest the idea of a larger "church" that is distributed in smaller gatherings (*Social World*, 75; and see BDAG for the distributive sense of *kata*).

35. Contra many scholars who claim there is no idea of the "universal church" in Paul (e.g., Dunn, *Theology of Paul*, 540–41; Wolter, *Paul*, 261).

36. E.g., Becker, *Paul: Apostle to the Gentiles*, 423.

37. Hurtado, "Paul's Messianic Christology," 98.

38. See esp. Young-Ho Park, *Paul's Ekklesia as a Civic Assembly: Understanding the People of God in Their Politico-Social World*, WUNT 2/393 (Tübingen: Mohr Siebeck, 2015), 98–124.

39. See, e.g., Lucien Cerfaux, *The Church in the Theology of St. Paul* (Freiburg: Herder & Herder, 1959), 289–97.

a development from the clear references to a universal church in his earlier letters.[40] Tracing this development is more difficult. Peter T. O'Brien, working from the focus in the word *ekklēsia* on a physical gathering, suggests that the word can be applied universally if we posit a "heavenly assembly" standing behind Paul's conception: "Men and women were called into membership of this one church of Christ, the heavenly assembly, through the preaching of the gospel. They were brought into fellowship with God's Son, and to speak of their membership of this heavenly gathering assembled around Christ is another way of referring to this new relationship with him."[41] However, the evidence may more easily be explained by positing influence from the two different backgrounds I identified earlier.

3.2 "Images of the Church" in Paul[42]

Paul's theology of the *concept* "church," or "new-realm people of God," must be grounded on much more than simply his use of the *word* "church." Wolfgang Kraus, for instance, lists fifteen terms that he thinks are relevant: *ekklēsia*, "holy ones," "called," "chosen," "loved of God," "children of God," "heirs," "children/seed of Abraham," "people of God," "building/planting/temple of God," "body of Christ," "fellowship," "brothers and sisters," "the righteous," "new creation."[43] Some of these terms overlap considerably with others, while others on the list have more to do with individuals within the church rather than the church itself. Three of the terms in the list, or concepts suggested by them, are worth particular attention: the church as a household, a temple, and a body.

3.2.1 "God's Household"

The title of this section is taken from Paul's well-known characterization of the church in 1 Timothy 3:15: "If I am delayed, you will know how people ought to conduct themselves in God's household, which is the church of the living God, the pillar and foundation of the truth." As I have noted above, most scholars think that early Christians typically met in private homes. It would not be surprising, then, if that setting influenced the way believers thought about the nature of their communal gatherings.[44] Thus Paul can refer to gentiles who are in Christ as "members of [God's]

40. See, e.g., Sigurd Grindheim, "A Deutero-Pauline Mystery? Ecclesiology in Colossians and Ephesians," in *Paul and Pseudepigraphy*, ed. Stanley E. Porter and Gregory P. Fewster, Pauline Studies 8 (Leiden: Brill, 2013), 173–95.

41. Peter T. O'Brien, "Church," in Hawthorne and Martin, *Dictionary of Paul and His Letters*, 126; see also idem, "The Church as a Heavenly and Eschatological Entity," in *The Church in the Bible and the World*, ed. D. A. Carson (Grand Rapids: Baker, 1987), 88–119, 307–11.

42. I borrow the title of this section from Paul S. Minear's classic *Images of the Church in the New Testament* (Philadelphia: Westminster, 1960).

43. Wolfgang Kraus, *Das Volk Gottes: zur Grundlegung der Ekklesiologie bei Paulus*, WUNT 2/85 (Tübingen: Mohr Siebeck, 1996), 111–19.

44. See Meeks, *Social World*, 75–77; Roger W. Gehring, *House Church and Mission: The Importance of Household Structures in Early Christianity* (Peabody, MA: Hendrickson, 2004), esp. 119–228.

household" (Eph 2:19). The clearest evidence for viewing the church in terms of the household comes in the Pastoral Epistles. In addition to 1 Timothy 3:15, Paul also suggests the parallel in requiring leaders of the church to be effective leaders in their own home (1 Tim 3:5, 12). But the overwhelmingly more important evidence for this conception of the church comes in Paul's usual way of referring to Christians (132 times): *adelphos*, "brother," "fellow believer," or *adelphoi*, "brothers and sisters." Feeding into this household conception also is Paul's regular depiction of believers as "sons" or "children" of God (Rom 8:14–17, 19, 21; 9:26; 1 Cor 4:14; 2 Cor 6:18; Gal 3:7, 26; 4:1–7, 19, 28, 31; 5:1, 8; Phil 2:15; 1 Thess 5:5), with Christ occasionally portrayed as *the* Son, who stamps his character on his brothers and sisters (Rom 8:29). Paul also uses familial imagery to depict his relationship to his converts. They are his "dear children" (1 Cor 4:14), and he is both like a "father" (1 Cor 4:15; 1 Thess 2:11) and a "mother" (1 Thess 2:7) to them. Timothy, Titus, and Onesimus, for instance, are his "sons" in the faith (1 Cor 4:17; 1 Tim 1:2, 18; 2 Tim 1:2; 2:1; Titus 1:4; Phlm 10; see also Phil 2:22). Nor should we overlook—as it is easy to do—the ubiquitous reference to God himself as "Father." See especially 2 Corinthians 6:18 (quoting 2 Sam 7:14): "And, 'I will be a Father to you, and you will be my sons and daughters, says the Lord Almighty.'"

Familial imagery is pervasive in Paul.[45] Not all of it applies directly to the church, but much of it does. By using it for the church, Paul implies that the intimate and loving nature of the home is to be duplicated in the church. Paul paints a picture of the church as a place where individuals, whatever their background and circumstances, can experience a depth of community that their society—and often their own families—does not provide. Paul uses the familiar word *koinōnia* and cognates to denote the intimate "fellowship" that characterized the churches. This fellowship is both vertical ("with his Son"; 1 Cor 1:9), manifested in the Eucharist (1 Cor 10:16), and horizontal (e.g., between Paul and Philemon; Phlm 6). "Fellowship" has concrete application: Paul uses the same word to refer to the community's "sharing" of its money with other believers and churches (Rom 15:26; 2 Cor 8:4; 9:13; Phil 4:15). The individual who believes is instantly joined with others in a family-like setting. It is at this point that we must recognize the important point made by those who insist that *ekklēsia* carries with it notions of actual physical assembly. The church is not just a "mystical" entity; it is a *gathering* of family members to worship their God in Christ and by the Spirit, a place where brothers and sisters can support, challenge, and love each other.[46] As the comparison Paul uses in 1 Timothy 3 suggests, the church as "family" also might imply that, just as the Greco-Roman household displayed a certain hierarchy,

45. Paul Trebilco, *Self-Designations and Group Identity in the New Testament* (Cambridge: Cambridge University Press, 2012), 16–67.

46. See on this Brian S. Rosner, *Known by God: A Biblical Theology of Personal Identity*, Biblical Theology for Life (Grand Rapids: Zondervan, 2017), 162–66.

so the church rightly recognizes its leaders as important for its flourishing.[47] However, whatever "hierarchy" we might find in the church is a hierarchy radically altered and newly configured in light of the gospel (see below, pp. 629–30).[48]

3.2.2 Temple

As I noted above (pp. 500–501), the temple or, more generally, "sacred space," has played an important role in recent biblical theology.[49] This focus seems warranted in light of the thematic importance of God's presence in the Old Testament.[50] The story begins with Adam and Eve enjoying God's presence in the garden, only to forfeit that privilege because of sin. The rest of the biblical story is, in one sense, about how that original fellowship could be regained—and, indeed, enhanced. Sanctuary and temple are physical manifestations both of God's presence with the people and of the distance yet remaining between a holy God and sinful people. The prophets anticipated the time when God would again dwell with his people, a fellowship sometimes pictured in terms of a rebuilt eschatological temple (e.g., Ezek 40–48; Mic 4:1–2; Zech 6:12–13; Mal 3:1). Jesus claims that the expectations of a renewed presence of God are fulfilled in him, "God with us" (Matt 1:23), the one whose body is the temple (John 2:21).[51] Paul picks up this theme of the fulfillment of the eschatological presence of God with his people in various ways. He does not, as Peter does, explicitly cite the central Old Testament call to be holy because God is holy (1 Pet 1:16), but his very frequent reference to believers as "holy ones" (*hagioi*) probably presumes this intimate relationship with the holy God. Of course, Paul's most explicit appropriation of the biblical theme of God's presence occurs in his references to the temple. Beale finds allusions to the restored-temple idea in Paul in various texts: 2 Corinthians 4:16–5:5 ("we have . . . an eternal house in heaven" [5:1]); Col 1:6, 9 ("bearing fruit and growing," alluding to Gen 1:28 and God's image); Col 1:19 (God's fullness dwelling in Christ).[52] Perrin adds to these implicit allusions the references to "pillars" in Galatians 2:9 and to "foundation" in Romans 15:20. The architectural allusions here may well have as their background the tabernacle or temple. "Pillar" (Gk. *stylos*) often refers to part of the tabernacle or the temple in the Old Testament (see also 1 Tim 3:15), and Paul explicitly uses "foundation" with reference to the temple elsewhere (Eph 2:20–21; see also 1 Cor 3:10–12).[53]

---

47. See, e.g., Burke, *Family Matters*; idem, "Paul's Role as 'Father' to the Corinthian 'Children' in Socio-Historical Context (1 Cor. 4:14–21)," in *Paul and the Corinthians: A Community in Conflict. Essays in Honour of Margaret Thrall*, ed. T. J. Burke and J. K. Elliott, NovTSup 109 (Leiden: Brill, 2003), 95–113.

48. See esp. J. Moo, who challenges Burke's reading of 1 Cor 4:15–16 and convincingly argues that Paul's familial imagery is focused on mutuality rather than hierarchy ("Of Parents and Children," 57–73).

49. See, e.g., Beale, *Temple and the Church's Mission*.

50. For a good overview of the theme in Scripture, see T. Desmond Alexander, *From Eden to the New Jerusalem: An Introduction to Biblical Theology* (Grand Rapids: Kregel, 2008).

51. For one exploration of this theme in the Gospels, see Nicholas Perrin, *Jesus the Temple* (Grand Rapids: Baker, 2010).

52. Beale, *Temple and the Church's Mission*, 256–59, 263–68.

53. Perrin, *Jesus the Temple*, 65–70.

However, the clearest Pauline connection to this rich biblical-theological theme comes in his explicit references to the church as a temple: 1 Corinthians 3:16–17; 2 Corinthians 6:16; Ephesians 2:21; and perhaps 2 Thessalonians 2:4.[54] This last text is debated (see p. 108): Is "God's temple," in which "the man of lawlessness" manifests himself, a physical building or, as I think more likely, the church?[55] In 1 Corinthians 3, Paul reminds the divisive believers that their attitudes may "destroy" "God's temple," composed of those believers themselves. And it is God's Spirit dwelling in their midst that justifies the claim about it being the temple. Paul makes a similar point in his second letter to the Corinthians, where his purpose is to warn the believers about improper associations with idolatry (2 Cor 6:16–17). "We are the temple of the living God," Paul proclaims (v. 16), fulfilling the Old Testament promise that God will "live with" his people and "walk among them" (see Lev 26:12; Jer 32:38; Ezek 37:27). In Ephesians 2:11–22, Paul employs a variety of metaphors to depict the inclusion of gentiles in the new-realm people of God. Having been "brought near by the blood of Christ," they are now "fellow citizens with God's people," "members of his household," forming, with Jewish believers, "one new man" (NIV "one new humanity"). Capping off these descriptions is the claim that Christians are "built on the foundation of the apostles and prophets, with Christ Jesus himself as the chief cornerstone," thereby becoming a building that "rises to become a holy temple in the Lord" (vv. 20–21). A connection with Paul's fundamental union with Christ conception is clear here; it is "in him [Christ Jesus]" that this temple comes into being.[56] Paul again cites the presence of the Spirit in the midst of the people as basis for the creation of this new temple. Putting these texts together, we see that Paul cites the Spirit as a basis for the creation of the new temple and uses the temple conception (1) to announce the fulfillment of God's Old Testament promise about God dwelling with his people; (2) to emphasize that gentiles, in fulfillment again of Old Testament prophecy, are joined with believing Jews in this new temple; and (3) to stress the need for this new community to exhibit the holiness that characterizes the God who now dwells among them. Christ has given himself for the church "to make her holy, cleansing her by the washing with water through the word, and to present her to himself as a radiant church, without stain or wrinkle or any other blemish, but holy and blameless" (Eph 5:25–27). The negative side of this concern for holiness is manifested in Paul's insistence that the church cleanse itself from those who would seriously pollute it (1 Cor 5:1–7; 2 Thess 3:14–15).

3.2.3 Body

Perhaps Paul's most distinctive contribution to the theology of the church is his characterization of the new-realm people of God as a "body." It is also one of the

---

54. As I noted earlier (p. 125), the temple in 1 Cor 6:19 is almost certainly the individual believer, not the community.

55. See esp. Beale, *Temple and the Church's Mission*, 269–92.
56. Macaskill, *Union with Christ*, 147–91.

more complicated. As Thiselton remarks, "Few terms have undergone so many twists and turns in the history of Pauline scholarship than *body* and *body of Christ*."[57] Such is the complexity, indeed, that we should speak of Paul's use of body with respect to the church not as a "doctrine" but as a "powerful image."[58] The following are the relevant texts:[59]

> Is not the cup of thanksgiving for which we give thanks a participation in the blood of Christ? And is not the bread that we break a participation in the body of Christ? Because there is one loaf, we, who are many, are one body, for we all share the one loaf. (1 Cor 10:16–17)

> And when he had given thanks, he broke it and said, "This is my body, which is for you; do this in remembrance of me." (1 Cor 11:24)

> So then, whoever eats the bread or drinks the cup of the Lord in an unworthy manner will be guilty of sinning against the body and blood of the Lord. Everyone ought to examine themselves before they eat of the bread and drink from the cup. For those who eat and drink without discerning the body of Christ eat and drink judgment on themselves. (1 Cor 11:27–29)[60]

> Just as a body, though one, has many parts, but all its many parts form one body, so it is with Christ. For we were all baptized by one Spirit so as to form one body— whether Jews or Gentiles, slave or free—and we were all given the one Spirit to drink. Even so the body is not made up of one part but of many.
>   Now if the foot should say, "Because I am not a hand, I do not belong to the body," it would not for that reason stop being part of the body. And if the ear should say, "Because I am not an eye, I do not belong to the body," it would not for that reason stop being part of the body. If the whole body were an eye, where would the sense of hearing be? If the whole body were an ear, where would the sense of smell be? But in fact God has placed the parts in the body, every one of them, just as he wanted them to be. If they were all one part, where would the body be? As it is, there are many parts, but one body.
>   The eye cannot say to the hand, "I don't need you!" And the head cannot say to the feet, "I don't need you!" On the contrary, those parts of the body that seem to be

---

57. Thiselton, *First Epistle to the Corinthians*, 990 (emphasis original).

58. Beker, *Paul the Apostle*, 307.

59. I exclude Rom 7:4—"So, my brothers and sisters, you also died to the law through the body of Christ, that you might belong to another, to him who was raised from the dead, in order that we might bear fruit for God"—judging, with most commentators, that the reference is to Jesus's physical body.

60. Verse 29, of course, is much debated, but I hesitantly think a reference to the church as the "body" might be most likely.

weaker are indispensable, and the parts that we think are less honorable we treat with special honor. And the parts that are unpresentable are treated with special modesty, while our presentable parts need no special treatment. But God has put the body together, giving greater honor to the parts that lacked it, so that there should be no division in the body, but that its parts should have equal concern for each other. If one part suffers, every part suffers with it; if one part is honored, every part rejoices with it.

Now you are the body of Christ, and each one of you is a part of it. (1 Cor 12:12–27)

For just as each of us has one body with many members, and these members do not all have the same function, so in Christ we, though many, form one body, and each member belongs to all the others. (Rom 12:4–5)

And he is the head of the body, the church; he is the beginning and the firstborn from among the dead, so that in everything he might have the supremacy. (Col 1:18)

Now I rejoice in what I am suffering for you, and I fill up in my flesh what is still lacking in regard to Christ's afflictions, for the sake of his body, which is the church. (Col 1:24)

Therefore do not let anyone judge you by what you eat or drink, or with regard to a religious festival, a New Moon celebration or a Sabbath day. These are a shadow of the things that were to come; the reality [or "body"; Gk. *sōma*], however, is found in Christ. (Col 2:16–17)

They have lost connection with the head, from whom the whole body, supported and held together by its ligaments and sinews, grows as God causes it to grow. (Col 2:19)

Let the peace of Christ rule in your hearts, since as members of one body you were called to peace. And be thankful. (Col 3:15)

And God placed all things under his feet and appointed him to be head over everything for the church, which is his body, the fullness of him who fills everything in every way. (Eph 1:22–23)

For he himself is our peace, who has made the two groups one and has destroyed the barrier, the dividing wall of hostility, by setting aside in his flesh the law with its commands and regulations. His purpose was to create in himself one new humanity out of the two, thus making peace, and in one body to reconcile both of them to God through the cross, by which he put to death their hostility. (Eph 2:14–16)

Make every effort to keep the unity of the Spirit through the bond of peace. There is one body and one Spirit, just as you were called to one hope when you were called; one Lord, one faith, one baptism; one God and Father of all, who is over all and through all and in all. (Eph 4:3–6)

So Christ himself gave the apostles, the prophets, the evangelists, the pastors and teachers, to equip his people for works of service, so that the body of Christ may be built up until we all reach unity in the faith and in the knowledge of the Son of God and become mature, attaining to the whole measure of the fullness of Christ. (Eph 4:11–13)

From him the whole body, joined and held together by every supporting ligament, grows and builds itself up in love, as each part does its work. (Eph 4:16)

For the husband is the head of the wife as Christ is the head of the church, his body, of which he is the Savior. (Eph 5:23)

After all, no one ever hated their own body, but they feed and care for their body, just as Christ does the church—for we are members of his body. (Eph 5:29–30)

As can readily be seen, these texts fall into four basic categories. First, we find passages that refer to the physical body of Christ in the Eucharist (1 Cor 10:16–17; 11:24, 27–29). Second are texts that *compare* the church to *a* body; for example, "just as the body . . . so it is with Christ" (1 Cor 12:12 and context; see also Rom 12:4–5; Eph 4:4[?]). Third, we find texts that *identify* the church with *Christ's* body; for example, "the church, which is his body" (Eph 1:22–23; see also Eph 2:16[?]; 4:12, 16[?]; 5:23; 5:30; Col 1:24; 2:17, 19[?]; 3:15[?]). And, fourth, we find a more extended metaphor, with Christ as "head" added to the body metaphor (Col 1:18; Eph 5:23; see also Eph 1:22–23; 4:15). The four types I have isolated do not occupy watertight compartments—there are, at the least, connections that can be traced. The simile of "church like a body" (1 Cor 12:12–26) slips quickly into metaphor—"you *are* the body of Christ" (1 Cor 12:27). Indeed, a careful reading of 1 Corinthians 12 reveals that metaphor and simile have been bound together from the beginning of Paul's argument.[61] For the concluding clause in verse 12—"so it is with Christ"—makes sense only if "Christ" here is functionally equivalent to "body"; that is, "as a [human] body so it is with [the body of] Christ." Affirmations of believers as making up the body of Christ therefore bookend the paragraph (vv. 12 and 27). There is no doubt that one can

---

61. E.g., Aletti, *Essai sur l'écclesiologie*, 56–67.

trace a certain development in Paul's use of "body" for the church. The number and complexity of references in Ephesians especially stand out. Yet the relatively mature use of the language as early as 1 Corinthians suggests, again (see above on *ekklēsia*), that we are not dealing here with a shift from the perspective of Paul to a later follower of his but with a development in Paul's use of a complex metaphor.[62]

The close proximity of 1 Corinthians 10:16–17, 11:24 (and perhaps 12:29) to 1 Corinthians 12:27 might suggest that identifying the church with Christ's body is a development from the church's partaking of Christ's body in the Eucharist.[63] Yet the preparation for the explicit imagery of chapter 12 goes back to an earlier stage of the letter.[64] In chapter 6, Paul prohibits Christian men from having sex with prostitutes because such activity "unites" "the members of Christ" with that prostitute; they become "one with her in body" (vv. 15–16). The word "member" (*melos*) is most often used in the New Testament of a part of the human body. Calling believers "members of Christ," then, comes close to implying that Christ is himself like a body.[65] Another significant background to the explicit body metaphor in chapter 12 is Paul's understanding of baptism as the locus in which believers become "one body" (v. 13). This verse, in turn, picks up key motifs from Galatians 3:27–29 (baptism, erasure of social and gender distinctions, "oneness" in Christ): "For all of you who were baptized into Christ have clothed yourselves with Christ. There is neither Jew nor Gentile, neither slave nor free, nor is there male and female, for you are all one in Christ Jesus. If you belong to Christ, then you are Abraham's seed, and heirs according to the promise." These specific passages, in turn, direct our attention to a central christological idea in Paul: Christ the Messiah as a corporate person, "the new man" (Eph 2:15 [NIV "one new humanity"]; 4:24; Col 3:10–11 ["new self"]), in whom all believers find themselves included. All this suggests that a plausible explanation of Paul's identification of believers together as "the body of Christ" may be this fundamental and widespread corporate conception of Christ.[66]

However, we need briefly to consider other possible sources for Paul's imagery of the church as "the body of Christ." Some can be dismissed quite quickly as inadequately explaining Paul's distinctive use of the imagery, such as gnostic speculations about an "*Ur-anthropos*," Stoic notions of the cosmos as a single "body," or an extension of Christ's actual physical body (perhaps mediated in the Eucharist).[67] Much more likely

---

62. See, e.g., Aletti, *Essai sur l'écclesiologie*, 189–90. As is often noted, Colossians occupies something of a transitional stage in this development.

63. A connection between Paul's imagery of body for the church and the Eucharist is widely posited (often combined with other backgrounds; e.g., Stuhlmacher, *Biblische Theologie*, 2:357–58; Aletti, *Essai sur l'écclesiologie*, 67–73; Cerfaux, *Church*, 262–82).

64. See, e.g., Ciampa and Rosner, *First Corinthians*, 594–95.

65. Ernest Best, *One Body in Christ: A Study in the Relationship of the Church to Christ in the Epistles of the Apostle Paul* (London: SPCK, 1955), 94–95.

66. Some scholars trace this identification back to Paul's conversion, when the risen Christ asked Paul about his persecution of the church: "Saul, Saul, why do you persecute *me*?" (Acts 9:4; e.g., Kim, *Origin of Paul's Gospel*, 253).

67. For a survey and discussion of these options, see esp.

is the influence of political rhetoric in Paul's day, where comparisons of a political entity (a city-state, the empire) with a "body" were common. Like Paul, writers used the imagery to highlight the unity of the political entity. To take one example: the first-century Roman Seneca encourages understanding in human relationships on the basis that "we are the parts of one great body" (*Epistulae morales* 95.51–52). And, like Paul, these comparisons sometimes both identified a political leader with the body at the same time as they differentiated the leader. Again, Seneca refers to Emperor Nero as "the soul of the republic which is your body" (*De clementia* 1.5.1)—a close parallel to Paul's claim that the church is Christ's body and that he is also the head of the body. These comparisons even mentioned some of the same body parts that Paul refers to in 1 Corinthians 12:15–26: foot, hand, eye, and ear (see, e.g., Plutarch, *Moralia* 478D).[68] The similarity between Paul and these texts, which are spread over several centuries and found in both secular and Jewish sources, makes it overwhelmingly likely that it has played some role in his use of the imagery.[69] It is also possible that Paul deliberately turns on its head the typical way this imagery was used. The Greco-Roman authors use it to justify the superiority of certain kinds of people within the "body politic"; Paul uses it to elevate the "lowest" members of the community.

Believers are "in Christ"; they "put on" Christ. He is the "new man" who gathers up in himself all who belong to him. Along a similar corporate line of thinking in Paul, we could find the apostle moving from the claim that the church is the temple, to Jesus's assertion that the renewed temple is his body (John 2:21), to the syllogistic conclusion that the church is Christ's body. It can readily be seen how Paul could extend this basic corporate conception by borrowing the popular Greco-Roman imagery of the body to express the "diversity within unity" of the new-realm people of God.[70] Of course, what is ultimately most important is what Paul says about the new people of God by means of this language. What stands out here first of all is the stress on unity. Paul accentuates this point by referring several times to the *one* body (1 Cor 12:12, 13, 20; Eph 2:16; 4:4; Col 3:15). The "one body" includes all kinds of people with many different gifts (1 Cor 12; Rom 12). Scholars continue to debate the socioeconomic diversity in the Pauline churches, but whatever the relative percentages of different

---

Matthias Walter, *Gemeinde als Leib Christi: Untersuchungen zum Corpus Paulinium und zu den "Apostolischen Vätern,"* NTOA 49 (Göttingen: Vandenhoeck & Ruprecht, 2001); see also, e.g., Thiselton, *First Epistle to the Corinthians,* 990–94; Lincoln, *Ephesians,* 68–72; Gundry, *Sōma,* 228–41; Whitely, *Theology,* 191–94.

68. See esp. Mitchell, *Paul and the Rhetoric of Reconciliation,* 157–59, for a survey of the relevant texts.

69. So also, e.g., Wolter, *Paul,* 281–83; Dunn, *Theology of Paul,* 548–52; Aletti, *Essai sur l'ecclesiologie,* 67–73.

70. For a similar conclusion, see Ernst Percy, *Der Leib Christi*

(Soma Christou) in den Paulinischen Homologumena und Antilegomena, Lunds Universitets Årsskrift 1/38 (Lund: Gleerup, 1942), 18–46; Thompson, *Church according to Paul,* 70–73. Others who highlight the significance of the corporate Christ for Paul's body imagery are, e.g., C. F. D. Moule, *The Origin of Christology* (Cambridge: Cambridge University Press, 1977), 68–69; Constantine R. Campbell, "Metaphor, Reality, and Union with Christ," in Thate, Vanhoozer, and Campbell, *"In Christ" in Paul,* 68–69; Wright, *Resurrection,* 295.

classes, the churches were obviously diverse. They included the wealthy and the poor, the upper class and the lower class—and, of course, everything in between.[71] And, in an emphasis particularly important for Paul, this body includes gentiles and Jews (Eph 2:11–22). Without in any way diminishing, then, diversity—indeed, Paul celebrates it—the diversity of the church should never lead to a rival community—there is *one* body—nor should it lead to disparaging others who are different than we are. The "one body" imagery, therefore, is a powerful reminder that *all* believers belong together and must find ways of accepting and, indeed, honoring one another.

As we have seen, Paul adds a level of complexity to his use of this metaphor when he portrays Christ not simply as the body but as the "head" of the body. In 1 Corinthians 12:12–26, the head of the body has no particular significance, simply mentioned along with other body parts (v. 21). But in Colossians (1:18; 2:10, 19) and Ephesians (1:22; 4:15; 5:23), the head is identified with Christ. The addition of the idea that Christ is the *head* of the body (e.g., Col 1:18: "he is the head of the body, the church") to the idea that Christ *is* the body (e.g., 1 Cor 12:27: "you are the body of Christ") creates a slight tension.[72] But such tensions are often found in the use of metaphor. Paul uses body language both to stress the uniqueness and oneness of the church and to identify the unique role of Christ in this body.[73] "Head" (Gk. *kephalē*) is, of course, one of the debated terms in Paul's theology. As I have noted elsewhere (e.g., pp. 140–41 on 1 Cor 11:3–4), Paul appears to use the word to connote preeminence, with the related notions of sustenance and authority. These ideas are clear in the contexts in which Paul characterizes Christ as "head." Because he is the "head of the church," believers must submit to him (Eph 5:23–24). Yet in that same context, Paul also suggests that Christ's headship involves his "saving" of the church (v. 23), a notion of spiritual sustenance that is more explicit already in Ephesians 4:15–16, where Christ is identified as the head of the body from whom "the whole body, joined and held together by every supporting ligament, grows and builds itself up in love, as each part does its work" (see also the close parallel in Col 2:19).

4 THE LIFE OF THE CHURCH

"The church community is God's eschatological beachhead, the place where the power of God has invaded the world."[74] Richard Hays reminds us that the church is the place

---

71. On this subject, see, e.g., Edwin A. Judge, *The Social Pattern of Early Christian Groups in the First Century* (London: Tyndale, 1960); idem, "The Social Identity of the First Christians: A Question of Method in Religious History," *JRH* 11 (1980): 201–17; idem, with David M. Scholer, *Social Distinctives of the Christians in the First Century: Pivotal Essays* (Peabody, MA:

Hendrickson, 2008); Horrell, *Solidarity and Difference*, 92–103 (with particular focus on the Corinthians).
72. See *TDNT* 3:508.
73. See, e.g., Percy, *Leib Christi*, 47–54.
74. Hays, *Moral Vision*, 27.

where the power and character of the God the church worships is displayed. Paul, of course, has a great deal to say about the life of the church in terms of the "everyday" worship to which believers are called (Rom 12:1–2). And it is not always easy to distinguish references to the life of the church in its daily experience and the life of the church as it is gathered for worship. But there are enough clear references to the corporate experience of the Christian worship service to also give us a window through which we can see some aspects of the meetings of Christians in the Pauline churches. He assumes that Christians in their own locations regularly "come together" (1 Cor 11:17–18, 20, 33, 34; 14:23, 26), probably usually on the "first day of every week" (1 Cor 16:2). It is unclear whether Paul presumes one gathering, in the context of which the Lord's Supper was celebrated (1 Cor 11:17–34), or whether he assumes two separate "gatherings."[75] Evidence from early Christianity does not enable us to identify one particular pattern that we can plausibly trace back to the New Testament churches.[76] However, most scholars think that 1 Corinthians 11:17–34 implies a celebration of the Eucharist in close proximity to the eating of a regular meal. However many stages these gatherings had, we can also assume that in them gifts were exercised, and unbelievers were apparently welcomed (1 Cor 14:22–35). Prayer was clearly an important component of these meetings (1 Cor 11:4–5; 1 Tim 2:1–2, 8). We may also presume that the gathering of the church included instruction in and meditation on the "message of Christ," both in formal teaching (a particular focus in the Pastoral Epistles: 1 Tim 4:13; 6:2b; 2 Tim 4:2; Titus 2:1–3, 6, 9) and informally, in "psalms, hymns, and songs from the Spirit" (Col 3:16; see Eph 5:19). An important goal in this gathering, which was to dictate the components of the gathering and the conduct of those gathered, was "edification," or "building up" (*oikodomē*; see 1 Cor 14:1–17; and also Eph 4:12–16). In addition to these glimpses into the life of the gathered church, Paul sheds light on two theological aspects of the community that deserve separate consideration: its observance of baptism and the Lord's Supper, and its leadership.

4.1 Sacraments[77]

The two ritual acts that were ultimately recognized by Protestants as "sacraments"— baptism and the Lord's Supper, or Eucharist—are both mentioned by Paul, and in a way that suggests they were important in the life of the church. They were visible means by which the community maintained cohesion and vision.[78] References to baptism far outweigh references to the Lord's Supper. Paul refers to the latter in only one letter (1 Cor 10:16–17; 11:17–34), while he mentions baptism in five letters (Rom 6:3–4;

---

75. Dunn, e.g., thinks the latter is more likely (*Theology of Paul*, 618–19).

76. See, e.g., "Eucharist," *IDB* 2:354.

77. I use the word "sacrament" because I think that both baptism and the Lord's Supper are each rightly viewed as "a visible sign of an invisible grace," to quote the classic definition, going back to Augustine (*Epistles* 138).

78. Horrell, *Solidarity and Difference*, 86.

1 Cor 1:13–17; 12:13; 15:29 [and see 10:2]; Gal 3:27; Eph 4:5; Col 2:12). To be sure, it is possible that Paul refers to the sacraments much more often than these explicit references indicate.[79] Indeed, the whole issue of the importance and significance of the sacraments in the New Testament is fraught with subjectivity and circular reasoning. Thus, some argue, in effect, that baptism was very important in the early church, so of course virtually every reference to water is an allusion to baptism; and we know it was important because of all these allusions to baptism. Others argue in the other direction. Finding one's way in negotiating the evidence in Paul is not easy, and one should admit that one's convictions about the sacraments based on larger theological and ecclesiastical commitments will play a significant role in one's analysis. For these reasons, we must be very modest about what we can conclude theologically from Paul's scattered references.

Baptism, as noted above, receives more attention in Paul than the Lord's Supper. First Corinthians 1:13–17 at least indicates that Paul did not view it as a central element in his own ministry. Yet this might only mean, for instance, that he thought it was better administered by local church leaders than by an itinerant apostle. Certainly Paul's casual allusions to baptism suggest that it typically accompanied one's entrance into the Christian community (Rom 6:3–4; 1 Cor 12:13; Gal 3:27; Col 2:12). To be sure, some minimize or deny the relevance of these texts for our subject by arguing that "baptize" (*baptizō*) or "baptism" (*baptismos* or *baptisma*) refer not to a church ritual involving water but to "immersion" in the Spirit or into Christ. And, of course, the Greek words have this basic meaning, while texts such as Mark 10:38–39 and parallels attest to New Testament use of the language in a metaphorical sense.[80] However, one of the Greek words Paul uses—*baptisma*—always elsewhere refers to an experience in water, and in general there is enough New Testament evidence to show that the language of baptism in Paul's day had taken on a technical sense, denoting a ritual of immersion in water that accompanied conversion. In putting the matter this way, I am distancing myself from the view, popular in some modern contexts, that locates baptism on the road of discipleship rather than at the point of conversion. Paul's use of the language indicates pretty clearly that baptism, for him, signifies entrance into Christ and his community. Paul connects being baptized with being "clothed with Christ" (Gal 3:27) and being "buried with him" (Rom 6:3–4; Col 2:12)—and these are given at conversion. If, as I hesitantly think, 1 Corinthians 12:13 is also a reference

---

79. Many interpreters think that Paul alludes to baptism in 1 Cor 6:11b ("But you were washed, you were sanctified, you were justified in the name of the Lord Jesus Christ and by the Spirit of our God"); Eph 1:13 ("When you believed, you were marked in him with a seal, the promised Holy Spirit"); 5:26 ("Cleansing her [the church] by the washing with water through the word"); Titus 3:5 ("He saved us through the washing of rebirth and renewal by the Holy Spirit").

80. See esp. Eckhard J. Schnabel, "The Language of Baptism: The Meaning of Βαπτίζω in the New Testament," in Köstenberger and Yarbrough, *Understanding the Times*, 217–46.

to water baptism ("baptized [in water] by [*en*] one Spirit"; see p. 147), baptism also has a communal focus, serving to integrate the new believer into the body of Christ. Paul's use of baptism language therefore reflects the picture we find in the book of Acts, where being baptized appears to be interchanged with faith and repentance. Baptism is more than a symbol of a dying and rising with Christ that had already happened; it functions in Paul as the instrument (see "through [*dia*] baptism" in Rom 6:4) that brings people into union with Christ's death, burial, and resurrection (see also Col 2:12).[81] However, this does *not* mean that Paul viewed water baptism as such as having the power to effect salvation or entry into the community.[82] He is altogether too emphatic about the power of faith—and faith alone—to make this a reasonable reading of his letters. Rather, borrowing James Dunn's very helpful language, we should think of water baptism as one component of "conversion-initiation."[83] Water baptism, administered by the church to believers shortly after their conversion—by faith—puts a seal on that conversion experience.[84]

Colossians 2:12 is often thought to present baptism as a parallel to circumcision, and scholars draw various theological conclusions from this association. However, the association is looser than is sometimes thought. Paul does not compare baptism with (literal) circumcision; he identifies baptism as the "place" where our spiritual circumcision takes place. Paul's logic runs like this: "You have been spiritually 'circumcised.' This 'circumcision' took place when you were buried with Christ and raised with him. And this burial and resurrection with Christ happened when you were baptized." As this paraphrase of Paul's argument also reveals, the relationship between baptism and circumcision is indirect. At the same time, this text also highlights again Paul's tendency to associate baptism with conversion rather than with discipleship.[85]

Teasing out anything approaching a "theology of the Eucharist" in Paul is even more difficult. He refers to the rite in only two passages—1 Corinthians 10:14–22 and 11:17–34—and in neither case is his focus on that rite itself. In chapter 10, Paul warns the Corinthians against joining in pagan temple meals, asserting that if they were to do so, they would become "participants [*koinōnous*] with demons" (v. 20). This "table of demons" stands in stark contrast to the "Lord's table" (v. 21), where believers enjoy

---

81. Contra, e.g., Flemington, *Doctrine of Baptism*, 59.

82. Baptism as a sacrament of salvation, a manifestation of grace that in itself saves, is, of course, a widely held view. See, e.g., Rudolf Schnackenburg, *Baptism in the Thought of St. Paul: A Study in Pauline Theology* (Oxford: Basil Blackwell, 1964), 105–7; Schnelle, *Apostle Paul*, 479–80.

83. Dunn, *Baptism in the Holy Spirit*, 372.

84. I go into greater detail on this theology, and its foundation in Rom 6:3–4, in my *Romans* (NICNT), 385–91. See also, for a full exposition of this general view, Beasley-Murray, *Baptism in the New Testament*. Dunn helpfully suggests that "baptism" in

Paul is a "concertina" word, referring narrowly to the water rite but perhaps also, by synecdoche, to the larger conversion process (see also Wolter, *Paul*, 125–46). Horton pertinently remarks that there is too often in the contemporary church a separation between baptism into Christ, Spirit baptism, and the sacrament of baptism that robs the sacrament of its meaning and power (*Rediscovering the Holy Spirit*, 189–90). He rightly notes that in many churches the sacraments are treated as a "means of commitment" in place of a "means of grace" (*People and Place*, 171).

85. For this last paragraph, see Moo, *Colossians*, 202.

"participation" (*koinōnia*) in the body of Christ, mediated by the bread, and in the blood of Christ, mediated by the "cup of thanksgiving" (*eulogia*; v. 16). This passage makes the first explicit reference to the Supper, but it is likely that Paul's language about the Israelites eating "spiritual food" and drinking "spiritual drink" (vv. 3–4) evokes the Supper also. Having experienced both a "baptism" (into Moses, v. 2) and having regularly partaken of spiritual meals, most of the people of Israel nevertheless fell under the judgment of God. This is naturally read as a warning to the Corinthians about their inappropriate dependence on the sacraments for spiritual deliverance (see vv. 6–13). We must be careful not to read too much into Paul's allusive remarks here, but it might be fair to conclude that Paul does not view the sacraments as possessing the power, in themselves, to communicate saving grace.[86]

Paul sounds a further note in his discussion of the Eucharist in chapter 10, reminding the Corinthians that because there is "one loaf" (or "one bread"), believers are also "one body" (v. 17). This emphasis on unity, which is somewhat out of place in this context, probably indicates that this theme of oneness was a standard focus in Paul's teaching about the Eucharist. And, of course, this note is developed into a whole melody in chapter 11, where Paul rebukes the Corinthians for their selfish behavior in the context of celebration of the Eucharist. The text clearly assumes that the Corinthian celebration involved a meal, although the precise scenario eludes us. Most interpreters, partly in light of later Christian practice, think that the believers would have gathered first for a regular meal, followed by the celebration of the Eucharist. Some of the Corinthians were behaving selfishly at the common meal, tainting their celebration of the Eucharist—indeed, it is "not the Lord's Supper you eat" (11:20). It is in this context that Paul repeats the words of institution from the Last Supper, citing them in language closer to Luke than to Mark and Matthew (vv. 23–26). The Last Supper meal was, in fact, a Passover meal that Jesus reinterpreted in light of his own impending death. Jews who celebrated the Passover were encouraged to put themselves into the shoes of the original participants in the exodus. So also, we can assume, Jesus called on his followers to celebrate his Supper with a view toward identifying with his own redemptive work. Believers "*participate* in the deliverance of the cross *as if they were 'there.*"[87] However, Paul does little to indicate this rich theological sense of the meal. His concern, as I have noted, is not in the rite itself but in the selfish attitudes and divisive behavior of the Corinthians. Paul, then, provides only minimal help in developing a robust Eucharistic theology. That theology will have to be worked out at a level above and beyond Paul's meager evidence. Paul's contribution is his warning that celebration of what can rightly

---

86. Contra, e.g., Pitre, Barber, and Kincaid, *Paul: A New Covenant Jew*, 211–50, who argue that Paul's discussion in 1 Corinthians 10 implies that the substance of the bread and wine possesses gracious power.

87. Thiselton, *Hermeneutics of Doctrine*, 528 (emphasis original).

be called "the Lord's Supper" can only take place if believers eat and drink with the right disposition. This disposition will include the kind of inward reflection so often encouraged when the Eucharist is celebrated today. But, as this context makes clear, our "outward"-looking disposition is also crucially important. Getting right with God as we celebrate cannot happen unless we are right with one another.

4.2 Ministry and Leadership

Paul clearly assumes that believers will be active in ministry, or "service" (*diakonia*) to others within their community. The gifted people Christ gives the church are designed "to equip his people for works of service" (Eph 4:12); "From him [Christ] the whole body, joined and held together by every supporting ligament, grows and builds itself up in love, *as each part does its work*" (Eph 4:16); "Now *to each one* the manifestation of the Spirit is given for the common good" (1 Cor 12:7). Yet Paul also recognizes that certain believers will be called to a special form of service: "Acknowledge those who work hard among you, who care for you in the Lord and who admonish you" (1 Thess 5:12). And, of course, Paul also frequently mentions some individuals who joined with him in significant ministry, sometimes associating them with the letters he writes as well as sending letters to encourage and instruct them in ministry (e.g., Timothy and Titus). We can learn much about the nature of ministry from these examples, although we must also be sensitive to the possible differences between their ministry (having perhaps a unique authority derived from Paul) and ours. Here I focus on what Paul teaches about the leadership and organization of his churches.

Decisions about the number of letters to integrate fully into Paul's theology has a greater impact on this issue than on any other. Since the majority of Pauline scholars, including those who have written Pauline theologies, attribute the Pastoral Epistles to someone writing after Paul's day in his name, the Pastoral Epistles' evidence about church ministry and leadership is either ignored or relegated to a secondary level of importance.[88] The impact of this decision is quite breathtaking, since these letters offer by far the most data about this issue within the "Pauline" corpus. My decision to attribute the Pastorals to Paul means that I will seek to fully integrate their witness into the Pauline theology of ministry and leadership.

The teaching of the Pastoral Epistles about this issue is, of course, one of the main reasons that scholars think a later Paulinist must be responsible for them. Gone from these letters is the free-wheeling, Spirit-led church ministry that we find in, for example, 1 Corinthians. Gifts of the Spirit, distributed by the Spirit as he wills, are replaced

---

88. E.g., the Pastoral Epistles are not mentioned in the treatment of Paul's view of women in the ministry of the church in Hays, *Moral Vision*, 52–56.

with people appointed to offices in highly organized churches. Marshall summarizes the scholarly consensus:

> The P[astoral] E[pistles] represent the development of an early catholic view of the church which was occasioned by the rise of heresy and the consequent need to preserve apostolic teaching by an appeal to the "deposit" handed down from Paul, by the development of structures to ensure that teaching was in the hands of trustworthy leaders, and by the development of a discipline to restrain the opponents.[89]

The movement from less (or no) structure to much more structure is often traced to the "delay of the parousia." According to this scenario, Jesus taught, and the earliest church believed, that the Lord would be returning from heaven within a short time to gather Christians to himself. With so strong an expectation of quick deliverance, Christians felt no need to organize their churches. However, as time went on, and this expectation of Christ's quick return waned, believers began to recognize the need for mechanisms to preserve the truth of the faith and to provide for the ongoing life of the church.[90] I cast doubt on this whole "delay of the parousia" scheme earlier. Paul is pretty consistent in his letters about viewing the Lord's return as potentially able to take place within a very short time. But the evidence that this expectation ever morphed into a belief that the Lord would definitely return within x number of years is simply not forthcoming. That there is development in Paul's assumptions and teaching about church leadership is fairly clear. However, as I have repeatedly argued with respect to a host of issues, this development is a matter of organic growth rather than a shift from one view to another. The analogy is the growth of a tree versus the replacement of one tree with another. In what follows, then, I will look generally at Paul's teaching about ministry and leadership across his letters, with particular attention to his teaching about gifts of the Spirit and church "offices."

Paul refers to gifts given for the edification of the church in four passages: Romans 12:6–8; 1 Corinthians 12:4–11, 28–31a; and Ephesians 4:11.[91] In the 1 Corinthians and Romans passages, Paul uses the Greek *charisma*, while in Ephesians he uses *doma* (with dependence on Ps 68:18).[92] *Charisma* comes from the verb *charizomai*, "give

---

89. Marshall and Towner, *Pastoral Epistles*, 516. Marshall provides a succinct survey of the history of the discussion (512–21). See Dunn, *Unity and Diversity*, 109–16, for a version of this perspective on Paul's letters.

90. As Marshall notes in the quotation above, the movement toward an organizational church is often called (by Protestants, at least!) "early Catholicism": a sort of halfway house between the free-wheeling churches of the "authentic" Paul and the later, more institutional structures we find in the early church.

91. For a useful general overview, see H. Schürmann, "Die geistlichen Gnadengaben in den paulinischen Gemeiden," in *Ursprung und Gestalt: Erörterungen und Besinnungen zum Neuen Testament* (Düsseldorf: Patmos, 1970), 236–73.

92. The word *pneumatikos* in 1 Cor 12:1 probably also refers to spiritual gifts (so most translations), although some think it refers to "spiritual people." It is also possible, as, e.g., Thiselton thinks (*Hermeneutics of Doctrine*, 425), that Paul replaces the Corinthians' "Spirit" focus with his own emphasis on "gracious gift."

graciously," and is related, of course, to the important theological word *charis*, "grace."[93] Paul makes clear that the relationship is not just a matter of etymology. In Romans 12, Paul introduces his discussion of gifts by saying, "We have different gifts [*charismata*], according to the grace [*charis*] given to each of us" (v. 6a; see also Eph 4:7). We regularly refer to these gifts as "gifts of the Spirit," and 1 Corinthians 12:7 justifies this language: "Now to each one the manifestation of the Spirit is given for the common good" (and note the references to the Spirit throughout vv. 8–11).[94] However, Paul also claims that gifts are given by God (1 Cor 12:28) and by Christ (Eph 4:11). The passages referring to gifts have different rhetorical purposes. In 1 Corinthians 12, Paul celebrates the diversity of people and their gifts and ministries; see, for example, verse 27: "Now you are the body of Christ, and each one of you is a part of it." He lists several gifts in the passage following this verse to urge that the church recognize this diversity. But in the chapter as a whole, his more fundamental purpose seems to be to assert the unity of the "one body of Christ." The references to gifts in verses 7–11 serve this purpose by tracing them all back to the "same Spirit." In Romans 12, Paul's concern is with pride— perhaps with an eye to the arrogance and intolerance that he rebukes in chapter 11 and in 14:1–15:7. The "many" members of Christ, Paul reminds them, "form one body," and "each member belongs to all the others" (v. 5). Paul then urges believers to use the various gifts they have been given so that they rightly serve each other. In Ephesians 4, as in 1 Corinthians 12, Paul accentuates the unity of the church. The various gifts bestowed by the risen Christ are designed to build up that single body, "until we all reach unity in the faith and in the knowledge of the Son of God, becoming a mature man" (Eph 4:12–13; the last phrase is my own translation).

In none of these passages is Paul's overall purpose to enumerate a set list of gifts. Gifts are mentioned in service of other purposes. These "lists," then, are all somewhat ad hoc. We have no reason to think that Paul provides us with a comprehensive list of all the available gifts of the Spirit. His concern, rather, as we have seen, is with the way those gifts, and the diversity they exemplify, ultimately serve to edify and unify the one body of Christ.

This is not the place to delve into the question of the specific nature of each of the gifts. I will comment briefly on only two of them, prophecy and tongues. What exactly they entail is difficult to determine, since Paul assumes his readers know what he is talking about.

"Prophecy" was obviously an important phenomenon in Paul's churches, as the number of references indicate.[95] He refers to New Testament "prophets" (using *prophētēs*)

93. Turner, *Holy Spirit*, 264.

94. However, Kenneth Berding has a point when he argues that we have smuggled "spiritual" into our language of gifts too often, leading to a focus on abilities rather than, as is the case arguably in Paul, on ministries ("Confusing Word and Concept in 'Spiritual Gifts': Have We Forgotten James Barr's Exhortations?," *JETS* 43 [2000]: 37–51).

95. Thiselton has an excellent overview of the discussion of this gift (*First Epistle to the Corinthians*, 956–65). See also Turner, *Holy Spirit*, 196–220.

or "prophecy" (*prophēteia*) in Romans 12:6; 1 Corinthians 12:10, 28, 29; 13:2, 8; Eph 4:11; 1 Thess 5:20; 1 Tim 1:18; 4:14. In the lists in 1 Corinthians 12:28–31 and Ephesians 4:11, prophets are listed just after apostles. This suggestion of their prominence is enhanced if Paul's reference to "apostles and prophets" as the "foundation" of the new household of God (Eph 2:20; see 3:5) includes New Testament prophets. Some deny this, claiming either that the prophets are Old Testament prophets or that Paul has only one group in mind: apostles who prophesy.[96] But a reference to two foundational New Testament figures, apostles and prophets, is more likely.[97] Of course, the most specific information about prophets comes in 1 Corinthians 14, where Paul is seeking to diminish the attention being given in Corinth to tongues by contrasting this gift with the gift of prophecy. Prophecy, unlike tongues, communicates directly and clearly to believers. It therefore has a greater potential to edify the church, which is Paul's criterion in judging the value of gifts (1 Cor 14:3–5). Later in this chapter, Paul appears to suggest that prophecy involves communicating something to the church that comes through a sudden revelation. Clearly speaking about prophecy (see vv. 29–31), Paul refers to "a revelation" coming "to someone who is sitting down."[98] He goes on to urge the church (or perhaps other prophets) to "weigh carefully" what a prophet says (v. 29; see also 1 Thess 5:20–21). These verses suggest to some that Paul views New Testament prophets as people who channel special and occasional revelations from God to the community.[99] They do not possess the kind of authority wielded by the Old Testament prophet or by the apostles. However, the majority of interpreters, noting the evidence about the importance of prophets I looked at above, view New Testament prophecy as broader in scope, involving the communication of fundamental theological truth to the community, perhaps in a more specific or applied form than "teaching."[100]

The gift of tongues, of course, is particularly controversial.[101] Paul's references to this gift are confined to 1 Corinthians: 12:10, 28, 30; 13:1, 8; chapter 14 passim. As we have seen, Paul is particularly concerned to wean the Corinthians away from what was apparently an overvaluation of tongues—perhaps because of the perceived status it may have given the tongues-speaker. The word for "tongues" (*glōssa*) is the ordinary Greek word for the organ of speech (like our "tongue"; see Rom 14:11; Phil 2:11) and

96. For the former, see, e.g., John Calvin, *Galatians, Ephesians, Philippians and Colossians* (repr., Grand Rapids: Eerdmans, 1975), 154–55; for the latter (based partly on the single article governing the two words), see Grudem, *Gift of Prophecy*, 45–63.

97. This is the view of most scholars; see esp. O'Brien, *Ephesians*, 214–16.

98. As many interpreters have noted, the "revelation" communicated by prophets need not be spontaneous; revelation is compatible with preparation or study. But it is the particular language of something "being revealed to another who is seated" (*ean de allō apokalyphthē kathēmenō*) that strikes the note of spontaneity.

99. See esp. Grudem, *Gift of Prophecy*; and also see David E. Aune, *Prophecy in Early Christianity and the Ancient Mediterranean World* (Grand Rapids: Eerdmans, 1983); Forbes, *Prophecy and Inspired Speech*, 218–37. One reason to take this view of prophecy is that Paul consistently distinguishes between "teaching" and "prophecy"; see, e.g., Smith, *Pauline Communities*, 239–53.

100. See, e.g., Thiselton, *First Epistle to the Corinthians*, 960–61.

101. Once again, Thiselton (*First Epistle to the Corinthians*, 972–88) offers a valuable survey of options. See also Carson, *Showing the Spirit*, 77–88.

also for what we would call a "language" (e.g., Rev 5:9). Since, then, Acts 2 appears to characterize "tongues" in terms of a Spirit-enabled ability to speak a known human language that one previously did not know ("xenoglossia"; Acts 2:4, 11; see also 10:46; 19:6), it is possible that Paul also considers tongues to involve speaking in a known human language.[102] And it would make a lot of sense to think that these two New Testament authors, using the same word to describe the gift, would be referring to the same phenomenon. However, the idea that Paul thinks of tongues as a known human language is difficult to square with his description of the gift. In 1 Corinthians 14:2, he says that "anyone who speaks in a tongue does not speak to people but to God. Indeed, no one understands them; they utter mysteries by the Spirit." The purpose of the gift in Acts 2, of course, is just the opposite: to enable the disciples to communicate the good news of Jesus to people from other lands who speak other languages. Most interpreters, then, are convinced that tongues in Paul is a "prayer language," a series of utterances that, while being generally language-like, do not conform to any human language.[103] Since Paul himself refers to "different kinds of tongues" (*genē glōssōn*, 1 Cor 12:10), it is possible that the gift of tongues took two or more forms in the early church.[104]

The controversial nature of gifts such as tongues, along with a concern that claims to prophetic speech might undercut orthodox teaching (as, e.g., in the Montanist crisis), have fostered the view that Paul views some of the gifts as intended to last only until the time when the church would be fully established.[105] Sometimes labeled "cessationism," this view is sometimes based on a reading of 1 Corinthians 13:10 as indicating a cessation of gifts like prophecy when the "completed canon" is in place. However, the key word here, *teleios*, almost certainly refers to the very end of history, when "we shall see face to face" (v. 12).[106] The stronger arguments for cessationism are historical (many of the gifts fell out of usage over time) and theological. However, none of them is ultimately convincing. There is little reason to think that Paul puts any kind of time limit on the availability of any of the gifts.[107]

While our evidence comes from only three epistles, they are diverse enough in time and destination to suggest that gifts were an important means of the ministry and leadership of the Pauline churches. However, it is important to correct any impression

---

102. E.g., Turner, *Holy Spirit*, 221–39; Horton, *Rediscovering the Holy Spirit*, 236–39. Some argue that the "miracle" in Acts 2 is not one of speaking but of hearing.

103. See esp. Forbes, *Prophecy and Inspired Speech*, 47–65.

104. E.g., Thiselton, *Hermeneutics of Doctrine*, 444.

105. The view is particularly associated with some modern evangelicals (see, e.g., Robert L. Thomas, *Understanding Spiritual Gifts: A Verse-by-Verse Study of 1 Corinthians 12–14* [Grand Rapids: Kregel, 1999]); but it has a rather long history in the church. See, in the nineteenth century, Benjamin B. Warfield, *Counterfeit Miracles* (repr., Edinburgh: Banner of Truth, 1972).

For further evaluation and debate, see Wayne A. Grudem, ed., *Are Miraculous Gifts for Today? Four Views*, Counterpoints (Grand Rapids: Zondervan, 1996).

106. See, e.g., James W. Scott, "The Time When Revelatory Gifts Cease (1 Cor 13:8–12)," *WTJ* 72 (2010): 267–89, who argues that Paul refers to people in his day who will exercise their gifts until the parousia. See also Carson, *Showing the Spirit*, 66–72.

107. See Turner, *Holy Spirit*, 286–302. This, of course, is a long way from claiming that the Spirit makes all gifts available in every time and at every place.

that this focus on gifts meant that Paul and the churches had no concern for order. Paul manifests this concern in his discussion of gifts in 1 Corinthians 14:33–40. Paul encourages the use of gifts—even tongues—but he also insists that the gifts be used in "a fitting and orderly way" (v. 40). Nor were leaders absent from the churches. In one of Paul's earliest letters, he commands the people "to acknowledge those who work hard among you, who care for you in the Lord and who admonish you. Hold them in the highest regard in love because of their work" (1 Thess 5:12–13). The verb translated in the NIV as "care for" (*proistēmi*) is translated in most other English versions as a reference to leadership—"preside over you" (NET), "lead you" (CSB)—and this meaning fits better with Paul's other uses of the verb (1 Tim 3:4, 5, 12; 5:17; in Titus 3:8 and 14 it means "show concern"; Rom 12:8 is ambiguous). There is no reason, then, to think that Paul's appointment of "elders" as early as the end of his first missionary journey (Acts 14:23) is a Lukan invention. Recognized leaders and a concern for "order" were found side by side with gifts given by the Spirit in the earliest Pauline communities.[108]

It is, however, only in Paul's later letters that we find specifics about leadership positions in the churches. In his letter to the Philippians, Paul adds to his usual address of "God's holy people" (*hagiois*) a reference to "the overseers and deacons [*episkopois kai diakonois*]." The mention of these specific leaders may reflect a development in the churches (Philippians, I have argued, was probably written in AD 61 or so—see pp. 296–97). However, it could also be due simply to the specific occasion of this letter. The leaders may have had a significant role in collecting and sending money to Paul (see Phil 4:10–20). In any case, no more is heard of these leaders in the rest of the letter, so we do not learn much about these leadership roles from this letter.

Paul's first letter to Timothy and his letter to Titus give us quite a bit more information about these roles. The occasion of the letters may again have something to do with this. It would be natural for letters written to ministry associates to focus more than usual on issues of church leadership and organization. Perhaps the more significant impetus for this focus, however, is Paul's realization that his time of ministry is drawing to a close. Paul's second letter to Timothy, of course, indicates that he believes his death is imminent (4:6–8), and this recognition of the relatively short time Paul has left for ministry pervades the other Pastoral Epistles as well, though perhaps not as intensely. Paul, in other words, must provide guidance for the church and his ministry associates for the time when he, and the other apostles—the "foundation" of the church (Eph 2:20)—are no longer around. Who will lead the new-realm people of God in these postapostolic circumstances? How will "the truth of the gospel" be maintained in the

---

108. Richard Last has suggested that parallels with other Greco-Roman associations, along with some hints in the letter itself, suggest that the Corinthian church may well have had "officers" in leadership roles (*The Pauline Church and the Corinthian Ekklēsia: Greco-Roman Associations in Comparative Context*, SNTSMS 164 [Cambridge: Cambridge University Press, 2016], 183–212); see also Thiselton, *Hermeneutics of Doctrine*, 496–99.

face of false teaching in those days? Church leaders with these kinds of responsibilities, as we have seen, were probably in place since churches were first established. But the circumstances of the Pastoral Epistles require that Paul devote more concentrated attention to this leadership question. "After the key issues of the nature of the gospel had received clarification . . . the next step was to insure the *maintenance* of these hard-won traditions. This stage is in no way an *alternative* to mission; it is part of the conditions for preserving the vision in order to continue mission."[109]

In addition to his extensive advice to Timothy and Titus for their own ministries, and his recognition of the ministries of God's people in general, Paul isolates three particular ministry positions by name: elders, overseers, and deacons. "Elder" in Greek (*presbyteros*), as in English, denotes, generally, an "older man" (see, e.g., 1 Tim 5:1), and it is possible that the use of the word as a title morphed from the natural associations of age and authority in the ancient world. "Elders" are mentioned many times in the Old Testament, usually in leadership or judicial roles. See, e.g., Deuteronomy 31:9: "So Moses wrote down this law and gave it to the Levitical priests, who carried the ark of the covenant of the LORD, and to all the elders [Heb. *zaqen*; Gk. *presbyteros*] of Israel." In the New Testament, *presbyteros* is overwhelmingly used to refer to some kind of leadership position (almost sixty times). The Gospels and Acts refer often to the "elders of the Jews" (e.g., Luke 7:3) or "the elders of the people" (e.g., Matt 21:23), or simply the "elders."[110] The leadership role of the elders is indicated by the way they are mentioned along with other leaders ("the elders, the chief priests and the teachers of the law," Matt 16:21) and by the roles attributed to them (e.g., the elders joined the high priest in bringing charges against Paul [Acts 24:1]). The use of "elders" in this way in the Jewish world was adopted by the early church in Jerusalem, where they are often paired with "apostles" (Acts 15:2, 4, 6, 22, 23; 16:4; cf. 11:30; 21:18). "Elders" then appear in other churches, perhaps as an extension from the "mother" church (Paul and Barnabas appoint elders in the churches founded on the first missionary journey [Acts 14:23], and Paul meets with the "elders" of the Ephesian church [20:17]; see also 1 Pet 5:1–4; Jas 5:14).

The position of "elder" is mentioned in two texts in the Pastoral Epistles, 1 Timothy 5:17, 19 and Titus 1:5. In the latter text, Titus is instructed to appoint elders "in every town," that is, in churches located in the various towns on Crete. The parallel with Acts 14:23 is clear. In 1 Timothy 5, Paul encourages recognition of the elders "who direct the affairs of the church," "especially those whose work is preaching and teaching" (v. 17), and discourages accusations against them unless supported by "two or three witnesses"

---

109. Thiselton, *Hermeneutics of Doctrine*, 508.

110. The Gospels also use "elders" to denote earlier generations of Jews (e.g., Matt 15:2), and Revelation refers to a mysterious group of twenty-four elders (e.g., Rev 4:4). The author of 2 and 3 John also calls himself an "elder" (2 John 1; 3 John 1).

(v. 19). We can add to the profile of the "elder" by looking also at the description of the "overseers." The close relationship of these positions is indicated by their juxtaposition in two texts. In Titus 1, Paul speaks of appointing "elders" (v. 5) but then, apparently unconsciously, shifts to "overseer" in verse 7. Something similar happens in Acts 20. Paul refers to the "elders of the church" at Ephesus (v. 17) as "overseers" (v. 28; and note they are also called "shepherds"). To be sure, some scholars think that these words denote separate ministry positions, or that perhaps the "overseer" is an elder who leads the elders.[111] But it is simpler to view them as referring in different ways to the same position.[112] This has the advantage of bringing Philippians 1:1 into conformity with the Pastorals, with both mentioning two leadership positions: elders/overseers and deacons. Paul, as we have seen, mentions "the overseer" in Titus 1:7 and sets out qualifications for those who aspire to "the office of overseer" (ESV; Gk. *episkopē*) in 1 Timothy 3:1–7. If "elder" is a title taken from the Jewish world, "overseer"[113] may reflect the Greco-Roman world.[114] However, the conceptual background of the term may be traced to the Qumran community's use of *mebaqqer* to denote a leader of the community.[115] This individual had responsibility for smaller entities within the community, admitting new members, instructing them, and caring (financially and otherwise) for needy members. The *mebaqqer* thus had both religious and administrative functions, and this combination seems also to characterize, at least to some extent, Paul's "elder/overseer."[116]

Paul's few references to the "elder/overseer" do not enable us to build a completely clear profile of this position. However, as we have seen, 1 Timothy 5:17 refers to elders who "direct the affairs" of the church; the Greek verb Paul uses here (*proistēmi*) is the same one he uses in 1 Thessalonians 5:12 to refer to those who lead the believers (see above). The leadership responsibility of the overseer/elder is suggested also in the analogy with the household that Paul uses in referring to the qualifications of the overseer: "He must manage [*proistēmi* again] his own family well and see that his children obey him, and he must do so in a manner worthy of full respect. (If anyone does not know how to manage his own family, how can he take care of [*epimeleomai*] God's church?)" (1 Tim 3:4–5). First Timothy 5:17 also indicates that at least some of the elders/overseers teach the church. When we combine these references with the associations in other texts between elders and "shepherds" (Acts 20:28; 1 Pet 5:1–4), we have some secure basis for identifying the elders/overseers as the spiritual leaders of the church.

---

111. E.g., Clarke, *Pauline Theology of Church Leadership*, 47–60; Towner, *Timothy and Titus*, 246–47.

112. Benjamin L. Merkle, *The Elder and the Overseer: One Office in the Early Church*, SBL 57 (New York: Peter Lang, 2003).

113. The cognate verb *episkopeō* is used to describe the responsibility of "shepherds" of the church in 1 Pet 5:2. The word *episkopos* occurs also in 1 Pet 2:25 as a reference to Christ, "the Shepherd and Overseer of your souls."

114. See, e.g., Marshall and Towner, *Pastoral Epistles*, 174–75.

115. See, e.g., 1QS 6.12, 20; CD 9.16–23; 13.7–19; 14.8–12.

116. See esp. B. E. Theiring, "*Mebaqqer* and *Episkopos* in the Light of the Temple Scroll," *JBL* 100 (1981): 59–74.

If the profile of the elder/overseer is not entirely clear, that of the "deacon" is even murkier. "Deacon" is the English word we use to refer to a particular position of ministry in the church. However, the Greek word behind it is simply the generic *diakonos*, which is widely used in the New Testament to denote a "minister" or "servant" of God and of the church. Scholars disagree over which texts use *diakonos* in a more technical sense. This sense is clear in Philippians 1:1 and 1 Timothy 3:8, 12; and it likely has this sense also in Romans 16:1, where Phoebe is designated a "*diakonos* of the church in Cenchreae."[117] It is common to appeal to Acts 6 to fill out the picture of the New Testament "deacon," but it is not at all clear that this passage is referring to an established position in the church. It is also common to appeal to the usage of *diakonos* in the Greco-Roman world to denote people who wait on tables, but the association of the word with this rather menial form of service has been challenged.[118] With little New Testament evidence to go by except what can be inferred from the qualifications of deacons set out in 1 Timothy 3:8–12, we must be cautious about drawing conclusions. Most scholars suspect, partly on the basis of later evidence, that "deacons" were particularly responsible for financial and logistical aspects of the church, especially the distribution of welfare for needy believers.

The implications of these ministry positions for the overall shape of church organization in the New Testament is debated. Some scholars, whether attributing the Pastoral Epistles to Paul or not, privilege what is claimed to be the "freedom and social radicalism" of the early Pauline letters, looking askance at any notion of "leaders" in the traditional sense.[119] Others read the Pastoral Epistles as providing clear and required structures of leadership. Clearly what is needed is a balance that combines the mutuality inherent in the gifts the Spirit distributes to all the community with recognized structures of leadership. When the entire sweep of Paul's letters are considered, we can identify a harmonious integration of gifts, ministry, and "office." God, Christ, and the Spirit give gifts. As people discover and use those gifts, they naturally gravitate to certain kinds of ministries. As people engage in these ministries over time, churches (or church leaders) take official notice of the ministries by appointing these people to suitable "offices." The teaching of Paul on this matter across his thirteen letters displays differences in emphasis and development, yet these developments do not entail contradiction. It is also vital to stress that any "authority" exercised by human leaders is an indirect and derived authority. The gospel (and the Scripture that attests to it) is the

---

117. See Moo, *Romans* (NICNT), 929–30.

118. See esp. Collins, *Diakonia*. See also the collection of essays in Bart J. Koet, Edwina Murphy, and Esko Ryökäs, eds., *Deacons and Diakonia in Early Christianity: The First Two Centuries*, WUNT 2/479 (Tübingen: Mohr Siebeck, 2018).

119. Mark Strom, *Reframing Paul: Conversations in Grace and Community* (Downers Grove, IL: InterVarsity Press, 2000), 178–81 (phrase quoted from p. 181). See also Robert Banks, *Paul's Idea of Community: The Early House Churches in Their Cultural Setting*, rev. ed. (Peabody, MA: Hendrickson, 1994), 104–5 (who notes on p. 3 that he will not be integrating the evidence of the Pastoral Epistles in his overview).

ultimate authority, and it is only as leaders faithfully reflect and transmit its teaching that their authority is legitimized.[120]

What pattern of church leadership emerges from the evidence of the Pastoral Epistles? There are three main options. First, we can view Timothy and Titus as having authority over a group of churches, with elders/overseers serving under them in particular churches. Second, we can view Timothy and Titus as "pastors" of individual churches, perhaps to be identified with the "elder," with deacons serving as lay leaders under them. Or, third, we can view Timothy and Titus as "apostolic delegates," having no permanent role in the leadership of the church, with each church being led by a group of elders/overseers and assisted by deacons.[121] This last option fits the data of the Pastoral Epistles best, and also fits well with the picture we find elsewhere: "elders" appointed in each first-missionary-journey church (Acts 14:23), "elders/overseers" shepherding the church in Ephesus (Acts 20:17–28), "overseers and deacons" in the church at Philippi (Phil 1:1), elders "shepherding" the church in 1 Peter 5:1–4. What emerges, then, from the Pauline (and NT) evidence is a rather consistent picture of church leadership.[122] However, it is important to point out that this leadership structure is nowhere mandated but is simply assumed. That being the case, it might be that the New Testament gives freedom to believers in different times and places to "organize" their communities in ways that best fit their particular circumstances.

A final point about leadership in the Pauline communities needs to be mentioned: Are these leadership positions open to men and women alike? I touch here, of course, on one of the more incendiary issues in the modern church, and this is not the place to evaluate or even list the bewildering array of exegetical, hermeneutical, and theological aspects of the debate. I will look more generally at the broader issue of gender in Paul in the next chapter (pp. 633–35). The issue is not, it must emphatically be said, whether women engaged in significant ministry. Paul names many such women, including some who "worked alongside" Paul, including, for example, Priscilla (Rom 16:3) and Junia who, with her husband Andronicus, was "outstanding among the apostles" (v. 7; or "esteemed by the apostles," see NIV footnote; see p. 243n136).[123] Unfortunately, these texts are not clear about the nature of these women's ministries. So these texts cannot settle the issue of leadership (even "apostle" in Rom 16:7 is unclear). It is possible—in my view, probable—that Paul also recognizes women as deacons. Phoebe (Rom 16:1) is probably a deacon, the church recognizing her organizational ability and (probably) her use of her wealth to support the church. I also think it is slightly more likely that the

---

120. See esp. John Howard Schütz, *Paul and the Anatomy of Apostolic Authority*, SNTSMS 26 (Cambridge: Cambridge University Press, 1975).

121. See, e.g., Köstenberger, *Commentary on 1–2 Timothy and Titus*, 8–11, 376–82.

122. Knight, *Pastoral Epistles*, 175–77.

123. Others named as "co-workers" are Euodia and Syntyche (Phil 4:2–3), and women who served in ministry are Tryphena and Tryphosa, and Persis (Rom 16:12).

"women" mentioned in 1 Timothy 3:11 are deacons rather than the wives of deacons. At the same time, some texts suggest some degree of restriction on the ministries of women in the church. The classic, much-debated text has Paul telling Timothy that a woman is not "to teach or to assume authority over a man" (1 Tim 2:12). I discuss the exegetical issues in this text in my exposition (pp. 325–27). Here I want simply to summarize what seem to me to be the two main hermeneutical/theological attempts to reconcile these two sets of texts (what I might term with popular but somewhat misleading language, the "egalitarian" and "complementarian" perspectives). First, we might privilege those passages that appear to grant unqualified equality to men and women in the new realm (e.g., Gal 3:28) and view the restrictions found in other texts as temporary, culture-bound requirements that are not in force for the church everywhere and at all times.[124] Second, we might view restrictions Paul imposes as theologically grounded limitations on the way equality in Christ is to be expressed. Good exegetical and theological arguments can be mustered for each of these viewpoints, but I slightly prefer the latter.[125]

124. For a series of essays arguing for this general view, see Ronald W. Pierce and Rebecca Merrill Groothuis, eds., *Discovering Biblical Equality: Complementarity without Hierarchy* (Downers Grove, IL: InterVarsity Press, 2004); and see also the essay on 1 Tim 2:11–15 by Linda L. Belleville in this volume ("Teaching and Usurping Authority," 205–23). I have found very useful the overall conceptualization of this issue in William J. Webb, *Slaves, Women, and Homosexuals: Exploring the Hermeneutics of Cultural Analysis* (Downers Grove, IL: InterVarsity Press, 2001).

125. See esp. the series of essays in Köstenberger and Schreiner, *Women in the Church*; and also Craig L. Blomberg, "Neither Hierarchicalist nor Egalitarian: Gender Roles in Paul," in *Paul and His Theology*, ed. Stanley E. Porter, Pauline Studies 3 (Leiden: Brill, 2006), 283–326; Douglas J. Moo, "1 Timothy 2:11–15: Meaning and Significance," *TrinJ* 1 (1980): 62–83; idem, "The Interpretation of 1 Timothy 2:11–15: A Rejoinder," *TrinJ* 2 (1981): 198–222 (I would not now, however, endorse all the positions I take in these articles).

Chapter 24

LIVING IN THE NEW REALM

For the grace of God has appeared that offers salvation to all people. *It teaches us to say "No" to ungodliness and worldly passions, and to live self-controlled, upright and godly lives in this present age*, while we wait for the blessed hope— the appearing of the glory of our great God and Savior, Jesus Christ, who gave himself for us to redeem us from all wickedness and to purify for himself a people that are his very own, *eager to do what is good.*

—TITUS 2:11–14

I N THIS VOLUME I have attempted to show that Paul's letters reveal a coherent body of thought. However, we must remember that Paul is rarely interested in that structure of thought, rooted in and always related to God—and hence we denote this "theo-logy"—for its own sake. His letters, written to churches and individuals who face particular issues and challenges, are ultimately intended to mold behavior. "If the transformation of believers is the ultimate goal of Paul's work, it is also the focal point of his theology."[1] We find so much theology in Paul's letters because he is convinced that he can only mold his readers' behavior if he first molds their thinking—their mindset, their worldview. And this has been my focus for most of the book. But we would miss the whole point of that theology if we did not spend some time looking at the way Paul expects the new-realm people of God to live out that theology. Indeed, Larry Hurtado has made the case that Christianity was somewhat distinct from other "religions" in the early Roman Empire precisely in the degree to which it imposed behavioral demands on its followers.[2]

Of course, it is another question to ask if this concern with ethics, or moral teaching, is rightly included in a study of Paul's *theology*. Some Pauline scholars, indeed, claim

---

1. Thompson, *Moral Formation*, 2.

2. Hurtado, *Destroyer of the Gods*, 133–81. See also, along these lines, N. T. Wright's comments at the beginning of his massive two-volume *magnum opus*: "A worldview such as his [Paul's], granted what it does and doesn't contain, needs theology in a way that (some?) other worldviews do not. It can only be sustained by constantly, thoughtfully and prayerfully clarifying the question of who the one true God actually is, what this God has done and is doing, and what this all means for the lives of the community and the particular Messiah-follower" (*Paul and the Faithfulness of God*, 1:36; see pp. 21–36).

that we cannot distinguish theology and ethics. For example, Richard Hays writes: "There is no meaningful distinction between theology and ethics in Paul's thought, because Paul's theology is fundamentally an account of God's work of transforming his people into the image of Christ."[3] But erasing any distinction in this way goes too far.[4] What people think and how they behave are two different things. To be sure, they overlap and impinge on each other, as the close ties between Paul's theological teaching and his ethical instruction make clear.[5] But a distinction can, and probably should, be made. Schnelle's simple definition of ethics implicitly makes the point: "The theme of ethics is what the new being (the new life in the sphere of Christ) looks like as expressed in what one does and the way one lives."[6]

In this final chapter, then, I survey Paul's basic ethical teaching. A thorough discussion, of course, would need to be both more extensive and more intensive than what follows: extensive, in looking at the many specific issues Paul has to deal with because of the particular circumstances of different readers; and intensive, in going into far more depth on some of the difficult and controversial issues he raises. However, in a book on Paul's theology generally, I hope I will be excused for the necessarily superficial treatment of Paul's ethics that follows.

1 THE NEW-REALM FRAMEWORK

Commenting on the relationship between Jesus's teaching on the kingdom and his ethical teaching, T. W. Manson writes, "The notion that we can wander at will through the teaching of Jesus as through a garden, plucking here and there an ethical flower to weave a chaplet for the adornment of our own philosophy of life, is an idea that is doomed to disappoint, for the nature of plucked flowers is to wither."[7] The point that Manson makes so picturesquely for Jesus's teaching applies with equal weight to Paul's. How we live in the new realm is inextricably tied to the nature of that realm—which, of course, is determined by the theological teaching about that realm. And the key aspects of that theology for this particular issue all cluster around Paul's eschatology.

1.1 Eschatology

"Eschatology," as we have come to understand it from Paul's letters, is not simply the teaching about the end of the world. Rather, it has to do with Paul's foundational conviction that with the coming of Messiah Jesus and the outpouring of God's Spirit, the "last days" have arrived. God's people live in a new realm. However, that new

---

3. Hays, *Moral Vision of the New Testament*, 46.

4. So, rightly, Witherington, *Indelible Image*, 1:243.

5. See on this Engberg-Pedersen's conclusion in his book on *Paul and the Stoics*, 295.

6. Schnelle, *Theology of the New Testament*, 321.

7. T. W. Manson, *The Teaching of Jesus: Studies in Its Form and Content* (repr., Cambridge: Cambridge University Press, 1967), 286.

realm has not arrived in its final form, and a climactic inbreaking of that new realm is expected. This "already"/"not yet" salvation-historical perspective undergirds all Paul's theology, but nowhere does it have a greater impact than on his pastoral exhortations. As many others have done, we may compare the stages of salvation history to the acts of a play. Believers come on the stage to play their part in salvation history in a particular act of that play. "Paul sees the community of faith being caught up into the story of God's remaking of the world through Jesus Christ. Thus, to make ethical discernments is, for Paul, simply to recognize our place within the epic story of redemption."[8] Several acts of the drama have already been played out: Act I, creation, Act II, the fall, Act III, Israel, and Act IV, Jesus's first coming. Act VI, the consummation, is yet to come. God's new-realm people, the church, have entered the drama in Act V, inaugurated by the Spirit's descent at Pentecost and to be climaxed by Jesus's descent at his parousia. In order to play our roles well, we must understand both what God has already done and what God is yet committed to do. Summarizing his general exhortations to God's people in Romans, Paul says they are to "do this [all that he has said in 12:1–13:10], understanding the present time" (Rom 13:11). Specifically, believers are to recognize that, on the one hand, they are people living in "the day" (v. 13 NRSV), but that, on the other hand, they are waiting for a "day" that is "almost here" (v. 12). The "day of the Lord," the time of God's decisive intervention to save his people, has dawned. God has sent his Son to die and to be raised to cure the human sin problem, a problem introduced in Act II and which Israel, in Act III, did not solve. Yet that "day" has not yet come in its full and final splendor. Sin has been atoned for, but not removed; sickness and suffering continue to dog God's people; Satan, the demons, and all their manifestations of evil have not yet been finally judged and destroyed. In Act V, then, believers look back in joy and thankfulness for God's mighty acts of redemption in the past and look ahead to the culmination of his plan in the future.[9]

If, then, believers "understand the present time," they will boldly seek to implement the will of God in their lives, recognizing all the things God has already done to enable the obedience he calls for. But they will recognize also that their obedience in this life will never be perfect, that they will have to constantly seek forgiveness for failures, looking all the time with eager expectation for the work of God for them and for the world to be finished. Many of the specific pastoral problems Paul addresses can be plausibly traced back, at least to some extent, to believers' failure to rightly understand the present time. While it is not the whole story in Galatians (as we have seen), the debate between Paul and the agitators involves different answers to the question, "What time is it?" The agitators have not understood that a new day in salvation history has dawned;

---

8. Hays, *Moral Vision*, 45–46.

9. For an overview of the significance of this eschatological framework for gospel living, see Benjamin L. Gladd and Matthew

S. Harmon, *Making All Things New: Inaugurated Eschatology for the Life of the Church* (Grand Rapids: Baker, 2016).

or, at least they have not sufficiently appreciated what that new day means. They are therefore insisting on "business as usual," wanting to force gentile converts to come under the reign of Torah. For Paul, however, the time of fulfillment has arrived, a time when the purpose of Torah has been realized in the preservation of a people and when it is no longer to play a decisive role in governing the people of God. The opposite problem seems to be at least one of the factors giving rise to the bevy of problems in Corinth, as seen in Paul's first letter to them. As I have noted, the Corinthians seem to have been guilty of an "overrealized eschatology." "Realized" eschatology is, of course, an entirely appropriate viewpoint for God's people in Act V of his salvation-historical drama. "Now is the time of God's favor, now is the day of salvation" (2 Cor 6:2). However, when realized eschatology becomes the focus at the expense of "future eschatology," an imbalance in appreciating both the time in general and the believer's position in particular sets in. The tendency will be to focus so intently on one's existing spiritual state that its necessary incompleteness is overlooked, leading to an arrogance about one's own state of spirituality. "Already . . . we are reigning," the Corinthians seem to be claiming (1 Cor 4:8), and if that is the case, the body, so much a part of the old reality of this world, really does not matter so much anymore. What one does with it—whether engaging in sex with prostitutes (6:12–20), or withholding sex from one's spouse (7:1–16), or thinking it had already been transformed (cf. ch. 15; and note also 2 Tim 2:18)—really does not matter anymore. These two letters may stand as illustrations of a general principle: a right understanding of eschatology is vital to right gospel living.

1.1.1 The Impact of the "Already" on New-Realm Living

According to an old saying whose source I cannot identify, many Christians believe in "justification by faith" and "sanctification by struggle." Getting into relationship with Christ is possible only by the power God's grace, enabling sinners to believe and so appropriate the benefits of Christ. Once "in," however, living out that relationship often is thought to be a matter of one's own responsibility and initiative. Of course, there is an element of truth here. Paul's letters are full of commands in which he charges believers to think and act in certain ways. He clearly views Christians as responsible moral agents. But he is equally clear in grounding the believer's response in God's own enabling power. This dynamic is evident in many texts. Note, for example:

> Therefore, brothers and sisters, we have an obligation—but it is not to the flesh, to live according to it. For if you live according to the flesh, you will die; but if by the Spirit you put to death the misdeeds of the body, you will live. (Rom 8:12–13)

> Therefore, my dear friends, as you have always obeyed—not only in my presence, but now much more in my absence—work toward your salvation with fear and

trembling, for it is God who works in you to will and to act in order to fulfill his good purpose. (Phil 2:12–13; my translation [see pp. 309–10])

If in these texts Paul puts believers on the spot by requiring them to produce works that will lead to their final salvation, he at the same time makes quite clear that these works are ultimately only possible because of God's own working in them. It is "by the Spirit" that "you put to death the misdeeds of the body"; we are to "work toward salvation" at the same time as—and, importantly, *because*—"it is God who works in you to will and to act in order to fulfill his good purpose."

To put it in the terms frequently used in this discussion, then, for Paul the "indicative" precedes and grounds the "imperative." What God now commands his people to do—imperatives, the "thou shalts"—is based on and empowered by what God has already done for his people—captured in the indicative mood, the "he has done."[10] This pattern is exhibited very clearly in one of Paul's classic texts on the believer's new life, Romans 6:1–14. Here Paul responds to the claim that his celebration of the power of God's grace (5:20) might lead believers to think they could "live in sin." Quite the contrary, Paul responds. In being joined to Christ, believers are set free not only from the penalty of sin, condemnation (see Rom 5:12–21), but from sin's power as well. They have "died to sin" (Rom 6:2). Paul unpacks just what "dying to sin" means in the rest of the chapter, again and again using the imagery of slavery to make his point. Believers, as he puts it in verse 6, are "no longer . . . slaves to sin." This is what God has done for us—put us in a wholly new relationship to sin. It is, then, on the basis of this "indicative"—what God has done—that Paul can issue his imperatives: "Count yourselves dead to sin" (v. 11); "do not let sin reign" (v. 12).

We should note also that this release from sin's power takes place through our union with Christ. "With" Christ is a key motif in Romans 6:3–8, coming to its climax in verse 6. I quoted the last part of that verse above, but its first part expresses the source of that freedom from sin: "Our old self was crucified with him." There has been considerable misunderstanding of Paul's "old self" or "old man" (Gk. *palaios anthrōpos*), which, with its counterpart "the new man," occurs also in Ephesians 4:22–24 and Colossians 3:9–11 (cf. also Eph 2:15 and 4:13). Many popular discussions of Paul's doctrine of the Christian life argue, or assume, that Paul distinguishes with these phrases between two parts or "natures" of a person. With this interpretation as the premise, it is then debated whether the "old nature" is replaced with the "new nature" at conversion, or whether the "new nature" is added to the "old nature." But, as I argue above (p. 452), the assumption that "old man" and "new man" refer to parts, or natures, of a person is

10. Bultmann's statement of this view is classic and influential (*Theology of the New Testament*, 1:332). See also Furnish, *Theology and Ethics in Paul*, esp. 208–26; Dunn, *Theology of Paul*, 628–31.

incorrect, betraying an assumption of individualism not shared by Paul. Rather, they designate the person as a whole, considered in relation to the corporate structure to which he or she belongs. "Old man" and "new man" are not ontological but relational or positional in orientation. They do not, at least in the first place, speak of a change in nature but of a change in relationship. Our "old man" is not our sin "nature" that is judged and dethroned on the cross,[11] to which is added in the believer another "nature," "the new man." Rather, the "old man" is what we were "in Adam." As John R. W. Stott puts it, "What was crucified with Christ was not a part of me called my old nature, but the whole of me as I was before I was converted."[12]

It is only by interpreting "old man" and "new man" in this manner that we are able to integrate two apparently conflicting viewpoints in Paul. On the one hand, this verse and Colossians 3:9–11 make clear that the believer has ceased to be "old man" and has become "new man"; on the other hand, Paul in Ephesians 4:22–24 commands Christians to "put off the old man" and "put on the new man" (my translations). Attempts to reconcile these have often taken the form either of taking the "crucifixion" of the old man to be only a preliminary judgment (see above) or of denying that Paul is giving commands in Ephesians 4:22–24.[13] Neither approach is exegetically sound.[14] If, however, these phrases look at the person as one who belongs to the old age or the new, respectively, then this conflict is resolved. Paul makes clear that the believer has been transferred from the old age of sin and death to the new age of righteousness and life (Rom 6:6 and Col 3:9–11), just as he indicates that the "powers" of that old age continue to influence the believer and must be continually resisted—hence the imperatives of Ephesians 4:22–24. At the heart of the contrast between "old man" and "new man" is the eschatological tension between the inauguration of the new age in the life of the believer—he or she belongs to the "new creation" (2 Cor 5:17)—and the culmination of that new age in glorification with Christ (Rom 8:17). What we *were* "in Adam" is no more; but, until heaven, the temptation to *live* in Adam always remains. Hence, Paul exhorts believers to "put off" the old man and "put on" the new (Eph 4:22–24); or, as he puts it in Romans 13:14, to "clothe yourselves with the Lord Jesus Christ." As is the case with every dimension of Paul's theology, living in the new realm means working out our "in Christ" identity.

To be sure, some scholars question whether this "indicative-imperative" scheme adequately captures Paul's ethical structure. And, of course, it is always going to be the

---

11. E.g., Ames, *Marrow of Theology*, 171: "The corrupted part which remains in the sanctified."

12. John R. W. Stott, *Men Made New: An Exposition of Romans 5–8* (London: Inter-Varsity Press, 1966), 45.

13. Cf., e.g., Murray, *Principles of Conduct*, 214–18.

14. Murray (see the previous note) and others take the infinitives *apothesthai* ("put off") and *endysasthai* ("put on") in Eph 4:22–24 as equivalent to indicatives. But their dependence on the verb *edidachthēte*, "were taught" (v. 21), makes an imperatival rendering more likely (cf., e.g., Bruce, *Colossians, Philemon and Ephesians*, 358–59n).

case that a single slogan will miss nuances. In this case, I think it is helpful to push the "indicative" side a bit to include "ethos." That is, the indicative of God's acts on our behalf includes the creation of a new set of relationships in which the believer lives, relationships both vertical—with Christ and the Spirit—and horizontal—with fellow believers. Believers respond to God's summons to a new life from the context of that new set of relationships. As Horrell puts it, "The apparently paradoxical nature of the Pauline indicative-imperative formulations can, then, be resolved when the indicatives in question are seen not as statements which can be held to be either 'true' or not but as identity-descriptors and group norms which need to be constantly affirmed."[15] If we are to use the "indicative-imperative" rubric to describe Paul's ethics, then, we must not confine the indicative to the past. God continues to work in the present, working by his Spirit within believers and within the community of faith. See, for example, the present tense of "God who works in you" in the Philippian quotation above (2:13). The customary summary of Paul's ethical framework is "become what you are"; but we should probably add to it "and what you are being made into."

God's grace, then, is active not only in securing initial salvation but is also the source of new-realm living. God's grace "teaches us to say 'No' to ungodliness and worldly passions, and to live self-controlled, upright and godly lives in this present age" (Titus 2:12). This teaching does not simply instruct us about what to do but also enables us to do what we need to do. As Paul pivots in Romans from his focus on entering the new realm (3:21–4:25) to living in the new realm (chs. 5–8), he claims that "having been justified [by grace]," believers now "stand" in this same grace (5:2). God has transferred his people into the realm of grace (see "under grace" in 6:14, 15), and they live under its reign (5:21). Paul testifies to the power of this grace in his own ministry. "By the grace God has given me, I laid a foundation as a wise builder, and someone else is building on it" (1 Cor 3:10). Expressing, as clearly as he does anywhere, the dynamic interplay of human effort and God's grace, Paul says, "But by the grace of God I am what I am, and his grace to me was not without effect. No, I worked harder than all of them—yet not I, but the grace of God that was with me" (15:10). And, of course, Paul often labels his ministry simply as "the grace God gave me" (e.g., Rom 15:15).

Empowering grace for living in the new realm is concentrated especially on the distinctive new-realm gift of God's Spirit. Paul uses the word *pneuma* 146 times, referring to spiritual beings, the human spirit, and God's Spirit. Some of his uses of *pneuma* are debated in terms of what it refers to, but Paul probably uses the word to refer to the Holy Spirit around 110 times. As we have seen, a new and unprecedented

---

15. Horrell, *Solidarity and Difference*, 103. See also, for similar emphases, Thompson, *Moral Formation*, 4–5, 44; Barclay, *Paul and the Gift*, 506–8; Allen, *Sanctification*, 246–55. Another who questions the usefulness of the "indicative-imperative" scheme is, e.g., Schnelle, *Apostle Paul*, 547–48.

effusion of the Spirit on the people of God is promised in the prophets (Isa 44:3; Ezek 11:9; 36:26–27; 37:14; Joel 2:28–29 [Acts 2:16–21]). These prophecies bear a strong resemblance to Jeremiah's new-covenant prophecy (Jer 31:31–34). Paul does not quote any of these texts, but he alludes to several of them. The prediction in Joel 2:28 that God would "pour out my Spirit on all people" influences Romans 5:5: "God's love has been poured out into our hearts through the Holy Spirit, who has been given to us." The combination of Spirit and blessing that we find in Isaiah 44:3—"I will pour out my Spirit on your offspring, and my blessing on your descendants"—is picked up by Paul in Galatians 3:14: "He redeemed us in order that the blessing given to Abraham might come to the Gentiles through Christ Jesus, so that by faith we might receive the promise of the Spirit." Ezekiel 37:14—"I will put my Spirit in you and you will live"—lies behind passages such as Romans 8:10–11: "But if Christ is in you, then even though your body is subject to death because of sin, the Spirit gives life because of righteousness. And if the Spirit of him who raised Jesus from the dead is living in you, he who raised Christ from the dead will also give life to your mortal bodies because of his Spirit who lives in you" (see also 2 Cor 3:6). In light of the central role this expectation has in Paul's letters, one scholar has appropriately entitled his book on Paul's ethics, *New Covenant Morality in Paul*.[16] Central to the new covenant that God promises to "cut" with his people in the last days is his own provision for the peoples' obedience—an obedience that was singularly lacking in the history of Israel under the Torah. A Spirit-fueled conformity to God's will is therefore a central and distinguishing characteristic of new-realm living.

In an earlier section of the book, I noted that God's gift of the Spirit is a key blessing of the new realm, acting, indeed, as a signal indicator that this new realm has arrived. Paul often attributes to the Spirit the standing in the new realm that believers enjoy. Less often—indeed, less often than one would expect—he cites the Spirit as the means for enabling believers to live lives pleasing to God in that new realm (perhaps only ten or so verses). Nevertheless, the point is clear enough. The letter to the Galatians reveals this connection better than any other. After reminding the Galatians that they received the Spirit, the mark of new-covenant belonging, by their faith (3:2, 5), he calls on them to "walk by the Spirit" (5:16) and "keep in step with the Spirit" (v. 25) so that the "fruit of the Spirit" might be manifested among them (v. 22). However, we look in vain for concentrated teaching in Paul about the Spirit. N. T. Wright has aptly compared the Spirit in Paul to the way in which worldview functions for most people: "It isn't what you look *at*, it's what you look *through*." He goes on to say that "the Spirit was not, for Paul and his contemporaries, a 'doctrine' or 'dogma' to be discussed, but the breath of life which put them in a position to discuss everything else—and, more

---

16. Deidun, *New Covenant Morality in Paul*.

to the point, to worship, pray, love and work. We should not, then, be surprised at the relative absence of discourse, including monotheistic discourse, *about* the Spirit."[17] The Spirit, then, is located at the center of Paul's theological web, joining the believer's past and their future, justification and sanctification, individual and community.[18] As James Dunn puts it, "'By faith alone' could be matched by the equivalent phrase 'by the Spirit alone' as the heart of Paul's gospel."[19] To add textual substantiation to this point, see, for example, Galatians 5:5: "For *through the Spirit* we eagerly await *by faith* the righteousness for which we hope."

Paul is not very clear in helping us understand just *how* the Spirit transforms believers. Volker Rabens has explored this issue, taking as his foil a view he calls "substance-ontological," according to which the Spirit is viewed as a semi-material or physical entity implanted in believers (often connected with the sacraments). In contrast, Rabens persuasively argues that transformation occurs as the Spirit brings believers into an intimate relationship with God and with the community.[20] He singles out 2 Corinthians 3:18 as a key text: "And we all, who with unveiled faces contemplate the Lord's glory, are being transformed into his image with ever-increasing glory, which comes from the Lord, who is the Spirit." Putting aside for now the debated identity of the "Lord" in the last part of the verse, this text links transformation with the Spirit. A key point for Rabens, which I endorse, is that for Paul the work of the Spirit is not a mystical process separated from other "means of grace." Rather, the Spirit works in the context of the believer's ever-deeper engagement with Scripture and ever-deeper relationship with God and Christ to transform believers.

1.1.2 The Impact of the "Not Yet" on New-Realm Living

As Romans 8:12–13 and Philippians 2:12–13, quoted above, indicate, believers are called on to produce good works with a view toward their final salvation. Only if believers "put to death the misdeeds of the body" will they "live"—experience ultimate salvation.[21] Believers must "work" toward their final salvation. In an earlier part of the book, I listed a series of Pauline texts that, in my view, teach that believers' works will be scrutinized in the judgment and that this judgment has to do with eternal life and eternal destruction. But I also stressed—and I stress again here—that we cannot allow these warnings about judgment to erase or detract from the confidence in the judgment

17. Wright, *Paul and the Faithfulness of God*, 1:710.
18. Schnelle, *Apostle Paul*, 487–90.
19. James D. G. Dunn, "The Christian Life from the Perspective of Paul's Letter to the Galatians," in McKnight and Modica, *Apostle Paul and the Christian Life*, 11.
20. Volker Rabens, *Holy Spirit and Ethics in Paul*. See also, idem, "Ethics and the Spirit in Paul (1): Religious-Ethical Empowerment through Infusion-Transformation?," *ExpTim* 125 (2014):

209–19; idem, "Ethics and the Spirit in Paul (2): Religious-Ethical Empowerment through Infusion-Transformation?," *ExpTim* 125 (2014): 272–81.
21. The promise of "life" in Rom 8:13 clearly refers to spiritual life, as the logic of the argument (the "life" must be something that one can only achieve by putting evil deeds away) and the context (vv. 2, 6, 10, 11) make clear. See p. 227.

that believers have because they have been justified by faith alone. When we ask, then, about the significance of the "not yet" for Paul's ethical teaching, a dual focus emerges. On the one hand, Paul urges believers to respond faithfully to God's grace in light of the serious scrutiny that they will face when Christ returns. Romans 8:12–13, to mention this text once again, makes this clear. On the other hand, Paul repeatedly encourages believers to look with joy and anticipation to the day when their work on earth will be over and the judgment rendered over them in justification is ratified. In Philippians 1, for example, Paul remembers the Philippian believers with thanks because he is "confident of this, that he who began a good work in you will carry it on to completion until the day of Christ Jesus" (Phil 1:6). Looking at these two foci at the same time means that it is difficult to bring into sharp focus Paul's view of believers in the judgment. Part of our problem arises from our failure to appreciate Paul's rhetorical aims—that is, what he is trying to "do" with his words in these texts. But another part of the problem is the difficulty of integrating these two perspectives into a neat, logically coherent view. Nevertheless, I think a fair exegesis of the relevant texts leads to this "double vision." Perhaps we could summarize by suggesting that Paul encourages believers to take up an attitude toward the "not yet" of their salvation that we could characterize as "an assurance accompanied by humility and a call to appropriate that assurance."

1.2 Renewing the Mind: Direction for New-Realm Living

Romans 12:1–2 is a classic expression of what it means to live in the new realm:

> Therefore, I urge you, brothers and sisters, in view of God's mercy, to offer your bodies as a living sacrifice, holy and pleasing to God—this is your true and proper worship. Do not conform to the pattern of this world, but be transformed by the renewing of your mind. Then you will be able to test and approve what God's will is—his good, pleasing and perfect will.

"World" in verse 2 translates Greek *aiōn*, which could also be translated "age" or "era." There is here, then, an implicit contrast between the life of the "old age" and that of the "new age." In this new age, or world that has now dawned, Paul claims that discerning God's will comes by means of the "renewing of your mind."[22] This language brings to clear expression a fundamental principle in Paul's ethics. In the new realm, God's people discern the right way to live through the transforming work of God's Spirit as he replaces the mindset of this world with the mindset of the

---

22. Gk. *tē anakainōsei tou noos*. The dative case here indicates the means by which a believer is "transformed." See 2 Cor 4:16, Col 3:10, and Titus 3:5 for similar uses of "renewal." This "renewal" here picks up language of "newness" (*kainotēs*) that Paul has used earlier in Romans: "newness of life" (6:4 NRSV) and "newness produced by the Spirit" (7:6, my translation). See also Eph 4:23: "Be renewed [*ananeousthai*] in [or by] the spirit of your minds [*noos*]" (NRSV).

new world.[23] See, in this regard, Romans 8:4–9, where the "mind" (*phronēma*) of the Spirit is the link between "being" in the Spirit and "walking" according to the Spirit. Paul elsewhere uses words from this same *phron-* root to make the same point (*phroneō*, "think," in Romans 12:3 [twice]; 15:5; 2 Cor 13:11; Gal 5:10; Phil 2:2 [twice], 5; 3:15 [twice], 19; 4:2; Col 3:2; *phronēsis* in Eph 1:8). This principle of internal transformation is another key aspect of the new covenant, as it is spelled out in the prophets. The old covenant revealed the depths of human sinfulness, manifested in the people's inability to accomplish God's will. And so God promises that he will "put a new S/spirit" in his people, replacing the "heart of stone" with a "heart of flesh," with the result that they would "follow my decrees and . . . keep my laws" (Ezek 36:26–27). It is this conformity to God's will that Spirit-fueled renewal of the mind produces—a renewing process that takes shape in, and is itself stimulated by, involvement in the life of the new-realm community.

As Romans 12:1–2 suggests, a transformed mind not only provides the power to "walk in the Spirit" but also directs the believer in the path he or she should walk in. How one should live faithfully in the new realm is dictated by the values of that realm as they are absorbed by those who have been transferred into it. This reorientation of values, as we have seen, is very much tied to the work of the Spirit in the hearts of believers. But it is also strongly influenced by the believer's participation in the new community. The "message of Christ" will dwell "among" the people of God as they "teach and admonish one another with all wisdom through psalms, hymns, and songs from the Spirit" (Col 3:16). As David Horrell has emphasized, Paul's letters are "community-forming," as they seek to create a "symbolic universe" that shapes thinking and practice: "We should view the Pauline material as a development of a body of tradition, based on a specific narrative myth, which gave meaning and order to the lives of those who 'inhabited' it. This mythology is enacted in ritual performance and shapes the lives of its adherents."[24]

Granted this approach to the transformation of people in the new realm, it is no surprise that Paul's specific injunctions to his churches often take the form of "exhortations." This English word is the traditional rendering of the Greek word *parakaleō*. This word has a wide semantic range, often meaning "encourage" or "comfort," but Paul uses it twenty-eight times to introduce his advice to the churches or to his ministry associates. Contemporary English versions often render it as "urge" or "appeal" (it is the Gk. word behind "urge" in Rom 12:1, quoted above). As in Romans 12:1, this word sometimes functions to make a transition into parts of Paul's letters that focus on advice to the community.[25] This word also is the basis for the designation of Paul's ethical

23. "Mind" translates *nous*, "way of thinking" (BDAG).

24. Horrell, *Solidarity and Difference*, 91–100 (quotation from p. 100).

25. See Carl J. Bjerkelund, *Parakalô. Form, Funktion und Sinn der Parakalô-Sätze in den Paulinischen Briefen*, Bibliotheca Theologica Norvegica (Oslo: Universitetsforlaget, 1967), for a form-critical study of this word in its contexts. See also Furnish, *Theology and Ethics in Paul*, 92–98.

teaching as taking the form of *paraklēsis*.[26] This language suggests that Paul is interested not so much in imposing commands on his churches but in encouraging believers to allow their renewed minds, guided and empowered by the Spirit, to direct their lives into channels that align with the will of God. Indeed, Paul occasionally expresses a somewhat surprising openness to give scope to his readers to make their own moral choices. See, for example, Philippians 3:15–16: "All of us, then, who are mature should take such a view of things. And if on some point you think differently, that too God will make clear to you. Only let us live up to what we have already attained."

However, this *paraklēsis* focus does not tell the whole story. Paul is quite comfortable issuing "commands" to his churches and advising his ministry associates to do the same. He introduces moral advice to believers with the verb "command," *parangellō*, six times (1 Cor 11:17; 1 Thess 4:11; 2 Thess 3:4, 6, 10, 12) and encourages Timothy to do the same (1 Tim 1:3; 4:11; 5:7; 6:17). On the other side of the relationship, Paul commends and calls for Christians to be "obedient" (using *hypakoē/hypakouō*: Rom 1:5; 6:16, 17; 10:16; 15:18; 16:19, 26; 2 Cor 7:15; 10:5, 6; Phil 2:12; 2 Thess 1:8; 3:14; Phlm 21 [Philemon]; using *peithō*: Gal 5:7). Moreover, without entirely dismissing the point about *paraklēsis* we made above, even Paul's "appeals" are apostolic appeals, with some of the authority of his unique office clinging to them. Reinforcing this sense of authority in his appeals, Paul will cite Christ or the Spirit as the agents, or means, of his appeal. See 2 Corinthians 5:20: "We are therefore Christ's ambassadors, as though God were making his appeal through us" (and also Rom 15:30; 1 Cor 1:10; 2 Cor 10:1; 1 Thess 4:1; 2 Thess 3:12). Paul therefore walks a careful line between the "appeal" mode and the "command" mode. Much of his ethical teaching falls somewhere in the middle.

2 SOURCES OF MORAL GUIDANCE

Paul views Christian conformity to the will of God in all matters of life as arising from, and stimulated by, the believer's new life in Christ. It is the Spirit working within believers and among them to renew minds that characterizes Paul's "new-covenant morality." However, while the minds of believers are, indeed, being renewed, that process is an ongoing one. In Romans 12:2, Paul speaks not of the "renew*ed* mind" but of the "renew*ing* of the mind." This focus on process rather than finished work is suggested in Ephesians 4 also, where renewing the mind is a command issued to believers (v. 23). I return here, then, to a fundamental point I made earlier: Paul is quite aware that Christian transformation will not be complete until the "not yet" of the

---

26. *Paraenesis* is also a word frequently used to denote this ethical teaching, but it comes burdened with too much questionable baggage (e.g., the idea [held in the past, at least] that *paraenesis* consists of scattered exhortations without any coherence). See, e.g., Anton Grabner-Haider, *Paraklese und Eschatologie bei Paulus*, NTAbh (Göttingen: Vandenhoeck & Ruprecht, 1968), 4, passim.

parousia. It is because believers are acting out their roles in this particular stage of the salvation-historical drama that the renewing of their minds requires specific guidance. We badly misunderstand Paul's vision for the Christian moral life if we do not give primary place to the Spirit's work of transformation. Indeed, if we lived in a time when the new realm had completely ousted the old, we would have no need of guidance. Our perfectly renewed minds would infallibly guide us to think, say, and do just what would most please God in every situation. And Paul makes clear that believers should be constantly seeking to remold their very way of thinking so that it is oriented by the Spirit to the things of God. But we are not there yet. Our imperfectly renewed minds therefore require external guidance. Hence the quite specific and clear commands that Paul sprinkles throughout his letters. It is as if he is saying in these texts, "If you think this behavior is what your renewed mind commends, you are wrong."

Paul is clear, then. "Keeping God's commands" (1 Cor 7:19) has a role to play in Christian moral formation. Where, however, are these commands found? One obvious answer is in the teaching of Jesus. As we have seen (pp. 26–27), the degree to which Paul knew and used in his own teaching the words of Jesus is debated. Paul only rarely cites Jesus's teaching to instruct believers in their behavior (1 Cor 7:10; 9:14; 1 Tim 5:18), but there is evidence that the content and occasionally the wording (e.g., Rom 12:14; cf. Matt 5:44; Luke 6:27–28) has influenced Paul's own instructions.[27]

Another source for Paul's commands would seem obvious: the Old Testament law. However, there is considerable debate about the role of the law in Paul's ethical teaching. Specifically, does Paul teach that the commands of the Torah continue to have authority in directing the lives of the new-realm people of God? Answers to this question vary quite significantly. Note, for instance, these two statements:

> The Christian must observe even the minute details of God's law. . . . The NT believers are responsible to keep the older Testament law, for it has abiding validity until the world passes away.[28]

> Christians are free from obligation to the law. . . . The will of God is no longer defined as an obligation to observe the law's statutes.[29]

Historically, the issue has been couched in terms of the "third use of the law." Reformed theologians, especially, identified three functions of God's law: (1) to restrain wickedness; (2) to reveal human guilt; and (3) to guide Christian conduct.

---

27. Paul is also inevitably influenced by various ethical teachings from his Greco-Roman environment (see, e.g., Furnish, *Theology and Ethics in Paul*, 44–50), but Paul, of course, filters all these through the grid of Christ.

28. Greg L. Bahnsen, *Theonomy in Christian Ethics* (Nutley, NJ: Craig Press, 1984), 490.

29. Westerholm, *Israel's Law and the Church's Faith*, 208, 209.

The Reformation tradition itself is quite divided over this third use of the law.[30] Luther, for instance, appears to have dismissed this "use" of the law, while Calvin elevated it to the most important function of the law.[31] Following the lead of Calvin, then, one influential theological stream, covenant theology, distinguishes between the law as a "covenant of works" and the law in its regulatory significance, arguing that believers are freed from the former but are still obliged to the latter.[32] Many Pauline scholars advocate this general approach, claiming that Paul views the "moral" law of the Torah as authoritative for believers (the "moral law" often being summarized by the Decalogue). Others, as we have seen (see pp. 433–35), argue that Paul may exempt gentile Christians from Torah observance but expects Jewish Christians to continue to observe "their" law (though usually not the sacrificial law). At the other end of the spectrum are those who argue that Paul no longer views the Torah as providing direct guidance for believers (see the quote from Westerholm above). Exegesis of several crucial texts is, of course, vital to settle this matter. But the issue is particularly difficult and divisive because it is both influenced by and has a strong influence on larger construals of how the Old Testament and the New Testament relate to each other. In what follows, I will briefly outline an argument for seeing more discontinuity than continuity between the Testaments on this particular issue. Specifically, I argue that Paul, while dependent in many ways for his ethics on the Old Testament law, no longer views that law as an authoritative guide for new-realm living.[33]

An important preliminary point is one that I implicitly make in the previous paragraph, by shifting from (and between) "law" and "Torah." Debates on this matter are occasionally confused by a failure to define what "law" we are talking about. In theological circles, the word "law," particularly under the influence of Luther's theology, often means "whatever God commands us to do"—whether that "law" is

---

30. As Otto Weber notes, the issue of the third use of the law is complicated by different conceptions of what it means to claim the law has directive force for the church (*Foundations of Dogmatics*, 2 vols. [Grand Rapids: Eerdmans, 1981, 1983], 2:394–97).

31. See "How Christians Should Regard Moses" [1525] in *Word and Sacrament 1*, vol. 35 of *Luther's Works*, ed. E. Theodore Bachmann (Philadelphia: Muhlenberg, 1960), 162–71. To be sure, discovering Luther's view on any subject is challenging because of the occasional nature of most of his writings and because he tends to express himself in extremes. But most scholars do not think that Luther taught a third use of the law, as usually defined (see, e.g., G. Ebeling, "On the Doctrine of the *Triplex Usus Legis* in the Theology of the Reformation," in *Word and Faith*, trans. J. W. Leitch [Philadelphia: Fortress, 1963], 62–64; H. Bornkamm, *Luther and the Old Testament* [Philadelphia: Fortress, 1969], 124–28). But a "third use of the law" is suggested in Zwingli (G. W. Locher, "The Characteristic Features of Zwingli's Theology in Comparison with Luther and Calvin," in *Zwingli's Thought: New Perspectives*,

Studies in the History of Christian Thought 25 [Leiden: Brill, 1981], 197–99), is clear in Calvin (for whom the "third use" is the "chief use"), in Melanchthon (*Loci Communes* 7; see also the Formula of Concord, Art. 6), and is generally taught in Reformed theology.

32. Turretin, for instance, distinguishes between two senses of being "under the law": the law as a "covenant to acquire life" and the law as a "rule of life" (*Institutes of Elenctic Theology*, topic 11, Q. 33 part 7). See also, e.g., John Ball, *A Treatise of the Covenant of Grace* (London, 1645), 15; Bolton, *True Bounds of Christian Freedom*, 28.

33. I argue this basic view in more detail in two articles: "The Law of Moses or the Law of Christ," in Feinberg, *Continuity and Discontinuity*, and "The Law of Christ as the Fulfillment of the Law of Moses: A Modified Lutheran View," in *Five Views on Law and Gospel* (Grand Rapids: Zondervan, 1996), 319–76. See also relevant sections of my commentaries on Romans and Galatians for more detailed exegesis of key passages.

found in Deuteronomy, Matthew, or 1 Corinthians.[34] Paul clearly thinks believers are under some form of "law" in this wider sense: "the commandments of God" matter. The charge of "antinomianism" does not stick, then, to Paul or to those who hold the position for which I am arguing. The issue we are discussing is a narrower salvation-historical-oriented question: Are new-covenant believers obligated to obey the law of Moses, the Torah? This is the question Paul directly addresses and reflects on in various ways. As we have seen (pp. 424–26), Paul's *nomos* is almost always a reference to this particular form of law, the law that he was so intimately familiar with and that became a pressing issue when gentiles, never "under" the law, entered the new-covenant people of God.

The argument for the view I am advocating can be simply summarized. Paul views the law of Moses as a body of commandments given to Israel for a limited time and for a particular purpose. With the coming of Christ and the inauguration of a new phase in salvation history, the era when the Torah governed God's people has come to an end. Believers, therefore, while they profitably read and learn from the law, are no longer "under" it—obliged to follow it as a rule for their lives. This argument rests on and presumes a particular reading of Paul's presentation of salvation history, a reading I have grounded in Paul's teaching earlier (pp. 27–34). So I will here only very briefly summarize that data.

Paul's response to the agitators in Galatia focuses especially on what he views as their failure to grasp the significance of the salvation-historical shift that has occurred. For them, it is "business as usual": Messiah has come, but Torah still governs the people of God, and those who want to be included within that people, whether Jew or gentile, must conform to it. In response, Paul argues that the Torah entered into salvation history at a particular point in time ("430 years" after the promise to Abraham [3:17]; see "added" in v. 19) and, especially importantly, was intended to rule God's people only until "the Seed to whom the promise referred had come" (v. 19). The Torah functioned to "guard" Israel during that earlier time; but "now that this faith has come, we are no longer under a guardian" (v. 25). The purpose of the law expressed in this language of "guardian" (Gk. *paidagōgos*) is indicated in a variation of this formula that Paul uses several times: "under the law" (Rom 6:14, 15; 1 Cor 9:20 [4x]; Gal 3:23; 4:4, 5, 21; 5:18). Paul's "under" in these kinds of contexts generally denotes "under the power of." To be "under the law," then, is to be under the authority of the law.[35] It refers to one basic aspect of what it meant to be the old-covenant people of God, governed by the law

---

34. "The knowledge of this topic, the distinction between the Law and the Gospel, is necessary to the highest degree; for it contains a summary of all Christian doctrine" (Luther, *Lectures on Galatians*, on 2:14 [*Luther's Works*, vol. 26, ed. Jaroslav Pelikan {Saint Louis: Concordia, 1963}, 117]).

35. For this view, see, e.g., Belleville, ""Under Law,'" 53–78. A number of scholars argue, in contrast, that the phrase refers to being under the "curse," or condemnation of the law (e.g., Schreiner, *Law and Its Fulfillment*, 77–81).

that God graciously gave his people. Romans 7:4 makes a similar point: believers have been "put to death with respect to the law" (my translation). As the parallel with death to sin in Romans 6 makes clear, being "put to death with respect to the law" means to be released from its binding authority (see v. 6). Paul's famous statement about the law in Romans 10:4 should also be interpreted in the context of this salvation-historical scheme. When Paul claims that "Christ is the *telos* of the law," he is not saying simply that Christ "ends" the law. Rather, *telos* is best translated "climax" or "culmination" (see NIV). Paul is reminding his readers that Christ is what the law was all along pointing toward: he is, as it were, the finish line of the race Israel had been running. Now that the finish line has been reached, the race is over, and the law is no longer the "guardian" of God's people.[36] Thus Paul asserts that the coming of Christ, like the finish line in a race, marks the intended outcome or culmination of the law, the race that Israel had been running.

These texts suggest that Paul views the Torah as "old-covenant law," and, as such, no longer a source of direct moral guidance for the new-covenant people of God. Of course, his many appeals to the Old Testament make clear that the Old Testament, as a whole, remains a source of authority for God's new-realm people (see below). The question here is in what sense the Torah of Moses is authoritative for the church. By relegating the Torah to a past stage of salvation history, Paul implies that it does not have a determinative role in guiding new-realm conduct. With this basic perspective in place, we now need to address several follow-up issues.

First, I need to acknowledge the many serious arguments that fine scholars who hold a different view than I do have advanced, and briefly explain why I do not think they overturn the general approach outlined above. One line of argument can, I think, be quickly dismissed. In order to avoid the force of many of Paul's "negative" claims about the law, some scholars argue that *nomos* in these texts refers not to the law as God gave it but the law as abused by people in a legalistic manner.[37] Paul, of course, does confront legalism in places, but there is no basis to think he refers to it by means of the simple word *nomos*. As context makes clear, Paul's references to *nomos* are references to the law as it is enshrined in Scripture (see, e.g., Gal 3:17). And Heikki Räisänen makes the pertinent point: "It is hard to understand why a method as drastic as the death both of Christ and of the Christians would have been necessary to get rid of a mere misunderstanding about the law. A new revelation about its true meaning would have sufficed."[38] Another response is to argue that Paul's teaching about the law's end refers

---

36. See p. 233 and Moo, *Romans* (NICNT), 654–60, for further argument. Romans 10:4 is, on this view, making a point very similar to what Jesus is claiming when he refers to his "fulfilling" the law in Matt 5:17 (for Matt 5:17, see my "Jesus and the Authority of the Mosaic Law," *JSNT* 20 [1984]: 3–49).

37. E.g., Cranfield, "St. Paul and the Law," 43–68; Fuller, *Gospel and Law*. In response, see Moo, "'Law,' 'Works of the Law,' and Legalism in Paul."

38. Räisänen, *Paul and the Law*, 46.

to only parts of the law, to specific functions of the law, or to the law viewed in a certain way. It has been, for instance, popular in Christian history to divide the law into three parts: civil, ceremonial, and moral. The former two parts of the law lose their direct authority over God's people with the coming of Christ, but the "moral law" (again, often confined to the Decalogue) remains in force. The recent focus on inclusion of the gentiles as a prime motivator of Paul's theology leads recent scholars to a variation on this time-honored view: Paul applies to believers those aspects of the law "shorn of those ritual elements that exclude Gentiles."[39] However, while it can be helpful to categorize the many specific commandments and prohibitions in the Torah, no neat division into the traditional categories of "moral," "ceremonial," and "civil" is possible. More importantly, there is no evidence that Jews in Paul's day or New Testament authors assumed such categories. Indeed, two New Testament texts imply that early Christians viewed the law as a single entity (Gal 5:3; Jas 2:10). This makes it very difficult to think that any particular occurrence of "law" (without clear contextual clues) would be intended to mean "ceremonial law" or "moral law." As I noted above, a distinction between the law as direction for life and the law as pronouncing condemnation on those who disobey it is also popular as a way of dismissing the view I have argued.[40] However, again, I am unconvinced that there is adequate lexical or contextual evidence to show that Paul uses "law" to refer to such a distinct function of the law. Recently, many scholars have identified two different perspectives on the law in Paul by focusing on texts in which Paul refers to contrasting "laws" (Rom 3:27; 7:22–23; 8:2; 9:31–32). On this view, "the law of sin and death," for instance, in Romans 8:2 refers to the law as an instrument of sin that leads to death, whereas "the law of the Spirit who gives life" in that same verse refers to that same law as it functions in the hands of the new-covenant Spirit. However, as I argue in my exposition of each of these texts, the contrast in "laws" in these texts is probably between the Torah, on the one hand, and new-covenant "law" or "authority" on the other.

A second line of argument that raises questions about the view I have defended above is based on passages in Paul which affirm the continuing importance of the law. In Romans 3:31, Paul claims that his emphasis on faith does not "nullify the law"; rather, he "upholds the law." The question, of course, is in what sense Paul upholds the law. Murray thinks Paul upholds the law by reinstating it as a moral guide for believers.[41] Most interpreters, however, think Paul anticipates the argument following in chapter 4: by highlighting faith, Paul upholds that same emphasis in Genesis 15:6.[42] However,

---

39. Scobie, *Ways of Our God*, 780 (discussion on pp. 742–80); Dunn, *Theology of Paul*, 631–58; see also, in general, the basic argument of Pollmann, *Gesetzeskritische Motive im Judentum*.

40. E.g., R. Longenecker, for instance, suggests that we carefully distinguish "the law, as the standard and judgment of God" and "the law as contractual obligation" (*Paul, Apostle of Liberty*, 131–39).

41. Murray, *Romans*, 124–26.

42. See esp. Rhyne, *Faith Establishes the Law*.

it might be more likely that Paul anticipates a point even further ahead in Romans. Paul's teaching of faith upholds the law because faith joins us to Christ, who has himself perfectly upheld the law in our place. This, I argue, is what Paul means in Romans 8:4 by claiming that the "righteous requirement of the law" is "fulfilled in us" (NRSV). The language here of "fulfill" brings into our purview two other texts in which Paul affirms that love "fulfills the law" (Rom 13:8–10; Gal 5:14). Some interpreters argue that "fulfill" (*plēroō*) in these texts is a rough synonym for other words that Paul uses to speak about "doing" the law. This text may then teach that Christians are to "do" the law by obeying the love command (the law is "reduced" to this one command)[43] or to keep the law truly by making love preeminent in their broader "doing" of the law.[44] But the distinctive theological significance of this verb in the New Testament suggests that it is not referring simply to obedience to the law but to an eschatological completion of the law. Christians bring the whole law to its conclusive and intended "end" by loving others. The whole law aims at "doing good" to others, and if one loves truly and consistently, all that the law is aiming at is also accomplished.

A final pair of texts to consider in this regard, which will also help us transition into another point, is Galatians 6:2 and 1 Corinthians 9:19–22:

Carry each other's burdens, and in this way you will fulfill the law of Christ.

Though I am free and belong to no one, I have made myself a slave to everyone, to win as many as possible. To the Jews I became like a Jew, to win the Jews. To those under the law I became like one under the law (though I myself am not under the law), so as to win those under the law. To those not having the law I became like one not having the law (though I am not free from God's law but am under Christ's law), so as to win those not having the law. To the weak I became weak, to win the weak. I have become all things to all people so that by all possible means I might save some.

Both texts refer to "law" (*nomos*) in relationship to Christ. In Galatians, we find the simple genitive construction, *ton nomon tou Christou*, "the law of Christ," while in 1 Corinthians 9 we have the adjective *ennomos* qualified by *Christou*: "in-lawed to Christ." In Galatians 6:2, two major directions of interpretation can be identified. First, some argue that, as in Galatians consistently to this point, "law" must refer to the law of Moses, which, Paul is here claiming, is fulfilled by, or interpreted by, or focused on, Christ.[45] On this reading, Paul could be indicating that the law of Moses, seen in light of Christ, has continuing authority over believers. But a second option may be

43. E.g., Räisänen, *Paul and the Law*, 26–28; Thielman, *Paul and the Law*, 140.
44. E.g., Schreiner, *Law and Its Fulfillment*, 38, 110.
45. In addition to the scholars cited in my exposition of this text (pp. 82–83), see esp. Chester, *Messiah and Exaltation*, 537–601. He also provides a thorough overview of the options.

the more likely interpretation. Paul refers to a law distinct from that of Moses, a law that is taught by, or has relation to Christ. In light of 5:14, this "law" might be the love command, which Jesus, of course, put forward as one of the "great commandments." However, while not excluding the love command, I think it more likely that Paul uses "law of Christ" as a rhetorical counterpart to the law of Moses to describe broadly the moral implications of being bound to Christ. The teaching of Christ and the apostles would be included;[46] but also included would be, for instance, the implications of Christ's example for his followers (see, e.g., Phil 2:5), the various ways God's Spirit induces certain values and forms of behavior in Christ followers (e.g., Gal 5:16–25), and the working out of the renewed mind.[47]

The probability that Galatians 6:2 refers to "Christian law" is enhanced when we look at 1 Corinthians 9:19–22. Here, as André Feuillet has shown, Paul breaks the broad entity "law of God" into two parts: the law that was valid for Jews and that Paul is no longer "under"; and the law of Christ, to which Paul is obligated.[48] As in Galatians 6:2, "law of Christ" is best seen as a contrast to the law of Moses, a neat way of referring to the moral constraints of the new covenant that Paul and other believers are obliged to obey. They now encounter the "law of God" (the big category) not as *the* law (of Moses) but as "the law of Christ."

Finally, I want to add an important nuance to the view I have been arguing in this section. Paul, I have been maintaining, claims that the Torah, the law of Moses, as "old-covenant law," is not an immediate, authoritative source for Christian conduct. However, our final view of this matter must do justice to passages where Paul does seem to cite the Old Testament law as normative for Christian conduct (e.g., 1 Cor 9:10; and esp. Eph 6:2). I do not think these texts overturn the case I have made for our view. But they are, in a sense, the "tip of the iceberg," revealing that Paul in many ways continues to integrate Old Testament law into his moral teaching. Paul seems to assume with his readers a shared sense of basic "right" and "wrong," what it means to "do good" (e.g., Rom 2:7) versus what doing "evil" means (e.g., 2:8; for both, see 12:9). These shared moral norms probably reflect "natural law," a moral compass that God has built into the world he has made and manifest in the conscience (2:14–15; see pp. 205–6). But these moral norms undoubtedly reflect Paul's deep familiarity with the Old Testament

---

46. For the case that Paul, and other NT writers, think believers are responsible for specific commandments, see esp. Wolfgang Schrage, *Die Konkreten Einzelgebote in der Paulinische Paränese: Ein Beitrag zur Neutestamentlichen Ethik* (Gütersloh: Gerd Mohn, 1961).

47. For this more expansive view of the law of Christ, see, e.g., Richard B. Hays, "Christology and Ethics in Galatians: The Law of Christ," *CBQ* 49 (1987): 268–90; Heinz Schürmann, "'Das Gesetz des Christus' (Gal 6,2): Jesu Verhalten und Wort als Letztgültige Sittliche Norm nach Paulus," in *Neues Testament und*

Kirche (Freiburg: Herder, 1974), 282–300; Horrell, *Solidarity and Difference*, 244–54; Jipp, *Christ Is King*, 43–76. See, for details and bibliography, pp. 82–83 and Moo, *Galatians*, 376–78. Furnish outlines the various influences on Paul's ethics (*Theology and Ethics in Paul*, 25–67).

48. André Feuillet, "Loi de Dieu, Loi du Christ et Loi de L'esprit d'après les Epîtres Pauliniennes: Les rapports de sec trois avec la Loi Mosaique," *NovT* 22 (1980): 29–63. There are, as one would expect, dissenting opinions about the meaning and significance of this verse (see my discussion on pp. 135–36).

law. Brian Rosner has highlighted the many ways in which Paul assumes the teaching of the law in his own teaching, and comes to a conclusion that I find quite compelling. While not imposing the law as an authoritative norm, Paul reappropriates the law as "wisdom," integrating its essential core into his own teaching.[49]

Our discussion of "the commandments of God" in these last paragraphs is not intended to detract from our earlier emphasis on internal transformation as the core of Paul's ethics—a transformation accomplished by the Spirit renewing the mind of each believer and by each believer's "absorption" of new-realm values through their participation in the life of the community. The shape of the new life is dictated by this transforming work, but as we have seen, it is dictated also by specific commandments to which believers are responsible. Another directive force in Paul's ethical teaching is the example of others. Paul calls on believers to "imitate" (*mimeomai*) or be "imitators" (*mimētēs, symmimētēs*) of God (Eph 5:1), Christ (1 Cor 11:1), Paul himself (1 Cor 4:16; 11:1; Phil 3:17; 1 Thess 1:6; 2 Thess 3:7, 9), and other believers (1 Thess 2:14). He also encourages believers to orient their thinking and behavior according to various "models" (*typos, hypotypōsis*): other believers generally (Phil 3:17; 1 Thess 1:7), Paul (2 Thess 3:9), Timothy (1 Tim 4:12), Titus (Titus 2:7), and, of course, Christ (1 Tim 1:16). Of course, the best-known text along these lines is Philippians 2, where Paul encourages believers to "think" as Christ "thought." Paul also presents his own history, attitudes, and behavior as something to be imitated. The Corinthian believers are to privilege the needs of others over their own "rights," just as Paul gives up his own rights for the sake of the gospel (1 Cor 9). Paul's decision to turn away from the status and privileges he enjoyed under the law in order to follow Christ is an object lesson in the priorities of the new realm (Phil 3:2–11; see Rom 7:7–25; Gal 2:17–20). David Horrell is probably right, then, when he claims that imitation plays a larger role in Paul's ethical teaching than is often recognized. However, he is also probably correct to stress that this imitation is not simply a kind of external "do as you see me doing" but also involves a deeper conformity to the pattern of living exhibited by Christ—especially his giving up of himself for others.[50]

3 FUNDAMENTAL VALUES OF THE NEW REALM

The ethos of the new realm can be described in terms of its essential characteristics—what we may call the values of the new realm. Before briefly exploring these values, it is

49. Rosner, *Paul and the Law*. For the influence of the Torah on Paul's teaching, see also Markus Bockmuehl, *Jewish Law in Gentile Churches: Halakah and the Beginning of Christian Public Ethics* (Edinburgh: T&T Clark, 2000), 145–74; Thompson, *Moral Formation*, 111–34.

50. Horrell, *Solidarity and Difference*, 255–70; see also Fee, *First Corinthians*, 203–4; John M. G. Barclay, "Paul's Story: Theology as Testimony," in Longenecker, *Narrative Dynamics in Paul*, 155–56.

worth returning to an issue that has been controversial in recent study of Paul's theology and that is especially germane to our present subject: the interplay of individual and corporate foci in Paul's theology. I argued earlier that we must carefully balance these perspectives. On the one hand, interpreters located in the West (as I am), have tended to focus too exclusively on the individual at the expense of the corporate. We need to rid ourselves of the culturally inbred notions of the "rugged individual" perspective. Recent interpreters have worked hard to shift this balance, and this is appropriate. However, as is usually the case, a balance shifted from one side has been pushed too far to the other side. Paul is vitally interested in the community, and he knows well that individuals are shaped in very fundamental ways by their communities and other associations. However, his theological teaching is, on the whole, directed to individuals, who are responsible to listen and shape their own thinking in accordance with that theology and then work out the implications of that theology—yes, often in community. So, then, with Paul's ethics. He calls on believers to "renew" their minds (Rom 12:2). These "minds" are the organs of practical reasoning possessed by individuals.[51] The individual is responsible to let the Spirit have his way in "reprogramming" our ways of thinking. As Dunson puts it, "The prominence of cognitively focused exhortations in 12:1–3 points to the indispensably personal and individual nature, as well as the inward location (in the mind [νοῦς]), of the moral revolution that is to take place among every individual Roman believer."[52] However, it is important to note that Paul almost immediately stresses how that renewed mind will be worked out in community. He calls on "every" (*pas*) believer in the Roman Christian community to "think" (*phroneō*) of themselves in the right way (v. 3). By doing so, they will take their proper position in relationship to other believers (v. 3) and become effective "members" of the one body of which they are a part (vv. 4–5). We may summarize Paul's approach in this way: each believer is responsible to embrace and live out new-realm values. As each believer does so, the community will become a place where those values are taught and lived. The believer's ongoing participation in that body will then enhance the appropriation of new-realm values in the life of each believer.

3.1 Holiness

A central new-realm value is holiness.[53] Paul, as is well known, uses the "holiness" word group (including words usually translated into English as "saint," "sanctify," or "sanctification") in two basic senses. One is a definitive, or positional sense; believers become "holy," separated for God, the moment they believe. However, in yet another

---

51. Contra Arland J. Hultgren, *Paul's Letter to the Romans: A Commentary* (Grand Rapids: Eerdmans, 2011), 441, who thinks the reference is to a shared community mind.

52. Dunson, *Individual and Corporate*, 167 (see 166–70).

53. The prominence of the word group and the concept to which it points is emphasized by Hanna Stettler, *Heiligung bei Paulus: Ein Beitrag aus biblisch-theologischer Sicht*, WUNT 2/368 (Tübingen: Mohr Siebeck, 2014); see, e.g., p. 621.

manifestation of Paul's "already/not yet" eschatology, he also cites "holiness" as a state that God has destined believers to attain (*hagiōsynē*: 2 Cor 7:1; 1 Thess 3:13). Similarly, while Paul customarily uses the adjective *hagios* to describe the present state of God's people ("saints" in many English versions), he can also use it, like *hagiōsynē*, to refer to this ultimate state of believers (Eph 1:4; 2:21; 5:27; Col 1:22). I have described this important "blessing" of the new realm above and surveyed the language Paul uses to describe it (pp. 499–501). But our interest here is on the stage between initial and final holiness, that is, progressive sanctification. As Paul prays in 1 Thessalonians 5:23, "May God himself, the God of peace, sanctify you through and through. May your whole spirit, soul and body be kept blameless at the coming of our Lord Jesus Christ." Paul uses the verb *hagiazō* three other times with reference to the progressive sanctification of believers (see also Rom 15:16; Eph 5:26[?]; 2 Tim 2:21). More common are two nouns from this same root: *hagiasmos* and *hagiōsynē*. Both are usually translated "holiness" or "sanctification." According to the pattern of Greek word formation, the former noun, ending in *-mos*, would naturally have an active sense—"being made holy"—whereas the latter would focus more on a state. The more active connotation of *hagiasmos* can be seen in 1 Thessalonians 4:3: "It is God's will that you should be sanctified [*hagiasmos*]: that you should avoid sexual immorality" (see also vv. 4, 7; and Rom 6:19, 22; 1 Tim 2:15). "Holiness," then, like several other key words in Paul, has "three tenses" or "moments": we *are* "holy," we *are to be* "holy," we *are destined* to be "holy."

"Holiness," of course, is a concept Paul draws from the Old Testament, where it is a central concept in God's relationship with Israel (the word group occurs over a thousand times in the LXX). God's call to Israel to "be holy, because I am holy" in Leviticus (11:44–45; cf. 19:2; 20:7, 26) expresses both the standard by which Israel is to measure its life and the direction that life should take. We often hear that being "holy" or "sanctified" means to be set apart *from* the world. And Paul can certainly use the vocabulary with this nuance. See, for example, 2 Corinthians 7:1: "Therefore, since we have these promises, dear friends, let us purify ourselves *from* everything that contaminates body and spirit, perfecting holiness out of reverence for God." But Paul does not usually explicitly mention this "negative" side of holiness, and this nuance has been overemphasized in many traditional treatments of the concept. Sanctification focuses as much on the positive as the negative, connoting our being "set apart" *for* God and his purposes. As it is put in the *NIDNTTE*, referring to the concept in the Old Testament: "It may be that the basic idea is a positive one: the divine-human encounter that inevitably demands certain modes of response."[54] It is not by chance that Paul regularly refers to the Spirit as the *Holy* Spirit (once also "the Spirit of holiness" [Rom 1:4]). By doing so, he reminds us that we are people indwelt by One who is

---

54. *NIDNTTE* 1:125.

intrinsically holy, mediating to us the holiness of all the persons of the Godhead. At the same time, Paul implies, the only possible source of Christian holiness comes through "the sanctifying [*hagiasmō*] work of the Spirit" (2 Thess 2:13).

I note, finally, that holiness, in keeping with the interplay I identified above, is both an individual and corporate matter. The call for sexual purity in 1 Thessalonians 4:4–5 is directed to "each of you." But the holiness of individual believers will ultimately result in, and, in turn, be influenced by the community; Paul wants the "whole building" "to become a holy temple in the Lord" (Eph 2:21).

Holiness is the believer's ultimate goal, which Paul calls on believers to work toward in this life—appropriating and working out the holy status already given to us. Holiness is what we need in order to stand before a holy God; without it "no one will see the Lord" (Heb 12:14). Standing in contrast to holiness is idolatry, which we might simply describe as being dedicated to anyone or anything that is not God. Christians are people who have turned "from idols to serve the living and true God" (1 Thess 1:9; see 1 Cor 5:10–11; 6:9; 12:2; Gal 5:20). There can be no agreement between "the temple of God and idols" (2 Cor 6:16); and so, as the church becomes a "holy temple in the Lord," its members must shun idols. That is the reason Paul forbids the Corinthians from eating meals in pagan temples (1 Cor 8:7; 10:14, 19; cf. 10:7). It is quite valid, and helpful in terms of application in our own day, to expand idolatry to include anything that becomes a rival to God in our affections. However, while he can agree with the Corinthians that "an idol is nothing at all in the world" (1 Cor 8:4), he also warns them about the possibility of demonic activity lurking behind the idols (10:20). We should not "demythologize" idols to the extent that we fail to recognize the reality of spiritual beings who take the form of idols. "Our struggle is . . . against the rulers, against the authorities, against the powers of this dark world and against the spiritual forces of evil in the heavenly realms" (Eph 6:12).

3.2 Other Regard (Love)

Jesus, of course, summarizes obedience to the law in two "great commandments": loving God and loving the neighbor. Paul, as we will see below, also highlights the command to love the neighbor. However, while he occasionally refers to believers as people who "love God" (Rom 8:28; 1 Cor 2:9; 8:3; 16:22; Eph 6:24; 2 Tim 3:4), he never commands love for God. Love of other humans obviously stands out as one central (if not *the* central) value of the new realm. The new realm is permeated by the atmosphere of love, so it is natural that Paul should so often commend believers for their love and equally often call on them to manifest that love to others. Paul, of course, refers to God's love, or Christ's love for his people; and, reciprocally, our love for God (e.g., Rom 8:28). But in over sixty verses, Paul refers to believers' love for others (overwhelmingly with the noun *agapē* and verb *agapaō*; but once with *philostorgos* and twice with *philadelphia*). Perhaps more significant than the number of occurrences is the way Paul so often singles out love as *the* defining value of new-realm living:

> For the entire law is fulfilled in keeping this one command: "Love your neighbor as yourself." (Gal 5:14)

> Let no debt remain outstanding, except the continuing debt to love one another, for whoever loves others has fulfilled the law. The commandments, "You shall not commit adultery," "You shall not murder," "You shall not steal," "You shall not covet," and whatever other command there may be, are summed up in this one command: "Love your neighbor as yourself." Love does no harm to a neighbor. Therefore love is the fulfillment of the law. (Rom 13:8–10)

> And now these three remain: faith, hope and love. But the greatest of these is love. (1 Cor 13:13)

> For in Christ Jesus neither circumcision nor uncircumcision has any value. The only thing that counts is faith expressing itself through love. (Gal 5:6)

> And over all these virtues put on love, which binds them all together in perfect unity. (Col 3:14)

After this introduction, it will appear strange when I suggest that I prefer to refer to this value in other language. The problem with "love" is that it is debased currency. The term is used so often and in so many different ways that it has lost its meaning. So without in any way diminishing the importance of love—indeed, precisely to highlight it—I prefer, following other recent interpreters, to use the language of "other regard."[55] "Other regard" is, we might say, what it means to love—the fundamental posture toward others that genuine love fosters. Paul uses this language in several texts, but Philippians 2:1–4 is one of the most important:

> Therefore if you have any encouragement from being united with Christ, if any comfort from his love, if any common sharing in the Spirit, if any tenderness and compassion, then make my joy complete by being like-minded, having the same love, being one in spirit and of one mind. Do nothing out of selfish ambition or

---

55. I suspect the phrase has a long history; but I became familiar with it in David Horrell's excellent book *Solidarity and Difference*.

vain conceit. Rather, in humility *value others above yourselves, not looking to your own interests but each of you to the interests of the others.*

This exhortation for "other regard" is, of course, grounded in the "other regard" of Christ, who chose to "make himself nothing" for the sake of others (vv. 5–11). We find a similar pattern in 2 Corinthians 8:8–9, where Paul wants "to test the sincerity of your love" by the Corinthians' willingness to give to others, exhibiting the same love shown by Jesus, who "for your sake . . . became poor." In addition to other texts that reflect this regard for the "other" (e.g., Rom 13:8 [with love]; 15:1–3; 1 Cor 10:24; 14:17; 15:13; Phil 2:21), Paul alludes to this value in other language as well; for example, "Always strive to do what is good for each other and for everyone else" (1 Thess 5:15). Moreover, the value of "other regard" is woven into the fabric of Paul's exhortations to the churches. Paul's long exhortations to the Corinthians about eating idol meat (1 Cor 8:1–11:1) and to the Romans about disputes over observing aspects of the Torah (Rom 14:1–15:13) have at their heart the need to privilege other people's needs and interests over one's own "liberty." Paul rebukes the Corinthians for the way they celebrate the Lord's Supper because they do not display concern for others (1 Cor 11:17–34). His "bottom line" in the instruction about the use of gifts is to focus on what will best edify others (e.g., 1 Cor 14:17). The "law of Christ" is fulfilled when believers bear the burdens of others (Gal 6:2).

The centrality of "other regard" in Paul's ethics is reinforced by the opposite value he often warns about: arrogance, or being "puffed up." Paul singles out this vice as a root problem behind many of the issues plaguing the church in Corinth (1 Cor 1:31; 3:18; 4:6–7, 18; 8:1–2; 12:21–25; 13:1–5; 14:36). The other passage in which arrogance is prominently mentioned is Romans 11–12 (11:18, 20, 25; 12:3, 10b, 16). Paul's warning about "think[ing] of yourself more highly than you ought" (12:3), an attitude being displayed especially by gentile Christians with respect to their Jewish-Christian brothers and sisters, while important in its own right, also prepares the way for his rebuke of the critical spirit being displayed by both the "strong" and the "weak" (Rom 14:1–15:13).[56] "Self-regard" is the attitude of those who are "enemies of the cross of Christ" (Phil 3:18–19; cf. Rom 16:18).

Another specific manifestation of "self-regard" is greed, or covetousness. Greed is one of the sins that Paul most often criticizes.[57] In addition to the number of references, Paul also goes out of his way to single out this sin by identifying it with idolatry

---

56. As Craig Keener notes, "Paul's emphasis on the right way to think . . . fits his larger emphasis on unity" (*The Mind of the Spirit: Paul's Approach to Transformed Thinking* [Grand Rapids: Baker, 2016], 170).

57. He refers to "greed" (*pleonexia*) six times (Rom 1:29;

2 Cor 9:5; Eph 4:19; 5:3; Col 3:5; 1 Thess 2:5), to "greedy people" (*pleonektēs*) four times (1 Cor 5:10, 11; 6:10; Eph 5:5); and to the act of "cheating" or "exploiting" (*pleonekteō*) five times (2 Cor 2:11; 7:2; 12:17, 18; 1 Thess 4:6).

(Eph 5:5; Col 3:5). This close association of greed with idolatry has its roots in the Old Testament and has parallels in Second Temple Judaism and in the New Testament. The Old Testament frequently sets wealth in competition with God as a source of security (e.g., Ps 52:7; Prov 10:15; Jer 48:7). The Jewish philosopher and theologian Philo, a rough contemporary of the apostle Paul, claimed that the first commandment prohibits "money-lovers" (*Special Laws* 1.23). And the New Testament frequently highlights the love of material possessions as offering a particularly enticing and entrapping alternative to the love of God (e.g., Matt 6:25–34; 1 Tim 6:17; Heb 13:5).[58] Because greed is the inappropriate desire to accumulate more and more, it is a fundamental attitude that underlies and gives greater impetus to other sins (see Eph 4:19). "For the love of money is a root of all kinds of evil. Some people, eager for money, have wandered from the faith and pierced themselves with many griefs" (1 Tim 6:10).

4 SOME SPECIFIC ASPECTS OF NEW-REALM LIVING

Paul has a great deal to say about how believers are to live—more than we can accommodate in a book on his theology. However, I want at least to touch on several key specific issues he addresses. The challenge of constructing a "theology of Paul" out of his occasional letters is nowhere greater than on this topic. The issues Paul addresses do not arise from his concerns but from the specific needs of the churches and individuals he addresses. However, (1) many of the issues, at root, that arise in the letters are ones that appear to be common to Christians in every age; and (2) while always having his readers in view, Paul will sometimes focus more on general behavioral patterns that should characterize their lives as new-realm participants.

Romans 12 is a case in point. Paul begins at the most basic level; believers are to be transformed by the renewing of their minds (v. 2). He then tackles attitudes that are interfering with the unity of the body (vv. 3–8). In a series of rapid-fire commands in verses 9–21, he unpacks some ways the believer's transformation is to manifest itself. Sincere love (v. 9a) is the heading for what follows. This sincere love has distinct moral direction: believers are to "hate what is evil" and "cling to what is good" (v. 9b; see also v. 21). Then in verses 10–21 Paul quickly moves through a number of ways love is to be manifest, in relationships both with believers (vv. 10–13, 15–16) and unbelievers (vv. 14, 17–21). The dominant note in these verses is "other regard." This focus frames Paul's exhortations to believers—they are to "honor one another above yourselves" (v. 10) and to avoid pride (v. 16). In their interaction with unbelievers, "other regard"

---

58. See on this topic especially Brian S. Rosner, *Greed as Idolatry: The Origin and Meaning of a Pauline Metaphor* (Grand Rapids: Eerdmans, 2007).

takes the form of giving up one's natural desire to return evil for evil (v. 17) and seek, rather, to "live at peace with everyone" (v. 18).

In addition to such passages, Paul's so-called "vice" and "virtue" lists also give us some insight into his general ethical concerns.[59] Paul uses these lists in various kinds of contexts to illustrate behavior he either condemns or commends. They sometimes display a certain structure, either conceptual or literary, and sometimes appear to be geared toward issues in the context. However, more often they appear to be rather random lists that arguably reflect Paul's basic and regular ethical concerns. These lists include seventy-six sins (based on the Greek roots used), and, as one might imagine, they cover the whole range of sinful behavior. Most of the terms denote sinfulness in general; for example, "wickedness," "evil," "lust," "ungodly," "unholy." The specific area of sin that Paul mentions most often is sexual immorality (twenty-one references). Speech comes shortly behind, with fourteen references. Many of the terms in this category describe critical and abusive speech. We might, then, combine these with references to factionalism and party spirit to bring out one of Paul's underlying concerns, the unity of the community. These lists also manifest persistent concerns with idolatry (six references), greed (seven references), and anger (six).

Paul calls on believers to live out their new-realm identity in all their spheres of life: their own physical families, their new spiritual family, and the larger world. I will use these spheres of life to organize my discussion of Paul's key ethical concerns. However, while Paul tends to bring up these concerns especially often in the context of one of these spheres or the other, he of course often intends that they be displayed in other spheres as well.

4.1 The Earthly Family

Before looking briefly at Paul's admonitions related to family life, we need to mention a foundational issue that has implications for our interpretation of Paul's teaching for this sphere of life and for the life of the believer in the world.

As I have noted at various places, the widespread assumption that some of the letters that appear in our New Testament under Paul's name were not, in fact, written by him, often carries large implications for our interpretation of "the theology of Paul" (pp. 49–51). We have seen, for instance, how Paul's theology of church leadership can take quite different shapes depending on how much of the material in the thirteen Pauline letters is allowed to inform that theology (pp. 592–93). The same is true for

---

59. These lists take different forms and are integrated into their contexts in different ways, so we are not dealing with a very defined form. The following is a rather expansive enumeration of these lists. Vice lists: Rom 1:29–31; 13:13; 1 Cor 5:10, 11; 6:9; Gal 5:19–21; Eph 4:19, 31; 5:3–5; Col 3:5, 8; 1 Tim 1:9–10; 2 Tim 3:2–4; Titus 3:3. Virtue lists: Gal 5:22–23a; Phil 4:8. See the study of E. Kamlah, *Die Form der katalogischen Paränese im Neuen Testament*, WUNT 1/7 (Tübingen: Mohr Siebeck, 1964); Thompson, *Moral Formation*, 87–109.

Paul's teaching about family relationships and about his advice to Christians about their place in the wider world. On one view, for instance, the "authentic Paul" held what we might call a "liberationist" view, affirming full equality in marriage (e.g., Gal 3:28), and a negative attitude toward authorities in general. The "radical" Paul of the seven authentic letters, however, gave way to a "conservative" viewpoint in Colossians and Ephesians and then finally to a "reactionary" view in the Pastoral Epistles.[60] The progression of letters exhibits, then, an increasing concern to "domesticate" the passion and radical vision of Paul himself, imposing hierarchy in the home (seen in the "household codes" of Col 3:18–4:1; Eph 5:22–6:9, and throughout the Pastorals) and encouraging believers to accommodate to the institutions of the world (e.g., 1 Tim 2:1–8). I will not repeat here the reasons why I am convinced that Paul did, in fact, write all the letters attributed to him; nor will I again explain why I am convinced that, while Paul's theology developed, it did not fundamentally change. What this means is that *all* the evidence of Paul's letters on these issues must be taken seriously, and our task is to develop comprehensive viewpoints that take into full account both the alleged "libertarian" passages as well as the alleged "authoritarian" passages.

The view of marriage that emerges from Paul's letters is a case in point.[61] The challenge here is to integrate what Paul says in 1 Corinthians 7 and Ephesians 5. In the former passage, Paul expresses a preference that believers, like him, would stay single (1 Cor 7:6, 28, 38, 40). He appears to view marriage as an unfortunately necessary accommodation to channel one's sexual lust (v. 9). In the latter passage, on the other hand, Paul holds up the one-flesh union of man and woman as an analogy to the relationship of Christ and the church (Eph 5:32). However, what appears to be a contradictory understanding of marriage results from overreading both passages. An extreme view of 1 Corinthians 7 is that Paul commends an ascetic lifestyle in light of the nearness of the end ("because of the present crisis" [v. 26]; "the time is short" [v. 29]). However, as I argue above (pp. 541–45), Paul's teaching is governed not by a belief that the world would end soon but by a conviction that the nature of the world had changed. And he certainly does not argue against sex or marriage. On the contrary, in response to the Corinthians, who are claiming "it is good for a man not to have sexual relations with a woman" (v. 1), Paul asserts the appropriateness, indeed, the "rightness," of sex within marriage (vv. 3–5) and affirms marriage as a valid option for "spiritual" people like the Corinthian Christians. Moreover, Paul is not in 1 Corinthians 7 setting forth "a theology of marriage." Rather, he is trying to move the Corinthians away from an ascetic position, rooted perhaps in a poor view of the body.[62] To do so, he signals

---

60. These phases are identified in these terms by Borg and Crossan, *First Paul*, 14–15. See also, e.g., Elliott, *Liberating Paul*, esp. 25–54, 84–90; Wolter, *Paul*, 314–15.

61. See, e.g., Beattie, who argues that the differing view of

marriage in Ephesians vis-à-vis 1 Corinthians shows that the former is pseudepigraphical (*Women and Marriage*).

62. See, e.g., Dunn, *Theology of Paul*, 693–98.

agreement with them on the appropriateness of believers choosing the single state; yet he is also very clear in affirming sex and marriage as valid options for believers. In Ephesians 5, on the other hand, a very high view of marriage is often grounded in a certain interpretation of verse 32—ascribing the word "mystery" to the marriage relationship and then interpreting the Greek word behind "mystery" (*mystērion*) to mean "sacrament." However, it is more likely that the mystery refers to the union of believers with Christ. If this is so, Paul in Ephesians 5 says nothing about marriage *per se*; his focus is entirely on the kind of relationship that should mark the marriage of believers. Taken as a whole, then, Paul clearly upholds the appropriateness of marriage for believers; indeed, he often appears to assume that the Christians to whom he writes will be married.[63] On the other hand, he is also clear in affirming that remaining single is a valid choice, a decision that can free up the believer to serve Christ without so many distractions. This last perspective is, sadly, often lost in our contemporary churches, where singles are isolated and assumed to be on their way to a married relationship.

Another issue related to marriage that surfaces in 1 Corinthians 7 is Paul's view of the permanence of marriage. His teaching here is so brief and directed to so specific an issue that it would be inappropriate to draw conclusions about divorce from this passage. But he appears to make three basic points: (1) Christians should not divorce (vv. 10–11); (2) Christians married to non-Christians should seek to remain married (vv. 12–14); (3) if an unbelieving partner insists on divorce, the believer is not bound to the marriage (v. 15).

Discussion of marriage leads naturally into some words on sex. In Paul's day, as in ours, sex was an area in which biblical standards clashed especially harshly with contemporary mores. We are not surprised, then, that he warns his gentile converts about their conduct in this sphere of life. As I noted above, sex is the area of sinfulness that Paul most often mentions in his vice lists. First Thessalonians 4 is particularly pointed. Paul here rehearses what he taught these mainly gentile converts in his short time with them about how they are "to live in order to please God" (v. 1). The first thing he mentions, identifying it with their sanctification (v. 3), is the need to "avoid sexual immorality" (*porneia*, the Gk. word referring to inappropriate sexual behavior). As I argued above, Paul fleshes this out by urging believers to use their sexual organs "in a way that is holy and honorable" (v. 4). Paul follows Jewish precedent in identifying inappropriate sexual conduct as an especially clear indication of the way humans have turned from the worship of God (Rom 1:24–27). While written to gentiles, this passage also reveals Paul's indebtedness to the Old Testament in his ethical teaching. The passage is suffused with calls to holiness (1 Thess 4:3, 4, 7), echoing the familiar Old Testament call to holiness (e.g., Lev 11:44; see above). Paul's reference to the gift

---

63. Granted Paul's cultural context, it is clear that he assumes marriage is between one man and one woman. Attempts to find traction in Paul for a more expansive view of marriage (e.g., Campbell, *Pauline Dogmatics*, 594–641) are not convincing.

of the Holy Spirit in verse 8 recalls the promise of Ezekiel 36:25–27, that God would "cleanse" his people from "impurity" and idolatry (see 1 Thess 1:9) by a new effusion of his Spirit.[64] Perhaps the clearest theological foundation for Paul's call for sexual purity is found in 1 Corinthians 6:12–20. Here, in response to a Corinthian view that apparently viewed the body as unimportant for the spiritual life, Paul affirms the importance of the body and therefore underscores the need to use the body appropriately in the sexual realm. One must not join with prostitutes, because this would violate the intimate and exclusive union believers have with Christ (vv. 15–17). Our bodies, in fact, are "temples of the Holy Spirit" (v. 19). Believers must, Paul concludes, "honor God with your bodies" (v. 20)—and that, of course, means using them in the sexual realm in ways pleasing to God.

Paul never enumerates any kind of comprehensive list of sexual sins. He often warns in general about serious sexual sin (*porneia*; see 1 Thess 4:3 above; also 1 Cor 5:1; 6:13, 18; 7:2; 2 Cor 12:21; Gal 5:19; Eph 5:3; Col 3:5; also *pornos*, a sexually immoral person [1 Cor 5:9, 10, 11; 6:9; Eph 5:5; 1 Tim 1:10] and *porneuō*, "to commit sexual immorality" [1 Cor 6:18; 10:8]). The number of occurrences manifests the importance of this issue in Paul's churches. "Impurity" (*akatharsia*), while not restricted to sexual sin, certainly includes it (Gal 5:19; Eph 4:19; 5:3; Col 3:5); see also "lust" (Col 3:5) and "lovers of pleasure" (2 Tim 3:4). Paul assumes that incest is a form of serious sexual sin (1 Cor 5:1). In more specific terms, Paul condemns "orgies" (Gal 5:21), "adulterers" (1 Cor 6:9), and "those practicing homosexuality" (1 Tim 1:10) or "men who have sex with men" (1 Cor 6:9). These last references invite a brief further discussion. Contemporary shifts in culture have placed same-sex relations high on the list of controversial issues, leading to a number of revisionist interpretations of the biblical evidence. For instance, various nuanced and restrictive definitions of the word used in 1 Corinthians 6:9 and 1 Timothy 1:10—*arsenokoitēs*—have been suggested. But the word seems clearly to mean "men who lie with men," that is, people who engage in same-sex sexual relations (see p. 124). A lot of attention has also been given to the other key text, Romans 1:26–27. Paul here refers to people who have sex with those of their own gender as an illustration of the sin that pervades the gentile world. Some dismiss the significance of Paul's teaching here by claiming that he simply follows his Jewish precedents.[65] Paul does seem to agree with Old Testament and Second Temple Jewish teaching on this matter, and his appeal to it in this text signals further that he himself endorses it. Others argue that Paul condemns only same-sex relationships that run counter to the "nature" of the individual.[66] But Paul uses "nature" here, as do most

64. See Weima, "'How You Must Walk to Please God,'" 98–119.

65. E.g., Scroggs, *New Testament and Homosexuality*, 17–118; Brownson, *Bible, Gender, Sexuality*, 224–31.

66. E.g., J. Boswell, *Christianity, Social Tolerance, and Homo-sexuality* (Chicago: University of Chicago Press, 1980). John Nolland ("Romans 1:26–27 and the Homosexuality Debate," *HBT* 22 [2000]: 32–57) responds well to alternative interpretations of the Romans passage (though his article is now a bit dated).

Jewish authors, particularly Philo, to make clear that sexual morality is part of "natural law" and therefore a divine mandate applicable to all people. Paul includes same-sex sexual practices within the category of "serious sexual sin."[67] However, it is also important not to overinterpret the significance of Romans 1:26–27. Paul does not include homosexual acts in his depiction of the gentile world here because they are particularly heinous sins but because they are an especially clear and graphic manifestation of the way people have turned away from God.

Paul's teaching on family relationships emerges most clearly in the "household codes" of Colossians 3:18–4:1 and Ephesians 5:22–6:9 (and see also Titus 2:1–10).[68] These passages address the three basic relationships found within the Greco-Roman household: husbands and wives, fathers (or parents) and children, and masters and slaves. This kind of instruction for the good ordering of the household has parallels in Paul's Greco-Roman world and was adapted by Philo and Josephus in the Jewish world. In other words, this basic framework of teaching was "in the air," and it is unsurprising that Paul utilizes it to instruct early Christians in their household responsibilities.[69]

In keeping with their antecedents in the wider culture, Paul's household codes require certain household members (wives, children, slaves) to "submit to" or "obey" others. These exhortations reflect the Roman household pattern, according to which the husband/father/slaveowner, the *paterfamilias*, exercised *patria potestas*, "paternal power," over the household.

Wives, Paul urges, are to "submit" to their husbands (Col 3:18; Eph 5:22; Titus 2:5). This submission reflects the submission of the church to Christ (Eph 5:24). The verb being translated is *hypotassō*, which etymologically could be rendered "order" (*tassō*) "under" (*hypo*). Paul uses the verb twenty-three times in a variety of contexts, most often in the sense of a voluntary "putting oneself under" one kind of authority or another. The force of the verb is much debated in current scholarship, reflecting larger, rather intense, debates about Paul's view of women and marriage. The verse immediately preceding Paul's command that women "submit" to their husbands in Ephesians (5:22) urges believers to "submit to one another out of reverence for Christ."[70] As I commented earlier (pp. 291–92), this call for mutual submission requires believers to defer to one another—to adopt a consistent "other regard." It is this gospel-based deference that Paul asks of Christian wives in verse 22 (and in Col 3:18 and Titus 2:5). The wife "puts herself under" her husband in recognizing and living out an

---

67. On the issue of homosexuality in the teaching of Paul (and the NT generally), see esp. Hays, *Moral Vision*, 379–406; Gagnon, *Bible and Homosexual Practice*. For a competing view, see Johnson, *Interpreting Paul*, 313–36.

68. The content, and occasionally the wording, of these next paragraphs is taken from Moo, *Colossians*, 293–98.

69. See esp. Balch, "Household Codes."

70. The close relationship of the verses is suggested by the fact that v. 22, in fact, has no verb in the Greek text. "Submit" is (appropriately) read as a carryover from the verb in v. 21.

"order" established by God himself within the marriage relationship.[71] In contrast to "obedience," submission suggests a voluntary willingness to recognize and put oneself under the leadership of another.[72] The call for wives to submit to husbands must also be put in a larger context. Submission to any human is always conditioned by the ultimate submission that each believer owes to God. In any hierarchy we can imagine, God stands at the "top of the chart."

In Ephesians 5:23, Paul grounds his call for wives to submit by reminding them that the husband is "the head" (*kephalē*) of his wife—just as Christ is the "head" of the church.[73] The husband, Paul suggests, has the difficult and challenging role of being the final authority in the relationship. However, the exercise of that "authority" is significantly tempered by Paul's injunction to husbands to love their wives (Col 3:19; Eph 5:25, 28). We see here the clearest revision of the usual Greco-Roman household code. Those codes asserted the authority of the head of the family in order to maintain order in the household; "love" of husband for wives was never mentioned. Paul's inclusion of this command to the husband reflects the influence of the basic "Christ story" that is so important a grounding for Paul's ethics. The kind of love the husband is to have for his wife is the self-sacrificial love of the one who "gave himself up" on behalf of the church. The husband's love for his wife will therefore often mean that he defers to her needs (Eph 5:21). The mutuality implied by the one-flesh union of husband and wife and the husband's love of the wife must be given full weight, even as the need for wives to recognize the headship of their husbands is upheld. We should also note that, contrary to what is sometimes claimed, Paul does call on wives (at least "younger" ones) to "love their husbands and children" (Titus 2:4).

We must pause here to put Paul's requirement that wives submit to husbands in a larger theological context. These exhortations in the household codes are matched by some other passages in which Paul appears in some sense to subordinate wives to husbands or women to men (1 Cor 14:33b–35; 1 Tim 2:11–15). This strand of teaching, however, appears to contradict Paul's sweeping claim about relationships in Christ—where "there is neither Jew nor Gentile, neither slave nor free, nor is there male and female" (Gal 3:28). I commented briefly on this issue in the previous chapter (pp. 600–602), but it needs to be addressed again here. This "egalitarian" thrust in Paul is often considered incompatible with calls to wives, or women, to be in submission, or with restrictions on what women can do in the church. Many scholars therefore dismiss such passages by denying they were written by Paul.[74] However, as I have indicated in

---

71. For a different view, see, e.g., Lynn H. Cohick, "Tyranny, Authority, Service: Leadership and Headship in the New Testament," *ExAud* 28 (2014): 74–89.

72. The middle form may connote this; cf. G. Delling, *TDNT* 8:42; Schweizer, *Colossians*, 221; O'Brien, *Colossians, Philemon*, 224.

73. See pp. 140–41 for a discussion of the metaphorical sense of "head" in these kinds of contexts.

74. Three arguments are used to pry these texts loose from Paul: they are textually suspect (e.g., 1 Cor 14:34a–35 [see my comments in the exposition]); they are a set of texts interpolated

various places, I am not convinced that we can dismiss these passages. Of course, many fine scholars would agree with me on this point but argue nonetheless on exegetical and/or hermeneutical grounds that they should be interpreted in such a way as not to diminish a fully egalitarian viewpoint.[75] However, again, I am generally not convinced by this line of exegesis (see my comments on relevant texts in the exposition).

On my view, then, Paul juxtaposes passages asserting some kind of "oneness" or equality for men and women with others requiring that women "submit" or in some way work out their faith in Christ in ways different than men. One way of bringing these perspectives together is to view exhortations to submission as deliberate accommodations to the prevailing culture. People in the Greco-Roman world were suspicious of new religious movements, particularly ones that proclaimed revolutionary ideas such as the equality of all people. Paul and other New Testament writers urge Christians to respect the hierarchical structure of the Greco-Roman household as a means of defending the new faith from charges that it was intent on overthrowing existing social structures.[76] This concern to allay suspicion about the gospel was indeed one motivation for some of these passages (see Titus 2:10). But it is doubtful that these texts can be explained simply as an accommodation to the culture. Paul grounds many of his specific injunctions in these texts on Christian principles. While, then, the household codes are obviously directed toward, and thereby reflect, the culture of that time (e.g., by addressing slavery; see pp. 643–45), they appear to embody authoritative Pauline teaching that is not limited to his time or circumstances. These passages do not contradict the "egalitarian" principle of Galatians 3:28 (and other passages); they rather indicate what "equality" means and how it is to be worked out.

In the Colossian and Ephesian household codes, Paul turns next to parents and children. The reciprocity that characterizes these codes surfaces here again; in contrast to most ancient moral treatises, the children are "addressed as responsible persons within the congregation."[77] The admonition to fathers (or parents) in Ephesians 6:4 to "bring them up in the training and instruction of the Lord" suggests that the concern is with young children. Paul urges children to "obey" their parents (see also Rom 1:30; 1 Tim 3:4; 2 Tim 3:2; Titus 1:6). "Submission" and "obedience" are distinct but overlapping concepts. Submission is the broader concept, implying a general "order" in a particular relationship that renders it appropriate for one party to defer to another. Obedience is the specific form that submission will often take. The expectation that children would

into Paul's letters (e.g., Winsome Munro, *Authority in Paul and Peter: The Identification of a Pastoral Stratum in the Pauline Corpus and 1 Peter*, SNTSMS 45 [Cambridge: Cambridge University Press, 1983]); or they are located in letters not written by Paul.

75. For a recent treatment along these lines, see Westfall, *Paul and Gender*.

76. On Col 3:18–4:1, see Robert W. Wall, *Colossians and Philemon*, IVPNTC (Downers Grove, IL: InterVarsity Press, 1993), 158. See also, on the Pastoral Epistles, Verner, *Household of God*; John G. Stackhouse Jr., *Partners in Christ: A Conservative Case for Egalitarianism* (Downers Grove, IL: InterVarsity Press, 2015).

77. O'Brien, *Colossians, Philemon*, 224.

obey their parents is widespread in the ancient world and is, of course, firmly rooted in the Old Testament—as Paul's quotation of the Decalogue commandment (Eph 6:2–3) reminds us. But Paul again breaks, or at least stretches the mold, by warning fathers (or parents)[78] about exercising their authority in a way that "exasperates" (Eph 6:4) or "embitters" (Col 3:21) their children.

The third relationship Paul addresses in his household codes is that of slave and master. Paul here reflects the fact that the ancient household often included domestic slaves. Again, at first sight, Paul appears simply to endorse the status quo of his time by requiring slaves to obey their masters (Col 3:22; Eph 6:5; see also 1 Tim 6:1; Titus 2:9–10). But what Paul says in these passages also subtly undermines it. That Paul addresses slaves at all is significant, as he implies not only that they are assembled with other Christians to hear the letters being read but that they are responsible people who need to choose a certain kind of behavior. Paul clearly relativizes the status of the slave's master by repeatedly reminding both slave and master of the ultimate "master" to whom both are responsible, the Lord Jesus Christ. I discuss the larger issue of the institution of slavery below (pp. 643–45).

While not included in the household codes, care for widows is another family obligation. Paul refers in 1 Timothy 5:3–16 to arrangements in the church to care for widows; but he puts the initial obligation for their care on their larger family members (v. 8; see v. 16).

In concluding this section on the family, I return to the issue with which I started. Rather than viewing Paul's advice about the home, women, and the institutions of the world (see below) as unfortunate accommodations to the structures of the world of Paul's day, we may instead view them as a response to an unbalanced appropriation of the "all one in Christ" principle. While the principle is exceedingly important, setting forth a fundamental dimension of the new realm, it was never intended to eradicate all distinctions between men and women, husbands and wives, children and parents. Yet some Christians in the early church apparently interpreted the principle in just this way, suggesting, it seems, that marriage, for instance, was an institution of this world best avoided by "liberated," Spirit-filled Christians or that, if one were married, at least sex should be avoided (1 Cor 7; 1 Tim 4:3). In response, Paul reminds believers that certain institutions of this world are provisions of God's common grace for our good and that believers need to relate appropriately to one another within these institutions. The new family of God gave believers their fundamental identity, but the spiritual family did not eliminate the continuing significance of the physical family and the relations appropriate to its smooth functioning.

---

78. The Greek *pateres* in Col 3:21 and Eph 6:4 usually means "fathers," but it can also refer to "parents" (see BDAG).

4.2 The Spiritual Family

If the earthly family retains its importance as a provision of God for human flourishing, it is, of course, the spiritual family to which Paul devotes most of his attention. As I have pointed out, the trend in recent scholarship is to view the formation of a Christian community as *the* goal of Paul's theology. While I have qualified that viewpoint slightly by giving due regard to the formation of individual Christians in Paul's teaching, it is still fair to see community formation as a central concern for Paul. Indeed, it is so central that we could do justice to this focus only by repeating the theology of Paul as we have surveyed it throughout this volume. In this regard, I should note that the ethical issues I have already addressed, while focused on the family, have relevance for the community also. For instance, after urging believers to avoid sexual immorality in 1 Thessalonians 4:3–5, Paul goes on to say "in this matter no one should wrong or take advantage of a brother or sister" (v. 6). Illicit sex is a violation of God's holy requirements (v. 7), but it is also an offense against the community.

In David Horrell's book on Pauline ethics, he highlights "community solidarity" as one of Paul's two "metanorms" ("other regard" being the other metanorm; see above). I am not sure if it should be elevated to quite so significant a place in Paul's ethics, but the unity of the body of Christ is certainly a significant concern for Paul. One important explanation for this focus is related to one of the dominant concerns of his ministry, namely, to integrate gentiles into the new-realm people of God. Paul, for instance, urges the Christians in Rome to recognize that, despite their differences, they "form one body" (Rom 12:5), and this general appeal ultimately grounds Paul's exhortation to the "weak" (mainly Jewish Christians) and the "strong" (mainly gentiles) to "accept one another" and to have "the same attitude of mind toward each other . . . so that with one mind and one voice you may glorify the God and Father of our Lord Jesus Christ" (15:5–7). A similar concern emerges in Ephesians 2:11–22. But Paul's concern for unity goes beyond the Jew-gentile divide, as he urges believers to subordinate their earthly identities and habits to their common identity in Christ. Factionalism, following one leader in opposition to others, is a prominent issue in 1 Corinthians (chs. 1–4; 11:17–34), and as we have seen, some interpreters think it is *the* concern of the letter (pp. 112–14). Paul's letter to the Philippians also focuses on unity (1:27–2:4; 4:2–3).

As I have repeatedly pointed out, this concern to integrate Jewish and gentile believers into "one body" has been highlighted in recent study of Paul. And, while I have argued that the focus on this issue should not push out or minimize other concerns in Paul, there is no doubt that the full and equal inclusion of different kinds of people into the body of Christ is an important concern in his letters. Of course, many of us do not directly face the Jewish-gentile division that was so important in

Paul's days. But Christians in our day across the world, in varying ways, encounter similar divisions, as people divide into factions based on race, ethnic identity, gender, social standing, etc. Paul's "principle of inclusion" should be adopted and lived out in our churches. The local body of believers should be a countercultural example of inclusion, and the voice of believers who are called to uphold this principle needs to be heard in our cultures.

As I suggested above (pp. 586–87), Paul seeks unity, not uniformity. He allows for, indeed celebrates, the rich diversity of the body. Male and female, Jew and gentile, and slave and free are indeed one in Christ, and Paul is very forceful about insisting on this oneness. But men remain men, women remain women, Jews remain Jews, gentiles remain gentiles, slaves remain slaves, and free people remain free, and Paul recognizes that each kind of person will work out their faith in Christ and responsibilities to the single body in different ways.

Two obvious barriers to unity are arrogance and critical speech. As I noted above, arrogance is the opposite of "other regard." Philippians 1:27–2:4 is a passage where Paul clearly traces disunity to its root problem in people who think too much of themselves. Arrogance, in turn, often manifests itself in critical speech. Sins of speech come second in terms of frequency of reference in Paul's vice lists (Eph 4:25, 29; 5:4; Col 3:8–9; 1 Tim 1:6; 3:11; 5:13; 6:4; 2 Tim 2:14, 16, 23; Titus 1:10; 2:3; 3:2, 9; and see above, p. 629). Of course, the issues that occasion Paul's letters have a lot to do with this focus. The large number of texts in the list above from the Pastoral Epistles arises from the need to confront false teachers who were guilty of unfruitful and divisive speech. But the references Paul makes to this sin, when it does not appear to be a presenting problem in the church, show that it was a constant issue that he felt necessary to mention.

The fundamental posture of "other regard" is displayed toward other believers in many ways. But one of the most tangible expressions is the use of our resources to help others. Paul highlights the importance of generosity toward others in several ways. Negatively, his focus on greed as one of the outstanding characteristics of life in the old realm (see above) implies that new-realm members should exhibit the opposite. In place of the "acquisitive urge," the desire to accumulate more and more for ourselves, there should be a desire to use our resources to help others. Paul's own lifestyle provided an example of one whose use of resources was oriented to the good of others. He refused support from some of his churches out of apparent concern that he might be thought to be preaching the gospel for personal gain. Instead, he "worked night and day in order not to be a burden to anyone" (1 Thess 2:9; 2 Thess 3:7–10; see also 1 Cor 9:6–18; 2 Cor 11:7–9, 20–21; 12:13). Paul is explicit that his practice of supporting himself was to be seen as an example for others to imitate (2 Thess 3:7–10). However, Paul is also clear that ministers of the gospel can appropriately expect support from other Christians

(1 Cor 9:5–14; Gal 6:6; 1 Tim 5:17), and he himself sometimes expresses thanks for gifts sent to him (see esp. Phil 4:10–20).[79]

Most of Paul's teaching about the importance of believers' generosity comes in his exhortations about the "collection," that is, his third-missionary-journey project to get believers in his mainly gentile churches to send money to impoverished Jewish believers in Jerusalem (Rom 15:25–33; 1 Cor 16:1–4; 2 Cor 8–9). This collection was several things at once. It was a simple mechanism to help Christians in need, an act of worship, and a tangible expression of the unity of God's people.[80] "Money talks," the saying goes. Paul did not know the saying, but he understood the sentiment. He hopes that a gift of money from the gentiles to the Jews might speak very loudly about their oneness in Christ. And so he encourages gentile believers to give and prays that Jewish believers will receive (something he was not sanguine about; see Rom 15:31). Paul also views this gift of money as an appropriate return to the Jews for the spiritual benefits they have provided to the gentiles (v. 27). But the greatest motivation for giving is the recognition of just how much believers have themselves been given: "For you know the grace of our Lord Jesus Christ, that though he was rich, yet for your sake he became poor, so that you through his poverty might become rich" (2 Cor 8:9; cf. 9:11). As Barclay puts it, "Placing the Corinthians within the flow of divine grace ensures that their relationship to Jerusalem is 'triangulated' by reference to God."[81] While noting the kind of obligation that gentiles stand under, he is also clear in wanting the giving to be voluntary (8:8). While Paul makes these points about the collection, they are applicable to Paul's general teaching about money and giving.

Paul's collection project is a specific, large-scale application of the general principle enunciated in Galatians 2:10 to "remember the poor." Indeed, some interpreters think this exhortation from the "pillar" apostles in Jerusalem to Paul, Barnabas, and Titus refers to the collection. But this is unlikely.[82] Paul says this remembering of the poor was something "I had been eager to do all along," suggesting that it has already been his practice—perhaps as early as the first missionary journey, if my dating of Galatians is accepted (pp. 54–56). Paul seems to assume that generosity to the poor would characterize the church. As Bruce Longenecker puts it, "Essential to the core identity of Jesus-followers is a corporate generosity that ensures that the economically

---

79. For an excellent survey of Paul's own practices with respect to money, see Verbrugge and Krell, *Paul and Money*, 34–103.

80. See, on the collection, Dieter Georgi, *Remembering the Poor: The History of Paul's Collection for Jerusalem* (Nashville: Abingdon, 1992); Nickle, *Collection*; David J. Downs, *The Offering of the Gentiles: Paul's Collection for Jerusalem in Its Chronological, Cultural, and Cultic Contexts*, WUNT 2/248 (Tübingen: Mohr Siebeck, 2008). The collection has also been thought to represent Paul's attempt to fulfill the prophetic idea of a pilgrimage of the nations to Jerusalem in the last days (Samuel Auler, "More Than a Gift: Revisiting Paul's Collection for Jerusalem and the Pilgrimage of Gentiles," *JSPL* 6 [2016]: 143–60).

81. John M. G. Barclay, "Paul and the Gift to Jerusalem: Overcoming the Problems of the Long-Distance Gift," in *Poverty in the Early Church and Today: A Conversation*, ed. Steve Walton and Hannah Swithinbank (London: T&T Clark, 2019), 95.

82. Dunn, *Beginning from Jerusalem*, 935; Moo, *Galatians*, 139.

poor are 'remembered' within groups of Jesus-followers, even if not all Jesus-followers are in a position to demonstrate economic generosity themselves."[83] These initiatives to help the poor were "incarnations of a divine order that was invading the very structures of the not-yet-restored world."[84]

4.3 The World

Paul's theology is directed toward the building up of Christians and of the communities they are members of. As we saw in Paul's provision for the collection of money for the Jerusalem believers, he also implies that Christians have certain obligations to believers in other churches and locations. But, of course, he also reckons with the reality that the church exists in an unredeemed world and that believers will have to figure out how to live as members of the new realm amid the old realm. As Paul reminds the Corinthians, they have not left the world, and association with the people and institutions of that world will still be necessary (1 Cor 5:10). Therefore, while Paul does not say a lot about how Christians should relate to the larger structures of their society and world, this is not to say he has nothing to say about these matters. In this section, I will briefly survey what Paul says about Christian/non-Christian relationships generally and then look at Paul's teaching about government, slavery, and the natural world.

4.3.1 "Doing Good to All"

In two roughly parallel summary verses, Paul suggests the relative weight of the two main spheres of life believers relate to:

Therefore, as we have opportunity, let us do good to all people, especially to those who belong to the family of believers. (Gal 6:10)

Make sure that nobody pays back wrong for wrong, but always strive to do what is good for each other and for everyone else. (1 Thess 5:15)

Believers' primary obligation is to live faithfully with other "members of the household of faith" (Gal 6:10, my translation of *tous oikeious tēs pisteōs*), and as we have seen, Paul has a great deal to say about doing good to "each other" (*allēlous*; a word Paul frequently uses to refer to the shared life of believers in their new-realm communities). Paul's prohibition about not paying back someone "wrong for wrong"

---

83. Longenecker, *Remember the Poor*, 284. In Longenecker's analysis, most believers in the Pauline churches were either near or at subsistence level economically (294–97). Many of these believers would not have been expected, or able, to give financially to others.

84. Longenecker, *Remember the Poor*, 290. See also, on this issue, Craig L. Blomberg, *Neither Poverty nor Riches: A Biblical Theology of Material Possessions*, NSBT (Downers Grove, IL: IVP Academic, 1999).

in 1 Thessalonians 5:15 reminds us of his similar advice about the right response to unbelievers in Romans 12:14, 17–21 (see above). Paul alludes in passing to various points of contact between believers and unbelievers. Believers will occasionally eat with unbelievers (1 Cor 10:27–30), believers may have spouses who are not believers (7:12–16), and unbelievers may be present at worship services (14:23–25). The importance of good relations with unbelievers is suggested by the expectation that overseers "have a good reputation with outsiders" (1 Tim 3:7). This concern for positive and amicable relations with unbelievers is, in fact, a certain motif in the Pastoral Epistles (1 Tim 2:1–2; 6:1; Titus 2:5, 10, 3:1–2). Moreover, it is possible that Paul intends to include unbelievers in the scope of other general exhortations; see, for example, his command to share with "those in need" (Eph 4:28), his request that Timothy teach believers to "do good, to be rich in good deeds, and to be generous and willing to share" (1 Tim 6:18), or his command that believers "devote themselves to doing what is good" (Titus 3:14). These few references provide slim evidence about the specifics of how Paul wants believers to interact with unbelievers. However, the fact that he includes both believers and unbelievers in his call to "do good" suggests that many of his exhortations to the family of God apply also to the larger population. At the same time, while Paul is not explicit about it, several texts (Phil 1:5, 14, 27, 30; 2:16; Eph 6:10–20) suggest that he expected his converts to be engaged in active evangelism.[85]

4.3.2 Government

The Roman Empire, especially in its various local instantiations, was one of the overwhelming realities in the world of the early Christians. We are not surprised, then, that Paul would address this reality. On the whole, reflecting some of Paul's own experiences with Roman officials (e.g., Acts 18:12–16; 19:35–41; 21:31–32), he urges that Christians should seek to live amicably within the Empire (e.g., 1 Tim 2:1–2; Titus 3:1–2). This stream of teaching is one aspect of the alleged "reactionary" posture of post-Pauline books such as the Pastoral Epistles. We have countered this way of reading these books and other similar texts above (pp. 49–51). On this issue, of course, we have to add the weight of Paul's most famous passage on this topic, Romans 13:1–7—a text that comes, of course, in a letter almost universally attributed to Paul himself. To be sure, a few interpreters have suggested the passage might be a later interpolation in the letter, but this radical move has attracted little following. The basic thrust of the paragraph is clear, coming to expression in verses 1 and 5: believers are to "submit" to governing authorities because (1) all such authorities are appointed by God (vv. 1a–2);

---

85. Peter T. O'Brien, *Gospel and Mission in the Writings of Paul: an Exegetical and Theological Analysis* (Grand Rapids: Baker, 1995), 109–31; Gorman, *Becoming the Gospel*, 36–49.

and (2) believers should fear the authorities' punishment for wrongdoing (v. 5). As I explain in my exposition of the text (pp. 239–40), this call for submission is not absolute. Particular governments or government authorities may so lose their legitimacy under God that they no longer command our obedience; and the call to "submit" to lower authorities is always conditioned by the call to submit to God, the ultimate authority. Christians, Paul claims, are citizens of a higher kingdom that claims their ultimate allegiance—"our citizenship is in heaven" (Phil 3:20).[86]

This generally positive view of the Roman Empire and of government in general may however, need to be qualified by another, more subtle aspect of Paul's teaching. Interpreters have recently drawn attention to the growing influence in Paul's day of the imperial cult.[87] As a way of securing allegiance from people within the empire, the emperor was being accorded greater and greater honors, to the point where worship of him as a god was being expected. Such a movement would naturally run smack into Christian claims about the exclusive demands of their God. Paul never explicitly refers to the imperial cult; nor, of course, therefore, does he speak against it. However, scholars have recently suggested that Paul might subtly counteract the claims of the emperor by the way he uses certain key words. For instance, undermining the emperor's claim to be "Lord" is Paul's insistence that Jesus is Lord. In contrast to the emperor's claim to bring "good news," Paul attributes "good news" to Christ. It is not the "coming" (*parousia*) of the emperor we should hope for but the "coming" of Christ. Paul, it is alleged, is using a device familiar to oppressed people: "hidden transcripts," a kind of coded language that critiques the powers without naming them.[88]

This "Paul and Empire" movement has undoubtedly overreached in some of its claims. We have little evidence that Paul's letters would have been in danger of being intercepted by the authorities; "hidden transcripts" were hardly needed. Most of the key terms alleged to be critiquing the emperor's pretensions can be explained without recourse to imperial rhetoric (on "good news," see pp. 349–51). Moreover, the "powers" that Paul is really concerned about appear to be spiritual beings, sin, and death.[89]

---

86. This perspective may inform Paul's advice to the Corinthians to settle their own matters, without recourse to secular law courts (1 Cor 6:1–8).

87. See esp. S. R. F. Price, *Rituals and Power: The Roman Imperial Cult in Asia Minor* (Cambridge: Cambridge University Press, 1984); I. Gradel, *Emperor Worship and Roman Religion* (Oxford: Clarendon, 2002); Winter, *Divine Honours for the Caesars*. For relevant texts, see Mark Reasoner, *Roman Imperial Texts: A Sourcebook* (Minneapolis: Fortress, 2013). N. T. Wright provides a useful, readable summary of the growth of the imperial cult (*Paul and the Faithfulness of God*, 1:279–347).

88. On anti-imperial rhetoric in Paul in general, see esp. Richard A. Horsley, ed., *Paul and Empire: Religion and Power in Roman Imperial Society* (Harrisburg, PA: Trinity Press International,

1997); Wright, *Paul: In Fresh Perspective*, 59–79. It should be noted that talk of "*the* imperial cult" can conceal the reality that the cult took many different forms in first-century Roman life (see K. Galinski, "The Cult of the Roman Emperor: Uniter or Divider?," in *Rome and Religion: A Cross-Disciplinary Dialogue on the Imperial Cult*, ed. J. Brodd and J. L. Reed [Atlanta: SBL, 2011], 1–21). On "hidden transcripts," see the survey in James R. Harrison, *Paul and the Imperial Authorities at Thessalonica and Rome*, WUNT 2/273 (Tübingen: Mohr Siebeck, 2011), 2–44. For a critical examination of the criteria used to identify such codes, see esp. C. Heilig, *Hidden Criticism? The Methodology and Plausibility of the Search for a Counter-Imperial Subtext in Paul*, WUNT 2/392 (Tübingen: Mohr Siebeck, 2015).

89. See esp. John M. G. Barclay, "Paul, Roman Religion

And, of course, as we have just seen, Paul's one explicit and extensive discussion of government appears strongly to endorse it as an institution being used by God for his own purposes.[90] Nevertheless, granted the overwhelming social reality of the imperial cult, it is also hard to think that Paul's readers would not have heard in his claim "Jesus is Lord," at least faintly, the implication "and Caesar is not."[91]

Larger questions about the way believers are to relate to governing authorities or to other institutions of our world are left unanswered in Paul. Certainly Paul can be read as stressing the importance of the church "being the church." As we have seen, one of his central concerns is to build up Jesus-following communities so that they would embody and exemplify the values of the new realm. On the other hand, Paul's silence about Christians being involved in the political process or engaging in social action or the like should not be taken as determinative. Living in the world of authoritarian government that he did, some of the questions many of us have today about political or social involvement were simply not on the agenda. These questions will have to be answered at a level of theological discussion beyond Paul.

4.3.3 Slavery[92]

One socioeconomic institution of Paul's day that does potentially come within the purview of his teaching is slavery. In my exposition of Philemon above (pp. 262–65), I argued that Paul's desire that Philemon receive his slave Onesimus back as a brother in Christ (v. 17) is central to the purpose of the letter. I also argue that verse 21, where Paul expresses confidence that Philemon "will do even more than I ask," probably suggests that Paul hopes that Philemon will free Onesimus. Yet Paul does not come out and say so, and it is especially interesting that Paul never commands masters to free their slaves, even though, as we have seen above, he addresses Christian slave masters on this issue.[93] This silence urgently raises the question of the implications of Paul's theology for this issue.[94] As Stuhlmacher has noted, the history of interpretation on this matter reveals tendencies toward opposite extremes.[95] On the one hand, beginning with Chrysostom in the early church, continuing with Luther at the time of the Reformation, and seen in its most extreme form among defenders of slavery in nineteenth-century United States, there is an "anti-enthusiastic" or "conservative" tendency to stress the

---

and the Emperor: Mapping the Point of Conflict," in *Pauline Churches and Diaspora Jews* (Tübingen: Mohr Siebeck, 2011), 345–62; Kim, *Christ and Caesar*; White, "Anti-Imperial Subtexts in Paul," 305–33.

90. See, e.g., Johnson, *Constructing Paul*, 163–69.

91. For a series of articles on this issue from various perspectives, see McKnight and Modica, *Jesus Is Lord, Caesar Is Not.*

92. The content and, occasionally, the wording of this section parallel my treatment in *Colossians and Philemon*, 369–77. Used with permission.

93. Paul might, on the other hand, urge slaves to take advantage of any opportunity to gain their freedom (1 Cor 7:21), but we cannot be sure because the meaning of the text is uncertain (see p. 129).

94. For an exploration of this issue, see esp. John M. G. Barclay, "Paul, Philemon and the Dilemma of Christian Slave-Ownership," *NTS* 37 (1991): 161–86.

95. Stuhlmacher, *Brief an Philemon*, 58–69.

degree to which Paul upholds the status quo.[96] Paul, of course, urges slaves to obey their masters (see above), and argues that believers should be unconcerned about their earthly status (1 Cor 7:17–24). Moreover, we perhaps need to recognize that many of us come to this issue with a modern valuation of "freedom" as an ultimate virtue. This is by no means so clear in Paul's world, especially since slaves could often count on being provided for by masters, whereas their "freedom" might lead to starvation. At the other end of the spectrum are interpreters who espouse liberation as a dominating value and seek to find in Paul a basis for their program. Most scholars have steered a middle course, acknowledging, for the reasons I have given above, that Paul makes no frontal attack on the institution of slavery but that, in Lightfoot's classic way of putting it, in Philemon, for instance, "a principle is boldly enunciated, which must in the end prove fatal to slavery."[97] While there is some truth to this, we must also recognize that the basic principle Paul works from in Philemon is a distinctly Christian one: Philemon and Onesimus are "brothers." It is not clear that the principle can validly be extended to slavery in general.[98]

I have neither the space nor the expertise to address this issue adequately, but I will make two general points. First, it is important to stress that Paul never suggests that he approves of the *institution* of slavery. He instructs masters and slaves about how they should relate together within one of the most fundamental institutions in the world of his day. So the problem is not with texts that endorse slavery but with the absence of texts that condemn it. Second, then, we note three basic ways that scholars have dealt with this silence:

1. The New Testament is silent on the matter because it does not, in fact, condemn at least some forms of slavery; nor should we.[99]
2. The New Testament is silent on the matter because it does not condemn slavery; but, of course, we must. This shows that the New Testament is not adequate for providing ethical direction today.[100]

96. Many conservative theologians in early nineteenth-century America defended slavery on the basis of sustained biblical and theological arguments. For an overview of these defenses, see, e.g., Larry E. Tise, *Proslavery: A History of the Defense of Slavery in America 1701–1840* (Athens, GA: University of Georgia Press, 1987); Elizabeth Fox-Genovese and Eugene D. Genovese, "The Divine Sanction of Social Order: Religious Foundations of the Southern Slaveholders' World View," *JAAR* 55 (1987): 211–33.

97. Lightfoot, *Colossians and Philemon*, 325. There is debate over the degree of influence that Christianity had on the amelioration of slavery in the later Roman Empire (e.g., Westermann, *Slave Systems*, 159–62). And it is also pointedly asked why, if the principle was so clear, it took so long for slavery to be eradicated (and against the arguments of some of the most biblically oriented

Christians of the time; see Meeks, "The 'Haustafeln' and American Slavery," 249–50).

98. Although note Marshall's suggestion that "once it has been realized that Christian masters must treat their Christian slaves as brothers and sisters in the flesh and in Christ, is it not inevitable that they should treat their other slaves as brothers and sisters in the flesh—with all that implies?" (I. H. Marshall, "The Theology of Philemon," in Donfried and Marshall, *Theology of the Shorter Pauline Letters*, 190).

99. E.g., Murray, *Principles of Conduct*, 91–106.

100. E.g., K. Giles, "The Biblical Argument for Slavery: Can the Bible Mislead? A Case Study in Hermeneutics," *EvQ* 66 (1994): 3–17.

3. The New Testament is silent on the matter because, although it sets forth principles that are incompatible with slavery,
    a. slavery was part of the fabric of first-century society; and
    b. the New Testament was not fundamentally interested in "earthly" liberation.

I think the third explanation correctly stresses the incompatibility between biblical theology and slavery, but we question whether it adequately explains the silence of the New Testament. With respect to point (a) under this third option, as I have suggested above in the text, while it provides a generally convincing explanation of why the New Testament does not condemn the *institution* of slavery, it does not explain why it does not require Christian slave-owners to free their slaves. Point (b) (again, with reference to the third option), on the other hand, while preserving a measure of truth (again, see the text above), tends uncomfortably toward a dualistic, "two-kingdom" ethic according to which the New Testament speaks to the spiritual side of life but not to the physical and earthly side of life. I therefore very tentatively suggest that William Webb's "redemptive-movement hermeneutic" may have something to offer at this point.[101] Webb basically argues that the New Testament itself is part of a trajectory of teaching on ethical issues in Scripture, and that the New Testament may not therefore offer to us an "ideal ethic" on all issues. I have reservations with this way of thinking of New Testament and Pauline ethics, but it may help explain why Paul never takes the step of forbidding Christians from owning slaves.

4.3.4 The Natural World[102]
If the political and social institutions of his day are largely ignored by Paul, the same would seem to be the case for the natural world. Paul's focus is on the formation of Christians and Christian communities, and these communities are located in urban settings where the natural world has little impact. However, while Paul does not say a lot about the natural world, he does say more than is sometimes recognized.[103] And it is important, in order to correct misapprehensions about Paul, and the New Testament in general, to give space to this teaching.

101. Webb, *Slaves, Women, and Homosexuals.* For criticism, see, e.g., Wayne A. Grudem, "Should We Move beyond the New Testament to a Better Ethic?," *JETS* 47 (2004): 299–346.
102. The concepts and, occasionally, the wording of this section are found also in my following publications: "Creation and New Creation"; "Eschatology and Environmental Ethics: On the Importance of Biblical Theology to Creation Care," in *Keeping God's Earth: The Global Environment in Theological Perspective*, ed. Noah J. Toly and Daniel I. Block (Downers Grove, IL: InterVarsity Press, 2010), 23–45; "Creation and New Creation: Transforming Christian Perspectives," in *Creation in Crisis: Christian Perspectives on Sustainability*, ed. Robert S. White (London: SPCK, 2009), 241–54; "Nature in the New Creation"; *Creation Care* (with J. Moo).
103. Sean McDonough has noted how interrelated in the ancient world and in Paul are concerns for the moral world and for the natural world (*Christ as Creator*, 51–64).

The place to begin is with Paul's use of the language of "new creation" in 2 Corinthians 5:17 and Galatians 6:15. I briefly discuss this phrase in chapter 20 (pp. 466–67), but it deserves a fuller treatment here. In neither context where the phrase occurs does Paul elaborate on its meaning, suggesting that he can assume a meaning for the phrase from its background usage. This background is probably to be found especially in the later chapters of Isaiah, where God's restoration project is pictured in cosmic terms. The prophet does not use the phrase "new creation"—indeed, it appears nowhere in the Old Testament—but he does famously predict the coming of a "new heavens and a new earth" (Isa 65:17–22; cf. 66:22–24). This expectation that God's final salvation would embrace the whole cosmos became widespread in Second Temple Jewish literature, especially in apocalyptic. The phrase "new creation" refers in this literature to the *concept* of cosmic renewal (e.g., Jub. 1.29; 4.26; 1 En. 72.1; 1QS 4.25; 2 Bar. 44.12).

We would expect, then, that "new creation" in these two Pauline texts would at least include reference to the natural world itself. To be sure, the phrase encompasses more than this. Paul appears to use it as a kind of final reminder to believers that, with Christ, a whole new state of affairs has been inaugurated. So some allusion to the renewed person or the renewed community may be intended. But reference also to a final renovation of the world of nature is also present. As Herman Ridderbos puts it, "When he [Paul] speaks here of 'new creation,' this is not meant merely in an individual sense (a 'new creature'), but one is to think of the new world of re-creation that God has made to dawn in Christ, and in which everyone who is in Christ is included."[104]

Two other passages confirm that the natural world is not forgotten in Paul's portrayal of the "world" that believers must interact with. Romans 8:19–22 is the clearest and most important. I will not here repeat the exposition (see pp. 227–28). But, to summarize, this passage indicates that "the creation" (the natural world) is destined to be liberated. It is destined not for destruction but for renovation. "New creation" in this phase of inaugurated eschatology is taking the form of renewed people and communities. But the intention is that "new creation" would ultimately embrace the entire universe; and, in keeping with Paul's understanding of the relation between the "already" and the "not yet," what God ultimately intends for his created world should be anticipated, to the degree possible, by believers here and now.[105] Colossians 1:20, with its claim that God's purpose is to "reconcile to himself all things" makes a similar point. As I have argued elsewhere (pp. 252–53), the "all things" in this text includes the natural world. By referring here to "making peace," Paul taps into a widespread Old Testament

104. Ridderbos, *Paul*, 45. See also Mark S. Gignilliat, *Paul and Isaiah's Servants: Paul's Theological Reading of Isaiah 40–66 in 2 Corinthians 5:14–6:10* (London: T&T Clark, 2007), 98–99.

105. Bauckham, *Bible and Ecology*, 99–100. On this passage, see esp. Harry Alan Hahne, *The Corruption and Redemption of Creation: Nature in Romans 8:19–22 and Jewish Apocalyptic Literature*, LNTS 336 (London: T&T Clark, 2006).

expectation that God would one day establish *shalom*.[106] The "headship" of Christ over all creation (Col 2:10) will manifest itself universally as every part of creation is brought within the scope of God's reclamation work in Christ. Renovation of the cosmos as a whole is again an important component of Paul's eschatological expectation.

There are other texts that may contribute to this teaching in Paul (e.g., Rom 4:13; 2 Cor 5:19 [for which, see my exposition]), but the passages we have considered are sufficient to show that Paul retains the Old Testament and Second Temple Jewish expectation of a renewed cosmos. Interpreted within the framework of Paul's inaugurated eschatology, "new creation" finds its initial fulfillment in the salvation of individual human beings and the creation of a new humanity, and its ultimate consummation in a renewed universe. As Richard Hays puts it, "Paul's image of 'new creation' stands . . . as a shorthand signifier for the dialectical eschatology that runs throughout the New Testament."[107]

While Paul's teaching about "new creation" is in the "indicative" mode, the implications for how one is to live in the inaugurated new creation are clear enough. The natural world, created by God, remains a focus of his concern. It should therefore be a concern to believers as well, who now, in Christ, *the* "image of God," can likewise image God by being the faithful stewards of this world they were created to be.[108] Moreover, humans can only flourish in environments that are conducive to their well-being. Environments polluted by human misuse or damaged by a rapidly changing climate are not conducive to human flourishing. Loving other humans—"other regard"—then, will mean seeking to provide for them the best environment possible.

We appropriately conclude, then, on a note that reminds us of the cosmic-wide scope of Paul's vision of transformation. The apostle's focus on individual humans—their sin, their plight, their renewal, their destiny—does not mean that they are all he cares about. Rather, it is by renewing humans that the relationships among humans can be mended, that the universe itself can be transformed, and that God, in and through all of this, can be glorified.

---

106. See esp. Isa 52:6–10; and also (among others) Isa 9:7; 26:3, 12; 27:5; 52:7; 55:12; 66:12; Jer 29:11; 30:10; 33:6, 9; 46:27; Ezek 34:29; 37:26; Mic 5:5; Hag 2:9; Zech 9:10.

107. Hays, *Moral Vision*, 198.

108. On the relationship between "image of God" and this issue, see above, pp. 371–72. The "steward" analogy, despite its problems, is still, in my view, the best single way to depict human beings' role with respect to the created world. For the spectrum of opinion on the stewardship imagery, see esp. the collection of essays in R. J. Berry, ed., *Environmental Stewardship: Critical Perspectives—Past and Present* (London: T&T Clark, 2006).

Part 4

FINAL MATTERS

Chapter 25

CONCLUSION

AS I REACH the end of this volume, I am half tempted to go back to the beginning and start all over again. I am keenly aware of the many lacunae left in my attempt to describe the theology of the apostle Paul and his letters. I am also very conscious of the degree to which I have approached Paul from a particular perspective. Because I entered seminary only nine months after my conversion, my seminary days became very influential in forming my theological perspective. The seminary I attended—Trinity Evangelical Divinity School—was very deliberately (under the wise leadership of Kenneth Kantzer) a broadly evangelical institution, with an attempt to represent various theological traditions. Nevertheless, the theology I was taught there was broadly Reformational, with an emphasis on the Reformed side of this broad movement. At the same time, my involvement with the church I was attending and, ultimately, serving, exposed me to the baptist (small "b") tradition. I therefore emerged a Reformed Baptist—although the "Reformed" part eventually was modified a bit with Lutheran influences.

The point of this autobiography is to register my awareness that I have written this volume from a particular perspective. I emphasize that I have worked hard—yes, even struggled—to let the text have its way, to allow it to take me wherever it was leading. I hope I have, at least in some measure, allowed that to happen. And the careful reader of this volume will note the many places where I depart from "Reformed Baptist" orthodoxy in the interpretations I adopt and views I argue for.

Another aspect of this volume that makes me want to start all over again—or at least revise significantly—is my failure to integrate Paul's theology with other New Testament "theologies." As an evangelical, I am committed to the ultimate unity of New Testament theology—without, of course, ignoring or dismissing the very real diversity we find. Yet I also had to recognize, as I worked on this volume, that I was not writing a New Testament theology, and that others have taken up this task and done it very well.

I write this theology of Paul at a time when two somewhat contrasting directions of emphasis are evident in the theological academy. On the one hand, as I mentioned in the introduction (thus, creating a sort of *inclusio*), books and articles on Paul and his theology are pouring off the presses like a waterfall at flood stage. On the other hand, however, many today think that Paul's theology has been given too large a role in shaping our theology as a whole—whether at the academic, pastoral, or personal level. This accusation is somewhat fair. We who stand in the Reformation tradition have often been guilty of working implicitly with a "canon within the canon," privileging Paul's own way of communicating the significance of Christ and then either ignoring other New Testament voices or forcing them to sing Paul's own tune. I hear and understand this complaint. And yet, my years of studying Paul have convinced me yet again about just how much he has to contribute to our vision of Christ and the life that flows from our relationship with him. Paul's is not the only voice, and perhaps not even the foundational voice, but his is one very important voice.

My prayer for myself over these years of working on Paul is that my study would accomplish for me the goal Paul himself sets forth—a renewed mind (Rom 12:2). It is my prayer that this would be the effect on those who read this volume.

Bibliography

Aageson, James W. *Paul, the Pastoral Epistles, and the Early Church*. Library of Pauline Studies. Peabody, MA: Hendrickson, 2008.

Abasciano, Brian J. "Corporate Election in Romans 9: A Reply to Thomas Schreiner." *JETS* 49 (2006): 351–71.

Abbott, T. K. *A Critical and Exegetical Commentary on the Epistles to the Ephesians and to the Colossians*. ICC. Edinburgh: T&T Clark, 1897.

Adams, Edward. *Constructing the World: A Study in Paul's Cosmological Language*. SNTW. Edinburgh: T&T Clark, 2000.

Aernie, Jeffrey W. "Tablets of Fleshly Hearts: Paul and Ezekiel in Concert." *JSPL* 6 (2016): 55–73.

Aletti, Jean Noël. *Colossiens 1,15–20: Genre et Exégèse du texte—function de la thématique sapientielle*. AnBib 91. Rome: Pontifical Biblical Institute, 1981.

———. *Essai sur l'ecclesiologie des Lettres de Saint-Paul*. Études Bibliques 2.60. Paris: Gabalda, 2009.

———. *Justification by Faith in the Letters of Saint Paul: Keys to Interpretation*. AnBib Studia 5. Rome: Gregorian & Biblical Press, 2015.

Alexander, T. Desmond. *From Eden to the New Jerusalem: An Introduction to Biblical Theology*. Grand Rapids: Kregel, 2008.

———. "Further Observations on the Term 'Seed' in Genesis." *TynBul* 48 (1997): 363–67.

Alford, Henry. *The Greek Testament*. Rev. ed. 8 vols. Chicago: Moody, 1958.

Allen, R. Michael. *The Christ's Faith: A Dogmatic Account*. T&T Clark Studies in Systematic Theology. London: T&T Clark, 2009.

———. "'From the Time He Took on the Form of a Servant': The Christ's Pilgrimage of Faith." *International Journal of Systematic Theology* 16 (2014): 4–24.

———. *Justification and the Gospel: Understanding the Contexts and Controversies*. Grand Rapids: Baker, 2013.

———. *Sanctification*. New Studies in Dogmatics. Grand Rapids: Zondervan Academic, 2017.

Allen, R. Michael, and Daniel J. Treier. "Dogmatic Theology and Biblical Perspectives on Justification: A Reply to Leithart." *WTJ* 70 (2008): 105–10.

Allison, Dale C., Jr. "Jesus and the Covenant: A Response to E. P. Sanders." *JSNT* 29 (1987): 57–78.

Allo, E. Bernard. *Saint Paul: Première épître aux Corinthiens*. Études Bibliques. Paris: Gabalda, 1934.

———. *Saint Paul: Seconde épître aux Corinthiens*. Études Bibliques. Paris: Gabalda, 1937.

American Heritage Dictionary of the English Language. 4th ed. Boston: Houghton Mifflin Harcourt, 2009.

Ames, William. *The Marrow of Theology*. Repr., Durham, NC: Labyrinth, 1983.

Anderson, Garwood P. *Paul's New Perspective: Charting a Soteriological Journey*. Downers Grove, IL: InterVarsity Press, 2016.

Archer, Gleason L. "The Case for the Mid-Seventieth-Week Rapture Position." Pages 113–46 in *Three Views on the Rapture: Pre-, Mid-, or Post-Tribulation*. By Richard R. Reiter, Paul D. Feinberg, Gleason L. Archer, and Douglas J. Moo. Repr., Grand Rapids: Zondervan, 1994.

Arnold, Clinton E. *The Colossian Syncretism: The Interface between Christianity and Folk Belief in Colossae*. WUNT 2/77. Tübingen: Mohr Siebeck, 1995. Repr., Grand Rapids: Baker, 1996.

———. *Ephesians*. ZECNT. Grand Rapids: Zondervan, 2010.

———. *Ephesians: Power and Magic. The Concept of Power in Ephesians and Its Historical Setting*. Grand Rapids: Baker, 1992.

————. "Jesus Christ: 'Head' of the Church (Colossians and Ephesians)." Pages 346–66 in *Jesus of Nazareth, Lord and Christ: Essays on the Historical Jesus and New Testament Christology*. Edited by Joel B. Green and Max Turner. Grand Rapids: Eerdmans, 1994.

————. *Powers of Darkness: Principalities and Powers in Paul's Letters*. Downers Grove, IL: InterVarsity Press, 1992.

Arzt-Grabner, Peter. *2. Korinther*. Papyrologische Kommentare Zum Neuen Testament 4. Göttingen: Vandenhoeck & Ruprecht, 2014.

————. "Onesimus Erro: Zur Vorgeschichte des Philemonbriefes." *ZNW* 95 (2004): 131–43.

Aulén, Gustav. *Christus Victor: An Historical Study of the Three Main Types of the Idea of Atonement*. New York: Macmillan, 1931.

Auler, Samuel. "More Than a Gift: Revisiting Paul's Collection for Jerusalem and the Pilgrimage of Gentiles." *JSPL* 6 (2016): 143–60.

Aune, David E. *Prophecy in Early Christianity and the Ancient Mediterranean World*. Grand Rapids: Eerdmans, 1983.

Avemarie, Friedrich. "Erwählung und Vergeltung: Zur optionalen Struktur rabbischer Soteriologie." *NTS* 45 (1999): 108–26.

————. *Torah und Leben: Untersuchungen zur Heilsbedeutung der Torah in der frühen Rabbinischen Literatur*. WUNT 2/92. Tübingen: Mohr Siebeck, 1996.

————. "Die Werke des Gesetzes im Spiegel des Jakobusbriefs: A Very Old Perspective on Paul." *ZTK* 98 (2001): 282–309.

Averbeck, Richard. "Crucial Features of Sin Offering Atonement in Leviticus 4–5 and 16." Unpublished manuscript.

Bachmann, Michael. "The Church and the Israel of God: On the Meaning and Ecclesiastical Relevance of the Benediction at the End of Galatians." Pages 101–23 in *Anti-Judaism in Galatians? Exegetical Studies on a Polemical Letter and on Paul's Theology*. Grand Rapids: Eerdmans, 2008.

————. "Keil oder Mikroskop? Zur jüngeren Diskussion um den Ausdruck 'Werke des Gesetzes.'" Pages 72–102 in *Lutherische und Neue Perspektive: Beiträge zu einem Schüsselproblem der gegenwärtigen exegetischen Diskussion*. Edited by Michael Bachmann. WUNT 2/182. Tübingen: Mohr Siebeck, 2005.

Bahnsen, Greg L. *Theonomy in Christian Ethics*. Nutley, NJ: Craig Press, 1984.

Bailey, Daniel P. "Biblical and Greco-Roman Uses of *Hilastērion* in Romans 3:25 and 4 Maccabees 17:22 (Codex S)." Pages 824–67 in *Biblical Theology of the New Testament*. By Peter Stuhlmacher. Edited by Daniel P. Bailey. Grand Rapids: Eerdmans, 2018.

————. "Concepts of *Stellvertretung* in the Interpretation of Isaiah 53." Pages 88–103 in *Jesus and the Suffering Servant: Isaiah 53 and Christian Origins*. Edited by William H. Bellinger Jr. and William R. Farmer. Harrisburg, PA: Trinity Press International, 1998.

Balch, David L. "Household Codes." Pages 25–35 in *Greco-Roman Literature and the New Testament: Selected Forms and Genres*. Edited by David Aune. Atlanta: Scholars Press, 1988.

Ball, John. *A Treatise of the Covenant of Grace*. London, 1645.

Balla, Peter. "2 Corinthians." Pages 753–83 in *Commentary on the New Testament Use of the Old Testament*. Edited by G. K. Beale and D. A. Carson. Grand Rapids: Baker, 2007.

————. *Challenges to New Testament Theology*. Peabody, MA: Hendrickson, 1997.

Bandstra, Andrew John. *The Law and the Elements of the World: An Exegetical Study in Aspects of Paul's Teaching*. Kampen: Kok, 1964.

Banks, Robert. *Paul's Idea of Community: The Early House Churches in their Cultural Setting*. Rev. ed. Peabody, MA: Hendrickson, 1994.

Barclay, John M. G. "Apocalyptic Allegiance and Disinvestment in the World: A Reading of 1 Corinthians 7:25–35." Pages 257–74 in *Paul and the Apocalyptic Imagination*. Edited by Ben C. Blackwell, John K. Goodrich, and Jason Maston. Minneapolis: Fortress, 2016.

————. *Colossians and Philemon*. NTG. Sheffield: Sheffield Academic, 1997.

————. "Conflict in Thessalonica." *CBQ* 55 (1993): 512–30.

————. *Obeying the Truth: A Study of Paul's Ethics in Galatians*. Edinburgh: T&T Clark, 1988.

————. "Ordinary But Different: Colossians and Hidden Moral Identity." *ABR* 49 (2001): 34–52.

————. *Paul and the Gift*. Grand Rapids: Eerdmans, 2015.

————. "Paul and the Gift to Jerusalem: Overcoming the Problems of the Long-Distance Gift." Pages 88–97 in *Poverty in the Early Church and Today: A Conversation*. Edited by Steve Walton and Hannah Swithinbank. London: T&T Clark, 2019.

———. "Paul, Judaism, and the Jewish People." Pages 188–201 in *The Blackwell Companion to Paul*. Edited by Stephen Westerholm. Chichester: Wiley-Blackwell, 2011.

———. "Paul, Philemon and the Dilemma of Christian Slave-Ownership." *NTS* 37 (1991): 161–86.

———. "Paul, Roman Religion and the Emperor: Mapping the Point of Conflict." Pages 345–62 in *Pauline Churches and Diaspora Jews*. Tübingen: Mohr Siebeck, 2011.

———. "Paul's Story: Theology as Testimony." Pages 133–56 in *Narrative Dynamics in Paul: A Critical Assessment*. Edited by Bruce Longenecker. Louisville: Westminster John Knox, 2002.

———. "Paul, the Gift and the Battle over Gentile Circumcision: Revisiting the Logic of Galatians." *ABR* 58 (2010): 36–56.

Barker, Paul A. *The Triumph of Grace in Deuteronomy: Faithless Israel, Faithful Yahweh in Deuteronomy*. Paternoster Biblical Monographs. Waynesboro, GA: Paternoster, 2004.

Barnett, Paul. *Jesus and the Rise of Early Christianity: A History of New Testament Times*. Downers Grove, IL: InterVarsity Press, 1999.

———. *Paul: Missionary of Jesus*. Grand Rapids: Eerdmans, 2008.

———. *The Second Epistle to the Corinthians*. NICNT. Grand Rapids: Eerdmans, 1997.

Barr, James. *The Concept of Biblical Theology: An Old Testament Perspective*. Minneapolis: Augsburg Fortress, 1999.

Barrett, C. K. "The Allegory of Abraham, Sarah, and Hagar in the Argument of Galatians." Pages 1–16 in *Rechtfertigung: Festschrift für Ernst Käsemann zum 70. Geburtstag*. Edited by Johannes Friedrich, Wolfgang Pöhlmann, and Peter Stuhlmacher. Göttingen: Vandenhoeck & Ruprecht, 1976.

———. *The Epistle to the Romans*. HNTC. New York: Harper & Row, 1958.

———. *The First Epistle to the Corinthians*. BNTC. London: Black, 1993.

———. *From First Adam to Last: A Study in Pauline Theology*. Hewett Lectures 1961. London: Adam & Charles Black, 1962.

———. "Paul's Opponents in II Corinthians." *NTS* 17 (1971): 233–54.

Barrosse, T. "Death and Sin in Saint Paul's Epistle to the Romans." *CBQ* 15 (1953): 449–55.

Bartchy, S. Scott. *Mallon Chrēsai: First-Century Slavery and the Interpretation of 1 Corinthians 7:21*. SBLDS 11. Missoula: SBL, 1973.

Barth, Karl. *Church and State*. London: SCM, 1939.

———. *Church Dogmatics*. 14 vols. Edinburgh: T&T Clark, 1936–1977.

———. *The Epistle to the Romans*. London: Oxford University Press, 1933.

Barth, Markus. *Ephesians: Introduction, Translation, and Commentary on Chapters 1–3*. AB 34. Garden City: Doubleday, 1974.

———. *Ephesians: Translation and Commentary on Chapters 4–6*. AB 34A. Garden City: Doubleday, 1974.

Barth, Markus, and Helmut Blanke. *Colossians*. AB 34B. New York: Doubleday, 1994.

———. *The Letter to Philemon*. ECC. Grand Rapids: Eerdmans, 2000.

Bartholomew, Craig G. *Where Mortals Dwell: A Christian View of Place for Today*. Grand Rapids: Baker, 2011.

Bassler, Jouette M. "Paul's Theology: Whence and Whither?" Pages 3–17 in *Pauline Theology, Vol. 2: 1 & 2 Corinthians*. Edited by David M. Hay. Minneapolis: Augsburg Fortress, 1993.

Bates, Matthew W. *Salvation by Allegiance Alone*. Grand Rapids: Baker, 2017.

Bauckham, Richard. "Barnabas in Galatians." *JSNT* 2 (1979): 61–70.

———. *The Bible and Ecology: Rediscovering the Community of Creation*. Waco, TX: Baylor University Press, 2010.

———. "Colossians 1:24 Again: The Apocalyptic Motif." *EvQ* 47 (1975): 168–70.

———. *Gospel of Glory: Major Themes in Johannine Theology*. Grand Rapids: Eerdmans, 2015.

———. "James and the Jerusalem Church." Pages 468–70 in *The Book of Acts in Its Palestinian Setting*. Edited by Richard Bauckham. Vol. 4 of *The Book of Acts in Its First Century Setting*. Edited by Bruce W. Winter. Grand Rapids: Eerdmans, 1995.

———. "James, Peter, and the Gentiles." Pages 91–142 in *The Missions of James, Peter and Paul: Tensions in Early Christianity*. Edited by Bruce Chilton and Craig Evans. Leiden: Brill, 2004.

———. *Jesus and the Eyewitnesses: The Gospels as Eyewitness Testimony*. 2nd ed. Grand Rapids: Eerdmans, 2017.

———. *Jesus and the God of Israel: God Crucified and Other Studies on the New Testament's Christology of Divine Identity*. Grand Rapids: Eerdmans, 2008.

———. "The Millennium." Pages 123–48 in *God Will Be All in All: The Eschatology of Jürgen Moltmann*. Edited by Richard Bauckham. Minneapolis: Fortress, 2001.

———. "The Parting of the Ways: What Happened and Why?" *ST* 47 (1993): 135–51.

———. "The Story of the Earth according to Paul: Romans 8:18–23." *RevExp* 108 (2011): 91–97.

———. "The Throne of God and the Worship of Jesus." Pages 43–69 in *The Jewish Roots of Christological Monotheism*. Edited by C. C. Newman, J. R. Davila, and G. S. Lewis. Supplements to the Journal for the Study of Judaism 63. Leiden: Brill, 1999.

———. "Universalism: A Historical Survey." *Them* 4.2 (1979): 47–54.

———. "Where Is Wisdom to Be Found? Colossians 1.15–20 (2)." Pages 129–38 in *Reading Texts, Seeking Wisdom: Scripture and Theology*. Edited by David F. Ford and Graham Stanton. Grand Rapids: Eerdmans, 2003.

Baugh, Steven M. "The Poetic Form of Col 1:15–20." *WTJ* 47 (1985): 227–44.

Baum, Armin D. "Content and Form: Authorship Attribution and Pseudonymity in Ancient Speeches, Letters, Lectures, and Translations—A Rejoinder to Bart Ehrman." *JBL* 136 (2017): 381–403.

———. "Paul's Conflicting Statements on Female Public Speaking (1 Cor. 11:5) and Silence (1 Cor. 14:34–35): A New Suggestion." *TynBul* 65 (2014): 247–74.

———. *Pseudepigraphie und literarische Falschung im frühen Christentum*. WUNT 2/138. Tübingen: Mohr Siebeck, 2001.

Bavinck, Herman. *Reformed Dogmatics*. 4 vols. Grand Rapids: Baker, 2008.

Beale, G. K. *1–2 Thessalonians*. IVPNTC 13. Downers Grove, IL: InterVarsity Press, 2003.

———. "The Background of Ἐκκλησία Revisited." *JSNT* 38 (2015): 151–68.

———. "The Cognitive Peripheral Vision of Biblical Authors." *WTJ* 76 (2014): 263–93.

———. *Colossians and Philemon*. BECNT. Grand Rapids: Baker Academic, 2019.

———. "The Eschatological Conception of New Testament Theology." Pages 11–52 in *"The Reader Must Understand": Eschatology in Bible and Theology*. Edited by K. E. Brower and M. W. Elliott. Leicester: Inter-Varsity Press, 1997.

———. *Handbook on the New Testament Use of the Old Testament: Exegesis and Interpretation*. Grand Rapids: Baker, 2012.

———. "Myth, History, and Inspiration: A Review Article of *Inspiration and Incarnation*." *JETS* 49 (2006): 287–312.

———. *A New Testament Biblical Theology: The Unfolding of the Old Testament in the New*. Grand Rapids: Baker, 2011.

———. "The Old Testament Background of Reconciliation in 2 Corinthians 5–7 and Its Bearing on the Literary Problem of 2 Corinthians 6:14–7:1." *NTS* 35 (1989): 550–81.

———. "Peace and Mercy upon the Israel of God: The Old Testament Background of Galatians 6,16b." *Bib* 80 (1999): 204–23.

———. *The Right Doctrine from the Wrong Texts? Essays on the Use of the Old Testament in the New*. Grand Rapids: Baker, 1994.

———. *The Temple and the Church's Mission: A Biblical Theology of the Dwelling Place of God*. NSBT. Downers Grove, IL: InterVarsity Press, 2004.

Beale, G. K., and D. A. Carson, eds. *Commentary on the New Testament Use of the Old Testament*. Grand Rapids: Baker, 2007.

Beard, Mary. *The Roman Triumph*. Cambridge: Harvard University Press, 2007.

Beasley-Murray, G. R. *Baptism in the New Testament*. Grand Rapids: Eerdmans, 1962.

Beattie, Gillian. *Women and Marriage in Paul and His Early Interpreters*. JSNTSup 296. London: T&T Clark, 2005.

Becker, Jürgen. *Paul: Apostle to the Gentiles*. Louisville: Westminster John Knox, 1993.

Beetham, Christopher A. *Echoes of Scripture in the Letter of Paul to the Colossians*. BibInt 96. Leiden: Brill, 2009. Repr., Atlanta: Society of Biblical Literature, 2010.

Beker, J. Christiaan. "Echoes and Intertextuality: On the Role of Scripture in Paul's Theology." Pages 64–69 in *Paul and the Scriptures of Israel*. Edited by Craig A. Evans and James A. Sanders. JSNTSup 83. Sheffield: JSOT, 1993.

———. *Paul the Apostle: The Triumph of God in Life and Thought*. Philadelphia: Fortress, 1980.

———. "Recasting Pauline Theology: The Coherence-Contingency Scheme as Interpretive Model." Pages 15–24 in *Pauline Theology, Vol. 1: Thessalonians, Philippians, Galatians, Philemon*. Edited by Jouette M. Bassler. Minneapolis: Augsburg Fortress, 1991.

Bell, Richard H. *Deliver Us from Evil: Interpreting the Redemption from the Power of Satan in New Testament Theology*. WUNT 2/216. Tübingen: Mohr Siebeck, 2007.

———. *No One Seeks for God: An Exegetical and Theological Study of Romans 1.18–3.20.* WUNT 2/106. Tübingen: Mohr Siebeck, 1998.

———. "Sacrifice and Christology in Paul." *JTS* 53 (2002): 1–27.

Belleville, Linda. *Reflections of Glory: Paul's Polemical Use of the Moses-Doxa Tradition in 2 Corinthians 3:1–18.* JSNTSup 52. Sheffield: JSOT, 1991.

———. "Teaching and Usurping Authority." Pages 205–23 in *Discovering Biblical Equality: Complementarity without Hierarchy.* Edited by Ronald W. Pierce and Rebecca Merrill Groothuis. Downers Grove, IL: InterVarsity Press, 2004.

———. "'Under Law': Structural Analysis and the Pauline Concept of Law in Galatians 3:21–4:11." *JSNT* 26 (1986): 53–78.

Bengel, J. A. *Gnomon of the New Testament.* 5 vols. Repr., Edinburgh: T&T Clark, 1860.

Bennett, Thomas Andrew. *Labor of God: The Agony of the Cross and Birth of the Church.* Waco, TX: Baylor University Press, 2017.

Berding, Kenneth. "Confusing Word and Concept in 'Spiritual Gifts': Have We Forgotten James Barr's Exhortations?" *JETS* 43 (2000): 37–51.

Berkhof, Louis. *Systematic Theology.* Grand Rapids: Eerdmans, 1938.

Berry, R. J., ed. *Environmental Stewardship: Critical Perspectives—Past and Present.* London: T&T Clark, 2006.

Bertschmann, Dorothea H. *Bowing before Christ—Nodding to the State? Reading Paul Politically with Oliver O'Donovan and John Howard Yoder.* LNTS 502. London: Bloomsbury, 2014.

Best, Ernest. *A Critical and Exegetical Commentary on Ephesians.* ICC. Edinburgh: T&T Clark, 1998.

———. *The First and Second Epistles to the Thessalonians.* BNTC. Peabody, MA: Hendrickson, 1993.

———. *One Body in Christ: A Study in the Relationship of the Church to Christ in the Epistles of the Apostle Paul.* London: SPCK, 1955.

Best, T. F. "The Apostle Paul and E. P. Sanders: The Significance of Paul and Palestinian Judaism." *RestQ* 25 (1982): 65–74.

Betz, Hans Dieter. *Galatians: A Commentary on Paul's Letter to the Churches in Galatia.* Hermeneia. Minneapolis: Fortress, 1979.

Betz, Otto. "Der Katechon." *NTS* 9 (1963): 276–91.

Bevere, Allan R. *Sharing in the Inheritance: Identity and the Moral Life in Colossians.* JSNTSup 226. Sheffield: Sheffield Academic, 2003.

Bieringer, Reimund. "Dying and Being Raised For: Shifts in the Meaning of Hyper in 2 Cor 5:14–15." Pages 163–75 in *Theologizing in the Corinthian Conflict: Studies in the Exegesis and Theology of 2 Corinthians.* Edited by M. S. Ibita, D. Kurek-Chomycz, R. Bieringer, and T. Vollmer. Leuven: Peeters, 2013.

Billings, J. Todd. *Calvin, Participation, and the Gift: The Activity of Believers in Union with Christ.* Changing Paradigms in Historical and Systematic Theology. Oxford: Oxford University Press, 2007.

Bird, Michael F. *An Anomalous Jew: Paul among Jews, Greeks, and Romans.* Grand Rapids: Eerdmans, 2016.

———. *Evangelical Theology: A Biblical and Systematic Introduction.* Grand Rapids: Zondervan, 2013.

———. "Justification as Forensic Declaration and Covenant Membership: A Via Media between Reformed and Revisionist Readings of Paul." *TynBul* 57.1 (2006): 109–30.

———. *Romans.* Story of God Bible Commentary. Grand Rapids: Zondervan, 2016.

———. *The Saving Righteousness of God: Studies on Paul, Justification and the New Perspective.* Paternoster Biblical Monographs. Waynesboro, GA: Paternoster, 2007.

Bird, Michael F., and Scott Harrower, eds. *Trinity without Hierarchy: Reclaiming Nicene Orthodoxy in Evangelical Theology.* Grand Rapids: Kregel, 2018.

Bird, Michael F., and Preston M. Sprinkle, eds. *The Faith of Jesus Christ: Exegetical, Biblical, and Theological Studies.* Peabody, MA: Hendrickson, 2009.

Bjerkelund, Carl J. *Parakalô. Form, Funktion und Sinn der Parakalô-Sätze in den Paulinischen Briefen.* Bibliotheca Theologica Norvegica 1. Oslo: Universitetsforlaget, 1967.

Blackwell, Ben C. *Christosis: Soteriology in Light of Deification in Irenaeus and Cyril of Alexandria.* WUNT 2/314. Tübingen: Mohr Siebeck, 2011.

———. "Paul and Judaism." *JSPL* 5 (2016): 157–67.

Blackwell, Ben C., John K. Goodrich, and Jason Maston. "Paul and the Apocalyptic Imagination: An Introduction." Pages 3–22 in *Paul and the Apocalyptic Imagination.* Edited by Ben C. Blackwell, John K. Goodrich, and Jason Maston. Minneapolis: Fortress, 2016.

Blaising, Craig A., and Darryl L. Bock, eds. *Dispensationalism, Israel and the Church: The Search for Definition*. Grand Rapids: Zondervan, 1992.

Blaising, Craig A., Alan Hultberg, and Douglas J. Moo. *Three Views on the Rapture: Pretribulation, Prewrath, or Posttribulation*. Edited by Alan Hultberg. Counterpoints. Grand Rapids: Zondervan, 2010.

Blank, Josef. *Paulus und Jesus: Eine theologische Grundlegung*. SANT 18. Munich: Kösel, 1968.

Blass, F., A. Debrunner, and R. W. Funk. *A Greek Grammar of the New Testament*. Chicago: University of Chicago Press, 1961.

Blinzler, Joseph. "Lexikalisches zu dem τὰ στοιχεῖα τοῦ κόσμου bei Paulus." Pages 429–43 in vol. 2 of *Studiorum Paulinorum Congressus Internationalis Catholicus 1961*. AnBib 17–18. Rome: Pontifical Biblical Institute, 1963.

———. "Zur Auslegung von I Kor 7,14." Pages 23–41 in *Neutestamentliche Aufsätze: Festschrift für Josef Schmid*. Edited by Joseph Blinzler, Otto Kuss, and Franz Mussner. Regensburg: Friedrich Puster, 1963.

Blocher, Henri A. G. *"Agnus Victor*: The Atonement as Victory and Vicarious Punishment." Pages 67–91 in *What Does It Mean to Be Saved? Broadening Evangelical Horizons of Salvation*. Edited by John G. Stackhouse Jr. Grand Rapids: Baker Academic, 2002.

———. "Biblical Metaphors and the Doctrine of the Atonement." *JETS* 47 (2004): 629–45.

———. "Everlasting Punishment and the Problem of Evil." Pages 283–312 in *Universalism and the Doctrine of Hell*. Edited by Nigel M. de S. Cameron. Carlisle: Paternoster, 1992.

———. "Justification of the Ungodly (Sola Fide): Theological Reflections." Pages 465–500 in *The Paradoxes of Paul*. Vol. 2 of *Justification and Variegated Nomism*. Edited by D. A. Carson, Peter T. O'Brien, and Mark A. Seifrid. WUNT 2/140. Tübingen: Mohr Siebeck, 2004.

———. "Old Covenant, New Covenant." Pages 240–70 in *Always Reforming: Explorations in Systematic Theology*. Edited by A. T. B. McGowan. Downers Grove, IL: InterVarsity Press, 2006.

Blomberg, Craig L. "Degrees of Reward in the Kingdom of Heaven?" *JETS* 35 (1992): 159–72.

———. "Neither Hierarchicalist nor Egalitarian: Gender Roles in Paul." Pages 283–326 in *Paul and His Theology*. Edited by Stanley E. Porter. Pauline Studies 3. Leiden: Brill, 2006.

———. *Neither Poverty nor Riches: A Biblical Theology of Material Possessions*. NSBT. Downers Grove, IL: IVP Academic, 1999.

———. "Quotations, Allusions, and Echoes of Jesus in Paul." Pages 129–43 in *Studies in the Pauline Epistles: Essays in Honor of Douglas J. Moo*. Edited by Matthew S. Harmon and Jay E. Smith. Grand Rapids: Zondervan, 2014.

Boccaccini, Gabriele. "The Three Paths to Salvation of Paul the Jew." Pages 1–19 in *Paul the Jew: Rereading the Apostle as a Figure of Second Temple Judaism*. Edited by Gabriele Boccaccini and Carlos A. Segovia. Minneapolis: Fortress, 2016.

Boccaccini, Gabriele, and Carlos A. Segovia, eds. *Paul the Jew: Rereading the Apostle as a Figure of Second Temple Judaism*. Minneapolis: Fortress, 2016.

Bock, Darrell L. "'The New Man' as Community in Colossians and Ephesians." Pages 157–67 in *Integrity of Heart, Skillfulness of Hands: Biblical and Leadership Studies in Honor of Donald K. Campbell*. Edited by C. Dyer and R. B. Zuck. Grand Rapids: Baker, 1994.

Bockmuehl, Markus N. A. *A Commentary on the Epistle to the Philippians*. BNTC 11. Peabody, MA: Hendrickson, 1998.

———. *Jewish Law in Gentile Churches: Halakah and the Beginning of Christian Public Ethics*. Edinburgh: T&T Clark, 2000.

———. *Revelation and Mystery in Ancient Judaism and Pauline Christianity*. WUNT 2/36. Tübingen: Mohr Siebeck, 1990.

Boda, Mark J. *A Severe Mercy: Sin and Its Remedy in the Old Testament*. Winona Lake, IN: Eisenbrauns, 2009.

Boersma, Hans. *Violence, Hospitality, and the Cross: Reappropriating the Atonement Tradition*. Grand Rapids: Baker, 2004.

Bolton, Samuel. *The True Bounds of Christian Freedom*. Repr., London: Banner of Truth, 1964 (1645).

Boman, Thorlief. "Die dreifache Würde des Völkerapostels." *ST* 29 (1975): 63–69.

Bonnard, Pierre. *L'épître de saint Paul aux Galates*. 2nd ed. CNT 9. Neuchatel: Delachaux & Niestle, 1972.

Borg, Marcus J., and John Dominic Crossan. *The First Paul: Reclaiming the Radical Visionary behind the Church's Conservative Icon*. New York: HarperCollins, 2009.

Boring, M. Eugene. *I and II Thessalonians: A Commentary*. NTL. Louisville: Westminster John Knox, 2015.

———. "The Language of Universal Salvation in Paul." *JBL* 105 (1986): 269–92.

Bornkamm, Gunther. "The Letter to the Romans as Paul's Last Will and Testament." Pages 16–28 in *The Romans Debate*. Edited by K. P. Donfried. Rev. and exp. ed. Peabody, MA: Hendrickson, 1991.

Bornkamm, H. *Luther and the Old Testament*. Philadelphia: Fortress, 1969.

Boswell, J. *Christianity, Social Tolerance, and Homosexuality*. Chicago: University of Chicago Press, 1980.

Bousset, Wilhelm. *Kyrios Christos: A History of the Belief in Christ from the Beginnings of Christianity to Irenaeus*. Nashville: Abingdon, 1970.

Bouttier, Michel. *En Christ; Étude d'exégèse et de Théologie Pauliniennes*. Etudes d'histoire et de Philosophie Religieuses 54. Paris: Presses universitaires de France, 1962.

Bowens, Lisa M. *African American Readings of Paul: Reception, Resistance, and Transformation*. Grand Rapids: Eerdmans, 2020.

Boyarin, Daniel. *A Radical Jew: Paul and the Politics of Identity*. Berkeley: University of California Press, 1994.

Brannon, M. J. *The Heavenlies in Ephesians: A Lexical, Exegetical, and Conceptual Analysis*. LNTS 447. London: T&T Clark, 2011.

Breytenbach, Cilliers. "'Christus Starb für uns': Zur Tradition und paulinischen Rezeption der sogenannten 'Sterbeformeln.'" *NTS* 49 (2003): 447–75.

———. *Versöhnung: Eine Studie zur paulinischen Soteriologie*. WMANT 60. Neukirchen-Vluyn: Neukirchener, 1989.

Brown, Jared. "'The Obedience of Faith' in Romans: An Exegetical and Rhetorical Case for Polyvalence." PhD diss., Wheaton College, 2019.

Brown, Raymond E. *An Introduction to the New Testament*. New York: Doubleday, 1997.

———. *The Semitic Background of the Term "Mystery" in the New Testament*. Philadelphia: Fortress, 1968.

Brownson, James V. *Bible, Gender, Sexuality: Reframing the Church's Debate on Same-Sex Relationships*. Grand Rapids: Eerdmans, 2013.

Bruce, F. F. *I and II Corinthians*. NCB. Grand Rapids: Eerdmans, 1971.

———. *1 and 2 Thessalonians*. WBC 45. Dallas: Word, 1982.

———. *The Epistle to the Galatians: A Commentary on the Greek Text*. NIGTC. Grand Rapids: Eerdmans, 1982.

———. *The Epistles to the Colossians, to Philemon, and to the Ephesians*. NICNT. Grand Rapids: Eerdmans, 1984.

———. *The Letter of Paul to the Romans*. TNTC. Grand Rapids: Eerdmans, 1985.

———. *Paul, Apostle of the Heart Set Free*. Grand Rapids: Eerdmans, 1978.

———. "The Romans Debate—Continued." Pages 175–94 in *The Romans Debate*. Edited by K. P. Donfried. Rev. ed. Peabody, MA: Hendrickson, 1991.

Brueggemann, Walter. *The Land: Place as Gift, Promise, and Challenge in Biblical Faith*. 2nd ed. Minneapolis: Fortress, 2002.

Bryan, Steven M. *Jesus and Israel's Traditions of Judgement and Restoration*. SNTSMS 117. Cambridge: Cambridge University Press, 2002.

Buck, Charles, and Greer Taylor. *Saint Paul: A Study of the Development of His Thought*. New York: Scribner's Sons, 1969.

Bultmann, Rudolf. *Theology of the New Testament*. 2 Vols. New York: Scribner's Sons, 1951, 1955.

Burge, Gary M. *Jesus and the Land: The New Testament Challenge to "Holy Land" Theology*. Grand Rapids: Baker, 2010.

Burger, Christoph. *Schöpfung und Versöhnung: Studien zum Liturgischen Gut im Kolosser- und Epheserbrief*. WMANT 46. Neukirchener-Vluyn: Neukirchener, 1975.

Burke, Trevor J. *Adopted into God's Family: Exploring a Pauline Metaphor*. NSBT 22. Downers Grove, IL: InterVarsity Press, 2006.

———. *Family Matters: A Socio-Historical Study of Kinship Metaphors in 1 Thessalonians*. JSNTSup 247. London: T&T Clark, 2003.

———. "Paul's Role as 'Father' to the Corinthian 'Children' in Socio-Historical Context (1 Cor. 4:14–21)." Pages 95–113 in *Paul and the Corinthians: A Community in Conflict. Essays in Honour of Margaret Thrall*. Edited by T. J. Burke and J. K. Elliott. NovTSup 109. Leiden: Brill, 2003.

Burnett, Gary W. *Paul and the Salvation of the Individual*. BibInt 57. Leiden: Brill, 2001.

Burtchaell, Tunstead. *Philemon's Problem: A Theology of Grace*. Grand Rapids: Eerdmans, 1998.

Burton, Ernest de Witt. *A Critical and Exegetical Commentary on the Epistle to the Galatians*. ICC. Edinburgh: T&T Clark, 1921.

Byrne, Brendan. "Interpreting Romans Theologically in a Post-'New Perspective' Perspective." *HTR* 94 (2001): 227–41.

———. "The Problem of Nomos and the Relationship with Judaism in Romans." *CBQ* 62 (2000): 294–309.

———. *"Sons of God"—"Seed of Abraham": A Study of the Idea of the Sonship of God of All Christians in Paul against the Jewish Background.* AnBib 83. Rome: Biblical Institute Press, 1979.

Byrskog, Samuel. "Co-Senders, Co-Authors and Paul's Use of the First Person Plural." *ZNW* 87 (1996): 230–50.

Cable, Paul. "'We Await a Savior': 'Salvation' in Philippians." PhD diss., Wheaton College, 2017.

Caird, G. B., completed and edited by L. D. Hurst. *New Testament Theology.* Oxford: Clarendon, 1994.

Callan, Terrance. *Dying and Rising with Christ: The Theology of Paul the Apostle.* New York: Paulist, 2006.

Calvin, John. *Commentaries on the Epistle of Paul the Apostle to the Romans.* Repr., Grand Rapids: Eerdmans, 1947.

———. *Commentaries on the Epistles of Paul to the Galatians and Ephesians.* Edinburgh: Thomas Clark, 1854.

———. *Galatians, Ephesians, Philippians, and Colossians.* Repr., Grand Rapids: Eerdmans, 1975.

Cambier, J.-M. *L'évangile de la justice et de la grace.* Vol. 1 of *L'évangile de Dieu selon l'épître aux Romains: Exégèse et théologie biblique.* StudNeot 3. Brussels: Desclée de Brouwer, 1967.

Campbell, Constantine R. "Metaphor, Reality, and Union with Christ." Pages 61–86 in *"In Christ" in Paul: Explorations in Paul's Theology of Union and Participation.* Edited by Michael J. Thate, Kevin J. Vanhoozer, and Constantine R. Campbell. WUNT 2/384. Tübingen: Mohr Siebeck, 2014.

———. *Paul and the Hope of Glory: An Exegetical and Theological Study.* Grand Rapids: Zondervan Academic, 2020.

———. *Paul and Union with Christ: An Exegetical and Theological Study.* Grand Rapids: Zondervan, 2012.

Campbell, Douglas A. *The Deliverance of God : An Apocalyptic Rereading of Justification in Paul.* Grand Rapids: Eerdmans, 2009.

———. *Framing Paul: An Epistolary Biography.* Grand Rapids: Eerdmans, 2014.

———. *Pauline Dogmatics: The Triumph of God's Love.* Grand Rapids: Eerdmans, 2020.

———. *The Quest for Paul's Gospel: A Suggested Strategy.* London: T&T Clark, 2005.

———. "Rereading Paul's ΔIKAIO-Language." Pages 196–213 in *Beyond Old and New Perspectives on Paul: Reflections on the Work of Douglas Campbell.* Edited by Chris Tilling. Eugene, OR: Cascade, 2014.

Campbell, William S. *Paul and the Creation of Christian Identity.* London: T&T Clark, 2008.

———. *Paul's Gospel in an Intercultural Context: Jew and Gentile in the Letter to the Romans.* Frankfurt: Peter Lang, 1991.

———. "Why Did Paul Write Romans?" *ExpTim* 85 (1974): 264–69.

Caneday, Ardel B. "The Faithfulness of Jesus Christ as a Theme in Paul's Theology in Galatians." Pages 185–205 in *The Faith of Jesus Christ: Exegetical, Biblical, and Theological Studies.* Edited by Michael F. Bird and Preston M. Sprinkle. Peabody, MA: Hendrickson, 2009.

Capes, David B. *The Divine Christ: Paul, the Lord Jesus, and the Scriptures of Israel.* Grand Rapids: Baker, 2018.

Caragounis, Chrys C. *The Development of Greek and the New Testament: Morphology, Syntax, Phonology, and Textual Transmission.* WUNT 2/167. Tübingen: Mohr Siebeck, 2004.

———. *The Ephesian Mysterion: Meaning and Content.* ConBNT 8. Lund: Gleerup, 1977.

Carr, Wesley. *Angels and Principalities: The Background, Meaning, and Development of the Pauline Phrase hai archai kai hai exousiai.* SNTSMS 42. Cambridge: Cambridge University Press, 1981.

Carraway, George. *Christ Is God over All: Romans 9:5 in the Context of Romans 9–11.* LNTS 489. London: Bloomsbury, 2013.

Carson, D. A. *Divine Sovereignty and Human Responsibility: Biblical Perspectives in Tension.* Grand Rapids: Baker, 1994.

———. *From Triumphalism to Maturity: An Exposition of 2 Corinthians 10–13.* Grand Rapids: Baker, 1984.

———. "Mystery and Fulfillment: Toward a More Comprehensive Paradigm of Paul's Understanding of the Old and the New." Pages 393–436 in *The Paradoxes of Paul.* Vol. 2 of *Justification and Variegated Nomism.* Edited by D. A. Carson, Peter T. O'Brien, and Mark A. Seifrid. WUNT 2/140. Tübingen: Mohr Siebeck, 2004.

———. *Showing the Spirit: A Theological Exposition of 1 Corinthians 12–14.* Grand Rapids: Baker, 1987.

———. "Summaries and Conclusions." Pages 543–48 in *The Complexities of Second Temple Judaism.* Vol. 1 of *Justification and Variegated Nomism.* Edited by D. A. Carson, Peter T. O'Brien, and Mark A. Seifrid. Tübingen: Mohr Siebeck, 2001.

———. "Systematic Theology and Biblical Theology." Pages 89–104 in *New Dictionary of Biblical Theology.* Edited by T. Desmond Alexander and Brian S. Rosner. Downers Grove, IL: InterVarsity Press, 2000.

———. "The Vindication of Imputation: On Fields of Discourse and, of Course, Semantic Fields." Pages 58–66 in *Justification: What's at Stake in the Current Debates?* Edited by M. A. Husbands and D. J. Treier. Downers Grove, IL: InterVarsity Press, 2004.

———. "What Is the Gospel—Revisited." Pages 147–70 in *For the Fame of God's Name: Essays in Honor of John Piper*. Edited by Sam Storms and Justin Taylor. Wheaton, IL: Crossway, 2010.

Carson, D. A., and Douglas J. Moo. *An Introduction to the New Testament*. 2nd ed. Grand Rapids: Zondervan, 2005.

Carson, D. A., Peter T. O'Brien, and Mark A. Seifrid, eds. *The Complexities of Second Temple Judaism*. Vol. 1 of *Justification and Variegated Nomism*. WUNT 2/140. Tübingen: Mohr Siebeck, 2001.

Cerfaux, Lucien. *Christ in the Theology of St. Paul*. New York: Herder and Herder, 1959.

———. *The Church in the Theology of St. Paul*. Freiburg: Herder and Herder, 1959.

Cervin, Richard. "Does Κεφαλή Mean 'Source' or 'Authority Over' in Greek Literature? A Rebuttal." *TrinJ* 10 (1989): 85–112.

Charlesworth, James H. "From Messianology to Christology: Problems and Prospects." Pages 3–35 in *The Messiah: Developments in Earliest Judaism and Christianity*. Edited by James H. Charlesworth. Minneapolis: Fortress, 2009.

Chester, Andrew. "The Christ of Paul." Pages 109–21 in *Redemption and Resistance: The Messianic Hopes of Jews and Christians in Antiquity*. Edited by Markus Bockmuehl and James Carleton Paget. London: T&T Clark, 2007.

———. *Messiah and Exaltation: Jewish Messianic and Visionary Traditions and New Testament Christology*. WUNT 2/207. Tübingen: Mohr Siebeck, 2007.

Chester, Stephen J. *Conversion at Corinth: Perspectives on Conversion in Paul's Theology and the Corinthian Church*. SNTW. London: T&T Clark, 2003.

———. "It Is No Longer I Who Live: Justification by Faith and Participation in Christ in Martin Luther's Exegesis of Galatians." *NTS* 55 (2009): 315–37.

———. "Paul and the Galatian Believers." Pages 63–78 in *The Blackwell Companion to Paul*. Edited by Stephen Westerholm. Chichester: Wiley-Blackwell, 2011.

———. *Reading Paul with the Reformers*. Grand Rapids: Eerdmans, 2017.

———. "The Retrospective View of Romans 7: Paul's Past in Present Perspective." Pages 57–103 in *Perspectives on Our Struggle with Sin: 3 Views of Romans 7*. Edited by T. L. Wilder. Nashville: B&H, 2011.

Cheung, Alex T. *Idol Food in Corinth: Jewish Background and Pauline Legacy*. JSNTSup 176. Sheffield: Sheffield Academic Press, 1999.

Childs, Brevard S. *The New Testament as Canon: An Introduction*. Philadelphia: Fortress, 1985.

Chow, John K. *Patronage and Power: A Study of Social Networks in Corinth*. JSNTSup 75. Sheffield: JSOT, 1992.

Christiansen, Ellen Juhl. *The Covenant in Judaism and Paul: A Study of Ritual Boundaries as Identity Markers*. AGJU 27. Leiden: Brill, 1995.

Ciampa, Roy E. *The Presence and Function of Scripture in Galatians 1 and 2*. WUNT 2/102. Tübingen: Mohr Siebeck, 1998.

Ciampa, Roy E., and Brian S. Rosner. *The First Letter to the Corinthians*. PNTC. Grand Rapids: Eerdmans, 2010.

Clark, Bruce. *Completing Christ's Afflictions: Christ, Paul, and the Reconciliation of All Things*. WUNT 2/383. Tübingen: Mohr Siebeck, 2015.

Clark, Stephen B. *Man and Woman in Christ: An Examination of the Roles of Men and Women in Light of Scripture and the Social Sciences*. Edinburgh: T&T Clark, 1980.

Clarke, Andrew D. *A Pauline Theology of Church Leadership*. T&T Clark Library of Biblical Studies. London: T&T Clark, 2008.

———. *Secular and Christian Leadership in Corinth: A Socio-Historical and Exegetical Study of 1 Corinthians 1–6*. AGJU 18. Leiden: Brill, 1993.

Cohick, Lynn H. *The Letter to the Ephesians*. NICNT. Grand Rapids: Eerdmans, 2020.

———. "Philippians and Empire: Paul's Engagement with Imperialism and the Imperial Cult." Pages 166–82 in *Jesus Is Lord, Caesar Is Not: Evaluating Empire in New Testament Studies*. Edited by Scot McKnight and Joseph B. Modica. Downers Grove, IL: InterVarsity Press, 2013.

———. "Tyranny, Authority, Service: Leadership and Headship in the New Testament." *Ex Auditu* 28 (2014): 74–89.

Cole, Graham A. *Christ the Peacemaker: How Atonement Brings Shalom*. NSBT 25. Downers Grove, IL: InterVarsity Press, 2009.

Collange, Jean-François. *L'épître de Saint Paul à Philémon*. CNT 11C. Geneva: Labor et Fides, 1987.

Collins, Adela Yarbro. "Jesus as Messiah and Son of God in the Letters of Paul." Pages 101–22 in *King and Messiah as Son of God: Divine, Human, and Angelic Messianic Figures in Biblical and Related Literature*. Edited by John J. Collins and Adela Yarbro Collins. Grand Rapids: Eerdmans, 2008.

Collins, C. John. "Galatians 3:16: What Kind of Exegete Was Paul?" *TynBul* 54 (2003): 75–86.

Collins, John N. *DIAKONIA: Re-interpreting the Ancient Sources*. Oxford: Oxford University Press, 1990.

Collins, Raymond F. *Studies on the First Letter to the Thessalonians*. BETL 66. Leuven: Leuven University Press, 1984.

Conzelmann, Hans. *An Outline of the Theology of the New Testament*. London: SCM, 1969.

Cooper, John W. *Body, Soul, and Life Everlasting: Biblical Anthropology and the Monism-Dualism Debate*. Grand Rapids: Eerdmans, 2000.

Corley, Bruce. "Interpreting Paul's Conversion: Then and Now." Pages 1–17 in *The Road from Damascus: The Impact of Paul's Conversion on His Life, Thought and Ministry*. Edited by Richard N. Longenecker. Grand Rapids: Eerdmans, 1997.

Cortez, Marc. *ReSourcing Theological Anthropology: A Constructive Account of Humanity in the Light of Christ*. Grand Rapids: Zondervan, 2017.

Cosgrove, Charles H. "Justification in Paul: A Linguistic and Theological Reflection." *JBL* 106 (1987): 653–70.

Cotton, John. *A Treatise of the Covenant of Grace*. 3rd ed. London, 1671.

Cottrell, Jack. "Conditional Election." Pages 51–73 in *Grace Unlimited*. Edited by Clark H. Pinnock. Minneapolis: Bethany, 1975.

Cousar, Charles B. "Continuity and Discontinuity: Reflections on Romans 5–8." Pages 196–210 in *Pauline Theology, Vol. 3: Romans*. Edited by David M. Hay and E. Elizabeth Johnson. Minneapolis: Fortress, 1995.

Couser, Greg A. "The Sovereign Savior of 1 and 2 Timothy and Titus." Pages 105–36 in *Entrusted with the Gospel: Paul's Theology in the Pastoral Epistles*. Edited by Andreas J. Köstenberger and Terry L. Wilder. Nashville: B&H, 2010.

Cranfield, Charles E. B. *A Critical and Exegetical Commentary on the Epistle to the Romans*. ICC. 2 vols. Edinburgh: T&T Clark, 1975, 1979.

———. "St. Paul and the Law." *SJT* 17 (1964): 43–68.

———. "'The Works of the Law' in the Epistle to the Romans." *JSNT* 43 (1991): 89–101.

Cremer, Hermann, and Ernst Kappeler. *Die paulinische Rechtfertigungslehre im Zusammenhange ihrer geschichtlichen Voraussetzungen*. Gütersloh: C. Bertelsmann, 1900.

Crockett, W. V. "The Ultimate Restoration of all Mankind: 1 Corinthians 15:22." Pages 83–87 in *Studia Biblica 1978: Papers on Paul and Other New Testament Authors*. Edited by E. A. Livingstone. Sheffield: Academic, 1980.

Cullmann, Oscar. *Christ and Time: The Primitive Christian Conception of Time and History*. Philadelphia: Westminster, 1950.

———. *The Christology of the New Testament*. Philadelphia: Westminster, 1963.

———. *Salvation in History*. London: SCM, 1967.

———. *The State in the New Testament*. New York: Scribner's Sons, 1956.

Culver, Robert D. "A Neglected Millennial Passage from St. Paul." *BSac* 113 (1956): 141–52.

Cummins, Stephen A. *Paul and the Crucified Christ: Maccabean Martyrdom and Galatians 1 and 2*. SNTSMS 114. Cambridge: Cambridge University Press, 2001.

Dahl, Nils Alstrup. "The Messiahship of Jesus in Paul." Pages 37–47 in *The Crucified Messiah*. Minneapolis: Augsburg, 1974.

———. "Der Name Israel: Zur Auslegung von Gal 6,16." *Judaica* 6 (1950): 161–70.

———. *Studies in Paul: Theology for the Early Christian Mission*. Minneapolis: Augsburg, 1977.

Darko, Daniel K. *No Longer Living as the Gentiles: Differentiation and Shared Ethical Values in Ephesians 4:17–6:9*. LNTS 375. London: T&T Clark, 2008.

Das, A. Andrew. "Oneness in Christ: The *Nexus Indivulsus* between Justification and Sanctification in Paul's Letter to the Galatians." *Concordia Journal* 21 (1995): 173–86.

———. *Paul and the Jews*. Peabody, MA: Hendrickson, 2004.

———. *Paul and the Stories of Israel: Grand Thematic Narratives in Galatians*. Minneapolis: Fortress, 2016.

———. "Paul and Works of Obedience in Second Temple Judaism: Romans 4:4–5 as a 'New Perspective' Case Study." *CBQ* 71 (2009): 795–812.

———. *Solving the Romans Debate*. Minneapolis: Fortress, 2007.

Davidson, Richard M. *Typology in Scripture: A Study of Hermeneutical Typos Structures*. Andrews University Seminary Doctoral Dissertation Series. Berrien Springs, MI: Andrews University Press, 1981.

Davies, J. P. *Paul among the Apocalypses? An Evaluation of the "Apocalyptic Paul" in the Context of Jewish and Christian Apocalyptic*. LNTS 562. London: Bloomsbury, 2016.

Davies, R. E. "Christ in Our Place—The Contribution of the Prepositions." *TynBul* 21 (1970): 71–91.

Davies, William D. *The Gospel and the Land: Early Christianity and Jewish Territorial Doctrine*. Berkeley: University of California Press, 1974.

———. *Paul and Rabbinic Judaism: Some Rabbinic Elements in Pauline Theology*. 4th ed. Philadelphia: Fortress, 1980.

———. "Paul and the Gentiles: A Suggestion concerning Romans 11.13–24." Pages 153–63 in *Jewish and Pauline Studies*. Philadelphia: Fortress, 1984.

Davis, James A. *Wisdom and Spirit: An Investigation of 1 Cor. 1:18–3:20 against the Background of Jewish Sapiential Traditions in the Greco-Roman World*. Lanham, MD: University Press of America, 1984.

Dawes, Gregory W. *The Body in Question: Metaphor and Meaning in the Interpretation of Ephesians 5:21–33*. BibInt 30. Leiden: Brill, 1998.

de Boer, Martinus C. *Galatians: A Commentary*. NTL. Louisville: Westminster John Knox, 2011.

———. "Paul and Jewish Apocalyptic Eschatology." Pages 169–90 in *Apocalyptic and the New Testament: Essays in Honor of J. Louis Martyn*. Edited by Joel Marcus and Marion L. Soards. JSNTSup 24. Sheffield: Sheffield Academic, 1989.

———. "Salvation History in Galatians: A Response to Bruce W. Longenecker and Jason Maston." *JSPL* 2 (2012): 105–14.

de Lacey, Douglas. "The Sabbath/Sunday Question and the Law in the Pauline Corpus." Pages 159–96 in *From Sabbath to Lord's Day: A Biblical, Historical and Theological Investigation*. Edited by D. A. Carson. Grand Rapids: Zondervan, 1982.

de Roo, Jacqueline C. R. *Works of the Law at Qumran and in Paul*. New Testament Monographs 13. Sheffield: Sheffield Phoenix, 2007.

Deidun, T. J. *New Covenant Morality in Paul*. AnBib 89. Rome: Pontifical Biblical Institute, 1981.

Deissmann, Adolf. "ἱλαστήριος und ἱλαστήριον: Eine lexikalische Studie." *ZNW* 4 (1903): 195–211.

Deming, W. *Paul in Marriage and Celibacy: The Hellenistic Background of 1 Corinthians 7*. SNTSMS 83. Cambridge: Cambridge University Press, 1995.

Denney, James. *The Death of Christ: Its Place and Interpretation in the New Testament*. New York: A. C. Armstrong and Son, 1903.

———. "St. Paul's Epistle to the Romans." Pages 555–725 in *The Expositor's Greek Testament*. Vol. 2. Edited by W. Robertson Nicoll. London: Hodder and Stoughton, 1900.

———. *Studies in Theology*. 4th ed. London: Hodder & Stoughton, 1895.

DeRouchie, Jason S. "Father of a Multitude of Nations: New Covenant Ecclesiology in OT Perspective." Pages 7–38 in *Progressive Covenantalism: Charting a Course between Dispensational and Covenant Theology*. Edited by Stephen J. Wellum and Brent E. Parker. Nashville: B&H Academic, 2016.

deSilva, David A. *The Letter to the Galatians*. NICNT. Grand Rapids: Eerdmans, 2018.

Dibelius, Martin. *Die Pastoralbriefe*. 2nd ed. HNT 13. Tübingen: Mohr Siebeck, 1931.

Dick, Karl. *Der schriftstellerische Plural bei Paulus*. Halle: Ehrhardt Karras, 1899.

Dietzfelbinger, Christian. *Der Sohn: Skizzen zur Christologie und Anthropologie des Paulus*. BTS 118. Neukirchen-Vluyn: Neukirchener, 2011.

Dodd, C. H. *According to the Scriptures: The Substructure of New Testament Theology*. London: Nisbet, 1953.

———. *The Bible and the Greeks*. London: Hodder & Stoughton, 1935.

———. "ΙΛΑΣΚΕΣΘΑΙ, Its Cognates, Derivatives, and Synonyms, in the Septuagint." *JTS* 32 (1931): 352–60. Repr., Pages 82–95 in *The Bible and the Greeks*. By C. H. Dodd. London: Hodder & Stoughton, 1935.

———. "The Law." Pages 25–41 in *The Bible and the Greeks*. London: Hodder & Stoughton, 1935.

Donaldson, Terrence L. "The Juridical, the Participatory and the 'New Perspective' on Paul." Pages 233–40 in *Reading Paul in Context: Explorations in Identity Formation. Essays in Honour of William S. Campbell*. Edited by Kathy Ehrensperger and J. Brian Tucker. London: T&T Clark, 2010.

———. "Paul, Abraham's Gentile 'Offspring,' and the Torah." Pages 135–50 in *Torah Ethics and Early Christian Identity*. Edited by S. J. Wendel and D. M. Miller. Grand Rapids: Eerdmans, 2016.

———. *Paul and the Gentiles: Remapping the Apostle's Convictional World*. Minneapolis: Fortress, 1997.

———. "Paul within Judaism: A Critical Evaluation from a 'New Perspective' Perspective." Pages 277–301 in *Paul within Judaism: Restoring the First-Century Context to the Apostle*. Edited by Mark Nanos and Magnus Zetterholm. Minneapolis: Fortress, 2015.

Donfried, Karl P., and I. Howard Marshall. *The Theology of the Shorter Pauline Letters*. Cambridge: Cambridge University Press, 1993.

Downs, David J. *The Offering of the Gentiles: Paul's Collection for Jerusalem in Its Chronological, Cultural, and Cultic Contexts.* WUNT 2/248. Tübingen: Mohr Siebeck, 2008.

Downs, David J., and Benjamin J. Lappenga. *The Faithfulness of the Risen Christ: Pistis and the Exalted Lord in the Pauline Letters.* Waco, TX: Baylor University Press, 2019.

Drane, John. "Why Did Paul Write Romans?" Pages 212–23 in *Pauline Studies: Essays Presented to F. F. Bruce.* Edited by Donald A. Hagner and Murray J. Harris. Exeter: Paternoster, 1980.

du Toit, Andre. "The Centrality of Grace in the Theology of Paul." Pages 77–94 in *Focusing on Paul: Persuasion and Theological Design in Romans and Galatians.* Edited by Cilliers Breytenbach and David S. du Toit. BZNW 151. New York: de Gruyter, 2007.

———. "Faith and Obedience in Paul." Pages 117–27 in *Focusing on Paul: Persuasion and Theological Design in Romans and Galatians.* Edited by Cilliers Breytenbach and David S. du Toit. BZNW 151. New York: de Gruyter, 2007.

———. "'In Christ,' 'in the Spirit' and Related Prepositional Phrases: Their Relevance for a Discussion on Pauline Mysticism." Pages 129–45 in *Focusing on Paul: Persuasion and Theological Design in Romans and Galatians.* Edited by Cilliers Breytenbach and David S. du Toit. New York: de Gruyter, 2007.

Duff, Paul B. "Transformed 'from Glory to Glory': Paul's Appeal to the Experience of His Readers in 2 Corinthians 3:18." *JBL* 127 (2008): 759–80.

Duguid, I. M. "Israel." Pages 391–97 in *Dictionary of the Old Testament Prophets.* Edited by Mark J. Boda and J. Gordon McConville. Downers Grove, IL: InterVarsity Press, 2012.

Dumbrell, William J. *The Faith of Israel: A Theological Survey of the Old Testament.* 2nd ed. Grand Rapids: Baker, 2002.

Dunn, James D. G. "2 Corinthians III.17—'The Lord is the Spirit.'" *JTS* 21 (1970): 309–20.

———. *Baptism in the Holy Spirit: A Re-Examination of the New Testament Teaching on the Gift of the Spirit in Relation to Pentecostalism Today.* SBT 15. London: SCM, 1970.

———. *Beginning from Jerusalem.* Vol. 2 of *Christianity in the Making.* Grand Rapids: Eerdmans, 2009.

———. "The Christian Life from the Perspective of Paul's Letter to the Galatians." Pages 1–18 in *The Apostle Paul and the Christian Life: Ethical and Missional Implications of the New Perspective.* Edited by Scot McKnight and Joseph B. Modica. Grand Rapids: Baker, 2016.

———. *Christology in the Making: A New Testament Inquiry into the Origins of the Doctrine of the Incarnation.* London: SCM, 1980.

———. *Did the First Christians Worship Jesus? The New Testament Evidence.* Louisville: Westminster John Knox, 2010.

———. "Echoes of Intra-Jewish Polemic in Paul's Letter to the Galatians." *JBL* 112 (1993): 459–77.

———. "*Ek Pisteos*: A Key to the Meaning of *Pistis Christou.*" Pages 351–66 in *The Word Leaps the Gap: Essays on Scripture and Theology in Honor of Richard B. Hays.* Edited by J. Ross Wagner, Kavin C. Rowe, and Katherine Grieb. Grand Rapids: Eerdmans, 2008.

———. *The Epistle to the Galatians.* BNTC. Peabody, MA: Hendrickson, 1993.

———. *The Epistles to the Colossians and to Philemon.* NIGTC. Grand Rapids: Eerdmans, 1996.

———. "The Gospel according to Paul." Pages 139–53 in *The Blackwell Companion to Paul.* Edited by Stephen Westerholm. Chichester: Wiley-Blackwell, 2011.

———. "In Search of the Historical Paul." Pages 15–48 in *Celebrating Paul: Festschrift in Honor of Jerome Murphy-O'Connor, O.P., and Joseph A. Fitzmyer, S. J.* Edited by P. Spitaler. CBQMS 48. Washington, DC: Catholic Biblical Association of America, 2011.

———. "The Incident at Antioch (Gal 2:11–18)." *JSNT* 18 (1983): 3–57.

———. "Jesus—Flesh and Spirit: An Exposition of Romans I.3–4." *JTS* 24 (1973): 44–51.

———. *Jesus, Paul, and the Law: Studies in Mark and Galatians.* Louisville: Westminster John Knox, 1990.

———. "Jesus the Judge: Further Thoughts of Paul's Christology and Soteriology." Pages 389–405 in *The New Perspective on Paul.* WUNT 2/185. Tübingen: Mohr Siebeck, 2005.

———. "The New Perspective on Paul." *BJRL* 65 (1983): 95–122.

———. "The New Perspective on Paul: Whence, What, Whither?" Pages 1–88 in *The New Perspective on Paul: Collected Essays.* Tübingen: Mohr Siebeck, 2005.

———. "A New Perspective on the New Perspective on Paul." *Early Christianity* 4 (2013): 157–82.

———. "New Perspective Response" (to the "Deification View"). Page 256 in *Justification: Five Views.* Edited by J. K. Beilby and P. R. Eddy. Downers Grove, IL: InterVarsity Press, 2011.

————. "New Perspective View." Pages 176–201 in *Justification: Five Views*. Edited by J. K. Beilby and P. R. Eddy. Downers Grove, IL: InterVarsity Press, 2011.

————. *New Testament Theology: An Introduction*. Library of Biblical Theology. Nashville: Abingdon, 2009.

————. *The Partings of the Ways: Between Judaism and Christianity and their Significance for the Character of Christianity*. Philadelphia: Trinity Press International, 1991.

————. "Paul's Conversion: A Light to Twentieth Century Disputes." Pages 347–65 in *The New Perspective on Paul: Collected Essays*. WUNT 2/185. Tübingen: Mohr Siebeck, 2005.

————. "Paul's Knowledge of the Jesus Tradition: The Evidence of Romans." Pages 193–207 in *Christus Bezeugen: Festschrift für Wolfgang Trilling zum 65. Geburtstag*. Edited by Karl Kertelge, Traugott Holtz, and Claus-Peter März. Leipzig: Benno, 1989.

————. "Philippians 3.2–14 and the New Perspective on Paul." Pages 463–84 in *The New Perspective on Paul: Collected Essays*. WUNT 2/185. Tübingen: Mohr Siebeck, 2005.

————. "Rom 7,14–25 in the Theology of Paul." *TZ* 5 (1975): 257–73.

————. *Romans 1–8*. WBC 38A. Dallas: Word, 1988.

————. *Romans 9–16*. WBC 38B. Dallas: Word, 1988.

————. *A Theology of Paul the Apostle*. Grand Rapids: Eerdmans, 1998.

————. *The Theology of Paul's Letter to the Galatians*. Cambridge: Cambridge University Press, 1993.

————. *Unity and Diversity in the New Testament: An Inquiry into the Character of Earliest Christianity*. 3rd ed. London: SCM, 2006.

————. "What's Right about the Old Perspective on Paul." Pages 214–29 in *Studies in the Pauline Epistles: Essays in Honor of Douglas J. Moo*. Edited by Matthew Harmon and Jay Smith. Grand Rapids: Zondervan, 2014.

Dunson, Ben C. "Faith in Romans: The Salvation of the Individual or Life in Community?" *JSNT* 34 (2011): 19–46.

————. *Individual and Community in Paul's Letter to the Romans*. WUNT 2/332. Tübingen: Mohr Siebeck, 2012.

Dupont, Jacques. *La réconciliation dans la théologie de Saint Paul*. ALBO 2/32. Louvain: Publications universitaires de Louvain, 1953.

Eastman, Susan Grove. "Israel and the Mercy of God: A Re-Reading of Galatians 6.16 and Romans 9–11." *NTS* 56 (2010): 367–95.

————. "Oneself in Another: Participation and the Spirit in Romans 8." Pages 103–25 in *"In Christ" in Paul: Explorations in Paul's Theology of Union and Participation*. Edited by Michael J. Thate, Kevin J. Vanhoozer, and Constantine R. Campbell. WUNT 2/384. Tübingen: Mohr Siebeck, 2014.

————. *Paul and the Person: Reframing Paul's Anthropology*. Grand Rapids: Eerdmans, 2017.

————. *Recovering Paul's Mother Tongue: Language and Theology in Galatians*. Grand Rapids: Eerdmans, 2007.

Ebeling, G. "On the Doctrine of the *Triplex Usus Legis* in the Theology of the Reformation." Pages 62–78 in *Word and Faith*. Philadelphia: Fortress, 1963.

Eckert, Jost. *Die urchristliche Verkündigung im Streit zwischen Paulus und seinen Gegnern nach dem Galaterbrief*. Regensburg: Friedrich Pustet, 1971.

Eckstein, Hans-Joachim. *Verheissung und Gesetz: Eine exegetische Untersuchung zu Galater 2,15–4,7*. WUNT 2/86. Tübingen: Mohr Siebeck, 1996.

Edsall, Benjamin, and Jennifer R. Strawbridge. "The Songs We Used to Sing? Hymn 'Traditions' and Reception in the Pauline Letters." *JSNT* 37 (2015): 290–311.

Edwards, Mark J., ed. *Galatians, Ephesians, Philippians*. ACCS 8. Downers Grove, IL: InterVarsity Press, 1999.

Ehrensperger, Kathy. *That We May Be Mutually Encouraged: Feminism and the New Perspective in Pauline Studies*. London: T&T Clark, 2004.

Eisenbaum, Pamela. *Paul Was Not a Christian: The Original Message of a Misunderstood Apostle*. New York: Harper, 2009.

Elliott, Mark Adam. *The Survivors of Israel: A Reconsideration of the Theology of Pre-Christian Judaism*. Grand Rapids: Eerdmans, 2000.

Elliott, Mark W. "Judaism, Reformation Theology, and Justification." Pages 143–58 in *Galatians and Christian Theology: Justification, the Gospel, and Ethics in Paul's Letter*. Edited by Mark W. Elliott, Scott J. Hafemann, N. T. Wright, and John Frederick. Grand Rapids: Baker, 2014.

————. "Πίστις Χριστοῦ in the Church Fathers and Beyond." Pages 277–89 in *The Faith of Jesus Christ: Exegetical, Biblical, and Theological Studies*. Edited by Michael F. Bird and Preston M. Sprinkle. Peabody, MA: Hendrickson, 2009.

Elliott, Neil. *Liberating Paul: The Justice of God and the Politics of the Apostle*. Maryknoll, NY: Orbis, 1994.

Ellis, E. Earle. "II Corinthians V.1–10 in Pauline Eschatology." *NTS* 6 (1960): 211–24.

———. *Paul's Use of the Old Testament*. Edinburgh: Oliver & Boyd, 1957.

Engberg-Pedersen, Troels. *Paul and the Stoics*. Louisville: Westminster John Knox, 2000.

Enns, Peter. *The Evolution of Adam: What the Bible Does and Doesn't Say about Human Origins*. Grand Rapids: Brazos, 2012.

———. "Expansions of Scripture." Pages 73–98 in *The Complexities of Second Temple Judaism*. Vol. 1 of *Justification and Variegated Nomism*. Edited by D. A. Carson, Peter T. O'Brien, and Mark Seifrid. WUNT 2/140. Tübingen: Mohr Siebeck, 2001.

Eschner, Christina. *Gestorben und hingegeben "für" die Sünder: Die griechische Konzeption des Unheil abwendenden Sterbens und deren Paulinische Aufnahme für die Deutung des Todes Jesu Christi*. 2 vols. WMANT 122. Neukirchen-Vluyn: Neukirchener, 2010.

Eskola, Timo. "How to Write a Synthesis: Wright and the Problem of Continuity in New Testament Theology." Pages 237–52 in *Exile: A Conversation with N. T. Wright*. Edited by James M. Scott. Downers Grove, IL: InterVarsity Press, 2017.

———. *Theodicy and Predestination in Pauline Soteriology*. WUNT 2/100. Tübingen: Mohr Siebeck, 1998.

Esler, Philip. *Galatians*. London: Routledge, 1998.

Evans, Craig A. "The Colossian Mystics." *Bib* 63 (1982): 197–201.

———. "Paul and 'Works of the Law' Language in Late Antiquity." Pages 201–26 in *Paul and His Opponents*. Edited by Stanley E. Porter. Pauline Studies 2. Leiden: Brill, 2005.

Evans, William B. "Déjà Vu All over Again? The Contemporary Reformed Soteriological Controversy in Historical Perspective." *WTJ* 72 (2010): 135–51.

———. *Imputation and Impartation: Union with Christ in American Reformed Theology*. Studies in Christian History and Thought. Eugene, OR: Wipf & Stock, 2008.

Fee, Gordon D. "II Corinthians VI.14–VII.1 and Food Offered to Idols." *NTS* 23 (1977): 140–61.

———. *The First and Second Letters to the Thessalonians*. NICNT. Grand Rapids: Eerdmans, 2009.

———. *The First Epistle to the Corinthians*. 2nd ed. NICNT. Grand Rapids: Eerdmans, 2014.

———. *Galatians*. Pentecostal Commentary. Blandford Forum, UK: Deo, 2007.

———. *God's Empowering Presence: The Holy Spirit in the Letters of Paul*. Peabody, MA: Hendrickson, 1994.

———. *Pauline Christology: An Exegetical-Theological Study*. Peabody, MA: Hendrickson, 2007.

———. *Paul's Letter to the Philippians*. NICNT. Grand Rapids: Eerdmans, 1995.

Fee, Gordon, and Douglas Stuart. *How to Read the Bible for All Its Worth*. 4th ed. Grand Rapids: Zondervan, 2014.

Feinberg, J. "God Ordains All Things." Pages 17–43 in *Predestination and Free Will: Four Views of Divine Sovereignty and Human Freedom*. Spectrum Multiview Book Series. Edited by David Basinger and Randall Basinger. Downers Grove, IL: InterVarsity Press, 1986.

Ferguson, Sinclair B. *The Holy Spirit*. Downers Grove, IL: InterVarsity Press, 1996.

Feuillet, André. "Loi de Dieu, Loi du Christ et Loi de L'esprit d'après les Epîtres Pauliniennes: Les Rapports de sec trois avec la Loi Mosaique." *NovT* 22 (1980): 29–63.

Finlan, Stephen. *The Background and Content of Paul's Cultic Atonement Metaphors*. AcBib 19. Atlanta: SBL, 2004.

Fiorenza, Elizabeth Schüssler. *In Memory of Her: A Feminist Theological Reconstruction of Christian Origins*. New York: Crossroad, 1983.

Fitzmyer, Joseph A. "The Consecutive Meaning of *eph' hō* in Romans 5.12." *NTS* 39 (1993): 321–39.

———. *First Corinthians: A New Translation with Introduction and Commentary*. AB 32. New Haven: Yale University Press, 2008.

——— *The Letter to Philemon: A New Translation with Introduction and Commentary*. AB 34C. New York: Doubleday, 2000.

———. "Reconciliation in Pauline Theology." Pages 155–77 in *No Famine in the Land: Studies in Honor of John L. McKenzie*. Edited by James W. Flanagan and Anita Weisbrod Robinson. Missoula, MT: Scholars Press, 1975.

———. *Romans: A New Translation with Introduction and Commentary*. AB 33. Garden City: Doubleday, 1993.

———. "The Semitic Background of the New Testament *Kyrios*-Title." Pages 115–42 in *A Wandering Aramean: Collected Aramaic Essays*. SBLDS 25. Missoula, MT: Scholars Press, 1979.

Flemington, William Frederick. *The New Testament Doctrine of Baptism*. London: SPCK, 1957.

Fletcher-Louis, Crispin H. T. "The Worship of Divine Humanity as God's Image and the Worship of Jesus." Pages 112–28 in *The Jewish Roots of Christological Monotheism*. Edited by C. C. Newman, J. R. Davila, and G. S. Lewis. Supplements to the Journal for the Study of Judaism 63. Leiden: Brill, 1999.

Forbes, Christopher. *Prophecy and Inspired Speech in Early Christianity and Its Hellenistic Environment*. WUNT 2/75. Tübingen: Mohr Siebeck, 1995.

Ford, Desmond. *The Abomination of Desolation in Biblical Eschatology*. Washington, DC: University Press of America, 1979.

Forman, Mark. *The Politics of Inheritance in Romans*. SNTSMS 148. Cambridge: Cambridge University Press, 2011.

Foster, Paul. *Colossians*. BNTC. London: Bloomsbury, 2016.

Fotopoulos, John. *Food Offered to Idols in Roman Corinth: A Social-Rhetorical Reconsideration of 1 Corinthians 8:1–11:1*. WUNT 2/151. Tübingen: Mohr Siebeck, 2003.

Fowl, Stephen E. *Ephesians: A Commentary*. NTL. Louisville: Westminster John Knox, 2012.

———. *The Story of Christ in the Ethics of Paul: An Analysis of the Hymnic Material in the Pauline Corpus*. JSNTSup 36. Sheffield: Sheffield Academic, 1990.

Fox-Genovese, Elizabeth, and Eugene D. Genovese. "The Divine Sanction of Social Order: Religious Foundations of the Southern Slaveholders' World View." *JAAR* 55 (1987): 211–33.

Frame, James E. *A Critical and Exegetical Commentary on the Epistles of St. Paul to the Thessalonians*. ICC. New York: Scribner's Sons, 1912.

Frame, John. "Review of David VanDrunen's *A Biblical Case for Natural Law*." *The Works of John Frame & Vern Poythress*. May 10, 2012. https://frame-poythress.org /review-of-david-van-drunen-a-biblical-case-for-natural -law.

Francis, Fred O. "Humility and Angel Worship in Col. 2:18." *ST* 16 (1962): 109–34.

Francis, Fred O., and Wayne A. Meeks, eds. *Conflict at Colossae: A Problem in the Interpretation of Early Christianity Illustrated by Selected Modern Studies*. Sources for Biblical Study 4. Atlanta: SBL, 1975.

Frankemölle, H. *Das Taufverständnis des Paulus: Taufe, Tod und Auferstehung nach Röm 6*. SBS 47. Stuttgart: Katholisches, 1970.

Fredriksen, Paula. *Paul: The Pagan's Apostle*. New Haven: Yale University Press, 2017.

Freundorfer, Joseph. *Erbsünde und Erbtod beim Apostel Paulus: Eine religionsgeschichtliche und exegetische Untersuchung über Römerbrief 5,12–21*. NTAbh 13. Münster: Aschendorff, 1927.

Frey, Jörg. "Der Philipperbrief im Rahmen der Paulusforschung." Pages 1–31 in *Der Philipperbrief des Paulus in der hellenistisch-römischen Welt*. Edited by Jörg Frey and Benjamin Schliesser. Tübingen: Mohr Siebeck, 2015.

———. "Probleme der Deutung des Todes Jesu in der Neutestamentlichen Wissenschaft: Streiflichter zur exegetischen Diskussion." Pages 3–50 in *Deutungen des Todes Jesu im Neuen Testament*. Edited by Jörg Frey and Jens Schröter. Tübingen: Mohr Siebeck, 2005.

Froom, LeRoy Edwin. *The Conditionalist Faith of Our Fathers*. 2 vols. Washington: Review and Herald, 1966.

Fudge, Edward. *The Fire That Consumes: A Biblical and Historical Survey of Final Punishment*. Houston, TX: Providential, 1982.

Fuller, Daniel P. *Gospel and Law: Contrast or Continuum?* Grand Rapids: Eerdmans, 1980.

Fung, Ronald Y. K. *The Epistle to the Galatians*. NICNT. Grand Rapids: Eerdmans, 1988.

Furnish, Victor Paul. *II Corinthians*. AB 32A. Garden City: Doubleday, 1984.

———. "The Jesus-Paul Debate: From Baur to Bultmann." *BJRL* 47 (1965): 342–81.

———. *Theology and Ethics in Paul*. Louisville: Westminster John Knox, 2009.

———. "Theology in 1 Corinthians." Pages 59–89 in *Pauline Theology, Vol. 2: 1 & 2 Corinthians*. Edited by David M. Hay. Minneapolis: Augsburg Fortress, 1993.

———. *The Theology of the First Letter to the Corinthians*. New Testament Theology. Cambridge: Cambridge University Press, 1999.

Gabathuler, Hans Jakob. *Jesus Christus: Haupt der Kirche, Haupt der Welt—Der Christushymnus Colosser 1,15–20 in der theologischen Forschung der letzten 130 Jahre*. ATANT 45. Zurich: Zwingli, 1965.

Gablenz, Pablo. *Called from the Jews and from the Gentiles: Pauline Ecclesiology in Romans 9–11*. WUNT 2/267. Tübingen: Mohr Siebeck, 2009.

Gäckle, Volker. "Die Relevanz des Landes Israel bei Paulus." *ZTK* 112 (2015): 141–63.

Gaffin, Richard B., Jr. "Atonement in the Pauline Corpus: 'The Scandal of the Cross.'" Pages 140–62 in *The Glory of the Atonement: Biblical, Historical and Practical Perspectives: Essays in Honor of Roger Nicole*. Edited by Charles E. Hill and Frank A. James III. Downers Grove, IL: InterVarsity Press, 2004.

———. *By Faith, Not by Sight: Paul and the Order of Salvation*. Waynesboro, GA: Paternoster, 2006.

———. *Resurrection and Redemption: A Study in Paul's Soteriology*. BBMS. Grand Rapids: Baker, 1978. Repr., of *The Centrality of the Resurrection : A Study in Paul's Soteriology*.

Gager, John. *Reinventing Paul*. Oxford: Oxford University Press, 2000.

Gagnon, Robert A. J. *The Bible and Homosexual Practice: Texts and Hermeneutics*. Nashville: Abingdon, 2001.

———. "Heart of Wax and a Teaching That Stamps: ΤΥΠΟΣ ΔΙΔΑΧΗΣ (Rom 6:17b) Once More." *JBL* 112 (1994): 671–73.

Galinski, K. "The Cult of the Roman Emperor: Uniter or Divider?" Pages 1–21 in *Rome and Religion: A Cross-Disciplinary Dialogue on the Imperial Cult*. Edited by J. Brodd and J. L. Reed. Atlanta: SBL, 2011.

Gane, Roy E. *Cult and Character: Purification Offerings, Day of Atonement, and Theodicy*. Winona Lake, IN: Eisenbrauns, 2005.

Garcia, Mark A. "Debating Justification Productively: A Review." *Scottish Bulletin of Evangelical Theology* 31 (2013): 211–26.

———. "Imputation and the Christology of Union with Christ: Calvin, Osiander, and the Contemporary Quest for a Reformed Model." *WTJ* 68 (2006): 219–51.

Gardner, Paul D. *1 Corinthians*. ZECNT. Grand Rapids: Zondervan, 2018.

Garland, David E. *1 Corinthians*. BECNT. Grand Rapids: Baker Academic, 2003.

———. *2 Corinthians*. NAC 29. Nashville: Broadman & Holman, 1999.

———. *Colossians and Philemon*. NIVAC. Grand Rapids: Zondervan, 1998.

———. "The Compositon and Unity of Philippians: Some Neglected Literary Factors." *NovT* 27 (1985): 141–73.

Garlington, Don B. "'Even We Have Believed': Galatians 2:15–16 Revisited." *CTR* 7 (2009): 3–28.

———. *An Exposition of Galatians: A New Perspectival/Reformational Reading*. Eugene, OR: Wipf & Stock, 2003.

———. *Faith, Obedience, and Perseverance: Aspects of Paul's Letter to the Romans*. WUNT 2/79. Tübingen: Mohr Siebeck, 1994.

———. "The New Perspective on Paul: Two Decades On." Pages 1–30 in *Studies in the New Perspective on Paul: Essays and Reviews*. Eugene, OR: Wipf & Stock, 2008.

———. *"The Obedience of Faith": A Pauline Theme in Historical Context*. WUNT 2/38. Tübingen: Mohr Siebeck, 1991.

Garner, David B. *Sons in the Son: The Riches and Reach of Adoption in Christ*. Phillipsburg, NJ: P&R, 2017.

Gaston, Lloyd. *Paul and the Torah*. Vancouver: University of British Columbia Press, 1987.

Gathercole, Simon. "The Cross and Substitutionary Atonement." *Scottish Bulletin of Evangelical Theology* 21 (2003): 152–65.

———. *Defending Substitution: An Essay on Atonement in Paul*. Grand Rapids: Baker, 2015.

———. "The Doctrine of Justification in Paul and Beyond: Some Proposals." Pages 219–41 in *Justification in Perspective: Historical Developments and Contemporary Challenges*. Edited by Bruce L. McCormack. Grand Rapids: Baker, 2006.

———. "Early Judaism and Covenantal Nomism: A Review Article." *EvQ* 76 (2004): 153–62.

———. "Justified by Faith, Justified by His Blood: The Evidence of Romans 3:21–4:25." Pages 147–84 in *The Paradoxes of Paul*. Vol. 2 of *Justification and Variegated Nomism*. Edited by D. A. Carson, Peter T. O'Brien, and Mark A. Seifrid. WUNT 2/140. Tübingen: Mohr Siebeck, 2001.

———. "A Law unto Themselves: The Gentiles in Romans 2.14–15 Revisited." *JSNT* 85 (2002): 27–49.

———. "Paul's Christology." Pages 172–87 in *The Blackwell Companion to Paul*. Edited by Stephen Westerholm. Oxford: Blackwell, 2011.

———. "The Petrine and Pauline Sola Fide in Galatians 2." Pages 309–27 in *Lutherische und Neue Perspektive: Beiträge Zu Einem Schüsselproblem Der Gegenwärtigen Exegetischen Diskussion*. Edited by Michael Bachmann. WUNT 2/182. Tübingen: Mohr Siebeck, 2005.

———. "'Sins' in Paul." *NTS* 64 (2018): 143–61.

———. "Torah, Life, and Salvation: Leviticus 18:5 in Early Judaism and the New Testament." Pages 126–45 in *From Prophecy to Testament: The Function of the Old Testament in the New*. Edited by Craig A. Evans. Peabody, MA: Hendrickson, 2004.

———. *Where Is Boasting? Early Jewish Soteriology and Paul's Response in Romans 1–5*. Grand Rapids: Eerdmans, 2002.

Gaukesbrink, Martin. *Die Sühnetradition bei Paulus: Rezeption und theologischer Stellenwert*. FB 32. Würzburg: Echter, 1999.

Gaventa, Beverly Roberts. "Galatians 1 and 2: Autobiography as Paradigm." *NovT* 28 (1986): 309–26.

———. *Our Mother Saint Paul*. Louisville: Westminster John Knox, 2007.

———. "The Singularity of the Gospel: A Reading of Galatians." Pages 147–59 in *Pauline Theology, Vol. 1:*

Thessalonians, Philippians, Galatians, Philemon. Edited by Jouette M. Bassler. Minneapolis: Augsburg Fortress, 1991.

———. *When in Romans: An Invitation to Linger with the Gospel according to Paul.* Grand Rapids: Baker, 2016.

Geeraerts, Dirk, ed. *Cognitive Linguistics: Basic Readings.* New York: Mouton de Gruyter, 2006.

Gehring, Roger W. *House Church and Mission: The Importance of Household Structures in Early Christianity.* Peabody, MA: Hendrickson, 2004.

Gentry, Peter J., and Stephen J. Wellum. *Kingdom through Covenant: A Biblical-Theological Understanding of the Covenants.* Wheaton, IL: Crossway, 2012.

George, Timothy. *Galatians.* NAC 10. Nashville: Broadman & Holman, 1994.

Georgi, Dieter. *The Opponents of Paul in Second Corinthians.* Philadelphia: Fortress, 1986.

———. *Remembering the Poor: The History of Paul's Collection for Jerusalem.* Repr., Nashville: Abingdon, 1992.

Gese, H. "Atonement." Pages 93–116 in *Essays in Biblical Theology.* Minneapolis: Augsburg, 1981.

Gese, Michael. *Das Vermächtnis des Apostels: Die Rezeption der paulinischen Theologie im Epheserbrief.* WUNT 2/99. Tübingen: Mohr Siebeck, 1997.

Giblin, Charles Homer. *The Threat to Faith: An Exegetical and Theological Reexamination of 2 Thessalonians 2.* AnBib 31. Rome: Pontifical Biblical Institute, 1967.

Gibson, Jonathan. "The Glorious, Indivisible, Trinitarian Work of God in Christ: Definite Atonement in Paul's Theology of Salvation." Pages 331–74 in *From Heaven He Came and Sought Her: Definite Atonement in Historical, Biblical, Theological, and Pastoral Perspective.* Edited by David Gibson and Jonathan Gibson. Wheaton, IL: Crossway, 2013.

Gignilliat, Mark S. *Paul and Isaiah's Servants: Paul's Theological Reading of Isaiah 40–66 in 2 Corinthians 5:14–6:10.* London: T&T Clark, 2007.

Giles, K. "The Biblical Argument for Slavery: Can the Bible Mislead? A Case Study in Hermeneutics." *EvQ* 66 (1994): 3–17.

Gilliard, Frank D. "The Problem of the Antisemitic Comma between 1 Thessalonians 2.14 and 15." *NTS* 35 (1989): 481–502.

Gladd, Benjamin L., and Matthew S. Harmon. *Making All Things New: Inaugurated Eschatology for the Life of the Church.* Grand Rapids: Baker, 2016.

Gnilka, Joachim. *Der Epheserbrief.* 4th ed. HThKNT 10.2. Freiburg: Herder, 1990.

———. *Der Philipperbrief.* 4th ed. HThKNT. Freiburg: Herder, 1987.

Godet, Frederic Louis. *Commentary on Romans.* Repr., Grand Rapids: Kregel, 1977.

Gombis, Timothy G. *The Drama of Ephesians.* Downers Grove, IL: InterVarsity Press, 2010.

———. "Participation in the New-Creation People of God in Christ by the Spirit." Pages 103–24 in *The Apostle Paul and the Christian Life: Ethical and Missional Implications of the New Perspective.* Edited by Scot McKnight and Joseph B. Modica. Grand Rapids: Baker, 2016.

———. *Paul: A Guide for the Perplexed.* London: T&T Clark, 2010.

Goodspeed, Edgar J. *The Key to Ephesians.* Chicago: University of Chicago Press, 1956.

Goppelt, Leonhard. *Theology of the New Testament.* 2 vols. Grand Rapids: Eerdmans, 1981, 1982.

Gordley, Matthew E. *New Testament Christological Hymns: Exploring Texts, Contexts, and Significance.* Downers Grove, IL: InterVarsity Press, 2018.

Gorman, Michael J. *Apostle of the Crucified Lord: A Theological Introduction to Paul and His Letters.* 2nd ed. Grand Rapids: Eerdmans, 2017.

———. *Becoming the Gospel: Paul, Participation, and Mission.* Grand Rapids: Eerdmans, 2015.

———. *The Death of the Messiah and the Birth of the New Covenant: A (Not So) New Model of the Atonement.* Eugene, OR: Cascade, 2014.

———. *Inhabiting the Cruciform God: Kenosis, Justification, and Theosis in Paul's Narrative Soteriology.* Grand Rapids: Eerdmans, 2009.

———. "The Lord of Peace: Christ Our Peace in Pauline Theology." *JSPL* 3 (2013): 219–53.

———. "Romans: The First Christian Treatise on Theosis." *Journal of Theological Interpretation* 5 (2011): 13–34.

Grabner-Haider, Anton. *Paraklese und Eschatologie bei Paulus.* NTAbh. Göttingen: Vandenhoeck & Ruprecht, 1968.

Gradel, I. *Emperor Worship and Roman Religion.* Oxford: Clarendon, 2002.

Green, Bradley G. *Covenant and Commandment: Works, Obedience and Faithfulness in the Christian Life.* NSBT 33. Downers Grove, IL: InterVarsity Press, 2014.

Green, Gene L. *The Letters to the Thessalonians*. PNTC. Grand Rapids: Eerdmans, 2002.

Green, Joel B. *Body, Soul, and Human Life*. Grand Rapids: Baker, 2008.

Green, Joel B., and Mark D. Baker. *Recovering the Scandal of the Cross: Atonement in New Testament and Contemporary Contexts*. Downers Grove, IL: InterVarsity Press, 2000.

Green, William Scott. "Introduction: Messiah in Judaism: Rethinking the Question." Pages 1–14 in *Judaisms and Their Messiahs at the Turn of the Christian Era*. Edited by Jacob Neusner, William Scott Green, and Ernest S. Frerichs. Cambridge: Cambridge University Press, 1987.

Greenspoon, Leonard. "By the Letter? Word for Word? Scriptural Citation in Paul." Pages 9–24 in *Paul and Scripture: Extending the Conversation*. Edited by Christopher D. Stanley. Early Christianity and Its Literature 9. Atlanta: SBL, 2012.

Grindheim, Sigurd. "A Deutero-Pauline Mystery? Ecclesiology in Colossians and Ephesians." Pages 173–95 in *Paul and Pseudepigraphy*. Edited by Stanley E. Porter and Gregory P. Fewster. Pauline Studies 8. Leiden: Brill, 2013.

———. "The Law Kills But the Gospel Gives Life: The Letter-Spirit Dualism in 2 Corinthians 3.5–18." *JSNT* 84 (2001): 97–115.

———. "A Theology of Glory: Paul's Use of Δόξα Terminology in Romans." *JBL* 136 (2017): 451–65.

———. "Wisdom for the Perfect: Paul's Challenge to the Corinthian Church (1 Corinthians 2:6–16)." *JBL* 121 (2002): 689–709.

Grosheide, F. W. *Commentary on the First Epistle to the Corinthians*. NICNT. Grand Rapids: Eerdmans, 1953.

Grudem, Wayne A. "Does Κεφαλή Mean 'Source' or 'Authority Over' in Greek Literature? A Survey of 2,336 Examples." *TJ* 6 (1985): 38–59.

———. *The Gift of Prophecy in the New Testament and Today*. Westchester, IL: Crossway, 1988.

———. "The Meaning of Κεφαλή ('Head'): A Response to Recent Studies." *TJ* 11 (1990): 3–72.

———. "The Meaning of Κεφαλή ('Head'): An Evaluation of New Evidence, Real and Alleged." *JETS* 44 (2001): 25–65.

———. "Should We Move beyond the New Testament to a Better Ethic?" *JETS* 47 (2004): 299–346.

Grudem, Wayne A., ed. *Are Miraculous Gifts for Today? Four Views*. Counterpoints. Grand Rapids: Zondervan, 1996.

Gundry, Robert H. *Church and Tribulation: A Biblical Examination of Posttribulationism*. Grand Rapids: Zondervan, 1999.

———. "Grace, Works, and Staying Saved in Paul." *Bib* 66 (1985): 1–38.

———. "The Inferiority of the New Perspective on Paul." Pages 195–224 in *The Old Is Better: New Testament Essays in Support of Traditional Interpretations*. By Robert H. Gundry. WUNT 2/178. Tübingen: Mohr Siebeck, 2005.

———. "The Nonimputation of Christ's Righteousness." Pages 225–51 in *The Old Is Better: New Testament Essays in Support of Traditional Interpretations*. WUNT 2/178. Tübingen: Mohr Siebeck, 2005.

———. *Sōma in Biblical Theology: With Emphasis on Pauline Anthropology*. SNTSMS 29. Cambridge: Cambridge University Press, 1976.

———. "Style and Substance in Philippians 2:6–11." Pages 272–91 in *The Old Is Better: New Testament Essays in Support of Traditional Interpretations*. By Robert H. Gundry. WUNT 2/178. Tübingen: Mohr Siebeck, 2005.

Gundry Volf, Judith M. "Male and Female in Creation and New Creation: Interpretations of Galatians 3:28c in 1 Corinthians 7." Pages 95–121 in *To Tell the Mystery: Essays on New Testament Eschatology in Honor of Robert H. Gundry*. Edited by T. E. Schmidt and Moisés Silva. Sheffield: JSOT Press, 1994.

———. *Paul and Perseverance: Staying In and Falling Away*. Louisville: Westminster John Knox, 1990.

Gupta, Nijay K. *1 and 2 Thessalonians*. Zondervan Critical Introductions to the New Testament. Grand Rapids: Zondervan Academic, 2019.

———. *Paul and the Language of Faith*. Grand Rapids: Eerdmans, 2020.

Gupta, Nijay K., John K. Goodrich, eds. *Sin and Its Remedy in Paul*. Eugene, OR: Cascade, 2020.

Guthrie, Donald. *New Testament Introduction*. 3rd ed. Downers Grove, IL: InterVarsity Press, 1970.

———. *New Testament Theology*. Downers Grove, IL: InterVarsity Press, 1981.

Guthrie, George H. *2 Corinthians*. BECNT. Grand Rapids: Baker Academic, 2015.

Hafemann, Scott. *2 Corinthians*. NIVAC. Grand Rapids: Zondervan, 2000.

———. "Paul and the Exile of Israel in Galatians 3–4." Pages 333–51 in *Exile: Old Testament, Jewish, and Christian Conceptions*. Edited by James M. Scott. Supplements to the Journal for the Study of Judaism 56. Leiden: Brill, 1997.

———. "Reading Paul's ΔΙΚΑΙΟ-Language: A Response to Douglas Campbell's 'Rereading Paul's

ΔIKAIO-Language.'" Pages 214–29 in *Beyond Old and New Perspectives on Paul: Reflections on the Work of Douglas Campbell*. Edited by Chris Tilling. Eugene, OR: Cascade, 2014.

———. *Suffering and Ministry in the Spirit: Paul's Defense of His Ministry in II Corinthians 2:14–3:3*. Grand Rapids: Eerdmans, 1990.

Hagner, Donald A. *How New Is the New Testament?* Grand Rapids: Baker, 2019.

———. "Paul and Judaism: The Jewish Matrix of Early Christianity: Issues in the Current Debate." *BBR* 3 (1993): 111–30.

———. "Paul's Quarrel with Judaism." Pages 128–50 in *Anti-Semitism and Early Christianity: Issues of Polemic and Faith*. Edited by Craig A. Evans and Donald A. Hagner. Minneapolis: Fortress, 1993.

Hahn, Ferdinand. *Theologie des Neuen Testaments*. 3rd ed. 2 vols. Uni-Taschenbücher 3500. Tübingen: Mohr Siebeck, 2011.

———. "Zum Verständnis von Römer 11.26a: '. . . und so wird ganz Israel gerettet werden.'" Pages 221–34 in *Paul and Paulinism: Essays in Honour of C. K. Barrett*. Edited by Morna D. Hooker and Stephen G. Wilson. London: SPCK, 1982.

Hahne, Harry Alan. *The Corruption and Redemption of Creation: Nature in Romans 8:19–22 and Jewish Apocalyptic Literature*. LNTS 336. London: T&T Clark, 2006.

Haller, William. *The Rise of Puritanism*. Philadelphia: University of Pennsylvania Press, 1972.

Hallonsten, Gösta. "Theosis in Recent Research: A Renewal of Interest and a Need for Clarity." Pages 281–93 in *Partakers in the Divine Nature: The History and Development of Deification in the Christian Traditions*. Edited by Michael J. Christensen and Jeffery A. Wittung. Cranbury, NJ: Farleigh Dickinson University Press, 2007.

Hamilton, Neill Quinn. *The Holy Spirit and Eschatology in Paul*. Scottish Journal of Theology Occasional Papers 6. Edinburgh: Oliver & Boyd, 1957.

Hansen, Bruce. *All of You Are One: The Social Vision of Galatians 3.28, 1 Corinthians 12.13 and Colossians 3.11*. LNTS 409. London: T&T Clark, 2010.

Hansen, G. Walter. *Abraham in Galatians: Epistolary and Rhetorical Contexts*. JSNTSup 29. Sheffield: JSOT, 1989.

———. *Galatians*. IVPNTC 9. Downers Grove, IL: InterVarsity Press, 1994.

———. *The Letter to the Philippians*. PNTC. Grand Rapids: Eerdmans, 2009.

Hanson, Anthony Tyrrell. *The Wrath of the Lamb*. London: SPCK, 1957.

Hardin, Justin K. *Galatians and the Imperial Cult: A Critical Analysis of the First-Century Social Context of Paul's Letter*. WUNT 2/237. Tübingen: Mohr Siebeck, 2008.

Harding, Susan. *Paul's Eschatological Anthropology: The Dynamics of Human Transformation*. Minneapolis: Fortress, 2015.

Harink, Douglas, ed. *Paul, Philosophy, and the Theopolitical Vision: Critical Engagements with Agamben, Badiou, Žižek, and Others*. Theopolitcal Visions Book 7. Eugene, OR: Cascade, 2010.

Harmon, Matthew S. *Philippians*. Mentor Commentary. Fearn, Ross-shire: Mentor, 2015.

———. *She Must and Shall Go Free: Paul's Isaianic Gospel in Galatians*. BZNW 168. Berlin: de Gruyter, 2010.

Harris, Murray J. *Colossians & Philemon*. Exegetical Guide to the Greek New Testament 1. Grand Rapids: Eerdmans, 1991.

———. *From Grave to Glory: Resurrection in the New Testament*. Grand Rapids: Zondervan, 1990.

———. *Jesus as "God": The New Testament Use of Theos in Reference to Jesus*. Grand Rapids: Baker, 1992.

———. *Prepositions and Theology in the Greek New Testament*. Grand Rapids: Zondervan, 2012.

———. *Raised Immortal: Resurrection and Immortality in the New Testament*. Grand Rapids: Eerdmans, 1985.

———. *The Second Epistle to the Corinthians: A Commentary on the Greek Text*. NIGTC. Grand Rapids: Eerdmans, 2005.

———. *Slave of Christ: A New Testament Metaphor for Total Devotion to Christ*. NSBT 8. Downers Grove, IL: InterVarsity Press, 1999.

Harris, W. Hall, III. *Descent of Christ: Ephesians 4:7–11 and Traditional Hebrew Imagery*. AGJU 32. Leiden: Brill, 1996.

Harrison, James R. *Paul and the Imperial Authorities at Thessalonica and Rome*. WUNT 2/273. Tübingen: Mohr Siebeck, 2011.

———. "Paul and the Imperial Gospel in Thessalonika." *JSNT* 25 (2002): 71–96.

———. *Paul's Language of Grace in Its Graeco-Roman Context*. WUNT 2/172. Tübingen: Mohr Siebeck, 2003.

Hart, Trevor. "Eschatology." Pages 262–77 in *The Oxford Handbook of Evangelical Theology*. Edited by Gerald R. McDermott. Oxford: Oxford University Press, 2010.

———. "Redemption and Fall." Pages 189–206 in *The Cambridge Companion to Christian Doctrine*. Edited by Colin E. Gunton. Cambridge: Cambridge University Press, 1997.

Hartman, Lars. *Prophecy Interpreted: The Formation of Some Jewish Apocalyptic Texts and of the Eschatological Discourse Mark 13 Par*. ConBNT 1. Lund: Gleerup, 1966.

Hatch, William Henry Paine. *The Pauline Idea of Faith in Its Relation to Jewish and Hellenistic Religion*. HTS 2. Cambridge: Harvard University Press, 1917.

Häusser, Detlef. *Christusbekenntnis und Jesusüberlieferung bei Paulus*. WUNT 2/210. Tübingen: Mohr Siebeck, 2006.

Hawthorne, Gerald F. *Philippians*. WBC 43. Waco, TX: Word, 1983.

Hawthorne, Gerald F., and Ralph P. Martin. *Philippians*. Rev. ed. WBC 43. Nashville: Nelson, 2004.

Hays, Richard B. "Christology and Ethics in Galatians: The Law of Christ." *CBQ* 49 (1987): 268–90.

———. *The Conversion of the Imagination: Paul as Interpreter of Israel's Scripture*. Grand Rapids: Eerdmans, 2005.

———. "The Conversion of the Imagination: Scripture and Eschatology in 1 Corinthians." *NTS* 45 (1999): 391–412.

———. "Crucified with Christ: A Synthesis of the Theology of 1 and 2 Thessalonians, Philemon, Philippians, and Galatians." Pages 227–46 in *Pauline Theology, Vol. 1: Thessalonians, Philippians, Galatians, Philemon*. Edited by Jouette M. Bassler. Minneapolis: Augsburg Fortress, 1991.

———. *Echoes of Scripture in the Letters of Paul*. New Haven: Yale University Press, 1989.

———. *The Faith of Jesus Christ: The Narrative Substructure of Galatians 3:1–4:11*. 2nd ed. Grand Rapids: Eerdmans, 2002.

———. *First Corinthians*. Interpretation. Louisville: Westminster John Knox, 1997.

———. "Galatians." Pages 181–348 in vol. 11 of *The New Interpreter's Bible*. Edited by L. Keck. Nashville: Abingdon, 2000.

———. *The Moral Vision of the New Testament: A Contemporary Introduction to New Testament Ethics*. San Francisco: HarperSanFrancisco, 1996.

———. ΠΙΣΤΙΣ and Pauline Christology: What Is at Stake?" Pages 714–29 in *Society of Biblical Literature 1991 Seminar Papers*. Edited by E. H. Lovering Jr. Atlanta: Scholars Press, 1991.

———. "Victory over Violence: The Significance of N. T. Wright's Jesus for New Testament Ethics." Pages 142–48 in *Jesus and the Restoration of Israel: A Critical Assessment of N. T. Wright's Jesus and the Victory of God*. Edited by Carey C. Newman. Downers Grove, IL: InterVarsity Press, 1999.

Heilig, Christoph. *Hidden Criticism? The Methodology and Plausibility of the Search for a Counter-Imperial Subtext in Paul*. WUNT 2/392. Tübingen: Mohr Siebeck, 2015.

Heim, Erin. M. *Adoption in Galatians and Romans: Contemporary Metaphor Theories and the Pauline Huiothesia*. BibInt 153. Leiden: Brill, 2017.

Heininger, Bernhard. "Contemporary Religions and Philosophical Schools." Pages 23–56 in *Paul: Life, Setting, Work, Letters*. Edited by Oda Wischmeyer. London: T&T Clark, 2012.

Hellerman, Joseph H. *Philippians*. EGGNT. Nashville: Broadman & Holman, 2015.

———. *Reconstructing Honor at Philippi: Carmen Christi as Cursus Pudorum*. SNTSMS 132. Cambridge: Cambridge University Press, 2005.

Hemer, Colin J. *The Book of Acts in the Setting of Hellenistic History*. Edited by Conrad H. Gempf. WUNT 2/49. Tübingen: Mohr Siebeck, 1989.

Hendriksen, William. *Exposition of I and II Thessalonians*. New Testament Commentary. Grand Rapids: Baker, 1955.

Hengel, Martin. *The Atonement: The Origins of the Doctrine in the New Testament*. Philadelphia: Fortress, 1981.

———. "Heilsgeschichte." Pages 1–33 in *Theologicsche, Historische und Biographische Skizzen: Kleine Schriften VII*. Edited by Claus-Jürgen Thorton. WUNT 2/253. Tübingen: Mohr Siebeck, 2010.

———. *Judaism and Hellenism: Studies in Their Encounter in Palestine during the Early Hellenistic Period*. 2 vols. Tübingen: Mohr Siebeck, 1974.

———. *The Son of God: The Origin of Christology and the History of Jewish-Hellenistic Religion*. Philadelphia: Fortress, 1976.

Hengel, Martin, and Anna Maria Schwemer. *Paul between Damascus and Antioch: The Unknown Years*. Louisville: Westminster John Knox, 1997.

Heppe, Heinrich. *Reformed Dogmatics: Set Out and Illustrated from the Source*. Edited and revised by Ernst Bizer. Grand Rapids: Baker, 1978.

Hering, Jean. "'Serviteurs de Dieu': Contribution à l'exégèse pratique de Romains 13,3–4." *RHPR* 30 (1950): 31–40.

Hick, John. *Evil and the God of Love*. London: Macmillan, 1966.

Hill, David. *Greek Words and Hebrew Meanings: Studies in the Semantics of Soteriological Terms*. SNTSMS 5. Cambridge: Cambridge University Press, 1967.

Hill, Wesley. *Paul and the Trinity: Persons, Relations, and the Pauline Letters*. Grand Rapids: Eerdmans, 2015.

Hillbert, Sven. *Limited and Universal Salvation: A Text-Oriented and Hermeneutical Study of Two Perspectives in Paul*. ConBNT 31. Stockholm: Almqvist & Wiksell, 1999.

Hoehner, Harold W. *Ephesians: An Exegetical Commentary*. Grand Rapids: Baker Academic, 2002.

Hoekema, Anthony A. *Created in God's Image*. Grand Rapids: Eerdmans, 1986.

Hoffmann, Paul. *Die Toten in Christus. Eine religionsgeschichtliche und exegetische Untersuchung zur paulinischen Eschatologie*. NTAbh 2. Münster: Aschendorff, 1966.

Hofius, Otfried. "Erwägungen zur Gestalt und Herkunft des paulinischen Versöhnungs Gedankens." Pages 1–14 in *Paulusstudien*. WUNT 2/51. Tübingen: Mohr Siebeck, 1989.

———. "The Lord's Supper and the Lord's Supper Tradition: Reflections on 1 Cor. 11:23b–25." Pages 75–115 in *One Loaf, One Cup: Ecumenical Studies of 1 Cor. 11 and Other Eucharistic Texts*. Edited by Ben F. Meyer. Macon, GA: Mercer University Press, 1988.

———. "Sühne und Versöhnung: Zum Paulinischen Verständnis des Kreuzestodes Jesu." Pages 33–49 in *Paulusstudien*. WUNT 2/51. Tübingen: Mohr Siebeck, 1994.

———. "'Werke des Gesetzes': Untersuchungen zu der paulinischen Rede von den ἔργα νόμου." Pages 271–310 in *Paulus and Johannes: Exegetische Studien zur paulinischen und johanneischen Theologie und Literatur*. Edited by D. Sänger and U. Mell. WUNT 2/198. Tübingen: Mohr Siebeck, 2006.

Hoglund, Jonathan. *Called by Triune Grace: Divine Rhetoric and the Effectual Call*. Downers Grove, IL: InterVarsity Press, 2016.

Holland, Tom. *Contours of Pauline Theology: A Radical New Survey of the Influences on Paul's Biblical Writings*. Fearn, Scotland: Mentor, 2004.

———. *Romans: The Divine Marriage. A Biblical Theological Commentary*. Eugene, OR: Pickwick, 2011.

Holleman, Joost. *Resurrection and Parousia: A Traditio-Historical Study of Paul's Eschatology in 1 Corinthians 15*. NovTSup 84. Leiden: Brill, 1996.

Hollis, Wendall. "Become Full in the Spirit: A Linguistic, Contextual, and Theological Study of ΠΛΗΡΟΥΣΘΕ 'ΕΝ ΠΝΕΥΜΑΤΙ." PhD diss., Trinity International University, 2001.

Holtz, Gottfried. *Die Pastoralbriefe*. THKNT 13. Berlin: Evangelische Verlagsanstalt, 1986.

Holtz, Traugott. *Der erste Brief an die Thessalonicher*. EKKNT 13. Zürich: Benziger, 1986.

Hong, In-Gyu. "Being 'under the Law' in Galatians." *Evangelical Review of Theology* 26 (2002): 354–72.

———. *The Law in Galatians*. JSNTSup 8. Sheffield: JSOT, 1993.

Hood, Jason. "The Cross in the New Testament: Two Theses in Conversation with Recent Literature (2000–2007)." *WTJ* 71 (2009): 281–95.

Hooker, Morna D. "Authority on Her Head: An Examination of 1 Corinthians 11.10." *NTS* 10 (1963–1964): 410–16.

———. "Interchange and Atonement." Pages 13–25 in *From Adam to Christ: Essays on Paul*. Cambridge: Cambridge University Press, 1990.

———. "Interchange in Christ." *JTS* 22 (1971): 349–61.

———. "On Becoming the Righteousness of God: Another Look at 2 Corinthians 5:21." *NovT* 50 (2008): 358–75.

———. "Paul and 'Covenantal Nomism.'" Pages 47–56 in *Paul and Paulinism: Essays in Honour of C. K. Barrett*. Edited by M. D. Hooker and S. G. Wilson. London: SPCK, 1982.

———. "Philippians 2.6–11." Pages 88–100 in *From Adam to Christ: Essays on Paul*. Cambridge: Cambridge University Press, 1990.

———. "Were There False Teachers in Colossae?" Pages 315–31 in *Christ and Spirit in the New Testament: Studies in Honour of Charles Francis Digby Moule*. Edited by Barnabas Lindars and Stephen S. Smalley. Cambridge: Cambridge University Press, 1973.

Hoover, Roy W. "The HARPAGMOS Enigma: A Philological Solution." *HTR* 64 (1971): 95–119.

Horn, Friedrich Wilhelm. "Juden und Heiden. Aspekte der Verhältnisbestimmung in den paulinischen Briefen. Ein Gespräch mit Krister Stendahl." Pages 17–39 in *Lutherische und Neue Perspektive: Beiträge zu einem Schüsselproblem der gegenwärtigen exegetischen Diskussion*. Edited by Michael Bachmann. WUNT 2/182. Tübingen: Mohr Siebeck, 2005.

Horrell, David G. "Ethnicisation, Marriage and Early Christian Identity: Critical Reflections on 1 Corinthians 7, 1 Peter 3 and Modern New Testament Scholarship." *NTS* 62 (2016): 439–60.

———. *The Social Ethos of the Corinthian Correspondence: Interests and Ideology from 1 Corinthians to 1 Clement.* Edinburgh: T&T Clark, 1996.

———. *Solidarity and Difference: A Contemporary Reading of Paul's Ethics.* 2nd ed. London: T&T Clark, 2015.

Horsley, Richard A. "Gnosis in Corinth: 1 Corinthians 8:1–6." *NTS* 27 (1980): 37–39.

Horsley, Richard A., ed. *Paul and Empire: Religion and Power in Roman Imperial Society.* Harrisburg: Trinity Press International, 1997.

Horton, Michael S. *The Christian Faith: A Systematic Theology for Pilgrims on the Way.* Grand Rapids: Zondervan, 2011.

———. *Covenant and Salvation: Union with Christ.* Louisville: Westminster John Knox, 2007.

———. "Ephesians 4:1–16: The Ascension, the Church, and the Spoils of War." Pages 129–53 in *Theological Commentary: Evangelical Perspectives.* Edited by R. Michael Allen. London: T&T Clark, 2011.

———. *Justification.* 2 vols. New Studies in Dogmatics. Grand Rapids: Zondervan, 2018.

———. *Lord and Servant: A Covenant Christology.* Louisville: Westminster John Knox, 2005.

———. *People and Place: A Covenant Ecclesiology.* Louisville: Westminster John Knox, 2008.

———. *Rediscovering the Holy Spirit: God's Perfecting Presence in Creation, Redemption, and Everyday Life.* Grand Rapids: Zondervan, 2017.

———. "Traditional Reformed Response." Pages 244–49 in *Justification: Five Views.* Edited by James K. Beilby and Paul Rhodes Eddy. Downers Grove, IL: InterVarsity Press, 2011.

Howard, G. E. "'The Faith of Christ.'" *ExpTim* 85 (1973–1974): 212–14.

Hubbard, Moyer V. *New Creation in Paul's Letters and Thought.* SNTSMS 119. Cambridge: Cambridge University Press, 2002.

Hübner, Hans. *Law in Paul's Thought: Studies of the New Testament and Its World.* Edinburgh: T&T Clark, 1984.

———. *An Philemon, an die Kolosser, an die Epheser.* HNT 12. Tübingen: Mohr Siebeck, 1997.

Huddleston, Rodney, and Geoffrey K. Pullum. *The Cambridge Grammar of the English Language.* Cambridge: Cambridge University Press, 2002.

Hughes, Philip Edgcumbe. *The Second Epistle to the Corinthians.* NICNT. Grand Rapids: Eerdmans, 1962.

———. *The True Image: The Origin and Destiny of Man in Christ.* Grand Rapids: Eerdmans, 1989.

Hultberg, Alan. "The Case for a Prewrath Rapture." Pages 109–54 in *Three Views on the Rapture: Pretribulation, Prewrath, or Posttribulation.* Edited by Alan Hultberg. Counterpoints. Grand Rapids: Zondervan, 2010.

Hultgren, Arland J. *Paul's Gospel and Mission: The Outlook from His Letter to the Romans.* Philadelphia: Fortress, 1985.

———. *Paul's Letter to the Romans: A Commentary.* Grand Rapids: Eerdmans, 2011.

Hultgren, Stephen. "Hilasterion (Rom. 3:25) and the Union of Divine Justice and Mercy Part I: The Convergence of Temple and Martyrdom Theologies." *JTS* 70 (2019): 69–109.

———. "Hilasterion (Rom. 3:25) and the Union of Divine Justice and Mercy Part II: Atonement in the Old Testament and in Romans 1–5." *JTS* 70 (2019): 546–99.

Humphrey, Edith M. "Apocalyptic as Theoria in the Letters of St. Paul: A New Perspective on Apocalyptic as Mother of Theology." Pages 87–100 in *Paul and the Apocalyptic Imagination.* Edited by Ben C. Blackwell, John K. Goodrich, and Jason Maston. Minneapolis: Fortress, 2016.

———. "Becoming the Righteousness of God: The Potency of the New Creation in the World (2 Cor 5:16–21)." Pages 125–57 in *Participation, Justification, and Conversion: Eastern Orthodox Interpretation of Paul and the Debate between "Old and New Perspectives on Paul."* Edited by Athanasios Despotis. Tübingen: Mohr Siebeck, 2017.

Hunn, Debbie. "*Pistis Christou* in Galatians 2:16: Clarification from 3:1–6." *TynBul* 57 (2006): 23–33.

Hurd, John Coolidge. *The Origin of 1 Corinthians.* New York: Seabury, 1965.

Hurley, James B. *Man and Woman in Biblical Perspective.* Grand Rapids: Zondervan, 1981.

Hurtado, Larry W. "The Binitarian Shape of Early Christian Worship." Pages 187–213 in *The Jewish Roots of Christological Monotheism.* Edited by C. C. Newman, J. R. Davila, and G. S. Lewis. Supplements to the Journal for the Study of Judaism 63. Leiden: Brill, 1999.

———. "Convert, Apostate or Apostle to the Nations: The 'Conversion' of Paul in Recent Scholarship." *SR* 22 (1993): 273–84.

———. *Destroyer of the Gods: Early Christian Distinctiveness in the Roman World.* Waco, TX: Baylor University Press, 2016.

———. "Jesus' Divine Sonship in Paul's Epistle to the Romans." Pages 217–33 in *Romans and the People of God: Essays in Honor of Gordon D. Fee on the Occasion of His 65th Birthday.* Edited by Sven Soderlund and N. T. Wright. Grand Rapids: Eerdmans, 1999.

———. *Lord Jesus Christ: Devotion to Jesus in Earliest Christianity.* Grand Rapids: Eerdmans, 2003.

———. *One God, One Lord: Early Christian Devotion and Ancient Jewish Monotheism*. 3rd ed. London: Bloomsbury T&T Clark, 2015.

———. "Paul's Messianic Christology." Pages 107–31 in *Paul the Jew: Rereading the Apostle as a Figure of Second Temple Judaism*. Edited by Gabriele Boccaccini and Carlos A. Segovia. Minneapolis: Fortress, 2016.

Instone-Brewer, David. "1 Corinthians 7 in the Light of the Graeco-Roman Marriage and Divorce Papyri." *TynBul* 52 (2001): 101–16.

———. "1 Corinthians 9:9–11: A Literal Interpretation of 'Do Not Muzzle the Ox.'" *NTS* 38 (1992): 225–43.

Irons, Charles Lee. *The Righteousness of God: A Lexical Examination of the Covenant-Faithfulness Interpretation*. WUNT 2/386. Tübingen: Mohr Siebeck, 2015.

Jackson, T. Ryan. *New Creation in Paul's Letters: A Study of the Historical and Social Setting of a Pauline Concept*. WUNT 2/272. Tübingen: Mohr Siebeck, 2010.

Jacob, Haley Goranson. *Conformed to the Image of His Son: Reconsidering Paul's Theology of Glory in Romans*. Downers Grove, IL: InterVarsity Press, 2018.

Janowski, Bernd. *Stellvertretung: Alttestamentliche Studien zu einem theologischen Grundbegriff*. SBS 165. Stuttgart: Katholisches Bibelwerk, 1997.

Jeremias, Joachim. *The Eucharistic Words of Jesus*. London: SCM, 1966.

Jervis, L. Ann. *The Purpose of Romans: A Comparative Letter Structure Investigation*. JSNTSup 55. Sheffield: JSOT Press, 1991.

Jewett, Robert. *A Chronology of Paul's Life*. Philadelphia: Fortress, 1979.

———. "Conflicting Movements in the Early Church as Revealed in Philippians." *NovT* 12 (1970): 362–90.

———. *The Thessalonian Correspondence: Pauline Rhetoric and Millenarian Piety*. Philadelphia: Fortress, 1986.

Jewett, Robert, with Roy D. Kotansky. *Romans*. Hermeneia. Minneapolis: Fortress, 2007.

Jipp, Joshua W. *Christ Is King: Paul's Royal Ideology*. Minneapolis: Fortress, 2015.

Johnson, Adam J. *Atonement: A Guide to the Perplexed*. London: Bloomsbury T&T Clark, 2015.

Johnson, Adam J., ed. *Five Views on the Extent of the Atonement*. Grand Rapids: Zondervan, 2019.

Johnson, Luke Timothy. *Constructing Paul*. Vol. 1 of *The Canonical Paul*. Grand Rapids: Eerdmans, 2020.

———. *The First and Second Letters to Timothy: A New Translation with Introduction and Commentary*. AB 35A. New York: Doubleday, 2001.

———. "A Historiographical Response to Wright's Jesus." Pages 206–26 in *Jesus and the Restoration of Israel: A Critical Assessment of N. T. Wright's Jesus and the Victory of God*. Edited by Carey C. Newman. Downers Grove, IL: InterVarsity Press, 1999.

———. *Interpreting Paul*. Vol. 2 of *The Canonical Paul*. Grand Rapids: Eerdmans, 2021.

———. "The Paul of the Letters: A Catholic Perspective." Pages 65–96 in *Four Views of the Apostle Paul*. Edited by Michael F. Bird. Grand Rapids: Zondervan, 2012.

———. "Rom 3:21–26 and the Faith of Jesus." *CBQ* 44 (1982): 77–90.

———. *The Writings of the New Testament: An Interpretation*. 3rd ed. Minneapolis: Fortress, 2010.

Jowers, Dennis W., and H. Wayne House, eds. *The New Evangelical Subordinationism? Perspectives on the Equality of God the Father and God the Son*. Eugene, OR: Pickwick, 2012.

Judant, D. *Les deux Israël: Essai sur le mystère du salut d'Israël selon l'économie des deux Testaments*. Paris: Cerf, 1960.

Judge, Edwin A. "The Social Identity of the First Christians: A Question of Method in Religious History." *JRH* 11 (1980): 201–17.

———. *The Social Pattern of Early Christian Groups in the First Century*. London: Tyndale, 1960.

Judge, Edwin A., with David M. Scholer. *Social Distinctives of the Christians in the First Century: Pivotal Essays*. Peabody, MA: Hendrickson, 2008.

Juncker, Günther. "'Children of Promise': Spiritual Paternity and Patriarch Theology in Galatians and Romans." *BBR* 17 (2007): 131–60.

Jüngel, Eberhard. *Justification: The Heart of the Christian Faith: A Theological Study with Ecumenical Purpose*. Edinburgh: T&T Clark, 2001.

Kaiser, Walter C., Jr. *Toward an Old Testament Theology*. Grand Rapids: Zondervan, 1978.

Kamlah, E. *Die Form der katalogischen Paränese im Neuen Testament*. WUNT 1/7. Tübingen: Mohr, 1964.

Kärkkäinen, Veli-Matti. *Salvation as Deification and Justification*. Collegeville, MN: Liturgical, 2004.

Käsemann, Ernst. "Die Heilsbedeutung des Todes Jesu nach Paulus." Pages 11–34 in *Zur Bedeutung des Todes Jesu. Exegetische Beiträge*. Edited by Hans Conzelmann, Ellen Fesseman-van-Leer, and Ernst Haenchen. Gütersloh: Gütersloher, 1967.

———. "Kritische Analyse von Phil. 2,5–11." *ZTK* 47 (1950): 313–60.

———. *New Testament Questions of Today*. Philadelphia: Fortress, 1969.

———. *Perspectives on Paul*. Philadelphia: Fortress, 1971.

———. "'The Righteousness of God' in Paul." Pages 168–82 in *New Testament Questions of Today*. By Ernst Käsemann. Philadelphia: Fortress, 1969.

———. "Some Thoughts on the Theme 'The Doctrine of Reconciliation in the New Testament.'" Pages 51–64 in *The Future of Our Religious Past: Essays in Honor of Rudolf Bultmann*. Edited by James M. Robinson. London: SCM, 1971.

Katembo, Fabrice S. *The Mystery of the Church: Applying Paul's Ecclesiology in Africa*. Carlisle: Langham, 2020.

Kaye, Bruce Norman. *The Thought Structure of Romans with Special Reference to Chapter 6*. Austin, TX: Schola, 1979.

Keck, Leander E. *Christ's First Theologian: The Shape of Paul's Thought*. Waco, TX: Baylor University Press, 2015.

Keener, Craig S. *1–2 Corinthians*. New Cambridge Bible Commentary. Cambridge: Cambridge University Press, 2005.

———. *Acts: An Exegetical Commentary. Volume 3: Acts 13:1–23:35*. Grand Rapids: Baker, 2014.

———. *Galatians: A Commentary*. Grand Rapids: Baker, 2019.

———. *The Mind of the Spirit: Paul's Approach to Transformed Thinking*. Grand Rapids: Baker, 2016.

———. *Paul, Women and Wives: Marriage and Women's Ministry in the Letters of Paul*. Peabody, MA: Hendrickson, 1992.

Keesmaat, Silvia C. "Exodus and the Intertextual Transformation of Tradition in Romans 8.14–30." *JSNT* 54 (1994): 29–56.

———. *Paul and His Story: (Re)interpreting the Exodus Tradition*. JSNTSup 181. Sheffield: Sheffield Academic Press, 1999.

Keil, C. F., and F. Delitzsch. *Commentary on the Old Testament: The Pentateuch*. Grand Rapids: Eerdmans, 1969.

Kertelge, Karl. "Gesetz und Freiheit im Galaterbrief." *NTS* 30 (1984): 389–90.

Kibbe, Michael. "'The Obedience of Christ': A Reassessment of Τὴν Ὑπακοὴν Τοῦ Χριστοῦ in 2 Corinthians 10:5." *JSPL* 2 (2012): 41–56.

Kidd, Reggie M. *Wealth and Beneficence in the Pastoral Epistles*. SBLDS 122. Atlanta: Scholars Press, 1990.

Kilner, John F. *Dignity and Destiny: Humanity in the Image of God*. Grand Rapids: Eerdmans, 2015.

Kim, Mitchell. "Respect for Context and Authorial Intention: Setting the Epistemological Bar." Pages 115–29 in *Paul and Scripture: Extending the Conversation*. Edited by Christopher D. Stanley. Early Christianity and Its Literature 9. Atlanta: SBL, 2012.

Kim, Seyoon. *Christ and Caesar: The Gospel and the Roman Empire in the Writings of Paul and Luke*. Grand Rapids: Eerdmans, 2008.

———. *The Origin of Paul's Gospel*. WUNT 2/4. Tübingen: Mohr Siebeck, 1981.

———. *Paul and the New Perspective: Second Thoughts on the Origin of Paul's Gospel*. Grand Rapids: Eerdmans, 2001.

———. "Paul's Entry (εἴσοδος) and the Thessalonians' Faith (1 Thessalonians 1–3)." *NTS* 51 (2005): 519–42.

Kinzer, Mark S. *Post-Missionary Messianic Judaism: Redefining Christian Engagement with the Jewish People*. Grand Rapids: Baker, 2005.

Kirby, J. T. "The Syntax of Romans 5.12: A Rhetorical Approach." *NTS* 33 (1987): 283–86.

Kirby, Peter. "The Muratorian Fragment." *Early Christian Writings*. www.earlychristianwritings.com /text/muratorian -metzger.html.

Kirk, Alexander N. *The Departure of an Apostle: Paul's Death Anticipated and Remembered*. WUNT 2/406. Tübingen: Mohr Siebeck, 2015.

Kirk, J. R. Daniel. *Jesus Have I Loved, but Paul? A Narrative Approach to the Problem of Pauline Christianity*. Grand Rapids: Baker, 2011.

———. *Unlocking Romans: Resurrection and the Justification of God*. Grand Rapids: Eerdmans, 2008.

Kittredge, Cynthia Briggs. "Feminist Approaches: Rethinking History and Resisting Ideologies." Pages 117–33 in *Studying Paul's Letters: Contemporary Perspectives and Methods*. Edited by Joseph A. Marchal. Minneapolis: Fortress, 2012.

Kiuchi, Nobuyoshi. *Leviticus*. AOTC. Downers Grove, IL: InterVarsity Press, 2007.

Klaiber, Walter. *Rechtfertigung und Gemeinde: Eine Untersuchung zum Paulinischen Kirchenverständnis*. FRLANT 127. Göttingen: Vandenhoeck & Ruprecht, 1982.

Klein, William W. *The New Chosen People: A Corporate View of Election*. Eugene, OR: Wipf & Stock, 2015.

Klink, Edward W., and Darian R. Lockett. *Understanding Biblical Theology: A Comparison of Theory and Practice.* Grand Rapids: Zondervan, 2012.

Knight, George W., III. *The Faithful Sayings in the Pastoral Epistles.* Grand Rapids: Baker, 1979.

———. "Husbands and Wives as Analogues of Christ and the Church: Ephesians 5:21–33 and Colossians 3:18–19." Pages 161–75 in *Recovering Biblical Manhood and Womanhood: A Response to Evangelical Feminism.* Edited by John Piper and Wayne Grudem. Wheaton, IL: Crossway, 1991.

———. *The Pastoral Epistles.* NIGTC. Grand Rapids: Eerdmans, 1992.

Knöppler, Thomas. *Sühne im Neuen Testament: Studien zum urchristlichen Verständnis der Heilsbedeutung des Todes Jesu.* WMANT 88. Neukirchen-Vluyn: Neukirchener, 2001.

Knox, John. *Philemon among the Letters of Paul.* London: Collins, 1960.

Koch, Dietrich-Alex. *Die Schrift als Zeuge des Evangeliums: Untersuchungen zur Verwendung und zum Verständnis der Schrift bei Paulus.* BHT. Tübingen: Mohr Siebeck, 1986.

Koet, Bart J., Edwina Murphy, and Esko Ryökäs. *Deacons and Diakonia in Early Christianity: The First Two Centuries.* WUNT 2/479. Tübingen: Mohr Siebeck, 2018.

Korner, Ralph J. "*Ekklēsia* as a Jewish Synagogue Term: Some Implications for Paul's Socio-Religious Location." *Journal of the Jesus Movement in Its Jewish Setting* 2 (2015): 53–78.

———. *The Origin and Meaning of Ekklesia in the Early Jesus Movement.* Ancient Judaism and Early Christianity 98. Leiden: Brill, 2017.

Köstenberger, Andreas J. *A Commentary on 1–2 Timothy and Titus.* BTCP. Nashville: B&H Academic, 2017.

———. "A Complex Sentence: The Syntax of 1 Timothy 2:12." Pages 117–61 in *Women in the Church: An Interpretation and Application of 1 Timothy 2:9–15.* Edited by Andreas J. Köstenberger and Thomas R. Schreiner. Wheaton, IL: Crossway, 2016.

———. "The Identity of the ΙΣΡΑΗΛ ΤΟΥ ΘΕΟΥ (Israel of God) in Galatians 6:16." *Faith and Mission* 19 (2001): 3–24.

———. "The Mystery of Christ and the Church: Head and Body, 'One Flesh.'" *TrinJ* 12 (1991): 79–94.

Köstenberger, Andreas J., and Thomas R. Schreiner, eds. *Women in the Church: An Interpretation and Application of 1 Timothy 2:9–15.* 3rd ed. Wheaton, IL: Crossway, 2016.

Kraus, Wolfgang. *Das Volk Gottes: Zur Grundlegung der Ekklesiologie bei Paulus.* WUNT 2/85. Tübingen: Mohr Siebeck, 1996.

Kreinecker, Christina M. *2 Thessaloniker.* Papyrologische Kommentare zum Neuen Testament 3. Göttingen: Vandenhoeck & Ruprecht, 2010.

Kreitzer, L. Joseph. *Jesus and God in Paul's Eschatology.* JSNTSup 19. Sheffield: JSOT, 1987.

Kruger, Michael J. *Canon Revisited: Establishing the Origins and Authority of the New Testament Books.* Wheaton, IL: Crossway, 2012.

Kruse, Colin. *Paul's Letter to the Romans.* PNTC. Grand Rapids: Eerdmans, 2012.

Kümmel, Werner Georg. *Introduction to the New Testament.* 2nd ed. London: SCM, 1975.

———. *The Theology of the New Testament.* Nashville: Abingdon, 1973.

Kwon, Yon-Gyong. *Eschatology in Galatians: Rethinking Paul's Response to the Crisis in Galatia.* WUNT 2/183. Tübingen: Mohr Siebeck, 2004.

Laato, Timo. *Paul and Judaism: An Anthropological Approach.* SFSHJ 115. Atlanta: Scholars Press, 1995.

———. "Paul's Anthropological Considerations: Two Problems." Pages 343–60 in *The Paradoxes of Paul.* Vol. 2 of *Justification and Variegated Nomism.* Edited by D. A. Carson, Peter T. O'Brien, and Mark A. Seifrid. WUNT 2/140. Tübingen: Mohr Siebeck, 2004.

———. *Paulus und das Judentum: Anthropologische Erwägungen.* Åbo: Åbo Academy, 1991.

———. "*Simul Iustus et Peccator* through the Lenses of Paul." *JETS* 61 (2018): 735–66.

Ladd, George Eldon. *The Blessed Hope.* Grand Rapids: Eerdmans, 1956.

———. *A Theology of the New Testament.* Rev. ed. with assistance of Donald A. Hagner. Grand Rapids: Eerdmans, 1993.

Lähnemann, Johannes. *Der Kolosserbrief: Komposition, Situation und Argumentation.* SNT 3. Gütersloh: Gütersloher Verlagshaus, 1971.

Lambrecht, Jan. "'Reconcile Yourselves . . .': A Reading of 2 Corinthians 5:11–21." Pages 363–412 in *Studies on 2 Corinthians.* Edited by R. Bieringer and J. Lambrecht. BETL 112. Leuven: Leuven University Press, 1994.

Lampe, Peter. *From Paul to Valentinus: Christians at Rome in the First Two Centuries.* Minneapolis: Fortress, 2003.

———. "Keine 'Sklavenflucht' des Onesimus." *ZNW* 76 (1985): 135–37.

———. "The Roman Christians of Romans 16." Pages 216–30 in *The Romans Debate*. Edited by Karl P. Donfried. Rev. ed. Grand Rapids: Baker, 1991.

———. *Die stadtrömischen Christen in den ersten beiden Jahrhunderten: Untersuchungen zur Sozialgeschichte*. WUNT 2/18. Tübingen: Mohr Siebeck, 1987.

Last, Richard. *The Pauline Church and the Corinthian Ekklēsia: Greco-Roman Associations in Comparative Context*. SNTSMS 164. Cambridge: Cambridge University Press, 2016.

Lau, Andrew Y. *Manifest in Flesh: The Epiphany Christology of the Pastoral Epistles*. WUNT 2/86. Tübingen: Mohr Siebeck, 1996.

Lee, Chee-Chiew. *The Blessing of Abraham, the Spirit, and Justification in Galatians: Their Relationship and Significance for Paul's Theology*. Eugene, OR: Pickwick, 2013.

———. "*Goyim* in Genesis 35:11 and the Abrahamic Promise of Blessing for the Nations." *JETS* 52 (2009): 467–82.

Lee, Yongbom. *Paul, Scribe of Old and New: Intertextual Insights for the Jesus-Paul Debate*. LNTS 512. London: Bloomsbury, 2015.

Légasse, Simon. *L'épître de Paul aux Galates*. LD 9. Paris: Cerf, 2000.

Leighton, Matthew B. "'Mosaic Covenant' as a Possible Referent for ΝΟΜΟΣ in Paul." *TynBul* 69 (2018): 161–81.

Leithart, Peter J. *Delivered from the Elements of the World: Atonement, Justification, Mission*. Grand Rapids: Baker, 2016.

Letham, Robert. *Union with Christ in Scripture, History, and Theology*. Phillipsburg, NJ: Presbyterian and Reformed, 2011.

Lightfoot, J. B. "The Destination of the Epistle to the Ephesians." Pages 377–96 in *Biblical Essays*. London: Macmillan, 1893.

———. *Saint Paul's Epistle to the Galatians: A Revised Text with Introduction, Notes, and Dissertations*. 7th ed. London: Macmillan, 1881.

———. *Saint Paul's Epistle to the Philippians*. London: Macmillan, 1888.

———. *Saint Paul's Epistles to the Colossians and to Philemon*. London: MacMillan, 1897. Repr., Grand Rapids: Zondervan, 1971.

Lilburne, Geoffrey A. *A Sense of Place: A Christian Theology of the Land*. Nashville: Abingdon, 1989.

Lim, Timothy H. *Holy Scripture in the Qumran Commentaries and Pauline Letters*. Oxford: Clarendon, 1997.

Lincoln, Andrew T. *Ephesians*. WBC 42. Nashville: Thomas Nelson, 1990.

———. "The Letter to the Colossians." Pages 553–669 in volume 11 of *The New Interpreter's Bible*. Edited by Leander E. Keck. Nashville: Abingdon, 2000.

———. *Paradise Now and Not Yet: Studies in the Role of the Heavenly Dimension in Paul's Thought with Special Reference to His Eschatology*. SNTSMS 43. Cambridge Cambridge University Press, 1981.

Lindemann, Andreas. *Die Aufhebung der Zeit: Geschichtsverständnis und Eschatologie im Epheserbrief*. SNT 12. Gütersloh: Gütersloh Mohn, 1975.

———. *Der Epheserbrief*. ZBK 8. Zurich: TVZ, 1985.

Lindsay, Dennis R. *Josephus and Faith: Pistis and Pisteuein as Faith Terminology in the Writings of Flavius Josephus and in the New Testament*. AGJU 19. Leiden: Brill, 1993.

———. "Works of Law, Hearing of Faith and *Pistis Christou* in Galatians 2:16–3:5." *Stone-Campbell Journal* 3 (2000): 79–88.

Linebaugh, Jonathan A. *God, Grace and Righteousness in Wisdom of Solomon and Paul's Letter to the Romans*. NovTSup 152. Leiden: Brill, 2013.

Litfin, Duane. *Paul's Theology of Preaching: The Apostle's Challenge to the Art of Persuasion in Ancient Corinth*. Downers Grove, IL: IVP Academic, 2015.

———. *St. Paul's Theology of Proclamation: 1 Corinthians 1–4 and Greco-Roman Rhetoric*. SNTSMS 79. Cambridge: Cambridge University Press, 1994.

Lloyd-Jones, D. Martyn. *Romans: Exposition of Chapter 6, The New Man*. Edinburgh: Banner of Truth, 1972.

Locher, G. W. "The Characteristic Features of Zwingli's Theology in Comparison with Luther and Calvin." Pages 142–232 in *Zwingli's Thought: New Perspectives*. Studies in the History of Christian Thought 25. Leiden: Brill, 1981.

Lohmeyer, Ernst. *Christuskult und Kaiserkult*. Tübingen: Mohr Siebeck, 1919.

———. *Kyrios Jesus: Eine Untersuchung zu Phil. 2, 5–11*. Sitzungsberichte der Heidelberger Akademie der Wissenschaften. Philosophisch-historische Klasse. Jahrgang 1927/8.4. Heidelberg: Winter, 1961.

Lohse, Eduard. *Der Brief an die Römer*. KEK. Göttingen: Vandenhoeck & Ruprecht, 2003.

———. *Colossians and Philemon*. Hermeneia. Philadelphia: Fortress, 1971.

———. *Märtyrer und Gottesknecht: Untersuchungen zur urchristlichen Verkündigung vom Sühntod Jesu Christi*. FRLANT 46. Göttingen: Vandenhoeck & Ruprecht, 1963.

Loke, Andrew Ter Ern. *The Origin of Divine Christology*. SNTSMS 169. Cambridge: Cambridge University Press, 2017.

Longenecker, Bruce W. "Different Answers to Different Issues: Israel, the Gentiles and Salvation History in Romans 9–11." *JSNT* 36 (1989): 95–123.

———. *Eschatology and the Covenant: A Comparison of 4 Ezra and Romans 1–11*. JSNTSup 57. Sheffield: Sheffield Academic Press, 1991.

———. *Remember the Poor: Paul, Poverty, and the Greco-Roman World*. Grand Rapids: Eerdmans, 2010.

———. "Salvation History in Galatians and the Making of a Pauline Discourse." *JSPL* 2 (2012): 65–87.

———. *The Triumph of Abraham's God: The Transformation of Identity in Galatians*. Edinburgh: T&T Clark, 1998.

Longenecker, Bruce W., and Todd D. Still. *Thinking through Paul: A Survey of His Life, Letters, and Theology*. Grand Rapids: Zondervan, 2015.

Longenecker, Richard N. *The Christology of Early Jewish Christianity*. Grand Rapids: Baker, 1970.

———. *The Epistle to the Romans: A Commentary on the Greek Text*. NIGTC. Grand Rapids: Eerdmans, 2016.

———. *Galatians*. WBC 41. Dallas: Word, 1990.

———. "The Obedience of Christ in the Theology of the Early Church." Pages 142–52 in *Reconciliation and Hope: New Testament Essays on Atonement and Eschatology Presented to L. L. Morris on his 60th Birthday*. Edited by Robert Banks. Grand Rapids: Eerdmans, 1974.

———. *Paul, Apostle of Liberty: The Origin and Nature of Paul's Christianity*. New York: Harper & Row, 1964. Repr., Grand Rapids: Eerdmans, 2015.

Lopez, Davina Casperina. *Apostle to the Conquered: Reimagining Paul's Mission*. Minneapolis: Fortress, 2008.

Louth, Andrew. "The Place of *Theosis* in Orthodox Theology." Pages 32–44 in *Partakers of the Divine Nature: The History and Development of Deification in the Christian Tradition*. Edited by Michael J. Christensen and Jeffery A. Wittung. Grand Rapids: Baker, 2007.

Lövestam, Evald. *Spiritual Wakefulness in the New Testament*. LUÅ 55.3. Lund: Gleerup, 1963.

Luckensmeyer, David. *The Eschatology of First Thessalonians*. NTOA/SUNT 71. Göttingen: Vandenhoeck & Ruprecht, 2009.

Lüdemann, Gerd. *Paul, Apostle to the Gentiles: Studies in Chronology*. Philadelphia: Fortress, 1984.

Luraghi, S. *On the Meaning of Prepositions and Cases: The Expression of Semantic Roles in Ancient Greek*. Studies in Language Companion Series. Amsterdam: John Benjamin, 2003.

Luther, Martin. "How Christians Should Regard Moses." Pages 162–71 in *Word and Sacrament I*. Vol. 35 of *Luther's Works*. Edited by Theodore Bachmann. Philadelphia: Fortress, 1960.

———. *Lectures on Galatians 1535, Chapters 1–4*. Vol. 26 of *Luther's Works*. Edited by Jaroslav Pelikan. St. Louis: Concordia, 1963.

———. *Lectures on Galatians 1535, Chapters 5–6, and Lectures on Galatians 1519, Chapters 1–6*. Vol. 27 of *Luther's Works*. Edited by Jaroslav Pelikan. Saint Louis: Concordia, 1964.

———. "Preface to the Epistle of St. Paul to the Romans." Page 365 in *Word and Sacrament I*, vol. 35 of *Luther's Works*. Edited by Theodore Bachmann. Philadelphia: Fortress, 1960.

Luz, Ulrich. "Der Brief an die Kolosser." Pages 181–244 in *Die Briefe an die Galater, Epheser, und Kolosser*. By Jürgen Becker and Ulrich Luz. NTD 8.1. Göttingen: Vandenhoeck & Ruprecht, 1998.

———. *Das Geschichtsverständnis des Paulus*. BEvT 49. Munich: Chr. Kaiser, 1968.

Lyall, Francis. "Roman Law in the Writings of Paul: Adoption." *JBL* 88 (1969): 458–66.

———. *Slaves, Citizens, Sons: Legal Metaphors in the Epistles*. Grand Rapids: Zondervan, 1984.

Lyons, George. *Pauline Autobiography: Toward a New Understanding*. SBLDS 73. Atlanta: Scholars Press, 1985.

Macaskill, Grant. *Union with Christ in the New Testament*. Oxford: Oxford University Press, 2013.

MacDonald, Lee Martin, and Stanley E. Porter. *Early Christianity and Its Sacred Literature*. Peabody, MA: Hendrickson, 2000.

MacDonald, Margaret Y. *Colossians and Ephesians*. SP 17. Collegeville, MN: Liturgical, 2000.

MacGregor, G. H. C. "The Concept of the Wrath of God in the New Testament." *NTS* 7 (1960–1961): 101–9.

Madueme, Hans, and Michael Reeves, eds. *Adam, the Fall, and Original Sin: Theological, Biblical, and Scientific Perspectives*. Grand Rapids: Baker, 2014.

Magee, Gregory S. *Portrait of an Apostle: A Case for Paul's Authorship of Colossians and Ephesians.* Eugene, OR: Pickwick, 2013.

Malherbe, Abraham J. "'Gentle as a Nurse': The Cynic Background to 1 Thess 2." *NovT* 12 (1970): 203–17.

———. *The Letters to the Thessalonians.* AB 32B. New Haven: Yale University Press, 2004.

Manson, T. W. "St. Paul's Letter to the Romans—and Others." Pages 3–15 in *The Romans Debate.* Edited by Karl P. Donfried. Rev. ed. Grand Rapids: Baker Academic, 1991.

———. *The Teaching of Jesus: Studies in Its Form and Content.* Repr., Cambridge: Cambridge University Press, 1967.

Marshall, I. Howard. *1 & 2 Thessalonians.* NCB. Grand Rapids: Eerdmans, 1983.

———. *Aspects of the Atonement: Cross and Resurrection in the Reconciling of God and Humanity.* London: Paternoster, 2007.

———. "The Development of the Concept of Redemption in the New Testament." Pages 153–69 in *Reconciliation and Hope: New Testament Essays on Atonement and Eschatology Presented to L. L. Morris on His 60th Birthday.* Edited by R. Banks. Grand Rapids: Eerdmans, 1974.

———. "The Meaning of 'Reconciliation.'" Pages 117–32 in *Unity and Diversity in New Testament Theology: Essays in Honor of George E. Ladd.* Edited by Robert A. Guelich. Grand Rapids: Eerdmans, 1978.

———. *New Testament Theology: Many Witnesses, One Gospel.* Downers Grove, IL: InterVarsity Press, 2010.

———. "Romans 16:25–27: An Apt Conclusion." Pages 170–84 in *Romans and the People of God: Essays in Honor of Gordon D. Fee on the Occasion of His 65th Birthday.* Edited by Sven K. Soderlund and N. T. Wright. Grand Rapids: Eerdmans, 1999.

———. "Salvation, Grace and Works in the Later Writings of the Pauline Corpus." *NTS* 42 (1996): 339–58.

———. "The Theology of Philemon." Pages 175–91 in *The Theology of the Shorter Pauline Letters.* By I. Howard Marshall and Karl P. Donfried. Cambridge: Cambridge University Press, 1993.

Marshall, I. Howard, with Philip H. Towner. *A Critical and Exegetical Commentary on the Pastoral Epistles.* ICC. London: T&T Clark, 1999.

Martens, Elmer A. *Plot and Purpose in the Old Testament.* Downers Grove, IL: InterVarsity Press, 1981.

Martin, Brice L. *Christ and the Law in Paul.* NovTSup 62. Leiden: Brill, 1989.

Martin, Dale B. *The Corinthian Body.* New Haven: Yale University Press, 1999.

Martin, Neil. *Regression in Galatians.* WUNT 2/530. Tübingen: Mohr Siebeck, 2020.

———. "Returning to the *Stoicheia tou Kosmou:* Enslavement to the Physical Elements in Galatians 4.3 and 9?" *JSNT* 40 (2018): 434–52.

Martin, Oren R. *Bound for the Promised Land: The Land Promise in God's Redemptive Plan.* NSBT 34. Downers Grove, IL: InterVarsity Press, 2015.

Martin, Ralph P. *2 Corinthians.* WBC 40. Nashville: Thomas Nelson, 2010.

———. *Carmen Christi: Philippians ii.5–11 in Recent Interpretation and in the Setting of Early Christian Worship.* SNTSMS 4. Cambridge: Cambridge University Press, 1967. Repr., *A Hymn of Christ: Philippians 2:5–11 in Recent Interpretation and in the Setting of Early Christian Worship.* Downers Grove, IL: InterVarsity Press, 1997.

———. "New Testament Hymns: Background and Development." *ExpTim* 94 (1983): 132–36.

———. *Reconciliation: A Study of Paul's Theology.* New Foundations Theological Library. Atlanta: John Knox, 1981.

Martyn, J. Louis. "Apocalyptic Antinomies in Paul's Letter to the Galatians." *NTS* 31 (1985): 410–24.

———. *Galatians: A New Translation and Introduction with Commentary.* AB 33A. New York: Doubleday, 1997.

Marxsen, Willi. *Introduction to the New Testament: An Approach to Its Problems.* Philadelphia: Fortress, 1968.

Mason, Steve. "Jews, Judaeans, Judaizing, Judaism: Problems of Categorization in Ancient History." *JSJ* 38 (2007): 457–512.

———. "N. T. Wright on Paul the Pharisee and Ancient Jews in Exile." *SJT* 69 (2016): 432–52.

Masson, Charles. *L'Épître de Saint Paul aux Philippiens; L'Épître de Saint Paul aux Colossiens.* CNT 10. Neuchatel: Delachaux & Niestle, 1950.

Maston, Jason. "Christ or Adam: The Ground for Understanding Humanity." *Journal of Theological Interpretation* 11 (2017): 277–93.

———. *Divine and Human Agency in Second Temple Judaism and Paul: A Comparative Study.* WUNT 2/297. Tübingen: Mohr Siebeck, 2010.

———. "The Nature of Salvation History in Galatians." *JSPL* 2 (2012): 89–103.

Matera, Frank J. "The Death of Christ and the Cross in Paul's Letter to the Galatians." *LS* 18 (1993): 283–96.

———. *Galatians*. SP 9. Collegeville, MN: Liturgical, 1992.

———. *God's Saving Grace: A Pauline Theology*. Grand Rapids: Eerdmans, 2012.

———. *New Testament Theology: Exploring Diversity and Unity*. Louisville: Westminster John Knox, 2007.

Mathew, Susan. *Women in the Greetings of Romans 16.1–16: A Study of Mutuality and Women's Ministry in the Letter to the Romans*. LNTS 471. London: Bloomsbury T&T Clark, 2013.

Matlock, R. Barry. "The Arrow and the Web: Critical Reflections on a Narrative Approach to Paul." Pages 44–57 in *Narrative Dynamics in Paul: A Critical Assessment*. Edited by Bruce W. Longenecker. Louisville: Westminster John Knox, 2002.

———. "Saving Faith: The Rhetoric and Semantics of πίστις in Paul." Pages 73–89 in *The Faith of Jesus Christ: Exegetical, Biblical, and Theological Studies*. Edited by Michael F. Bird and Preston M. Sprinkle. Peabody, MA: Hendrickson, 2009.

———. *Unveiling the Apocalyptic Paul: Paul's Interpreters and the Rhetoric of Criticism*. JSNTSup 127. Sheffield: Sheffield Academic Press, 1996.

Mattern, Liselotte. *Das Verständnis des Gerichtes bei Paulus*. ATANT 47. Zürich: Zwingli, 1966.

McCall, Thomas H. *Against God and Nature: The Doctrine of Sin*. Foundations of Evangelical Theology. Wheaton, IL: Crossway, 2019.

McCaulley, Esau. *Reading While Black: African American Biblical Interpretation as an Exercise in Hope*. Downers Grove, IL: InterVarsity Press, 2020.

McConville, J. Gordon. *Grace in the End: A Study in Deuteronomic Theology*. Grand Rapids: Zondervan, 1993.

McDermott, Gerald, and Harold Netland. *A Trinitarian Theology of Religions: An Evangelical Proposal*. Oxford: Oxford University Press, 2014.

McDonald, Gregory. *The Evangelical Universalist*. Eugene, OR: Cascade, 2006.

McDonough, Sean M. *Christ as Creator: Origins of a New Testament Doctrine*. Oxford: Oxford University Press, 2009.

———. "Competent to Judge: The Old Testament Connection between 1 Corinthians 5 and 6." *JTS* 56 (2005): 99–102.

———. *Creation and New Creation: Understanding God's Creation Project*. Peabody, MA: Hendrickson, 2016.

McFadden, Kevin W. "Does Πίστις Mean 'Faith(Fulness)' in Paul?" *TynBul* 66 (2015): 251–70.

———. *Faith in the Son of God: Christ-Oriented Faith in Pauline Theology*. Wheaton, IL: Crossway, 2020.

———. *Judgment according to Works in Romans: The Meaning and Function of Divine Judgment in Paul's Most Important Letter*. Minneapolis: Fortress, 2013.

McGrath, Alistair. *Iustitia Dei: A History of the Christian Doctrine of Justification*. 2 vols. Cambridge: Cambridge University Press, 1998.

McKnight, Scot. *A Community Called Atonement*. Nashville: Abingdon, 2007.

———. *The Letter to the Colossians*. NICNT. Grand Rapids: Eerdmans, 2018.

McKnight, Scot, and Joseph B. Modica, eds. *Jesus Is Lord, Caesar Is Not: Evaluating Empire in New Testament Studies*. Downers Grove, IL: InterVarsity Press, 2013.

Meek, Russell L. "Intertexuality, Inner-Biblical Exegesis, and Inner-Biblical Allusion: The Ethics of a Methodology." *Bib* 95 (2014): 280–91.

Meeks, Wayne A. *The First Urban Christians: The Social World of the Apostle Paul*. New Haven: Yale, 1983.

———. "The 'Haustafeln' and American Slavery: A Hermeneutical Challenge." Pages 232–53 in *Theology and Ethics in Paul and His Interpreters: Essays in Honor of Victor Paul Furnish*. Edited by Eugene H. Lovering Jr. and Jerry L. Sumney. Nashville: Abingdon, 1996.

Melanchthon, P. *Commentary on Romans*. Repr., St. Louis: Concordia, 1992.

Mell, Ulrich. *Neue Schöpfung: Eine traditionsgeschichtliche und exegetische Studie zu einem soteriologischen Grundsatz paulinischer Theologie*. BZNW 56. Berlin: de Gruyter, 1989.

Merkle, Benjamin L. "Ecclesiology in the Pastoral Epistles." Pages 173–98 in *Entrusted with the Gospel: Paul's Theology in the Pastoral Epistles*. Edited by Andreas J. Köstenberger and Terry L. Wilder. Nashville: B&H, 2010.

———. *The Elder and the Overseer: One Office in the Early Church*. SBL 57. New York: Peter Lang, 2003.

———. "Romans 11 and the Future of Ethnic Israel." *JETS* 43 (2000): 709–21.

Metzger, Bruce M. *A Textual Commentary on the Greek New Testament: A Companion Volume to the United Bible Societies' Greek New Testament (Fourth Revised Edition)*. 2nd ed. Stuttgart: United Bible Societies, 1994.

Michel, Otto. *Der Brief an die Römer*. KEK 4. Göttingen: Vandenhoeck & Ruprecht, 1966.

Middleton, J. Richard. *The Liberating Image: The Imago Dei in Genesis 1*. Grand Rapids: Baker, 2005.

Milgrom, Jacob. *Leviticus 1–16: A New Translation with Introduction and Commentary*. AB 3. New Haven: Yale University Press, 1998.

Milligan, George. *St. Paul's Epistles to the Thessalonians*. London: Macmillan, 1908.

Minear, Paul S. *Images of the Church in the New Testament*. Philadelphia: Westminster, 1960.

Mitchell, A. C. "Rich and Poor in the Courts of Corinth: Litigiousness and Status in 1 Corinthians." *NTS* 39 (1993): 562–86.

Mitchell, Margaret M. *Paul and the Rhetoric of Reconciliation: An Exegetical Investigation of the Language and Composition of 1 Corinthians*. Louisville: Westminster John Knox, 1991.

———. *Paul, the Corinthians and the Birth of Christian Hermeneutics*. Cambridge: Cambridge University Press, 2010.

Moessner, David P., ed. *Paul and the Heritage of Israel: Paul's Claim upon Israel's Legacy in Luke and Acts in the Light of the Pauline Letters*. LNTS 452. London: T&T Clark, 2012.

Moffit, David. *Atonement and the Logic of Resurrection in the Epistle to the Hebrews*. SupNovT 14. Leiden: Brill, 2011.

Monkemeier, Matthew. "'A Righteous God and Savior': Romans 1:17 and the Old Testament Concept of God's Righteousness." PhD diss., Wheaton College, 2020.

Montanari, Franco. *The Brill Dictionary of Ancient Greek*. Edited by Madeleine Goh and Chad Schroeder. Leiden: Brill Academic, 2015.

Montefiore, C. G. *Judaism and St. Paul: Two Essays*. New York: E. P. Dutton, 1915.

Moo, Douglas J. "1 Timothy 2:11–15: Meaning and Significance." *TJ* 1 (1980): 62–83.

———. "A Case for the Posttribulation Rapture." Pages 185–241 in *Three Views on the Rapture: Pretribulation, Prewrath, or Posttribulation*. Edited by Alan Hultberg. Counterpoints. Grand Rapids: Zondervan, 2010.

———. "Creation and New Creation." *BBR* 20 (2010): 39–60.

———. "Creation and New Creation: Transforming Christian Perspectives." Pages 241–54 in *Creation in Crisis: Christian Perspectives on Sustainability*. Edited by Robert S. White. London: SPCK, 2009.

———. *Encountering the Book of Romans. A Theological Survey*. 2nd ed. Grand Rapids: Baker, 2014.

———. *The Epistle to the Romans*. 1st ed. NICNT. Grand Rapids: Eerdmans, 1996.

———. *The Epistle to the Romans*. 2nd ed. NICNT. Grand Rapids: Eerdmans, 2018.

———. "Eschatology and Environmental Ethics: On the Importance of Biblical Theology to Creation Care." Pages 23–45 in *Keeping God's Earth: The Global Environment in Theological Perspective*. Edited by Noah J. Toly and Daniel I. Block. Downers Grove, IL: InterVarsity Press, 2010.

———. "'Flesh' in Romans: A Problem for the Translator." Pages 365–79 in *The Challenge of Bible Translation: Communicating God's Word to the World. Essays in Honor of Ronald F. Youngblood*. Edited by Glen S. Scorgie, Mark L. Strauss, and Steven M. Voth. Grand Rapids: Zondervan, 2003.

———. *Galatians*. BECNT. Grand Rapids: Baker Academic, 2013.

———. "Genesis 15:6 in the New Testament." Pages 147–62 in *From Creation to New Creation: Biblical Theology and Exegesis. Essays in Honor of G. K. Beale*. Edited by Daniel M. Gurtner and Benjamin L. Gladd. Peabody, MA: Hendrickson, 2013.

———. "The Interpretation of 1 Timothy 2:11–15: A Rejoinder." *TrinJ* 2 (1981): 198–222.

———. "Jesus and the Authority of the Mosaic Law." *JSNT* 20 (1984): 3–49.

———. "John Barclay's *Paul and the Gift* and the New Perspective on Paul." *Them* 41.2 (2016): 279–88. http://themelios.thegospelcoalition.org/article/john-barclays-paul-and-the-gift-and-the-new-perspective-on-paul.

———. "Justification in Galatians." Pages 160–95 in *Understanding the Times: New Testament Studies in the 21st Century. Essays in Honor of D. A. Carson on the Occasion of his 65th Birthday*. Edited by Andreas J. Köstenberger and Robert W. Yarbrough. Wheaton, IL: Crossway, 2011.

———. "The Law of Christ as the Fulfillment of the Law of Moses: A Modified Lutheran View." Pages 319–76 in *Five Views on Law and Gospel*. Grand Rapids: Zondervan, 1996.

———. "The Law of Moses or the Law of Christ." Pages 203–18, 373–76 in *Continuity and Discontinuity: Perspectives on the Relationship between the Old and New Testament. Essays in Honor of S. Lewis Johnson Jr.* Edited by John S. Feinberg. Westchester, IL: Crossway, 1988.

———. "'Law,' 'Works of the Law,' and Legalism in Paul." *WTJ* 45 (1983): 73–100.

———. *The Letters to the Colossians and to Philemon*. PNTC. Grand Rapids: Eerdmans, 2008.

———. "Nature in the New Creation: New Testament Eschatology and the Environment." *JETS* 49 (2006): 449–88.

———. *The Old Testament in the Gospel Passion Narratives*. Sheffield: Almond, 1983. Repr., Eugene, OR: Wipf & Stock, 2008.

———. "Paul's Universalizing Hermeneutic in Romans." *The Southern Baptist Journal of Theology* 11 (Fall 2007): 62–90.

———. Review of *The Deliverance of God: An Apocalyptic Rereading of Justification in Paul*, by Douglas A. Campbell. *JETS* 53 (2010): 143–50.

———. Review of *Kingdom through Covenant: A Biblical-Theological Understanding of the Covenants*, by Peter J. Gentry and Stephen J. Wellum. The Gospel Coalition. September 12, 2012. www.thegospelcoalition.org /reviews/kingdom-covenant-douglas-moo.

———. *Romans*. NIVAC. Grand Rapids: Zondervan, 2000.

———. "Sin in Paul." Pages 107–30 in *Fallen: A Theology of Sin*. Edited by Christopher W. Morgan and Robert A. Peterson. Wheaton, IL: Crossway, 2013.

———. "'The Type of the One to Come': Adam in Paul's Theology." *TJ* 40 (2019): 145–64.

———. "What Does Paul Teach about Hell?" Pages 91–109 in *Hell under Fire*. Edited by Chris Morgan and Robert Peterson. Grand Rapids: Zondervan, 2004.

Moo, Douglas J., and Andrew D. Naselli. "The Problem of the New Testament's Use of the Old Testament." Pages 702–46 in *The Enduring Authority of the Christian Scriptures*. Edited by D. A. Carson. Grand Rapids: Eerdmans, 2016.

Moo, Douglas J., and Jonathan A. Moo, *Creation Care: A Biblical Theology of the Natural World*. Biblical Theology for Life. Grand Rapids: Zondervan, 2018.

Moo, Jonathan A. "Of Parents and Children: 1 Corinthians 4:15–16 and Life in the Family of God." Pages 57–73 in *Studies in the Pauline Epistles: Essays in Honor of Douglas J. Moo*. Edited by Matthew S. Harmon and Jay E. Smith. Grand Rapids: Zondervan, 2014.

———. "Romans 8.19–22 and Isaiah's Cosmic Covenant." *NTS* 54 (2008): 74–89.

Moore, Arthur L. *The Parousia in the New Testament*. NovTSup 13. Leiden: Brill, 1966.

Moore, George Foot. *Judaism in the First Centuries of the Christian Era: The Age of the Tannaim*. 3 vols. Cambridge: Harvard University Press, 1927.

Morgan, Teresa. *Roman Faith and Christian Faith: Pistis and Fides in the Early Roman Empire and Early Christianity*. Oxford: Oxford University Press, 2015.

Moritz, Thorsten. *A Profound Mystery: The Use of the Old Testament in Ephesians*. NovTSup 85. Leiden: Brill, 1996.

Morris, Leon. *The Apostolic Preaching of the Cross*. Grand Rapids: Eerdmans, 1955.

———. *The Atonement: Its Meaning and Significance*. Downers Grove, IL: InterVarsity Press, 1983.

———. *The First and Second Epistles to the Thessalonians*. Rev. ed. NICNT. Grand Rapids: Eerdmans, 1991.

———. *The First Epistle of Paul to the Corinthians*. TNTC. Grand Rapids: Eerdmans, 1985.

———. "Forgiveness." Pages 311–13 in *Dictionary of Paul and His Letters*. Edited by Gerald F. Hawthorne and Ralph P. Martin. Downers Grove, IL: InterVarsity Press, 1993.

Moses, Robert Ewusie. *Practices of Power: Revisiting the Principalities and Powers in the Pauline Letters*. Minneapolis: Fortress, 2014.

Motyer, Stephen. "Righteousness by Faith in the New Testament." Pages 33–56 in *Here We Stand: Justification by Faith Today*. Edited by J. I. Packer. London: Hodder and Stoughton, 1986.

———. "Two Testaments, One Biblical Theology." Pages 143–64 in *Between Two Horizons: Spanning New Testament Studies and Systematic Theology*. Edited by Joel B. Green and Max Turner. Grand Rapids: Eerdmans, 2000.

Moule, C. F. D. *The Epistles of Paul the Apostle to the Colossians and to Philemon*. CGTC. Cambridge: Cambridge University Press, 1968.

———. "Further Reflections on Philippians 2:5–11." Pages 264–76 in *Apostolic History and the Gospel: Biblical and Historical Essays Presented to F. F. Bruce on His 60th Birthday*. Edited by W. Ward Gasque and Ralph P. Martin. Grand Rapids: Eerdmans, 1970.

———. *An Idiom Book of New Testament Greek*. Cambridge: Cambridge University Press, 1953.

———. *The Origin of Christology*. Cambridge: Cambridge University Press, 1977.

Mounce, William D. *The Pastoral Epistles*. WBC 46. Nashville: Thomas Nelson, 2000.

Moyise, Steve. "Does Paul Respect the Context of His Quotations?" Pages 97–114 in *Paul and Scripture: Extending the Conversation*. Edited by Christopher D. Stanley. ECL 9. Atlanta: Society of Biblical Literature, 2012.

———. *Paul and Scripture: Studying the New Testament Use of the Old Testament*. Grand Rapids: Baker, 2010.

Muddiman, John. *A Commentary on the Epistle to the Ephesians*. BNTC. London: Continuum, 2001.

Müller, Ulrich B. *Der Brief des Paulus an die Philipper*. THKNT 11/1. Leipzig: Evangelische, 1993.

Munck, Johannes. *Christ and Israel: An Interpretation of Romans 9–11*. Philadelphia: Fortress, 1967.

———. *Paul and the Salvation of Mankind*. Richmond, VA: John Knox, 1959.

Mundle, Wilhelm. *Der Glaubensbegriff des Paulus: Eine Untersuchung zur Dogmengeschichte des ältesten Christentums*. Darmstadt: Wissenschaftliche Buchgesellschaft, 1977.

Munro, Winsome. *Authority in Paul and Peter: The Identification of a Pastoral Stratum in the Pauline Corpus and 1 Peter*. SNTSMS 45. Cambridge: Cambridge University Press, 1983.

Murphy-O'Connor, Jerome. *Paul: A Critical Life*. Oxford: Oxford University Press, 1996.

———. *The Theology of the Second Letter to the Corinthians*. Cambridge: Cambridge University Press, 1991.

Murray, John. *The Epistle to the Romans*. Two volumes in one. NICNT. Grand Rapids: Eerdmans, 1968.

———. *The Imputation of Adam's Sin*. Phillipsburg: Presbyterian and Reformed, 1959.

———. *Principles of Conduct*. Grand Rapids: Eerdmans, 1957.

———. *Redemption Accomplished and Applied*. Grand Rapids: Eerdmans, 1955.

Mussner, Franz. *Der Galaterbrief*. 5th ed. HThKNT 9. Freiburg: Herder, 1988.

Nanos, Mark D. *The Irony of Galatians: Paul's Letter in First-Century Context*. Minneapolis: Fortress, 2002.

———. "A Jewish View." Pages 159–93 in *Four Views of the Apostle Paul*. Edited by Michael F. Bird. Grand Rapids: Zondervan, 2012.

———. *The Mystery of Romans: The Jewish Context of Paul's Letter*. Minneapolis: Fortress, 1996.

———. "Paul and Judaism: Why Not Paul's Judaism?" Pages 117–60 in *Paul Unbound: Other Perspectives on the Apostle*. Edited by Mark D. Given. Peabody, MA: Hendrickson, 2010.

———. "Paul and the Jewish Tradition: The Ideology of the *Shema*." Pages 62–80 in *Celebrating Paul: Festschrift in Honor of Jerome Murphy-O'Connor, O.P., and Joseph A. Fitzmyer, S. J.* Edited by P. Spitaler. CBQMS 48. Washington, DC: Catholic Biblical Association of America, 2011.

———. "The Question of Conceptualization: Qualifying Paul's Position on Circumcision in Dialogue with Josephus's Advisors to King Izates." Pages 105–52 in *Paul within Judaism: Restoring the First-Century Context to the Apostle*. Edited by Mark Nanos and Magnus Zetterholm. Minneapolis: Fortress, 2015.

Nanos, Mark D., and Magnus Zetterholm, eds. *Paul within Judaism: Restoring the First-Century Context to the Apostle*. Minneapolis: Fortress, 2015.

Naselli, Andrew David. "Is Every Sin outside the Body Except Immoral Sex? Weighing Whether 1 Corinthians 6:18b Is Paul's Statement or a Corinthian Slogan." *JBL* 136 (2017): 969–87.

———. "The Structure and Theological Message of 1 Corinthians." *Presb* 44 (2018): 98–114.

Nebe, Gottfried. *"Hoffnung" bei Paulus: Elpis und ihre Synonyme im Zusammenhang der Eschatologie*. SUNT 16. Göttingen: Vandenhoeck & Ruprecht, 1983.

Netland, Harold. *Encountering Religious Pluralism: The Challenge to Christian Faith and Mission*. Downers Grove, IL: InterVarsity Press, 2001.

Neugebauer, F. *In Christus (EN XPIΣTΩI). Eine Untersuchung zum paulinischen Glaubenverständnis*. Göttingen: Vandenhoeck & Ruprecht, 1961.

Neusner, Jacob. *Judaic Law from Jesus to the Mishnah*. SFSHJ 84. Atlanta: Scholars Press, 1993.

———. "The Use of the Later Rabbinic Evidence for the Study of Paul." Pages 47–52 in *Approaches to Ancient Judaism*. Vol. 2. Edited by W. S. Green. BJS 9. Chico, CA: Scholars Press, 1980.

Newman, Carey C. *Paul's Glory-Christology: Tradition and Rhetoric*. NovTSup 69. Leiden: Brill, 1992.

Newman, Carey C., ed. *Jesus and the Restoration of Israel: A Critical Assessment of N. T. Wright's Jesus and the Victory of God*. Downers Grove, IL: InterVarsity Press, 1999.

Newton, Derek. *Deity and Diet: The Dilemma of Sacrificial Food in Corinth*. JSNTSup 169. Sheffield: Sheffield Academic, 1998.

Nicholl, Colin. *From Hope to Despair in Thessalonica: Situating 1 and 2 Thessalonians*. SNTSMS 126. Cambridge: Cambridge University Press, 2004.

Nicklas, T. "Paulus und die Erretung Israels: Röm 11,25–36 in der exegetischen Diskussion und im jüdisch-christlichen Dialog." *Early Christianity* 2 (2011): 173–97.

Nickle, Keith F. *The Collection: A Study in Paul's Strategy*. SBT 48. London: SCM, 1966.

Niehaus, Jeffrey J. "An Argument against Theologically Constructed Covenants." *JETS* 50 (2007): 259–73.

Nolland, John. "Romans 1:26–27 and the Homosexuality Debate." *HBT* 22 (2000): 32–57.

Norden, Eduard. *Agnostos Theos: Untersuchungen zur Formengeschichte religiöser Rede*. 4th ed. Darmstadt: Wissenschaftliche Buchgesellschaft, 1956.

Norris, Laurie. "The Function of New Testament Warning Passages: A Speech Act Theory Approach." PhD diss., Wheaton College, 2011.

Novenson, Matthew V. "Can the Messiahship of Jesus Be Read off Paul's Grammar? Nils Dahl's Criteria 50 Years Later." *NTS* 56 (2010): 396–412.

———. *Christ among the Messiahs: Christ Language in Paul and Messiah Language in Ancient Judaism*. Oxford: Oxford University Press, 2012.

———. "The Jewish Messiahs, the Pauline Christ, and the Gentile Question." *JBL* 128 (2009): 357–73.

———. "Paul's Former Occupation in Ioudaismos." Pages 24–39 in *Galatians and Christian Theology: Justification, the Gospel, and Ethics in Paul's Letter*. Edited by Mark W. Elliott, Scott J. Hafemann, N. T. Wright, and John Frederick. Grand Rapids: Baker, 2014.

Nygren, Anders. *Commentary on Romans*. Repr., Philadelphia: Fortress, 1949.

Oakes, Peter. *Philippians: From People to Letter*. SNTSMS 110. Cambridge: Cambridge University Press, 2001.

Oberlinner, Lorenz. *Erster Timotheusbrief*. Vol. 1 of *Die Pastoralbriefe*. HThKNT 11.2. Freiburg im Breisgau: Herder, 1994.

———. *Kommentar zum Titusbrief*. Vol. 3 of *Die Pastoralbriefe*. HThKNT 11.2. Freiburg im Breisgau: Herder, 1996.

———. *Zweiter Timotheusbrief*. Vol. 2 of *Die Pastoralbriefe*. HThKNT 11.2. Freiburg im Breisgau: Herder, 1995.

O'Brien, Peter T. "Church." Pages 123–31 in *Dictionary of Paul and His Letters*. Edited by Gerald F. Hawthorne and Ralph P. Martin. Downers Grove, IL: InterVarsity Press, 1993.

———. "The Church as a Heavenly and Eschatological Entity." Pages 88–119 in *The Church in the Bible and the World: An International Study*. Edited by D. A. Carson. Grand Rapids: Baker, 1987.

———. *Colossians, Philemon*. WBC 44. Waco, TX: Word, 1982.

———. *The Epistle to the Philippians: A Commentary on the Greek Text*. NIGTC. Grand Rapids: Eerdmans, 1991.

———. *Gospel and Mission in the Writings of Paul: An Exegetical and Theological Analysis*. Grand Rapids: Baker, 1995.

———. *Introductory Thanksgivings in the Letters of Paul*. Eugene, OR: Wipf & Stock, 1977.

———. "Justification in Paul and Some Crucial Issues of the Last Two Decades." Pages 69–95 in *Right with God: Justification in the Bible and the World*. Edited by D. A. Carson. Grand Rapids: Baker, 1992.

———. *The Letter to the Ephesians*. PNTC. Grand Rapids: Eerdmans, 1999.

———. "Was Paul a Covenantal Nomist?" Pages 249–96 in *The Paradoxes of Paul*. Vol. 2 of *Justification and Variegated Nomism*. Edited by D. A. Carson, Peter T. O'Brien, and Mark A. Seifrid. WUNT 2/140. Tübingen: Mohr Siebeck, 2004.

———. "Was Paul Converted?" Pages 361–91 in *The Paradoxes of Paul*. Vol. 2 of *Justification and Variegated Nomism*. Edited by D. A. Carson, Peter T. O'Brien, and Mark A. Seifrid. WUNT 2/140. Tübingen: Mohr Siebeck, 2004.

Oden, Thomas C. *The Justification Reader*. Grand Rapids: Eerdmans, 2002.

———. "Without Excuse: Classic Christian Exegesis of General Revelation." *JETS* 41 (1998): 55–68.

O'Donovan, Oliver. *Resurrection and the Moral Order: An Outline for Evangelical Ethics*. 2nd ed. Grand Rapids: Eerdmans, 1994.

Oepke, Albrecht. *Der Brief des Paulus an die Galater*. THKNT. Berlin: Evangelische Verlagsanstalt, 1973.

Orchard, J. B. "Thessalonians and the Synoptic Gospels." *Bib* 19 (1938): 19–42.

Oropeza, B. J. *Jews, Gentiles, and the Opponents of Paul*. Apostasy in the New Testament Communities. Vol. 2. Eugene, OR: Cascade, 2012.

———. *Paul and Apostasy: Eschatology, Perseverance, and Falling Away in the Corinthian Congregation*. WUNT 2/115. Tübingen: Mohr Siebeck, 2000.

Orr, Peter. *Christ Absent and Present: A Study in Pauline Christology*. WUNT 2/354. Tübingen: Mohr Siebeck, 2014.

Ortlund, Dane C. "Justified by Faith, Judged according to Works: Another Look at a Pauline Paradox." *JETS* 52 (2009): 323–39.

———. *Zeal without Knowledge: The Concept of Zeal in Romans 10, Galatians 1, and Philippians 3*. LNTS 472. London: T&T Clark, 2012.

Osborne, Grant R. "The Flesh without the Spirit: Romans 7 and Christian Experience." Pages 6–48 in *Perspectives on Our Struggle with Sin: 3 Views of Romans 7*. Edited by Terry L. Wilder. Nashville: B&H, 2011.

———. "Hermeneutics and Paul: Psalm 68:18 in Ephesians 4:7–10 as a Test Case." Pages 159–77 in *Studies in the Pauline Epistles: Essays in Honor of Douglas J. Moo*. Edited by Matthew S. Harmon and Jay E. Smith. Grand Rapids: Zondervan, 2014.

Oswalt, John. *The Book of Isaiah*. 2 vols. NICOT. Grand Rapids: Eerdmans, 1986.

Ouoba, Elisee. "Paul's Use of Isaiah 27:9 and 59:20–21 in Romans 11:25–27." PhD diss., Wheaton College, 2010.

Paddison, Angus. *Theological Hermeneutics and 1 Thessalonians*. SNTSMS 133. Cambridge: Cambridge University Press, 2005.

Pao, David W. *Colossians and Philemon*. ZECNT. Grand Rapids: Zondervan, 2012.

———. *Thanksgiving: An Investigation of a Pauline Theme*. NSBT 13. Downers Grove, IL: InterVarsity Press, 2002.

Park, Sung-Ho. *Stellvertretung Jesu Christi im Gericht: Studien zum Verhältnis von Stellvertretung und Kreuztod Jesu bei Paulus*. WMANT 143. Neukircken-Vluyn: Neukirchener, 2015.

Park, Young-Ho. *Paul's Ekklesia as a Civic Assembly: Understanding the People of God in Their Politico-Social World*. WUNT 2/393. Tübingen: Mohr Siebeck, 2015.

Parker, Brent E. "The Israel-Christ-Church Relationship." Pages 39–68 in *Progressive Covenantalism: Charting a Course between Dispensational and Covenant Theology*. Edited by Stephen J. Wellum and Brent E. Parker. Nashville: B&H Academic, 2016.

Parry, Donald W., and Emanuel Tov, eds. *The Dead Sea Scrolls Reader, Part 2: Exegetical Texts*. Leiden: Brill, 2004.

Pate, C. Marvin, and Douglas W. Kennard. *Deliverance Now and Not Yet: The New Testament and the Great Tribulation*. StBibLit 54. New York: Peter Lang, 2003.

Payne, Philip B. *Man and Woman, One in Christ: An Exegetical and Theological Study of Paul's Letters*. Grand Rapids: Zondervan, 2009.

Payton, James R., Jr. *The Victory of the Cross: Salvation in Eastern Orthodoxy*. Downers Grove, IL: InterVarsity Press, 2019.

Peake, A. S. "The Quintessence of Paulinism." *BJRL* 4 (1917–1918): 285–311.

Pearson, Birger A. "1 Thessalonians 2:13–16: A Deutero-Pauline Interpolation." *HTR* 64 (1971): 79–94.

———. *The Pneumatikos-Psychikos Terminology in 1 Corinthians: A Study in The Theology of the Corinthian Opponents of Paul and Its Relationship to Gnosticism*. SBLDS 12. Missoula, MT: Scholars Press, 1973.

Pegler, Stephen. "The Nature of Paul's Universal Salvation Language in Romans." PhD diss., Trinity Evangelical Divinity School, 2002.

Percy, Ernst. *Der Leib Christi (Soma Christou) in den paulinischen Homologumena und Antilegomena*. Lunds Universitets Årsskrift 1.38. Lund: Gleerup, 1942.

———. *Die Probleme der Kolosser- und Epheserbriefe*. Lund: Gleerup, 1946.

Perriman, A. C. "The Head of a Woman: The Meaning of Κεφαλή in 1 Cor 11:3." *JTS* 45 (1994): 602–22.

Perrin, Nicholas. *Jesus the Temple*. Grand Rapids: Baker, 2010.

Peterman, Gerald W. "Plural You: On the Use and Abuse of the Second Person." *BBR* 20 (2010): 201–14.

Peterson, David. *Possessed by God: A New Testament Theology of Sanctification and Holiness*. NSBT 1. Downers Grove, IL: InterVarsity Press, 1995.

Peterson, Norman R. *Rediscovering Paul: Philemon and the Sociology of Paul's Narrative World*. Philadelphia: Fortress, 1985.

Peterson, Robert A. *Election and Free Will: God's Choice and Our Responsibility*. Wheaton, IL: Crossway, 2007.

———. *Hell on Trial: The Case for Eternal Punishment*. Phillipsburg, NJ: P&R, 1995.

Peterson, Ryan S. *The Imago Dei as Human Identity: A Theological Interpretation*. JTISup 14. Winona Lake, IN: Eisenbrauns, 2016.

Pickett, Raymond. *The Cross in Corinth: The Social Significance of the Death of Jesus*. JSNTSup 143. Sheffield: Sheffield Academic, 1997.

Pierce, Ronald W., and Rebecca Merrill Groothuis, eds. *Discovering Biblical Equality: Complementarity without Hierarchy*. Downers Grove, IL: InterVarsity Press, 2004.

Pietersen, Lloyd K. *The Polemic of the Pastoral Epistles: A Sociological Examination of the Development of Pauline Christianity*. JSNTSup 264. London: T&T Clark, 2004.

Pifer, Jeannette Hagen. *Faith as Participation: An Exegetical Study of Some Key Pauline Texts*. WUNT 2/486. Tübingen: Mohr Siebeck, 2019.

Piper, John. *Counted Righteous in Christ: Should We Abandon the Imputation of Christ's Righteousness?* Wheaton, IL: Crossway, 2002.

———. *The Future of Justification: A Response to N. T. Wright*. Wheaton, IL: Crossway, 2007.

———. *The Justification of God: An Exegetical and Theological Study of Romans 9:1–23*. Grand Rapids: Baker, 1993.

Pitre, Brant. *Jesus, the Tribulation, and the End of the Exile: Restoration Eschatology and the Origin of the Atonement.* Grand Rapids: Baker, 2005.

Pitre, Brant, Michael P. Barber, and John A. Kincaid. *Paul, A New Covenant Jew: Rethinking Pauline Theology.* Grand Rapids: Eerdmans, 2019.

Plevnik, Joseph. *Paul and the Parousia: An Exegetical and Theological Investigation.* Eugene, OR: Wipf & Stock, 1997.

Pokorný, Petr. *Colossians: A Commentary.* Peabody, MA: Hendrickson, 1991.

Polaski, Sandra Hack. *A Feminist Introduction to Paul.* St. Louis: Chalice, 2005.

Polkinghorne, John. "Eschatology: Some Questions and Some Insights from Science." Pages 31–40 in *The End of the World and the Ends of God: Science and Theology on Eschatology.* Edited by John Polkinghorne and Michael Welker. Harrisburg, PA: Trinity Press International, 2000.

———. *The God of Hope and the End of the World.* New Haven: Yale University Press, 2002.

Pollmann, Ines. *Gesetzeskritische Motive im Judentum und die Gesetzeskritik des Paulus.* NTOA/SUNT 98. Göttingen: Vandenhoeck & Ruprecht, 2012.

Porter, Stanley E. *The Apostle Paul: His Life, Thought, and Letters.* Grand Rapids: Eerdmans, 2016.

———. *Καταλλάσσω in Ancient Greek Literature, with Reference to the Pauline Writings.* EFN 5. Cordoba: Ediciones el Almendro, 1994.

———. *The Letter to the Romans: A Linguistic and Literary Commentary.* New Testament Monographs 37. Sheffield: Sheffield Phoenix, 2015.

———. *Paul in Acts.* Library of Pauline Studies. Grand Rapids: Baker, 2000.

———. "Paul of Tarsus and His Letters." Pages 533–85 in *Handbook of Classical Rhetoric in the Hellenistic Period 330 B.C.–A.D. 400.* Edited by Stanley E. Porter. Leiden: Brill, 1997.

———. "Reconciliation and 2 Cor 5:18–21." Pages 693–705 in *The Corinthian Correspondence.* Edited by R. Bieringer. BETL 125. Leiden: Brill, 1996.

Porter, Stanley E., ed. *Paul and His Opponents.* Pauline Studies 2. Leiden: Brill, 2005.

Porter, Stanley E., and Bryan R. Dyer, eds. *Paul and Ancient Rhetoric: Theory and Practice in the Hellenistic Context.* Cambridge: Cambridge University Press, 2016.

Porter, Stanley E., and Sean A. Adams, eds. *Paul and the Ancient Letter Form.* Pauline Studies 6. Leiden: Brill, 2010.

Poythress, Vern S. "The Meaning of μάλιστα in 2 Timothy 4:13 and Related Verses." *JTS* 53 (2002): 523–32.

———. "The Nature of Corinthian Glossolalia: Possible Options." *WTJ* 40 (1977): 130–36.

Prat, Ferdinand. *The Theology of St. Paul.* 2 vols. Westminster, MD: Newman, 1961.

Price, S. R. F. *Rituals and Power: The Roman Imperial Cult in Asia Minor.* Cambridge: Cambridge University Press, 1984.

Prothro, James B. *Both Judge and Justifier: Biblical Legal Language and the Act of Justifying in Paul.* WUNT 2/461. Tübingen: Mohr Siebeck, 2018.

Quarles, Charles L. "The Soteriology of R. Akiba and E. P. Sanders' *Paul and Palestinian Judaism.*" *NTS* 42 (1996): 185–95.

Rabens, Volker. "Ethics and the Spirit in Paul (1): Religious-Ethical Empowerment through Infusion-Transformation?" *ExpTim* 125 (2014): 209–19.

———. "Ethics and the Spirit in Paul (2): Religious-Ethical Empowerment through Infusion-Transformation?" *ExpTim* 125 (2014): 272–81.

———. *The Holy Spirit and Ethics in Paul: Transformation and Empowering for Religious-Ethical Life.* WUNT 2/283. Tübingen: Mohr Siebeck, 2010.

Rainbow, Paul A. *The Way of Salvation: The Role of Christian Obedience in Justification.* Milton Keynes: Paternoster, 2005.

Räisänen, Heikki. *Paul and the Law.* WUNT 2/29. Tübingen: Mohr Siebeck, 1983.

———. "Paul's Theological Difficulties with the Law." Pages 301–20 in *Studia Biblica 1978.* Vol. 3. Edited by E. A. Livingstone. JSNTSup 2. Sheffield: JSOT, 1980.

Rapinchuk, Mark. "Universal Sin and Salvation in Romans 5:12–21." *JETS* 42 (1999): 427–41.

Rapske, Brian M. "The Prisoner Paul in the Eyes of Onesimus." *NTS* 37 (1991): 187–203.

Reasoner, Mark. *Roman Imperial Texts: A Sourcebook.* Minneapolis: Fortress, 2013.

———. "The Salvation of Israel in Romans 9–11." Pages 256–79 in *The Call of Abraham: Essays on the Election of Israel in Honor of John D. Levinson.* Edited by Gary A. Anderson and Joel S. Kaminsky. Notre Dame: University of Notre Dame Press, 2013.

Refoulé, F. ". . . Et ainsi tout Israël sera sauvé": Romains 11,25–32. LD 117. Paris: Cerf, 1984.

Rehfeld, Emmanuel L. Relationale Ontologie bei Paulus: Die ontische Wirksamkeit des Christusbezogenheit im Denken des Heidenapostels. WUNT 2/326. Tübingen: Mohr Siebeck, 2012.

Reicke, Bo. Re-examining Paul's Letters: The History of the Pauline Correspondence. Edited by David P. Moessner and Ingalisa Reicke. Harrisburg, PA: Trinity Press International, 2001.

Reid, J. K. S. Our Life in Christ. London: SCM, 1963.

Reumann, John. Philippians. AB 33B. New Haven: Yale University Press, 2008.

———. Righteousness in the New Testament. Philadelphia: Fortress, 1982.

Reyes, Luis Carlos. "The Structure and Rhetoric of Colossians 1:15–20." Filologia Neotestamentaria 12 (1999): 140–46.

Reymond, Robert L. Paul, Missionary Theologian: A Survey of His Missionary Labours and Theology. Fearn: Christian Focus, 2000.

Rhyne, C. Thomas. Faith Establishes the Law. SBLDS 55. Chico, CA: Scholars Press, 1981.

Richards, E. R. Paul and First-Century Letter Writing: Secretaries, Composition and Collection. Downers Grove, IL: InterVarsity Press, 2004.

Richards, William A. Difference and Distance in Post-Pauline Christianity: An Epistolary Analysis of the Pastorals. StBibLit 44. New York: Peter Lang, 2002.

Richardson, Peter. Israel in the Apostolic Church. SNTSMS 10. Cambridge: Cambridge University Press, 1969.

Ridderbos, Herman. Paul: An Outline of His Theology. Grand Rapids: Eerdmans, 1975.

Riesner, Rainer. "Pauline Chronology." Pages 1–29 in The Blackwell Companion to Paul. Edited by Stephen Westerholm. Chichester: Wiley-Blackwell, 2011.

———. Paul's Early Period: Chronology, Mission Strategy, Theology. Grand Rapids: Eerdmans, 1998.

Rigaux, Beda. Saint Paul: Les Epitres aux Thessaloniciens. EB. Paris: Gabalda, 1956.

Robertson, Archibald, and Alfred Plummer. A Critical and Exegetical Commentary on the First Epistle of St. Paul to the Corinthians. ICC. Edinburgh: T&T Clark, 1914.

Robertson, Paul M. Paul's Letters and Contemporary Greco-Roman Literature: Theorizing a New Taxonomy. NovTSup 167. Leiden: Brill, 2016.

Robinson, D. W. B. "II Thess. 2:6: 'That Which Restrains' or 'That Which Holds Sway'?" Pages 635–38 in Studia Evangelica II. Edited by Frank L. Cross. TU 87. Berlin: Akademie, 1964.

———. "'Faith of Jesus Christ'—A New Testament Debate." RTR 29 (1970): 71–81.

Robinson, H. W. Corporate Personality in Ancient Israel. Repr., Philadelphia: Fortress, 1980.

Robinson, J. Armitage. St. Paul's Epistle to the Ephesians. 2nd ed. London: Macmillan, 1907.

Robinson, John A. T. The Body: A Study in Pauline Theology. Philadelphia: Westminster, 1977.

———. Redating the New Testament. London: SCM, 1976.

Roetzel, Calvin J. Judgement in the Community: A Study of the Relationship between Eschatology and Ecclesiology in Paul. Leiden: Brill, 1972.

Rogerson, J. W. "The Hebrew Conception of Corporate Personality: A Reexamination." JTS 21 (1970): 1–16.

Rohde, Joachim. Der Brief des Paulus an die Galater. THKNT 9. Berlin: Evangelische Verlagsanstalt, 1989.

Rohr, J. von. The Covenant of Grace in Puritan Thought. AARSR 45. Atlanta: Scholars Press, 1986.

Röhser, Günter. "Paulus und die Herrschaft der Sünde." ZNW 103 (2012): 84–110.

———. Stellvertretung im Neuen Testament. SBS 195. Stuttgart: Katholisches, 2002.

Roloff, J. Der ester Brief an Timotheus. EKKNT. Neukirchen-Vluyn: Neukirchener, 1988.

Rondez, Pascale. "Ein Zentrum paulinischer Theologie? Eine pneumatologische Erschliessung des Zusammenhangs von Soteriologie und Christologie Anhand von Gal 5,25." Pages 59–79 in Kreuztheologie im Neuen Testament. Edited by Andreas Dettwiler and Jean Zumstein. Tübingen: Mohr Siebeck, 2002.

Ropes, J. H. "'Righteousness' and 'The Righteousness of God' in the Old Testament and in St. Paul." JBL 22 (1903): 211–27.

Rosner, Brian S. "Biblical Theology." Pages 3–11 in New Dictionary of Biblical Theology. Edited by T. Desmond Alexander and Brian S. Rosner. Downers Grove, IL: InterVarsity Press, 2000.

———. Greed as Idolatry: The Origin and Meaning of a Pauline Metaphor. Grand Rapids: Eerdmans, 2007.

———. Known by God: A Biblical Theology of Personal Identity. Biblical Theology for Life. Grand Rapids: Zondervan, 2017.

———. Paul and the Law: Keeping the Commandments of God. NSBT 31. Downers Grove, IL: InterVarsity Press, 2013.

Rousselle, Aline. "Body Politics in Ancient Rome." Pages 296–337 in *From Ancient Goddesses to Christian Saints*. Edited by Pauline Schmitt Pantel. Vol. 1 of *A History of Women in the West*. Edited by Georges Duby and Michelle Perrot. Cambridge: Harvard University Press, 1992.

Rowe, C. Kavin. "Biblical Pressure and Trinitarian Hermeneutics." *ProEccl* 11 (2002): 295–312.

———. *One True Life: The Stoics and Early Christians as Rival Traditions*. New Haven: Yale University Press, 2016.

Rowley, H. H. *The Faith of Israel: Aspects of Old Testament Thought*. London: SCM, 1956.

Rudolph, David J. *A Jew to the Jews: Jewish Contours of Pauline Flexibility in 1 Corinthians 9.19–23*. WUNT 2/304. Tübingen: Mohr Siebeck, 2011.

Rudolph, David J., and Joel Willitts, eds. *Introduction to Messianic Judaism: Its Ecclesial Context and Biblical Foundations*. Grand Rapids: Zondervan, 2013.

Runesson, Anders. "The Question of Terminology: The Architecture of Contemporary Discussions of Paul." Pages 53–77 in *Paul within Judaism: Restoring the First-Century Context to the Apostle*. Edited by Mark Nanos and Magnus Zetterholm. Minneapolis: Fortress, 2015.

Rusam, Dietrich. "Neue Belege zu den *Stoicheia tou Kosmou* (Gal 4,3.9, Kol 2,8.20)." *ZNW* 83 (1992): 119–25.

Russell, N. *The Doctrine of Deification in the Greek Patristic Tradition*. Oxford: Oxford University Press, 2004.

Rutledge, Fleming. *Crucifixion: Understanding the Death of Jesus*. Grand Rapids: Eerdmans, 2015.

Ryrie, Charles. *Dispensationalism Today*. Chicago: Moody, 1965.

Sanders, E. P. "Did Paul's Theology Develop?" Pages 325–50 in *The Word Leaps the Gap: Essays on Scripture and Theology in Honor of Richard B. Hays*. Edited by J. Ross Wagner, Kavin C. Rowe, and Katherine Grieb. Grand Rapids: Eerdmans, 2008.

———. "Jewish Association with Gentiles and Galatians 2:11–14." Pages 170–88 in *The Conversation Continues: Studies in Paul and John in Honor of J. Louis Martyn*. Edited by Robert T. Fortna and Beverly R. Gaventa. Nashville: Abingdon, 1990.

———. *Judaism: Practice and Belief, 63 BCE–66 CE*. Philadelphia: TPI, 1992.

———. *Paul and Palestinian Judaism: A Comparison of Patterns of Religion*. Philadelphia: Fortress, 1977.

———. *Paul: The Apostle's Life, Letters, and Thought*. Minneapolis: Fortress, 2015.

———. *Paul, the Law, and the Jewish People*. Minneapolis: Fortress, 1983.

———. "Puzzling Out Rabbinic Judaism." Pages 69–75 in *Approaches to Ancient Judaism*. Vol. 2. Edited by W. S. Green. BJS 9. Chico, CA: Scholars Press, 1980.

Sandmel, Samuel. *The Genius of Paul: A Study in History*. Philadelphia: Fortress, 1979.

Sandnes, Karl Olav. *Paul—One of the Prophets? A Contribution to the Apostle's Self-Understanding*. WUNT 2/43. Tübingen: Mohr Siebeck, 1991.

———. *Paul Perceived: An Interactionist Perspective on Paul and the Law*. WUNT 2/412. Tübingen: Mohr Siebeck, 2018.

Sappington, Thomas J. *Revelation and Redemption at Colossae*. JSNTSup 53. Sheffield: JSOT Press, 1991.

Savage, Timothy B. *Power through Weakness: Paul's Understanding of the Christian Ministry in 2 Corinthians*. SNTSMS 86. Cambridge: Cambridge University Press, 1996.

Schechter, S. *Aspects of Rabbinic Theology*. New York: Schocken, 1961 (original ed. 1909).

Schellenberg, Ryan S. "Rhetorical Terminology in Paul: A Critical Reappraisal." *ZNW* 104 (2013): 177–91.

Schlatter, Adolf. *Romans: The Righteousness of God*. Peabody, MA: Hendrickson, 1995.

———. *The Theology of the Apostles*. Translated by Andreas J. Köstenberger. Grand Rapids: Baker, 1999 [1922].

Schlier, Heinrich. *Der Brief an die Galater*. 15th ed. KEK 7. Göttingen: Vandenhoeck & Ruprecht, 1989.

Schliesser, Benjamin. *Abraham's Faith in Romans 4: Paul's Concept of Faith in Light of the History of Reception of Genesis 15:6*. WUNT 2/224. Tübingen: Mohr Siebeck, 2007.

———. "Faith in Early Christianity: An Encyclopedic and Bibliographical Outline." Pages 3–50 in *Glaube: Das Verständnis des Glaubens im frühen Christentum und in seiner jüdischen und Hellenistisch-Römischen Umwelt*. Edited by Jörg Frey, Benjamin Schliesser, and Nadine Ueberschaer. WUNT 2/373. Tübingen: Mohr Siebeck, 2017.

Schlueter, Carol J. *Filling Up the Measure: Polemical Hyperbole in 1 Thessalonians 2.14–16*. JSNTSup 98. Sheffield: JSOT, 1994.

Schmeller, Thomas. *Der zweite Brief an die Korinther*. EKKNT 8. Neukirchen-Vluyn: Neukirchener, 2010.

Schmithals, Walter. *Gnosticism in Corinth: An Investigation of the Letters to the Corinthians*. Nashville: Abingdon, 1971.

Schnabel, Eckhard J. *Acts*. ZECNT. Grand Rapids: Zondervan, 2016.

———. *Der Brief des Paulus an die Römer*. 2 vols. Historisch Theologische Auslegung: Neues Testament. Giessen: Brunnen, 2015, 2016.

———. *Der erste Brief des Paulus an die Korinther*. Historisch Theologische Auslegung: Neues Testament. Giessen: Brockhaus, 2006.

———. "Die Gemeinde des Neuen Bundes in Kontinuität mit Diskontinuität zur Gemeinde des Alten Bundes." Pages 145–213 in *Israel in Geschichte und Gegenwart: Beiträge zur Geschichte Israels und zum jüdisch-christlichen Dialog*. Edited by Gerhard Maier. Wuppertal: Theologische, 1996.

———. "The Language of Baptism: The Meaning of Βαπτίζω in the New Testament." Pages 217–46 in *Understanding the Times: New Testament Studies in the 21st Century. Essays in Honor of D. A. Carson on the Occasion of his 65th Birthday*. Edited by Andreas J. Köstenberger and Robert W. Yarbrough. Wheaton, IL: Crossway, 2011.

———. *Paul and the Early Church*. Vol. 2 of *Early Christian Mission*. Downers Grove, IL: InterVarsity Press, 2004.

Schnackenburg, Rudolf. *Baptism in the Thought of St. Paul: A Study in Pauline Theology*. Oxford: Basil Blackwell, 1964.

———. *The Church in the New Testament*. New York: Seabury, 1965.

———. *Ephesians: A Commentary*. Edinburgh: T&T Clark, 1991.

Schnelle, Udo. *Apostle Paul: His Life and Theology*. Grand Rapids: Baker, 2005.

———. *The Theology of the New Testament*. Grand Rapids: Baker, 2007.

Schoeps, Hans Joachim. *Paul: The Theology of the Apostle in the Light of Jewish Religious History*. Philadelphia: Westminster, 1961.

Schrage, Wolfgang. *Der erste Brief an die Korinther*. 2nd ed. EKKNT 7. Zürich: Benziger Verlag, 2008.

———. *Die Konkreten Einzelgebote in der Paulinische Paränese: Ein Beitrag zur Neutestamentlichen Ethik*. Gütersloh: Gerd Mohn, 1961.

———. "Probleme paulinischer Ethik anhand von Gal 5,25–6,10." Pages 183–88 in *La foi agissant par l'amour (Galates 4,12–6,16)*. Edited by Albert Vanhoye. Rome: Abbaye de S. Paul, 1996.

Schreiner, Thomas R. *1 Corinthians: An Introduction and Commentary*. TNTC 7. Downers Grove, IL: InterVarsity Press, 2018.

———. "Corporate and Individual Election in Romans 9: A Response to Brian Abasciano." *JETS* 49 (2006): 373–86.

———. "Did Paul Believe in Justification by Works? Another Look at Romans 2." *BBR* 3 (1993): 131–55.

———. "Does Romans 9 Teach Individual Election unto Salvation? Some Exegetical and Theological Reflections." *JETS* 36 (1993): 25–40.

———. *Faith Alone: The Doctrine of Justification*. Grand Rapids: Zondervan, 2015.

———. *Galatians*. ZECNT. Grand Rapids: Zondervan, 2010.

———. "Is Perfect Obedience to the Law Possible: A Re-Examination of Galatians 3:10." *JETS* 27 (1984): 151–60.

———. *The Law and Its Fulfillment: A Pauline Theology of Law*. Grand Rapids: Baker, 1993.

———. "Paul and Perfect Obedience to the Law: An Evaluation of the View of E. P. Sanders." *WTJ* 47 (1985): 245–78.

———. *Paul: Apostle of God's Glory in Christ*. Downers Grove, IL: InterVarsity, 2001.

———. "'Problematic Texts' for Definite Atonement in the Pastoral and General Epistles." Pages 375–99 in *From Heaven He Came and Sought Her: Definite Atonement in Historical, Biblical, Theological, and Pastoral Perspective*. Edited by David Gibson and Jonathan Gibson. Wheaton, IL: Crossway, 2013.

———. "Proclaiming a Magnificent God: The Pauline Mission." Pages 37–72 in *Paul: Apostle of God's Glory in Christ*. Downers Grove, IL: InterVarsity Press, 2001.

———. *Romans*. 2nd ed. BECNT. Grand Rapids: Baker Academic, 2018.

———. "'Works of Law' in Paul." *NovT* 33 (1991): 217–44.

Schreiner, Thomas R., and Ardel B. Caneday. *The Race Set before Us: A Biblical Theology of Perseverance and Assurance*. Downers Grove, IL: InterVarsity Press, 2001.

Schrenk, Gottlob. "Der Segenwunsch nach der Kampfepistel." *Judaica* 6 (1950): 170–90.

———. "Was bedeutet 'Israel Gottes'?" *Judaica* 5 (1949): 81–94.

Schröter, Jens. "Sühne, Stellvertretung und Opfer: Zur Verwendung Analytischer Kategorien zur Deutung des Todes Jesu." Pages 51–71 in *Deutungen des Todes Jesu im Neuen Testament*. Edited by Jörg Frey and Jens Schröter. Tübingen: Mohr Siebeck, 2005.

Schultz, Richard J. "Intertextuality, Canon and 'Undecidability': Understanding Isaiah's 'New Heavens and New Earth' (Isaiah 65:17–25)." *BBR* 20 (2010): 19–38.

Schürmann, Heinz. "Die geistlichen Gnadengaben in den paulinischen Gemeiden." Pages 263–73 in *Ursprung und Gestalt: Erörterungen und Besinningen zum Neuen Testament*. Düsseldorf: Patmos, 1970.

———. "'Das Gesetz des Christus' (Gal 6,2): Jesu Verhalten und Wort als Letztgültige Sittliche Norm nach Paulus." Pages 282–300 in *Neues Testament und Kirche*. Freiburg: Verlag Herder, 1974.

Schütz, John Howard. *Paul and the Anatomy of Apostolic Authority*. SNTSMS 26. Cambridge: Cambridge University Press, 1975.

Schwarz, Roland. *Bürgerliches Christentum im Neuen Testament? Eine Studien zu Ethik, Amt, und Recht in den Pastoralbriefen*. Kolsternburg: OBS, 1983.

Schweitzer, Albert. *The Mysticism of Paul the Apostle*. New York: Macmillan, 1956.

———. *Paul and His Interpreters: A Critical History*. London: Adam and Charles Black, 1912.

Schweizer, Eduard. "Die 'Elemente der Welt' Gal 4,3.9; Kol 2,8.20." Pages 245–59 in *Verborum Veritas: Festschrift für Gustav Stählin zum 70. Geburtstag*. Edited by Otto Böcher and Klaus Haacker. Wuppertal: Brockhaus, 1970.

———. *The Letter to the Colossians: A Commentary*. Minneapolis: Augsburg, 1982.

Scobie, Charles H. H. "History of Biblical Theology." Pages 11–20 in *New Dictionary of Biblical Theology*. Edited by T. Desmond Alexander and Brian S. Rosner. Downers Grove, IL: InterVarsity Press, 2000.

———. *The Ways of Our God: An Approach to Biblical Theology*. Grand Rapids: Eerdmans, 2003.

Scornaienchi, Lorenzo. *Sarx und Soma bei Paulus: Der Mensch zwischen Destruktivität und Konstruktivität*. NTOA 67. Göttingen: Vandenhoeck & Ruprecht, 2008.

Scott, C. A. Anderson. *Christianity according to St. Paul*. Cambridge: Cambridge University Press, 1927.

Scott, Ian W. *Implicit Epistemology in the Letters of Paul: Story, Experience and the Spirit*. WUNT 2/205. Tübingen: Mohr Siebeck, 2006.

———. *Paul's Way of Knowing: Story, Experience, and the Spirit*. Grand Rapids: Baker, 2009.

Scott, James M. *Adoption as Sons of God: An Exegetical Investigation into the Background of Huiothesia in the Pauline Corpus*. WUNT 2/48. Tübingen: Mohr Siebeck, 1992.

———. "'For as Many as Are of Works of the Law Are under a Curse' (Galatians 3.10)." Pages 187–221 in *Paul and the Scriptures of Israel*. Edited by Craig A. Evans and James A. Sanders. JSNTSup 83. Sheffield: Sheffield Academic, 1993.

Scott, James M., ed. *Exile: A Conversation with N. T. Wright*. Downers Grove, IL: InterVarsity Press, 2017.

Scott, James W. "The Time When Revelatory Gifts Cease (1 Cor 13:8–12)." *WTJ* 72 (2010): 267–89.

Scott, Matthew. *The Hermeneutics of Christological Psalmody in Paul: An Intertextual Enquiry*. SNTSMS 158. Cambridge: Cambridge University Press, 2014.

Scroggs, Robin. *The New Testament and Homosexuality: Contextual Background for Contemporary Debate*. Philadelphia: Fortress, 1983.

———. "Paul and the Eschatological Women." *JAAR* 40 (1972): 283–303.

Sechrest, Love L. *A Former Jew: Paul and the Dialectics of Race*. LNTS 410. London: T&T Clark, 2009.

Seifrid, Mark. *Christ, Our Righteousness: Paul's Theology of Justification*. NSBT 9. Downers Grove, IL: InterVarsity Press, 2000.

———. *Justification by Faith: The Origin and Development of a Central Pauline Theme*. NovTSup 68. Leiden: Brill, 1992.

———. "The Narrative of Scripture and Justification by Faith: A Fresh Response to N. T. Wright." *CTQ* 72 (2008): 19–44.

———. "The New Perspective *from* Paul." *The Southern Baptist Journal of Theology* 14 (2010): 20–35.

———. "Paul's Use of Righteousness Language against Its Hellenistic Background." Pages 39–74 in *The Paradoxes of Paul*. Vol. 2 of *Justification and Variegated Nomism*. Edited by D. A. Carson, Peter T. O'Brien, and Mark A. Seifrid. Tübingen: Mohr Siebeck, 2004.

———. "Righteousness Language in the Hebrew Scriptures and Early Judaism." Pages 415–42 in *The Complexities of Second Temple Judaism*. Vol. 1 of *Justification and Variegated Nomism*. Edited by D. A. Carson, Peter T. O'Brien, and Mark A. Seifrid. Tübingen: Mohr Siebeck, 2001.

———. *The Second Letter to the Corinthians*. PNTC. Grand Rapids: Eerdmans, 2014.

———. "The Text of Romans and the Theology of Melanchthon: The Preceptor of the Germans and the Apostle to the Gentiles." Pages 97–120 in *Reformation Readings of Paul: Explorations in History and Exegesis*. Edited by Michael Allen and Jonathan A. Linebaugh. Downers Grove, IL: InterVarsity Press, 2015.

Seitz, Christopher R. *The Character of Christian Scripture: The Significance of a Two-Testament Bible*. STI. Grand Rapids: Baker, 2011.

———. "Jewish Scripture for Gentile Churches: Human Destiny and the Future of the Pauline Correspondence. Part I: Romans." *ProEccl* 23 (2014): 294–308.

Shank, Robert. *Elect in the Son: A Study of the Doctrine of Election.* Springfield: Westcott, 1970.

Shaw, D. A. "Apocalyptic and Covenant: Perspectives on Paul or Antinomies at War?" *JSNT* 36 (2013): 155–71.

Sherwood, Aaron. *Paul and the Restoration of Humanity in Light of Ancient Jewish Traditions.* Ancient Judaism and Early Christianity 82. Boston: Brill, 2013.

Shogren, Gary S. *1 & 2 Thessalonians.* ZECNT. Grand Rapids: Zondervan, 2012.

Siebenthal, H. von. *Griechische Grammatik zum Neuen Testament.* Giessen: Brunnen, 2011.

Silva, Moises. "Faith Versus Works of the Law in Galatians." Pages 217–48 in *The Paradoxes of Paul.* Vol. 2 of *Justification and Variegated Nomism.* Edited by D. A. Carson, Peter T. O'Brien, and Mark A. Seifrid. WUNT 2/140. Tübingen: Mohr Siebeck, 2004.

———. "Galatians." Pages 785–812 in *Commentary on the New Testament Use of the Old Testament.* Edited by G. K. Beale and D. A. Carson. Grand Rapids: Baker Academic, 2006.

———. "Galatians 1:1–2:16a." Unpublished manuscript, 2003.

———. *Interpreting Galatians: Explorations in Exegetical Method.* 2nd ed. Grand Rapids: Baker, 2001.

———. "The Law and Christianity: Dunn's 'New Synthesis.'" *WTJ* 53 (1991): 339–53.

———. *Philippians.* BECNT. Grand Rapids: Baker Academic, 2005.

———. "Philippians." Pages 835–39 in *Commentary on the New Testament Use of the Old Testament.* Edited by G. K. Beale and D. A. Carson. Grand Rapids: Baker Academic, 2006.

Sirard, Leas. "La Parousie de l'Antéchrist, 2 Thess 2, 3–9." Pages 2:94–99 in *Studiorum Paulinorum Congressus Internationalis Catholicus 1961.* AnBib 17–18. Rome: Pontifical Biblical Institute, 1963.

Sklar, Jay. *Leviticus: An Introduction and Commentary.* TOTC. Downers Grove, IL: InterVarsity Press, 2014.

Smedes, Lewis B. *Union with Christ: A Biblical View of the New Life in Jesus Christ.* Grand Rapids: Eerdmans, 1983.

Smith, Barry D. *The Meaning of Jesus' Death: Reviewing the New Testament's Interpretations.* London: Bloomsbury, 2017.

Smith, Claire S. *Pauline Communities as "Scholastic Communities."* WUNT 2/335. Tübingen: Mohr Siebeck, 2012.

Smith, Craig A. *Timothy's Task and Paul's Prospect: A New Reading of 2 Timothy.* New Testament Monographs 12. Sheffield: Sheffield Phoenix, 2006.

Smith, Gary V. "Paul's Use of Psalm 68:18 in Ephesians 4:8." *JETS* 18 (1975): 181–89.

Smith, Ian K. *Heavenly Perspective: A Study of the Apostle Paul's Response to a Jewish Mystical Movement at Colossae.* LNTS 346. Edinburgh: T&T Clark, 2006.

Smith, Jay E. "Another Look at 4Q416 2 ii.21: A Critical Parallel to First Thessalonians 4:4." *CBQ* 63 (2001): 499–504.

———. "A Slogan in 1 Corinthians 6:18b: Pressing the Case." Pages 74–98 in *Studies in the Pauline Epistles: Essays in Honor of Douglas J. Moo.* Edited by Matthew S. Harmon and Jay E. Smith. Grand Rapids: Zondervan, 2014.

Smith, Mark D. "Ancient Bisexuality and the Interpretation of Romans 1:26–27." *JAAR* 64 (1996): 223–56.

Snodgrass, Klyne R. "Justification by Grace—to the Doers: An Analysis of the Place of Romans 2 in the Theology of Paul." *NTS* 32 (1986): 72–93.

———. "Spheres of Influence: A Possible Solution for the Problem of Paul and the Law." *JSNT* 32 (1988): 93–113.

Soskice, Janet Martin. *Metaphor and Religious Language.* Oxford: Clarendon, 1985.

Sprinkle, Preston M. *Law and Life: The Interpretation of Leviticus 18:5 in Early Judaism and in Paul.* WUNT 2/241. Tübingen: Mohr Siebeck, 2007.

———. *Paul and Judaism Revisited: A Study of Divine and Human Agency in Salvation.* Downers Grove, IL: InterVarsity Press, 2013.

———. "*Pistis Christou* as Eschatological Event." Pages 165–84 in *The Faith of Jesus Christ: Exegetical, Biblical, and Theological Studies.* Edited by Michael F. Bird and Preston M. Sprinkle. Peabody, MA: Hendrickson, 2009.

———. "Romans 1 and Homosexuality: A Critical Review of James Brownson's *Bible, Gender, Sexuality.*" *BBR* 24 (2014): 515–28.

Spychalla, Peter D. "The Use of the Old Testament in 1 Corinthians 10:4: Paul's Combining of the Water-from-Rock and YHWH-as-Rock Motifs." PhD diss., Wheaton College, 2008.

Stacey, David. *The Pauline View of Man: In Relation to Its Judaic and Hellenistic Background.* London: Macmillan, 1956.

Stackhouse, John G., Jr. *Partners in Christ: A Conservative Case for Egalitarianism*. Downers Grove, IL: InterVarsity Press, 2015.

Stalder, Kurt. *Das Werk des Geistes in der Heiligung bei Paulus*. Zürich: EVZ, 1962.

Stanley, Christopher D. *Arguing with Scripture: The Rhetoric of Quotations in the Letters of Paul*. New York: T&T Clark, 2004.

———. *Paul and the Language of Scripture: Citation Techniques in the Pauline Epistles and Contemporary Literature*. SNTSMS 69. Cambridge: Cambridge University Press, 1992.

———. "'Under a Curse': A Fresh Reading of Galatians 3:10–14." *NTS* 36 (1990): 481–511.

Stanton, Graham N. *Jesus and Gospel*. Cambridge: Cambridge University Press, 2004.

———. "The Law of Moses and the Law of Christ: Galatians 3:1–6:2." Pages 99–116 in *Paul and the Mosaic Law*. Edited by James D. G. Dunn. Tübingen: Mohr Siebeck, 1996.

Starling, David I. *Not My People: Gentiles as Exiles in Pauline Hermeneutics*. BZNW 184. Berlin: de Gruyter, 2011.

Stendahl, Krister. "The Apostle Paul and the Introspective Conscience of the West." *HTR* 56 (1963): 199–215.

———. "Biblical Theology, Contemporary." Pages 418–32 in vol. 1 of *The Interpreter's Dictionary of the Bible*. Edited by George A. Buttrick. New York: Abingdon, 1962.

———. "Christ's Lordship and Religious Pluralism." Pages 233–44 in *Meanings: The Bible as Document and as Guide*. By Krister Stendahl. Philadelphia: Fortress, 1984.

———. *Final Account: Paul's Letter to the Romans*. Minneapolis: Fortress, 1995.

———. "Paul among Jews and Gentiles." Pages 1–71 in *Paul among Jews and Gentiles, and Other Essays*. Philadelphia: Fortress, 1976.

———. *Paul among Jews and Gentiles, and Other Essays*. Philadelphia: Fortress, 1976.

Stettler, Christian. *Das Endgericht bei Paulus: Framesemantische und Exegetische Studien zur paulinischen Eschatologie und Soteriologie*. WUNT 2/317. Tübingen: Mohr Siebeck, 2017.

———. *Der Kolosserhymnus: Untersuchungen zu Form, Traditionsgeschictlichen Hintergrund und Aussage Von Kol 1,15–20*. WUNT 2/131. Tübingen: Mohr Siebeck, 2000.

Stettler, Hanna. *Die Christologie der Pastoralbriefe*. WUNT 2/105. Tübingen: Mohr Siebeck, 1998.

———. *Heiligung bei Paulus: Ein Beitrag aus biblisch-theologischer Sicht*. WUNT 2/368. Tübingen: Mohr Siebeck, 2014.

———. "An Interpretation of Colossians 1:24 in the Framework of Paul's Mission Theology." Pages 192–208 in *Mission of the Early Church to Jews and Gentiles*. Edited by Jostein Adna and Hans Kvalbein. WUNT 2/127. Tübingen: Mohr Siebeck, 2000.

Stevens, George Barker. *The Theology of the New Testament*. New York: Scribner's Sons, 1947.

Stewart, James Stuart. *A Man in Christ: The Vital Elements of St. Paul's Religion*. New York: Harper and Brothers, 1935.

Still, Todd D. *Conflict at Thessalonica: A Pauline Church and Its Neighbors*. JSNTSup 183. Sheffield: JSOT, 1999.

Stockhausen, Carol Kern. *Moses' Veil and the Glory of the New Covenant: The Exegetical Substructure of II Cor. 3,1–4,6*. AnBib 116. Rome: Pontifical Biblical Institute, 1989.

Storms, Sam. *Chosen for Life: The Case for Divine Election*. Wheaton, IL: Crossway, 2007.

Stott, John R. W. *Men Made New: An Exposition of Romans 5–8*. London: Inter-Varsity Press, 1966.

———. *The Message of Ephesians: God's New Society*. Bible Speaks Today. Downers Grove, IL: InterVarsity Press, 1979.

Stowers, Stanley K. "Friends and Enemies in the Politics of Heaven: Reading Theology in Philippians." Pages 105–21 in *Pauline Theology, Vol. 1: Thessalonians, Philippians, Galatians, Philemon*. Edited by Jouette M. Bassler. Minneapolis: Augsburg Fortress, 1991.

Strecker, Georg. *Theology of the New Testament*. Louisville: Westminster John Knox, 1996.

Strom, Mark. *Reframing Paul: Conversations in Grace and Community*. Downers Grove, IL: InterVarsity Press, 2000.

Stuckenbruck, Loren T. "Posturing 'Apocalyptic' in Pauline Theology: How Much Contrast to Jewish Tradition?" Pages 245–56 in *The Myth of the Rebellious Angels: Studies in Second Temple Judaism and New Testament Texts*. WUNT 2/355. Tübingen: Mohr Siebeck, 2014.

Stuhlmacher, Peter. "The Apostle Paul's View of Righteousness." Pages 68–93 in *Reconciliation, Law, and Righteousness: Essays in Biblical Theology*. Philadelphia: Fortress, 1986.

———. *Biblical Theology of the New Testament*. Grand Rapids: Eerdmans, 2018.

———. *Der Brief an Philemon*. EKKNT 18. Neukirchen-Vluyn: Neukirchener, 2004.

———. "Erwägungen zum ontologischen Charakter der *kainē ktisis* bei Paulus." *EvT* 27 (1967): 1–35.

———. *Grundlegung: Von Jesus zu Paulus*. Vol. 2 of *Biblische Theologie des Neuen Testaments*. Göttingen: Vandenhoeck & Ruprecht, 2005.

———. "The Hermeneutical Significance of 1 Cor 2:6–16." Pages 328–43 in *Tradition and Interpretation in the New Testament: Essays in Honor of E. Earle Ellis*. Edited by Gerald F. Hawthorne and Otto Betz. Grand Rapids: Eerdmans, 1987.

———. "Jesustradition im Römerbrief? Eine Skizze." *TBei* 14 (1983): 240–50.

———. *Das Paulinische Evangelium. 1. Vorgeschichte*. FRLANT 95. Göttingen: Vandenhoeck & Ruprecht, 1968.

———. "Recent Exegesis on Romans 3:24–26." Pages 94–109 in *Reconciliation, Law, and Righteousness: Essays in Biblical Theology*. Philadelphia: Fortress, 1986.

———. "The Theme of Romans." Pages 333–45 in *The Romans Debate*. Edited by K. P. Donfried. Rev. and exp. ed. Peabody, MA: Hendrickson, 1991.

Swartley, Willard M. *Covenant of Peace: The Missing Peace in New Testament Theology and Ethics*. Grand Rapids: Eerdmans, 2006.

Swinson, L. Timothy. *What Is Scripture? Paul's Use of Graphe in the Letters to Timothy*. Eugene, OR: Wipf & Stock, 2014.

Talbert, Charles H. "Paul, Judaism, and the Revisionists." *CBQ* 63 (2001): 1–22.

———. *Reading Corinthians: A Literary and Theological Commentary on 1 and 2 Corinthians*. New York: Crossroad, 1987.

Tannehill, Robert C. *Dying and Rising with Christ: A Study in Pauline Theology*. BZNW 32. Berlin: Töpelmann, 1967.

Tatum, Gregory. *New Chapters in the Life of Paul: The Relative Chronology of His Career*. CBQMS 41. Washington: Catholic Biblical Association, 2006.

Theiring, B. E. "*Mebaqqer* and *Episkopos* in the Light of the Temple Scroll." *JBL* 100 (1981): 59–74.

Theissen, Gerd. *The Social Setting of Pauline Christianity: Essays on Corinth*. Philadephia: Fortress, 1982.

Thielman, Frank. *Ephesians*. BECNT. Grand Rapids: Baker Academic, 2010.

———. *From Plight to Solution: A Jewish Framework for Understanding Paul's View of the Law in Galatians and Romans*. NovTSup 41. Leiden: Brill, 1989.

———. "God's Righteousness as God's Fairness in Romans 1:17: An Ancient Perspective on a Significant Phrase." *JETS* 54 (2011): 35–48.

———. *Paul and the Law: A Contextual Approach*. Downers Grove, IL: InterVarsity Press, 1994.

———. *Romans*. ZECNT. Grand Rapids: Zondervan, 2018.

———. "The Story of Israel and the Theology of Romans 5–8." Pages 169–95 in *Pauline Theology, Vol. 3: Romans*. Edited by David M. Hay and E. Elizabeth Johnson. Minneapolis: Fortress, 1995.

Thiessen, Matthew. *Paul and the Gentile Problem*. Oxford: Oxford University Press, 2016.

Thiselton, Anthony C. *The First Epistle to the Corinthians*. NIGTC. Grand Rapids: Eerdmans, 2013.

———. *The Hermeneutics of Doctrine*. Grand Rapids: Eerdmans, 2007.

———. *Life after Death: A New Approach to the Last Things*. Grand Rapids: Eerdmans, 2012.

———. "Realized Eschatology at Corinth." *NTS* 24 (1977–1978): 510–26.

———. *The Two Horizons: New Testament Hermeneutics and Philosophical Description with Special Reference to Bultmann, Heidegger, Gadamer, and Wittgenstein*. Grand Rapids: Eerdmans, 1979.

Thomas, M. J. *Paul's "Works of the Law" in the Perspective of Second Century Reception*. WUNT 2/468. Tübingen: Mohr Siebeck, 2018.

Thomas, Robert L. *Understanding Spiritual Gifts: A Verse-by-Verse Study of 1 Corinthians 12–14*. Grand Rapids: Kregel, 1999.

Thompson, G. H. P. *The Letters of Paul to the Ephesians, to the Colossians, and to Philemon*. CBC. Cambridge: Cambridge University Press, 1967.

Thompson, James W. *The Church according to Paul: Rediscovering the Community Conformed for Christ*. Grand Rapids: Baker, 2014.

———. *Moral Formation according to Paul: The Context and Coherence of Pauline Ethics*. Grand Rapids: Baker, 2011.

Thompson, Marianne Meye. *Colossians and Philemon*. The Two Horizons New Testament Commentary. Grand Rapids: Eerdmans, 2005.

Thompson, Michael B. *Clothed with Christ: The Example and Teaching of Jesus in Romans 12.1–15.13*. JSNTSup 59. Sheffield: Sheffield Academic, 1991.

Thornhill, A. Chadwick. *The Chosen People: Election, Paul and Second Temple Judaism*. Downers Grove, IL: InterVarsity Press, 2015.

Thorsteinsson, Runar M. *Paul's Interlocutor in Romans 2: Function and Identity in the Context of Ancient Epistolography*. ConBNT 40. Stockholm: Almqvist & Wiksell, 2003.

Thrall, Margaret. *Greek Particles in the New Testament: Linguistic and Exegetical Studies*. NTTS 3. Leiden: Brill, 1962.

———. *Second Epistle to the Corinthians*. ICC. London: T&T Clark, 1994.

Thurén, Lauri. *Derhetorizing Paul: A Dynamic Perspective on Pauline Theology and the Law*. WUNT 2/124. Tübingen: Mohr Siebeck, 2000.

Tilling, Chris. *Paul's Divine Christology*. WUNT 2/323. Tübingen: Mohr Siebeck, 2012.

Tilling, Chris, ed. *Beyond Old and New Perspectives on Paul: Reflections on the Work of Douglas Campbell*. Eugene, OR: Cascade, 2014.

Timmins, Will N. "A Faith Unlike Abraham's: Matthew Bates on Salvation by Allegiance Alone." *JETS* 61 (2018): 595–615.

———. *Romans 7 and Christian Identity: A Study of the "I" in Its Literary Context*. SNTSMS 170. Cambridge: Cambridge University Press, 2017.

Tise, Larry E. *Proslavery: A History of the Defense of Slavery in America 1701–1840*. Athens, GA: University of Georgia Press, 1987.

Tolmie, D. François. *Persuading the Galatians: A Text-Centred Rhetorical Analysis of a Pauline Letter*. WUNT 2/190. Tübingen: Mohr Siebeck, 2005.

Tomson, Peter J. *Paul and the Jewish Law: Halakha in the Letters of the Apostle to the Gentiles*. CRINT. Minneapolis: Fortress, 1991.

Toney, Carl N. *Paul's Inclusive Ethic: Resolving Community Conflicts and Promoting Mission in Romans 14–15*. WUNT 2/252. Tübingen: Mohr Siebeck, 2008.

Torrance, Thomas F. "One Aspect of the Biblical Conception of Faith." *ExpTim* 68 (1956–1957): 111–14.

———. *Space, Time and Resurrection*. Edinburgh: T&T Clark, 1976.

Towner, Philip H. *The Goal of Our Instruction: The Structure of Theology and Ethics in the Pastoral Epistles*. JSNTSup 34. Sheffield: JSOT Press, 1989.

———. *The Letters to Timothy and Titus*. NICNT. Grand Rapids: Eerdmans, 2006.

Travis, Stephen H. *Christ and the Judgement of God: The Limits of Divine Retribution in New Testament Thought*. 2nd ed. Peabody, MA: Hendrickson, 2008.

———. "Christ as Bearer of Divine Judgment in Paul's Thought about the Atonement." Pages 332–45 in *Jesus of Nazareth: Lord and Christ: Essays on the Historical Jesus and New Testament Christology*. Edited by Michael Green and Max Turner. Grand Rapids: Eerdmans, 1994.

Treat, Jeremy. *The Crucified King: Atonement and Kingdom in Biblical and Systematic Theology*. Grand Rapids: Zondervan, 2014.

Trebilco, Paul. *Self-Designations and Group Identity in the New Testament*. Cambridge: Cambridge University Press, 2012.

Trilling, Wolfgang. *Untersuchungen zum zweiten Thessalonicherbrief*. ETS 27. Leipzig: St.-Benno, 1972.

Tuckett, C. M. "The Corinthians Who Say 'There Is No Resurrection of the Dead' (1 Cor 15,12)." Pages 247–75 in *The Corinthian Correspondence*. Edited by R. Bieringer. BETL 125. Leuven: Leuven University Press, 1996.

Turner, James T. *On the Resurrection of the Dead: A New Metaphysics of Afterlife for Christian Thought*. Routledge New Critical Thinking in Religion, Theology and Biblical Studies. New York: Routledge, 2019.

Turner, Max. *The Holy Spirit and Spiritual Gifts: Then and Now*. Carlisle: Paternoster, 1996.

———. "Mission and Meaning in Terms of 'Unity' in Ephesians." Pages 138–66 in *Mission and Meaning: Essays Presented to Peter Cotterell*. Edited by Antony Billington, Tony Lane, and Max Turner. Carlisle: Paternoster, 1995.

Turner, Nigel. *Syntax*. Vol. 3 of *A Grammar of New Testament Greek*. By J. H. Moulton. Edinburgh: T&T Clark, 1963.

Turretin, Francis. *Institutes of Elenctic Theology*. 3 vols. Philippsburg, NJ: P&R, 1997 (1679–1685).

Twelftree, Graham H. *Paul and the Miraculous: A Historical Reconstruction*. Grand Rapids: Baker, 2013.

Ulrichs, Karl Friedrich. *Christusglaube: Studien zum Syntagma Pistis Christou und zum paulinischen Verständnis von Glaube und Rechtfertigung*. WUNT 2/227. Tübingen: Mohr Siebeck, 2007.

Urbach, E. E. *The Sages: Their Concepts and Beliefs*. 2 vols. Jerusalem: Magnes, 1979.

van Bruggen, Jakob. *Die geschichtliche Einordnung der Pastoralbriefe*. Wuppertal: Brockhaus, 1982.

van der Horst, Peter W. "Only Then Will All Israel Be Saved: A Short Note on the Meaning of Καὶ Οὕτως in Romans 11:26." *JBL* 119 (2000): 521–25.

van Dülmen, Andrea. *Die Theologie des Gesetzes bei Paulus*. SBM 5. Stuttgart: Katholisches Bibelwerk, 1968.

van Kooten, George. "Ἐκκλησία τοῦ θεοῦ: The 'Church of God' and the Civic Assemblies [ἐκκλησίαι] of the Greek Cities in the Roman Empire: A Response to Paul Trebilco and Richard A. Horsley." *NTS* 58 (2012): 522–48.

van Nes, Jermo. *Pauline Language and the Pastoral Epistles: A Study of Linguistic Variation in the Corpus Paulinium*. Linguistic Biblical Studies 16. Leiden: Brill, 2018.

van Neste, Ray. *Cohesion and Structure in the Pastoral Epistles*. JSNTSup 280. London: T&T Clark, 2004.

van Roon, A. *The Authenticity of Ephesians*. NovTSup 39. Leiden: Brill, 1974.

van Unnik, Willem C. *Tarsus or Jerusalem: The City of Paul's Youth*. 2nd ed. Eugene, OR: Wipf & Stock, 2009.

VanderKam, James C. "Exile in Jewish Apocalyptic Literature." Pages 89–109 in *Exile: Old Testament, Jewish, and Christian Conceptions*. Edited by James M. Scott. Supplements to the Journal for the Study of Judaism 56. Leiden: Brill, 1997.

VanDrunen, David. *Divine Covenants and Moral Order: A Biblical Theology of Natural Law*. Emory University Studies in Law and Religion. Grand Rapids: Eerdmans, 2014.

Vanhoozer, Kevin J. "The Atonement in Postmodernity: Guilt, Goats, and Gifts." Pages 367–404 in *The Glory of the Atonement: Biblical, Historical, and Practical Perspectives: Essays in Honor of Roger R. Nicole*. Edited by Charles E. Hill and Frank A. James III. Downers Grove, IL: InterVarsity Press, 2004.

———. "Christ and Concept: Doing Theology and the 'Ministry' of Philosophy." Pages 99–145 in *Doing Theology in Today's World: Essays in Honor of Kenneth S. Kantzer*. Edited by John D. Woodbridge and Thomas Edward McComiskey. Grand Rapids: Zondervan, 1991.

———. "Exegesis and Hermeneutics." Pages 52–64 in *New Dictionary of Biblical Theology*. Edited by T. Desmond Alexander and Brian S. Rosner. Downers Grove, IL: InterVarsity Press, 2000.

———. "Wrighting the Wrongs of the Reformation? The State of the Union with Christ in St. Paul and Protestant Soteriology." Pages 235–59 in *Jesus, Paul and the People of God: A Theological Dialogue with N. T. Wright*. Edited by Nicholas Perrin and Richard B. Hays. Downers Grove, IL: InterVarsity Press, 2011.

VanLandingham, Chris. *Judgment and Justification in Early Judaism and the Apostle Paul*. Peabody, MA: Hendrickson, 2006.

Verbrugge, Verlyn D. "Greek Grammar and the Translation of Philippians 2:12." Pages 113–26 in *Studies in the Pauline Epistles: Essays in Honor of Douglas J. Moo*. Edited by Matthew S. Harmon and Jay E. Smith. Grand Rapids: Zondervan, 2014.

Verbrugge, Verlyn D., and Keith R. Krell. *Paul and Money: A Biblical and Theological Analysis of the Apostle's Teachings and Practices*. Grand Rapids: Zondervan, 2015.

Verner, David C. *The Household of God: The Social World of the Pastoral Epistles*. SBLDS 71. Chico, CA: Scholars Press, 1983.

Verseput, Donald J. "Paul's Gentile Mission and the Jewish Christian Community: A Study of the Narrative in Galatians 1 and 2." *NTS* 39 (1993): 36–58.

Via, Dan O. *What Is New Testament Theology?* GBS. Minneapolis: Fortress, 2002.

Vickers, Brian. *Jesus' Blood and Righteousness: Paul's Theology of Imputation*. Wheaton, IL: Crossway, 2006.

Vlach, Michael J. *Has the Church Replaced Israel? A Theological Evaluation*. Nashville: B&H Academic, 2010.

Vlachos, Chris Alex. *The Law and the Knowledge of Good & Evil: The Edenic Background of the Catalytic Operation of the Law in Paul*. Eugene, OR: Pickwick, 2009.

Vögtle, A. *Die Tugend- und Lasterkataloge im Neuen Testament, exegetisch, religions- und formgeschichtlich untersucht*. NTAbh 16. Münster: Aschendorff, 1936.

Volf, Miroslav. *Exclusion and Embrace: A Theological Exploration of Identity, Otherness, and Reconciliation*. Nashville: Abingdon, 1996.

Vollenweider, Samuel. "Der 'Raub' der Gottgleichheit: Ein religionsgeschichtlicher Vorschlag zu Phil 2.6[–11]." *NTS* 45 (1999): 413–33.

Vos, Geerhardus. *The Pauline Eschatology*. Princeton: Princeton University Press, 1930. Repr., Philipsburg, NJ: P&R, 1994.

Vouga, François. *An die Galater*. HNT. Tübingen: Mohr Siebeck, 1998.

Wagner, J. Ross. *Heralds of the Good News: Isaiah and Paul 'in Concert' in the Letter to the Romans*. NovTSup 101. Leiden: Brill, 2002.

———. "Paul and Scripture." Pages 154–71 in *The Blackwell Companion to Paul*. Edited by Stephen Westerholm. Chichester: Wiley-Blackwell, 2011.

Wakefield, Andrew H. *Where to Live: The Hermeneutical Significance of Paul's Citations from Scripture in Galatians 3:1–14*. AcBib 14. Atlanta: SBL, 2003.

Walker, William O., Jr. *Interpolations in the Pauline Letters*. JSNTSup 213. London: Sheffield Academic, 2001.

Wall, Robert W. *Colossians and Philemon*. IVPNTC. Downers Grove, IL: InterVarsity Press, 1993.

Wall, Robert W., with Richard B. Steele. *1 and 2 Timothy and Titus*. Two Horizons New Testament Commentary. Grand Rapids: Eerdmans, 2012.

Wallace, Daniel. *Greek Grammar Beyond the Basics: An Exegetical Syntax of the New Testament*. Grand Rapids: Zondervan, 1996.

———. "The Relation of θεόπνευστος to γραφή in 2 Timothy 3:16." *Bible.org*. July 14, 2019. https://bible.org/article/relation-font-facegreekqeovpneusto-grafhv-font-2-timothy-316.

Wallis, I. G. *The Faith of Jesus Christ in Early Christian Traditions*. SNTSMS 84. Cambridge: Cambridge University Press, 1995.

Wallis, Wilber. "The Problem of an Intermediate Kingdom in 1 Corinthians 15:20–28." *JETS* 18 (1975): 229–40.

Walter, Matthias. *Gemeinde als Leib Christi: Untersuchungen zum Corpus Paulinium und zu den "Apostolischen Vätern."* NTOA 49. Göttingen: Vandenhoeck & Ruprecht, 2001.

Waltke, Bruce K. *Genesis*. Grand Rapids: Zondervan, 2001.

Waltke, Bruce K., with Charles Yu. *An Old Testament Theology: An Exegetical, Canonical, and Thematic Approach*. Grand Rapids: Zondervan, 2007.

Walton, Steve. *Leadership and Lifestyle: The Portrait of Paul in the Miletus Speech and 1 Thessalonians*. SNTSMS 108. Cambridge: Cambridge University Press, 2000.

Wanamaker, Charles A. *The Epistles to the Thessalonians*. NIGTC. Grand Rapids: Eerdmans, 1990.

Warfield, Benjamin B. *Counterfeit Miracles*. Repr., Edinburgh: Banner of Truth, 1972.

———. *Revelation and Inspiration*. Oxford: Oxford University Press, 1927.

Watson, Francis. "Constructing an Antithesis: Pauline and Other Jewish Perspectives on Divine and Human Agency." Pages 99–116 in *Divine and Human Agency in Paul and His Cultural Environment*. Edited by John M. G. Barclay and Simon Gathercole. LNTS 335. Edinburgh: T&T Clark, 2006.

———. "Is There a Story in These Texts?" Pages 231–39 in *Narrative Dynamics in Paul: A Critical Assessment*. Edited by Bruce Longenecker. Louisville: Westminster John Knox, 2002.

———. *Paul and the Hermeneutics of Faith*. 2nd ed. Edinburgh: T&T Clark, 2016.

———. *Paul, Judaism, and the Gentiles: A Sociological Approach*. SNTSMS 56. Cambridge: Cambridge University Press, 1986.

———. "The Triune Divine Identity: Reflections on Pauline God-Language, in Disagreement with J. D. G. Dunn." *JSNT* 80 (2000): 99–124.

Watts, Rikki E. "'For I Am Not Ashamed of the Gospel': Romans 1:16–17 and Habakkuk 2:4." Pages 3–25 in *Romans and the People of God: Essays in Honor of Gordon D. Fee on the Occasion of His 65th Birthday*. Edited by Sven Soderlund and N. T. Wright. Grand Rapids: Eerdmans, 1999.

Webb, William J. *Slaves, Women, and Homosexuals: Exploring the Hermeneutics of Cultural Analysis*. Downers Grove, IL: InterVarsity Press, 2001.

Weber, Otto. *Foundations of Dogmatics*. 2 vols. Grand Rapids: Eerdmans, 1981, 1983.

Webster, John. "Karl Barth." Pages 205–23 in *Reading Romans through the Centuries: From the Early Church to Karl Barth*. Edited by Jeffrey P. Greenman and Timothy Larsen. Grand Rapids: Baker, 2011.

———. *Word and Church*. Edinburgh: T&T Clark, 2001.

Wedderburn, A. J. M. *Baptism and Resurrection: Studies in Pauline Theology against Its Graeco-Roman Background*. WUNT 2/44. Tübingen: Mohr Siebeck, 1987.

———. *The Death of Jesus: Some Reflections on Jesus-Traditions and Paul*. WUNT 2/299. Tübingen: Mohr Siebeck, 2013.

———. *The Reasons for Romans*. London: T&T Clark, 1991.

———. "Some Observations on Paul's Use of the Phrases 'in Christ' and 'with Christ.'" *JSNT* 25 (1985): 83–90.

———. "The Theological Structure of Romans V.12." *NTS* 19 (1972–1973): 339–54.

Weima, Jeffrey A. D. *1–2 Thessalonians*. BECNT. Grand Rapids: Baker Academic, 2014.

———. "'How You Must Walk to Please God': Holiness and Discipleship in 1 Thessalonians." Pages 98–119 in *Patterns of Discipleship in the New Testament*. Edited by R. N. Longenecker. McMaster New Testament Studies. Grand Rapids: Eerdmans, 1996.

———. *Neglected Endings: The Significance of the Pauline Letter Closings*. JSNTSup 101. Sheffield: Sheffield Academic, 1994.

———. *Paul the Ancient Letter Writer: An Introduction to Epistolary Analysis*. Grand Rapids: Baker, 2016.

———. "'Peace and Security' (1 Thess 5.3): Prophetic Warning or Political Propaganda?" *NTS* 58 (2012): 33–59.

Weiser, Alfons. *Der zweite Brief an Timotheus*. EKKNT 16/1. Düsseldorf: Benziger, 2003.

Wells, Kyle B. *Grace and Agency in Paul and Second Temple Judaism: Interpreting the Transformation of the Heart*. NovTSup 157. Leiden: Brill, 2015.

Wells, Tom, and Fred Zaspel. *New Covenant Theology: Description, Definition, Defense*. Frederick, MD: New Covenant Media, 2002.

Wenham, David. "Acts and the Pauline Corpus II. The Evidence of Parallels." Pages 215–58 in *The Book of Acts in Its Literary Setting*. Vol. 1 of *The Book of Acts in Its First Century Setting*. Edited by B. W. Winter and Andrew D. Clarke. Grand Rapids: Eerdmans, 1993.

———. *From Good News to Gospels: What Did the First Christians Say about Jesus?* Grand Rapids: Eerdmans, 2018.

———. "Paul and the Synoptic Apocalypse." Pages 345–75 in *Studies of History and Tradition in the Four Gospels*. Edited by R. T. France and David Wenham. Gospel Perspectives 2. Sheffield: JSOT, 1981.

———. *Paul: Follower of Jesus or Founder of Christianity?* Grand Rapids: Eerdmans, 1995.

———. *The Rediscovery of Jesus' Eschatological Discourse*. Gospel Perspectives 4. Eugene, OR: Wipf & Stock, 1984.

Wenham, Gordon J. "The Theology of Old Testament Sacrifice." Pages 75–87 in *Sacrifice in the Bible*. Edited by Roger T. Beckwith and Martin J. Selman. Carlisle: Paternoster, 1995.

Wenham, J. W. "The Case for Conditional Immortality." Pages 161–91 in *Universalism and the Doctrine of Hell*. Edited by Nigel M. de S. Cameron. Grand Rapids: Baker, 1992.

Westerholm, Stephen. "Canonical Paul and the Law." Pages 207–22 in *Torah Ethics and Early Christian Identity*. Edited by Susan J. Wendel and David M. Miller. Grand Rapids: Eerdmans, 2016.

———. *Israel's Law and the Church's Faith: Paul and His Recent Interpreters*. Grand Rapids: Eerdmans, 1988.

———. *Justification Reconsidered: Rethinking a Pauline Theme*. Grand Rapids: Eerdmans, 2013.

———. "The Law and the 'Just Man' (1 Tim 1,3–11)." *ST* 36 (1982): 79–95.

———. "Paul's Anthropological 'Pessimism' in Its Jewish Context." Pages 71–98 in *Divine and Human Agency in Paul and His Cultural Environment*. Edited by John M. G. Barclay and Simon Gathercole. LNTS 335. Edinburgh: T&T Clark, 2006.

———. *Perspectives Old and New on Paul: The "Lutheran" Paul and His Critics*. Grand Rapids: Eerdmans, 2004.

———. "*Torah, Nomos*, and Law: A Question of 'Meaning.'" *SR* 15 (1986): 327–36.

Westermann, William Linn. *The Slave Systems of Greek and Roman Antiquity*. Memoirs of the American Philosophical Society 40. Philadelphia: American Philosophical Society, 1955.

Westfall, Cynthia Long. "A Moral Dilemma? The Epistolary Body of 2 Timothy." Pages 213–52 in *Paul and the Ancient Letter Form*. Edited by Stanley E. Porter and Sean A. Adams. Pauline Studies 6. Leiden: Brill, 2010.

———. *Paul and Gender: Reclaiming the Apostle's Vision for Men and Women in Christ*. Grand Rapids: Baker, 2016.

White, Joel. "Anti-Imperial Subtexts in Paul: An Attempt at Building a Firmer Foundation." *Bib* 90 (2009): 305–33.

———. "Paul's Cosmology: The Witness of Romans, 1 and 2 Corinthians, and Galatians." Pages 90–106 in *Cosmology and New Testament Theology*. Edited by Jonathan T. Pennington and Sean M. McDonough. LNTS 355. London: T&T Clark, 2008.

Whitely, D. E. H. *The Theology of St. Paul*. Philadelphia: Fortress, 1972.

Wieland, George. *The Significance of Salvation: A Study of Salvation Language in the Pastoral Epistles*. Paternoster Biblical Monographs. Milton Keynes: Paternoster, 2006.

Wilckens, Ulrich. *Der Brief an die Römer*. EKKNT. 3 vols. Neukirchen-Vluyn: Neukirchener; Zürich: Benziger, 1978–1981.

———. *Die Briefe des Urchristentums: Paulus und seine Schüler, Theologen aus dem Bereich judenchristlicher Heidenmission*. Vol. 3 of *Geschichte der urchristlichen Theologie*. Part 1 of *Theologie des Neuen Testament*. 3rd ed. Neukirchen-Vluyn: Neukirchener, 2014.

———. *Theologie des Neuen Testaments*. 6 vols. 2nd, 3rd, and 4th eds. Neukirchen-Vluyn: Neukirchener, 2014.

———. "Über Abfassungszweck und Aufbau des Römerbriefes." Pages 110–43 in *Rechtfertigung als Freiheit: Paulusstudien*. Neukirchen-Vluyn: Neukirchener, 1974.

Wilder, Terry L. "Pseudonymity, the New Testament, and the Pastoral Epistles." Pages 28–51 in *Entrusted with the Gospel: Paul's Theology in the Pastoral Epistles*. Edited by Andreas J. Köstenberger and Terry L. Wilder. Nashville: B&H, 2010.

Wilder, Terry L., ed. *Perspectives on Our Struggle with Sin: 3 Views of Romans 7*. Nashville: B&H, 2011.

Wiles, M. F. *The Divine Apostle: The Interpretation of St. Paul's Epistles in the Early Church.* Cambridge: Cambridge University, 1967.

Williams, Garry. "Penal Substitution: A Response to Recent Criticisms." Pages 172–91 in *The Atonement Debate: Papers from the London Symposium on the Theology of the Atonement.* Edited by David Hilborn, Justin Thacker, and Derek Tidball. Grand Rapids: Zondervan, 2008.

Williams, Jarvis J. *For Whom Did Christ Die? The Extent of the Atonement in Paul's Theology.* Paternoster Biblical Monographs. Milton Keynes: Paternoster, 2012.

———. *Maccabean Martyr Traditions in Paul's Theology of Atonement: Did Martyr Theology Shape Paul's Conception of Jesus's Death?* Eugene, OR: Wipf & Stock, 2010.

———. *One New Man: The Cross and Racial Reconciliation in Pauline Theology.* Nashville: B&H, 2010.

Williams, Sam K. "Again *Pistis Christou.*" *CBQ* 49 (1987): 431–47.

———. "The Hearing of Faith: *Akoe Pisteos* in Galatians 3." *NTS* 35 (1989): 82–93.

———. "The 'Righteousness of God' in Romans." *JBL* 99 (1980): 241–90.

Williams, Stephen N. *The Election of Grace: A Riddle Without a Resolution?* Grand Rapids: Eerdmans, 2015.

———. "The Question of Hell and Salvation: Is There a Fourth View?" *TynBul* 57 (2006): 263–83.

Williamson, Paul. "Promise and Fulfillment: The Territorial Inheritance." Pages 17–32 in *The Land of Promise: Biblical, Theological and Contemporary Perspectives.* Edited by Philip Johnston and Peter Walker. Downers Grove, IL: InterVarsity Press, 2000.

Willitts, Joel. "Isa 54,1 in Gal 4,27b–27: Reading Genesis in Light of Isaiah." *ZNW* 96 (2005): 188–210.

Wilson, Andrew J. *The Warning-Assurance Relationship in 1 Corinthians.* WUNT 2/452. Tübingen: Mohr Siebeck, 2017.

Wilson, Robert McL. *A Critical and Exegetical Commentary on Colossians and Philemon.* ICC. Edinburgh: T&T Clark, 2005.

Wilson, Todd A. *The Curse of the Law and the Crisis in Galatia: Reassessing the Purpose of Galatians.* WUNT 2/225. Tübingen: Mohr Siebeck, 2007.

———. "The Law of Christ and the Law of Moses: Reflections on a Recent Trend in Interpretation." *CurBR* 5 (2006): 123–44.

Windsor, Lionel J. *Paul and the Vocation of Israel: How Paul's Jewish Identity Informs His Apostolic Ministry, with Special Reference to Romans.* BZNW 205. Berlin: de Gruyter, 2014.

Winger, Michael. *By What Law?: The Meaning of Nomos in the Letters of Paul.* SBLDS 128. Atlanta: Scholars Press, 1992.

Wink, Walter. *Engaging the Powers: Discernment and Resistance in a World of Domination.* Philadelphia: Fortress, 1992.

———. *Naming the Powers: The Language of Power in the New Testament.* Philadelphia: Fortress, 1984.

———. *Unmasking the Powers: The Invisible Forces that Determine Human Existence.* Philadelphia: Fortress, 1986.

Winter, Bruce W. *After Paul Left Corinth: The Influence of Secular Ethics and Social Change.* Grand Rapids: Eerdmans, 2001.

———. *Divine Honours for the Caesars: The First Christians' Responses.* Grand Rapids: Eerdmans, 2015.

———. "The Lord's Supper at Corinth: An Alternative Reconstruction." *RTR* 37 (1978): 73–82.

———. *Philo and Paul among the Sophists: Alexandrian and Corinthian Responses to a Julio-Claudian Movement.* 2nd ed. Grand Rapids: Eerdmans, 2002.

———. *Roman Wives, Roman Widows: The Appearance of New Women and the Pauline Communities.* Grand Rapids: Eerdmans, 2003.

———. *Seek the Welfare of the City: Christians as Benefactors and Citizens.* First Century Christians in the Graeco-Roman World. Grand Rapids: Eerdmans, 1994.

Witherington, Ben, III. *1 and 2 Thessalonians: A Socio-Rhetorical Commentary.* Grand Rapids: Eerdmans, 2006.

———. "The Case of the Imprisonment That Did Not Happen: Paul at Ephesus." *JETS* 60 (2017): 525–32.

———. *Conflict & Community in Corinth: A Socio-Rhetorical Commentary on 1 and 2 Corinthians.* Grand Rapids: Eerdmans, 1995.

———. *Grace in Galatia: A Commentary on Paul's Letter to the Galatians.* Grand Rapids: Eerdmans, 1998.

———. *The Indelible Image: The Theological and Ethical World of the New Testament.* 2 vols. Downers Grove, IL: InterVarsity Press, 2009.

———. *Jesus the Sage: The Pilgrimage of Wisdom.* Minneapolis: Fortress, 1994.

———. *Jesus the Seer: The Progress of Prophecy.* Peabody, MA: Hendrickson, 1999.

————. *The Paul Quest: The Renewed Search for the Jew of Tarsus*. Downers Grove, IL: InterVarsity Press, 1998.

Witherington, Ben, III, with D. Hyatt. *Paul's Letter to the Romans: A Socio-Rhetorical Commentary*. Grand Rapids: Eerdmans, 2004.

Wojtkowiak, Heiko. *Christologie und Ethik im Philipperbrief: Studien zur Handlungsorienteirung einer frühchristlichen Gemeinde in Paganer Umwelt*. FRLANT 243. Göttingen: Vandenhoeck & Ruprecht, 2012.

Wolfe, B. Paul. "The Sagacious Use of Scripture." Pages 199–218 in *Entrusted with the Gospel: Paul's Theology in the Pastoral Epistles*. Edited by Andreas J. Köstenberger and Terry L. Wilder. Nashville: B&H, 2010.

Wolff, Christian. "True Apostolic Knowledge of Christ: Exegetical Reflections on 2 Corinthians 5:14ff." Pages 81–98 in *Paul and Jesus: Collected Essays*. Edited by A. J. M. Wedderburn. JSNTSup 37. Sheffield: Sheffield Academic, 1989.

Wolter, Michael. *Der Brief an die Kolosser. Der Brief an Philemon*. ÖTK 12. Gütersloh: Gerd Mohn, 1993.

————. *Der Brief an die Römer*. EKKNT 6. Neukirchen-Vluyn: Neukirchener, 2014.

————. "The Development of Pauline Christianity from a 'Religion of Conversion' to a 'Religion of Tradition.'" Pages 49–69 in *Paul and the Heritage of Israel: Paul's Claim upon Israel's Legacy in Luke and Acts in the Light of the Pauline Letters*. Edited by David P. Moessner, Daniel Marguerat, Mikeal C. Parsons, and Michael Wolter. LNTS 452. London: T&T Clark, 2012.

————. *Die Pastoralbriefe als Paulustradition*. FRLANT 146. Göttingen: Vandenhoeck & Ruprecht, 1988.

————. *Paul: An Outline of His Theology*. Waco, TX: Baylor University Press, 2015.

Wolters, Al. "The Meaning of Αὐθεντέω." Pages 65–115 in *Women in the Church: An Interpretation and Application of 1 Timothy 2:9–15*. Edited by Andreas J. Köstenberger and Thomas R. Schreiner. 3rd ed. Wheaton, IL: Crossway, 2016.

Wrede, Wilhelm. *Paul*. Boston: American Unitarian Association, 1908.

Wright, Christopher J. H. *Old Testament Ethics for the People of God*. Leicester: Inter-Varsity Press, 2004.

Wright, N. T. "Adam, Israel and the Messiah." Pages 18–40 in *The Climax of the Covenant: Christ and the Law in Pauline Theology*. Minneapolis: Fortress, 1991.

————. ΧΡΙΣΤΟΣ as 'Messiah' in Paul: Philemon 6." Pages 41–55 in *The Climax of the Covenant: Christ and the Law in Pauline Theology*. Minneapolis: Fortress, 1991.

————. "Christ, the Law and the People of God: The Problem of Romans 9–11." Pages 231–57 in *The Climax of the Covenant: Christ and the Law in Pauline Theology*. Minneapolis: Fortress, 1991.

————. "Curse and Covenant: Galatians 3.10–14." Pages 137–56 in *The Climax of the Covenant: Christ and the Law in Pauline Theology*. Minneapolis: Fortress, 1991.

————. *The Day the Revolution Began: Reconsidering the Meaning of Jesus' Crucifixion*. New York: HarperOne, 2016.

————. *The Epistles of Paul to the Colossians and to Philemon: An Introduction and Commentary*. TNTC 12. Grand Rapids: Eerdmans, 1986.

————. "Jesus Christ Is Lord: Philippians 2.5–11." Pages 56–98 in *The Climax of the Covenant: Christ and the Law in Pauline Theology*. Minneapolis: Fortress, 1991.

————. *Justification: God's Plan and Paul's Vision*. Downers Grove, IL: InterVarsity Press, 2009.

————. "Justification: Yesterday, Today, and Forever." *JETS* 54 (2011): 49–63.

————. "New Exodus, New Inheritance: The Narrative Substructure of Romans 3–8." Pages 26–35 in *Romans and the People of God: Essays in Honor of Gordon D. Fee on the Occasion of His 65th Birthday*. Edited by Sven Soderlund and N. T. Wright. Grand Rapids: Eerdmans, 1999.

————. "A New Perspective on Käsemann? Apocalyptic, Covenant, and the Righteousenss of God." Pages 243–58 in *Studies in the Pauline Epistles: Essays in Honor of Douglas J. Moo*. Edited by Matthew S. Harmon and Jay E. Smith. Grand Rapids: Zondervan, 2014.

————. "New Perspectives on Paul." Pages 243–64 in *Justification in Perspective: Historical Developments and Contemporary Challenges*. Edited by Bruce McCormack. Grand Rapids: Baker, 2006.

————. *The New Testament and the People of God*. Vol. 1 of Christian Origins and the Question of God. Minneapolis: Fortress, 1992.

————. *Paul and His Recent Interpreters: Some Contemporary Debates*. Minneapolis: Fortress, 2015.

————. *Paul and the Faithfulness of God*. 2 vols. Minneapolis: Fortress, 2013.

————. *Paul: In Fresh Perspective*. Minneapolis: Fortress, 2005.

————. "The Paul of History and the Apostle of Faith." *TynBul* 29 (1978): 61–88.

————. "Poetry and Theology in Colossians 1.15–20." Pages 99–119 in *The Climax of the Covenant: Christ and the Law in Pauline Theology*. Minneapolis: Fortress, 1991.

———. *The Resurrection of the Son of God*. Vol. 3 of Christian Origins and the Question of God. Minneapolis: Fortress, 2003.

———. "Romans." Pages 395–770 in vol. 8 of *The New Interpreter's Bible*. Edited by Leander E. Keck. Nashville: Abingdon, 2002.

———. *Suprised by Hope: Rethinking Heaven, the Resurrection, and the Mission of the Church*. New York: HarperOne, 2008.

———. *What Saint Paul Really Said: Was Paul of Tarsus the Real Founder of Christianity?* Grand Rapids: Eerdmans, 1997.

Yarbrough, Robert W. "Atonement." Pages 388–93 in *New Dictionary of Biblical Theology*. Edited by T. Desmond Alexander and Brian S. Rosner. Downers Grove, IL: InterVarsity Press, 2000.

———. *The Letters to Timothy and Titus*. PNTC. Grand Rapids: Eerdmans, 2018.

———. "Salvation History (*Heilsgeschichte*) and Paul: Comments on a Disputed but Essential Category." Pages 181–97 in *Studies in the Pauline Epistles: Essays in Honor of Douglas J. Moo*. Edited by Matthew S. Harmon and Jay E. Smith. Grand Rapids: Zondervan, 2014.

———. "Sexual Gratification in 1 Thess 4,1–8." *TrinJ* 20 (1999): 215–32.

Yinger, Kent L. *Paul, Judaism, and Judgment according to Deeds*. SNTSMS 105. Cambridge: Cambridge University Press, 1999.

Zamfir, Korinna. *Men and Women in the Household of God: A Contextual Approach to Roles and Ministries in the Pastoral Epistles*. NTOA/SNTSU 103. Göttingen: Vandenhoeck & Ruprecht, 2013.

Zeller, Dieter. "Israel unter dem Ruf Gottes (Röm 9–11)." *IKZ* 2 (1973): 289–301.

Zetterholm, Magnus. *Approaches to Paul: A Student's Guide to Recent Scholarship*. Minneapolis: Fortress, 2009.

Ziesler, John A. *The Meaning of Righteousness in Paul: A Linguistic and Theological Enquiry*. SNTSMS 20. Cambridge: Cambridge University Press, 1972.

Zumstein, Jean. "Das Wort von Kreuz als Mitte der Paulinischen Theologie." Pages 27–41 in *Kreuztheologie im Neuen Testament*. Edited by Andreas Dettwiler and Jean Zumstein. Tübingen: Mohr Siebeck, 2002.

SCRIPTURE INDEX

JEREMIAH

INDEX OF EXTRABIBLICAL LITERATURE

SUBJECT INDEX

worldview, 12, 15, 24, 27, 28, 31, 33–35, 133, 152, 269,
    413–14, 568, 603, 610
  Christian, 113, 414
  Jewish, 466
  pagan, 131
worship, 93, 132, 153, 203, 246, 256, 283, 308, 373, 409,
    423, 462, 575, 579, 611, 631, 639, 642

  false, 256, 351, 428
  of angels, 246, 256–58
  of idols, 132, 139, 203, 409
  service, 139–42, 145, 151–52, 198, 325, 588, 641
wrath, 93–94, 100, 200, 202–3, 210–11, 214, 217–18, 231,
    259, 277–80, 290, 398, 403, 408, 411–13, 422–24,
    428, 462, 468–69, 488, 495–96, 547, 550, 561

Author Index

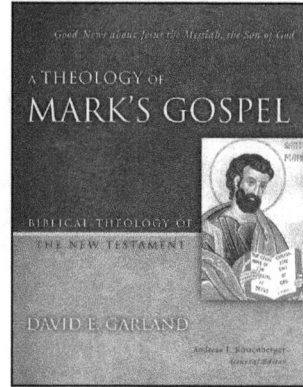

A Theology of Luke and Acts

God's Promised Program,
Realized for All Nations

Darrell L. Bock
Andreas J. Köstenberger, general editor

This groundbreaking work by Darrell Bock thoroughly explores the theology of Luke's Gospel and the book of Acts. In his writing, Luke records the story of God working through Jesus to usher in a new era of promise and Spirit-enablement so that the people of God can be God's people even amid a hostile world. It is a message the church still needs today. Bock both covers major Lukan themes and sets forth the distinctive contribution of Luke-Acts to the New Testament and the canon of Scripture, providing readers with an in-depth and holistic grasp of Lukan theology in the larger context of the Bible.

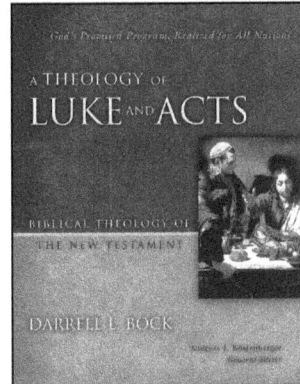

Available in stores and online!

ZONDERVAN®
.com

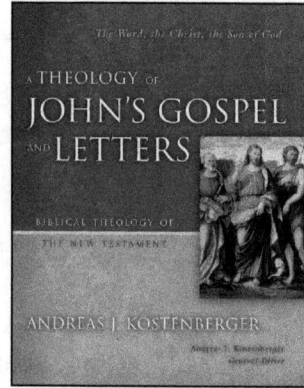